COLLEGE ENGLISH

8th Edition

COLLEGE ENGLISH

8th Edition

Alton C. Morris (late)

Biron Walker

Philip Bradshaw
University of Florida

John C. Hodges (late)
University of Tennessee

Mary E. Whitten
North Texas State University

Harcourt Brace Jovanovich, Inc.

New York   San Diego   Chicago   San Francisco   Atlanta
London   Sydney   Toronto

CONTENTS

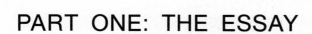

PART TWO: THE SHORT STORY   187

PART THREE: DRAMA 317

PART FOUR: POETRY 551

THE POET AS STORYTELLER 559

THE POET AS ELEGIST 581

592

THE POET AS WIT AND HUMORIST

THE POET AS PORTRAYER OF CHARACTER 591

THE POET AS CRITIC AND PHILOSOPHER   602

PREFACE

The fundamental objectives of the seven preceding editions of *College English* have guided the editors in the preparation of the eighth: to foster awareness of the broad range of ideas and attitudes in literature; to encourage the development of skill in critical reading; to make the connection between critical reading and writing; and to provide a source of ideas for writing and discussion. The basic premise of this book is that the competent writer must also be a skillful reader, able to apprehend and articulate the ideas and forms that writers use. More selections are included here than will probably be needed in any course, allowing instructors considerable flexibility. An *Instructor's Manual* offers teaching suggestions for most of the selections.

The eighth edition of *College English* has five parts: Parts One through Four contain essays, short stories, plays, and poems; Part Five presents the ninth edition of the *Harbrace College Handbook* in its entirety. Part One consists of 44 thematically arranged essays of varying length and difficulty, of which 26 are new to this edition. Similarly, nearly half the short stories and poems are new, and the drama section has been expanded to include Shakespeare's *King Lear*, Molière's *Tartuffe*, and Pinter's *The Birthday Party*.

The ninth edition of the *Harbrace College Handbook* has been thoroughly revised and expanded, especially Section 32, which presents the steps in planning and writing an essay, and Section 33, devoted to the research paper. These two sections use sample essays to demonstrate the importance of a writer's attitude toward subject and audience, how to gather and organize ideas, write a first draft, and revise the first and second drafts. In short, the *Harbrace College Handbook* and the essay section of *College English* make up a highly useful rhetoric-reader, and the five parts of *College English*, taken as a whole, present in one volume all the materials required in a freshman English class.

It is fitting to acknowledge the work and influence of our late senior co-editor, co-author, colleague, and friend, Alton C. Morris, who between 1940 and his death in 1979 saw twenty or more titles to press, including the first seven editions of *College English*.

Thanks are due Beverly Thomas, Santa Fe Community College, Gainesville, Florida, for her sound advice on the plays in the drama section, based on her extensive study, teaching, and direction. Also thanks to Linda Williams, English teacher and curriculum and materials consultant, for her advice on the table of contents. And special thanks are due Stephen C. Williams, University of North Florida at Jacksonville, for his substantial contribution to this edition. His knowledge of literature, unique teaching experience, and high editorial competence have made him a virtual co-editor. We also wish to thank the following reviewers for their helpful comments and suggestions: Christine E. Anderson, Miami-Dade Community College; Eileen Evans, Western Michigan University; Oliver Evans, Western Michigan University; Marjorie M. Kaiser, University of Louisville; Virginia J. Lovett, Cumberland College; Lowell Lynde, Louisiana Tech University; Jack Rucker, Northeastern Oklahoma Agriculture and Mechanical College; and C. E. Young, Northwood Institute, Midland, Michigan. Finally, to all our editors and friends of long standing at Harcourt Brace Jovanovich who have helped shape the eight editions of *College English,* we are indebted and grateful for their advice, guidance, expertise, and concern.

B. W.
P. B.

HENRY DAVID THOREAU

On Reading (from *Walden*)

No wonder that Alexander carried the Iliad with him on his expeditions in a precious casket. A written word is the choicest of relics. It is something at once more intimate with us and more universal than any other work of art. It is the work of art nearest to life itself. It may be translated into every language, and not only be read but actually breathed from all human lips;—not be represented on canvas or in marble only, but be carved out of the breath of life itself. The symbol of an ancient man's thought becomes a modern man's speech. Two thousand summers have imparted to the monuments of Grecian literature, as to her marbles, only a maturer golden and autumnal tint, for they have carried their own serene and celestial atmosphere into all lands to protect them against the corrosion of time. Books are the treasured wealth of the world and the fit inheritance of generations and nations.

INTRODUCTION TO LITERATURE

The chief purpose in reading literature is to intensify our awareness of the variety and quality of other people's perceptions of human experience; and to see how variously writers use their art to communicate them. A literary work—essay, short story, novel, play, poem—therefore possesses greatness by virtue of the power it is able to exert, through means peculiar to its particular form, over the imaginative as well as the real life of attentive readers. Literary works have a wide range of complexity. At one end of the scale is a brief expression of personal emotion, such as Edna St. Vincent Millay's "Wild Swans" (p. 600). The middle reaches are represented by the contained fervor of E. M. Forster's familiar essay "What I Believe" (p. 150) and by the buoyance of Eudora Welty's "A Worn Path" (p. 254). At the other end stands such accumulated force and complexity as in Sophocles' tragedy *Antigonê* (p. 323) or Shakespeare's *King Lear* (p. 347). But however modest or grand in scope an essay, short story, novel, or play may be, readers must participate actively and eagerly by contributing from their own experience and thinking to that of the author's as recorded in his or her writing to get the full realization of the presented experience. Persons who have read much with understanding have shared in many lives, places, and events, historical or imagined. Each life or place has been vividly different from the others and each has added to the richness and perspective of these readers' sum total of experience—to the outer and inner events of their lives.

Experience, it is said, is a good but costly teacher. Direct experience is often desirable, despite its danger or cost, but not all experience can or need be participated in directly. It is possible to avoid disaster, for instance, and yet lay hold of the quality of character that disaster sometimes creates, or at least reveals. The imaginative projection of ourselves into the consciousness of others through literature yields experiences that would be too strenuous to endure without hazard in actual life, and yet these experiences can chasten and humanize us, bringing us to a better understanding of ourselves and others. The range of such indirect experiences is surprisingly large and varied—from the outrageous to the sublime—but they are most meaningful to readers when they complement their own experiences. Those who have even vaguely felt themselves beckoned by something beyond their daily lives, for example, or who regret not having greater experience and pleasure from living will find special meaning in

Steinbeck's "The Chrysanthemums" (p. 239), Yeat's "Down by the Salley Gardens" (p. 569), and Eliot's "The Love Song of J. Alfred Prufrock" (p. 579).

But literature, however closely allied to actual experience, is not an exact reproduction or transcript of lives, places, or events. That is, literature is not so much a photograph of life as it is a series of portraits or paintings. Life is so crowded with details as to seem nearly chaotic to most at times, but each work of literature is a selection from among the many details combined to suggest a coherent impression of a life, actual or historical, literary or imagined. Writers do not give masses of unassimilated experience but rather impose form upon the materials available and, through this form, suggest meanings. Organization, grammar, rhetoric, logic (sometimes a special logic peculiar to the writer or the kind of truth used), diction, and other components of writing give a sense of the meanings implied. An analysis of any one of the essays, short stories, or poems in this book will reveal how little in the way of details—of description or character or action—the author actually gives, and how much is only suggested or implied, thus leaving readers to add from their store of knowledge and experience to make full the meaning from their reading.

The central importance of the selection and organization of materials is especially well illustrated by the short story, because its brief limits require the author to select and order material with unusual care and skill. For example, when E. B. White in "The Door" (p. 236) wishes to show the disorienting effects of modern life upon human perception and psyche, he chooses a single stretch of stream-of-consciousness reaction by one character who spends a few minutes in a room of technological simulations of natural materials and objects. But selectivity goes beyond the simple limitation of character, incident, and setting; it involves also the choice of those personalities and events that most quickly and richly symbolize the theme of the story.

The meaning that emerges from organization and selection in any work of literature cannot be adequately conveyed in a summary. To perceive the full quality of the experience interpreted, we must become very sensitive to every part and its relationship, as if we were writer rather than only reader; and the comprehension finally achieved will depend in part on the scope of our own consciousness. As a critic has suggested, the effect of a work of art on the consciousness of the reader is like the effect of pebbles falling into a pool of water: the ripples always move out from the point of fall to the far edge of the pool, but some pools are larger than others. For example, in Chesterton's poem "The Donkey," (p. 575) the poet's meaning emerges only when the reader grasps the special connotation of one word, *palms*, rather than its usual denotation. Slowly we realize that the poet is not writing merely a humorous poem in which the donkey is praising himself despite his evolutionary history and unprepossessing appearance. Pondering the validity of this initial meaning, we suddenly realize that *palms* may have a special reference: to a Sabbath long ago when a religious leader entered Jerusalem riding on a donkey. Otherwise the poem has a different tone, one of humor and not of irony, and the donkey is only a ridiculous creature praising himself despite his ungainly and ugly being. It is a singular poem, because, unlike most poems, its full meaning turns on the full understanding the very special connotation of a single word.

Literature appeals to both the mind and the heart. Therefore, the whole consciousness of the reader must respond to it. Sometimes full comprehension of a piece of literature, for example, Maugham's "Appointment in Samarra" (p. 187), comes in the sudden insight generated by new connotation or ironic circumstances or other devices that enlarge our perception of an otherwise conventional experience. This lifts the reader to a different plane of being. Robert Frost records such an incident in the following lines:

> The way a crow
> Shook down on me
> The dust of snow
> From a hemlock tree
> Has given my heart
> A change of mood
> And saved some part
> Of a day I had rued.*

The sudden insight communicated here yields a deep understanding, an unusual illumination, a discovery applicable to oneself. No doubt all of us have such moments of poetic or literary insight when past knowledge and present awareness come to focus upon a single point of understanding: these are among our most memorable experiences. Readers of literature may share these moments with the writer, and then determine to try to create these results in their own writing. Just as speaking and listening are directly related, because a speaker must have a listener and the listener a speaker, so the same relationship necessarily exists between a writer and reader. Creative reading at its best includes this awareness that reader and writer are inevitably linked: each must know the art of the other, and being actively and sensitively engaged in the one directly enhances competence in the other.

PART 1

The Essay

THOMAS CARLYLE

from **The Hero as Man of Letters**

All that mankind has done, thought, gained or
been: it is lying as in magic preservation in the
pages of books. . . . If we think of it, all that a university, or final highest school can do for us is still
but what the first school began doing—teach us to
read. We learn to *read*, in various languages, in
various sciences; we learn the alphabet and letters
of all manner of books. But the place where we
are to get knowledge, even theoretic knowledge, is
the books themselves!

genre
poetry
fiction
Drama
Essay

Probably no form of literature records the varied interests, patterns of thinking, and temper of a time more completely and accurately than the essay. The essays of Bacon and Montaigne, sixteenth-century originators of the form, reflect the taste of the Renaissance for philosophical speculation and practical knowledge. Eighteenth-century essays present the lively world of the English Enlightenment: the wit, gossip, and learned talk of London's coffee houses and drawing rooms appeared in the essays of Addison and Steele, and the social and political history of the time was recorded in the essays, diaries, and biographies of Johnson, Boswell, and Defoe. In the nineteenth century the essays of Lamb, Pater, Newman, Carlyle, Darwin, Thoreau, and Emerson reveal the social, religious, literary, artistic, and scientific ferment in England and America. Today the genre has an even broader range of subjects, a wider variety of types or mixtures of types, and a greater audience. It not only reflects the interests of the contemporary world and the complexity of this century, but provides a sounding board for ideas, aspirations, and fears. Thus the essay continues to increase in popularity and usefulness as a means for readers to obtain information, ideas, opinion, and counsel, and for writers to practice their prose art and to see how other writers work.

The essay received its name from the title of Montaigne's first collection of short nonfiction prose writings—*Essais* (or in English, *Attempts*)—and from its beginning was an "attempt" to communicate. The term still retains this meaning—indeed, it is every writer's hope to communicate with someone else (an audience)—but today signifies a short, nonfiction prose selection that has a worthwhile idea and an artistic presentation (style). The terms *article* (as in "magazine article") or *story* (as in "reporter's story" or "newspaper story") may or may not be synonymous with *essay*. The term *article* often suggests either a timely treatment written on demand and hastily (often with a word limit) or a piece of writing that did not achieve the lasting or universal quality required of an essay. Though important and useful for a time, such an article or story may soon lose its readership. If it becomes a piece that continues to be read and reread because of its intellectual pertinence or literary merit, it is likely to be considered an essay.

Essays have traditionally been classified for rhetorical convenience into four main types, depending on their writer's purpose: (1) to narrate (narration), (2) to describe (description), (3) to explain or analyze (exposition), or (4) to argue (argumentation or persuasion). Though an essay may be limited fairly rigidly to narration or one of the other types, most modern essays often contain a mixture of two or more of the types.

For example, George Orwell's "Shooting an Elephant" (p. 103) uses narration, description, and exposition to make its point. In Whipple's "Machinery, Magic, and Art" (p. 89) exposition and argumentation are fused to communicate the author's main idea. Thus, the classification scheme of the traditional rhetoricians no longer seems followed in practice. Though numerous terms have been used to categorize essays, perhaps two are sufficient—*informal* (personal, familiar) and *formal.* The informal essay has an almost instinctive flow of ideas rather than the formal essay's classically logical structure. It is also conversational in tone, often frankly given to reminiscing, and seems to be uncalculating in achieving its effect, while the formal essay uses language, structure, and logic to maintain more objectivity and distance from both subject and reader. The White and Maslow essays (p. 142 and p. 146) on the demise of the Model T Ford and the MG sports car are informal or, more accurately, personal or familiar essays. Healy's "The Donne Thing" (p. 9) and Bowen's "We've Never Asked a Woman Before" (p. 136) would be classified as informal, because they too are personal and familiar. In contrast, Woolfson's "Speech Is More than Language" (p. 27) and Tuchman's "Mankind's Better Moments" (p. 160) are formal essays. In current publications, most of the formal essays are found in scholarly, professional, scientific, and technical journals and books. Informal essays are published in the more widely circulated magazines and in newspapers.

Whether formal or informal, essays are a repository of ideas from many areas of knowledge and are also samples of the essay writer's art. Though reading essays may demand more background knowledge, greater objectivity, steadier concentration, and greater reading skill than other literary forms require, the reader's rewards are increased knowledge and understanding, an appreciation of the vital ideas, opinions, and judgments of the ablest writers of the time—and, for the student, useful insights into the art of writing. By analyzing the way authors limit their subjects, develop their ideas, use language in their chosen sentence and paragraph structures, and reveal through writing their purpose in writing, a reader can turn to writing with success.

HOWARD NEMEROV

To David,
about His Education

The world is full of mostly invisible things,
And there is no way but putting the mind's eye,
Or its nose, in a book, to find them out,
Things like the square root of Everest
Or how many times Byron goes into Texas,
Or whether the law of the excluded middle
Applies west of the Rockies. For these
And the like reasons, you have to go to school
And study books and listen to what you are told,
And sometimes try to remember. Though I don't know
What you will do with the mean annual rainfall
On Plato's Republic, or the calorie content
Of the Diet of Worms, such things are said to be
Good for you, and you will have to learn them
In order to become one of the grown-ups
Who sees invisible things neither steadily nor whole,
But keeps gravely the grand confusion of the world
Under his hat, which is where it belongs,
And teaches small children to do this in their turn.

WILLIE MORRIS

The Awakening

Willie Morris (1934–   ) was born in Jackson, Mississippi, and educated at the University of Texas and at New College, Oxford University, England, where he was a Rhodes Scholar from 1956 to 1959. In 1960 he was appointed editor of the Texas *Observer* in Austin, and later was made editor-in-chief. He then moved to *Harper's* magazine, first as associate editor, then executive editor, then vice-president of the corporation. He has written *The South Today: 100 Years after Appomattox*, 1965; *North toward Home*, 1967, his autobiography, which won the Collins Non-Fiction Award and the Houghton Mifflin Literary Award; *Yazoo: Integration in a Deep Southern Town*, 1971; *The Last of the Southern Girls*, 1975; and *James Jones: A Friendship*, 1978, a memorial to the American novelist whose major work was *From Here to Eternity*.

In "The Awakening," from his autobiography, Morris captures the fears, distractions, and demands that confront many students starting their collegiate careers.

1. What strikes me most in reading books like Alfred Kazin's haunting poetic reminiscences of boyhood in an immigrant Jewish neighborhood in the East is the vast gulf which separates that kind of growing up and the childhood and adolescence of those of us who came out of the towns of the American South and Southwest a generation later. With the Eastern Jewish intellectuals who play such a substantial part in American cultural life, perhaps in the late 1960s a dominant part, the struggle as they grew up in the 1930s was for one set of ideas over others, for a fierce acceptance or rejection of one man's theories or another man's poetry—and with all this a driving determination to master the language which had not been their parents' and to find a place in a culture not quite theirs. For other Eastern intellectuals and writers whom I later was to know, going to the Ivy League schools involved, if not a finishing, then a deepening of perceptions, or of learning, or culture.

2. But for so many of us who converged on Austin, Texas, in the early 1950s, from places like Karnes City or Big Spring or Abilene or Rockdale or Yazoo City, the awakening we were to experience, or to have jolted into us, or to undergo by some more subtle chemistry, did not mean a mere finishing or deepening, and most emphatically did not imply the victory of one set of ideologies over another, one way of viewing literature or politics over another, but something more basic and simple. This was the acceptance of ideas themselves as something worth living by. It was a matter, at the age of eighteen or nineteen, not of discovering *certain* books, but the simple *presence* of books, not the nuances of idea and feeling, but idea and feeling on their own terms. It is this late coming to this kind of awareness that still gives the intellectuals from the small towns of our region a hungry, naïve quality, as opposed to the sharp-elbowed overintellectuality of some Easterners, as if those from down there who made it were lucky, or chosen, out of all the disastrous alternatives of their isolated lower- or middle-class upbringings, to enjoy and benefit from the fruits of simply being educated and liberal-minded.

3. What we brought to the University of Texas in the 1950s, to an enormous, only partially formed state university, was a great awe before the splendid quotations on its buildings and the walls of its libraries, along with an absolutely prodigious insensitivity as to what they implied beyond decoration. Minds awakened slowly, painfully, and with pretentious and damaging inner searches. Where an Alfred Kazin at the age of nineteen might become aroused in the subway by reading a review by John Chamberlain in the *New York Times* and rush to his office to complain, we at eighteen or nineteen were only barely beginning to learn that there *were* ideas, much less ideas to arouse one from one's self. If places like City College or Columbia galvanized the young New York intellectuals already drenched in literature and polemics, the University of Texas had, in its halting, unsure, and often frivolous way, to teach those of us with good minds and small-town high school diplomas that we were intelligent human beings, with minds and hearts of our own that we might learn to call our own, that there were some things, many things—ideas, values, choices of action—worth committing one's self to and fighting for, that a man in some instances might become morally committed to honoring every manifestation of individual conscience and courage. Yet the hardest task at the University of Texas, as many of us were to learn, was to separate all the extraneous and empty things that can drown a young person there, as all big universities can drown its young people, from the few simple things that are worth living a life by. Without wishing to sound histrionic, I believe I am thinking of something approaching the Western cultural tradition; yet if someone had suggested that to me that September night in 1952, as I stepped off the bus in Austin to be greeted by three fraternity men anxious to look me over, I would have thought him either a fool or a con man.

4. I emerged from that bus frightened and tired, after having come 500 miles non-stop over the red hills of Louisiana and the pine forests of East Texas. The three men who met me—appalled, I was told later, by my green trousers and the National Honor Society medal on my gold-plated watch chain—were the kind that I briefly liked and admired, for their facility at small talk, their clothes, their manner, but whom I soon grew to deplore and finally to be bored by. They were the kind who made fraternities tick, the favorites of the Dean of Men at the time, respectable B or C-plus students, tolerable athletes, good with the Thetas or the Pi Phis; but one would find later, lurking there inside of them, despite—or maybe because of—their good fun and jollity, the ideals of the insurance salesman and an aggressive distrust of anything approaching thought. One of them later told me, with the seriousness of an early disciple, that my table manners had become a source of acute embarrassment to all of them. That night they drove me around the campus, and they were impressed that I knew from my map-reading where the University library was, for two of them were not sure.

FRANCIS BACON

Of Studies

Francis Bacon (1561–1626), English nobleman, was educated at Trinity College, Cambridge University, England, and became a lawyer and member of Parliament in 1584, from which he was removed in 1621 for corruption and neglect. Confined briefly in the Tower of London, he later devoted his remaining years to literary, philosophical, and professional writing in Latin and English. He wanted to replace the Aristotelian system of philosophy with one based on his own interpretation of nature. Among his works are his *Essays,* published in 1597 and revised in final form in 1625; *Advancement of Learning,* 1605; *Novum Organum,* 1620; and *De Augmentis,* 1623.

In "Of Studies" Bacon points out why one should become a student and stresses what books to choose and how to read them.

1. Studies serve for delight, for ornament, and for ability. Their chief use for delight is in privateness and retiring; for ornament, is in discourse; and for ability, is in the judgment and disposition of business. For expert men can execute and perhaps judge of particulars, one by one; but the general counsels and the plots and marshaling of affairs come best from those that are learned. To spend too much time in studies is sloth; to use them too much for ornament is affectation; to make judgment wholly by their rules is the humor of a scholar. They perfect nature, and are perfected by experience; for natural abilities are like natural plants, that need proyning by study; and studies themselves do give forth directions too much at large, except they be bounded in by experience. Crafty men contemn studies, simple men admire them, and wise men use them; for they teach not their own use; but that is a wisdom without them and above them, won by observation. Read not to contradict and confute, nor to believe and take for granted, nor to find talk and discourse, but to weigh and consider. Some books are to be tasted, others to be swallowed, and some few to be chewed and digested; that is, some books are to be read only in parts, others to be read, but not curiously, and some few to be read wholly, and with diligence and attention. Some books also may be read by deputy, and extracts made of them by others; but that would be only in the less important arguments, and the meaner sort of books; else distilled books are like common distilled waters, flashy things. Reading maketh a full man, conference a ready man, and writing an exact man. And therefore, if a man write little, he had need have a great memory; if he confer little, he had need have a present wit; and if he read little, he had need have much cunning, to seem to know that he doth not. Histories make men wise; poets, witty; the mathematics, subtle; natural philosophy, deep; moral, grave; logic and rhetoric, able to contend. *Abeunt studia in mores.* Nay, there is no stond or impediment in the wit but may be wrought out by fit studies; like as diseases of the body may have appropriate exercises. Bowling is good for the stone and reins, shooting for the lungs and breast, gentle walking for the stomach, riding for the head, and the like. So if a man's wit be wandering, let him study the mathematics; for in demonstrations, if his wit be called away never so little, he must begin again; if his wit be not apt

to distinguish or find differences, let him study the schoolmen, for they are *cymini sectores;* if he be not apt to beat over matters, and to call one thing to prove and illustrate another, let him study the lawyers' cases. So every defect of the mind may have a special receipt.

TIMOTHY S. HEALY

The Donne Thing

Timothy S. Healy (1923–   ), educated at Woodstock College, Louvain in Belgium, Fordham University, and Oxford University in England, was ordained a Jesuit priest in 1953. He has taught Latin, English, and Comparative Literature at Fordham. In 1965 he became executive vice-president of the City University of New York, then, in 1974, special assistant to the Chancellor of the State University of New York. In 1976 he was named Professor of English and President of Georgetown University, Washington, D.C. His publications include *Ignatius, His Conclave,* 1969, and with Helen Gardner, *John Donne's Selected Poems,* 1967. He has been a member of the board of directors of the *Journal of the History of Ideas* since 1975.

In the informal and familiar essay "The Donne Thing," he expresses the fears and hopes every teacher has upon first meeting a new class and concludes with the observation that wisdom begins when students and teacher come to know and love one another.

1. About the front lawn and on the steps of buildings are draped agile figures in undergraduate uniform—jeans and T-shirts. In the rather more formal University Board Room, I wait for my first class of the year. It gathers, 31 strong, around the long, gleaming table. Above us, in the frozen self-possession only age can give, hang a gaggle of red and purple ecclesiastical greats to remind us drab moderns of our littleness.

2. Despite my 30 years teaching, any first session is always nervous, stiff with the pent-up energy that finds release in talk. Underneath pulses a sense of choice, of possibilities, of all the ways I can help an old poet speak to new minds. I wonder at the new beginning and at the newness of the beginners.

3. I've forgotten my own expectations when I was 18. It's too long ago. This lot is faintly awed by the setting, but that won't last. They wonder what the year will be like, how I will handle it, how they will "do". Most of them are seniors, and so are less nervous and trust the system to deliver recognizable intellectual goods. I'm the system, and I'm not so sure.

4. I start with a brief introduction, to give them a chance to hear my voice and to see what it sounds like myself. Then I give out cards so I can have phone numbers and know which college and what year each is in; the minor backwash of registration. Nervous chatter gets the year started, eases us over the introductory pangs. We dance around each other warily. We're going to work together, but it takes time to settle into harness one with another.

5. Our work is the poetry of John Donne. My job is to summon this splendid ghost out of his far century. We begin with what he wrote as a young man, 17 to 19, roughly the age of the students sitting in front of me. The young Elizabe-

THE DONNE THING   Reprinted by permission of the author.

than at the Inns of Court seems so much older and more knowing than young Americans from Des Moines, Bronxville and McLean. Will they ever come to understand his religious struggle and strength? Will they ever take to themselves the mercy of his later comment, "Thou seest this man's fall, but thou sawest not his wrastling"?

6. Today it's not with the great Dean in his long-since-burned-out cathedral that we deal. This Donne is the young poet, full of life and energy, writing outrageous and rough lines in imitation of Roman satire.

7. Poetry is to be said, and Donne's is no exception. So we speak it out loud; mostly they do. Jeff, a senior, is hesitant and needs to beat the lines out with a pencil. He stumbles over the colloquialisms:

We went, till one (which did excell
Th' Indians, in drinking his Tobacco well)
Met us; they talk'd; I whispered, 'Let us goe,
'T may be you smell him not, truely, I do'.

8. A few eyes smile at the familiar problem and on we go. Donne waxes sardonic even about poetry. Anne, with an easy voice, reads this, clearly and well:

Though Poetry indeed be such a sinne
As I thinke that brings dearth and Spaniards in,
Though like the Pestilence and old fashion'd love,
Ridlingly it catch men; and doth remove
Never, till it be serv'd out; yet their state
Is poore, disarm'd, like Papists, not worth hate.

9. As the voices rise and fall, an awareness grows around the table that over long time and under the stiff clarity of Elizabethan speech this man is saying something.

10. For me, his meaning is as close as the sunlight outside the windows. I listen to Mark's voice (he leads the choir so he gets the rhythm right):

To stand inquiring right, is not to stray;
    . . . On a huge hill,
Cragged and steep, Truth stands, and hee that will
Reach her, about must, and about must goe;
And what th' hill's suddenness resists winne so;

11. How often these four years will all of them go "about and about". On their young and level plain they can't know how high and hurtful truth stands, nor how much the "hill's suddenness" will slow them. None can understand yet that it grows steeper with time.

12. But this is no time for foreboding. My joys are too strong. First, the joy of recovery: a working back to a great artist of another time; meeting him with fresh imaginations; watching the long roots start down, even for the young. A second joy is of peace in a job: the students settling in, the familiar pull on the wits, the rich sound of the verse, and all of us knowing that the harness fits and that we will be comfortable in it. It's a good trade, teaching. With any luck, across this table, in talk and laughter and insight, we will come to the beginning of wisdom, that is, to know and love each other.

BEN JONSON

On Style and the Best Kind of Writing

Ben Jonson (1572–1637), bricklayer, dramatist, and essayist, was the first poet laureate of England, having been named by James I in 1616. His chief works were plays and masques: *Every Man Out of His Humour*, 1595; *Every Man in His Humour,* 1598, in which Shakespeare acted; *Sejanus,* his first tragedy, 1603; *Volpone,* his most famous play (recently produced on Broadway and on television as *The Sly Fox*), 1606. Among the actors, writers, and artists of his time, he had a host of friends, including Inigo Jones, Francis Bacon, Francis Beaumont, John Fletcher, John Donne, William Shakespeare, Richard Herrick, and John Suckling. It was they who had inscribed upon his tomb in Westminster Abbey "O Rare Ben Jonson."

In "On Style and the Best Kind of Writing" Jonson points out the components of good writing and the way to achieve the ability to write well.

1. For a man to write well, there are required three necessaries—to read the best authors, observe the best speakers, and much exercise of his own style. In style, to consider what ought to be written, and after what manner, he must first think and excogitate his matter, then choose his words, and examine the weight of either. Then take care, in placing and ranking both matter and words, that the composition be comely; and to do this with diligence and often. No matter how slow the style be at first, so it be labored and accurate; seek the best, and be not glad of the froward conceits, or first words, that offer themselves to us; but judge of what we invent, and order what we approve. Repeat often what we have formerly written; which beside that it helps the consequence, and makes the juncture better, it quickens the heat of imagination, that often cools in the time of setting down, and gives it new strength as if it grew lustier by the going back. As we see in the contention of leaping, they jump farthest that fetch their race largest; or, as in throwing a dart or javelin, we force back our arms to make our loose the stronger. Yet, if we have a fair gale of wind, I forbid not the steering out of our sail, so the favor of the gale deceive us not. For all that we invent doth please us in the conception of birth, else we would never set it down. But the safest is to return to our judgment, and handle over again those things the easiness of which might make them justly suspected. So did the best writers in their beginnings; they imposed upon themselves care and industry; they did nothing rashly. They obtained first to write well, and then custom made it easy and a habit. By little and little their matter showed itself to them more plentifully; their words answered, their composition followed; and all, as in a well-ordered family, presented itself in the place. So that the sum of all is, ready writing makes not good writing, but good writing brings on ready writing. Yet, when we think we have got the faculty, it is even then good to resist it, as to give a horse a check sometimes with a bit, which doth not so much stop his course as stir his mettle. Again, whither a man's genius is best able to reach, thither it should more and more contend, lift, and dilate itself; as men of low stature raise themselves on their toes, and so ofttimes get even, if not eminent. Besides, as it is fit for grown and able writers to stand of themselves, and work with their own strength, to trust and endeavor by their own faculties, so it is fit for the beginner and learner to study others and the best. For the mind

and memory are more sharply exercised in comprehending another man's things than our own; and such as accustom themselves and are familiar with the best authors shall ever and anon find somewhat of them in themselves, and in the expression of their minds, even when they feel it not, be able to utter something like theirs, which

hath an authority above their own. Nay, sometimes it is the reward of a man's study, the praise of quoting another man fitly; and though a man be more prone and able for one kind of writing than another, yet he must exercise all. For as in an instrument, so in style, there must be a harmony and consent of parts.

ISAAC ASIMOV

A Cult of Ignorance

Isaac Asimov (1920–   ) was born in Russia and came to the United States in 1923, becoming a citizen in 1928. In 1948 he received a Ph.D. from Columbia University. His professional career began at Boston University Medical School in 1949, where he continues to be affiliated. He is the author of more than 217 books, making him one of the most prolific authors of all time, and surely the most versatile, for he has written on scientific, political, and literary subjects and in all literary forms. He is especially famous for his limericks (see L. L. Miller's "A Limerick" (p. 586)—not "polite" ones only but "Lecherous Limericks" too—on one volume of which he collaborated with John Ciardi. He wrote in one of his many books, "I have been avid to learn and avid to teach. . . . I have been fortunate to be born with a restless and efficient brain, with capacity for clear thought and an ability to put thought into words. I am the beneficiary of a lucky break in the genetic sweepstakes."

In his pithy essay he gets at the heart of many problems—the inability to read effectively and efficiently. More and more the citizenry needs to read steadily and much, but they do not know how and so the "right to know is only a meaningless slogan."

1. It's hard to quarrel with that ancient justification of the free press: "America's right to know." It seems almost cruel to ask, ingenuously, "America's right to know what, please? Science? Mathematics? Economics? Foreign languages?"

2. None of those things, of course. In fact, one might well suppose that the popular feeling is that Americans are a lot better off without any of that tripe.

3. There is a cult of ignorance in the United States, and there always has been. The strain of anti-intellectualism has been a constant thread

winding its way through our political and cultural life, nurtured by the false notion that democracy means that "my ignorance is just as good as your knowledge."

4. Politicians have routinely striven to speak the language of Shakespeare and Milton as ungrammatically as possible in order to avoid offending their audiences by appearing to have gone to school. Thus, Adlai Stevenson, who incautiously allowed intelligence and learning and wit to peep out of his speeches, found the American people flocking to a Presidential candidate who invented a version of the English language that was all his own and that has been the despair of satirists ever since.

5. George Wallace, in his speeches, had, as one of his prime targets, the "pointy-headed professor," and with what a roar of approval that phrase was always greeted by his pointy-headed audience.

6. Now we have a new slogan on the part of the obscurantists: "Don't trust the experts!" Ten years ago, it was "Don't trust anyone over 30." But the shouters of that slogan found that the inevitable alchemy of the calendar converted them to the untrustworthiness of the over-30, and, apparently, they determined never to make that mistake again. "Don't trust the experts!" is absolutely safe. Nothing, neither the passing of time nor exposure to information, will convert these shouters to experts in any subject that might conceivably be useful.

7. We have a new buzzword, too, for anyone who admires competence, knowledge, learning and skill, and who wishes to spread it around. People like that are called "elitists." That's the funniest buzzword ever invented because people who are not members of the intellectual elite don't know what an "elitist" is, or how to pronounce the word. As soon as someone shouts "elitist" it becomes clear that he or she is a closet elitist who is feeling guilty about having gone to school.

8. All right, then, forget my ingenuous question. America's right to know does not include knowledge of elitist subjects. America's right to know involves something we might express vaguely as "what's going on." America has the right to know "what's going on" in the courts, in Congress, in the White House, in industrial councils, in the regulatory agencies, in labor unions—in the seats of the mighty, generally.

9. Very good, I'm for that, too. But how are you going to let people know all that?

10. Grant us a free press, and a corps of independent and fearless investigative reporters, comes the cry, and we can be sure that the people will know.

11. Yes, *provided they can read!*

12. As it happens, reading is one of those elitist subjects I have been talking about, and the American public, by and large, in their distrust of experts and in their contempt for pointy-headed professors, can't read and don't read.

13. To be sure, the average American can sign his name more or less legibly, and can make out the sports headlines—but how many nonelitist Americans can, without undue difficulty, read as many as a thousand consecutive words of small print, some of which may be trisyllabic?

14. Moreover, the situation is growing worse. Reading scores in the schools decline steadily. The highway signs, which used to represent elementary misreading lessons ("Go Slo," "Xroad") are steadily being replaced by little pictures to make them internationally legible and incidentally to help those who know how to drive a car but, not being pointy-headed professors, can't read.

15. Again, in television commercials, there are frequent printed messages. Well, keep your eyes on them and you'll find out that no advertiser ever believes that anyone but an occasional elitist can read that print. To ensure that more than this mandarin minority gets the message, every word of it is spoken out loud by the announcer.

16. If that is so, then how have Americans got the right to know? Grant that there are certain publications that make an honest effort to tell the public what they should know, but ask yourselves how many actually read them.

17. There are 200 million Americans who have inhabited schoolrooms at some time in their lives and who will admit that they know how to read (provided you promise not to use their names and shame them before their neighbors), but most decent periodicals believe they are doing amazingly well if they have circulations of half a million. It may be that only 1 per cent—or less—of Americans make a stab at exercising their right to know. And if they try to do anything on that basis they are quite likely to be accused of being elitists.

18. I contend that the slogan "America's right to know" is a meaningless one when we have an ignorant population, and that the function of a free press is virtually zero when hardly anyone can read.

19. What shall we do about it?

20. We might begin by asking ourselves whether ignorance is so wonderful after all, and whether it makes sense to denounce "elitism."

21. I believe that every human being with a physically normal brain can learn a great deal and can be surprisingly intellectual. I believe that what we badly need is social approval of learning and social rewards for learning.

22. We can *all* be members of the intellectual elite and then, and only then, will a phrase like "America's right to know" and, indeed, any true concept of democracy, have any meaning.

WILLIAM G. PERRY, JR.

Examsmanship and the Liberal Arts

William G. Perry, Jr. (1913–   ) is a member of the faculty and director of the Bureau of Study Counsel at Harvard University. He and Charles Preston Whitlock coproduced a set of sixteen reading films in 1949 and twice since have revised them, the most recent revision in 1959. Mr. Perry has contributed to many professional journals, including Harvard Educational Review *and* Journal of General Education. *This essay was his contribution to* Examining in Harvard College: A Collection of Essays by Members of the Harvard Faculty.

Mr. Perry examines here two diametrically opposed definitions of knowledge: one, represented by the term "cow," is the application of facts without understanding; the other, "bull," is the application of understanding with few or no facts.

1. "But sir, I don't think I really deserve it, it was mostly bull, really." This disclaimer from a student whose examination we have awarded a straight "A" is wondrously depressing. Alfred North Whitehead invented its only possible rejoinder: "Yes sir, what you wrote is nonsense, utter nonsense. But ah! Sir! It's the right *kind* of nonsense!"

2. Bull, in this university, is customarily a source of laughter, or a problem in ethics. I shall step a little out of fashion to use the subject as a take-off point for a study in comparative epistemology. The phenomenon of bull, in all the honor and opprobrium with which it is regarded by students and faculty, says something, I think, about our theories of knowledge. So too, the grades which we assign on examinations communicate to students what these theories may be.

3. We do not have to be out-and-out logical-positivists to suppose that we have something to learn about "what we think knowledge is" by having a good look at "what we do when we go about measuring it." We know the straight "A" examination when we see it, of course, and we have reason to hope that the student will understand why his work receives our recognition. He doesn't always. And those who receive lesser honor? Perhaps an understanding of certain anomalies in our customs of grading good bull will explain the students' confusion.

4. I must beg patience, then, both of the reader's humor and of his morals. Not that I ask him to suspend his sense of humor but that I shall ask him to go beyond it. In a great university the picture of a bright student attempting to outwit his professor while his professor takes pride in not being outwitted is certainly ridiculous. I shall report just such a scene, for its implications bear upon my point. Its comedy need not present a serious obstacle to thought.

5. As for the ethics of bull, I must ask for a suspension of judgment. I wish that students could suspend theirs. Unlike humor, moral commitment is hard to think beyond. Too early a moral judgment is precisely what stands between

EXAMSMANSHIP AND THE LIBERAL ARTS Reprinted by permission of the publishers from William G. Perry, Jr. in *Examining at Harvard College;* Cambridge, Mass.: Harvard University. Distributed by Harvard University Press.

many able students and a liberal education. The stunning realization that the Harvard Faculty will often accept, as evidence of knowledge, the cerebrations of a student who has little data at his disposal, confronts every student with an ethical dilemma. For some it forms an academic focus for what used to be thought of as "adolescent disillusion." It is irrelevant that rumor inflates the phenomenon to mythical proportions. The students know that beneath the myth there remains a solid and haunting reality. The moral "bind" consequent on this awareness appears most poignantly in serious students who are reluctant to concede the competitive advantage to the bullster and who yet feel a deep personal shame when, having succumbed to "temptation," they themselves receive a high grade for work they consider "dishonest."

6. I have spent many hours with students caught in this unwelcome bitterness. These hours lend an urgency to my theme. I have found that students have been able to come to terms with the ethical problem, to the extent that it is real, only after a refined study of the true nature of bull and its relation to "knowledge." I shall submit grounds for my suspicion that we can be found guilty of sharing the students' confusion of moral and epistemological issues.

I

7. I present as my "premise," then, an amoral *fabliau*. Its hero-villain is the Abominable Mr. Metzger '47. Since I celebrate his virtuosity, I regret giving him a pseudonym, but the peculiar style of his bravado requires me to honor also his modesty. Bull in pure form is rare; there is usually some contamination by data. The community has reason to be grateful to Mr. Metzger for having created an instance of laboratory purity, free from any adulteration by matter. The more credit is due him, I think, because his act was free from premeditation, deliberation, or hope of personal gain.

8. Mr. Metzger stood one rainy November day in the lobby of Memorial Hall. A junior, concentrating in mathematics, he was fond of diverting himself by taking part in the drama, a penchant which may have had some influence on the events of the next hour. He was waiting to take part in a rehearsal in Sanders Theatre, but, as sometimes happens, no other players appeared.

Perhaps the rehearsal had been canceled without his knowledge? He decided to wait another five minutes.

9. Students, meanwhile, were filing into the Great Hall opposite and taking seats at the testing tables. Spying a friend crossing the lobby toward the Great Hall's door, Metzger greeted him and extended appropriate condolences. He inquired, too, what course his friend was being tested in. "Oh, Soc. Sci. something-or-other." "What's it all about?" asked Metzger, and this, as Homer remarked of Patroclus, was the beginning of evil for him.

10. "It's about Modern Perspectives on Man and Society and All That," said his friend. "Pretty interesting, really."

11. "Always wanted to take a course like that," said Metzger. "Any good reading?"

12. "Yeah, great. There's this book"—his friend did not have time to finish.

13. "Take your seats please" said a stern voice beside them. The idle conversation had somehow taken the two friends to one of the tables in the Great Hall. Both students automatically obeyed; the proctor put blue books before them; another proctor presented them with copies of the printed hour-test.

14. Mr. Metzger remembered afterwards a brief misgiving that was suddenly overwhelmed by a surge of curiosity and puckish glee. He wrote "George Smith" on the blue book, opened it, and addressed the first question.

15. I must pause to exonerate the Management. The Faculty has a rule that no student may attend an examination in a course in which he is not enrolled. To the wisdom of this rule the outcome of this deplorable story stands witness. The Registrar, charged with the enforcement of the rule, has developed an organization with procedures which are certainly the finest to be devised. In November, however, class rosters are still shaky, and on this particular day another student, named Smith, was absent. As for the culprit, we can reduce his guilt no further than to suppose that he was ignorant of the rule, or, in the face of the momentous challenge before him, forgetful.

16. We need not be distracted by Metzger's performance on the "objective" or "spot" questions on the test. His D on these sections can be explained by those versed in the theory of probability. Our interest focuses on the quality of his

essay. It appears that when Metzger's friend picked up his own blue book a few days later, he found himself in company with a large proportion of his section in having received on the essay a C+. When he quietly picked up "George Smith's" blue book to return it to Metzger, he observed that the grade for the essay was A—. In the margin was a note in the section man's hand. It read "Excellent work. Could you have pinned these observations down a bit more closely? Compare . . . in . . . pp. . . . ."

17. Such news could hardly be kept quiet. There was a leak, and the whole scandal broke on the front page of Tuesday's *Crimson*. With the press Metzger was modest, as becomes a hero. He said that there had been nothing to it at all, really. The essay question had offered a choice of two books, Margaret Mead's *And Keep Your Powder Dry* or Geoffrey Gorer's *The American People*. Metzger reported that having read neither of them, he had chosen the second "because the title gave me some notion as to what the book might be about." On the test, two critical comments were offered on each book, one favorable, one unfavorable. The students were asked to "discuss." Metzger conceded that he had played safe in throwing his lot with the more laudatory of the two comments, "but I did not forget to be balanced."

18. I do not have Mr. Metzger's essay before me except in vivid memory. As I recall, he took his first cue from the name Geoffrey, and committed his strategy to the premise that Gorer was born into an "Anglo-Saxon" culture, probably English, but certainly "English speaking." Having heard that Margaret Mead was a social anthropologist, he inferred that Gorer was the same. He then entered upon his essay, centering his inquiry upon what he supposed might be the problems inherent in an anthropologist's observation of a culture which was his own, or nearly his own. Drawing in part from memories of table-talk on cultural relativity and in part from creative logic, he rang changes on the relation of observer to observed, and assessed the kind and degree of objectivity which might accrue to an observer through training as an anthropologist. He concluded that the book in question did in fact contribute a considerable range of " 'objective,' and even 'fresh,' " insights into the nature of our culture. "At the same time," he warned, "these observations must be understood within the context of their generation by a person only partly freed from his embeddedness in the culture he is observing, and limited in his capacity to transcend those particular tendencies and biases which he has himself developed as a personality in his interaction with this culture since his birth. In this sense the book portrays as much the character of Geoffrey Gorer as it analyzes that of the American people." It is my regrettable duty to report that at this moment of triumph Mr. Metzger was carried away by the temptations of parody and added, "We are thus much the richer."

19. In any case, this was the essay for which Metzger received his honor grade and his public acclaim. He was now, of course, in serious trouble with the authorities.

20. I shall leave him for the moment to the mercy of the Administrative Board of Harvard College and turn the reader's attention to the section man who ascribed the grade. He was in much worse trouble. All the consternation in his immediate area of the Faculty and all the glee in other areas fell upon his unprotected head. I shall now undertake his defense.

21. I do so not simply because I was acquainted with him and feel a respect for his intelligence; I believe in the justice of his grade! Well, perhaps "justice" is the wrong word in a situation so manifestly absurd. This is more a case in "equity." That is, the grade is equitable if we accept other aspects of the situation which are equally absurd. My proposition is this: if we accept as valid those C grades which were accorded students who, like Metzger's friend, demonstrated a thorough familiarity with the details of the book without relating their critique to the methodological problems of social anthropology, then "George Smith" deserved not only the same, but better.

22. The reader may protest that the C's given to students who showed evidence only of diligence were indeed not valid and that both these students and "George Smith" should have received E's. To give the diligent E is of course not in accord with custom. I shall take up this matter later. For now, were I to allow the protest, I could only restate my thesis: that "George Smith's" E would, in a college of liberal arts, be properly a "better" E.

23. At this point I need a short-hand. It is a curious fact that there is no academic slang for

the presentation of evidence of diligence alone. "Parroting" won't do; it is possible to "parrot" bull. I must beg the reader's pardon, and, for reasons almost too obvious to bear, suggest "cow."

24. Stated as nouns, the concepts look simple enough:

> cow (pure): data, however relevant, without relevancies.
>
> bull (pure): relevancies, however relevant, without data.

25. The reader can see all too clearly where this simplicity would lead. I can assure him that I would not have imposed on him this way were I aiming to say that knowledge in this university is definable as some neuter compromise between cow and bull, some infertile hermaphrodite. This is precisely what many diligent students seem to believe: that what they must learn to do is to "find the right mean" between "amounts" of detail and "amounts" of generalities. Of course this is not the point at all. The problem is not quantitative, nor does its solution lie on a continuum between the particular and the general. Cow and bull are not poles of a single dimension. A clear notion of what they really are is essential to my inquiry, and for heuristic purposes I wish to observe them further in the celibate state.

26. When the pure concepts are translated into verbs, their complexities become apparent in the assumptions and purposes of the students as they write:

To cow (*v. intrans.*) or the act of cowing:

To list data (or perform operations) without awareness of, or comment upon, the contexts, frames of reference, or points of observation which determine the origin, nature, and meaning of the data (or procedures). To write on the assumption that "a fact is a fact." To present evidence of hard work as a substitute for understanding, without any intent to deceive.

To bull (*v. intrans.*) or the act of bulling:

To discourse upon the contexts, frames of reference and points of observation which would determine the origin, nature, and meaning of data if one had any. To present evidence of an understanding of form in the hope that the reader may be deceived into supposing a familiarity with content.

27. At the level of conscious intent, it is evident that cowing is more moral, or less immoral, than bulling. To speculate about unconscious intent would be either an injustice or a needless elaboration of my theme. It is enough that the impression left by cow is one of earnestness, diligence, and painful naiveté. The grader may feel disappointment or even irritation, but these feelings are usually balanced by pity, compassion, and a reluctance to hit a man when he's both down and moral. He may feel some challenge to his teaching, but none whatever to his one-ups-manship. He writes in the margin: "See me."

28. We are now in a position to understand the anomaly of custom: As instructors, we always assign bull an E, *when we detect it;* whereas we usually give cow a C, *even though it is always obvious.*

29. After all, we did not ask to be confronted with a choice between morals and understanding (or did we?). We evince a charming humanity, I think, in our decision to grade in favor of morals and pathos. "I simply *can't* give this student an E after he has *worked* so hard." At the same time we tacitly express our respect for the bullster's strength. We recognize a colleague. If he knows so well how to dish it out, we can be sure that he can also take it.

30. Of course it is just possible that we carry with us, perhaps from our own schooldays, an assumption that if a student is willing to work hard and collect "good hard facts" he can always be taught to understand their relevance, whereas a student who has caught onto the forms of relevance without working at all is a lost scholar.

31. But this is not in accord with our experience.

32. It is not in accord either, as far as I can see, with the stated values of a liberal education. If a liberal education should teach students "how to think," not only in their own fields but in fields outside their own—that is, to understand "how the other fellow orders knowledge," then bulling, even in its purest form, expresses an important part of what a pluralist university holds dear, surely a more important part than the collecting of "facts that are facts" which schoolboys learn to do. Here then, good bull appears not as ignorance at all but as an aspect of knowledge. It is both relevant and "true." In a university setting good bull is therefore of more value than

"facts," which, without a frame of reference, are not even "true" at all.

33. Perhaps this value accounts for the final anomaly: as instructors, we are inclined to reward bull highly, *where we do not detect its intent*, to the consternation of the bullster's acquaintances. And often we do not examine the matter too closely. After a long evening of reading blue books full of cow, the sudden meeting with a student who at least understands the problems of one's field provides a lift like a draught of refreshing wine, and a strong disposition toward trust.

34. This was, then, the sense of confidence that came to our unfortunate section man as he read "George Smith's" sympathetic considerations.

II

35. In my own years of watching over students' shoulders as they work, I have come to believe that this feeling of trust has a firmer basis than the confidence generated by evidence of diligence alone. I believe that the theory of a liberal education holds. Students who have dared to understand man's real relation to his knowledge have shown themselves to be in a strong position to learn content rapidly and meaningfully, and to retain it. I have learned to be less concerned about the education of a student who has come to understand the nature of man's knowledge, even though he has not yet committed himself to hard work, than I am about the education of the student who, after one or two terms at Harvard, is working desperately hard and still believes that collected "facts" constitute knowledge. The latter, when I try to explain to him, too often understands me to be saying that he "doesn't *put in enough generalities*." Surely he has "put in *enough* facts."

36. I have come to see such quantitative statements as expressions of an entire, coherent epistemology. In grammar school the student is taught that Columbus discovered America in 1492. The *more* such items he gets "right" on a given test the more he is credited with "knowing." From years of this sort of thing it is not unnatural to develop the conviction that knowledge consists of the accretion of hard facts by hard work.

37. The student learns that the more facts and procedures he can get "right" in a given course, the better will be his grade. The more courses he takes, the more subjects he has "had," the more credits he accumulates, the more diplomas he will get, until, after graduate school, he will emerge with his doctorate, a member of the community of scholars.

38. The foundation of this entire life is the proposition that a fact is a fact. The necessary correlate of this proposition is that a fact is either right or wrong. This implies that the standard against which the rightness or wrongness of a fact may be judged exists *someplace*—perhaps graven upon a tablet in a Platonic world outside and above *this* cave of tears. In grammar school it is evident that the tablets which enshrine the spelling of a word or the answer to an arithmetic problem are visible to my teacher who need only compare my offerings to it. In high school I observe that my English teachers disagree. This can only mean that the tablets in such matters as the goodness of a poem are distant and obscured by clouds. They surely exist. The pleasing of befuddled English teachers degenerates into assessing their prejudices, a game in which I have no protection against my competitors more glib of tongue. I respect only my science teachers, authorities who *really know*. Later I learn from them that "this is only what we think *now*." But eventually, surely. . . . Into this epistemology of education, apparently shared by teachers in such terms as "credits," "semester hours" and "years of French" the student may invest his ideals, his drive, his competitiveness, his safety, his self-esteem, and even his love.

39. College raises other questions: by whose calendar is it proper to say that Columbus discovered America in 1492? How, when and by whom was the year 1 established in this calendar? What of other calendars? In view of the evidence for Leif Ericson's previous visit (and the American Indians), what historical ethnocentrism is suggested by the use of the word "discover" in this sentence? As for Leif Ericson, in accord with what assumptions do you order the evidence?

40. These questions and their answers are not "more" knowledge. They are devastation. I do not need to elaborate upon the epistemology, or rather epistemologies, they imply. A fact has become at last "an observation or an operation performed in a frame of reference." A liberal

education is founded in an awareness of frame of reference even in the most immediate and empirical examination of data. Its acquirement involves relinquishing hope of absolutes and of the protection they afford against doubt and the glib-tongued competitor. It demands an ever widening sophistication about systems of thought and observation. It leads, not away from, but *through* the arts of gamesmanship to a new trust.

41. This trust is in the value and integrity of systems, their varied character, and the way their apparently incompatible metaphors enlighten, from complementary facets, the particulars of human experience. As one student said to me: "I used to be cynical about intellectual games. Now I want to know them thoroughly. You see I came to realize that it was only when I knew the rules of the game cold that I could tell whether what I was saying was tripe."

42. We too often think of the bullster as cynical. He can be, and not always in a lighthearted way. We have failed to observe that there can lie behind cow the potential of a deeper and more dangerous despair. The moralism of sheer work and obedience can be an ethic that, unwilling to face a despair of its ends, glorifies its means. The implicit refusal to consider the relativity of both ends and means leaves the operator in an unconsidered proprietary absolutism. History bears witness that in the pinches this moral superiority has no recourse to negotiation, only to force.

43. A liberal education proposes that man's hope lies elsewhere: in the negotiability that can arise from an understanding of the integrity of systems and of their origins in man's address to his universe. The prerequisite is the courage to accept such a definition of knowledge. From then on, of course, there is nothing incompatible between such an epistemology and hard work. Rather the contrary.

44. I can now at last let bull and cow get together. The reader knows best how a productive wedding is arranged in his own field. This is the nuptial he celebrates with a straight A on examinations. The masculine context must embrace the feminine particular, though itself "born of woman." Such a union is knowledge itself, and it alone can generate new contexts and new data which can unite in their turn to form new knowledge.

45. In this happy setting we can congratulate

in particular the Natural Sciences, long thought to be barren ground to the bullster. I have indeed drawn my examples of bull from the Social Sciences, and by analogy from the Humanities. Essay-writing in these fields has long been thought to nurture the art of bull to its prime. I feel, however, that the Natural Sciences have no reason to feel slighted. It is perhaps no accident that Metzger was a mathematician. As part of my researches for this paper, furthermore, a student of considerable talent has recently honored me with an impressive analysis of the art of amassing "partial credits" on examinations in advanced physics. Though beyond me in some respects, his presentation confirmed my impression that instructors of Physics frequently honor on examinations operations structurally similar to those requisite in a good essay.

46. The very qualities that make the Natural Sciences fields of delight for the eager gamesman have been essential to their marvelous fertility.

III

47. As priests of these mysteries, how can we make our rites more precisely expressive? The student who merely cows robs himself, without knowing it, of his education and his soul. The student who only bulls robs himself, as he knows full well, of the joys of inductive discovery—that is, of engagement. The introduction of frames of reference in the new curricula of Mathematics and Physics in the schools is a hopeful experiment. We do not know yet how much of these potent revelations the very young can stand, but I suspect they may rejoice in them more than we have supposed. I can't believe they have never wondered about Leif Ericson and that word "discovered," or even about 1492. They have simply been too wise to inquire.

48. Increasingly in recent years better students in the better high schools and preparatory schools *are* being allowed to inquire. In fact they appear to be receiving both encouragement and training in their inquiry. I have the evidence before me.

49. Each year for the past five years all freshmen entering Harvard and Radcliffe have been asked in freshman week to "grade" two essays answering an examination question in History. They are then asked to give their reasons for their grades. One essay, filled with dates, is 99%

cow. The other, with hardly a date in it, is a good essay, easily mistaken for bull. The "official" grades of these essays are, for the first (alas!) C+ "because he has worked so hard," and for the second (soundly, I think) B+. Each year a larger majority of freshmen evaluate these essays as would the majority of the faculty, and for the faculty's reasons, and each year a smaller minority give the higher honor to the essay offering data alone. Most interesting, a larger number of students each year, while not overrating the second essay, award the first the straight E appropriate to it in a college of liberal arts.

50. For us who must grade such students in a university, these developments imply a new urgency, did we not feel it already. Through our grades we describe for the students, in the showdown, what we believe about the nature of knowledge. The subtleties of bull are not peripheral to our academic concerns. That they penetrate to the center of our care is evident in our feelings when a student whose good work we have awarded a high grade reveals to us that he does not feel he deserves it. Whether he disqualifies himself because "there's too much bull in it," or worse because "I really don't think I've worked that hard," he presents a serious educational problem. Many students feel this sleaziness; only a few reveal it to us.

51. We can hardly allow a mistaken sense of fraudulence to undermine our students' achievements. We must lead students beyond their concept of bull so that they may honor relevancies that are really relevant. We can willingly acknowledge that, in lieu of the date 1492, a consideration of calendars and of the word "discovered," may well be offered with intent to deceive. We must insist that this does not make such considerations intrinsically immoral, and that, contrariwise, the date 1492 may be no substitute for them. Most of all, we must convey the impression that we grade understanding qua understanding. To be convincing, I suppose we must concede to ourselves in advance that a bright student's understanding is understanding even if he achieved it by osmosis rather than by hard work in our course.

52. These are delicate matters. As for cow, its complexities are not what need concern us. Unlike good bull, it does not represent partial knowledge at all. It belongs to a different theory of knowledge entirely. In our theories of knowledge it represents total ignorance, or worse yet, a knowledge downright inimical to understanding. I even go so far as to propose that we award no more C's for cow. To do so is rarely, I feel, the act of mercy it seems. Mercy lies in clarity.

53. The reader may be afflicted by a lingering curiosity about the fate of Mr. Metzger. I hasten to reassure him. The Administrative Board of Harvard College, whatever its satanic reputations, is a benign body. Its members, to be sure, were on the spot. They delighted in Metzger's exploit, but they were responsible to the Faculty's rule. The hero stood in danger of probation. The debate was painful. Suddenly one member, of a refined legalistic sensibility, observed that the rule applied specifically to "examinations" and that the occasion had been simply an hour-test. Mr. Metzger was merely "admonished."

Read ~~by~~ for Friday.

LANCELOT LAW WHYTE

Where Do Those Bright Ideas Come From?

Lancelot Law Whyte (1896–1972), a British physicist and jet propulsion engineer who was also a social scientist and philosopher, was deeply concerned with the need for a continuing flow of new ideas. He published in his professional field and on other subjects of special interest— *Archimedes, or the Future of Physics,* 1927; *Everyman Looks Forward,* 1948; *The Next Development in Man,* 1948; *The Unitary Principle in Physics and Biology,* 1949; *Aspects of Form,* 1951; *Accent on Form,* 1954; *The Atomic Problem: A Challenge to Physicists and Mathematicians,* 1961.

In answering the question about the origin of creative thought, Mr. Whyte makes suggestions about the conditions which may stimulate the unconscious process.

> *. . . as imagination bodies forth*
> *The forms of things unknown, . . .*
> —A MIDSUMMER NIGHT'S DREAM

1. There are few experiences quite so satisfactory as getting a good idea. You've had a problem, you've thought about it till you were tired, forgotten it and perhaps slept on it, and then flash! when you weren't thinking about it suddenly the answer has come to you, as a gift from the gods. You're pleased with it, and feel good. It may not be right, but at least you can try it out.

2. Of course all ideas don't come like that, but the interesting thing is that so many do, particularly the most important ones. They burst into the mind, glowing with the heat of creation. How they do it is a mystery. Psychology does not yet understand even the ordinary processes of conscious thought, but the emergence of new

ideas by a "leap in thought," as Dewey put it, is particularly intriguing, because they must have come from somewhere. For the moment let us assume that they come from the "unconscious." This is reasonable, for the psychologists use this term to describe mental processes which are unknown to the subject, and creative thought consists precisely in what was unknown becoming known.

3. We have all experienced this sudden arrival of a happy idea, but it is easiest to examine it in the great creative figures, many of whom experienced it in an intensified form and have put it on record in their memoirs and letters. One can draw examples from genius in any realm, from religious mysticism, philosophy, and literature to art and music, and even in mathematics, science, and technical invention, though these are often thought to rest solely on logic and experiment. It seems that all truly creative activity depends in some degree on these signals from the unconscious, and the more highly intuitive the person, the sharper and more dramatic the signals become.

4. Here, for example, is Richard Wagner conceiving the prelude to "Rhinegold," as told by Wagner himself and recounted by Newman in his biography. Wagner had been occupied with the general idea of the "Ring" for several years, and for many weary months had been struggling to make a start with the actual composition. On September 4, 1863, he reached Spezia sick with dysentery, crawled to a hotel, could not sleep for noise without and fever within, took a long walk the next day, and in the afternoon flung himself on a couch intending to sleep. And then at last the miracle happened for which his subconscious mind had been crying out for so many months. Falling into a trance-like state, he suddenly felt, he says, as though he were sinking in a mighty flood of water:

> The rush and roar soon took musical shape within my brain as the chord of E-flat major, surging incessantly in broken chords. . . . Yet the pure triad of E-flat major never changed, but seemed by its steady persistence to impart infinite significance to the element in which I was sinking. I awoke from my half-sleep in terror, feeling as though the waves were rushing high above my head. I at once recognized that the orchestral prelude to the "Rhinegold," which for a long time I must have carried about within me, yet had never been able to fix definitely, had at last come to being within me; and I quickly understood the very essence of my own nature: the stream of life was not to flow to me from without, but from within.

5. In this example, which is exceptional only in the violence of the emotions, the conscious mind at the moment of creation knew nothing of the actual processes by which the solution was found. As a contrast we may take a famous story: the discovery by Henri Poincaré, the great French mathematician, of a new mathematical method called the Fuchsian functions. For here we see the conscious mind, in a person of the highest ability, actually watching the unconscious at work, if that paradox may be allowed. Poincaré describes how he came to write his first treatise on these functions.

> For a fortnight I had been attempting to prove that there could not be any function analogous to what I have since called the Fuchsian func-

tions. I was at that time very ignorant. Every day I sat down at my table and spent an hour or two trying a great number of combinations, and I arrived at no result. One night I took some black coffee, contrary to my custom, and was unable to sleep. A host of ideas kept surging in my head; I could almost feel them jostling one another, until two of them coalesced, so to speak, to form a stable combination. When morning came, I had established the existence of one class of Fuchsian functions. . . . I had only to verify the results, which took only a few hours.

6. While the Wagner story illustrates the sudden explosion of a new conception into consciousness, in this one we see the conscious mind observing the new combinations being formed in that part of the mind whose operations are normally beyond the range of conscious attention. A third type of creative experience is exemplified by the dreams which came to Descartes at the age of twenty-three and determined the path he was to follow for the rest of his life. Descartes tells how he had vainly searched for certainty, first in the world of books, and then in the world of men, and how in a triple dream on November 10, 1619, he made the crucial discovery that he could only find certainty in his own thoughts, *cogito ergo sum*. This dream filled him with intense religious enthusiasm, because it had brought to him the "simple and fertile idea, all sparkling with angelic luster" (Maritain), which provided the foundation of the "admirable science" which it was his mission to create. Freud classified this dream as one of those whose content is very close to conscious thought.

7. Wagner's, Poincaré's, and Descartes' experiences are representative of countless others in every realm of culture. The unconscious is certainly the source of instinctive activity and therefore sometimes of conflict with the demands of reason, as Freud emphasized. But in creative thought the unconscious is responsible, not for conflict, but for the production of new organized forms from relatively disorganized elements.

8. The processes of creative activity display several striking features. One of the most frequent is the occurrence of flashes of insight outside the hours of regular work, during periods of physical activity or at odd moments of reverie or relaxation when the mind is daydreaming.

Poincaré tells how the further steps of his discovery of the Fuchsian functions came to him, with a sense of absolute certainty, "just as I put my foot on the step" (of a wagonette), and again, "as I was crossing the street." Similar examples are endless, and give comforting glimpses of the ordinary daily life of genius. Mozart got the idea for the melody of the "Magic Flute" quintet while playing billiards, Berlioz found himself humming a musical phrase he had long sought in vain as he rose from a dive while bathing in the Tiber, Sir William Hamilton, a great mathematical physicist, thought of quaternions (a new mathematical method) while strolling with his wife in the streets of Dublin, and the chemist Kekulé saw the atoms dancing in mid-air and so conceived his theory of atomic groupings while riding on the top of a London bus.

9. So familiar is this phenomenon that many have taken advantage of it and have developed techniques to woo their shy genius. The prolific Haydn, with 125 symphonies and hundreds of other compositions to his credit, says, "When my work does not advance I retire into the oratory with my rosary, and say an Ave; immediately ideas come to me." Many, like Hamilton, have found that walking encourages the appearance of ideas. Thus Mozart tells how "taking a drive or walking after a good meal, or in the night when I cannot sleep, thoughts crowd into my mind as easily as you could wish"; James Watt saw how the waste of heat in a steam engine could be avoided by condensing steam, in a flash of inspiration on a walk to the golf house; Helmholtz, the German scientist and philosopher, records how "happy ideas . . . come particularly readily during the slow ascent of hills on a sunny day"; and many persons devoted to creative work have carried scraps of paper with them everywhere so that nothing of the precious flashes of revelation shall be lost.

10. "Sleeping on it" also produces good results. Sir Walter Scott used to say to himself, "Never mind, I shall have it at seven o'clock tomorrow morning." Gauss, one of the greatest mathematicians, put as heading to his paper on the "Law of Induction" the note: "Found 23rd January 1835—7.0 A.M. before rising." And Helmholtz says, "Often they come as soon as one wakes up in the morning."

11. The suddenness with which ideas come is often stressed. "You feel a little electric shock striking you in the head . . . that is the moment of genius"; so Buffon, the French biologist. In the "Hymn to Intellectual Beauty" Shelley writes:

> Sudden, thy shadow fell on me:
> I shrieked, and clasped my hands in ecstasy.

In Chopin, according to George Sand, who knew him intimately, "creation was spontaneous, miraculous . . . it would come sudden, sublime."

12. Thinkers, artists, and scientists have all described the sense of precision and inevitability, the loss of freedom of choice, or feeling of possession by an impersonal force which accompanies the creative moment. Blake declares, "I have written the poem . . . without premeditation, and even against my will," and Jacob Boehme, the German mystic of the early seventeenth century, says: "Before God I do not know how the thing arises in me, without the participation of my will. I do not even know that which I must write." Van Gogh describes how he had "a terrible lucidity at moments, when nature is so glorious. In those days, I am hardly conscious of myself and the picture comes to me like a dream." Walt Whitman says that the "fruition of beauty is no chance of hit or miss—it is as inevitable as life—it is as exact and plumb as gravitation." Russel Wallace, who published the theory of natural selection simultaneously with Darwin, expresses the views of many thinkers in saying, "Ideas and beliefs are not voluntary acts."

13. Moreover the new ideas come before they can be justified or applied. Thus Bernard Shaw's Joan of Arc says, "The voices come first, and I find the reasons after." This feature is most remarkable in the realm of science and of mathematics. Sir Isaac Newton wrote of a geometrical theorem: "It is plain to me by the fountain I draw it from, though I will not undertake to prove it to others." Like most intuitive mathematicians, he usually got the result before he could prove it; indeed one discovery of his (on the roots of equations) was only proved two hundred years later. Gauss says of one of his mathematical discoveries:

> At last I succeeded, not by painful effort, but so to speak by the grace of God. As a sudden flash of truth the enigma was solved. For my part I am not in a position to point to the

thread which joins what I knew previously to what I have succeeded in doing.

14. In the field of applied mathematics intuitive guessing sometimes proves superior to ordinary calculation. Edison says:

> In all the work connected with the building of the first Central Station, the greatest bugbears I had to contend with were the mathematicians. I found after a while that I could guess a good deal closer than they could figure, so I went on guessing.

A similar example is to be found in the design of complex electric valves, where practical, intuitive knowledge has played a major role, and one of the best living valve engineers is said to use only the multiplication table! The genius of many great experimenters, such as Faraday and Rutherford, lay in an exceptionally powerful intuition resulting from a passionate and sustained interest in a definite field of inquiry.

15. Owing to the heightened interest in psychology many studies of creative thought have been made recently, and the majority of these trace the creative element to the unconscious in the individual mind. This interpretation is supported by the recorded views of many creative personalities. Schiller held that "poetry sets out from the unconscious," and since the middle of the nineteenth century countless others have ascribed their inspiration to the working of the unconscious. But this must not be interpreted in a one-sided manner, for all thought depends on the cooperation of conscious and unconscious. The supreme type of creative thought, in certain realms at least, appears to depend on an intimate blending of unconscious and conscious processes, when both work in harmony.

16. A few writers, disliking the conception of the unconscious, have held that all true mental work is conscious, that new ideas arise by the chance association of previously formed ideas, and that "inspiration" is a romantic fiction. But this view is scarcely tenable, for an important part of all mental activity takes place behind the scenes. The working of memory and association normally lies outside the field of conscious atten-

tion, and it is only their results which flash into our awareness.

17. Graham Wallas, an English sociologist, divided the process of creative thought into four stages: conscious *Preparation,* unconscious *Incubation,* the flash of *Illumination,* and the conscious *Verification* (or application). There is as yet no accepted psychological or physiological theory of the operations of the unconscious which lead to the creation of new patterns during the period of incubation, perhaps because the sharp separation of "physical" and "mental" processes in our dualistic language has delayed the advance of a science of thought. But it seems clear that no mere rearrangement of unchanged elements can account for what happens in the unconscious creative processes. The conscious mind performs such mechanical rearrangements all the time. But the creative imagination does more: it actually changes the character of the separate elements given to it, in course of molding them into a new unity.

18. Hadamard, a French mathematician now in the United States, suggests that mathematical invention is choice guided by the aesthetic sense. That is not wide enough to cover all creation, which sometimes involves not merely choice, but in addition the molding of the elements so that they can combine to form a new whole. The coalescence, or growing together, of elements into a new unit may *change* them. This creative reshaping is evident in all branches of culture. The new unity grows out of the old and is as different from the elements that were used to make it, as the living organism is from the foodstuffs which it absorbs and assimilates. Indeed the creative processes of the mind share many features with the synthetic processes which occur throughout all living organisms.

19. It is therefore natural that the analogy of growth has often been used for creative thought. Keats liked the symbol of plant growth: "Let us open our leaves like a flower and be passive and receptive—budding patiently under the eye of Apollo." Tchaikovsky speaks of the

> germ of a future composition [coming] suddenly. . . . If the soil is ready . . . it takes root with extraordinary force and rapidity, shoots up through the earth, puts forth branches, leaves, and finally blossoms. I cannot describe

the creative process in any other way than by this simile.

20. But growth requires a seed, and the heart of the creative process lies in the production of the original fertile nucleus from which growth can proceed. This initial step in all creation consists in the establishment of a new unity from disparate elements, of order out of disorder, of shape from what was formless. The mind achieves this by the plastic reshaping, so as to form a new unit, of a selection of the separate elements derived from experience and stored in memory. Intuitions arise from richly unified experience. Henry James spoke of the "deep well of unconscious cerebration," and Coleridge of the "inward creatrix" which "establishes a center, as it were, a sort of nucleus in this reservoir of the soul."

21. Professor Lowes, in *The Road to Xanadu*, a superb study of the ways of the poetic imagination, speaks of the "incredible facility with which in the wonder-working depths of the unconscious the fragments which sink incessantly below the surface fuse and assimilate and coalesce."

22. This process of the establishment of new forms must occur in patterns of nervous activity in the brain, lying below the threshold of consciousness, which interact and combine to form more comprehensive patterns. Experimental physiology has not yet identified this process, for its methods are as yet insufficiently refined, but it may be significant that a quarter of the total bodily consumption of energy during sleep goes to the brain, even when the sense organs are at rest, to maintain the activity of ten thousand million brain cells. These cells, acting together as a single organ, achieve the miracle of the production of new patterns of thought. No calculating machine can do that, for such machines can "only do what we know how to design them to do," and these formative brain processes obey laws which are still unknown.

23. Can any practical conclusions be drawn from the experience of genius? Is there an art of thought for the ordinary person? Certainly there is no single road to success; in the world of the imagination each has to find his own way to use his own gifts. Yet a study of those who have been successful suggests some elementary hints towards a hygiene of the unconscious mind.

24. A wide range of interests is an advantage, since valuable clues may be drawn from unexpected fields. High specialism may lead to sterility.

25. When a particular task makes no progress, one can go on with something else and return to the first later on. It may pay to keep several jobs running in parallel.

26. Periods of relaxation are important, such as an hour or two alone, when no definite task is undertaken and the time is kept free for pondering over anything that comes into one's mind.

27. Finally, the less haste the better. New ideas come less easily when the mind is strained by anxiety or tense with impatience to achieve a definite result. The new grows at its own pace—"as inevitable as life."

ROBERT GRAVES

The Cool Web

Children are dumb to say how hot the day is,
How hot the scent is of the summer rose,
How dreadful the black wastes of evening sky,
How dreadful the tall soldiers drumming by.

But we have speech, to chill the angry day,
And speech, to dull the rose's cruel scent.
We spell away the overhanging night,
We spell away the soldiers and the fright.

There's a cool web of language winds us in,
Retreat from too much joy or too much fear:
We grow sea-green at last and coldly die
In brininess and volubility.

But if we let our tongues lose self-possession,
Throwing off language and its watery clasp
Before our death, instead of when death comes,
Facing the wide glare of the children's day,
Facing the rose, the dark sky and the drums,
We shall go mad no doubt and die that way.

PETER WOOLFSON

Speech Is More than Language

Peter Woolfson (1936–   ) was born in Toronto, Ontario, and educated at the University of Toronto and the State University of New York at Buffalo. He is now professor of anthropology and chairman of the Department of Anthropology at the University of Vermont. His many publications have appeared in journals of speech, linguistics, and anthropology. He also serves frequently as a consultant on bilingual and bicultural matters, especially as they concern upper New England and its French-speaking population.

His "Speech Is More Than Language" points out that language is but one of the large number of communication systems through which we interact with others, because speech includes language, paralanguage, and kinesics.

1. When we think of communication among humans, we automatically think of language: the intricate system of sounds that differentiates between words that fit into a grammatical framework that makes sense. Yet human communication is multi-dimensional, occurring within the setting of human interaction and functioning within that complex blueprint of life's activities called *culture*. Culture, itself, can be considered "an interacting set of communications."[1] It is made up of a network of communication systems in which humans interact and participate. We can see on an obvious level how all aspects of culture communicate when we walk into a doctor's office, a barbershop, a supermarket, a library, or a schoolroom. Each place has a special character that indicates its function immediately to the senses.

2. E. T. Hall in a classic work, *The Silent Language*,[2] effectively illustrates the concept of cul-

ture as communication, especially in terms of systems of time and space (*proxemics*). By examining the idea of lateness, Hall argues that there is an informal system of expectations, varying from culture to culture, that requires different responses. In America, significant units of lateness are: mumble-something periods (after five minutes); mild apology periods (after fifteen minutes); and full apology periods (after a half hour). By examining the concepts of space in different cultures, he argues that the distance between men in talking to one another and in behaving with each other provides significant information. For example, in America if a man approaches another man more closely than one arm-length—approximately two feet—the former becomes uneasy, because the violation of his territory could be interpreted as aggressiveness.

3. Although all culture communicates, the communication complex designed to carry the weight of interaction and participation is speech. *Speech* is a complex network of three interdependent communication systems: *language, paralanguage,* and *kinesics. Language* is the central and apparently most highly developed of the three communication systems, yet in actual speech it is always accompanied by the other two. *Paralanguage,* the system of extra-linguistic

[1] George L. Trager, "Paralanguage: A First Approximation," in *Language in Culture and Society,* ed. Dell Hymes (New York: Harper & Row, 1964), p. 275.
[2] Edward T. Hall, *The Silent Language* (Garden City, N.Y.: Doubleday & Company, 1959).

noises, is often thought of as "tone of voice." *Kinesics*, the system of postures, facial expressions, and bodily motions, is thought of as "body language." The three systems make an interlocking and interpenetrating communication set.

4. *Paralanguage,* as a system, was developed principally by George Trager along lines analogous to those he established for the analysis of language. One of the difficulties of paralinguistic analysis is distinguishing between language sounds and paralinguistic noises. Language sounds fall into distinctive and contrastive classes called *phonemes* that identify and distinguish among the various grammatical units of the language. Paralinguistic noises, by definition, are excluded from these classes. They function in a complementary capacity—they accompany, interpenetrate, or even substitute for language, but they are not part of it.

5. There are apparently two main classes of paralinguistic noises: *voice qualities* and *vocalizations. Voice qualities* operate as background characteristics of a person's voice: his pitch range, his articulation control, his tempo, and his rhythm. Much information is conveyed—usually without much conscious notice—by the voice qualities: an overhigh pitch can indicate nervous excitement; sloppy articulation can indicate a "high" on drugs or alcohol; a jerky rhythm can indicate insecurity. *Vocalizations* are classified into three groups: *vocal characterizers, vocal qualifiers,* and *vocal segregates. Vocal characterizers* represent such phenomena as laughing, crying, groaning, moaning, giggling, whispering, yelling. They are useful, of course, for indicating attitude. If you say the sentence "John went to the bank" using each of the characterizers listed above, you will convey a different message each time. It is this level that is meant when someone says, "It was not *what* he said that bothered me, but the *way* that he said it!" *Vocal qualifiers* represent modifications of utterances in terms of intensity (loud or soft), pitch height (high or low), and extent (drawl or clipping). They, too, indicate attitude, but not overall attitude; rather they indicate attitudes to specific lexical items. If you say the phrase "Get out" with loudness, high pitch, and clipping, you will probably be demonstrating agitated anger; however, if you say it with softness, low pitch, and drawl, you will probably be demonstrating controlled, dangerous anger. *Vocal segregates* represent such phenomena as *uh-uh, shh, tsk,* and *brr*. Vocal segregates substitute for language; for example, you can express disgust or contempt by extending the tip of your tongue and trilling your lips—an excellent way to make a "Bronx cheer."

6. *Kinesics,* as a science, was developed by Ray Birdwhistell along the lines he found in linguistics. Thus, *kines* are parallel to *phones, kinemes* to *phonemes, kinemorphs* to *morphs,* and *kinemorphemes* to *morphemes.* Kinesic messages are expressed through a variety of gestures. Doubt, for example, can be expressed in a number of ways: scratching the scalp, biting the lip, knitting the brows, pulling the ear, pulling the nose, scratching the chin, and scratching the cheek. There are all kinds of movements which have message potentials from crossing your legs to curling your toes. The kinesicist has a relatively complex system of *kinegraphs* for describing body motion within each of eight basic sections of the body: the total head, the face, the neck, the trunk, the shoulder (including arm and wrist), the hand (including finger activity), the hip (including leg and ankle), and the foot.

7. *Kinesic markers* are particularly interesting gestures because, in addition to communicating in themselves, they also complement language. In their complementary function they usually reinforce the verbal message; occasionally, however, they contradict it. For example, consider a woman who says "But I love him" while shaking her head in a negative manner. Kinesic markers are of various types. There are *pronominal markers* where the hand is directed toward an object or event and accompanies a word like *he, she, it, any,* and *some.* There are *pluralization markers* indicated by a slight sweep of the hand or head accompanying a word like *we, us, they, these,* and *our.* There are *verboid markers* which involve movement of the body forward or backward accompanying references to future or past time. There are *area markers* signaled by a movement of the body and accompanying words like *on, over, under, by, through,* and *behind.* And there are *manner markers* involving jerky or smooth motions which accompany words like *slowly, smoothly,* and *quickly.*

8. In summary, the act of speech requires a speaker and a hearer; both are members of society and participants in a culture. The communication interaction between them is very complex—they act according to the expectations

of their social roles by a blueprint provided by their culture. They speak to each other not only in words, their language, but with space, gestures, facial expressions, and body movements; with extralinguistic noises, changes in pitch, loudness, and length; accompanied by giggling, laughing, crying, moaning, groaning, whispering, and yelling. Although we are not consciously aware of many of these activities, they are a necessary part of the communication act. Speech is more than language: it is a complex network of interpenetrating communication systems.

STUART CHASE

Words and the World View

Stuart Chase (1888–   ), a well-known writer on social and economic subjects, abandoned an accountant's life to pursue a writing career. His popular books on such topics as labor relations, conservation, consumer education, and semantics have given thousands of readers an insight into the influence of these subjects on their lives. Among his books are *The Tyranny of Words*, 1938; *The Proper Study of Mankind*, 1948; *Power of Words*, 1954; *Some Things Worth Knowing: A Generalizer's Guide to Useful Knowledge*, 1958; *Live and Let Live*, 1960; *American Credos*, 1962; *Money to Grow On*, 1964; and *Danger—Men Talking*, 1969.

In this essay, from *Power of Words*, Mr. Chase discusses the broad implications of language systems—how these actually control our thoughts and our cultural outlook.

1. Linguistics as a study of patterned sounds has been called the most exact of all the social sciences. One can predict with it, and prediction is the ultimate test of any science. From this rigorous base, some linguists, especially the late Benjamin Lee Whorf, graduated into a larger inquiry: How does a given language mold the thought of the man whose mother tongue it is, and his view of nature and the world? In this inquiry the vistas are even more exciting, though prediction is probably lower.

2. Whorf, had he lived, might have become another Franz Boas or William James, so brilliant were his powers of projecting scientific data into fruitful generalizations. He died in 1941 at the age of forty-four. A graduate of M.I.T., he became an executive of the Hartford Fire Insurance Company, and took up linguistics as a hobby. Presently it became his consuming interest. His skill in deciphering Mexican inscriptions brought him to the attention of the scientific world and the close friendship of Edward Sapir. In 1930 the Social Science Research Council gave him a grant to go to Yucatan. Maya and Aztec languages led him to the live speech of American Indians, and he spent two years on Hopi alone.

3. Whorf's only book is a Hopi dictionary, an unpublished manuscript, now in the possession of Clyde Kluckhohn. He published some thirty articles in the learned journals, and might well have gone on to give the world one of the great classics of social science.

4. The forms of a man's thoughts, he said, are controlled by patterns learned early, of which the man is mostly unconscious. Thinking is a language process, whether in English, Russian, or Hopi. Every language is a complex system, with three main functions.

WORDS AND THE WORLD VIEW From *Power of Words*, copyright, 1954, by Stuart Chase. Reprinted by permission of Harcourt Brace Jovanovich, Inc.

(1) To communicate with other persons.
(2) To communicate with oneself, or, as we say, think.
(3) To mold one's whole outlook on life.

5. As he uses words, "a person notices or neglects types of relationships and phenomena, he channels his reasoning, and builds the house of his consciousness." This conclusion, says Whorf, has been largely neglected by the philosophers, but stands on unimpeachable evidence.

6. Thinking follows the tracks laid down in one's own language; these tracks will converge on certain phases of "reality," and completely bypass phases which may be explored in other languages. In English, for instance, we say, "look at that wave." But a wave in nature never occurs as a single phenomenon. In the Hopi language they say, "look at that slosh." The Hopi word, whose nearest equivalent in English is "slosh," gives a closer fit to the actual physics of wave motion, connoting movement in a mass. (This is only one of several tough matters in physics where Hopi does better than English.)

7. Perhaps the majority of linguists today, though they are not prepared to follow Whorf all the way, do recognize the vital part which language plays in thought and culture. The study of *metalinguistics*, as they call it, is thus described by Trager and Smith:

Not only does it deal with *what* people talk about and *why*, but also considers *how* they use the linguistic system, and how they react to its use. This leads further to the consideration of how the linguistic system affects the behavior, both conscious and unconscious, and the world-view, of the speaker. . . .

Contrasted with microlinguistics, which takes a long time to reach a unit as large as the sentence, the meta- or super-linguistics considers the "organization of sentences into discourse, and the relation of the discourse to the rest of the culture."

UNCONSCIOUS ASSUMPTIONS

8. Most of us were brought up to believe that talking is merely a tool which something deeper called "thinking" puts to work. Thinking, we have assumed, depends on laws of reason and logic common to all mankind. These laws are said to be implicit in the mental machinery of humans, whether they speak English or Choctaw. Languages, it follows, are simply parallel methods for expressing this universal logic. On this assumption it also follows that any logical idea can be translated unbroken, or even unbent, into any language. A few minutes in the glass palace of the United Nations in New York will quickly disabuse one of this quaint notion. Even such a common concept as "democracy" may not survive translation.

9. Another set of assumptions underlying Western culture, says Whorf, imposes upon the universe two grand cosmic forms: *space* and *time*. *Space* in our thinking is static, three-dimensional, and infinite; beyond the last area is always another area. *Time* is kinetic and one-dimensional, flowing perpetually and smoothly from the past to the present and into the future. It took the genius of Einstein to correct these cosmic assumptions, and most of us are still firmly wedded to them.

10. The assumptions underlying the culture of the Hopi also impose two grand cosmic forms upon the universe: the *objective* and the *subjective;* the manifest and the unmanifest. The first is everything accessible to the human senses, without distinction between past and present. The second is "the realm of expectancy, of desire and purpose, of vitalizing life, of efficient causes, of thought thinking itself out . . . into manifestation." It exists in the hearts and minds of animals, plants, mountains, as well as men. This subjective realm is intensely real to a Hopi, "quivering with life, power and potency."

11. All languages contain terms of cosmic grandeur. English includes "reality," "matter," "substance," "cause," "energy," as well as "space" and "time." Hopi includes the cosmic term *tunátya*, meaning a special and exalted kind of "hope." It is a verb, not a noun—the action of hoping, the stirring toward hope—and is bound up with communal ceremonies, like prayers for the harvest, and for the forming of rain clouds.

12. The ancient Greeks believed, among other things, in a universal rule of reason. This came easily because their language structure, like all Indo-European tongues, followed what is called the "subject-predicate" form. If there is a verb there must be a noun to make it work; it could not exist in its own right as pure action. The

ancient Greeks, as well as all Western peoples today, say "the light flashed." Something has to be there to make the flash; "light" is the subject; "flash" is the predicate. The whole trend of modern physics, however, with its emphasis on the *field,* is away from subject-predicate propositions. A Hopi Indian, accordingly, is the better physicist when he says *"Reh-pi"*—"flash!"—one word for the whole performance, no subject, no predicate, and no time element. (Children tend to do this too.) In Western languages we are constantly reading into nature ghostly entities which flash and perform other miracles. Do we supply them because our verbs require substantives in front of them?

13. Again, the Hopi language does not raise the question whether things in a distant village exist at the same present moment as things in one's own village. Thus it avoids the idea of *simultaneity,* which has plagued Western scientists for generations, and was only banished by relativity. The thoughts of a Hopi about events always include *both* space and time, for neither is found alone in his world view. Thus his language gets along adequately without tenses for its verbs, and permits him to think habitually in terms of space-time. For a Westerner really to understand relativity, he must abandon his spoken tongue altogether and take to the special language of calculus. But a Hopi, Whorf implies, has a sort of calculus built into him.

LINGUISTIC RELATIVITY

14. Whorf emphasizes that Hopi is only one language of one small tribe, and that there are thousands of other tongues, each imposing a unique view of nature and the cosmos upon those who speak it. Here is still another kind of relativity, a very important kind. No human is free to describe nature with strict objectivity; for he is a prisoner of his language. A trained linguist can do better because he, at least, is aware of the bondage, and can look at nature through a variety of frames. A physicist can do better by using the language of mathematics. Semanticists are now painfully learning how to do better. It is not easy for anybody. Says Whorf:

We are thus introduced to a new principle of relativity, which holds that all observers are not led by the same physical evidence to the same picture of the universe, unless their linguistic backgrounds are similar, or can in some way be calibrated.

15. Indo-European languages can be calibrated with each other: English, Italian, Spanish, French, Russian, German, Latin, Greek, and the rest, back to Indo-Hittite, all use the subject-predicate form. All speakers of these languages are capable of observing the world in a roughly similar way, at least on the high levels of "time," "space," and "matter." Hopi cannot be calibrated with them; neither can Chinese, nor thousands of other languages, living and dead.

CHINESE AND WESTERN LANGUAGES

16. Speakers of Chinese dissect nature and the universe very differently from Western speakers, with a profound effect upon their systems of belief. A Chinese writer, Chang Tung-sun, vigorously supports the relativity thesis in a monograph comparing his culture with that of the West.[1]

17. Kant imagined that he was dealing in universal categories in *The Critique of Pure Reason,* but actually, says Chang, he was only discussing standard forms of Western thought, a very limited approach. Kant's logic was of the subject-predicate variety, which is not normal in Chinese. An intelligent Chinese gentleman does not know what Kant is talking about—unless he learns some Western tongue in which to read Kant's words. (To some readers this will raise another interesting question: Did Kant himself know what he was talking about?)

18. Our Western verb "to be," observes Chang, used with an adjective predicate, implies the existence of the adjective as an independent quality. When we say "this is yellow and hard," we tend to assume the existence of two qualities, "yellowness" and "hardness," which suggests to a Chinese something Chang calls a "cosmic substance." "The substance is characterized by its attributes, and the attributes are attributed to the substance," says Chang, in considerable astonishment at such a circular performance. The verb "to be" creates great congeries of identities, and blossoms in Aristotle's laws of logic, of which the first is the law of identity, "A is A." . . .

19. No such law is possible in the Chinese

[1] *ETC,* Spring 1952.

language, where logic follows a quite different path. In Chinese, one does not attribute existence to "yellowness" and "hardness," or to polar words like "longness" and "shortness." Rather one says: "the long and the short are mutually related"; "the difficult and easy are mutually complementary"; "the front and the rear are mutually accompanying."

20. In the West we say, "This is the front of the car, and that is the rear, and let's have no more nonsense about it!" But in the Chinese view, Westerners are guilty of considerable nonsense in creating "frontness" and "rearness" as entities. Even a Westerner can see that if a car is torn in two in a crash, the part with the radiator grille becomes the "front," and the part toward the now severed windshield becomes the "rear"—*of that segment*. We can see, if we work hard enough, that there are no such entities as "frontness" or "rearness," "difficulty" or "easiness," "length" or "shortness," by themselves out there. The Chinese language has this useful correction built in; we Westerners have to sweat it out with the help of linguistics, semantics, and mathematics.

21. Linguists have also emphasized that Chinese is a "multi-valued" language, not primarily two-valued like English and Western languages generally. We say that things must be "good" or "bad," "right" or "wrong," "clean" or "dirty," "capitalistic" or "socialistic," "black" or "white"—ignoring shades of gray. When an economist talks about a middle road between "Socialism" and "Capitalism," both camps vie in their ferocity to tear him apart. (I have been that unhappy economist.)

22. Speakers of Chinese set up no such grim dichotomies; they see most situations in shades of gray, and have no difficulty in grasping the significance of a variety of middle roads. As a result, Chinese thought has been traditionally tolerant, not given to the fanatical ideologies of the West. Racial, religious, and doctrinal conflicts have been hard to maintain in China, because a Chinese speaker does not possess an unshakable confidence that he is totally right and that you are totally wrong. Observe that this is not a moral judgment, but structural in the language.

MARXISM IN CHINA?

23. This happy lack of bi-polar thinking raises a most interesting question. Communism, as formulated by Marx and developed by Lenin, is rigidly bi-polar. The heroic worker stands against the wicked capitalist and one or the other must go down. There is no place for shades of gray or for innocent bystanders in this two-valued struggle. Those who are not with us are against us! Look at almost any bulletin of the National Association of Manufacturers, or at any issue of the *Daily Worker*. Which side are you on?

24. Russian is an Indo-European language, and the two-sided choice is readily accepted by its speakers. The choice was accepted, too, by top leaders of the Chinese Communists today, for they went to Moscow to be indoctrinated, and to learn the Russian language. But 400 million Chinese have not been to Moscow or learned Russian, or any other Indo-European language, and there is small prospect of their doing so.

25. How, then, can the Chinese people become good ideological Communists, if it is impossible for them to take seriously the central idea of Marxism? Professor Nathaniel Peffer, of Columbia University, a specialist on the Far East, observes that the Chinese culture has endured many conquerors but has always managed to absorb them. Then he asks a related question: Will not the little group of "Reds" in control of the Chinese state be absorbed too? At first these leaders were accepted, he says, as part of the process of the great Chinese revolution which began in 1911. After its completion, the world may find that it was a *Chinese* revolution, not a communist one. In any event the language barrier to Marxism is formidable.

MORE SIDELIGHTS ON ENGLISH

26. The Wintu Indians of North America are even more shy of the law of identity (A is A) than the Chinese, says D. D. Lee, writing in the *International Journal of American Linguistics*.[2] We say, "this *is* bread," but in Wintu they say, "we call this bread." They avoid the "is of identity," and so are less likely to confuse words with things. When a Wintu speaks of an event not within his own experience, he never affirms it but only suggests, "perhaps it is so." When Lee asked her informant the word for "body," she was given a term signifying "the whole person." Thus the Wintus seem to have antedated the psychosomatic school.

[2] 1944. Quoted by L. Doob.

27. The Coeur d'Alene Indians of Idaho have long antedated other modern scientists. They do not speak in terms of simple cause-and-effect relations as we do, but rather in terms of *process,* as Western scientists are now painfully learning to do. Their language requires speakers to discriminate between three causal processes, denoted by three verb forms: growth, addition, secondary addition. "If, given a more sophisticated culture," says Whorf, "their thinkers erected these now unconscious discriminations into a theory of triadic causality, fitted to scientific observations, they might thereby produce a valuable intellectual tool for science." Our specialists can do this by taking thought, fortified with mathematics, but the Coeur d'Alenes seem to do it automatically.

28. In Nootka, a language of Vancouver Island Indians, a number of English nouns turn into verbs. A speaker does not say "a house," but "a house occurs." The suffixes indicate the duration of the house-event: "a long-lasting house," "a temporary house," "a future house," "a house that used to be," "what started out to be a house."

29. Eskimo, as we have noted, breaks down our single term "snow" into many words for different kinds of snow. Aztec, however, goes in the opposite direction; here we find one word, though with different terminations, for "snow," "ice," and "cold"! In Hopi, "wave," "flame," "meteor," and "lightning" are all verbs, suiting their dynamic quality. Looking into the August sky, a Hopi says: *"Reh-pi."* "It meteors!"

30. It is easier to recite the story of William Tell in the Algonquin language than in English, because it has enough possessive pronouns to make a distinction between "his," as applied to Tell, and as applied to his son. As a writer I must continually watch my step with English pronouns, lest they trip me up.

31. Linguistic relativity makes it clear that Newton took his concepts of Absolute Space and Absolute Time, not so much out of profound cogitation, as out of the language he spoke. They had been lying there for thousands of years. Both "time" and "space" affect the behavior of everyone in Western culture.

32. "Time," especially, causes us to be oriented toward calendars, dates, "the course of history," timetables, clocks, time wages, races against time, accounting, compound interest, actuarial statistics, annals, diaries, the age of the rocks, of the earth, of the solar system, of the universe. The concept of time impels us to look ahead in planning programs, schedules, appropriations, balanced budgets. Our love affair with time causes other cultures, whose languages permit a less hurried outlook, to regard us as somewhat mad.

SUMMARY OF LINGUISTICS

33. The linguists are making us realize that language is not a tool with which to uncover a deeper vein of reason, universal to all thinkers, but a shaper of thought itself. Shaping the thought, it helps to shape the culture, as in the Western cult of time. They are making us realize that we get our view of the world outside our heads probably as much from the words inside as from independent observation. When we try to become independent observers, furthermore, these words, unless we take special precautions, may distort the vision. There is no reason to suppose that English, French, Spanish, or any other Western language, with its two-valued logic, its subject-predicate form, and its law of identity, is the ultimate in a communication system.

34. A study of other cultures and their languages brings humility, together with a deeper understanding of human behavior. It brings a new concept of human brotherhood. Though the language systems differ widely, yet in their order, harmony, and subtle power of apprehending reality, they show that all men are equal. This equality, Whorf observes, is invariant and independent of race, civilization, ethical development, degree of sophistication, science, art. Such a conclusion may shock those who hold that progress is linear, with Western man on its topmost rung; but it is the conclusion to which the study of linguistics strongly points.

35. Scientists have continually collided with the unconscious assumptions imbedded in language. If their work was to continue in an orderly way, they had to improve communication. So they have invented new languages, such as tensor calculus and multivalued logic; they have erected new concepts such as the operational definition; they have sharpened ordinary language to the most exact and economical statement possible. The results of this housecleaning have been spectacular.

RICHARD MITCHELL

Darkling Plain English

Richard Mitchell (1930–   ) is a professor of English at Glassboro State College in New Jersey. His concern for the state of the English language led him to set up his own printing press on which he prints *The Underground Grammarian*, in which, often humorously, he criticizes the language of bureaucrats and academicians. His first book, *Less Than Words Can Say*, 1978, expressed his opinion that a mind can be overthrown by words and that poor use of the language is "immoral." In 1981, in his book *The Graves of Academe*, he turned his anger specifically to schools as the source of the trouble because of their lack of concern and poor teaching of the language. One critic said that in this book Mitchell turns from being a comedian to a "scourging prophet." In his most recent work, *Darkling Plain English*, from which this essay is taken, Mitchell says that the problem lies in the shift from cognitive psychology as the basis for teaching to affective psychology that deals with feelings rather than with thinking. Because of this shift, students have lost their power to reason and discriminate.

In the essay reprinted here, the author says that writers can write either so that no one can understand them or so that everyone can understand them. However, he feels that the solution is not only to improve writing, but to teach all students to read so well that they can read any English written.

1. We have all been charmed and gratified in recent times by what seems to be an official attempt to stamp out jargon and gobbledygook. From a President himself we have heard a call for plain English, and state legislatures here and there are drafting and passing laws requiring simplicity in the wording of contracts and regulations. We are delighted to see that lawyers and moneylenders, also landlords and insurance companies, are opposed to the process. Anything that displeases those odious enemies of clarity and good sense must be desirable, and the cause of plain English is beginning to attract not only politicians who see in it a safe way to please the public but many of those good-hearted citizens who used to be members of SANE.

2. Here is an example of the sort of thing that infuriates the advocates of plain English. It's an extract from one of those handbooks put out by the Occupational Safety and Health Administration, an outfit notorious not only for its torture of English but for the fact that many of its thousands of rules and regulations render each other what they call in Washington "inoperative." It's hard to decide whether the people at OSHA are simply ineffectual bumblers or supremely talented satirists boring from within. Here, for instance, is how they define an exit: "That portion of a means of egress which is separated from all other spaces of the building or structure by construction or equipment as required in this subpart to provide a protected way of travel to the exit discharge." That's not all. Now they elaborate on "means of egress": "A continuous and unobstructed way of exit travel from any point in a building or structure to a public way [which]

consists of three separate and distinct parts: the way of exit access, the exit, and the way of exit discharge."

3. That's certainly ugly, and it makes us wonder whether an exit has to be defined at all, and, if it does, why couldn't it just be called a way to get out. Then we wonder why a "means of egress" has to be defined at all, and, if it does, why couldn't it be called a way to get to the exit. If these reservations seem reasonable to you, it's because you're just not thinking. You are assuming that any ghastly mess of verbiage that comes from a bureaucracy needs to be simplified because it is needlessly complicated to begin with. Wrong. As it happens, that horrid prose serves its aims perfectly. Regulations of this nature have one clear purpose, and that is to answer, before the fact, any imaginable questions that might be asked in a court of law. For that purpose it's not enough to assume that everyone knows what an exit is. Is a door an exit? Maybe, but maybe not, if a drill press just happens to be standing in front of it. Is a hole in the wall acceptable as an exit? Do you really get out of the building (let's say it's ready to blow up) if you go through a door and find yourself in an enclosed courtyard instead of a "public way"? You don't have to be very clever to think of lots of other such questions, and the writer of this regulation is thinking about your questions. He had done a good job, although he has written something very ugly. But it's *only* ugly; it's not wrong, it's not more complicated than it has to be. It doesn't need simplification; it needs simply to be kept pretty much out of sight, lest it provide some plain English fanatics with what they think is a useful example.

4. There are, of course, lots of things that ought to be written in such English as the citizens may understand, but there are lots of citizens who ought to learn to read the English in which it is necessary to say some things. This is not a distinction that the plain English faddist is always able to make. For many of them, though, it doesn't really matter.

5. The marvelous thing about the plain English fad, for a politician, is that there's no way it can hurt him. If he fights for automobile safety or for gun control, he's bound to lose some votes and some campaign contributions. On the other hand, if he comes out against automobile safety and against gun control, he's bound to lose some votes and some campaign contributions. Politi-

cians have to balance things like this all the time, always hoping to make a little more on the peanuts than they have to lose on the popcorn. It's not easy, and they're delighted, actually, whenever they can find a cause with a high yield of profit and very little overhead. Plain English is just such a cause.

6. True, there are a few opponents of the simplification of legal and public language, but just look at them—a pack of notorious scoundrels. You can always show a profit when you castigate lawyers, moneylenders, and landlords. Not only are these enemies of good sense unpopular, but their case against plain English is difficult to present and difficult to understand, and, coming from them, sounds suspiciously self-serving. The case for plain English, on the other hand, is so easy to state and seems so reasonable that it now ranks with those splendid self-evident truths so dear to all Americans.

7. How can we tell whether or not something is written in plain English? It's simple. We have a couple of systems available that call for counting words and syllables in the average sentence and dividing something by something or maybe multiplying something by something after we have divided something by something. And there you have it—a rational, concrete index in the form of a number, a plain English score. A "good" score means, naturally, that lots of Americans can understand it, and a "bad" score means that few Americans can understand it. Theoretically it ought to be possible to write in such a way that *no* Americans can understand your English, or so that *all* Americans can understand your English. In fact, the former is common, but when we find it we rarely discover that its difficulty has anything to do with sentence length or numbers of words and syllables. The latter, however, is impossible, since there are so many Americans who can read nothing at all. Those various indexing systems are not meant to deal with the extremes. They want only to say, of this or that piece of prose, that it probably calls for an eighth-grade ability to read, or a college graduate's ability to read, or something like that. Let's hope that the scale is adjusted year by year, since this year's eighth graders, like this year's college graduates, don't read quite as well as last year's, although they do read a bit better than next year's. Unless the indexers give this some thought, we'll be faced with a continual downward revision of all

those laws and contracts and regulations, because this year's newly revised and simplified driver's license application form that almost any high school graduate can read will be, in 1994, incomprehensible to those who hold master's degrees in sociology or doctorates in education.

8. The problem has some entertaining qualities. We have found ways to produce every year more and more high school graduates who can barely read. More and more of the citizens are finding, accordingly, that more and more documents are hard to read. The automatic populists, now common among us, see an obvious solution to this problem. If the people are having trouble understanding what is written, then we must write it more simply. It's analogous to the view that if the people haven't got the brains to buckle their seat belts or to refrain from sticking their hands into the blades of their lawn mowers, then we must redesign the seat belts and the lawn mowers. We reveal thus that our national commitment to education is pious hypocrisy. If we really believed that the people could be taught, we would teach them the worth of buckling their seat belts and keeping their hands out of the lawn mower blades. We would even teach them to read, not just enough to puzzle out some slightly complicated prose, but to read, when necessary, the inevitably complicated expression of complicated ideas. It's as though you went to the hospital with a broken arm and the people in the emergency room, instead of setting the thing, got busy on the telephone trying to find you some other line of work, something that requires only one arm.

9. Like all cockeyed social notions, the plain English movement invites us to look around and see who's going to make a profit from it. A paranoid observer might think to detect a massive conspiracy. And here's how it goes: First we start providing the schools with lots of taxpayers' money to support research into quaint and curious innovations in teaching children how to read. This results in some extraordinary gimmick, and a very profitable one, not only for some professionals of education who are paid to cook it up but especially for that massive educational-industrial complex that makes and sells at high prices books and flash cards and sets of gadgets to go with every new fad. These people, of course, would like to see as many new fads as possible, because each one makes all the old stuff obsolete.

What the gimmick is, is not important, for a while, and in some schools still, it was the weird notion that reading would be better taught without reference to the sounds of letters but rather through identifying whole words as symbols of something. The latest gimmick seems to be speed reading, which will make it possible, at a stiff price, to read a complete gothic romance in three minutes and forty seconds, thus ensuring a steady market for gothic romances. A well-trained keypunch operator could go through sixteen of them on her lunch hour, provided of course that she ate something like a sandwich or a slice of pizza. Speed reading does require the use of at least one hand.

10. Let the gimmick be whatever it is. Think of your own, if you need an example, something like printing vowels in different colors or providing new and tricky shapes for certain letters. These, of course, have been done, so you'll have to stretch a bit; and, when you do come up with something that seems unspeakably zany, keep your mouth shut. If you mention it in public, it won't be long before someone offers to fund it. It's best to avoid offering the occasion for sin. But enough. Let's say we have a gimmick.

11. Now we experiment, being careful to use methods and controls that would make a first-year chemistry student blush and stating the problems and the expected results (those we call "outcomes") in the silliest possible jargon. Don't worry, we'll "prove" the efficacy of our gimmick (remember the new math?). As a result, or outcome, although we'd rather not use that word in the singular, more and more students in the public schools will read less and less.

12. Do not make the mistake of thinking that this means that our gimmick has failed. Pay attention. This means that the gimmick has succeeded. Remember, we have taken the role of dentists handing out lollipops to ensure that there will be no falling off of customers. Now that things are worse than ever, we view with alarm the "reading problem" in the schools. It's time for a new round of grants, projects, experimental proposals, expensive consultants, packets of materials, instruction booklets, sets of visual aids, more teachers, carpeted classrooms, air conditioning, just about anything you can imagine. It's all good for the education business, and if it seems to have been exaggerated, just you go footing around yourself and find anybody anywhere

who proposes that we can teach reading (or anything else) better by spending less money.

13. If there were a conspiracy that worked all these wonders, you can imagine the joy of the conspirators in the windfall that the plain English agitation has brought them. In one way it's a happy result of that conspiracy, and perhaps, therefore, not unexpected. Naturally, as fewer and fewer literate people move out of the schools and start signing leases and borrowing money for Corvettes and stereo systems, it more and more appears that the documents put before them are just too hard. They're always too hard for somebody; it's just that now we have more and more of those somebodies, and the problem grows more visible. It becomes a cause; it suddenly seems that we can make a case for rudimentary English as one of an American's inalienable rights. You deprive him of that—it's practically like forbidding the sale of classic comics or those benoveled versions of movies. It's a splendid cause for politicians and educationists, especially, because anyone who opposes it must do so either out of some devious special interest by which he lives or out of a positively un-American elitism intended to maintain a rigid class structure and deprive the ignorant of access to professorships in philosophy and literature. Both politicians and educationists will profit from the cause, the politicians at once, in good will and support from the public, and the educationists somewhat later, in more grants, and because they will sooner or later be the very ones called on to do the necessary simplifying.

14. The bureaucrats who have produced most of our dismal official English will, at first, be instructed to fix it. They will try, but *nihil ex nihilo.* That English is the mess it is because they did it in the first place and they'll never be able to fix it. They write that kind of stuff because that is the kind of stuff that they write. Ultimately, in desperation, they will call on those people who say they know about these things—the professionals of reading and writing. There will be lucrative jobs and consultancies available in every branch and department of government for remedial-reading teachers. The foxes will be made the guardians of the hen house.

15. Here is an example of what the bureaucrats will do when left to their own devices. The following passage is from a document called "Draft Regulations to Implement the National Environmental Policy Act." It *has* been rewritten into what they call plain English, and a covering letter from the chairman of the President's Council on Environmental Quality says that it "represents an extraordinary improvement over the existing guidelines":

> The agency need make the finding of no significant impact available for public review for thirty days before the agency makes its final determination whether to prepare an environmental impact statement and before the action may begin only in one of the following limited circumstances: . . .

Remember, this has been simplified; the original is hard to imagine. There are no difficult words in this passage—even the five syllables of "determination" do not make it a difficult word, whatever they might do to the passage's score. What these people *mean* by "determination" might be better served by "judgment" or even "decision," but still, most readers will not be baffled by "determination." In fact, there's nothing at all—neither word nor thought—nothing at all difficult for any moderately educated reader in that passage. Why then is it so hard to understand? Why do you have to read it over a couple of times, should you really care to know what it means? Does this passage, already simplified from God knows what, need further simplification? No. All it needs is a little attention to the stuff that used to be taught to sixth-grade students back in the days when sixth-grade students actually wrote compositions.

16. People who have learned even a little about how English works have all heard about modifiers. They know that a modifier is something that tells us something about something, and that there are many kinds of modifiers, some with tricky names. The way we teach things like this, as though they were subject to arbitrary rules like the rules of basketball, is so stupid and tedious that most people block out modifiers as soon as possible. The English system of modification, however, does not exist in a set of paltry rules that do what they can, and fail, to describe some very elaborate operations not simply of the language but of the mind. To say that an adjective modifies a noun is worth nothing unless we see that sticking adjectives on nouns is the outward equivalent of some mysterious inward

process that goes on in the mind. It's not entirely absurd to think that somewhere in the past of mankind someone, for the first time, did in his mind the equivalent of putting an adjective to a noun, and saw, not only a relationship, but *this* special relationship between two things of different kinds. That moment was more important to our history than the flight of the Wright brothers. In sum, all the seemingly complicated kinds of modification in English are just ways of thinking and seeing how things go with each other or reflect each other. Modifiers in our language are not *aids* to understanding relationships; they are *the ways* to understand relationships. A mistake in this matter either comes from or causes a clouded mind. Usually it's both.

17. This passage clouds our minds not because what it means to say is difficult, not because the matter is too technical for most of us, but for a very simple reason. In effect, it says that the agency need do something only under certain circumstances. That's a clear thought. They need do A only when B. The nature of the relationship between A and B is tucked into the words "need . . . only." In the passage, thirty-four words intervene between "need" and "only," so that by the time we see "only" we have forgotten to expect any further modification of "need." It's like finding one more step when you thought you had reached the landing. Between those two words, furthermore, we may have been a bit bewildered by something that sounds like a modification but isn't: "impact available for public review." It takes a moment to look back and see that "available for public review" is actually supposed to go with "finding." When we add to those two failures—failures of the writing to match the modification systems of the mind—the tedious parade of words and clauses not yet related to any idea that we can identify, the passage becomes what it is, awkward, puzzling, and exasperating. It requires of us more attention and backtracking than its ideas are worth.

18. This passage does not need simplification or even a change in its choice of words. It needs merely to have been written by someone with elementary skills in finding the right thing to do on the page to call forth certain things in the mind. The idea is not complicated; the prose, in fact, is not complicated—it's just bad. Nevertheless, it *could* be simplified even using that vocabulary. Here's how it might go:

In some cases, a finding of no significant impact *does* have to be made available for public review. Public review means that you have to give the public thirty days to look it over before you can even decide whether to write an environmental impact statement, and certainly before any action is taken. Here are the cases in which you do have to provide the public review:

There. All we need now is to draw little pictures.

19. The people who write like this write like this simply because they are the people who write like this. Even when you can convince them that there is something wrong with what they have written, you cannot make them into people who wouldn't write like this. If you send them to go and fix it, you'll get what you deserve—it's like hoping the termites will build you a new house out of the glop they have made of your old one.

20. So the bureaucrats will need help, and lo, help is at hand. The educational establishment that has provided the problem will come forward to be paid for the solution. Thus firefighters sometimes set fires so that they can try out the new pumper. Hosts of advisers and consultants will be added to bureaucracies of all kinds. New courses of study will appear in the schools to prepare people for such lucrative and respectable labors. New courses of study will appear in the teacher-training academies to prepare the teachers for the teaching of new courses of study that will prepare the advisers and consultants. New journals of the new study will blossom; new workshops and conferences will convene from Tacoma to Key West; new federal grants will support studies that will find new findings. If you had any sense at all, you'd buy some stock right now.

21. There is, of course, an alternative to the plain English fad, but it's almost too dangerous to discuss in public. We could simply decide to educate all Americans to such a degree that they could read and understand even the OSHA definition of an exit. We could even educate them well enough so that they could understand why OSHA has to say things like that and why it doesn't matter much. We could have the schools devote lots of time, especially in the early grades, to spelling and vocabulary and even writing so that the next generation will grow up able to

grasp relative clauses and complex sentences at sight and understand at once the meaning of "reciprocal" and "indemnify" and even "mitigate." This sounds so easy and so right that there must be a catch, and indeed there is. When we consider the inevitable consequences of such a policy, we can see that it is probably too dangerous to contemplate.

22. Just think what happens in the mind of the person who knows the difference between restrictive and nonrestrictive clauses. Anyone who understands that distinction is on the brink of seeing the difference between simple fact and elaborative detail and may well begin to make judgments about the logic of such relationships. He may start bothering his head about the difference between things essential and things accidental, a disorder that often leads to the discovery of tautologies. Furthermore, anyone who sees the difference between restrictive and nonrestrictive clauses is likely to understand *why* modifiers should be close to the things they modify and thus begin to develop a sense of the way in which ideas grow from one another. From that, it's not a long way to detecting non sequiturs and unstated premises and even false analogies.

23. Unfortunately, we just don't know how to teach skillful reading and writing without developing many undesirable and socially destructive side effects. Should we raise up a generation of literate Americans, very little of the America that we know would survive. We depend on a steady background level of ignorance and stupid-

ity. A skillful reader, for instance, cannot be depended upon to buy this after-shave rather than some other because he is always weighing and considering statements that just weren't meant to be weighed and considered. He may capriciously and irresponsibly switch not only from one after-shave to another but even from one hot comb to another. Our industries depend on what we call "brand loyalty," and thoughtful readers will all be brand traitors. They may, even probably will, go the next step and become brand nihilists who decide not to buy any aftershave or hot comb at all. It may even occur to them that the arguments for the ownership of trash compacters and toaster ovens are specious, and then they won't buy any trash compacters or toaster ovens. Economic chaos will follow.

24. The next thing you know they'll start listening very carefully to the words and sentences of the politicians, and they'll decide that there isn't one of them worth voting for anywhere on the ballot. There's no knowing where this will end. The day will come when a President is elected only because those few feebleminded citizens who still vote just happened to bump up against his lever more often than they bumped up against the other guy's lever. A President, of course, doesn't care how he gets elected, but he might lose clout among world leaders when they remind him that he owes his high office to the random twitchings of thirty-seven imbeciles. That will be the end of network election coverage as we know it.

BERGEN EVANS

Grammar for Today

Bergen Evans (1904–1978), who was professor of English at Northwestern University, had a special interest in radio and television programs, having served as a lively moderator of a popular television show entitled "Down You Go." The appearance in 1957 of *A Dictionary of Contemporary American Usage,* a volume he and his sister Cornelia edited, created much criticism, both favorable and unfavorable. His books include *Dictionary of Quotations,* 1968; and *Dictionary of Mythology,* 1970.

In this essay he gives his reasons for believing that contemporary descriptive grammar is more valid than the traditional prescriptive grammar.

1. In 1747 Samuel Johnson issued a plan for a new dictionary of the English language. It was supported by the most distinguished printers of the day and was dedicated to the model of all correctness, Philip Dormer Stanhope, Fourth Earl of Chesterfield. Such a book, it was felt, was urgently needed to "fix" the language, to arrest its "corruption" and "decay," a degenerative process which, then as now, was attributed to the influence of "the vulgar" and which, then as now, it was a mark of superiority and elegance to decry. And Mr. Johnson seemed the man to write it. He had an enormous knowledge of Latin, deep piety, and dogmatic convictions. He was also honest and intelligent, but the effect of these lesser qualifications was not to show until later.

2. Oblig'd by hunger and request of friends, Mr. Johnson was willing to assume the role of linguistic dictator. He was prepared to "fix" the pronunciation of the language, "preserve the purity" of its idiom, brand "impure" words with a "note of infamy," and secure the whole "from being overrun by . . . low terms."

3. There were, however, a few reservations. Mr. Johnson felt it necessary to warn the oversanguine that "Language is the work of man, a being from whom permanence and stability cannot be derived." English "was not formed from heaven . . . but was produced by necessity and enlarged by accident." It had, indeed, been merely "thrown together by negligence" and was in such a state of confusion that its very syntax could no longer "be taught by general rules, but [only] by special precedents."

4. In 1755 the *Dictionary* appeared. The noble patron had been given a great deal more immortality than he had bargained for by the vigor of the kick Johnson had applied to his backside as he booted him overboard. And the *Plan* had been replaced by the *Preface,* a sadder but very much wiser document.

5. Eight years of "sluggishly treading the track of the alphabet" had taught Johnson that the hopes of "fixing" the language and preserving its "purity" were but "the dreams of a poet doomed at last to wake a lexicographer." In "the boundless chaos of living speech," so copious and energetic in its disorder, he had found no guides except "experience and analogy." Irregularities were "inherent in the tongue" and could not be "dismissed or reformed" but must be permitted

"to remain untouched." "Uniformity must be sacrificed to custom . . . in compliance with a numberless majority" and "general agreement." One of the pet projects of the age had been the establishment of an academy to regulate and improve style. "I hope," Johnson wrote in the *Preface*, that if "it should be established . . . the spirit of English liberty will hinder or destroy [it]."

6. At the outset of the work he had flattered himself, he confessed, that he would reform abuses and put a stop to alterations. But he had soon discovered that "sounds are too volatile and subtle for legal restraints" and that "to enchain syllables and to lash the wind are equally undertakings of pride unwilling to measure its desires by its strength." For "the causes of change in language are as much superior to human resistance as the revolutions of the sky or the intumescence of the tide."

7. There had been an even more profound discovery: that grammarians and lexicographers "do not form, but register the language; do not teach men how they should think, but relate how they have hitherto expressed their thoughts." And with this statement Johnson ushered in the rational study of linguistics. He had entered on his task a medieval pedant. He emerged from it a modern scientist.

8. Of course his discoveries were not strikingly original. Horace had observed that use was the sole arbiter and norm of speech and Montaigne had said that he who would fight custom with grammar was a fool. Doubtless thousands of other people had at one time or another perceived and said the same thing. But Johnson introduced a new principle. Finding that he could not lay down rules, he gave actual examples to show meaning and form. He offered as authority illustrative quotations, and in so doing established that language is what usage makes it and that custom, in the long run, is the ultimate and only court of appeal in linguistic matters.

9. This principle, axiomatic today in grammar and lexicography, seems to exasperate a great many laymen who, apparently, find two hundred and five years too short a period in which to grasp a basic idea. They insist that there are absolute standards of correctness in speech and that these standards may be set forth in a few simple rules. To a man, they believe, of course, that they speak and write "correctly" and they

are loud in their insistence that others imitate them.

10. It is useless to argue with such people because they are not, really, interested in language at all. They are interested solely in demonstrating their own superiority. Point out to them—as has been done hundreds of times—that forms which they regard as "corrupt," "incorrect," and "vulgar" have been used by Shakespeare, Milton, and the Bible and are used daily by 180 million Americans and accepted by the best linguists and lexicographers, and they will coolly say, "Well, if they differ from me, they're wrong."

11. But if usage is not the final determinant of speech, what is? Do the inhabitants of Italy, for example, speak corrupt Latin or good Italian? Is Spanish superior to French? Would the Breton fisherman speak better if he spoke Parisian French? Can one be more fluent in Outer Mongolian than in Inner Mongolian? One has only to ask such questions in relation to languages other than one's own, language within which our particular snobberies and struggles for prestige have no stake, to see the absurdity of them.

12. The language that we do speak, if we are to accept the idea of "corruption" and "decay" in language, is a horribly decayed Anglo-Saxon, grotesquely corrupted by Norman French. Furthermore, since Standard English is a development of the London dialect of the fourteenth century, our speech, by true aristocratic standards, is woefully middle-class, commercial, and vulgar. And American speech is lower middle-class, reeking of counter and till. Where else on earth, for instance, would one find crime condemned because it didn't *pay!*

13. In more innocent days a great deal of time was spent in wondering what was the "original" language of mankind, the one spoken in Eden, the language of which all modern tongues were merely degenerate remnants. Hector Boethius tells us that James I of Scotland was so interested in this problem that he had two children reared with a deaf and dumb nurse on an island in order to see what language they would "naturally" speak. James thought it would be Hebrew, and in time, to his great satisfaction, it was reported that the children were speaking Hebrew!

14. Despite this experiment, however, few people today regard English as a corruption of

Hebrew. But many seem to think it is a corruption of Latin and labor mightily to make it conform to this illusion. It is they and their confused followers who tell us that we can't say "I am mistaken" because translated into Latin this would mean "I am misunderstood," and we can't say "I have enjoyed myself" unless we are egotistical or worse.

15. It is largely to this group—most of whom couldn't read a line of Latin at sight if their lives depended on it—that we owe our widespread bewilderment concerning *who* and *whom*. In Latin the accusative or dative form would always be used, regardless of the word's position in the sentence, when the pronoun was the object of a verb or a preposition. But in English, for at least four hundred years, this simply hasn't been so. When the pronoun occurs at the beginning of a question, people who speak natural, fluent, literary English use the nominative, regardless. They say "Who did you give it to?" not "Whom did you give it to?" But the semiliterate, intimidated and bewildered, are mouthing such ghastly utterances as a recent headline in a Chicago newspaper: WHOM'S HE KIDDING?

16. Another group seems to think that in its pure state English was a Laputan tongue, with logic as its guiding principle. Early members of this sect insisted that *unloose* could only mean "to tie up," and present members have compelled the gasoline industry to label its trucks *Flammable* under the disastrous insistence, apparently, that the old *Inflammable* could only mean "not burnable."

17. It is to them, in league with the Latinists, that we owe the bogey of the double negative. In all Teutonic languages a doubling of the negative merely emphasizes the negation. But we have been told for a century now that two negatives make a positive, though if they do and it's merely a matter of logic, then three negatives should make a negative again. So that if "It doesn't make no difference" is wrong merely because it includes two negatives, then "It doesn't never make no difference" ought to be right again.

18. Both of these groups, in their theories at least, ignore our idiom. Yet idiom—those expressions which defy all logic but are the very essence of a tongue—plays a large part in English. We go to school and college, but we go to *the* university. We buy two dozen eggs but a couple of dozen. *Good and* can mean *very* ("I am good and mad!") and "a hot cup of coffee" means that the coffee, not the cup, is to be hot. It makes a world of difference to a condemned man whether his reprieve is *upheld* or *held up*.

19. There are thousands of such expressions in English. They are the "irregularities" which Johnson found "inherent in the tongue" and which his wisdom perceived could not and should not be removed. Indeed, it is in the recognition and use of these idioms that skillful use of English lies.

20. Many words in the form that is now mandatory were originally just mistakes, and many of these mistakes were forced into the language by eager ignoramuses determined to make it conform to some notion of their own. The *s* was put in *island*, for instance, in sheer pedantic ignorance. The second *r* doesn't belong in *trousers*, nor the *g* in *arraign*, nor the *t* in *deviltry*, nor the *n* in *passenger* and *messenger*. Nor, so far as English is concerned, does that first *c* in *arctic* which so many people twist their mouths so strenuously to pronounce.

21. And grammar is as "corrupted" as spelling or pronunciation. "You are" is as gross a solecism as "me am." It's recent, too; you won't find it in the Authorized Version of the Bible. *Lesser, nearer,* and *more* are grammatically on a par with *gooder. Crowed* is the equivalent of *knowed* or *growed,* and *caught* and *dug* (for *catched* and *digged*) are as "corrupt" as *squoze* for *squeezed* or *snoze* for *sneezed*.

22. Fortunately for our peace of mind most people are quite content to let English conform to English, and they are supported in their sanity by modern grammarians and linguists.

23. Scholars agree with Puttenham (1589) that a language is simply speech "fashioned to the common understanding and accepted by consent." They believe that the only "rules" that can be stated for a language are codified observations. They hold, that is, that language is the basis of grammar, not the other way round. They do not believe that any language can become "corrupted" by the linguistic habits of those who speak it. They do not believe that anyone who is a native speaker of a standard language will get into any linguistic trouble unless he is misled by snobbishness or timidity or vanity.

24. He may, of course, if his native language

is English, speak a form of English that marks him as coming from a rural or an unread group. But if he doesn't mind being so marked, there's no reason why he should change. Johnson retained a Staffordshire burr in his speech all his life. And surely no one will deny that Robert Burns' rustic dialect was just as good a form of speech as, and in his mouth infinitely better as a means of expression than, the "correct" English spoken by ten million of his southern contemporaries.

25. The trouble is that people are no longer willing to be rustic or provincial. They all want to speak like educated people, though they don't want to go to the trouble of becoming truly educated. They want to believe that a special form of socially acceptable and financially valuable speech can be mastered by following a few simple rules. And there is no lack of little books that offer to supply the rules and promise "correctness" if the rules are adhered to. But, of course, these offers are specious because you don't speak like an educated person unless you are an educated person, and the little books, if taken seriously, will not only leave the lack of education showing but will expose the pitiful yearning and the basic vulgarity as well, in such sentences as "Whom are you talking about?"

26. As a matter of fact, the educated man uses at least three languages. With his family and his close friends, on the ordinary, unimportant occasions of daily life, he speaks, much of the time, a monosyllabic sort of shorthand. On more important occasions and when dealing with strangers in his official or business relations, he has a more formal speech, more complete, less allusive, politely qualified, wisely reserved. In addition he has some acquaintance with the literary speech of his language. He understands this when he reads it, and often enjoys it, but he hesitates to use it. In times of emotional stress hot fragments of it may come out of him like lava, and in times of feigned emotion, as when giving a commencement address, cold, greasy gobbets of it will ooze forth.

27. The linguist differs from the amateur grammarian in recognizing all of these variations and gradations in the language. And he differs from the snob in doubting that the speech of any one small group among the language's more than 300 million daily users constitutes a model for all the rest to imitate.

28. The methods of the modern linguist can be illustrated by the question of the grammatical number of *none*. Is it singular or plural? Should one say "None of them is ready" or "None of them are ready"?

29. The prescriptive grammarians are emphatic that it should be singular. The Latinists point out that *nemo*, the Latin equivalent, is singular. The logicians triumphantly point out that *none* can't be more than one and hence can't be plural.

30. The linguist knows that he hears "None of them are ready" every day, from people of all social positions, geographical areas, and degrees of education. He also hears "None is." Furthermore, literature informs him that both forms were used in the past. From Malory (1450) to Milton (1650) he finds that *none* was treated as a singular three times for every once that it was treated as a plural. That is, up to three hundred years ago men usually said *None is*. From Milton to 1917, *none* was used as a plural seven times for every four times it was used as a singular. That is, in the past three hundred years men often said *None is*, but they said *None are* almost twice as often. Since 1917, however, there has been a noticeable increase in the use of the plural, so much so that today *None are* is the preferred form.

31. The descriptive grammarian, therefore, says that while *None is* may still be used, it is becoming increasingly peculiar. This, of course, will not be as useful to one who wants to be cultured in a hurry as a short, emphatic permission or prohibition. But it has the advantage of describing English as it is spoken and written here and now and not as it ought to be spoken in some Cloud-Cuckoo-Land.

32. The descriptive grammarian believes that a child should be taught English, but he would like to see the child taught the English actually used by his educated contemporaries, not some pedantic, theoretical English designed chiefly to mark the imagined superiority of the designer.

33. He believes that a child should be taught the parts of speech, for example. But the child should be told the truth—that these are functions of use, not some quality immutably inherent in this or that word. Anyone, for instance, who tells a child—or anyone else—that *like* is used in English only as a preposition has grossly misinformed him. And anyone who complains that

its use as a conjunction is a corruption introduced by Winston cigarettes ought, in all fairness, to explain how Shakespeare, Keats, and the translators of the Authorized Version of the Bible came to be in the employ of the R. J. Reynolds Tobacco Company.

34. Whether formal grammar can be taught to advantage before the senior year of high school is doubtful; most studies—and many have been made—indicate that it can't. But when it is taught, it should be the grammar of today's English, not the obsolete grammar of yesterday's prescriptive grammarians. By that grammar, for instance, *please* in the sentence "Please reply" is the verb and *reply* its object. But by modern meaning *reply* is the verb, in the imperative, and *please* is merely a qualifying word meaning "no discourtesy intended," a mollifying or de-imperatival adverb, or whatever you will, but not the verb.

35. This is a long way from saying "Anything goes," which is the charge that, with all the idiot repetition of a needle stuck in a groove, the uninformed ceaselessly chant against modern grammarians. But to assert that usage is the sole determinant in grammar, pronunciation, and meaning is *not* to say that anything goes. Custom is illogical and unreasonable, but it is also tyrannical. The latest deviation from its dictates is usually punished with severity. And because this is so, children should be taught what the current and local customs in English are. They should not be taught that we speak a bastard Latin or a vocalized logic. And they should certainly be disabused of the stultifying illusion that after God had given Moses the Commandments He called him back and pressed on him a copy of Woolley's *Handbook of English Grammar.*

36. The grammarian does not see it as his function to "raise the standards" set by Franklin, Lincoln, Melville, Mark Twain, and hundreds of millions of other Americans. He is content to record what they said and say.

37. Insofar as he serves as a teacher, it is his business to point out the limits of the permissible, to indicate the confines within which the writer may exercise his choice, to report that which custom and practice have made acceptable. It is certainly not the business of the grammarian to impose his personal taste as the only norm of good English, to set forth his prejudices as the ideal standard which everyone should copy. That would be fatal. No one person's standards are broad enough for that.

ARTHUR BERGER

Hot Language and Cool Lives

Arthur Berger (1933–   ), who received his Ph.D. in American Studies from the University of Minnesota, currently teaches at San Francisco State University. A recognized expert on popular culture, Berger is also the film and television review editor for *Society* and writes a television column for *Focus*. Among his published works in the field of popular culture are *The Comic Stripped American*, 1974, and *The TV-Guided American*, 1975.

"Hot Language and Cool Lives" examines the use of exaggeration or hyperbole in modern English. Berger suggests that perhaps a schism between our "jazzed up" language and mundane existences has begun to develop.

HOT LANGUAGE AND COOL LIVES   Reprinted from *ETC.*, Vol. XXVIII, No. 3 (1971), by permission of the International Society for General Semantics.

1. There is a fish that always delights me whenever I take my children to the aquarium. It is a slender rather trivial thing that has the ability to puff itself up into a big ball and scare off (hopefully) other fish that might wish to attack it. It is literally a big windbag, yet this defense mechanism works—well enough, at least, for other windbags to be born and survive.

2. The whole business is quite absurd except that it does work, and what is more fantastic, with people as well as with fishes. A lot of people are leading rather luke-warm lives, if not cool (and not in the sense of "good" as some use the term) or tepid lives, yet they describe themselves and their actions in terms of what might be called "hot" language.

3. I can recall once overhearing two bored youths at a tennis court. Said one of them, "Let's split," a phrase much in usage these days, in fitting with the schizophrenic nature of the times. Somehow "splitting" from a place is much more exciting than "going someplace else" or "leaving."

4. Is it not possible that there is a direct correlation between a growing sense of powerlessness and futility in our lives and the jazzed-up language we use? The more you feel yourself diminished the more you "build yourself up" by using hot language, showing that you are in some kind of an "in" group, and know what's going on. It is only natural to try to represent oneself in the best possible light, but if we study the way people do this, we find that this hot or inflated language is somewhat self-defeating.

5. As everything becomes inflated and *tremendous*, the word loses its currency. What is normal becomes tremendous. What then do we say about something that really is tremendous? It seems that the more we use hot language to add color to our otherwise colorless lives, the less utility the hot language has; it becomes devalued, and we have to work harder for less, so to speak. What used to be large is now "giant king size," and we have reached the point of no return.

6. Perhaps there is some kind of a searching for the infinite at work. In a recent advertisement from a humane society, various kinds of memberships were announced: Annual $5, Patron $10, Life $100, Perpetual $250. A lifetime is no longer enough. We must have a rate for those who would be immortal. On the opposite side of the fence death must be made more final, some-how. Thus we find ads for insecticides claiming that they "kill bugs *dead!*"

7. It may be that we can now think of killing without death—for as everything grows out of control and the fantastic becomes the commonplace (men on the moon on prime-time television), the old words like the old lifestyle become, somehow, inadequate. We need more and more emphasis and must be told that when something is killed it will be dead.

8. Television commercials have bred within the average American a skepticism that must somehow be overcome. We find all about us claims that are obviously absurd: on menus, travel brochures, book jackets, etc. The law of diminishing returns is at work. Since people now believe less and less, you have to promise more and more to come out even. In this sense advertising is self-defeating for it (more than anything else) has created this skepticism, which it keeps attacking and forcing at the same time.

9. The use of this hot language is symptomatic of a certain malaise affecting people, which leads them to believe that life must at all times be exciting, vital, dazzling, full of "fabulous" experiences. This is nonsense, obviously. Everyone—even "world historical figures" such as leaders of great nations or movie celebrities—spends a great deal of his time doing routine, ordinary things. Thus, the use of hot language makes us *devalue* our lives, since we take a rather absurd conception of what is normal, measure our lives against this false norm, and find ourselves wanting. We all want to lead Giant King Size lives in an age when there are few giants or kings. Since we cannot, we then define ourselves as leading lives of quiet desperation, describe life as absurd and meaningless, and try to escape from all this by consumerism, drugs, or some other kind of narcoticism.

10. A distinguished sociologist, Leo Lowenthal, has discussed a form of hot language, the use of "superlatives," in the following manner:

> This wholesale distribution of highest ratings defeats its own purpose. Everything is presented as something unique, unheard of, outstanding. Thus nothing is unique, unheard of, outstanding. Totality of the superlative means totality of the mediocre. It levels the presentation of human life to the presentation of merchandise.

He wrote this in reference to the tendency of contemporary writers to use superlatives in biographies done for popular magazines. Lowenthal noticed that there was a change from early biographies that didn't use superlatives and dealt with heroes of production to recent biographies (around 1940) that used superlatives and were about heroes of consumption. On first sight the superlatives didn't seem very significant, until their real function was discovered. This was, Lowenthal suggested, to create "a reign of psychic terror, where the masses have to realize the pettiness and insignificance of their everyday life. The already weakened consciousness of being an individual is struck another heavy blow by the pseudo-individualizing forces of the superlative."

11. This was written in the forties, when we had "stars." How does the ordinary man feel in the seventies, in an era when being a "star" is no longer significant, since we now have *"superstars"?* When the star is relegated to mediocrity, what do we say about the average citizen? The fact is significant that we now use terms such as the "little guy"; his stature and significance are diminishing greatly, and he is on the verge of becoming a "forgotten" American.

Author's postscript: It is curious but behind such terms as "groovy," "my bag," and "heavy," there is a suggestion of containment and control. Could it be that many of the "now" generation are really seeking a bit of guidance and direction?

RICHARD N. OSTLING

Unmanning the Holy Bible

The Sexual-Textual Revolution Comes to Scripture

Richard N. Ostling (1940–   ) was educated at the University of Michigan, Northwestern University, and George Washington University. He was reporter and copyreader for a newspaper in Wilmington, Delaware in 1963–64; assistant news editor of *Christianity Today* in 1965–67 and news editor in 1967–69. He became religion correspondent for *Time* magazine in 1969 and is now *Time's* religion editor. He wrote *Secrecy in the Church: A Reporter's Case for the Christian's Right to Know* in 1974.

In "Unmanning the Holy Bible," Ostling, in collaboration with a colleague, John Kohan, discusses an issue of linguistic, religious, and social importance—a matter certain to receive varied responses—removing sexist language from new translations of the Bible.

What is a human being that you are mindful of him, and a mortal that you care for him?
1. Sound familiar but somehow flat? The more famous rendering of *Psalms 8: 4* is rather more

ringing: "What is man that thou art mindful of him, and the son of man that thou dost care for him?" But Christians in the English-speaking world had better get used to the neutered wording, for it may appear in the new edition of the Revised Standard Version of the Bible due a decade from now. The reworked RSV will include hundreds of such language changes made in the cause of stripping Scripture of "sexism."

2. The use of "inclusive language," intended to put women on a textual par with men, has long since been accepted in many areas of U.S. publishing, such as school textbooks and children's fables. But its application to the Bible is already stirring an unholy row. The immediate point of contention is the RSV, now being updated by a committee of 25 scholars and translators. Their efforts will have far-reaching importance. With millions of copies sold worldwide since it first appeared in 1952, the RSV is by far the most broadly used Bible translation in modern English.

3. Precisely because of its influence, the RSV is now a target of Protestant feminists and other critics who want to purge it of the male chauvinism that they find running all through its pages, Says the Rev. Jeanne Audrey Powers, a United Methodist mission official: "People are becoming increasingly sensitive to language that renders half the human race invisible." As it happens, such sentiment is strong in the National Council of Churches (N.C.C.), whose education division is overseeing the RSV revision. But the N.C.C.'s leaders have hesitated to alter the RSV radically, partly because the organization gets the royalties. The RSV has been a success largely because of its preservation of much of the evocative language of its antecedent, the King James Bible of 1611. So after the education division decided to prepare a new edition of the RSV, it instructed its translators to get rid of as much "masculine-biased language" as possible while retaining the King James "flavor."

4. The man in charge of the RSV revision is the Rev. Bruce M. Metzger, 66, a gentlemanly New Testament professor at Princeton Theological Seminary. While Metzger is conservative on matters of doctrine, he is willing to avoid male nouns and pronouns—where the original Hebrew and Greek texts allow it. Thus the reference in *Romans 14: 1* to "the *man* who is weak in faith" will likely become "the *one* who is weak . . ." In *Psalms*, the first verse will read "Blessed *are those* who walk not in the counsel of the wicked," rather than "Blessed *is the man* who walks not . . ." In *Psalms* alone, more than 200 male pronouns will be dropped.

5. Even these limited word changes are too much for many traditionalists, among them the Rev. E. Earle Ellis of New Brunswick Theological Seminary in New Jersey, who quit Metzger's group in protest. With all the sensitivity over sexism, he complains, the emerging Bible "is taking on the nature of a paraphrase," and the rewrites are sacrificing important nuances in meaning. For instance, Ellis grants that the use of "human being" instead of "man" in the new *Psalms 8: 4* is defensible as a perfectly literal translation from the original Hebrew. But he argues that the change is reckless since in the context of the psalm, "man" could also imply Adam, an ideal king, or some other individual. So could the banished phrase "son of man," a New Testament title associated with Jesus as the Messiah. Declares Ellis: "Whatever we think, the text has a right to be heard. You cannot cover over words just because the meaning is an embarrassment to certain modern movements."

6. For their part, militants on Bible sexism protest that Metzger's translators are too fastidious in holding to traditional language about God and Christ. An eight-man, five-woman Bible translation "task force" that includes officials and scholars from six N.C.C. denominations has declared that Metzger's committee should "move more boldly." Among suggested changes, they want women to get equal billing in passages where the original text names only males: Sarah should be included along with mentions of Abraham, for example, and Eve ought to appear when Adam does. Moreover, the hard-liners propose that Jesus should be called the "Child of God" instead of the "Son of God." Also, the impersonal pronoun *it* should replace *he* in references to the Spirit of God when the original Greek is neuter, notwithstanding Christian teaching that the Spirit is a person. Finally, since God has no gender, use of *he, him* and *his* should be minimized; a properly de-sexed *Romans 8: 29*, for instance, would say, "Those whom *God* foreknew, *God* also predestined to be conformed to the image of *God's child* . . ."

7. During a meeting at the N.C.C.'s New York City headquarters last week, leaders of the education division rejected such radical proposals but did agree to add feminists to Metzger's group as vacancies occur. Discussion of how to tackle alleged "racism, classism and anti-Semitism" in the Bible was postponed. Metzger assailed the militants' approach as unscholarly and "intolerable." As for the inclusive-language issue, he said firmly, "I do not find much clamor for this in the

churches. Most people find sexist language in regard to persons irrelevant and, concerning God, irreverent."

8. Nonetheless, the education division did approve a recommendation to work on a different Bible translation that would more fully meet feminist demands. The first step toward what some religious wags are already calling the "Unisex Bible" will be translation of a new lectionary, the series of Bible readings listed for worship each week in many denominations. The N.C.C. expects to show whether a "completely inclusive-language Bible translation" is feasible.

9. As the skirmishing over Bible bias continues, some church feminists are beginning to voice an argument made by traditionalist foes: at bottom, the ancient texts are what they are. Roman Catholic Sister Ann Patrick Ware, of New York City, a top theology executive at the N.C.C., points out resignedly: "There are parts of Scripture that are sexist, and there is nothing you can do about them." Of course, she adds, "you don't have to read them, either."

THEODORE ROETHKE

Double Feature

With Buck still tied to the log, on comes the light.
Lovers disengage, move sheepishly toward the aisle
With mothers, sleep-heavy children, stale perfume, past the manager's smile
Out through the velvety chains to the cool air of night.

I dawdle with groups near the rickety pop-corn stand;
Dally at shop windows, still reluctant to go;
I teeter, heels hooked on the curb, scrape a toe;
Or send off a car with vague lifts of a hand.

A wave of Time hangs motionless on this particular shore.
I notice a tree, arsenical grey in the light, or the slow
Wheel of the stars, the Great Bear glittering colder than snow,
And remember there was something else I was hoping for.

CARLL TUCKER

Writing in the Dark

Carll Tucker (1951–   ), author and editor, was born in New York City and educated at Yale University. He began his career in 1969 as a columnist for the *Patent Trader*, a local newspaper in the suburbs north of New York. Then he became theatre critic and book columnist for the *Village Voice* from 1974 to 1977, and was then named editor of the *Saturday Review*, for which he had been writing a regular feature, "The Back Door."

In "Writing in the Dark," Tucker shows the importance of print, and by implication the importance of those who write what gets into print. He concludes that print and freedom of thought are inextricably linked—that we cannot live without freedom of thought, and that it is maintained by print.

1. Moments of transition jog us to reflection. They remind us that though we may sometimes ignore time, it never returns the favor. Having to face the transitoriness of all things forces us to ask ourselves whether what we do with our time has value.

2. It is a healthful exercise. Journalists, like many other souls, tend to *assume* that their occupation is important, without bothering to explore the proposition. The risk of such negligence is that it prevents the development of values. Unless one knows one's underlying goals, one cannot judge whether one is making progress toward them, whether one is doing well or poorly.

3. In my view, print journalism has never been so necessary to the health of our body politic as it is today. History shows that there are invariable swings between ages of "reason" or reliance on man's intellect and ability to solve his problems and ages of "faith" or superstition, when man is viewed as a slave to some higher Purpose. Ages of reason tend to be characterized by optimism and human accomplishments; ages of faith tend

to be gloomy, oppressive, and stagnant. In broadest outline, Western history has experienced three such swings: the emergence of a man-centered world view in Greece and Rome, followed by the Dark Ages, followed by a renaissance of belief in man. The Industrial Revolution was fueled by optimism that man could achieve a better world through technology. The United States was founded on the radical faith that ordinary men working together could manage their mutual destiny better than any king or priest.

4. Today, the signs suggest a return to an era of unreason. The worldwide rise of fundamentalism bespeaks a disillusion with man-made solutions. In overthrowing the Shah, the Iranian revolutionaries rejected not only a tyrant but the notion of progress altogether. The indifference of the American people to the electoral process suggests that we no longer share the Founding Fathers' buoyant belief that our votes matter. The murderous violence reported in last month's Miami riots, where individuals were brutally mutilated for the hell of it, is evidence of a deep malaise in the American soul. There is a vast difference between social action, however violent,

and barbarism: The one is born of optimism, the other of utter hopelessness.

5. A degree of discouragement is understandable. For decades, American industry has promised us Nirvana-via-consumption; better things must result in better living. Meanwhile, television has vivified the disparities between rich and poor, sharpening frustrations. And we have all come to realize that for many social problems there are no quick fixes. Indeed, solutions often spawn worse problems than those they were intended to solve. It is not impossible to sympathize with Ayatollah Khomeini's assertions that Western technology and commerce are inventions of the Devil. His pronouncements about greedy industrialists raping the earth might be echoed by the residents of Love Canal.

6. It is natural enough in such a perplexed environment for the thought to take hold that if man can't solve his problems, maybe Somebody Else can. It is tempting to try to rid oneself of the problems by placing one's faith in a Superman.

7. The importance of print in such a time is to persuade us of the implausibility of any such desperate solutions. Print is the least emotional means of communication. Television and radio are dramatic media: We end up buying Ultra-Brite or Walter Cronkite because of their appeal to our gut, not our intellect. As Orson Welles demonstrated in 1938, the electronic media have the terrifying capacity to persuade us instantly that Martians have landed.

8. Print is an analytic medium. With print one can dissect complicated problems into their component parts. The more imposing the problem, the more important it is that its solution be predicated on analysis. Whatever momentary satisfactions the Iranian rulers derived from exiling Western technocrats or taking hostages, the impoverishment of the Iranian people is too high a price to pay for them. If the Iranian leaders had analyzed their objectives, they surely would have selected a different course.

9. Print is, furthermore, an enduring medium. The truth in print survives. Demagogues invariably detest print if they cannot control it. In an era of uncertainty, when our confidence is wobbly and our convictions are shaken by emotional gusts, print serves as an anchor to our reason, reminding us that there are no easy or instant solutions.

10. The dangers I perceive are not imminent. I do not expect the majority of Americans in the next few months to go crazy, like the Miami rioters, or, like Mount St. Helens, to blow their tops. The pendulum swings imperceptibly, by increments. Surely the dissatisfaction with technology is widening. Our faith in reasonable solutions has been buffeted. Either we will build a postindustrial world sensitively and sensibly, or we will rebel against sense altogether. In either event, print will help to protect our freedom of thought—the only freedom without which we cannot live.

FRANK TRIPPETT

The Growing Battle of the Books

Frank Trippett (1926–   ) grew up in Columbus, Mississippi, and attended Mississippi College, the University of Mississippi, and Duke University. He was a reporter for several Southern newspapers before moving to *Newsweek* in 1961 as associate editor for national affairs, and then to *Look* magazine as senior editor in 1968. Since 1971 he has been a free-lance editor and writer, and now is a senior writer for *Time* magazine.

In this essay, Trippett says that "censorship can place people in bondage more efficiently than chains." He cites the alarming increase in numbers of overt incidents of book censorship in this country, many of them caused by people who have not read the books they want to "burn." Apparently the motive for urging censorship is more often a need to exert power over others than a wish to destroy a particular book.

1. Written words running loose have always presented a challenge to people bent on ruling others. In times past, religious zealots burned heretical ideas and heretics with impartiality. Modern tyrannies promote the contentment and obedience of their subjects by ruthlessly keeping troubling ideas out of their books and minds. Censorship can place people in bondage more efficiently than chains.

2. Thanks to the First Amendment, the U.S. has been remarkably, if not entirely, free of such official monitoring. Still, the nation has always had more than it needs of voluntary censors, vigilantes eager to protect everybody from hazards like ugly words, sedition, blasphemy, unwelcome ideas and, perhaps worst of all, reality. Lately, however, it has been easy to assume that when the everything-goes New Permissiveness gusted forth in the 1960s, it blew the old book-banning spirit out of action for good.

3. Quite the contrary. In fact, censorship has been on the rise in the U.S. for the past ten years.

Every region of the country and almost every state has felt the flaring of the censorial spirit. Efforts to ban or squelch books in public libraries and schools doubled in number, to 116 a year, in the first five years of the 1970s over the last five of the 1960s—as Author L. B. Woods documents in *A Decade of Censorship in America—The Threat to Classrooms and Libraries, 1966-1975.* The upsurge in book banning has not since let up, one reason being that some 200 local, state and national organizations now take part in skirmishes over the contents of books circulating under public auspices. The American Library Association, which has been reporting an almost yearly increase in censorial pressures on public libraries, has just totted up the score for 1980. It found, without surprise, yet another upsurge: from three to five episodes a week to just as many in a day. Says Judith Krug, director of the A.L.A.'s Office for Intellectual Freedom: "This sort of thing has a chilling effect."

4. That, of course, is precisely the effect that censorship always intends. And the chill, whether intellectual, political, moral or artistic, is invariably hazardous to the open traffic in ideas that not

only nourishes a free society but defines its essence. The resurgence of a populist censorial spirit has, in a sense, sneaked up on the nation. National attention has focused on a few notorious censorship cases, such as the book-banning crusade that exploded into life-threatening violence in Kanawha County, W. Va., in 1974. But most kindred episodes that have been cropping up all over have remained localized and obscure. The Idaho Falls, Idaho, school book review committee did not make a big splash when it voted, 21 to 1, to ban *One Flew Over the Cuckoo's Nest*—in response to one parent's objection to some of the language. It was not much bigger news when Anaheim, Calif., school officials authorized a list of *approved* books that effectively banned many previously studied books, including Richard Wright's classic *Black Boy*. And who recalls the Kanawha, Iowa, school board's banning *The Grapes of Wrath* because some scenes involved prostitutes?

5. Such cases, numbering in the hundreds, have now been thoroughly tracked down and sorted out by English Education Professor Edward B. Jenkinson of Indiana University in a study, *Censors in the Classroom—The Mind Benders*. He began digging into the subject after he became chairman of the Committee Against Censorship of the National Council of Teachers of English. His 184-page report reviews hundreds of cases (notorious and obscure), suggests the scope of censorship activity (it is ubiquitous), discusses the main censorial tactics (usually pure power politics) and points to some of the subtler ill effects. Popular censorship, for one thing, induces fearful teachers and librarians to practice what Jenkinson calls "closet censorship." The targets of the book banners? Jenkinson answers the question tersely: "Nothing is safe."

6. Case histories make that easy to believe. The books that are most often attacked would make a nice library for anybody with broad-gauged taste. Among them: *Catcher in the Rye, Brave New World, Grapes of Wrath, Of Mice and Men, Catch-22, Soul on Ice,* and *To Kill a Mockingbird. Little Black Sambo* and *Merchant of Venice* ran into recurring protests based on suspicions that the former is anti-black, the latter anti-Semitic. One school board banned *Making It with Mademoiselle,* but reversed the decision after finding out it was a how-to pattern book for youngsters hoping to learn dressmaking. Authori-

ties in several school districts have banned the *American Heritage Dictionary* not only because it contains unacceptable words but because some organizations, the Texas Daughters of the American Revolution among them, have objected to the sexual intimations of the definition of the word bed as a transitive verb.

7. Censorship can, and often does, lead into absurdity, though not often slapstick absurdity like the New Jersey legislature achieved in the 1960s when it enacted a subsequently vetoed antiobscenity bill so explicit that it was deemed too dirty to be read in the legislative chambers without clearing out the public first. The mother in Whiteville, N.C., who demanded that the Columbus County library keep adult books out of the hands of children later discovered that her own daughter had thereby been made ineligible to check out the Bible. One group, a Florida organization called Save Our Children, has simplified its censorship goals by proposing to purge from libraries all books by such reputed homosexuals as Emily Dickinson, Willa Cather, Virginia Woolf, Tennessee Williams, Walt Whitman and John Milton.

8. Most often, censors wind up at the ridiculous only by going a very dangerous route. The board of the Island Trees Union Free School District on Long Island, N.Y., in a case still being contested by former students in court, banned eleven books as "anti-American, anti-Christian, anti-Semitic and just plain filthy." Later they discovered that the banished included two Pulitzer prizewinners: Bernard Malamud's *The Fixer* and Oliver La Farge's *Laughing Boy.* For censors to ban books they have never read is commonplace. For them to deny that they are censoring is even more so. Said Attorney George W. Lipp Jr., announcing plans to continue the legal fight for the Island Trees board: "This is not book burning or book banning but a rational effort to transmit community values."

9. Few censors, if any, tend to see that censorship itself runs counter to certain basic American values. But why have so many people with such an outlook begun lurching forth so aggressively in recent years? They quite likely have always suffered the censorial impulse. But they have been recently emboldened by the same resurgent moralistic mood that has enspirited evangelical fundamentalists and given form to the increas-

ingly outspoken constituency of the Moral Majority. At another level, they probably hunger for some power over something, just as everybody supposedly does these days. Thus they are moved, as American Library Association President Peggy Sullivan says, "by a desperation to feel some control over what is close to their lives."

10. Americans are in no danger of being pushed back to the prudery of the 19th century. The typical U.S. newsstand, with its sappy pornutopian reek, is proof enough of that, without even considering prime-time TV. But the latter-day inflamed censor is no laughing matter. One unsettling feature of the current censorial vigilantism is its signs of ugly inflammation. There is, for instance, the cheerily incendiary attitude expressed by the Rev. George A. Zarris, chairman of the Moral Majority in Illinois. Says Zarris: "I would think moral-minded people might object to books that are philosophically alien to what they believe. If they have the books and feel like burning them, fine." The notion of book burning is unthinkable to many and appalling to others, if only because it brings to mind the rise of Adolf Hitler's Germany—an event marked by widespread bonfires fed by the works of scores of writers including Marcel Proust, Thomas Mann, H. G. Wells and Jack London.

11. Unthinkable? In fact, the current wave of censorship has precipitated two of the most outrageous episodes of book burning in the U.S. since 1927, when Chicago Mayor William ("Big Bill") Thompson, an anglophobe miffed by a view sympathetic to the British, had a flunky put the torch on the city hall steps to one of Historian Arthur Schlesinger Sr.'s books. In Drake, N. Dak., the five-member school board in 1973 ordered the confiscation and burning of three books that, according to Professor Jenkinson, none of the members had read: Kurt Vonnegut's *Slaughterhouse Five,* James Dickey's *Deliverance* and an anthology of short stories by writers like Joseph Conrad, John Steinbeck and William Faulkner. Said the school superintendent later: "I don't regret it one bit, and we'd do it again. I'm just sorry about all the publicity that we got." In Warsaw, Ind., a gaggle of citizens in 1977 publicly burned 40 copies of *Values Clarifications,* a textbook, as a show of support for a school board that decided to ban both written matter and independent-minded teachers from its system. Said William I. Chapel, a member of that board: "The bottom line is: Who will control the minds of the students?"

12. An interesting question. It baldly reveals the ultimate purpose of all censorship—mind control—just as surely as the burning of books dramatizes a yearning latent in every consecrated censor. The time could not be better for recalling something Henry Seidel Canby wrote after Big Bill Thompson put Arthur Schlesinger to the flame. Said Canby: "There will always be a mob with a torch ready when someone cries, 'Burn those books!'" The real bottom line is: How many more times is he going to be proved right?

JOHN CULHANE

Leapin' Lizards! What's Happening to the Comics?

John Culhane (1934–   ), a free-lance writer and recognized film historian, is absorbed with comedy, clowns, comics, and animated cartoons. He was asked to teach the first courses for credit about the history of the animated cartoon. In November, 1978, he was master of ceremonies at the Library of Congress for the fiftieth-anniversary commemoration of the first appearance of Mickey Mouse from the Walt Disney Studios. He writes frequently for the *New York Times Magazine, Saturday Review,* and *Reader's Digest.* He was coauthor of the script "Noah's Animals," an animated cartoon for television, and author of *Special Effects in the Movies: How They Do It,* 1981.

In this essay Culhane explains the decline of the serious serial comic strip, such as "Little Orphan Annie," and hails the arrival of "the new generation of sophisticated funnies" like "Doonesbury," which provide us with present-day images of our aspirations and do not promote nostalgia.

1. After mass, the newsboys would have their stacks of Sunday papers piled up at the bottom of the broad stone steps leading down to the sidewalk from old St. Mary's, competing for our patronage in the good old free enterprise way. My father read The Chicago Herald & Examiner and The Rockford Morning Star, so we kids were assured of their comic sections; but unless we could also persuade him to buy The Chicago Tribune, we could not follow the adventures of "Terry and the Pirates," "Smilin' Jack," "Dick Tracy" and "Little Orphan Annie." Even though Dad disliked The Tribune for being anti-Roosevelt, he would usually indulge us; then we could keep the Sunday boredom at bay until the good radio shows started in the evening, lying flat on our stomachs on the living room rug, with the color comics of three newspapers spread out before us. Believe it or not, we had no difficulty keeping in mind from week to week the continuing adven-

tures of several dozen heroes on land ("Joe Palooka"), sea ("Don Winslow of the Navy") and air ("Smilin' Jack"), and in the past ("Prince Valiant"), present ("Gasoline Alley") and future ("Flash Gordon" and "Buck Rogers, 25th Century A.D.")

2. But then, at Thanksgiving of 1943, my Dad went into the Army. My mother, trying to get along on his allotment check, stopped getting any Sunday paper except the local one—which was needed to know who had been reported killed, missing or wounded in action. From that time on, I had to wait for the periodic paper drives, when I could collect old newspapers, turn to their comic sections and catch up on the funnies before turning them in up at the schoolhouse. This scrambled continuity didn't make any difference in reading "Blondie," but it made it very difficult for me to follow the adventure strips. For example, it was nearly Easter of 1944 before I found the installment of "Little Orphan Annie" for Christmas of 1943. It sticks in my mind because it seemed to express my political

views so perfectly. It showed Annie kneeling before her bed and praying: "Bless Uncle Spike and Auntie Sally . . . and bless 'Daddy' . . . and all our men out there . . . whose courage makes it possible for millions o' us kids to grow up here in decency and *peace!*" In the next picture, "Daddy" Warbucks paused while hacking his way through what in those days we called a "Jap-infested jungle" to look up at the evening star and say to his faithful Punjab and Asp: "Christmas Eve! Back home she'll be saying her prayers . . . From Herod to Hitler and Hirohito! But the prayers of all the Little Annies are greater than all the Herods of all time!"

3. Leapin' Lizards! Since that wartime Christmas at Easter, 30 years have gone by! Us millions o' kids did grow up here in decency and peace, and we begat many millions more, while Little Orphan Annie stayed the same age (11 or 12) that she was when she first appeared on a comic page 50 years ago next August 5. For all these years, she has faced up to one danger after another with blunked-out eyes. But this year, she finally succumbed to the one kind of danger no comic-strip hero can survive. Two weeks ago [in April, 1974], at the 50-year-old age of 11 or 12, Little Orphan Annie died of circulation trouble.

4. The condition resulted from complications following television. First, there was the competition from television for the time the audience has to spend being entertained. Why follow one story in "Little Orphan Annie" for eight weeks when you can get eight stories in eight weeks on "Kung Fu"? How can a newspaper adventure strip compete with a television program that is essentially an adventure strip that moves, in color, on a panel eight columns wide and four comic strips high? To make the competition more unequal, television has also caused an economic crisis in the newspaper business; this, aggravated by recent newsprint shortages, has resulted in less space for comic strips—a condition that hits story strips hardest because it takes away the space they need for dialogue, settings and props. And, lastly, television has been a major factor in social changes since the Second World War which have rendered most prewar heroes obsolete.

5. At least five story men and artists tried to keep Annie alive after the death of her creator, Harold Gray, in 1968. But the formula that made the strip popular for so long belonged to another

time. Underscoring this truth was the decision of the Chicago Tribune–New York News Syndicate, which owns "Little Orphan Annie," to offer reruns of old Harold Gray strips to newspapers, starting with her 1936 adventures on the road during the Great American Depression. This decision to "go to reruns," as they say in TV-land, served to make "Little Orphan Annie" a thing of the past even more than her simple disappearance might have. For the syndicate's idea, according to its president, Robert S. Reed, is to appeal to "the current mood of nostalgia for the good things of the past."

6. The decline of "Little Orphan Annie" is no small event, for it was one of the most popular comic strips of all time. A survey conducted by the Opinion Research Corporation in 1962 found it the third most popular strip in the comics—after "Blondie" and "Dick Tracy." In those days, when The Washington Post tried to drop the strip, angry Annie fans picketed the paper. At its peak (in the forties) it was running in over 500 papers.

7. Furthermore, Annie's demise is part of a wider trend—the general decline of the serious adventure serial comic strip. Last year, for example, on Feb. 25, the Chicago Tribune–New York News Syndicate ended the 38-year run of "Terry and the Pirates" rather than seeking a successor for the artist, George Wunder, who resigned. Wunder conceded that the strip's readership had been declining for some time. "People just don't seem to follow continuity strips any more the way they used to," he says. And less than two months later, on April 1, the syndicate also ended the 40-year run of its other flying-adventure strip, "Smilin' Jack." Its creator, Zack Mosley, in his sixties as was Wunder, was retiring, and the syndicate did not name a successor.

8. Those who put out surviving adventure strips are far from sanguine these days. Chester Gould, 73-year-old creator of "Dick Tracy," warns that adventure strips will have to be better and better to stay alive. "The strip that stands still will be tossed out in the face of competition," he says. And Milton Caniff, who had created the syndicate-owned "Terry and the Pirates" but abandoned it in 1946 for the chance to own his own story strip, "Steve Canyon," has admitted that he is running scared. He says he's cut the length of his episodes from twelve weeks down to eight in an effort to hold readers.

9. Robert Gillespie, promotion director of the Chicago Tribune–New York News Syndicate, says flatly that "the comics are in a state of change. The joke strip is in, the story strip's in trouble. The strong ones still survive, but the weaker ones die or run in fewer papers, and there have been few new continuity strips over the last five years."

. . .

10. In 1957, Leo Bogart, director of research for the American Newspaper Publishers Association, made a study of New York readers and found that "Annie" had "a strong appeal to persons who feel weak or frustrated. For them, the strip . . . permits regression to the happy days of childhood by introducing an all-powerful father-image who can always be counted upon to set things right." Well, that fits me, all right. I loved "Little Orphan Annie" at a time when I wanted my own daddy to come home and take charge and make everything come out all right. But he was off to war, so my mother and us kids had to do the best we could. As a result, I couldn't justify my actions with "Father Knows Best," and could hardly understand the Watergate defendants who justified actions they would ordinarily consider wrong by pleading that the President's office had authorized them, and the President should know best.

11. Instead of the authoritarianism of the unfunny funnies, there is about the sophisticated funnies a skepticism that I find healthy. You see it in Pogo's famous comment when he found his beloved swamp polluted with garbage. Instead of blaming it on any of the hate objects and objects of righteous superiority feelings that Gray used as enemies (politicians, bureaucrats, spies and other foreigners), he simply said, "We have met the enemy, and they is us."

12. Kelly, of course, was more than a cartoonist; he was a philosopher. He expounded his philosophy in fun—his goal was always the laugh that liberates—but he had as much common sense in his strips as Harold Gray had humbug. As president of the National Cartoonists Society in 1954 (his peers had chosen him cartoonist of the year for 1952), he campaigned to cut down on the crime and horror in comic strips. It was an idea whose time had come: "Superman was created in the Depression as an icon, a Nietzsche superman," Carmine Infantino, editorial director of National Comics, explained in 1970. "At that time, people needed a perfect being." In other words, we were scared. As Walt Kelly wrote, "Laughter can always be depended upon to well up out of the balanced mind and the courage of truth, right where it started many thousands of years ago. Wit shrivels and laughter dies when we submerge ourselves in images of perfection, in fear and trembling." And as harsh experiences have destroyed our innocence, we have seen that the heroes of the unfunny funnies are the real jokes.

13. "Doonesbury" is the perfect example of the new generation of sophisticated funnies. The artist, Gary Trudeau, was born in 1948, the year that Walt Kelly launched "Pogo," and he has grown up on comics that get their laughs out of wit rather than slapstick. "Charles Schulz and Walt Kelly had the most profound influence on me as far as the writing goes, and Jules Feiffer had the most important influence on me as far as drawing goes—particularly in my early cartoons," says Trudeau. His early cartoons were for The Yale Daily News in 1969, when he was a Yale undergraduate majoring in art. "The strip was called 'Bull Tales' and it was about a football player named B.D., who was based on Brian Dowling, the Yale quarterback. Most of the episodes took place in a huddle."

14. The strip was a campus sensation, which was duly noted in a story in The New York Times, and that story was duly noted by John McMeel, who was about to become president of the Universal Press Syndicate, which was founded in 1970 and which acquired Sheed & Ward, the religious publishing house, and led it into secular pastures. "We had just launched Garry Wills as a columnist and we were looking for good young talent. So we subscribed to college newspapers, trying to find a writer who deserved to be syndicated nationally. My partner, Jim Andrews, who is the editor of the syndicate and is about my age [38], spotted this strip in The Yale Daily News and wanted to syndicate it, and I remembered the story in The Times, so we decided to gamble. We started selling it in 1970 with a release date of Oct. 26. We started with only 27 or 28 papers, but they included The Washington Post, The Boston Globe and The Chicago Tribune, which went all the way in promoting it."

15. "Doonesbury" now runs in 347 papers, with an estimated daily readership of 18 million persons. "'Doonesbury's' well-earned popularity is based on the pithy way its characters sink their teeth into contemporary subjects," said The Washington Post. "The strip is created with sure-handed sophistication." An example was during the Vietnam war, when B.D. dropped out of school and joined the Army to avoid a term paper. B.D. got sent to Vietnam, where he got lost and was captured by a Viet Cong terrorist named Phred. They became dependent upon each other for survival, and Phred saved them both from starvation by finding a cache of Schlitz that the Viet Cong had stolen from the U.S. supply depot. In the end they become the best of friends. "It seemed the way I could make a statement about the war most effectively," said Trudeau. "I placed two individuals who, under normal circumstances, would be the bitterest of enemies into a situation where their mutual survival depended on their understanding of their common humanity."

16. "Sweetness and light—who the hell wants it?" groused Harold Gray in 1964, as the trend toward joke strips got stronger and stronger. "What's news in the newspapers? Murder, rape and arson. That's what stories are made of."

17. That's true enough; but the kind of heroes the comic page offers no longer provide us with images of our aspirations. We no longer believe in the hero as soldier, as fighter pilot, as astronaut: Television has shown them all too close up. The hero as detective is bigger than ever in this guilt-ridden society, so Dick Tracy survives; but life-styles have changed, and it is hard to imagine him sharing a squad car with Frank Serpico. And as for "Daddy" Warbucks, the hero as billionaire is absolutely out. To the newspaper reader of the thirties and forties, Howard Hughes was a dashing aviator-movie producer who won round-the-world airplane races and pioneered depth cleavage in a Jane Russell movie called "The Outlaw." To the readers of the seventies, Hughes is a comic and/or sinister recluse who makes huge, anonymous political contributions and served as a model for the kidnaped billionaire saved by James Bond in "Diamonds Are Forever." What My Lai and Watergate have shown is that Americans have grown up from being blind hero-worshipers. We no longer confuse the man with his role, and we believe in the man only as long as he acts ethically. (Is that the reason that Gray wouldn't let Annie grow up—because she might have caught on to "Daddy"?) What we need now is not heroes but lots of citizens with a respect for truth, a sense of balance and a sense of humor.

18. So good-by, "Little Orphan Annie," living symbol with blunked-out eyes; and hello, "Little Orphan Annie," shade of Gray. And welcome back to the funnies, funnies. Perhaps, in whatever Valhalla is reserved for defunct comic-strip heroes, there is Depression, World War and Cold War forever, and "Daddy" can spend eternity justifying the ways of robber baron capitalism to God. As for me, I'll take the living present and "Doonesbury." Nostalgia for the way we were doesn't mean we want to go back. We been there before.

JUDITH WHEELER

The Electronic Age

Judith Wheeler (1934–   ) is a senior research associate with The Carnegie Study of the Education of Educators. Her article "The Electronic Age" grew out of her collaboration with Charles E. Silberman on a series of articles on automation first published in *Fortune* and now available as a book entitled *The Myths of Automation*, 1966. She and Mr. Silberman have also collaborated in a critique of the writings of Marshall McLuhan.

"The Electronic Age" asserts that writers are increasingly needed as interpreters because the world represents more and more experience that "lies beyond the limits of our personal lives."

1. Donald Barthelme's story, "The Balloon," in a recent issue of *The New Yorker,* conjured a gigantic balloon that expanded during a night and a morning over a large part of Manhattan. There had been "a flood of original ideas in all media, works of singular beauty as well as significant milestones in the history of inflation, but at that moment there was only *this balloon,* concrete particular, hanging there." It transformed the lives of the people. They talked of little else; they tested it for toxic effect, analyzed it for philosophical significance, and found in it the explanation of their psychic disturbances. Discussion of the *meaning* of the balloon, however, was quickly abandoned because meanings "are rarely even looked for now, except in cases involving the simplest, safest phenomena." It was easier to adapt to the balloon, to be submerged by it.

2. In a way, "the electronic age" is our gigantic, overblown balloon, hanging there. Its manifestations intrude during more and more of the hours of our days, and there are few sanctuaries left. We have approached it from all angles, yet its meaning eludes us.

3. It is not as though it came upon us in a night and a morning, however: in 1942 General David Sarnoff gave notice that television would "bring to the home a complete means of instantaneous participation in the sights and sounds of the outer world." It was, he said, the "ultimate form of communication." Whether television has quite lived up to this promise is not settled, but it is clear that it can offer the illusion of "real life" better than any other medium. And its "truthfulness" transforms the impact of other media. A New York taxi-driver says he doesn't care if *all* the newspapers go out of business: "I like the news on TV. There you can see for yourself what's happening." Television's "sights and sounds of the outer world" have proved they can mystify, excite, instruct, horrify, even ennoble their audience. We seem to have all the values of art along with the comforting/awesome awareness that *those* people are *real.*

4. Perhaps this is why critic John Aldridge, in his new book *Time to Murder and Create*, finds that the novel is no longer "the primary source of our information about the varieties of experience that lie beyond the limits of our personal

THE ELECTRONIC AGE By Judith Wheeler, from the *Saturday Review*, June 4, 1966. Reprinted by permission of the author and the publisher.

lives. . . ." Mr. Aldridge is right. But it is also true that we don't need more information; we are in the midst of a data explosion. The possibilities for conveying information have proliferated to such an extent, and they feed so voraciously on "reality," that as Marshall McLuhan, director of the Center for Culture and Technology at the University of Toronto, says, the world itself has become "a sort of museum of objects that have been encountered before in some other medium."

5. Yet, paradoxically, the more we encounter these "objects," the more inscrutable they seem to be. Each rendition of the object in a different medium, or in the same medium at different times, or in several media at the same time, seems to give it luster. Familiarity breeds unfamiliarity just as a word repeated over and over suddenly sounds mysterious. We have more and more information, and suddenly no understanding. We experience a great deal that lies "beyond the limits of our personal lives," and things are more unreasonable than ever. A tourist promotion film on South Africa shows a stately parade of welldressed citizens (white) at garden parties, in skyscraper offices, at splendid resorts. Toward the end the narrator describes South Africa's abundant crop yields, and on the screen are the only Negroes in the film—women with baskets of fruit on their heads waiting in line to have their loads checked. This film was shown in New York theaters during the weeks when television offered the 1964 Harlem and Rochester race riots.

6. The incongruousness of this film would have gone unremarked twenty years ago, and not because there was less sensitivity about race relations. As the taxi-driver said, you can see for yourself—and the whole world is watching. One American first heard that there was rioting in Watts last summer from a priest in the cathedral at Palma, Majorca, who had seen the "difficul-

ties," as he politely called them, on television. How do you think about a world where the news of an ongoing riot 6,000 miles distant is dropped into the immense dark silence of a fourteenth-century Spanish cathedral?

7. The point is, can we still talk about something that lies beyond the limits of our personal lives? The old limits of time and space have been drastically altered, and the new limits are not obvious. Nor is it clear any longer what "authentic" experience is. Mr. Aldridge writes, "We are vicariously informed about experience to the point where we do not need to *have* experience, and if we do have it, we very often feel it to be less compelling than the secondhand version of it that we already possess." This is an odd statement to make in a decade of activism. But perhaps mere activity is not experience. To a large extent we think of "an experience" as something personal, raised out of the flux of daily life by virtue of having a beginning, a middle, and an end, very like a book or a play. But more and more, with the bombardment of information, experience becomes process without end. And direct personal experience becomes indistinguishable from the vicarious, the compelling secondhand version, when the doings of the outer world are brought to us on television, as they happen. We know at the same moment as the astronaut whether his shot is successful. It is not only real life; it is real time.

8. A writer can make this museum of objects, this collection of random sights and sounds, relevant to each of us. He separates us from the "mass audience," and makes us feel important. He even makes us feel wise. Television shows us what we do; writers try to tell us why. Television turns reality into news; writers make news into reality. As we probe farther into physical space, deeper into human awareness; as we devour our world, the only one left may be the one the writers make.

JOYCE CARY

The Mass Mind: Our Favorite Folly

Joyce Cary (1888–1957) was born in Ireland and educated at Oxford University. Appointed a colonial officer in Africa in 1913, he served there until ill health resulting from a wound received in the Cameroons Campaign of 1915–16 caused him to resign in 1920 and to return to England, where he settled down to be a writer. Among his twenty books are many novels—*Aissa Saved*, 1932; a trilogy—*Herself Surprised*, 1941, *To Be a Pilgrim*, 1942, and *The Horse's Mouth*, 1944; *A Fearful Joy*, 1949; and *Prisoner of Grace*, 1952. It was *The Horse's Mouth* that brought him recognition as a novelist of stature in both England and America. A critical work, *Art and Reality*, 1958, was published posthumously.

In "The Mass Mind: Our Favorite Folly" Cary utilizes his African experiences to dispute the current dogma that standardized production, education, and amusements have produced a standardized individual.

1. Every age, they say, has its special bit of nonsense. The eighteenth century had its noble savage, and the nineteenth, its automatic progress. Now we have this modern nonsense about the "mass man." We are all told constantly that people are becoming more and more standardized. That mass education, mass amusements, mass production, ready-made clothes, and a popular dress are destroying all individuality—turning civilization into a nice, warmed, sterilized orphan asylum where all the little lost souls wear the same uniforms, eat the same meals, think the same thoughts, and play the same games.

2. This belief is now so completely accepted that it underlies half the writing and thinking of the time, like chalk under the downs. You don't see it but it gives shape to what you do see. If you deny it you will get exactly the same response as Galileo when he said that the earth moved through the sky. You will be told, "Use

your eyes. And don't talk nonsense. Look at the crowds in the street or at any football match. Go to the films, read the newspapers. Consider the disappearance of national dress all over the world—the immense development of laws restricting individual liberty, standardizing our lives. Go on a tour to famous sights—year by year there will be bigger crowds of morons gaping at them and listening to the spiel of some bored guide—a piece nicely designed to satisfy the mass mind."

3. And you will be referred to history and old travel accounts to learn how various and delightful the world was, in dress and thought and individuality, one hundred or even fifty years ago.

4. I was convinced of all this myself till I went to administer the affairs of a primitive tribe in Africa. There I found that the tribal mind was much more truly a mass mind than anything I had known in Europe. The nearest approximation to it was among illiterate peasantry in remote country districts. Tribesmen and primitive peasants are intensely narrow and conservative. Their very simple ideas and reactions

guide them in a mysterious and dangerous world.

5. I found that young chiefs with enterprise and ambition were keen to learn about the world outside the tribe. If they got away with it, they tended to put on European dress. To them, European dress was not a mark of the mass mind, but of the free and independent mind.

6. Likewise, when a European peasantry becomes educated and enterprising, it breaks away from the national dress which seems a badge of servitude and backwardness. To tourists, no doubt, this is a misfortune. As a keen tourist and sight-seer, I wish all Scotsmen would wear the kilt and all Turks the tarboosh. I'm delighted that some are beginning to do so again. But these are individualists, eccentrics, nationalists—national dress is not a tribal uniform to them, but a proclamation of difference, an assertion of self.

7. Education, contact with other peoples, breaks up tribal uniformity of thought and custom, brings in new ideas. That is, it makes for difference. The celebrated eccentrics of former centuries were either lunatics—or educated men.

8. New ideas also make for conflict. Old African chiefs hated roads and railways: they said they brought in strangers who corrupted the young people with new ideas and made them rebellious. They were quite right. It is far easier to rule a primitive tribe than a modern democracy where every individual is ready to criticize the government, where everyone has his own ideas about politics and religion, and where dozens of societies, unions, religious sects claim independence and support ambitious leaders who are ready to fight at any time for their "rights."

9. The more education a man has the more likely he is to be independent in his views and obstinate in sticking to them. A committee of professors, I can assure you, is much harder to manage than a council of African chiefs.

10. And this throws light on another argument brought forward to prove that individuality is vanishing from the world—the enormous increase of law and regulation, the growing power of the police. In any primitive African tribe, law enforcement was in the hands of village chiefs. There was very little theft. I could leave my bungalow wide open and unguarded for three weeks at a time and nothing was ever taken. We had crimes of passion and crimes of witchcraft, but no criminal class, no crooks as you know them in the big city, no cranks, no anarchists—so we did not require an elaborate structure of law.

11. You do not need traffic police where there is no wheeled traffic. You do not need postal bylaws where no one knows how to write. But the modern state, simply because of the independence of its citizens, the complication of their demands, needs a huge machine of law and police. This is not a proof of the mass mind but the exact opposite—of a growing number of people who think and act for themselves, and, rightly or wrongly, are ready to defy the old simple rules founded on custom.

12. Thus, the modern state has lost its mass mind in getting education. But, you will say, this education destroys the primitive mass mind only to replace it with a number of mob minds: in the crowds which queue for the films or a match, read the same newspapers, and shout for the same spellbinders. Mass education is driving out the sound, traditional culture to bring in a lot of half-baked slogans. It produces the shallow brain seeking only to be distracted from serious reflection.

13. But these "mobs" have no resemblance to those of the tribal world where every individual does the same thing at the same time—hunts, dances, drinks in the mass. Even if he had the will to do anything else, it would not be there to do. The modern individual has an immense choice of occupation and amusement. So that the "mass" of sight-seers at any show place today is actually composed of individuals who have freely chosen to join the crowd and will join a different one tomorrow. What looks like a proof of the mob mind is really evidence of spreading interests among the people and a variety of occupations. And if some of these interests are "popular," aimed at a crowd which is not very critical or reflective, they are a good deal more so than interests which were the only recourse of their ancestors—dog-fighting, bear-baiting, the fit-up melodrama or one-night stand, once a year, and booze.

14. In the best educated countries, you find the biggest demand for something new in amusement as well as for instruction. Education enlarges all the interests of a man. Apart from what he learns, he acquires a general curiosity and a wider taste.

15. Compare the press of today with that of a hundred or even fifty years ago. You will find a far greater variety of subjects appealing to a

greater variety of tastes. You will find instructive articles on matters formerly dealt with only in the special magazines. Perhaps they don't aim at a learned audience, but they help the general reader to get some idea of what the experts are doing in atomic research or medicine or even astronomy. If you want to write a best seller, your best subject nowadays is probably cosmology.

16. But if a hundred thousand people are ready to buy a book on the nature of the universe, you have a mass demand at bookshops. The mass demand is not a proof of falling standards: it means that millions are being educated who would formerly have been left in the illiterate mass. There are "masses" reading learned works just as there are other "masses" going to popular films. The number of people with a good university education is many hundred times what it was fifty years ago, and that explains the immense development of arts and literature in experimental forms that would have had no chance of appreciation before. And in the millions in the next category who have just become literate in the last generation, whose reactions to education have given rise to this illusion of an increasing "mass mind," what we are seeing is not a collapse of standards, but a very rapid improvement. The crowds at the cinemas and the bus loads on the sight-seeing tours are on the way up. They have already left the mass; they are individuals seeking ideas for themselves.

17. The mass mind idea is not only a bit of nonsense, it is a dangerous nonsense. It leads to a profound defeatism, to the secret and unacknowledged belief that the dictators hold all the trumps.

18. The reasoning, when you bring it to light, is something like this. There are two kinds of education in the world: the free, which develops the individual according to his nature, and the specialized, which turns out doctors, scientists, mechanics—useful servants of the state or of industry. In a democracy each individual has both types. In the Soviet he gets only the specialized—the whole plan is to make him a state slave.

19. But it seems that free education merely debases the standards of thought and life by producing mob minds without spiritual strength. Meanwhile the Soviet acquires millions of workers, docile as serfs, yet skillful as our own craftsmen. Aiming deliberately at the creation of a mass mind it will easily defeat the free world, where opinions are shallow and divided.

20. But this is based on bad psychology. The West is not producing a mass mind, but a variety of strong minds with the richest sense of adventure and will for discovery. The East is not succeeding in obtaining a mass mind either—it is going in the opposite direction. Merely by process of education, it is producing every year people who can at least think a little more freely than illiterate peasants, who are very likely therefore to think critical thoughts, however much they may hide them. That is why the task of dictatorship becomes constantly more difficult, why it is obliged to stiffen its grip, to hire more police, to bribe more spies, and to purge its own party, every year or so, of "deviators."

21. What I suggest is that no kind of education, however narrow, can produce the mass mind. The reason is that minds are creative, that thoughts wander by themselves and cannot be controlled by the cleverest police. All education is free in this sense; it cannot be shut up within walls. To teach people to think, if only to make them more useful as soldiers and mechanics, is to open all thoughts to them—a whole world of new ideas. And though the dictator may wish to think of them as a proletariat they have already begun to leave the proletariat.

22. The "mass mind" is a delusion. How many dictators have been amazed when their rule, which seemed so strong, has collapsed in a few hours, without a friend?

ALVIN TOFFLER

The Death of the Mass Media?

Alvin Toffler (1920–   ) was born in New York City and graduated from New York University in 1949. He has since been the recipient of many honorary degrees. From 1957 to 1959 he was a correspondent in Washington, D.C. for various newspapers, and then became associated with *Fortune* magazine as an editor. In 1965 he joined the faculty of the New School for Social Research, and in 1969–70 he was visiting scholar for the Russell Sage Foundation. That same year he became a professor at Cornell University. Toffler also serves as a consultant to the Rockefeller Brothers Fund, the Institute for the Future, and the American Telephone and Telegraph Company. He contributes regularly to several periodicals, including *Art News*.

His writings, for which he has been given several awards, include *The Culture Consumers,* 1964; *Schoolhouse in the City,* 1968; *Future Shock,* 1970; *The Futurists,* 1972; *Learning for Tomorrow,* 1974; *The Eco-Spasm Report,* 1975; and *The Third Wave,* 1980.

In the essay included here, Toffler questions whether the mass media will retain a mass audience or will, instead, turn to regional and specialized audiences who are dissatisfied with the standardization of culture and the loss of individualism.

1. Are we witnessing the death of the mass media?

2. Starting nearly two hundred years ago, the media—newspapers, magazines, radio, television, and the movies—have increasingly influenced daily life in all the industrial nations. Filling our ears with mass-produced music, our eyes with mass-produced graphics, and our minds with mass-produced folk tales about football heroes and Hollywood stars, they form the sea of popular culture in which all of us swim.

3. Their basic principle was simple: Like a factory that stamped out products, they stamped out images, then disseminated them. Sets of images, carefully engineered by professional writers, editors, artists, newscasters, actors or copywriters, were packaged into programs, articles, or films, and then pumped wholesale into the mind-stream of the nation, or for that matter, the world.

4. The result was a standardization of the culture of the world's industrial societies, the homogenization of ideas, values, and lifestyles. The mass media helped create what sociologists came to call "mass society."

5. The *Ladies Home Journal,* for example, was the world's first truly mass magazine, achieving a circulation of around one million at the turn of the century. When the LHJ carried an article on how to decorate your living room, it influenced taste (and furniture sales) from California to New England, helping in this way to create a national market for standardized, mass manufactured goods.

6. Even today, the mass media retain enormous mind-shaping power. Nevertheless, there

are signs that the mass media are in their death throes and that a revolutionary new information system is being born. What we are witnessing is nothing less than the de-massification of the mass media.

7. Since the 1950s some of the world's largest magazines—*Life, Look,* and the *Saturday Evening Post,* to name a few—have died or shrunk into ghostly reincarnations of their former selves. Some media gurus declared that this was because people were no longer reading, that television produced a "post-literate" generation.

8. Yet after a decade or more of so-called post-literacy, people are reading as much as, if not more than, ever before. Ask the publishers. People are reading. But their word diet is no longer limited to standardized messages aimed at a universal, mass audience. The place of the great mega-magazines has increasingly been taken by hundreds of mini-magazines carrying highly specialized messages to small segments of the public.

9. On one newsstand in Omaha, not long ago, I found 15 different magazines aimed at aviation enthusiasts alone. In addition, the stands are filled with cheaply produced, offset printed, specialized magazines for hot-rodders, scuba-divers, ecologists, collectors of antique cameras, UFO freaks, religious cultists, political splinter groups, ethnic subcultures, businesses, professions, and for every age group from toddlers to those in their "golden years."

10. Long before we had national magazines at all, we had regional and local magazines that reflected the regional and local basis of our technology and economy. As technology grew more powerful, and national markets emerged, these local and regional publications disappeared and the national magazine took their place.

11. Today, we see a revival of regional and local publications in every part of the country. There are even magazines that slice up the reading public two ways at once: by region and by interest. Thus we find, for example, *South,* a magazine aimed exclusively at Southern businessmen.

12. What does all this mean? The death of the mass-interest magazines heralds a basic change in our popular culture. The decline of the mass magazines and the proliferation of specialized magazines means that fewer standardized, culture-wide messages are flowing into our minds,

and that more specialized messages are reaching different sub-groups within the society. This is accelerating the break-up of the old mass society and the formation of a new social, political and cultural diversity.

13. With the arrival of cheap copying machines, as media critic Marshall McLuhan has suggested, every individual can be his or her own "publisher," and we are now freely circulating images, messages, signs, and symbols to very small groups, indeed. The Xeroxed Christmas message that goes to family and friends is an example of this form of "personalized" publishing. It represents the ultimate de-massification of the mass media.

14. But parallel trends are racing through the audio media as well. Take, for example, the tape recorder. The radio broadcaster operates a "sound factory" distributing the same sounds to millions of ears simultaneously. The tape recorder makes each of us a broadcaster, or more accurately, a narrow-caster. We choose what we wish to record, of all the sounds around us, and we can duplicate them and pass them around to friends or through chain-letters, if we like.

15. Radio, putting us in the position of passive listener, and carrying messages from the few to the many, is inherently undemocratic. Tape recorders are inherently democratic. (Soviet dissidents—poets and singers who cannot get on the state-controlled airwaves—pass messages along the tape-vine.)

16. Television remains today the great standardizing medium, and Barbara Walters can still command $1 million a year because it is thought she can maximize the mass audience for her network. But television is still a primitive technology. (We mistakenly think TV is more "advanced" than printing, but it has gone through fewer successive generations of improvement.)

17. As we move toward wider use of cable and video cassette, the number of channels and the number of different messages will rise, just as it is already doing in both print and oral communications. Here, too, we shall increasingly generate images, ideas, and symbols to be shared by a few, rather than by the culture as a whole.

18. These changes in our media and in our popular culture reflect even deeper shifts in our society. Industrialism produced a mass society. We are now swiftly moving beyond industrialism to a new stage of civilization that will be techno-

logical, but not industrial. This new society will be the mass society de-massified.

19. We see this de-massification taking place at many levels. We see it in the rise of ethnic consciousness, in the rise of secessionism in Quebec, Scotland, or Brittany, in the breakup of monolithic Communism into nationally oriented Marxist movements, in the growing sectionalism in the United States, and in many other social, political, and artistic manifestations.

20. This centrifugal process will undoubtedly bring with it many problems. But it will also open vast new opportunities for us to reach toward greater individuality.

21. Popular culture, instead of being mass-machined at a few centers, then mass-distributed to passive culture consumers, will take in a new richness and variety, as we become producers as well as consumers of our own imagery and symbolism, our own values and life-styles.

22. Surely some powerful national mass media will survive this long-term shift. No doubt there will continue to be some national or even global hook-ups to spread certain important ideas, news, and metaphors simultaneously to us all.

23. But instead of getting most of our popular culture from the mass media in pre-packaged form, as it were, we will increasingly design and create our own culture, as communities did in the distant, pre-industrial past. We are moving swiftly into the future.

24. We are about to witness the death of the mass media as we have known them.

THE ARTS

GEORGE GORDON, LORD BYRON

from Childe Harold

'Tis to create, and in creating live
A being more intense, that we endow
With form our fancy, gaining as we give
The life we image, even as I do now.
What am I? Nothing: but not so art thou,
Soul of my thought! with whom I traverse earth,
Invisible but gazing, as I glow
Mix'd with thy spirit, blended with thy birth,
And feeling still with thee in my crush'd feelings' dearth.

JAMES ALAN McPHERSON

On Becoming an American Writer

James Alan McPherson (1943–   ), teacher of English, lecturer, fiction writer, and contributing editor of *The Atlantic,* graduated from the Harvard Law School in 1968. In addition to articles and short stories, he has published a collection of short stories, *Hue and Cry,* 1969. His most recent work, *Elbow Room,* 1977, won the Pulitzer prize for fiction.

In "On Becoming an American Writer," McPherson, who originally delivered parts of this essay at a Chautauqua lecture, argues that it is not race but culture which dominates all Americans, who must be made aware of the components of the culture and of its complexity, for it is much more complex than generally supposed. Regardless of race, what is important is learning to become a person, a citizen, within the diversity, variety, and "craziness" of American culture.

1. In 1974, during the last months of the Nixon Administration, I lived in San Francisco, California. My public reason for leaving the East and going there was that my wife had been admitted to the San Francisco Medical Center School of Nursing, but my private reason for going was that San Francisco would be a very good place for working and for walking. Actually, during that time San Francisco was not that pleasant a place. We lived in a section of the city called the Sunset District, but it rained almost every day. During the late spring Patricia Hearst helped to rob a bank a few blocks from our apartment, a psychopath called "the Zebra Killer" was terrorizing the city, and the mayor seemed about to declare martial law. Periodically the FBI would come to my apartment with pictures of the suspected bank robbers. Agents came several times, until it began to dawn on me that they had become slightly interested in why, of all the people in a working-class neighborhood, I alone sat at home every day. They never asked any questions on this point, and I never volunteered that I was trying to keep my sanity by working very hard on a book dealing with the relationship between folklore and technology in nineteenth-century America.

2. In the late fall of the same year a friend came out from the East to give a talk in Sacramento. I drove there to meet him, and then drove him back to San Francisco. This was an older black man, one whom I respect a great deal, but during our drive an argument developed between us. His major worry was the recession, but eventually his focus shifted to people in my age group and our failures. There were a great many of these, and he listed them point by point. He said, while we drove through a gloomy evening rain, "When the smoke clears and you start counting, I'll bet you won't find that many more black doctors, lawyers, accountants, engineers, dentists. . . ." The list went on. He remonstrated a bit more, and said, "White people are very generous. When they start a thing they usually finish it. But after all this chaos, imagine how mad and tired they must be. Back in the fifties, when this

thing started, they must have known anything could happen. They must have said, 'Well, we'd better settle in and hold on tight. Here come the niggers.'" During the eighteen months I spent in San Francisco, this was the only personal encounter that really made me mad.

3. In recent years I have realized that my friend, whom I now respect even more, was speaking from the perspective of a tactician. He viewed the situation in strict bread-and-butter terms: a commitment had been made to redefine the meaning of democracy in this country, certain opportunities had been provided, and people like him were watching to see what would be made of those opportunities and the freedom they provided. From his point of view, it was simply a matter of fulfilling a contractual obligation: taking full advantage of the educational opportunities that had been offered to achieve middle-class status in one of the professions. But from my point of view, one that I never shared with him, it was not that simple. Perhaps it was because of the differences in our generations and experiences. Or perhaps it was because each new generation, of black people at least, has to redefine itself even while it attempts to grasp the new opportunities, explore the new freedom. I can speak for no one but myself, yet maybe in trying to preserve the uniqueness of my experience, as I tried to do in *Elbow Room*, I can begin to set the record straight for my friend, for myself, and for the sake of the record itself.

4. In 1954, when *Brown* v. *Board of Education* was decided, I was eleven years old. I lived in a lower-class black community in Savannah, Georgia, attended segregated public schools, and knew no white people socially. I can't remember thinking of this last fact as a disadvantage, but I do know that early on I was being conditioned to believe that I was not *supposed* to know any white people on social terms. In our town the children of the black middle class were expected to aspire to certain traditional occupations; the children of the poor were expected not to cause too much trouble.

5. There was in those days a very subtle, but real, social distinction based on gradations of color, and I can remember the additional strain under which darker-skinned poor people lived. But there was also a great deal of optimism, shared by all levels of the black community. Besides a certain reverence for the benign inten-

tions of the federal government, there was a belief in the idea of progress, nourished, I think now, by the determination of older people not to pass on to the next generation too many stories about racial conflict, their own frustrations and failures. They censored a great deal. It was as if they had made basic and binding agreements with themselves, or with their ancestors, that for the consideration represented by their silence on certain points they expected to receive, from either Providence or a munificent federal government, some future service or remuneration, the form of which would be left to the beneficiaries of their silence. Lawyers would call this a contract with a condition precedent. And maybe because they did tell us less than they knew, many of us were less informed than we might have been. On the other hand, because of this same silence many of us remained free enough of the influence of negative stories to take chances, be ridiculous, perhaps even try to form our own positive stories out of whatever our own experiences provided. Though ours was a limited world, it was one rich in possibilities for the future.

6. If I had to account for my life from segregated Savannah to this place and point in time, I would probably have to say that the contract would be no bad metaphor. I am reminded of Sir Henry Maine's observation that the progress of society is from status to contract. Although he was writing about the development of English common law, the reverse of his generalization is most applicable to my situation: I am the beneficiary of a number of contracts, most of them between the federal government and the institutions of society, intended to provide people like me with a certain status.

7. I recall that in 1960, for example, something called the National Defense Student Loan Program went into effect, and I found out that by my agreeing to repay a loan plus some little interest, the federal government would back my enrollment in a small Negro college in Georgia. When I was a freshman at that college, disagreement over a seniority clause between the Hotel & Restaurant Employees and Bartenders Union and the Great Northern Railway Company, in St. Paul, Minnesota, caused management to begin recruiting temporary summer help. Before I was nineteen I was encouraged to move from a segregated Negro college in the South and through

that very beautiful part of the country that lies between Chicago and the Pacific Northwest. That year—1962—the World's Fair was in Seattle, and it was a magnificently diverse panorama for a young man to see. Almost every nation on earth was represented in some way, and at the center of the fair was the Space Needle. The theme of the United States exhibit, as I recall, was drawn from Whitman's *Leaves of Grass:* "Conquering, holding, daring, venturing as we go the unknown ways."

8. When I returned to the South, in the midst of all the civil rights activity, I saw a poster advertising a creative-writing contest sponsored by *Reader's Digest* and the United Negro College Fund. To enter the contest I had to learn to write and type. The first story I wrote was lost (and very badly typed); but the second, written in 1965, although also badly typed, was awarded first prize by Edward Weeks and his staff at *The Atlantic Monthly.* That same year I was offered the opportunity to enter Harvard Law School. During my second year at law school, a third-year man named Dave Marston (who was in a contest with Attorney General Griffin Bell earlier this year) offered me, through a very conservative white fellow student from Texas, the opportunity to take over his old job as a janitor in one of the apartment buildings in Cambridge. There I had the solitude, and the encouragement, to begin writing seriously. Offering my services in that building was probably the best contract I ever made.

9. I have not recalled all the above to sing my own praises or to evoke the black American version of the Horatio Alger myth. I have recited these facts as a way of indicating the haphazard nature of events during that ten-year period. I am the product of a contractual process. To put it simply, the 1960s were a crazy time. Opportunities seemed to materialize out of thin air; and if you were lucky, if you were in the right place at the right time, certain contractual benefits just naturally accrued. You were assured of a certain status; you could become a doctor, a lawyer, a dentist, an accountant, an engineer. Achieving these things was easy, if you applied yourself.

10. But a very hard price was extracted. It seems to me now, from the perspective provided by age and distance, that certain institutional forces, acting impersonally, threw together black peasants and white aristocrats, people who oper-ated on the plane of the intellect and people who valued the perspective of the folk. There were people who were frightened, threatened, and felt inferior; there were light-skinned people who called themselves "black" and darker-skinned people who could remember when this term had been used negatively; there were idealists and opportunists, people who seemed to want to be exploited and people who delighted in exploiting them. Old identities were thrown off, of necessity, but there were not many new ones of a positive nature to be assumed. People from backgrounds like my own, those from the South, while content with the new opportunities, found themselves trying to make sense of the growing diversity of friendships, of their increasing familiarity with the various political areas of the country, of the obvious differences between their values and those of their parents. We *were* becoming doctors, lawyers, dentists, engineers; but at the same time our experiences forced us to begin thinking of ourselves in new and different ways. We never wanted to be "white," but we never wanted to be "black" either. And back during that period there was the feeling that we could be whatever we wanted. But, we discovered, unless we joined a group, subscribed to some ideology, accepted some provisional identity, there was no contractual process for defining and stabilizing what it was we wanted to be. We also found that this was an individual problem, and in order to confront it one had to go inside one's self.

11. Now I want to return to my personal experience, to one of the contracts that took me from segregated Savannah to the Seattle World's Fair. There were many things about my earliest experiences that I liked and wanted to preserve, despite the fact that these things took place in a context of segregation; and there were a great many things I liked about the vision of all those nations interacting at the World's Fair. But the two seemed to belong to separate realities, to represent two different world views. Similarly, there were some things I liked about many of the dining-car waiters with whom I worked, and some things I liked about people like Dave Marston whom I met in law school. Some of these people and their values were called "black" and some were called "white," and I learned very quickly that all of us tend to wall ourselves off from experiences different from our

own by assigning to these terms greater significance than they should have. Moreover, I found that trying to maintain friendships with, say, a politically conservative white Texan, a liberal-to-radical classmate of Scottish-Italian background, my oldest black friends, and even members of my own family introduced psychological contradictions that became tense and painful as the political climate shifted. There were no contracts covering such friendships and such feelings, and in order to keep the friends and maintain the feelings I had to force myself to find a basis other than race on which such contradictory urgings could be synthesized. I discovered that I had to find, first of all, an identity as a writer, and then I had to express what I knew or felt in such a way that I could make something whole out of a necessarily fragmented experience.

12. While in San Francisco, I saw in the image of the nineteenth-century American locomotive a possible cultural symbol that could represent my folk origins and their values, as well as the values of all the people I had seen at the World's Fair. During that same time, unconsciously, I was also beginning to see that the American language, in its flexibility and variety of idioms, could at least approximate some of the contradictory feelings that had resulted from my experience. Once again, I could not find any contractual guarantee that this would be the most appropriate and rewarding way to hold myself, and my experience, together. I think now there are no such contracts.

13. I quoted earlier a generalization by Sir Henry Maine to the effect that human society is a matter of movement from status to contract. Actually, I have never read Sir Henry Maine. I lifted his statement from a book by a man named Henry Allen Moe— a great book called *The Power of Freedom*. In that book, in an essay entitled "The Future of Liberal Arts Education," Moe goes on to say that a next step, one that goes beyond contract, is now necessary, but that no one seems to know what that next step should be. Certain trends suggest that it may well be a reversion to status. But if this happens it will be a tragedy of major proportions, because most of the people in the world are waiting for some nation, some people, to provide the model for the next step. And somehow I felt, while writing the last stories in *Elbow Room*, that the condition precedent the old folks in my hometown wanted

in exchange for their censoring was not just status of a conventional kind. I want to think that after having waited so long, after having seen so much, they must have at least expected some new stories that would no longer have to be censored to come out of our experience. I felt that if anything, the long experience of segregation could be looked on as a period of preparation for a next step. Those of us who are black and who have had to defend our humanity should be obliged to continue defending it, on higher and higher levels—not of power, which is a kind of tragic trap, but on higher levels of consciousness.

14. All of this is being said in retrospect, and I am quite aware that I am rationalizing many complex and contradictory feelings. Nevertheless, I do know that early on, during my second year of law school, I became conscious of a model of identity that might help me transcend, at least in my thinking, a provisional or racial identity. In a class in American constitutional law taught by Paul Freund, I began to play with the idea that the Fourteenth Amendment was not just a legislative instrument devised to give former slaves legal equality with other Americans. Looking at the slow but steady way in which the basic guarantees of the Bill of Rights had, through judicial interpretation, been incorporated into the clauses of that amendment, I began to see the outlines of a new identity.

15. You will recall that the first line of Section 1 of the Fourteenth Amendment makes an all-inclusive definition of citizenship: "All persons born or naturalized in the United States and subject to the jurisdiction thereof, are citizens of the United States. . . ." The rights guaranteed to such a citizen had themselves traveled from the provinces to the World's Fair: from the trial and error of early Anglo-Saxon folk rituals to the rights of freemen established by the Magna Carta, to their slow incorporation into early American colonial charters, and from these charters (especially George Mason's Virginia Declaration of Rights) into the U.S. Constitution as its first ten amendments. Indeed, these same rights had served as the basis for the Charter of the United Nations. I saw that through the protean uses made of the Fourteenth Amendment, in the gradual elaboration of basic rights to be protected by federal authority, an outline of something much more complex than "black" and "white" had been begun.

16. It was many years before I was to go to the Library of Congress and read the brief of the lawyer-novelist Albion W. Tourgée in the famous case *Plessy* v. *Ferguson.* Argued in 1896 before the United States Supreme Court, Tourgée's brief was the first meaningful attempt to breathe life into the amendment. I will quote here part of his brief, which is a very beautiful piece of literature:

> This provision of Section 1 of the Fourteenth Amendment *creates a new* citizenship of the United States embracing *new* rights, privileges and immunities, derivable in a *new* manner, controlled by *new* authority, having a *new* scope and extent, depending on national authority for its existence and looking to national power for its preservation.

17. Although Tourgée lost the argument before the Supreme Court, his model of citizenship—and it is not a racial one—is still the most radical idea to come out of American constitutional law. He provided the outline, the clothing, if you will, for a new level of status. What he was proposing in 1896, I think was that each United States citizen would attempt to approximate the ideals of the nation, be on at least conversant terms with all its diversity, carry the mainstream of the culture inside himself. As an American, by trying to wear these clothes he would be a synthesis of high and low, black and white, city and country, provincial and universal. If he could live with these contradictions, he would be simply a representative American.

18. This was the model I was aiming for in my book of stories. It can be achieved with or without intermarriage, but it will cost a great many mistakes and a lot of pain. It is, finally, a product of culture and not of race. And achieving it will require that one be conscious of America's culture and the complexity of all its people. As I tried to point out, such a perspective would provide a minefield of delicious ironies. Why, for example, should black Americans raised in Southern culture *not* find that some of their responses are geared to country music? How else, except in terms of cultural diversity, am I to account for the white friend in Boston who taught me much of what I know about black American music? Or the white friend in Virginia who, besides developing a homegrown aesthetic he calls "crackertude," knows more about black American folklore than most black people? Or the possibility that many black people in Los Angeles have been just as much influenced by Hollywood's "star system" of the forties and fifties as they have been by society's response to the color of their skins? I wrote about people like these in *Elbow Room* because they interested me, and because they help support my belief that most of us are products of much more complex cultural influences than we suppose.

19. What I have said above will make little sense until certain contradictions in the nation's background are faced up to, until personal identities are allowed to partake of the complexity of the country's history as well as of its culture. Last year, a very imaginative black comedian named Richard Pryor appeared briefly on national television in his own show. He offended a great many people, and his show was canceled after only a few weeks. But I remember one episode that may emphasize my own group's confusion about its historical experience. This was a satiric takeoff on the popular television movie *Roots,* and Pryor played an African tribal historian who was selling trinkets and impromptu history to black American tourists. One tourist, a middle-class man, approached the tribal historian and said, "I want you to tell me who my great-great-granddaddy was." The African handed him a picture. The black American looked at it and said, "But that's a *white* man!" The tribal historian said, "That's right." Then the tourist said, "Well, I want you to tell me where I'm from." The historian looked hard at him and said, "You're from Cleveland, nigger." I think I was trying very hard in my book to say the same thing, but not just to black people.

20. Today I am not the lawyer my friend in San Francisco thought I should be, but this is the record I wanted to present to him that rainy evening back in 1974. It may illustrate why the terms of my acceptance of society's offer had to be modified. I am now a writer, a person who has to learn to live with contradictions, frustrations, and doubts. Still, I have another quote that sustains me, this one from a book called *The Tragic Sense of Life,* by a Spanish philosopher named Miguel de Unamuno. In a chapter called "Don Quixote Today," Unamuno asks, "How is it that among the words the English have borrowed

from our language there is to be found this word *desperado?*" And he answers himself: "It is despair, and despair alone, that begets heroic hope, absurd hope, mad hope."

21. I believe that the United States is complex enough to induce that sort of despair that begets heroic hope. I believe that if one can experience its diversity, touch a variety of its people, laugh at its craziness, distill wisdom from its tragedies, and attempt to synthesize all this inside oneself without going crazy, one will have earned the right to call oneself "citizen of the United States," even though one is not quite a lawyer, doctor, engineer, or accountant. If nothing else, one will have learned a few new stories and, most important, one will have begun on that necessary movement from contract to the next step, from province to the World's Fair, from a hopeless person to a desperado. I wrote about my first uncertain steps in this direction in *Elbow Room* because I have benefited from all the contracts, I have exhausted all the contracts, and at present it is the only new direction I know.

JOSEPHINE HENDIN

Grinds in the Modern Novel

Josephine Hendin (1946–   ) is a novelist, critic, and a professor of English at New York University. She also taught at the New School of Social Research in 1973–74. In 1970 the Indiana University Press published her critical work *The World of Flannery O'Connor*. On a Guggenheim Fellowship she wrote *Vulnerable People: A View of American Fiction Since 1945*, which was published in 1978. The American Library Association voted *Vulnerable People* one of the notable books of 1978, and, earlier, *Choice* magazine had selected *The World of Flannery O'Conner* as one of the outstanding academic publications of 1970. She has written frequently for *Harper's* magazine, *Psychology Today*, the *New York Times Book Review* and *Saturday Review*.

In the essay reprinted here, Hendin expresses her conviction that modern novelists have lost the motivations of strong feeling, hope, and desire and no longer are able to believe in themselves or in the creation of heroes by the culture.

1. Donald Barthelme once wrote of an artist laboring up a glass mountain in Manhattan with the aid of two toilet plungers. The climber wants to free an "enchanted symbol" at the top. The streets around the mountain are studded with excrement and filled with a crowd shouting obscenities, demanding that he jump, and cheering for him to fall. The artist climbs on, able to reach the top only by incredible effort. When he arrives, he finds the "enchanted symbol" is a beautiful princess. He flings her down the mountain to the crowd, who "can be relied upon to deal with her." This parable captures the troubles of people who reject fairy-tale endings.

2. Speaking to our mistrust of enchantment, Barthelme's cautionary story warns the reader against chasing after perfection. It casts an icy eye on the charming creature who does not take the artist out of his rage, but only confronts him

GRINDS IN THE MODERN NOVEL From *Psychology Today*, March 1979. Copyright © 1979 by Josephine Hendin. Reprinted by permission of the author.

with his limitations in love. The artist has been burned before; he refuses to be seduced. His murder of the enchanted princess breaks up the tale, in line with his broken expectations. He is the man who is too sophisticated to believe there is gold at the end of any rainbow, and too sensitive to resign himself to living in the crowd of ordinary men, those cursing angries who never think of enchantment at all. What is such a man to do?

3. The "working stiff," once a creature from the depths of working-class life and fiction, is surfacing in novels of the middle class as the professional who is resigned to the meaninglessness of his work. In Joseph Heller's bitterly funny new novel, *Good as Gold*, Bruce Gold is a professor of English who doesn't believe in education, academic freedom, or sexual or political liberty. An opinionmaker for virtually all causes, he advocates "fiery caution and crusading inertia." His lack of genuine interest in teaching or government permits him to wax eloquent about both without convictions inhibiting him. He delivers the same speech to a "reactionary religious group that he had given the day before with equal success to a congress of teen-aged Maoists." Without illusions of saying anything, he is infatuated with expressing himself, with probing the petty, competitive envy he feels and can inspire in his colleagues. What he finds in his sophistry is a means of controlling both his anger and his belief, a game plan that keeps attachments in check.

4. Bruce Gold is a more publicly cynical version of Bob Slocum, the narrator of Heller's previous (second) novel *Something Happened*. Slocum is an executive in a division of people who believe in nothing and are concerned with "collecting . . . interpreting statistical information about the public, the market, the country and the world." They are expected to suggest ingenious ways of disguising reality. "I am very good with these techniques of deception," he thinks, and all the better for not deceiving himself, for the man who believes "begin(s) relying on what he now thinks is the truth and loses his talent for devising good lies."

5. Without the pull of strong feeling, of hope and desire, some people grind to a halt like cars out of gas. When John Barth's Jake Horner in *The End of the Road* wants to change his life, he has so little desire available to him he can only drop out into insensibility. Stuck, as if paralyzed, in a bus station, he has no desire to go anywhere. The psychiatrist for this new condition turns up. He does not prescribe reviving Horner's heart, but suggests he keep what little imagination he has left from running away. He advises him to find another rut.

6. "You will teach prescriptive grammar," the psychiatrist says. "No description at all. No optional situations. Teach the rules." He tells him to study the almanac, memorize the seating capacity of the Cleveland Municipal Stadium and other bits of knowledge, because "the world is everything that is the case." You shall know trivia, he implies, and that knowledge shall make you free.

7. A culture creates its heroes even as its writers create culture. The grind, committed to busywork, may be a sign of a wider loss of faith in the results of human effort, in the declining belief that expertise will solve in a large and satisfying way any of the problems that confront us. The man of energetic despair works out a way of seeing that is a way of not seeing. He avoids the temptation of belief, in princesses or in successes, which remains a persistent part of—and perhaps a persistent con in—American life. By refusing to believe anything enchanting can happen to him, and by refusing to let it happen, he works out an innovative nihilism, one that optimistically insists that something can come out of nothing. Recoiling from the emphasis on self-fulfillment and self-expression once associated with the avant-garde hero, he remains engaged in ongoing relations, plugging ever onward. Steadiness keeps him from breaking apart, from despair, and gives his life at least an external, social cohesiveness.

8. Technology is often condemned as a cause of human trouble. But the new heroes speak of the extent to which people can come to envy machines and wish to be like them. To see life as primarily a mechanical process they wish to be part of is to begin an infatuation with the IBMized personality. Dreaming of themselves as machines that can be switched on and off, as robots, or as rats in mazes, many of the new heroes work out affinities to nonhuman things. In depersonalization, once considered wholly negative, they find a liberating process. As categorizers of information, as collectors of cultural trivia, they build walls between themselves and the memory of enchantment.

9. Behind the hero's energetic despair is the experience of disillusionment with the promises and possibilities of life. The sight of a princess, the spectacle of men who believe in their work, arouse cynical resentment in proportion to a sense of loss. The hero attempts to make this experience of loss a revolutionary act, insisting on tracking, diminishing, limiting expectations until they reach an alignment with minimal human possibilities. As literary figures, the new heroes stand against the tradition of the romantic hero who was, in his violence, his appetites, hopes, and even in his evil, voracious. As mirrors of ourselves, they call into question the dimensions of our capacity for trust, love, and attachment all the more acutely because they do not attack the "system" but follow it, acknowledge they are its products, and continue to function in it without believing in its value. They dramatize what is becoming a standard brand of American cynicism.

10. Men on a treadmill save their sanity, save themselves from disappointment, by expecting nothing. By not leaving the beaten track, they may rescue themselves from chance. In the magnitude of their submission to what they see as the unalterable narrowness of life, they achieve a kind of dignity. But the price they pay is sweeping and consuming, in shrinking the joy of life and in diminishing even the simpler, smaller joy of not being dead.

EUGENE RASKIN

Walls and Barriers

Eugene Raskin (1909–   ) studied architecture at Columbia University and the University of Paris. He was a practicing architect in New York from 1937 to 1939, then an architectural consultant and critic from 1939 to 1942, and from 1942 to 1976 professor of architecture at Columbia University. He is also a playwright, novelist, and composer, having won the Gold Record Award in 1969 for the song "Those Were the Days," which remains a great popular success. He wrote two film scripts, one of which, "How to Look at a City," was filmed and won first prize at the American Film Festival in 1964. His publications include *Architecturally Speaking*, 1954; *Sequel to Cities: The Post-Urban Society*, 1969; a play, *Last Island*, produced at the Margo Jones Theatre in Dallas, 1954; a novel, *Stranger in My Arms*, 1971; and *Architecture and People*, 1975.

In Raskin's essay "Walls and Barriers," the symbolism of walls is explored and explained. He concludes that "our changing conceptions of ourselves" determine the kinds of walls we build.

1. My father's reaction to the bank building at 43rd Street and Fifth Avenue in New York City was immediate and definite: "You won't catch me putting my money in *there!*" he declared. "Not in that glass box!"

2. Of course, my father is a gentleman of the old school, a member of the generation to whom a good deal of modern architecture is unnerving; but I suspect—I more than suspect, I am convinced—that his negative response was not so

much to the architecture as to a violation of his concept of the nature of money.

3. In his generation money was thought of as a tangible commodity—bullion, bank notes, coins—that could be hefted, carried, or stolen. Consequently, to attract the custom of a sensible man, a bank had to have heavy walls, barred windows, and bronze doors, to affirm the fact, however untrue, that money would be safe inside. If a building's design made it appear impregnable, the institution was necessarily sound, and the meaning of the heavy wall as an architectural symbol dwelt in the prevailing attitude toward money, rather than in any aesthetic theory.

4. But that attitude toward money has of course changed. Excepting pocket money, cash of any kind is now rarely used; money as a tangible commodity has largely been replaced by credit, a book-keeping-banking matter. A deficit economy, accompanied by huge expansion, has led us to think of money as a product of the creative imagination. The banker no longer offers us a *safe*, he offers us a *service*—a service in which the most valuable elements are dash and a creative flair for the invention of large numbers. It is in no way surprising, in view of this change in attitude, that we are witnessing the disappearance of the heavy-walled bank. The Manufacturers Trust, which my father distrusted so heartily, is a great cubical cage of glass whose brilliantly lighted interior challenges even the brightness of a sunny day, while the door to the vault, far from being secluded and guarded, is set out as a window display.

5. Just as the older bank asserted its invulnerability, this bank *by its architecture* boasts of its imaginative powers. From this point of view it is hard to say where architecture ends and human assertion begins. In fact, there is no such division; the two are one and the same.

6. It is in the understanding of architecture as a medium for the expression of human attitudes, prejudices, taboos, and ideals that the new architectural criticism departs from classical aesthetics. The latter relied upon pure proportion, composition, etc., as bases for artistic judgment. In the age of sociology and psychology, walls are not simply walls but physical symbols of the barriers in men's minds.

7. In a primitive society, for example, men pictured the world as large, fearsome, hostile, and beyond human control. Therefore they built heavy walls of huge boulders, behind which they could feel themselves to be in a delimited space that was controllable and safe; these heavy walls expressed man's fear of the outer world and his need to find protection, however illusory. It might be argued that the undeveloped technology of the period precluded the construction of more delicate walls. This is of course true. Still, it was not technology, but a fearful attitude toward the world, which made people want to build walls in the first place. The greater the fear, the heavier the wall, until in the tombs of ancient kings we find structures that are practically all wall, the fear of dissolution being the ultimate fear.

8. And then there is the question of privacy—for it *has* become questionable. In some Mediterranean cultures it was not so much the world of nature that was feared, but the world of men. Men were dirty, prying, vile, and dangerous. One went about, if one could afford it, in guarded litters; women went about heavily veiled, if they went about at all. One's house was surrounded by a wall, and the rooms faced not out, but in, toward a patio, expressing the prevalent conviction that the beauties and values of life were to be found by looking inward, and by engaging in the intimate activities of a personal as against a public life. The rich intricacies of the decorative arts of the period, as well as its contemplative philosophies, are as illustrative of this attitude as the walls themselves.

9. We feel different today. For one thing, we place greater reliance upon the control of human hostility, not so much by physical barriers, as by the conventions of law and social practice—as well as the availability of motorized police. We do not cherish privacy as much as did our ancestors. We are proud to have our women seen and admired, and the same goes for our homes. We do not seek solitude; in fact, if we find ourselves alone for once, we flick a switch and invite the whole world in through the television screen. Small wonder, then, that the heavy surrounding wall is obsolete, and we build, instead, membranes of thin sheet metal or glass.

10. The principal function of today's wall is to separate possibly undesirable outside air from the controlled conditions of temperature and humidity which we have created inside. Glass may accomplish this function, though there are apparently a good many people who still have

qualms about eating, sleeping, and dressing under conditions of high visibility; they demand walls that will at least give them a sense of adequate screening. But these shy ones are a vanishing breed. The Philip Johnson house in Connecticut, which is much admired and widely imitated, has glass walls all the way around, and the only real privacy is to be found in the bathroom, the toilette taboo being still unbroken, at least in Connecticut.

11. To repeat, it is not our advanced technology, but our changing conceptions of ourselves in relation to the world that determine how we shall build our walls. The glass wall expresses man's conviction that he can and does master nature and sociey. The "open plan" and the unobstructed view are consistent with his faith in the eventual solution of all problems through the expanding efforts of science. This is perhaps why it is the most "advanced" and "forwardlooking" among us who live and work in glass houses. Even the fear of the cast stone has been analyzed out of us.

F. L. LUCAS

Tragedy

Frank Laurence Lucas (1894–1970), fellow and former lecturer at King's College, Cambridge, was born in Yorkshire and educated at Cambridge. He was a distinguished poet, scholar, translator, anthologist, and literary critic. The variety and scope of his knowledge are reflected in the titles of his works, among them: *Greek Poetry for Everyman*, 1951; *Tennyson*, 1957; *Literature and Psychology*, 1957; *The Greatest Problem, and Other Essays*, 1960; and *The Drama of Ibsen and Strindberg*, 1962.

Following the tenets of Aristotle's *Poetics*, Lucas suggests that all great tragedy relies upon the imitation of some serious aspect of life. We view tragedy, however, neither to purge ourselves of tragic feelings nor to learn from the experience, but primarily to experience the event ourselves.

1. Life is fascinating to watch, whatever it may be to experience. In *Iliad VII*, when Hector is about to challenge the Achaeans to single combat, Apollo and Athene perch in the shape of eagles on a great oak in the Trojan Plain, "delighting in the deeds of men"—the first of Greek tragic audiences. And so we too go to tragedies not in the least to get rid of emotions, but to have them more abundantly; to banquet, not to purge. Our lives are often dull; they are always brief in duration and confined in scope; but in drama or

TRAGEDY From *Tragedy*, rev. ed., by F. L. Lucas. © F. L. Lucas 1962. Reprinted with permission of Macmillan Publishing Co., Inc.

fiction, even the being "whose dull morrow cometh and is as to-day is" can experience, vicariously, something more. To be "tragic", however, the experience must have in addition a certain peculiar quality—"must", not for moral or philosophic reasons, but because if the experience were not of that kind, we should use a different word for it. Some other forms of art may be merely beautiful; by Tragedy, I think, we imply also something fundamentally true to life. It need not be the whole truth, but it must be true. Twice at the theatre I can remember having felt in the midst of a play, "Yes, this is the very essence of Tragedy": once, in Turgenev's *A*

Month in the Country, where the slow disillusionment of years is crowded into one agonized scene, and a girl frozen into a woman before our eyes. Were the truth and the beauty of it less perfect, we should feel it less keenly; were they more perfect, we might feel it more keenly than we could bear. As it is, we mutter, "How unbearable!—and yet, yes, that is how it happens, the inevitable change that comes on all of us, made visible here as never before. This is life. This is growing up. How appallingly—how fascinatingly true!" And so again in the work of another Russian, *The Three Sisters* of Chekhov. A series of petty, futile disasters has passed across these women's lives; and now nothing is left them, not even (it might seem) anything tragic, only a monotony of hopelessness, like the flapping of burnt paper in an empty grate, as all that had lent meaning to their existence passes away from them with the music of the departing regiment—that music which goes marching on so gaily, so confidently, as if it at least had no part in these weary doubts, and knew whither it was going and why men are born. There is, for me, no more really tragic ending in all drama; for as we see these wasted figures stand before us, as we hear fife and bugle go dancing so light-heartedly upon their way, in that contrast seems embodied, for one eternal moment, the paradox of the tragedy of life, its hopefulness and its despair, its calling trumpets and its after silences. And here too the only consolation is the utter truthfulness: we have seen for an instant through its mists the sheer mountainface of life.

2. So the essence of Tragedy reduces itself to this—the pleasure we take in a rendering of life both serious and true. It must be serious, whether or no it has incidentally comic relief. It must seem to matter, or else the experience would belong to a different category and need a different name. And it must also seem true, or it will not move us. This is all. It may be good for us, but that is not why we go to it. And watching scenes like those of Turgenev, the mind revolts with a sudden anger at the thought of the besetting narrowness of philosophers, who can so seldom be disinterested, who so often make life a reformatory, and beauty useful, and art a pill. Tragedy may teach us to live more wisely; but that is not why we go to it; we go to have the experience, not to use it.

3. But is there, beyond this, no definite attitude to life in general which we may call tragic, something in fact common to *The Oresteia* and *Othello,* *The Bacchæ* and *The Master Builder,* some common impression which they leave? Is there in tragedy something corresponding to that fundamental paradox of comedy, which men have seen supremely embodied in Falstaff—the eternal incongruity between the divine wit and the animal grossness of man? The answer is, I think, "Yes." And this paradox of Hamlet which answers that of Falstaff? It is the very same. "What a piece of work is man!" cries the Tragic Muse; and Comedy echoes with a laugh, "What a piece of work!" Nietzsche's tragic antithesis seems nearer to the truth than his predecessors' simpler answers. For in Tragedy is embodied the eternal contradiction between man's weakness and his courage, his stupidity and his magnificence, his frailty and his strength. It is the transcendent commonplace of Pope:

> Placed on this isthmus of a middle state,
> A being darkly wise, and rudely great:
> With too much knowledge for the Sceptic side,
> With too much weakness for the Stoic's pride,
> He hangs between; in doubt to act, or rest,
> In doubt to deem himself a God, or Beast;
> In doubt his Mind or Body to prefer,
> Born but to die, and reas'ning but to err . . .
> Created half to rise, and half to fall:
> Great lord of all things, yet a prey to all;
> Sole judge of Truth, in endless Error hurl'd:
> The glory, jest, and riddle of the world!

4. That is the essential theme of Tragedy. The dramatist may be a pessimist like Euripides, or a Jansenist like Racine, or we know not what, like Shakespeare. There may be a god out of a machine to come hereafter, a happy epilogue; but *Hamlet* or *Phèdre* call for neither of these; they need nothing to perfect them. They stand alone and we forget the rest—the after-life with its readjustments, the martyr's crown, the lost in their livery of flame. Here is a mirror held up to the fashion of this world; we can look in it and bear to look, without being turned to stone. Here the problem of evil and of suffering is set before us; often it is not answered, but always there is something that makes it endurable. It may be the thought that the hero, like Oedipus or Hamlet or Samson, has at last got nobly off the stage, away from the fitful fever of life.

Vex not his ghost, O let him passe, he hates him
That would upon the wracke of this tough world
Stretch him out longer.

It may be simply the consolation of perfect language, as when Antigone passes with that last
great cry down to her living tomb:

O tomb, O bridal-chamber, prison-house
Deep-delved, sure-guarded ever; whither I
Pass and am gathered to my kin, all those
Persephone has numbered with her dead!

It may be the sense that human splendour is
greater and finer even in defeat than the blind
universe that crushes it; as in the last cry of
Synge's Deirdre—"It's a pitiful thing, Conchubor,
you have done this night in Emain; yet a thing

will be a joy and triumph to the ends of life and
time."

5. Or it may be simply the consolation of the
sheer integrity which faces life as it is. The characters may no longer be heroes sublime even in
their fall, they may be the ordinary men and
women of Ibsen and Chekhov, over whose lack of
tragic splendour critics have mourned so needlessly. Complaining of the want of great personalities in this play or that, they forgot the author.
For the characters may be poor in spirit and
feeble in desire, and the play remain tragic in
spite of it, if we feel that the author is himself
none of these things and has never cheated or
paltered in his picture of men as they are. Tragedy, then, is a representation of human unhappi-
ness which pleases us notwithstanding, by the
truth with which it is seen and the fineness with
which it is communicated. . . .

ERIC BENTLEY

The Classic Theatre in Modern Life

Eric Bentley (1916–   ) was born in England and educated at Oxford and Yale University. He
has received several honorary degrees in addition to his earned ones. Bentley has had a long
and distinguished career in drama and dramatic criticism, and he has received many important
awards and fellowships. A Fellow of the American Academy of Arts and Sciences, he has been
Katherine Cornell Professor of Theatre, the State University of New York at Buffalo since 1974.
His writings include at least a score of books, and he has been adapter or translator of several
plays, including Bertolt Brecht's *Mother Courage*. In 1944 he wrote *A Century of Hero-Worship*
and *The Playwright as Thinker*. Other titles include *Bernard Shaw*, 1947; *In Search of Theatre*,
1953; *What is Theatre*, 1956; *The Theatre of Commitment*, 1967; *A Time to Die*, 1970; *Theatre of
War*, 1972; *Lord Alfred's Lover*, 1978; *The Brecht Commentaries*, 1981; and *The Fall of the
Amazons*, 1982.

In the essay reprinted here, Bentley wishes for the theatre to be a major force in the present
cultural revolution so as to make dramatic art accessible to all, and he feels that there is a large
audience ready for those dramatic works never before available. He cites the Théâtre Nationale Populaire as having met the need well in France and thinks the same could be done here.

THE CLASSIC THEATRE IN MODERN LIFE Reprinted by permission of the author.

1. The world is in a troubling but fascinating period of transition between aristocratic culture and a culture that, in some sense of the term, will be democratic. It is surely not surprising if many features of this transition are bizarre or just plain deplorable, yet people who cite the bizarre and deplorable things nearly always assume that aristocratic culture was characterized throughout by truly aristocratic qualities. What about the aristocrats of Tsarist Russia? They are depicted by the aristocrat Leo Tolstoy in his novel *Resurrection*. The aristocrats of nineteenth-century England were characterized by Matthew Arnold as the Barbarians. Milton described those of the seventeenth century as drunk with insolence and wine. Mozart's life was one long indignity as a result of their callousness.

2. True, those who hoped for a flowering of culture with the onset of democracy have been disappointed. They supposed that once the working man had leisure he would take to arts and crafts; and actually he takes to automobiles and television. Some people will never recover from their surprise and disgust at this fact. That is why they either refuse to contemplate any more heartening phenomena, or hasten to "explain" them. The explaining is mere explaining away, as when one is invited to attribute the new interest of Americans in classical music to the personal glamour of Mr. Leonard Bernstein. And why must we cast a cold eye on personal glamour? Mr. Bernstein makes the wide public feel welcome in the halls of culture. Is that bad? On the contrary, it helps us to see that what stood between that public and the enjoyment of great music was partly a social apparatus that made them feel excluded. Opera and symphony were addressed to dowagers. The working man didn't have the right clothes for the occasion, or the right accent, or the right kind of chit-chat. Invited to a concert he could hardly be expected not to feel a pariah.

3. Much the same is true of theatre. That institution (as most of us know it) is still amazingly upper-class in its mores, and extraordinarily inconvenient in its prices and its schedule for anyone who earns a modest living. How true this is one only realizes fully when the prices and the schedule and the social atmosphere abruptly change, as they did on the creation of the Federal Theatre in the thirties. Millions of Americans who "never go to the theatre" suddenly went to the theatre.

4. It is easy to be overcome with gloom as we contemplate the recent history of what has come to be called Mass Culture. Indeed, stronger than all the evidence provided by writers on the subject is the despondency in the writers themselves—covered, though it conventionally is, by a devastating smartness of tone. But the prospects for anything good are always black. The good things were impossible until they happened—it is only afterward that they were found to have been inevitable. If we bow to what is inevitable beforehand, what we shall get is George Orwell's 1984.

5. Bertolt Brecht is supposed to have said that you don't paint a still life when the ship is going down. One is tempted to retort that you don't paint at all when the ship is going down. But perhaps you do. When, after all, is the ship *not* going down? What other chance has anyone got to paint a still life? And sometimes there are enough lifeboats. Sometimes, even, land is in sight.

6. Alongside Broadway, alongside TV, there exists a certain hunger for high art. That does not mean that art is always liked, let alone understood. But one would have to be a fanatic pessimist to assert that is is uniformly *dis*liked and *mis*understood. Those of us who have a professional interest in culture are inclined to let our irritation at modern vulgarities blind us to any concomitant achievement. We are acutely aware, for example, that many of the classical phonograph records that are bought are not really listened to but are used as a background to work or conversation. We are less inclined to concede that some listening does occur. We note the incongruous context of classical paintings when they are reproduced in *Life* magazine. We perhaps overlook entirely the fact that a serious interest in painting might stem from a reading of such a magazine.

7. Or consider the notorious bad taste of the large public. One form it takes is that of a naïve earnestness which leads it to regard the latest domestic drama on Broadway as being just as profound as Ibsen or even Shakespeare.

8. Mr. Lionel Trilling recently made a cutting remark about the dramatists who write these plays of modern life. It was to the effect that he studiously refrains from seeing their work. The remark was, I think, a deserved rebuke to the pretentiousness of certain playwrights and to the ignorance of such devotees of theirs as do not

know that the same sort of thing has been done much better by others. A play like *Death of a Salesman* gets to be taken more seriously than it deserves to be.

9. Mr. Trilling, I gather, sees the public's undiscriminating earnestness as a wholly negative factor and has proposed as a sort of alternative a light comedy called *Two for the Seesaw*. Here I believe his sophistication has betrayed him. The fact that he will see or read so few Broadway plays has permitted him to believe that *Two for the Seesaw* has some little distinction. It really hasn't. Such items abound on the Broadway program; when you've seen three you've seen the lot. More important: the earnestness which Mr. Trilling rejects out of hand is not all bad. At bottom it is a demand for high seriousness and as such not only a good thing but a supremely encouraging thing to anyone with the interests of the theatre at heart. It is because this demand is imperious—because the public will not take No for an answer—that something has to present itself as Highly Serious several times every season. Much is passed off as sublime that is in fact only earnest—something that no one has failed to notice who has given Broadway more than a cursory look. The public, as is well known, is likely to find *Death of a Salesman* just as noble and profound as *King Lear.* The invalidity of this proposition has prevented critical people from seeing the corollary: *King Lear* is just as noble and profound as *Death of a Salesman*—in other words, the mass public has nothing, finally, against *King Lear,* but is willing to be as moved and impressed by it as by a much more easily accessible modern work.

10. In the cultural revolution that is under way all over the world, the theatre could play a leading part for the reason that high theatrical art is more accessible to the new untrained audiences than perhaps any other high art whatsoever. Most of music and painting is impenetrable except to people of a certain training. The same is true of poetry. Fiction is a little more approachable. I know people who left school at thirteen whose reading for pleasure embraces most of Tolstoy. But the drama—not in its printed form but on the stage—is the most attractive of all high arts. That fact seems to me to give it a certain responsibility. And here I do not have in mind a drama that is in any intentional or overt way didactic. I am thinking, rather, of

plays that speak to the heart. But then good plays all speak to the heart, not least those of the supposedly "cerebral" playwrights, such as Shaw. The masterpieces of dramatic art may have subtleties in them that it takes generations of scholars to decipher. They certainly have a characteristic that is far more important socially: they are emotionally powerful, and their principal emotions are such as make an immediate impact on a crowd. I think one might even say that the subtleties are at the periphery and that the center of each great drama is a certain simplicity. I do not, of course, mean superficiality, but rather that inessentials are so fully eliminated that we face an elemental and universal subject in its nudity. In this sense, the story of the Crucifixion is simple as told in the Gospels, even though men still disagree as to what it means.

11. One of the most sophisticated of modern plays is Pirandello's *Henry IV* and much has been written of its philosophy. At the core of the play, however, is something that all men feel keenly about: growing old. This is a play about a man of forty who clings to the image of himself at twenty. And so this is a play about Everyman. Writing for a literary magazine, you assume that this fact is clear to all and you proceed to argue about the philosophy; and many writers for literary magazines come to identify the non-obvious with the essential. A theatre audience does the opposite, and is, I think, less wrong. Certainly, it has a better starting point for judgment: a primary emotional experience. *King Lear* may contain all manner of Elizabethan lore concerning kingship for scholars to talk about, but if they have not started from actually feeling what Shakespeare says here about fathers and children, they have not started from the center. A public that picked up the points about parents and children would have responded more properly to the play than one that picked up points about Elizabethan culture. And that is understating my thesis, for it is not really a matter of points to be picked up, but of spontaneity versus sophistication. You hear a Beethoven quartet by having a sensibility and listening, not by knowing all about quartets.

12. As for great drama, I am saying something even simpler: that while there are barriers between it and the mass public, these barriers can often be broken down by the fact of theatre, the act of performance. Without any jazzing up or

deliberate popularization. Literary people complain that in performance the subtle passages whizz past before one can take them in. For nonliterary people that is an advantage. A play whose value lies in the subtlety of separate passages is not a popular play. Nor have any plays of that sort ever, I think, been considered great. When a subtle play is popular it is because behind the subtlety lies a human simplicity, a limited number of universal and powerful emotions. People will tolerate any amount of subtlety provided they can ignore it, and they can ignore it with pleasure if they are borne along by even one unsubtle, strong emotion. In the theatre, who ever notices that the first act of *Hamlet* contains much more information than he can retain? We are preoccupied by the one, simple, central situation: the death of the father, the remarriage of the mother, the desolation of the son, the appearance of the father's ghost.

13. Despite the movies, radio, and TV, there is still, even in America, a lot of interest in the theatre. Indeed, it has never conclusively been shown that this interest has declined. Losses in one respect seem to have been recouped in another. "Theatre," notoriously, is mostly mass entertainment of low artistic quality. Some mass entertainment is of high artistic quality—one thinks of some of the comedians who have been the darlings of the modern masses—yet, by and large, the artistic theatre is a thing apart for people with not only an education but a special interest or hobby. This apartness implies a division in modern society as a whole and indeed has been widely discussed in such terms as highbrow and lowbrow. The discussions are unpleasant. Both high and lowbrows are ferocious champions, and the middlebrows, as becomes them, have milder ones—or perhaps only snider ones. No real discussion is possible because the statements of the various teams imply accusations that are also insults. The champion of the highbrows implies that his opponents have no taste. The champion of the lowbrows implies that his opponents are undemocratic—the most violent epithet in the American vocabulary.

14. The returns are not all in. Much has yet to be learned about the nature of popular taste, as also about the possibilities of so-called highbrow theatre among those presumed to be lowbrows. When this kind of theatre was suddenly made available in America at prices the mass audience could pay, and in places where the mass audience lives, the mass audience attended the theatre and paid. I refer again to the Federal Theatre.

15. Jean Vilar's Théâtre Nationale Populaire has been having "high-brow" successes with huge popular audiences in France, and has also been making discoveries about popular predilections. His audiences like best the plays which are not of the type known as popular. They like the plays they are supposed to dislike. A prime instance is Kleist's *Prince of Homburg*. Frenchmen don't like Germans, especially not Prussians, and especially not Prussian Junkers; but Kleist was a German and a Prussian and a Junker and suddenly this play of his, considered in Germany somewhat esoteric, appeals to a mass audience in France. I should add that it was produced with the greatest possible austerity—that is, quite without all the devices of deliberate popularization.

16. Another case in point is that of Paul Claudel. To the Communist press, he is a Catholic apologist, and the working-class audience in France is powerfully influenced by the Communist press. Claudel's style, furthermore, is what an English critic has called Mandarin—it bears all the marks of the highbrow caste. Yet the plays of Claudel have been captivating mass audiences in France.

17. Various conclusions could be drawn. What occurs to me is that, though the motive of going to the theatre is "to be entertained," a great deal more than entertainment may be painlessly added once the curtain is up. The common man's demand not to be bored is a reasonable one. But once you have succeeded in not boring him, you have indeed "captivated" him. You can do what you want with him; he may even approve. For it is possible that, once relieved of boredom, even the least artistic person will want to be treated as a work of art will treat him. After all, it is not necessarily the substance of a great work that the public fears. People who cannot read Racine may just be scared of words—those endless lines, lines, lines. If this is the case, the passions which are the real substance of Racine's work have never been rejected by the mass audience: they have never been brought to the attention of the mass audience. The omission is repaired by such institutions as the Théâtre Nationale Populaire.

JOHN CIARDI

Robert Frost: The Way to the Poem

John Ciardi (1916–   ) can be heard on National Public Radio, and he is also director of the Bread Loaf Writers' Conference. From 1953 to 1961 he taught English at Rutgers University. His first volume of poetry—*Homeward to America*, 1940—won him the Hopwood Award for Poetry, and he has received numerous other honors for his poetry. Among his publications are *Other Skies*, 1947; *As If*, 1955; *I Marry You*, 1958; *How Does a Poem Mean?*, 1959; *In the Stoneworks*, 1961; and a long poem, *The King Who Saved Himself from Being Saved*, 1965. He has also translated Dante's *Inferno and Purgatorio*, 1954, and Dante's *Paradiso*, 1971. His most recent books are *Lives of X*, 1971; *Fast and Slow*, 1975; *The Little That Is All*, 1975; and with Isaac Asimov, *Limericks*, 1978.

In this essay Ciardi says the most important, or first, consideration in reading a poem is not to look for *what* the poem says but instead to try to see *how* it says it. A poem usually begins simply enough—seemingly—but at the end suggests meanings far beyond what is actually in print before one's eyes. A reader must know that the insights into a poem and the technical devices that are used to make the poem are inseparable. In Ciardi's words: "Each feeds the other." If readers will look at what goes into the making of a poem, then its meaning will emerge, although not all at once.

Stopping by Woods on a Snowy Evening

Whose woods these are I think I know.
His house is in the village though;
He will not see me stopping here
To watch his woods fill up with snow.

My little horse must think it queer
To stop without a farmhouse near
Between the wood and frozen lake
The darkest evening of the year.

He gives his harness bells a shake
To ask if there is some mistake.
The only other sound's the sweep
Of easy wind and downy flake.

The woods are lovely, dark and deep.
But I have promises to keep,
And miles to go before I sleep,
And miles to go before I sleep.

1. The School System has much to say these days of the virtue of reading widely, and not enough about the virtues of reading less but in depth. There are any number of reading lists for

poetry, but there is not enough talk about individual poems. Poetry, finally, is one poem at a time. To read any one poem carefully is the ideal preparation for reading another. Only a poem can illustrate how poetry works.

2. Above, therefore, is a poem—one of the master lyrics of the English language, and almost certainly the best-known poem by an American poet. What happens in it?—which is to say, not *what* does it mean, but *how* does it mean? How does it go about being a human reenactment of a human experience? The author—perhaps the thousandth reader would need to be told—is Robert Frost.

3. Even the TV audience can see that this poem begins as a seemingly simple narration of a seemingly simple incident but ends by suggesting meanings far beyond anything specifically referred to in the narrative. And even readers with only the most casual interest in poetry might be made to note the additional fact that, though the poem suggests those larger meanings, it is very careful never to abandon its pretense to being simple narration. There is duplicity at work. The poet pretends to be talking about one thing, and all the while is he is talking about many others.

4. Many readers are forever unable to accept the poet's essential duplicity. It is almost safe to say that a poem is never about what it seems to be about. As much could be said of the proverb. The bird in the hand, the rolling stone, the stitch in time never (except by an artful double-deception) intend any sort of statement about birds, stones, or sewing. The incident of this poem, one must conclude, is at root a metaphor.

5. Duplicity aside, this poem's movement from the specific to the general illustrates one of the basic formulas of all poetry. Such a grand poem as Arnold's "Dover Beach" and such lesser, though unfortunately better known, poems as Longfellow's "The Village Blacksmith" and Holmes's "The Chambered Nautilus" are built on the same progression. In these three poems, however, the generalization is markedly set apart from the specific narration, and even seems additional to the telling rather than intrinsic to it. It is this sense of division one has in mind in speaking of "a tacked-on moral."

6. There is nothing wrong-in-itself with a tacked-on moral. Frost, in fact, makes excellent use of the device at times. In this poem, however, Frost is careful to let the whatever-the-moral-is grow out of the poem itself. When the action ends the poem ends. There is no epilogue and no explanation. Everything pretends to be about the narrated incident. And that pretense sets the basic tone of the poem's performance of itself.

7. The dramatic force of that performance is best observable, I believe, as a progression in three scenes.

8. In scene one, which coincides with stanza one, a man—a New England man—is driving his sleigh somewhere at night. It is snowing, and as the man passes a dark patch of woods he stops to watch the snow descend into the darkness. We know, moreover, that the man is familiar with these parts (he knows who owns the woods and where the owner lives), and we know that no one has seen him stop. As scene one forms itself in the theater of the mind's eye, therefore, it serves to establish some as yet unspecified relation between the man and the woods.

9. It is necessary, however, to stop here for a long parenthesis: Even so simple an opening statement raises any number of questions. It is impossible to address all the questions that rise from the poem stanza by stanza, but two that arise from stanza one illustrate the sort of thing one might well ask of the poem detail by detail.

10. Why, for example, does the man not say what errand he is on? What is the force of leaving the errand generalized? He might just as well have told us that he was going to the general store, or returning from it with a jug of molasses he had promised to bring Aunt Harriet and two suits of long underwear he had promised to bring the hired man. Frost, moreover, can handle homely detail to great effect. He preferred to leave his motive generalized. Why?

11. And why, on the other hand, does he say so much about knowing the absent owner of the woods and where he lives? Is it simply that one set of details happened-in whereas another did not? To speak of things "happening-in" is to assault the integrity of a poem. Poetry cannot be discussed meaningfully unless one can assume that everything in the poem—every last comma and variant spelling—is in it by the poet's specific act of choice. Only bad poets allow into their poems what is haphazard or cheaply chosen.

12. The errand, I will venture a bit brashly for lack of space, is left generalized in order the more aptly to suggest *any* errand in life and,

therefore, life itself. The owner is there because he is one of the forces of the poem. Let it do to say that the force he represents is the village of mankind (that village at the edge of winter) from which the poet finds himself separated (has separated himself?) in his moment by the woods (and to which, he recalls finally, he has promises to keep). The owner is he-who-lives-in-his-village-house, thereby locked away from the poet's awareness of the-time-the-snow-tells as it engulfs and obliterates the world the village man allows himself to believe he "owns." Thus, the owner is a representative of an order of reality from which the poet has divided himself for the moment, though to a certain extent he ends by re-uniting with it. Scene one, therefore, establishes not only a relation between the man and the woods, but the fact that the man's relation begins with his separation (though momentarily) from mankind.

13. End parenthesis one, begin parenthesis two.

14. Still considering the first scene as a kind of dramatic performance of forces, one must note that the poet has meticulously matched the simplicity of his language to the pretended simplicity of the narrative. Clearly, the man stopped because the beauty of the scene moved him, but he neither tells us that the scene is beautiful nor that he is moved. A bad writer, always ready to overdo, might have written: "The vastness gripped me, filling my spirit with the slow steady sinking of the snow's crystalline perfection into the glimmerless profundities of the hushed primeval wood." Frost's avoidance of such a spate illustrates two principles of good writing. The first, he has stated himself in "The Mowing": "Anything *more* than the truth would have seemed too weak" (italics mine). Understatement is one of the basic sources of power in English poetry. The second principle is to let the action speak for itself. A good novelist does not tell us that a given character is good or bad (at least not since the passing of the Dickens tradition): he shows us the character in action and then, watching him, we know. Poetry, too, has fictional obligations: even when the characters are ideas and metaphors rather than people, they must be *characterized in action*. A poem does not *talk about* ideas; it *enacts* them. The force of the poem's performance, in fact, is precisely to act out (and thereby to make us act out empathically,

that is, to *feel out*, that is, to *identify with*) the speaker and why he stopped. The man is the principal actor in this little "drama of why" and in scene one he is the only character, though as noted, he is somehow related to the absent owner.

15. End second parenthesis.

16. In scene two (stanzas two and three) a *foil* is introduced. In fiction and drama, a foil is a character who "plays against" a more important character. By presenting a different point of view or an opposed set of motives, the foil moves the more important character to react in ways that might not have found expression without such opposition. The more important character is thus more fully revealed—to the reader and to himself. The foil here is the horse.

17. The horse forces the question. Why did the man stop? Until it occurs to him that his "little horse must think it queer" he had not asked himself for reasons. He had simply stopped. But the man finds himself faced with the question he imagines the horse to be asking: what *is* there to stop for out there in the cold, away from bin and stall (house and village and mankind?) and all that any self-respecting beast could value on such a night? In sensing that other view, the man is forced to examine his own more deeply.

18. In stanza two the question arises only as a feeling within the man. In stanza three, however (still scene two), the horse acts. He gives his harness bells a shake. "What's wrong?" he seems to say. "What are we waiting for?"

19. By now, obviously, the horse—without losing its identity as horse—has also become a symbol. A symbol is something that stands for something else. Whatever that something else may be, it certainly begins as that order of life that does not understand why a man stops in the wintry middle of nowhere to watch the snow come down. (Can one fail to sense by now that the dark and the snowfall symbolize a death-wish, however momentary, *i.e.*, that hunger for final rest and surrender that a man may feel, but not a beast?)

20. So by the end of scene two the performance has given dramatic force to three elements that work upon the man. There is his relation to the world of the owner. There is his relation to the brute world of the horse. And there is that third presence of the unownable world, the movement of the all-engulfing snow across all the

orders of life, the man's, the owner's, and the horse's—with the difference that the man knows of that second dark-within-the-dark of which the horse cannot, and the owner will not, know.

21. The man ends scene two with all these forces working upon him simultaneously. He feels himself moved to a decision. And he feels a last call from the darkness: "the sweep / Of easy wind and downy flake." It would be so easy and so downy to go into the woods and let himself be covered over.

22. But scene three (stanza four) produces a fourth force. This fourth force can be given many names. It is certainly better, in fact, to give it many names than to attempt to limit it to one. It is social obligation, or personal commitment, or duty, or just the realization that a man cannot indulge a mood forever. All of these and more. But, finally, he has a simple decision to make. He may go into the woods and let the darkness and the snow swallow him from the world of beast and man. Or he must move on. And unless he is going to stop here forever, it is time to remember that he has a long way to go and that he had best be getting there. (So there is something to be said for the horse, too.)

23. Then and only then, his question driven more and more deeply into himself by these cross-forces, does the man venture a comment on what attracted him: "The woods are lovely, dark and deep." His mood lingers over the thought of that lovely dark-and-deep (as do the very syllables in which he phrases the thought), but the final decision is to put off the mood and move on. He has his man's way to go and his man's obligations to tend to before he can yield. He has miles to go before his sleep. He repeats that thought and the performance ends.

24. But why the repetition? The first time Frost says "And miles to go before I sleep," there can be little doubt that the primary meaning is: "I have a long way to go before I get to bed tonight." The second time he says it, however, "miles to go" and "sleep" are suddenly transformed into symbols. What are those "something-elses" the symbols stand for? Hundreds of people have tried to ask Mr. Frost that question and he has always turned it away. He has turned it away *because he cannot answer it.* He could answer some part of it. But some part is not enough.

25. For a symbol is like a rock dropped into a pool: it sends out ripples in all directions, and the ripples are in motion. Who can say where the last ripple disappears? One may have a sense that he knows the approximate center point of the ripples, the point at which the stone struck the water. Yet even then he has trouble marking it surely. How does one make a mark on water? Oh, very well—the center point of that second "miles to go" is probably approximately in the neighborhood of being close to meaning, perhaps, "the road of life"; and the second "before I sleep" is maybe that close to meaning "before I take my final rest," the rest in darkness that seemed so temptingly dark-and-deep for the moment of the mood. But the ripples continue to move and the light to change on the water, and the longer one watches the more changes he sees. Such shifting-and-being-at-the-same-instant is of the very sparkle and life of poetry. One experiences it as one experiences life, for every time he looks at an experience he sees something new, and sees it change as he watches it. And that sense of continuity in fluidity is one of the primary kinds of knowledge, one of man's basic ways of knowing, and one that only the arts can teach, poetry foremost among them.

26. Frost himself certainly did not ask what the repeated last line meant. It came to him and he received it. He "felt right" about it. And what he "felt right" about was in no sense a "meaning" that, say, an essay could apprehend, but an act of experience that could be fully presented only by the dramatic enactment of forces which is the performance of the poem.

27. Now look at the poem in another way. Did Frost know what he was going to do when he began? Considering the poem simply as an act of skill, as a piece of juggling, one cannot fail to respond to the magnificent turn at the end where, with one flip, seven of the simplest words in the language suddenly dazzle full of never-ending waves of thought and feeling. Or, more precisely, of felt-thought. Certainly an equivalent stunt by a juggler—could there be an equivalent—would bring the house down. Was it to cap his performance with that grand stunt that Frost wrote the poem?

28. Far from it. The obvious fact is that *Frost could not have known he was going to write those lines until he wrote them.* Then a second fact must be registered: *he wrote them because, for the fun of it, he had got himself into trouble.*

29. Frost, like every good poet, began by playing a game with himself. The most usual way of writing a four line stanza with four feet to the line is to rhyme the third line with the first, and the fourth line with the second. Even that much rhyme is so difficult in English that many poets and almost all of the anonymous ballad makers do not bother to rhyme the first and third lines at all, settling for two rhymes in four lines as good enough. For English is a rhyme-poor language. In Italian and in French, for example, so many words end with the same sounds that rhyming is relatively easy—so easy that many modern French and Italian poets do not bother to rhyme at all. English, being a more agglomerate language, has far more final sounds, hence fewer of them rhyme. When an Italian poet writes a line ending with "vita" (life) he has literally hundreds of rhyme choices available. When an English poet writes "life" at the end of a line he can summon "strife, wife, knife, fife, rife," and then he is in trouble. Now "life-strife" and "life-rife" and "life-wife" seem to offer a combination of possible ideas that can be related by more than just the rhyme. Inevitably, therefore, the poets have had to work and rework these combinations until the sparkle has gone out of them. The reader is normally tired of such rhyme-led associations. When he encounters "life-strife" he is certainly entitled to suspect that the poet did not really want to say "strife"—that had there been in English such a word as, say, "hife," meaning "infinite peace and harmony," the poet would as gladly have used that word instead of "strife." Thus, the reader feels that the writing is haphazard, that the rhyme is making the poet say things he does not really feel, and which therefore the reader does not feel except as boredom. One likes to see the rhymes fall into place, but he must end with the belief that it is the poet who is deciding what is said and not the rhyme scheme that is forcing the saying.

30. So rhyme is a kind of game, and an especially difficult one in English. As in every game, the fun of the rhyme is to set one's difficulties high and then to meet them skillfully. As Frost himself once defined freedom, it consists of "moving easy in harness."

31. In "Stopping by Woods on a Snowy Evening" Frost took a long chance. He decided to rhyme not two lines in each stanza, but three. Not even Frost could have sustained that much rhyme in a long poem (as Dante, for example, with the advantage of writing in Italian, sustained triple rhyme for thousands of lines in "The Divine Comedy"). Frost would have known instantly, therefore, when he took the original chance, that he was going to write a short poem. He would have had that much foretaste of it.

32. So the first stanza emerged rhymed a-a-b-a. And with the sure sense that this was to be a short poem, Frost decided to take an additional chance and to redouble: in English three rhymes in four lines is more than enough; there is no need to rhyme the fourth line. For the fun of it, however, Frost set himself to pick up that loose rhyme and to weave it into the pattern, thereby accepting the all but impossible burden of quadruple rhyme.

33. The miracle is that it worked. Despite the enormous freight of rhyme, the poem not only came out as a neat pattern, but managed to do so with no sense of strain. Every word and every rhyme falls into place as naturally and as inevitably as if there were no rhyme restricting the poet's choices.

34. That ease-in-difficulty is certainly inseparable from the success of the poem's performance. One watches the skill-man juggle three balls, then four, then five, and every addition makes the trick more wonderful. But unless he makes the hard trick seem as easy as an easy trick, then all is lost.

35. The real point, however, is not only that Frost took on a hard rhyme-trick and made it seem easy. It is rather as if the juggler, carried away, had tossed up one more ball than he could really handle, and then amazed himself by actually handling it. So with the real triumph of this poem. Frost could not have known what a stunning effect his repetition of the last line was going to produce. He could not even know he was going to repeat the line. He simply found himself up against a difficulty he almost certainly had not foreseen and he had to improvise to meet it. For in picking up the rhyme from the third line of stanza one and carrying it over into stanza two, he had created an endless chain-link form within which each stanza left a hook sticking out for the next stanza to hang on. So by stanza four, feeling the poem rounding to its end, Frost had to do something about that extra rhyme.

36. He might have tucked it back into a third line rhyming with the *know-though-snow* of

stanza one. He could thus have rounded the poem out to the mathematical symmetry of using each rhyme four times. But though such a device might be defensible in theory, a rhyme repeated after eleven lines is so far from its original rhyme sound that its feeling as rhyme must certainly be lost. And what good is theory if the reader is not moved by the writing?

37. It must have been in some such quandary that the final repetition suggested itself—a suggestion born of the very difficulties the poet had let himself in for. So there is that point beyond mere ease in handling a hard thing, the point at which the very difficulty offers the poet the opportunity to do better than he knew he could. What, aside from having that happen to oneself, could be more self-delighting than to participate in its happening by one's reader-identification with the poem?

38. And by now a further point will have suggested itself: that the human insight of the poem and the technicalities of its poetic artifice are inseparable. Each feeds the other. That interplay is the poem's meaning, a matter not of WHAT DOES IT MEAN, for no one can ever say entirely what a good poem means, but of HOW DOES IT MEAN, a process one can come much closer to discussing.

39. There is a necessary epilogue. Mr. Frost has often discussed this poem on the platform, or more usually in the course of a long-evening-after a talk. Time and again I have heard him say that he just wrote it off, that it just came to him, and that he set it down as it came.

40. Once at Bread Loaf, however, I heard him add one very essential piece to the discussion of how it "just came." One night, he said, he had sat down after supper to work at a long piece of blank verse. The piece never worked out, but Mr. Frost found himself so absorbed in it that, when next he looked up, dawn was at his window. He rose, crossed to the window, stood looking out for a few minutes, and *then* it was that "Stopping by Woods" suddenly "just came," so that all he had to do was cross the room and write it down.

41. Robert Frost is the sort of artist who hides his traces. I know of no Frost worksheets anywhere. If someone has raided his wastebasket in secret, it is possible that such worksheets exist somewhere, but Frost would not willingly allow anything but the finished product to leave him. Almost certainly, therefore, no one will ever know what was in that piece of unsuccessful blank verse he had been working at with such concentration, but I for one would stake my life that could that worksheet be uncovered, it would be found to contain the germinal stuff of "Stopping by Woods"; that what was a-simmer in him all night without finding its proper form, suddenly, when he let his still-occupied mind look away, came at him from a different direction, offered itself in a different form, and that finding that form exactly right the impulse proceeded to marry itself to the new shape in one of the most miraculous performances of English lyricism.

42. And that, too—whether or not one can accept so hypothetical a discussion—is part of HOW the poem means. It means that marriage to the perfect form, the poem's shaped declaration of itself, its moment's monument fixed beyond all possibility of change. And thus, finally, in every truly good poem, "How does it mean?" must always be answered "Triumphantly." Whatever the poem "is about," *how* it means is always how Genesis means: the word become a form, and the form become a thing, and—when the becoming is true—the thing become a part of the knowledge and experience of the race forever.

T. K. WHIPPLE

Machinery, Magic, and Art

Thomas King Whipple (1890–1939), who was a professor of English at the University of California for several years, published magazine articles such as this one in the *Saturday Review*. In 1928 his *Spokesmen*, a book appraising the chief American authors of the 1920s, made its appearance.

In this article, Whipple maintains that art must serve a useful purpose. Only when it does so, he holds, will art and the artist regain their proper importance in society.

1. Some people seem to feel, vaguely and perhaps uncomfortably, that the arts somehow ought to be thought of as important. We permit our children in school to give their time to music and drawing. Our self-made men often devote part of their hard-won earnings to paintings or old books. As soon as our cities accumulate a little spare capital, they start public libraries and orchestras and art galleries. Nevertheless, the lot of the arts is not an altogether happy one. The practitioner of any art is apt to feel that the homage paid the arts is largely sham, and that he is in reality surrounded by a vast ocean of indifference and incomprehension. He and his cohorts are inclined to take to scolding the public or the nation. And the public, on the other hand, when at intervals it is seized with compunction and decides to investigate what is happening in the arts, is likely to find itself puzzled and vexed, and forced to the conclusion that the modern painter or musician or poet "only does it to annoy." It gladly returns to its old favorites, or to its old unconcern.

2. Meanwhile, becalmed upon this windless sea of neglect, the artists and their hangers-on degenerate into connoisseurs and virtuosos and technicians, and quarrel over the functions and purposes of their several arts, and lament the crassness of the modern age. Yet the responsibility for the present unsatisfactory state of affairs must be charged chiefly to the artists. The modern age—for all the disparagement of it which we hear from those who do not belong to it in spirit—is as good as another, if not better. And the public is on the whole right—right in its sense both that the arts ought to be important, and that they somehow aren't. Surely, everyone has a drastic, vital need of art—for reasons which I shall try to set forth later on. And for a long time now the arts have done little to fill this need. In other words, they neglect their most important function.

3. Both artists and critics are apparently unaware of the function I have in mind. In the theoretical discussions which rage among the specialists, many purposes are propounded—and these, it is true, the arts fulfil: they give much pleasure, they afford self-expression to many, they supply a representation, an interpretation, a criticism, of life. At their best, they do what Robert Frost says art should do—"strip life to form." Yet the fact remains that nowadays painting and music and literature are luxury products, epiphenomena—and this condition, I insist, is both wrong and needless. It is due to the arts having forsaken their essential office.

4. To turn to the one art that really flourishes

MACHINERY, MAGIC, AND ART From the *Saturday Review*, July 11, 1931. Reprinted by permission of the publishers.

in our time is instructive—engineering, and especially mechanical engineering. The fact that this is not a fine art, but a utilitarian one, long prevented it from being recognized as an art at all. However, the presupposition that nothing useful can be art, a notion general among both the esthetic clans and the laity, is directly opposite to truth, and has wrought great harm. On the contrary, there ought to be no fine arts, but only useful ones. And mechanical engineering has prospered because there is no doubt as to what it accomplishes, and because that is something everybody wants done: it transmits and regulates power, and everyone wants command of power, ever more power. Thus, this one art that thrives has two lessons to teach the fine arts: that any art can flourish if it will satisfy a strong universal desire; and that what men crave is power. In other words, I suggest that artists set themselves the same end as mechanicians, the communication and control of power. This is the all-important function which modern art has abandoned.

5. Of late there has been some talk, and very interesting talk, too, about machines as works of art. Why not reverse the process, and look at works of art as machines? Such an identification of art and machinery is not unwarranted. In the beginning, they were one and the same thing, they served the same single object, the gaining and ruling of power. This was in the days when they were both indistinguishable parts of primitive magic. As they have developed and differentiated, however, machinery has remained true to its original purpose, but has specialized in handling only physical power. Art, on the other hand, which should specialize in conveying psychological power, has relinquished its office. Consequently, it finds itself in the doldrums, although it has vital work to do that can be done by no other agency. The world has urgent need of it; both the world and art would benefit if the arts could be persuaded to resume their original and proper business, to play once again the rôle they played in early magic.

6. The mention of magic ought not to be too surprising. It has long been recognized that in primitive magic lies a chief source of both science and art. Magic is the savage's engineering, his technology. It is his effort to get command of power and direct it to his own purpose. By mimicry, incantation, and the other methods of magic, he undertakes to control the wind and the rains, to induce fecundity in his tribe, to make his crops grow. Always he has in view, according to his lights, what Bacon foretold as the chief service of natural science, "the relief of man's estate." And it must be remembered that to him magic is in a sense not magic, and certainly not to be divided from science and art. To divert the waters of a stream to his cornfield, to sprinkle it with holy meal, and to make a song or a statue for the benefit of his grain, are for him not only equally valid, but essentially similar means of attaining his end.

7. Furthermore, it must be remembered also that, not discriminating as we do between objective and subjective, he sees physical and psychological energy as all one. He conceives of a universal potency in which all things share to a greater or lesser degree; the terms of the Maori and of the Sioux for this potency, *mana* and *wakanda* respectively have come into wide use among anthropologists. The common American word is "medicine." Just as we wish above everything to get at what we call energy and use it for ourselves, so the savage wishes to avail himself of what he calls *mana*—the two words mean much the same thing. From the individual's private relations with the Powers Above and Below to the communal rites of the whole tribe, runs the same motive, the winning and directing of power.

8. After all, the ways of the savage are not so utterly different from our own. In time of war, for instance, as we invent new explosives and machine guns, he makes himself the best bow and arrows that he can. His fighters do their war dances; our soldiers march and sing. He paints the Thunderbird and other mighty spirits on his equipment to get their assistance; we try to reassure ourselves in our churches that Omnipotence is with us. It is curious to reflect how many of our devices for keeping up our morale, or for sustaining our tribal *wakanda*, are like those of the savage—that is, are magical. And very effective these devices are, too, as everybody knows.

9. For unquestionably there is truth in magic, as well as delusion—but it is psychological, not scientific truth. The love song or the war song, the amulet in which he has faith, beyond doubt render a man more irresistible in love or war, if only by heartening him. By similar means, it is probable, medicine men have succeeded in

curing many illnesses. In the fertility rites of spring, we may question the efficacy of the ceremony with reference to the crops, but we have no reason to question its efficacy with reference to the tribe itself. In relation to external objects, we know that magic fails; but we ought to know also that with reference to the practitioners themselves it is likely to succeed: by means of it, they gain an access of energy—they gain the power they desire.

10. No one, I am sure, who has ever witnessed a genuine magical ceremony will question its effectiveness. Even the ignorant and infidel bystander gains from it a tremendous lift, a renewal, and an enhancement of strength. After all, we have our bodies, we are part animal, and to get a proper relation to our bodily animal energies, instincts, powers—the groundwork of our lives—is of enormous benefit.

11. Magic, then, insofar as it is efficacious and true, might be described as a kind of psychological machinery—that is, a set of devices by which the human being is enabled to avail himself of augmented psychological power, to raise his vitality. "Psychic energy," to be sure, may be only a metaphor, a figure of speech which we use to cover our ignorance, because we know too little to speak literally and exactly. Indeed, we might as well use the primitive terms, and call it *mana, wakanda,* "medicine," mysterious potency. But the phenomenon itself, in some form or other, I am sure, is familiar to everyone; everyone, that is, must be conscious at times of possessing a peculiar abundance of vigor, and at other times of its dearth. We have various methods of securing this vigor; the primitive secures it by the practice of magic.

12. Among the means by which magic works, the two most important, I suspect, are images and rhythm. The savage sings, he dances, he beats his drum—magical practices are replete with rhythmical activities. And rhythmical activity, as we all know from our own experience, sets free our latent energies. Probably it affects our breathing, the beating of our hearts, and the other bodily processes which are themselves rhythmical, speeding them up or toning them down, heightening them and making them more regular. At any rate, whatever the cause, the effect of rhythm is familiar enough, from the savage's war dance to the congregational singing in church and to modern dancing.

13. As for images, their potency is perhaps less generally recognized. But consider the part played by images in magical procedure—in the typical case, for instance, of the warrior's magic, whether individual or communal. First of all, he holds before his mind an image of success, of victory; he pictures himself irresistibly slaying huge numbers of the enemy. Thus he gains confidence, and therefore power. Furthermore, he imagines himself receiving aid from nature; he keeps in his mind an image of Wind or Sun, thus associating and identifying himself with forces mightier than his own. So his own little "medicine" is enlarged by drawing upon the great "medicines" of the world, and he is bucked up, he feels that "virtue" has entered into him. A war song of the Blackfeet, rendered by Miss Eda Lou Walton, illustrates the process:

> The earth is my home,
> It is powerful.
> Water speaks in foam,
> It is powerful.
> There sits a hill,
> It is powerful.
> I go now to kill,
> I am powerful!

14. Strong as the image in the mind may be, however, its strength is immensely increased if it is embodied in something, and so objectified and externalized. The mere association of it with some external object seems to be of much help: the possession of a wolf's tooth or an eagle's feather, for example, aids in addressing prayer for ferocity or speed to the Wolf or Eagle Spirit—aids, presumably, by making more vivid and real the images involved. Still more effective is a drawing, a picture, a carving of wood or stone—any such representation of the Power to be won. This is the "image" in the sense of effigy or likeness, as in the Biblical phrase, "graven image." It is noteworthy that no religion has been able to get along without such images for long—a testimonial to the inability of most people to hold a mental image without help, and to the superior efficacy of the objective image. To the methods of achieving this result should be added the embodying of an image in the mimicry and movements of a dance, and the snaring of it in the words and music of a song. These last methods are of special consequence, because they unite strikingly the two most effec-

tual of the instruments of magic, rhythm, and image.

15. According to the civilized view, the savage, in the act of creating his charm, whether fetish or song or dance, frees and utilizes latent energy in himself; and thereafter the charm has the capacity at proper moments again to make latent energy available, through working upon him with imagery and rhythm. But this, of course, is not at all the savage's view. He believes that the charm itself possesses the *mana;* and he further believes that once the charm is made, its *mana* becomes transferable. The original owner and maker, by giving his talisman to someone else, or by teaching his song or his dance to another, can pass on with it its "medicine." Thus, a man, for instance, who makes a good hunting dance or song may be thought a great benefactor of his tribe. And quite properly, too, for these charms do no doubt produce much the same psychological effect upon others as upon the creators of them. So the man who devises a good war dance may make better fighters of all his clansmen, by enhancing their belligerent ardor.

16. It must be clear by this time what a large part magic has played in the origin of the arts. Other sources also may have contributed: probably wood was carved and pictures drawn for the mere fun of it; probably from the beginning some songs were sheer outbursts of spontaneous feeling. But serious art, art that mattered, was pretty well tied up with magic; a work of art was a magical machine, a contrivance for capturing *mana,* potency. Songs and dances were spells, charms; rituals and pantomimes developed into drama and opera and choral singing; modern fiction is related to the ceremonial rehearsing of sacred myths; and painting and sculpture began mainly in primitive fetishes and idols. Bach and Beethoven are lineal descendants of early shamans and medicine men. Art as well as science has grown out of the basic impulse which underlies magic. But whereas science, at least applied science, has remained true to its first aim, the arts, in our world, have drifted far away.

17. That is my complaint of them. In surrendering their practical usefulness, they have relinquished their chief excuse for being. And only, I am sure, when they return to their first function, when they become again channels of power, will they regain the robust vitality and the wide acceptance and understanding which they have forfeited. For everyone craves more vital energy, more medicine or *wakanda,* and when artists supply it, they will no longer have cause to complain of public indifference. The triumphs and services of science and engineering are no more momentous, I venture to say, in utilizing natural resources, than might be the triumphs and services of art in utilizing human resources.

18. All art that amounts to much has been true to its original function, and has attained its end by magical means—by rhythm and images, embodied, externalized images. The Greek tragedies were not performed, nor the Gothic cathedrals built, we may be sure, merely to gratify the esthetic sense, but to do something, to perform work on the beholders. Later artists, too, have been conscious of this aspect of their work. When Browning describes the effect on a band of pirates of listening to poetry, he says:

> And then, because Greeks are Greeks,
> And hearts are hearts, and *poetry is power,*
> They all outbrake in a great joyous laughter
> With much love.

The effect of, say, imagist verse on bands of Americans is very different from that. And before deciding that Americans are insensitive, let us ask "Is this poetry power?" Of all qualities demanded of poetry nowadays, we hear least of this, that it communicate power. And most of the poets, too, seem to have forgotten this purpose. But Browning was well aware of it, as witness his "Saul," in which David by singing wins Saul back from death to life, and in which Browning himself exemplifies the fact that poetry can be power, can be charged and surcharged with tremendous "medicine."

19. From the artist's point of view, Byron has said the last word: as the artist gives shape and body to his imaginings, he gets back from them the vitality he imparts, and thus increases the life that is in him:

> 'Tis to create, and in creating live
> A being more intense, that we endow
> With form our fancy, gaining as we give
> The life we image.

20. The artist expends much energy, but somehow he gets back more. This is the magical and mysterious effect of artistic creation. It is as if the images, hidden in his mind, contained great

stores of energy, but locked up, latent, inert, which are set free and made available. To take a conspicuous example of figures which have the kind of power in question, think of Michael Angelo's Night or his Adam: these figures, we may suppose, lay secretly in Michael Angelo's mind, unknown to himself, rich in inactive power; then, as they rose before his mind at the moment of conception, and still more, vastly more, as he projected them in marble and in paint, this power was liberated and flooded his consciousness, so that, in Byron's words, he gained, as he gave it, the life he imaged, and lived "a being more intense." In other words, we may be sure that Night or Adam had for Michael Angelo the value that his fetish or his charm has for a savage—an embodiment and a source of supernal energy, of *wakanda*, of mysterious potency. Just as the primitive carves or paints or sings to get at this potency, so does the artist.

21. And just as the charm, together with its power, is transferable, so also—luckily for most of us—is the work of art. It is as if a great musical composition or building or play were an inexhaustible reservoir or store of energy. It transmits to us the power which its creator poured into it. Upon it we can draw for a heightening of vitality, for more abundant life. Nor should it be assumed that only the stately and sublime works of art possess this quality; on the contrary, much popular art has it, and indeed I question whether any art or artist that altogether lacks it can be widely popular. For example, I should say that "The Big Parade" and Charlie Chaplin and Fannie Brice and "Old Man River" and Zane Grey all have more or less of it. Perhaps, indeed, at present the lowbrow arts have more of it than the highbrow. But at any time people will flock to the artist who will move them, do something to them—who will give them that enhancement of life which we all crave. We care so much for it that we will even suffer to get it—and this, I am sure, is why we enjoy tragic art. In spite of the pain involved, the tragic spectacle exalts our own sense of life; it transmits to us the artist's passion and energy, and so gives us a lift, an augmented vitality. Freudians, and others before them, have maintained that all art, and tragedy in particular, is of service chiefly in cleansing bosoms of perilous stuff. But surely art's function is less important as a purgative or a safety-valve than as an unbounded source of energy.

22. I have suggested that art works upon us as magic works upon the savage—by rhythm, and by embodied images. But I think the effect of art is more understandable if for *rhythm* the larger term, *order* or *harmony*, is substituted. If a poem, a statue, or a building is patterned or ordered in form as it should be, if it is a harmonious embodiment of power, it conveys that power to us in order and harmony, and so induces a corresponding harmony in ourselves. Now most of us are seldom in a wholly harmonious state; most of the time much of our energy is absorbed and wasted in strains and conflicts, outer and inner; we do not often, so to speak, hit on all cylinders. Therefore, to be harmonized is for us to be energized—to be "put in order," literally, is to experience an increase of power. This is why form is all-important in art; it corresponds to efficiency in a machine; the power involved, instead of being lost, is communicated so as to do the work it ought to do.

23. If the form enables the power to be transmitted, the carrier of that power is the image. The importance of imagination is grossly underestimated today, probably because for various reasons modern life is marked by an exaggerated objectivity. But for all our externality, our running away from ourselves into outer circumstances and hectic activity, our lives are still largely ruled by images. We imagine ourselves wealthy, or powerful, or learned, or famous, or irresistible in love, or having exciting adventures, and we set ourselves to acquire what we have imagined. Many men and women, possessed by imagination, have cast themselves for rôles beyond their capacities, and striven to be superhuman heroes or saints or sages. For weal or woe, images have dominion over us, and it is of the utmost consequence that we be aware of them, conscious of what is happening, that we be not obsessed by them but judge their fitness for ourselves and our situation. And art, by embodying them in some external medium, helps us to this awareness, enables us to avoid obsession, to distinguish between ourselves and these images. It does not shear them of their power, but it changes that power from obsessive to beneficial.

24. Miss Rebecca West's phrase, "the potent image," is a good one. I have not meant to imply that any or every image is potent; most of them are not. One may imagine oneself walking downstairs or washing one's face, but the image has

no special value for oneself or anyone else. And only potent images have value for art. The most valuable are those which are racial or national, or still better universal. The figure of Don Quixote has been of enormous worth to Spain; the figure of Robin Hood has had a particular attraction for Englishmen. Perhaps the nearest that America has come to such "potent images" is in Lincoln or Jesse James—the mythical, not the historical figures—or in the Indian. The Viking appeals to all northern races. Such figures as Prometheus, the Fire-bringer, or Faust, the man who sold himself to the devil, have a world-wide significance. The potent image, however, need not be human or even naturalistic. Oddly enough, it may even be mathematical. The embodiments in architecture and in music of abstract imagination, of pure form, can be as moving as any. There is no way, so far as I know, of telling which images will have potency, and which will not—but the quality itself is unmistakable.

25. Sometimes it looks as if modern artists by preference busied themselves with impotent images. They seem to avoid images which profoundly move themselves or anyone else, to be distrustful of imagination and above all of emotion. And they have their reward, in comparative neglect and misunderstanding. The public cannot be expected to comprehend, much less to care violently about, subtle problems of technique. But meanwhile, unfortunately, the public suffers even more than the artists from this state of affairs. To be sure, there is all the art of the past to draw upon, but somehow with the lapse of time works of art suffer a gradual loss of power. By no means a total loss, of course, or we should be hard put to it—but it would be absurd to suppose that the "Bacchae" of Euripides or "Le Misanthrope" of Molière can mean as much to us as to their original audiences. The images which were potent in ancient Greece or under the Ancien Régime are naturally much less potent in the twentieth century United States.

26. For these reasons, if we are to get the power which only art can give us, we must have artists of our own to convey it. And we are not without them. There is little ground to complain of our architects. Some of our writers perform their functions. Musicians seem less satisfactory; and only a few sculptors or painters in the United States aim at transmitting power. Just now, this function has been largely relegated to the cheapest practitioners—in literature, for instance, to Zane Grey and Edgar Rice Burroughs. However, there is no reason to suppose that the public prefers inadequate and incompetent art. O'Neill has not lacked his audiences, and even a poem—witness "John Brown's Body"—if it will do its job, can attract hordes of readers. But the public in its demands has been faithful to the original purpose of art; it asks magic and power, and if good artists deny it, it turns to bad ones.

27. The result is deplorable all round. While the artists take for their motto "No compromise with the public taste" and wither away in minute elaboration of their individual, private, and insignificant moods and sensations and skills, the public feeds on husks and straw. Yet I cannot believe that our artists are incapable of conceiving powerful forms and images of more than personal significance, which would profoundly stir them, and therefore us too. I believe rather that, misapprehending their function, they do not solicit such forms and images. For too long they have thought of themselves as playing no social rôle. It is as if a savage, instead of using his magic for the major purpose of living, were to use it only for private entertainment; as if a mechanical engineer, instead of helping get the world's work done, were to design only toys to amuse himself. We need the artists, as we need imperatively the kind of life and power which only they can supply. Let us beg them not to desert us utterly.

PAUL R. WENDT

The Language of Pictures

Paul R. Wendt (1905–   ), professor emeritus of Education at Southern Illinois University, has been associated for many years at several universities with the use of audio-visual aid materials in teaching. He is a member of the Illinois Audio-Visual Association, the American Library Association, the American Education Association, and the Association for Supervision and Curriculum Development. He has published articles in several journals and one monograph, *Development of the Eye Camera for Use with Motion Pictures,* 1953.

In this essay Wendt explains the ways in which pictures speak a language and the semantic pitfalls in our interpretations of that language.

1. Man has been communicating by pictures longer than he has been using words. With the development of photography in this century we are using pictures as a means of communication to such an extent that in some areas they overshadow verbal language. The science of semantics has studied the conveyance of meaning by language in considerable detail. Yet very little is known as to how pictures convey meaning and what their place is in the life of man.

2. Perhaps this neglect may be due to the poor repute pictures have in our society as a means of communication. For example, in the field of education, pictures, as a part of the group of audio-visual materials available to teachers, are still considered supplementary rather than complementary to other teaching materials such as textbooks or other purely verbal materials. The term audio-visual "aids" persists, although a number of educators have tried for a decade to persuade their colleagues to discontinue its use on the basis of its connotation of (1) something used by poor teachers who cannot teach without gadgets, (2) a luxury to be trimmed off the budget in hard times, and (3) a mental crutch for backward pupils.

3. Pictures are of course surrogates for experience. As such they may be said to be closer to extensional meaning than to intensional meaning. At least their position lies in between these two. They are not always close to the actual experience even though the school of "you press the button and we do the rest" implies that merely pointing the camera at Aunt Minnie results in a good likeness to cherish when she is not around. Neither are pictures symbols as words are symbols, since even Aunt Minnie's nephew, age four, can recognize her snapshot though he cannot read.

4. Pictures are a language in themselves. They are not merely limited representations of reality operating within narrow limits of expression. On the contrary photography is a very flexible medium with a wide range whose limits have not yet been sighted. The range extends from absorbing realism to a fairly high level of abstraction. Let us consider the realistic end of the scale.

5. The tendency today is to say that the heyday of the movies is over. Television is gnawing at the vitals of Hollywood. But the powerfully realistic effect of the film remains. The other day the writer showed to one of his classes

THE LANGUAGE OF PICTURES   From *The Use and Misuse of Language* edited by S. I. Hayakawa. Reprinted by permission of Paul R. Wendt.

a film, *The Cinematographer*, which purports to show the work of the director of photography in a large studio. Excerpts from several dramatic films were shown to illustrate the different types of sciences a cinematographer encounters. None of these excerpts was longer than one minute. After the film ended some members of the class complained that the excerpts were so realistic and exciting that they "lost" themselves in the content of the episodes and completely forgot that the purpose of the film showing was to study cinematography. Each episode in turn caught these students up in a rich representation of reality. The excerpts were very dissimilar in content so that it was a wrench to change from one scene to another. Nevertheless the students were deeply involved in each excerpt in turn, and only when the lights came on in the classroom did they remember where they were.

6. Motion pictures are a powerful medium of persuasion. Hitler's films of the bombing of Warsaw were such terribly realistic records that they could be used as a tool of conquest. At times a motion picture may seem even more realistic than the real experience.

7. At the other end of the scale from realism to abstraction, pictures have many qualities of language. Like words every picture has a content of meaning partly intensional, partly extensional. Whether this meaning is more or less extensionally clear or abstractly difficult to understand depends of course on many factors inherent in the viewer, such as his past experience. But it also is dependent on factors in the picture itself which we might call the grammar of photography.

8. Composition is all important. In chirographic, or handmade pictures, composition is achieved sometimes by selection of the point of view but more often by manipulation of space relationships of objects perceived or imagined. The still photographer, unless he is using techniques which are essentially chirographic, such as retouching, montage, or collage, is bound by the objects of reality as the eye of his camera sees them. He achieves composition by painstaking selection of the camera angle, by using a variety of lenses, by choice of filters and emulsions, and by controlling lighting on the subject or scene. Choosing a camera angle may take a professional photographer days of continuous effort, even though television camera operators may be

forced to do it in seconds. The angle and the lens used for the shot determine the basic composition. The lighting, however, gives the photographer an enormous range of control over the representation of reality. High key photography in which all the values are crowded toward the whites and light grays, gives the impressions of light, of lightness, or happiness, or innocent pleasures. Low key photography with many shadows and low values is appropriate for mystery, danger, depression. Every textbook in photography contains the series of portraits of a model taken with different lighting effects, showing how one face can be made to look like many strange people. Pictures have affective connotations.

9. These constitute the grammar of photographs. The analogy holds even down to details such as synizesis. Two crucial objects in a picture, like two syllables, can be blended and not discriminated from each other, thereby changing the meaning entirely. Even though the photographer uses lighting and other techniques to separate the two objects, the viewer may still misread the picture because of lack of experience or poor viewing conditions. Always it is important to remember that pictures, like words, are merely surrogates for reality, not reality itself.

10. In motion pictures we find the syntax of photography. Motion pictures present a flowing discourse in picture surrogates. Like a paragraph, a motion picture sequence is a highly structured time-space analysis and synthesis of reality. Using individual "shots" like words, the sequence inflects the static frame of film by motion. One scene with motion by actors or by the camera resembles a sentence. Short dynamic scenes have the same effect as blunt statements. Longer scenes with complicated changes in composition created by camera movement have somewhat the effect of compound sentences.

11. Pictures, like words, must make a logical continuity, according to accepted rules. For example, a motion picture showing two people conversing must first show them more or less side-to, to establish their relative positions. Then as each speaks he is shown over the other's shoulder. This is the familiar "reverse-angle" shot. That this is a culturally based convention of film syntax is shown by the experience of representatives of the U.S. Office of Information who have found that natives of foreign countries who have not seen motion pictures cannot "under-

stand" the reverse-angle shot. They cannot adjust to our stereotyped representations of reality. They don't understand our language of pictures. Similarly, most of the action in a motion picture must be "matched." That is, if an actor is shown walking up to a door in a distant shot, the following close-up should show him approximately in the same position as he was in the last frame of the long shot. "Matching the action" is a convention in cinematography, part of the film language. It is not always used. When the tempo of the film is fast it is common practice for the editor to elide some of the action, as an author does when he wants the same effect. And of course films *can* compress time dramatically.

12. Paragraphing is accomplished by the traditional fade-out and fade-in, or by the dissolve or optical effect as soft or hard "wipes." The pace of the narrative is determined more by the film editor than by the script. The editor of words clarifies the presentation of content by eliminating words, sentences, paragraphs, and even chapters. The film editor clips out frames, scenes, sequences, and even large parts of a film (resulting sometimes in "the face on the cutting room floor"). The book editor may achieve lucidity by rearranging the author's text, moving paragraphs and chapters. The film editor boldly changes the order of film sequences. Both the book editor and the film editor can have a decisive influence on the style of the finished work. Both can call for rewriting or new photography. Both can affect the pace of the manuscript or the "rough cut." Both are experts in grammar, syntax, and style.

13. More important than the mechanical analogy to words are the semantic dimensions of pictures. Every photograph is an abstraction of an object or an event. Even the amateur, ignorant of the plasticity of the medium, makes an abstraction of Aunt Minnie when he presses the button. Only a few of Aunt Minnie's characteristics are recorded on the film.

14. The professional photographer in control of his medium knows he is abstracting. If he is competent he abstracts to a purpose. Knowing he cannot possibly record the whole event, he sees to it that the abstracting preserves those features he wants to present to the picture-reader. By manipulation of the variables at his command, he lets us "see" the event as he thinks it should be "seen." If he is a news photographer he probably wants to present a "realistic" event,

full of details, although often he is working under such handicaps of haste that the picture as we see it in the newspaper has become simplified and perhaps indistinct. Then it lacks background or environment, it lacks the richness and crispness which a realistic picture must have. Some news pictures are so simplified that they look like symbolizations. They fit the definition of a symbol as "that which suggests something else by convention."

15. The fashion photographer, however, preparing for an advertisement in *The New Yorker*, controls the photographic medium to produce a simple, stylized figure, often against a blank background. This picture is realistic only to a limited extent and approaches the characteristics of a symbol. Carried even further a photograph can be almost purely symbolic, devoid of the very characteristics that are usually associated with photography. Take as an example the famous combat photo of the planting of the American flag by Marines on the summit of Mount Suribachi. There is nothing in the frame but the men struggling to raise the flag and a few rocks of the mountain top. This picture has been accepted as a symbol. It has even been reproduced in bronze in Washington, D.C., as a memorial to the Marines. We accept a statue as a symbol. But here is a case where the statue was copied directly *with little change* from a press shot.

16. At this point we may consider a paradox. *Life* magazine a few years ago ran a series of photographs called "What's in a Picture." One showed a tired interne in a hospital having a quick cup of coffee while still in his surgical gown. Another showed a boy and his dog walking the railroad track. In a third Cardinal Mindszenty was on trial in Hungary. A fourth showed the exhaustion in the face of a combat Marine. There is no doubt that these pictures rate among the most graphic that have ever been taken. In fact, this is why *Life* ran them as a separate series, to show that some of the best pictures need no explanation. This, however, is a characteristic of symbols, and these pictures achieve their greatness because they present symbols— the American doctor, a typical boy, the horror of brain-washing behind the Iron Curtain, and the life of a frontline soldier. It is a paradox that these most graphic pictures are symbolic. They are *at the same time* very real and very symbolic.

17. A picture is a map, since there is not a

one-to-one correspondence between elements of the picture and elements of the event. We might say, as J. J. Gibson says about the retinal image, that a picture is a good correlate *but not a copy* of the scene photographed. A picture definitely has structure. It is a configuration of symbols which make it possible for us to interpret the picture, provided that we have enough experience with these symbols to read the picture.

18. Pictures can be manipulated like words so as to seem to change their referents. The motion picture editor can lengthen and shorten individual scenes and place them in such a juxtaposition in a carefully planned tempo as to create an impression foreign to the events photographed. It would be possible to assemble a number of pictures of active American businessmen and cut them together to give the impression of frantic competition for money when this did not exist in the actual situations.

19. Once we have established the fact that photographs of events are *not* the events, that they show by intent or accident only a few characteristics of events, we have the perspective to question some reactions of people to pictures. In spite of decades of visual education there still are teachers who will not use teaching films when they are easily available. This refusal has been dismissed as conservatism, laziness, and poor teaching. Could it be that some of these teachers, projecting films in undarkened rooms on a wall (for want of a proper screen) and with a screen image not large enough to give a realistic effect, have unconsciously concluded that motion pictures are not enough different from words to bother with? Obviously the great asset of films is realism, which gives the pupils a chance to identify with characters on the screen and "lose" themselves in the picture. When this realism is wiped out by poor reproduction or poor projection, the faint images on the wall lose details, become more outlined and stylized, and have little advantage, if any, over words. Like words they are so vague that they can be interpreted individually by each viewer. Pictures, unlike words, depend very much indeed on the quality of their reproduction for the kind and amount of meaning the picture-reader gets from them.

20. Because of the plasticity of the photographic medium it is well that there are few pictures that do not have captions. In a sense these are indices like Interne$_1$, Interne$_2$. We feel the need of captions on pictures as we do not feel the need for indices on words. Yet we usually feel that pictures are much more likely to be completely self-explanatory than words.

21. General semanticists know it is hard to make the average person realize that he brings meaning to the word, that the word does *not* contain any meaning. A word is just a series of hen tracks which we are told authoritatively stands for a certain concept.

22. It is still harder to convince anyone that we also bring meaning to a picture. If the picture is well within our previous experience it means something. What it means depends on the kind of our experience. The picture of any political figure is interpreted in radically different manner by opposing parties. City children react differently to a picture of a cow than do farm children. Thus pictures can reinforce stereotypes because the characteristics of people or events which the photographer presents through the medium are not strong enough to overcome the "embedded canalizations" in the reader.

23. When the picture is not within the range of our experience we react to it almost as little as to an unknown word. Scenes of mass calisthenics performed by ten thousand Russians mean to us little more than "mass conformity," whereas they may originally have been meant to express "ideals." Strange animals are to us just configurations of light and shade on paper. If they moved on the screen we can apply more of our experience to understanding what we see. Professional photographers, like teachers, have their readers carefully estimated. Like teachers, they see to it that their pictures contain plenty of the familiar (to their particular reader) and some of the unusual. We are able to reach out a short distance into the unknown from the solid base of our own experience. The difference here between words and pictures is that the distinction between the known and the unknown is sharpened by pictures. If we read that an emu is like an ostrich, only larger, we have a vague idea about it. If we see a picture of an emu we remember more clearly the features similar to an ostrich and perhaps notice how the emu is different and new.

24. Pictures are multiordinal. They are interpreted on different levels of abstraction. We have seen this happen in the *Life* series mentioned above. Our Aunt Minnie is just another aunt to

strangers; they think she looks like the Genus Aunt. The fact that pictures are interpreted on different levels is the basis for some items in some common intelligence scales. The lowest level is that in which the child merely enumerates objects and people: "I see a woman and a girl and a stove," etc. This is analogous to the descriptive level of words. A higher level of reaction would be description and interpretation such as, "The woman is probably the girl's mother and she is cooking her supper."

25. A picture causing a semantic disturbance is familiar to everyone. "Oh, that doesn't look like me at all. What a terrible picture!" Or the vacationers who have rented a lake cottage on the basis of glamorous pictures in an advertising folder get a shock when they find that the lake is much smaller than they thought, that the trees are scrubby, and that the cottage is in disrepair. Visitors to California complain that the "blue Pacific" is not always blue, as the postcards invariably show it. Or they say, "Is *that* Velma Blank, the great movie star?" It is in situations like these that we can best realize that pictures, although somewhat better than words, are only maps of the territory they represent.

26. Pictures can be self-reflexive. A photograph of a photograph is a standard method of reproduction, for example, in the making of filmstrips. It is by such reproduction that it is possible to present to congressional committees photographs which seem to show members of the cabinet or senators in conversation with persons with whom they never exchanged more than a word.

27. Pictures, then, have many of the characteristics of language, not in the figurative sense of "the language of flowers" but in the very real characteristics of structure (syntax, grammar, style) and of semantics. The most crucial characteristic is that pictures are abstractions of reality. A picture can present only a few of the aspects of the event. It may, under the strict control of the photographer, become as abstract as a symbol.

28. It is most urgent that there should be more awareness of the abstracting power of photography, that pictures *do lie*. Instead we find great naïveté. People believe what they see in pictures. "One picture is worth a thousand words" not only because it is more graphic but because it is believed to be the gospel truth, an incontrovertible fact. A teacher may present her pupils in a big city with a side view of a cow. They should then know what a cow is! Little do they dream that to a farm boy a cow is a complex of associations which even four hours of movies could not present. We find pictures used as "illustrations." They are inserted in textbooks as a last resort to relieve the copy. One picture of Iowa in the geography text must suffice for Iowa. The author says, "This is Iowa." The general semanticists would recognize this as the error of "allness," ascribing to a word all the characteristics of the thing abstracted from. The danger of "allness" is so much more lively in the case of pictures than in the case of words because everyone assumes pictures *are* reality.

29. Of course pictures provide us with more cues from reality itself (cues for eliciting the meaning we bring to the picture) than the arbitrary hen tracks we call "words." But the basic error is to fail to realize that the meanings of pictures are not in the pictures, but rather in what we bring to them.

ROBERT FROST

Desert Places

Snow falling and night falling fast, oh, fast
In a field I looked into going past,
And the ground almost covered smooth in snow,
But a few weeds and stubble showing last.

The woods around it have it—it is theirs.
All animals are smothered in their lairs.
I am too absent-spirited to count;
The loneliness includes me unawares.

And lonely as it is, that loneliness
Will be more lonely ere it will be less—
A blanker whiteness of benighted snow
With no expression, nothing to express.

They cannot scare me with their empty spaces
Between stars—on stars where no human race is.
I have it in me so much nearer home
To scare myself with my own desert places.

THE NEW YORKER

"Each of Us Is an Odysseus. . . . "

This essay first appeared in *The New Yorker's* "Talk of the Town," a regular column authored anonymously by various writers.

"Each of Us Is an Odysseus. . . ." discusses an often ignored aspect of modern individualism— the dissolution of the traditional bonds between and among individuals.

1. A friend of ours has written us as follows: One afternoon this spring, on the upper East Side of Manhattan, about eighty people sat in pews in a low-ceilinged, rectangular room that had been converted into a chapel. The chapel was an annex of the main church, and, though it was expensively fitted out, had an impersonal, functional character that made one think of the word "service" not in the sense of a religious ritual but in the sense in which the word is linked to "commodity." The presiding minister went well with this impression. The commodity he was providing that afternoon was a funeral, and he delivered the psalms and led the hymns with a professional sincerity that resonated through voids of lost faith. The mood of the congregation, however, was strikingly intent. I would not describe it as either religious or secular; it seemed, rather, to be a sharply focussed mood, bearing witness to a life and death. This focus of feeling cohered within the boundaries of the ceremony like a liquid contained by a centripetal force of its own within a broken, leaky vessel.

2. I had not been close to the woman whose funeral this was. Let's call her Mary Jones. She and her husband, Robert, had spent their summers in the community in which I, two generations younger, was growing up, and this meant that I had seen her often during my life but did

not mean, as far as I could remember, that I had ever had a substantial conversation with her. She was, however, part of a privately held image; and it was in honor of this image that I was there, and with it that I contributed to the centripetal force in the room. Every summer for as far back as I could remember, I had watched Robert and Mary Jones walking down the beach to the water for a swim: she a tall, big-boned woman, clearly beautiful when young, a person with a languorous, faintly ironic style suggesting both character and humor; he a small man, distinguished (although not as glamorous as she), upright (in spirit and body), cheerfully earnest, energetic. A slightly comical couple because of their difference in size, they would walk at a leisurely pace, several feet apart, conversing. I never overheard much of what they said, but it was apparent that the conversation ranged from serious discussion to banter. Often it was punctuated with laughter; I remember the laughter most vividly. When they reached the water, they would wade in, still talking, losing their balance somewhat on the rocks underfoot, talk some more, and, finally, sink in and swim around a little—in a semi-upright position that allowed them to continue talking. Their enjoyment of each other was arresting— sharp as pepper, golden. I have seen other happy old couples, but this picture of the Joneses, renewed many times, came to represent to me an essence of human exchange—something indescribably moving and precious, which comes to fruition only toward the end of a lifelong marriage. Whatever that essence is, I find it dazzling. It has always struck me as one of the great possibilities life has to offer.

3. All through the successive movements of personal emancipation which have been washing across our world in the last century, and particularly in the last decade—drawing power from the most profound intellectual currents of the century, but for the first time forming the values and governing the lives of most of a generation—I have held on to this image of the Joneses. That was not because I disagreed with the principles: the spirit of emancipation has also touched deep nerves of truth, has also opened windows on life's great possibilities. I kept hold of the image not as a refutation of my generation's values but because it reminded me of their limitations: of the blind side of our age, and the cost of the blindness; of a perhaps fatal stupidity intertwined with our enlightenment. The idea of emancipation, after all, has to do with an escape from bonds, not a strengthening of bonds. Emancipation has to do with power, not love; and a view of life in terms of emancipation—or liberation—will tend to be a political view, or, at least, it will interpret life with the political metaphor. Finally, the object of emancipation is the individual, not the connection between individuals; the doctrines of this emancipation stress terms like "self-awareness," "self-fulfillment," "self-discovery," "self-determination," and "self-sufficiency"—terms that crowd anybody other than the "self" right out of one's imagination. The doctrines claim that the relationships between people will be better, on the whole, for the participants' having been emancipated, but even if this is sometimes true, it is fairly plain that the better relationship is not a goal in itself; what is considered worth working for is the individual self-fulfillment possible within the better relationship. (When the relationship—no matter how good—gets in the way of self-fulfillment, it is clear which one has to go.) This may seem to be a purely academic difference of emphasis, but I don't think it is. I don't think that it's a coincidence, for example, that more and more people are living alone these days, that more are getting divorced, that fewer are getting married; it's no coincidence, in other words, that in the age of emancipation—all the talk about "healthier" relationships notwithstanding—there are going to be fewer and fewer Robert and Mary Joneses.

4. During Mary Jones's funeral, I basked in the thought of her marriage, hoarding the warmth against the astral chill of an unknown future. The future chilled me not because I think it promises to eradicate long, happy marriages from the face of the earth; only the most tyrannical social system could accomplish that. What chilled me was a more general sense of the transformation of our society from one that strengthens the bonds between people to one that is, at best, indifferent to them; a sense of an inevitable fraying of the net of connections betwen people at many critical intersections, of which the marital knot is only one. Each fraying accelerates others. A break in one connection, such as attachment to a stable community, puts pressure on other connections: marriage, the relationship between parents and children, religious affiliation, a feeling of connection with the past—even citizenship, that sense of membership in a large community which grows best when it is grounded in membership in a small one. If one examines these points of disintegration separately, one finds they have a common cause—the overriding value placed on the idea of individual emancipation and fulfillment, in the light of which, more and more, the old bonds are seen not as enriching but as confining. We are coming to look upon life as a lone adventure, a great personal odyssey, and there is much in this view which is exhilarating and strengthening, but we seem to be carrying it to such an extreme that if each of us is an Odysseus, he is an Odysseus with no Telemachus to pursue him, with no Ithaca to long for, with no Penelope to return to—an Odysseus on a journey that has been rendered pointless by becoming limitless. The pointlessness of unlimited dispersal: that was the chill against which I hoarded a small, indirect warmth, against which all the people in the room seemed to be exercising, through sheer power of attention, a centripetal, connective force. Death, as always, had reminded me, and perhaps all of us there, of the passionate loneliness at the center of each destiny, and this has no doubt always been a side of human awareness. But the other side—that we give form and meaning to those solitary destinies through our associations with others—has been allowed to fade away, leaving us exposed to a new kind of cold; leaving us to be bound occasionally by the fleeting miracle of coinciding emotions—as in that chapel this spring—but otherwise to hold together through the sheer quixotic effort of individual will alone.

GEORGE ORWELL

Shooting an Elephant

George Orwell (1903–50), whose real name was Eric Blair, was a British novelist, essayist, and satirist. He was born in Bengal, India, and after attending Eton from 1917 to 1921, he served for five years with the Indian Imperial Police in Burma. During the 1930s, Orwell spent several years writing fiction in Paris and one year fighting in the Spanish Civil War, in which he was badly wounded. Among his many books are *Animal Farm,* 1945; *Nineteen Eighty-Four,* 1949; *Shooting an Elephant,* 1950; *Homage to Catalonia,* 1952; and *Such, Such Were the Joys,* 1953.

In his reactions to human experience and behavior Orwell was primarily satirical. "Shooting an Elephant" is a stirring account of an experience that gave him an insight into the real nature of imperialism.

1. In Moulmein, in Lower Burma, I was hated by large numbers of people—the only time in my life that I have been important enough for this to happen to me. I was subdivisional police officer of the town, and in an aimless, petty kind of way anti-European feeling was very bitter. No one had the guts to raise a riot, but if a European woman went through the bazaars alone somebody would probably spit betel juice over her dress. As a police officer I was an obvious target and was baited whenever it seemed safe to do so. When a nimble Burman tripped me up on the football field and the referee (another Burman) looked the other way, the crowd yelled with hideous laughter. This happened more than once. In the end the sneering yellow faces of young men that met me everywhere, the insults hooted after me when I was at a safe distance, got badly on my nerves. The young Buddhist priests were the worst of all. There were several thousands of them in the town and none of them seemed to have anything to do except stand on street corners and jeer at Europeans.

2. All this was perplexing and upsetting. For at that time I had already made up my mind that imperialism was an evil thing and the sooner I chucked up my job and got out of it the better. Theoretically—and secretly, of course—I was all for the Burmese and all against their oppressors, the British. As for the job I was doing, I hated it more bitterly than I can perhaps make clear. In a job like that you see the dirty work of Empire at close quarters. The wretched prisoners huddling in the stinking cages of the lock-ups, the grey, cowed faces of the long-term convicts, the scarred buttocks of the men who had been flogged with bamboos—all these oppressed me with an intolerable sense of guilt. But I could get nothing into perspective. I was young and ill-educated and I had had to think out my problems in the utter silence that is imposed on every Englishman in the East. I did not even know that the British Empire is dying, still less did I know that it is a great deal better than the younger empires that are going to supplant it. All I knew was that I was stuck between my hatred of the

empire I served and my rage against the evil-spirited little beasts who tried to make my job impossible. With one part of my mind I thought of the British Raj as an unbreakable tyranny, as something clamped down, in *saecula saeculorum*, upon the will of prostrate peoples; with another part I thought that the greatest joy in the world would be to drive a bayonet into a Buddhist priest's guts. Feelings like these are the normal by-products of imperialism; ask any Anglo-Indian official, if you can catch him off duty.

3. One day something happened which in a roundabout way was enlightening. It was a tiny incident in itself, but it gave me a better glimpse than I had had before of the real nature of imperialism—the real motives for which despotic governments act. Early one morning the sub-inspector at a police station the other end of the town rang me up on the 'phone and said that an elephant was ravaging the bazaar. Would I please come and do something about it? I did not know what I could do, but I wanted to see what was happening and I got on to a pony and started out. I took my rifle, an old .44 Winchester and much too small to kill an elephant, but I thought the noise might be useful *in terrorem*. Various Burmans stopped me on the way and told me about the elephant's doings. It was not, of course, a wild elephant, but a tame one which had gone "must." It had been chained up, as tame elephants always are when their attack of "must" is due, but on the previous night it had broken its chain and escaped. Its mahout, the only person who could manage it when it was in that state, had set out in pursuit, but had taken the wrong direction and was now twelve hours' journey away, and in the morning the elephant had suddenly reappeared in the town. The Burmese population had no weapons and were quite helpless against it. It had already destroyed somebody's bamboo hut, killed a cow and raided some fruit-stalls and devoured the stock; also it had met the municipal rubbish van and, when the driver jumped out and took to his heels, had turned the van over and inflicted violences upon it.

4. The Burmese sub-inspector and some Indian constables were waiting for me in the quarter where the elephant had been seen. It was a very poor quarter, a labyrinth of squalid bamboo huts, thatched with palm-leaf, winding all over a steep hillside. I remember that it was a cloudy, stuffy morning at the beginning of the rains. We began questioning the people as to where the elephant had gone and, as usual, failed to get any definite information. That is invariably the case in the East; a story always sounds clear enough at a distance, but the nearer you get to the scene of events the vaguer it becomes. Some of the people said that the elephant had gone in one direction, some said that he had gone in another, some professed not even to have heard of any elephant. I had almost made up my mind that the whole story was a pack of lies, when we heard yells a little distance away. There was a loud, scandalized cry of "Go away, child! Go away this instant!" and an old woman with a switch in her hand came round the corner of a hut, violently shooing away a crowd of naked children. Some more women followed, clicking their tongues and exclaiming; evidently there was something that the children ought not to have seen. I rounded the hut and saw a man's dead body sprawling in the mud. He was an Indian, a black Dravidian coolie, almost naked, and he could not have been dead many minutes. The people said that the elephant had come suddenly upon him round the corner of the hut, caught him with its trunk, put its foot on his back and ground him into the earth. This was the rainy season and the ground was soft, and his face had scored a trench a foot deep and a couple of yards long. He was lying on his belly with arms crucified and head sharply twisted to one side. His face was coated with mud, the eyes wide open, the teeth bared and grinning with an expression of unendurable agony. (Never tell me, by the way, that the dead look peaceful. Most of the corpses I have seen looked devilish.) The friction of the great beast's foot had stripped the skin from his back as neatly as one skins a rabbit. As soon as I saw the dead man I sent an orderly to a friend's house nearby to borrow an elephant rifle. I had already sent back the pony, not wanting it to go mad with fright and throw me if it smelt the elephant.

5. The orderly came back in a few minutes with a rifle and five cartridges, and meanwhile some Burmans had arrived and told us that the elephant was in the paddy fields below, only a few hundred yards away. As I started forward practically the whole population of the quarter flocked out of the houses and followed me. They had seen the rifle and were all shouting excitedly

that I was going to shoot the elephant. They had not shown much interest in the elephant when he was merely ravaging their homes, but it was different now that he was going to be shot. It was a bit of fun to them, as it would be to an English crowd; besides they wanted the meat. It made me vaguely uneasy. I had no intention of shooting the elephant—I had merely sent for the rifle to defend myself if necessary—and it is always unnerving to have a crowd following you. I marched down the hill, looking and feeling a fool, with the rifle over my shoulder and an ever-growing army of people jostling at my heels. At the bottom, when you got away from the huts, there was a metalled road and beyond that a miry waste of paddy fields a thousand yards across, not yet ploughed but soggy from the first rains and dotted with coarse grass. The elephant was standing eight yards from the road, his left side towards us. He took not the slightest notice of the crowd's approach. He was tearing up bunches of grass, beating them against his knees to clean them and stuffing them into his mouth.

6. I had halted on the road. As soon as I saw the elephant I knew with perfect certainty that I ought not to shoot him. It is a serious matter to shoot a working elephant—it is comparable to destroying a huge and costly piece of machinery—and obviously one ought not to do it if it can possibly be avoided. And at that distance, peacefully eating, the elephant looked no more dangerous than a cow. I thought then and I think now that his attack of "must" was already passing off; in which case he would merely wander harmlessly about until the mahout came back and caught him. Moreover, I did not in the least want to shoot him. I decided that I would watch him for a little while to make sure that he did not turn savage again, and then go home.

7. But at that moment I glanced round at the crowd that had followed me. It was an immense crowd, two thousand at the least and growing every minute. It blocked the road for a long distance on either side. I looked at the sea of yellow faces above the garish clothes—faces all happy and excited over this bit of fun, all certain that the elephant was going to be shot. They were watching me as they would watch a conjurer about to perform a trick. They did not like me, but with the magical rifle in my hands I was momentarily worth watching. And suddenly I realized that I should have to shoot the elephant after all. The people expected it of me and I had got to do it; I could feel their two thousand wills pressing me forward, irresistibly. And it was at this moment, as I stood there with the rifle in my hands, that I first grasped the hollowness, the futility of the white man's dominion in the East. Here was I, the white man with his gun, standing in front of the unarmed native crowd—seemingly the leading actor of the piece; but in reality I was only an absurd puppet pushed to and fro by the will of those yellow faces behind. I perceived in this moment that when the white man turns tyrant it is his own freedom that he destroys. He becomes a sort of hollow, posing dummy, the conventionalized figure of a sahib. For it is the condition of his rule that he shall spend his life in trying to impress the "natives," and so in every crisis he has got to do what the "natives" expect of him. He wears a mask, and his face grows to fit it. I had got to shoot the elephant. I had committed myself to doing it when I sent for the rifle. A sahib has got to act like a sahib; he has got to appear resolute, to know his own mind and do definite things. To come all that way, rifle in hand, with two thousand people marching at my heels, and then to trail feebly away, having done nothing—no, that was impossible. The crowd would laugh at me. And my whole life, every white man's life in the East, was one long struggle not to be laughed at.

8. But I did not want to shoot the elephant. I watched him beating his bunch of grass against his knees, with that preoccupied grandmotherly air that elephants have. It seemed to me that it would be murder to shoot him. At that age I was not squeamish about killing animals, but I had never shot an elephant and never wanted to. (Somehow it always seems worse to kill a *large* animal.) Besides, there was the beast's owner to be considered. Alive, the elephant was worth at least a hundred pounds; dead, he would only be worth the value of his tusks, five pounds, possibly. But I had got to act quickly. I turned to some experienced-looking Burmans who had been there when we arrived, and asked them how the elephant had been behaving. They all said the same thing: he took no notice of you if you left him alone, but he might charge if you went too close to him.

9. It was perfectly clear to me what I ought

to do. I ought to walk up to within, say, twenty-five yards of the elephant and test his behavior. If he charged, I could shoot; if he took no notice of me, it would be safe to leave him until the mahout came back. But also I knew that I was going to do no such thing. I was a poor shot with a rifle and the ground was soft mud into which one would sink at every step. If the elephant charged and I missed him, I should have about as much chance as a toad under a steam-roller. But even then I was not thinking particularly of my own skin, only of the watchful yellow faces behind. For at that moment, with the crowd watching me, I was not afraid in the ordinary sense, as I would have been if I had been alone. A white man musn't be frightened in front of "natives"; and so, in general, he isn't frightened. The sole thought in my mind was that if anything went wrong those two thousand Burmans would see me pursued, caught, trampled on and reduced to a grinning corpse like that Indian up the hill. And if that happened it was quite probable that some of them would laugh. That would never do. There was only one alternative. I shoved the cartridges into the magazine and lay down on the road to get a better aim.

10. The crowd grew very still, and a deep, low, happy sigh, as of people who see the theatre curtain go up at last, breathed from innumerable throats. They were going to have their bit of fun after all. The rifle was a beautiful German thing with cross-hair sights. I did not then know that in shooting an elephant one would shoot to cut an imaginary bar running from ear-hole to ear-hole. I ought, therefore, as the elephant was sideways on, to have aimed straight at his ear-hole; actually I aimed several inches in front of this, thinking the brain would be further forward.

11. When I pulled the trigger I did not hear the bang or feel the kick—one never does when a shot goes home—but I heard the devilish roar of glee that went up from the crowd. In that instant, in too short a time, one would have thought, even for the bullet to get there, a mysterious, terrible change had come over the elephant. He neither stirred nor fell, but every line of his body had altered. He looked suddenly stricken, shrunken, immensely old, as though the frightful impact of the bullet had paralysed him without knocking him down. At last, after what seemed a long time—it might have been five seconds, I dare say—he sagged flabbily to his

knees. His mouth slobbered. An enormous senility seemed to have settled upon him. One could have imagined him thousands of years old. I fired again into the same spot. At the second shot he did not collapse but climbed with desperate slowness to his feet and stood weakly upright, with legs sagging and head drooping. I fired a third time. That was the shot that did for him. You could see the agony of it jolt his whole body and knock the last remnant of strength from his legs. But in falling he seemed for a moment to rise, for as his hind legs collapsed beneath him he seemed to tower upward like a huge rock toppling, his trunk reaching skyward like a tree. He trumpeted, for the first and only time. And then down he came, his belly towards me, with a crash that seemed to shake the ground even where I lay.

12. I got up. The Burmans were already racing past me across the mud. It was obvious that the elephant would never rise again, but he was not dead. He was breathing very rhythmically with long rattling gasps, his great mound of a side painfully rising and falling. His mouth was wide open—I could see far down into caverns of pale pink throat. I waited a long time for him to die, but his breathing did not weaken. Finally I fired my two remaining shots into the spot where I thought his heart must be. The thick blood welled out of him like red velvet, but still he did not die. His body did not even jerk when the shots hit him, the tortured breathing continued without a pause. He was dying, very slowly and in great agony, but in some world remote from me where not even a bullet could damage him further. I felt that I had got to put an end to that dreadful noise. It seemed dreadful to see the great beast lying there, powerless to move and yet powerless to die, and not even to be able to finish him. I sent back for my small rifle and poured shot after shot into his heart and down his throat. They seemed to make no impression. The tortured gasps continued as steadily as the ticking of a clock.

13. In the end I could not stand it any longer and went away. I heard later that it took him half an hour to die. Burmans were bringing dahs and baskets even before I left, and I was told they had stripped his body almost to the bones by the afternoon.

14. Afterwards, of course, there were endless discussions about the shooting of the elephant.

The owner was furious, but he was only an Indian and could do nothing. Besides, legally I had done the right thing, for a mad elephant has to be killed, like a mad dog, if its owner fails to control it. Among the Europeans opinion was divided. The older men said I was right, the younger men said it was a damn shame to shoot an elephant for killing a coolie, because an ele-phant was worth more than any damn Coringhee coolie. And afterwards I was very glad that the coolie had been killed; it put me legally in the right and it gave me a sufficient pretext for shooting the elephant. I often wondered whether any of the others grasped that I had done it solely to avoid looking a fool.

JAMES BALDWIN

Stranger in the Village

James Baldwin (1924–) was born in Harlem the son of a minister. Recipient of numerous writing fellowships and awards, he has become one of the best black authors of this century. His *Go Tell It on the Mountain*, 1953, tells of his early religious experience. He has written several novels—*Giovanni's Room*, 1956; *Another Country*, 1962; and *Tell Me How Long the Train's Been Gone*, 1968; as well as several volumes of essays—*Notes of a Native Son*, 1955, a long autobiographical essay for which he is best known; *Nobody Knows My Name*, 1961; and *The Fire Next Time*, 1963. His recent writings are a volume of short stories, *Going to Meet the Man*, 1965; two full-length plays—*Blues for Mister Charley*, 1964; and *The Amen Corner*, 1968—*Another Country*, 1970; *If Beale Street Could Talk*, 1974; *The Devil Finds Work*, 1976; and *Just Above My Head*, 1979.

"Stranger in the Village" perceptively tells of Baldwin's experience during a stay in a Swiss village, where he feels directly and indirectly the age-old hostility between blacks and whites.

1. From all available evidence no black man had ever set foot in this tiny Swiss village before I came. I was told before arriving that I would probably be a "sight" for the village; I took this to mean that people of my complexion were rarely seen in Switzerland, and also that city people are always something of a "sight" outside of the city. It did not occur to me—possibly because I am an American—that there could be people anywhere who had never seen a Negro.

2. It is a fact that cannot be explained on the basis of the inaccessibility of the village. The village is very high, but it is only four hours from Milan and three hours from Lausanne. It is true that it is virtually unknown. Few people making plans for a holiday would elect to come here. On the other hand, the villagers are able, presumably, to come and go as they please—which they do: to another town at the foot of the mountain, with a population of approximately five thousand, the nearest place to see a movie or go to the bank. In the village there is no movie house, no bank, no library, no theater; very few radios, one jeep, one station wagon; and, at the moment, one typewriter, mine, an invention

STRANGER IN THE VILLAGE From *Notes of a Native Son* by James Baldwin. Copyright © 1955 by James Baldwin. Reprinted by permission of the Beacon Press.

which the woman next door to me here had never seen. There are about six hundred people living here, all Catholic—I conclude this from the fact that the Catholic church is open all year round, whereas the Protestant chapel, set off on a hill a little removed from the village, is open only in the summertime when the tourists arrive. There are four or five hotels, all closed now, and four or five *bistros*, of which, however, only two do any business during the winter. These two do not do a great deal, for life in the village seems to end around nine or ten o'clock. There are a few stores, butcher, baker, *épicerie*, a hardware store, and a money-changer—who cannot change travelers' checks, but must send them down to the bank, an operation which takes two or three days. There is something called the *Ballet Haus*, closed in the winter and used for God knows what, certainly not ballet, during the summer. There seems to be only one schoolhouse in the village, and this for the quite young children; I suppose this to mean that their older brothers and sisters at some point descend from these mountains in order to complete their education—possibly, again, to the town just below. The landscape is absolutely forbidding, mountains towering on all four sides, ice and snow as far as the eye can reach. In this white wilderness, men and women and children move all day, carrying washing, wood, buckets of milk or water, sometimes skiing on Sunday afternoons. All week long boys and young men are to be seen shoveling snow off the rooftops, or dragging wood down from the forest in sleds.

3. The village's only real attraction, which explains the tourist season, is the hot spring water. A disquietingly high proportion of these tourists are cripples, or semicripples, who come year after year—from other parts of Switzerland, usually—to take the waters. This lends the village, at the height of the season, a rather terrifying air of sanctity, as though it were a lesser Lourdes. There is often something beautiful, there is always something awful, in the spectacle of a person who has lost one of his faculties, a faculty he never questioned until it was gone, and who struggles to recover it. Yet people remain people, on crutches or indeed on deathbeds; and wherever I passed, the first summer I was here, among the native villagers or among the lame, a wind passed with me—of astonishment, curiosity, amusement, and outrage. That

first summer I stayed two weeks and never intended to return. But I did return in the winter, to work; the village offers, obviously, no distractions whatever and has the further advantage of being extremely cheap. Now it is winter again, a year later, and I am here again. Everyone in the village knows my name, though they scarcely ever use it, knows that I come from America—though, this, apparently, they will never really believe: black men come from Africa—and everyone knows that I am the friend of the son of a woman who was born here, and that I am staying in their chalet. But I remain as much a stranger today as I was the first day I arrived, and the children shout *Neger! Neger!* as I walk along the streets.

4. It must be admitted that in the beginning I was far too shocked to have any real reaction. In so far as I reacted at all, I reacted by trying to be pleasant—it being a great part of the American Negro's education (long before he goes to school) that he must make people "like" him. This smile-and-the-world-smiles-with-you routine worked about as well in this situation as it had in the situation for which it was designed, which is to say that it did not work at all. No one, after all, can be liked whose human weight and complexity cannot be, or has not been, admitted. My smile was simply another unheard-of phenomenon which allowed them to see my teeth—they did not, really, see my smile and I began to think that, should I take to snarling, no one would notice any difference. All of the physical characteristics of the Negro which had caused me, in America, a very different and almost forgotten pain were nothing less than miraculous—or infernal—in the eyes of the village people. Some thought my hair was the color of tar, that it had the texture of wire, or the texture of cotton. It was jocularly suggested that I might let it all grow long and make myself a winter coat. If I sat in the sun for more than five minutes some daring creature was certain to come along and gingerly put his fingers on my hair, as though he were afraid of an electric shock, or put his hand on my hand, astonished that the color did not rub off. In all of this, in which it must be conceded there was the charm of genuine wonder and in which there was certainly no element of intentional unkindness, there was yet no suggestion that I was human: I was simply a living wonder.

5. I knew that they did not mean to be unkind, and I know it now; it is necessary, nevertheless, for me to repeat this to myself each time that I walk out of the chalet. The children who shout *Neger!* have no way of knowing the echoes this sound raises in me. They are brimming with good humor and the more daring swell with pride when I stop to speak with them. Just the same, there are days when I cannot pause and smile, when I have no heart to play with them; when, indeed, I mutter sourly to myself, exactly as I muttered on the streets of a city these children have never seen, when I was no bigger than these children are now: *Your* mother *was a nigger.* Joyce is right about history being a nightmare—but it may be the nightmare from which no one *can* awaken. People are trapped in history and history is trapped in them.

6. There is a custom in the village—I am told it is repeated in many villages—of "buying" African natives for the purpose of converting them to Christianity. There stands in the church all year round a small box with a slot for money, decorated with a black figurine, and into this box the villagers drop their francs. During the *carnaval* which precedes Lent, two village children have their faces blackened—out of which bloodless darkness their blue eyes shine like ice—and fantastic horsehair wigs are placed on their blond heads; thus disguised, they solicit among the villagers for money for the missionaries in Africa. Between the box in the church and the blackened children, the village "bought" last year six or eight African natives. This was reported to me with pride by the wife of one of the *bistro* owners and I was careful to express astonishment and pleasure at the solicitude shown by the village for the souls of black folk. The *bistro* owner's wife beamed with a pleasure far more genuine than my own and seemed to feel that I might now breathe more easily concerning the souls of at least six of my kinsmen.

7. I tried not to think of these so lately baptized kinsmen, of the price paid for them, or the peculiar price they themselves would pay, and said nothing about my father, who having taken his own conversion too literally never, at bottom, forgave the white world (which he described as heathen) for having saddled him with a Christ in whom, to judge at least from their treatment of him, they themselves no longer believed. I thought of white men arriving for the first time in an African village, strangers there, as I am a stranger here, and tried to imagine the astounded populace touching their hair and marveling at the color of their skin. But there is a great difference between being the first white man to be seen by Africans and being the first black man to be seen by whites. The white man takes the astonishment as tribute, for he arrives to conquer and to convert the natives, whose inferiority in relation to himself is not even to be questioned; whereas I, without a thought of conquest, find myself among a people whose culture controls me, has even, in a sense, created me, people who have cost me more in anguish and rage than they will ever know, who yet do not even know of my existence. The astonishment with which I might have greeted them, should they have stumbled into my African village a few hundred years ago, might have rejoiced their hearts. But the astonishment with which they greet me today can only poison mine.

8. And this is so despite everything I may do to feel differently, despite my friendly conversations with the *bistro* owner's wife, despite their three-year-old son who has at last become my friend, despite the *saluts* and *bonsoirs* which I exchange with people as I walk, despite the fact that I know that no individual can be taken to task for what history is doing, or has done. I say that the culture of these people controls me—but they can scarcely be held responsible for European culture. America comes out of Europe, but these people have never seen America, nor have most of them seen more of Europe than the hamlet at the foot of their mountain. Yet they move with an authority which I shall never have; and they regard me, quite rightly, not only as a stranger in their village but as a suspect latecomer, bearing no credentials, to everything they have—however unconsciously—inherited.

9. For this village, even were it incomparably more remote and incredibly more primitive, is the West, the West onto which I have been so strangely grafted. These people cannot be, from the point of view of power, strangers anywhere in the world; they have made the modern world, in effect, even if they do not know it. The most illiterate among them is related, in a way that I am not, to Dante, Shakespeare, Michelangelo, Aeschylus, Da Vinci, Rembrandt, and Racine; the cathedral at Chartres says something to them which it cannot say to me, as indeed would New

York's Empire State Building, should anyone here ever see it. Out of their hymns and dances come Beethoven and Bach. Go back a few centuries and they are in their full glory—but I am in Africa, watching the conquerors arrive.

10. The rage of the disesteemed is personally fruitless, but it is also absolutely inevitable; this rage, so generally discounted, so little understood even among the people whose daily bread it is, is one of the things that makes history. Rage can only with difficulty, and never entirely, be brought under the domination of the intelligence and is therefore not susceptible to any arguments whatever. This is a fact which ordinary representatives of the *Herrenvolk*, having never felt this rage and being unable to imagine it, quite fail to understand. Also, rage cannot be hidden, it can only be dissembled. This dissembling deludes the thoughtless, and strengthens rage and adds, to rage, contempt. There are, no doubt, as many ways of coping with the resulting complex of tensions as there are black men in the world, but no black man can hope ever to be entirely liberated from this internal warfare—rage, dissembling, and contempt having inevitably accompanied his first realization of the power of white men. What is crucial here is that, since white men represent in the black man's world so heavy a weight, white men have for black men a reality which is far from being reciprocal; and hence all black men have toward all white men an attitude which is designed, really, either to rob the white man of the jewel of his naïveté, or else to make it cost him dear.

11. The black man insists, by whatever means he finds at his disposal, that the white man cease to regard him as an exotic rarity and recognize him as a human being. This is a very charged and difficult moment, for there is a great deal of will power involved in the white man's naïveté. Most people are not naturally reflective any more than they are naturally malicious, and the white man prefers to keep the black man at a certain human remove because it is easier for him thus to preserve his simplicity and avoid being called to account for crimes committed by his forefathers, or his neighbors. He is inescapably aware, nevertheless, that he is in a better position in the world than black men are, nor can he quite put to death the suspicion that he is hated by black men therefore. He does not wish to be hated, neither does he wish to change

places, and at this point in his uneasiness he can scarcely avoid having recourse to those legends which white men have created about black men, the most usual effect of which is that the white man finds himself enmeshed, so to speak, in his own language which describes hell, as well as the attributes which lead one to hell, as being as black as night.

12. Every legend, moreover, contains its residuum of truth, and the root function of language is to control the universe by describing it. It is of quite considerable significance that black men remain, in the imagination, and in overwhelming numbers in fact, beyond the disciplines of salvation; and this despite the fact that the West has been "buying" African natives for centuries. There is, I should hazard, an instantaneous necessity to be divorced from this so visibly unsaved stranger, in whose heart, moreover, one cannot guess what dreams of vengeance are being nourished; and, at the same time, there are few things on earth more attractive than the idea of the unspeakable liberty which is allowed the unredeemed. When, beneath the black mask, a human being begins to make himself felt one cannot escape a certain awful wonder as to what kind of human being it is. What one's imagination makes of other people is dictated, of course, by the laws of one's own personality and it is one of the ironies of black-white relations that, by means of what the white man imagines the black man to be, the black man is enabled to know who the white man is.

13. I have said, for example, that I am as much a stranger in this village today as I was the first summer I arrived, but this is not quite true. The villagers wonder less about the texture of my hair than they did then, and wonder rather more about me. And the fact that their wonder now exists on another level is reflected in their attitudes and in their eyes. There are the children who make those delightful, hilarious, sometimes astonishingly grave overtures of friendship in the unpredictable fashion of children; other children, having been taught that the devil is a black man, scream in genuine anguish as I approach. Some of the older women never pass without a friendly greeting, never pass, indeed, if it seems that they will be able to engage me in conversation; other women look down or look away or rather contemptuously smirk. Some of the men drink with me and suggest that I learn how to ski—partly,

I gather, because they cannot imagine what I would look like on skis—and want to know if I am married, and ask questions about my *métier*. But some of the men have accused *le sale nègre*—behind my back—of stealing wood and there is already in the eyes of some of them that peculiar, intent, paranoiac malevolence which one sometimes surprises in the eyes of American white men when, out walking with their Sunday girl, they see a Negro male approach.

14. There is a dreadful abyss between the streets of this village and the streets of the city in which I was born, between the children who shout *Neger!* today and those who shouted *Nigger!* yesterday—the abyss is experience, the American experience. The syllable hurled behind me today expresses, above all, wonder: I am a stranger here. But I am not a stranger in America and the same syllable riding on the American air expresses the war my presence has occasioned in the American soul.

15. For this village brings home to me this fact: that there was a day, and not really a very distant day, when Americans were scarcely Americans at all but discontented Europeans, facing a great unconquered continent and strolling, say, into a marketplace and seeing black men for the first time. The shock this spectacle afforded is suggested, surely, by the promptness with which they decided that these black men were not really men but cattle. It is true that the necessity on the part of the settlers of the New World of reconciling their moral assumptions with the fact—and the necessity—of slavery enhanced immensely the charm of this idea, and it is also true that this idea expresses, with a truly American bluntness, the attitude which to varying extents all masters have had toward all slaves.

16. But between all former slaves and slave-owners and the drama which begins for Americans over three hundred years ago at Jamestown, there are at least two differences to be observed. The American Negro slave could not suppose, for one thing, as slaves in past epochs had supposed and often done, that he would ever be able to wrest the power from his master's hands. This was a supposition which the modern era, which was to bring about such vast changes in the aims and dimensions of power, put to death; it only begins, in unprecedented fashion, and with dreadful implications, to be resurrected today. But even had this supposition persisted with undiminished force, the American Negro slave could not have used it to lend his condition dignity, for the reason that this supposition rests on another: that the slave in exile yet remains related to his past, has some means—if only in memory—of revering and sustaining the forms of his former life, is able, in short, to maintain his identity.

17. This was not the case with the American Negro slave. He is unique among the black men of the world in that his past was taken from him, almost literally, at one blow. One wonders what on earth the first slave found to say to the first dark child he bore. I am told that there are Haitians able to trace their ancestry back to African kings, but any American Negro wishing to go back so far will find his journey through time abruptly arrested by the signature on the bill of sale which served as the entrance paper for his ancestor. At the time—to say nothing of the circumstances—of the enslavement of the captive black man who was to become the American Negro, there was not the remotest possibility that he would ever take power from his master's hands. There was no reason to suppose that his situation would ever change, nor was there, shortly, anything to indicate that his situation had ever been different. It was his necessity, in the words of E. Franklin Frazier, to find a "motive for living under American culture or die." The identity of the American Negro comes out of this extreme situation, and the evolution of this identity was a source of the most intolerable anxiety in the minds and the lives of his masters.

18. For the history of the American Negro is unique also in this: that the question of his humanity, and of his rights therefore as a human being, became a burning one for several generations of Americans, so burning a question that it ultimately became one of those used to divide the nation. It is out of this argument that the venom of the epithet *Nigger!* is derived. It is an argument which Europe has never had, and hence Europe quite sincerely fails to understand how or why the argument arose in the first place, why its effects are so frequently disastrous and always so unpredictable, why it refuses until today to be entirely settled. Europe's black possessions remained—and do remain—in Europe's colonies, at which remove they represented no threat whatever to European identity. If they

posed any problem at all for the European conscience, it was a problem which remained comfortingly abstract: in effect, the black man, *as a man*, did not exist for Europe. But in America, even as a slave, he was an inescapable part of the general social fabric and no American could escape having an attitude toward him. Americans attempt until today to make an abstraction of the Negro, but the very nature of these abstractions reveals the tremendous effects the presence of the Negro has had on the American character.

19. When one considers the history of the Negro in America it is of the greatest importance to recognize that the moral beliefs of a person, or a people, are never really as tenuous as life— which is not moral—very often causes them to appear; these create for them a frame of reference and a necessary hope, the hope being that when life has done its worst they will be enabled to rise above themselves and to triumph over life. Life would scarcely be bearable if this hope did not exist. Again, even when the worst has been said, to betray a belief is not by any means to have put oneself beyond its power; the betrayal of a belief is not the same thing as ceasing to believe. If this were not so there would be no moral standards in the world at all. Yet one must also recognize that morality is based on ideas and that all ideas are dangerous—dangerous because ideas can only lead to action and where the action leads no man can say. And dangerous in this respect: that confronted with the impossibility of remaining faithful to one's beliefs, and the equal impossibility of becoming free of them, one can be driven to the most inhuman excesses. The ideas on which American beliefs are based are not, though Americans often seem to think so, ideas which originated in America. They came out of Europe. And the establishment of democracy on the American continent was scarcely as radical a break with the past as was the necessity, which Americans faced, of broadening this concept to include black men.

20. This was, literally, a hard necessity. It was impossible, for one thing, for Americans to abandon their beliefs, not only because these beliefs alone seemed able to justify the sacrifices they had endured and the blood that they had spilled, but also because these beliefs afforded them their only bulwark against a moral chaos as absolute as the physical chaos of the continent it was their destiny to conquer. But in the situation in which Americans found themselves, these beliefs threatened an idea which, whether or not one likes to think so, is the very warp and woof of the heritage of the West, the idea of white supremacy.

21. Americans have made themselves notorious by the shrillness and the brutality with which they have insisted on this idea, but they did not invent it; and it has escaped the world's notice that those very excesses of which Americans have been guilty imply a certain, unprecedented uneasiness over the idea's life and power, if not, indeed, the idea's validity. The idea of white supremacy rests simply on the fact that white men are the creators of civilization (the present civilization, which is the only one that matters; all previous civilizations are simply "contributions" to our own) and are therefore civilization's guardians and defenders. Thus it was impossible for Americans to accept the black man as one of themselves, for to do so was to jeopardize their status as white men. But not so to accept him was to deny his human reality, his human weight and complexity, and the strain of denying the overwhelmingly undeniable forced Americans into rationalizations so fantastic that they approached the pathological.

22. At the root of the American Negro problem is the necessity of the American white man to find a way of living with the Negro in order to be able to live with himself. And the history of this problem can be reduced to the means used by Americans—lynch law and law, segregation and legal acceptance, terrorization and concession—either to come to terms with this necessity, or to find a way around it, or (most usually) to find a way of doing both these things at once. The resulting spectacle, at once foolish and dreadful, led someone to make the quite accurate observation that "the Negro-in-America is a form of insanity which overtakes white men."

23. In this long battle, a battle by no means finished, the unforeseeable effects of which will be felt by many future generations, the white man's motive was the protection of his identity; the black man was motivated by the need to establish an identity. And despite the terrorization which the Negro in America endured and endures sporadically until today, despite the cruel and totally inescapable ambivalence of his status in his country, the battle for his identity has long ago been won. He is not a visitor to

the West, but a citizen there, an American; as American as the Americans who despise him, the Americans who fear him, the Americans who love him—the Americans who became less than themselves, or rose to be greater than themselves by virtue of the fact that the challenge he represented was inescapable. He is perhaps the only black man in the world whose relationship to white men is more terrible, more subtle, and more meaningful than the relationship of bitter possessed to uncertain possessor. His survival depended, and his development depends, on his ability to turn his peculiar status in the Western world to his own advantage and, it may be, to the very great advantage of that world. It remains for him to fashion out of his experience that which will give him sustenance, and a voice.

24. The cathedral at Chartres, I have said, says something to the people of this village which it cannot say to me; but it is important to understand that this cathedral says something to me which it cannot say to them. Perhaps they are struck by the power of the spires, the glory of the windows; but they have known God, after all, longer than I have known him, and in a different way, and I am terrified by the slippery bottomless well to be found in the crypt, down which heretics were hurled to death, and by the obscene, inescapable gargoyles jutting out of the stone and seeming to say that God and the devil can never be divorced. I doubt that the villagers think of the devil when they face a cathedral because they have never been identified with the devil. But I must accept the status which myth, if nothing else, gives me in the West before I can hope to change the myth.

25. Yet, if the American Negro has arrived at his identity by virtue of the absoluteness of his estrangement from his past, American white men still nourish the illusion that there is some means of recovering the European innocence, of returning to a state in which black men do not exist. This is one of the greatest errors Americans can make. The identity they fought so hard to protect has, by virtue of that battle, undergone a change:

Americans are as unlike any other white people in the world as it is possible to be. I do not think, for example, that it is too much to suggest that the American vision of the world—which allows so little reality, generally speaking, for any of the darker forces in human life, which tends until today to paint moral issues in glaring black and white—owes a great deal to the battle waged by Americans to maintain between themselves and black men a human separation which could not be bridged. It is only now beginning to be borne in on us—very faintly, it must be admitted, very slowly, and very much against our will—that this vision of the world is dangerously inaccurate, and perfectly useless. For it protects our moral high-mindedness at the terrible expense of weakening our grasp of reality. People who shut their eyes to reality simply invite their own destruction, and anyone who insists on remaining in a state of innocence long after that innocence is dead turns himself into a monster.

26. The time has come to realize that the interracial drama acted out on the American continent has not only created a new black man, it has created a new white man, too. No road whatever will lead Americans back to the simplicity of this European village where white men still have the luxury of looking on me as a stranger. I am not, really, a stranger any longer for any American alive. One of the things that distinguishes Americans from other people is that no other people has ever been so deeply involved in the lives of black men, and vice versa. This fact faced, with all its implications, it can be seen that the history of the American Negro problem is not merely shameful, it is also something of an achievement. For even when the worst has been said, it must also be added that the perpetual challenge posed by this problem was always, somehow, perpetually met. It is precisely this black-white experience which may prove of indispensable value to us in the world we face today. This world is white no longer, and it will never be white again.

CARLOS FUENTES

Dealing with the Damn Yanqui

Carlos Fuentes (1928-   ), is Mexico's greatest and best-known contemporary writer and, since 1974, his country's ambassador to France. Educated at the University of Mexico and the Institute of International Studies in Geneva, Switzerland, he began his diplomatic career as assistant head of the Mexican Ministry of Foreign Affairs; he then became assistant director of cultural dissemination in the same ministry, and later head of the Department of Cultural Relations. In 1974 he was named a fellow at the Woodrow Wilson International Center for Scholars in Washington, D.C. Among Fuentes' works in English are *Whither Latin America*, 1963; *Don Quixote, or The Critique of Reading*, 1974; and *Terra Nostra*, 1974. He is a constant contributor to magazines and journals in several languages.

In "Dealing with the Damn Yanqui" Fuentes details the problems between Mexico and the United States—their history, cultural bases, and their significance—and provides a precise solution. He says: "Understanding is a two-way street and when we travel it . . . we tend to greet each other as human beings. But being human is being singular, shaped by history and culture, being different." Learning to accept those who are different is at the heart of most international problems, because those problems are really intercultural problems.

1. The very first problem Mexico has with the United States of America is right here in this sentence. What should we call you? For most Mexicans, the United States of America is not a name. It is a description as imprecise as the Shop Around the Corner, a location as hazy as the one Where Angels Fear to Tread.

2. There is the question of usurpation. The Americas stretch from the Arctic to the Antarctic, not from Oregon to Florida or from Central Park South to Canal Street. The unfriendly ghost of hegemony peers down at us from this monopoly of a continent's name in the name of one of its nations—constantly reminding us that you are the most powerful, the wealthiest, the most cavalier. It is as if Russia decided to call itself the European Union of Republics, and left fifty million Frenchmen and a few citizens of Andorra to wince and stew.

3. Perhaps it is fitting that the two mightiest nations in today's world should have no real name but rather what amount to acronyms, U.S.A. and U.S.S.R. Mexico does have a name, and it is heavy with meaning. First, it is the name of a people, the Mexitli, who came down from the north in search of a lake, an eagle and a serpent, and there founded a city in the center of Mexico and with the name of Mexico. This word means "navel of the moon" and reflects the innermost conflict of the original Mexicans (also known as Aztecs), those latecomers to the sacred highland from which Mexico has been ruled for more than a thousand years.

4. "Mexico" is the name of a nation that has forever harbored the suspicion that nothing begins today, that all things and all peoples are charged with a past that must be dealt with per-

DEALING WITH THE DAMN YANQUI   Reprinted by permission of the author.

petually, because redemption is to be found more in the origin than in the future. Take the case of the Aztecs. When they reached the Valley of Mexico in the early fourteenth century, they claimed for themselves the legitimacy of the sacred center, the summit of the pyramid, but still had the feeling of being satellites of the Toltec tradition (somewhat like the Romans' relationship to the Greeks); usurpers of the Toltec morality of brotherhood and freedom, which centered around the cult of Quetzalcoatl, the Plumed Serpent, and which the Aztecs debased and transformed into a politics of domination.

5. So the name Mexico, from its very beginning, is a place and a meaning, center and moon, a fleeting power, a tragic fate, a culture of omens subject to the return of Quetzalcoatl and his judgment on what men had done with his heritage. The Plumed Serpent returned precisely on the day foreseen by the augurs and its name was Cortés. The Aztec Empire succumbed out of sheer astonishment that the prophecies should have come true. It yielded the navel of the moon to the sons of Quetzalcoatl, the white, bearded Spaniards.

6. The more sensual companions-in-arms of Cortés tried to entice him to settle in the eternal spring of the valley of Cuernavaca and forget the lofty, suffocating grandeur of the capital of the vanquished. The wily conquistador knew better; he razed the Indian metropolis and built the Spanish city on top of it, cathedral on top of pyramid, viceregal palace on top of the ruins of Moctezuma's abode. So was Mexico born. This is what "Mexico" means.

7. But the "United States of America"? They are not even the only "United States" on this continent. Venezuela was a United States until, discouraged, it let the moniker drop and with it the pervading confusion. But constitutionally both Brazil and Mexico are United States—that is, federal republics, as opposed to the unitary regimes of countries such as Colombia or Bolivia.

8. Bolivia: there's a name. Christened for the great liberator Simón Bolívar, this landlocked, penurious, never-say-die nation has honored its name-giver by having at least one military coup every nine or ten months, more governments than years in its history—and a refusal to be, eventually, anything but a democracy. Its military proclaim that they are saving Bolivia's dignity each time they drag Bolivia's dignity around

Lake Titicaca and lose all their wars with Chile or Paraguay. But Bolivia, like the little Chinaman with the leaden belly, just springs back for more every time it is knocked down. I have always wondered if this is the steadfast way in which Bolivians honor their name.

9. So what's in a name? There is nothing very inspiring, at least originally, in being called "Americans." We are honoring, it is true, the first man who said that this was really a New World and not, as Columbus had thought, the outer reaches of Cipango and Cathay. Amerigo Vespucci was a pragmatic Florentine with a questioning mind, halfway between the plodding bookkeeper and the utopian dreamer. In this sense, perhaps, the people living to the south of Canada and the north of Mexico deserve to be called "Americans," though an equally good case could be made for calling them Columbians, for when the American Dream sours, the real Christopher Columbus stands up and is identified. He is hallucinated by paradise, propaganda and puritanism. This must be Heaven, but only because there are gold nuggets the size of beans, and an essentially pagan but asexual people are panting to be converted.

10. One feels like pattering off in Cole Porter fashion, you say American and I say Columbian, you say Christophoran and I say Vespucian. We should not call you "North Americans," since that would exclude—or include, if you wish— the Canadians. So we call you "Yankees," but that only speaks for a slim geographic sector of your nation. So then we call you "gringos," which can be said with a pejorative inflection, as when we deal with history, or with a tender one, as when we deal with women. Gringos want to get hold of our oil, Gringas should be serenaded.

11. Yet, as we move further south in the hemisphere, even this singularity of denomination is lost. A "gringo" in Argentina is any foreigner of European stock, whether he hails from Warsaw or Washington or even, as is more and more the case these days, from both towns. The word itself is a corruption of the ditty sung by the British troops that occupied Buenos Aires in 1812, "Green grow the rushes-o." The same song was chanted by the armies of Winfield Scott in Mexico City in 1847, so the name stuck and triumphed over more profane descriptions of the WASPS whom the Mexicans first encountered not as curious tourists, but as invading soldiers:

"güeros" (blondies), "pecosos" (freckles), "patudos" (big feet), and místeres" (which I have always heard as "mysteries" rather than the plural of the English mister; your *señores* are our *mysteries*).

12. So if music is to be the criterion, perhaps we should follow the suggestion of the brillant Cuban writer, Cabrera Infanta, and call you "Anglo-saxofons." Anglo-America? What about Canada: Gallic-Anglo-America? And Haiti: Gallic-Afro-America? Or, in all truth, Argentina: Hispanic-Italo-America? Not to speak of multiracial Brazil: Lusitanic-Italo-Germanic-Niponic-Indo-Afro-America? Many people in Latin (Afro? Iberian? Gallic? Indo?) America prefer to call you, horror of horrors, *Estadounidenses*, "Unitedstaters" or "Unitedstatees" if not "Unitedstationers." The confusion becomes so devastating at this point that we shrug our collective shoulders and call your country, among ourselves, "Gringolandia."

13. Since this is nothing but a national private joke, we are back at square one. We are, in effect, left with the international consensus that calls only *these* United States *the* United States and only *this* American nation *America*. We know what Mrs. Thatcher means when she says "America," Giscard d'Estaing when he says "*l'Amérique*," or Franz Kafka when he writes *Amerika*. Well, "England," "France," and "Germany" are proper names that evoke both time and place, culture and history. The nameless U.S. of A. is handicapped in our minds by the absence of any such symbiosis. Nameless in the depths of our suspicious Mexican souls, the U.S.A. is like a river without a course, a vast menacing rush of drowned images that go from the arbitrary to the reflexive, from the instinctual to the intellectual, from the extremes of refusal to those of bootlicking surrender.

14. If we were to polarize Mexican attitudes toward you, one extreme would be that of total negation, the other of abject abeyance. The Mexicans who live in negation of the U.S.A. proclaim that nothing good can be expected of you, only deceit, exploitation and disdain. Otherwise intelligent Mexicans go berserk when your country is mentioned under any of its nominative guises. Their screams of horror resemble those of Fay Wray in the grasp of King Kong. The U.S.A. appears as the permanent menace, the ravisher of our national virginity.

15. The countries of the New World are curiously entangled in the concept of virginity. Where Europeans would quickly disclaim any indulgence in the virgin ideal, Americans north and south like to think of themselves as Noble Savages at one remove. Pocahontas and La Malinche are perennially about to be deflowered by the corruption of the Old World. You don't have to be Henry James to find a Daisy Miller in every citizen of the U.S.A. as soon as he or she comes into contact with the other, the strange. In addition, the U.S.A. needs enemies. Its Manichean mentality would not survive if it did not have the bad guy, the black hat, the white whale or the red egghead to meet at High Noon in an eternal Dodge City of the mind. This is indeed one of your great problems, to have a handy enemy, for once the enemy of yesterday becomes the ally of today, you must quickly invent a new enemy to feel good.

16. Mexico does not have this problem. If the U.S.A. is a virgin about to be raped by a motley crowd of ideological buccaneers in green fatigues and outlandish headgear at one time favored only by Rudolf Valentino, Mexicans in the extremes of negation are always about to be devoured by a hungry wolf who speaks English and looks like Uncle Sam in lupine drag. We do not have to think twice: anything that goes wrong in Mexico, from salt in the Mexicali valley to drought in the Zacatecas cornfields, can and should be blamed on the gringos. Ridiculousness may be the reward for such trembling vigilance. A Mexican writer and bureaucrat of some note has declared that he refuses to learn English so as to remain untainted by the Empire. No matter that he is tainted by our very own Republic. Our national vices, it seems, will not hurt us, but reading Faulkner, or, for that matter, Shakespeare, will.

17. This sort of irrational hate pose clouds the very good reasons Mexicans have to be wary of U.S. attitudes and initiatives and to be mindful of our own past history. The fact is that we *should* be wary and vigilant. If Mexico often reacts like a scalded cat it is because it has been in contact too many times with hot water poured on it from the North. The history of relations between the U.S.A. and Mexico has been an unhappy one. We were not yet an independent republic when Jefferson was explaining to Monroe what manifest destiny was all about. The new republic founded in Philadelphia had an almost divine right to ex-

pand at the expense of Spain's possessions in the New World. From Joel R. Poinsett to Henry Lane Wilson, Washington's envoys have acted in a manner befitting a Roman proconsul out to gain his laurels. The young Mexican republic was quickly undermined by the fifth column that filtered into our Texas territory. Polk's war, denounced by Lincoln and Thoreau, ended in the total humiliation of a poor and divided Mexican nation and the loss of half our national territory.

18. The Mexican Revolution of 1910 was certainly the first and probably the greatest opportunity offered the U.S.A. to confront and define its policies toward what we now call the Third World. Mexico was ripe for revolution. It was not just a question of justice and exploitation, freedom and oppression. It was also one of self-definition, of permitting the real face of the nation—brutal and disagreeable as it might be—to show itself for the first time. It was a question of self-revelation, of violently plumbing the cultural reality of Mexico. In 1910 a revolution could not be blamed on an international communist conspiracy. The U.S.A. had the opportunity to deal with a movement nurtured on the very complex strains of Mexico's own history—not an "imported" revolution, if such a thing exists.

19. The response of the successive administrations in Washington, from Taft's to Hoover's, was one of bafflement disguised as moral outrage. Woodrow Wilson proclaimed that he would teach the Mexicans to elect good men to office. Yet when, in the first free vote in thirty years, Mexico elected a good man, Francisco Madero, Ambassador Henry Lane Wilson (no kin to the President) promptly entered into a conspiracy with all the forces threatened by Madero's rather mild democratic reforms: the army, the landed gentry, the foreign investors.

20. Typical of U.S. policy toward revolutionary Mexico was the shelling and occupation of Veracruz by the Marines in 1914, intended as an act of moral quarantine against Huerta, the counterrevolutionary dictator who stepped into Madero's place thanks to Ambassador Wilson's efforts. The result was to unite Mexican nationalists of all stripes against this new proof of U.S. interventionism. In 1917 Wilson again forced Carranza to admit a punitive expedition, headed by General Pershing, in search of Pancho Villa in the mountains of Chihuahua. Villa was never caught; he knew those mountains like a wolf. But

Carranza, who was fashioning constitutional stability out of chaos in Mexico, was severly undermined in his efforts. So was Mexican democracy. Once more, unfortunately, Mexicans were driven by the U.S.A. to believe that national self-preservation took precedence over democratic pluralism.

21. Mexico should have been the crucible of an intelligent policy toward what is now called the Third World—and was then only the "White Man's Burden." Instead, we were constantly harassed by the successive administrations, by Congress, by the press, by private interests, for the "crimes," as Secretary of State Kellogg called them, of reclaiming our basic resources, freeing the peasants from bondage to the hacienda and introducing literacy, health and communications to the vast Mexican hinterland. What were we to think of the nation and the people that so ferociously opposed our own development on our own terms and who waved imcomprehensible slogans at us—private property is sacred, elect good men to office, try to be like *us*? Mexicans were left wondering if social property was not worthy of respect, if a good man for Vermont was also a good man for Veracruz—and whether we had ever asked the U.S.A. to be like *us*?

22. The feasibility of another policy, a policy serving the interests of both Mexico and the U.S.A., was demonstrated when President Cárdenas nationalized the foreign oil holdings in 1938. President Roosevelt felt the dragons of intervention, sanctions and even war breathing down his neck. He refused to fall into the pit that later caught Eisenhower in Guatemala, Kennedy in Cuba, Johnson in the Dominican Republic and Nixon in Chile. He decided to respect Mexico's sovereign decision to expel the companies which had failed to recognize judicial rulings on equal salaries and union rights for workers in the oil fields, and to recover the right to rationally exploit a basic, non-renewable resource.

23. In the light of events forty-two OPEC years later, you may well understand why Cárdenas is a national hero in Mexico and Roosevelt the most respected gringo since Lincoln. We are but returning the respect F.D.R. showed toward Mexico and his decision to bet on Mexico's capacity to rule itself and become—as it did—a steadfast ally in the approaching war, a fundamental source of raw materials, labor and strategic vigilance against Axis aggression. Roosevelt

listened to the cool and far-sighted counsel of two great diplomats, Ambassador Josephus Daniels and Undersecretary Sumner Welles. Are statesmen of this caliber no longer around? I know they are. The question is, are they being sufficiently consulted?

24. The U.S.A. feels no real need to be vigilant toward Mexico. Rarely has a country such as yours taken a neighbor so much for granted. Our own vigilance is justified not only by the lessons of the past but by the shocks of the present. It has been said that Mexico has a low representative capacity in the U.S.A. and does not fully employ the multiple channels of approach offered by your highly diversified decision-making process. But this does not justify a policy of torts compounded by outright surprises. Let me mention only the dumping of saline waters from the Colorado river on Baja California's Mexicali valley, Nixon's Operation Intercept, cotton dumping, commercial restrictions, Carter's Tortilla Wall. These were all sprung as surprises in a rapidly deteriorating relationship. (I will not discuss here the European and Japanese complaint that Mexico is not the only nation to live under the surprise shocks of U.S. policy.) We are simply very much aware that the White House and the State Department rarely spring surprises on the Chinese or the Soviets. It would be good to recall what former Mexican President Luis Echeverría asked both houses of your Congress in 1972: Why can you not treat your friends with the consideration that you show your enemies?

25. At the other end of the psychological spectrum, there is another, much more dangerous frame of mind, and that is the extreme of Mexican servility toward things and persons that bear the imprint "Made in U.S.A." These minorities of *entreguistas* or "give-alls," as we call them, have always existed in our history. By their fawning celebration of every single U.S. policy, attitude or fad, they demean our relations even more than the negativists do. At least the latter group has a historical justification, of sorts.

26. Policy makers in Washington, Sacramento or Austin should fear the boot-lickers more than the stone-throwers. The U.S.A. might be throwing rocks with the latter group some day. I mean by this to suggest that if the U.S.A. is to have a stable neighbor in a highly volatile world, it will have to become a friend, or at least demonstrate an understanding of what we can loosely term the Mexican liberals, the honest nationalists, the citizens who fight for justice in my own country.

27. The Mexican *entreguistas* have a long and dishonorable history. They wanted to remain a Spanish colony and fought against independence in the first half of the nineteenth century. They wanted to retain their aristocratic privileges against the liberal reforms of Benito Juárez in the second half and asked for French intervention to protect them. They left the country wide open to foreign exploitation during the long Porfirio Díaz dictatorship that culminated in revolution in 1910. Now they will go on their knees to the government offices and corporate suites of the U.S.A. asking for pressures to ward off reforms that are indispensable to a growing, mature and stable society, but which might hurt their pocketbooks.

28. Mexican plutocrats would scream and thunder and cry Bolshevism if they were hit by the regulations, taxes and demands for social solidarity which capitalists in the U.S. consider perfectly normal. The Mexican government, for fear of conservative reaction, has yet to enact many distributive policies that the U.S.A. absorbed between the ages of Jackson and the two Roosevelts. The reformist regime of Echeverría was almost knocked out in 1976 by severe reprisals from Mexico's private sector which included layoffs, shutdowns, flights of foreign currency, panic withdrawals from banks and rumor campaigns which culminated in the sharp devaluation of the Mexican peso.

29. What I mean is that both extremes, total rejection and abject submission, not only disfigure our own very good national reasons for greater independence and self-identification; they also pervert the very good reasons the U.S.A. should have for overcoming the remnants of its provincialism and entering the world of diversified aspirations, multipolar burgeonings, and cultural pluralism that will be the mark of the coming century.

30. I have evoked names, and not in vain; I believe that the misunderstandings between Mexico and the U.S.A. begin at a very basic semantic level. We use identical words that have, nevertheless, totally different cultural and historical meanings for our respective national psyches.

31. History and God, law and state, life and death, center and periphery, progress and ori-

gins, space and time, past and future, reason and dream, have severely different connotations in Mexico and the U.S. All these words are shot through with highly symbolic, that is, cultural meanings. For a Mexican they are intimately linked to the experience of pre-Columbian cosmogonies, Indian theocracies, conquest and genocide, Renaissance utopias doing battle with the European Counter-Reformation, religious syncretism, a vertically ordained authority, a rigid hierarchy between man and God, the baroque sensuality of forms and the economic folly of spending what you do not have in the name of aesthetic compensation. An extreme faith in the Roman tradition of the law: what is written *is*, whether it is obeyed or not.

32. The Anglo-Saxon New World would simply represent the opposite of what I have just outlined. Yet, you are the children of the heretic Pelagius, who believed in direct grace between God and man; we, of the orthodox Saint Augustine and his hieratic intermediaries. You are the children of the constipation of Augsburg and Geneva; we, of the diarrhea of Madrid and Trent. You are founded on the thrift of capitalism, the parsimony of Calvin and Ben Franklin. We are founded on an autocratic and popular dispensation; we spend our wealth on altars and fireworks, as Moctezuma and Philip II did. Your art is the nameless simplicity of a New England church; ours is the baroque abundance of gold leaf in a flea-bitten village. You want to live better. We want to die better. You feel you must redeem the future. We are convinced we must redeem the past. Your past is assimilated; ours is still battling for our souls. You are accustomed to success; we, to failure. Or, rather, your failures drive you into a self-flagellating malaise of incomprehension. Mexico measures its successes with the tragic misgivings of experience; all things are limited and fleeting, especially success.

33. This is why Mexico is so valuable a country in terms of your own national experience. The frontier between Mexico and the U.S.A. is not only the troubled, conflicting, and challenging frontier between two nations. It is the frontier between the U.S.A. and the totality of Latin America, which begins right here on that border—in a way, the marches of Chile and Argentina are on the Rio Grande. It is the only frontier between the U.S.A. and the Third World. In fact, it is the frontier between the industrialized and the developing worlds. Even more interestingly, it is the most dramatic frontier between the two great cultural and historical strains of the Old World in the New World.

34. In the borderland between our two nations we face well-known problems which will, rightly, hold our attention during the coming years. But while dealing with them in all their facticity, these problems, the problems of immigrant workers, trade and energy supplies, should always be considered as indexes of a larger solution, that of relations between the industrialized North and the underdeveloped South. As Mexico and the U.S.A. resolve their differences, so will a vast majority of the world's peoples and governments react, in anticipation, to the attitudes you will reserve toward them.

35. But Mexico is above all a valuable country because it so clearly contrasts your own basic cultural assumptions. It is important to know that we are not only what we think we are but what others think we are, not only what we see in our own mirrors but what we are seen to be in the mirrors of others. Our political mechanisms, as I indicated before, are to a great extent a response to the challenge of the U.S.A., a sort of holding fast against the pressure from the Colossus of the North. You have shaped us in this constant tension, this harassment, even this brutality of your dealings with us. Let me recognize that you have also given us something precious: a constant awareness of ourselves, a searing search for identity and for the preservation of the traits that distinguish us, doubly valuable because they are what we are and also what you are not.

36. But if this is true, then we, as Mexicans, must be wary of falling into the easy trap of denying the U.S.A. any historical or cultural reality. If, first, I refuse to learn English, the second step is then to say that in any case it is unnecessary because "the gringos have no history and have not produced any cultural values."

37. To state this is to deny ourselves the very enriching experience of contrasting our values with those of the U.S.A. How can we do so if the U.S.A. has no values? I like to deflate the chauvinism of my compatriots from time to time by reminding them that just one of the United States of America, Missouri, has produced more literary geniuses—Mark Twain, T. S. Eliot, Marianne Moore and Tennessee Williams—than Mexico in all its history.

38. When two cultures deny each other, they deny themselves, for culture is nothing if it is not the capacity to relate to the other, to what is different. What many Mexicans see as a curse—extreme proximity to the U.S.A.—could actually be a blessing in disguise. There is neither tragedy nor fatality in our geographical situation, but rather a unique opportunity for ourselves, for the U.S.A. and for the world. Distance and ignorance kept the cultural diversity of the world hidden from view, or perhaps patronizingly regarded, for most of the modern age. Now a shrinking world refuses to accommodate those who have mechanically shrunk it; we will not be like you, we shall be like ourselves *with you.* No two nations personify this challenge as sharply as Mexico and the U.S.A.

39. Relations between Mexico and the U.S.A. are the first test of the feasibility of the world to come. No two other peoples have a greater common experience in dealing with each other as practically ideal representatives of two different experiences of Western culture. The U.S., in its relations with Mexico, can certainly re-orient itself in the light of the experience it has gained through contact with a country driven by the forces of nationalism, material deprivation, and cultural abundance. And perhaps Mexico, beyond the extremes of negativism and *entreguismo*, will also come to understand and appreciate, more and more, the true values of your society: tolerance, pluralism, respect for local initiative, the greatest possible diffusion of human rights and a working judicial system.

40. Understanding is a two-way street, and when we travel it, all denominations, pejorative or otherwise, fall by the wayside, and we tend to greet each other as human beings. But being human is being singular, shaped by history and culture, being *different.* No one is human in the abstract. Mexico and the U.S.A. are humanly conceivable as neighboring nations in the exact measure that their peoples learn to identifiy, respect and understand one another.

JANE HOWARD

All Happy Clans Are Alike

Jane Howard (1935–   ) graduated from the University of Michigan in 1956 and was a reporter for *Life* magazine from 1958 to 1963, becoming in turn assistant editor, associate editor, and staff writer in 1967. She was a visiting lecturer at the Iowa Writer's Workshop, University of Iowa, then at the University of Georgia, and later at Yale University in 1976. Her first book, *Please Touch*, 1970, established her as an author. Since then she has written *A Different Woman*, 1973, and *Families*, 1978.

Howard says that every human being needs a group—family, clan, tribe, or other collection of people—but the group does not have to be based on blood ties. Friends can often take the place of relatives and display the ten characteristics of a good family in surrogate fashion.

1. Call it a clan, call it a network, call it a tribe, call it a family. Whatever you call it, who-

ever you are, you need one. You need one because you are human. You didn't come from nowhere. Before you, around you, and presumably after you, too, there are others. Some of these others must matter a lot—to you, and if you are very lucky, to one another. Their welfare must be nearly as important to you as your own. Even if you live alone, even if your solitude is elected and ebullient, you still cannot do without a clan or a tribe.

2. The trouble with the clans and tribes many of us were born into is not that they consist of meddlesome ogres but that they are too far away. In emergencies we rush across continents and if need be oceans to their sides, as they do to ours. Maybe we even make a habit of seeing them, once or twice a year, for the sheer pleasure of it. But blood ties seldom dictate our addresses. Our blood kin are often too remote to ease us from our Tuesdays to our Wednesdays. For this we must rely on our families of friends. If our relatives are not, do not wish to be, or for whatever reasons cannot be our friends, then by some complex alchemy we must try to transform our friends into our relatives. If blood and roots don't do the job, then we must look to water and branches, and sort ourselves into new constellations, new families.

3. These new families, to borrow the terminology of an African tribe (the Bangwa of the Cameroons), may consist either of friends of the road, ascribed by chance, or friends of the heart, achieved by choice. Ascribed friends are those we happen to go to school with, work with, or live near. They know where we went last weekend and whether we still have a cold. Just being around gives them a provisional importance in our lives, and us in theirs. Maybe they will still matter to us when we or they move away; quite likely they won't. Six months or two years will probably erase us from each other's thoughts, unless by some chance they and we have become friends of the heart.

4. Wishing to be friends, as Aristotle wrote, is quick work, but friendship is a slowly ripening fruit. An ancient proverb he quotes in his *Ethics* had it that you cannot know a man until you and he together have eaten a peck of salt. Now a peck, a quarter of a bushel, is quite a lot of salt—more, perhaps, than most pairs of people ever have occasion to share. We must try though. We must sit together at as many tables as we can. We must steer each other through enough seasons and weathers so that sooner or later it crosses our minds that one of us, God knows which or with what sorrow, must one day mourn the other.

5. We must devise new ways, or revive old ones, to equip ourselves with kinfolk. Maybe such an impulse prompted whoever ordered the cake I saw in my neighborhood bakery to have it frosted to say "HAPPY BIRTHDAY SURRO-GATE." I like to think that this cake was decorated not for a judge but for someone's surrogate mother or surrogate brother: loathsome jargon, but admirable sentiment. If you didn't conceive me or if we didn't grow up in the same house, we can still be related, if we decide we ought to be. It is never too late, I like to hope, to augment our families in ways nature neglected to do. It is never too late to choose new clans.

6. The best-chosen clans, like the best friendships and the best blood families, endure by accumulating a history solid enough to suggest a future. But clans that don't last have merit too. We can lament them but we shouldn't deride them. Better an ephemeral clan or tribe than none at all. A few of my life's most tribally joyous times, in fact, have been spent with people whom I have yet to see again. This saddens me, as it may them too, but dwelling overlong on such sadness does no good. A more fertile exercise is to think back on those times and try to figure out what made them, for all their brevity, so stirring. What can such times teach us about forming new and more lasting tribes in the future?

7. New tribes and clans can no more be willed into existence, of course, than any other good thing can. We keep trying, though. To try, with gritted teeth and girded loins, is after all American. That is what the two Helens and I were talking about the day we had lunch in a room way up in a high-rise motel near the Kansas City airport. We had lunch there at the end of a two-day conference on families. The two Helens were social scientists, but I liked them even so, among other reasons because they both objected to that motel's coffee shop even more than I did. One of the Helens, from Virginia, disliked it so much that she had brought along homemade whole wheat bread, sesame butter, and honey from her parents' farm in South Dakota, where she had visited before the conference. Her picnic was the best thing that happened, to me at least, those whole two days.

8. "If you're voluntarily childless and alone," said the other Helen, who was from Pennsylvania by way of Puerto Rico, "it gets harder and harder with the passage of time. It's stressful. That's why

you need support systems." I had been hearing quite a bit of talk about "support systems." The term is not among my favorites, but I can understand its currency. Whatever "support systems" may be, the need for them is clearly urgent, and not just in this country. Are there not thriving "megafamilies" of as many as three hundred people in Scandinavia? Have not the Japanese for years had an honored, enduring—if perhaps by our standards rather rigid—custom of adopting nonrelatives to fill gaps in their families? Should we not applaud and maybe imitate such ingenuity?

9. And consider our own Unitarians. From Santa Barbara to Boston they have been earnestly dividing their congregations into arbitrary "extended families" whose members are bound to act like each other's relatives. Kurt Vonnegut, Jr. plays with a similar train of thought in his fictional *Slapstick*. In that book every newborn baby is assigned a randomly chosen middle name, like Uranium or Daffodil or Raspberry. These middle names are connected with hyphens to numbers between one and twenty, and any two people who have the same middle name are automatically related. This is all to the good, the author thinks, because "human beings need all the relatives they can get—as possible donors or receivers not of love but of common decency." He envisions these extended families as "one of the four greatest inventions by Americans," the others being *Robert's Rules of Order,* the Bill of Rights, and the principles of Alcoholics Anonymous.

10. This charming notion might even work, if it weren't so arbitrary. Already each of us is born into one family not of our choosing. If we're going to devise new ones, we might as well have the luxury of picking the members ourselves. Clever picking might result in new families whose benefits would surpass or at least equal those of the old. As a member in reasonable standing of six or seven tribes in addition to the one I was born to, I have been trying to figure which characteristics are common to both kinds of families.

11. (1) Good families have a chief, or a heroine, or a founder—someone around whom others cluster, whose achievements, as the Yiddish word has it, let them *kvell*, and whose example spurs them on to like feats. Some blood dynasties pro-

duce such figures regularly; others languish for as many as five generations between demigods, wondering with each new pregnancy whether this, at last, might be the messianic baby who will redeem them. Look, is there not something gubernatorial about her footstep, or musical about the way he bangs with his spoon on his cup? All clans, of all kinds, need such a figure now and then. Sometimes clans based on water rather than blood harbor several such personages at one time. The Bloomsbury Group in London six decades ago was not much hampered by its lack of a temporal history.

12. (2) Good families have a switchboard operator—someone who cannot help but keep track of what all the others are up to, who plays Houston Mission Control to everyone else's Apollo. This role is assumed rather than assigned. The person who volunteers for it often has the instincts of an archivist, and feels driven to keep scrapbooks and photograph albums up to date, so that the clan can see proof of its own continuity.

13. (3) Good families are much to all their members, but everything to none. Good families are fortresses with many windows and doors to the outer world. The blood clans I feel most drawn to were founded by parents who are nearly as devoted to what they do outside as they are to each other and their children. Their curiosity and passion are contagious. Everybody, where they live, is busy. Paint is spattered on eyeglasses. Mud lurks under fingernails. Person-to-person calls come in the middle of the night from Tokyo and Brussels. Catcher's mitts, ballet slippers, overdue library books, and other signs of extrafamilial concerns are everywhere.

14. (4) Good families are hospitable. Knowing that hosts need guests as much as guests need hosts, they are generous with honorary memberships for friends, whom they urge to come early and often and to stay late. Such clans exude a vivid sense of surrounding rings of relatives, neighbors, teachers, students, and godparents, any of whom at any time might break or slide into the inner circle. Inside that circle a wholesome, tacit emotional feudalism develops: you give me protection, I'll give you fealty. Such pacts begin with, but soon go far beyond, the jolly exchange of pie at Thanksgiving or cake on a birthday. They mean that you can ask me to supervise your children for the fortnight you will

be in the hospital, and that however inconvenient this might be for me, I shall manage to do so. It means I can phone you on what for me is a dreary, wretched Sunday afternoon and for you is the eve of a deadline, knowing you will tell me to come right over, if only to watch you type. It means we need not dissemble. ("To yield to seeming," as Martin Buber wrote, "is man's essential cowardice, to resist it is his essential courage . . . one must at times pay dearly for life lived from the being, but it is never too dear.")

15. (5) Good families deal squarely with direness. Pity the tribe that doesn't have, and cherish, at least one flamboyant eccentric. Pity too the one that supposes it can avoid for long the woes to which all flesh is heir. Lunacy, bankruptcy, suicide, and other unthinkable fates sooner or later afflict the noblest of clans with an undertow of gloom. Family life is a set of givens, someone once told me, and it takes courage to see certain givens as blessings rather than as curses. It surely does. Contradictions and inconsistencies are givens, too. So is the battle against what the Oregon patriarch Kenneth Babbs calls malarkey. "There's always malarkey lurking, bubbles in the cesspool, fetid bubbles that pop and smell. But I don't put up with malarkey, between my stepkids and my natural ones or anywhere else in the family."

16. (6) Good families prize their rituals. Nothing welds a family more than these. Rituals are vital especially for clans without histories, because they evoke a past, imply a future, and hint at continuity. No line in the seder service at Passover reassures more than the last: "Next year in Jerusalem!" A clan becomes more of a clan each time it gathers to observe a fixed ritual (Christmas, birthdays, Thanksgiving, and so on), grieves at a funeral (anyone may come to most funerals; those who do declare their tribalness), and devises a new rite of its own. Equinox breakfasts can be at least as welding as Memorial Day parades. Several of my colleagues and I used to meet for lunch every Pearl Harbor Day, preferably to eat some politically neutral fare like smorgasbord, to "forgive" our only ancestrally Japanese friend, Irene Kubota Neves. For that and other things we became, and remain, a sort of family.

17. "Rituals," a California friend of mine said, "aren't just externals and holidays. They are the performances of our lives. They are a kind of shorthand. They can't be decreed. My mother used to try to decree them. She'd make such a goddamn fuss over what we talked about at dinner, aiming at Topics of Common Interest, topics that celebrated our cohesion as a family. These performances were always hollow, because the phenomenology of the moment got sacrificed for the *idea* of the moment. Real rituals are discovered in retrospect. They emerge around constitutive moments, moments that only happen once, around whose memory meanings cluster. You don't choose those moments. They choose themselves." A lucky clan includes a born mythologizer, like my blood sister, who has the gift for apprehending such a moment when she sees it, and who cannot help but invent new rituals everywhere she goes.

18. (7) Good families are affectionate. This of course is a matter of style. I know clans whose members greet each other with gingerly handshakes or, in what pass for kisses, with hurried brushes of jawbones, as if the object were to touch not the lips but the ears. I don't see how such people manage. "The tribe that does not hug," as someone who has been part of many *ad hoc* families recently wrote to me, "is no tribe at all. More and more I realize that everybody, regardless of age, needs to be hugged and comforted in a brotherly or sisterly way now and then. Preferably now."

19. (8) Good families have a sense of place, which these days is not achieved easily. As Susanne Langer wrote in 1957, "Most people have no home that is a symbol of their childhood, not even a definite memory of one place to serve that purpose . . . all the old symbols are gone." Once I asked a roomful of supper guests if anyone felt a strong pull to any certain spot on the face of the earth. Everyone was silent, except for a visitor from Bavaria. The rest of us seemed to know all too well what Walker Percy means in *The Moviegoer* when he tells of the "genie-soul of a place, which every place has or else is not a place [and which] wherever you go, you must meet and master or else be met and mastered." All that meeting and mastering saps plenty of strength. It also underscores our need for tribal bases of the sort which soaring real estate taxes and splintering families have made all but obsolete.

20. So what are we to do, those of us whose habit and pleasure and doom is our tendency, as a Georgia lady put it, to "fly off at every other whipstitch?" Think in terms of movable feasts, that's what. Live here, wherever here may be, as if we were going to belong here for the rest of our lives. Learn to hallow whatever ground we happen to stand on or land on. Like medieval knights who took their tapestries along on Crusades, like modern Afghanis with their yurts, we must pack such totems and icons as we can to make short-term quarters feel like home. Pillows, small rugs, watercolors can dispel much of the chilling anonymity of a motel room or sublet apartment. When we can, we should live in rooms with stoves or fireplaces or at least candlelight. The ancient saying is still true: Extinguished hearth, extinguished family.

21. Round tables help too, and as a friend of mine once put it, so do "too many comfortable chairs, with surfaces to put feet on, arranged so as to encourage a maximum of eye contact." Such rooms inspire good talk, of which good clans can never have enough.

22. (9) Good families, not just the blood kind, find some way to connect with posterity. "To forge a link in the humble chain of being, encircling heirs to ancestors," as Michael Novak has written, "is to walk within a circle of magic as primitive as humans knew in caves." He is talking of course about babies, feeling them leap in wombs, giving them suck. Parenthood, however, is a state which some miss by chance and others by design, and a vocation to which not all are called. Some of us, like the novelist Richard P. Brickner, look on as others "name their children and their children in turn name their own lives, devising their own flags from their parents' cloth." What are we who lack children to do? Build houses? Plant trees? Write books or symphonies or laws? Perhaps, but even if we do these things, there should be children on the sidelines if not at the center of our lives.

23. It is a sadly impoverished tribe that does not allow access to, and make much of, some children. Not too much, of course; it has truly been said that never in history have so many educated people devoted so much attention to so few children. Attention, in excess, can turn to fawning, which isn't much better than neglect. Still, if we don't regularly see and talk to and laugh with people who can expect to outlive us by twenty years or so, we had better get busy and find some.

24. (10) Good families also honor their elders. The wider the age range, the stronger the tribe. Jean-Paul Sartre and Margaret Mead, to name two spectacularly confident former children, have both remarked on the central importance of grandparents in their own early lives. Grandparents are now in much more abundant supply than they were a generation or two ago, when old age was more rare. If actual grandparents are not at hand, no family should have too hard a time finding substitute ones to whom to pay unfeigned homage. The Soviet Union's enchantment with day-care centers, I have heard, stems at least in part from the state's eagerness to keep children away from their presumably subversive grandparents. Let that be a lesson to clans based on interest as well as to those based on genes.

25. Of course there are elders and elders. Most people in America, as David T. Bazelon has written, haven't the slightest idea of what to do with the extra thirty years they have been given to live. Few are as briskly secure as Alice Roosevelt Longworth, who once, when I visited her for tea, showed a recent photograph and asked whether I didn't think it made her look like "a malevolent Eurasian concubine—an *aged* malevolent Eurasian concubine." I admitted that it did, which was just what she wanted to hear. But those of us whose fathers weren't Presidents may not grow old, if at all, with such style.

26. Sad stories abound. The mother of one friend of mine languished for years, never far from a coma, in a nursing home. Only when her husband and children sang one of her favorite old songs, such as "Lord Jeffrey Amherst," would a smile fleet across her face. But a man I know of in New Jersey, who couldn't stand the state of Iowa or babies, changed his mind on both counts when his daughter, who lived in Iowa, had a baby. Suddenly he took to inventing business trips to St. Louis, by way of Cedar Rapids, phoning to say he would be at the airport there at 11:31 P.M., and "Be sure to bring Jake!" That cheers me. So did part of a talk I had with a woman in Albuquerque, whom I hadn't seen since a trip some years before to the Soviet Union.

27. "Honey," she said when I phoned her during a short stopover and asked how she was, "if I were any better I'd blow up and *bust*! I can't *tell* you how *neat* it is to put some age on! A lot of it,

of course, has to do with going to the shrink, getting uncorked, and of course it doesn't hurt to have money—no, we *don't* have a ranch; it's only 900 acres, so we call it a farm. But every year, as far as age is concerned, I seem to get better, doing more and more stuff I love to do. The only thing I've ever wanted and don't have is a good marriage. Nothing I do ever pleases the men I marry. The only reason I'm still married now is it's too much trouble not to be. But my girls are growing up to be just *neat* humans, and the men they're sharing their lives with are too. They pick nice guys, my girls. I wish I could say the same. But I'm a lot better off than many women my age. I go to parties where sixty-year-olds with blue bouffant hairdos are still telling the same jokes they told twenty-five or thirty years ago. Complacent? No, that's not it, exactly. What they are is sad—sad as the dickens. They don't seem to be *connected*."

28. Some days my handwriting resembles my mother's, slanting hopefully and a bit extravagantly eastward. Other days it looks more like my father's: resolute, vertical, guardedly free of loops. Both my parents will remain in my nerves and muscles and mind until the day I die, and so will my sister, but they aren't the only ones. If I were to die tomorrow, the obituary would note that my father and sister survived me. True, but not true enough. Like most official lists of survivors, this one would be incomplete.

29. Several of the most affecting relationships I have ever known of, or been part of, have sprung not from genes or contracts but from serendipitous, uncanny bonds of choice. I don't think enough can be said for the fierce tenderness such bonds can generate. Maybe the best thing to say is nothing at all, or very little. Midwestern preachers used to hold that "a heavy rain doesn't seep into the ground but rolls off—when you preach to farmers, your sermon should be a drizzle instead of a downpour." So too with any cause that matters: shouting and lapel-grabbing and institutionalizing can do more harm than good. A quiet approach works better.

30. "I wish it would hurry up and get colder," I said one warm afternoon several Octobers ago to a black man with whom I was walking in a park.

31. "Don't worry," he told me. "Like my grandmother used to say when I was a boy, 'Hawk'll be here soon enough.'"

32. "What does she mean by 'hawk'?"

33. "Hawk meant winter, cold, trouble. And she was right: the hawk always came."

34. With regards to families, many would say that the hawk has long been here, hovering. "I'd rather put up with being lonely now than have to put up with being still more lonely in the future," says a character in Natsume Soseki's novel *Kokoro.* "We live in an age of freedom, independence, and the self, and I imagine this loneliness is the price we have to pay for it." Seven decades earlier, in *Either/Or,* Sören Kierkegaard had written, "Our age has lost all the substantial categories of family, state, and race. It must leave the individual entirely to himself, so that in a stricter sense he becomes his own creator."

35. If it is true that we must create ourselves, maybe while we are about it we can also devise some new kinds of families, new connections to supplement the old ones. The second verse of a hymn by James Russell Lowell says,

"New occasions bring new duties;
Time makes ancient goods uncouth."

Surely one outworn "good" is the maxim that blood relatives are the only ones who can or should greatly matter. Or look at it another way: go back six generations, and each one of us has sixty-four direct ancestors. Go back twenty—only four or five centuries, not such a big chunk of human history—and we each have more than a million. Does it not stand to reason, since the world population was then so much smaller, that we all have a lot more cousins—though admittedly distant ones—than we were brought up to suspect. And don't these cousins deserve our attention?

36. One day after lunch at a friend's apartment I waited in his lobby while he collected his mail. Out of the elevator came two nurses supporting a wizened, staring woman who couldn't have weighed much more than seventy pounds. It was all the woman could do to make her way down the three steps to the sidewalk and the curb where a car was waiting. Those steps must have been to that woman what a steep mountain trail would be to me. The nurses guided her down them with infinite patience.

37. "Easy darlin'," one nurse said to the woman.

38. "That's a good girl," said the other. The woman, my friend's doorman told us, was ninety. That morning she had fallen and hurt herself. On her forehead was something which, had it not been a bruise, we might have thought beautiful: a marvel of mauve and lavender and magenta. This woman, who was then being taken to a nursing home, had lived in my friend's apartment building for forty years. All her relatives were dead and her few surviving friends no longer chose to see her.

39. "But how can that be?" I asked my friend. "We could never be that alone, could we?"

40. "Don't be so sure," said my friend, who knows more of such matters than I do. "Even if we were to end up in the same nursing home, if I was in markedly worse shape than you were, you might not want to see me either."

41. "But I can't imagine not wanting to see you."

42. "It happens," my friend said.

43. Maybe we can keep it from happening. Maybe the hawk can be kept at bay, if we give more thought to our tribes and our clans and our several kinds of families. No aim seems to me more urgent, nor any achievement more worthy of a psalm. So *hosanna in excelsis,* and blest be the tie that binds. And please pass the salt.

HARVEY COX

Eastern Cults and Western Culture: Why Young Americans Are Buying Oriental Religions

Harvey Cox (1929–   ), a clergyman, teacher, and author, studied divinity at Harvard University after graduating from the University of Pennsylvania. He became Protestant chaplain at Temple University and later director of religious activities at Oberlin College in Ohio. He then went overseas for the Gossner Mission, East Berlin, East Germany in 1962–63. He has taught at Andover-Newton Theological Seminary, and joined the faculty of the Harvard Divinity School in 1966, where he has been chairman of the Department of Applied Theology and Victor Thomas Professor of Divinity. He wrote *The Secular City,* 1965; *God's Revolution and Man's Responsibility,* 1965; *The Seduction of the Spirit,* 1973; and *Turning East: The Promise and Peril of the New Orientalism,* 1977, from which this essay is taken.

Cox answers the question of why Americans are turning to Eastern religions by saying that the crisis in the West causes people to decide that solutions are elsewhere—in this case, the East. But, he goes on, eventually after probing the cultures and religions of other people, they may find that the real satisfaction they are seeking will be found in their own culture.

An old Zen story tells of a pilgrim who mounted his horse and crossed formidable mountains and swift rivers seeking a famous roshi, or wise man, in order to ask him how to find true enlightenment. After months of searching, the pilgrim located the teacher in a cave. The roshi listened to the question, and said nothing. The seeker waited. Finally, after hours of silence, the roshi looked at the steed on which the pilgrim had arrived, and asked the pilgrim why he was not looking for a horse instead of enlightenment. The pilgrim responded that obviously he already had a horse. The roshi smiled, and retreated to his cave.

1. In the past decade, this country has seen dozens of Eastern religious cults and movements spring up and flourish, attracting thousands of American youths who are searching for truth, brotherhood, and authority. What has provoked this neo-Oriental religious revival? Who are the people caught up in it? Why have they left some more conventional religious life—or none at all—to become seekers or adherents in these new spiritual movements? What does it all mean for American culture?

2. Large numbers of people are involved in this quest, not just a fringe group. And the extent of their interest has no precedent in American religious history. Although overall estimates vary widely—partly because the movements themselves tend to overstate their membership—I would guess that by now several million Americans have been touched one way or another by some form of neo-Oriental thought or devotional practice. I base this guess not only on the number of actual adherents, but also on those who practice—regularly or sporadically—various forms of meditation, or whose practice of karate or the martial arts goes beyond self-defense to their underlying Buddhist philosophy.

3. To learn why people join these movements and practice these disciplines, I and some of my students at Harvard Divinity School spent three years informally studying dozens of such groups currently operating in Cambridge, Massachusetts. Some of the students were already involved in the movements, while most of them were just curious about what meaning they had to their adherents, why people had joined, and what they were looking for.

4. To find out, we visited the centers to observe, participate in the meetings and the rituals, and talk with the devotees.

5. Cambridge is known throughout the country primarily as the home of Harvard University. But in recent years it has also become a thriving center of Eastern religious cults and movements, prompting one of my friends to call it "Benares-on-the-Charles."

6. Within walking distance of Harvard Square, one can find dozens of different neo-Oriental religious movements. A few blocks away stands the Zen center, furnished with black silk cushions, bells, an appropriately wizened and wise-looking resident master, and a visiting Zen swordplay instructor. In the basement of a nearby Episcopal church, the Sufi dancers meet twice a week to twist and turn like the legendary whirling dervishes in a ritual circle, chanting verses from the Koran. Down the street is the Ananda Marga center, specializing in a combination of meditation and community action.

7. A few blocks south sits the headquarters of the Hare Krishnas, officially known as the International Society for Krishna Consciousness. There, the devotees hold a weekly feast of savory Indian food and a somewhat less piquant introductory lecture on the mysteries of the Krishna devotion. The clean-shaven followers of the chubby young guru, the Maharaj Ji, have a meeting place near Central Square. A group of self-styled Sikhs, immaculately clad in white robes, turbans, and daggers, have opened a vegetarian restaurant called the Golden Temple of Conscious Cookery. Nearby is the International Student Meditation Center, founded several years ago by the Maharishi Mahesh Yoga, the best known of the swamis of the late '60s, where one can learn the art of "transcendental meditation." Recent arrivals include the followers of guru Sri Chinmoy, a former postal clerk living in Queens; the Dharma House, founded by Chogyam Trungpa Rinpoche, the Tibetan Buddhist lama; and dozens of smaller, less stable groups devoted to yoga, Tai Chi, and other exotic pursuits.

8. I knew that no matter how hard I tried to maintain scholarly objectivity, my inner distrust for all "opiates of the people" might continue to influence me. But I decided to do the study anyway. Although my prejudice against some of the movements was undeniable, I was at least fully aware of it.

9. During the first several weeks of the study my students and I all had a marvelous time. Together and separately we attended dozens of meditation sessions, feasts, satsangs, introductory lectures, inquirers' meetings, worship services, and study circles. The groups we visited were invariably hospitable. We asked questions, read stacks of tracts and pamphlets, watched, listened, and filled up stacks of tape cartridges. For once we were getting something straight from the source instead of from textbooks.

10. With all our research, however, I felt something was lacking. As the notebooks piled up, I began to wonder what it would feel like to be on the inside of one of the movements. No one can hope to experience another person's faith as he does. And as a Christian and a professional theologian I realized I was neither a genuine Oriental pilgrim nor an authentic seeker. I was intrigued, curious, fascinated, but not a devotee. Still, I realized I would have to pursue some kind of "inside" knowing and feeling if I were going to understand the disciples I was studying. So I tried to become as much of a participant as I could. I did not merely observe the Sufi dancers; I whirled too. I did not just read about Zen, or visit centers; I "sat." I chanted with the Hare Krishnas. I stood on my head, stretched my torso, and breathed deeply with the yoga practitioners. I spent hours softly intoning a mantra to myself in a favorite form of Hindu devotional practice.

11. I became a participant not because I thought there was actually something in it for me, but because I wanted to nourish my capacity for empathy. I wanted to find out what I could about the lure of the East on the visceral level. This participant-observer phase of my inquiry took me far away from Benares-on-the-Charles. It led me to spiritual centers in California, Colorado, Texas, and Vermont, and into conversations with Zen abbots, Sufi drummers, and Divine Light devotees.

12. Only after my search became personal did I finally hit on an approach which seemed both faithful to the movements, and helpful in interpreting them to other people. I had become interested in Eastern spirituality for personal reasons, with a host of internal reservations. My purposes were clearly different from those advanced by the teachers themselves. I was quite that mine was a most unusual case. I soon vered, however, it was not. Once I got to know them, nearly all the people I met turned out to have personal reasons that often had little to do with the official teaching of the movement's leaders. This discovery provided me with the clue I needed. I decided to concentrate not on what the movements and their leaders claim to offer, but on what the individuals who turn to them actually find.

13. The "East turners" we found in these movements have not moved to India to live in an ashram. They have not left home for the Orient to dwell in a Tibetan temple or a Zen monastery. They still live in Texas or Ohio or New York or somewhere else in the United States. They have not *gone* East, they have *turned* East. There are true seekers and frivolous dilettantes, converts and fellow travelers. Their interest comes in widely varying degrees of seriousness and persistence: some merely sneak a glance at a paperback edition of the *I Ching* or try some yoga postures; others find that one of the Eastern practices becomes important to them; others leave everything behind and sleep on mats in a Hare Krishna temple.

14. One way to find out what kind of people join these movements is to determine the standard sociological data of their social class, age, race, sex, education, and ethnic background. Such studies have been done, but they leave much unsaid. The participants tend to be young, in their late teens or early 20s. Although some early teen-agers learn how to do yoga, or read a little Eastern philosophy, few become seriously involved until late adolescence. The 20s are the prime turning time.

15. The Eastern religious movements are made up almost exclusively of white, educated, middle- and upper-middle-class young people. Most have at least begun college, although some have dropped out after a year or two. Men and women seem to participate in fairly equal numbers, but men control the leadership groups. There is no predominance of any particular regional background, although more of the devotees seem to come from urban than from rural areas, probably because the movements are generally based in cities.

16. These young people come from all religious denominations, with relatively more from liberal Protestant and reform Jewish backgrounds than the proportion of these groups in the general population would suggest. This is not

surprising, considering the urban, middle-class, educated milieu in which these groups recruit most of their members. Few come from strongly atheistic or unusually pious homes. They seem to have received some religion from their parents, but not enough to satisfy them.

17. Despite all these statistics and data and categories, we still don't know much about the actual human beings who have made this decisive choice. So my students and I asked the people themselves to tell us in their own words what they found in the groups they belonged to. Their answers varied, but as we sorted through them, several definite patterns emerged.

18. (1) Most of the members of these movements seem to be looking for simple human *friendship.* The reply we heard most often, especially from those actually living in religious communes or ashrams, told a story of loneliness, isolation, and the search for a supportive community. To paraphrase a large number of replies: *They seem to care for me here. I was bummed out, confused, just wandering around. When I first came here I didn't know what they were talking about. They all seemed crazy, and I told them. But that didn't seem to bother them. They took me in. They made me feel at home. Now I feel like I'm a part of it, an important part, too. I belong here. It's where I was meant to be.*

19. The newer the convert, the more likely this reply. After a few weeks, however, the novices begin to learn a more theologically proper answer, such as, *Krishna called me here,* or *It was my karma.* Many seekers who drift into such movements looking for intimacy quickly learn to express their reasons in the group argot. But the need for plain friendship is clearly their chief motivation. They are looking for warmth, affection, and close ties of feeling. They don't find it at work, at school, in churches they attend, or even at home. But they do seem to find it, at least for a while, in the community of devotees. The groups we visited provide an island of companionship in what the adherents feel is a world devoid of fraternity.

20. (2) The East turners are also looking for a way to experience life directly, without the intervention of ideas and concepts. They seek a kind of *immediacy* they have not been able to find elsewhere. Even though some young people drift from movement to movement, they do not

seem to be looking for just another kick or "trip" to add to their collection.

21. Most are serious, and want a real, personal encounter with God, or simply with life, nature, and other people: *All I got at any church I ever went to were sermons or homilies about God, about "the peace that passes understanding." Words, words, words. It was all up in the head. I never really* felt *it. It was all abstract, never direct, always somebody else's account of it. It was dull and boring. I'd sit or kneel or stand. I'd listen to or read prayers. But it seemed lifeless. It was like reading the label instead of eating the contents.*

22. *But here it really happened to me. I experienced it myself. I don't have to take someone else's word for it.*

23. This testimony of direct experience became more understandable when we noticed that nearly all the neo-Oriental movements include instruction in some form of spiritual discipline. Initiates learn the primary techniques of prayer, chanting, contemplation, or meditation. Teachers rely not only on words, as in most Western religious training, but also on actual techniques—either quite simple, as in transcendental meditation, or complex, as in Zen—for inducing the desired forms of consciousness. At the local Zen center, for example, the teachers sit you down immediately to face a blank wall, and smilingly refuse to answer all but the most elementary questions until you have taken the practical step of trying to meditate. Even after that they keep the ideas to a minimum. Practice and direct exposure are the keys to the kingdom.

24. (3) Some East turners are looking for *authority.* They have turned East to find truth, to lay hold on a message or teaching they can believe and trust. They join these groups as refugees from uncertainty and doubt. They often stress the role of the particular swami or guru whose wisdom or charismatic power has caused such a change in their lives: *I tried everything. I read all the books, went to lectures, listened to different teachers. But all that happened was that I got more confused. I couldn't think straight any more. I couldn't get myself together or make any decisions. Then I met him, and what he said finally made sense. Everything finally clicked. I knew he was for real. I could tell just from the way he spoke that he knew. Now my confusion is over.*

25. The quest for authority results from a wide range of factors documented by dozens of sociologists: the dissolution of conventional moral codes; the erosion of traditional authorities; the emergence of what Alvin Toffler, the author of *Future Shock*, once called "over-choice." As a result, large numbers of people have begun to suffer a kind of choice-fatigue. They hunger for an authority that will simplify, straighten out, assure; something or somebody that will make their choices fewer and less arduous. For some, the search for authority ends at the swami's feet.

26. (4) A smaller number of people told us in one way or another that they had turned to the East because somehow it seemed more *natural*. These people also seem to have changed their faith-orientation more self-consciously than others, and with deliberate rejection of what they consider the effete, corrupt, or outworn religious tradition of the West. They see in Eastern spirituality a kind of unspoiled purity. In contrast to Western faith, the East seems artless, simple, and fresh. They could often tell us why they had turned *from* some Western religion more clearly than they could say why they had turned *toward* the East.

27. *Western civilization is shot. It is nothing but technology and power and rationalization, corrupted to its core by power and money. It has no contact with nature, feeling, spontaneity. What we need to do now is learn from the Oriental peoples who have never been ruined by machines and science, who have kept close to their ancestors' simplicity. Western religion has invalidated itself. Now only the East is possible.*

28. The people who talked to us in this vein were often the most widely read and best educated of the East turners. They could often cite evidence more specifically and phrase their arguments more clearly than the others. Though they did not put it this way themselves, to me their decision to turn East often seemed to have some of the quality of a purification ritual. It was as though they were going through the Western equivalent of a bath in the Ganges, shedding the tainted and the impure.

29. These then are the reasons most East turners cite for their choice: they seek friendship; a direct experience of God and the world; a way out of intellectual and moral confusion; and a kind of innocence, or a way of life unmarred by technological overkill. This list of goals shows that East turners are really not very different from anyone else. They are looking for what many other people in America are looking for today. They have merely chosen a more visible and dramatic way of looking. The real question, of course, is will they find it?

30. The ironic aspect of the Turn East is that it is occurring just as many millions of Asians are involved in an epochal "Turn West" toward Western science and technology, Western political systems, and Western cultural forms. Just as this great awakening to history has begun to occur in the real Asia, millions of Americans have fallen in love with an Asia that is disappearing, or maybe never existed: the "mysterious Orient" of the old Western myth. In fact, those who yearn for what they call an "Oriental" approach today are really opting for an archaic rather than a historical way of life. They may be turning back instead of turning East.

31. Two kinds of replies from East turners disturb me because they reveal a quest that will lead not just to disillusionment but to frustration and bitterness. One can sympathize with those who hope to regain a lost innocence—a world free of complications, a world of black and white choices. But eventually they will find out that no such world will ever be found. For maturity means learning to live in a complex, shades-of-gray world.

32. I feel similar qualms about those who long for an authority so unquestionable and total that they would not have to make hard decisions or chew through choices on their own.

33. At first, converts to these movements often do seem to find a kind of new innocence. They are "blissed out" with their hassle-free life. The emphasis many of these groups place on the inner life, plus their relegation of secular society to an inferior form of reality, means that adhering to their teachings will remove the uncomfortable tensions of school, work, or home. Since money, power, and, in some cases, even the capacity to make choices are viewed as illusory or insignificant, the causes of most political tussles disappear. The problem is that the nasty issues of work, politics, and the rest do not really disappear, and even East turners must eventually grapple with them. But as devotees they must do so with a world view that gives them little help, because it refuses to recognize that the problems even exist.

34. I am also troubled by the pursuit of an absolute religious and moral authority that will relieve the discomfort of making decisions. People who hunger for this kind of authority over them suffer from the wounds dealt out by parents, schools, and jobs where they have never been encouraged to flex their decision-making capabilities. But in order to mature, the last thing they need is one more perfect master to solve their problems for them.

35. They need friends and families and larger settings in which their confidence in their own capacities will be strengthened.

36. What the East turners are doing is hardly a prescription for a general cure; rather, it is a symptom of a malaise with which we must all contend. Religious remedies to the ills of culture take two basic forms: one tries to get at the underlying causes of the malady; the other provides a way for people to live in spite of the illness, usually by providing them with an alternative miniworld, sufficiently removed from the one outside so that its perils are kept away from the gate. The East turners have almost all chosen this second form. The only solution they offer to other people is to join them in their miniworld.

37. But if we all join them, it would soon be a maxiworld with all the problems back again. Part of the answer is that these movements cannot be the answer for everyone. Some East turners have found a haven from the impersonality and vacuousness of the larger society, and, some would say, of its churches. They have rightly located the most severe symptoms of our ailing era. But their solution, though it may work for them individually, at least for a while, is ultimately no solution for the rest of us.

38. As for the movements themselves, I also worry about their future. For the business of America is business, and that includes the religion business. The greatest irony of the Eastern religious movements is that in their effort to present an alternative to the Western way of life, most have succeeded in adding only one more line of spiritual products to the American religious marketplace. They have become a part of the consumer culture they set out to call in question.

39. This consumerization of the new religious movements should not surprise us. After all, the genius of any consumer society is its capacity for changing anything, including its critics, into items for distribution and sale. Religious teachings and diciplines—Eastern or Western—can be transformed into commodities, assigned prices, packaged attractively, and made available to prospective buyers.

40. Conspicuous consumption is no longer a mark of distinction. What we have in its place is something I call the new gluttony, which transforms the entire range of human ideas and emotions into a well-stocked pantry. Today, only the old-fashioned glutton still stuffs his mouth with too many entrees. The new glutton craves experiences: in quantity and variety, more and better, increasingly exotic, and even spiritual. Today's money does not lust after houses, cars, and clothes, but travel, drugs, unusual sights and sounds, exotic tastes, therapies, and new emotional states. If disgrace haunts the affluent, it is not apt to be for failing to *have* something, but rather for failing to have *tried* something. The very thought that out there lurks an experience one has not had now sends the affluent into panic.

41. No doubt economists as well as theologians could advance explanations for why we are moving from a greed for things to a gluttony of experience. In a system based on encouraging greed, people eventually become sated. It is hard to sell still another television set to the family that already has one in every room. There is a limit somewhere to what most people can stack up.

42. With experiences, however, there seems to be no such limit, and the experience merchants do not need to plan obsolescence or invent style changes. Their product self-destructs immediately, except for one's memory. Last year's model is unusable not for any reason as trivial as changing hemlines but because it is gone.

43. Economists can explain the new gluttony in the classical terms of a movement from goods to services. It is the old story of expanding markets, finding new resources and developing novel products. But now the product is an experience that can be sold and delivered to a customer. The resources are virtually infinite for the imaginative entrepreneur, and the market is that growing group of people whose hunger for accumulating mere things has begun to decline.

44. I think there is an element of spiritual gluttony in the current fascination with Oriental spirituality. We should not blame this on the Ori-

ental traditions themselves, most of which are highly sensitive to the pitfalls of spiritual pride. Nor can we blame the often anguished people who are driven by forces they can neither control nor understand toward searching out more and more exhilarating spiritual experiences.

45. If there is any fault to be allocated, it lies not with the victims but with the buyer-seller nexus within which the new religious wave is marketed. Despite what may be good intentions all around, the consumer mentality can rot the fragile fruits of Eastern spirituality as soon as they are unpacked. The process is both ironic and pathetic. What begins in Benares as a protest against possessiveness ends up in Boston as still another possession.

46. No deity, however terrible, no devotion, however deep, no ritual, however spendid, is exempt from the voracious process of trivialization. The smiling Buddha himself and the worldly wise Krishna can be transformed by the new gluttony into collectors' trinkets. It was bad enough for King Midas that everything he touched turned to gold. The acquisition-accumulation pattern of the new gluttony does even more. Reversing the alchemist's course, it transforms rubies and emeralds into plastic, the sacred into the silly, the holy into the hokey.

47. The gods of the Orient mean one thing there, and something quite different here. This is not to be blamed either on the gods themselves, or on their original devotees, or on their new seekers. It happens because when the gods migrate, or are transported to a civilization where everything is to some extent a commodity, they become commodities too.

48. The culture barrier that a commodity culture erects against the possibility of genuine interreligious exchange is formidable. It raises the question of whether we in the West can ever hear the voice of the East, can ever learn about the Buddhist or Hindu paths without corrupting them in the process.

49. Although America today *seems* uncommonly receptive to spiritual ideas and practices from the East, the truth is that we are not really receptive to them at all. True, no stone walls have been erected to keep the pagans out. No

orders of Knights Templar have ridden forth to hurl back the infidels. The gates are open, and the citizens seem ready to listen. No wonder many Eastern teachers view America as a fertile ground in which to sow their seeds.

50. But curiously it is precisely America's receptivity, its eagerness to hear, explore, and experience, that creates the most difficult barrier to our actually learning from Eastern spirituality. The very insatiable hunger for novelty, for intimacy, even for a kind of spirituality that motivates so many Americans to turn toward the East also virtually guarantees that the turn will ultimately fail.

51. The final paradox is that Easterners have never claimed to be able to save the West. Frequently they deny having any interest in doing so, even if they could. They rarely send missionaries here, and they accept Western novices with reluctance. Although the Westernized versions of Eastern faiths often claim to bring salvation to the West, at this point they betray the spirit of their sources, and actually worsen the Western dilemma by advertising more than they can deliver.

52. The spiritual crisis of the West will not be resolved by spiritual importations or individual salvation. It is the crisis of a whole civilization, and one of its major symptoms is the belief that the answer must come from Elsewhere. The crisis can be met only when the West sets aside myths of the Orient, and returns to its own primal roots.

53. Eventually the spiritual disciplines of the Orient will make a profound contribution to our consciousness and our way of life. Some day, somewhere, we will hear the message the East has for us. But we can only begin to know the real Orient when we are willing to let go of the mythical one. And we can only begin to hear the message of the Oriental religious traditions when we are willing to confront the inner dislocations in our own civilization that caused us to invent the myth of the East in the first place. And when we are willing to do that, we may realize, like the truth seeker in the Zen parable, that what we are seeking so frantically elsewhere may turn out to be the horse we have been riding all along.

GLORIA STEINEM

Why Women Work

Gloria Steinem (1934–   ) is a writer, editor, lecturer, and an important campaigner for women's rights. After her graduation from Smith College in 1956, she became a Chester Bowles Asian Fellow and wrote *Ten Thousand Indians,* 1957, and *The Beach Book,* 1963. In 1968 she was co-founder and contributing editor of *New York* magazine, and in 1971 she was co-founder of *Ms.* magazine. She has been active in civil rights, peace and women's rights movements, and always an active supporter of the Democratic presidential nominee. *McCall's* magazine named her Woman of the Year in 1972. She was awarded a fellowship at the Woodrow Wilson International Center for Scholars in 1977. She is a regular contributor to major magazines and journals.

Steinem's answer to the question she poses as to why women work is that every person has a right to a decent job, although she says the most often given answer is that women work because they have to earn or help to earn a living.

1. Last year, the *Wall Street Journal* devoted an eight-part, front-page series to "the working woman" as the greatest change in American life since the Industrial Revolution.

2. Many women readers greeted both the news and the definition with cynicism. After all, women have always worked. If all the vital work that women do in the home were valued at its replacement cost, the gross national product would go up by 26 percent. It's just that now, we are more likely than ever before to leave our poorly rewarded, low-security, high-risk job of homemaking (though we're still trying to explain that it's a perfectly good one, that the problem is society's definition of it as both limitless and valueless) for more secure, independent and better-paid jobs outside the home.

3. Obviously, the real revolution won't come until all productive work is rewarded—including child-rearing and other jobs done in the home—

and men are integrated into so-called women's work, as well as vice versa. But the radical change being reported by the *Journal* and others is one part of that long integration process: the unprecedented flood of women into salaried jobs; that is, into the national work force as it has been male-defined. We are already more than 41 percent of it; the highest proportion in history. Given the fact that women also make up a whopping 69 percent of the "discouraged labor force" (that is, people who need jobs but are not counted in the unemployment statistics because they've given up looking)—plus our official unemployment rate that is already substantially higher than men's—it's clear that we could expand to become fully half of the national work force by 1990.

4. Faced with this determination of women to find some way of being paid and honored for our work, experts have rushed to ask "Why?" It's a question rarely directed at male workers; their basic motivations of survival through personal satisfaction are largely taken for granted. (In-

WHY WOMEN WORK Reprinted with permission of Ms. Foundation for Communication and Education; © 1979.

deed, men are regarded as "odd" and therefore subjects for sociological study only when they don't have work of their own, even if they are rich, or can't find jobs, even if they are poor and untrained.) Nonetheless, pollsters and sociologists have gone to great expense to prove that women work outside the home mainly out of dire financial need if there is no man supporting us, or out of some semi-frivolous desire to buy "luxuries" or "little extras" for our families if we persist despite the presence of a wage-earning male.

5. Even relatives or job interviewers may still ask women the big "why?" that they would never ask men; all the more so if we have small children at home or are in some job regarded as "men's work." Condescending or accusatory versions of "What's a nice girl like you doing in a place like this?" have definitely not gone out of style in the workplace.

6. And just how do we answer these assumptions that we could only be "working" out of some external or peculiar need? Do we feel okay about arguing that it's as natural for us to have a salaried job as for our husband—even though we have young children at home? Can we have strong career ambitions without fearing that we will be thought unfeminine? When we confront the growing resentment against women in the work force (often in the form of guilt-producing accusations that we are "taking men's jobs away" or destroying our children), do we simply state that a decent job is a basic human right? I'm afraid that the answer is very often no. As individuals and as a movement, we tend to retreat into some version of an incomplete and tactically questionable defense: "womenworkbecausewehaveto." It's become one word, one key on the typewriter; an economic form of the acceptably "feminine" stance of passivity and self-sacrifice. Under attack, we have a habit of presenting ourselves as the creation of external economic necessity—whether the need is for basic survival or for "little extras" for our families. "Weworkbecausewehaveto" seems to have become the easiest thing to say.

7. It isn't that this truism is difficult to prove with statistics. Of course, economic need is the most consistent of work motives—for women as well as men. In 1976, for instance, 43 percent of all women in the paid labor force were single, widowed, separated or divorced, and working to support themselves and their dependents. An additional 21 percent were married to men who earned less than $10,000 in the previous year, the minimum required to support a family of four. In fact, if you take pensions and various forms of accumulated wealth into account, a good statistical case can be made that there are more women who "have" to work (that is, who have neither the accumulated wealth in pension or any other form, nor husbands who are able to support them for the rest of their lives) than there are men with the same need to work.

8. But the first weakness of the whole "havetowork" defense is its deceptiveness. Anyone who has ever experienced dehumanized life on welfare or any other confidence-shaking dependency knows that the will to work on one's own can go down as desperation and obsession with daily survival go up. That may be related to the fact that—contrary to the "have to" rationale—wives of men who earn less than $3,000 a year are actually *less* likely to be employed than wives whose husbands make $10,000 a year or more.

9. Furthermore, the greatest proportion of employed wives is found among families with a total income of $25,000 to $50,000 a year. This is the statistical underpinning used by some sociologists to prove that women's work is most important in boosting families into the middle or upper-middle class, and that our incomes are largely used for buying "luxuries" and "little extras"; a neat doublewhammy that renders us secondary and our salaries expendable at the same time. We may even go along with this interpretation, since it preserves any husbandly ego-need to be seen as the primary bread-winner, yet still allows us the protective "feminine" stance of working for the family.

10. But there may be other rewards we're not confessing. As noted in *The Two-Career Couple,* an upcoming book by Francine and Douglas Hall: "Women who hold jobs by choice, even blue-collar routine jobs, are more satisfied with their lives than are the full-time housewives."

11. Personal satisfaction is crucial, but there is also the question of society's need for all its members' talents. Suppose that jobs were given out on only a "havetowork" basis to both women and men; perhaps one job per household. It would be unthinkable to lose the unique abilities of, for instance, Eleanor Holmes Norton, the distinguished head of the Equal Employment Opportunity Commission. But would we then be forced

to question the important work of her husband, Edward Norton, who is a lawyer for HUD?

12. It was this kind of waste of human talents on a society-wide, populist scale that traumatized millions of unemployed or underemployed Americans during the depression. Then, of course, the one-job-per-household seemed to be justified, yet the concept was generally used to displace women workers and create intolerable dependencies. (As it still would be. If only one salary is allowable per family, guess who is likely to get it?) That depression experience, plus the energy and example of women who were finally allowed to work during the World War II man-shortage, led Congress to reinterpret the meaning of the country's full-employment goal in the Economic Act of 1946. It became "employment of those who want to work, without regard to whether their employment is, by some definition, necessary. This goal applies equally to men and to women."

13. Clearly, anything less than a government commitment to employment as a basic right will leave the less powerful groups, whoever they may be, out in the unemployed cold. And almost as important as the financial penalty is the suffering that comes from being shut out of productive work; of the ability to prove that we are alive by making some difference in the world.

14. But it won't be easy to give up the passive defense of "womenworkbecausewehaveto."

15. When a woman who is struggling to support her children and grandchildren on welfare sees her neighbor working as a waitress, even though that neighbor's husband has a job, it makes sense for her to feel resentful. Yet unless we establish the obligation to provide a job for everyone who is willing and able to work, that welfare woman may herself be penalized by social policies that are currently inclined to give out only one public-service job per household. Not only will she have to decide whether she or her daughter will have that precious job, but the whole household may have to survive on only one salary.

16. A job as a human right is a principle that applies to men as well as women. But we have more cause to fight for it. The phenomenon of the "working woman" has been held responsible for everything from male impotence to the rising cost of steak (because, according to one explanation, we are no longer staying home to prepare the cheaper, slower-cooking cuts, as good wives should). Unless we include a job as part of every citizen's right to autonomy and personal fulfillment, we will continue to be vulnerable to someone else's idea of what "need" is.

17. In a way, women who do not have to work for simple survival, but who choose to do so nonetheless, are on the frontier of asserting this right. Those with well-to-do husbands or other sources of income outside their work are dangerously easy to resent and put down. It's easier still to resent women from families of inherited wealth. But to prevent a wealthy woman from earning her own keep—and from gaining the personal confidence that comes with that ability—is to keep her needful of that unearned power, and less willing to disperse it. Moreover, it is to lose her unique talents.

18. Perhaps second-wave feminists have sometimes been guilty of a kind of reverse snobbism that keeps us from reaching out to the wives and daughters of wealthy men; yet it was exactly such women who refused the restrictions of class and used their money to finance the first wave of feminist revolution.

19. For most of us, however, "womenworkbecausewehaveto" has more than enough truth in it to be a seductive defense. But if we use it without also staking out the larger human right to work, we may never achieve that right.

20. And worst of all, we may never learn to take work for granted as part of ourselves and one of life's pleasures.

CATHERINE DRINKER BOWEN

We've Never Asked a Woman Before

Catherine Drinker Bowen (1897–1973) wrote biographies as well as books about her experiences as a biographer. Among her biographies are *Yankee from Olympus,* 1944, on Justice Oliver Wendell Holmes; *John Adams and the American Revolution,* 1950; *The Lion and the Throne,* 1957, on Sir Edward Coke; *Francis Bacon: The Temper of a Man,* 1963; and *Miracle at Philadelphia* (a Book of the Month selection), 1966. Her writings about the art of biography include *Adventures of a Biographer,* 1959; *Biography: The Craft and the Calling,* 1969; and a biography of her family, *Family Portrait,* published in 1974.

In this essay Bowen discusses a problem of timely and nationwide interest to both women and men.

1. For thirty years I have been writing about lawyers and the law. And for almost as many years I have been the recipient of invitations to stand on platforms and address large assemblies of legal experts. I enjoy receiving these invitations; it shows that people are reading my books. Yet I often hesitate; the program means serious preparation. A non-lawyer—and a non-man—cannot stand up and talk drivel for thirty minutes or fifty (as specified) to a hall bristling with five hundred or so hard-minded professional gentlemen. Therefore I hold off, saying into the telephone that I haven't the time; I am writing a new book and must stay home by myself, where writers belong. Perhaps the committee will send a letter, giving details? "Mrs. Bowen!" says an urgent voice from Houston or San Francisco. "This is our law society's big annual celebration. We've had Senator Fulbright as speaker, and Wechsler of Columbia, and the Lord Chief Justice of England [and God and Santa Claus]. But we've never asked a woman before."

2. At this moment all my latent feminism rises up. Why haven't they asked a woman before—

aren't there any women lawyers? Impossible to refuse this challenge! In Washington there exists a prestigious group called the American Law Institute. The cream of the profession belongs to it; the work they do is significant to the country at large. After I spoke at the institute's annual dinner, women lawyers crowded to shake my hand. They said they had sat for years watching those men at the head table; they wanted me to know what it meant to see a woman sitting there. It made me very glad that I had come.

3. The word feminism is outmoded. "The movement," young women call it today. We know of the ferocity with which the goal is pursued. We have heard of the extremists—ten thousand strong—called Women's Liberation, how they crop their hair short, wear baggy trousers and loose sweaters to conceal the more notable evidences of sex. "Abolish sexism!" is their slogan. Brassieres must go, and beauty contests. "Miss America!" say their banners. "Men make money off *your* body too. Pornography, Bunnies, Playboy Magazine are as degrading to women as racism is to blacks."

4. But of course! And why, one asks oneself, has it taken the sisters so long to find this out, so long to proclaim that for women sex is neither cute nor funny and can result in pain, disgrace, or

years of virtual—though respectable—servitude? Sex jokes are a male invention. It is indeed a naïve girl who grows up in our society unaware of what her world considers the primary function of women. To suggest that women don't have to be beautiful is the worst kind of heresy; it means women have more important functions than pleasing men.

5. How does all this affect women writers? The answer is, profoundly. Nobody writes from a vacuum; writers compose from their life experience. They use what they know and feel in the environment round about, the stuff of life as it has been handed out or as they have been able to grasp it, hold it up and look at it with courage and with truth. For many centuries girls have been told that their business is wifehood, motherhood—and nothing else. "When children cease to be altogether desirable, women cease to be altogether necessary," said John Langdon Davis in *A Short History of Women.* I once had a husband who liked to say that nothing is expected of a wife-and-mother but respectability. Yet writers, male and female, belong in the category artist. (Muriel Rukeyser, the poet, puts women into four classes: whores, saints, wives, and artists.) No artist can operate lacking belief in his mission. *His* mission; the very pronoun confesses an age-old situation. I hope the young activists in the movement wipe out that generalized pronoun, so bland, so denigrating to the woman professional in any field.

6. Without a clear view of their capabilities, men and women cannot function. Convince a two-legged man that he has but one leg, and he will not be able to walk. A writer must know her horizon, how wide is the circle within which she, as artist, extends. The world still professes to wonder why there has been no female Shakespeare or Dante, no woman Plato or Isaiah. Yet people do what society looks for them to do. The Quaker Meeting House has existed for centuries, but it has produced no Bach and no B Minor Mass. Music was not desired by Quakers, it was frowned on. Poetry, fiction, playwriting have been expected from women only recently, as history counts time. Of the brilliant, erratic Margaret Cavendish, her husband, the Duke of Newcastle, remarked, circa 1660, "A very wise woman is a very foolish thing." As lately as 1922, Christina Rossetti's biographer wrote of her, that "like most poetesses, she was purely subjective,

and in no sense creative." What a beautiful triple sneer, and how it encompasses the entire second sex! One recalls the fiery poet*ess*, Lady Winchelsea, born 1661, said to be "lost in melancholy"—and small wonder:

> Debarred from all improvements of the mind
>   [she wrote],
> And to be dull, expected and designed. . . .
> Alas! a woman that attempts the pen,
> Such a presumptuous creature is esteemed,
> The fault can by no virtue be redeemed.
> Good breeding, fashion, dancing, dressing,
>   play,
> Are the accomplishments we should desire;
> To write, or read, or think, or to enquire,
> Would cloud our beauty, and exhaust our time,
> And interrupt the conquests of our prime,
> Whilst the dull manage of a servile house
> Is held by some our utmost art and use.

7. Because I write about the law and the Constitution I am often asked why I entered "a man's field." Men tell me I write like a man. "Mrs. Bowen," they say with pleased smiles, "you *think* like a man." No, gentlemen, thank you, I do not, I write like a woman. I enjoy being a woman and thinking like a woman, which means using my mind and using it hard. Women have an advantage as writers because they are trained from childhood to notice the relationships between people. Upon such perceptions all their later welfare can depend. Is it not a mother's business, a wife's business to soothe hurt feelings, pacify the male, keep peace within her household? She is vitally concerned therefore with human motivation, what trial lawyers call *intent.* In my own field, intent lies at the base of the entire structure; the motivation of mankind makes up the plot of every biography that is written.

8. Women writers do not think like men. It is when I am told so that I remember Lady Winchelsea, remember also the ladies who had to use men's names on their books: George Eliot, George Sand, Currer Bell and her sisters, the Brontës.

9. I have used the word ladies in speaking of artists. I ask their forgiveness. No writer, no artist, is a lady. She can't afford to be. The novelist, biographer, historian, looks bleakly at life, lingers to squint at its sorrier aspects, reaches out

to touch the dirty places, and raises the hand to the nostrils to make sure. Charles Beard once told me, "You have to have a strong stomach to study history." Happily, I was early indoctrinated against being a lady. At sixteen, the family decided to send me to boarding school, in order to correct certain provincialisms of speech and deportment picked up from schoolmates in the Lehigh Valley town where we lived. I didn't want to go, and protested furiously. A brother, Cecil, ten years my senior, protested also. "That place," he told me morosely, "is called a finishing school. They want to make a lady of you, Katz. But you're born for something better, and don't you ever forget it."

10. I did not forget it. I was the youngest of six; the four brothers were considerably older. They taught me their skills; in fact, they insisted that I learn. "Push out, Katz, with that right skate. *Don't be scared!* Get your whole body into it." I grew up believing that girls were supposed to compete with boys, not just compete *for* boys. Our mother devoted herself wholly to domesticity. Yet she told my sister and me that a girl could be just as independent and well educated as a boy, there was no reason not. My Aunt Cecilia Beaux was earning a living painting portraits by the time she was twenty-five, though Cecilia, my mother said, resented being referred to in the newspapers as a woman painter. "They don't talk about a *man* painter," Cecilia Beaux said. Aunt Beaux made money enough to buy six acres in Gloucester, Massachusetts, and build a house and studio there called Green Alley.

11. It would be hard to exaggerate the effect this had on a girl of twelve, fourteen, eighteen. I have been told that women feel guilty competing intellectually with men. Anaïs Nin, the writer, so confesses in her diary, and I have seen graphs drawn by psychologists, showing that girls do badly in what the professors call "achievement-orientated situations vis-à-vis boys." Guilt at competing? To me it is a contradiction in terms. I would have thought myself guilty in *not* competing. My parents expected high marks at school examinations, and if I brought home a bad paper, "What's wrong?" my brother Cecil would ask, "lose your nerve this time, Katz, or just lazy?" As for Beaux's Green Alley, it has become the family summer place. I have written four books there, in Aunt Beaux's studio by the bay; her spirit sustained me while I wrote. "We think back through

our mothers if we are women." It was Virginia Woolf who said it.

12. Nevertheless, the female brain does not reside in the uterus, though women as well as men try their best so to persuade us. A recent newspaper showed Grace Kelly on a platform receiving an award from the YWCA. Glittering in sequins, she announced complacently that today's women, pushing into a man's world, were sacrificing their femininity. (Nothing was said about the twenty-nine million American women who work for their living.) A day or so later, a woman newspaper columnist eagerly affirmed this by recounting at length the joys of motherhood, ending with the dictum that once the children grow up and depart the scene, mothers never again experience a like happiness and sense of fulfillment. Wives too come forward with proud claims: the self-sacrifice, the best years given. "There is no career more exciting or exacting for a woman than marriage to a great man." So writes a recent biographer of Mrs. Gladstone, and a female biographer at that.

13. Against this flood of bilge water I am fortified by a line in my great-great-grandmother's diary. Elizabeth Drinker, having given birth to nine and reared five, wrote in the year 1790 that she had often thought a woman's best years came after she left off bearing and rearing. I myself happen to be the mother of two and grandmother of four. I always expected to be married and looked forward to it—but not as sole career; never, never as sole career. It is not the maternal chores that oppress but the looming of the altar which has been erected to motherhood, its sacrosanctity, the assumption that nothing but motherhood is important. For the woman artist this ideal can prove as bewildering as the onset of a national war. Nothing matters but this patriotism, this motherhood. One is praised and petted for being a mother, all other values put in the discard. When the baby comes: "You have joined the human race!" women cry, bringing gifts, adding gleefully that you won't have time *now* for writing (or sculpting or painting or playing the violin). When my two children, a girl and then a boy, came along, I had already published two small books and twelve magazine articles. A local newspaper, the Easton *Daily Express*, paid me a dollar a day for a three-hundred-word column, handsomely boxed in. I looked on the pay as munificent and was terrified that I wouldn't be

worth it. When time came for the first baby to be born I wrote two weeks' columns ahead, told the editor, a red-headed Irishman, that I'd be back in a fortnight, received his blessing, and never wrote another line until both children were in nursery school, five years later, and the mornings were once more my own. It was about this time that I came on Katherine Mansfield's thrice-blessed words: "Mothers of children grow on every bush."

14. A writer's regimen can reduce certain nagging moralisms to dust—the notion, for instance, that housework is ennobling to women, or at least instinctive to them as scuffing leaves to clean his bed is instinctive to a dog. Love of cooking is thought by many to be a secondary female sex characteristic. So is the exercise of following little children interminably about the yard. If I had not been a writer, these moralistic conceptions would have defeated me before I reached the age of thirty. Writing saved me. The housework still had to be done and done cheerfully. The children still had to be followed around the yard. But these activities, repeated day after day for years, were no longer defeating because they were no longer the be-all and end-all of existence.

15. "How fortunate, dear, that you have this hobby of writing to occupy you while your husband is away!" Thus my mother-in-law in September of the year 1941. I was two years along with *Yankee from Olympus*. My husband, a surgeon and member of the Naval Reserve, had gone to Honolulu on a hospital ship. By this time I had published six books and become inured to married women's attitudes toward the professional writer, so I merely told my mother-in-law, yes, it *was* lucky, and I had better get upstairs to my typewriter. Back and forth in the family the question raged: Should I take our daughter out of college, our son from school, and migrate to Honolulu? Hawaii was paradise! people said. We'd all love it, and what an opportunity! I could do my Holmes research in the Honolulu University's splendid library. Palm trees and warm sea—a paradise!

16. The notion of Oliver Wendell Holmes of New England revealing himself at the University of Honolulu belonged, of course, in the realms of fantasy. Also, my daughter loved Radcliffe and my son Haverford School. I listened to women spelling out my duty (what today they call a

husband-supportive program), and I developed stomachaches, a pain in the lower back. Then one night I had a dream that settled everything, so vivid I can see it today. I sat in a room filled with people; my father, white-haired, white-whiskered, and long since dead, stood across the carpet. He raised an arm and pointed at me. "Thou shalt not go to Paradise!" he said.

17. Next morning I announced we were staying home, and went on with *Yankee from Olympus*. Nor did I suffer further qualms, Dr. Freud notwithstanding.

18. *Subject A*, young women call it today, bringing me the age-old query: How to manage a career, a husband, and children. Despite "the movement" and the liberation fronts, the problem is still here, sharp and demanding. I am likely to give a twofold answer. "You manage it by doing double work, using twice the energy other wives use: housework *and* writing. Or you do what Mrs. Eleanor Roosevelt told me. I quote her, verbatim: 'If a woman wants to pursue her own interests after marriage, she must choose the right husband. Franklin stood back of me in everything I wanted to do.'"

19. Competition was bred in my bones. Yet I never wrote to rival men; such a thing would not have occurred to me. Actually it was a man—my first husband—who started me writing, in my twenties. And once I saw my product in print, nothing mattered but to get on with the work, get on with studying history and with learning how to write sentences that said what I wanted to say. Many writers hate writing. I happen to love it. With my hands on the typewriter I feel like the war-horse in the Bible that smells the battle far off and saith among the trumpets, Ha, ha. Writers have in them a vast ambition . . . hunger . . . egotism—call it what you will. A writer wants to be read, wants to be known. If there is talent, it must come out or it will choke its host, be she three times wife-and-mother. Scholarship also is a hungry thing, the urge to know. A great legal historian, Maitland, spoke of "the blessing which awaits all those who have honestly taught themselves anything."

20. A woman biographer must, like anybody else, earn her place in the sun. When I turned from writing about musical subjects to legal subjects, I entered a man's world with a vengeance, though some time passed before I was fully

aware of it. The Holmes Papers were guarded by two literary executors, John Gorham Palfrey (father of the tennis champion) and Felix Frankfurter, of the United States Supreme Court. In the six years since Holmes's death, quite evidently the executors had expected hordes of hungry biographers to descend. It came as a shock that the first to approach was a non-Bostonian, a non-lawyer, and a non-man. Nevertheless, Mr. Palfrey handed me five hundred of Holmes's letters, neatly copied in typescript, saying I could take all the notes I wished. I procured four court stenographers—this was before the days of Xerox—who copied profusely. In Washington I saw Felix Frankfurter, who greeted me jovially (he was an old friend), said of course I didn't plan to present the big cases, the Lochner dissent, Rosika Schwimmer, the Gitlow dissent—the great issues of free speech, the ten-hour day, and so on? I said of course I did, why else would I be writing the book?

21. I went home and back to work. Two months later a letter came from Mr. Palfrey, enclosing what he called "some of the more unfavorable replies" to his queries among Holmes's legal friends and associates. Nothing in Mrs. Bowen's previous experience, these said, qualified her to write about a lawyer, a New Englander, or indeed an American. In short, the executors had decided to deny access to all unpublished material, even for the purpose of establishing chronology or telling me where Holmes had been at a given time. My work and my Boston visits, Mr. Palfrey said, had spurred the executors to appoint the "definitive biographer," Mark Howe of the Harvard Law School, secretary to the Justice the year before he died.

22. Plainly, the executors hoped to stop me from writing the book. I let the initial shock wear off and laid plans. Scores of men and women existed who had known Holmes. Whatever I needed from those letters I must get by legwork—even when letters had been sent me by recipients, like Rosika Schwimmer and others. I must persuade the writers to tell me what the Justice had said and done on the occasions their letters described. This exercise took perhaps an added year, but was well worth it. Meanwhile, Frankfurter wrote from time to time. He heard I had been at the Supreme Court building and had left some unsolved questions with the Marshal. Was I actually making an effort to attain accuracy,

ceasing to be an artist and becoming merely a thinker? The letters were wonderful and awful. They kindled the anger that sends one on ever harder quests; Frankfurter could be a formidable antagonist. I talked with Irving Olds of United States Steel, Attorney General Francis Biddle, and ten other legal secretaries of Holmes's, choosing them not because of their worldly prominence but because their particular secretarial year coincided with an important Supreme Court case. I think my book benefited from the program, rigorous though it was, and by the denial of those hundreds of letters. A biography can smother under too much quoted material.

23. When finally the Book-of-the-Month chose my manuscript, Frankfurter sent me a long congratulatory telegram: "I always knew you could do it." I did not see him, however, until ten years and several biographies later. After my book on Sir Edward Coke was published, the director of the Folger Shakespeare Library, Louis Wright, invited me to speak in their Washington theater. He said Justice Frankfurter had telephoned, asking to introduce me, and why was this? Frankfurter never made such requests, Louis said.

24. On the appointed evening, the Justice sat on the platform with me; I had no notion of his intentions. He got up and told the audience that he had done all he could to stop Mrs. Bowen from writing *Yankee from Olympus*, but there were people who worked better under difficulties and I was one of them. He had not read the book, he would never read it, though he had read my other biographies. But he wished to make public apology, public amends. Then he bowed, grinned at me where I sat, and returned to his chair.

25. It was handsome of Frankfurter. Yet I had wondered how much of the entire feud, and its climax, could be laid to the fact of my sex. I do not know. But as time passed and I proceeded to other legal biographies—John Adams, Sir Edward Coke, Francis Bacon, *Miracle at Philadelphia*—I know that the rigors I underwent with *Yankee* stood me in good stead, toughened me, made me ready for whatever might come. With John Adams I was again refused unpublished material and again went on my quest, though this time it had to be in research libraries and took five years. Sir Edward Coke's college was Trinity, at Cambridge University. And even Bluebeard did not consider women more expendable than does a Cambridge don. All but one of the law and

history professors I met there brushed aside my project and did it smiling, with the careless skill of the knowledgeable Englishman. "Are you planning to write a popular book about Coke?" they asked. I smiled in turn, and said by popular they no doubt meant cheap, and that only the finished manuscript could answer their question. "At least," remarked another, "Mrs. Bowen has been shrewd enough to see that a book about Edward Coke will sell. And a person has to begin to learn *somewhere.*" After inquiring how many copies my other biographies had sold, one history professor looked glum. "Someday," he said, snapping his fingers, "I'm going to take a year off and write a popular book."

26. Seven years later the Acting Master of Trinity wrote to me in Philadelphia, saying he had read the English edition of my Coke biography, *The Lion and the Throne.* Did I recall how he had not, initially, been enthusiastic about the project? He went on to say kind things about the book, acknowledging that he had been mistaken. And next time I was in Cambridge, would I permit him to give a small celebration in my honor?

27. Again, I cannot know how much of the battle—the defeats and the victories—can be laid to my being a woman. I know only that I spent days of anger, of outrage, and that I enjoyed the challenge. How could one not enjoy it? *"We never invited a woman before . . . ."*

28. One honors those who march in the streets for a cause; one knows that social liberation does not come peacefully. I have not taken part in the movement, though feminine activists greet me as a sister. I think they know that the woman writer who stays outside the movement by no means dodges the issue. She takes a risk too, though of another kind. Instead of the dangers of marching, she assumes the risks of lifelong dedication to her profession—a program that runs counter to many cherished slogans. As a young woman conversing with young men, I learned to caution myself: "Let him win! When a woman wins she loses." Yet even as I said it I knew that such capitulation was merely for the purposes of flirtation, where a woman can afford the delicious indulgence of yielding. Only when men—or women—block and balk her progress in the professions must a woman strike back, and then she must use every weapon in her artillery.

29. To bear and rear a child is all that it is said to be; it is joy and sorrow, the very heart of living. There is no comparing it with a woman's profession beyond the home. Simply, the two things do not bear comparison. It is false to say the home comes first, the career second. For the woman writer, there can be no first or second about these matters; even to think it is an offense. For myself I enjoy housekeeping, by which I mean I like living in an attractive house and entertaining my friends. I look on house and garden as the most delightful toys, and take pleasure in every facet. But I know also that if house-and-garden should interfere seriously with work, with writing, house-and-garden would go.

30. Women in the professions must make their choices. That many refuse, sidestepping to easy pursuits, is a reason why American women have not kept pace with their sisters in India and Russia. The United States Senate of 100 has one woman member.

31. Perhaps the real turn in the road will come—and I predict it is coming soon—when more than two children to a family will seem bad taste, like wearing mink in a starving village. No woman can devote a life to the rearing of two; she cannot even make a pretense of it. When the mother image loses its sanctity, something will take its place on the altar. And any writer knows that when the image of the heroine changes, the plot changes with her. Such an event could alter, for both men and women, the whole picture of American life.

LEE STROUT WHITE (E. B. WHITE)

Farewell, My Lovely!

The reader will search in vain for a writer named Lee Strout White. This charming tribute to an old car was the joint effort of two individuals, Richard Lee Strout and E. B. White. Richard Lee Strout (1898–   ) was educated at Harvard University. He began his newspaper work in England with the Sheffield *Independent*, and was later a reporter for the Boston *Post*. In 1921 he joined the *Christian Science Monitor* and since 1925 has been with its Washington Bureau. One of the leading journalists of our day, Strout also publishes in the *New Republic* and other magazines. (A biographical sketch of E. B. White appears in the headnote to "The Door," page 236.)

E. B. White has probably contributed more to the preservation of the familiar essay than any other American writer. Underlying his light-hearted style and his good-natured satire are a seriousness of purpose, increasingly evident since the Second World War, and a quiet idealism, suggesting courage, honesty, and sympathy. In this essay he and Strout have given perfect expression to a subject admirably suited to the essay form. No "institution" is historically more significant or more thoroughly indigenous to the United States than the Model T. As these writers say, ". . . the old Ford practically *was* the American scene."

1. I see by the new Sears Roebuck catalogue that it is still possible to buy an axle for a 1909 Model T Ford, but I am not deceived. The great days have faded, the end is in sight. Only one page in the current catalogue is devoted to parts and accessories for the Model T; yet everyone remembers springtimes when the Ford gadget section was larger than men's clothing, almost as large as household furnishings. The last Model T was built in 1927, and the car is fading from what scholars call the American scene—which is an understatement, because to a few million people who grew up with it, the old Ford practically *was* the American scene.

2. It was the miracle God had wrought. And it was patently the sort of thing that could only happen once. Mechanically uncanny, it was like nothing that had ever come to the world before. Flourishing industries rose and fell with it. As a vehicle, it was hardworking, commonplace, heroic; and it often seemed to transmit those qualities to the persons who rode in it. My own generation identifies it with Youth, with its gaudy, irretrievable excitements; before it fades into the mist, I would like to pay it the tribute of the sigh that is not a sob, and set down random entries in a shape somewhat less cumbersome than a Sears Roebuck catalogue.

3. The Model T was distinguished from all other makes of cars by the fact that its transmission was a type known as planetary—which was half metaphysics, half sheer friction. Engineers accepted the word "planetary" in its epicyclic

sense, but I was always conscious that it also meant "wandering," "erratic." Because of the peculiar nature of this planetary element, there was always, in Model T, a certain dull rapport between engine and wheels, and even when the car was in a state known as neutral, it trembled with a deep imperative and tended to inch forward. There was never a moment when the bands were not faintly egging the machine on. In this respect it was like a horse, rolling the bit on its tongue, and country people brought to it the same technique they used with draft animals.

4. Its most remarkable quality was its rate of acceleration. In its palmy days the Model T could take off faster than anything on the road. The reason was simple. To get under way, you simply hooked the third finger of the right hand around a lever on the steering column, pulled down hard, and shoved your left foot forcibly against the low-speed pedal. These were simple, positive motions; the car responded by lunging forward with a roar. After a few seconds of this turmoil, you took your toe off the pedal, eased up a mite on the throttle, and the car, possessed of only two forward speeds, catapulted directly into high with a series of ugly jerks and was off on its glorious errand. The abruptness of this departure was never equalled in other cars of the period. The human leg was (and still is) incapable of letting in a clutch with anything like the forthright abandon that used to send Model T on its way. Letting in a clutch is a negative, hesitant motion, depending on delicate nervous control; pushing down the Ford pedal was a simple, country motion—an expansive act, which came as natural as kicking an old door to make it budge.

5. The driver of the old Model T was a man enthroned. The car, with top up, stood seven feet high. The driver sat on top of the gas tank, brooding it with his own body. When he wanted gasoline, he alighted, along with everything else in the front seat; the seat was pulled off, the metal cap unscrewed, and a wooden stick thrust down to sound the liquid in the well. There were always a couple of these sounding sticks kicking around in the ratty sub-cushion regions of a flivver. Refueling was more of a social function then, because the driver had to unbend, whether he wanted to or not. Directly in front of the driver was the windshield—high, uncompromisingly erect. Nobody talked about air resistance,

and the four cylinders pushed the car through the atmosphere with a simple disregard of physical law.

6. There was this about a Model T: the purchaser never regarded his purchase as a complete, finished product. When you bought a Ford, you figured you had a start—a vibrant, spirited framework to which could be screwed an almost limitless assortment of decorative and functional hardware. Driving away from the agency, hugging the new wheel between your knees, you were already full of creative worry. A Ford was born naked as a baby, and a flourishing industry grew up out of correcting its rare deficiencies and combatting its fascinating diseases. Those were the great days of lily-painting. I have been looking at some old Sears Roebuck catalogues, and they bring everything back so clear.

7. First you bought a Ruby Safety Reflector for the rear, so that your posterior would glow in another's car's brilliance. Then you invested thirty-nine cents in some radiator Moto Wings, a popular ornament which gave the Pegasus touch to the machine and did something godlike to the owner. For nine cents you bought a fanbelt guide to keep the belt from slipping off the pulley.

8. You bought a radiator compound to stop leaks. This was as much a part of everybody's equipment as aspirin tablets are of a medicine cabinet. You bought special oil to prevent chattering, a clamp-on dash light, a patching outfit, a tool box which you bolted to the running board, a sun visor, a steering-column brace to keep the column rigid, and a set of emergency containers for gas, oil, and water—three thin, disc-like cans which reposed in a case on the running board during long, important journeys—red for gas, gray for water, green for oil. It was only a beginning. After the car was about a year old, steps were taken to check the alarming disintegration. (Model T was full of tumors, but they were benign.) A set of anti-rattlers (ninety-eight cents) was a popular panacea. You hooked them on to the gas and spark rods, to the brake pull rod, and to the steering-rod connections. Hood silencers, of black rubber, were applied to the fluttering hood. Shock-absorbers and snubbers gave "complete relaxation." Some people bought rubber pedal pads, to fit over the standard metal pedals. (I didn't like these, I remember.) Persons of a suspicious or pugnacious turn of mind bought a

rear-view mirror; but most Model T owners weren't worried by what was coming from behind because they would soon enough see it out in front. They rode in a state of cheerful catalepsy. Quite a large mutinous clique among Ford owners went over to a foot accelerator (you could buy one and screw it to the floor board), but there was a certain madness in these people, because the Model T, just as she stood, had a choice of three foot pedals to push, and there were plenty of moments when both feet were occupied in the routine performance of duty and when the only way to speed up the engine was with the hand throttle.

9. Gadget bred gadget. Owners not only bought ready-made gadgets, they invented gadgets to meet special needs. I myself drove my car directly from the agency to the blacksmith's, and had the smith affix two enormous iron brackets to the port running board to support an army trunk.

10. People who owned closed models builded along different lines: they bought ball grip handles for opening doors, window anti-rattlers; and de-luxe flower vases of the cut-glass anti-splash type. People with delicate sensibilities garnished their car with a device called the Donna Lee Automobile Disseminator—a porous vase guaranteed, according to Sears, to fill the car with a "faint clean odor of lavender." The gap between open cars and closed cars was not as great then as it is now: for $11.95, Sears Roebuck converted your touring car into a sedan and you went forth renewed. One agreeable quality of the old Fords was that they had no bumpers, and their fenders softened and wilted with the years and permitted the driver to squeeze in and out of tight places.

11. Tires were $30 \times 3\frac{1}{2}$, cost about twelve dollars, and punctured readily. Everybody carried a Jiffy patching set, with a nutmeg grater to roughen the tube before the goo was spread on. Everybody was capable of putting on a patch, expected to have to, and did have to.

12. During my association with Model T's, self-starters were not a prevalent accessory. They were expensive and under suspicion. Your car came equipped with a serviceable crank, and the first thing you learned was how to Get Results. It was a special trick, and until you learned it (usually from another Ford owner, but sometimes by a period of appalling experimentation) you might as well have been winding up an awning. The trick was to leave the ignition switch off, proceed to the animal's head, pull the choke (which was a little wire protruding through the radiator) and give the crank two or three nonchalant upward lifts. Then, whistling as though thinking about something else, you would saunter back to the driver's cabin, turn the ignition on, return to the crank, and this time, catching it on the down stroke, give it a quick spin with plenty of That. If this procedure was followed, the engine almost always responded—first with a few scattered explosions, then with a tumultuous gunfire, which you checked by racing around to the driver's seat and retarding the throttle. Often, if the emergency brake hadn't been pulled all the way back, the car advanced on you the instant the first explosion occurred and you would hold it back by leaning your weight against it. I can still feel my old Ford nuzzling me at the curb, as though looking for an apple in my pocket.

13. In zero weather, ordinary cranking became an impossibility, except for giants. The oil thickened, and it became necessary to jack up the rear wheels, which, for some planetary reason, eased the throw.

14. The lore and legend that governed the Ford were boundless. Owners had their own theories about everything; they discussed mutual problems in that wise, infinitely resourceful way old women discuss rheumatism. Exact knowledge was pretty scarce, and often proved less effective than superstition. Dropping a camphor ball into the gas tank was a popular expedient; it seemed to have a tonic effect on both man and machine. There wasn't much to base exact knowledge on. The Ford driver flew blind. He didn't know the temperature of his engine, the speed of his car, the amount of his fuel, or the pressure of his oil (the old Ford lubricated itself by what was amiably described as the "splash system"). A speedometer cost money and was an extra, like a windshield-wiper. The dashboard of the early models was bare save for an ignition key; later models, grown effete, boasted an ammeter which pulsated alarmingly with the throbbing of the car. Under the dash was a box of coils, with vibrators which you adjusted, or thought you adjusted. Whatever the driver learned of his motor, he learned not through instruments but through sudden developments. I remember that the timer was one of the vital organs about which there was ample doctrine. When everything else

had been checked, you "had a look" at the timer. It was an extravagantly odd little device, simple in construction, mysterious in function. It contained a roller, held by a spring, and there were four contact points on the inside of the case against which, many people believed, the roller rolled. I have had a timer apart on a sick Ford many times. But I never really knew what I was up to—I was just showing off before God. There were almost as many schools of thought as there were timers. Some people, when things went wrong, just clenched their teeth and gave the timer a smart crack with a wrench. Other people opened it up and blew on it. There was a school that held that the timer needed large amounts of oil; they fixed it by frequent baptism. And there was a school that was positive it was meant to run dry as a bone; these people were continually taking it off and wiping it. I remember once spitting into a timer; not in anger, but in a spirit of research. You see, the Model T driver moved in the realm of metaphysics. He believed his car could be hexed.

15. One reason the Ford anatomy was never reduced to an exact science was that, having "fixed" it, the owner couldn't honestly claim that the treatment had brought about the cure. There were too many authenticated cases of Fords fixing themselves—restored naturally to health after a short rest. Farmers soon discovered this, and it fitted nicely with their draft-horse philosophy: "Let 'er cool off and she'll snap into it again."

16. A Ford owner had Number One Bearing constantly in mind. This bearing, being at the front end of the motor, was the one that always burned out, because the oil didn't reach it when the car was climbing hills. (That's what I was always told, anyway.) The oil used to recede and leave Number One dry as a clam flat; you had to watch that bearing like a hawk. It was like a weak heart—you could hear it start knocking, and that was when you stopped to let her cool off. Try as you would to keep the oil supply right, in the end Number One always went out. "Number One Bearing burned out on me and I had to have her replaced," you would say, wisely; and your companions always had a lot to tell about how to protect and pamper Number One to keep her alive.

17. Sprinkled not too liberally among the millions of amateur witch doctors who drove Fords and applied their own abominable cures were the heaven-sent mechanics who could really make the car talk. These professionals turned up in undreamed-of spots. One time, on the banks of the Columbia River in Washington, I heard the rear end go out of my Model T when I was trying to whip it up a steep incline onto the deck of a ferry. Something snapped; the car slid backward into the mud. It seemed to me like the end of the trail. But the captain of the ferry, observing the withered remnant, spoke up.

18. "What's got her?" he asked.

19. "I guess it's the rear end," I replied, listlessly. The captain leaned over the rail and stared. Then I saw that there was a hunger in his eyes that set him off from other men.

20. "Tell you what," he said, carelessly, trying to cover up his eagerness, "let's pull the son of a bitch up onto the boat, and I'll help you fix her while we're going back and forth on the river."

21. We did just this. All that day I plied between the towns of Pasco and Kennewick, while the skipper (who had once worked in a Ford garage) directed the amazing work of resetting the bones of my car.

22. Springtime in the heyday of the Model T was a delirious season. Owning a car was still a major excitement, roads were still wonderful and bad. The Fords were obviously conceived in madness: any car which was capable of going from forward into reverse without any perceptible mechanical hiatus was bound to be a mighty challenging thing to the human imagination. Boys used to veer them off the highway into a level pasture and run wild with them, as though they were cutting up with a girl. Most everybody used the reverse pedal quite as much as the regular foot brake—it distributed the wear over the bands and wore them all down evenly. That was the big trick, to wear all the bands down evenly, so that the final chattering would be total and the whole unit scream for renewal.

23. The days were golden, the nights were dim and strange. I still recall with trembling those loud, nocturnal crises when you drew up to a signpost and raced the engine so the lights would be bright enough to read destinations by. I have never been really planetary since. I suppose it's time to say goodbye. Farewell, my lovely!

JONATHAN EVAN MASLOW

Requiem for a Sports Car

Jonathan Evan Maslow (1948–   ) has been a contributing editor to the "Sporting Life" section of *Saturday Review* and has also written for *Ramparts, The Nation,* and *The New Republic.*

In a personal essay about the MGB sports car, reminiscent of E. B. White's earlier sigh for the Model T Ford, Maslow laments that what the MG did to "persuade its driver . . . that the world was a bright and happy place" is gone and will never return.

1. When the news came over the wireless that British Leyland had sold the Morris garage marque to Aston-Martin, Ltd., makers of the 007-mobile and other automobile fantasies, I was standing in the driveway in dreg-encrusted jeans sanding down the new fiber-glass patches on the rear fenders of my '65 MG. Since I had put in half an average life expectancy's worth of labor on my MG's restoration, not to mention considerable costs in parts and domestic tranquility, I took British Leyland's decision to get rid of the MG rather personally. As well might MG's 25,000 workers, who must still be holding their breath, given the precarious nature of the British auto industry.

2. If I could stick it out with my old MG, why couldn't British Leyland? To hell with streamlining operations and costcutting; this was "the sports car the world fell in love with," the nymphet of the automotive world they were handing over to strangers. This was youth and exuberance and precocious charm on rollers they were abandoning!

3. The MGB, last and longest-lived of its line, was the direct descendent and legitimate heir of those classic postwar MG touring cars, justly remembered for their squared-off grilles, fire engine-red finishes, leather-strapped hoods, and rear-mounted spare wheels. Those were the little dreams your debonair bachelor Uncle Basil bobbed round in come summer, if you had an Uncle Basil. (I did not. I had an Uncle Emile, a used-car dealer from the Bronx, who dispensed this wisdom in the time of Dwight Eisenhower: "When you buy a foreign car, you're buying yourself trouble." But that is another story.)

4. The MGB reached these shores in an era when big was still beautiful. The highways were the domain of the V-8s, with their Dinah Shore styling and goliathan appendages. When the Philistines of Detroit looked about and saw the MG, they disdained it:

For he was but a youth, and ruddy, and of a fair countenance.

5. But the MG stole hearts and minds over to the idea that small, too, had its special appeal. The MGB had the longest run of any single model that could legitimately be called a sports car.

6. The MGB was MG's export model, big seller, and smash success, the first European sports car redesigned for the American market. This basically meant they replaced the isinglass

side curtains with roll-up glass windows, substituted door handles for guide wires, and improved the convertible top to the point where you could almost get it up into place before your date got drenched.

7. The colors the MGB came in looked like a Carnaby Street Teddy boy's idea of Alice's acid trip in the Colonies. Not that they were bad colors. On the contrary. They were, up until then, the most beaudacious colors to have graced sheet metal. They were plain eccentric. They included a gorgeous robin's egg blue; a fleshy beige; lemon yellow; and, my own favorite, a rosy-hued pink, the shade of a Balzac heroine's cheeks as she sits in her box at the Opéra Comique under the gaze of an ardent chevalier.

8. But thereabouts ended compromises in the name of new-world comfort and tastes. For the rest, the MGB brought along the essential elements of the true sports car. Its first order of business was to lower the driver's butt so close to the ground that one felt every twig, pebble, and road surface imperfection. It took all four limbs, coordinated by the split-second decisiveness of a smoothly functioning brain, to run through the four gears and start cruising, while the eyes had to mind an instrument panel only slightly more complex than your average Boeing. With the top up, the engine rumbled through every nerve ending of your body. With the top down, it purred, and you felt yourself mesh with its rhythms.

9. For its size, which was very small, and its weight, which was very light, the MGB had an indecent amount of power in its four-cylinder, dual-carbureted, overhead valve engine. Neither the MGA nor the MGB did a whole lot more than 120 mph, fast enough for me, and the Midget strained at 90. But lowered into the driver's crevice, with that Orson Welles-sized, leather-covered steering wheel wrapped around your chest and your legs thrust straight ahead for the pedals, even at more humble velocities you felt like Icarus roaring for the sun on waxed wings.

10. Despite British Leyland's barmy ad campaigns to convince the American public that the MG was just the thing for trendy executives and busy housewives, nobody was fooled, and the MGB made little pretense about its utter lack of utility. The luggage compartment (endearingly known as "the boot") had room for a packet of Kleenex and a paperback novel, provided that work did not stretch beyond 150 pages. You

could wedge a can of tennis balls in between the bucket seats and the inadequate space provided behind them for storage of the convertible top. But you were smart to lay in metric wrenches instead.

11. A journey of more than 100 miles in an MG was nearly every bit as challenging—or foolhardy—as Scott's last venture to the Antarctic. Semis and tractor-trailers took an instant dislike to MGs and tried to trash you every chance they got. Then, too, you had to possess the confidence and skill to weather the breakdown. The *inevitable* breakdown. Providence and British engineering so conspired that for every MG there could be only one person who understood its problems and could set them right.

12. One MG required gentle rocking in second gear to engage the starter motor. Another wanted a stiff ratchet clout on the regulator to get moving. A third needed tending of the groundwire on the fuel pump, located, of all places, up behind the right rear tire, where said tending was nearly impossible unless you happened to be the jointless wretch from the Ringling Brothers' sideshow. Some MGs didn't catch in wet weather, and more refused to budge if it looked like snow, but who could blame them? I don't know anyone who claimed to have detected heat coming out of an MG heater.

13. In any case, whatever your MG needed, you had to supply it personally. No strange mechanic was going to diagnose the auto's malaise. As with the family dog, you often had the certain impression that your MG could speak. But arrive at an unfamiliar garage and the little darling suddenly clammed up. It is beyond scientific doubt that MGs responded more favorably to sweet tokens of attention, such as new racing plugs and super-high-octane gas.

14. I'm not here to tell you the MGB was the most beautiful sports car in the world; that it had any single curve to match the dimple front fenders of the old Jaguar XK-140 or a figure to shame a teardrop Porsche.

15. What the MG did, and did better than the rest, was persuade its driver for the duration that the world was a bright and happy place and belonged to him, or her, or in many cases, them. To take an MGB down a twisting country road with the sun dancing in your eyes, a fine breeze on your hair, the silver fluting of leaves flashing by,

and children squealing as you passed, was to grow dizzy on the pleasures of life. It was nearly impossible to set out for an aimless spin without feeling all the joys and possibilities of creation unfolding before you. At 30 miles to the gallon and a price tag then under $3,000, it put those tantalizing gifts of rejuvenation within the reach of the toiling classes.

16. All that's changed now. Every $6,000 subcompact has rack and pinion steering and disc brakes. Every box-on-fours peddles the "sporty" image, and as a British Leyland spokesman told me the other day, "The MGB has grown too long in the tooth." No one knows for certain what Aston-Martin intends for MG, but my guess is an expensive *gran turismo*, and that the MGB is gone forever. Some people will insist that the MG has had its day and now must exit. Others will say that we've grown up.

WALTER PATER

"This Hard, Gemlike Flame . . ."

Walter Pater (1838–1894) ranks with Matthew Arnold and John Ruskin as one of the nineteenth century's finest essayists. Born in Shadwell, East London, he attended Queen's College, Oxford, and in 1864 became a Fellow at Brasenose College, Oxford. Pater wrote numerous rhetorical set pieces, brilliantly self-contained essays, on a multitude of artistic concerns. During his later career he was profoundly influenced by the Pre-Raphaelites, especially by Dante Gabriel Rossetti and Algernon Charles Swinburne and their conception of "art for art's sake." Pater's own works include *Studies in the History of the Renaissance*, 1873, from which this essay is taken; *Marius the Epicurean*, 1885; and *Plato and Platonism*, 1893.

Noting the brevity of life, Pater decries the passive, uneventful existence, suggesting that to live such a life is merely to "sleep before the evening." Avoiding routine, the successful life contains as many "ecstatic moments" as possible—moments, Pater argues, found not in the ephemeral pleasures of the physical appetite but in "the desire of beauty, the love of art for its own sake."

1. To regard all things and principles of things as inconstant modes or fashions has more and more become the tendency of modern thought. Let us begin with that which is without—our physical life. Fix upon it in one of its more exquisite intervals, the moment, for instance, of delicious recoil from the flood of water in summer heat. What is the whole physical life in that moment but a combination of natural elements to which science gives their names? But those elements, phosphorus and lime and delicate fibers, are present not in the human body alone: we detect them in places most remote from it. Our physical life is a perpetual motion of them—the passage of the blood, the waste and repairing of the lenses of the eye, the modification of the tissues of the brain under every ray of light and sound—processes which science reduces to simpler and more elementary forces. Like the elements of which we are composed, the action of these forces extends beyond us: it rusts iron and ripens corn. Far out on every side of us those elements are broadcast, driven in many currents; and birth and gesture and death and the springing of violets from the grave are but a few out of ten thousand resultant combinations. That clear, perpetual outline of face and limb is but an image of ours, under which we group them—a

design in a web, the actual threads of which pass out beyond it. This at least of flame-like our life has, that it is but the concurrence, renewed from moment to moment, of forces parting sooner or later on their ways.

2. Or if we begin with the inward world of thought and feeling, the whirlpool is still more rapid, the flame more eager and devouring. There it is no longer the gradual darkening of the eye, the gradual fading of color from the wall—movements of the shoreside, where the water flows down indeed, though in apparent rest—but the race of the mid-stream, a drift of momentary acts of sight and passion and thought. At first sight experience seems to bury us under a flood of external objects, pressing upon us with a sharp and importunate reality, calling us out of ourselves in a thousand forms of action. But when reflection begins to play upon those objects they are dissipated under its influence; the cohesive force seems suspended like some trick of magic; each object is loosed into a group of impressions—color, odor, texture—in the mind of the observer. And if we continue to dwell in thought on this world, not of objects in the solidity with which language invests them, but of impressions, unstable, flickering, inconsistent, which burn and are extinguished with our consciousness of them, it contracts still further: the whole scope of observation is dwarfed into the narrow chamber of the individual mind. Experience, already reduced to a group of impressions, is ringed round for each one of us by that thick wall of personality through which no real voice has ever pierced on its way to us, or from us to that which we can only conjecture to be without. Every one of those impressions is the impression of the individual in his isolation, each mind keeping as a solitary prisoner its own dream of a world. Analysis goes a step farther still, and assures us that those impressions of the individual mind to which, for each one of us, experience dwindles down, are in perpetual flight; that each of them is limited by time, and that as time is infinitely divisible, each of them is infinitely divisible also; all that is actual in it being a single moment, gone while we try to apprehend it, of which it may ever be more truly said that it has ceased to be than that it is. To such a tremulous wisp constantly re-forming itself on the stream, to a single sharp impression, with a sense in it, a relic more or less fleeting, of such moments gone by, what is real in our life

fines itself down. It is with this movement, with the passage and dissolution of impressions, images, sensations, that analysis leaves off—that continual vanishing away, that strange, perpetual weaving and unweaving of ourselves.

3. *Philosophiren*, says Novalis, *ist dephlegmatisiren vivificiren*. The service of philosophy, of speculative culture, towards the human spirit, is to rouse, to startle it to a life of constant and eager observation. Every moment some form grown perfect in hand or face; some tone on the hills or the sea is choicer than the rest; some mood of passion or insight or intellectual excitement is irresistibly real and attractive to us,—for that moment only. Not the fruit of experience, but experience itself, is the end. A counted number of pulses only is given to us of a variegated, dramatic life. How may we see in them all that is to be seen in them by the finest senses? How shall we pass most swiftly from point to point, and be present always at the focus where the greatest number of vital forces unite in their purest energy?

4. To burn always with this hard, gemlike flame, to maintain this ecstasy, is success in life. In a sense it might even be said that our failure is to form habits: for, after all, habit is relative to a stereotyped world, and meantime it is only the roughness of the eye that makes any two persons, things, situations seem alike. While all melts under our feet, we may well grasp at any exquisite passion, or any contribution to knowledge that seems by a lifted horizon to set the spirit free for a moment, or any stirring of the senses, strange dyes, strange colors, and curious odors, or work of the artist's hands, or the face of one's friend. Not to discriminate every moment some passionate attitude in those about us, and in the very brilliancy of their gifts some tragic dividing of forces on their ways, is, on this short day of frost and sun, to sleep before evening. With this sense of the splendor of our experience and of its awful brevity, gathering all we are into one desperate effort to see and touch, we shall hardly have time to make theories about the things we see and touch. What we have to do is to be forever curiously testing new opinions and courting new impressions, never acquiescing in a facile orthodoxy of Comte, or of Hegel, or of our own. Philosophical theories or ideas, as points of view, instruments of criticism, may help us to gather up what might otherwise pass unregarded by us.

"Philosophy is the microscope of thought." The theory or idea or system which requires of us the sacrifice of any part of this experience, in consideration of some interest into which we cannot enter, or some abstract theory we have not identified with ourselves, or of what is only conventional, has no real claim upon us.

5. One of the most beautiful passages of Rousseau is that in the sixth book of the *Confessions*, where he describes the awakening in him of the literary sense. An undefinable taint of death had clung always about him, and now in early manhood he believed himself smitten by mortal disease. He asked himself how he might make as much as possible of the interval that remained; and he was not biased by anything in his previous life when he decided that it must be by intellectual excitement, which he found just then in the clear, fresh writings of Voltaire. Well! we are all *condamnés*, as Victor Hugo says: we are all under sentence of death but with a sort of indefinite reprieve—*les hommes sont tous condamnés à mort avec des sursis indéfinis:* we have an interval, and then our place knows us no more. Some spend this interval in listlessness, some in high passions, the wisest, at least among "the children of this world," in art and song. For our one chance lies in expanding that interval, in getting as many pulsations as possible into the given time. Great passions may give us this quickened sense of life, ecstasy and sorrow of love, the various forms of enthusiastic activity, disinterested or otherwise, which come naturally to many of us. Only be sure it is passion—that it does yield you this fruit of a quickened, multiplied consciousness. Of such wisdom, the poetic passion, the desire of beauty, the love of art for its own sake, has most. For art comes to you proposing frankly to give nothing but the highest quality of your moments as they pass, and simply for those moments' sake.

E. M. FORSTER

What I Believe

Edward Morgan Forster (1879–1970) was one of England's most distinguished writers and lecturers and an honorary member of the American Academy of Arts and Letters. The holder of many awards, among which was membership in the Order of Companions of Honour to the Queen, he is best known as a novelist and literary critic. His books include *A Room with a View*, 1908; *Howard's End*, 1910; *A Passage to India*, 1924; *Abinger Harvest*, 1926; *Aspects of the Novel*, 1927; and two volumes of short stories, *The Celestial Omnibus*, 1911, and *The Eternal Moment*, 1928. A collection of his essays, *Two Cheers for Democracy*, appeared in 1951. In 1962 he wrote the libretto for the opera *Billy Budd*. *Fairy Tales for Computers* appeared in 1969; *Eternal Moment and Other Stories* in 1970; and a novel, *Maurice*, 1971, was published posthumously.

In "What I Believe," Mr. Forster presents his liberal beliefs on a wide range of subjects—faith, democracy, use of force, hero-worship, aristocracy, and Christianity.

1. I do not believe in Belief. But this is an age of faith, and there are so many militant creeds that, in self-defence, one has to formulate a creed of one's own. Tolerance, good temper and sympathy are no longer enough in a world which is rent by religious and racial persecution, in a world where ignorance rules, and science, who ought to have ruled, plays the subservient pimp. Tolerance, good temper and sympathy—they are what matter really, and if the human race is not to collapse they must come to the front before long. But for the moment they are not enough, their action is no stronger than a flower, battered beneath a military jack-boot. They want stiffening, even if the process coarsens them. Faith, to my mind, is a stiffening process, a sort of mental starch, which ought to be applied as sparingly as possible. I dislike the stuff. I do not believe in it, for its own sake, at all. Herein I probably differ from most people, who believe in Belief, and are only sorry they cannot swallow even more than they do. My law-givers are Erasmus and Montaigne, not Moses and St. Paul. My temple stands not upon Mount Moriah but in that Elysian Field where even the immoral are admitted. My motto is: "Lord, I disbelieve—help thou my unbelief."

2. I have, however, to live in an Age of Faith—the sort of epoch I used to hear praised when I was a boy. It is extremely unpleasant really. It is bloody in every sense of the word. And I have to keep my end up in it. Where do I start?

3. With personal relationships. Here is something comparatively solid in a world full of violence and cruelty. Not absolutely solid, for Psychology has split and shattered the idea of a "Person," and has shown that there is something incalculable in each of us, which may at any moment rise to the surface and destroy our normal balance. We don't know what we are like. We can't know what other people are like. How, then, can we put any trust in personal relationships, or cling to them in the gathering political storm? In theory we cannot. But in practice we can and do. Though A is not unchangeably A or B unchangeably B, there can still be love and loyalty between the two. For the purpose of living one has to assume that the personality is solid, and the "self" is an entity, and to ignore all contrary evidence. And since to ignore evidence is one of the characteristics of faith, I certainly can proclaim that I believe in personal relationships.

4. Starting from them, I get a little order into the contemporary chaos. One must be fond of people and trust them if one is not to make a mess of life, and it is therefore essential that they should not let one down. They often do. The moral of which is that I must, myself, be as reliable as possible, and this I try to be. But reliability is not a matter of contract—that is the main difference between the world of personal relationships and the world of business relationships. It is a matter for the heart, which signs no documents. In other words, reliability is impossible unless there is a natural warmth. Most men possess this warmth, though they often have bad luck and get chilled. Most of them, even when they are politicians, *want* to keep faith. And one can, at all events, show one's own little light here, one's own poor little trembling flame, with the knowledge that it is not the only light that is shining in the darkness, and not the only one which the darkness does not comprehend. Personal relations are despised today. They are regarded as bourgeois luxuries, as products of a time of fair weather which is now past, and we are urged to get rid of them, and to dedicate ourselves to some movement or cause instead. I hate the idea of causes, and if I had to choose between betraying my country and betraying my friend, I hope I should have the guts to betray my country. Such a choice may scandalise the modern reader, and he may stretch out his patriotic hand to the telephone at once and ring up the police. It would not have shocked Dante, though. Dante places Brutus and Cassius in the lowest circle of Hell because they had chosen to betray their friend Julius Caesar rather than their country Rome. Probably one will not be asked to make such an agonizing choice. Still, there lies at the back of every creed something terrible and hard for which the worshipper may one day be required to suffer, and there is even a terror and a hardness in this creed of personal relationships, urbane and mild though it sounds. Love and loyalty to an individual can run counter to the claims of the State. When they do—down with the State, say I, which means that the State would down me.

5. This brings me along to Democracy, "even Love, the Beloved Republic, which feeds upon Freedom and lives." Democracy is not a Beloved

Republic really, and never will be. But it is less hateful than other contemporary forms of government, and to that extent it deserves our support. It does start from the assumption that the individual is important, and that all types are needed to make a civilisation. It does not divide its citizens into the bossers and the bossed—as an efficiency-regime tends to do. The people I admire most are those who are sensitive and want to create something or discover something, and do not see life in terms of power, and such people get more of a chance under a democracy than elsewhere. They found religions, great or small, or they produce literature and art, or they do disinterested scientific research, or they may be what is called "ordinary people," who are creative in their private lives, bring up their children decently, for instance, or help their neighbours. All these people need to express themselves; they cannot do so unless society allows them liberty to do so, and the society which allows them most liberty is a democracy.

6. Democracy has another merit. It allows criticism, and if there is not public criticism there are bound to be hushed-up scandals. That is why I believe in the Press, despite all its lies and vulgarity, and why I believe in Parliament. Parliament is often sneered at because it is a Talking Shop. I believe in it *because* it is a talking shop. I believe in the Private Member who makes himself a nuisance. He gets snubbed and is told that he is cranky or ill-informed, but he does expose abuses which would otherwise never have been mentioned, and very often an abuse gets put right just by being mentioned. Occasionally, too, a well-meaning public official starts losing his head in the cause of efficiency, and thinks himself God Almighty. Such officials are particularly frequent in the Home Office. Well, there will be questions about them in Parliament sooner or later, and then they will have to mind their steps. Whether Parliament is either a representative body or an efficient one is questionable, but I value it because it criticises and talks, and because its chatter gets widely reported.

7. So Two Cheers for Democracy: one because it admits variety and two because it permits criticism. Two cheers are quite enough: there is no occasion to give three. Only Love the Beloved Republic deserves that.

8. What about Force, though? While we are trying to be sensitive and advanced and affectionate and tolerant, an unpleasant question pops up: does not all society rest upon force? If a government cannot count upon the police and the army, how can it hope to rule? And if an individual gets knocked on the head or sent to a labour camp, of what significance are his opinions?

9. This dilemma does not worry me as much as it does some. I realise that all society rests upon force. But all the great creative actions, all the decent human relations, occur during the intervals when force has not managed to come to the front. These intervals are what matter. I want them to be as frequent and as lengthy as possible, and I call them "civilisation." Some people idealise force and pull it into the foreground and worship it, instead of keeping it in the background as long as possible. I think they make a mistake, and I think that their opposites, the mystics, err even more when they declare that force does not exist. I believe that it exists, and that one of our jobs is to prevent it from getting out of its box. It gets out sooner or later, and then it destroys us and all the lovely things which we have made. But it is not out all the time, for the fortunate reason that the strong are so stupid. Consider their conduct for a moment in the Niebelung's Ring. The giants there have the guns, or in other words the gold; but they do nothing with it, they do not realise that they are all-powerful, with the result that the catastrophe is delayed and the castle of Walhalla, insecure but glorious, fronts the storms. Fafnir, coiled round his hoard, grumbles and grunts; we can hear him under Europe today; the leaves of the wood already tremble, and the Bird calls its warnings uselessly. Fafnir will destroy us, but by a blessed dispensation he is stupid and slow, and creation goes on just outside the poisonous blast of his breath. The Nietzschean would hurry the monster up, the mystic would say he did not exist, but Wotan, wiser than either, hastens to create warriors before doom declares itself. The Valkyries are symbols not only of courage but of intelligence; they represent the human spirit snatching its opportunity while the going is good, and one of them even finds time to love. Brünnhilde's last song hymns the recurrence of love, and since it is the privilege of art to exaggerate, she goes even further, and proclaims the

love which is eternally triumphant and feeds upon freedom, and lives.

10. So that is what I feel about force and violence. It is, alas! the ultimate reality on this earth, but it does not always get to the front. Some people call its absences "decadence"; I call them "civilisation" and find in such interludes the chief justification for the human experiment. I look the other way until fate strikes me. Whether this is due to courage or to cowardice in my own case I cannot be sure. But I know that if men had not looked the other way in the past, nothing of any value would survive. The people I respect most behave as if they were immortal and as if society was eternal. Both assumptions are false: both of them must be accepted as true if we are to go on eating and working and loving, and are to keep open a few breathing holes for the human spirit. No millennium seems likely to descend upon humanity; no better and stronger League of Nations will be instituted; no form of Christianity and no alternative to Christianity will bring peace to the world or integrity to the individual; no "change of heart" will occur. And yet we need not despair, indeed, we cannot despair; the evidence of history shows us that men have always insisted on behaving creatively under the shadow of the sword; that they have done their artistic and scientific and domestic stuff for the sake of doing it, and that we had better follow their example under the shadow of the aeroplanes. Others, with more vision or courage than myself, see the salvation of humanity ahead, and will dismiss my conception of civilisation as paltry, a sort of tip-and-run game. Certainly it is presumptuous to say that we *cannot* improve, and that Man, who has only been in power for a few thousand years, will never learn to make use of his power. All I mean is that, if people continue to kill one another as they do, the world cannot get better than it is, and that since there are more people than formerly, and their means for destroying one another superior, the world may well get worse. What is good in people—and consequently in the world—is their insistence on creation, their belief in friendship and loyalty for their own sakes; and though Violence remains and is, indeed, the major partner in this muddled establishment, I believe that creativeness remains too, and will always assume direction when violence sleeps. So, though I am not an optimist, I cannot agree with Sophocles that it were better never to have been born. And although, like Horace, I see no evidence that each batch of births is superior to the last, I leave the field open for the more complacent view. This is such a difficult moment to live in, one cannot help getting gloomy and also a bit rattled, and perhaps short-sighted.

11. In search of a refuge, we may perhaps turn to hero-worship. But here we shall get no help, in my opinion. Hero-worship is a dangerous vice, and one of the minor merits of a democracy is that it does not encourage it, or produce that unmanageable type of citizen known as the Great Man. It produces instead different kinds of small men—a much finer achievement. But people who cannot get interested in the variety of life, and cannot make up their own minds, get discontented over this, and they long for a hero to bow down before and to follow blindly. It is significant that a hero is an integral part of the authoritarian stock-in-trade today. An efficiency-regime cannot be run without a few heroes stuck about it to carry off the dullness—much as plums have to be put into a bad pudding to make it palatable. One hero at the top and a smaller one each side of him is a favourite arrangement, and the timid and the bored are comforted by the trinity, and, bowing down, feel exalted and strengthened.

12. No, I distrust Great Men. They produce a desert of uniformity around them and often a pool of blood too, and I always feel a little man's pleasure when they come a cropper. Every now and then one reads in the newspapers some such statement as: "The coup d'état appears to have failed, and Admiral Toma's whereabouts is at present unknown." Admiral Toma had probably every qualification for being a Great Man—an iron will, personal magnetism, dash, flair, sexlessness—but fate was against him, so he retires to unknown whereabouts instead of parading history with his peers. He fails with a completeness which no artist and no lover can experience, because with them the process of creation is itself an achievement, whereas with him the only possible achievement is success.

13. I believe in aristocracy, though—if that is the right word, and if a democrat may use it. Not an aristocracy of power, based upon rank and influence, but an aristocracy of the sensitive, the considerate and the plucky. Its members are to be found in all nations and classes, and all

through the ages, and there is a secret understanding between them when they meet. They represent the true human tradition, the one permanent victory of our queer race over cruelty and chaos. Thousands of them perish in obscurity, a few are great names. They are sensitive for others as well as for themselves, they are considerate without being fussy, their pluck is not swankiness but the power to endure, and they can take a joke. I give no examples—it is risky to do that—but the reader may as well consider whether this is the type of person he would like to meet and to be, and whether (going farther with me) he would prefer that this type should *not* be an ascetic one. I am against asceticism myself. I am with the old Scotsman who wanted less chastity and more delicacy. I do not feel that my aristocrats are a real aristocracy if they thwart their bodies, since bodies are the instruments through which we register and enjoy the world. Still, I do not insist. This is not a major point. It is clearly possible to be sensitive, considerate and plucky and yet be an ascetic too; if anyone possesses the first three qualities, I will let him in! On they go—an invincible army, yet not a victorious one. The aristocrats, the elect, the chosen, the Best People—all the words that describe them are false, and all attempts to organise them fail. Again and again Authority, seeing their value, has tried to net them and to utilise them as the Egyptian Priesthood or the Christian Church or the Chinese Civil Service or the Group Movement, or some other worthy stunt. But they slip through the net and are gone; when the door is shut, they are no longer in the room; their temple, as one of them remarked, is the Holiness of the Heart's Affection, and their kingdom, though they never possess it, is the wide-open world.

14. With this type of person knocking about, and constantly crossing one's path if one has eyes to see or hands to feel, the experiment of earthly life cannot be dismissed as a failure. But it may well be hailed as a tragedy, the tragedy being that no device has been found by which these private decencies can be transmitted to public affairs. As soon as people have power they go crooked and sometimes dotty as well, because the possession of power lifts them into a region where normal honesty never pays. For instance, the man who is selling newspapers outside the Houses of Parliament can safely leave his papers to go for a drink and his cap beside them: anyone who takes a paper is sure to drop a copper into the cap. But the men who are inside the Houses of Parliament—they cannot trust one another like that; still less can the Government they compose trust other governments. No caps upon the pavement here, but suspicion, treachery and armaments. The more highly public life is organised the lower does its morality sink; the nations of today behave to each other worse than they ever did in the past, they cheat, rob, bully and bluff, make war without notice, and kill as many women and children as possible; whereas primitive tribes were at all events restrained by taboos. It is a humiliating outlook—though the greater the darkness, the brighter shine the little lights, reassuring one another, signalling: "Well, at all events, I'm still here. I don't like it very much, but how are you?" Unquenchable lights of my aristocracy! Signals of the invincible army! "Come along—anyway, let's have a good time while we can." I think they signal that too.

15. The Saviour of the future—if ever he comes—will not preach a new Gospel. He will merely utilise my aristocracy, he will make effective the good will and the good temper which are already existing. In other words, he will introduce a new technique. In economics, we are told that if there was a new technique of distribution, there need be no poverty, and people would not starve in one place while crops were being ploughed under in another. A similar change is needed in the sphere of morals and politics. The desire for it is by no means new; it was expressed, for example, in theological terms by Jacopone da Todi over six hundred years ago. "Ordina questo amore, O tu che m'ami," he said; "O thou who lovest me—set this love in order." His prayer was not granted, and I do not myself believe that it ever will be, but here, and not through a change of heart, is our probable route. Not by becoming better, but by ordering and distributing his native goodness, will Man shut up Force into its box, and so gain time to explore the universe and to set his mark upon it worthily. At present he only explores it at odd moments, when Force is looking the other way, and his divine creativeness appears as a trivial by-product, to be scrapped as soon as the drums beat and the bombers hum.

16. Such a change, claim the orthodox, can only be made by Christianity, and will be made

by it in God's good time: man always has failed and always will fail to organise his own goodness, and it is presumptuous of him to try. This claim—solemn as it is—leaves me cold. I cannot believe that Christianity will ever cope with the present world-wide mess, and I think that such influence as it retains in modern society is due to the money behind it, rather than to its spiritual appeal. It was a spiritual force once, but the indwelling spirit will have to be restated if it is to calm the waters again, and probably restated in a non-Christian form. Naturally a lot of people, and people who are not only good but able and intelligent, will disagree here; they will vehemently deny that Christianity has failed, or they will argue that its failure proceeds from the wickedness of men, and really proves its ultimate success. They have Faith, with a large F. My faith has a very small one, and I only intrude it because these are strenuous and serious days, and one likes to say what one thinks while speech is comparatively free: it may not be free much longer.

17. The above are the reflections of an individualist and a liberal who has found liberalism crumbling beneath him and at first felt ashamed. Then, looking around, he decided there was no special reason for shame, since other people, whatever they felt, were equally insecure. And as for individualism—there seems no way of getting off this, even if one wanted to. The dictator-hero can grind down his citizens till they are all alike, but he cannot melt them into a single man. That is beyond his power. He can order them to merge, he can incite them to mass-antics, but they are obliged to be born separately, and to die separately, and, owing to these unavoidable termini, will always be running off the totalitarian rails. The memory of birth and the expectation of death always lurk within the human being, making him separate from his fellows and consequently capable of intercourse with them. Naked I came into the world, naked I shall go out of it! And a very good thing too, for it reminds me that I am naked under my shirt, whatever its colour.

RICHARD WILBUR

Advice to a Prophet

When you come, as you soon must, to the streets of our city,
Mad-eyed from stating the obvious,
Not proclaiming our fall but begging us
In God's name to have self-pity,

Spare us all word of the weapons, their force and range,
The long numbers that rocket the mind;
Our slow, unreckoning hearts will be left behind,
Unable to fear what is too strange.

Nor shall you scare us with talk of the death of the race.
How should we dream of this place without us?—
The sun mere fire, the leaves untroubled about us,
A stone look on the stone's face?

Speak of the world's own change. Though we cannot conceive
Of an undreamt thing, we know to our cost
How the dreamt cloud crumbles, the vines are blackened by frost,
How the view alters. We could believe,

If you told us so, that the white-tailed deer will slip
Into perfect shade, grown perfectly shy,
The lark avoid the reaches of our eye,
The jack-pine lose its knuckled grip

On the cold ledge, and every torrent burn
As Xanthus once, its gliding trout
Stunned in a twinkling. What should we be without
The dolphin's arc, the dove's return,

These things in which we have seen ourselves and spoken?
Ask us, prophet, how we shall call
Our natures forth when that live tongue is all
Dispelled, that glass obscured or broken

In which we have said the rose of our love and the clean
Horse of our courage, in which beheld
The singing locust of the soul unshelled,
And all we mean or wish to mean.

Ask us, ask us whether with the worldless rose
Our hearts shall fail us; come demanding
Whether there shall be lofty or long standing
When the bronze annals of the oak-tree close.

MARK O'DONNELL

From Here to Eternity

In Which We Rummage through Destiny's Pocket

Mark O'Donnell (1954–   ) was born in Ohio, an identical twin. He studied at the American Academy of Dramatic Arts in New York and then attended Harvard University from which he graduated magna cum laude in 1976. During his time at Harvard he was editor of the *Harvard Lampoon.* He writes essays, plays, and poems for newspapers and magazines, among them *House and Garden, Saturday Review, New Times* ("Portrait of the Artist as a Young Manic"), and the *New York Times* ("Old Codger's 1979 Almanac" and "April Fool's Day"). He has been co-editor of *Tools of Power,* 1980, and contributing author for several books, among them *Junk Food,* 1980, a collection of scathing satirical pieces, which includes his "Xmas Dinner."

Especially appropriate for anyone who is tired of the past, disappointed with the present, and ready to take any future is O'Donnell's essay, which with gloom and horror and glee tells us that "the future . . . is all we have left, and it doesn't even exist."

Tomorrow is the biggest word in the English language.
> —an unknown civics teacher,
> 1948, and every year thereafter

1. Otherwise untalented men from Nostradamus on down have sought to prefurnish Tomorrow's vast, cleanly corridors with crowds of garish, overstuffed Possibilities, and today's future is no exception. A new decade yawns before futurologists—as who wouldn't?—and they are meeting its challenge by strip-mining the prairies of Potentiality and showing off their swag like moon rocks won at poker.

2. What will tomorrow hold for us Present Day types? More importantly, what of that will it accidentally drop? What do the futurologists see of war, of peace, in times to come? Why are they selling all their waterfront property?

3. Before we unwrap Time's veiling bandages, however, remember that the future is like a doe venturing from the woods to lick salt from your hand, or possibly to root around in your garbage. In that case it's like a raccoon. But it's more like a deer, usually. Maybe two deer. Anyway, you can't rush the future. Slowly, the sweet by-and-by will come up behind you (assuming, like most, you're facing the past) and nuzzle the small of your back, bringing with its shy, wet overtures anything from tall, dark strangers to nuclear cataclysm.

4. Those who cannot learn from the future are condemned to experience it. Let us review the coming years, and vow never to repeat them.

5. In the near future, the family as we know it will cease to exist, even on important holidays. More and more dual-career couples will move into beige apartments in a single, continent-spanning renovated city. Instead of having children, they will have stereos, plants, and magazines. In fact, magazines called *Son* and *Daughter* will

substitute for child-rearing, featuring articles and photographs of a boy or girl that will age along with the subscription.

6. People will become so neurotically independent that they will have their spouses regularly arrested for invasion of privacy. Boutiques full of other people's old photographs, mementos, and clothing will proliferate, and Salvation Army Chic will give the Willfully Inexperienced Generation its chance to feel witty and childlike by donning the broken flotsam of lives it is unequipped to imagine. Everyone will be a lawyer who dislikes his job.

7. The world's nations will aggregate into three enormous Megalands, each of which will talk about the third when it isn't around. Paper money will become meaningless, but you wouldn't know it to hear it talk. Submarines with cowcatchers will plow the ocean floor for plankton and kelp to feed our enemies. We'll wear clothes with batteries and inhale protein vapors instead of eating.

8. For entertainment, people will be surgically transplanted to someone else's life for a few days, although this probably won't include check-signing privileges. Robots will attend movies for us and give us print-out capsule summaries that will allow us more free time to contemplate our increasingly smooth and hairless skin. Electrified animals will do our tax forms for us, and out-of-work literate chimpanzees will write our diaries in our stead. However, the extra leisure hours gained from all these services will be largely absorbed by the new style of leisure: Games, parties, and even sexual episodes will take twice as long, since we'll watch the videotapes afterward.

9. Exclusive nurseries for adults will spring up in warehouses and old hotels, allowing those who have released every other discipline to dismiss what remains of bodily control.

10. In a trillion years or so (and this will come sooner than you think, especially if you agree to have dinner then with someone you don't like),

man will have evolved into balls of light or just plain Pure Being. We may fuss around with extra fingers and turnip-shaped heads, but ultimately we'll go with the Pure Being look. Hammock sales will go down drastically. Man will not need toiletries or antacids or even a mailing address—he will just sort of hum or pulsate and meld with the universe. There will be greater voter awareness, and at sing-alongs everyone will know all the words. There will be no more ugliness, although there may be occasional rudeness in checkout lines. Man will have transcended love and revenge but some people may still put XXXs at the end of telegrams or publicly embarrass someone else's Pure Being.

11. On the sports scene, a solar holocaust will incinerate our planet, so there will be no professional athletics for a while. Eventually they will get the Davis Cup going again, but without a sun to measure time, a lot of the participants will arrive late. As man phases out his physical side, there will be only touch football, and even that will get just pathetic as we near the Pure Being state. After that, it will be mostly Twenty Questions.

12. Beyond a trillion years in the future, there's no one you'd know, and here many futurologists lose interest in watching, but several foresee a dark era in the history of the earth, followed by a very successful revival of *Show Boat*.

13. Why does man relish these whiffs of that eternally dangling carrot, Tomorrow? Most of us are tired of the past—if not of our own, then certainly of others' versions of theirs—and the present is a mere flash of tangled rope as we slide down the tightening slip knot of time. The future, when you come down to it, is all we have left, and it doesn't even exist. No wonder futurologists say (at least after a few drinks), "Tomorrow is like a woman: So long as she keeps you waiting, you assume she's beautiful." If only her kid brother Today didn't pester us while we wait.

BARBARA W. TUCHMAN

Mankind's Better Moments

Barbara Tuchman (1912–   ) was born in New York City and graduated from Radcliffe College. She is a distinguished and internationally accepted historian who has won two Pulitzer prizes, for *Stilwell and the American Experience in China, 1911–1945*, 1971 and for *The Guns of August*, 1976. *A Distant Mirror: The Calamitous Fourteenth Century*, 1978, is a monumental study of that century as one of violence, bewilderment, suffering, and disintegration. She sees parallels with the twentieth century but thinks we should not be overwhelmed by our present troubles, as every age has had its own special problems.

In this essay, "Mankind's Better Moments," taken from a longer essay published in *The American Scholar* in 1980 and originally given as a lecture for the National Endowment for the Humanities' Jefferson lecture, the preceding spring, Tuchman tempers her pessimism in *A Distant Mirror* by looking at some of history's better moments instead of its flaws and corruption. She concludes essentially that times of "gloom and doom" are times when new eras are beginning to be born.

1. For a change from prevailing pessimism, I should like to recall for you some of the positive and even admirable capacities of the human race. We hear very little of them lately. Ours is not a time of self-esteem or self-confidence as was, for instance, the 19th century, whose self-esteem may be seen oozing from its portraits. Victorians, especially the men, pictured themselves as erect, noble, and splendidly handsome. Our self-image looks more like Woody Allen or a character from Samuel Beckett. Amid a mass of world-wide troubles and a poor record for the 20th century, we see our species—with cause—as functioning very badly, as blunderers when not knaves, as violent, ignoble, corrupt, inept, incapable of mastering the forces that threaten us, weakly subject to our worst instincts; in short, decadent.

2. The catalogue is familiar and valid, but it is growing tiresome. A study of history reminds one that mankind has its ups and downs and during the ups has accomplished many brave and beautiful things, exerted stupendous endeavors, explored and conquered oceans and wilderness, achieved marvels of beauty in the creative arts and marvels of science and social progress, loved liberty with a passion that throughout history led men to fight and die for it over and over again, pursued knowledge, exercised reason, enjoyed laughter and pleasures, played games with zest, shown courage, heroism, altruism, honor, and decency, experienced love, known comfort, contentment, and occasionally happiness. All these qualities have been part of human experience, and if they have not had as important notice as the negatives nor exerted as wide and persistent as influence as the evils we do, they nevertheless deserve attention, for they are currently all but forgotten.

GREAT ENDEAVORS

3. Among the great endeavors, we have in our own time carried men to the moon and brought them back safely—surely one of the most remarkable achievements in history. Some may disapprove of the effort as unproductive, as too costly, and a wrong choice of priorities in relation to greater needs, all of which may be true but does not, as I see it, diminish the achievement.

4. If you look carefully, all positives have a negative underside, sometimes more, sometimes less, and not all admirable endeavors have admirable motives. Some have sad consequences. Although most signs presently point from bad to worse, human capacities are probably what they have always been. If primitive man could discover how to transform grain into bread, and reeds growing by the river bank into baskets, if his successors could invent the wheel, harness the insubstantial air to turn a two-ton millstone, transform sheep's wool, flax, and worm's cocoons into fabric, we, I imagine, will find a way to manage the energy problem.

5. Consider how the Dutch accomplished the miracle of making land out of the sea. By progressive enclosure of the Zuyder Zee over the last 60 years, they have added half a million acres to their country, enlarging its area by 8 percent and providing homes, farms, and towns for close to a quarter of a million people. The will to do the impossible, the spirit of Can-Do that overtakes our species now and then was never more manifest than in this earth-altering act by the smallest of the major European nations. . . .

6. Great endeavor requires vision and some kind of compelling impulse, not necessarily practical as in the case of the Dutch, but something less definable, more exalted, as in the case of the Gothic cathedrals of the Middle Ages. The architectural explosion that produced this multitude of soaring vaults—arched, ribbed, pierced with jeweled light, studded with thousands of figures of the stone-carvers' art—represents in size, splendor, and numbers one of the great, permanent artistic achievements of human hands. What accounts for it? Not religious fervor alone. . . .

7. Explanations of the extraordinary burst that produced the cathedrals are several. Art historians will tell you that it was the invention of the ribbed vault, permitting subdivision, independence of parts, replacement of solid walls by columns, multiplication of windows, and all the extrapolations that followed. But this does not explain the energies that took hold of and developed the rib. Religious historians say these were the product of an age of faith that believed that with God's favor anything was possible. In fact, it was not a period of untroubled faith but of heresies and Inquisition. Rather, one can only say that conditions were right. Social order under monarchy and the towns was replacing the anarchy of the barons, so that existence was no longer merely a struggle to stay alive but allowed a surplus of goods and energies and greater opportunity for mutual effort. Banking and commerce were producing capital, roads making possible wheeled transport, universities nourishing ideas and communication. It was one of history's high tides, an age of vigor, confidence, and forces converging to quicken the blood.

8. Even when the general tide was low, a particular group of doers could emerge in exploits that still inspire awe. Shrouded in the mists of the 8th century, long before the cathedrals, Viking seamanship was a wonder of daring, stamina, and skill. Pushing relentlessly outward in open boats, they sailed southward around Spain to North Africa and Arabia, north to the top of the world, west across uncharted seas to American coasts. They hauled their boats overland from the Baltic to make their way down Russian rivers to the Black Sea. Why? We do not know what engine drove them, only that it was part of the human endowment.

MAN AT PLAY

9. What of the founding of our own country? We take the Mayflower for granted, yet think of the boldness, the enterprise, the determined independence, the sheer grit it took to leave the known and set out across the sea for the unknown where no houses or food, no stores, no cleared land, no crops or livestock, none of the equipment of settlement or organized living awaited. . . .

10. Happily, man has a capacity for pleasure too, and, in contriving ways to entertain and amuse himself, has created brilliance and delight. Pageants, carnivals, festivals, fireworks, music, dancing and drama, parties and picnics, sports and games, the comic spirit and its gift of laugh-

ter, all the range of enjoyment from grand ceremonial to the quiet solitude of a day's fishing, has helped to balance the world's infelicity. *Homo ludens,* man at play, is surely as significant a figure as man at war or at work. In human activity, the invention of the ball may be said to rank with the invention of the wheel. Imagine America without baseball, Europe without soccer, England without cricket, the Italians without boccie, China without ping-pong, and tennis for no one. Even stern John Calvin, the exemplar of Puritan denial, was once discovered playing bowls on Sunday, and in 1611 an English supply ship arriving at Jamestown found the starving colonists suppressing their misery in the same game. Cornhuskings, log-rollings, barn-raisings, horse races, wrestling and boxing matches have engaged America as, somewhat more passively, the armchair watching of football and basketball does today.

11. Play was invented for diversion, exertion, and escape from routine cares. In colonial New York, sleighing parties preceded by fiddlers on horseback drove out to country inns, where, according to a participant, "we danced, sang, romped, ate and drank and kicked away care from morning to night." John Audubon, present at a barbecue and dance on the Kentucky frontier, wrote, "Every countenance beamed with joy, every heart leaped with gladness . . . care and sorrow were flung to the winds. . . ."

12. It was a case of men and women engaged in the art of enjoyment, a function common to all times, although one would hardly know it from today's image of ourselves as wretched creatures forever agonizing over petty squalors of sex and alcohol as if we had no other recourse or destiny.

13. The greatest recourse and mankind's most enduring achievement is art. At its best, it reveals the nobility that coexists in human nature along with flaws and evils, and the beauty and truth it can perceive. Whether in music or architecture, literature, painting, or sculpture, art opens our eyes and ears and feelings to something beyond ourselves, something we cannot experience without the artist's vision and the genius of his craft.

ART AND PROGRESS

14. The placing of Greek temples like the Temple of Poseidon on the promontory at Sunium, outlined against the piercing blue of the Aegean Sea, Poseidon's home; the majesty of Michaelangelo's sculptured figures in stone; Shakespeare's command of language and knowledge of the human soul; the intricate order of Bach, the enchantment of Mozart; the purity of Chinese monochrome pottery, with the lovely names—celadon, oxblood, peach blossom, clair de lune; the exuberance of Tiepolo's ceilings where, without the picture frames to limit movement, a whole world in exquisitely beautiful colors lives and moves in the sky; the prose and poetry of all the writers from Homer to Cervantes to Jane Austen, and John Keats to Dostoyevsky and Chekhov—who made all these things? We—our species—did. The range is too vast and various to do justice to it in this space, but the random samples I have mentioned, and all the rest they suggest, are sufficient reason to honor mankind.

15. If we have, as I think, lost beauty and elegance in the modern world, we have gained much, through science and technology and democratic pressures, in the material well-being of the masses. The change in the lives of, and society's attitude toward, the working class marks the great divide between the modern world and the old regime.

16. From the French Revolution through the brutal labor wars of the 19th and 20th centuries, the change was earned mainly by force against fierce and often vicious opposition. While this was a harsh process, it developed and activated a social conscience hardly operative before. Slavery, beggary, unaided misery and want have, on the whole, been eliminated in the developed nations of the West. That much is a credit in the human record even if the world is uglier as a result of adapting to mass values. History generally arranges these things so that gain is balanced by loss, perhaps in order to make the gods jealous. . . .

17. Although the Enlightenment may have overestimated the power of reason to guide human conduct, it nevertheless opened to men and women a more humane view of their fellow passengers. Slowly the harshest habits gave way to reform—in treatment of the insane, reduction of death penalties, mitigation of the fierce laws against debtors and poachers, and in the passionately fought cause for abolition of the slave trade.

18. The humanitarian movement was not charity, which always carries an overtone of

being done in the donor's interest, but a more disinterested benevolence-altruism, that is to say, motivated by conscience. It was personified in William Wilbeforce who, in the later 18th century, stirred the great rebellion of the English conscience against the trade in human beings. His eloquence, charm of character, and influence over devoted followers could have carried him to the Prime Minister's seat if personal power had been his goal, but he channeled his life instead toward a goal for mankind. He instigated, energized, inspired a movement whose members held meetings, organized petitions, collected information on the horrors of the middle passage, showered pamphlets on the public, gathered Nonconformist middle-class sentiment into a swelling tide that "melted," in Trevelyan's phrase, "the hard prudence of statesmen."

SUMMONING COURAGE

19. Abolition of the slave trade under the British flag was won in 1807, against, it must be said, American resistance. The British Navy was used to enforce the ban by searches on the high seas and regular patrols of the African coast. When Portugal and Spain were persuaded to join in the prohibition, they were paid a compensation of £300,000 and £400,000, respectively, by the British taxpayer. Violations and smuggling continued, convincing the abolitionists that in order to stop the trade, slavery itself had to be abolished. Agitation resumed. By degrees over the next quarter century, compensation reduced the opposition of the West Indian slave-owners and their allies in England until emancipation of all slaves in the British Empire was enacted in 1833. The total cost to the British taxpayer was reckoned at £20 million.

20. Through recent unpleasant experiences, we have learned to expect ambition, greed, or corruption to reveal itself behind every public act, but, as we have just seen, it is not invariably so. Human beings do possess better impulses, and occasionally act upon them, even in the 20th century. Occupied Denmark, during World War II, outraged by Nazi orders for deportation of its Jewish fellow-citizens, summoned the courage of defiance and transformed itself into a united underground railway to smuggle virtually all 8,000 Danish Jews out to Sweden. Far away and unconnected, a village in southern France, Le Chambon-sur-Lignon, devoted itself to rescuing

Jews and other victims of the Nazis at the risk of the inhabitants' own lives and freedom. "Saving lives became a hobby of the people of Le Chambon," said one of them. The larger record of the time was admittedly collaboration, passive or active. We cannot reckon on the better impulses predominating in the world; only that they will always appear.

21. The strongest of these in history, summoner of the best in men, has been zeal for liberty. Time after time, in some spot somewhere in the globe, people have risen in what Swinburne called the "divine right of insurrection"—to overthrow despots, repel alien conquerors, achieve independence, and so it will be until the day power ceases to corrupt—not a near expectation.

22. The ancient Jews rose three times against alien rulers, beginning with the revolt of the Maccabees against the effort of Antiochus to outlaw observance of the Jewish faith. . . . In the next century, the uprising of zealots against Roman rule was fanatically and hopelessly pursued through famine, sieges, the fall of Jerusalem, and destruction of the Temple, until a last stand of less than a thousand on the rock of Masada ended in a group suicide in preference to surrender. After 60 years as an occupied province, Judea rose again under Simeon Bar Koziba, who regained Jerusalem for a brief moment of Jewish control but could not withstand the arms of Hadrian. The rebellion was crushed, but the zeal of self-hood, smoldering in exile through 18 centuries, was to revive and regain its home in our time.

23. The phenomenon continues today in various forms, by Algerians, Irish, Vietnamese, and peoples of Africa and the Middle East. Seen at close quarters and more often than not manipulated by outsiders, these contemporary movements seem less pure and heroic than those polished by history's gloss—for instance, the Scots of the Middle Ages against the English, the Swiss against the Hapsburgs, or the American colonists against the mother country.

24. I have always cherished the spirited rejoinder of one of the great colonial landowners of New York who, on being advised not to risk his property by signing the Declaration of Independence, replied "Damn the property; give me the pen!" On seeking confirmation for the purpose of this essay, I am deeply chagrined to report that the saying appears to be apocryphal. Yet not its

spirit, for the signers well knew they were risking their property, not to mention their heads, by putting their names to the Declaration. . . .

HISTORY'S LESSONS

25. So far I have considered qualities of the group rather than of the individual, except for art, which is always a product of the single spirit. Happiness, too, is a matter of individual capacity. It springs up here or there, haphazard, random, without origin or explanation. It resists study, laughs at sociology, flourishes, vanishes, reappears somewhere else. Take Izaac Walton, author of *The Compleat Angler,* that guide to contentment as well as fishing of which Charles Lamb said, "It would sweeten any man's temper at any time to read it." Although Walton lived in distracted times of Revolution and regicide, though he adhered to the losing side of the Civil War, though he lost in their infancy all seven children by his first wife and the eldest son of his second marriage, though he was twice a widower, his misfortunes could not sour an essentially buoyant nature. "He passed through turmoil," in the words of a biographer, "ever accompanied by content. . . ."

26. *The Compleat Angler,* published when the author was 60, glows in the sunshine of his character. In it are humor and piety, grave advice on the idiosyncracies of fish and the niceties of landing them, delight in nature and in music. Walton saw five editions reprinted in his lifetime, while innumerable later editions secured him immortality. He wrote his last work, a life of his friend Robert Sanderson, at 85, and died at 90 after being celebrated in verse by one of his circle as a "happy old man" whose life "showed how to compass true felicity." Let us think of him when we grumble.

27. Is anything to be learned from my survey? I raise the question only because most people *want* history to teach them lessons, which I believe it can do, although I am less sure we can use them when needed. I gathered these examples not to teach but merely to remind people in a despondent era that the good in mankind operates even if the bad gets more attention. I am aware that selecting out the better moments does not result in a realistic picture. Turn them over and there is likely to be a darker side, as when

Project Apollo, our journey to the moon, was authorized because its glamor could obtain subsidies for rocket and missile development that otherwise might not have been forthcoming. That is the way things are.

28. Whole philosophies have evolved over the question whether the human species is predominantly good or evil. I only know that it is mixed, that you cannot separate good from bad, that wisdom, courage, benevolence exist alongside knavery, greed, and stupidity; heroism and fortitude alongside vainglory, cruelty, and corruption.

29. It is a paradox of our time that never have so many people been so relatively well off and never has society been more troubled. Yet I suspect that humanity's virtues have not vanished, although the experiences of our century seem to suggest they are in abeyance. A century that took shape in the disillusion that followed the enormous effect and hopes of World War I, that saw revolution in Russia congeal into the same tyranny it overthrew, saw a supposedly civilized nation revert under the Nazis into organized and unparalleled savagery, saw the craven appeasement by the democracies, is understandably suspicious of human nature. A literary historian, Van Wyck Brooks, discussing the 1920s and '30s, spoke of "an eschatalogical despair of the world." Whereas Whitman and Emerson, he wrote, "had been impressed by the worth and good sense of the people, writers of the new time" were struck by their lusts, cupidity, and violence, and had come to dislike their fellow men. The same theme reappeared in a recent play in which a mother struggled against her two "pitilessly contemptuous" children. Her problem was that she wanted them to be happy and they did not want to be. They preferred to watch horrors on television. In essence, this is our epoch. It insists upon the flaws and corruptions, without belief in valor or virtue or the possibility of happiness. It keeps turning to look back on Sodom and Gomorrah; it has no view of the Delectable Mountains.

30. We must keep a balance, and I know of no better prescription than a phrase from Condorcet's eulogy on the death of Benjamin Franklin: "He pardoned the present for the sake of the future."

ALBERT ROSENFELD

How Anxious Should Science Make Us?

Albert H. Rosenfeld (1920–   ) was educated at New Mexico State University and served as New Mexico correspondent for *Time* magazine from 1956 to 1959. He was also science editor briefly for *Family Health*, medical editor for *Time-Life* video and radio services, science interviewer for CBS, and senior editor for *Saturday Review*.

Rosenfeld's reply to the question in the title of his essay is that the age of anxiety produced by the age of science—a continuing battle between "pure" science and its "impure" technology—feeds our anxieties, both personal and cosmic. As intelligent and free human beings we can control these anxieties by knowing our options to be informed and to be heard (he says "be healthily worried"), or we can become totally neurotic—afraid to leave our immediate "neighborhood." We should try, however, to meet the challenge by being "co-authors of our own future."

1. In early human history a Stone Age, a Bronze Age, or an Iron Age came into unhurried gestation and endured for centuries or even millennia; and as one technology gradually displaced or merged with another, the changes wrought in any single lifetime were easily absorbed, if noticed at all. But a transformation has come about in our own time. A centenarian born in 1879 has seen, in the years of his own life, scientific and technological advances more sweeping and radical than those that took place in all the accumulated past. He has witnessed—and felt the personal impact of—the Age of Electricity, the Automobile Age, the Aviation Age, the Electronic Age, the Atomic Age, the Space Age, and the Computer Age, to name but a few of the "ages" that have been crowding in upon us at such an unprecedented rate, sometimes arriving virtually side by side. Let us use the shortcut designation the "Age of Science" to encompass them all.

2. Our era has also been widely known as the Age of Anxiety, especially since the publication of W. H. Auden's poem of that title in 1947. Not that the poet was responsible for generating the feeling. He merely captured it, gave it a name, and made us more aware of its pervasiveness. Thirty-two years later, the anxiety has not gone away; if anything it has been heightened. How much of it can be attributed to the accelerated acquisition of scientific knowledge and its widespread application? Plenty.

3. It would be an exaggeration to say that the Age of Anxiety was brought on by the Age of Science. There is no way to measure precisely how much of our anxiety is directly related to science and how much to other factors in our lives. But there seems little doubt that science (and I include technology) has been a major producer of anxiety.

4. Science's contribution to anxiety did not begin with this past century. When Copernicus and Galileo finally got their messages through, for example, we could no longer believe in a stationary earth around which the sun, moon, and

planets moved against the background of a stationary starscape. Once we understood the earth was not at the center of the universe, could we be so sure man was at the center?

5. Then Darwin and the geologists came along to offer impressive evidence that our planet had been around much longer than previously estimated and that our own species was a rather late arrival upon its face. The theory of evolution implied that we were not the products of a special creation but just one more vulnerable—albeit superior—species that had evolved from precursor creatures.

6. In physics, Newton's absolutes were overthrown by Einstein, and we were given relativity, the fourth dimension, mass-energy equivalence, and the space-time continuum. In our ever-deeper penetration into the heart of the atom, we arrived at Heisenberg's Uncertainty Principle, where "facts" could ultimately be stated only as probability values, where an electron could only be said to have "tendencies to exist" but not to exist for sure at any given place and time.

7. As we moved our intellectual explorations outward to the galaxies, we learned that the universe was vaster than we had ever imagined and that it was, moreover, expanding; that the earth would one day be colder than ice, but only after it had been burnt to a crisp in the death throes of the sun; that the universe itself would one day die.

8. On a personal level, meanwhile, Freud had appeared on the scene to reveal to us our messy Unconscious and to introduce us to the world of childhood sexuality. It is hard to say to what extent he and his successors—including Kinsey and Masters and Johnson—contributed to the current relativity of our sexual morality, but we scarcely seem to know anymore when we are sinning and, if so, against what.

9. Even a quick, cursory glance at recent scientific history, then, suffices to demonstrate how thoroughly our perceptions of our selves and of our world have been overhauled. But to talk of the anxiety-producing factors implicit in scientific insight and discovery is only half the story.

10. The other half lies in what science and technology have directly *done* to us. Merely to think about nuclear energy is to be aware of anxiety all the way from the bang at Hiroshima to the near-whimper at Three Mile Island. We feel menaced on all sides by countless substances that have polluted our air, water, and food, substances that—either separately or acting together in synergy—might trigger or accelerate a spectrum of health-draining syndromes and diseases. The rapid computerization of almost everything has made us fear a trend toward depersonalization and dehumanization, not to mention the accessibility of our most secret dossiers to any curious inquirer. Technology has speeded up the pace of our lives, adding a host of new pressures and stresses. The biological revolution arrives now, too, with its test-tube babies and genetic engineering. Not to be anxious would be foolhardy.

11. We must remember, of course, that science can be—and has often been—the *reliever* of anxieties as well. It has provided, for instance, the means to keep our bodies, homes, and workplaces warm in the coldest climates and to keep them cool when it is hot outside. Science lights up our darkest nights. It puts us in quick touch with anyone near a telephone. It provides easy transportation to carry us wherever we might wish to go. It produces an endless array of products for our pleasure and enlightenment. It offers cultural delights to the masses that were once available only to the elite.

12. One anxiety-producer has always been the prospect of illness and premature death, for ourselves and for those we love. In this area biomedical science has been credited with allaying or removing any number of specific anxieties—through vaccines and drugs against any infectious diseases, through a sharp reduction in infant mortality and a considerable extension of the average life expectancy.

13. As a matter of fact, until very recently in this heady century, we tended to emphasize the blessings of science and technology, to accept the benefits without much question while paying little attention to the risks—content to identify every new smokestack, every escalation of velocity or power, as a sign of progress. By and large, we entertained the conviction that, whatever problems might arise, we could count on science to solve them.

14. Disillusionment has only recently set in with the realization that we had been blithely charging ahead without giving any serious thought to the long-range consequences of our technological decisions. The earth had always

seemed so large, its atmosphere and oceans so boundless, its energy resources so unlimited. What contaminants could not be blown aloft by the winds or carried away by swift-running currents to the sea depths? But now we have been made painfully aware that the planet is finite, as are its supplies of air, water, and energy, as well as its capacity to absorb pollutants.

15. We know that the aerosol suspensions from our spray cans may endanger the ozone layer, that asbestos-dust particles may give us lung cancer. And we have reacted violently against science, becoming suspicious of what we once so admired. Some of us have become virtual neo-Luddites in our antipathy to all things technological. The doomsayers have never been more strident than now, and we listen to them intently and with ever increasing anxiety.

16. There are at least two kinds of anxiety that afflict us. One is our specific anxiety about the personal circumstances of our everyday lives. The other is the existential, cosmic anxiety having to do with the human condition in the universe. Science and technology have copiously fed both.

17. What does a human being need, anyway? The psychoanalysts who write about anxiety—among them Rollo May, Heinz Kohut, Robert Jay Lifton, and Willard Gaylin—all emphasize the importance of a healthy self-esteem and a strong self-concept, along with at least minimal feelings of security and stability and a sense that what one does matters in the world. These qualities and convictions are difficult enough to attain under any circumstances. But under the stressful conditions that govern the lives of so many parents today, it is doubly difficult for their children to develop the characteristics best suited to cope with anxiety. Moreover, the circumstances of the children's lives, as they become adults, render it yet more difficult to retain self-esteem and a strong self-concept, to feel secure and stable in a world that changes with such bewildering rapidity, to feel that what they do matters when they are so often at the mercy of forces outside their control, of decisions arrived at without their consultation.

18. We may imagine how different our outlook might be if we still lived in a pre-Copernican world, with the earth fixed in place, the unquestioned center of the universe, created for us to have dominion over, and we ourselves the main purpose and focus of creation and of the Creator. We would still possess a sure sense of right and wrong (though we might deviate occasionally from the rules). Even amid these certainties, however, there would be anxiety; even in pre-Copernican days there was plenty of reason for it.

19. How much harder is it, then, to maintain a modicum of serenity, knowing that we are the transient all-too-mortal inhabitants—members of a perhaps ephemeral species—riding an unresting speck of cosmic dust, itself mortal; lost in an insignificant corner of just another galaxy, one of billions like it and billions unlike it, all moving away from one another at astonishing velocities. And what if, on that speck of dust, we understand that our life-support systems may be running out? And that our more irrational fellow passengers on our isolated planetary spaceship may now command the means to accelerate its demise? What kind of person does it take to maintain, in the face of such knowledge, a high self-esteem, a strong self-concept, a sense of security and stability, a faith that there will even be a future?

20. Analysts and child-development experts tell us that one of the deepest anxieties of our infancy and early childhood is separation anxiety—the fear that we will be separated from those whose love and support we depend on. Most of us probably never altogether master our separation anxiety; it keeps resurfacing at critical moments. As for adulthood, one of its overriding anxieties is tied to the knowledge of death. "The omnipresence of anxiety," says Rollo May, "arises from the fact that, when all is said and done, anxiety is our human awareness of the fact that each of us is *a being confronted with non-being.*" The knowledge lies heavy upon us, though we usually keep it somewhere off in the periphery of our consciousness, along with our malaise about our planet's fate.

21. Meanwhile, we seem destined to continue living with science and technology. There is no going home again—if home it ever was—to the pre-Copernican era, or even to the pre-nuclear era. We also seem destined to continue living with anxiety. How can we minimize it? How should we deal with it? And with science and technology?

22. There is of course no sure set of recipes to offer. But there are clues to be gleaned from psy-

chiatric case histories as well as from more systematic studies. It seems clear, for instance, that an *absence* of anxiety is almost as great a handicap as over-anxiety. In a study of patients preparing to undergo surgery, Irving Janis at Yale found that those who were not anxious at all fared almost as poorly as those who were excessively anxious. Those who came out best were the patients with normal, realistic anxieties that enabled them to carry out what Janis called the necessary "work of worrying."

23. There is a range of anxieties, the analysts tell us, that runs from the *pathological* through several degrees of the *neurotic* to the *normal*—including the anxiety that one might call *healthy* anxiety. To be somewhat anxious about the dangers of travel is not abnormal; but to be so anxious as to fear to travel away from one's own immediate neighborhood—the situation described, for instance, by the poet William Ellery Leonard in his psychological autobiography, *The Locomotive God*—certainly rates as pathological anxiety.

24. Ants are not anxious. They require neither thought nor awareness; all their answers are inscribed in their genes. But we are intelligent creatures, aware of our fate. We are also free—or at least relatively so—and anxiety is what freedom costs us. We do tend to be uneasy with freedom, and that suggests yet another way in which science has induced anxiety: It has given us a bewildering array of options. It seems pathological to back away from these options merely because we can never entirely foresee the risks; like William Ellery Leonard, we would never dare leave the neighborhood. (And then, how safe is the neighborhood?) A healthy anxiety would rather encompass a certain exhilaration at the challenges and opportunities freedom offers.

25. As Willard Gaylin suggests in *Feelings*, one way to alleviate anxiety—which tends to be a vague and unfocused feeling—is to turn it wherever possible into *worry*. A worry usually centers on a specific problem or concern. "Worry is easier to handle," says Gaylin. "We can tell ourselves to stop worrying because it *is* about something," and hence we may be able to do something about it.

26. In a sense we turned our anxieties about pollution and overpopulation into worries by organizing movements such as Earth Day and Zero Population Growth. It is amazing, in retrospect, to think how rapidly such activities succeeded in mobilizing the public's environmental awareness, galvanizing the government to set up protective agencies and actually reducing the fertility rate. We can certainly hope for a continuation of nuclear détente, and, even before the meltdown scare at Three Mile Island, we were slowing the pace of nuclear-power generation and instilling in the public a healthy anxiety as to its safety.

27. There are many ways to use our imaginations to bring about the kinds of change in awareness Rollo May recommended to achieve a healthy, normal anxiety. At a recent conference I attended in Monterey, California, for example, Barbara Marx Hubbard of the Committee for the Future recalled some examples which were originally put forth by that little appreciated space genius, Krafft Ehricke: He has imagined a primordial time when the first precursors of green plants were starting to photosynthesize, thereby producing oxygen. Oxygen, in those days, would have had to be classified as a pollutant. Had there been at hand a pathologically anxious organism with the power to stop this hazardous activity, there would today not only be no plants but no animals either. Ehricke also hypothesizes a tiny, intelligent organism that resides inside a developing fetus, with no experience of anything else and of course no concept of what birth is like. As the fetus passes through the eighth month of pregnancy and begins to crowd its uterine space, the anxious organism might well point out the obvious limits to the fetus's growth, predict the running-out of its life-support systems, and declare that the fetus must halt its growth or face disaster.

28. Every period of crisis may be a prelude either to disaster or to marvelous growth. An often-cited example is that of a silkworm en route to becoming a butterfly. Lying dormant in its cocoon, its substance apparently undergoing disintegration (actually reorganization), it could easily be perceived as being in its death throes. For all we know, the turmoil of our own chaotic time may be a harbinger of a beautiful butterfly era of civilization ahead.

29. I am not suggesting that we be fatuous about facing our very real threats and dangers; only that we should not draw negative conclusions hastily based purely on logic and experience. A healthy anxiety, dealing with things as

they are and applying imagination to things as they might become, can lead us to hope and even good cheer.

30. As for our self-image: If, in contemplating our puniness in the immensities of the cosmos, we feel diminished, we should remember that the entire universe out there is merely a construct of our own intellect, extrapolated from data gleaned by dissecting starlight in our spectroscopes. A creature who can bring off such a feat should never lack for self-esteem.

31. "The freedom of the healthy individual," says Rollo May in *The Meaning of Anxiety*, "inheres in his capacity to avail himself of new possibilities in the meeting and overcoming of threats to his existence. By moving through anxiety-creating experiences, one seeks and partially achieves realization of himself."

32. We seem to be on the verge of learning so much more than we presently know, or ever thought we might know, that it would be a pity to draw back now—especially from the knowledge of life's processes. Such understanding holds the promise of alleviating, curing, or preventing most of our crippling and lethal illnesses, of adding a greater quality of vigor and enjoyment to the later years of life, even of extending the life span.

33. One of the problems with scientific and technological advances and the anxieties they have produced so far is that much of what has been done has been done without our prior understanding and consent. There has, fortunately, been a trend lately toward not only explaining to the public what is planned but also inviting it to participate in the discussions.

34. In the field of recombinant-DNA research—the moving frontier of genetic engineering—there have, for example, been extended public debates. In this instance, the scientists themselves had alerted the public to the potential hazards. Now, after considerable examination and re-examination, the work proceeds, but under strict safety guidelines. Handled in this manner, the research may still evoke some healthy worries about specific possible dangers—with the consequent likelihood that we'll keep a sharp eye out. But the public process will have allayed the nagging anxiety that comes with exposure to unexamined and little understood dangers that no one bothered to explain to us or consult us about.

35. As the Ages of Science and Anxiety proceed in tandem, then, we will perhaps be best served by listening to our healthy anxieties, letting them surface, then doing all we can to minimize our neurotic anxieties by keeping ourselves informed and by insisting on being heard—knowing that we can decide *not* to do what we choose not to; cloning, for instance, may be an example of what we choose not to do. If we can be both informed and heard, we can watch scientific research proceed apace, not only with our permission but with our encouragement and applause. We should stay healthily worried all the way but not so pathologically anxious as to foreclose a proper exploration of our options—some of which could provide the solutions to our stickier dilemmas. To the extent that we succeed with this balancing act, we can keep our self-esteem and self-concept strong, and—though we must live with ambiguity rather than certainty—we can feel that what we do does matter after all, that we are not powerless to be co-authors of our own future.

DAN STRICKLAND

The Eskimo vs. the Walrus vs. the Government

Dan Strickland (1953–   ) was born in West Point, New York, and studied at the University of California at Davis and, after he moved to Alaska in 1972, at the University of Alaska at Fairbanks. A game biologist who has worked in Eskimo villages for the Alaska Department of Fish and Game, he is now a commercial salmon fisherman in Prince William Sound. For several years he has witnessed the annual harvest of walruses off the islands of St. Lawrence and Little Diomede, and he has been struck by its effects on the life and economy of the Eskimos. Strickland is also a free-lance writer, whose work has been published in *Natural History, Alaska Magazine, Alaskafest, Defenders of Wildlife, Alaska Today,* and *Alaska Farm Magazine.* In his free time, he backpacks and skis cross-country in the Alaskan wilderness.

In this essay, reprinted from *Natural History,* Strickland resolves the walrus-hunting controversy in which he is involved into three components: the walrus, the Eskimo, and the U.S. Government. He has learned that the Eskimos perceive animals and life quite differently than the Government does and that the Eskimos' way of life is being threatened by the twentieth-century technology on which the government bases its controls of hunting and fishing in Alaskan areas.

1. The walrus-skin boat glided silently forward, its pliable bow pushing small chunks of ice to either side. The Eskimos were tense but ready, their eyes directed ahead, gloved hands checking rifles and cartridges.

2. "Take your cap off!" John whispered fiercely. "Walrus don't like red. They see that, they're gone."

3. I slid the wool cap from my head and stuffed it into a pocket, feeling immediately the gelid touch of the wind.

4. It was after midnight, but the Arctic sun hung stubbornly above the northern horizon. Its rays turned the pack ice to amber and seemed to gild the sea itself with a placid sheen. Across the disintegrating pack ice of this late spring night Little Diomede Island rose abruptly, a stark sentinel at the crossroads of the Bering and Chukchi seas off the coast of western Alaska.

5. John gripped my arm and directed me to one side of the umiak. "We'll approach in this way," he explained, illustrating with his hands. "Broadside, so everyone can shoot."

6. The umiak skirted a cake of ice and came suddenly on the walruses. Twenty massive bulls lay together on a large ice floe—grunting, bellowing, thrusting at each other with their heavy ivory tusks. Only one or two of the more wary animals glared at us as we drifted in closer and closer. We were scarcely fifteen yards away.

7. Edgar used the stilled motor as a rudder and the umiak turned slowly broadside to the walruses. John whispered a signal and firing erupted from the boat. There was a moment of confused hesitation before the enormous bulls began lumbering toward the edge of the ice. They slipped gracefully but ponderously into the sea, churning the water into a frothy turbulence.

THE ESKIMO VS. THE WALRUS VS. THE GOVERNMENT With permission from *Natural History,* Volume 90, No. 2. Copyright the American Museum of Natural History, 1981.

8. Four bulls remained, motionless in death. The umiak's bow touched the ice and the crew leaped nimbly onto the floe. Long knives, carried in scabbards made from the skin of the *oogruk*, or bearded seal, were drawn and sharpened on whetstones. With a rapidity and skill born of years of experience the Eskimos laid the carcasses open and cut them into pieces that could be lifted easily, dragged to the skin boat, and heaved aboard. All the meat from the animals was salvaged, including the intestines, stomach, liver, and heart. Four sets of white ivory tusks were thrown in last, on top of the steaming meat. As we pulled away, little more than a red stain colored the ice.

9. The walrus-hunting season—heralded by the annual spring retreat of the ice to more northern waters—was only beginning for the Diomede people. The village was emerging from winter with a limited supply of fresh walrus meat. On these early hunting trips, great quantities of walrus and seal are brought back to the village by the crews. This meat is distributed among the people to fill their depleted caches. I wondered how much meat would be retrieved as the season progressed and greater numbers of walrus were harvested.

10. In 1977 and again in 1978, while working for the Alaska Department of Fish and Game, I visited many of the state's coastal and island villages to gather specimens from the walruses and seals harvested in the spring hunts. Hunting with the Diomede people gave me a vivid picture of the world in which they live, a world dramatically different from any I have known. In particular, I learned that the Eskimos have a perception of animals—indeed, of life itself—that is all their own.

11. In August 1728 Vitus Bering sailed through the strait that Capt. James Cook would name for him fifty years later. Bering christened two islands in the strait after Saint Diomede. Despite their proximity (less than three miles apart), Big and Little Diomede are split by the international dateline and mark the boundaries of two different worlds. Big Diomede belongs to the Soviet Union; Little Diomede, called Ignaluk by the inhabitants, is the northwesternmost extension of Alaska and has been home to a hardy group of Eskimos for centuries. Although many of these people came originally from Siberia and Big Diomede, visits between the islands have been curtailed since 1948.

12. The Little Diomeders are embroiled in a newer and more explosive issue than détente between governments. They are a hunting people. The waters of the Bering and Chukchi seas are treacherous, but abundantly rich in marine life. Walruses, seals, polar bears, whales, and sea birds have provided the Eskimos with skins and oil, meat and sinew, and with the inspiration for hauntingly beautiful legends, powerful dances, and traditional ivory carvings. But the Diomeders no longer subsist, as they once did, solely on the marine plants and animals of their islands and of the Bering and Chukchi seas. Twentieth-century technology has transformed their way of life and their relation to the natural world.

13. Contact with the outside world came when Russian and English explorers penetrated the northern seas in the 1700s. In the nineteenth century, Yankee whalers pushed north in quest of bowhead whales. The whaling ships sailed into the northern Bering Sea in late April to early May. Waiting for the ice to recede northward so they could pursue the bowheads into the Beaufort and Chukchi seas, the whalers traded with the natives for hunting implements, skin clothing, furs, and raw and carved ivory. This contact spurred a desire among the Eskimos for goods that were novel and delightful but always expensive. Coffee, tea, and sugar became as much staples for the Eskimos as they were for the whalers.

14. The coastal Eskimos could trade a wide variety of items, including baleen, fur, fish, ivory, and jade. The Diomeders, however, had mainly ivory. For centuries the strategic location of their island prompted these people to carve and trade, initially, for fish and furs from the mainland, then for glass beads and Asian trade goods via Siberia. Finally, the tempting novelties of the Yankee whalers were added to the flourishing trade.

15. The Diomeders became specialists at carving exquisite bracelets of ivory and baleen, lifelife walrus images, and representations of other animals and spirits that shaped their culture. Carving evolved over the decades. Ivory tusks drilled and etched into cribbage boards and such trinkets as swizzle sticks, gherkin forks, napkin rings, and statuettes of copulating polar bears joined the more traditional carvings of whales, walruses, and seals. Ivory became the basis of the Diomeders' economy.

16. In recent years the soaring inflation that has swept the lower forty-eight states has

reached the Eskimo villages of Alaska, spurring an even greater effort among the Diomeders to acquire ivory. The cost of living in rural Alaska is exorbitant, but it pales beside the prices Diomeders must pay for what have become necessities of life. During the spring of 1979 gasoline cost $154 for a 55-gallon drum; by midsummer it rose to $206 a drum or $3.75 a gallon. Butter now sells for $2.55 per pound, and five pounds of sugar cost $2.90.

17. Diomede's high prices are largely the result of its inaccessability—it lies across twenty-four inhospitable miles of ocean from mainland Alaska. Groceries and mail arrive by skin boat during the summer. During the winter months supplies are brought by planes that land on the sea ice in front of the village, but these deliveries are at the mercy of capricious winds and shifting ice.

18. The remoteness of the island was poignantly impressed upon me one evening as we were hunting. A friend from Anchorage had joined our crew. He urged John to accompany him on a fall moose hunt in interior Alaska.

19. "When will this be?" John asked.

20. "We'll go in October," answered Joe.

21. Shaking his head, John sighed, "No, I have to be home in October. Otherwise I might not get in for the winter."

22. The brutally high cost of living has forced the Eskimos to rely heavily upon their one marketable commodity—ivory. On Little Diomede the yearly harvest of walrus has long since surpassed the number required to supply the meat needs of the village. After each spring's initial hunting trips, very little meat is retrieved from the animals killed. Other villages, such as Savoonga and Gambell on Saint Lawrence Island, have been slower to change, but now they too are turning inexorably toward increased walrus hunting for ivory rather than for food. The two ivory tusks carried by both male and female walruses, and the penis bone (baculum) of the male are retrieved, but the carcass is abandoned on the ice or pushed into the sea. Ivory carvings find a ready market in Nome or Anchorage. The art can be a profitable one. A young man from Diomede told me he could make $260 a day carving ivory, more if he really worked at it.

23. Hunting as a means of providing an income from ivory has touched off a blazing controversy in Alaska, one that has drawn national and international attention. Headless walrus carcasses washing up on Russian shores have placed Americans in an embarrassing light. The Soviet Union also harvests walrus annually, but the hunt is carried out under strict regulations and in a nonwasteful manner.

24. The killing of walrus for ivory alone stirs passionate emotions outside the Eskimo community, as well as within. The natives commonly either refuse to admit the practice exists or claim vehemently that this is bonafide subsistence. "We have hunted walrus for thousands of years," an elderly Eskimo recounted. "They have provided us with what we needed in the past, and they provide us with what we need now." What they need now, however, includes snowmobiles, television sets, slide viewers, generators, and outboard motors.

25. The softly spoken words of an old Eskimo emphasized the changes that have come to the villages. "When I was young," he said, "the village was quiet all the time and the whales and walrus would come very close to shore." He turned from the sea and glanced disdainfully at the roaring village generators. "Now we have snowmobiles, generators, six-wheelers . . . too much noise. The game never comes close anymore."

26. The changes are indeed great. Although skin boats are used by Diomeders and occasionally in the other villages, aluminum skiffs with powerful outboards have become the preferred craft. (The skiffs are faster than the skin boats, but they are more vulnerable to the crushing ice pack.) High-powered rifles have long since replaced the ivory lances and harpoons of earlier years. CB radios, binoculars, and compasses are acquisitions that have turned the Eskimo into a more effective hunter.

27. Yankee whalers certainly set a miserable example of restraint. When bowhead stocks declined in the 1870s, the whalers took walrus by the thousands. The ivory was chopped from the skull and the blubber rendered down for the valuable oil. In a ten-year period 100,000 walruses may have been harvested by whaling crews.

28. This intensive hunting sent the walrus population into a dramatic decline, from an estimated 200,000 animals to a low of 50,000 in the 1940s. The walrus herds were so decimated that it became uneconomical to hunt them and the industry died. Commercial walrus hunting was

officially closed in 1941 with the passage of the Walrus Act, which prohibited the export of raw ivory from Alaska. The walrus population began to increase in the 1950s and today the herds in the Bering and Chukchi seas number between 140,000 and 200,000 animals. Walrus are "hauling out," or resting on shores and islands where they have not been seen for decades, indicating a rising population. Now the contention that the walrus population is dangerously high is voiced loudly and unanimously in most villages.

29. With the passage in December 1972 of the Marine Mammal Protection Act, the federal government took over marine mammal control from the state of Alaska. All hunting of marine mammals was abruptly stopped, bringing to an end the sport hunting of walrus allowed by the state. Eskimos, Indians, and Aleuts, however, were granted an exemption that allowed them to harvest these animals for subsistence purposes or for the creation of authentic articles of native handicraft. In January 1973, Alaska petitioned for return of the management of nine species of marine mammals important to coastal residents, both Eskimos and nonnatives. In April 1976 the federal government hesitantly yielded jurisdiction only over walrus, mandating that the annual harvest must not exceed 3,000 animals. If this number was exceeded, control of walrus hunting would revert to the federal government.

30. When the state of Alaska resumed management of walrus in 1976 it accepted a volatile situation. The number of animals killed in the spring hunt began to rise as more and more walrus were taken for their ivory. According to the Alaska Department of Fish and Game, Alaskan Eskimos took roughly 1,600 walrus in 1962; 2,300 in 1974; 2,600 in 1975; and nearly 3,000 in 1976.

31. As the number of walrus harvested approached the federal ceiling of 3,000, a limit was imposed and village quotas were set. Past dependence upon walrus was considered, as well as the availability of wage-earning jobs to meet the cash needs of the Eskimos. The villages of Gambell, Savoonga, and Little Diomede—historically the most dependent upon walrus—were initially accorded 450 walrus per year. The quota system was poorly received, difficult to enforce, and unpopular with both natives and those state representatives working in the villages. Hunting limits imposed by those who had ruthlessly de-

pleted their seas of whales and walruses seemed ludicrous and high-handed to the Eskimos.

32. "You don't know what it is to be Eskimo," claimed one young man. "Out here hunting is our way of life. Carving ivory is our livelihood. We don't want welfare supporting us and we don't want to be forced from the villages.

33. "There are too many walrus now," he continued. "The Eskimos know this. There is no reason for these quotas. You do not understand how we live."

34. A biologist who has spent much time with the Eskimo people and is liked by them had this to say: "People speak of the noble, ideal Eskimo who wastes nothing. Unfortunately, that concept is fictitious, just as is the other voiced extreme that would have them all unscrupulous renegades. The truth lies in the middle. They are a people and a culture worthy of respect, but they are being bludgeoned by change. They are reacting as any of us would, taking each step in response to what they have and what they can do. Some are tougher than others. They hold up under pressure while others break."

35. The swiftness with which changes have come to the Eskimos has generated problems long associated with the acculturation of one society into another. The Eskimos are not consciously turning from traditional ways. They are responding naturally to the choices offered them. The new variety of foods found in the stores is appealing, snowmobiles are faster and easier to handle than dog teams, and winter clothes and hunting gear are more readily bought than made in the painstakingly traditional fashion. Yet these changes are eroding traditions that have been a source of dignity and pride to the Eskimos.

36. In the past the Eskimos had no alternatives to facing the rigors of the Arctic environment. Hunting was a daily necessity that provided the Eskimo culture with a powerful, unifying theme. Legends portraying hunters and dances depicting courageous sea journeys were inspiring and supportive, fostering strong village ties. But modern technology and an ivory-based economy (which wastes valuable animal protein) have introduced competition among the hunters. Moreover, there are now alternatives to hunting. The Arctic continues to be a rugged home, however, and without the constant endeavor of hunting, the long winters can weigh heavily. Intriguing new life styles, conveyed vividly by weekly

movies and taped television programs, impart a restlessness and dissatisfaction to the younger Eskimos. The legends and dances are still there, but their influence is weakening, yielding to that of bingo and basketball.

37. Unfortunately, some of the social transitions affecting the villages are more serious. Although most communities have voted themselves dry, liquor is easily obtained, and alcoholism, with all its associated problems, is a prevalent disease. Drug abuse is making inroads in the tiniest, most remote communities. Last year a youth died of an overdose of angel dust in the isolated village of Scammon Bay, north of the Kuskokwim River on Alaska's coast. The suicide rate is overwhelmingly high, a tragic index of the depression plaguing the Eskimos, especially the younger individuals.

38. John Iyapana was the captain of the crew I joined. Although the hunts were often long and arduous, John enlivened them with stories of past hunts and adventures. He and the others in the crew pointed out rocks and landmarks on the Russian and American mainlands, giving their Eskimo names and indicating where it was wise to watch for changing weather. Late one afternoon we were hunting close to Little Diomede. We had not seen any walrus or seal and decided to run in against the island and have *yo kuk* ("coffee break"). As we lay on the rocks waiting for the water to boil, John raised his hand toward the cliffs above us and said, "The old people say this is the best place on the island for boot liners. Come on, I'll show you how to gather the grass." We climbed the hillside and filled a large bag with the soft, dry grass.

39. "Bend this gently in a figure eight, without breaking it," John explained. "Then lay it on the bottom of your mukluks [skin boots]." He smiled, "It's warmer and softer than any wool sock."

40. The camaraderie and rapport between myself and the Eskimos was only occasionally subdued by reference to hunting walrus for their ivory. The hunters are somewhat defensive about this activity, an attitude prevalent throughout the villages. It envelops the entire issue in a smothering shame that only serves to make more difficult the search for solutions. The hunting of walrus solely for ivory is an understandable, albeit lamentable, result of an expanding ivory market. If the guilt were to be lifted from the Eskimos, perhaps by a realization that their posi-

tion has been shaped as much by our culture as by theirs, the managing agency and natives could work together more harmoniously.

41. Which agency will manage the walrus harvest is going to be a puzzling question. The state of Alaska returned control of walrus to the federal government on July 1, 1979. The federal restrictions placed upon state management were felt to be untenable and cumbersome by the state biologists involved. Just prior to this action the Alaska State Board of Game rescinded the walrus quotas, acknowledging that the walrus herds may be undergoing population stress. On a biological basis, then, the state gave tacit approval for an increased harvest of animals.

42. Under federal control the Eskimos are again being allowed unlimited subsistence hunting. Walrus will no longer be subjected to sport hunting by non-natives, which the state had allowed shortly after it resumed management in 1976. The number of walrus harvested by sport hunters in 1976 was about 150 out of the yearly take of 3,000. The Eskimos are divided over the issue of sport hunting because guiding associated with these hunts brought substantial money into the Eskimo community.

43. Management by the federal government creates an additional dilemma. Under the Marine Mammal Protection Act the native exemption is granted for subsistence and handicraft use only. The state recognized that walrus hunting is closer to a commercial endeavor and was seeking markets for the surplus products. Walrus meat is strong and rich but quite palatable. Certainly in a world starving for protein this meat could be utilized. The thick hides of the bull walrus, although heavy, cumbersome, and difficult to retrieve, are used in industry on buffering wheels. Walrus stomachs can be scraped, dried, and made into the traditional skin drum of the Eskimos. This spring, coastal villages were buying prepared stomachs for $75 a piece from the Diomede hunters. This search for commercial outlets may be impeded, depending upon the most recent interpretation of the Marine Mammal Protection Act. Although the wording of the act is vague regarding what constitutes waste of an animal, the native exemption is obviously aimed at subsistence use and not commercial enterprise. Programs such as the installation of large community freezers in some villages to hold excess walrus meat are suddenly left on un-

steady ground. Although these freezers would hold additional meat for the Eskimos' use, they are meant primarily to facilitate the commercial sale of walrus meat. Restaurants in Nome and Anchorage have expressed interest, and the Japanese have made inquiries.

44. It is difficult to foresee what walrus management will be like under the federal government. If the present Eskimo hunting practices are interpreted as wasteful, a herculean effort will be required to curtail their harvest. The ivory trade could be outlawed, but a flourishing black market already exists, as evidenced by the illegal traffic in polar bear skins traced to Alaskan Eskimo villages. And the Eskimos would not be easily dissuaded from hunting. They feel no one has the right to take that from them. Biological evidence further complicates the picture: The walrus population may be at a level where it could absorb the Eskimos' harvest without serious impact.

45. In the clear light of an Arctic evening I watched a drama unfold on the ice, one that summed up the complexity and intricacy of implementing effective walrus management. Our crew had fired into a walrus pod. Most of the animals plunged into the sea, leaving behind three dead companions and a young, wounded bull, with tusks protruding a scant six inches, which struggled valiantly to reach the water. Normally, hunters quickly dispatch a wounded walrus, and I looked at our crew, expecting a rapid reaction to the bull left alive on the ice. But no one moved.

46. As the Eskimos continued to watch the walrus intently, I realized that they were hoping the animal would reach the water. If it was not retrieved, the walrus would not be included in the village quota.

47. I looked back to the young walrus and thought sadly what a strange ritual was being performed. Because limits had been imposed on the number of animals harvested, this walrus might have been wasted simply because his ivory was small. And the hunters, a people who have lived from the animals of the sea for centuries, have been placed in this situation where they permit this to happen.

48. The walrus writhed a few more times. At last, one of the hunters raised his rifle and fired. The animal lay still. We moved in to butcher the carcasses, an embarrassed quietness pervading the air. It was an impressive example of well-intentioned regulations having unforeseen effects when actually applied.

49. When the cold winds begin to sweep down from the Beaufort and Chukchi seas this fall, the walrus herds will funnel through Bering Strait and move into their wintering grounds farther south. Spring will come again to the Bering Sea Eskimo villages, and with it, the walrus hunting that is so much a part of these people and their lives. Progress can be made toward a more efficient harvest, but the steps toward that end should be carefully weighed and closely scrutinized. The Eskimo way of life, whether it be called traditional or twentieth-century mainstream, is at stake.

FREDERIC GOLDEN

Superzapping in Computer Land

Frederic Golden (1933–   ) is Science and Environment Editor for *Time* magazine, and he has written for *International Wildlife* and *Reader's Digest*. Born in Germany, he was educated at New York University, the Columbia University Graduate School of Journalism, and Duke University, where he was a *Time*-Duke Fellow in 1980. Golden also writes books for young people, including most recently *Colonies in Space*, 1977. The honors he has received for his writing include the National Space Club Award, the American Institute of Physics–Westinghouse Science Writing Award, and the Aviation-Space Writers Award.

In this brief essay Golden writes of the vulnerability of computer systems to "computer crooks who have developed a whole bag of electronic tricks," of which the ultimate is "superzapping," penetrating a system to make it reveal all of its data. Though much of this activity was at first considered in the category of pranks, computer owners are not sure what constitutes only a prank and what is a crime; nor is it an easy and quick problem to solve fully.

1. The customer, calling from Ottawa, was furious. Someone, he complained to officials of Telenet, a telecommunications network based in Vienna, Va., was using its lines to penetrate his company's computer. As a result, his operations were fouled up. The next week another computer network, named Datapac and tied to Telenet, got a similar call from a firm in Montreal. Its circuits too were being plagued by electronic interlopers.

2. Operating out of unknown terminals, possibly hundreds of miles away, the intruders had tapped into—or "accessed," in computer jargon—one of the company's computers. Even worse, they had actually "seized control" of the electronic brain, blocking the network's legitimate users from getting on line, and were systematically destroying data. The raids continued for more than a week. During one foray, 10 million "bits" of information, almost one-fifth of the

computer's storage capacity, were temporarily lost.

3. It was an electronic sting with international repercussions: the Royal Canadian Mounted Police joined with the FBI to catch the criminals. By tracing phone calls, they soon got their man. Or rather boys. The culprits, only 13 years old, were four clever students at New York's Dalton School, a posh private institution on Manhattan's Upper East Side.

4. The bit-size bandits, perhaps the youngest computer con men ever nabbed, had obtained the Telenet phone number, coupled their school terminals to the line, and probably by nothing more than trial and error punched out the right combinations—in this case only five letters and numbers—to link up with the computers. More shrewd guesswork got them the "password" to log onto and operate the machines.

5. It was a schoolboy lark. None of the Dalton gang, even its eighth-grade leader, was prosecuted. But computer specialists were not amused. Besides costing the firms thousands of

dollars in computer time, the incident was one more irritating example of the vulnerability of systems that can have price tags in the millions and store information of incalculable value. It was also a sign of the growing incidence of computer crime.

6. No one can say exactly how much such crime costs; often the losses are not even reported by embarrassed companies. But the larceny clearly is far from petty. It may well run to hundreds of millions of dollars a year. Last January, California became the first state to enact a computer-fraud law, allowing fines of up to $5,000 and three years' imprisonment. Still, warns Donn Parker of SRI International, a leading scholar of electronic theft: "By the end of the 1980s, computer crimes could cause economic chaos."

7. An exaggeration perhaps. But as computers spread into all facets of life, from controlling the flow of money to manning factories and missile defenses, the potential for troublemaking seems boundless. Already computer thieves, often striking from within, have embezzled millions of dollars. In 1978 a consultant got a Los Angeles bank's computer to transfer $10.2 million to his out-of-town account. Only a confederate's tip led to his discovery. To be a computer-age thief, you need nothing more than an inexpensive home computer, a telephone and a few light-fingered skills. As in the Dalton case, computer passwords are often short and simple. Besides, computer networks like Telenet or Datapac, frequently publicize their numbers to attract customers. Once into the computer system, there are other barriers to crash, and other techniques for purloining information.

8. Computer crooks have developed a whole bag of electronic tricks. One is the so-called Trojan Horse. Like the famed ruse used by the Greeks to penetrate Troy, it helps an interloper get into forbidden recesses of a computer. The mischiefmaker slyly slips some extra commands into a computer program (the instructions by which the machine performs a given task). Then when another programmer with higher clearance runs the program, he will unwittingly trigger the covert instructions. These unlock the guarded areas, just as the Greek soldiers hidden in the horse unlocked Troy's gates. The culprit might then transfer money to his own account, steal private information or sabotage the system itself. Other colorfully named ploys: superzapping (penetrating a computer by activating its own emergency master program, an act comparable to opening a door with a stolen master key); scavenging (searching through stray data or "garbage" for clues that might unlock still other secrets); and piggybacking (riding into a system behind a legitimate user).

9. Faced with such ingenuity, some computer owners are resorting to complex coding devices that scramble information before it is transmitted or stored. They are also changing passwords. Some even rely on detectors that identify legitimate individual computer users by fingerprints or voice patterns.

10. Yet as the safeguards go up, so does the urge to crash the barriers, especially among students. In a celebrated Princeton University case, students snatched grades and housing data from the school's computers and, by their account, briefly shut them down. Last September, two Illinois high school students dialed their way into one of DePaul University's computers and threatened to immobilize it unless they got access to a special program that would have let them communicate with the machine more directly. Said an investigator who helped catch the teen-agers: "They did it because everyone said it couldn't be done." Maybe so. But computer owners wonder: Where does the fun end and the crime begin?

LOREN EISELEY

How Natural Is "Natural"?

Loren Eiseley (1907–1977) was a professor of anthropology, writer on science, and curator of the Early Man section of the University of Pennsylvania Museum. The author of many popular articles, books, short stories, and poems, as well as a contributor to scientific journals, he received a number of prestigious literary awards and medals. In 1957 he published his first book, *The Immense Journey*, a speculative book on evolution. It was this book that established him as the leading "literary naturalist," made him and the poet W. H. Auden firm friends and led Auden to write that Eiseley was very likely the heir of Henry David Thoreau. His finest works include *Darwin's Century: Evolution and the Men Who Discovered It*, 1958; *The Firmament of Time*, 1960; *Francis Bacon and the Modern Dilemma*, 1961; *The Mind as Nature*, 1962; *Invisible Pyramid*, 1970; *Night Country*, 1971; *The Innocent Assassins*, 1973; *All the Strange Hours*, 1975; *The Star Thrower* (with an introduction by Auden), 1977; and *Darwin and the Mysterious Mr. X*, 1979. At the time of his death he had at least half a dozen books in preparation, including a science-fiction novel, *The Snow Wolf*.

Eiseley asks the question, "How natural is 'natural'?" and follows with a second question: "Is there anything we can call a natural world at all?" He answers: "Natural is a magician's word," and then shows that what is natural is only what we now know and seem to understand but that new phenomena will lead us beyond the "natural" of today to the "natural" of tomorrow, and it will, doubtless, be different.

I

1. In the more obscure scientific circles which I frequent there is a legend circulating about a late distinguished scientist who, in his declining years, persisted in wearing enormous padded boots much too large for him. He had developed, it seems, what to his fellows was a wholly irrational fear of falling through the interstices of that largely empty molecular space which common men in their folly speak of as the world. A stroll across his living-room floor had become, for him, something as dizzily horrendous as the activities of a window washer on the Empire State Building. Indeed, with equal reason he could have passed a ghostly hand through his own ribs.

2. The quivering network of his nerves, the awe-inspiring movement of his thought, had become a vague cloud of electrons interspersed with the light-year distances that obtain between us and the farther galaxies. This was the natural world which he had helped to create, and in which, at last, he had found himself a lonely and imprisoned occupant. All around him the ignorant rushed on their way over the illusion of substantial floors, leaping, though they did not see it, from particle to particle, over a bottomless abyss. There was even a question as to the reality of the particles which bore them up. It did not, however, keep insubstantial newspapers from being sold, or insubstantial love from being made.

3. Not long ago I became aware of another world perhaps equally natural and real, which man is beginning to forget. My thinking began in New England under a boat dock. The lake I speak of has been pre-empted and civilized by man. All day long in the vacation season high-speed motorboats, driven with the reckless abandon common to the young Apollos of our society, speed back and forth, carrying loads of equally attractive girls. The shores echo to the roar of the powerful motors and the delighted screams of young Americans with uncounted horsepower surging under their hands. In truth, as I sat there under the boat dock, I had some desire to swim or to canoe in the older ways of the great forest which once lay about this region. Either notion would have been folly. I would have been gaily chopped to ribbons by teen-age youngsters whose eyes were always immutably fixed on the far horizons of space or upon the dials which indicated the speed of their passing. There was another world, I was to discover, along the lake shallows and under the boat dock, where the motors could not come.

4. As I sat there one sunny morning when the water was peculiarly translucent, I saw a dark shadow moving swiftly over the bottom. It was the first sign of life I had seen in this lake, whose shores seemed to yield little but washed-in beer cans. By and by the gliding shadow ceased to scurry from stone to stone over the bottom. Unexpectedly, it headed almost directly for me. A furry nose with gray whiskers broke the surface. Below the whiskers green water foliage trailed out in an inverted V as long as his body. A muskrat still lived in the lake. He was bringing in his breakfast.

5. I sat very still in the strips of sunlight under the pier. To my surprise the muskrat came almost to my feet with his little breakfast of greens. He was young, and it rapidly became obvious to me that he was laboring under an illusion of his own, and that he thought animals and men were still living in the Garden of Eden. He gave me a friendly glance from time to time as he nibbled his greens. Once, even, he went out into the lake again and returned to my feet with more greens. He had not, it seemed, heard very much about men. I shuddered. Only the evening before I had heard a man describe with triumphant enthusiasm how he had killed a rat in the garden because the creature had dared to nibble his petunias. He had even showed me the murder weapon, a sharp-edged brick.

6. On this pleasant shore a war existed and would go on until nothing remained but man. Yet this creature with the gray, appealing face wanted very little: a strip of shore to coast up and down, sunlight and moonlight, some weeds from the deep water. He was an edge-of-the-world dweller, caught between a vanishing forest and a deep lake pre-empted by unpredictable machines full of chopping blades. He eyed me near-sightedly, a green leaf poised in his mouth. Plainly he had come with some poorly instructed memory about the lion and the lamb.

7. "You had better run away now," I said softly, making no movement in the shafts of light. "You are in the wrong universe and must not make this mistake again. I am really a very terrible and cunning beast. I can throw stones." With this I dropped a little pebble at his feet.

8. He looked at me half blindly, with eyes much better adjusted to the wavering shadows of his lake bottom than to sight in the open air. He made almost as if to take the pebble up into his forepaws. Then a thought seemed to cross his mind—a thought perhaps telepathically received, as Freud once hinted, in the dark world below and before man, a whisper of ancient disaster heard in the depths of a burrow. Perhaps after all this was not Eden. His nose twitched carefully; he edged toward the water.

9. As he vanished in an oncoming wave, there went with him a natural world, distinct from the world of girls and motorboats, distinct from the world of the professor holding to reality by some great snowshoe effort in his study. My muskrat's shoreline universe was edged with the dark wall of hills on one side and the waspish drone of motors farther out, but it was a world of sunlight he had taken down into the water weeds. It hovered there, waiting for my disappearance. I walked away, obscurely pleased that darkness had not gained on life by any act of mine. In so many worlds, I thought, how natural is "natural"—and is there anything we can call a natural world at all?

II

Nature, contended John Donne in the seventeenth century, is the common law by which God governs us. Donne was already aware of the new science and impressed by glimpses of those vast abstractions which man was beginning to build across the gulfs of his ignorance. Donne makes, however, a reservation which rings strangely in the modern ear. If nature is the common law, he said, then Miracle is God's Prerogative.

10. By the nineteenth century, this spider web of common law had been flung across the deeps of space and time. "In astronomy," meditated Emerson, "vast distance, but we never go into a foreign system. In geology, vast duration, but we are never strangers. Our metaphysic should be able to follow the flying force through all its transformations."

11. Now admittedly there is a way in which all these worlds are real and sufficiently natural. We can say, if we like, that the muskrat's world is naïve and limited, a fraction, a bare fraction, of the world of life: a view from a little pile of wet stones on a nameless shore. The view of the motor speedsters in essence is similar and no less naïve. All would give way to the priority of that desperate professor, striving like a tired swimmer to hold himself aloft against the soft and fluid nothingness beneath his feet. In terms of the modern temper, the physicist has penetrated the deepest into life. He has come to that place of whirling sparks which are themselves phantoms. He is close upon the void where science ends and the manifestation of God's Prerogative begins. "He can be no creature," argued Donne, "Who is present at the first creation."

12. Yet there is a way in which the intelligence of man in this era of science and the machine can be viewed as having taken the wrong turning. There is a dislocation of our vision which is, perhaps, the product of the kind of creatures we are, or at least conceive ourselves to be. Man, as a two-handed manipulator of the world about him, has projected himself outward upon his surroundings in a way impossible to other creatures. He has done this since the first half-human man-ape hefted a stone in his hand. He has always sought mastery over the materials of his environment, and in our day he has pierced so deeply through the screen of appearances that the age-old distinctions between matter and energy have been dimmed to the point of disappearance. The creations of his clever intellect ride in the skies and the sea's depths; he has hurled a great fragment of metal at the moon, which he once feared. He holds the heat of suns within his hands and threatens with it both the lives and the happiness of his unborn descendants.

13. Man, in the words of one astute biologist, is "caught in a physiological trap and faced with the problem of escaping from his own ingenuity." Pascal, with intuitive sensitivity, saw this at the very dawn of the modern era in science. "There is nothing which we cannot make natural," he wrote, and then, prophetically, comes the full weight of his judgment upon man: "there is nothing natural which we do not destroy." *Homo faber*, the toolmaker, is not enough. There must be another road and another kind of man lurking in the mind of this odd creature, but whether the attraction of that path is as strong as the age-old primate addiction to taking things apart remains to be seen.

14. We who are engaged in the life of thought are likely to assume that the key to an understanding of the world is knowledge, both of the past and of the future—that if we had that knowledge we would also have wisdom. It is not my intention here to decry learning, but only to say that we must come to understand that learning is endless and that nowhere does it lead us behind the existent world. It may reduce the prejudices of ignorance, set our bones, build our cities. In itself it will never make us ethical men. Yet because ours, we conceive, is an age of progress, and because we know more about time and history than any men before us, we fallaciously equate ethical advance with scientific progress in a point-to-point relationship. Thus as society improves physically, we assume the improvement of the individual and are all the more horrified at those mass movements of terror which have so typified the first half of the twentieth century.

15. On the morning of which I want to speak, I was surfeited with the smell of mortality and tired of the years I had spent in archaeological dustbins. I rode out of a camp and across a mountain. I would never have believed, before it happened, that one could ride into the past on horseback. It is true I rode with a purpose, but that purpose was to settle an argument within myself.

16. It was time, I thought, to face up to what was in my mind—to the dust and the broken teeth and the spilled chemicals of life seeping away into the sand. It was time I admitted that life was of the earth, earthy, and could be turned

into a piece of wretched tar. It was time I consented to the proposition that man had as little to do with his fate as a seed blown against a grating. It was time I looked upon the world without spectacles and saw love and pride and beauty dissolve into effervescing juices. I could be an empiricist with the best of them. I would be deceived by no more music. I had entered a black cloud of merciless thought, but the horse, as it chanced, worked his own way over that mountain.

17. I could hear the sudden ring of his hooves as we came cautiously treading over a tilted table of granite, past the winds that blow on the high places of the world. There were stones there so polished that they shone from the long ages that the storms had rushed across them. We crossed the divide then, picking our way in places scoured by ancient ice action, through boulder fields where nothing moved, and yet where one could feel time like an enemy hidden behind each stone.

18. If there was life on those heights, it was the thin life of mountain spiders who caught nothing in their webs, or of small gray birds that slipped soundlessly among the stones. The wind in the pass caught me head on and blew whatever thoughts I had into a raveling stream behind me, until they were all gone and there was only myself and the horse, moving in an eternal dangerous present, free of the encumbrances of the past.

19. We crossed a wind that smelled of ice from still higher snowfields, we cantered with a breeze that came from somewhere among cedars, we passed a gust like Hell's breath that had risen straight up from the desert floor. They were winds and they did not stay with us. Presently we descended out of their domain, and it was curious to see, as we dropped farther through gloomy woods and canyons, how the cleansed and scoured mind I had brought over the mountain began, like the water in those rumbling gorges, to talk in a variety of voices, to debate, to argue, to push at stones or curve subtly around obstacles. Sometimes I wonder whether we are only endlessly repeating in our heads an argument that is going on in the world's foundations among crashing stones and recalcitrant roots.

20. "Fall, fall, fall," cried the roaring water and the grinding pebbles in the torrent. "Let go, come with us, come home to the place without light." But the roots clung and climbed and the trees pushed up, impeding the water, and forests filled even the wind with their sighing and grasped after the sun. It is so in the mind. One can hear the rattle of falling stones in the night, and the thoughts like trees holding their place. Sometimes one can shut the noise away by turning over on the other ear, sometimes the sounds are as dreadful as a storm in the mountains, and one lies awake, holding, like the roots that wait for daylight. It was after such a night that I came over the mountain, but it was the descent on the other side that suddenly struck me as a journey into the aeons of the past.

21. I came down across stones dotted with pink and gray lichens—a barren land dreaming life's last dreams in the thin air of a cold and future world.

22. I passed a meadow and a meadow mouse in a little shower of petals struck from mountain flowers. I dismissed it—it was almost my own time—a pleasant golden hour in the age of mammals, lost before the human coming. I rode heavily toward an old age far backward in the reptilian dark.

23. I was below timber line and sinking deeper and deeper into the pine woods, whose fallen needles lay thick and springy over the ungrassed slopes. The brown needles and the fallen cones, the stiff, endless green forests, were a mark that placed me in the Age of Dinosaurs. I moved in silence now, waiting a sign. I saw it finally, a green lizard on a stone. We were far back, far back. He bobbed his head uncertainly at me, and I reined in with the nostalgic intent, for a moment, to call him father, but I saw soon enough that I was a ghost who troubled him and that he would wish me, though he had not the voice to speak, to ride on. A man who comes down the road of time should not expect to converse—even with his own kin. I made a brief, uncertain sign of recognition, to which he did not respond, and passed by. Things grew more lonely. I was coming out upon the barren ridges of an old sea beach that rose along the desert floor. Life was small and grubby now. The hot, warning scarlet of peculiar desert ants occasionally flashed among the stones. I had lost all trace of myself and thought regretfully of the lizard who might have directed me.

24. A turned-up stone yielded only a scorpion who curled his tail in a kind of evil malice. I

surveyed him reproachfully. He was old enough to know the secret of my origin, but once more an ancient, bitter animus drawn from that poisoned soil possessed him and he possessed me. I turned away. An enormous emptiness by degrees possessed me. I was back almost, in a different way, to the thin air over the mountain, to the end of all things in the cold starlight of space.

25. I passed some indefinable bones and shells in the salt-crusted wall of a dry arroyo. As I reined up, only sand dunes rose like waves before me and if life was there it was no longer visible. It was like coming down to the end—to the place of fires where we began. I turned about then and let my gaze go up, tier after tier, height after height, from crawling desert bush to towering pine on the great slopes far above me.

26. In the same way animal life had gone up that road from these dry, envenomed things to the deer nuzzling a fawn in the meadows far above. I had come down the whole way into a place where one could lift sand and ask in a hollow, dust-shrouded whisper, "Life, what is it? Why am I here? Why am I here?"

27. And my mind went up that figurative ladder of the ages, bone by bone, skull by skull, seeking an answer. There was none, except that in all that downrush of wild energy that I had passed in the canyons there was this other stranger organized stream that marched upward, gaining a foothold here, tossing there a pine cone a little farther upward into a crevice in the rock.

28. And again one asked, not of the past this time, but of the future, there where the winds howled through open space and the last lichens clung to the naked rock, "Why did we live?" There was no answer I could hear. The living river flowed out of nowhere into nothing. No one knew its source or its departing. It was an apparition. If one did not see it there was no way to prove that it was real.

29. No way, that is, except within the mind itself. And the mind, in some strange manner so involved with time, moving against the cutting edge of it like the wind I had faced on the mountain, has yet its own small skull-borne image of eternity. It is not alone that I can reach out and receive within my head a handsbreadth replica of the far fields of the universe. It is not because I can touch a trilobite and know the fall of light in ages before my birth. Rather, it lies in the fact that the human mind can transcend time, even though trapped, to all appearances, within that medium. As from some remote place, I see myself as child and young man, watch with a certain dispassionate objectivity the violence and tears of a remote youth who was once I, shaping his character, for good or ill, toward the creature he is today. Shrinking, I see him teeter at the edge of abysses he never saw. With pain I acknowledge acts undone that might have saved and led him into some serene and noble pathway. I move about him like a ghost, that vanished youth. I exhort, I plead. He does not hear me. Indeed, he too is already a ghost. He has become me. I am what I am. Yet the point is, we are not wholly given over to time—if we were, such acts, such leaps through that gray medium, would be impossible. Perhaps God himself may rove in similar pain up the dark roads of his universe. Only how would it be, I wonder, to contain at once both the beginning and the end, and to hear, in helplessness perhaps, the fall of worlds in the night?

30. This is what the mind of man is just beginning to achieve—a little microcosm, a replica of whatever it is that, from some unimaginable "outside," contains the universe and all the fractured bits of seeing which the world's creatures see. It is not necessary to ride over a mountain range to experience historical infinity. It can descend upon one in the lecture room.

31. I find it is really in daylight that the sensation, I am about to describe is apt to come most clearly upon me, and for some reason I associate it extensively with crowds. It is not, you understand, an hallucination. It is a reality. It is, I can only say with difficulty, a chink torn in a dimension life was never intended to look through. It connotes a sense beyond the eye, though the twenty years' impressions are visual. Man, it is said, is a time-binding animal, but he was never intended for this. Here is the way it comes.

32. I mount the lecturer's rostrum to address a class. Like any workworn professor fond of his subject, I fumble among my skulls and papers, shuffle to the blackboard and back again, begin the patient translation of three billion years of time into chalk scrawls and uncertain words ventured timidly to a sea of young, impatient faces. Time does not frighten them, I think enviously. They have, most of them, never lain awake and

grasped the sides of a cot, staring upward into the dark while the slow clock strokes begin.

33. "Doctor." A voice diverts me. I stare out nearsightedly over the class. A hand from the back row gesticulates. "Doctor, do you believe there is a direction to evolution? Do you believe, Doctor . . . Doctor, do you believe? . . ." Instead of the words, I hear a faint piping, and see an eager scholar's face squeezed and dissolving on the body of a chest-thumping ape. "Doctor, is there a direction?"

34. I see it then—the trunk that stretches monstrously behind him. It winds out of the door, down dark and obscure corridors to the cellar, and vanishes into the floor. It writhes, it crawls, it barks and snuffles and roars, and the odor of the swamp exhales from it. That pale young scholar's face is the last bloom on a curious animal extrusion through time. And who among us, under the cold persuasion of the archeological eye, can perceive which of his many shapes is real, or if, perhaps, the entire shape in time is not a greater and more curious animal than its single appearance?

35. I too am aware of the trunk that stretches loathsomely back of me along the floor. I too am a many-visaged thing that has climbed upward out of the dark of endless leaf falls, and has slunk, furred, through the glitter of blue glacial nights. I, the professor, trembling absurdly on the platform with my book and spectacles, am the single philosophical animal. I am the unfolding worm, and mud fish, the weird tree of Igdrasil shaping itself endlessly out of darkness toward the light.

36. I have said this is not an illusion. It is when one sees in this manner, or a sense of strangeness halts one on a busy street to verify the appearance of one's fellows, that one knows a terrible new sense has opened a faint crack into the Absolute. It is in this way alone that one comes to grips with a great mystery, that life and time bear some curious relationship to each other that is not shared by inanimate things.

37. It is in the brain that this world opens. To our descendants it may become a commonplace, but me, and others like me, it has made a castaway. I have no refuge in time, as others do who troop homeward at nightfall. As a result, I am one of those who linger furtively over coffee in the kitchen at bedtime or haunt the all-night restaurants. Nevertheless, I shall say without regret: there are hazards in all professions.

III

38. It may seem at this point that I have gone considerably round about in my examination of the natural world. I have done so in the attempt to indicate that the spider web of law which has been flung, as Emerson indicated, across the deeps of time and space and between each member of the living world has brought us some quite remarkable, but at the same time disquieting, knowledge. In rapid summary, man has passed from a natural world of appearances invisibly controlled by the caprice of spirits to an astronomical universe visualized by Newton, through the law of gravitation, as operating with the regularity of a clock.

39. Newton, who remained devout, assumed that God, at the time of the creation of the solar system, had set everything to operating in its proper orbit. He recognized, however, certain irregularities of planetary movement which, in time, would lead to a disruption of his perfect astronomical machine. It was here, as a seventeenth-century scholar, that he felt no objection to the notion that God interfered at periodic intervals to correct the deviations of the machine.

40. A century later Laplace had succeeded in dispensing with this last vestige of divine intervention. Hutton had similarly dealt with supernaturalism in earth-building, and Darwin, in the nineteenth century, had gone far toward producing a similar mechanistic explanation of life. The machine that began in the heavens had finally been installed in the human heart and brain. "We can make everything natural," Pascal had truly said, and surely the more naïve forms of worship of the unseen are vanishing.

41. Yet strangely, with the discovery of evolutionary, as opposed to purely durational, time, there emerges into this safe-and-sane mechanical universe something quite unanticipated by the eighteenth-century rationalists—a kind of emergent, if not miraculous, novelty.

42. I know that the word "miraculous" is regarded dubiously in scientific circles because of past quarrels with theologians. The word has been defined, however, as an event transcending the known laws of nature. Since, as we have seen, the laws of nature have a way of being altered from one generation of scientists to the next, a little taste for the miraculous in this broad sense

will do us no harm. We forget that nature itself is one vast miracle transcending the reality of night and nothingness. We forget that each one of us in his personal life repeats that miracle.

43. Whatever may be the power behind those dancing motes to which the physicist has penetrated, it makes the light of the muskrat's world as it makes the world of the great poet. It makes, in fact, all of the innumerable and private worlds which exist in the heads of men. There is a sense in which we can say that the planet, with its strange freight of life, is always just passing from the unnatural to the natural, from that Unseen which man has always reverenced to the small reality of the day. If all life were to be swept from the world, leaving only its chemical constituents, no visitor from another star would be able to establish the reality of such a phantom. The dust would lie without visible protest, as it does now in the moon's airless craters, or in the road before our door.

44. Yet this is the same dust which, dead, quiescent, and unmoving, when taken up in the process known as life, hears music and responds to it, weeps bitterly over time and loss, or is oppressed by the looming future that is, on any materialist terms, the veriest shadow of nothing. How natural was man, we may ask, until he came? What forces dictated that a walking ape should watch the red shift of light beyond the island universes or listen by carefully devised antennae to the pulse of unseen stars? Who, whimsically, conceived that the plot of the world should begin in a mud puddle and end—where, and with whom? Men argue learnedly over whether life is chemical chance or antichance, but they seem to forget that the life *in* chemicals may be the greatest chance of all, the most mysterious and unexplainable property in matter.

45. "The special value of science," a perceptive philosopher once wrote, "lies not in what it makes of the world, but in what it makes of the knower." Some years ago, while camping in a vast eroded area in the West, I came upon one of those unlikely sights which illuminate such truths.

46. I suppose that nothing living had moved among those great stones for centuries. They lay toppled against each other like fallen dolmens. The huge stones were beasts, I used to think, of a kind that man ordinarily lived too fast to understand. They seemed inanimate because the tempo of the life in them was slow. They lived ages in one place and moved only when man was not looking. Sometimes at night I would hear a low rumble as one drew itself into a new position and subsided again. Sometimes I found their tracks ground deeply into the hillsides.

47. It was with considerable surprise that while traversing this barren valley I came, one afternoon, upon what I can only describe as a very remarkable sight. Some distance away, so far that for a little space I could make nothing of the spectacle, my eyes were attracted by a dun-colored object about the size of a football, which periodically bounded up from the desert floor. Wonderingly, I drew closer and observed that something ropelike which glittered in the sun appeared to be dangling from the ball-shaped object. Whatever the object was, it appeared to be bouncing faster and more desperately as I approached. My surroundings were such that this hysterical dance of what at first glance appeared to be a common stone was quite unnerving, as though suddenly all the natural objects in the valley were about to break into a jig. Going closer, I penetrated the mystery.

48. The sun was sparkling on the scales of a huge blacksnake which was partially looped about the body of a hen pheasant. Desperately the bird tried to rise, and just as desperately the big snake coiled and clung, though each time the bird, falling several feet, was pounding the snake's body in the gravel. I gazed at the scene in astonishment. Here in this silent waste, like an emanation from nowhere, two bitter and desperate vapors, two little whirlwinds of contending energy, were beating each other to death because their plans—something, I suspected, about whether a clutch of eggs was to turn into a thing with wings or scales—this problem, I say, of the onrushing nonexistent future, had catapulted serpent against bird.

49. The bird was too big for the snake to have had it in mind as prey. Most probably, he had been intent on stealing the pheasant's eggs and had been set upon and pecked. Somehow in the ensuing scuffle he had flung a loop over the bird's back and partially blocked her wings. She could not take off, and the snake would not let go. The snake was taking a heavy battering among the stones, but the high-speed metabolism and tremendous flight exertion of the mother bird were rapidly exhausting her. I stood a moment and saw

the bloodshot glaze deepen in her eyes. I suppose I could have waited there to see what would happen when she could not fly; I suppose it might have been worth scientifically recording. But I could not stand that ceaseless, bloody pounding in the gravel. I thought of the eggs somewhere about, and whether they were to elongate and writhe into an armor of scales or eventually to go whistling into the wind with their wild mother.

50. So I, the mammal, in my way supple, and less bound by instinct, arbitrated the matter. I unwound the serpent from the bird and let him hiss and wrap his battered coils around my arm. The bird, her wings flung out, rocked on her legs and gasped repeatedly. I moved away in order not to drive her farther from her nest. Thus the serpent and I, two terrible and feared beings, passed quickly out of view.

51. Over the next ridge, where he could do no more damage, I let the snake, whose anger had subsided, slowly uncoil and slither from my arm. He flowed away into a little patch of bunch grass—aloof, forgetting, unaware of the journey he had made upon my wrist, which throbbed from his expert constriction. The bird had contended for birds against the oncoming future; the serpent writhing into the bunch grass had contended just as desperately for serpents. And I, the apparition in that valley—for what had I contended?—I who contained the serpent and the bird and who read the past long written in their bodies.

52. Slowly, as I sauntered dwarfed among overhanging pinnacles, as the great slabs which were the visible remnants of past ages laid their enormous shadows rhythmically as life and death across my face, the answer came to me. Man could contain more than himself. Among these many appearances that flew, or swam in the waters, or wavered momentarily into being, man alone possessed that unique ability.

53. The Renaissance thinkers were right when they said that man, the Microcosm, contains the Macrocosm. I had touched the lives of creatures other than myself and had seen their shapes waver and blow like smoke through the corridors of time. I had watched, with sudden concentrated attention, myself, this brain, unrolling from the seed like a genie from a bottle, and casting my eyes forward, I had seen it vanish again into the formless alchemies of the earth.

54. For what then had I contended, weighing the serpent with the bird in that wild valley? I had struggled, I am now convinced, for a greater, more comprehensive version of myself.

IV

55. I am a man who has spent a great deal of his life on his knees, though not in prayer. I do not say this last pridefully, but with the feeling that the posture, if not the thought behind it, may have had some final salutary effect. I am a naturalist and a fossil hunter, and I have crawled most of the way through life. I have crawled downward into holes without a bottom, and upward, wedged into crevices where the wind and the birds scream at you until the sound of a falling pebble is enough to make the sick heart lurch. In man, I know now, there is no such thing as wisdom. I have learned this with my face against the ground. It is a very difficult thing for a man to grasp today, because of his power; yet in his brain there is really only a sort of universal marsh, spotted at intervals by quaking green islands representing the elusive stability of modern science—islands frequently gone as soon as glimpsed.

56. It is our custom to deny this; we are men of precision, measurement and logic; we abhor the unexplainable and reject it. This, too, is a green island. We wish our lives to be one continuous growth in knowledge; indeed, we expect them to be. Yet well over a hundred years ago Kierkegaard observed that maturity consists in the discovery that "there comes a critical moment where everything is reversed, after which the point becomes to understand more and more that there is something which cannot be understood."

57. When I separated the serpent from the bird and released them in that wild upland, it was not for knowledge; not for anything I had learned in science. Instead, I contained, to put it simply, the serpent and the bird, I would always contain them. I was no longer one of the contending vapors; I had embraced them in my own substance and, in some insubstantial way, reconciled them, as I had sought reconciliation with the muskrat on the shore. I had transcended feather and scale and gone beyond them into another sphere of reality. I was trying to give birth to a different self whose only expression lies again in the deeply religious words of

Pascal, "You would not seek me had you not found me."

58. I had not known what I sought, but I was aware at last that something had found me. I no longer believed that nature was either natural or unnatural, only that nature now appears natural to man. But the nature that appears natural to man is another version of the muskrat's world under the boat dock, or the elusive sparks over which the physicist made his trembling passage. They were appearances, specialized insights, but unreal because in the constantly onrushing future they were swept away.

59. What had become of the natural world of that gorilla-headed little ape from which we sprang—that dim African corner with its chewed fish bones and giant Ice Age pigs? It was gone more utterly than my muskrat's tiny domain, yet it had given birth to an unimaginable thing—ourselves—something overreaching the observable laws of that far epoch. Man since the beginning seems to be awaiting an event the nature of which he does not know. "With reference to the near past," Thoreau once shrewdly commented, "we all occupy the region of common sense, but in the prospect of the future we are, by instinct, transcendentalists." This is the way of the man who makes nature "natural." He stands at the point where the miraculous comes into being, and after the event he calls it "natural." The imagination of man, in its highest manifestations, stands close to the doorway of the infinite, to the world beyond the nature that we know. Perhaps, after all, in this respect man constitutes the exertion of that act which Donne three centuries ago called God's Prerogative.

60. Man's quest for certainty is, in the last analysis, a quest for meaning. But the meaning lies buried within himself rather than in the void he has vainly searched for portents since antiquity. Perhaps the first act in its unfolding was taken by a raw beast with a fearsome head who dreamed some difficult and unimaginable thing denied his fellows. Perhaps the flashes of beauty and insight which trouble us so deeply are no less prophetic of what the race might achieve. All that prevents us is doubt—the power to make everything natural without the accompanying gift to see, beyond the natural, to that inexpressible realm in which the words "natural" and "supernatural" cease to have meaning.

61. Man, at last, is face to face with himself in natural guise. "What we make natural, we destroy," said Pascal. He knew, with superlative insight, man's complete necessity to transcend the worldly image that this word connotes. It is not the outward powers of man the toolmaker that threaten us. It is a growing danger which has already afflicted vast areas of the world—the danger that we have created an unbearable last idol for our worship. That idol, that uncreate and ruined visage which confronts us daily, is no less than man made natural. Beyond this replica of ourselves, this countenance already grown so distantly inhuman that it terrifies us, still beckons the lonely figure of man's dreams. It is a nature, not of this age, but of the becoming—the light once glimpsed by a creature just over the threshold from a beast, a despairing cry from the dark shadow of a cross on Golgotha long ago.

62. Man is not totally compounded of the nature we profess to understand. Man is always partly of the future, and the future he possesses a power to shape. "Natural" is a magician's word—and like all such entities, it should be used sparingly lest there arise from it, as now, some unglimpsed, unintended world, some monstrous caricature called into being by the indiscreet articulation of worn syllables. Perhaps, if we are wise, we will prefer to stand like those forgotten humble creatures who poured little gifts of flints into a grave. Perhaps there may come to us then, in some such moment, a ghostly sense that an invisible doorway has been opened—a doorway which, widening out, will take man beyond the nature that he knows.

PART 2
The Short Story

W. SOMERSET MAUGHAM

Appointment in Samarra

There was a merchant in Bagdad who sent his servant to market to buy provisions, and in a little while the servant came back, white and trembling, and said, "Master, just now when I was in the market-place I was jostled by a woman in the crowd and when I turned I saw it was Death that jostled me. She looked at me and made a threatening gesture; now, lend me your horse, and I will ride away from this city and avoid my fate. I will go to Samarra and there Death will not find me." The merchant lent him his horse, and the servant mounted it, and he dug his spurs in its flanks and as fast as the horse could gallop he went. Then the merchant went down to the market-place and he saw Death standing in the crowd and he came to Death and said, "Why did you make a threatening gesture to my servant when you saw him this morning?" "That was not a threatening gesture," Death said. "It was only a start of surprise. I was astonished to see him in Bagdad, for I had an appointment with him tonight in Samarra."

The art of story-telling certainly predates the earliest written records of civilization; even the modern short story, the most recent of the major literary types, has an ancient lineage. Perhaps the oldest and most direct ancestor of the short story is the *anecdote*—an illustrative story that goes straight to the point. But the form also shares characteristics with the ancient *parable* and *fable*, starkly brief narratives used to delineate some moral or spiritual truth. These types anticipate the brevity and unity of many short stories written today. Other ancestors of the short story emerged during the Middle Ages, including the Scandinavian *saga*, a long tale centered around the life of a particular family. Among the shorter medieval forms were the *exemplum*, a brief story used to support the text of a sermon, and the *ballad*, folk verse narrating a dramatic episode. During the sixteenth, seventeeth, and eighteenth centuries numerous forerunners of the short story appeared, such as the sketch and the *tale*—loosely constructed prose narratives, not so compact, intense, or comprehensive as the short story. Though these early narratives sometimes bear close superficial resemblance to the modern short story, few, if any, exemplify its specialized artistry.

THE DEVELOPMENT OF THE SHORT STORY

The short story as it is known today began with Nathaniel Hawthorne and Edgar Allan Poe. The first typical story of each of these writers was published in 1835—Poe's "Berenice" and Hawthorne's "The Ambitious Guest." Though it now seems naive, Poe's horror story demonstrated the author's mastery of a new type of narrative. The strange characters, plots far removed from ordinary experience, the fantastic scenes—all these Poe subordinates to narrative suspense and emotional effect.

Hawthorne's stories are as closely knit and unified as Poe's. But Hawthorne, unlike Poe, is primarily a moralist, and his constant focus on a moral problem—selfishness, pride, ambition—is usually the unifying factor of his stories. It was this quality that caused Poe, when reviewing Hawthorne's *Twice-Told Tales* in 1842, to observe:

A skillful literary artist has constructed a tale. If wise, he has not fashioned his thoughts to accommodate his incidents; but having conceived, with deliberate care, a certain unique or single effect to be wrought out, he then invents such incidents—he then combines such events as may best aid him in establishing this preconceived effect. If his very initial sentence tend not to the outbringing of this effect, then he has failed in his first step. In the whole composition there should be no word written, of which the tendency, direct or indirect, is not to the one preestablished design.

This celebrated passage is now generally considered the first significant definition of the type. And, along with another restriction in the same essay—a story must not be so long that it "cannot be read at one sitting"—Poe's phrase "a certain unique or single effect" remains, with remarkable accuracy, the hallmark of the short story even today. By 1842, then, Hawthorne and Poe had isolated and defined the essential characteristics of the short story—brevity, unity, intensity. Forty years later an American critic, Brander Matthews, rephrased Poe's definition and supplied a label: the short story, called the "short-story" (spelled with a hyphen) to "emphasize the distinction between the short-story and the story which is merely short." In the meantime, two other American writers had made significant contributions to this literary form: Bret Harte, with his stories of early life in California, started a vogue of local-color stories, and Henry James produced the first of his long series of peculiarly modern psychological investigations of the human mind and heart.

While later developments of the short-story form remained primarily within the scope set forth by these writers and critics, two foreign writers, Guy de Maupassant and Anton Chekhov, did have far-reaching effect on the focus of the American short story in particular. Maupassant showed remarkable ingenuity in inventing means to gain dramatic compression and considerable boldness in relentlessly subordinating everything to a central effect. The structural neatness of countless "plotted" stories owes, ultimately, something to Maupassant's technique. Chekhov's practice of presenting a segment of life, objective and seemingly plotless yet highly suggestive and penetrating, has been another influence on the short story—perhaps second to none in recent years. Many writers agree with Chekhov that life poses questions but provides no answers. The artist, they believe, is therefore obliged only to give a unified impression of some part of life. The major development in the short story in recent decades has, in fact, been the work of a group of writers who seek to create an "impression." In addition to Chekhov and James, the great masters who influenced this group are Gustave Flaubert, Stephen Crane, James Joyce, and D. H. Lawrence. Some of the best known of this group are Sean O'Faolain, Franz Kafka, Frank O'Connor, Albert Camus, Marcel Aymé, and Friedrich Dürrenmatt in Great Britain and Europe, and Ernest Hemingway, William Faulkner, John Steinbeck, and Eudora Welty in the United States.

The flowering of the short story was one of the principal literary events of the first half of the twentieth century, especially in the United States, where the rapid growth of periodicals and the tempo and pressure of American life were both compatible with the form's structure and length. Scores of writers discovered dynamic materials in the isolated communities and forgotten backwoods, the humdrum towns, the congested cities; they presented the lost generation, the gangster, the neglected artist, the immigrant, the lingering pioneer; they wrote about Harlem, Chicago, Winesburg, the prairies, the Appalachian Mountains, the deep South.

THE ART OF THE SHORT STORY

An awareness of the essential characteristics already pointed out—brevity, unity, intensity—increases the reader's understanding and enjoyment of a short story. In addition, some knowledge of the specialized techniques by which these qualities are produced makes communication between writer and reader more satisfying.

Scene In all forms of fiction, from the longest novel to the shortest short story, the basic elements are the same: scene, character, and action. Of these, usually, the least important is scene, which in most instances merely "sets the stage" and, because of the premium on space in the short story, is handled as quickly as possible. Yet in some stories the scene is of fundamental importance—in Crane's "The Open Boat," for example, the sea becomes the central force in the men's existence. Many of the most skillful authors integrate scene entirely into the story in such a way that it significantly contributes to the story's intensity. Conrad, for example, in "The Lagoon," treats scene as a central element within the story's context.

Character The primary concern of most authors is character: "Take care of character," Galsworthy said; "action and dialogue will take care of themselves." Theme and meaning evolve from the interrelation between a character and the circumstances of the character's life. Yet the short story has neither time nor space to describe fully development or disintegration; this is the province of the novel. Furthermore, the short story's focus is usually on one character; the other characters serve only to emphasize his personality and predicament. In most stories the main character is easily discovered. Identifying the main character early in the story enables the reader to more accurately understand the intricate relationships among the characters and consequently gain a fuller appreciation of what they do and say.

Action For many readers action is the most important element of fiction. In fact, the success of some stories—those of Saki, for example—rests largely on the action of an ingenious plot. Yet many of the best short-story writers today often minimize action, lest it destroy that delicate balance of all the elements upon which their total achievement depends. Still, everyone agrees that some plot is indispensable. But the action by which plot is developed must, in the short story, be limited to a critical moment in the life of the chief character. His or her whole life history cannot be told; that again is the province of the novel. The essential facet of plot is conflict; it alone causes tension and creates suspense. The conflict may be of various kinds: it may be an inner conflict (as in "The Chrysanthemums"), a conflict among people (as in "Wash"), or a conflict between the characters and their surroundings (as in "The Open Boat"). Ordinarily action follows a definable pattern. It begins with the first point of conflict (*incentive moment*), develops through a series of entanglements (*complication*), reaches a peak of intensity (*climax*), and finally becomes disentangled (*resolution*). It would hardly be wise to graph the action of a story, fixing precisely the incentive moment, the climax, and the last moment of suspense; it is helpful, however, even in casual reading, to note the beginning of the conflict, to follow the increasing tension to the highest point of interest, and to watch the suspense subside and ultimately come to rest.

Scene, character, and plot are combined into a continuum of existence, an illusion of reality, so that readers willingly suspend disbelief and enter into the experience of the story. In working these elements into a pattern of continuous experience, writers make use chiefly of two techniques—summary and drama (sometimes referred to as the "long view" and the "short view"). If they decide to hurry over a certain part of the story, they simply describe or summarize the action. But those parts of the story that are crucial they present in vivid detail. In such parts the characters usually break into dialogue. Thus by using the long view writers economize, and by using the short view they gain the intensity that marks the short story.

Although the elements of scene, character, and plot may be isolated in analyzing a story, they are in reality inseparable; and the art of the short story in no small degree depends on the skill of the writer in integrating all three so as to illuminate the theme of the story. Furthermore, the action of the story itself must be related to the life that existed before the story began and will continue to exist after the story ends. It is the relation between the specific action of the story and this enveloping action that affords the shock of discovery in the resolution and gives the story meaning.

Though the major devices that constitute the art of the short story concern the handling of the basic elements of scene, character, and action, there are a few special techniques of particular importance to the reader.

Enveloping Action Since the short story presents only a fragment of experience, the writer employs special techniques in order to give the reader a feeling that the fragment is a part of a continuous experience. Sometimes the story begins or ends with a sentence or phrase that refers to the larger experience. More often, however, the momentary events of the story are interwoven with the routine action of the characters' lives in order to create this impression. Through cumulative references to past events the writer is able to impart to the reader an impression of continuous experience from which the specific experience has been extracted.

Point of View For both the writer and reader, point of view—that is, through whose eyes the story is seen and by whose consciousness the material is interpreted—is an important consideration. All stories are told from one of two broad points of view or from some variation of the two. In the first of these, the *first-person* point of view, the author tells the story as if only one character—the narrator, speaking as the "I" in the story—knew about the story's events and characters. This one character to whose knowledge and understanding the reader is intentionally limited may be a main character, a minor character, or even an outside observer. "Guests of the Nation" and "An Old Manuscript" are told from the first-person, main-character point of view, and "The Man on the Threshold" from the first-person, ouside-observer point of view.

The second of the two broad points of view—generally called the *omniscient*—is used in various special ways not adequately described by the terminology. The word "omniscient" signifies that the author knows everything—not merely the externalities some spectator might see but also the inner workings of the minds of the characters. All omniscient stories are necessarily third-person stories. With these two ideas in mind, the reader can distinguish the three primary types of the omniscient story. First, *third person* is the designation given to the omniscient story in which the author freely moves inside and outside the minds of any and all characters, knowing all and doing as he or she chooses. "The Lagoon" is a typical third-person story. The second prominent type of the omniscient story, known as the *central intelligence,* limits the author to moving inside and outside the consciousness of only one character, either a major or minor one. In "The Open Boat" the journalist is the central intelligence, the one character whose mind Crane enters or withdraws from at will. The third most prominent variety is the *scenic.* Although the scenic is actually an omniscient and third-person point of view, its features are subtly obscured. They are present, however; to deny them is equivalent to saying that a story can be told without a teller. It is enough to say that the scenic story does not invade the consciousness of any character; by being presented almost entirely through dialogue, it calls no attention to the identity of the teller. In effect, the teller is effaced almost to the point of non-existence. This technique is used in "A Clean Well-Lighted Place," a technique much the same as that used in Strindberg's play "The Stronger."

These narrative methods vary chiefly in two respects—the amount of freedom they allow and the degree of directness they permit. For writers, fixing on a point of view is of utmost importance, since, if they are to realize the full value of their material, they must choose a convenient position from which to tell the story. For readers, an awareness of point of view is also highly important, for once they have discovered through whose eyes they are to see what happens, the story unfolds more logically and can be more readily interpreted.

Language   In the modern short story, language is a critical component—hardly less decisive than in poetry. Since a story is constructed about a particular isolated experience, the language in which it is told must suggest the quality of that experience: the language must be incisive, suggestive, and alert. The first few sentences of a well-written story will include words that reveal its unique quality. Since so much of a short story is often presented dramatically, the language of dialogue is of particular importance. For example, in "A Late Encounter with the Enemy," the dialogue of General and Sally Poker Sash accurately and vividly reveals their characters and roles, which largely constitute the story.

Ethical Insight   To many readers the highest test of fiction is ethical insight into a world of universal and ideal truth. Modern short stories may still depend on adventure, but not necessarily on the adventure of action in strange and dangerous places. More typically they are concerned with adventure in understanding human nature—complex and contradictory, amusing and surprising, comic and tragic. As noted above, the theme is developed by showing how the limited action of the story is related to the enveloping action of its background in life. It is the struggle between these two forces that constitutes the main tension, the resolution of which makes the point of the story.

For writers to attain the unity required of a successful short story, their feeling toward scene, character, action, and theme must be consistent. Since short stories are usually read at one sitting, and since their focus is so narrow, writers must be extraordinarily skillful in utilizing all the potential of their materials. It was, indeed, this central point of the art of the short story with which Poe was concerned when he observed that a "skillful literary artist" conceives "with deliberate care, a certain unique or single effect to be wrought out."

EDGAR ALLAN POE

The Tell-Tale Heart

Edgar Allan Poe (1809–1849), recognized (along with Nathaniel Hawthorne) as the major American developer of the short-story form, was born in Boston and attended the University of Virginia after the death of his actor parents. Forced to withdraw from the university because of gambling, Poe published anonymously his first work, *Tamerlane and Other Poems*, 1827. After marrying his cousin, Virginia Clemm, in 1836, Poe published works that have since defined the modern horror and detective genres: *The Fall of the House of Usher*, 1839; *Tales of the Grotesque and Arabesque*, 1840; *The Murders in the Rue Morgue*, 1841; and *The Purloined Letter*, 1845. Despite his prolific prose writings, in Europe Poe is best remembered as a poet whose works and ideas later influenced Mallarmé and the French symbolists.

"The Tell-Tale Heart," told in the first person by a murderer and madman, illustrates Poe's blending of the physical and the psychological to create both mood and plot. Like the narrator, the reader is drawn into a world wherein the boundaries between the real and unreal are blurred.

True!—nervous—very, very dreadfully nervous I had been and am; but why *will* you say that I am mad? The disease had sharpened my senses—not destroyed—not dulled them. Above all was the sense of hearing acute. I heard all things in the heaven and in the earth. I heard many things in hell. How, then, am I mad? Hearken! and observe how healthily—how calmly I can tell you the whole story.

It is impossible to say how first the idea entered my brain; but once conceived, it haunted me day and night. Object there was none. Passion there was none. I loved the old man. He had never wronged me. He had never given me insult. For his gold I had no desire. I think it was his eye! yes, it was this! One of his eyes resembled that of a vulture—a pale blue eye, with a film over it. Whenever it fell upon me, my blood ran cold; and so by degrees—very gradually—I made up my mind to take the life of the old man, and thus rid myself of the eye forever.

Now this is the point. You fancy me mad. Madmen know nothing. But you should have seen *me*. You should have seen how wisely I proceeded—with what caution—with what foresight—with what dissimulation I went to work! I was never kinder to the old man than during the whole week before I killed him. And every night, about midnight, I turned the latch of his door and opened it—oh, so gently! And then, when I had made an opening sufficient for my head, I put in a dark lantern, all closed, closed, so that no light shone out, and then I thrust in my head. Oh, you would have laughed to see how cunningly I thrust it in! I moved it slowly—very, very slowly, so that I might not disturb the old man's sleep. It took me an hour to place my whole head within the opening so far that I could see him as he lay upon his bed. Ha!—would a madman have been so wise as this? And then, when my head was well in the room, I undid the lantern cautiously—oh, so cautiously—cautiously (for the hinges creaked)—I undid it just so much that a single thin ray fell upon the vulture eye. And this I did for seven long nights—every night just at midnight—but I found the eye always closed; and so it was impossible to do the work; for it was not the old man who vexed me, but his Evil Eye. And every morning, when the day broke, I went boldly into the chamber, and spoke courageously to him, calling him by name in a hearty tone, and inquiring how he had passed the night. So you see he would have been a very profound old man, indeed, to suspect that every night, just at twelve, I looked in upon him while he slept.

Upon the eighth night I was more than usually cautious in opening the door. A watch's minute hand moves more quickly than did mine. Never before that night had I *felt* the extent of my own powers—of my sagacity. I could scarcely contain my feelings of triumph. To think that there I was, opening the door, little by little, and he not even to dream of my secret deeds or thoughts. I fairly chuckled at the idea; and perhaps he heard me; for he moved on the bed suddenly, as if startled. Now you may think that I drew back—but no. His room was as black as pitch with the thick darkness (for the shutters were close fastened, through fear of robbers), and so I knew that he could not see the opening of the door, and I kept pushing it on steadily, steadily.

I had my head in, and was about to open the lantern, when my thumb slipped upon the tin fastening, and the old man sprang up in the bed, crying out—"Who's there?"

I kept quite still and said nothing. For a whole hour I did not move a muscle, and in the meantime I did not hear him lie down. He was still sitting up in the bed listening;—just as I have done, night after night, hearkening to the death watches in the wall.

Presently I heard a slight groan, and I knew it was the groan of mortal terror. It was not a groan of pain or of grief—oh, no!—it was the low stifled sound that arises from the bottom of the soul when overcharged with awe. I knew the sound well. Many a night, just at midnight, when all the world slept, it was welled up from my own bosom, deepening, with its dreadful echo, the terrors that distracted me. I say I knew it well. I knew what the old man felt, and pitied him, although I chuckled at heart. I knew that he

had been lying awake ever since the first slight noise, when he had turned in the bed. His fears had been ever since growing upon him. He had been trying to fancy them causeless, but could not. He had been saying to himself—"It is nothing but the wind in the chimney—it is only a mouse crossing the floor," or "it is merely a cricket which has made a single chirp." Yes, he has been trying to comfort himself with these suppositions; but he had found all in vain. *All in vain;* because Death, in approaching him, had stalked with his black shadow before him, and enveloped the victim. And it was the mournful influence of the unperceived shadow that caused him to feel—although he neither saw nor heard—to *feel* the presence of my head within the room.

When I had waited a long time, very patiently, without hearing him lie down, I resolved to open a little—a very, very little crevice in the lantern. So I opened it—you cannot imagine how stealthily, stealthily—until, at length, a single dim ray, like the thread of the spider, shot from out the crevice and full upon the vulture eye.

It was open—wide, wide open—and I grew furious as I gazed upon it. I saw it with perfect distinctness—all a dull blue, with a hideous veil over it that chilled the very marrow in my bones; but I could see nothing else of the old man's face or person: for I had directed the ray as if by instinct, precisely upon the damned spot.

And now have I not told you that what you mistake for madness is but over-acuteness of the senses?—now, I say, there came to my ears a low, dull, quick sound, such as a watch makes when enveloped in cotton. I knew *that* sound well too. It was the beating of the old man's heart. It increased my fury, as the beating of a drum stimulates the soldier into courage.

But even yet I refrained and kept still. I scarcely breathed. I held the lantern motionless. I tried how steadily I could maintain the ray upon the eye. Meantime the hellish tattoo of the heart increased. It grew quicker and quicker, and louder and louder every instant. The old man's terror *must* have been extreme! It grew louder, I say, louder every moment!—do you mark me well? I have told you that I am nervous: so I am. And now at the dead hour of the night, amid the dreadful silence of that old house, so strange a noise as this excited me to uncontrollable terror. Yet, for some minutes longer I refrained and stood still. But the beating grew louder, louder! I thought the heart must burst. And now a new anxiety seized me—the sound would be heard by a neighbor! The old man's hour had come! With a loud yell, I threw open the lantern and leaped into the room. He shrieked once—once only. In an instant I dragged him to the floor, and pulled the heavy bed over him. I then smiled gaily, to find the deed so far done. But, for many minutes, the heart beat on with a muffled sound. This, however, did not vex me; it would not be heard through the wall. At length it ceased. The old man was dead. I removed the bed and examined the corpse. Yes, he was stone, stone dead. I placed my hand upon the heart and held it there many minutes. There was no pulsation. He was stone dead. His eye would trouble me no more.

If still you think me mad, you will think so no longer when I describe the wise precautions I took for the concealment of the body. The night waned, and I worked hastily, but in silence. First of all I dismembered the corpse. I cut off the head and the arms and the legs.

I then took up three planks from the flooring of the chamber, and deposited all between the scantlings. I then replaced the boards so cleverly, so cunningly, that no human eye—not even *his*—could have detected any thing wrong. There was nothing to wash out—no stain of any kind—no blood-spot whatever. I had been too wary for that. A tub had caught all—ha! ha!

When I had made an end of these labors, it was four o'clock—still dark as midnight. As the bell sounded the hour, there came a knocking at the street door. I went down to open it with a light heart,—for what had I *now* to fear? There entered three men, who introduced themselves, with perfect suavity, as officers of the police. A shriek had been heard by a neighbor during the night; suspicion of foul play had been aroused; information had been lodged at the police office, and they (the officers) had been deputed to search the premises.

I smiled—for *what* had I to fear? I bade the gentlemen welcome. The shriek, I said, was my own in a dream. The old man, I mentioned, was absent in the country. I took my visitors all over the house. I bade them search—search *well*. I led them, at length, to *his* chamber. I showed them his treasures, secure, undisturbed. In the enthusi-

asm of my confidence, I brought chairs into the room, and desired them *here* to rest from their fatigues, while I myself, in the wild audacity of my perfect triumph, placed my own seat upon the very spot beneath which reposed the corpse of the victim.

The officers were satisfied. My *manner* had convinced them. I was singularly at ease. They sat, and while I answered cheerily, they chatted familiar things. But, ere long, I felt myself getting pale and wished them gone. My head ached, and I fancied a ringing in my ears: but still they sat and still chatted. The ringing became more distinct:—it continued and became more distinct: I talked more freely to get rid of the feeling: but it continued and gained definitiveness—until, at length, I found that the noise was *not* within my ears.

No doubt I now grew *very* pale;—but I talked more fluently, and with a heightened voice. Yet the sound increased—and what could I do? It was *a low, dull, quick sound—much such a sound as a watch makes when enveloped in cotton*. I gasped for breath—and yet the officers heard it not. I talked more quickly—more vehemently; but the noise steadily increased. I arose and argued about trifles, in a high key and with violent gesticulations, but the noise steadily increased. Why *would* they not be gone? I paced the floor to and fro with heavy strides, as if excited to fury by the observation of the men—but the noise steadily increased. Oh God! what *could* I do? I foamed—I raved—I swore! I swung the chair upon which I had been sitting, and grated it upon the boards, but the noise arose over all and continually increased. It grew louder—louder—*louder!* And still the men chatted pleasantly, and smiled. Was it possible they heard not? Almighty God!—no, no! They heard!—they suspected!—they *knew!*—they were making a mockery of my horror!—this I thought, and this I think. But any thing was better than this agony! Any thing was more tolerable than this derision! I could bear those hypocritical smiles no longer! I felt that I must scream or die!—and now—again!—hark! louder! louder! louder! *louder!*—

"Villains!" I shrieked, "dissemble no more! I admit the deed!—tear up the planks!—here, here!—it is the beating of his hideous heart!"

NATHANIEL HAWTHORNE

Young Goodman Brown

Nathaniel Hawthorne (1804–1864), American writer of short stories and novels, was born into a Puritan family in Salem, Mass. After graduating from Bowdoin College in 1825, Hawthorne, desirous of becoming a writer, isolated himself in his uncle's house in Salem. During this period he produced *Fanshawe*, 1828, and wrote many of the tales later collected in *Twice-Told Tales*, 1837. In 1842 he married Sophia Peabody and moved to Concord, Mass. Despite his masterfully crafted short stories, Hawthorne is perhaps today best remembered as a novelist; yet he was 46 years old before he published his first major novel, *The Scarlet Letter*, 1850, which brought him immediate national acclaim. Soon afterwards he wrote *The House of the Seven Gables*, 1851, and *The Blithedale Romance*, 1852. His last work was *The Marble Faun*, 1860.

Hawthorne's highly allegorical "Young Goodman Brown" recounts the temptation of a young Salem Puritan. Although paralleling Christ's temptation in the wilderness, Young Goodman Brown's night in the Salem woods ends quite differently.

Young Goodman Brown came forth at sunset, into the street of Salem village, but put his head back, after crossing the threshold, to exchange a parting kiss with his young wife. And Faith, as the wife was aptly named, thrust her own pretty head into the street, letting the wind play with the pink ribbons of her cap, while she called to Goodman Brown.

"Dearest heart," whispered she, softly and rather sadly, when her lips were close to his ear, "prithee, put off your journey until sunrise, and sleep in your own bed to-night. A lone woman is troubled with such dreams and such thoughts, that she's afeard of herself, sometimes. Pray, tarry with me this night, dear husband, of all nights in the year!"

"My love and my Faith," replied young Goodman Brown, "of all nights in the year, this one night must I tarry away from thee. My journey, as thou callest it, forth and back again, must needs be done 'twixt now and sunrise. What, my sweet, pretty wife, dost thou doubt me already, and we but three months married!"

"Then God bless you!" said Faith with the pink ribbons, "and may you find all well, when you come back."

"Amen!" cried Goodman Brown. "Say thy prayers, dear Faith, and go to bed at dusk, and no harm will come to thee."

So they parted; and the young man pursued his way, until, being about to turn the corner by the meeting-house, he looked back and saw the head of Faith still peeping after him, with a melancholy air, in spite of her pink ribbons.

"Poor little Faith!" thought he, for his heart smote him. "What a wretch am I, to leave her on such an errand! She talks of dreams, too. Methought, as she spoke, there was trouble in her face, as if a dream had warned her what work is to be done to-night. But no, no! 't would kill her to think it. Well, she's a blessed angel on earth; and after this one night, I'll cling to her skirts and follow her to Heaven."

With this excellent resolve for the future, Goodman Brown felt himself justified in making more haste on his present evil purpose. He had taken a dreary road, darkened by all the gloomiest trees of the forest, which barely stood aside to let the narrow path creep through, and closed immediately behind. It was all as lonely as could be; and there is this peculiarity in such a solitude, that the traveller knows not who may be concealed by the innumerable trunks and the thick boughs overhead; so that, with lonely footsteps, he may yet be passing through an unseen multitude.

"There may be a devilish Indian behind every tree," said Goodman Brown to himself; and he glanced fearfully behind him, as he added, "What if the devil himself should be at my very elbow!"

His head being turned back, he passed a crook of the road, and looking forward again, beheld the figure of a man, in grave and decent attire, seated at the foot of an old tree. He arose at Goodman Brown's approach, and walked onward, side by side with him.

"You are late, Goodman Brown," said he. "The clock of the Old South was striking, as I came through Boston; and that is full fifteen minutes agone."

"Faith kept me back awhile," replied the young man, with a tremor in his voice, caused by the sudden appearance of his companion, though not wholly unexpected.

It was now deep dusk in the forest, and deepest in that part of it where these two were journeying. As nearly as could be discerned, the second traveller was about fifty years old, apparently in the same rank of life as Goodman Brown, and bearing a considerable resemblance to him, though perhaps more in expression than features. Still, they might have been taken for father and son. And yet, though the elder person was as simply clad as the younger, and as simple in manner too, he had an indescribable air of one who knew the world, and would not have felt abashed at the governor's dinner-table, or in King William's court, were it possible that his affairs should call him thither. But the only thing about him that could be fixed upon as remarkable, was his staff, which bore the likeness of a great black snake, so curiously wrought, that it might almost be seen to twist and wriggle itself like a living serpent. This, of course, must have been an ocular deception, assisted by the uncertain light.

"Come, Goodman Brown!" cried his fellow-traveller, "this is a dull pace for the beginning of a journey. Take my staff, if you are so soon weary."

"Friend," said the other, exchanging his slow pace for a full stop, "having kept covenant by meeting thee here, it is my purpose now to return whence I came. I have scruples, touching the matter thou wot'st of."

"Sayest thou so?" replied he of the serpent, smiling apart. "Let us walk on, nevertheless, reasoning as we go, and if I convince thee not, thou shalt turn back. We are but a little way in the forest, yet."

"Too far, too far!" exclaimed the goodman, unconsciously resuming his walk. "My father never went into the woods on such an errand, nor his father before him. We have been a race of honest men and good Christians, since the days of the martyrs. And shall I be the first of the name of Brown that ever took this path and kept—"

"Such company, thou wouldst say," observed the elder person, interrupting his pause. "Well said, Goodman Brown! I have been as well acquainted with your family as with ever a one among the Puritans; and that's no trifle to say. I helped your grandfather, the constable, when he lashed the Quaker woman so smartly through the streets of Salem. And it was I that brought your father a pitch-pine knot, kindled at my own hearth, to set fire to an Indian village, in King Phillip's war. They were good friends, both; and many a pleasant walk have we had along this path, and returned merrily after midnight. I would fain be friends with you, for their sake."

"If it be as thou sayest," replied Goodman Brown, "I marvel they never spoke of these matters. Or, verily, I marvel not, seeing that the least rumor of the sort would have driven them from New England. We are a people of prayer, and good works to boot, and abide no such wickedness."

"Wickedness or not," said the traveller with twisted staff, "I have a very general acquaintance here in New England. The deacons of many a church have drunk the communion wine with me; the selectmen, of divers towns, make me their chairman; and a majority of the Great and General Court are firm supporters of my interest. The governor and I, too—but these are state secrets."

"Can this be so!" cried Goodman Brown, with a stare of amazement at his undisturbed companion. "Howbeit, I have nothing to do with the governor and council; they have their own ways, and are no rule for a simple husbandman like me. But, were I to go on with thee, how should I meet the eye of that good old man, our minister, at Salem village? Oh, his voice would make me tremble, both Sabbath-day and lecture-day!"

Thus far, the elder traveller had listened with due gravity, but now burst into a fit of irrepressible mirth, shaking himself so violently, that his snakelike staff actually seemed to wriggle in sympathy.

"Ha! ha! ha!" shouted he, again and again; then composing himself, "Well, go on, Goodman Brown, go on; but, prithee, don't kill me with laughing!"

"Well, then, to end the matter at once," said Goodman Brown, considerably nettled, "there is my wife, Faith. It would break her dear little heart; and I'd rather break my own!"

"Nay, if that be the case," answered the other, "e'en go thy ways, Goodman Brown. I would not, for twenty old women like the one hobbling before us, that Faith should come to any harm."

As he spoke, he pointed his staff at a female figure on the path, in whom Goodman Brown recognized a very pious and exemplary dame, who had taught him his catechism in youth, and was still his moral and spiritual adviser, jointly with the minister and Deacon Gookin.

"A marvel, truly, that Goody Cloyse should be so far in the wilderness, at nightfall!" said he. "But, with your leave friend, I shall take a cut through the woods, until we have left this Christian woman behind. Being a stranger to you, she might ask whom I was consorting with, and whither I was going."

"Be it so," said his fellow-traveller. "Betake you to the woods, and let me keep the path."

Accordingly, the young man turned aside, but took care to watch his companion, who advanced softly along the road, until he came within a staff's length of the old dame. She, meanwhile, was making the best of her way, with singular speed for so aged a woman, and mumbling some indistinct words; a prayer, doubtless, as she went. The traveller put forth his staff, and touched her withered neck with what seemed the serpent's tail.

"The devil!" screamed the pious old lady.

"Then Goody Cloyse knows her old friend?" observed the traveller, confronting her, and leaning on his writhing stick.

"Ah, forsooth, and is it your worship, indeed?" cried the good dame. "Yea, truly is it, and in the very image of my old gossip, Goodman Brown, the grandfather of the silly fellow that now is. But, would your worship believe it? my broomstick hath strangely disappeared, stolen, as I suspect, by that unhanged witch, Goody Cory, and that, too, when I was all anointed with the juice of smallage and cinque-foil and wolf's bane—"

"Mingled with fine wheat and the fat of a new-born babe," said the shape of old Goodman Brown.

"Ah, your worship knows the recipe," cried the old lady, cackling aloud. "So, as I was saying, being all ready for the meeting, and no horse to ride on, I made up my mind to foot it; for they tell me there is a nice young man to be taken into communion to-night. But now your good worship will lend me your arm, and we shall be there in a twinkling."

"That can hardly be," answered her friend. "I may not spare you my arm, Goody Cloyse, but here is my staff, if you will."

So saying, he threw it down at her feet, where, perhaps, it assumed life, being one of the rods which its owner had formerly lent to the Egyptian Magi. Of this fact, however, Goodman Brown could not take cognizance. He had cast up his eyes in astonishment, and looking down again, beheld neither Goody Cloyse nor the serpentine staff, but his fellow-traveller alone, who waited for him as calmly as if nothing had happened.

"That old woman taught me my catechism!" said the young man; and there was a world of meaning in this simple comment.

They continued to walk onward, while the elder traveller exhorted his companion to make good speed and persevere in the path, discoursing so aptly, that his arguments seemed rather to spring up in the bosom of his auditor, than to be suggested by himself. As they went he plucked a branch of maple, to serve for a walking-stick, and began to strip it of the twigs and little boughs, which were wet with evening dew. The moment his fingers touched them, they became strangely withered and dried up, as with a week's sunshine. Thus the pair proceeded, at a good free pace, until suddenly, in a gloomy hollow of the road, Goodman Brown sat himself down on the stump of a tree, and refused to go any farther.

"Friend," said he, stubbornly, "my mind is

made up. Not another step will I budge on this errand. What if a wretched old woman do choose to go to the devil, when I thought she was going to Heaven! Is that any reason why I should quit my dear Faith, and go after her?"

"You will think better of this by and by," said his acquaintance, composedly. "Sit here and rest yourself awhile; and when you feel like moving again, there is my staff to help you along."

Without more words, he threw his companion the maple stick, and was as speedily out of sight as if he had vanished into the deepening gloom. The young man sat a few moments by the road-side, applauding himself greatly, and thinking with how clear a conscience he should meet the minister, in his morning walk, nor shrink from the eye of good old Deacon Gookin. And what calm sleep would be his, that very night, which was to have been spent so wickedly, but purely and sweetly now, in the arms of Faith! Amidst these pleasant and praiseworthy meditations, Goodman Brown heard the tramp of horses along the road, and deemed it advisable to conceal himself within the verge of the forest, conscious of the guilty purpose that had brought him thither, though now so happily turned from it.

On came the hoof-tramps and the voices of the riders, two grave old voices, conversing soberly as they drew near. These mingled sounds appeared to pass along the road, within a few yards of the young man's hiding-place; but owing, doubtless, to the depth of the gloom, at that particular spot, neither the travellers nor their steeds were visible. Though their figures brushed the small boughs by the wayside, it could not be seen that they intercepted, even for a moment, the faint gleam from the strip of bright sky, athwart which they must have passed. Goodman Brown alternately crouched and stood on tiptoe, pulling aside the branches, and thrusting forth his head as far as he durst, without discerning so much as a shadow. It vexed him the more, because he could have sworn, were such a thing possible, that he recognized the voices of the minister and Deacon Gookin, jogging along quietly, as they were wont to do, when bound to some ordination or ecclesiastical council. While yet within hearing, one of the riders stopped to pluck a switch.

"Of the two, reverend Sir," said the voice like the deacon's, "I had rather miss an ordination dinner than to-night's meeting. They tell me that some of our community are to be here from Falmouth and beyond, and others from Connecticut and Rhode Island; besides several of the Indian powwows, who, after their fashion, know almost as much deviltry as the best of us. Moreover, there is a goodly young woman to be taken into communion."

"Mighty well, Deacon Gookin!" replied the solemn old tones of the minister. "Spur up, or we shall be late. Nothing can be done, you know, until I get on the ground."

The hoofs clattered again, and the voices, talking so strangely in the empty air, passed on through the forest, where no church had ever been gathered, nor solitary Christian prayed. Whither, then, could these holy men be journeying, so deep into the heathen wilderness? Young Goodman Brown caught hold of a tree, for support, being ready to sink down on the ground, faint and over-burthened with the heavy sickness of his heart. He looked up to the sky, doubting whether there really was a Heaven above him. Yet, there was the blue arch, and the stars brightening in it.

"With Heaven above, and Faith below, I will yet stand firm against the devil!" cried Goodman Brown.

While he still gazed upward, into the deep arch of the firmament, and had lifted his hands to pray, a cloud, though no wind was stirring, hurried across the zenith, and hid the brightening stars. The blue sky was still visible, except directly overhead, where this black mass of cloud was sweeping swiftly northward. Aloft in the air, as if from the depths of the cloud, came a confused and doubtful sound of voices. Once, the listener fancied that he could distinguish the accents of town's-people of his own, men and women, both pious and ungodly, many of whom he had met at the communion-table, and had seen others rioting at the tavern. The next moment, so indistinct were the sounds, he doubted whether he had heard aught but the murmur of the old forest, whispering without a wind. Then came a stronger swell of those familiar tones, heard daily in the sunshine, at Salem village, but never, until now, from a cloud at night. There was one voice, of a young woman, uttering lamentations, yet with an uncertain sorrow, and entreating for some favor, which, perhaps, it would grieve her to obtain. And all the unseen multitude, both saints and sinners, seemed to encourage her onward.

"Faith!" shouted Goodman Brown, in a voice of agony and desperation; and the echoes of the forest mocked him, crying—"Faith! Faith!" as if bewildered wretches were seeking her, all through the wilderness.

The cry of grief, rage, and terror was yet piercing the night, when the unhappy husband held his breath for a response. There was a scream, drowned immediately in a louder mumur of voices fading into far-off laughter, as the dark cloud swept away, leaving the clear and silent sky above Goodman Brown. But something fluttered lightly down through the air, and caught on the branch of a tree. The young man seized it and beheld a pink ribbon.

"My Faith is gone!" cried he, after one stupefied moment. "There is no good on earth and sin is but a name. Come, devil! for to thee is this world given."

And maddened with despair, so that he laughed loud and long, did Goodman Brown grasp his staff and set forth again, at such a rate, that he seemed to fly along the forest path, rather than to walk or run. The road grew wilder and drearier, and more faintly traced, and vanished at length, leaving him in the heart of the dark wilderness, still rushing onward, with the instinct that guides mortal man to evil. The whole forest was peopled with frightful sounds; the creaking of the trees, the howling of wild beasts, and the yell of Indians; while, sometimes, the wind tolled like a distant church bell, and sometimes gave a broad roar around the traveller, as if all Nature were laughing him to scorn. But he was himself the chief horror of the scene, and shrank not from its other horrors.

"Ha! ha! ha!" roared Goodman Brown, when the wind laughed at him. "Let us hear which will laugh loudest! Think not to frighten me with your deviltry! Come witch, come wizard, come Indian powwow, come devil himself! and here comes Goodman Brown. You may as well fear him as he fear you!"

In truth, all through the haunted forest, there could be nothing more frightful than the figure of Goodman Brown. On he flew, among the black pines, brandishing his staff with frenzied gestures, now giving vent to an inspiration of horrid blasphemy, and now shouting forth such laughter, as set all the echoes of the forest laughing like demons around him. The fiend in his own shape is less hideous, than when he rages in the breast of man. Thus sped the demoniac on his course, until, quivering among the trees, he saw a red light before him, as when the felled trunks and branches of a clearing have been set on fire, and throw up their lurid blaze against the sky, at the hour of midnight. He paused, in a lull of the tempest that had driven him onward, and heard the swell of what seemed a hymn, rolling solemnly from a distance, with the weight of many voices. He knew the tune. It was a familiar one in the choir of the village meeting-house. The verse died heavily away, and was lengthened by a chorus, not of human voices, but of all the sounds of the benighted wilderness, pealing in awful harmony together. Goodman Brown cried out; and his cry was lost to his own ear, by its unison with the cry of the desert.

In the interval of silence, he stole forward, until the light glared full upon his eyes. At one extremity of an open space, hemmed in by the dark wall of the forest, arose a rock, bearing some rude, natural resemblance either to an altar or a pulpit, and surrounded by four blazing pines, their tops aflame, their stems untouched, like candles at an evening meeting. The mass of foliage, that had overgrown the summit of the rock, was all on fire, blazing high into the night, and fitfully illuminating the whole field. Each pendent twig and leafy festoon was in a blaze. As the red light arose and fell, a numerous congregation alternately shone forth, then disappeared in shadow, and again grew, as it were, out of the darkness, peopling the heart of the solitary woods at once.

"A grave and dark-clad company!" quoth Goodman Brown.

In truth, they were such. Among them, quivering to-and-fro, between gloom and splendor, appeared faces that would be seen, next day, at the council-board of the province, and others which, Sabbath after Sabbath, looked devoutly heavenward, and benignantly over the crowded pews, from the holiest pulpits in the land. Some affirm that the lady of the governor was there. At least, there were high dames well known to her, and wives of honored husbands, and widows a great multitude, and ancient maidens, all of excellent repute, and fair young girls, who trembled lest their mothers should espy them. Either the sudden gleams of light, flashing over the obscure field, bedazzled Goodman Brown, or he recognized a score of the church members of Salem village, famous for their especial sanctity. Good old Deacon Gookin had arrived, and waited at the skirts of that venerable saint, his reverend pastor. But, irreverently consorting with these grave, reputable, and pious people, these elders of the church, these chaste dames and dewy virgins, there were men of dissolute lives and women of spotted fame, wretches given over to all mean and filthy vice, and suspected even of horrid crimes. It was strange to see, that the good shrank not from the wicked, nor were the sinners abashed by the saints. Scattered, also, among their pale-faced enemies, were the Indian priests, or powwows, who had often scared their native forest with more hideous incantations than any known to English witchcraft.

"But, where is Faith?" thought Goodman Brown; and, as hope came into his heart, he trembled.

Another verse of the hymn arose, a slow and mournful strain, such as the pious love, but joined to words which expressed all that our nature can conceive of sin, and darkly hinted at far more. Unfathomable to mere mortals is the lore of fiends. Verse after verse was sung, and still the chorus of the desert swelled between, like the deepest tone of a mighty organ. And, with the final peal of that dreadful anthem, there came a sound, as if the roaring wind, the rushing streams, the howling beasts, and every other voice of the unconverted wilderness were mingling and according with the voice of guilty man, in homage to the prince of all. The four blazing pines threw up a loftier flame, and obscurely discovered shapes and visages of horror on the smoke-wreaths, above the impious assembly. At the same moment, the fire on the rock shot redly forth, and formed a glowing arch above its base, where now appeared a figure. With reverence be it spoken, the apparition bore no slight similitude, both in garb and manner, to some grave divine of the New England churches.

"Bring forth the converts!" cried a voice, that echoed through the field and rolled into the forest.

At the word, Goodman Brown stepped forth from the shadow of the trees, and approached the congregation, with whom he felt a loathful brotherhood, by the sympathy of all that was wicked in his heart. He could have well-nigh sworn, that the shape of his own dead father beckoned him to advance, looking downward from a smoke-wreath, while a woman, with dim features of despair, threw out her hand to warn him back. Was it his mother? But he had no power to retreat one step, nor to resist, even in thought, when the minister and good old Deacon Gookin seized his arms, and led him to the blazing rock. Thither came also the slender form of a veiled female, led between Goody Cloyse, that pious teacher of the catechism, and Martha Carrier, who had received the devil's promise to be queen of hell. A rampant hag was she! And there stood the proselytes, beneath the canopy of fire.

"Welcome, my children," said the dark figure, "to the communion of your race! Ye have found, thus young, your nature and your destiny. My children, look behind you!"

They turned; and flashing forth, as it were, in a sheet of flame, the fiend-worshippers were seen; the smile of welcome gleamed darkly on every visage.

"There," resumed the sable form, "are all whom ye have reverenced from youth. Ye deemed them holier than yourselves, and shrank from your own sin, contrasting it with their lives of righteousness and prayerful aspirations heavenward. Yet, here are they all, in my worshipping assembly! This night it shall be granted you to know their secret deeds; how hoary-bearded elders of the church have whispered wanton words to the young maids of their households; how many a woman, eager for widow's weeds, has given her husband a drink at bedtime, and let him sleep his last sleep in her bosom; how beardless youths have made haste to inherit their father's wealth; and how fair damsels—blush not, sweet ones!—have dug little graves in the garden, and bidden me, the sole guest, to an infant's funeral. By the sympathy of your human hearts for sin, ye shall scent out all the places—whether in church, bed-chamber, street, field, or forest—where crime has been committed, and shall exult to behold the whole earth one stain of guilt, one mighty blood-spot. Far more than this! It shall be yours to penetrate, in every bosom, the deep mystery of sin, the fountain of all wicked arts, and which inexhaustibly supplies more evil impulses than human power—than my power, at its utmost!—can make manifest in deeds. And now, my children, look upon each other."

They did so; and, by the blaze of the hell-kindled torches, the wretched man beheld his Faith, and the wife her husband, trembling before that unhallowed altar.

"Lo! there ye stand, my children," said the figure, in a deep and solemn tone, almost sad, with its despairing awfulness, as if his once angelic nature could yet mourn for our miserable race. "Depending upon one another's hearts, ye had still hoped that virtue were not all a dream! Now are ye undeceived!—Evil is the nature of mankind. Evil must be your only happiness. Welcome, again, my children, to the communion of your race!"

"Welcome!" repeated the fiend-worshippers, in one cry of despair and triumph.

And there they stood, the only pair, as it seemed, who were yet hesitating on the verge of wickedness, in this dark world. A basin was hollowed, naturally, in the rock. Did it contain water, reddened by the lurid light? or was it blood? or, perchance, a liquid flame? Herein did the Shape of Evil dip his hand, and prepare to lay the mark of baptism upon their foreheads, that they might be partakers of the mystery of sin, more conscious of the secret guilt of others, both in deed and thought, than they could now be of their own. The husband cast one look at his pale wife, and Faith at him. What polluted wretches would the next glance show them to each other, shuddering alike at what they disclosed and what they saw!

"Faith! Faith!" cried the husband. "Look up to Heaven, and resist the Wicked One!"

Whether Faith obeyed, he knew not. Hardly had he spoken, when he found himself amid calm night and solitude, listening to a roar of the wind, which died heavily away through the forest. He staggered against the rock, and felt it chill and damp, while a hanging twig, that had been all on fire, besprinkled his cheek with the coldest dew.

The next morning, young Goodman Brown came slowly into the street of Salem village staring around him like a bewildered man. The good old minister was taking a walk along the graveyard, to get an appetite for breakfast and meditate his sermon, and bestowed a blessing, as he passed, on Goodman Brown. He shrank from the venerable saint, as if to avoid an anathema. Old Deacon Gookin was at domestic worship, and the holy words of his prayer were heard through the open window. "What God doth the wizard pray to?" quoth Goodman Brown. Goody Cloyse, that excellent old Christian, stood in the early sunshine, at her own lattice, catechising a little girl, who had brought her a pint of morning's milk. Goodman Brown snatched away the child, as from the grasp of the fiend himself. Turning the corner by the meetinghouse, he spied the head of Faith, with the pink ribbons, gazing anxiously forth, and bursting into such joy at sight of him that she skipt along the street, and almost kissed her husband before the whole village. But Goodman Brown looked sternly and sadly into her face, and passed on without a greeting.

Had Goodman Brown fallen asleep in the forest, and only dreamed a wild dream of a witch-meeting?

Be it so, if you will. But, alas! it was a dream of evil omen for young Goodman Brown. A stern, a sad, a darkly meditative, a distrustful, if not a desperate man did he become, from the night of that fearful dream. On the Sabbath day, when the congregation were singing a holy psalm, he could not listen, because an anthem of sin rushed loudly upon his ear, and drowned all the blessed strain. When the minister spoke from the pulpit, with power and fervid eloquence, and with his hand on the open Bible, of the sacred truths of our religion, and of saint-like lives and triumphant deaths, and of future bliss or misery unutterable, then did Goodman Brown turn pale, dreading lest the roof should thunder down upon the gray blasphemer and his hearers. Often, awaking suddenly at midnight, he shrank from the bosom of Faith, and at morning or eventide, when the family knelt down at prayer, he scowled, and muttered to himself, and gazed sternly at his wife, and turned away. And when he had lived long, and was borne to his grave, a hoary corpse, followed by Faith, an aged woman, and children and grandchildren, a goodly procession, besides neighbors not a few, they carved no hopeful verse upon his tombstone; for his dying hour was gloom.

LEO TOLSTOY

The Three Hermits

TRANSLATED FROM THE RUSSIAN BY LOUISE AND AYLMER MAUDE

Leo Nikolaevich Tolstoy (1828–1910), Russian nobleman and writer, known for two of the world's greatest novels—*War and Peace* and *Anna Karenina*—abandoned the restrictions of his aristocratic class to become an intellectual, assuming very liberal positions on many moral and religious questions. Tolstoy's influence spread far beyond the borders of his homeland, pervading Western culture to such an extent that George Bernard Shaw was moved to call him a masterful voice in art and literature. In addition to his great novels, Tolstoy also wrote short stories, plays, essays, and a study of economics. His works reflect his strong moral convictions, his realism, and his heightened sense of imaginative perspective.

"The Three Hermits," written in 1886, displays Tolstoy's use of folktales to illustrate his ironic vision of conventional interpretations of religious beliefs.

And in praying use not vain repetitions, as the Gentiles do: for they think that they shall be heard for their much speaking. Be not therefore like unto them: for your Father knoweth what things ye have need of, before ye ask Him.

MATTHEW 6:7–8

A bishop was sailing from Archangel to the Solovétsk Monastery, and on the same vessel were a number of pilgrims on their way to visit the shrines at that place. The voyage was a smooth one, the wind favourable and the weather fair. The pilgrims lay on deck, eating, or sat in groups talking to one another. The Bishop, too, came on deck, and as he was pacing up and down he noticed a group of men standing near the prow and listening to a fisherman, who was pointing to the sea and telling them something. The Bishop stopped, and looked in the direction in which the man was pointing. He could see

THE THREE HERMITS From *Twenty-three Tales by Leo Tolstoy*, translated by Louise and Aylmer Maude (1906). Reprinted by permission of Oxford University Press.

nothing, however, but the sea glistening in the sunshine. He drew nearer to listen, but when the man saw him, he took off his cap and was silent. The rest of the people also took off their caps and bowed.

"Do not let me disturb you, friends," said the Bishop. "I came to hear what this good man was saying."

"The fisherman was telling us about the hermits," replied one, a tradesman, rather bolder than the rest.

"What hermits?" asked the Bishop, going to the side of the vessel and seating himself on a box. "Tell me about them. I should like to hear. What were you pointing at?"

"Why, that little island you can just see over there," answered the man, pointing to a spot ahead and a little to the right. "That is the island where the hermits live for the salvation of their souls."

"Where is the island?" asked the Bishop. "I see nothing."

"There, in the distance, if you will please look along my hand. Do you see that little cloud?

Below it, and a bit to the left, there is just a faint streak. That is the island."

The Bishop looked carefully, but his unaccustomed eyes could make out nothing but the water shimmering in the sun.

"I cannot see it," he said. "But who are the hermits that live there?"

"They are holy men," answered the fisherman. "I had long heard tell of them, but never chanced to see them myself till the year before last."

And the fisherman related how once, when he was out fishing, he had been stranded at night upon that island, not knowing where he was. In the morning, as he wandered about the island, he came across an earth hut, and met an old man standing near it. Presently two others came out, and after having fed him and dried his things, they helped him mend his boat.

"And what are they like?" asked the Bishop.

"One is a small man and his back is bent. He wears a priest's cassock and is very old; he must be more than a hundred, I should say. He is so old that the white of his beard is taking a greenish tinge, but he is always smiling, and his face is as bright as an angel's from heaven. The second is taller, but he also is very old. He wears a tattered peasant coat. His beard is broad, and of a yellowish grey colour. He is a strong man. Before I had time to help him, he turned my boat over as if it were only a pail. He too is kindly and cheerful. The third is tall, and has a beard as white as snow and reaching to his knees. He is stern, with overhanging eyebrows; and he wears nothing but a piece of matting tied round his waist."

"And did they speak to you?" asked the Bishop.

"For the most part they did everything in silence, and spoke but little even to one another. One of them would just give a glance, and the others would understand him. I asked the tallest whether they had lived there long. He frowned, and muttered something as if he were angry; but the oldest one took his hand and smiled, and then the tall one was quiet. The oldest one only said: 'Have mercy upon us,' and smiled."

While the fisherman was talking, the ship had drawn nearer to the island.

"There, now you can see it plainly, if your Lordship will please to look," said the tradesman, pointing with his hand.

The Bishop looked, and now he really saw a dark streak—which was the island. Having looked at it a while, he left the prow of the vessel, and going to the stern, asked the helmsman:

"What island is that?"

"That one," replied the man, "has no name. There are many such in this sea."

"Is it true that there are hermits who live there for the salvation of their souls?"

"So it is said, Your Lordship, but I don't know if it's true. Fisherman say they have seen them; but of course they may only be spinning yarns."

"I should like to land on the island and see these men," said the Bishop. "How could I manage it?"

"The ship cannot get close to the island," replied the helmsman, "but you might be rowed there in a boat. You had better speak to the captain."

The captain was sent for and came.

"I should like to see these hermits," said the Bishop. "Could I not be rowed ashore?"

The captain tried to dissuade him.

"Of course it could be done," said he, "but we should lose much time. And if I might venture to say so to your Lordship, the old men are not worth your pains. I have heard say that they are foolish old fellows, who understand nothing, and never speak a word, any more than the fish in the sea."

"I wish to see them," said the Bishop, "and I will pay you for your trouble and loss of time. Please let me have a boat."

There was no help for it; so the order was given. The sailors trimmed the sails, the steersman put up the helm, and the ship's course was set for the island. A chair was placed at the prow for the Bishop, and he sat there, looking ahead. The passengers all collected at the prow, and gazed at the island. Those who had the sharpest eyes could presently make out the rocks on it, and then a mud hut was seen. At last one man saw the hermits themselves. The captain brought a telescope and, after looking through it, handed it to the Bishop.

"It's right enough. There are three men standing on the shore. There, a little to the right of that big rock."

The Bishop took the telescope, got it into position, and he saw the three men: a tall one, a shorter one, and one very small and bent, standing on the shore and holding each other by the hand.

The captain turned to the Bishop.

"The vessel can get no nearer in than this, your Lordship. If you wish to go ashore, we must ask you to go in the boat, while we anchor here."

The cable was quickly let out; the anchor cast, and the sails furled. There was a jerk, and the vessel shook. Then, a boat having been lowered, the oarsmen jumped in, and the Bishop descended the ladder and took his seat. The men pulled at their oars and the boat moved rapidly towards the island. When they came within a stone's throw, they saw three old men: a tall one with only a piece of matting tied round his waist, a shorter one in a tattered peasant coat, and a very old one bent with age and wearing an old cassock—all three standing hand in hand.

The oarsmen pulled in to the shore, and held on with the boathook while the Bishop got out.

The old men bowed to him, and he gave them his blessing, at which they bowed still lower. Then the Bishop began to speak to them.

"I have heard," he said, "that you, godly men, live here saving your own souls and praying to our Lord Christ for your fellow men. I, an unworthy servant of Christ, am called, by God's mercy, to keep and teach His flock. I wished to see you, servants of God, and to do what I can to teach you, also."

The old men looked at each other, smiling, but remained silent.

"Tell me," said the Bishop, "what you are doing to save your souls, and how you serve God on this island."

The second hermit sighed, and looked at the oldest, the very ancient one. The latter smiled, and said:

"We do not know how to serve God. We only serve and support ourselves, servant of God."

"But how do you pray to God?" asked the Bishop.

"We pray in this way," replied the hermit. "'Three are ye, three are we, have mercy upon us.'"

And when the old man said this, all three raised their eyes to heaven, and repeated:

"Three are ye, three are we, have mercy upon us!"

The Bishop smiled.

"You have evidently heard something about the Holy Trinity," said he. "But you do not pray aright. You have won my affection, godly men. I see you wish to please the Lord, but you do not know how to serve Him. That is not the way to pray; but listen to me, and I will teach you. I will teach you, not a way of my own, but the way in which God in the Holy Scriptures has commanded all men to pray to Him."

And the Bishop began explaining to the hermits how God had revealed Himself to men; telling them of God the Father, and God the Son, and God the Holy Ghost.

"God the Son came down on earth," said he, "to save men, and this is how He taught us all to pray. Listen, and repeat after me: 'Our Father.'"

And the first old man repeated after him, "Our Father," and the second said, "Our Father," and the third said, "Our Father."

"Which art in heaven," continued the Bishop.

The first hermit repeated, "Which art in heaven," but the second blundered over the words, and the tall hermit could not say them properly. His hair had grown over his mouth so that he could not speak plainly. The very old hermit, having no teeth, also mumbled indistinctly.

The Bishop repeated the words again, and the old men repeated them after him. The Bishop sat down on a stone, and the old men stood before him, watching his mouth, and repeating the words as he uttered them. And all day long the Bishop laboured, saying a word twenty, thirty, a hundred times over, and the old men repeated it after him. They blundered, and he corrected them, and made them begin again.

The Bishop did not leave off till he had taught them the whole of the Lord's Prayer so that they could not only repeat it after him, but could say it by themselves. The middle one was the first to know it, and to repeat the whole of it alone. The Bishop made him say it again and again, and at last the others could say it too.

It was getting dark and the moon was appearing over the water, before the Bishop rose to return to the vessel. When he took leave of the old men they all bowed down to the ground before him. He raised them, and kissed each of them, telling them to pray as he had taught them. Then he got into the boat and returned to the ship.

And as he sat in the boat and was rowed to the ship he could hear the three voices of the hermits loudly repeating the Lord's Prayer. As the boat drew near the vessel their voices could no longer be heard, but they could still be seen in the moonlight, standing as he had left them on the shore, the shortest in the middle, the tallest on the right, the middle one on the left. As soon as the Bishop had reached the vessel and got on board, the anchor was weighed and the sails unfurled. The wind filled them and the ship sailed away, and the Bishop took a seat in the stern and watched the island they had left. For a time he could still see the hermits, but presently they disappeared from sight, though the island was still visible. At last it too vanished, and only the sea was to be seen, rippling in the moonlight.

The pilgrims lay down to sleep, and all was quiet on deck. The Bishop did not wish to sleep, but sat alone at the stern, gazing at the sea where the island was no longer visible, and thinking of the good old men. He thought how pleased they had been to learn the Lord's Prayer; and he thanked God for having sent him to teach and help such godly men.

So the Bishop sat, thinking, and gazing at the sea where the island had disappeared. And the moonlight flickered before his eyes, sparkling, now here, now there, upon the waves. Suddenly he saw something white and shining, on the bright path which the moon cast across the sea. Was it a seagull, or the little gleaming sail of some small boat? The Bishop fixed his eyes on it, wondering.

"It must be a boat sailing after us," thought he, "but it is overtaking us very rapidly. It was far, far away a minute ago, but now it is much nearer. It cannot be a boat, for I can see no sail; but whatever it may be, it is following us and catching us up."

And he could not make out what it was. Not a boat, nor a bird, nor a fish! It was too large for a man, and besides a man could not be out there in the midst of the sea. The Bishop rose, and said to the helmsman:

"Look there, what is that, my friend? What is it?" the Bishop repeated, though he could now see plainly what it was—the three hermits running upon the water, all gleaming white, their grey beards shining, and approaching the ship as quickly as though it were not moving.

The steersman looked, and let go the helm in terror.

"Oh Lord! The hermits are running after us on the water as though it were dry land!"

The passengers, hearing him, jumped up and crowded to the stern. They saw the hermits coming along hand in hand, and the two outer ones beckoning the ship to stop. All three were gliding along upon the water without moving their feet. Before the ship could be stopped, the hermits had reached it, and raising their heads, all three as with one voice, began to say:

"We have forgotten your teaching, servant of God. As long as we kept repeating it we remembered, but when we stopped saying it for a time, a word dropped out, and now it has all gone to pieces. We can remember nothing of it. Teach us again."

The Bishop crossed himself, and leaning over the ship's side, said:

"Your own prayer will reach the Lord, men of God. It is not for me to teach you. Pray for us sinners."

And the Bishop bowed low before the old men; and they turned and went back across the sea. And a light shone until daybreak on the spot where they were lost to sight.

STEPHEN CRANE

The Open Boat

Stephen Crane (1871–1900), novelist, poet, journalist, and biographer, began his literary career by writing a startlingly realistic novel, *Maggie: A Girl of the Streets,* 1892. His second novel, *The Red Badge of Courage,* published in 1895, brought him fame. He was a war correspondent for Hearst's New York *Journal* during the Greco-Turkish War. After returning from Greece, Crane married and went to live in England, where he became a friend of Joseph Conrad. In 1898 he distinguished himself by his objective reporting from Cuba of the Spanish-American War. He contracted tuberculosis and died when he was only twenty-nine.

Crane's strongly realistic style did much to revolutionize the technique and style of American fiction. Carl and Mark Van Doren have commented, "Modern American fiction may be said to begin with Stephen Crane." H. G. Wells called "The Open Boat" the "finest short story in English." The story is based on an actual experience of Crane's, as indicated in the original subtitle—"A Fate Intended to Be After the Fact: Being the Experience of Four Men from the Sunk Steamer *Commodore.*" Thoughtful readers will agree with Conrad, who commented, "The simple humanity of its presentation seems somehow to illustrate the essentials of life itself, like a symbolic tale."

None of them knew the color of the sky. Their eyes glanced level, and were fastened upon the waves that swept toward them. These waves were of the hue of slate, save for the tops, which were of foaming white, and all of the men knew the colors of the sea. The horizon narrowed and widened, and dipped and rose, and at all times its edge was jagged with waves that seemed thrust up in points like rocks.

Many a man ought to have a bath-tub larger than the boat which here rode upon the sea. These waves were most wrongfully and barbarously abrupt and tall, and each froth-top was a problem in small-boat navigation.

The cook squatted in the bottom and looked with both eyes at the six inches of gunwale which separated him from the ocean. His sleeves were

THE OPEN BOAT From *Stephen Crane: An Omnibus,* edited by Robert Wooster Stallman, by permission of Alfred A. Knopf, Inc. Copyright 1952 by Alfred A. Knopf, Inc.

rolled over his fat forearms, and the two flaps of his unbuttoned vest dangled as he bent to bail out the boat. Often he said: "Gawd! That was a narrow clip." As he remarked it he invariably gazed eastward over the broken sea.

The oiler, steering with one of the two oars in the boat, sometimes raised himself suddenly to keep clear of water that swirled in over the stern. It was a thin little oar and it seemed often ready to snap.

The correspondent, pulling at the other oar, watched the waves and wondered why he was there.

The injured captain, lying in the bow, was at this time buried in that profound dejection and indifference which comes, temporarily at least, to even the bravest and most enduring when, willy-nilly, the firm fails, the army loses, the ship goes down. The mind of the master of a vessel is rooted deep in the timbers of her, though he command for a day or a decade, and this captain had on him the stern impression of a scene in the grays of dawn of seven turned faces, and later a stump of a top-mast with a white ball on it that slashed to and fro at the waves, went low and lower, and down. Thereafter there was something strange in his voice. Although steady, it was deep with mourning, and of a quality beyond oration or tears.

"Keep 'er a little more south, Billie," said he.

"A little more south, sir," said the oiler in the stern.

A seat in this boat was not unlike a seat upon a bucking bronco, and, by the same token, a bronco is not much smaller. The craft pranced and reared, and plunged like an animal. As each wave came, and she rose for it, she seemed like a horse making at a fence outrageously high. The manner of her scramble over these walls of water is a mystic thing, and, moreover, at the top of them were ordinarily these problems in white water, the foam racing down from the summit of each wave, requiring a new leap, and a leap from the air. Then, after scornfully bumping a crest, she would slide, and race, and splash down a long incline, and arrive bobbing and nodding in front of the next menace.

A singular disadvantage of the sea lies in the fact that after successfully surmounting one wave you discover that there is another behind it just as important and just as nervously anxious to do something effective in the way of swamping boats. In a ten-foot dinghy one can get an idea of the resources of the sea in the line of waves that is not probable to the average experience which is never at sea in a dinghy. As each slaty wall of water approached, it shut all else from the view of the men in the boat, and it was not difficult to imagine that this particular wave was the final outburst of the ocean, the last effort of the grim water. There was a terrible grace in the move of the waves, and they came in silence, save for the snarling of the crests.

In the wan light, the faces of the men must have been gray. Their eyes must have glinted in strange ways as they gazed steadily astern. Viewed from a balcony, the whole thing would doubtless have been weirdly picturesque. But the men in the boat had no time to see it, and if they had had leisure there were other things to occupy their minds. The sun swung steadily up the sky, and they knew it was broad day because the color of the sea changed from slate to emerald-green, streaked with amber lights, and the foam was like tumbling snow. The process of the breaking day was unknown to them. They were aware only of this effect upon the color of the waves that rolled toward them.

In disjointed sentences the cook and the correspondent argued as to the difference between a life-saving station and a house of refuge. The cook had said: "There's a house of refuge just north of the Mosquito Inlet Light, and as soon as they see us, they'll come off in their boat and pick us up."

"As soon as who see us?" said the correspondent.

"The crew," said the cook.

"Houses of refuge don't have crews," said the correspondent. "As I understand them, they are only places where clothes and grub are stored for the benefit of shipwrecked people. They don't carry crews."

"Oh, yes, they do," said the cook.

"No, they don't," said the correspondent.

"Well, we're not there yet, anyhow," said the oiler, in the stern.

"Well," said the cook, "perhaps it's not a house of refuge that I'm thinking of as being near Mosquito Inlet Light. Perhaps it's a life-saving station."

"We're not there yet," said the oiler, in the stern.

II

As the boat bounced from the top of each wave, the wind tore through the hair of the hatless men, and as the craft plopped her stern down again the spray slashed past them. The crest of each of these waves was a hill, from the top of which the men surveyed, for a moment, a broad tumultuous expanse, shining and wind-driven. It was probably splendid. It was probably glorious, this play of the free sea, wild with lights of emerald and white and amber.

"Bully good thing it's an on-shore wind," said the cook. "If not, where would we be? Wouldn't have a show."

"That's right," said the correspondent.

The busy oiler nodded his assent.

Then the captain, in the bow, chuckled in a way that expressed humor, contempt, tragedy, all in one. "Do you think we've got much of a show now, boys?" said he.

Whereupon the three were silent, save for a trifle of hemming and hawing. To express any particular optimism at this time they felt to be childish and stupid, but they all doubtless possessed this sense of the situation in their mind. A young man thinks doggedly at such times. On the other hand, the ethics of their condition was decidedly against any open suggestion of hopelessness. So they were silent.

"Oh, well," said the captain, soothing his children, "we'll get ashore all right."

But there was that in his tone which made them think, so the oiler quoth: "Yes! If this wind holds!"

The cook was bailing: "Yes! If we don't catch hell in the surf."

Canton flannel gulls flew near and far. Sometimes they sat down on the sea, near patches of brown seaweed that rolled over the waves with a movement like carpets on a line in a gale. The birds sat comfortably in groups, and they were envied by some in the dinghy, for the wrath of the sea was no more to them than it was to a covey of prairie chickens a thousand miles inland. Often they came very close and stared at the men with black bead-like eyes. At these times they were uncanny and sinister in their unblinking scrutiny, and the men hooted angrily at them, telling them to be gone. One came, and evidently decided to alight on the top of the captain's head. The bird flew parallel to the boat and did not circle, but made short sidelong jumps in the air in chicken-fashion. His black eyes were wistfully fixed upon the captain's head. "Ugly brute," said the oiler to the bird. "You look as if you were made with a jackknife." The cook and the correspondent swore darkly at the creature. The captain naturally wished to knock it away with the end of the heavy painter; but he did not dare do it, because anything resembling an emphatic gesture would have capsized this freighted boat, and so, with his open hand, the captain gently and carefully waved the gull away. After it had been discouraged from the pursuit the captain breathed easier on account of his hair, and others breathed easier because the bird struck their minds at this time as being somehow gruesome and ominous.

In the meantime the oiler and the correspondent rowed. And also they rowed.

They sat together in the same seat, and each rowed an oar. Then the oiler took both oars; then the correspondent took both oars; then the oiler; then the correspondent. They rowed and they rowed. The very ticklish part of the business was when the time came for the reclining one in the stern to take his turn at the oars. By the very last star of truth, it is easier to steal eggs from under a hen than it was to change seats in the dinghy. First the man in the stern slid his hand along the thwart and moved with care, as if he were of Sèvres. Then the man in the rowing seat slid his hand along the other thwart. It was all done with the most extraordinary care. As the two sidled past each other, the whole party kept watchful eyes on the coming wave, and the captain cried: "Look out now! Steady there!"

The brown mats of seaweed that appeared from time to time were like islands, bits of earth. They were traveling, apparently, neither one way nor the other. They were, to all intents, stationary. They informed the men in the boat that it was making progress slowly toward the land.

The captain, rearing cautiously in the bow, after the dinghy soared on a great swell, said that he had seen the lighthouse at Mosquito Inlet. Presently the cook remarked that he had seen it. The correspondent was at the oars then, and for some reason he too wished to look at the lighthouse, but his back was toward the far shore and the waves were important, and for some time he could not seize an opportunity to turn his head. But at last there came a wave more gentle than the others, and when at the crest of it he swiftly scoured the western horizon.

"See it?" said the captain.

"No," said the correspondent slowly, "I didn't see anything."

"Look again," said the captain. He pointed. "It's exactly in that direction."

At the top of another wave, the correspondent did as he was bid, and this time his eyes chanced on a small still thing on the edge of the swaying horizon. It was precisely like the point of a pin. It took an anxious eye to find a lighthouse so tiny.

"Think we'll make it, captain?"

"If this wind holds and the boat don't swamp, we can't do much else," said the captain.

The little boat, lifted by each towering sea, and splashed viciously by the crests, made progress that in the absence of seaweed was not apparent to those in her. She seemed just a wee thing wallowing, miraculously top up, at the mercy of five oceans. Occasionally, a great spread of water, like white flames, swarmed into her.

"Bail her, cook," said the captain serenely.

"All right, captain," said the cheerful cook.

III

It would be difficult to describe the subtle brotherhood of men that was here established on the seas. No one said that it was so. No one mentioned it. But it dwelt in the boat, and each man felt it warm him. They were a captain, an oiler, a cook, and a correspondent, and they were friends, friends in a more curiously iron-bound degree than may be common. The hurt captain, lying against the water-jar in the bow, spoke always in a low voice and calmly, but he could never command a more ready and swiftly obedient crew than the motley three of the dinghy. It was more than a mere recognition of what was best for the common safety. There was surely in it a quality that was personal and heartfelt. And after this devotion to the commander of the boat there was this comradeship that the correspondent, for instance, who had been taught to be cynical of men, knew even at the time was the best experience of his life. But no one said that it was so. No one mentioned it.

"I wish we had a sail," remarked the captain. "We might try my overcoat on the end of an oar and give you two boys a chance to rest." So the cook and the correspondent held the mast and spread wide the overcoat. The oiler steered, and the little boat made good way with her new rig. Sometimes the oiler had to scull sharply to keep a sea from breaking into the boat, but otherwise sailing was a success.

Meanwhile the lighthouse had been growing slowly larger. It had now almost assumed color, and appeared like a little gray shadow on the sky. The man at the oars could not be prevented from turning his head rather often to try for a glimpse of this little gray shadow.

At last, from the top of each wave the men in the tossing boat could see land. Even as the lighthouse was an upright shadow on the sky, this land seemed but a long black shadow on the sea. It certainly was thinner than paper. "We must

be about opposite New Smyrna," said the cook, who had coasted this shore often in schooners. "Captain, by the way, I believe they abandoned that life-saving station there about a year ago."

"Did they?" said the captain.

The wind slowly died away. The cook and the correspondent were not now obliged to slave in order to hold high the oar. But the waves continued their old impetuous swooping at the dinghy, and the little craft, no longer under way, struggled woundily over them. The oiler or the correspondent took the oars again.

Shipwrecks are apropos of nothing. If men could only train for them and have them occur when the men had reached pink condition, there would be less drowning at sea. Of the four in the dinghy none had slept any time worth mentioning for two days and two nights previous to embarking in the dinghy, and in the excitement of clambering about the deck of a foundering ship they had also forgotten to eat heartily.

For these reasons, and for others, neither the oiler nor the correspondent was fond of rowing at this time. The correspondent wondered ingenuously how in the name of all that was sane could there be people who thought it amusing to row a boat. It was not an amusement; it was a diabolical punishment, and even a genius of mental aberrations could never conclude that it was anything but a horror to the muscles and a crime against the back. He mentioned to the boat in general how the amusement of rowing struck him, and the weary-faced oiler smiled in full sympathy. Previously to the foundering, by the way, the oiler had worked double-watch in the engine-room of the ship.

"Take her easy, now, boys," said the captain. "Don't spend yourselves. If we have to run a surf you'll need all your strength, because we'll sure have to swim for it. Take your time."

Slowly the land arose from the sea. From a black line it became a line of black and a line of white, trees and sand. Finally, the captain said that he could make out a house on the shore. "That's the house of refuge, sure," said the cook. "They'll see us before long, and come out after us."

The distant lighthouse reared high. "The keeper ought to be able to make us out now, if he's looking through a glass," said the captain. "He'll notify the life-saving people."

"None of those other boats could have got

ashore to give word of the wreck," said the oiler, in a low voice. "Else the lifeboat would be out hunting us."

Slowly and beautifully the land loomed out of the sea. The wind came again, It had veered from the north-east to the south-east. Finally, a new sound struck the ears of the men in the boat. It was the low thunder of the surf on the shore. "We'll never be able to make the lighthouse now," said the captain. "Swing her head a little more north, Billie."

"A little more north, sir," said the oiler.

Whereupon the little boat turned her nose once more down the wind, and all but the oarsmen watched the shore grow. Under the influence of this expansion doubt and direful apprehension were leaving the minds of the men. The management of the boat was still most absorbing, but it could not prevent a quiet cheerfulness. In an hour, perhaps, they would be ashore.

Their backbones had become thoroughly used to balancing in the boat, and they now rode this wild colt of a dinghy like circus men. The correspondent thought that he had been drenched to the skin, but happening to feel in the top pocket of his coat, he found therein eight cigars. Four of them were soaked with sea-water; four were perfectly scatheless. After a search, somebody produced three dry matches, and thereupon the four waifs rode impudently in their little boat, and with an assurance of an impending rescue shining in their eyes, puffed at the big cigars and judged well and ill of all men. Everybody took a drink of water.

IV

"Cook," remarked the captain, "there don't seem to be any signs of life about your house of refuge."

"No," replied the cook. "Funny they don't see us!"

A broad stretch of lowly coast lay before the eyes of the men. It was of low dunes topped with dark vegetation. The roar of the surf was plain, and sometimes they could see the white lip of a wave as it spun up the beach. A tiny house was blocked out black upon the sky. Southward, the slim lighthouse lifted its little gray length.

Tide, wind, and waves were swinging the dinghy northward. "Funny they don't see us," said the men.

The surf's roar was here dulled, but its tone was, nevertheless, thunderous and mighty. As the boat swam over the great rollers, the men sat listening to this roar. "We'll swamp sure," said everybody.

It is fair to say here that there was not a life-saving station within twenty miles in either direction, but the men did not know this fact, and in consequence they made dark and opprobrious remarks concerning the eyesight of the nation's life-savers. Four scowling men sat in the dinghy and surpassed records in the invention of epithets.

"Funny they don't see us."

The light-heartedness of a former time had completely faded. To their sharpened minds it was easy to conjure pictures of all kinds of incompetency and blindness and, indeed, cowardice. There was the shore of the populous land, and it was bitter and bitter to them that from it came no sign.

"Well," said the captain, ultimately, "I suppose we'll have to make a try for ourselves. If we stay out here too long, we'll none of us have strength left to swim after the boat swamps."

And so the oiler, who was at the oars, turned the boat straight for the shore. There was a sudden tightening of muscles. There was some thinking.

"If we don't all get ashore—" said the captain. "If we don't all get ashore, I suppose you fellows know where to send news of my finish?"

They then briefly exchanged some addresses and admonitions. As for the reflections of the men, there was a great deal of rage in them. Perchance they might be formulated thus: "If I am going to be drowned—if I am going to be drowned—if I am going to be drowned, why, in the name of the seven mad gods who rule the sea, was I allowed to come thus far and contemplate sand and trees? Was I brought here merely to have my nose dragged away as I was about to nibble the sacred cheese of life? It is preposterous. If this old ninny-woman, Fate, cannot do better than this, she should be deprived of the management of men's fortunes. She is an old hen who knows not her intention. If she has decided to drown me, why did she not do it in the beginning and save me all this trouble? The whole affair is absurd. . . . But no, she cannot mean to drown me. She dare not drown me. She cannot drown me. Not after all this work." Afterward the man might have had an impulse to shake his fist at the clouds: "Just you drown me, now, and then hear what I call you!"

The billows that came at this time were more formidable. They seemed always just about to break and roll over the little boat in a turmoil of foam. There was a preparatory and long growl in the speech of them. No mind unused to the sea would have concluded that the dinghy could ascend these sheer heights in time. The shore was still afar. The oiler was a wily surfman. "Boys," he said swiftly, "she won't live three minutes more, and we're too far out to swim. Shall I take her to sea again, captain?"

"Yes! Go ahead!" said the captain.

This oiler, by a series of quick miracles, and fast and steady oarsmanship, turned the boat in the middle of the surf and took her safely to sea again.

There was a considerable silence as the boat bumped over the furrowed sea to deeper water. Then somebody in gloom spoke. "Well, anyhow, they must have seen us from the shore by now."

The gulls went in slanting flight up the wind toward the gray desolate east. A squall, marked by dingy clouds, and clouds brick-red, like smoke from a burning building, appeared from the south-east.

"What do you think of those life-saving people? Ain't they peaches?"

"Funny they haven't seen us."

"Maybe they think we're out here for sport! Maybe they think we're fishin'. Maybe they think we're damned fools."

It was a long afternoon. A changed tide tried to force them southward, but wind and wave said northward. Far ahead, where coastline, sea, and sky formed their mighty angle, there were little dots which seemed to indicate a city on the shore.

"St. Augustine?"

The captain shook his head. "Too near Mosquito Inlet."

And the oiler rowed, and then the correspondent rowed. Then the oiler rowed. It was a weary business. The human back can become the seat of more aches and pains than are registered in books for the composite anatomy of a regiment. It is a limited area, but it can become the theater of innumerable muscular conflicts, tangles, wrenches, knots, and other comforts.

"Did you ever like to row, Billie?" asked the correspondent.

"No," said the oiler. "Hang it."

When one exchanged the rowing-seat for a place in the bottom of the boat, he suffered a bodily depression that caused him to be careless of everything save an obligation to wiggle one finger. There was cold sea-water swashing to and fro in the boat, and he lay in it. His head, pillowed on a thwart, was within an inch of the swirl of a wave crest, and sometimes a particularly obstreperous sea came in-board and drenched him once more. But these matters did not annoy him. It is almost certain that if the boat had capsized he would have tumbled comfortably out upon the ocean as if he felt sure that it was a great soft mattress.

"Look! There's a man on the shore!"

"Where?"

"There! See 'im? See 'im?"

"Yes, sure! He's walking along."

"Now he's stopped. Look! He's facing us!"

"He's waving at us!"

"So he is! By thunder!"

"Ah, now we're all right! Now we're all right! There'll be a boat out here for us in half an hour."

"He's going on. He's running. He's going up to that house there."

The remote beach seemed lower than the sea, and it required a searching glance to discern the little black figure. The captain saw a floating stick and they rowed to it. A bath-towel was by some weird chance in the boat, and, tying this on the stick, the captain waved it. The oarsman did not dare turn his head, so he was obliged to ask questions.

"What's he doing now?"

"He's standing still again. He's looking, I think. . . . There he goes again. Toward the house. . . . Now he stopped again."

"Is he waving at us?"

"No, not now! He was, though."

"Look! There comes another man!"

"He's running."

"Look at him go, would you!"

"Why, he's on a bicycle. Now he's met the other man. They're both waving at us. Look!"

"There comes something up the beach."

"What the devil is that thing?"

"Why, it looks like a boat."

"Why, certainly it's a boat."

"No, it's on wheels."

"Yes, so it is. Well, that must be the life-boat. They drag them along shore on a wagon."

"That's the life-boat, sure."

"No, by—, it's—it's an omnibus."

"I tell you it's a life-boat."

"It is not! It's an omnibus. I can see it plain. See? One of these big hotel omnibuses."

"By thunder, you're right. It's an omnibus, sure as fate. What do you suppose they are doing with an omnibus? Maybe they are going around collecting the life-crew, hey?"

"That's it, likely. Look! There's a fellow waving a little black flag. He's standing on the steps of the omnibus. There come those other two fellows. Now they're all talking together. Look at the fellow with the flag. Maybe he ain't waving it."

"That ain't a flag, is it? That's his coat. Why, certainly, that's his coat."

"So it is. It's his coat. He's taken it off and is waving it around his head. But would you look at him swing it."

"Oh, say, there isn't any life-saving station there. That's just a winter resort hotel omnibus that has brought over some of the boarders to see us drown."

"What's that idiot with the coat mean? What's he signaling, anyhow?"

"It looks as if he were trying to tell us to go north. There must be a life-saving station up there."

"No! He thinks we're fishing. Just giving us a merry hand. See? Ah, there, Billie."

"Well, I wish I could make something out of those signals. What do you suppose he means?"

"He don't mean anything. He's just playing."

"Well, if he'd just signal us to try the surf again, or to go to sea and wait, or go north, or go south, or go to hell—there would be some reason in it. But look at him. He just stands there and keeps his coat revolving like a wheel. The ass!"

"There come more people."

"Now there's quite a mob. Look! Isn't that a boat?"

"Where? Oh, I see where you mean. No, that's no boat."

"That fellow is still waving his coat."

"He must think we like to see him do that. Why don't he quit it? It don't mean anything."

"I don't know. I think he is trying to make

us go north. It must be that there's a life-saving station there somewhere."

"Say, he ain't tired yet. Look at 'im wave."

"Wonder how long he can keep that up. He's been revolving his coat ever since he caught sight of us. He's an idiot. Why aren't they getting men to bring a boat out? A fishing boat—one of those big yawls—could come out here all right. Why don't he do something?"

"Oh, it's all right, now."

"They'll have a boat out here for us in less than no time, now that they've seen us."

A faint yellow tone came into the sky over the low land. The shadows on the sea slowly deepened. The wind bore coldness with it, and the men began to shiver.

"Holy smoke!" said one, allowing his voice to express his impious mood, "if we keep on monkeying out here! If we've got to flounder out here all night!"

"Oh, we'll never have to stay here all night! Don't you worry. They've seen us now, and it won't be long before they'll come chasing out after us."

The shore grew dusky. The man waving a coat blended gradually into this gloom, and it swallowed in the same manner the omnibus and the group of people. The spray, when it dashed uproariously over the side, made the voyagers shrink and swear like men who were being branded.

"I'd like to catch the chump who waved that coat. I feel like soaking him one, just for luck."

"Why? What did he do?"

"Oh, nothing, but then he seemed so damned cheerful."

In the meantime the oiler rowed, and then the correspondent rowed, and then the oiler rowed. Gray-faced and bowed forward, they mechanically, turn by turn, plied the leaden oars. The form of the lighthouse had vanished from the southern horizon, but finally a pale star appeared, just lifting from the sea. The streaked saffron in the west passed before the all-merging darkness, and the sea to the east was black. The land had vanished, and was expressed only by the low and drear thunder of the surf.

"If I am going to be drowned—if I am going to be drowned—if I am going to be drowned, why, in the name of the seven mad gods who rule the sea, was I allowed to come thus far and contemplate sand and trees? Was I brought here merely to have my nose dragged away as I was about to nibble the sacred cheese of life?"

The patient captain, drooped over the water-jar, was sometimes obliged to speak to the oarsman.

"Keep her head up! Keep her head up!"

"'Keep her head up,' sir." The voices were weary and low.

This was surely a quiet evening. All save the oarsman lay heavily and listlessly in the boat's bottom. As for him, his eyes were just capable of noting the tall black waves that swept forward in a most sinister silence, save for an occasional subdued growl of a crest.

The cook's head was on a thwart, and he looked without interest at the water under his nose. He was deep in other scenes. Finally he spoke. "Billie," he murmured, dreamfully, "what kind of pie do you like best?"

V

"Pie," said the oiler and the correspondent, agitatedly. "Don't talk about those things, blast you!"

"Well," said the cook, "I was just thinking about ham sandwiches, and—"

A night on the sea in an open boat is a long night. As darkness settled finally, the shine of the light, lifting from the sea in the south, changed to full gold. On the northern horizon a new light appeared, a small bluish gleam on the edge of the waters. These two lights were the furniture of the world. Otherwise there was nothing but waves.

Two men huddled in the stern, and distances were so magnificent in the dinghy that the rower was enabled to keep his feet partly warmed by thrusting them under his companions. Their legs indeed extended far under the rowing-seat until they touched the feet of the captain forward. Sometimes, despite the efforts of the tired oarsman, a wave came piling into the boat, an icy wave of the night, and the chilling water soaked them anew. They would twist their bodies for a moment and groan, and sleep the dead sleep once more, while the water in the boat gurgled about them as the craft rocked.

The plan of the oiler and the correspondent was for one to row until he lost the ability, and then arouse the other from his sea-water couch in the bottom of the boat.

The oiler plied the oars until his head drooped forward, and the overpowering sleep blinded him. And he rowed yet afterward. Then he touched a man in the bottom of the boat, and called his name. "Will you spell me for a little while?" he said, meekly.

"Sure, Billie," said the correspondent, awakening and dragging himself to a sitting position. They exchanged places carefully, and the oiler, cuddling down in the sea-water at the cook's side, seemed to go to sleep instantly.

The particular violence of the sea had ceased. The waves came without snarling. The obligation of the man at the oars was to keep the boat headed so that the tilt of the rollers would not capsize her, and to preserve her from filling when the crests rushed past. The black waves were silent and hard to be seen in the darkness. Often one was almost upon the boat before the oarsman was aware.

In a low voice the correspondent addressed the captain. He was not sure that the captain was awake, although this iron man seemed to be always awake. "Captain, shall I keep her making for that light north, sir?"

The same steady voice answered him. "Yes. Keep it about two points off the port bow."

The cook had tied a life-belt around himself in order to get even the warmth which this clumsy cork contrivance could donate, and he seemed almost stove-like when a rower, whose teeth invariably chattered wildly as soon as he ceased his labor, dropped down to sleep.

The correspondent, as he rowed, looked down at the two men sleeping underfoot. The cook's arm was around the oiler's shoulders, and, with their fragmentary clothing and haggard faces, they were the babes of the sea, a grotesque rendering of the old babes in the wood.

Later he must have grown stupid at his work, for suddenly there was a growling of water, and a crest came with a roar and a swash into the boat, and it was a wonder that it did not set the cook afloat in his life-belt. The cook continued to sleep, but the oiler sat up, blinking his eyes and shaking with the new cold.

"Oh, I'm awful sorry, Billie," said the correspondent, contritely.

"That's all right, old boy," said the oiler, and lay down again and was asleep.

Presently it seemed that even the captain dozed, and the correspondent thought that he was the one man afloat on all the oceans. The wind had a voice as it came over the waves, and it was sadder than the end.

There was a long, loud swishing astern of the boat, and a gleaming trail of phosphorescence, like blue flame, was furrowed on the black waters. It might have been made by a monstrous knife.

Then there came a stillness, while the correspondent breathed with open mouth and looked at the sea.

Suddenly there was another swish and another long flash of bluish light, and this time it was alongside the boat, and might almost have been reached with an oar. The correspondent saw an enormous fin speed like a shadow through the water, hurling the crystalline spray and leaving the long glowing trail.

The correspondent looked over his shoulder at the captain. His face was hidden, and he seemed to be asleep. He looked at the babes of the sea. They certainly were asleep. So, being bereft of sympathy, he leaned a little way to one side and swore softly into the sea.

But the thing did not then leave the vicinity of the boat. Ahead or astern, on one side or the other, at intervals long or short, fled the long sparkling streak, and there was to be heard the *whiroo* of the dark fin. The speed and power of the thing was greatly to be admired. It cut the water like a gigantic and keen projectile.

The presence of this biding thing did not affect the man with the same horror that it would if he had been a picnicker. He simply looked at the sea dully and swore in an undertone.

Nevertheless, it is true that he did not wish to be alone with the thing. He wished one of his companions to awaken by chance and keep him company with it. But the captain hung motionless over the water-jar, and the oiler and the cook in the bottom of the boat were plunged in slumber.

VI

"If I am going to be drowned—if I am going to be drowned—if I am going to be drowned, why, in the name of the seven mad gods who rule the sea, was I allowed to come thus far and contemplate sand and trees?"

During this dismal night, it may be remarked that a man would conclude that it was really the intention of the seven mad gods to drown him, despite the abominable injustice of it. For it was certainly an abominable injustice to drown a man who had worked so hard, so hard. The man felt it would be a crime most unnatural. Other people had drowned at sea since galleys swarmed with painted sails, but still—

When it occurs to a man that nature does not regard him as important, and that she feels she would not maim the universe by disposing of him, he at first wishes to throw bricks at the temple, and he hates deeply the fact that there are no bricks and no temples. Any visible expression of nature would surely be pelleted with his jeers.

Then, if there be no tangible thing to hoot he feels, perhaps, the desire to confront a personification and indulge in pleas, bowed to one knee, and with hands supplicant, saying: "Yes, but I love myself."

A high cold star on a winter's night is the word he feels that she says to him. Thereafter he knows the pathos of his situation.

The men in the dinghy had not discussed these matters, but each had, no doubt, reflected upon them in silence and according to his mind. There was seldom any expression upon their faces save the general one of complete weariness. Speech was devoted to the business of the boat.

To chime the notes of his emotion, a verse mysteriously entered the correspondent's head. He had even forgotten that he had forgotten this verse, but it suddenly was in his mind.

A soldier of the Legion lay dying in Algiers,
There was lack of woman's nursing, there was dearth
   of woman's tears;
But a comrade stood beside him, and he took that
   comrade's hand,
And he said: "I shall never see my own, my native
   land."

In his childhood, the correspondent had been made acquainted with the fact that a soldier of the Legion lay dying in Algiers, but he had never regarded the fact as important. Myriads of his school-fellows had informed him of the soldier's plight, but the dinning had naturally ended by making him perfectly indifferent. He had never considered it his affair that a soldier of the Legion lay dying in Algiers, nor had it appeared to him as a matter for sorrow. It was less to him than the breaking of a pencil's point.

Now, however, it quaintly came to him as a human, living thing. It was no longer merely a picture of a few throes in the breast of a poet, meanwhile drinking tea and warming his feet at the grate; it was an actuality—stern, mournful, and fine.

The correspondent plainly saw the soldier. He lay on the sand with his feet out straight and still. While his pale left hand was upon his chest in an attempt to thwart the going of his life, the blood came between his fingers.

In the far Algerian distance, a city of low square forms was set against a sky that was faint with the last sunset hues. The correspondent, plying the oars and dreaming of the slow and slower movements of the lips of the soldier, was moved by a profound and perfectly impersonal comprehension. He was sorry for the soldier of the Legion who lay dying in Algiers.

The thing which had followed the boat and waited had evidently grown bored at the delay. There was no longer to be heard the slash of the cutwater, and there was no longer the flame of the long trail. The light in the north still glimmered, but it was apparently no nearer to the boat. Sometimes the boom of the surf rang in the correspondent's ears, and he turned the craft seaward then and rowed harder. Southward, someone had evidently built a watch-fire on the beach. It was too low and too far to be seen, but it made a shimmering, roseate reflection upon the bluff back of it, and this could be discerned from the boat. The wind came stronger, and sometimes a wave suddenly raged out like a mountain-cat, and there was to be seen the sheen and sparkle of a broken crest.

The captain, in the bow, moved on his water-jar and sat erect. "Pretty long night," he observed to the correspondent. He looked at the shore. "Those life-saving people take their time."

"Did you see that shark playing around?"

"Yes, I saw him. He was a big fellow, all right."

"Wish I had known you were awake."

Later the correspondent spoke into the bottom of the boat.

"Billie!" There was a slow and gradual disentanglement. "Billie, will you spell me?"

"Sure," said the oiler.

As soon as the correspondent touched the cold comfortable sea-water in the bottom of the boat and had huddled close to the cook's life-belt he was deep in sleep, despite the fact that his teeth played all the popular airs. This sleep was so good to him that it was but a moment before he heard a voice call his name in a tone that demonstrated the last stages of exhaustion. "Will you spell me?"

"Sure, Billie."

The light in the north had mysteriously vanished, but the correspondent took his course from the wide-awake captain.

Later in the night they took the boat farther out to sea, and the captain directed the cook to take one oar at the stern and keep the boat facing the seas. He was to call out if he should hear the thunder of the surf. This plan enabled the oiler and the correspondent to get respite together. "We'll give those boys a chance to get into shape again," said the captain. They curled down and, after a few preliminary chatterings and trembles, slept once more the dead sleep. Neither knew they had bequeathed to the cook the company of another shark, or perhaps the same shark.

As the boat caroused on the waves, spray occasionally bumped over the side and gave them a fresh soaking, but this had no power to break their repose. The ominous slash of the wind and the water affected them as it would have affected mummies.

"Boys," said the cook, with the notes of every reluctance in his voice, "she's drifted in pretty close. I guess one of you had better take her to sea again." The correspondent, aroused, heard the crash of the toppled crests.

As he was rowing, the captain gave him some whisky-and-water, and this steadied the chills out of him. "If I ever get ashore and anybody shows me even a photograph of an oar—"

At last there was a short conversation.

"Billie . . . Billie, will you spell me?"

"Sure," said the oiler.

VII

When the correspondent again opened his eyes, the sea and the sky were each of the gray hue of the dawning. Later, carmine and gold was painted upon the waters. The morning appeared finally, in its splendor, with a sky of pure blue, and the sunlight flamed on the tips of the waves.

On the distant dunes were set many little black cottages, and a tall white windmill reared above them. No man, nor dog, nor bicycle appeared on the beach. The cottages might have formed a deserted village.

The voyagers scanned the shore. A conference was held in the boat. "Well," said the captain, "if no help is coming, we might better try a run through the surf right away. If we stay out here much longer we will be too weak to do anything for ourselves at all." The others silently acquiesced in this reasoning. The boat was headed for the beach. The correspondent wondered if none ever ascended the tall wind-tower, and if then they never looked seaward. This tower was a giant, standing with its back to the plight of the ants. It represented in a degree, to the correspondent, the serenity of nature amid the struggles of the individual—nature in the wind, and nature in the vision of men. She did not seem cruel to him then, nor beneficent, nor treacherous, nor wise. But she was indifferent, flatly indifferent. It is, perhaps, plausible that a man in this situation, impressed with the unconcern of the universe, should see the innumerable flaws of his life, and have them taste wickedly in his mind and wish for another chance. A distinction between right and wrong seems absurdly clear to him, then, in this new ignorance of the grave-edge, and he understands that if he were given another opportunity he would mend his conduct and his words, and be better and brighter during an introduction or at a tea.

"Now, boys," said the captain, "she is going to swamp sure. All we can do is to work her in as far as possible, and then when she swamps, pile out and scramble for the beach. Keep cool now, and don't jump until she swamps sure."

The oiler took the oars. Over his shoulders he scanned the surf. "Captain," he said, "I think I'd better bring her about, and keep her head-on to the seas and back her in."

"All right, Billie," said the captain. "Back her in." The oiler swung the boat then and, seated in the stern, the cook and the correspondent were obliged to look over their shoulders to contemplate the lonely and indifferent shore.

The monstrous in-shore rollers heaved the boat high until the men were again enabled to see the white sheets of water scudding up the slanted beach. "We won't get in very close," said the captain. Each time a man could wrest his attention from the rollers, he turned his glance toward the shore, and in the expression of the eyes during this contemplation there was a singular quality. The correspondent, observing the others, knew that they were not afraid, but the full meaning of their glances was shrouded.

As for himself, he was too tired to grapple fundamentally with the fact. He tried to coerce his mind into thinking of it, but the mind was dominated at this time by the muscles, and the muscles said they did not care. It merely occurred to him that if he should drown it would be a shame.

There were no hurried words, no pallor, no plain agitation. The men simply looked at the shore. "Now, remember to get well clear of the boat when you jump," said the captain.

Seaward the crest of a roller suddenly fell with a thunderous crash, and the long white comber came roaring down upon the boat.

"Steady now," said the captain. The men were silent. They turned their eyes from the shore to the comber and waited. The boat slid up the incline, leaped at the furious top, bounced over it, and swung down the long back of the waves. Some water had been shipped and the cook bailed it out.

But the next crest crashed also. The tumbling boiling flood of white water caught the boat and whirled it almost perpendicular. Water swarmed in from all sides. The correspondent had his hands on the gunwale at this time, and when the water entered at that place he swiftly withdrew his fingers, as if he objected to wetting them.

The little boat, drunken with this weight of water, reeled and snuggled deeper into the sea.

"Bail her out, cook! Bail her out," said the captain.

"All right, captain," said the cook.

"Now, boys, the next one will do for us, sure," said the oiler. "Mind to jump clear of the boat."

The third wave moved forward, huge, furious, implacable. It fairly swallowed the dinghy, and almost simultaneously the men tumbled into the sea. A piece of life-belt had lain in the bottom of the boat, and as the correspondent went overboard he held this to his chest with his left hand.

The January water was icy, and he reflected immediately that it was colder than he had expected to find it off the coast of Florida. This appeared to his dazed mind as a fact important enough to be noted at the time. The coldness of the water was sad; it was tragic. This fact was somehow so mixed and confused with his opinion of his own situation that it seemed almost a proper reason for tears. The water was cold.

When he came to the surface he was conscious of little but the noisy water. Afterward he saw his companions in the sea. The oiler was ahead in the race. He was swimming strongly and rapidly. Off to the correspondent's left, the cook's great white and corked back bulged out of the water, and in the rear the captain was hanging with his one good hand to the keel of the overturned dinghy.

There is a certain immovable quality to a shore, and the correspondent wondered at it amid the confusion of the sea.

It seemed also very attractive, but the correspondent knew that it was a long journey, and he paddled leisurely. The piece of life-preserver lay under him, and sometimes he whirled down the incline of a wave as if he were on a hand-sled.

But finally he arrived at a place in the sea where travel was beset with difficulty. He did not pause swimming to inquire what manner of current had caught him, but there his progress ceased. The shore was set before him like a bit of scenery on a stage, and he looked at it and understood with his eyes each detail of it.

As the cook passed, much farther to the left, the captain was calling to him, "Turn over on your back, cook! Turn over on your back and use the oar."

"All right, sir." The cook turned on his back, and, paddling with an oar, went ahead as if he were a canoe.

Presently the boat also passed to the left of the correspondent with the captain clinging with one hand to the keel. He would have appeared like a man raising himself to look over a board fence, if it were not for the extraordinary gymnastics of the boat. The correspondent marveled that the captain could still hold to it.

They passed on, nearer to shore—the oiler, the cook, the captain—and following them went the water-jar, bouncing gaily over the seas.

The correspondent remained in the grip of this strange new enemy—a current. The shore, with its white slope of sand and its green bluff, topped with little silent cottages, was spread like a pic-

ture before him. It was very near to him then, but he was impressed as one who in a gallery looks at a scene from Brittany or Algiers.

He thought: "I am going to drown? Can it be possible? Can it be possible? Can it be possible?" Perhaps an individual must consider his own death to be the final phenomenon of nature.

But later a wave perhaps whirled him out of this small deadly current, for he found suddenly that he could again make progress toward the shore. Later still, he was aware that the captain, clinging with one hand to the keel of the dinghy, had his face turned away from the shore and toward him and was calling his name. "Come to the boat! Come to the boat!"

In his struggle to reach the captain and the boat, he reflected that when one gets properly wearied, drowning must really be a comfortable arrangement, a cessation of hostilities accompanied by a large degree of relief, and he was glad of it, for the main thing in his mind for some moments had been horror of the temporary agony. He did not wish to be hurt.

Presently he saw a man running along the shore. He was undressing with most remarkable speed. Coat, trousers, shirt, everything flew magically off him.

"Come to the boat," called the captain.

"All right, captain." As the correspondent paddled, he saw the captain let himself down to bottom and leave the boat. Then the correspondent performed his one little marvel of the voyage. A large wave caught him and flung him with ease and supreme speed completely over the boat and far beyond it. It struck him even then as an event in gymnastics, and a true miracle of the sea. An overturned boat in the surf is not a plaything to a swimming man.

The correspondent arrived in water that reached only to his waist, but his condition did not enable him to stand for more than a moment. Each wave knocked him into a heap, and the undertow pulled at him.

Then he saw the man who had been running and undressing, and undressing and running, come bounding into the water. He dragged ashore the cook, and then waded toward the captain, but the captain waved him away, and sent him to the correspondent. He was naked, naked as a tree in winter, but a halo was about his head, and he shone like a saint. He gave a strong pull, and a long drag, and a bully heave at the correspondent's hand. The correspondent, schooled in the minor formulae, said: "Thanks, old man." But suddenly the man cried: "What's that?" He pointed a swift finger. The correspondent said: "Go."

In the shallows, face downward, lay the oiler. His forehead touched sand that was periodically, between each wave, clear of the sea.

The correspondent did not know all that transpired afterward. When he achieved safe ground he fell, striking the sand with each particular part of his body. It was as if he had dropped from a roof, but the thud was grateful to him.

It seems that instantly the beach was populated with men, with blankets, clothes, and flasks, and women with coffee-pots and all the remedies sacred to their minds. The welcome of the land to the men from the sea was warm and generous, but a still and dripping shape was carried slowly up the beach, and the land's welcome for it could only be the different and sinister hospitality of the grave.

When it came night, the white waves paced to and fro in the moonlight, and the wind brought the sound of the great sea's voice to the men on shore, and they felt that they could then be interpreters.

JOSEPH CONRAD

The Lagoon

Joseph Conrad (1857–1924) was born of Polish parents in the Ukraine and was named Jozef Teodor Konrad Nalecz Korzeniowski. He spent his childhood and early youth in Russia as an exile with his parents, who left him an orphan at the age of twelve to be brought up by his uncle in Cracow, Poland. As a boy, Conrad was fascinated by romantic tales of adventure at sea, and at seventeen he went to sea in the French merchant service. In 1878 he changed over to the British service; by 1884 he had become a ship's master, a British citizen, and had acquired an extraordinary command of English—the language in which he did all his writing. His first novel, *Almayer's Folly*, was begun in 1889 but not published until 1895. It was followed by *An Outcast of the Islands*, 1896; *The Nigger of the Narcissus*, 1897; *Lord Jim*, 1900; and many other novels, several collections of short stories, reminiscences, and literary essays.

In "The Lagoon," as in all of his writings, Conrad is preoccupied with man's need for fidelity, honor, and courage. Here, as elsewhere, he is a master both at creating an atmosphere through richly realistic settings and at probing deep into the moral and psychological motives of his characters.

The white man, leaning with both arms over the roof of the little house in the stern of the boat, said to the steersman—

"We will pass the night in Arsat's clearing. It is late."

THE LAGOON From *Tales of Unrest* by Joseph Conrad. Reprinted by permission of J. M. Dent & Sons Ltd., publishers, and the Trustees of the Joseph Conrad Estate.

The Malay only grunted, and went on looking fixedly at the river. The white man rested his chin on his crossed arms and gazed at the wake of the boat. At the end of the straight avenue of forests cut by the intense glitter of the river, the sun appeared unclouded and dazzling; poised low over the water that shone smoothly like a band of metal. The forests, somber and dull, stood motionless and silent on each side of the broad stream. At the foot of big, towering trees, trunkless nipa palms rose from the mud of the bank, in bunches of leaves enormous and heavy, that hung unstirring over the brown swirl of eddies. In the stillness of the air every tree, every leaf, every bough, every tendril of creeper and every petal of minute blossoms seemed to have been bewitched into an immobility perfect and final. Nothing moved on the river but the eight paddles that rose flashing regularly, dipped together with a single splash; while the steersman swept right and left with a periodic and sudden flourish of his blade describing a glinting semicircle above his head. The churned-up water frothed alongside with a confused murmur. And the white man's canoe, advancing upstream in the short-lived disturbance of its own making, seemed to enter the portals of a land from which the very memory of motion had forever departed.

The white man, turning his back upon the setting sun, looked along the empty and broad expanse of the sea-reach. For the last three miles of its course the wandering, hesitating river, as if enticed irresistibly by the freedom of an open horizon, flows straight into the sea, flows straight to the east—to the east that harbors both light and darkness. Astern of the boat the repeated call of some bird, a cry discordant and feeble, skipped along over the smooth water and lost itself, before it could reach the other shore, in the breathless silence of the world.

The steersman dug his paddle into the stream, and held hard with stiffened arms, his body thrown forward. The water gurgled aloud; and suddenly the long straight reach seemed to pivot on its center, the forests swung in a semicircle, and the slanting beams of sunset touched the broadside of the canoe with a fiery glow, throwing the slender and distorted shadows of its crew upon the streaked glitter of the river. The white man turned to look ahead. The course of the boat had been altered at right-angles to the stream, and the carved dragon-head of its prow was pointing now at a gap in the fringing bushes of the bank. It glided through, brushing the overhanging twigs, and disappeared from the river like some slim and amphibious creature leaving the water for its lair in the forests.

The narrow creek was like a ditch: tortuous, fabulously deep; filled with gloom under the thin strip of pure and shining blue of the heaven.

Immense trees soared up, invisible behind the festooned draperies of creepers. Here and there, near the glistening blackness of the water, a twisted root of some tall tree showed amongst the tracery of small ferns, black and dull, writhing and motionless, like an arrested snake. The short words of the paddlers reverberated loudly between the thick and somber walls of vegetation. Darkness oozed out from between the trees, through the tangled maze of the creepers, from behind the great fantastic and unstirring leaves; the darkness, mysterious and invincible; the darkness scented and poisonous of impenetrable forests.

The men poled in the shoaling water. The creek broadened, opening out into a wide sweep of a stagnant lagoon. The forests receded from the marshy bank, leaving a level strip of bright green, reedy grass to frame the reflected blueness of the sky. A fleecy pink cloud drifted high above, trailing the delicate coloring of its image under the floating leaves and the silvery blossoms of the lotus. A little house, perched on high poles, appeared black in the distance. Near it, two tall nibong palms, that seemed to have come out of the forests in the background, leaned slightly over the ragged roof, with a suggestion of sad tenderness and care in the droop of their leafy and soaring heads.

The steersman, pointing with his paddle, said, "Arsat is there. I see his canoe fast between the piles."

The polers ran along the sides of the boat, glancing over their shoulders at the end of the day's journey. They would have preferred to spend the night somewhere else than on this lagoon of weird aspect and ghostly reputation. Moreover, they disliked Arsat, first as a stranger, and also because he who repairs a ruined house, and dwells in it, proclaims that he is not afraid to live amongst the spirits that haunt the places abandoned by mankind. Such a man can disturb the course of fate by glances or words; while his familiar ghosts are not easy to propitiate by casual wayfarers upon whom they long to wreak the malice of their human master. White men care not for such things, being unbelievers and in league with the Father of Evil, who leads them unharmed through the invisible dangers of this world. To the warnings of the righteous they oppose an offensive pretense of disbelief. What is there to be done?

So they thought, throwing their weight on the

end of their long poles. The big canoe glided on swiftly, noiselessly, and smoothly, towards Arsat's clearing, till, in a great rattling of poles thrown down, and the loud murmurs of "Allah be praised!" it came with a gentle knock against the crooked piles below the house.

The boatmen with uplifted faces shouted discordantly, "Arsat! O Arsat!" Nobody came. The white man began to climb the rude ladder giving access to the bamboo platform before the house. The juragan of the boat said sulkily, "We will cook in the sampan, and sleep on the water."

"Pass my blankets and the basket," said the white man, curtly.

He knelt on the edge of the platform to receive the bundle. Then the boat shoved off, and the white man, standing up, confronted Arsat, who had come out through the low door of his hut. He was a man young, powerful, with broad chest and muscular arms. He had nothing on but his sarong. His head was bare. His big, soft eyes stared eagerly at the white man, but his voice and demeanor were composed as he asked, without any words of greeting—

"Have you medicine, Tuan?"

"No," said the visitor in a startled tone. "No. Why? Is there sickness in the house?"

"Enter and see," replied Arsat, in the same calm manner, and turning short round, passed again through the small doorway. The white man, dropping his bundles, followed.

In the dim light of the dwelling he made out on a couch of bamboos a woman stretched on her back under a broad sheet of red cotton cloth. She lay still, as if dead; but her big eyes, wide open, glittered in the gloom, staring upwards at the slender rafters, motionless and unseeing. She was in a high fever, and evidently unconscious. Her cheeks were sunk slightly, her lips were partly open, and on the young face there was the ominous and fixed expression—the absorbed, contemplating expression of the unconscious who are going to die. The two men stood looking down at her in silence.

"Has she been long ill?" asked the traveler.

"I have not slept for five nights," answered the Malay, in a deliberate tone. "At first she heard voices calling her from the water and struggled against me who held her. But since the sun of today rose she hears nothing—she hears not me. She sees nothing. She sees not me—me!"

He remained silent for a minute, then asked softly—

"Tuan, will she die?"

"I fear so," said the white man, sorrowfully. He had known Arsat years ago, in a far country in times of trouble and danger, when no friendship is to be despised. And since his Malay friend had come unexpectedly to dwell in the hut on the lagoon with a strange woman, he had slept many times there, in his journeys up and down the river. He liked the man who knew how to keep faith in council and how to fight without fear by the side of his white friend. He liked him—not so much perhaps as a man likes his favorite dog—but still he liked him well enough to help and ask no questions, to think sometimes vaguely and hazily in the midst of his own pursuits, about the lonely man and the long-haired woman with audacious face and triumphant eyes, who lived together hidden by the forest—alone and feared.

The white man came out of the hut in time to see the enormous conflagration of sunset put out by the swift and stealthy shadows that, rising like a black and impalpable vapor above the tree-tops, spread over the heaven, extinguishing the crimson glow of floating clouds and the red brilliance of departing daylight. In a few moments all the stars came out above the intense blackness of the earth and the great lagoon, gleaming suddenly with reflected lights, resembled an oval patch of night sky flung down into the hopeless and abysmal night of the wilderness. The white man had some supper out of the basket, then collecting a few sticks that lay about the platform, made up a small fire, not for warmth, but for the sake of the smoke, which would keep off the mosquitoes. He wrapped himself in the blankets and sat with his back against the reed wall of the house, smoking thoughtfully.

Arsat came through the doorway with noiseless steps and squatted down by the fire. The white man moved his outstretched legs a little.

"She breathes," said Arsat in a low voice, anticipating the expected question. "She breathes and burns as if with a great fire. She speaks not; she hears not—and burns!"

He paused for a moment, then asked in a quiet, incurious tone—

"Tuan . . . will she die?"

The white man moved his shoulders uneasily and muttered in a hesitating manner—

"If such is her fate."

"No, Tuan," said Arsat, calmly. "If such is my

fate. I hear, I see, I wait. I remember . . . Tuan, do you remember the old days? Do you remember my brother?"

"Yes," said the white man. The Malay rose suddenly and went in. The other, sitting still outside, could hear the voice in the hut. Arsat said: "Hear me! Speak!" His words were succeeded by a complete silence. "O Diamelen!" he cried, suddenly. After that cry there was a deep sigh. Arsat came out and sank down again in his old place.

They sat in silence before the fire. There was no sound within the house, there was no sound near them; but far away on the lagoon they could hear the voices of the boatmen ringing fitful and distinct on the calm water. The fire in the bows of the sampan shone faintly in the distance with a hazy red glow. Then it died out. The voices ceased. The land and the water slept invisible, unstirring and mute. It was as though there had been nothing left in the world but the glitter of stars streaming, ceaseless and vain, through the black stillness of the night.

The white man gazed straight before him into the darkness with wide-open eyes. The fear and fascination, the inspiration and the wonder of death—of death near, unavoidable, and unseen, soothed the unrest of his race and stirred the most indistinct, the most intimate of his thoughts. The ever-ready suspicion of evil, the gnawing suspicion that lurks in our hearts, flowed out into the stillness round him—into the stillness profound and dumb, and made it appear untrustworthy and infamous, like the placid and impenetrable mask of an unjustifiable violence. In that fleeting and powerful disturbance of his being the earth enfolded in the starlight peace became a shadowy country of inhuman strife, a battlefield of phantoms terrible and charming, august or ignoble, struggling ardently for the possession of our helpless hearts. An unquiet and mysterious country of inextinguishable desires and fears.

A plaintive murmur rose in the night; a murmur saddening and startling, as if the great solitudes of surrounding woods had tried to whisper into his ear the wisdom of their immense and lofty indifference. Sounds hesitating and vague floated in the air around him, shaped themselves slowly into words; and at last flowed on gently in a murmuring stream of soft and monotonous sentences. He stirred like a man waking up and changed his position slightly. Arsat, motionless and shadowy, sitting with bowed head under the stars, was speaking in a low and dreamy tone—

". . . for where can we lay down the heaviness of our trouble but in a friend's heart? A man must speak of war and of love. You, Tuan, know what war is, and you have seen me in time of danger seek death as other men seek life! A writing may be lost; a lie may be written; but what the eye has seen is truth and remains in the mind!"

"I remember," said the white man, quietly. Arsat went on with mournful composure—

"Therefore I shall speak to you of love. Speak in the night. Speak before both night and love are gone—and the eye of day looks upon my sorrow and my shame; upon my blackened face; upon my burnt-up heart."

A sigh, short and faint, marked an almost imperceptible pause, and then his words flowed on, without a stir, without a gesture.

"After the time of trouble and war was over and you went away from my country in the pursuit of your desires, which we, men of the islands, cannot understand, I and my brother became again, as we had been before, the sword-bearers of the Ruler. You know we were men of family, belonging to a ruling race, and more fit than any to carry on our right shoulder the emblem of power. And in the time of prosperity Si Dendring showed us favor, as we, in time of sorrow, had showed to him the faithfulness of our courage. It was a time of peace. A time of deer-hunts and cock-fights; of idle talks and foolish squabbles between men whose bellies are full and weapons are rusty. But the sower watched the young rice-shoots grow up without fear, and the traders came and went, departed lean and returned fat into the river of peace. They brought news, too. Brought lies and truth mixed together, so that no man knew when to rejoice and when to be sorry. We heard from them about you also. They had seen you here and had seen you there. And I was glad to hear, for I remembered the stirring times, and I always remembered you, Tuan, till the time came when my eyes could see nothing in the past, because they had looked upon the one who is dying there—in the house."

He stopped to exclaim in an intense whisper, "O Mara bahia! O Calamity!" then went on speaking a little louder:

"There's no worse enemy and no better friend than a brother, Tuan, for one brother knows another, and in perfect knowledge is strength for good or evil. I loved my brother. I went to him and told him that I could see nothing but one face, hear nothing but one voice. He told me: 'Open your heart so that she can see what is in it—and wait. Patience is wisdom. Inchi Midah may die or our Ruler may throw off his fear of a woman!' . . . I waited! . . . You remember the lady with the veiled face, Tuan, and the fear of our Ruler before her cunning and temper. And if she wanted her servant, what could I do? But I fed the hunger of my heart on short glances and stealthy words. I loitered on the path to the bath-houses in the daytime, and when the sun had fallen behind the forest I crept along the jasmine hedges of the women's courtyard. Unseeing, we spoke to one another through the scent of flowers, through the veil of leaves, through the blades of long grass that stood still before our lips; so great was our prudence, so faint was the murmur of our great longing. The time passed swiftly . . . and there were whispers amongst women—and our enemies watched—my brother was gloomy, and I began to think of killing and of a fierce death. . . . We are of a people who take what they want—like you whites. There is a time when a man should forget loyalty and respect. Might and authority are given to rulers, but to all men is given love and strength and courage. My brother said, 'You shall take her from their midst. We are two who are like one.' And I answered, 'Let it be soon, for I find no warmth in sunlight that does not shine upon her.' Our time came when the Ruler and all the great people went to the mouth of the river to fish by torchlight. There were hundreds of boats, and on the white sand, between the water and the forests, dwellings of leaves were built for the households of the Rajahs. The smoke of cooking-fires was like a blue mist of the evening, and many voices rang in it joyfully. While they were making the boats ready to beat up the fish, my brother came to me and said, 'Tonight!' I looked to my weapons, and when the time came our canoe took its place in the circle of boats carrying the torches. The lights blazed on the water, but behind the boats there was darkness. When the shouting began and the excitement made them like mad we dropped out. The water swallowed our fire, and we floated back to the shore that was dark with only here and there the glimmer of embers. We could hear the talk of slave-girls amongst the sheds. Then we found a place deserted and silent. We waited there. She came. She came running along the shore, rapid and leaving no trace, like a leaf driven by the wind into the sea. My brother said gloomily, 'Go and take her; carry her into our boat.' I lifted her in my arms. She panted. Her heart was beating against my breast. I said, 'I take you from those people. You came to the cry of my heart, but my arms take you into my boat against the will of the great!' 'It is right,' said my brother. 'We are men who take what we want and can hold it against many. We should have taken her in daylight.' I said, 'Let us be off'; for since she was in my boat I began to think of our Ruler's many men. 'Yes. Let us be off,' said my brother. 'We are cast out and this boat is our country now— and the sea is our refuge.' He lingered with his foot on the shore, and I entreated him to hasten, for I remembered the strokes of her heart against my breast and thought that two men cannot withstand a hundred. We left, paddling downstream close to the bank; and as we passed by the creek where they were fishing, the great shouting had ceased, but the murmur of voices was loud like the humming of insects flying at noonday. The boats floated, clustered together, in the red light of torches, under a black roof of smoke; and men talked of their sport. Men that boasted, and praised, and jeered—men that would have been our friends in the morning, but on that night were already our enemies. We paddled swiftly past. We had no more friends in the country of our birth. She sat in the middle of the canoe with covered face; silent as she is now; unseeing as she is now—and I had no regret at what I was leaving because I could hear her breathing close to me—as I can hear her now."

He paused, listened with his ear turned to the doorway, then shook his head and went on:

"My brother wanted to shout the cry of challenge—one cry only—to let the people know we were freeborn robbers who trusted our arms and the great sea. And again I begged him in the name of our love to be silent. Could I not hear her breathing close to me? I knew the pursuit would come quick enough. My brother loved me. He dipped his paddle without a splash. He only said, 'There is half a man in you now—the other half is in that woman. I can wait. When you are a whole man again, you will come back with me here to shout defiance. We are sons of the same mother.' I made no answer. All my strength and all my spirit were in my hands that held the paddle—for I longed to be with her in a safe place beyond the reach of men's anger and of women's spite. My love was so great, that I thought it could guide me to a country where death was unknown, if I could only escape from Inchi Midah's fury and from our Ruler's sword. We paddled with haste, breathing through our teeth. The blades bit deep into the smooth water. We passed out of the river; we flew in clear channels amongst the shallows. We skirted the black coast; we skirted the sand beaches where the sea speaks in whispers to the land; and the gleam of white sand flashed back past our boat, so swiftly she ran upon the water. We spoke not. Only once I said, 'Sleep, Diamelen, for soon you may want all your strength.' I heard the sweetness of her voice, but I never turned my head. The sun rose and still we went on. Water fell from my face like rain from a cloud. We flew in the light and heat. I never looked back, but I knew that my brother's eyes, behind me, were looking steadily ahead, for the boat went as straight as a bushman's dart, when it leaves the end of the sumpitan. There was no better paddler, no better steersman than my brother. Many times, together, we had won races in that canoe. But we never had put out our strength as we did then—then, when for the last time we paddled together! There was no braver or stronger man in our country than my brother. I could not spare the strength to turn my head and look at him, but every moment I heard the hiss of his breath getting louder behind me. Still he did not speak. The sun was high. The heat clung to my back like a flame of fire. My ribs were ready to burst, but I could no longer get enough air into my chest. And then I felt I must cry out with my last breath, 'Let us rest!' . . . 'Good!' he answered; and his voice was firm. He was strong. He was brave. He knew not fear and no fatigue . . . My brother!"

A murmur powerful and gentle, a murmur vast and faint; the murmur of trembling leaves, of stirring boughs, ran through the tangled depths of the forests, ran over the starry smoothness of the lagoon, and the water between the piles lapped the slimy timber once with a sudden splash. A breath of warm air touched the two men's faces and passed on with a mournful sound—a breath loud and short like an uneasy sigh of the dreaming earth.

Arsat went on in an even, low voice.

"We ran our canoe on the white beach of a little bay close to a long tongue of land that seemed to bar our road; a long wooded cape going far into the sea. My brother knew that place. Beyond the cape a river has its entrance, and through the jungle of that land there is a narrow path. We made a fire and cooked rice. Then we lay down to sleep on the soft sand in the shade of our canoe, while she watched. No sooner had I closed my eyes than I heard her cry of alarm. We leaped up. The sun was halfway down the sky already, and coming in sight in the opening of the bay we saw a prau manned by many paddlers. We knew it at once; it was one of our Rajah's praus. They were watching the shore, and saw us. They beat the gong, and turned the head of the prau into the bay. I felt my heart become weak within my breast. Diamelen sat on the sand and covered her face. There was no escape by sea. My brother laughed. He had the gun you had given him, Tuan, before you went away, but there was only a handful of powder. He spoke to me quickly: 'Run with her along the path. I shall keep them back, for they have no firearms, and landing in the face of a man with a gun is certain death for some. Run with her. On the other side of that wood there is a fisherman's house—and a canoe. When I have fired all the shots I will follow. I am a great runner, and before they can come up we shall be gone. I will hold out as long as I can, for she is but a woman—that can neither run nor fight, but she has your heart in her weak hands.' He dropped behind the canoe. The prau was coming. She and I ran, and as we rushed along the path I heard shots. My brother fired—once—twice—and the booming of the gong ceased. There was silence behind us. That neck of land is narrow. Before I heard my brother fire the third shot I saw the shelving shore, and I saw the water again; the mouth of a broad river. We crossed a grassy glade. We ran down to the water. I saw a low hut above the black mud, and a small canoe hauled up. I heard another shot behind me. I thought, 'This is his last charge.' We rushed down to the canoe; a man came running from the hut, but I leaped on him, and we rolled together in the mud. Then I got up, and he lay still at my feet. I don't know whether I had killed him or not. I and Diamelen pushed the canoe afloat. I heard yells behind me, and I saw my brother run across the glade. Many men were bounding after him. I took her in my arms and threw her into the boat, then leaped in myself. When I looked back I saw that my brother had fallen. He fell and was up again, but the men were closing round him. He shouted, 'I am coming!' The men were close to him. I looked. Many men. Then I looked at her. Tuan, I pushed the canoe! I pushed it into deep water. She was kneeling forward looking at me, and I said, 'Take your paddle,' while I struck the water with mine. Tuan, I heard him cry. I heard him cry my name twice; and I heard voices shouting, 'Kill! Strike!' I never turned back. I heard him calling my name again with a great shriek, as when life is going out together with the voice—and I never turned my head. My own name! . . . My brother! Three times he called—but I was not afraid of life. Was she not there in that canoe? And could I not with her find a country where death is forgotten—where death is unknown!"

The white man sat up. Arsat rose and stood, an indistinct and silent figure above the dying embers of the fire. Over the lagoon a mist drifting and low had crept, erasing slowly the glittering images of the stars. And now a great expanse of white vapor covered the land: it flowed cold and gray in the darkness, eddied in noiseless whirls round the tree-trunks and about the platform of the house, which seemed to float upon a restless and impalpable illusion of a sea. Only far away the tops of the trees stood outlined on the twinkle of heaven, like a somber and forbidding shore—a coast deceptive, pitiless and black.

Arsat's voice vibrated loudly in the profound peace. "I had her there! I had her! To get her I would have faced all mankind. But I had her—and—"

His words went out ringing into the empty distances. He paused, and seemed to listen to them dying away very far—beyond help and beyond recall. Then he said quietly—

"Tuan, I loved my brother."

A breath of wind made him shiver. High above his head, high above the silent sea of mist the drooping leaves of the palms rattled together with a mournful and expiring sound. The white man stretched his legs. His chin rested on his chest, and he murmured sadly without lifting his head—

"We all love our brothers."

Arsat burst out with an intense whispering violence—

"What did I care who died? I wanted peace in my own heart."

He seemed to hear a stir in the house—listened—then stepped in noiselessly. The white man stood up. A breeze was coming in fitful puffs. The stars shone paler as if they had retreated into the frozen depths of immense space. After a chill gust of wind there were a few seconds of perfect calm and absolute silence. Then from behind the black and wavy line of the forests a column of golden light shot up into the heavens and spread over the semicircle of the eastern horizon. The sun had risen. The mist lifted, broke into drifting patches, vanished into thin flying wreaths; and the unveiled lagoon lay, polished and black, in the heavy shadows at the foot of the wall of trees. A white eagle rose over it with a slanting and ponderous flight, reached the clear sunshine and appeared dazzlingly brilliant for a moment, then soaring higher, became a dark and motionless speck before it vanished into the blue as if it had left the earth forever. The white man, standing gazing upwards before the doorway, heard in the hut a confused and broken murmur of distracted words ending with a loud groan. Suddenly Arsat stumbled out with outstretched hands, shivered, and stood still for some time with fixed eyes. Then he said—

"She burns no more."

Before his face the sun showed its edge above the treetops rising steadily. The breeze freshened; a great brilliance burst upon the lagoon, sparkled on the rippling water. The forests came out of the clear shadows of the morning, became distinct, as if they had rushed nearer—to stop short in a great stir of leaves, of nodding boughs, of swaying branches. In the merciless sunshine the whisper of unconscious life grew louder, speaking in an incomprehensible voice round the dumb darkness of that human sorrow. Arsat's eyes wandered slowly, then stared at the rising sun.

"I can see nothing," he said half aloud to himself.

"There is nothing," said the white man, moving to the edge of the platform and waving his hand to his boat. A shout came faintly over the lagoon and the sampan began to glide towards the abode of the friend of ghosts.

"If you want to come with me, I will wait all the morning," said the white man, looking away upon the water.

"No, Tuan," said Arsat, softly. "I shall not eat or sleep in this house, but I must first see my road. Now I can see nothing—see nothing! There is no light and no peace in the world; but there is death—death for many. We are sons of the same mother—and I left him in the midst of enemies; but I am going back now."

He drew a long breath and went on in a dreamy tone:

"In a little while I shall see clear enough to strike—to strike. But she has died, and . . . now . . . darkness."

He flung his arms wide open, let them fall along his body, then stood still with unmoved face and stony eyes, staring at the sun. The white man got down into his canoe. The polers ran smartly along the sides of the boat, looking over their shoulders at the beginning of a weary journey. High in the stern, his head muffled up in white rags, the juragan sat moody, letting his paddle trail in the water. The white man, leaning with both arms over the grass roof of the little cabin, looked back at the shining ripple of the boat's wake. Before the sampan passed out of the lagoon into the creek he lifted his eyes. Arsat had not moved. He stood lonely in the searching sunshine; and he looked beyond the great light of a cloudless day into the darkness of a world of illusions.

JAMES JOYCE

Eveline

James Joyce (1882–1941), born in Dublin, Ireland, is considered by many critics to have been the most influential novelist of the twentieth century. In 1904 Joyce exiled himself from Ireland in general and from "dear, dirty Dublin" in particular. Although he returned briefly in 1912, Joyce spent most of his adult life on the European continent. In 1914 he published his first major work, *Dubliners*, a collection of varied short stories describing facets of everyday life in Dublin. A highly autobiographical novel, *A Portrait of the Artist as a Young Man*, appeared in 1916 and *Finnegan's Wake*, a massive intermixing of dream and reality, was published in 1939. In 1922 Joyce published his masterwork, *Ulysses*, perhaps the most influential novel of modern times. *Ulysses*, paralleling Homer's *Odyssey* in many ways, recounts a single day in the life of Dubliner Leopold Bloom.

"Eveline," drawn from the *Dubliners* collection and based in part on the actual experiences of Dubliner Eveline Thornton, illustrates Joyce's view of the inertia and stagnation imposed by the city of Dublin and its culture upon its inhabitants.

She sat at the window watching the evening invade the avenue. Her head was leaned against

EVELINE From *Dubliners* by James Joyce. Originally published in 1916 by B. W. Heubsch. Definitive text Copyright © 1967 by the Estate of James Joyce. Reprinted by permission of Viking Penguin Inc.

the window curtains and in her nostrils was the odour of dusty cretonne. She was tired.

Few people passed. The man out of the last house passed on his way home; she heard his footsteps clacking along the concrete pavement and afterwards crunching on the cinder path before the new red houses. One time there used to be a field there in which they used to play every evening with other people's children. Then a man from Belfast bought the field and built houses in it—not like their little brown houses but bright brick houses with shining roofs. The children of the avenue used to play together in that field—the Devines, the Waters, the Dunns, little Keogh the cripple, she and her brothers and sisters. Ernest, however, never played: he was too grown up. Her father used often to hunt them in out of the field with his blackthorn stick; but usually little Keogh used to keep *nix* and call out when he saw her father coming. Still they seemed to have been rather happy then. Her father was not so bad then; and besides, her mother was alive. That was a long time ago; she and her brothers and sisters were all grown up; her mother was dead. Tizzie Dunn was dead, too, and the Waters had gone back to England. Everything changes. Now she was going to go away like the others, to leave her home.

Home! She looked round the room, reviewing all its familiar objects which she had dusted once a week for so many years, wondering where on earth all the dust came from. Perhaps she would never see again those familiar objects from which she had never dreamed of being divided. And yet during all those years she had never found out the name of the priest whose yellowing photograph hung on the wall above the broken harmonium beside the coloured print of the promises made to Blessed Margaret Mary Alacoque. He had been a school friend of her father. Whenever he showed the photograph to a visitor her father used to pass it with a casual word:

—He is in Melbourne now.

She had consented to go away, to leave her home. Was that wise? She tried to weigh each side of the question. In her home anyway she had shelter and food; she had those whom she had known all her life about her. Of course she had to work hard both in the house and at business. What would they say of her in the Stores when they found out that she had run away with a fellow? Say she was a fool, perhaps; and her place would be filled up by advertisement. Miss Gavan would be glad. She had always had an edge on her, especially whenever there were people listening.

—Miss Hill, don't you see these ladies are waiting?

—Look lively, Miss Hill, please.

She would not cry many tears at leaving the Stores.

But in her new home, in a distant unknown country, it would not be like that. Then she would be married—she, Eveline. People would treat her with respect then. She would not be treated as her mother had been. Even now, though she was over nineteen, she sometimes felt herself in danger of her father's violence. She knew it was that that had given her the palpitations. When they were growing up he had never gone for her, like he used to go for Harry and Ernest, because she was a girl; but latterly he had begun to threaten her and say what he would do to her only for her dead mother's sake. And now she had nobody to protect her. Ernest was dead and Harry, who was in the church decorating business, was nearly always down somewhere in the country. Besides, the invariable squabble for money on Saturday nights had begun to weary her unspeakably. She always gave her entire wages—seven shillings—and Harry always sent up what he could but the trouble was to get any money from her father. He said she used to squander the money, that she had no head, that he wasn't going to give her his hard-earned money to throw about the streets, and much more, for he was usually fairly bad of a Saturday night. In the end he would give her the money and ask her had she any intention of buying Sunday's dinner. Then she had to rush out as quickly as she could and do her marketing, holding her black leather purse tightly in her hand as she elbowed her way through the crowds and returning home late under her load of provisions. She had hard work to keep the house together and to see that the two young children who had been left to her charge went to school regularly and got their meals regularly. It was hard work—a hard life—but now that she was about to leave it she did not find it a wholly undesirable life.

She was about to explore another life with Frank. Frank was very kind, manly, openhearted. She was to go away with him by the night-boat to be his wife and to live with him in Buenos Ayres where he had a home waiting for her. How well she remembered the first time she had seen him; he was lodging in a house on the main road where she used to visit. It seemed a few weeks ago. He was standing at the gate, his peaked cap pushed back on his head and his hair tumbled forward over a face of bronze. Then they had come to know each other. He used to meet her outside the Stores every evening and see her home. He took her to see *The Bohemian Girl* and she felt elated as she sat in an unaccustomed part of the theatre with him. He was awfully fond of music and sang a little. People knew that they were courting and, when he sang about the lass that loves a sailor, she always felt pleasantly confused. He used to call her Poppens out of fun. First of all it had been an excitement for her to have a fellow and then she had begun to like him. He had tales of distant countries. He had started as a deck boy at a pound a month on a ship of the Allan Line going out to Canada. He told her the names of the ships he had been on and the names of the different services. He had sailed through the Straits of Magellan and he told her stories of the terrible Patagonians. He had fallen on his feet in Buenos Ayres, he said, and had come over to the old country just for a holiday. Of course, her father had found out the affair and had forbidden her to have anything to say to him.

—I know these sailor chaps, he said.

One day he had quarrelled with Frank and after that she had to meet her love secretly.

The evening deepened in the avenue. The white of two letters in her lap grew indistinct. One was to Harry; the other was to her father. Ernest had been her favourite but she liked Harry too. Her father was becoming old lately, she noticed; he would miss her. Sometimes he could be very nice. Not long before, when she had been laid up for a day, he had read her out a ghost story and made toast for her at the fire. Another day, when their mother was alive, they had all gone for a picnic to the Hill of Howth. She remembered her father putting on her mother's bonnet to make the children laugh.

Her time was running out but she continued to sit by the window, leaning her head against the window curtain, inhaling the odour of dusty cretonne. Down far in the avenue she could hear a street organ playing. She knew the air. Strange that it should come that very night to remind her of the promise to her mother, her promise to keep the home together as long as she could. She remembered the last night of her mother's illness; she was again in the close dark room at the other side of the hall and outside she heard a melancholy air of Italy. The organ-player had been ordered to go away and given sixpence. She re-

membered her father strutting back into the sickroom saying:

—Damned Italians! coming over here!

As she mused the pitiful vision of her mother's life laid its spell on the very quick of her being—that life of commonplace sacrifices closing in final craziness. She trembled as she heard again her mother's voice saying constantly with foolish insistence:

—Derevaun Seraun! Derevaun Seraun!

She stood up in a sudden impulse of terror. Escape! She must escape! Frank would save her. He would give her life, perhaps love, too. But she wanted to live. Why should she be unhappy? She had a right to happiness. Frank would take her in his arms, fold her in his arms. He would save her.

.　　.　　.

She stood among the swaying crowd in the station at the North Wall. He held her hand and she knew that he was speaking to her, saying something about the passage over and over again. The station was full of soldiers with brown baggages. Through the wide doors of the sheds she caught a glimpse of the black mass of the boat, lying in beside the quay wall, with illumined portholes. She answered nothing. She felt her cheek pale and cold and, out of a maze of distress, she prayed to God to direct her, to show her what was her duty. The boat blew a long mournful whistle into the mist. If she went, to-morrow she would be on the sea with Frank, steaming toward Buenos Ayres. Their passage had been booked. Could she still draw back after all he had done for her? Her distress awoke a nausea in her body and she kept moving her lips in silent fervent prayer.

A bell clanged upon her heart. She felt him seize her hand:

—Come!

All the seas of the world tumbled about her heart. He was drawing her into them: he would drown her. She gripped with both hands at the iron railing.

No! No! No! It was impossible. Her hands clutched the iron in frenzy. Amid the seas she sent a cry of anguish!

—Eveline! Evvy!

He rushed beyond the barrier and called to her to follow. He was shouted at to go on but he still called to her. She set her white face to him, passive, like a helpless animal. Her eyes gave him no sign of love or farewell or recognition.

FRANZ KAFKA

An Old Manuscript

Franz Kafka (1883–1924) was born in Prague of Czechoslovakian Jewish ancestry. He received a doctorate in jurisprudence from Karls-Ferdinand, a German university in Prague. A high-strung, sensitive individual, he continually sought new outlets for his intellectual interests and came under various influences—the Zionist Max Brod, Franz Werfel, Kierkegaard, and Pascal. With the encouragement of Brod, Kafka published his first books, *Observations* and *The Judgment,* in 1913. Thereafter he wrote steadily despite his ever declining health. *Metamorphosis* was published in 1915; *The Trial* in 1925; *The Castle* in 1926—the last two posthumously. In the summer of 1923 he married and enjoyed a few months of contentment, during which he wrote *A Little Woman.* By Christmas of 1923, however, he was again very ill and in June 1924 he died of tuberculosis.

Kafka was a part of a movement known as existentialism, which views the world essentially as cosmic chaos, absurd and hostile to man. His writings are rich in symbols that communicate his despairing attitude toward civilization. Typical of this aspect of Kafka's art, "An Old Manuscript" involves more than the literal meaning conveys.

It looks as if much has been neglected in our country's system of defense. We have not concerned ourselves with it until now and have gone about our daily work; but things that have been happening recently begin to trouble us.

I have a cobbler's workshop in the square that lies before the Emperor's palace. Scarcely have I taken my shutters down, at the first glimpse of dawn, when I see armed soldiers already posted in the mouth of every street opening on the square. But these soldiers are not ours, they are obviously nomads from the North. In some way that is incomprehensible to me they have pushed right into the capital, although it is a long way from the frontier. At any rate, here they are; it seems that every morning there are more of them.

As is their nature, they camp under the open sky, for they abominate dwelling houses. They busy themselves sharpening swords, whittling arrows and practicing horsemanship. This peaceful square, which was always kept scrupulously clean, they have made literally into a stable. We do try every now and then to run out of our shops and clear away at least the worst of the filth, but this happens less and less often, for the labor is in vain and brings us besides into danger of falling under the hoofs of the wild horses or of being crippled with lashes from the whips.

Speech with the nomads is impossible. They do not know our language, indeed they hardly have a language of their own. They communicate with each other much as jackdaws do. A screeching of jackdaws is always in our ears. Our way of living and our institutions they neither understand nor care to understand. And so they are unwilling to make sense even out of our sign language. You can gesture at them till you dislocate your jaws and your wrists and still they will not have understood you and will never understand. They often make grimaces; then the whites of their eyes turn up and foam gathers on their lips, but they do not mean anything by that, not even a threat; they do it because it is their nature to do it. Whatever they need, they take. You cannot call it taking by force. They grab at something and you simply stand aside and leave them to it.

From my stock, too, they have taken many good articles. But I cannot complain when I see how the butcher, for instance, suffers across the street. As soon as he brings in any meat the nomads snatch it all from him and gobble it up. Even their horses devour flesh; often enough a horseman and his horse are lying side by side, both of them gnawing at the same joint, one at either end. The butcher is nervous and does not dare to stop his deliveries of meat. We understand that, however, and subscribe money to keep him going. If the nomads got no meat, who knows what they might think of doing; who knows anyhow what they may think of, even though they get meat every day.

Not long ago the butcher thought he might at least spare himself the trouble of slaughtering, and so one morning he brought along a live ox. But he will never dare to do that again. I lay for a whole hour flat on the floor at the back of my workshop with my head muffled in all the clothes and rugs and pillows I had, simply to keep from hearing the bellowing of that ox, which the nomads were leaping on from all sides, tearing morsels out of its living flesh with their teeth. It had been quiet for a long time before I risked coming out; they were lying overcome round the remains of the carcass like drunkards round a wine cask.

This was the occasion when I fancied I actually saw the Emperor himself at a window of the palace; usually he never enters these outer rooms but spends all of his time in the innermost garden; yet on this occasion he was standing, or so at least it seemed to me, at one of the windows, watching with bent head the ongoings before his residence.

"What is going to happen?" we all ask ourselves. "How long can we endure this burden and torment? The Emperor's palace has drawn the nomads here but does not know how to drive them away again. The gate stays shut; the guards, who used to be always marching out and in with ceremony, keep close behind barred windows. It is left to us artisans and tradesmen to save our country; but we are not equal to such a task; nor have we ever claimed to be capable of it. This is a misunderstanding of some kind; and it will be the ruin of us."

KAY BOYLE

Astronomer's Wife

Kay Boyle (1903–   ), born in Minneapolis, has lived most of her life in Europe. She has written short stories, novels, and poems and has twice been awarded the O. Henry Memorial Award, in 1935 for "White Horses of Vienna," and in 1941 for "Defeat." A theme consistently present in her works written since 1945 has been the upheaval and disruption in Europe caused by World War II. Boyle's more recent works include: *Nothing Ever Breaks the Heart*, 1966; *The Long Walk at San Francisco State*, 1970; and *The Underground Woman*, 1975.

In "Astronomer's Wife" Boyle pinpoints the ironic distance between the actions and reactions of women and those of men. This ironic contrast is probed through the context of the "astronomer" and the "astronomer's wife."

ASTRONOMER'S WIFE From *The White Horses of Vienna and Other Stories* by Kay Boyle. Copyright 1936 by Kay Boyle. First published in *The New Yorker*. Reprinted by permission of the A. Watkins Agency, Inc.

There is an evil moment on awakening when all things seem to pause. But for women, they only falter and may be set in action by a single move: a lifted hand and the pendulum will swing, or the voice raised and through every room the pulse takes up its beating. The astronomer's wife felt the interval gaping and at once filled it to the brim. She fetched up her gentle voice and sent it warily down the stairs for coffee, swung her feet out upon the oval mat, and hailed the morning with her bare arms' quivering flesh drawn taut in rhythmic exercise: left, left, left my wife and fourteen children, right, right, right in the middle of the dusty road.

The day would proceed from this, beat by beat, without reflection, like every other day. The astronomer was still asleep, or feigning it, and she, once out of bed, had come into her own possession. Although scarcely ever out of sight of the impenetrable silence of his brow, she would be absent from him all the day in being clean, busy, kind. He was a man of other things, a dreamer. At times he lay still for hours, at others he sat upon the roof behind his telescope, or wandered down the pathway to the road and out across the mountains. This day, like any other, would go on from the removal of the spot left there from dinner on the astronomer's vest to the severe thrashing of the mayonnaise for lunch. That man might be each time the new arching wave, and woman the undertow that sucked him back, were things she had been told by his silence were so.

In spite of the earliness of the hour, the girl had heard her mistress's voice and was coming up the stairs. At the threshold of the bedroom she paused, and said: "Madame, the plumber is here."

The astronomer's wife put on her white and scarlet smock very quickly and buttoned it at the neck. Then she stepped carefully around the motionless spread of water in the hall.

"Tell him to come right up," she said. She laid her hands on the bannisters and stood looking down the wooden stairway. "Ah, I am Mrs. Ames," she said softly as she saw him mounting. "I am Mrs. Ames," she said softly, softly down the flight of stairs. "I am Mrs. Ames," spoken soft as a willow weeping. "The professor is still sleeping. Just step this way."

The plumber himself looked up and saw Mrs. Ames with her voice hushed, speaking to him. She was a youngish woman, but this she had for-gotten. The mystery and silence of her husband's mind lay like a chiding finger on her lips. Her eyes were gray, for the light had been extinguished in them. The strange dim halo of her yellow hair was still uncombed and sideways on her head.

For all of his heavy boots, the plumber quieted the sound of his feet, and together they went down the hall, picking their way around the still lake of water that spread as far as the landing and lay docile there. The plumber was a tough, hardy man; but he took off his hat when he spoke to her and looked her fully, almost insolently in the eye.

"Does it come from the wash-basin," he said, "or from the other . . . ?"

"Oh, from the other," said Mrs. Ames without hesitation.

In this place the villas were scattered out few and primitive, and although beauty lay without there was no reflection of her face within. Here all was awkward and unfit; a sense of wrestling with uncouth forces gave everything an austere countenance. Even the plumber, dealing as does a woman with matters under hand, was grave and stately. The mountains round about seemed to have cast them into the shadow of great dignity.

Mrs. Ames began speaking of their arrival that summer in the little villa, mourning each event as it followed on the other.

"Then, just before going to bed last night," she said, "I noticed something was unusual."

The plumber cast down a folded square of sack-cloth on the brimming floor and laid his leather apron on it. Then he stepped boldly onto the heart of the island it shaped and looked long into the overflowing bowl.

"The water should be stopped from the meter in the garden," he said at last.

"Oh, I did that," said Mrs. Ames, "the very first thing last night. I turned it off at once, in my nightgown, as soon as I saw what was happening. But all this had already run in."

The plumber looked for a moment at her red kid slippers. She was standing just at the edge of the clear, pure-seeming tide.

"It's no doubt the soil lines," he said severely. "It may be that something has stopped them, but my opinion is that the water seals aren't working. That's the trouble often enough in such cases. If you had a valve you wouldn't be caught like this."

Mrs. Ames did not know how to meet this rebuke. She stood, swaying a little, looking into the plumber's blue relentless eye.

"I'm sorry—I'm sorry that my husband," she said, "is still—resting and cannot go into this with you. I'm sure it must be very interesting. . . ."

"You'll probably have to have the traps sealed," said the plumber grimly, and at the sound of this Mrs. Ames' hand flew in dismay to the side of her face. The plumber made no move, but the set of his mouth as he looked at her seemed to soften. "Anyway, I'll have a look from the garden end," he said.

"Oh, do," said the astronomer's wife in relief. Here was a man who spoke of action and object as simply as women did! But however hushed her voice had been, it carried clearly to Professor Ames who lay, dreaming and solitary, upon his bed. He heard their footsteps come down the hall, pause, and skip across the pool of overflow.

"Katherine!" said the astronomer in a ringing tone. "There's a problem worthy of your mettle!"

Mrs. Ames did not turn her head, but led the plumber swiftly down the stairs. When the sun in the garden struck her face, he saw there was a wave of color in it, but this may have been anything but shame.

"You see how it is," said the plumber, as if leading her mind away. "The drains run from these houses right down the hill, big enough for a man to stand upright in them, and clean as a whistle too." There they stood in the garden with the vegetation flowering in disorder all about. The plumber looked at the astronomer's wife. "They come out at the torrent on the other side of the forest beyond there," he said.

But the words the astronomer had spoken still sounded in her in despair. The mind of man, she knew, made steep and sprightly flights, pursued illusion, took foothold in the nameless things that cannot pass between the thumb and finger. But whenever the astronomer gave voice to the thoughts that soared within him, she returned in gratitude to the long expanses of his silence. Desert-like they stretched behind and before the articulation of his scorn.

Life, life is an open sea, she sought to explain it in sorrow, and to survive women cling to the floating débris on the tide. But the plumber had suddenly fallen upon his knees in the grass and had crooked his fingers through the ring of the drains' trap-door. When she looked down she saw that he was looking up into her face, and she saw too that his hair was as light as gold.

"Perhaps Mr. Ames," he said rather bitterly, "would like to come down with me and have a look around?"

"Down?" said Mrs. Ames in wonder.

"Into the drains," said the plumber brutally. "They're a study for a man who likes to know what's what."

"Oh, Mr. Ames," said Mrs. Ames in confusion. "He's still—still in bed, you see."

The plumber lifted his strong, weathered face and looked curiously at her. Surely it seemed to him strange for a man to linger in bed, with the sun pouring yellow as wine all over the place. The astronomer's wife saw his lean cheeks, his high, rugged bones, and the deep seams in his brow. His flesh was as firm and clean as wood, stained richly tan with the climate's rigor. His fingers were blunt, but comprehensible to her, gripped in the ring and holding the iron door wide. The backs of his hands were bound round and round with ripe blue veins of blood.

"At any rate," said the astronomer's wife, and the thought of it moved her lips to smile a little, "Mr. Ames would never go down there alive. He likes going up," she said. And she, in her turn, pointed, but impudently, towards the heavens. "On the roof. Or on the mountains. He's been up on the tops of them many times."

"It's a matter of habit," said the plumber, and suddenly he went down the trap. Mrs. Ames saw a bright little piece of his hair still shining, like a star, long after the rest of him had gone. Out of the depths, his voice, hollow and dark with foreboding, returned to her. "I think something has stopped the elbow," was what he said.

This was speech that touched her flesh and bone and made her wonder. When her husband spoke of height, having no sense of it, she could not picture it nor hear. Depth or magic passed her by unless a name were given. But madness in a daily shape, as elbow stopped, she saw clearly and well. She sat down on the grasses, bewildered that it should be a man who had spoken to her so.

She saw the weeds springing up, and she did not move to tear them up from life. She sat powerless, her senses veiled, with no action taking shape beneath her hands. In this way some men sat for hours on end, she knew, tracking a single thought back to its origin. The mind of man could balance and divide, weed out, destroy. She sat on the full, burdened grasses, seeking to think, and dimly waiting for the plumber to return.

Whereas her husband had always gone up, as the dead go, she knew now that there were others who went down, like the corporeal being of the dead. That men were then divided into two bodies now seemed clear to Mrs. Ames. This knowledge stunned her with its simplicity and took the uneasy motion from her limbs. She could not stir, but sat facing the mountains' rocky flanks, and harking in silence to lucidity. Her husband was the mind, this other man the meat, of all mankind.

After a little, the plumber emerged from the earth: first the light top of his head, then the burnt brow, and then the blue eyes fringed with whitest lash. He braced his thick hands flat on the pavings of the garden-path and swung himself completely from the pit.

"It's the soil lines," he said pleasantly. "The gases," he said as he looked down upon her lifted face, "are backing up the drains."

"What in the world are we going to do?" said the astronomer's wife softly. There was a young and strange delight in putting questions to which true answers would be given. Everything the astronomer had ever said to her was a continuous query to which there could be no response.

"Ah, come, now," said the plumber, looking down and smiling. "There's a remedy for every ill, you know. Sometimes it may be that," he said as if speaking to a child, "or sometimes the other

thing. But there's always a help for everything a-miss."

Things come out of herbs and make you young again, he might have been saying to her; or the first good rain will quench any drought; or time of itself will put a broken bone together.

"I'm going to follow the ground pipe out right to the torrent," the plumber was saying. "The trouble's between here and there and I'll find it on the way. There's nothing at all that can't be done over for the caring," he was saying, and his eyes were fastened on her face in insolence, or gentleness, or love.

The astronomer's wife stood up, fixed a pin in her hair, and turned around towards the kitchen. Even while she was calling the servant's name, the plumber began speaking again.

"I once had a cow that lost her cud," the plumber was saying. The girl came out on the kitchen-step and Mrs. Ames stood smiling at her in the sun.

"The trouble is very serious, very serious," she said across the garden. "When Mr. Ames gets up, please tell him I've gone down."

She pointed briefly to the open door in the pathway, and the plumber hoisted his kit on his arm and put out his hand to help her down.

"But I made her another in no time," he was saying, "out of flowers and things and what-not."

"Oh," said the astronomer's wife in wonder as she stepped into the heart of the earth. She took his arm, knowing that what he said was true.

E. B. WHITE

The Door

Elwyn Brooks White (1899–   ), the well-known essayist, has written for *The New Yorker* for many years. A characteristic collection of his essays is *The Second Tree from the Corner*, 1954. In 1959 White revised William Strunk's *Elements of Style*, a composition textbook he had used as a student, and this revised edition has been in steady use by students ever since. As a writer of children's stories, White is unsurpassed: *Stuart Little*, 1945, and *Charlotte's Web*, 1952, continue to be best-sellers, as does *The Trumpet of the Swan*, 1970. His most recent titles include *Letters of E. B. White*, 1976, and *Essays of E. B. White*, 1977.

In "The Door" the effects of the ersatz and gimmicky world that technology has created are shown in the growing disorientation of the main character's personality.

Everything (he kept saying) is something it isn't. And everybody is always somewhere else. Maybe it was the city, being in the city, that made him feel how queer everything was and that it was something else. Maybe (he kept thinking) it was the names of the things. The names were tex and frequently koid. Or they were flex and oid or they were duroid (sani) or flexsan (duro), but everything was glass (but not quite glass) and the thing that you touched (the surface, washable, crease-resistant) was rubber, only it wasn't quite rubber and you didn't quite touch it but almost. The wall, which was glass but thrutex, turned out on being approached not to be a wall, it was something else, it was an opening or doorway— and the doorway (through which he saw himself approaching) turned out to be something else, it was a wall. And what he had eaten not having agreed with him.

He was in a washable house, but he wasn't sure. Now about those rats, he kept saying to himself. He meant the rats that the Professor had driven crazy by forcing them to deal with problems which were beyond the scope of rats, the

insoluble problems. He meant the rats that had been trained to jump at the square card with the circle in the middle, and the card (because it was something it wasn't) would give way and let the rat into a place where the food was, but then one day it would be a trick played on the rat, and the card would be changed, and the rat would jump but the card wouldn't give way, and it was an impossible situation (for a rat) and the rat would go insane and into its eyes would come the unspeakably bright imploring look of the frustrated, and after the convulsions were over and the frantic racing around, then the passive stage would set in and the willingness to let anything be done to it, even if it was something else.

He didn't know which door (or wall) or opening in the house to jump at, to get through, because one was an opening that wasn't a door (it was a void, or koid) and the other was a wall that wasn't an opening, it was a sanitary cupboard of the same color. He caught a glimpse of his eyes staring into his eyes, in the thrutex, and in them was the expression he had seen in the picture of the rats—weary after convulsions and the frantic racing around, when they were willing and did not mind having anything done to them. More and more (he kept saying) I am

THE DOOR From *The Second Tree from the Corner* by E. B. White. Copyright 1939, 1967 by E. B. White. Reprinted with the permission of Harper & Row, Publishers, Inc.

confronted by a problem which is incapable of solution (for this time even if he chose the right door, there would be no food behind it) and that is what madness is, and things seeming different from what they are. He heard, in the house where he was, in the city to which he had gone (as toward a door which might, or might not, give way), a noise—not a loud noise but more of a low prefabricated humming. It came from a place in the base of the wall (or stat) where the flue carrying the filterable air was, and not far from the Minipiano, which was made of the same material nailbrushes are made of, and which was under the stairs. "This, too, has been tested," she said, pointing, but not at it, "and found viable." It wasn't a loud noise, he kept thinking, sorry that he had seen his eyes, even though it was through his own eyes that he had seen them.

First will come the convulsions (he said), then the exhaustion, then the willingness to let anything be done. "And you better believe it *will* be."

All his life he had been confronted by situations which were incapable of being solved, and there was a deliberateness behind all this, behind this changing of the card (or door), because they would always wait till you had learned to jump at the certain card (or door)—the one with the circle—and then they would change it on you. There have been so many doors changed on me, he said, in the last twenty years, but it is now becoming clear that it is an impossible situation, and the question is whether to jump again, even though they ruffle you in the rump with a blast of air—to make you jump. He wished he wasn't standing by the Minipiano. First they would teach you the prayers and the Psalms, and that would be the right door (the one with the circle) and the long sweet words with the holy sound, and that would be the one to jump at to get where the food was. Then one day you jumped and it didn't give way, so that all you got was the bump on the nose, and the first bewilderment, the first young bewilderment.

I don't know whether to tell her about the door they substituted or not, he said, the one with the equation on it and the picture of the amoeba reproducing itself by division. Or the one with the photostatic copy of the check for thirty-two dollars and fifty cents. But the jumping was so long ago, although the bump is . . . how those old wounds hurt! Being crazy this way wouldn't be so bad if only, if only. If only when you put your foot forward to take a step, the ground wouldn't come up to meet your foot the way it does. And the same way in the street (only I may never get back to the street unless I jump at the right door), the curb coming up to meet your foot, anticipating ever so delicately the weight of the body, which is somewhere else. "We could take your name," she said, "and send it to you." And it wouldn't be so bad if only you could read a sentence all the way through without jumping (your eye) to something else on the same page; and then (he kept thinking) here was that man out in Jersey, the one who started to chop his trees down, one by one, the man who began talking about how he would take his house to pieces, brick by brick, because he faced a problem incapable of solution, probably, so he began to hack at the trees in the yard, began to pluck with trembling fingers at the bricks in the house. Even if a house is not washable, it is worth taking down. It is not till later that the exhaustion sets in.

But it is inevitable that they will keep changing the doors on you, he said, because that is what they are for; and the thing is to get used to it and not let it unsettle the mind. But that would mean not jumping, and you can't. Nobody can not jump. There will be no not-jumping. Among rats, perhaps, but among people never. Everybody has to keep jumping at a door (the one with the circle on it) because that is the way everybody is, specially some people. You wouldn't want me, standing here, to tell you, would you, about my friend the poet (deceased) who said, "My heart has followed all my days something I cannot name"? (It had the circle on it.) And like many poets, although few so beloved, he is gone. It killed him, the jumping. First, of course, there were the preliminary bouts, the convulsions, and the calm and the willingness.

I remember the door with the picture of the girl on it (only it was spring), her arms outstretched in loveliness, her dress (it was the one with the circle on it) uncaught, beginning the slow, clear, blinding cascade—and I guess we would all like to try that door again, for it seemed like the way and for a while it was the way, the door would open and you would go through winged and exalted (like any rat) and the food would be there, the way the Professor had it arranged, everything O.K., and you had chosen the right door for the world was young. The time they changed that door on me, my nose bled for a hundred hours—how do you like that, Madam? Or would you prefer to show me further through this so strange house, or you could take my name and send it to me, for although my heart has followed all my days something I cannot name, I am tired of the jumping and I do not know which way to go, Madam, and I am not even sure that I am not tired beyond the endurance of man (rat, if you will) and have taken leave of sanity. What are you following these days, old friend, after your recovery from the last bump? What is the name, or is it something you cannot name? The rats have a name for it by this time, perhaps, but I don't know what they call it. I call it plexikoid and it comes in sheets, something like insulating board, unattainable and ugli-proof.

And there was the man out in Jersey, because I keep thinking about his terrible necessity and the passion and trouble he had gone to all those years in the indescribable abundance of a householder's detail, building the estate and the planting of the trees and in spring the lawn-dressing and in fall the bulbs for the spring burgeoning, and the watering of the grass on the long light evenings in summer and the gravel for the driveway (all had to be thought out, planned) and the decorative borders, probably, the perennials and the bug spray, and the building of the house from plans of the architect, first the sills, then the studs, then the full corn in the ear, the floors laid on the floor timbers, smoothed, and then the carpets upon the smooth floors and the curtains and the rods therefor. And then, almost without warning, he would be jumping at the same old door and it wouldn't give: they had changed it

on him, making life no longer supportable under the elms in the elm shade, under the maples in the maple shade.

"Here you have the maximum of openness in a small room."

It was impossible to say (maybe it was the city) what made him feel the way he did, and I am not the only one either, he kept thinking—ask any doctor if I am. The doctors, they know how many there are, they even know where the trouble is only they don't like to tell you about the prefrontal lobe because that means making a hole in your skull and removing the work of centuries. It took so long coming, this lobe, so many, many years. (Is it something you read in the paper, perhaps?) And now, the strain being so great, the door having been changed by the Professor once too often . . . but it only means a whiff of ether, a few deft strokes, and the higher animal becomes a little easier in his mind and more like the lower one. From now on, you see, that's the way it will be, the ones with the small prefrontal lobes will win because the other ones are hurt too much by this incessant bumping. They can stand just so much, eh, Doctor? (And what is that, pray, that you have in your hand?) Still, you never can tell, eh, Madam?

He crossed (carefully) the room, the thick carpet under him softly, and went toward the door carefully, which was glass and he could see himself in it, and which, at his approach, opened to allow him to pass through; and beyond he half expected to find one of the old doors that he had known, perhaps the one with the circle, the one with the girl her arms outstretched in loveliness and beauty before him. But he saw instead a moving stairway, and descended in light (he kept thinking) to the street below and to the other people. As he stepped off, the ground came up slightly, to meet his foot.

JOHN STEINBECK

The Chrysanthemums

John Steinbeck (1902–1968) was born in Salinas, California, and attended Stanford University. *Pastures of Heaven*, 1932, a collection of short stories about a rural community in the Salinas Valley, foreshadowed his later style. *Tortilla Flat*, 1935, first brought him attention as a writer, and this success was followed by *In Dubious Battle*, 1936; *Of Mice and Men*, 1937; and *The Grapes of Wrath*, 1939, for which he received the Pulitzer Prize. During World War II he was a war reporter for the New York *Herald Tribune*. In 1941, with Edward F. Ricketts, he wrote *Sea of Cortez*, a report of their explorations in the Gulf of California. *East of Eden*, 1952, was his first major novel after the war. This was followed by *The Winter of Our Discontent*, 1961; and *Travels with Charley*, 1962, an account of his journey across America. *America and Americans* appeared in 1966. In 1962 he was awarded the Nobel Prize for Literature and in 1964 he received the Presidential Medal of Freedom.

Mr. Steinbeck's short stories and novels tend to begin realistically and conclude symbolically. This tendency is vividly displayed in *The Grapes of Wrath*. It is also shown in "The Chrysanthemums," where the reader senses a strong conflict but, because of indirection in the telling of the story, must draw his own inference.

The high grey-flannel fog of winter closed off the Salinas Valley from the sky and from all the rest of the world. On every side it sat like a lid on the mountains and made of the great valley a closed pot. On the broad, level land floor the gang plows bit deep and left the black earth shining like metal where the shares had cut. On the foothill ranches across the Salinas River, the yellow stubble fields seemed to be bathed in pale cold sunshine, but there was no sunshine in the valley now in December. The thick willow scrub along the river flamed with sharp and positive yellow leaves.

It was a time of quiet and of waiting. The air was cold and tender. A light wind blew up from the southwest so that the farmers were mildly hopeful of a good rain before long; but fog and rain did not go together.

Across the river, on Henry Allen's foothill ranch there was little work to be done, for the hay was cut and stored and the orchards were plowed up to receive the rain deeply when it should come. The cattle on the higher slopes were becoming shaggy and rough-coated.

Elisa Allen, working in her flower garden, looked down across the yard and saw Henry, her husband, talking to two men in business suits. The three of them stood by the tractor shed, each man with one foot on the side of the little Fordson. They smoked cigarettes and studied the machine as they talked.

Elisa watched them for a moment and then went back to her work. She was thirty-five. Her face was lean and strong and her eyes were as clear as water. Her figure looked blocked and heavy in her gardening costume, a man's black

THE CHRYSANTHEMUMS From *The Long Valley* by John Steinbeck. Copyright 1937, © renewed 1965 by John Steinbeck. Reprinted by permission of The Viking Press, Inc.

hat pulled low down over her eyes, clod-hopper shoes, a figured print dress almost completely covered by a big corduroy apron with four big pockets to hold the snips, the trowel and scratcher, the seeds and the knife she worked with. She wore heavy leather gloves to protect her hands while she worked.

She was cutting down the old year's chrysanthemum stalks with a pair of short and powerful scissors. She looked down toward the men by the tractor shed now and then. Her face was eager and mature and handsome; even her work with the scissors was over-eager, over-powerful. The chrysanthemum stems seemed too small and easy for her energy.

She brushed a cloud of hair out of her eyes with the back of her glove, and left a smudge of earth on her cheek in doing it. Behind her stood the neat white farm house with red geraniums close-banked around it as high as the windows. It was a hard-swept looking little house, with hard-polished windows, and a clean mud-mat on the front steps.

Elisa cast another glance toward the tractor shed. The strangers were getting into their Ford coupe. She took off a glove and put her strong fingers down into the forest of new green chrysanthemum sprouts that were growing around the old roots. She spread the leaves and looked down among the close-growing stems. No aphids were there, no sowbugs or snails or cutworms. Her terrier fingers destroyed such pests before they could get started.

Elisa started at the sound of her husband's voice. He had come near quietly, and he leaned over the wire fence that protected her flower garden from cattle and dogs and chickens.

"At it again," he said. "You've got a strong new crop coming."

Elisa straightened her back and pulled on the gardening glove again. "Yes. They'll be strong this coming year." In her tone and on her face there was a little smugness.

"You've got a gift with things," Henry observed. "Some of those yellow chrysanthemums you had this year were ten inches across. I wish you'd work out in the orchard and raise some apples that big."

Her eyes sharpened. "Maybe I could do it, too. I've a gift with things, all right. My mother had it. She could stick anything in the ground and make it grow. She said it was having planters' hands that knew how to do it."

"Well, it sure works with flowers," he said.

"Henry, who were those men you were talking to?"

"Why, sure, that's what I came to tell you. They were from the Western Meat Company. I sold those thirty head of three-year-old steers. Got nearly my own price, too."

"Good," she said. "Good for you."

"And I thought," he continued, "I thought how it's Saturday afternoon, and we might go into Salinas for dinner at a restaurant, and then to a picture show—to celebrate, you see."

"Good," she repeated. "Oh, yes. That will be good."

Henry put on his joking tone. "There's fights tonight. How'd you like to go to the fights?"

"Oh, no," she said breathlessly. "No, I wouldn't like fights."

"Just fooling, Elisa. We'll go to a movie. Let's see. It's two now. I'm going to take Scotty and bring down those steers from the hill. It'll take us maybe two hours. We'll go in town about five and have dinner at the Cominos Hotel. Like that?"

"Of course I'll like it. It's good to eat away from home."

"All right, then. I'll go get up a couple of horses."

She said, "I'll have plenty of time to transplant some of these sets, I guess."

She heard her husband calling Scotty down by the barn. And a little later she saw the two men ride up the pale yellow hillside in search of the steers.

There was a little square sandy bed kept for rooting the chrysanthemums. With her trowel she turned the soil over and over, and smoothed it and patted it firm. Then she dug ten parallel trenches to receive the sets. Back at the chrysanthemum bed she pulled out the little crisp shoots, trimmed off the leaves of each one with her scissors and laid it on a small orderly pile.

A squeak of wheels and plod of hoofs came from the road. Elisa looked up. The country road ran along the dense bank of willows and cottonwoods that bordered the river, and up this road came a curious vehicle, curiously drawn. It was an old spring-wagon, with a round canvas top on it like the cover of a prairie schooner. It was drawn by an old bay horse and a little grey-and-white burro. A big stubble-bearded man sat between the cover flaps and drove the crawling team. Underneath the wagon, between the hind wheels, a lean and rangy mongrel dog walked sedately. Words were painted on the canvas in clumsy, crooked letters. "Pots, pans, knives, sisors, lawn mores, Fixed." Two rows of articles, and the triumphantly definitive "Fixed" below. The black paint had run down in little sharp points beneath each letter.

Elisa, squatting on the ground, watched to see the crazy, loose-jointed wagon pass by. But it didn't pass. It turned into the farm road in front of her house, crooked old wheels skirling and squeaking. The rangy dog darted from between the wheels and ran ahead. Instantly the two ranch shepherds flew out at him. Then all three stopped, and with stiff and quivering tails, with taut straight legs, with ambassadorial dignity, they slowly circled, sniffing daintily. The caravan pulled up to Elisa's wire fence and stopped. Now the newcomer dog, feeling outnumbered, lowered his tail and retired under the wagon with raised hackles and bared teeth.

The man on the wagon seat called out, "That's a bad dog in a fight when he gets started."

Elisa laughed. "I see he is. How soon does he generally get started?"

The man caught up her laughter and echoed it heartily. "Sometimes not for weeks and weeks," he said. He climbed stiffly down, over the wheel. The horse and the donkey drooped like unwatered flowers.

Elisa saw that he was a very big man. Although his hair and beard were greying, he did not look old. His worn black suit was wrinkled and spotted with grease. The laughter had disappeared from his face and eyes the moment his laughing voice ceased. His eyes were dark, and they were full of the brooding that gets in the eyes of teamsters and of sailors. The calloused hands he rested on the wire fence were cracked, and every crack was a black line. He took off his battered hat.

"I'm off my general road, ma'am," he said. "Does this dirt road cut over across the river to the Los Angeles highway?"

Elisa stood up and shoved the thick scissors in her apron pocket. "Well, yes, it does, but it winds around and then fords the river. I don't think your team could pull through the sand."

He replied with some asperity, "It might surprise you what them beasts can pull through."

"When they get started?" she asked.

He smiled for a second. "Yes. When they get started."

"Well," said Elisa, "I think you'll save time if you go back to the Salinas road and pick up the highway there."

He drew a big finger down the chicken wire and made it sing. "I ain't in any hurry, ma'am. I go from Seattle to San Diego and back every year. Takes all my time. About six months each way. I aim to follow nice weather."

Elisa took off her gloves and stuffed them in the apron pocket with the scissors. She touched the under edge of her man's hat, searching for fugitive hairs. "That sounds like a nice kind of a way to live," she said.

He leaned confidentially over the fence. "Maybe you noticed the writing on my wagon. I mend pots and sharpen knives and scissors. You got any of them things to do?"

"Oh, no," she said quickly. "Nothing like that." Her eyes hardened with resistance.

"Scissors is the worst thing," he explained. "Most people just ruin scissors trying to sharpen 'em, but I know how. I got a special tool. It's a little bobbit kind of thing, and patented. But it sure does the trick."

"No. My scissors are all sharp."

"All right, then. Take a pot," he continued earnestly, "a bent pot, or a pot with a hole. I can make it like new so you don't have to buy no new ones. That's a saving for you."

"No," she said shortly. "I tell you I have nothing like that for you to do."

His face fell to an exaggerated sadness. His voice took on a whining undertone. "I ain't had a thing to do today. Maybe I won't have no supper tonight. You see I'm off my regular road. I know folks on the highway clear from Seattle to San Diego. They save their things for me to sharpen up because they know I do it so good and save them money."

"I'm sorry," Elisa said irritably. "I haven't anything for you to do."

His eyes left her face and fell to searching the ground. They roamed about until they came to the chrysanthemum bed where she had been working. "What's them plants, ma'am?"

The irritation and resistance melted from Elisa's face. "Oh, those are chrysanthemums, giant whites and yellows. I raise them every year, bigger than anybody around here."

"Kind of a long-stemmed flower? Looks like a quick puff of colored smoke?" he asked.

"That's it. What a nice way to describe them."

"They smell kind of nasty till you get used to them," he said.

"It's a good bitter smell," she retorted, "not nasty at all."

He changed his tone quickly. "I like the smell myself."

"I had ten-inch blooms this year," she said.

The man leaned farther over the fence. "Look. I know a lady down the road a piece, has got the nicest garden you ever seen. Got nearly every kind of flower but no chrysanthemums. Last time I was mending a copper-bottom washtub for her (that's a hard job but I do it good), she said to me, 'If you ever run acrost some nice chrysanthemums I wish you'd try to get me a few seeds.' That's what she told me."

Elisa's eyes grew alert and eager. "She couldn't have known much about chrysanthemums. You can raise them from seed, but it's much easier to root the little sprouts you see there."

"Oh," he said. "I s'pose I can't take none to her, then."

"Why yes you can," Elisa cried. "I can put some in damp sand, and you can carry them right along with you. They'll take root in the pot if you keep them damp. And then she can transplant them."

"She'd sure like to have some, ma'am. You say they're nice ones?"

"Beautiful," she said. "Oh, beautiful." Her eyes shone. She tore off the battered hat and shook out her dark pretty hair. "I'll put them in a flower pot, and you can take them right with you. Come into the yard."

While the man came through the picket fence Elisa ran excitedly along the geranium-bordered path to the back of the house. And she returned carrying a big red flower pot. The gloves were forgotten now. She kneeled on the ground by the starting bed and dug up the sandy soil with her fingers and scooped it into the bright new flower pot. Then she picked up the little pile of shoots she had prepared. With her strong fingers she pressed them into the sand and tamped around them with her knuckles. The man stood over her. "I'll tell you what to do," she said. "You remember so you can tell the lady."

"Yes, I'll try to remember."

"Well, look. These will take root in about a month. Then she must set them out, about a foot apart in good rich earth like this, see?" She lifted a handful of dark soil for him to look at. "They'll grow fast and tall. Now remember this. In July tell her to cut them down, about eight inches from the ground."

"Before they bloom?" he asked.

"Yes, before they bloom." Her face was tight with eagerness. "They'll grow right up again. About the last of September the buds will start."

She stopped and seemed perplexed. "It's the budding that takes the most care," she said hesitantly. "I don't know how to tell you." She looked deep into his eyes, searchingly. Her mouth opened a little, and she seemed to be listening. "I'll try to tell you," she said. "Did you ever hear of planting hands?"

"Can't say I have, ma'am."

"Well, I can only tell you what it feels like. It's when you're picking off the buds you don't want. Everything goes right down into your finger-tips. You watch your fingers work. They do it themselves. You can feel how it is. They pick and pick the buds. They never make a mistake. They're with the plant. Do you see? Your fingers and the plant. You can feel that, right up your arm. They know. They never make a mistake. You can feel it. When you're like that you can't do anything wrong. Do you see that? Can you understand that?"

She was kneeling on the ground looking up at him. Her breast swelled passionately.

The man's eyes narrowed. He looked away self-consciously. "Maybe I know," he said. "Sometimes in the night in the wagon there—"

Elisa's voice grew husky. She broke in on him. "I've never lived as you do, but I know what you mean. When the night is dark—why, the stars are sharp-pointed, and there's quiet. Why, you rise up and up! Every pointed star gets driven into your body. It's like that. Hot and sharp and—lovely."

Kneeling there, her hand went out toward his legs in the greasy black trousers. Her hesitant fingers almost touched the cloth. Then her hand dropped to the ground. She crouched low like a fawning dog.

He said, "It's nice, just like you say. Only when you don't have no dinner, it ain't."

She stood up then, very straight, and her face was ashamed. She held the flower pot out to him and placed it gently in his arms. "Here. Put it in your wagon, on the seat, where you can watch it. Maybe I can find something for you to do."

At the back of the house she dug in the can

pile and found two old and battered aluminum saucepans. She carried them back and gave them to him. "Here, maybe you can fix these."

His manner changed. He became professional. "Good as new I can fix them." At the back of his wagon he set a little anvil, and out of an oily tool box dug a small machine hammer. Elisa came through the gate to watch him while he pounded out the dents in the kettles. His mouth grew sure and knowing. At a difficult part of the work he sucked his under-lip.

"You sleep right in the wagon?" Elisa asked.

"Right in the wagon, ma'am. Rain or shine I'm dry as a cow in there."

"It must be nice," she said. "It must be very nice. I wish women could do such things."

"It ain't the right kind of a life for a woman."

Her upper lip raised a little, showing her teeth. "How do you know? How can you tell?" she said.

"I don't know, ma'am," he protested. "Of course I don't know. Now here's your kettles, done. You don't have to buy no new ones."

"How much?"

"Oh, fifty cents'll do. I keep my prices down and my work good. That's why I have all them satisfied customers up and down the highway."

Elisa brought him a fifty-cent piece from the house and dropped it in his hand. "You might be surprised to have a rival some time. I can sharpen scissors, too. And I can beat the dents out of little pots. I could show you what a woman might do."

He put his hammer back in the oily box and shoved the little anvil out of sight. "It would be a lonely life for a woman, ma'am, and a scarey life, too, with animals creeping under the wagon all night." He climbed over the singletree, steadying himself with a hand on the burro's white rump. He settled himself in the seat, picked up the lines. "Thank you kindly, ma'am," he said. "I'll do like you told me; I'll go back and catch the Salinas road."

"Mind," she called, "if you're long in getting there, keep the sand damp."

"Sand, ma'am? . . . Sand? Oh, sure. You mean around the chrysanthemums. Sure I will." He clucked his tongue. The beasts leaned luxuriously into their collars. The mongrel dog took his place between the back wheels. The wagon turned and crawled out the entrance road and back the way it had come, along the river.

Elisa stood in front of her wire fence watching the slow progress of the caravan. Her shoulders were straight, her head thrown back, her eyes half-closed, so that the scene came vaguely into them. Her lips moved silently, forming the words "Good-bye—good-bye." Then she whispered, "That's a bright direction. There's a glowing there." The sound of her whisper startled her. She shook herself free and looked about to see whether anyone had been listening. Only the dogs had heard. They lifted their heads toward her from their sleeping in the dust, and then stretched out their chins and settled asleep again. Elisa turned and ran hurriedly into the house.

In the kitchen she reached behind the stove and felt the water tank. It was full of hot water from the noonday cooking. In the bathroom she tore off her soiled clothes and flung them into the corner. And then she scrubbed herself with a little block of pumice, legs and thighs, loins and chest and arms, until her skin was scratched and red. When she had dried herself she stood in front of a mirror in her bedroom and looked at her body. She tightened her stomach and threw out her chest. She turned and looked over her shoulder at her back.

After a while she began to dress, slowly. She put on her newest underclothing and her nicest stockings and the dress which was the symbol of her prettiness. She worked carefully on her hair, pencilled her eyebrows and rouged her lips.

Before she was finished she heard the little thunder of hoofs and the shouts of Henry and his helper as they drove the red steers into the corral. She heard the gate bang shut and set herself for Henry's arrival.

His step sounded on the porch. He entered the house calling, "Elisa, where are you?"

"In my room, dressing. I'm not ready. There's hot water for your bath. Hurry up. It's getting late."

When she heard him splashing in the tub, Elisa laid his dark suit on the bed, and shirt and socks and tie beside it. She stood his polished shoes on the floor beside the bed. Then she went to the porch and sat primly and stiffly down. She looked toward the river road where the willow-line was still yellow with frosted leaves so that under the high grey fog they seemed a thin band of sunshine. This was the only color in the grey afternoon. She sat unmoving for a long time. Her eyes blinked rarely.

Henry came banging out of the door, shoving his tie inside his vest as he came. Elisa stiffened and her face grew tight. Henry stopped short and looked at her. "Why—why, Elisa. You look so nice!"

"Nice? You think I look nice? What do you mean by 'nice'?"

Henry blundered on. "I don't know. I mean you look different, strong and happy."

"I am strong? Yes, strong. What do you mean 'strong'?"

He looked bewildered. "You're playing some kind of a game," he said helplessly. "It's a kind of a play. You look strong enough to break a calf over your knee, happy enough to eat it like a watermelon."

For a second she lost her rigidity. "Henry! Don't talk like that. You didn't know what you said." She grew complete again. "I'm strong," she boasted. "I never knew before how strong."

Henry looked down toward the tractor shed, and when he brought his eyes back to her, they were his own again. "I'll get out the car. You can put on your coat while I'm starting."

Elisa went into the house. She heard him drive to the gate and idle down his motor, and then she took a long time to put on her hat. She pulled it here and pressed it there. When Henry turned the motor off she slipped into her coat and went out.

The little roadster bounced along on the dirt road by the river, raising the birds and driving the rabbits into the brush. Two cranes flapped heavily over the willow-line and dropped into the river-bed.

Far ahead on the road Elisa saw a dark speck. She knew.

She tried not to look as they passed it, but her eyes would not obey. She whispered to herself sadly, "He might have thrown them off the road. That wouldn't have been much trouble, not very much. But he kept the pot," she explained. "He had to keep the pot. That's why he couldn't get them off the road."

The roadster turned a bend and she saw the caravan ahead. She swung full around toward her husband so she could not see the little covered wagon and the mismatched team as the car passed them.

In a moment it was over. The thing was done. She did not look back. She said loudly, to be heard above the motor, "It will be good, tonight, a good dinner."

"Now you're changed again," Henry complained. He took one hand from the wheel and patted her knee. "I ought to take you in to dinner oftener. It would be good for both of us. We get so heavy out on the ranch."

"Henry," she asked, "could we have wine at dinner?"

"Sure we could. Say! That will be fine."

She was silent for a while; then she said, "Henry, at those prize fights, do the men hurt each other very much?"

"Sometimes a little, not often. Why?"

"Well, I've read how they break noses, and blood runs down their chests. I've read how the fighting gloves get heavy and soggy with blood."

He looked around at her. "What's the matter, Elisa? I didn't know you read things like that." He brought the car to a stop, then turned to the right over the Salinas River bridge.

"Do any women ever go to the fights?" she asked.

"Oh, sure, some. What's the matter, Elisa? Do you want to go? I don't think you'd like it, but I'll take you if you really want to go."

She relaxed limply in the seat. "Oh, no. No. I don't want to go. I'm sure I don't." Her face was turned away from him. "It will be enough if we can have wine. It will be plenty." She turned up her coat collar so he could not see that she was crying weakly—like an old woman.

WILLIAM FAULKNER

Wash

William Faulkner (1897–1962) spent most of his life near Oxford, Mississippi, the "Jefferson" of his writings. After serving in the Canadian Air Force during the First World War, he returned to Oxford, where he took a few courses at the University of Mississippi and began writing. His early novels brought him critical acclaim but little or no popularity or financial remuneration. *Sartoris*, 1929, was the first of his many novels centering loosely on the Sartoris family, suggested by his own wealthy Southern ancestors who had been reduced to genteel poverty by the Civil War. In 1931 Faulkner published *Sanctuary*, which he said was deliberately "horrific" to appeal to popular tastes and to earn enough money to support himself. In 1939 he received the O. Henry Memorial Award; in 1949, after the publication of *Intruder in the Dust*, 1948, he received the Nobel Prize for Literature "for his forceful and independently artistic contribution to modern American fiction"; and in 1954 he was awarded a Pulitzer Prize for *A Fable*. Faulkner, along with Hemingway, has received greater critical acclaim than any other contemporary American novelist. His better-known works include *The Sound and the Fury*, 1929; *Absalom, Absalom!*, 1936; *The Mansion*, 1959; and *The Reivers*, 1962.

Few writers have been able to achieve as much dramatic intensity in a story as William Faulkner. "Wash," for example, depicts with broad strokes the violent passions underlying the social and economic hierarchy of the Old South. The violent catastrophe resulting from the continual interaction between Sutpen's cruel egocentricity and Wash's fawning dependence typifies much of Faulkner's fiction.

Sutpen stood above the pallet bed on which the mother and child lay. Between the shrunken planking of the wall the early sunlight fell in long pencil strokes, breaking upon his straddled legs and upon the riding whip in his hand, and lay across the still shape of the mother, who lay looking up at him from still, inscrutable, sullen eyes, the child at her side wrapped in a piece of dingy though clean cloth. Behind them an old Negro woman squatted beside the rough hearth where a meager fire smoldered.

"Well, Milly," Sutpen said, "too bad you're not a mare. Then I could give you a decent stall in the stable."

WASH From *Collected Stories of William Faulkner*. Copyright 1934; renewed 1962 by William Faulkner. Reprinted by permission of Random House, Inc.

Still the girl on the pallet did not move. She merely continued to look up at him without expression, with a young, sullen, inscrutable face still pale from recent travail. Sutpen moved, bringing into the splintered pencils of sunlight the face of a man of sixty. He said quietly to the squatting Negress, "Griselda foaled this morning."

"Horse or mare?" the Negress said.

"A horse. A damned fine colt. . . . What's this?" He indicated the pallet with the hand which held the whip.

"That un's a mare, I reckon."

"Hah," Sutpen said. "A damned fine colt. Going to be the spit and image of old Rob Roy when I rode him North in '61. Do you remember?"

"Yes, Marster."

"Hah." He glanced back towards the pallet. None could have said if the girl still watched him or not. Again his whip hand indicated the pallet. "Do whatever they need with whatever we've got to do it with." He went out, passing out the crazy doorway and stepping down into the rank weeds (there yet leaned rusting against the corner of the porch the scythe which Wash had borrowed from him three months ago to cut them with) where his horse waited, where Wash stood holding the reins.

When Colonel Sutpen rode away to fight the Yankees, Wash did not go. "I'm looking after the Kernel's place and niggers," he would tell all who asked him and some who had not asked—a gaunt, malaria-ridden man with pale, questioning eyes, who looked about thirty-five, though it was known that he had not only a daughter but an eight-year-old granddaughter as well. This was a lie, as most of them—the few remaining men between eighteen and fifty—to whom he told it, knew, though there were some who believed that he himself really believed it, though even these believed that he had better sense than to put it to the test with Mrs. Sutpen or the Sutpen slaves. Knew better or was just too lazy and shiftless to try it, they said, knowing that his sole connection with the Sutpen plantation lay in the fact that for years now Colonel Sutpen had allowed him to squat in a crazy shack on a slough in the river bottom on the Sutpen place, which Sutpen had built for a fishing lodge in his bachelor days and which had since fallen in dilapidation from disuse, so that now it looked like an aged or sick wild beast crawled terrifically there to drink in the act of dying.

The Sutpen slaves themselves heard of his statement. They laughed. It was not the first time they had laughed at him, calling him white trash behind his back. They began to ask him themselves, in groups, meeting him in the faint road which led up from the slough and the old fish camp, "Why ain't you at de war, white man?"

Pausing, he would look about the ring of black faces and white eyes and teeth behind which derision lurked. "Because I got a daughter and family to keep," he said. "Git out of my road, niggers."

"Niggers?" they repeated; "niggers?" laughing now. "Who him, calling us niggers?"

"Yes," he said. "I ain't got no niggers to look after my folks if I was gone."

"Nor nothing else but dat shack down yon dat Cunnel wouldn't *let* none of us live in."

Now he cursed them; sometimes he rushed at them, snatching up a stick from the ground while they scattered before him, yet seeming to surround him still with that black laughing, derisive, evasive, inescapable, leaving him panting and impotent and raging. Once it happened in the very back yard of the big house itself. This was after bitter news had come down from the Tennessee mountains and from Vicksburg, and Sherman had passed through the plantation, and most of the Negroes had followed him. Almost everything else had gone with the Federal troops, and Mrs. Sutpen had sent word to Wash that he could have the scuppernongs ripening in the arbor in the back yard. This time it was a house servant, one of the few Negroes who remained; this time the Negress had to retreat up the kitchen steps, where she turned. "Stop right dar, white man. Stop right whar you is. You ain't never crossed dese steps whilst Cunnel here, and you ain't ghy' do hit now."

This was true. But there was this kind of pride: he had never tried to enter the big house, even though he believed that if he had, Sutpen would have received him, permitted him. "But I ain't going to give no black nigger the chance to tell me I can't go nowhere," he said to himself. "I ain't even going to give Kernel the chance to have to cuss a nigger on my account." This, though he and Sutpen had spent more than one afternoon together on those rare Sundays when there would be no company in the house. Perhaps his mind knew that it was because Sutpen had nothing else to do, being a man who could not bear his own company. Yet the fact remained that the two of them would spend whole afternoons in the scuppernong arbor, Sutpen in the hammock and Wash squatting against a post, a pail of cistern water between them, taking drink for drink from the same demijohn. Meanwhile on weekdays he would see the fine figure of the man—they were the same age almost to a day, though neither of them (perhaps because Wash had a grandchild while Sutpen's son was a youth in school) ever thought of himself as being so—on the fine figure of the black stallion, galloping about the plantation. For that moment his heart would be quiet and proud. It would seem to him that that world in which Negroes, whom the Bible told him had been created and cursed by God to be brute and vassal to all men of white skin, were better found and housed and even clothed than he and his; that world in which he sensed always about him mocking echoes of black laughter was but a dream and an illusion, and that the actual world was this one across which his own lonely apotheosis seemed to gallop on the black thoroughbred, thinking how the Book said also that all men were created in the image of God and hence all men made the same image in God's eyes at least; so that he could say, as though speaking of himself, "A fine proud man. If God Himself was to come down and ride the natural earth, that's what He would aim to look like."

Sutpen returned in 1865, on the black stallion. He seemed to have aged ten years. His son had been killed in action the same winter in which his wife had died. He returned with his citation for gallantry from the hand of General Lee to a ruined plantation, where for a year now his daughter had subsisted partially on the meager bounty of the man to whom fifteen years ago he had granted permission to live in that tumbledown fishing camp whose very existence he had at the time forgotten. Wash was there to meet him, unchanged: still gaunt, still ageless, with his pale, questioning gaze, his air diffident, a little servile, a little familiar. "Well, Kernel," Wash said, "they kilt us but they ain't whupped us yit, air they?"

That was the tenor of their conversation for the next five years. It was inferior whisky which they drank now together from a stoneware jug, and it was not in the scuppernong arbor. It was in the rear of the little store which Sutpen managed to set up on the highroad: a frame shelved room where, with Wash for clerk and porter, he dispensed kerosene and staple foodstuffs and stale gaudy candy and cheap beads and ribbons to Negroes or poor whites of Wash's own kind, who came afoot or on gaunt mules to haggle tediously for dimes and quarters with a man who at one time could gallop (the black stallion was still alive; the stable in which his jealous get lived was in better repair than the house where the master himself lived) for ten miles across his own fertile land and who had led troops gallantly in battle; until Sutpen in fury would empty the store, close and lock the doors from the inside. Then he and

Wash would repair to the rear and the jug. But the talk would not be quiet now, as when Sutpen lay in the hammock, delivering an arrogant monologue while Wash squatted guffawing against his post. They both sat now, though Sutpen had the single chair while Wash used whatever box or keg was handy, and even this for just a little while, because soon Sutpen would reach that stage of impotent and furious undefeat in which he would rise, swaying and plunging, and declare again that he would take his pistol and the black stallion and ride single-handed into Washington and kill Lincoln, dead now, and Sherman, now a private citizen. "Kill them!" he would shout. "Shoot them down like the dogs they are—"

"Sho, Kernel; sho, Kernel," Wash would say, catching Sutpen as he fell. Then he would commandeer the first passing wagon or, lacking that, he would walk the mile to the nearest neighbor and borrow one and return and carry Sutpen home: He entered the house now. He had been doing so for a long time, taking Sutpen home in whatever borrowed wagon might be, talking him into locomotion with cajoling murmurs as though he were a horse, a stallion himself. The daughter would meet them and hold open the door without a word. He would carry his burden through the once white formal entrance, surmounted by a fanlight imported piece by piece from Europe and with a board now nailed over a missing pane, across a velvet carpet from which all nap was now gone, and up a formal stairs, now but a fading ghost of bare boards between two strips of fading paint, and into the bedroom. It would be dusk by now, and he would let his burden sprawl onto the bed and undress it and then he would sit quietly in a chair beside. After a time the daughter would come to the door. "We're all right now," he would tell her. "Don't you worry none, Miss Judith."

Then it would become dark, and after a while he would lie down on the floor beside the bed, though not to sleep, because after a time—sometimes before midnight—the man on the bed would stir and groan and then speak. "Wash?"

"Hyer I am, Kernel. You go back to sleep. We ain't whupped yit, air we? Me and you kin do hit."

Even then he had already seen the ribbon about his granddaughter's waist. She was now fifteen, already mature, after the early way of her kind. He knew where the ribbon came from; he had been seeing it and its kind daily for three years, even if she had lied about where she got it, which she did not, at once bold, sullen, and fearful. "Sho now," he said "Ef Kernel wants to give hit to you, I hope you minded to thank him."

His heart was quiet, even when he saw the dress, watching her secret, defiant, frightened face when she told him that Miss Judith, the daughter, had helped her to make it. But he was quite grave when he approached Sutpen after they closed the store that afternoon, following the other to the rear.

"Get the jug," Sutpen directed.

"Wait," Wash said. "Not yit for a minute."

Neither did Sutpen deny the dress. "What about it?" he said.

But Wash met his arrogant stare; he spoke quietly. "I've knowed you for going on twenty years. I ain't never yit denied to do what you told me to do. And I'm a man nigh sixty. And she ain't nothing but a fifteen-year-old gal."

"Meaning that I'd harm a girl? I, a man as old as you are?"

"If you was ara other man, I'd say you was as old as me. And old or no old, I wouldn't let her keep that dress nor nothing else that come from your hand. But you are different."

"How different?" But Wash merely looked at him with his pale, questioning, sober eyes. "So that's why you are afraid of me?"

Now Wash's gaze no longer questioned. It was tranquil, serene. "I ain't afraid. Because you air brave. It ain't that you were a brave man at one minute or day of your life and got a paper to show hit from General Lee. But you air brave, the same as you air alive and breathing. That's where hit's different. Hit don't need no ticket from nobody to tell me that. And I know that whatever you handle or tech, whether hit's a regiment of men or a ignorant gal or just a hound dog, that you will make hit right."

Now it was Sutpen who looked away, turning suddenly, brusquely. "Get the jug," he said sharply.

"Sho, Kernel," Wash said.

So on that Sunday dawn two years later, having watched the Negro midwife, which he had walked three miles to fetch, enter the crazy door beyond which his granddaughter lay wailing, his heart was still quiet though concerned. He knew what they had been saying—the Negroes in cabins about the land, the white men who loafed all day long about the store, watching quietly the three of them: Sutpen, himself, his granddaughter with her air of brazen and shrinking defiance as her condition became daily more and more obvious, like three actors that came and went upon a stage. "I know what they say to one another," he thought. "I can almost hyear them: *Wash Jones has fixed old Sutpen at last. Hit taken him twenty years, but he has done hit at last.*"

It would be dawn after a while, though not yet. From the house, where the lamp shone dim beyond the warped doorframe, his granddaughter's voice came steadily as though run by a clock, while thinking went slowly and terrifically, fumbling, involved somehow with a sound of galloping hooves, until there broke suddenly free in mid-gallop the fine proud figure of the man on the fine proud stallion, galloping; and then that at which thinking fumbled, broke free too and quite clear, not in justification nor even explanation, but as the apotheosis, lonely, explicable, beyond all fouling by human touch: "He is bigger than all them Yankees that kilt his son and his wife and taken his niggers and ruined his land, bigger than this hyer durn country that he fit for and that has denied him into keeping a little country store; bigger than the denial which hit helt to his lips like the bitter cup in the Book. And how could I have lived this nigh to him for twenty years without being teched and changed by him? Maybe I ain't as big as him and maybe I ain't done none of the galloping. But at least I done been drug along. Me and him kin do hit, if so be he will show me what he aims for me to do."

Then it was dawn. Suddenly he could see the house, and the old Negress in the door looking at him. Then he realized that his granddaughter's voice had ceased. "It's a girl," the Negress said. "You can go tell him if you want to." She re-entered the house.

"A girl," he repeated; "a girl"; in astonishment, hearing the galloping hooves, seeing the proud galloping figure emerge again. He seemed to watch it pass, galloping through avatars which marked the accumulation of years, time, to the climax where it galloped beneath a brandished saber and a shot-torn flag rushing down a sky in color like thunderous sulphur, thinking for the first time in his life that perhaps Sutpen was an old man like himself. "Gittin a gal," he thought in that astonishment; then he thought with the pleased surprise of a child: "Yes, sir. Be dawg if I ain't lived to be a great-grandpaw after all."

He entered the house. He moved clumsily, on tiptoe, as if he no longer lived there, as if the infant which had just drawn breath and cried in light had dispossessed him, be it of his own blood too though it might. But even above the pallet he could see little save the blur of his granddaughter's exhausted face. Then the Negress squatting at the hearth spoke, "You better gawn tell him if you going to. Hit's daylight now."

But this was not necessary. He had no more than turned the corner of the porch where the scythe leaned which he had borrowed three months ago to clear away the weeds through which he walked, when Sutpen himself rode up on the old stallion. He did not wonder how Sutpen had got the word. He took it for granted that this was what had brought the other out at this hour on Sunday morning, and he stood while the other dismounted, and he took the reins from Sutpen's hand, an expression on his gaunt face almost imbecile with a kind of weary triumph, saying, "Hit's a gal, Kernel. I be dawg if you ain't as old as I am—" until Sutpen passed him and entered the house. He stood there with the reins in his hand and heard Sutpen cross the floor to the pallet. He heard what Sutpen said, and something seemed to stop dead in him before going on.

The sun was now up, the swift sun of Mississippi latitudes, and it seemed to him that he stood beneath a strange sky, in a strange scene, familiar only as things are familiar in dreams, like the dreams of falling to one who has never climbed. "I kain't have heard what I thought I heard," he thought quietly. "I know I kain't." Yet the voice, the familiar voice which had said the words was still speaking, talking now to the old Negress about a colt foaled that morning. "That's why he was up so early," he thought. "That was hit. Hit ain't me and mine. Hit ain't even hisn that got him outen bed."

Sutpen emerged. He descended into the weeds, moving with that heavy deliberation which would have been haste when he was younger. He had not yet looked full at Wash. He said, "Dicey will stay and tend to her. You better—" Then he seemed to see Wash facing him and paused. "What?" he said.

"You said—" To his own ears Wash's voice sounded flat and ducklike, like a deaf man's. "You

said if she was a mare, you could give her a good stall in the stable."

"Well?" Sutpen said. His eyes widened and narrowed, almost like a man's fists flexing and shutting, as Wash began to advance towards him, stooping a little. Very astonishment kept Sutpen still for the moment, watching that man whom in twenty years he had no more known to make any motion save at command than he had the horse which he rode. Again his eyes narrowed and widened; without moving he seemed to rear suddenly upright. "Stand back," he said suddenly and sharply. "Don't you touch me."

"I'm going to tech you, Kernel," Wash said in that flat, quiet, almost soft voice, advancing.

Sutpen raised the hand which held the riding whip; the old Negress peered around the crazy door with her black gargoyle face of a worn gnome. "Stand back, Wash," Sutpen said. Then he struck. The old Negress leaped down into the weeds with the agility of a goat and fled. Sutpen slashed Wash again across the face with the whip, striking him to his knees. When Wash rose and advanced once more he held in his hands the scythe which he had borrowed from Sutpen three months ago and which Sutpen would never need again.

When he reentered the house his granddaughter stirred on the pallet bed and called his name fretfully. "What was that?" she said.

"What was what, honey?"

"That ere racket out there."

"'Twarn't nothing," he said gently. He knelt and touched her hot forehead clumsily. "Do you want ara thing?"

"I want a sup of water," she said querulously. "I been laying here wanting a sup of water a long time, but don't nobody care enough to pay me no mind."

"Sho now," he said soothingly. He rose stiffly and fetched the dipper of water and raised her head to drink and laid her back and watched her turn to the child with an absolutely stonelike face. But a moment later he saw that she was crying quietly. "Now, now," he said, "I wouldn't do that. Old Dicey says hit's a right fine gal. Hit's all right now. Hit's all over now. Hit ain't no need to cry now."

But she continued to cry quietly, almost sullenly, and he rose again and stood uncomfortably above the pallet for a time, thinking as he had thought when his own wife lay so and then his daughter in turn: "Women. Hit's a mystry to me. They seem to want em, and yit when they git em they cry about hit. Hit's a mystry to me. To ara man." Then he moved away and drew a chair up to the window and sat down.

Through all that long, bright, sunny forenoon he sat at the window, waiting. Now and then he rose and tiptoed to the pallet. But his granddaughter slept now, her face sullen and calm and weary, the child in the crook of her arm. Then he returned to the chair and sat again, waiting, wondering why it took them so long, until he remembered that it was Sunday. He was sitting there at midafternoon when a half-grown white boy came around the corner of the house upon the body and gave a choked cry and looked up and glared for a mesmerized instant at Wash in the window before he turned and fled. Then Wash rose and tiptoed again to the pallet.

The granddaughter was awake now, wakened perhaps by the boy's cry without hearing it. "Milly," he said, "air you hungry?" She didn't answer, turning her face away. He built up the fire on the hearth and cooked the food which he had brought home the day before: fatback it was, and cold corn pone; he poured water into the stale coffee pot and heated it. But she would not eat when he carried the plate to her, so he ate himself, quietly, alone, and left the dishes as they were and returned to the window.

Now he seemed to sense, feel, the men who would be gathering with horses and guns and dogs—the curious, and the vengeful: men of Sutpen's own kind, who had made the company about Sutpen's table in the time when Wash himself had yet to approach nearer to the house than the scuppernong arbor—men who had also shown the lesser ones how to fight in battle, who maybe also had signed papers from the generals saying that they were among the first of the brave; who had also galloped in the old days arrogant and proud on the fine horses across the fine plantations—symbols also of admiration and hope; instruments too of despair and grief.

That was whom they would expect him to run from. It seemed to him that he had no more to run from than he had to run to. If he ran, he would merely be fleeing one set of bragging and evil shadows for another just like them, since they were all of a kind throughout all the earth which he knew, and he was old, too old to flee far even if he were to flee. He could never escape them, no matter how much or how far he ran: a man going on sixty could not run that far. Not far enough to escape beyond the boundaries of earth where such men lived, set the order and the rule of living. It seemed to him that he now saw for the first time, after five years, how it was that Yankees or any other living armies had managed to whip them: the gallant, the proud, the brave; the acknowledged and chosen best among them all to carry courage and honor and pride. Maybe if he had gone to the war with them he would have discovered them sooner. But if he had discovered them sooner, what would he have done with his life since? How could he have borne to remember for five years what his life had been before?

Now it was getting toward sunset. The child had been crying; when he went to the pallet he saw his granddaughter nursing it, her face still bemused, sullen, inscrutable. "Air you hungry yit?" he said.

"I don't want nothing."

"You ought to eat."

This time she did not answer at all, looking down at the child. He returned to his chair and found that the sun had set. "Hit kain't be much longer," he thought. He could feel them quite near now, the curious and the vengeful. He could even seem to hear what they were saying about him, the undercurrent of believing beyond the immediate fury: *Old Wash Jones he come a tumble at last. He thought he had Sutpen, but Sutpen fooled him. He thought he had Kernel where he would have to marry the gal or pay up. And Kernel refused.* "But I never expected that, Kernel!" he cried aloud, catching himself at the sound of his own voice, glancing quickly back to find his granddaughter watching him.

"Who you talking to now?" she said.

"Hit ain't nothing. I was just thinking and talked out before I knowed hit."

Her face was becoming indistinct again, again a sullen blur in the twilight. "I reckon so. I reckon you'll have to holler louder than that before he'll hear you, up yonder at that house. And I reckon you'll need to do more than holler before you get him down here too."

"Sho now," he said. "Don't you worry none." But already thinking was going smoothly on: "You know I never. You know how I ain't never expected or asked nothing from ara living man but what I expected from you. And I never asked that. I didn't think hit would need. I said, *I don't need to. What need has a fellow like Wash Jones to question or doubt the man that General Lee himself says in a handwrote ticket that he was brave?* Brave," he thought. "Better if nara one of them had never rid back home in '65"; thinking *Better if his kind and mine too had never drawn the breath of life on this earth. Better that all who remain of us be blasted from the face of earth than that another Wash Jones should see his whole life shredded from him and shrivel away like a dried shuck thrown onto the fire.*

He ceased, became still. He heard the horses, suddenly and plainly; presently he saw the lantern and the movement of men, the glint of gun barrels, in its moving light. Yet he did not stir. It was quite dark now, and he listened to the voices and the sounds of underbrush as they surrounded the house. The lantern itself came on; its light fell upon the quiet body in the weeds and stopped, the horses tall and shadowy. A man descended and stooped in the lantern light, above the body. He held a pistol; he rose and faced the house. "Jones," he said.

"I'm here," Wash said quietly from the window. "That you, Major?"

"Come out."

"Sho," he said quietly. "I just want to see to my granddaughter."

"We'll see to her. Come on out."

"Sho, Major. Just a minute."

"Show a light. Light your lamp."

"Sho. In just a minute." They could hear his voice retreat into the house, though they could not see him as he went swiftly to the crack in the chimney where he kept the butcher knife: the one thing in his slovenly life and house in which he took pride, since it was razor sharp. He approached the pallet, his granddaughter's voice:

"Who is it? Light the lamp, Grandpaw."

"Hit won't need no light, honey. Hit won't take but a minute," he said, kneeling, fumbling toward her voice, whispering now. "Where air you?"

"Right here," she said fretfully. "Where would I be? What is . . ." His hand touched her face. "What is . . . Grandpaw! Grand. . . ."

"Jones!" the sheriff said. "Come out of there!"

"In just a minute, Major," he said. Now he rose and moved swiftly. He knew where in the dark the can of kerosene was, just as he knew that it was full, since it was not two days ago that he had filled it at the store and held it there until he got a ride home with it, since the five gallons were heavy. There were still coals on the hearth; besides, the crazy building itself was like tinder: the coals, the hearth, the walls exploding in a single blue glare. Against it the waiting men saw him in a wild instant springing toward them with the lifted scythe before the horses reared and whirled. They checked the horses and turned them back toward the glare, yet still in wild relief against it the gaunt figure ran toward them with the lifted scythe.

"Jones!" the sheriff shouted; "stop! Stop, or I'll shoot. Jones! *Jones!*" Yet still the gaunt, furious figure came on against the glare and roar of the flames. With the scythe lifted, it bore down upon them, upon the wild glaring eyes of the horses and the swinging glints of gun barrels, without any cry, any sound.

ERNEST HEMINGWAY

A Clean, Well-Lighted Place

Ernest Hemingway (1898–1961), born in Oak Park, Illinois, volunteered for service in the ambulance corps in France during World War I. After the war Hemingway became a newspaper correspondent in Paris, where he met Ezra Pound and Gertrude Stein, who profoundly influenced his literary career. Hemingway's novels deeply reflect his wartime experiences. In 1926 he published *The Sun Also Rises;* in 1929, *A Farewell to Arms;* in 1940, *For Whom the Bell Tolls.* His last major work, *The Old Man and the Sea,* was published in 1952 and, in 1954, he received the Nobel Prize for Literature.

Hemingway's writings reflect his philosophy that man is a doomed creature, whose only hope is to face the inevitable stoically. In his short stories and in his novels there appears the famous Hemingway dialogue—short, clipped, and bare, the very essence of speech. "A Clean, Well-Lighted Place" is characteristic of both his philosophy and his technique.

It was late and every one had left the café except an old man who sat in the shadow the leaves of the tree made against the electric light. In the day time the street was dusty, but at night the dew settled the dust and the old man liked to sit late because he was deaf and now at night it was quiet and he felt the difference. The two waiters inside the café knew that the old man was a little drunk, and while he was a good client they knew that if he became too drunk he would leave without paying, so they kept watch on him.

"Last week he tried to commit suicide," one waiter said.

"Why?"

"He was in despair."

"Nothing."

"How do you know it was nothing?"

"He has plenty of money."

They sat together at a table that was close against the wall near the door of the café and looked at the terrace where the tables were all empty except where the old man sat in the shadow of the leaves of the tree that moved slightly in the wind. A girl and a soldier went by in the street. The street light shone on the brass number on his collar. The girl wore no head covering and hurried beside him.

"The guard will pick him up," one waiter said.

"What does it matter if he gets what he's after?"

"He had better get off the street now. The guard will get him. They went by five minutes ago."

The old man sitting in the shadow rapped on his saucer with his glass. The younger waiter went over to him.

"What do you want?"

The old man looked at him. "Another brandy," he said.

"You'll be drunk," the waiter said. The old man looked at him. The waiter went away.

"He'll stay all night, he said to his colleague. "I'm sleepy now. I never get into bed before three o'clock. He should have killed himself last week."

The waiter took the brandy bottle and another

saucer from the counter inside the café and marched out to the old man's table. He put down the saucer and poured the glass full of brandy.

"You should have killed yourself last week," he said to the deaf man. The old man motioned with his finger. "A little more," he said. The waiter poured on into the glass so that the brandy slopped over and ran down the stem into the top saucer of the pile. "Thank you," the old man said. The waiter took the bottle back inside the café. He sat down at the table with his colleague again.

"He's drunk now," he said.

"He's drunk every night."

"What did he want to kill himself for?"

"How should I know."

"How did he do it?"

"He hung himself with a rope."

"Who cut him down?"

"His niece."

"Why did they do it?"

"Fear for his soul."

"How much money has he got?"

"He's got plenty."

"He must be eighty years old."

"Anyway I should say he was eighty."

"I wish he would go home. I never get to bed before three o'clock. What kind of hour is that to go to bed?"

"He stays up because he likes it."

"He's lonely. I'm not lonely. I have a wife waiting in bed for me."

"He had a wife once too."

"A wife would be no good to him now."

"You can't tell. He might be better with a wife."

"His niece looks after him."

"I know. You said she cut him down."

"I wouldn't want to be that old. An old man is a nasty thing."

"Not always. This old man is clean. He drinks without spilling. Even now, drunk. Look at him."

"I don't want to look at him. I wish he would go home. He has no regard for those who must work."

The old man looked from his glass across the square, then over at the waiters.

"Another brandy," he said, pointing to his glass. The waiter who was in a hurry came over.

"Finished," he said, speaking with that omission of syntax stupid people employ when talking to drunken people or foreigners. "No more tonight. Close now."

"Another," said the old man.

"No. Finished." The waiter wiped the edge of the table with a towel and shook his head.

The old man stood up, slowly counted the saucers, took a leather coin purse from his pocket and paid for the drinks, leaving half a peseta tip.

The waiter watched him go down the street, a very old man walking unsteadily but with dignity.

"Why didn't you let him stay and drink?" the unhurried waiter asked. They were putting up the shutters. "It is not half-past two."

"I want to go home to bed."

"What is an hour?"

"More to me than to him."

"An hour is the same."

"You talk like an old man yourself. He can buy a bottle and drink at home."

"It's not the same."

"No, it is not," agreed the waiter with a wife. He did not wish to be unjust. He was only in a hurry.

"And you? You have no fear of going home before your usual hour?"

"Are you trying to insult me?"

"No, hombre, only to make a joke."

"No," the waiter who was in a hurry said, rising from pulling down the metal shutters. "I have confidence. I am all confidence."

"You have youth, confidence, and a job," the older waiter said. "You have everything."

"And what do you lack?"

"Everything but work."

"You have everything I have."

"No. I have never had confidence and I am not young."

"Come on. Stop talking nonsense and lock up."

"I am of those who like to stay late at the café," the older waiter said. "With all those who do not want to go to bed. With all those who need a light for the night."

"I want to go home and into bed."

"We are of two different kinds," the older waiter said. He was now dressed to go home. "It is not only a question of youth and confidence although those things are very beautiful. Each night I am reluctant to close up because there may be someone who needs the café."

"Hombre, there are bodegas open all night long."

"You do not understand. This is a clean and pleasant café. It is well lighted. The light is very good and also, now, there are shadows of the leaves."

"Good night," said the younger waiter.

"Good night," the other said. Turning off the electric light he continued the conversation with himself. It is the light of course but it is necessary that the place be clean and pleasant. You do not want music. Certainly you do not want music. Nor can you stand before a bar with dignity although that is all that is provided for these hours. What did he fear? It was not fear or dread. It was a nothing that he knew too well. It was all a nothing and a man was nothing too. It was only that and light was all it needed and a certain cleanness and order. Some lived in it and never felt it but he knew it all was nada y pues nada y nada y pues nada. Our nada who are in nada, nada be thy name thy kindom nada thy will be nada in nada as it is in nada. Give us this nada our daily nada and nada us our nada as we nada our nadas and nada us not into nada but deliver us from nada; pues nada. Hail nothing full of nothing, nothing is with thee. He smiled and stood before a bar with a shining steam pressure coffee machine.

"What's yours?" asked the barman.

"Nada."

"Otro loco mas," said the barman and turned away.

"A little cup," said the waiter.

The barman poured it for him.

"The light is very bright and pleasant but the bar is unpolished," the waiter said.

The barman looked at him but did not answer. It was too late at night for conversation.

"You want another copita?" the barman asked.

"No, thank you," said the waiter and went out. He disliked bars and bodegas. A clean, well-lighted café was a very different thing. Now, without thinking further, he would go home to his room. He would lie in the bed and finally, with daylight, he would go to sleep. After all, he said to himself, it is probably only insomnia. Many must have it.

EUDORA WELTY

A Worn Path

Eudora Welty (1909–   ) lives in Jackson, Mississippi, where she was born and where she and William Faulkner were acquainted. She attended Mississippi State College for Women, the University of Wisconsin, and Columbia University. After the publication of her first few short stories, mainly in the *Southern Review*, her work began to be widely anthologized. Her works include *A Curtain of Green*, 1941; *The Bride of Innisfallen*, 1955; *Losing Battles*, 1970; *The Optimist's Daughter*, 1972, which was awarded a Pulitzer Prize in 1973; and *The Collected Short Stories of Eudora Welty*, 1979. Welty's fiction has often been favorably compared with that of Jane Austen and Katherine Anne Porter.

"A Worn Path," typically Welty in its Southern setting and its familiar-grotesque main character, is among her best short stories. The odyssey of Phoenix Jackson is a warm and moving story as the difficulties of this frail old woman's life are transformed by her innocence and dignity into something close to joy.

It was December—a bright frozen day in the early morning. Far out in the country there was an old Negro woman with her head tied in a red rag, coming along a path through the pinewoods. Her name was Phoenix Jackson. She was very old and small and she walked slowly in the dark pine shadows, moving a little from side to side in her steps, with the balanced heaviness and lightness of a pendulum in a grandfather clock. She carried a thin, small cane made from an umbrella, and with this she kept tapping the frozen earth in front of her. This made a grave and persistent noise in the still air, that seemed meditative like the chirping of a solitary little bird.

She wore a dark striped dress reaching down to her shoe tops, and an equally long apron of bleached sugar sacks, with a full pocket: all neat and tidy, but every time she took a step she might have fallen over her shoelaces, which dragged from her unlaced shoes. She looked straight ahead. Her eyes were blue with age. Her skin had a pattern all its own of numberless branching wrinkles and as though a whole little tree stood in the middle of her forehead, but a golden color ran underneath, and the two knobs of her cheeks were illumined by a yellow burning under the dark. Under the red rag her hair came down on her neck in the frailest of ringlets, still black, and with an odor like copper.

Now and then there was a quivering in the thicket. Old Phoenix said, "Out of my way, all you foxes, owls, beetles, jack rabbits, coons and wild animals! . . . Keep out from under these feet, little bob-whites. . . . Keep the big wild hogs out of my path. Don't let none of those come running my direction. I got a long way." Under her small black-freckled hand her cane, limber as a buggy whip, would switch at the brush as if to rouse up any hiding things.

On she went. The woods were deep and still. The sun made the pine needles almost too bright to look at, up where the wind rocked. The cones dropped as light as feathers. Down in the hollow was the mourning dove—it was not too late for him.

The path ran up a hill. "Seem like there is chains about my feet, time I get this far," she said, in the voice of argument old people keep to use with themselves. "Something always take a hold of me on this hill—pleads I should stay."

After she got to the top she turned and gave a full, severe look behind her where she had come. "Up through pines," she said at length. "Now down through oaks."

Her eyes opened their widest, and she started down gently. But before she got to the bottom of the hill a bush caught her dress.

Her fingers were busy and intent, but her skirts were full and long, so that before she could pull them free in one place they were caught in another. It was not possible to allow the dress to tear. "I in the thorny bush," she said. "Thorns, you doing your appointed work. Never want to let folks pass, no sir. Old eyes thought you was a pretty little *green* bush."

Finally, trembling all over, she stood free, and after a moment dared to stoop for her cane.

"Sun so high!" she cried, leaning back and looking, while the thick tears went over her eyes. "The time getting all gone here."

At the foot of this hill was a place where a log was laid across the creek.

"Now comes the trial," said Phoenix.

Putting her right foot out, she mounted the log and shut her eyes. Lifting her skirt, leveling her cane fiercely before her, like a festival figure in some parade, she began to march across. Then she opened her eyes and she was safe on the other side.

"I wasn't as old as I thought," she said.

But she sat down to rest. She spread her skirts on the bank around her and folded her hands over her knees. Up above her was a tree in a pearly cloud of mistletoe. She did not dare to close her eyes, and when a little boy brought her a plate with a slice of marble-cake on it she spoke to him. "That would be acceptable," she said. But when she went to take it there was just her own hand in the air.

So she left that tree, and had to go through a barbed-wire fence. There she had to creep and crawl, spreading her knees and stretching her fingers like a baby trying to climb the steps. But she talked loudly to herself: she could not let her dress be torn now, so late in the day, and she could not pay for having her arm or her leg sawed off if she got caught fast where she was.

At last she was safe through the fence and risen up out in the clearing. Big dead trees, like black men with one arm, were standing in the purple stalks of the withered cotton field. There sat a buzzard.

"Who you watching?"

In the furrow she made her way along.

"Glad this not the season for bulls," she said, looking sideways, "and the good Lord made his snakes to curl up and sleep in the winter. A pleasure I don't see no two-headed snake coming around that tree, where it come once. It took a while to get by him, back in the summer."

She passed through the old cotton and went into a field of dead corn. It whispered and shook and was taller than her head. "Through the maze now," she said, for there was no path.

Then there was something tall, black, and skinny there, moving before her.

At first she took it for a man. It could have been a man dancing in the field. But she stood still and listened, and it did not make a sound. It was as silent as a ghost.

"Ghost," she said sharply, "who be you the ghost of? For I have heard of nary death close by."

But there was no answer—only the ragged dancing in the wind.

She shut her eyes, reached out her hand, and touched a sleeve. She found a coat and inside that an emptiness, cold as ice.

"You scarecrow," she said. Her face lighted. "I ought to be shut up for good," she said with laughter. "My senses is gone. I too old. I the oldest people I ever know. Dance, old scarecrow," she said, "while I dancing with you."

She kicked her foot over the furrow and, with mouth drawn down, shook her head once or twice in a little strutting way. Some husks blew down and whirled in streamers about her skirts.

Then she went on, parting her way from side to side with the cane, through the whispering field. At last she came to the end, to a wagon track where the silver grass blew between the red ruts. The quail were walking around like pullets, seeming all dainty and unseen.

"Walk pretty," she said. "This the easy place. This the easy going."

She followed the track, swaying through the quiet bare fields, through the little strings of trees silver in their dead leaves, past cabins silver from weather, with the doors and windows boarded shut, all like old women under a spell sitting there. "I walking in their sleep," she said, nodding her head vigorously.

In a ravine she went where a spring was silently flowing through a hollow log. Old Phoenix bent and drank. "Sweet-gum makes the water sweet," she said, and drank more. "Nobody know who made this well, for it was here when I was born."

The track crossed a swampy part where the moss hung as white as lace from every limb. "Sleep on, alligators, and blow your bubbles." Then the track went into the road.

Deep, deep the road went down between the high green-colored banks. Overhead the live-oaks met, and it was as dark as a cave.

A black dog with a lolling tongue came up out of the weeds by the ditch. She was meditating, and not ready, and when he came at her she only hit him a little with her cane. Over she went in the ditch, like a little puff of milkweed.

Down there, her senses drifted away. A dream visited her, and she reached her hand up, but nothing reached down and gave her a pull. So she lay there and presently went to talking. "Old woman," she said to herself, "that black dog come up out of the weeds to stall you off, and now there he sitting on his fine tail, smiling at you."

A white man finally came along and found her—a hunter, a young man, with his dog on a chain.

"Well, Granny!" he laughed. "What are you doing there?"

"Lying on my back like a June-bug waiting to be turned over, mister," she said, reaching up her hand.

He lifted her up, gave her a swing in the air, and set her down. "Anything broken, Granny?"

"No sir, them old dead weeds is springy enough," said Phoenix, when she had got her breath. "I thank you for your trouble."

"Where do you live, Granny?" he asked, while the two dogs were growling at each other.

"Away back yonder, sir, behind the ridge. You can't even see it from here."

"On your way home?"

"No sir, I going to town."

"Why, that's too far! That's as far as I walk when I come out myself, and I get something for my trouble." He patted the stuffed bag he carried, and there hung down a little closed claw. It was one of the bob-whites, with its beak hooked bitterly to show it was dead. "Now you go on home, Granny!"

"I bound to go to town, mister," said Phoenix. "The time come around."

He gave another laugh, filling the whole landscape. "I know you old colored people! Wouldn't miss going to town to see Santa Claus!"

But something held old Phoenix very still. The deep lines in her face went into a fierce and different radiation. Without warning, she had seen with her own eyes a flashing nickel fall out of the man's pocket onto the ground.

"How old are you, Granny?" he was saying.

"There is no telling, mister," she said, "no telling."

Then she gave a little cry and clapped her hands and said, "Git on away from here, dog! Look! Look at that dog!" She laughed as if in admiration. "He ain't scared of nobody. He a big black dog." She whispered, "Sic him!"

"Watch me get rid of that cur," said the man. "Sic him, Pete! Sic him!"

Phoenix heard the dogs fighting, and heard the man running and throwing sticks. She even heard a gunshot. But she was slowly bending forward by that time, further and further forward, the lids stretched down over her eyes, as if she were doing this in her sleep. Her chin was lowered almost to her knees. The yellow palm of her hand came out from the fold of her apron. Her fingers slid down and along the ground under the piece of money with the grace and care they would have in lifting an egg from under a setting hen. Then she slowly straightened up, she stood erect, and the nickel was in her apron pocket. A bird flew by. Her lips moved. "God watching me the whole time. I come to stealing."

The man came back, and his own dog panted about them. "Well, I scared him off that time," he said, and then he laughed and lifted his gun and pointed it at Phoenix.

She stood straight and faced him.

"Doesn't the gun scare you?" he said, still pointing it.

"No, sir, I seen plenty go off closer by, in my day, and for less than what I done," she said, holding utterly still.

He smiled, and shouldered the gun. "Well, Granny," he said, "you must be a hundred years old, and scared of nothing. I'd give you a dime if I had any money with me. But you take my advice and stay home, and nothing will happen to you."

"I bound to go on my way, mister," said Phoenix. She inclined her head in the red rag. Then they went in different directions, but she could hear the gun shooting again and again over the hill.

She walked on. The shadows hung from the oak trees to the road like curtains. Then she smelled wood-smoke, and smelled the river, and she saw a steeple and the cabins on their steep steps. Dozens of little black children whirled around her. There ahead was Natchez shining. Bells were ringing. She walked on.

In the paved city it was Christmas time. There were red and green electric lights strung and criss-crossed everywhere, and all turned on in the daytime. Old Phoenix would have been lost if she had not distrusted her eyesight and depended on her feet to know where to take her.

She paused quietly on the sidewalk where people were passing by. A lady came along in the crowd, carrying an armful of red-, green- and silver-wrapped presents; she gave off perfume like the red roses in hot summer, and Phoenix stopped her.

"Please, missy, will you lace up my shoe?" She held up her foot.

"What do you want, Grandma?"

"See my shoe," said Phoenix. "Do all right for out in the country, but wouldn't look right to go in a big building."

"Stand still then, Grandma," said the lady. She put her packages down on the sidewalk beside her and laced and tied both shoes tightly.

"Can't lace 'em with a cane," said Phoenix. "Thank you, missy, I doesn't mind asking a nice lady to tie up my shoe, when I gets out on the street."

Moving slowly and from side to side, she went into the big building, and into a tower of steps, where she walked up and around and around until her feet knew to stop.

She entered a door, and there she saw nailed up on the wall the document that had been stamped with the gold seal and framed in the gold frame, which matched the dream that was hung up in her head.

"Here I be," she said. There was a fixed and ceremonial stiffness over her body.

"A charity case, I suppose," said an attendant who sat at the desk before her.

But Phoenix only looked above her head. There was sweat on her face, the wrinkles in her skin shone like a bright net.

"Speak up, Grandma," the woman said. "What's your name? We must have your history, you know. Have you been here before? What seems to be the trouble with you?"

Old Phoenix only gave a twitch to her face as if a fly were bothering her.

"Are you deaf?" cried the attendant.

But then the nurse came in.

"Oh, that's just old Aunt Phoenix," she said. "She doesn't come for herself—she has a little grandson. She makes these trips just as regular as clockwork. She lives away back off the Old Natchez Trace." She bent down. "Well, Aunt Phoenix, why don't you just take a seat? We won't keep you standing after your long trip." She pointed.

The old woman sat down, bolt upright in the chair.

"Now, how is the boy?" asked the nurse.

Old Phoenix did not speak.

"I said, how is the boy?"

But Phoenix only waited and stared straight ahead, her face very solemn and withdrawn into rigidity.

"Is his throat any better?" asked the nurse. "Aunt Phoenix, don't you hear me? Is your grandson's throat any better since the last time you came for the medicine?"

With her hands on her knees, the old woman waited, silent, erect and motionless, just as if she were in armor.

"You musn't take up our time this way, Aunt Phoenix," the nurse said. "Tell us quickly about your grandson, and get it over. He isn't dead, is he?"

At last there came a flicker and then a flame of comprehension across her face, and she spoke.

"My grandson. It was my memory had left me. There I sat and forgot why I made my long trip."

"Forgot?" The nurse frowned. "After you came so far?"

Then Phoenix was like an old woman begging a dignified forgiveness for waking up frightened in the night. "I never did go to school, I was too old at the Surrender," she said in a soft voice. "I'm an old woman without an education. It was my memory fail me. My little grandson, he is just the same, and I forgot it in the coming."

"Throat never heals, does it?" said the nurse, speaking in a loud, sure voice to old Phoenix. By now she had a card with something written on it, a little list. "Yes. Swallowed lye. When was it?—January—two-three years ago—"

Phoenix spoke unasked now. "No, missy, he not dead, he just the same. Every little while his throat begin to close up again, and he not able to swallow. He not get his breath. He not able to help himself. So the time come around, and I go on another trip for the soothing medicine."

"All right. The doctor said as long as you came to get it, you could have it," said the nurse. "But it's an obstinate case."

"My little grandson, he sit up there in the house all wrapped up, waiting by himself," Phoenix went on. "We is the only two left in the world. He suffer and it don't seem to put him back at all. He got a sweet look. He going to last. He wear a little patch quilt and peep out holding his mouth open like a little bird. I remembers so plain now. I not going to forget him again, no, the whole enduring time. I could tell him from all the others in creation."

"All right." The nurse was trying to hush her now. She brought her a bottle of medicine. "Charity," she said, making a checkmark in a book.

Old Phoenix held the bottle close to her eyes, and then carefully put it into her pocket.

"I thank you," she said.

"It's Christmas time, Grandma," said the attendant. "Could I give you a few pennies out of my purse?"

"Five pennies is a nickel," said Phoenix stiffly.

"Here's a nickel," said the attendant.

Phoenix rose carefully and held out her hand. She received the nickel and then fished the other nickel out of her pocket and laid it beside the new one. She stared at her palm closely, with her head on one side.

Then she gave a tap with her cane on the floor.

"This is what come to me to do," she said. "I going to the store and buy my child a little windmill they sells, made out of paper. He going to find it hard to believe there such a thing in the world. I'll march myself back where he waiting, holding it straight up in this hand."

She lifted her free hand, gave a little nod, turned around, and walked out of the doctor's office. Then her slow step began on the stairs, going down.

JOHN COLLIER

Witch's Money

John Collier (1901–   ) is a widely read British short-story writer and critic, currently residing in Hollywood, California. His stories have been especially popular with movie and television producers. Among his books are *His Monkey Wife, or Married to a Chimp,* 1930; *Full Circle,* 1933; *Defy the Foul Fiend,* 1934; *The Touch of Nutmeg,* 1943; and *Fancies and Goodnights,* 1951. Most recently Collier has devoted his attention to the writing of critical works, including *New Facts Regarding the Life of Shakespeare* and *Shakespeare's Library,* both 1971.

Collier is a master of the ironic and fantastic tale into which is woven an underlying commentary on real people and real motivations. "Witch's Money" devastatingly describes the effects of sudden prosperity on a small village in the Pyrenees.

Foiral had taken a load of cork up to the high road, where he met the motor truck from Perpignan. He was on his way back to the village, walking harmlessly beside his mule, and thinking of nothing at all, when he was passed by a striding madman, half naked, and of a type never seen before in this district of the Pyrénées-Orientales.

He was not of the idiot sort, with the big head, like two or three of them down in the village. Nor was he a lean, raving creature, like Barilles's old father after the house burned down. Nor had he a little, tiny, shrunken-up, chattering head, like the younger Lloubes. He was a new sort altogether.

Foiral decided he was a kind of *bursting* madman, all blare and racket, as bad as the sun. His red flesh burst out of his little bits of coloured clothes; red arms, red knees, red neck, and a great round red face bursting with smiles, words, laughter.

Foiral overtook him at the top of the ridge. He was staring down into the valley like a man thunderstruck.

"My God!" he said to Foiral. "Just look at it!" Foiral looked at it. There was nothing wrong.

"Here have I," said the mad Jack, "been walking up and down these goddam Pyrénées for weeks—meadows, birch trees, pine trees, waterfalls—green as a dish of *haricots verts!* And here's what I've been looking for all the time. Why did no one tell me?"

There's a damned question to answer! However, madmen answer themselves. Foiral thumped his mule and started off down the track, but the mad fellow fell in step beside him.

"What is it, for God's sake?" said he. "A bit of Spain strayed over the frontier, or what? Might be a crater in the moon. No water, I suppose? God, look at that ring of red hills! Look at that pink and yellow land! Are those villages down there? Or the bones of some creatures that have died?

"I like it," he said. "I like the way the fig trees burst out of the rock. I like the way the seeds are bursting out of the figs. Ever heard of surrealism? This is surrealism come to life. What are those? Cork forests? They look like petrified ogres. Excellent ogres, who bleed when these impudent mortals flay you, with my little brush, on my little piece of canvas, I shall restore to you an important part of your life!"

Foiral, by no means devout, took the sensible precaution of crossing himself. The fellow went on and on, all the way down, two or three kilometres, Foiral answering with a "yes," a "no," and a grunt. "This is *my* country!" cried the lunatic. "It's *made* for me. Glad I didn't go to Morocco! Is this your village? Wonderful! Look at those houses—three, four stories. Why do they look as if they'd been piled up by cave-dwellers, cave-dwellers who couldn't find a cliff? Or are they caves from which the cliff has crumbled away, leaving them uneasy in the sunlight, huddling together? Why don't you have any windows? I like that yellow belfry. Sort of Spanish. I like the way the bell hangs in that iron cage. Black as your hat. Dead. Maybe that's why it's so quiet here. Dead noise, gibbeted against the blue! Ha! Ha! You're not amused, eh? You don't care for surrealism? So much the worse, my friend, because you're the stuff that sort of dream is made of. I like the black clothes all you people wear. Spanish touch again, I suppose? It makes you look like holes in the light."

"Goodbye," said Foiral.

"Wait a minute," said the stranger. "Where can I put up in this village? Is there an inn?"

"No," said Foiral, turning into his yard.

"Hell!" said the stranger. "I suppose someone has a room I can sleep in?"

"No," said Foiral.

That set the fellow back a bit. "Well," said he at last, "I'll have a look around, anyway."

So he went up the street. Foiral saw him talking to Madame Arago, and she was shaking her head. Then he saw him trying it on at the baker's, and the baker shook his head as well. However, he bought a loaf there, and some cheese and wine from Barilles. He sat down on the bench outside and ate it; then he went pottering off up the slope.

Foiral thought he'd keep an eye on him, so he followed to the top of the village, where he could see all over the hillside. The fellow was just mooning about; he picked up nothing, he did nothing. Then he began to drift over to the little farm-house, where the well is, a few hundred yards above the rest of the houses.

This happened to be Foiral's property, through his wife: a good place, if they'd had a son to live in it. Seeing the stranger edging that way, Foiral followed, not too fast, you understand, and not too slow either. Sure enough, when he got there, there was the fellow peering through the chinks in the shutters, even trying the door. He might have been up to anything.

He looked round as Foiral came up. "Nobody lives here?" he said.

"No," said Foiral.

"Who does it belong to?" said the stranger.

Foiral hardly knew what to say. In the end he had to admit it was his.

"Will you rent it to me?" said the stranger.

"What's that?" said Foiral.

"I want the house for six months," said the stranger.

"What for?" said Foiral.

"Damn it!" said the stranger. "To live in."

"Why?" said Foiral

The stranger holds up his hand. He picks hold of the thumb. He says, very slowly, "I am an artist, a painter."

"Yes," says Foiral.

Then the stranger lays hold of his forefinger. "I can work here. I like it. I like the view. I like those two ilex trees."

"Very good," says Foiral.

Then the stranger takes hold of his middle finger. "I want to stay here six months."

"Yes," says Foiral.

Then the stranger takes hold of his third finger. "In this house. Which, I may say, on this yellow ground, looks interestingly like a die on a desert. Or does it look like a skull?"

"Ah!" says Foiral.

Then the stranger takes hold of his little finger, and he says, "How much—do you want—to let me—live and work—in this house—for six months?"

"Why?" said Foiral.

At this the stranger began to stamp up and down. They had quite an argument. Foiral clinched the matter by saying that people didn't rent houses in that part of the world; everyone had his own.

"It is necessary," said the stranger, grinding his teeth, "for me to paint pictures here."

"So much the worse," said Foiral.

The stranger uttered a number of cries in some foreign gibberish, possibly that of hell itself. "I see your soul," said he, "as a small and exceed-ingly sterile black marble, on a waste of burning white alkali.''

Foiral, holding his two middle fingers under his thumb, extended the first and fourth in the direction of the stranger, careless of whether he gave offence.

"What will you take for the shack?" said the stranger. "Maybe I'll buy it."

It was quite a relief to Foiral to find that after all he was just a plain, simple, ordinary lunatic. Without a proper pair of pants to his back-side, he was offering to buy this excellent sound house, for which Foiral would have asked twenty thousand francs, had there been anyone of whom to ask it.

"Come on," said the stranger. "How much?"

Foiral, thinking he had wasted enough time, and not objecting to an agreeable sensation, said, "Forty thousand."

Said the stranger, "I'll give you thirty-five."

Foiral laughed heartily.

"That's a good laugh," said the stranger. "I should like to paint a laugh like that. I should express it by a *mélange* of the roots of recently extracted teeth. Well, what about it? Thirty-five? I can pay you a deposit right now." And, pulling out a wallet, this Croesus among madmen rustled one, two, three, four, five thousand-franc notes under Foiral's nose.

"It'll leave me dead broke," he said. "Still, I expect I can sell it again?"

"If God wills," said Foiral.

"Anyway, I could come here now and then," said the other. "My God! I can paint a showful of pictures here in six months. New York'll go crazy. Then I'll come back here and paint another show."

Foiral, ravished with joy, ceased attempting to understand. He began to praise his house furiously: he dragged the man inside, showed him the oven, banged the walls, made him look up the chimney, into the shed, down the well— "All right. All right," said the stranger. "That's grand. Everything's grand. Whitewash the walls. Find me some woman to come and clean and cook. I'll go back to Perpignan and turn up in a week with my things. Listen, I want that table chucked in, two or three of the chairs, and the bedstead. I'll get the rest. Here's your deposit."

"No, no," said Foiral. "Everything must be done properly, before witnesses. Then, when the lawyer comes, he can make out the papers. Come

back with me. I'll call Arago, he's a very honest man. Guis, very honest. Vigné, honest as the good earth. And a bottle of old wine. I have it. It shall cost nothing."

"Fine!" said the blessed madman, sent by God.

Back they went. In came Arago, Guis, Vigné, all as honest as the day. The deposit was paid, the wine was opened, the stranger called for more, others crowded in; those who were not allowed in stood outside to listen to the laughter. You'd have thought there was a wedding going on, or some wickedness in the house. In fact, Foiral's old woman went and stood in the doorway every now and then, just to let people see her.

There was no doubt about it, there was something very magnificent about this madman. Next day, after he had gone, they talked him over thoroughly. "To listen," said little Guis, "is to be drunk without spending a penny. You think you understand; you seem to fly through the air; you have to burst out laughing."

"I somehow had the delectable impression that I was rich," said Arago. "Not, I mean, with something in the chimney, but as if I—well, as if I were to spend it. And more."

"I like him," said little Guis. "He is my friend."

"Now you speak like a fool," said Foiral. "He is mad. And it is I who deal with him."

"I thought maybe he was not so mad when he said the house was like an old skull looking out of the ground," said Guis, looking sideways, as well he might.

"Nor a liar, perhaps?" said Foiral. "Let me tell you, he said also it was like a die on a desert. Can it be both?"

"He said in one breath," said Arago, "that he came from Paris. In the next, that he was an American."

"Oh, yes. Unquestionably a great liar," said Quès. "Perhaps one of the biggest rogues in the whole world, going up and down. But, fortunately, mad as well."

"So he buys a house," said Lafago. "If he had his wits about him, a liar of that size, he'd take it—like that. As it is, he buys it. Thirty-five-thousand francs!"

"Madness turns a great man inside out, like a sack," said Arago. "And if he is rich as well—"

"—money flies in all directions," said Guis.

Nothing could be more satisfactory. They waited impatiently for the stranger's return. Foiral whitewashed the house, cleaned the chimneys, put everything to rights. You may be sure he had a good search for anything that his wife's old man might have left hidden there years ago, and which this fellow might have heard of. They say they're up to anything in Paris.

The stranger came back, and they were all day with the mules getting his stuff from where the motor truck had left it. By the evening they were in the house, witnesses, helpers, and all—there was just the little matter of paying up the money.

Foiral indicated this with the greatest delicacy in the world. The stranger, all smiles and readiness, went into the room where his bags were piled up, and soon emerged with a sort of book in his hand, full of little *billets*, like those they try to sell for the lottery in Perpignan. He tore off the top one. "Here you are," he said to Foiral, holding it out. "Thirty thousand francs."

"No," said Foiral.

"What the hell now?" asked the stranger.

"I've seen that sort of thing," said Foiral. "And not for thirty thousand francs, my friend, but for three million. And afterwards—they tell you it hasn't won. I should prefer the money."

"This is the money," said the stranger. "It's as good as money anyway. Present this, and you'll get thirty thousand-franc notes, just like those I gave you."

Foiral was rather at a loss. It's quite usual in these parts to settle a sale at the end of a month. Certainly he wanted to run no risk of crabbing the deal. So he pocketed the piece of paper, gave the fellow good-day, and went off with the rest of them to the village.

The stranger settled in. Soon he got to know everybody. Foiral, a little uneasy, cross-examined him whenever they talked. It appeared, after all, that he *did* come from Paris, having lived there, and he *was* an American, having been born there. "Then you have no relations in this part of the world?" said Foiral.

"No relations at all."

Well! Well! Well! Foiral hoped the money was all right. Yet there was more in it than that. No relations! It was quite a thought. Foiral put it away at the back of his mind: he meant to extract the juice from it some night when he couldn't sleep.

At the end of the month, he took out his piece of paper, and marched up to the house again. There was the fellow, three parts naked, sitting under one of the ilex trees, painting away on a bit

of canvas. And what do you think he had chosen to paint? Roustand's mangy olives, that haven't borne a crop in living memory.

"What is it?" said the mad fellow. "I'm busy."

"This," said Foiral, holding out the bit of paper. "I need the money."

"Then why, in the name of the devil," said the other, "don't you go and get the money, instead of coming here bothering me?"

Foiral had never seen him in this sort of mood before. But a lot of these laughers stop laughing when it comes to hard cash. "Look here," said Foiral. "This is a very serious matter."

"Look here," said the stranger. "That's what's called a cheque. I give it to you. You take it to a bank. The bank gives you the money."

"Which bank?" said Foiral.

"Your bank. Any bank. The bank in Perpignan," said the stranger. "You go there. They'll do it for you."

Foiral, still hankering after the cash, pointed out that he was a very poor man, and it took a whole day to get to Perpignan, a considerable thing to such an extremely poor man as he was.

"Listen," said the stranger. "You know goddam well you've made a good thing out of this sale. Let me get on with my work. Take the cheque to Perpignan. It's worth the trouble. I've paid you plenty."

Foiral knew then that Guis had been talking about the price of the house. "All right, my little Guis, I'll think that over some long evening when the rains begin." However, there was nothing for it, he had to put on his best black, take the mule to Estagel, and there get the bus, and the bus took him to Perpignan.

In Perpignan they are like so many monkeys. They push you, look you up and down, snigger in your face. If a man has business—with a bank, let us say—and he stands on the pavement opposite to have a good look at it, he gets elbowed into the roadway half a dozen times in five minutes, and he's lucky if he escapes with his life.

Nevertheless, Foiral got into the bank at last. As a spectacle it was tremendous. Brass rails, polished wood, a clock big enough for a church, little cotton-backs sitting among heaps of money like mice in a cheese.

He stood at the back for about half an hour, waiting, and no one took any notice of him at all. In the end one of the little cotton-backs beckoned him up to the brass railing. Foiral delved in his pocket, and produced the cheque. The cotton-back looked at it as if it were a mere nothing. "Holy Virgin!" thought Foiral.

"I want the money for it," said he.

"Are you a client of the bank?"

"No."

"Do you wish to be?"

"Shall I get the money?"

"But naturally. Sign this. Sign this. Sign on the back of the cheque. Take this. Sign this. Thank you. Good-day."

"But the thirty thousand francs?" cried Foiral.

"For that, my dear sir, we must wait till the cheque is cleared. Come back in about a week."

Foiral, half dazed, went home. It was a bad week. By day he felt reasonably sure of the cash, but at night, as soon as he closed his eyes, he could see himself going into that bank, and all the cotton-backs swearing they'd never seen him before. Still, he got through it, and as soon as the time was up, he presented himself at the bank again.

"Do you want a cheque-book?"

"No. Just the money. The money."

"All of it? You want to close the account? Well! Well! Sign here. Sign here."

Foiral signed.

"There you are. Twenty-nine thousand eight hundred and ninety."

"But, sir, it was thirty thousand."

"But, my dear sir, the charges."

Foiral found it was no good arguing. He went off with his money. That was good. But the other hundred and ten! That sticks in a man's throat.

As soon as he got home, Foiral interviewed the stranger. "I am a poor man," said he.

"So am I," said the stranger. "A damned sight too poor to pay you extra because you can't get a cheque cashed in a civilized way."

This was a peculiarly villainous lie. Foiral had, with his own eyes, seen a whole block of these extraordinary thirty-thousand-franc *billets* in the little book from which the stranger had torn this one. But once more there was nothing to be done about it; a plain honest man is always being baffled and defeated. Foiral went home, and put his crippled twenty-nine thousand-odd into the little box behind the stone in the chimney. How different, if it had been a round thirty thousand! What barbarous injustice!

Here was something to think about in the evenings. Foiral thought about it a lot. In the end

he decided it was impossible to act alone, and called in Arago, Quès, Lafago, Vigné, Barilles. Not Guis. It was Guis who had told the fellow he had paid too much for the house, and put his back up. Let Guis stay out of it.

To the rest he explained everything very forcefully. "Not a relation in the whole country-side. And in that book, my dear friends—you have seen it yourselves—ten, twelve, fifteen, maybe twenty of these extraordinary little *billets*."

"And if somebody comes after him? Somebody from America?"

"He has gone off, walking, mad, just as he came here. Anything can happen to a madman, walking about, scattering money."

"It's true. Anything can happen."

"But it should happen before the lawyer comes."

"That's true. So far even the curé hasn't seen him."

"There must be justice, my good friends, society cannot exist without it. A man, an honest man, is not to be robbed of a hundred and ten francs."

"No, that is intolerable."

The next night, these very honest men left their houses, those houses whose tall uprights of white plaster and black shadow appear, in moonlight even more than in sunlight, like a heap of bleached ribs lying in the desert. Without much conversation they made their way up the hill and knocked upon the stranger's door.

After a brief interval they returned, still without much conversation, and slipped one by one into their extremely dark doorways, and that was all.

For a whole week, there was no perceptible change in the village. If anything, its darks and silences, those holes in the fierce light, were deeper. In every black interior sat a man who had two of these excellent *billets*, each of which commanded thirty thousand francs. Such a possession brightens the eyes, and enhances the savour of solitude, enabling a man, as the artist would have said, to partake of the nature of Fabre's tarantula, motionless at the angle of her tunnel. But they found it no longer easy to remember the artist. His jabbering, his laughter, even his final yelp, left no echo at all. It was all gone, like the rattle and flash of yesterday's thunderstorm.

So apart from the tasks of the morning and the evening, performing which they were camouflaged by habit, they sat in their houses alone. Their wives scarcely dared to speak to them, and they were too rich to speak to each other. Guis found it out, for it was no secret except to the world outside, and Guis was furious. But his wife rated him from morning till night, and left him no energy for reproaching his neighbours.

At the end of the week, Barilles sprang into existence in the doorway of his house. His thumbs were stuck in his belt, his face was flushed from lead colour to plum colour, his bearing expressed an irritable resolution.

He crossed to Arago's, knocked, leaned against a doorpost. Arago, emerging, leaned against the other. They talked for some little time of nothing at all. Then Barilles, throwing away the stump of his cigarette, made an oblique and sympathetic reference to a certain small enclosure belonging to Arago, on which there was a shed, a few vines, a considerable grove of olives. "It is the very devil," said Barilles, "how the worm gets into the olive in these days. Such a grove as that, at one time, might have been worth something."

"It is worse than the devil," said Arago. "Believe me or not, my dear friend, in some years I get no more than three thousand francs from that grove."

Barilles burst into what passes for laughter in this part of the world. "Forgive me!" he said. "I thought you said three thousand. Three hundred—yes. I suppose in a good year you might make that very easily."

This conversation continued through phases of civility, sarcasm, rage, fury and desperation until it ended with a cordial handshake, and a sale of the enclosure to Barilles for twenty-five thousand francs. The witnesses were called in; Barilles handed over one of his *billets*, and received five thousand in cash from the box Arago kept in his chimney. Everyone was delighted by the sale: it was felt that things were beginning to move in the village.

They were. Before the company separated, *pourparlers* were already started for the sale of Vigné's mules to Quès for eight thousand, the transfer of Lloubes's cork concession to Foiral for fifteen thousand, the marriage of Roustand's daughter to Vigné's brother with a dowry of twenty thousand, and the sale of a miscellaneous collection of brass objects belonging to Madame Arago for sixty-five francs, after some very keen bargaining.

Only Guis was left out in the cold, but on the way home, Lloubes, with his skin full of wine, ventured to step inside the outcast's doorway, and looked his wife Filomena up and down, from top to toe, three times. A mild interest, imperfectly concealed, softened the bitter and sullen expression upon the face of Guis.

This was a mere beginning. Soon properties began to change hands at a bewildering rate and at increasing prices. It was a positive boom. Change was constantly being dug out from under flagstones, from the strawy interiors of mattresses, from hollows in beams, and from holes in walls. With the release of these frozen credits the village blossomed like an orchid sprung from a dry stick. Wine flowed with every bargain. Old enemies shook hands. Elderly spinsters embraced young suitors. Wealthy widowers married young brides. Several of the weaker sort wore their best black every day. One of these was Lloubes, who spent his evenings in the house of Guis. Guis in the evenings would wander round the village, no longer sullen, and was seen cheapening a set of harness at Lafago's, a first-rate gun at Roustand's. There was talk of something very special by way of a fiesta after the grape harvest, but this was only whispered, lest the curé should hear of it on one of his visits.

Foiral, keeping up his reputation as leader, made a staggering proposal. It was nothing less than to improve the mule track all the way from the metalled road on the rim of the hills, so that motor trucks could visit the village. It was objected that the wage bill would be enormous. "Yes," said Foiral, "but we shall draw the wages ourselves. We shall get half as much again for our produce."

The proposal was adopted. The mere boys of the village now shared the prosperity. Barilles now called his little shop "Grand Café Glacier de l'Univers et des Pyrénées." The widow Loyau offered room, board, and clothing to certain unattached young women, and gave select parties in the evenings.

Barilles went to Perpignan and returned with a sprayer that would double the yield of his new olive grove. Lloubes went and returned with a positive bale of ladies' underclothing, designed, you would say, by the very devil himself. Two or three keen card players went and returned with new packs of cards, so lustrous that your hand seemed to be all aces and kings. Vigné went, and returned with a long face.

The bargaining, increasing all the time, called for more and more money. Foiral made a new proposal. "We will all go to Perpignan, the whole damned lot of us, march to the bank, thump down our *billets*, and show the little cotton-backs whom the money belongs to. Boys, we'll leave them without a franc."

"They will have the hundred and ten," said Quès.

"To hell with the hundred and ten!" said Foiral. "And, boys, after that—well—ha! ha!—all men sin once. They say the smell alone of one of those creatures is worth fifty francs. Intoxicating! Stair carpets, red hair, every sort of wickedness! Tomorrow!"

"Tomorrow!" they all cried, and on the morrow they went off, in their stiffest clothes, their faces shining. Every man was smoking like a chimney, and every man had washed his feet.

The journey was tremendous. They stopped the bus at every café on the road, and saw nothing they didn't ask the price of. In Perpignan they kept together in a close phalanx; if the townspeople stared, our friends stared back twice as hard. As they crossed over to the bank, "Where is Guis?" said Foiral, affecting to look for him among their number. "Has he nothing due to him?" That set them all laughing. Try as they might, they couldn't hold their faces straight. They were still choking with laughter when the swing doors closed behind them.

HERNANDO TÉLLEZ

Just Lather, That's All

Hernando Téllez (1908–1966) was born and educated in Bogotá, Colombia. Early he was interested in a career in journalism, and his work for some of his country's leading newspapers and magazines is the source of his reputation as a writer. In 1950 he published his short stories in a volume entitled *Cenizas al Viento* (*Seeds in the Wind*), a collection of tragicomic tales showing his ability as a keen observer sensitive to the contemporary scene in Hispanic America, and especially in Colombia.

This suspenseful, ironic, satirical story leaves the reader pondering the interpretation Téllez intended each of the characters to have: hero, coward, victim of circumstance, a person of great caution and reserve, or comedian?

He said nothing when he entered. I was passing the best of my razors back and forth on a strop. When I recognized him I started to tremble. But he didn't notice. Hoping to conceal my emotion, I continued sharpening the razor. I tested it on the meat of my thumb, and then held it up to the light. At that moment he took off the bullet-studded belt that his gun holster dangled from. He hung it up on a wall hook and placed his military cap over it. Then he turned to me, loosening the knot of his tie, and said, "It's hot as hell. Give me a shave." He sat in the chair.

JUST LATHER, THAT'S ALL Translated by Donald A. Yates. Reprinted by permission of Dell Publishing Company.

I estimated he had a four-day beard. The four days taken up by the latest expedition in search of our troops. His face seemed reddened, burned by the sun. Carefully, I began to prepare the soap. I cut off a few slices, dropped them into the cup, mixed in a bit of warm water, and began to stir with the brush. Immediately the foam began to rise. "The other boys in the group should have this much beard, too." I continued stirring the lather.

"But we did all right, you know. We got the main ones. We brought back some dead, and we've got some others still alive. But pretty soon they'll all be dead."

"How many did you catch?" I asked.

"Fourteen. We had to go pretty deep into the woods to find them. But we'll get even. Not one of them comes out of this alive, not one."

He leaned back on the chair when he saw me with the lather-covered brush in my hand. I still had to put the sheet on him. No doubt about it, I was upset. I took a sheet out of a drawer and knotted it around my customer's neck. He wouldn't stop talking. He probably thought I was in sympathy with his party.

"The town must have learned a lesson from what we did the other day," he said.

"Yes," I replied, securing the knot at the base of his dark, sweaty neck.

"That was a fine show, eh?"

"Very good," I answered, turning back for the brush. The man closed his eyes with a gesture of fatigue and sat waiting for the cool caress of the soap. I had never had him so close to me. The day he ordered the whole town to file into the patio of the school to see the four rebels hanging there, I came face to face with him for an instant. But the sight of the mutilated bodies kept me from noticing the face of the man who had directed it all, the face I was now about to take into my hands. It was not an unpleasant face, certainly. And the beard, which made him seem a bit older than he was, didn't suit him badly at all. His name was Torres. Captain Torres. A man of imagination, because who else would have thought of hanging the naked rebels and then holding target practice on certain parts of their bodies? I began to apply the first layer of soap. With his eyes closed, he continued. "Without any effort I could go straight to sleep," he said, "but there's plenty to do this afternoon." I stopped the lathering and asked with a feigned lack of interest: "A firing squad?" "Something like that, but a little slower." I got on with the job of lathering his beard. My hands started trembling again. The man could not possibly realize it, and this was in my favor. But I would have preferred that he hadn't come. It was likely that many of our faction had seen him enter. And an enemy under one's roof imposes certain conditions. I would be obliged to shave that beard like any other one, carefully, gently, like that of any customer, taking pains to see that no single pore emitted a drop of blood. Being careful to see that the little tufts of hair did not lead the blade astray. Seeing that his skin ended up clean, soft, and healthy, so that passing the back of my hand over it I couldn't feel a hair. Yes, I was secretly a rebel, but I was also a conscientious barber, and proud of the preciseness of my profession. And this four-days' growth of beard was a fitting challenge.

I took the razor, opened up the two protective arms, exposed the blade and began the job, from one of the sideburns downward. The razor responded beautifully. His beard was inflexible and hard, not too long, but thick. Bit by bit the skin emerged. The razor rasped along, making its customary sound as fluffs of lather mixed with bits of hair gathered along the blade. I paused a moment to clean it, then took up the strop again to sharpen the razor, because I'm a barber who does things properly. The man, who had kept his eyes closed, opened them now, removed one of his hands from under the sheet, felt the spot on his face where the soap had been cleared off, and said, "Come to the school today at six o'clock." "The same thing as the other day?" I asked horrified. "It could be better," he replied. "What do you plan to do?" "I don't know yet. But we'll amuse ourselves." Once more he leaned back and closed his eyes. I approached him with the razor poised. "Do you plan to punish them all?" I ventured timidly. "All." The soap was drying on his face. I had to hurry. In the mirror I looked toward the street. It was the same as ever: the grocery store with two or three customers in it. Then I glanced at the clock: two-twenty in the afternoon. The razor continued on its downward stroke. Now from the other sideburn down. A thick, blue beard. He should have let it grow like some poets or priests do. It would suit him well. A lot of people wouldn't recognize him. Much to his benefit, I thought, as I attempted to cover the neck area smoothly. There, for sure, the razor had to be handled masterfully, since the hair, although softer, grew into little swirls. A curly beard. One of the tiny pores could be opened up and issue forth its pearl of blood. A good barber such as I prides himself on never allowing this to happen to a client. And this was a first-class client. How many of us had he ordered shot? How many of us had he ordered mutilated? It was better not to think about it. Torres did not know that I was his enemy. He did not know it nor did the rest. It was a secret shared by very few, precisely so that I could inform the revolutionaries of what Torres was doing in the town and of what he was planning each time he undertook a rebel-hunting excursion. So it was going to be very difficult to explain that I had him right in my hands and let him go peacefully—alive and shaved.

The beard was now almost completely gone. He seemed younger, less burdened by years than when he had arrived. I suppose this always happens with men who visit barber shops. Under the stroke of my razor Torres was being rejuvenated—rejuvenated because I am a good barber, the best in the town, if I may say so. A little more lather here, under his chin, on his Adam's apple, on this big vein. How hot it is getting! Torres must be sweating as much as I. But he is not afraid. He is a calm man, who is not even thinking about what he is going to do with the prisoners this afternoon. On the other hand I, with this razor in my hands, stroking and restroking this skin, trying to keep blood from oozing from these pores, can't even think clearly. Damn him for coming, because I'm a revolutionary and not a murderer. And how easy it would be to kill him. And he deserves it. Does he? No! What the devil! No one deserves to have someone else make the sacrifice of becoming a murderer. What do you gain by it? Nothing. Others come along and still others, and the first ones kill the second ones, and they the next ones and it goes on like this until everything is a sea of blood. I could cut this throat just so, zip! zip! I wouldn't give him time to complain and since he has his eyes closed he wouldn't see the glistening knife blade or my glistening eyes. But I'm trembling like a real murderer. Out of his neck a gush of blood would

spout onto the sheet, on the chair, on my hands, on the floor. I would have to close the door. And the blood would keep inching along the floor, warm, ineradicable, uncontainable, until it reached the street, like a little scarlet stream. I'm sure that one solid stroke, one deep incision, would prevent any pain. He wouldn't suffer. But what would I do with the body? Where would I hide it? I would have to flee, leaving all I have behind, and take refuge far away, far, far away. But they would follow until they found me. "Captain Torres' murderer. He slit his throat while he was shaving him—a coward." And then on the other side. "The avenger of us all. A name to remember. (And here they would mention my name.) He was the town barber. No one knew he was defending our cause."

And what of all this? Murderer or hero? My destiny depends on the edge of this blade. I can turn my hand a bit more, press a little harder on the razor, and sink it in. The skin would give way like silk, like rubber, like the strop. There is nothing more tender than human skin and the blood is always there, ready to pour forth. A blade like this doesn't fail. It is my best. But I don't want to be a murderer, no sir. You come to me for a shave. And I perform my work honorably. . . . I don't want blood on my hands. Just lather, that's all. You are an executioner and I am only a barber. Each person has his own place in the scheme of things. That's right. His own place.

Now his chin had been stroked clean and smooth. The man sat up and looked into the mirror. He rubbed his hands over his skin and felt it fresh, like new.

"Thanks," he said. He went to the hanger for his belt, pistol and cap. I must have been very pale; my shirt felt soaked. Torres finished adjusting the buckle, straightened his pistol in the holster and after automatically smoothing down his hair, he put on the cap. From his pants pocket he took out several coins to pay me for my services. And he began to head toward the door. In the doorway he paused for a moment, and turning to me he said:

"They told me that you'd kill me. I came to find out. But killing isn't easy. You can take my word for it." And he headed on down the street.

CARSON McCULLERS

A Tree. A Rock. A Cloud.

Carson McCullers (1917–1968), was born in Columbus, Georgia, and began writing at an early age. Her first novel, *The Heart Is a Lonely Hunter*, 1940, was well received. Since then many other books have appeared: *Reflections in a Golden Eye*, 1941; *A Member of the Wedding*, a novel that was also produced as a play and a movie, 1946; *The Ballad of the Sad Cafe*, 1951; *Seven*, a volume of short stories, 1954; and *Clock Without Hands*, 1961.

This story presents, in a simple, direct, but moving way, the requirements for the growth of the emotion we call love.

It was raining that morning, and still very dark. When the boy reached the streetcar café he had almost finished his route and he went in for a cup of coffee. The place was an all-night café owned by a bitter and stingy man called Leo. After the raw, empty street the café seemed friendly and bright: along the counter there were a couple of soldiers, three spinners from the cotton mill, and in a corner a man who sat hunched over with his nose and half his face down in a beer mug. The boy wore a helmet such as aviators wear. When he went into the café he unbuckled the chin strap and raised the right flap up over his pink little ear; often as he drank his coffee someone would speak to him in a friendly way. But this morning Leo did not look into his face and none of the men were talking. He paid and was leaving the café when a voice called out to him:

"Son! Hey Son!"

He turned back and the man in the corner was crooking his finger and nodding to him. He had brought his face out of the beer mug and he seemed suddenly very happy. The man was long and pale, with a big nose and faded orange hair.

"Hey Son!"

A TREE. A ROCK. A CLOUD. From *The Ballad of the Sad Cafe* by Carson McCullers. Reprinted by permission of the publisher, Houghton Mifflin Company.

The boy went toward him. He was an undersized boy of about twelve, with one shoulder drawn higher than the other because of the weight of the paper sack. His face was shallow, freckled, and his eyes were round child eyes.

"Yeah Mister?"

The man laid one hand on the paper boy's shoulders, then grasped the boy's chin and turned his face slowly from one side to the other. The boy shrank back uneasily.

"Say! What's the big idea?"

The boy's voice was shrill; inside the café it was suddenly very quiet.

The man said slowly: "I love you."

All along the counter the men laughed. The boy, who had scowled and sidled away, did not know what to do. He looked over the counter at Leo, and Leo watched him with a weary, brittle jeer. The boy tried to laugh also. But the man was serious and sad.

"I did not mean to tease you, Son," he said. "Sit down and have a beer with me. There is something I have to explain."

Cautiously, out of the corner of his eye, the paper boy questioned the men along the counter to see what he should do. But they had gone back to their beer or their breakfast and did not notice him. Leo put a cup of coffee on the counter and a little jug of cream.

"He is a minor," Leo said.

The paper boy slid himself up onto the stool. His ear beneath the upturned flap of the helmet was very small and red. The man was nodding at him soberly. "It is important," he said. Then he reached in his hip pocket and brought out something which he held up in the palm of his hand for the boy to see.

"Look very carefully," he said.

The boy stared, but there was nothing to look at very carefully. The man held in his big, grimy palm a photograph. It was the face of a woman, but blurred, so that only the hat and the dress she was wearing stood out clearly.

"See?" the man asked.

The boy nodded and the man placed another picture in his palm. The woman was standing on a beach in a bathing suit. The suit made her stomach very big, and that was the main thing you noticed.

"Got a good look?" He leaned over closer and finally asked: "You ever seen her before?"

The boy sat motionless, staring slantwise at the man. "Not so I know of."

"Very well." The man blew on the photographs and put them back into his pocket. "That was my wife."

"Dead?" the boy asked.

Slowly the man shook his head. He pursed his lips as though about to whistle and answered in a long-drawn way: "Nuuu—" he said. "I will explain."

The beer on the counter before the man was in a large brown mug. He did not pick it up to drink. Instead he bent down and, putting his face over the rim, he rested there for a moment. Then with both hands he tilted the mug and sipped.

"Some night you'll go to sleep with your big nose in a mug and drown," said Leo. "Prominent transient drowns in beer. That would be a cute death."

The paper boy tried to signal to Leo. While the man was not looking he screwed up his face and worked his mouth to question soundlessly: "Drunk?" But Leo only raised his eyebrows and turned away to put some pink strips of bacon on the grill. The man pushed the mug away from him, straightened himself, and folded his loose crooked hands on the counter. His face was sad as he looked at the paper boy. He did not blink, but from time to time the lids closed down with delicate gravity over his pale green eyes. It was nearing dawn and the boy shifted the weight of the paper sack.

"I am talking about love," the man said. "With me it is a science."

The boy half slid down from the stool. But the man raised his forefinger, and there was something about him that held the boy and would not let him go away.

"Twelve years ago I married the woman in the photograph. She was my wife for one year, nine months, three days, and two nights. I loved her. Yes. . . ." He tightened his blurred, rambling voice and said again: "I loved her. I thought also that she loved me. I was a railroad engineer. She had all home comforts and luxuries. It never crept into my brain that she was not satisfied. But do you know what happened?"

"Mgneeow!" said Leo.

The man did not take his eyes from the boy's face. "She left me. I came in one night and the house was empty and she was gone. She left me."

"With a fellow?" the boy asked.

Gently the man placed his palm down on the counter. "Why naturally, Son. A woman does not run off like that alone."

The café was quiet, the soft rain black and endless in the street outside. Leo pressed down the frying bacon with the prongs of his long fork. "So you have been chasing the floozie for eleven years. You frazzled old rascal!"

For the first time the man glanced at Leo. "Please don't be vulgar. Besides, I was not speaking to you." He turned back to the boy and said in a trusting and secretive undertone: "Let's not pay any attention to him. O.K.?"

The paper boy nodded doubtfully.

"It was like this," the man continued. "I am a person who feels many things. All my life one thing after another has impressed me. Moonlight. The leg of a pretty girl. One thing after another. But the point is that when I had enjoyed anything there was a peculiar sensation as though it was laying around loose in me. Nothing seemed to finish itself up or fit in with the other things. Women? I had my portion of them. The same. Afterwards laying around loose in me. I was a man who had never loved."

Very slowly he closed his eyelids, and the gesture was like a curtain drawn at the end of a scene in a play. When he spoke again his voice was excited and the words came fast—the lobes of his large, loose ears seemed to tremble.

"Then I met this woman. I was fifty-one years old and she always said she was thirty. I met her at a filling station and we were married within three days. And do you know what it was like? I just can't tell you. All I had ever felt was gathered together around this woman. Nothing lay around loose in me any more but was finished up by her."

The man stopped suddenly and stroked his long nose. His voice sank down to a steady and reproachful undertone: "I'm not explaining this right. What happened was this. There were these beautiful feelings and loose little pleasures inside me. And this woman was something like an assembly line for my soul. I run these little pieces of myself through her and I come out complete. Now do you follow me?"

"What was her name?" the boy asked.

"Oh," he said. "I called her Dodo. But that is immaterial."

"Did you try to make her come back?"

The man did not seem to hear. "Under the circumstances you can imagine how I felt when she left me."

Leo took the bacon from the grill and folded two strips of it between a bun. He had a gray face, with slitted eyes, and a pinched nose saddled by faint blue shadows. One of the mill workers signaled for more coffee and Leo poured it. He did not give refills on coffee free. The spinner ate breakfast there every morning, but the better Leo knew his customers the stingier he treated them. He nibbled his own bun as though he grudged it to himself.

"And you never got hold of her again?"

The boy did not know what to think of the man, and his child's face was uncertain with mingled curiosity and doubt. He was new on the paper route; it was still strange to him to be out in the town in the black, queer early morning.

"Yes," the man said. "I took a number of steps to get her back. I went around trying to locate her. I went to Tulsa where she had folks. And to Mobile. I went to every town she had ever mentioned to me, and I hunted down every man she had formerly been connected with. Tulsa, Atlanta, Chicago, Cheehaw, Memphis. . . . For the better part of two years I chased around the country trying to lay hold of her."

"But the pair of them had vanished from the face of the earth!" said Leo.

"Don't listen to him," the man said confidentially. "And also just forget those two years. They are not important. What matters is that around the third year a curious thing begun to happen to me."

"What?" the boy asked.

The man leaned down and tilted his mug to take a sip of beer. But as he hovered over the mug his nostrils fluttered slightly; he sniffed the staleness of the beer and did not drink. "Love is a curious thing to begin with. At first I thought only of getting her back. It was a kind of mania. But then as time went on I tried to remember her. But do you know what happened?"

"No," the boy said.

"When I laid myself down on a bed and tried to think about her my mind became a blank. I couldn't see her. I would take out her pictures and look. No good. Nothing doing. A blank. Can you imagine it?"

"Say Mac!" Leo called down the counter. "Can you imagine this bozo's mind a blank!"

Slowly, as though fanning away flies, the man waved his hand. His green eyes were concentrated and fixed on the shallow little face of the paper boy.

"But a sudden piece of glass on a sidewalk. Or a nickel tune in a music box. A shadow on a wall at night. And I would remember. It might happen in a street and I would cry or bang my head against a lamppost. You follow me?"

"A piece of glass . . ." the boy said.

"Anything. I would walk around and I had no power of how and when to remember her. You think you can put up a kind of shield. But remembering don't come to a man face forward—it corners around sideways. I was at the mercy of everything I saw and heard. Suddenly instead of me combing the countryside to find her she begun to chase me around in my very soul. *She* chasing *me*, mind you! And in my soul."

The boy asked finally: "What part of the country were you in then?"

"Ooh," the man groaned. "I was a sick mortal. It was like smallpox. I confess, Son, that I boozed. I fornicated. I committed any sin that suddenly appealed to me. I am loath to confess it but I will do so. When I recall that period it is all curdled in my mind, it was so terrible."

The man leaned his head down and tapped his forehead on the counter. For a few seconds he stayed bowed over in this position, the back of his stringy neck covered with orange furze, his hands with their long warped fingers held palm to palm in an attitude of prayer. Then the man straightened himself; he was smiling and suddenly his face was bright and tremulous and old.

"It was in the fifth year that it happened," he said. "And with it I started my science."

Leo's mouth jerked with a pale, quick grin. "Well none of we boys are getting any younger," he said. Then with sudden anger he balled up a dishcloth he was holding and threw it down hard on the floor. "You draggletailed old Romeo!"

"What happened?" the boy asked.

The old man's voice was high and clear: "Peace," he answered.

"Huh?"

"It is hard to explain scientifically, Son," he said. "I guess the logical explanation is that she and I had fleed around from each other for so long that finally we just got tangled up together and lay down and quit. Peace. A queer and beautiful blankness. It was spring in Portland and the rain came every afternoon. All evening I just stayed there on my bed in the dark. And that is how the science come to me."

The windows in the streetcar were pale blue with light. The two soldiers paid for their beers and opened the door—one of the soldiers combed his hair and wiped off his muddy puttees before they went outside. The three mill workers bent silently over their breakfasts. Leo's clock was ticking on the wall.

"It is this. And listen carefully. I meditated on love and reasoned it out. I realized what is wrong with us. Men fall in love for the first time. And what do they fall in love with?"

The boy's soft mouth was partly open and he did not answer.

"A woman," the old man said. "Without science, with nothing to go by, they undertake the most dangerous and sacred experience in God's earth. They fall in love with a woman. Is that correct, Son?"

"Yeah," the boy said faintly.

"They start at the wrong end of love. They begin at the climax. Can you wonder it is so miserable? Do you know how men should love?"

The old man reached over and grasped the boy by the collar of his leather jacket. He gave him a gentle little shake and his green eyes gazed down unblinking and grave.

"Son, do you know how love should be begun?"

The boy sat small and listening and still. Slowly he shook his head. The old man leaned closer and whispered:

"A tree. A rock. A cloud."

It was still raining outside in the street: a mild, gray, endless rain. The mill whistle blew for the six o'clock shift and the three spinners paid and went away. There was no one in the café but Leo, the old man, and the little paper boy.

"The weather was like this in Portland," he said. "At the time my science was begun. I meditated and I started very cautious. I would pick up something from the street and take it home with me. I bought a goldfish and I concentrated on the goldfish and I loved it. I graduated from one thing to another. Day by day I was getting this technique. On the road from Portland to San Diego—"

"Aw shut up!" screamed Leo suddenly. "Shut up! Shut up!"

The old man still held the collar of the boy's jacket; he was trembling and his face was earnest and bright and wild. "For six years now I have gone around by myself and built up my science. And now I am a master. Son. I can love anything. No longer do I have to think about it even. I see a street full of people and a beautiful light comes in me. I watch a bird in the sky. Or I meet a traveler on the road. Everything, Son. And anybody. All stranger and all loved! Do you realize what a science like mine can mean?"

The boy held himself stiffly, his hands curled tight around the counter edge. Finally he asked: "Did you ever really find that lady?"

"What? What say, Son?"

"I mean," the boy asked timidly. "Have you fallen in love with a woman again?"

The old man loosened his grasp on the boy's collar. He turned away and for the first time his green eyes had a vague and scattered look. He lifted the mug from the counter, drank down the yellow beer. His head was shaking slowly from side to side. Then finally he answered: "No, Son. You see that is the last step in my science. I go cautious. And I am not quite ready yet."

"Well!" said Leo. "Well well well!"

The old man stood in the open doorway. "Remember," he said. Framed there in the gray damp light of the early morning he looked shrunken and seedy and frail. But his smile was bright. "Remember I love you," he said with a last nod. And the door closed quietly behind him.

The boy did not speak for a long time. He pulled down the bangs on his forehead and slid his grimy little forefinger around the rim of his empty cup. Then without looking at Leo he finally asked:

"Was he drunk?"

"No," said Leo shortly.

The boy raised his clear voice higher. "Then was he a dope fiend?"

"No."

The boy looked up at Leo, and his flat little face was desperate, his voice urgent and shrill. "Was he crazy? Do you think he was a lunatic?" The paper boy's voice dropped suddenly with doubt. "Leo? Or not?"

But Leo would not answer him. Leo had run a night café for fourteen years, and he held him-self to be a critic of craziness. There were the town characters and also the transients who roamed in from the night. He knew the manias of all of them. But he did not want to satisfy the questions of the waiting child. He tightened his pale face and was silent.

So the boy pulled down the right flap of his helmet and as he turned to leave he made the only comment that seemed safe to him, the only remark that could not be laughed down and despised:

"He sure has done a lot of traveling."

FLANNERY O'CONNOR

A Late Encounter with the Enemy

Flannery O'Connor (1925–1964) was born in Georgia and educated at Georgia State College for Women and the State University of Iowa, where she received a master's degree in fine arts in 1947. Her first novel, *Wise Blood*, appeared in 1952. After publishing stories in the *Partisan Review, Harper's Bazaar, Mademoiselle,* and other magazines, she published a collection of ten stories, *A Good Man Is Hard to Find and Other Stories*, 1955. For her story "Greenleaf" she won first prize in the 1957 O. Henry Memorial Awards. Her last works are a novel, *The Violent Bear It Away*, 1960, and a collection of stories, *Everything That Rises Must Converge*, 1965. A volume of her essays, edited by Sally and Robert Fitzgerald, appeared in 1969. *The Complete Stories of Flannery O'Connor*, 1971, won the National Book Award in fiction for that year.

"A Late Encounter with the Enemy" is typical of Miss O'Connor's work. In it, the reader finds bizarre, brutal, and often mindless characters who tend to be almost, but not quite, beyond the realm of one's experience.

General Sash was a hundred and four years old. He lived with his granddaughter, Sally Poker Sash, who was sixty-two years old and who prayed every night on her knees that he would live until her graduation from college. The General didn't give two slaps for her graduation but

he never doubted he would live for it. Living had got to be such a habit with him that he couldn't conceive of any other condition. A graduation exercise was not exactly his idea of a good time, even if, as she said, he would be expected to sit on the stage in his uniform. She said there would be a long procession of teachers and students in their robes but that there wouldn't be anything to equal *him* in his uniform. He knew this well enough without her telling him, and as for the damn procession, it could march to hell and back and not cause him a quiver. He liked parades with floats full of Miss Americas and Miss Daytona Beaches and Miss Queen Cotton Products. He didn't have any use for processions and a procession full of school-teachers was about as deadly as the River Styx to his way of thinking. However, he was willing to sit on the stage in his uniform so that they could see him.

Sally Poker was not as sure as he was that he would live until her graduation. There had not been any perceptible change in him for the last five years, but she had the sense that she might be cheated out of her triumph because she so often was. She had been going to summer school every year for the past twenty because when she started teaching, there were no such things as degrees. In those times, she said, everything was normal but nothing had been normal since she was sixteen, and for the past twenty summers, when she should have been resting, she had had to take a trunk in the burning heat to the state teacher's college; and though when she returned in the fall, she always taught in the exact way she had been taught not to teach, this was a mild revenge that didn't satisfy her sense of justice. She wanted the General at her graduation because she wanted to show what she stood for, or, as she said, "what all was behind her," and was not behind them. This *them* was not anybody in particular. It was just all the upstarts who had turned the world on its head and unsettled the ways of decent living.

She meant to stand on that platform in August with the General sitting in his wheel chair on the stage behind her and she meant to hold her head very high as if she were saying, "See him! See him! My kin, all you upstarts! Glorious upright old man standing for the old traditions! Dignity! Honor! Courage! See him!" One night in her sleep she screamed, "See him! See him!" and turned her head and found him sitting in his wheel chair behind her with a terrible expression on his face and with all his clothes off except the general's hat and she had waked up and had not dared to go back to sleep again that night.

For his part, the General would not have consented even to attend her graduation if she had not promised to see to it that he sit on the stage. He liked to sit on any stage. He considered that he was still a very handsome man. When he had

been able to stand up, he had measured five feet four inches of pure game cock. He had white hair that reached to his shoulders behind and he would not wear teeth because he thought his profile was more striking without them. When he put on his full-dress general's uniform, he knew well enough that there was nothing to match him anywhere.

This was not the same uniform he had worn in the War between the States. He had not actually been a general in that war. He had probably been a foot soldier; he didn't remember what he had been; in fact, he didn't remember that war at all. It was like his feet, which hung down now shriveled at the very end of him, without feeling, covered with a blue-gray afghan that Sally Poker had crocheted when she was a little girl. He didn't remember the Spanish-American War in which he had lost a son; he didn't even remember the son. He didn't have any use for history because he never expected to meet it again. To his mind, history was connected with processions and life with parades and he liked parades. People were always asking him if he remembered this or that—a dreary black procession of questions about the past. There was only one event in the past that had any significance for him and that he cared to talk about: that was twelve years ago when he had received the general's uniform and had been in the premiere.

"I was in that preemy they had in Atlanta," he would tell visitors sitting on his front porch. "Surrounded by beautiful guls. It wasn't a thing local about it. It was nothing local about it. Listen here. It was a nashnul event and they had me in it—up onto the stage. There was no bobtails at it. Every person at it had paid ten dollars to get in and had to wear his tuxseeder. I was in this uniform. A beautiful gul presented me with it that afternoon in a hotel room."

"It was in a suite in the hotel and I was in it too, Papa," Sally Poker would say, winking at the visitors. "You weren't alone with any young lady in a hotel room."

"Was, I'd a known what to do," the old General would say with a sharp look and the visitors would scream with laughter. "This was a Hollywood, California, gul," he'd continue. "She was from Hollywood, California, and didn't have any part in the pitcher. Out there they have so many beautiful guls that they don't need that they call them a extra and they don't use them for nothing but presenting people with things and having their pitchers taken. They took my pitcher with her. No, it was two of them. One on either side and me in the middle with my arms around each of them's waist and their waist ain't any bigger than a half a dollar."

Sally Poker would interrupt again. "It was Mr. Govisky that gave you the uniform, Papa, and he gave me the most exquisite corsage. Really, I wish you could have seen it. It was made with gladiola petals taken off and painted gold and put back together to look like a rose. It was exquisite. I wish you could have seen it, it was. . . ."

"It was as big as her head," the General would snarl. "I was tellin it. They gimme this uniform and they gimme this soward and they say, 'Now General, we don't want you to start a war on us. All we want you to do is march right up on that stage when you're innerduced tonight and answer a few questions. Think you can do that?' 'Think I can do it!' I say. 'Listen here. I was doing things before you were born,' and they hollered."

"He was the hit of the show," Sally Poker would say, but she didn't much like to remember the premiere on account of what had happened to her feet at it. She had bought a new dress for the occasion—a long black crepe dinner dress with a rhinestone buckle and a bolero—and a pair of silver slippers to wear with it, because she was supposed to go up on the stage with him to keep him from falling. Everything was arranged for them. A real limousine came at ten minutes to eight and took them to the theater. It drew up under the marquee at exactly the right time, after the big stars and the director and the author and the governor and the mayor and some less important stars. The police kept traffic from jamming and there were ropes to keep the people off who couldn't go. All the people who couldn't go watched them step out of the limousine into the lights. Then they walked down the red and gold foyer and an usherette in a Confederate cap and little short skirt conducted them to their special seats. The audience was already there and a group of UDC members began to clap when they saw the General in his uniform and that started everybody to clap. A few more celebrities came after them and then the doors closed and the lights went down.

A young man with blond wavy hair who said he represented the motion-picture industry came out and began to introduce everybody and each one who was introduced walked up on the stage and said how really happy he was to be here for this great event. The General and his granddaughter were introduced sixteenth on the program. He was introduced as General Tennessee Flintrock Sash of the Confederacy, though Sally Poker had told Mr. Govisky that his name was George Poker Sash and that he had only been a major. She helped him up from his seat but her heart was beating so fast she didn't know whether she'd make it herself.

The old man walked up the aisle slowly with his fierce white head high and his hat held over his heart. The orchestra began to play the Confederate Battle Hymn very softly and the UDC members rose as a group and did not sit down again until the General was on the stage. When he reached the center of the stage with Sally Poker just behind him guiding his elbow, the orchestra burst out in a loud rendition of the Battle Hymn and the old man, with real stage presence, gave a vigorous trembling salute and stood at attention until the last blast had died away. Two of the usherettes in Confederate caps and short skirts held a Confederate and a Union flag crossed behind them.

The General stood in the exact center of the spotlight and it caught a weird moon-shaped slice of Sally Poker—the corsage, the rhinestone buckle and one hand clenched around a white glove and handkerchief. The young man with the blond wavy hair inserted himself into the circle of light and said he was *really* happy to have here tonight for this great event, one, he said, who had fought and bled in the battles they would soon see daringly re-acted on the screen, and "Tell me, General," he asked, "how old are you?"

"Niiiiiinnttty-two!" the General screamed.

The young man looked as if this were just about the most impressive thing that had been said all evening. "Ladies and gentlemen," he said, "let's give the General the biggest hand we've got!" and there was applause immediately and the young man indicated to Sally Poker with a motion of his thumb that she could take the old man back to his seat now so that the next person could be introduced; but the General had not finished. He stood immovable in the exact center of the spotlight, his neck thrust forward, his mouth slightly open, and his voracious gray eyes drinking in the glare and the applause. He elbowed his granddaughter roughly away. "How I keep so young," he screeched, "I kiss all the pretty guls!"

This was met with a great din of spontaneous applause and it was at just that instant that Sally Poker looked down at her feet and discovered that in the excitement of getting ready she had forgotten to change her shoes: two brown Girl Scout oxfords protruded from the bottom of her dress. She gave the General a yank and almost ran with him off the stage. He was very angry that he had not got to say how glad he was to be here for this event and on the way back to his seat, he kept saying as loud as he could, "I'm glad to be here at this preemy with all these beautiful guls!" but there was another celebrity going up the other aisle and nobody paid any attention to him. He slept through the picture, muttering fiercely every now and then in his sleep.

Since then, his life had not been very interesting. His feet were completely dead now, his knees worked like old hinges, his kidneys functioned when they would, but his heart persisted doggedly to beat. The past and the future were the same thing to him, one forgotten and the other not remembered; he had no more notion of dying than a cat. Every year on Confederate Memorial Day, he was bundled up and lent to the Capitol City Museum where he was displayed from one to four in a musty room full of old photographs, old uniforms, old artillery, and historic documents. All these were carefully preserved in glass cases so that children would not put their hands on them. He wore his general's uniform from the premiere and sat, with a fixed scowl, inside a small roped area. There was nothing about him to indicate that he was alive except an occasional movement in his milky gray eyes, but once when a bold child touched his sword, his arm shot forward and slapped the hand off in an instant. In the spring when the old homes were opened for pilgrimages, he was invited to wear his uniform and sit in some conspicuous spot and lend atmosphere to the scene. Some of these times he only snarled at the visitors but sometimes he told about the premiere and the beautiful girls.

If he had died before Sally Poker's graduation, she thought she would have died herself. At the beginning of the summer term, even before she knew if she would pass, she told the Dean that her grandfather, General Tennessee Flintrock Sash of the Confederacy, would attend her graduation and that he was a hundred and four years old and that his mind was still clear as a bell. Distinguished visitors were always welcome and could sit on the stage and be introduced. She made arrangements with her nephew, John Wesley Poker Sash, a Boy Scout, to come wheel the General's chair. She thought how sweet it would be to see the old man in his courageous gray and the young boy in his clean khaki—the old and the new, she thought appropriately—they would be behind her on the stage when she received her degree.

Everything went almost exactly as she had planned. In the summer while she was away at school, the General stayed with other relatives and they brought him and John Wesley, the Boy Scout, down to the graduation. A reporter came to the hotel where they stayed and took the General's picture with Sally Poker on one side of him and John Wesley on the other. The General, who had had his picture taken with beautiful girls, didn't think much of this. He had forgotten precisely what kind of event this was he was going to attend but he remembered that he was to wear his uniform and carry the sword.

On the morning of the graduation, Sally Poker had to line up in the academic procession with the B.S.'s in Elementary Education and she couldn't see to getting him on the stage herself—but John Wesley, a fat blond boy of ten with an executive expression, guaranteed to take care of everything. She came in her academic gown to the hotel and dressed the old man in his uniform. He was as frail as a dried spider. "Aren't you just thrilled, Papa?" she asked. "I'm just thrilled to death!"

"Put the soward acrost my lap, damm you," the old man said, "where it'll shine."

She put it there and then stood back looking at him. "You look just grand," she said.

"God damm it," the old man said in a slow monotonous certain tone as if he were saying it to the beating of his heart. "God damm every goddam thing to hell."

"Now, now," she said and left happily to join the procession.

The graduates were lined up behind the Science building and she found her place just as the line started to move. She had not slept much the night before and when she had, she had dreamed of the exercises, murmuring, "See him, see him?" in her sleep but waking up every time just before she turned her head to look at him behind her. The graduates had to walk three blocks in the hot sun in their black wool robes and as she plodded stolidly along she thought that if anyone considered this academic procession something impressive to behold, they need only wait until they saw that old General in his courageous gray and that clean young Boy Scout stoutly wheeling his chair across the stage with the sunlight catching the sword. She imagined that John Wesley had the old man ready now behind the stage.

The black procession wound its way up the two blocks and started on the main walk leading to the auditorium. The visitors stood on the grass, picking out their graduates. Men were pushing back their hats and wiping their foreheads and women were lifting their dresses slightly from the shoulders to keep them from sticking to their backs. The graduates in their heavy robes looked as if the last beads of ignorance were being sweated out of them. The sun blazed off the fenders of automobiles and beat from the columns of the buildings and pulled the eye from one spot of glare to another. It pulled Sally Poker's toward the big red Coca-Cola machine that had been set up by the side of the auditorium. Here she saw the General parked, scowling and hatless in his chair in the blazing sun while John Wesley, his blouse loose behind, his hip and cheek pressed to the red machine, was drinking a Coca-Cola. She broke from the line and galloped to them and snatched the bottle away. She shook the boy and thrust in his blouse and put the hat on the old man's head. "Now get him in there!" she said, pointing one rigid finger to the side door of the building.

For his part the General felt as if there were a little hole beginning to widen in the top of his head. The boy wheeled him rapidly down a walk and up a ramp and into a building and bumped him over the stage entrance and into position where he had been told and the General glared in front of him at heads that all seemed to flow together and eyes that moved from one face to another. Several figures in black robes came and picked up his hand and shook it. A black procession was flowing up each aisle and forming to

stately music in a pool in front of him. The music seemed to be entering his head through the little hole and he thought for a second that the procession would try to enter it too.

He didn't know what procession this was but there was something familiar about it. It must be familiar to him since it had come to meet him, but he didn't like a black procession. Any procession that came to meet him, he thought irritably, ought to have floats with beautiful guls on them like the floats before the preemy. It must be something connected with history like they were always having. He had no use for any of it. What happened then wasn't anything to a man living now and he was living now.

When all the procession had flowed into the black pool, a black figure began orating in front of it. The figure was telling something about history and the General made up his mind he wouldn't listen, but the words kept seeping in through the little hole in his head. He heard his own name mentioned and his chair was shuttled forward roughly and the Boy Scout took a big bow. They called his name and the fat brat bowed. Goddam you, the old man tried to say, get out of my way, I can stand up!—but he was jerked back again before he could get up and take the bow. He supposed the noise they made was for him. If he was over, he didn't intend to listen to any more of it. If it hadn't been for the little hole in the top of his head, none of the words would have got to him. He thought of putting his finger up there into the hole to block them but the hole was a little wider than his finger and it felt as if it were getting deeper.

Another black robe had taken the place of the first one and was talking now and he heard his name mentioned again but they were not talking about him, they were still talking about history. "If we forget our past," the speaker was saying, "we won't remember our future and it will be as well for we won't have one." The General heard some of these words gradually. He had forgotten history and he didn't intend to remember it again. He had forgotten the name and face of his wife and the names and faces of his children or even if he had a wife and children, and he had forgotten the names of places and the places themselves and what had happened at them.

He was considerably irked by the hole in his head. He had not expected to have a hole in his head at this event. It was the slow black music that had put it there and though most of the music had stopped outside, there was still a little of it in the hole, going deeper and moving around in his thoughts, letting the words he heard into the dark places of his brain. He heard the words, Chickamauga, Shiloh, Johnston, Lee, and he knew he was inspiring all these words that meant nothing to him. He wondered if he had been a general at Chickamauga or at Lee. Then he tried to see himself and the horse mounted in the middle of a float full of beautiful girls, being driven slowly through downtown Atlanta. Instead, the old words began to stir in his head as if they were trying to wrench themselves out of place and come to life.

The speaker was through with that war and had gone on to the next one and now he was approaching another and all his words, like the black procession, were vaguely familiar and irritating. There was a long finger of music in the General's head, probing various spots that were words, letting in a little light on the words and helping them to live. The words began to come toward him and he said, Dammit! I ain't going to have it! and he started edging backwards to get out of the way. Then he saw the figure in the black robe sit down and there was a noise and the black pool in front of him began to rumble and to flow toward him from either side to the black slow music, and he said, Stop dammit! I can't do but one thing at a time! He couldn't protect himself from the words and attend to the procession too and the words were coming at him fast. He felt that he was running backwards and the words were coming at him like musket fire, just escaping him but getting

nearer and nearer. He turned around and began to run as fast as he could but he found himself running toward the words. He was running into a regular volley of them and meeting them with quick curses. As the music swelled toward him, the entire past opened up on him out of nowhere and he felt his body riddled in a hundred places with sharp stabs of pain and he fell down, returning a curse for every hit. He saw his wife's narrow face looking at him critically through her round gold-rimmed glasses; he saw one of his squinting baldheaded sons; and his mother ran toward him with an anxious look; then a succession of places—Chickamauga, Shiloh, Marthasville—rushed at him as if the past were the only future now and he had to endure it. Then suddenly he saw that the black procession was almost on him. He recognized it, for it had been dogging all his days. He made such a desperate effort to see over it and find out what comes after the past that his hand clenched the sword until the blade touched bone.

The graduates were crossing the stage in a long file to receive their scrolls and shake the president's hand. As Sally Poker, who was near the end, crossed, she glanced at the General and saw him sitting fixed and fierce, his eyes wide open, and she turned her head forward again and held it a perceptible degree higher and received her scroll. Once it was all over and she was out of the auditorium in the sun again, she located her kin and they waited together on a bench in the shade for John Wesley to wheel the old man out. That crafty scout had bumped him out the back way and rolled him at high speed down a flagstone path and was waiting now, with the corpse, in the long line at the Coca-Cola machine.

FRANK O'CONNOR

Guests of the Nation

Frank O'Connor (1903–1966), whose real name was Michael O'Donovan, was born in Cork, Ireland, and attended the Christian Brothers School there. He was financially unable to pursue a university education, but he educated himself and developed his ability as a writer while he worked as a librarian. In 1931 his first book of short stories, *Guests of the Nation,* was published; it was followed by many volumes of short stories and verse, by plays, criticism, a history of Michael Collins and the Irish Revolution, and his autobiography, *An Only Child,* 1961.

"Guests of the Nation," like all Mr. O'Connor's short stories, is noted for its technical skill. "Storytelling," he says, "is the nearest thing one can get to the quality of the pure lyric poem. It doesn't deal with problems; it doesn't have any solutions to offer; it just states the human condition."

At dusk the big Englishman, Belcher, would shift his long legs out of the ashes and say "Well, chums, what about it?" and Noble or me would say "All right, chum" (for we had picked up some of their curious expressions), and the little Englishman, Hawkins, would light the lamp and bring out the cards. Sometimes Jeremiah Donovan would come up and supervise the game and get excited over Hawkins's cards, which he always played badly, and shout at him as if he was one of our own "Ah, you divil, you, why didn't you play the trey?"

But ordinarily Jeremiah was a sober and contented poor devil like the big Englishman, Belcher, and was looked up to only because he was a fair hand at documents, though he was slow enough even with them. He wore a small cloth hat and big gaiters over his long pants, and you seldom saw him with his hands out of his pockets. He reddened when you talked to him, tilting from toe to heel and back, and looking down all

the time at his big farmer's feet. Noble and me used to make fun of his broad accent, because we were from the town.

I couldn't at the time see the point of me and Noble guarding Belcher and Hawkins at all, for it was my belief that you could have planted that pair down anywhere from this to Claregalway and they'd have taken root there like a native weed. I never in my short experience seen two men to take to the country as they did.

They were handed on to us by the Second Battalion when the search for them became too hot, and Noble and myself, being young, took over with a natural feeling of responsibility, but Hawkins made us look like fools when he showed that he knew the country better than we did.

"You're the bloke they calls Bonaparte," he says to me. "Mary Brigid O'Connell told me to ask you what you done with the pair of her brother's socks you borrowed."

For it seemed, as they explained it, that the Second used to have little evenings, and some of the girls of the neighbourhood turned in, and, seeing they were such decent chaps, our fellows

GUESTS OF THE NATION From *More Stories* by Frank O'Connor. Published 1954 by Alfred A. Knopf, Inc. Reprinted by permission of the publisher.

couldn't leave the two Englishmen out of them. Hawkins learned to dance "The Walls of Limerick," "The Siege of Ennis," and "The Waves of Tory" as well as any of them, though, naturally, we couldn't return the compliment, because our lads at that time did not dance foreign dances on principle.

So whatever privileges Belcher and Hawkins had with the Second they just naturally took with us, and after the first day or two we gave up all pretence of keeping a close eye on them. Not that they could have got far, for they had accents you could cut with a knife and wore khaki tunics and overcoats with civilian pants and boots. But it's my belief that they never had any idea of escaping and were quite content to be where they were.

It was a treat to see how Belcher got off with the old woman of the house where we were staying. She was a great warrant to scold, and cranky even with us, but before ever she had a chance of giving our guests, as I may call them, a lick of her tongue, Belcher had made her his friend for life. She was breaking sticks, and Belcher, who hadn't been more than ten minutes in the house, jumped up from his seat and went over to her.

"Allow me, madam," he says, smiling his queer little smile, "please allow me"; and he takes the bloody hatchet. She was struck too paralytic to speak, and after that, Belcher would be at her heels, carrying a bucket, a basket, or a load of turf, as the case might be. As Noble said, he got into looking before she leapt, and hot water, or any little thing she wanted, Belcher would have it ready for her. For such a huge man (and though I am five foot ten myself I had to look up at him) he had an uncommon shortness—or should I say lack?—of speech. It took us some time to get used to him, walking in and out, like a ghost, without a word. Especially because Hawkins talked enough for a platoon, it was strange to hear big Belcher with his toes in the ashes come out with a solitary "Excuse me, chum," or "That's right, chum." His one and only passion was cards, and I will say for him that he was a good card-player. He could have fleeced myself and Noble, but whatever we lost to him Hawkins lost to us, and Hawkins played with the money Belcher gave him.

Hawkins lost to us because he had too much old gab, and we probably lost to Belcher for the same reason. Hawkins and Noble would spit at one another about religion into the early hours of the morning, and Hawkins worried the soul out of Noble, whose brother was a priest, with a string of questions that would puzzle a cardinal. To make it worse, even in treating of holy subjects, Hawkins had a deplorable tongue. I never in all my career met a man who could mix such a variety of cursing and bad language into an argument. He was a terrible man, and a fright to argue. He never did a stroke of work, and when he had no one else to talk to, he got stuck in the old woman.

He met his match in her, for one day when he tried to get her to complain profanely of the drought, she gave him a great comedown by blaming it entirely on Jupiter Pluvius (a deity neither Hawkins nor I had ever heard of, though Noble said that among the pagans it was believed that he had something to do with the rain). Another day he was swearing at the capitalists for starting the German war when the old lady laid down her iron, puckered up her little crab's mouth, and said: "Mr. Hawkins, you can say what you like about the war, and think you'll deceive me because I'm only a simple poor countrywoman, but I know what started the war. It was the Italian Count that stole the heathen divinity out of the temple in Japan. Believe me, Mr. Hawkins, nothing but sorrow and want can follow the people that disturb the hidden powers."

A queer old girl, all right.

II

We had our tea one evening, and Hawkins lit the lamp and we all sat into cards. Jeremiah Donovan came in too, and sat down and watched us for a while, and it suddenly struck me that he had no great love for the two Englishmen. It came as a great surprise to me, because I hadn't noticed anything about him before.

Late in the evening a really terrible argument blew up between Hawkins and Noble, about capitalists and priests and love of your country.

"The capitalists," says Hawkins with an angry gulp, "pays the priests to tell you about the next world so as you won't notice what the bastards are up to in this."

"Nonsense, man!" says Noble, losing his temper. "Before ever a capitalist was thought of, people believed in the next world."

Hawkins stood up as though he was preaching a sermon.

"Oh, they did, did they?" he says with a sneer. "They believed all the things you believe, isn't that what you mean? And you believe that God created Adam, and Adam created Shem, and Shem created Jehoshophat. You believe all that silly old fairytale about Eve and Eden and the apple. Well, listen to me, chum. If you're entitled to hold a silly belief like that, I'm entitled to hold a silly belief—which is that the first thing your God created was a bleeding capitalist, with morality and Rolls-Royce complete. Am I right, chum?" he says to Belcher.

"You're right, chum," says Belcher with his amused smile, and got up from the table to stretch his long legs into the fire and stroke his moustache. So, seeing that Jeremiah Donovan was going, and that there was no knowing when the argument about religion would be over, I went out with him. We strolled down to the village together, and then he stopped and started blushing and mumbling and saying I ought to be behind, keeping guard on the prisoners. I didn't like the tone he took with me, and anyway I was bored with life in the cottage, so I replied by asking him what the hell we wanted guarding them at all for. I told him I'd talked it over with Noble, and that we'd both rather be out with a fighting column.

"What use are those fellows to us?" says I.

He looked at me in surprise and said: "I thought you knew we were keeping them as hostages."

"Hostages?" I said.

"The enemy have prisoners belonging to us," he says, "and now they're talking of shooting them. If they shoot our prisoners, we'll shoot theirs."

"Shoot them?" I said.

"What else did you think we were keeping them for?" he says.

"Wasn't it very unforeseen of you not to warn Noble and myself of that in the beginning?" I said.

"How was it?" says he. "You might have known it."

"We couldn't know it, Jeremiah Donovan," says I. "How could we when they were on our hands so long?"

"The enemy have our prisoners as long and longer," says he.

"That's not the same thing at all," says I.

"What difference is there?" says he.

I couldn't tell him, because I knew he wouldn't understand. If it was only an old dog that was going to the vet's, you'd try and not get too fond of him, but Jeremiah Donovan wasn't a man that would ever be in danger of that.

"And when is this thing going to be decided?" says I.

"We might hear tonight," he says. "Or tomorrow or the next day at latest. So if it's only hanging round here that's a trouble to you, you'll be free soon enough."

It wasn't the hanging round that was a trouble to me at all by this time. I had worse things to worry about. When I got back to the cottage the argument was still on. Hawkins was holding forth in his best style, maintaining that there was no next world, and Noble was maintaining that there was; but I could see that Hawkins had had the best of it.

"Do you know what, chum?" he was saying with a saucy smile. "I think you're just as big a bleeding unbeliever as I am. You say you believe in the next world, and you know just as much about the next world as I do, which is sweet damn-all. What's heaven? You don't know. Where's heaven? You don't know. You know sweet damn-all! I ask you again, do they wear wings?"

"Very well, then," says Noble, "they do. Is that enough for you? They do wear wings."

"Where do they get them, then? Who makes them? Have they a factory for wings? Have they a sort of store where you hands in your chit and takes your bleeding wings?"

"You're an impossible man to argue with," says Noble. "Now, listen to—" And they were off again.

It was long after midnight when we locked up and went to bed. As I blew out the candle I told Noble what Jeremiah Donovan was after telling me. Noble took it very quietly. When we'd been in bed about an hour he asked me did I think we ought to tell the Englishmen. I didn't think we should, because it was more than likely that the English wouldn't shoot our men, and even if they did, the brigade officers, who were always up and down with the Second Battalion and knew the Englishmen well, wouldn't be likely to want them plugged. "I think so too," says Noble. "It would be great cruelty to put the wind up them now."

"It was very unforeseen of Jeremiah Donovan anyhow," says I.

It was next morning that we found it so hard to face Belcher and Hawkins. We went about the house all day scarcely saying a word. Belcher didn't seem to notice; he was stretched into the ashes as usual, with his usual look of waiting in quietness for something unforeseen to happen, but Hawkins noticed and put it down to Noble's being beaten in the argument of the night before.

"Why can't you take a discussion in the proper spirit?" he says severely. "You and your Adam and Eve! I'm a Communist, that's what I am. Communist or anarchist, it all comes to much the same thing." And for hours he went round the house, muttering when the fit took him. "Adam and Eve! Adam and Eve! Nothing better to do with their time than picking bleeding apples!"

III

I don't know how we got through that day, but I was very glad when it was over, the tea things were cleared away, and Belcher said in his peaceable way: "Well, chums, what about it?" We sat round the table and Hawkins took out the cards, and just then I heard Jeremiah Donovan's footstep on the path and a dark presentiment crossed my mind. I rose from the table and caught him before he reached the door.

"What do you want?" I asked.

"I want those two soldier friends of yours," he says, getting red.

"Is that the way, Jeremiah Donovan?" I asked.

"That's the way. There were four of our lads shot this morning, one of them a boy of sixteen."

"That's bad," I said.

At that moment Noble followed me out, and the three of us walked down the path together, talking in whispers. Feeney, the local intelligence officer, was standing by the gate.

"What are you going to do about it?" I asked Jeremiah Donovan.

"I want you and Noble to get them out; tell them they're being shifted again; that'll be the quietest way."

"Leave me out of that," says Noble under his breath.

Jeremiah Donovan looks at him hard.

"All right," he says. "You and Feeney get a few tools from the shed and dig a hole by the far end of the bog. Bonaparte and myself will be after you. Don't let anyone see you with the tools. I wouldn't like it to go beyond ourselves."

We saw Feeney and Noble go round to the shed and went in ourselves. I left Jeremiah Donovan to do the explanations. He told them that he had orders to send them back to the Second Battalion. Hawkins let out a mouthful of curses, and you could see that though Belcher didn't say anything, he was a bit upset too. The old woman was for having them stay in spite of us, and she didn't stop advising them until Jeremiah Donovan lost his temper and turned on her. He had a nasty temper, I noticed. It was pitch-dark in the cottage by this time, but no one thought of lighting the lamp, and in the darkness the two Englishmen fetched their topcoats and said good-bye to the old woman.

"Just as a man makes a home of a bleeding place, some bastard at headquarters thinks you're too cushy and shunts you off," says Hawkins, shaking her hand.

"A thousand thanks, madam," says Belcher. "A thousand thanks for everything"—as though he'd made it up.

We went round to the back of the house and down towards the bog. It was only then that Jeremiah Donovan told them. He was shaking with excitement.

"There were four of our fellows shot in Cork this morning and now you're to be shot as a reprisal."

"What are you talking about?" snaps Hawkins. "It's bad enough being mucked about as we are without having to put up with your funny jokes."

"It isn't a joke," says Donovan. "I'm sorry, Hawkins, but it's true," and begins on the usual rigmarole about duty and how unpleasant it is.

I never noticed that people who talk a lot about duty find it much of a trouble to them.

"Oh, cut it out!" says Hawkins.

"Ask Bonaparte," says Donovan, seeing that Hawkins isn't taking him seriously. "Isn't it true, Bonaparte?"

"It is," I say, and Hawkins stops.

"Ah, for Christ's sake, chum!"

"I mean it, chum," I say.

"You don't sound as if you meant it."

"If he doesn't mean it, I do," says Donovan, working himself up.

"What have you against me, Jeremiah Donovan?"

"I never said I had anything against you. But why did your people take out four of our prisoners and shoot them in cold blood?"

He took Hawkins by the arm and dragged him on, but it was impossible to make him understand that we were in earnest. I had the Smith and Wesson in my pocket and I kept fingering it and wondering what I'd do if they put up a fight for it or ran, and wishing to God they'd do one or the other. I knew if they did run for it, that I'd never fire on them. Hawkins wanted to know was Noble in it, and when we said yes, he asked us why Noble wanted to plug him. Why did any of us want to plug him? What had he done to us? Weren't we all chums? Didn't we understand him and didn't he understand us? Did we imagine for an instant that he'd shoot us for all the so-and-so officers in the so-and-so British Army?

By this time we'd reached the bog, and I was so sick I couldn't even answer him. We walked along the edge of it in the darkness, and every now and then Hawkins would call a halt and begin all over again, as if he was wound up, about our being chums, and I knew that nothing but the sight of the grave would convince him that we had to do it. And all the time I was hoping that something would happen; that they'd run for it or that Noble would take over the responsibility from me. I had the feeling that it was worse on Noble than on me.

IV

At last we saw the lantern in the distance and made towards it. Noble was carrying it, and Feeney was standing somewhere in the darkness behind him, and the picture of them so still and silent in the bogland brought it home to me that we were in earnest, and banished the last bit of hope I had.

Belcher, on recognizing Noble, said: "Hallo, chum," in his quiet way, but Hawkins flew at him at once, and the argument began all over again, only this time Noble had nothing to say for himself and stood with his head down, holding the lantern between his legs.

It was Jeremiah Donovan who did the answering. For the twentieth time, as though it was haunting his mind, Hawkins asked if anybody thought he'd shoot Noble.

"Yes, you would," says Jeremiah Donovan.

"No, I wouldn't, damn you!"

"You would, because you'd know you'd be shot for not doing it."

"I wouldn't, not if I was to be shot twenty times over. I wouldn't shoot a pal. And Belcher wouldn't—isn't that right, Belcher?"

"That's right, chum," Belcher said, but more by way of answering the question than of joining in the argument. Belcher sounded as though whatever unforeseen thing he'd always been waiting for had come at last.

"Anyway, who says Noble would be shot if I wasn't? What do you think I'd do if I was in his place, out in the middle of a blasted bog?"

"What would you do?" asks Donovan.

"I'd go with him wherever he was going, of course. Share my last bob with him and stick by him through thick and thin. No one can ever say of me that I let down a pal."

"We had enough of this," says Jeremiah Donovan, cocking his revolver. "Is there any message you want to send?"

"No, there isn't."

"Do you want to say your prayers?"

Hawkins came out with a cold-blooded remark that even shocked me and turned on Noble again.

"Listen to me, Noble," he says. "You and me are chums. You can't come over to my side, so I'll come over to your side. That show you I mean what I say? Give me a rifle and I'll go along with you and the other lads."

Nobody answered him. We knew that was no way out.

"Hear what I'm saying?" he says. "I'm through with it. I'm a deserter or anything else you like. I don't believe in your stuff, but it's no worse than mine. That satisfy you?"

Noble raised his head, but Donovan began to speak and he lowered it again without replying.

"For the last time, have you any messages to send?" says Donovan in a cold, excited sort of voice.

"Shut up, Donovan! You don't understand me, but these lads do. They're not the sort to make a pal and kill a pal. They're not the tools of any capitalist."

I alone of the crowd saw Donovan raise his Webley to the back of Hawkins's neck, and as he did so I shut my eyes and tried to pray. Hawkins had begun to say something else when Donovan fired, and as I opened my eyes at the bang, I saw Hawkins stagger at the knees and lie out flat at Noble's feet, slowly and as quiet as a kid falling asleep, with the lantern-light on his lean legs and bright farmer's boots. We all stood very still, watching him settle out in the last agony.

Then Belcher took out a handkerchief and began to tie it about his own eyes (in our excitement we'd forgotten to do the same for Hawkins), and, seeing it wasn't big enough, turned and asked for the loan of mine. I gave it to him and he knotted the two together and pointed with his foot at Hawkins.

"He's not quite dead," he says. "Better give him another."

Sure enough, Hawkins's left knee is beginning to rise. I bend down and put my gun to his head; then, recollecting myself, I get up again. Belcher understands what's in my mind.

"Give him his first," he says. "I don't mind. Poor bastard, we don't know what's happening to him now."

I knelt and fired. By this time I didn't seem to know what I was doing. Belcher, who was fumbling a bit awkwardly with the handkerchiefs, came out with a laugh as he heard the shot. It was the first time I heard him laugh and it sent a shudder down my back; it sounded so unnatural.

"Poor bugger!" he said quietly. "And last night he was so curious about it all. It's very queer, chums, I always think. Now he knows as much about it as they'll ever let him know, and last night he was all in the dark."

Donovan helped him to tie the handkerchiefs about his eyes. "Thanks, chum," he said. Donovan asked if there were any messages he wanted sent.

"No, chum," he says. "Not for me. If any of you would like to write to Hawkins's mother, you'll find a letter from her in his pocket. He and his mother were great chums. But my missus left me eight years ago. Went away with another fellow and took the kid with her. I like the feeling of a home, as you may have noticed, but I couldn't start again after that."

It was an extraordinary thing, but in those few minutes Belcher said more than in all the weeks before. It was just as if the sound of the shot had started a flood of talk in him and he could go on the whole night like that, quite happily, talking about himself. We stood round like fools now that he couldn't see us any longer. Donovan looked at Noble, and Noble shook his head. Then Donovan raised his Webley, and at that moment Belcher gives his queer laugh again. He may have thought we were talking about him, or perhaps he noticed the same thing I'd noticed and couldn't understand it.

"Excuse me, chums," he says. "I feel I'm talking the hell of a lot, and so silly, about my being so handy about a house and things like that. But this thing came on me suddenly. You'll forgive me, I'm sure."

"You don't want to say a prayer?" asks Donovan.

"No, chum," he says. "I don't think it would help. I'm ready, and you boys want to get it over."

"You understand that we're only doing our duty?" says Donovan.

Belcher's head was raised like a blind man's, so that you could only see his chin and the tip of his nose in the lantern-light.

"I never could make out what duty was myself," he said. "I think you're all good lads, if that's what you mean. I'm not complaining."

Noble, just as if he couldn't bear any more of it, raised his fist at Donovan, and in a flash Donovan raised his gun and fired. The big man went over like a sack of meal, and this time there was no need of a second shot.

I don't remember much about the burying, but that it was worse than all the rest because we had to carry them to the grave. It was all mad lonely with nothing but a patch of lantern-light between ourselves and the dark, and birds hooting and screeching all round, disturbed by the guns. Noble went through Hawkins's belongings to find the letter from his mother, and then joined his hands together. He did the same with Belcher. Then, when we'd filled in the grave, we separated from Jeremiah Donovan and Feeney and took our tools back to the shed. All the way we didn't speak a word. The kitchen was dark and cold as we'd left it, and the old woman was sitting over the hearth, saying her beads. We walked past her into the room, and Noble struck a match to light the lamp. She rose quietly and came to the doorway with all her cantankerousness gone.

"What did ye do with them?" she asked in a whisper, and Noble started so that the match went out in his hand.

"What's that?" he asked without turning round.

"I heard ye," she said.

"What did you hear?" asked Noble.

"I heard ye. Do ye think I didn't hear ye, putting the spade back in the houseen?"

Noble struck another match and this time the lamp lit for him.

"Was that what ye did to them?" she asked.

Then, by God, in the very doorway, she fell on her knees and began praying, and after looking at her for a minute or two Noble did the same by the fireplace. I pushed my way out past her and left them at it. I stood at the door, watching the stars and listening to the shrieking of the birds dying out over the bogs. It is so strange what you feel at times like that that you can't describe it. Noble says he saw everything ten times the size, as though there were nothing in the whole world but that little patch of bog with the two Englishmen stiffening into it, but with me it was as if the patch of bog where the Englishmen were was a million miles away, and even Noble and the old woman, mumbling behind me, and the birds and the bloody stars were all far away, and I was somehow very small and very lost and lonely like a child astray in the snow. And anything that happened to me afterwards, I never felt the same about again.

RICHARD WRIGHT

The Man Who Was Almost a Man

Richard Wright (1908–1960), an American novelist and essayist of the first rank, was born in Mississippi. He was largely self-educated, having attended school for only a short time before he moved to Memphis, where he earned a living by doing odd jobs. Then, from 1935 to 1937, he was a writer for the Federal Writers Project in Chicago and New York. His first book, *Uncle Tom's Children,* came out in 1938, followed by his great novel *Native Son,* written on a Guggenheim Fellowship and published in 1940. It was the first Book-of-the-Month Club selection by a black writer. Now a steady flow of works appeared: *Twelve Million Black Voices: A Folk History of the Negro in the United States,* 1941; *Black Boy,* 1945 (this was also a Book-of-the-Month Club selection); *The Outsider,* 1953; *Black Power,* 1945; *White Man Listen,* 1957; *Eight Men,* 1961; *Lawd Today,* 1963. In 1978 the *Richard Wright Reader* was published. *Native Son* in a dramatic version became a very successful Broadway production and later an acclaimed film. Within ten years after *Native Son* was published, it had been translated into more than fifty languages.

"The Man Who Was Almost a Man" points out that barriers—especially those of color and poverty—to the fulfillment of maturity can cause one to take reckless action in the effort to become a mature human being.

Dave struck out across the fields, looking homeward through paling light. What's the use talkin wid em niggers in the field? Anyhow, his mother was putting supper on the table. Them niggers can't understan nothing. One of these days he was going to get a gun and practice shooting, then they couldn't talk to him as though he were a little boy. He slowed, looking at the ground. Shucks, Ah ain scareda them even ef they are biggern me! Aw, Ah know whut Ahma do. Ahm going by ol Joe's sto n git that Sears Roebuck catlog n look at them guns. Mebbe Ma will lemme buy one when she gits mah pay from ol man Hawkins. Ahma beg her t gimme some money. Ahm ol ernough to hava gun. Ahm seventeen. Almost a man. He strode, feeling his long loose-jointed limbs. Shucks, a man oughta hava little gun aftah he done worked hard all day.

He came in sight of Joe's store. A yellow lantern glowed on the front porch. He mounted steps and went through the screen door, hearing it bang behind him. There was a strong smell of coal oil and mackerel fish. He felt very confident until he saw fat Joe walk in through the rear door, then his courage began to ooze.

"Howdy, Dave! Whutcha want?"

"How yuh, Mistah Joe? Aw, Ah don wanna buy nothing. Ah jus wanted t see ef yuhd lemme look at tha catlog erwhile."

"Sure! You wanna see it here?"

"Nawsuh. Ah wans t take it home wid me. Ah'll bring it back termorrow when Ah come in from the fiels."

"You plannin on buying something?"

"Yessuh."

"Your ma lettin you have your own money now?"

"Shucks. Mistah Joe, Ahm gittin t be a man like anybody else!"

Joe laughed and wiped his greasy white face with a red bandanna.

"Whut you plannin on buyin?"

Dave looked at the floor, scratched his head, scratched his thigh, and smiled. Then he looked up shyly.

"Ah'll tell yuh, Mistah Joe, ef yuh promise yuh won't tell."

"I promise."

"Waal, Ahma buy a gun."

"A gun? Whut you want with a gun?"

"Ah wanna keep it."

"You ain't nothing but a boy. You don't need a gun."

"Aw, lemme have the catlog, Mistah Joe. Ah'll bring it back."

Joe walked through the rear door. Dave was elated. He looked around at barrels of sugar and flour. He heard Joe coming back. He craned his neck to see if he were bringing the book. Yeah, he's got it. Gawddog, he's got it!

"Here, but be sure you bring it back. It's the only one I got."

"Sho, Mistah Joe."

"Say, if you wanna buy a gun, why don't you buy one from me? I gotta gun to sell."

"Will it shoot?"

"Sure it'll shoot."

"Whut kind is it?"

"Oh, it's kinda old . . . a left-hand Wheeler. A pistol. A big one."

"Is it got bullets in it?"

"It's loaded."

"Kin Ah see it?"

"Where's your money?"

"Whut yuh wan fer it?"

"I'll let you have it for two dollars."

"Just two dollahs? Shucks, Ah could buy tha when Ah git mah pay."

"I'll have it here when you want it."

"Awright, suh. Ah be in fer it."

He went through the door, hearing it slam again behind him. Ahma git some money from Ma n buy me a gun! Only two dollahs! He tucked the thick catalogue under his arm and hurried.

"Where yuh been, boy?" His mother held a steaming dish of black-eyed peas.

"Aw, Ma, Ah jus stopped down the road t talk wid the boys."

"Yuh know bettah t keep suppah waitin."

He sat down, resting the catalogue on the edge of the table.

"Yuh git up from there and git to the well n wash yoself! Ah ain feedin no hogs in mah house!"

She grabbed his shoulder and pushed him. He stumbled out of the room, then came back to get the catalogue.

"Whut this?"

"Aw, Ma, it's jusa catlog."

"Who yuh git it from?"

"From Joe, down at the sto."

"Waal, thas good. We kin use it in the outhouse."

"Naw, Ma." He grabbed for it. "Gimme ma catlog, Ma."

She held onto it and glared at him.

"Quit hollerin at me! Whut's wrong wid yuh? Yuh crazy?"

"But Ma, please. It ain mine! It's Joe's! He tol me to bring it back t im termorrow."

She gave up the book. He stumbled down the back steps, hugging the thick book under his arm. When he had splashed water on his face and hands, he groped back to the kitchen and fumbled in a corner for the towel. He bumped into a chair; it clattered to the floor. The catalogue sprawled at his feet. When he had dried his eyes he snatched up the book and held it again under his arm. His mother stood watching him.

"Now, ef yuh gonna act a fool over that ol book, Ah'll take it n burn it up."

"Naw, Ma, please."

"Waal, set down n be still!"

He sat down and drew the oil lamp close. He thumbed page after page, unaware of the food his mother set on the table. His father came in. Then his small brother.

"Whutcha got there, Dave?" his father asked.

"Jusa catlog," he answered, not looking up.

"Yeah, here they is!" His eyes glowed at blue-and-black revolvers. He glanced up, feeling sudden guilt. His father was watching him. He eased the book under the table and rested it on his knees. After the blessing was asked, he ate. He scooped up peas and swallowed fat meat without chewing. Buttermilk helped to wash it down. He did not want to mention money before his father. He would do much better by cornering his mother when she was alone. He looked at his father uneasily out of the edge of his eye.

"Boy, how come yuh don quit foolin wid tha book n eat yo suppah?"

"Yessuh."

"How you n ol man Hawkins gittin erlong?"

"Suh?"

"Can't yuh hear? Why don yuh lissen? Ah ast yu how wuz yuh n ol man Hawkins gittin erlong?"

"Oh, swell, Pa. Ah plows mo lan than anybody over there."

"Waal, yuh oughta keep yo mind on whut yuh doin."

"Yessuh."

He poured his plate full of molasses and sopped it up slowly with a chunk of cornbread.

When his father and brother had left the kitchen, he still sat and looked again at the guns in the catalogue, longing to muster courage enough to present his case to his mother. Lawd, ef Ah only had tha pretty one! He could almost feel the slickness of the weapon with his fingers. If he had a gun like that he would polish it and keep it shining so it would never rust. N Ah'd keep it loaded, by Gawd!

"Ma?" His voice was hesitant.

"Hunh?"

"Ol man Hawkins give yuh mah money yit?"

"Yeah, but ain no usa yuh thinking bout throwin nona it erway. Ahm keepin tha money sos yuh kin have cloes t go to school this winter."

He rose and went to her side with the open catalogue in his palms. She was washing dishes, her head bent low over a pan. Shyly he raised the book. When he spoke, his voice was husky, faint.

"Ma, Gawd knows Ah wans one of these."

"One of whut?" she asked, not raising her eyes.

"One of these," he said again, not daring even to point. She glanced up at the page, then at him with wide eyes.

"Nigger, is yuh gone plumb crazy?"

"Aw, Ma—"

"Git outta here! Don yuh talk t me bout no gun! Yuh a fool!"

"Ma, Ah kin buy one for two dollahs."

"Not ef Ah knows it, yuh ain!"

"But yuh promised me one—"

"Ah don care whut Ah promised! Yuh ain nothing but a boy yit!"

"Ma, ef yuh lemme buy one Ah'll *never* ast yuh fer nothing no mo."

"Ah tol yuh t git outta here! Yuh ain gonna toucha penny of tha money fer no gun! Thas how come Ah has Mistah Hawkins t pay yo wages t me, cause Ah knows yuh ain got no sense."

"But, Ma, we needa gun. Pa ain't got no gun. We needa gun in the house. Yuh kin never tell whut might happen."

"Now don yuh try to maka fool outta me, boy! Ef we did hava gun, yuh wouldn't have it!"

He laid the catalogue down and slipped his arm around her waist.

"Aw, Ma, Ah done worked hard alla summer n ain ast yuh fer nothing, is Ah, now?"

"Thas whut yuh spose t do!"

"But Ma, Ah wans a gun. Yuh kin lemme have two dollahs outta mah money. Please, Ma. I kin give it to Pa . . . Please, Ma! Ah loves yuh, Ma."

When she spoke her voice came soft and low.

"Whut yu wan wida gun, Dave? Yuh don need no gun. Yuh'll git in trouble. N ef yo pa jus thought Ah let yuh have money t buy a gun he'd hava fit."

"Ah'll hide it, Ma. It ain but two dollahs."

"Lawd, chil, whut's wrong wid yuh?"

"Ain nothing wrong, Ma. Ahm almos a man now. Ah wans a gun."

"Who gonna sell yuh a gun?"

"Ol Joe at the sto."

"N it don cos but two dollahs?"

"Thas all, Ma. Jus two dollahs. Please, Ma."

She was stacking the plates away; her hands moved slowly, reflectively. Dave kept an anxious silence. Finally, she turned to him.

"Ah'll let yuh git tha gun ef yuh promise me one thing."

"Whut's tha, Ma?"

"Yuh bring it straight back t me, yuh hear? It be fer Pa."

"Yessum! Lemme go now, Ma."

She stooped, turned slightly to one side, raised the hem of her dress, rolled down the top of her stocking, and came up with a slender wad of bills.

"Here," she said. "Lawd knows yuh don need no gun. But yer pa does. Yuh bring it right back t me, yuh hear? Ahma put it up. Now ef yuh don, Ahma have yuh pa lick yuh so hard yuh won fergit it."

"Yessum."

He took the money, ran down the steps, and across the yard.

"Dave! Yuuuuuh Daaaaave!"

He heard, but he was not going to stop now. "Naw, Lawd!"

The first movement he made the following morning was to reach under his pillow for the gun. In the gray light of dawn he held it loosely, feeling a sense of power. Could kill a man with a gun like this. Kill anybody, black or white. And if he were holding his gun in his hand, nobody could run over him; they would have to respect him. It was a big gun, with a long barrel and a heavy handle. He raised and lowered it in his hand, marveling at its weight.

He had not come straight home with it as his mother had asked; instead he had stayed out in the fields, holding the weapon in his hand, aiming it now and then at some imaginary foe. But he

had not fired it; he had been afraid that his father might hear. Also he was not sure he knew how to fire it.

To avoid surrendering the pistol he had not come into the house until he knew that they were all asleep. When his mother had tiptoed to his bedside late that night and demanded the gun, he had first played possum; then he had told her that the gun was hidden outdoors, that he would bring it to her in the morning. Now he lay turning it slowly in his hands. He broke it, took out the cartridges, felt them, and then put them back.

He slid out of bed, got a long strip of old flannel from a trunk, wrapped the gun in it, and tied it to his naked thigh while it was still loaded. He did not go in to breakfast. Even though it was not yet daylight, he started for Jim Hawkins' plantation. Just as the sun was rising he reached the barns where the mules and plows were kept.

"Hey! That you, Dave?"

He turned. Jim Hawkins stood eying him suspiciously.

"What're yuh doing here so early?"

"Ah didn't know Ah wuz gittin up so early, Mistah Hawkins. Ah wuz fixin t hitch up ol Jenny n take her t the fiels."

"Good. Since you're so early, how about plowing that stretch down by the woods?"

"Suits me, Mistah Hawkins."

"O.K. Go to it!"

He hitched Jenny to a plow and started across the fields. Hot dog! This was just what he wanted. If he could get down by the woods, he could shoot his gun and nobody would hear. He walked behind the plow, hearing the traces creaking, feeling the gun tied tight to his thigh.

When he reached the woods, he plowed two whole rows before he decided to take out the gun. Finally, he stopped, looked in all directions, then untied the gun and held it in his hand. He turned to the mule and smiled.

"Know whut this is, Jenny? Naw, yuh wouldn know! Yuhs jusa ol mule! Anyhow, this is a gun, n it kin shoot, by Gawd!"

He held the gun at arm's length. Whut t hell, Ahma shoot this thing! He looked at Jenny again.

"Lissen here, Jenny! When Ah pulls this ol trigger, Ah don wan yuh t run n acka fool now!"

Jenny stood with head down, her short ears pricked straight. Dave walked off about twenty feet, held the gun far out from him at arm's length, and turned his head. Hell, he told himself, Ah ain afraid. The gun felt loose in his fingers; he waved it wildly for a moment. Then he shut his eyes and tightened his forefinger. Bloom! A report half deafened him and he thought his right hand was torn from his arm. He heard Jenny whinnying and galloping over the field, and he found himself on his knees, squeezing his fingers hard between his legs. His hand was numb; he jammed it into his mouth, trying to warm it, trying to stop the pain. The gun lay at his feet. He did not quite know what had happened. He stood up and stared at the gun as though it were a living thing. He gritted his teeth and kicked the gun. Yuh almos broke mah arm! He turned to look for Jenny; she was far over the fields, tossing her head and kicking wildly.

"Hol on there, ol mule!"

When he caught up with her she stood trembling, walling her big white eyes at him. The plow was far away; the traces had broken. Then Dave stopped short, looking, not believing, Jenny was bleeding. Her left side was red and wet with blood. He went closer. Lawd, have mercy! Wondah did Ah shoot this mule? He grabbed for Jenny's mane. She flinched, snorted, whirled, tossing her head.

"How on now! Hol on."

Then he saw the hole in Jenny's side, right between the ribs. It was round, wet, red. A crimson stream streaked down the front leg, flowing fast. Good Gawd! Ah wuzn't shootin at tha mule. He felt panic. He knew he had to stop that blood, or Jenny would bleed to death. He had never seen so much blood in all his life. He chased the mule for half a mile, trying to catch her. Finally she stopped, breathing hard, stumpy tail half arched. He caught her mane and led her back to where the plough and gun lay. Then he stooped and grabbed handfuls of damp black earth and tried to plug the bullet hole. Jenny shuddered, whinnied, and broke from him.

"Hol on! Hol on now!"

He tried to plug it again, but blood came anyhow. His fingers were hot and sticky. He rubbed dirt into his palms, trying to dry them. Then again he attempted to plug the bullet hole, but Jenny shied away, kicking her heels high. He stood helpless. He had to do something. He ran at Jenny; she dodged him. He watched a red stream of blood flow down Jenny's leg and form a bright pool at her feet.

"Jenny . . . Jenny," he called weakly.

His lips trembled. She's bleeding t death! He looked in the direction of home, wanting to go back, wanting to get help. But he saw the pistol lying in the damp black clay. He had a queer feeling that if he only did something, this would not be; Jenny would not be there bleeding to death.

When he went to her this time, she did not move. She stood with sleepy, dreamy eyes; and when he touched her she gave a low-pitched whinny and knelt to the ground, her front knees slopping in blood.

"Jenny . . . Jenny . . ." he whispered.

For a long time she held her neck erect; then her head sank, slowly. Her ribs swelled with a mighty heave and she went over.

Dave's stomach felt empty, very empty. He picked up the gun and held it gingerly between his thumb and forefinger. He buried it at the foot of a tree. He took a stick and tried to cover the pool of blood with dirt—but what was the use? There was Jenny lying with her mouth open and her eyes walled and glassy. He could not tell Jim Hawkins he had shot his mule. But he had to tell something. Yeah, Ah'll tell em Jenny started gitten wil n fell on the joint of the plow. . . . But that would hardly happen to a mule. He walked across the field slowly, head down.

It was sunset. Two of Jim Hawkins' men were over near the edge of the woods digging a hole in which to bury Jenny. Dave was surrounded by a knot of people, all of whom were looking down at the dead mule.

"I don't see how in the world it happened," said Jim Hawkins for the tenth time.

The crowd parted and Dave's mother, father, and small brother pushed into the center.

"Where Dave?" his mother called.

"There he is," said Jim Hawkins.

His mother grabbed him.

"Whut happened, Dave? Whut yuh done?"

"Nothin."

"C mon, boy, talk," his father said.

Dave took a deep breath and told the story he knew nobody believed.

"Waal," he drawled. "Ah brung ol Jenny down here sos Ah could do mah plowin. Ah plowed bout two rows, just like yuh see." He stopped and pointed at the long rows of upturned earth. "Then somethin musta been wrong wid ol Jenny.

She wouldn ack right a-tall. She started snortin n kickin her heels. Ah tried t hol her, but she pulled erway, rearin n goin in. Then when the point of the plow was stickin up in the air, she swung erroun n twisted herself back on it . . . She stuck herself n started t bleed. N fo Ah could do anything, she wuz dead."

"Did you ever hear of anything like that in all your life?" asked Jim Hawkins.

There were white and black standing in the crowd. They murmured. Dave's mother came close to him and looked hard into his face. "Tell the truth, Dave." she said.

"Looks like a bullet hole to me," said one man.

"Dave, whut yuh do wid the gun?" his mother asked.

The crowd surged in, looking at him. He jammed his hands into his pockets, shook his head slowly from left to right, and backed away. His eyes were wide and painful.

"Did he hava gun?" asked Jim Hawkins.

"By Gawd, Ah tol yuh tha wuz a gun wound," said a man, slapping his thigh.

His father caught his shoulders and shook him till his teeth rattled.

"Tell whut happened, yuh rascal! Tell whut . . ."

Dave looked at Jenny's stiff legs and began to cry.

"Whut yuh do wid tha gun?" his mother asked.

"Whut wuz he doin wida gun?" his father asked.

"Come on and tell the truth," said Hawkins. "Ain't nobody going to hurt you . . ."

His mother crowded close to him.

"Did yuh shoot tha mule, Dave?"

Dave cried, seeing blurred white and black faces.

"Ahh ddinn gggo tt sshooot hher . . . Ah ssswear ffo Gawd Ah ddin. . . . Ah wuz a-tryin t sssee ef the old gggun would sshoot—"

"Where yuh git the gun from?" his father asked.

"Ah got it from Joe, at the sto."

"Where yuh git the money?"

"Ma give it t me."

"He kept worryin me, Bob. Ah had t. Ah tol im t bring the gun right back t me . . . It was fer yuh, the gun."

"But how yuh happen to shoot that mule?" asked Jim Hawkins.

"Ah wuzn shootin at the mule, Mistah Hawkins. The gun jumped when Ah pulled the trigger . . . N fo Ah knowed anythin Jenny was there a-bleedin."

Somebody in the crowd laughed. Jim Hawkins walked close to Dave and looked into his face.

"Well, looks like you have bought you a mule, Dave."

"Ah swear fo Gawd, Ah didn go t kill the mule, Mistah Hawkins!"

"But you killed her!"

All the crowd was laughing now. They stood on tiptoe and poked heads over one another's shoulders.

"Well, boy, looks like yuh done bought a dead mule! Hahaha!"

"Ain tha ershame."

"Hohohohoho."

Dave stood, head down, twisting his feet in the dirt.

"Well, you needn't worry about it, Bob," said Jim Hawkins to Dave's father. "Just let the boy keep on working and pay me two dollars a month."

"Whut yuh wan fer yo mule, Mistah Hawkins?"

Jim Hawkins screwed up his eyes.

"Fifty dollars."

"Whut yuh do wid tha gun?" Dave's father demanded.

Dave said nothing.

"Yuh wan me t take a tree n beat yuh till yuh talk!"

"Nawsuh!"

"Whut yuh do wid it?"

"Ah throwed it erway."

"Where?"

"Ah . . . Ah throwed it in the creek."

"Waal, c mon home. N firs thing in the mawnin git to tha creek n fin tha gun."

"Yessuh."

"Whut yuh pay fer it?"

"Two dollahs."

"Take tha gun n git yo money back n carry it t Mistah Hawkins, yuh hear? N don fergit Ahma lam you black bottom good fer this? Now march yosef on home, suh!"

Dave turned and walked slowly. He heard people laughing. Dave glared, his eyes welling with tears. Hot anger bubbled in him. Then he swallowed and stumbled on.

That night Dave did not sleep. He was glad

that he had gotten out of killing the mule so easily, but he was hurt. Something hot seemed to turn over inside him each time he remembered how they had laughed. He tossed on his bed, feeling his hard pillow. N Pa says he's gonna beat me . . . He remembered other beatings, and his back quivered. Naw, naw, Ah sho don wan im t beat me tha way no mo. Dam em all! Nobody ever gave him anything. All he did was work. They treat me like a mule, n then they beat me. He gritted his teeth. N Ma had t tell on me.

Well, if he had to, he would take old man Hawkins that two dollars. But that meant selling the gun. And he wanted to keep that gun. Fifty dollars for a dead mule.

He turned over, thinking how he had fired the gun. He had an itch to fire it again. Ef other men kin shoota gun, by Gawd, Ah kin! He was still, listening. Mebbe they all sleepin now. The house was still. He heard the soft breathing of his brother. Yes, now! He would go down and get that gun and see if he could fire it! He eased out of bed and slipped into overalls.

The moon was bright. He ran almost all the way to the edge of the woods. He stumbled over the ground, looking for the spot where he had buried the gun. Yeah, here it is. Like a hungry dog scratching for a bone, he pawed it up. He puffed his black cheeks and blew dirt from the trigger and barrel. He broke it and found four cartridges unshot. He looked around; the fields were filled with silence and moonlight. He clutched the gun stiff and hard in his fingers. But, as soon as he wanted to pull the trigger, he shut his eyes and turned his head. Naw, Ah can't shoot wid mah eyes closed n mah head turned. With effort he held his eyes open; then he squeezed. *Blooooom!* He was stiff, not breathing. The gun

was still in his hands. Dammit, he'd done it! He fired again. *Blooooom!* He smiled. *Blooooom! Blooooom! Click, click.* There! It was empty. If anybody could shoot a gun, he could. He put the gun into his hip pocket and started across the fields.

When he reached the top of a ridge he stood straight and proud in the moonlight, looking at Jim Hawkins' big white house, feeling the gun sagging in his pocket. Lawd, ef Ah had just one mo bullet Ah'd taka shot at tha house. Ah'd like t scare ol man Hawkins jusa little . . . Jusa enough t let him know Dave Saunders is a man.

To his left the road curved, running to the tracks of the Illinois Central. He jerked his head, listening. From far off came a faint *hoooof-hoooof; hoooof-hoooof; hoooof-hoooof.* . . . He stood rigid. Two dollahs a mont. Les see now . . . Tha means it'll take bout two years. Shucks! Ah'll be dam!

He started down the road, toward the tracks. Yeah, here she comes! He stood beside the track and held himself stiffly. Here she comes, erroun the ben . . . C mon, yuh slow poke! C mon! He had his hand on his gun; something quivered in his stomach. Then the train thundered past, the gray and brown box cars rumbling and clinking. He gripped the gun tightly; then he jerked his hand out of his pocket. Ah betcha Bill wouldn't do it! Ah betcha . . . The cars slid past, steel grinding upon steel. Ahm riding yuh ternight, so help me Gawd! He was hot all over. He hesitated just a moment; then he grabbed, pulled atop of a car, and lay flat. He felt his pocket; the gun was still there. Ahead the long rails were glinting in the moonlight, stretching away, away to somewhere, somewhere where he could be a man . . .

GRAHAM GREENE

The Over-night Bag

Graham Greene (1904–   ), English journalist, playwright, and novelist, was born in Berkhamsted, England and attended Balliol College, Oxford. In 1925 he produced his first literary work, a collection of poems entitled *Babbling April*. The next year he converted to Roman Catholicism, a decision that is highly reflected in Greene's subsequent works of fiction, which Greene himself divides into "entertainments" and "novels". The former group consists of such tightly constructed thrillers as *Orient Express*, 1932; *The Confidential Agent*, 1939; and *The Third Man*, 1950. And the best-known representatives of the latter category include *The Power and the Glory*, 1940; *The Heart of the Matter*, 1948; *The Comedians*, 1966; and *The Human Factor*, 1978.

"The Over-night Bag" focuses upon the mysterious contents of traveler Henry Cooper's overnight bag. The author masterfully plays the irony inherent in the characters' reaction to Henry Cooper and his bag against the reader's curiosity as to the bag's contents.

The little man who came to the information desk in Nice airport when they demanded 'Henry Cooper, passenger on BEA flight 105 for London' looked like a shadow cast by the brilliant glitter of the sun. He wore a grey townsuit and black shoes; he had a grey skin which carefully matched his suit, and since it was impossible for him to change his skin, it was possible that he had no other suit.

'Are you Mr. Cooper?'

'Yes.' He carried a BOAC over-night bag and he laid it tenderly on the ledge of the information desk as though it contained something precious and fragile like an electric razor.

'There is a telegram for you.'

He opened it and read the message twice over. '*Bon voyage*. Much missed. You will be welcome home, dear boy. Mother.' He tore the telegram once across and left it on the desk, from which the girl in the blue uniform, after a discreet inter-

val, picked the pieces and with natural curiosity joined them together. Then she looked for the little grey man among the passengers who were now lining up at the tourist gate to join the Trident. He was among the last, carrying his blue BOAC bag.

Near the front of the plane Henry Cooper found a window-seat and placed the bag on the central seat beside him. A large woman in pale blue trousers too tight for the size of her buttocks took the third seat. She squeezed a very large handbag in beside the other on the central seat, and she laid a large fur coat on top of both. Henry Cooper said, 'May I put it on the rack, please?'

She looked at him with contempt. 'Put what?'

'Your coat.'

'If you want to. Why?'

'It's a very heavy coat. It's squashing my overnight bag.'

He was so small he could stand nearly upright under the rack. When he sat down he fastened the seat-belt over the two bags before he fastened his own. The woman watched him with suspicion. 'I've never seen anyone do that before,' she said.

'I don't want it shaken about,' he said. 'There are storms over London.'

'You haven't got an animal in there, have you?'

'Not exactly.'

'It's cruel to carry an animal shut up like that,' she said, as though she disbelieved him.

As the Trident began its run he laid his hand on the bag as if he were reassuring something within. The woman watched the bag narrowly. If she saw the least movement of life she had made up her mind to call the stewardess. Even if it were only a tortoise. . . . A tortoise needed air, or so she supposed, in spite of hibernation. When they were safely airborne he relaxed and began to read a *Nice-Matin*—he spent a good deal of time on each story as though his French were not very good. The woman struggled angrily to get her big cavernous bag from under the seat-belt. She muttered 'Ridiculous' twice for his benefit. Then she made up, put on thick horn-rimmed glasses and began to re-read a letter which began 'My darling Tiny' and ended 'Your own cuddly Bertha'. After a while she grew tired of the weight on her knees and dropped it on to the BOAC over-night bag.

The little man leapt in distress. 'Please,' he said, 'please.' He lifted her bag and pushed it quite rudely into a corner of the seat. 'I don't want it squashed,' he said. 'It's a matter of respect.'

'What have you got in your precious bag?' she asked him angrily.

'A dead baby,' he said. 'I thought I had told you.'

'On the left of the aircraft,' the pilot announced through the loud-speaker, 'you will see Montélimar. We shall be passing Paris in—'

'You are not serious,' she said.

'It's just one of those things,' he replied in a tone that carried conviction.

'But you can't take dead babies—like that—in a bag—in the economy class.'

'In the case of a baby it is so much cheaper than freight. Only a week old. It weighs so little.'

'But it should be in a coffin, not an over-night bag.'

'My wife didn't trust a foreign coffin. She said the materials they use are not durable. She's rather a conventional woman.'

'Then it's *your* baby?' Under the circumstances she seemed almost prepared to sympathize.

'My wife's baby,' he corrected her.

'What's the difference?'

He said sadly, 'There could well be a difference,' and turned the page of *Nice-Matin*.

'Are you suggesting . . . ?' But he was deep in a column dealing with a Lions Club meeting in Antibes and the rather revolutionary suggestion made there by a member from Grasse. She read over again her letter from 'cuddly Bertha', but it failed to hold her attention. She kept on stealing glances at the over-night bag.

'You don't anticipate trouble with the customs?' she asked him after a while.

'Of course I shall have to declare it,' he said. 'It was acquired abroad.'

When they landed, exactly on time, he said to her with old-fashioned politeness, 'I have enjoyed our flight.' She looked for him with a certain morbid curiosity in the customers—Channel 10—but then she saw him in Channel 12, for passengers carrying hand-baggage only. He was speaking, earnestly, to the officer who was poised, chalk in hand, over the over-night bag. Then she lost sight of him as her own inspector insisted on examining the contents of her cavernous bag, which yielded up a number of undeclared presents for Bertha.

Henry Cooper was the first out of the arrivals door and he took a hired car. The charge for taxis rose every year when he went abroad and it was his one extravagance not to wait for the airport-bus. The sky was overcast and the temperature only a little above freezing, but the driver was in a mood of euphoria. He had a dashing comradely air—he told Henry Cooper that he had won fifty pounds on the pools. The heater was on full blast, and Henry Cooper opened the window, but an icy current of air from Scandinavia flowed round his shoulders. He closed the window again and said, 'Would you mind turning off the heater?' It was as hot in the car as in a New York hotel during a blizzard.

'It's cold outside,' the driver said.

'You see,' Henry Cooper said, 'I have a dead baby in my bag.'

'Dead baby?'

'Yes.'

'Ah well,' the driver said, 'he won't feel the heat, will he? It's a he?'

'Yes. A he. I'm anxious he shouldn't—deteriorate.'

'They keep a long time,' the driver said. 'You'd be surprised. Longer than old people. What did you have for lunch?'

Henry Cooper was a little surprised. He had to cast his mind back. He said, '*Carré d'agneau à la provençale.*'

'Curry?'

'No, not curry, lamb chops with garlic and herbs. And then an apple-tart.'

'And you drank something I wouldn't be surprised?'

'A half bottle of *rosé*. And a brandy.'

'There you are, you see.'

'I don't understand.'

'With all that inside you, *you* wouldn't keep so well.'

Gillette Razors were half hidden in icy mist. The driver had forgotten or had refused to turn down the heat, but he remained silent for quite a while, perhaps brooding on the subject of life and death.

'How did the little perisher die?'' he asked at last.

'They die so easily,' Henry Cooper answered.

'Many a true word's spoken in jest,' the driver said, a little absent-mindedly because he had swerved to avoid a car which braked too suddenly, and Henry Cooper instinctively put his hand on the over-night bag to steady it.

'Sorry,' the driver said. 'Not my fault. Amateur drivers! Anyway, you don't need to worry—they can't bruise after death, or can they? I read something about it once in *The Cases of Sir Bernard Spilsbury*, but I don't remember now exactly what. That's always the trouble about reading.'

'I'd be much happier,' Henry Cooper said, 'if you would turn off the heat.'

'There's no point in your catching a chill, is there? Or me either. It won't help *him* where he's gone—if anywhere at all. The next thing you know you'll be in the same position yourself. Not in an over-night bag, of course. That goes without saying.'

The Knightsbridge tunnel as usual was closed because of flooding. They turned north through the park. The trees dripped on empty benches. The pigeons blew out their grey feathers the colour of soiled city snow.

'Is he yours?' the driver asked. 'If you don't mind my inquiring.'

'Not exactly.' Henry Cooper added briskly and brightly, 'My wife's, as it happens.'

'It's never the same if it's not your own,' the driver said thoughtfully. 'I had a nephew who died. He had a split palate—that wasn't the reason, of course, but it made it easier to bear for the parents. Are you going to an undertaker's now?'

'I thought I would take it home for the night and see about the arrangements tomorrow.'

'A little perisher like that would fit easily into the frig. No bigger than a chicken. As a precaution only.'

They entered the large whitewashed Bayswater square. The houses resembled the above-ground tombs you find in continental cemeteries, except that, unlike the tombs, they were divided into flatlets and there were rows and rows of bell-pushes to wake the inmates. The driver watched Henry Cooper get out with the over-night bag at a portico entitled Stare House. 'Bloody orful aircraft company,' he said mechanically when he saw the letters BOAC—without ill-will, it was only a Pavlov response.

Henry Cooper went up to the top floor and let himself in. His mother was already in the hall to greet him. 'I saw your car draw up, dear.' He put the over-night bag on a chair so as to embrace her better.

'You've come quickly. You got my telegram at Nice?'

'Yes, Mother. With only an over-night bag I walked straight through the customs.'

'So clever of you to travel light.'

'It's the drip-dry shirt that does it,' Henry Cooper said. He followed his mother into their sitting-room. He noticed she had changed the position of his favourite picture—a reproduction from *Life* magazine of a painting by Hieronymus Bosch. 'Just so that I don't see it from *my* chair, dear,' his mother explained, interpreting his glance. His slippers were laid out by his armchair and he sat down with an air of satisfaction at being home again.

'And now, dear,' his mother said, 'tell me how it was. Tell me everything. Did you make some new friends?'

'Oh yes, Mother, wherever I went I made friends.' Winter had fallen early on the House of Stare. The over-night bag disappeared in the darkness of the hall like a blue fish into blue water.

'And adventures? What adventures?'

Once, while he talked, his mother got up and tiptoed to draw the curtains and to turn on a reading lamp, and once she gave a little gasp of horror. 'A little toe' In the marmalade?'

'Yes, Mother.'

'It wasn't English marmalade?'

'No, Mother, foreign.'

'I could have understood a finger—an accident slicing the orange—but a toe!'

'As I understood it,' Henry Cooper said, 'in those parts they use a kind of guillotine worked by the bare foot of a peasant.'

'You complained, of course?'

'Not in words, but I put the toe very conspicuously at the edge of the plate.'

After one more story it was time for his mother to go and put the shepherd's pie into the oven and Henry Cooper went into the hall to fetch the over-night bag. 'Time to unpack,' he thought. He had a tidy mind.

SLAWOMIR MROZEK

On a Journey

Translated by Konrad Syrop

Slawomir Mrozek (1930–   ), son of a Polish postal clerk, was born in Borzcein, Poland, and studied architecture, oriental culture, and painting in Cracow before he began his writing career. A well-known cartoonist and satirist in his native Poland, Mrozek has written several stories and plays, including *Tango*, 1965. Few of his works, however, have been translated into English.

Although the plots of Mrozek's stories often seem fantastically improbable, the target of his satire usually is the implacable bureaucracy. Confronted with the strange substitution of men for machines, the young narrator of "On a Journey" must, for example, accept the authoritative statement of the coachman that this is the way things are.

Just after B—— the road took us among damp, flat meadows. Only here and there the expanse of green was broken by a stubble field. In spite of mud and potholes the chaise was moving at a brisk pace. Far ahead, level with the ears of the horses, a blue band of the forest was stretching across the horizon. As one would expect at that time of the year, there was not a soul in sight.

Only after we had travelled for a while did I

ON A JOURNEY   From *The Elephant* by Slawomir Mrozek, translated by Konrad Syrop. Reprinted by permission of Grove Press, Inc. Copyright © 1962 by MacDonald & Co., (Publishers) Ltd.

see the first human being. As we approached his features became clear; he was a man with an ordinary face and he wore a Post Office uniform. He was standing still at the side of the road, and as we passed he threw us an indifferent glance. No sooner had we left him behind than I noticed another one, in a similar uniform, also standing motionless on the verge. I looked at him carefully, but my attention was immediately attracted by the third and then the fourth still figure by the roadside. Their apathetic eyes were all fixed in the same direction, their uniforms were faded.

Intrigued by this spectacle I rose in my seat so that I could glance over the shoulders of the cabman; indeed, ahead of us another figure was standing erect. When we passed two more of them my curiosity became irresistible. There they were, standing quite a distance from each other, yet near enough to be able to see the next man, holding the same posture and paying as much attention to us as road signs do to passing travellers. And as soon as we passed one, another came into our field of vision. I was about to open my mouth to ask the coachman about the meaning of those men, when, without turning his head, he volunteered: "On duty."

We were just passing another still figure, staring indifferently into the distance.

"How's that?" I asked.

"Well, just normal. They are standing on duty," and he urged the horses on.

The coachman showed no inclination to offer any further elucidation; perhaps he thought it was superfluous. Cracking his whip from time to time and shouting at the horses, he was driving on. Roadside brambles, shrines and solitary willow trees came to meet us and receded again in the distance; between them, at regular intervals, I could see the now familiar silhouettes.

"What sort of duty are they doing?" I enquired.

"State duty, of course. Telegraph line."

"How's that? Surely for a telegraph line you need poles and wires!"

The coachman looked at me and shrugged his shoulders.

"I can see that you've come from far away," he said. "Yes, we know that for a telegraph you need poles and wires. But this is wireless telegraph. We were supposed to have one with wires but the poles got stolen and there's no wire."

"What do you mean, no wire?"

"There simply isn't any," he said, and shouted at the horses.

Surprise silenced me for the moment but I had no intention of abandoning my enquiries.

"And how does it work without wires?"

"That's easy. The first one shouts what's needed to the second, the second repeats it to the third, the third to the fourth and so on until the telegram gets to where it's supposed to. Just now they aren't transmitting or you'd hear them yourself."

"And it works, this telegraph?"

"Why shouldn't it work? It works all right. But often the message gets twisted. It's worst when one of them has had a drink too many. Then his imagination gets to work and various words get added. But otherwise it's even better than the usual telegraph with poles and wires. After all live men are more intelligent, you know. And there's no storm damage to repair and great saving on timber, and timber is short. Only in the winter there are sometimes interruptions. Wolves. But that can't be helped."

"And those men, are they satisfied?" I asked.

"Why not? The work isn't very hard, only they've got to know foreign words. And it'll get better still; the postmaster has gone to Warsaw to ask for megaphones for them so that they don't have to shout so much."

"And should one of them be hard of hearing?"

"Ah, they don't take such-like. Nor do they take men with a lisp. Once they took on a chap that stammered. He got his job through influence but he didn't keep it long because he was blocking the line. I hear that by the twenty kilometres' stone there's one who went to a drama school. He shouts most clearly."

His arguments confused me for a while. Deep in thought, I no longer paid attention to the men by the road verge. The chaise was jumping over potholes, moving towards the forest, which was now occupying most of the horizon.

"All right," I said carefully, "but wouldn't you prefer to have a new telegraph with poles and wires?"

"Good heavens, no." The coachman was shocked. "For the first time it's easy to get a job in our district in the telegraph, that is. And people don't have to rely only on their wages either. If someone expects a cable and is particularly anxious not to have it twisted, then he takes his chaise along the line and slips something into the pocket of each one of the telegraph boys. After all a wireless telegraph is something different from one with wires. More modern."

Over the rattle of the wheels I could hear a distant sound, neither a cry nor a shout, but a sort of sustained wailing.

"Aaaeeeaaauuueeeaaaeeeaayayay."

The coachman turned in his seat and put his hand to his ear.

"They are transmitting," he said. "Let's stop so that we can hear better."

When the monotonous noise of our wheels

ceased, total silence enveloped the fields. In that silence the wailing, which resembled the cry of birds on a moor, came nearer to us. His hand cupped to his ear, the telegraph man near by made ready to receive.

"It'll get here in a moment," whispered the coachman.

Indeed. When the last distant "ayayay" died away, from behind a clump of trees came the prolonged shout:

"Fa . . . th . . . er dea . . . d fu . . . ner . . . al Wed . . . nes . . . day."

"May he rest in peace," sighed the coachman and cracked his whip. We were entering the forest.

JOHN CHEEVER

The Swimmer

John Cheever (1912–1982) was born in Quincy, Massachusetts and attended Thayer Academy. Cheever's short fiction made him one of the outstanding figures in modern American fiction. While much of his fiction is regarded as social satire, Cheever, nevertheless, delivered moral judgments upon the deeds of his characters as he recorded what he felt to be the disintegration of middle-class America. His works include *The Way Some People Live*, 1942; *The Wapshot Chronicle*, 1957; *The Housebreaker of Shady Hill*, 1959; *The Wapshot Scandal*, 1964; *The Brigadier and the Golf Widow*, 1964; *The World of Apples*, 1973; *Falconer*, 1977; and *Oh What a Paradise It Seems*, 1979.

"The Swimmer," like many of Cheever's short stories, presents his concern with well-to-do suburbanites. Neddy Merrill, as *Time* put it, "turns an unsuspected corner and falls off the edge of things into outer darkness."

It was one of those midsummer Sundays when everyone sits around saying: "I *drank* too much last night." You might have heard it whispered by the parishioners leaving church, heard it from the lips of the priest himself, struggling with his cassock in the *vestiarium*, heard it from the golf links and the tennis courts, heard it from the wildlife preserve where the leader of the Audubon group was suffering from a terrible hangover. "I *drank* too much," said Donald Westerhazy. "We all *drank* too much," said Lucinda Merrill. "It must have been the wine," said Helen Westerhazy. "I *drank* too much of that claret."

This was at the edge of the Westerhazys' pool. The pool, fed by an artesian well with a high iron content, was a pale shade of green. It was a fine day. In the west there was a massive stand of cumulus cloud so like a city seen from a distance—from the bow of an approaching ship—that it might have had a name. Lisbon. Hackensack. The sun was hot. Neddy Merrill sat by the green water, one hand in it, one around a glass of gin. He was a slender man—he seemed to have the especial slenderness of youth—and while he was far from young he had slid down his banister that morning and given the bronze backside of Aphrodite on the hall table a smack, as he jogged toward the smell of coffee in his dining room.

He might have been compared to a summer's day, particularly the last hours of one, and while he lacked a tennis racket or a sail bag the impression was definitely one of youth, sport, and clement weather. He had been swimming and now he was breathing deeply, stertorously as if he could gulp into his lungs the components of that moment, the heat of the sun, the intenseness of his pleasure. It all seemed to flow into his chest. His own house stood in Bullet Park, eight miles to the south, where his four beautiful daughters would have had their lunch and might be playing tennis. Then it occurred to him that by taking a dogleg to the south-west he could reach his home by water.

His life was not confining and the delight he took in this observation could not be explained by its suggestion of escape. He seemed to see, with a cartographer's eye, that string of swimming pools, that quasi-subterranean stream that curved across the county. He had made a discovery, a contribution to modern geography; he would name the stream Lucinda after his wife. He was not a practical joker nor was he a fool but he was determinedly original and had a vague and modest idea of himself as a legendary figure. The day was beautiful and it seemed to him that a long swim might enlarge and celebrate its beauty.

He took off a sweater that was hung over his shoulders and dove in. He had an inexplicable contempt for men who did not hurl themselves into pools. He swam a choppy crawl, breathing either with every stroke or every fourth stroke and counting somewhere well in the back of his mind the one-two one-two of a flutter kick. It was not a serviceable stroke for long distances but the domestication of swimming had saddled the sport with some customs and in his part of the world a crawl was customary. To be embraced and sustained by the light green water was less a pleasure, it seemed, than the resumption of a natural condition, and he would have liked to swim without trunks, but this was not possible, considering his project. He hoisted himself up on the far curb—he never used the ladder—and started across the lawn. When Lucinda asked where he was going he said he was going to swim home.

The only maps and charts he had to go by were remembered or imaginary but these were clear enough. First there were the Grahams, the Hammers, the Lears, the Howlands, and the Crosscups. He would cross Ditmar Street to the Bunkers and come, after a short portage, to the Levys, the Welchers, and the public pool in Lancaster. Then there were the Hallorans, the Sachses, the Biswangers, Shirley Adams, the Gilmartins, and the Clydes. The day was lovely, and that he lived in a world so generously supplied with water seemed like a clemency, a beneficence. His heart was high and he ran across the grass. Making his way home by an uncommon route gave him the feeling that he was a pilgrim, an explorer, a man with a destiny, and he knew that he would find friends all along the way; friends would line the banks of the Lucinda River.

He went through a hedge that separated the Westerhazys' land from the Grahams', walked under some flowering apple trees, passed the shed that housed their pump and filter, and came out at the Grahams' pool. "Why, Neddy," Mrs. Graham said, "what a marvelous surprise. I've been trying to get you on the phone all morning. Here, let me get you a drink." He saw then, like any explorer, that the hospitable customs and traditions of the natives would have to be handled with diplomacy if he was ever going to reach his destination. He did not want to mystify or seem rude to the Grahams nor did he have the time to linger there. He swam the length of their pool and joined them in the sun and was rescued, a few minutes later, by the arrival of two carloads of friends from Connecticut. During the uproarious reunions he was able to slip away. He went down by the front of the Grahams' house, stepped over a thorny hedge, and crossed a vacant lot to the Hammers'. Mrs. Hammer, looking up from her roses, saw him swim by although she wasn't quite sure who it was. The Lears heard him splashing past the open windows of their living room. The Howlands and the Crosscups were away. After leaving the Howlands' he crossed Ditmar Street and started for the Bunkers', where he could hear, even at that distance, the noise of a party.

The water refracted the sound of voices and laughter and seemed to suspend it in midair. The Bunkers' pool was on a rise and he climbed some stairs to a terrace where twenty-five or thirty men and women were drinking. The only person in the water was Rusty Towers, who floated there on a rubber raft. Oh how bonny and lush were the banks of the Lucinda River! Prosperous men and women gathered by the sapphire-colored waters while caterer's men in white coats passed them cold gin. Overhead a red de Haviland trainer was circling around and around and around in the sky with something like the glee of a child in a swing. Ned felt a passing affection for the scene, a tenderness for the gathering, as if it was something he might touch. In the distance he heard thunder. As soon as Enid Bunker saw him she began to scream: "Oh look who's here! What a marvelous surprise! When Lucinda said that you couldn't come I thought I'd *die*." She made her way to him through the crowd, and when they had finished kissing she led him to the bar, a progress that was slowed by the fact that he stopped to kiss eight or ten other women and shake the hands of as many men. A smiling bartender he had seen at a hundred parties gave him a gin and tonic and he stood by the bar for a moment, anxious not to get stuck in any conversation that would delay his voyage. When he seemed about to be surrounded he dove in and swam close to the side to avoid colliding with Rusty's raft. At the far end of the pool he bypassed the Tomlinsons with a broad smile and jogged up the garden path. The gravel cut his feet but this was the only unpleasantness. The party was confined to the pool, and as he went toward the house he heard the brilliant, watery sound of voices fade, heard the noise of a radio from the Bunkers' kitchen, where someone was listening to a ballgame. Sunday afternoon. He made his way through the parked cars and down the grassy border of their driveway to Alewives' Lane. He did not want to be seen on the road in his bathing trunks but there was no traffic and he made the short distance to the Levys' driveway, marked with a private property sign and a green tube for the *New York Times*. All the doors and windows of the big house were open but there were no signs of life; not even a dog barked. He went around the side of the house to the pool and saw that the Levys had only recently left. Glasses and bottles and dishes of nuts were on a table at the deep end, where there was a bathhouse or gazebo, hung with Japanese lanterns. After swimming the pool he got himself a glass and poured a drink. It was his fourth or fifth drink and he had swum nearly half the length of the Lucinda River. He felt tired, clean, and pleased at that moment to be alone; pleased with everything.

It would storm. The stand of cumulus cloud—that city—had risen and darkened, and while he sat there he heard the percussiveness of thunder again. The de Haviland trainer was still circling overhead and it seemed to Ned that he could almost hear the pilot laugh with pleasure in the afternoon; but when there was another peal of thunder he took off for home. A train whistle blew and he wondered what time it had gotten to be. Four? Five? He thought of the provincial station at that hour, where a waiter, his tuxedo concealed by a raincoat, a dwarf with some flowers wrapped in newspaper, and a woman who had been crying would be waiting for the local. It was suddenly growing dark; it was that moment when the pin-headed birds seem to organize their song into some acute and knowledgeable recognition of the storm's approach. Then there was a fine noise of rushing water from the crown of an oak at his back, as if a spigot there had been turned. Then the noise of fountains came from the crowns of all the tall trees. Why did he love storms, what was the meaning of his excitement when the door sprang open and the rain wind fled rudely up the stairs, why had the simple task of shutting the windows of an old house seemed fitting and urgent, why did the first watery notes of a storm wind have for him the unmistakable sound of good news, cheer, glad tidings? Then there was an explosion, a smell of cordite, and rain lashed the Japanese lanterns that Mrs. Levy had bought in Kyoto the year before last, or was it the year before that?

He stayed in the Levys' gazebo until the storm had passed. The rain had cooled the air and he shivered. The force of the wind had stripped a maple of its red and yellow leaves and scattered them over the grass and the water. Since it was midsummer the tree must be blighted, and yet he felt a peculiar sadness at this sign of autumn. He braced his shoulders, emptied his glass, and started for the Welchers' pool. This meant crossing the Lindleys' riding ring and he was surprised to find it overgrown with grass and all the jumps dismantled. He wondered if the Lindleys had sold their horses or gone away for the summer and put them out to board. He seemed to remember having heard something about the Lindleys and their horses but the memory was unclear. On he went, barefoot through the wet grass, to the Welchers', where he found their pool was dry.

This breach in his chain of water disappointed him absurdly, and he felt like some explorer who seeks a torrential headwater and finds a dead stream. He was disappointed and mystified. It was common enough to go away for the summer but no one ever drained his pool. The Welchers had definitely gone away. The pool furniture was folded, stacked, and covered with a tarpaulin. The bathhouse was locked. All the windows of the house were shut, and when he went around to the driveway in front he saw a for-sale sign nailed to a tree. When had he last heard from the Welchers—when, that is, had he and Lucinda last regretted an invitation to dine with them? It seemed only a week or so ago. Was his memory failing or had he so disciplined it in the repression of unpleasant facts that he had damaged his sense of the truth? Then in the distance he heard the sound of a tennis game. This cheered him, cleared away all his apprehensions and let him regard the overcast sky and the cold air with indifference. This was the day that Neddy Merrill swam across the county. That was the day! He started off then for his most difficult portage.

Had you gone for a Sunday afternoon ride that day you might have seen him, close to naked, standing on the shoulders of route 424, waiting for a chance to cross. You might have wondered if he was the victim of foul play, had his car broken down, or was he merely a fool. Standing barefoot in the deposits of the highway—beer cans, rags, and blowout patches—exposed to all kinds of ridicule, he seemed pitiful. He had known when he started that this was a part of his journey—it had been on his maps—but confronted with the lines of traffic, worming through the summery light, he found himself unprepared. He was laughed at, jeered at, a beer can was thrown at him, and he had no dignity or humor to bring to the situation. He could have gone back, back to the Westerhazys', where Lucinda would still be sitting in the sun. He had signed nothing, vowed nothing, pledged nothing not even to himself. Why, believing as he did, that all human obduracy was susceptible to common sense, was he unable to turn back? Why was he determined to complete his journey even if it meant putting his life in danger? At what point had this prank, this joke, this piece of horseplay become serious? He could not go back, he could not even recall with any clearness the green water at the Westerhazys', the sense of inhaling the day's components, the friendly and relaxed voices saying that they had *drunk* too much. In the space of an hour, more or less, he had covered a distance that made his return impossible.

An old man, tooling down the highway at fifteen miles an hour, let him get to the middle of the road, where there was a grass divider. Here he was exposed to the ridicule of the northbound traffic, but after ten or fifteen minutes he was able to cross. From here he had only a short walk to the Recreation Center at the edge of the Village of Lancaster, where there were some handball courts and a public pool.

The effect of the water on voices, the illusion of brilliance and suspense, was the same here as it had been at the Bunkers' but the sounds here were louder, harsher, and more shrill, and as soon as he entered the crowded enclosure he was confronted with regimentation. "ALL SWIMMERS MUST TAKE A SHOWER BEFORE USING THE POOL. ALL SWIMMERS MUST USE THE FOOTBATH. ALL SWIMMERS MUST WEAR THEIR IDENTIFICATION DISKS." He took a shower, washed his feet in a cloudy and bitter solution and made his way to the edge of the water. It stank of chlorine and looked to him like a sink. A pair of lifeguards in a pair of towers blew police whistles at what seemed to be regular intervals and abused the swimmers through a public address system. Neddy remembered the sapphire water at the Bunkers' with longing and thought that he might contaminate himself—damage his own prosperousness and charm—by swimming in this murk, but he reminded himself that he was an explorer, a pilgrim, and that this was merely a stagnant bend in the Lucinda River. He dove, scowling with distaste, into the chlorine and had to swim with his head above water to avoid collisions, but even so he was bumped into, splashed and jostled. When he got to the shallow end both lifeguards were shouting at him: "Hey, you, you without the identification disk, get outa the water." He did, but they had no way of pursuing him and he went through the reek of suntan oil and chlorine out through the hurricane fence and passed the handball courts. By crossing the road he entered the wooded part of the Halloran estate. The woods were not cleared and the footing was treacherous and difficult until he reached the lawn and the clipped beech hedge that encircled their pool.

The Hallorans were friends, an elderly couple of enormous wealth who seemed to bask in the suspicion that they might be Communists. They were zealous reformers but they were not Communists, and yet when they were accused, as they sometimes were, of subversion, it seemed to gratify and excite them. Their beech hedge was yellow and he guessed this had been blighted like the Levys' maple. He called hullo, hullo, to warn the Hallorans of his approach, to palliate his invasion of their privacy. The Hallorans, for reasons that had never been explained to him, did not wear bathing suits. No explanations were in order, really. Their nakedness was a detail in their uncompromising zeal for reform and he stepped politely out of his trunks before he went through the opening in the hedge.

Mrs. Halloran, a stout woman with white hair and a serene face, was reading the *Times*. Mr. Halloran was taking beech leaves out of the water with a scoop. They seemed not surprised or displeased to see him. Their pool was perhaps the oldest in the county, a fieldstone rectangle, fed by a brook. It had no filter or pump and its waters were the opaque gold of the stream.

"I'm swimming across the county," Ned said.

"Why, I didn't know one could," exclaimed Mrs. Halloran.

"Well, I've made it from the Westerhazys'," Ned said. "That must be about four miles."

He left his trunks at the deep end, walked to the shallow end, and swam this stretch. As he was pulling himself out of the water he heard Mrs. Halloran say: "We've been *terribly* sorry to hear about all your misfortunes, Neddy."

"My misfortunes?" Ned asked. "I don't know what you mean."

"Why, we heard that you'd sold the house and that your poor children . . ."

"I don't recall having sold the house," Ned said, "and the girls are at home."

"Yes," Mrs. Halloran sighed. "Yes . . ." Her voice filled the air with an unseasonable melancholy and Ned spoke briskly. "Thank you for the swim."

"Well, have a nice trip," said Mrs. Halloran.

Beyond the hedge he pulled on his trunks and fastened them. They were loose and he wondered if, during the space of an afternoon, he could have lost some weight. He was cold and he was tired and the naked Hallorans and their dark water had depressed him. The swim was too

much for his strength but how could he have guessed this, sliding down the banister that morning and sitting in the Westerhazys' sun? His arms were lame. His legs felt rubbery and ached at the joints. The worst of it was the cold in his bones and the feeling that he might never be warm again. Leaves were falling down around him and he smelled woodsmoke on the wind. Who would be burning wood at this time of year?

He needed a drink. Whiskey would warm him, pick him up, carry him through the last of his journey, refresh his feeling that it was original and valorous to swim across the county. Channel swimmers took brandy. He needed a stimulant. He crossed the lawn in front of the Hallorans' house and went down a little path to where they had built a house for their only daughter Helen and her husband Eric Sachs. The Sachses' pool was small and he found Helen and her husband there.

"Oh, *Neddy*," Helen said. "Did you lunch at Mother's?"

"Not *really*," Ned said. "I *did* stop to see your parents." This seemed to be explanation enough. "I'm terribly sorry to break in on you like this but I've taken a chill and I wonder if you'd give me a drink."

"Why, I'd *love* to," Helen said, "but there hasn't been anything in this house to drink since Eric's operation. That was three years ago."

Was he losing his memory, had his gift for concealing painful facts let him forget that he had sold his house, that his children were in trouble, and that his friend had been ill? His eyes slipped from Eric's face to his abdomen, where he saw three pale, sutured scars, two of them at least a foot long. Gone was his navel, and what, Neddy thought, would the roving hand, bed-checking one's gifts at 3 A.M. make of a belly with no navel, no link to birth, this breach in the succession?

"I'm sure you can get a drink at the Biswangers'," Helen said. "They're having an enormous do. You can hear it from here. Listen!"

She raised her head and from across the road, the lawns, the gardens, the woods, the fields, he heard again the brilliant noise of voices over water. "Well, I'll get wet," he said, still feeling that he had no freedom of choice about his means of travel. He dove into the Sachses' cold water and, gasping, close to drowning, made his way from one end of the pool to the other. "Lucinda and I want *terribly* to see you," he said over his shoulder, his face set toward the Biswangers'. "We're sorry it's been so long and we'll call you *very* soon."

He crossed some fields to the Biswangers' and the sounds of revelry there. They would be honored to give him a drink, they would be happy to give him a drink, they would in fact be lucky to give him a drink. The Biswangers invited him and Lucinda for dinner four times a year, six weeks in advance. They were always rebuffed and yet they continued to send out their invitations, unwilling to comprehend the rigid and undemocratic realities of their society. They were the sort of people who discussed the price of things at cocktails, exchanged market tips during dinner, and after dinner told dirty stories to mixed company. They did not belong to Neddy's set—they were not even on Lucinda's Christmas card list. He went toward their pool with feelings of indifference, charity, and some unease, since it seemed to be getting dark and these were the longest days of the year. The party when he joined it was noisy and large. Grace Biswanger was the kind of hostess who asked the optometrist, the veterinarian, the real-estate dealer and the dentist. No one was swimming and the twilight, reflected on the water of the pool, had a wintry gleam. There was a bar and he started for this. When Grace Biswanger saw him she came toward him, not affectionately as he had every right to expect, but bellicosely.

"Why, this party has everything." she said loudly, "including a gate crasher."

She could not deal him a social blow—there was no question about this and he did not flinch. "As a gate crasher," he asked politely, "do I rate a drink?"

"Suit yourself," she said. "You don't seem to pay much attention to invitations."

She turned her back on him and joined some guests, and he went to the bar and ordered a whiskey. The bartender served him but he served him rudely. His was a world in which the caterer's men kept the social score, and to be rebuffed by a part-time barkeep meant that he had suffered some loss of social esteem. Or perhaps the man was new and uninformed. Then he heard Grace at his back say: "They went for broke overnight—nothing but income—and he showed up drunk one Sunday and asked us to loan him

five thousand dollars. . . ." She was always talking about money. It was worse than eating your peas off a knife. He dove into the pool, swam its length and went away.

The next pool on his list, the last but two, belonged to his old mistress, Shirley Adams. If he had suffered any injuries at the Biswangers' they would be cured here. Love—sexual roughhouse in fact—was the supreme elixir, the painkiller, the brightly colored pill that would put the spring back into his step, the joy of life in his heart. They had had an affair last week, last month, last year. He couldn't remember. It was he who had broken it off, his was the upper hand, and he stepped through the gate of the wall that surrounded her pool with nothing so considered as self-confidence. It seemed in a way to be his pool as the lover, particularly the illicit lover, enjoys the possessions of his mistress with an authority unknown to holy matrimony. She was there, her hair the color of brass, but her figure, at the edge of the lighted, cerulean water, excited in him no profound memories. It had been, he thought, a lighthearted affair, although she had wept when he broke it off. She seemed confused to see him and he wondered if she was still wounded. Would she, God forbid, weep again?

"What do you want?" she asked.

"I'm swimming across the county."

"Good Christ. Will you ever grow up?"

"What's the matter?"

"If you've come here for money," she said, "I won't give you another cent."

"You could give me a drink."

"I could but I won't. I'm not alone."

"Well, I'm on my way."

He dove in and swam the pool, but when he tried to haul himself up onto the curb he found that the strength in his arms and his shoulders had gone, and he paddled to the ladder and climbed out. Looking over his shoulder he saw, in the lighted bathhouse, a young man. Going out onto the dark lawn he smelled chrysanthemums or marigolds—some stubborn autumnal fragrance—on the night air, strong as gas. Looking overhead he saw that the stars had come out, but why should he seem to see Andromeda, Cepheus, and Cassiopeia? What had become of the constellations of midsummer? He began to cry.

It was probably the first time in his adult life that he had ever cried, certainly the first time in his life that he had ever felt so miserable, cold, tired, and bewildered. He could not understand the rudeness of the caterer's barkeep or the rudeness of a mistress who had come to him on her knees and showered his trousers with tears. He had swum too long, he had been immersed too long, and his nose and his throat were sore from the water. What he needed then was a drink, some company, and some clean dry clothes, and while he could have cut directly across the road to his home he went on to the Gilmartins' pool. Here, for the first time in his life, he did not dive but went down the steps into the icy water and swam a hobbled side stroke that he might have learned as a youth. He staggered with fatigue on his way to the Clydes' and paddled the length of their pool, stopping again and again with his hand on the curb to rest. He climbed up the ladder and wondered if he had the strength to get home. He had done what he wanted, he had swum the county, but he was so stupefied with exhaustion that his triumph seemed vague.

Stooped, holding onto the gateposts for support, he turned up the driveway of his own house.

The place was dark. Was it so late that they had all gone to bed? Had Lucinda stayed at the Westerhazys' for supper? Had the girls joined her there or gone someplace else? Hadn't they agreed, as they usually did on Sunday, to regret all their invitations and stay at home? He tried the garage doors to see what cars were in but the doors were locked and rust came off the handles onto his hands. Going toward the house, he saw that the force of the thunderstorm had knocked one of the rain gutters loose. It hung down over the front door like an umbrella rib, but it could be fixed in the morning. The house was locked, and he thought that the stupid cook or the stupid maid must have locked the place up until he remembered that it had been some time since they had employed a maid or a cook. He shouted, pounded on the door, tried to force it with his shoulder, and then, looking in at the windows, saw that the place was empty.

PÄR LAGERKVIST

Father and I

Pär Lagerkvist (1891–1974), Swedish dramatist, novelist, short-story writer and poet, a member of the Swedish Academy and winner of the Nobel Prize for Literature in 1951, grew up in a small Swedish town where his father worked for the railroad. Early in life he showed an interest in literature and went to study at the University of Uppsala. In 1912 he published his first poems and a short story. He came to Paris in 1913 and became involved with the artistic movement of the expressionists. *Angst*, 1916, secured his reputation as a leading Swedish literary figure. During World War I, Lagerkvist wrote several plays reflecting the influence of August Strindberg. He discerned the dangers of Nazism very early and wrote plays warning of the possibility of war and extolling the virtues of peace. Lagerkvist published more than thirty works, his best-known novel being *Barabbas*, 1950.

In "Father and I," perhaps autobiographical in inspiration, the child desires to see the future clearly, and the father, his vision fixed by the experiences of life, does not sense the fate of one with his life still before him.

FATHER AND I From *The Marriage Feast* by Pär Lagerkvist. Copyright © 1954 by Albert Bonniers Forlag. Reprinted by permission of Farrar, Straus & Giroux, Inc.

I remember one Sunday afternoon when I was about ten years old, Daddy took my hand and we went for a walk in the woods to hear the birds sing. We waved goodbye to mother, who was staying at home to prepare supper, and so couldn't go with us. The sun was bright and warm as we set out briskly on our way. We didn't take this bird-singing too seriously, as though it was something special or unusual. We were sensible people, Daddy and I. We were used to the woods and the creatures in them, so we didn't make any fuss about it. It was just because it was Sunday afternoon and Daddy was free. We went along the railway line where other people aren't allowed to go, but Daddy belonged to the railway and had a right to. And in this way we came direct into the woods and did not need to take a round-about way. Then the bird song and all the rest began at once. They chirped in the bushes; hedge-sparrows, thrushes, and warblers; and we heard all the noises of the little creatures as we came into the woods. The ground was thick with anemones, the birches were dressed in their new leaves, and the pines had young, green shoots. There was such a pleasant smell everywhere. The mossy ground was steaming a little, because the sun was shining upon it. Everywhere there was life and noise; bumble-bees flew out of their holes, midges circled where it was damp. The birds shot out of the bushes to catch them and then dived back again. All of a sudden a train came rushing along and we had to go down the embankment. Daddy hailed the driver with two fingers to his Sunday hat: the driver saluted and waved his hand. Everything seemed on the move. As we went on our way along the sleepers which lay and oozed tar in the sunshine, there was a smell of everything, machine oil and almond blossom, tar and heather, all mixed. We took big steps from sleeper to sleeper so as not to step among the stones, which were rough to walk on, and wore your shoes out. The rails shone in the sunshine. On both sides of the line stood the telephone poles that sang as we went by them. Yes! That was a fine day! The sky was absolutely clear. There wasn't a single cloud to be seen: there just couldn't be any on a day like this, according to what Daddy said. After a while we came to a field of oats on the right side of the line, where a farmer, whom we knew, had a clearing. The oats had grown thick and even; Daddy looked at it knowingly, and I could feel

that he was satisfied. I didn't understand that sort of thing much, because I was born in town. Then we came to the bridge over the brook that mostly hadn't much water in it, but now there was plenty. We took hands so that we shouldn't fall down between the sleepers. From there it wasn't far to the railway gate-keeper's little place, which was quite buried in green. There were apple trees and gooseberry bushes right close to the house. We went in there, to pay a visit, and they offered us milk. We looked at the pigs, the hens, and the fruit trees, which were in full blossom, and then we went on again. We wanted to go to the river, because there it was prettier than anywhere else. There was something special about the river, because higher up stream it flowed past Daddy's old home. We never liked going back before we got to it, and, as usual, this time we got there after a fair walk. It wasn't far to the next station, but we didn't go on there. Daddy just looked to see whether the signals were right. He thought of everything. We stopped by the river, where it flowed broad and friendly in the sunshine, and the thick leafy trees on the banks mirrored themselves in the calm water. It was all so fresh and bright. A breeze came from the little lakes higher up. We climbed down the bank, went a little way along the very edge. Daddy showed me the fishing spots. When he was a boy he used to sit there on the stones and wait for perch all day long. Often he didn't get a single bite, but it was a delightful way to spend the day. Now he never had time. We played about for some time by the side of the river, and threw in pieces of bark that the current carried away, and we threw stones to see who could throw farthest. We were, by nature, very merry and cheerful, Daddy and I. After a while we felt a bit tired. We thought we had played enough, so we started off home again.

Then it began to get dark. The woods were changed. It wasn't quite dark yet, but almost. We made haste. Maybe mother was getting anxious, and waiting supper. She was always afraid that something might happen, though nothing had. This had been a splendid day. Everything had been just as it should, and we were satisfied with it all. It was getting darker and darker, and the trees were so queer. They stood and listened for the sound of our footsteps, as though they didn't know who we were. There was a glow-worm under one of them. It lay down there in the dark and stared at us. I held Daddy's hand tight, but he didn't seem to notice the strange light: he just went on. It was quite dark when we came to the bridge over the stream. It was roaring down underneath us as if it wanted to swallow us up, as the ground seemed to open under us. We went along the sleepers carefully, holding hands tight so that we shouldn't fall in. I thought Daddy would carry me over, but he didn't say anything about it. I suppose he wanted me to be like him, and not think anything of it. We went on. Daddy was so calm in the darkness, walking with even steps without speaking. He was thinking his own thoughts. I couldn't understand how he could be so calm when everything was so ghostly. I looked round scared. It was nothing but darkness everywhere. I hardly dared to breathe deeply, because then the darkness comes into one, and that was dangerous, I thought. One must die soon. I remember quite well thinking so then. The railway embankment was very steep. It finished in black night. The telephone posts stood up ghostlike against the sky, mumbling deep inside as though someone were speaking, way down in the earth. The white china hats sat there scared, cowering with fear, listening. It was all so creepy. Nothing was real, nothing was natural, all seemed a mystery. I went closer to Daddy, and whispered: "Why is it so creepy when it's dark?"

"No child, it isn't creepy," he said, and took my hand.

"Oh, yes, but it is, Daddy."

"No, you mustn't think that. We know there is a God, don't we?" I felt so lonely, so abandoned. It was queer that it was only me that was frightened, and not Daddy. It was queer that we didn't feel the same about it. And it was queerer still that what he said didn't help, didn't stop me being frightened. Not even what he said about God helped. The thought of God made one feel creepy too. It was creepy to think that He was everywhere here in the darkness, down there under the trees, and in the telephone posts that mumbled so—probably that was Him everywhere. But all the same one could never see Him.

We went along silently, each of us thinking his own thoughts. My heart felt cramped as though the darkness had come in and was squeezing it.

Then, when we were in a bend, we suddenly heard a great noise behind us. We were startled out of our thoughts. Daddy pulled me down the embankment and held me tight, and a train rushed by; a black train. The lights were out in all the carriages, as it whizzed past us. What could it be? There shouldn't be any train now. We looked at it, frightened. The furnace roared in the big engine, where they shovelled in coal, and the sparks flew out into the night. It was terrible. The driver stood so pale and immovable, with such a stony look in the glare. Daddy didn't recognize him—didn't know who he was. He was just looking ahead as though he was driving straight into darkness, far into darkness which had no end.

Startled and panting with fear I looked after the wild thing. It was swallowed up in the night. Daddy helped me up on to the line, and we hurried home. He said, "That was strange! What train was that I wonder? And I didn't know the driver either." Then he didn't say any more.

I was shaking all over. That had been for me—for my sake. I guessed what it meant. It was all the fear which would come to me, all the unknown: all that Daddy didn't know about, and couldn't save me from. That was how the world would be for me, and the strange life I should live; not like Daddy's, where everyone was known and sure. It wasn't a real world, or a real life;—it just rushed burning into the darkness which had no end.

LANGSTON HUGHES

Thank You, M'am

Langston Hughes (1902–1967), poet and writer of fiction, drama, and biography; editor and lecturer, was born in Joplin, Missouri, and educated at Columbia University in New York and Lincoln University in Pennsylvania. His early activities were varied—merchant seaman, reader of poetry on nationwide tours, poet-in-residence, newspaper correspondent, and foreign correspondent during the Spanish Civil War. His first volume of poetry, *Weary Blues*, was published in 1926. Then followed *Dream Keeper*, 1932; *The Ways of White Folks*, 1934; *Shakespeare in Harlem* and *Fields of Wonder*, 1947; *Selected Poems*, 1959; *Best of Simple*, 1961; the first part of his autobiography, *The Big Sea*, 1963; the second part, *I Wonder as I Wander*, 1964; and *Five Plays*, 1963. *Don't Turn Back* and *Not Without Laughter* both appeared posthumously in 1969, and *The Langston Hughes Reader* in 1981. Hughes was awarded many prizes for his poetry and was a member of The National Institute of Arts and Letters.

The irony and pathos of this brief story show that misfortune and evil may be turned to good through sincerity, understanding, and kindness.

She was a large woman with a large purse that had everything in it but a hammer and nails. It had a long strap, and she carried it slung across her shoulder. It was about eleven o'clock at night, dark, and she was walking alone, when a boy ran up behind her and tried to snatch her purse. The strap broke with the sudden single tug the boy gave it from behind. But the boy's weight and the weight of the purse combined caused him to lose his balance. Instead of taking off full blast as he had hoped, the boy fell on his back on the sidewalk and his legs flew up. The large woman simply turned around and kicked him right square in his blue-jeaned sitter. Then she reached down, picked the boy up by his shirt front, and shook him until his teeth rattled.

After that the woman said, "Pick up my pocketbook, boy, and give it here."

She still held him tightly. But she bent down enough to permit him to stoop and pick up her purse. Then she said, "Now ain't you ashamed of yourself?"

Firmly gripped by his shirt front, the boy said, "Yes'm."

The woman said, "What did you want to do it for?"

The boy said, "I didn't aim to."

She said, "You a lie!"

By that time two or three people passed, stopped, turned to look, and some stood watching.

"If I turn you loose, will you run?" asked the woman.

"Yes'm," said the boy.

"Then I won't turn you loose," said the woman. She did not release him.

"Lady, I'm sorry," whispered the boy.

"Um-hum! Your face is dirty. I got a great mind to wash your face for you. Ain't you got nobody home to tell you to wash your face?"

"No'm," said the boy.

"Then it will get washed this evening," said the large woman, starting up the street, dragging the frightened boy behind her.

He looked as if he were fourteen or fifteen, frail and willow-wild, in tennis shoes and blue jeans.

The woman said, "You ought to be my son. I would teach you right from wrong. Least I can do right now is to wash your face. Are you hungry?"

"No'm," said the being-dragged boy. "I just want you to turn me loose."

"Was I bothering *you* when I turned that corner?" asked the woman.

"No'm."

"But you put yourself in contact with *me*," said the woman. "If you think that that contact is not going to last awhile, you got another thought coming. When I get through with you, sir, you are going to remember Mrs. Luella Bates Washington Jones."

Sweat popped out on the boy's face and he began to struggle. Mrs. Jones stopped, jerked him around in front of her, put a half nelson about his neck, and continued to drag him up the street. When she got to her door, she dragged the boy inside, down a hall, and into a large kitchenette-furnished room at the rear of the house. She switched on the light and left the door open. The boy could hear other roomers laughing and talking in the large house. Some of their doors were open, too, so he knew he and the woman were not alone. The woman still had him by the neck in the middle of her room.

She said, "What is your name?"

"Roger," answered the boy.

"Then, Roger, you go to that sink and wash your face," said the woman, whereupon she turned him loose—at last. Roger looked at the door—looked at the woman—looked at the door—*and went to the sink.*

"Let the water run until it gets warm," she said. "Here's a clean towel."

"You gonna take me to jail?" asked the boy, bending over the sink.

"Not with that face, I would not take you nowhere," said the woman. "Here I am trying to get home to cook me a bite to eat, and you snatch my pocketbook! Maybe you ain't been to your supper either, late as it be. Have you?"

"There's nobody home at my house," said the boy.

"Then we'll eat," said the woman. "I believe you're hungry—or been hungry—to try to snatch my pocketbook!"

"I want a pair of blue suede shoes," said the boy.

"Well, you didn't have to snatch *my* pocketbook to get some suede shoes," said Mrs. Luella Bates Washington Jones. "You could of asked me."

"M'am?"

The water dripping from his face, the boy looked at her. There was a long pause. A very long pause. After he had dried his face, and not knowing what else to do, dried it again, the boy turned around, wondering what next. The door was open. He could make a dash for it down the hall. He could run, run, run, *run!*

The woman was sitting on the daybed. After a while she said, "I were young once and I wanted things I could not get."

There was another long pause. The boy's mouth opened. Then he frowned, not knowing he frowned.

The woman said, "Um-hum! You thought I was going to say *but,* didn't you? You thought I was going to say, *but I didn't snatch people's pocketbooks.* Well, I wasn't going to say that." Pause. Silence. "I have done things, too, which I would not tell you, son—neither tell God, if He didn't already know. Everybody's got something in common. So you set down while I fix us something to eat. You might run that comb through your hair so you will look presentable."

In another corner of the room behind a screen was a gas plate and an icebox, Mrs. Jones got up and went behind the screen. The woman did not watch the boy to see if he was going to run now, nor did she watch her purse, which she left behind her on the daybed. But the boy took care to sit on the far side of the room, away from the purse, where he thought she could easily see him out of the corner of her eye if she wanted to. He did not trust the woman *not* to trust him. And he did not want to be mistrusted now.

"Do you need somebody to go to the store," asked the boy, "maybe to get some milk or something?"

"Don't believe I do," said the woman, "unless you just want sweet milk yourself. I was going to make cocoa out of this canned milk I got here."

"That will be fine," said the boy.

She heated some lima beans and ham she had

in the icebox, made the cocoa, and set the table. The woman did not *ask* the boy anything about where he lived, or his folks, or anything else that would embarrass him. Instead, as they ate, she told him about her job in a hotel beauty shop that stayed open late, what the work was like, and how all kinds of women came in and out, blondes, redheads, and Spanish. Then she cut him a half of her ten-cent cake.

"Eat some more, son," she said.

When they were finished eating, she got up and said, "Now here, take this ten dollars and buy yourself some blue suede shoes. And next time, do not make the mistake of latching onto

my pocketbook *nor nobody else's*—because shoes got by devilish ways will burn your feet. I got to get my rest now. But from here on in, son, I hope you will behave yourself."

She led him down the hall to the front door and opened it. "Good night! Behave yourself, boy!" she said, looking out into the street as he went down the steps.

The boy wanted to say something other than, "Thank you, m'am," to Mrs. Luella Bates Washington Jones, but although his lips moved, he couldn't even say that as he turned at the foot of the barren stoop and looked up at the large woman in the door. Then she shut the door.

URSULA K. LE GUIN

The Word of Unbinding

Ursula K. Le Guin (1929–   ), born in Berkeley, California, graduated from Radcliffe College and received a Master's Degree from Columbia University. Best known for her science fiction, Le Guin has been published in many magazines, including such diverse publications as *Playboy* and *The Harvard Advocate*. In 1970, for her novel *The Left Hand of Darkness*, she received the two most prestigious awards in the science-fiction field, the Hugo Award and the Nebula Award. Her other books include *The Lathe of Heaven*, 1971; *The Dispossessed*, 1974; and *A Wizard of Earthsea*, 1976.

In "The Word of Unbinding," Le Guin explores both the physical and psychological foundations of magic. The opposition of Festin and Voll reflects the opposition of the fundamental forces of the story's universe.

Where was he? The floor was hard and slimy, the air black and stinking, and that was all there was. Except a headache. Lying flat on the clammy floor Festin moaned, and then said, "Staff!" When his alderwood wizard's staff did not come to his hand, he knew he was in peril. He sat up, and not having his staff with which to make a proper light, he struck a spark between finger and thumb, muttering a certain Word. A blue will o' the wisp sprang from the spark and rolled

feebly through the air, sputtering. "Up," said Festin, and the fireball wobbled upward till it lit a vaulted trapdoor very high above, so high that Festin projecting into the fireball momentarily saw his own face forty feet below as a pale dot in the darkness. The light struck no reflections in the damp walls; they had been woven out of night, by magic. He rejoined himself and said, "Out." The ball expired. Festin sat in the dark, cracking his knuckles.

He must have been overspelled from behind, by surprise; for the last memory he had was of walking through his own woods at evening talking with the trees. Lately, in these lone years in the middle of his life, he had been burdened with a sense of waste, of unspent strength; so, needing to learn patience, he had left the villages and gone to converse with trees, especially oaks, chestnuts, and the grey alders whose roots are in profound communication with running water. It had been six months since he had spoken to a human being. He had been busy with essentials, casting no spells and bothering no one. So who had spellbound him and shut him in this reeking well? "Who?" he demanded of the walls, and slowly a name gathered on them and ran down to him like a thick black drop sweated out from pores of stone and spores of fungus: "Voll."

For a moment Festin was in a cold sweat himself.

He had heard first long ago of Voll the Fell, who was said to be more than wizard yet less than man; who passed from island to island of the Outer Reach, undoing the works of the Ancients, enslaving men, cutting forests and spoiling fields, and sealing in underground tombs any wizard or Mage who tried to combat him. Refugees from ruined islands told always the same tale, that he came at evening on a dark wind over the sea. His slaves followed in ships; these they had seen. But none of them had ever seen Voll. . . . There were many men and creatures of evil will among the Islands, and Festin, a young warlock intent on his training, had not paid much heed to these tales of Voll the Fell. "I can protect this island," he had thought, knowing his untried power, and had returned to his oaks and alders, the sound of wind in their leaves, the rhythm of growth in their round trunks and limbs and twigs, the taste of sunlight on leaves or dark groundwater around roots.—Where were they now, the trees, his old companions? Had Voll destroyed the forest?

Awake at last and up on his feet, Festin made two broad motions with rigid hands, shouting aloud a Name that would burst all locks and break open any manmade door. But these walls impregnated with night and the name of their builder did not heed, did not hear. The name re-echoed back, clapping in Festin's ears so that he fell on his knees, hiding his head in his arms till the echoes died away in the vaults above him. Then, still shaken by the backfire, he sat brooding.

They were right; Voll was strong. Here on his own ground, within this spell-built dungeon, his magic would withstand any direct attack; and

Festin's strength was halved by the loss of his staff. But not even his captor could take from him his powers, relative only to himself, of Projecting and Transforming. So, after rubbing his now doubly aching head, he transformed. Quietly his body melted away into a cloud of fine mist.

Lazy, trailing, the mist rose off the floor, drifting up along the slimy walls until it found, where vault met wall, a hairline crack. Through this, droplet by droplet, it seeped. It was almost all through the crack when a hot wind, hot as a furnace-blast, struck at it, scattering the mist-drops, drying them. Hurriedly the mist sucked itself back into the vault, spiraled to the floor, took on Festin's own form and lay there panting. Transformation is an emotional strain to introverted warlocks of Festin's sort; when to that strain is added the shock of facing unhuman death in one's assumed shape, the experience becomes horrible. Festin lay for a while merely breathing. He was also angry with himself. It had been a pretty simple-minded notion to escape as a mist, after all. Every fool knew that trick. Voll had probably just left a hot wind waiting. Festin gathered himself into a small black bat, flew up to the ceiling, retransformed into a thin stream of plain air, and seeped through the crack.

This time he got clear out and was blowing softly down the hall in which he found himself towards a window, when a sharp sense of peril made him pull together, snapping himself into the first small, coherent shape that came to mind—a gold ring. It was just as well. The hurricane of arctic air that would have dispersed his air-form in unrecallable chaos merely chilled his ring-form slightly. As the storm passed he lay on the marble pavement, wondering which form might get out the window quickest.

Too late, he began to roll away. An enormous blank-faced troll strode cataclysmically across the floor, stopped, caught the quick-rolling ring and picked it up in a huge, limestone-like hand. The troll strode to the trapdoor, lifted it by an iron handle and a muttered charm, and dropped Festin down into the darkness. He fell straight for forty feet and landed on the stone floor—clink.

Resuming his true form he sat up, ruefully rubbing a bruised elbow. Enough of this transformation on an empty stomach. He longed bitterly for his staff, with which he could have summoned up any amount of dinner. Without it, though he could change his own form and exert certain spells and powers, he could not transform or summon to him any material thing—neither lightning nor a lamb chop.

"Patience," Festin told himself, and when he had got his breath he dissolved his body into the infinite delicacy of volatile oils, becoming the aroma of a frying lamb chop. He drifted once more through the crack. The waiting troll sniffed suspiciously, but already Festin had regrouped himself into a falcon, winging straight for the window. The troll lunged after him, missed by yards, and bellowed in a vast stony voice, "The hawk, get the hawk!" Swooping over the enchanted castle towards his forest that lay dark to westward, sunlight and sea-glare dazzling his eyes, Festin rode the wind like an arrow. But a quicker arrow found him. Crying out, he fell. Sun and sea and towers spun around him and went out.

He woke again on the dank floor of the dungeon, hands and hair and lips wet with his own blood. The arrow had struck his pinion as a falcon, his shoulder as a man. Lying still, he mumbled a spell to close the wound. Presently he was able to sit up, and recollect a longer, deeper spell of healing. But he had lost a good deal of blood, and with it, power. A chill had settled in the marrow of his bones which even the healing-spell could not warm. There was darkness in his eyes, even when he struck a will o' the wisp and lit the reeking air: the same dark mist he had seen, as he flew, overhanging his forest and the little towns of his land.

It was up to him to protect that land.

He could not attempt direct escape again. He was too weak and tired. Trusting his power too much, he had lost his strength. Now whatever shape he took would share his weakness, and be trapped.

Shivering with cold, he crouched there, letting the fireball sputter out with a last whiff of methane—marsh gas. The smell brought to his mind's eye the marshes stretching from the forest wall down to the sea, his beloved marshes where no men came, where in fall the swans flew long and level, where between still pools and reed-islands the quick, silent seaward streamlets ran. Oh, to be a fish in one of those streams; or better yet to be farther upstream, near the springs, in the forest in the shadow of the trees, in the clear brown backwater under an alder's roots, resting hidden . . .

This was a great magic. Festin had no more performed it than has any man who in exile or danger longs for the earth and waters of his home, seeing and yearning over the doorsill of his house, the table where he has eaten, the branches outside the window of the room where he has slept. Only in dreams do any but the great Mages realize this magic of going home. But Festin, with the cold creeping out from his marrow into nerves and veins, stood up between the black walls, gathered his will together till it shone like a candle in the darkness of his flesh, and began to work the great and silent magic.

The walls were gone. He was in the earth, rocks and veins of granite for bones, groundwater for blood, the roots of things for nerves. Like a blind worm he moved through the earth westward, slowly, darkness before and behind. Then all at once coolness flowed along his back and belly, a buoyant, unresistant, inexhaustible caress. With his sides he tasted the water, felt current-flow; and with lidless eyes he saw before him the deep brown pool between the great buttress-roots of an alder. He darted forward, silvery, into shadow. He had got free. He was home.

The water ran timelessly from its clear spring. He lay on the sand of the pool's bottom letting running water, stronger than any spell of healing, soothe his wound and with its coolness wash away the bleaker cold that had entered him. But as he rested he felt and heard a shaking and trampling in the earth. Who walked now in his forest? Too weary to try to change form, he hid his gleaming trout-body under the arch of the alder root, and waited.

Huge grey fingers groped in the water, roiling the sand. In the dimness above water vague faces, blank eyes loomed and vanished, reappeared. Nets and hands groped, missed, missed again, then caught and lifted him writhing up into the air. He struggled to take back his own shape and could not; his own spell of homecoming bound him. He writhed in the net, gasping in the dry, bright, terrible air, drowning. The agony went on, and he knew nothing beyond it.

After a long time and little by little he became aware that he was in his human form again; some sharp, sour liquid was being forced down his throat. Time lapsed again, and he found himself sprawled face down on the dank floor of the vault. He was back in the power of his enemy. And, though he could breathe again, he was not very far from death.

The chill was all through him now; and the trolls, Voll's servants, must have crushed the fragile trout-body, for when he moved, his ribcage and one forearm stabbed with pain. Broken and without strength, he lay at the bottom of the well of night. There was no power in him to change shape; there was no way out, but one.

Lying there motionless, almost but not quite beyond the reach of pain, Festin thought: Why has he not killed me? Why does he keep me here alive?

Why has he never been seen? With what eyes can he be seen, on what ground does he walk?

He fears me, though I have no strength left.

They say that all the wizards and men of power whom he has defeated live on sealed in tombs like this, live on year after year trying to get free. . . .

But if one chose not to live?

So Festin made his choice. His last thought was, If I am wrong, men will think I was a coward. But he did not linger on this thought. Turning his head a little to the side he closed his eyes, took a last deep breath, and whispered the word of unbinding, which is only spoken once.

This was not transformation. He was not changed. His body, the long legs and arms, the clever hands, the eyes that had liked to look on trees and streams, lay unchanged, only still, perfectly still and full of cold. But the walls were gone. The vaults built by magic were gone, and the rooms and towers; and the forest, and the sea, and the sky of evening. They were all gone, and Festin went slowly down the far slope of the hill of being, under new stars.

In life he had had great power; so here he did not forget. Like a candle flame he moved in the darkness of the wider land. And remembering he called out his enemy's name: "Voll!"

Called, unable to withstand, Voll came towards him, a thick pale shape in the starlight. Festin approached, and the other cowered and screamed as if burnt. Festin followed when he fled, followed him close. A long way they went, over dry lava-flows from the great extinct volcanoes rearing their cones against the unnamed stars, across the spurs of silent hills, through valleys of short black grass, past towns or down their unlit streets between houses through whose windows no face looked. The stars hung in the sky; none set, none rose. There was no change here. No day would come. But they went on, Festin always driving the other before him, till they reached a place where once a river had run, very long ago: a river from the living lands. In the dry streambed, among boulders, a dead body lay: that of an old man, naked, flat eyes staring at the stars that are innocent of death.

"Enter it," Festin said. The Voll-shadow whimpered, but Festin came closer. Voll cowered away, stooped, and entered in the open mouth of his own dead body.

At once the corpse vanished. Unmarked, stainless, the dry boulders gleamed in starlight. Festin stood still a while, then slowly sat down among the great rocks to rest. To rest, not sleep; for he must keep guard here until Voll's body, sent back to its grave, had turned to dust, all evil power gone, scattered by the wind and washed seaward by the rain. He must keep watch over this place where once death had found a way back into the other land. Patient now, infinitely patient, Festin waited among the rocks where no river would ever run again, in the heart of the country which has no seacoast. The stars stood still above him; and as he watched them, slowly, very slowly he began to forget the voice of streams and the sound of rain on the leaves of the forests of life.

JORGE LUIS BORGES

The Man on the Threshold

Jorge Luis Borges (1899–   ), versatile Argentine essayist, poet, fiction writer, translator, and diplomat, has an international reputation based particularly on his short stories. *Ficciones,* which appeared in 1945 and was reissued in 1956; *Labyrinths,* 1962; and *Prologos,* 1975, are collections of some of his better-known stories and essays.

A curious and suspicious parallel exists between the immediate characters and events of the main story here and those of the tale within the tale, which is, supposedly, of the distant past.

Bioy Casares brought back with him from London to Buenos Aires a strange dagger with a triangular blade and a hilt in the shape of an H; a friend of ours, Christopher Dewey of the British Council, told us that such weapons were commonly used in India. This statement prompted him to mention that he had held a job in that country between the two wars. (*"Ultra Auroram et Gangen,"* I recall his saying in Latin, misquoting a line from Juvenal.) Of the stories he entertained us with that night, I venture to set down the one that follows. My account will be faithful; may Allah deliver me from the temptation of adding any circumstantial details or of weighing down with interpolations from Kipling the tale's Oriental character. It should be remarked that the story has a certain ancient simplicity that it would be a pity to lose—something perhaps straight out of the Arabian Nights.

The precise geography [Dewey said] of the events I am going to relate is of little importance.

THE MAN ON THE THRESHOLD From the book *The Aleph And Other Stories, 1933–1969* by Jorge Luis Borges. Edited and translated by Norman Thomas di Giovanni in collaboration with the author. English translation © 1968, 1969, 1970 by Emecé Editores, S.A., and Norman Thomas di Giovanni; © 1970 by Jorge Luis Borges, Adolfo Bioy-Casares and Norman Thomas di Giovanni. Published by E. P. Dutton and Co., and used with their permission.

Besides, what would the names of Amritsar or Oudh mean in Buenos Aires? Let me only say, then, that in those years there were disturbances in a Muslim city and that the central government sent out one of their best people to restore order. He was a Scotsman from an illustrious clan of warriors, and in his blood he bore a tradition of violence. Only once did I lay eyes on him, but I shall not forget his deep black hair, the prominent cheekbones, the somehow avid nose and mouth, the broad shoulders, the powerful set of a Viking. David Alexander Glencairn is what he'll be called in my story tonight; the names are fitting, since they belonged to kings who ruled with an iron sceptre. David Alexander Glencairn (as I shall have to get used to calling him) was, I suspect, a man who was feared; the mere news of his coming was enough to quell the city. This did not deter him from putting into effect a number of forceful measures. A few years passed. The city and the outlying district were at peace; Sikhs and Muslims had laid aside their ancient enmities, and suddenly Glencairn disappeared. Naturally enough, there was no lack of rumors that he had been kidnapped or murdered.

These things I learned from my superior, for the censorship was strict and the newspapers made no comment on (nor did they even record, for all I recall) Glencairn's disappearance. There's a saying that India is larger than the world; Glencairn, who may have been all-powerful in the city to which he was destined by a signature scrawled across the bottom of some document, was no more than a cog in the administration of Empire. The inquiries of the local police turned up nothing; my superior felt that a civilian might rouse less suspicion and achieve greater results. Three or four days later (distances in India are generous), I was appointed to my mission and was working my way without hope of success through the streets of the commonplace city that had somehow whisked away a man.

I felt, almost at once, the invisible presence of a conspiracy to keep Glencairn's fate hidden. *There's not a soul in this city* (I suspected) *who is not in on the secret and who is not sworn to keep it.* Most people upon questioning professed an unbounded ignorance; they did not know who Glencairn was, had never seen him, had never heard anyone speak of him. Others, instead, had caught a glimpse of him only a quarter of an hour before talking to So-and-So, and they even accompanied me to the house the two had entered and in which nothing was known of them, or which they had just that moment left. Some of those meticulous liars I went so far as to knock down. Witnesses approved my outbursts, and made up other lies. I did not believe them, but neither did I dare ignore them. One afternoon, I was handed an envelope containing a slip of paper on which there was an address.

The sun had gone down when I got there. The quarter was poor but not rowdy; the house was quite low; from the street I caught a glimpse of a succession of unpaved inner courtyards, and somewhere at the far end an opening. There, some kind of Muslim ceremony was being held; a blind man entered with a lute made of a reddish wood.

At my feet, motionless as an object, an old, old man squatted on the threshold. I'll tell what he was like, for he is an essential part of the story. His many years had worn him down and polished him as smooth as water polishes a stone, or as the generations of men polish a sentence. Long rags covered him, or so it seemed to me, and the cloth he wore wound around his head was one rag more. In the dusk, he lifted a dark face and a white beard. I began speaking to him without

preamble, for by now I had given up all hope of ever finding David Alexander Glencairn. The old man did not understand me (perhaps he did not hear me), and I had to explain that Glencairn was a judge and that I was looking for him. I felt, on speaking these words, the pointlessness of questioning this old man for whom the present was hardly more than a dim rumor. *This man might give me news of the Mutiny or of Akbar* (I thought) *but not of Glencairn.* What he told me confirmed this suspicion.

"A judge!" he cried with weak surprise. "A judge who has got himself lost and is being searched for. That happened when I was a boy. I have no memory for dates, but Nikal Seyn (Nicholson) had not yet been killed before the wall of Delhi. Time that has passed stays on in memory; I may be able to summon back what happened then. God, in his wrath, had allowed people to fall into corruption; the mouths of men were full of blasphemy and of deceit and of fraud. Yet not all were evil, and when it was known that the queen was about to send a man who would carry out in this land the law of England, those who were less evil were cheered, for they felt that law is better than disorder. The Christian came to us but it was not long before he too began deceiving and oppressing us, in concealing abominable crimes, and in selling decisions. We did not blame him in the beginning; the English justice he administered was not familiar to anyone, and the apparent excesses of the new judge may have obeyed certain valid arcane reasoning. Everything must have a justification in his book, we wished to think, but his kinship with all evil judges the world over was too obvious to be overlooked, and at last we were forced to admit that he was simply a wicked man. He turned out to be a tyrant, and the unfortunate people (in order to avenge themselves for the false hopes they had once placed in him) began to toy with the idea of kidnapping him and submitting him to judgment. To talk was not enough; from plans they had to move to action. Nobody, perhaps, save the very foolish or the very young, believed that that rash scheme could be carried out, but thousands of Sikhs and Muslims kept their word and one day they executed—incredulous—what to each of them had seemed impossible. They sequestered the judge and held him prisoner in a farmhouse beyond the outskirts of the town. Then they called together all those who had been wronged by him, or, in some cases, orphans and widows, for during those years the executioner's sword had not rested. In the end—this was perhaps the most difficult—they sought and named a judge to judge the judge."

At this point, the old man was interrupted by some women who were entering the house. Then he went on, slowly.

"It is well known that there is no generation that does not include in it four upright men who are the secret pillars of the world and who justify it before the Lord: one of these men would have made the perfect judge. But where are they to be found if they themselves wander the world lost and nameless, and do not know each other when they meet, and are unaware of the high destiny that is theirs? Someone then reasoned that if fate forbade us wise men we should seek out the witless. This opinion prevailed. Students of the Koran, doctors of law, Sikhs who bear the name of lions and who worship one God, Hindus who worship a multitude of gods, Mahavira monks who teach that the shape of the universe is that of a man with his legs spread apart, worshippers of fire, and black Jews made up the court, but the final ruling was entrusted to a madman."

Here he was interrupted by people who were leaving the ceremony.

"To a madman," he repeated, "so that God's wisdom might speak through his mouth and shame human pride. His name has been forgotten, or was never known, but he went naked through the streets, or was clothed in rags, counting his fingers with a thumb and mocking at the trees."

My common sense rebelled. I said that to hand over the verdict to a madman was to nullify the trial.

"The defendant accepted the judge," was his answer, "seeing, perhaps, that because of the risk the conspirators would run if they set him free, only from a man who was mad might he not expect a sentence of death. I heard that he laughed when he was told who the judge was. The trial lasted many days and nights, drawn out by the swelling of the number of witnesses."

The old man stopped. Something was troubling him. In order to bridge the lapse, I asked him how many days.

"At least nineteen," he replied.

People who were leaving the ceremony interrupted him again; wine is forbidden to Muslims, but the faces and voices were those of drunkards. One, on passing, shouted something to the old man.

"Nineteen days—exactly," he said, setting matters straight. "The faithless dog heard sentence passed, and the knife feasted on his throat."

He had spoken fiercely, joyfully. With a different voice now he brought the story to an end. "He died without fear; in the most vile of men there is some virtue."

"Where did all this happen?" I asked him. "In a farmhouse?"

For the first time, he looked into my eyes. Then he made things clear, slowly, measuring his words. "I said that he had been confined in a farmhouse, not that he was tried there. He was tried in this city, in a house like any other, like this one. One house differs little from another; what is important to know is whether the house is built in Hell or in Heaven."

I asked him about the fate of the conspirators.

"I don't know," he told me patiently. "These things took place and were forgotten many years ago now. Maybe what they did was condemned by men, but not by the Lord."

Having said this, he got up. I felt his words as a dismissal, and from that moment I no longer existed for him. Men and women from all the corners of the Punjab swarmed over us, praying and intoning, and nearly swept us away. I wondered how, from courtyards so narrow they were little more than long passageways, so many persons could be pouring out. Others were coming from the neighboring houses; it seems they had leaped over the walls. By shoving and cursing, I forced my way inside. At the heart of the innermost courtyard, I came upon a naked man, crowned with yellow flowers, whom everyone kissed and caressed, with a sword in his hand. The sword was stained, for it had dealt Glencairn his death. I found his mutilated body in the stables out back.

DONALD BARTHELME

How I Write My Songs by Bill B. White

Donald Barthelme (1931–   ) is widely acclaimed as a leader in experimental fiction techniques. He has published novels such as *Snow White*, 1967, but he is perhaps better known for his short stories, many of which appeared originally in *The New Yorker*. His most recent collections of stories are *City Life*, 1970, *Sadness*, 1972, and *Amateurs*, 1976.

"How I Write My Songs by Bill B. White" illustrates Barthelme's experimentation with the fictional form. Told in "how to" form, the story provides Barthelme with a vehicle for ironic commentary on the cliché-ridden popular-music industry.

Some of the methods I use to write my songs will be found in the following examples. Everyone has a song in him or her. Writing songs is a basic human trait. I am not saying that it is easy; like everything else worthwhile in this world it requires concentration and hard work. The methods I will outline are a good way to begin and have worked for me but they are by no means the only methods that can be used. There is no one set way of writing your songs, every way is just as good as the other as Kipling said. (I am talking now about the lyrics; we will talk about the melodies in a little bit.) The important thing is to put true life into your songs, things that people know and can recognize and truly feel. You have to be open to experience, to what is going on around you, the things of daily life. Often little things that you don't even think about at the time can be the basis of a song.

A knowledge of all the different types of songs that are commonly accepted is helpful. To give you an idea of the various types of songs there are I am going to tell you how I wrote various of my own, including "Rudelle," "Last Night,"

"Sad Dog Blues," and others—how I came to write these songs and where I got the idea and what the circumstances were, more or less, so that you will be able to do the same thing. Just remember, *there is no substitute for sticking to it* and listening to the work of others who have been down this road before you and have mastered their craft over many years.

In the case of "Rudelle" I was sitting at my desk one day with my pencil and yellow legal pad and I had two things that were irritating me. One was a letter from the electric company that said "The check for $75.60 sent us in payment of your bill has been returned to us by the bank unhonored etc. etc." Most of you who have received this type of letter from time to time know how irritating this kind of communication can be as well as embarrassing. The other thing that was irritating me was that I had a piece of white thread tied tight around my middle at navel height as a reminder to keep my stomach pulled in to strengthen the abdominals while sitting— this is the price you pay for slopping down too much beer when your occupation is essentially a sit-down one! Anyhow I had these two things itching me, so I decided to write a lost-my-mind song.

I wrote down on my legal pad the words:

When I lost my baby
I almost lost my mine

This is more or less a traditional opening for this type of song. Maybe it was written by somebody originally way long ago and who wrote it is forgotten. It often helps to begin with a traditional or well-known line or lines to set a pattern for yourself. You can then write the rest of the song and, if you wish, cut off the top part, giving you an original song. *Songs are always composed of both traditional and new elements.* This means that you can rely on the tradition to give your song "legs" while also putting in your own experience or particular way of looking at things for the new.

Incidentally the lines I have quoted may look pretty bare to you but remember you are looking at just one element, the words, and there is also the melody and the special way various artists will have of singing it which gives flavor and freshness. For example, an artist who is primarily a blues singer would probably give the "when" a lot of squeeze, that is to say, draw it out, and he might also sing "baby" as three notes, "bay-ee-bee," although it is only two syllables. Various artists have their own unique ways of doing a song and what may appear to be rather plain or dull on paper becomes quite different when it is a song.

I then wrote:

When I lost my baby
I almost lost my mine
When I lost my baby
I almost lost my mine
When I found my baby
The sun began to shine.
Copyright © 1972 by French Music, Inc.

You will notice I retained the traditional opening because it was so traditional I did not see any need to delete it. With the addition of various material about Rudelle and what kind of woman she was, it became gold in 1976.

Incidentally while we are talking about use of traditional materials here is a little tip: you can often make good use of colorful expressions in common use such as "If the good Lord's willin' and the creek don't rise" (to give you just one example) which I used in "Goin' to Get Together" as follows:

Goin' to get to-geth-er
Goin' to get to-geth-er
If the good Lord's willin' and the creek don't rise.
Copyright © 1974 by French Music, Inc.

These common expressions are expressive of the pungent ways in which most people often think—they are the salt of your song, so to say. Try it!

It is also possible to give a song a funny or humorous "twist":

Show'd my soul to the woman at the bank
She said put that thing away boy, put that thing away
Show'd my soul to the woman at the liquor store
She said put that thing away boy, 'fore it turns the wine
Show'd my soul to the woman at the 7-Eleven
She said: Is that all?
Copyright © 1974 by Rattlesnake Music, Inc.

You will notice that the meter here is various and the artist is given great liberties.

Another type of song which is a dear favorite of almost everyone is the song that has a message, some kind of thought that people can carry away with them and think about. Many songs of this type are written and gain great acceptance every day. Here is one of my own that I put to a melody which has a kind of martial flavor:

How do you spell truth? L-o-v-e is how you spell truth
How do you spell love? T-r-u-t-h is how you spell love
Where were you last night?
Where were you last night?
Copyright © 1975 by Rattlesnake Music/A.I.M. Corp.

When "Last Night" was first recorded, the engineer said "That's a keeper" on the first take and it was subsequently covered by sixteen artists including Walls.

The I-ain't-nothin'-but-a-man song is a good one to write when you are having a dry spell. These occur in songwriting as in any other profession and if you are in one it is often helpful to try your hand at this type of song which is particularly good with a heavy rhythm emphasis in the following pattern

Da da da da *da*
Whomp, whomp

where some of your instruments are playing da da da da *da*, hitting that last note hard, and the

others answer whomp, whomp. Here is one of
my own:

> I'm just an ordinary mane
> Da da da da *da*
> Whomp, whomp
> Just an ordinary mane
> Da da da da *da*
> Whomp, whomp
> Ain't nothin' but a mane
> Da da da da *da*
> Whomp, whomp
> I'm a grizzly mane
> Da da da da *da*
> Whomp, whomp
> I'm a hello-goodbye mane
> Da da da da *da*
> Whomp, whomp
> I''m a ramblin'-gamblin' mane
> Da da da da *da*
> Whomp, whomp
> I'm a *mane's* mane
> I'm a woeman's mane
> Da da da da *da*
> Whomp, whomp
> I'm an upstairs mane

> Da da da da *da*
> Whomp, whomp
> I'm a today-and-tomorrow mane
> Da da da da *da*
> Whomp, whomp
> I'm a Freeway mane
> Da da da da *da*
> Whomp, whomp

Copyright © 1977 by French Music, Inc.

Well, you see how it is done. It is my hope that
these few words will get you started. Remember
that although this business may seem closed and
standoffish to you, looking at it from the outside,
inside it has some very warm people in it, some
of the finest people I have run into in the course
of a varied life. The main thing is to persevere
and to believe in yourself, no matter what the
attitude of others may be or appear to be. I could
never have written my songs had I failed to believe in Bill B. White, not as a matter of conceit
or false pride but as a human being. I will continue to write my songs, for the nation as a whole
and for the world.

PART 3
Drama

JOHN KEATS

On Sitting Down to Read
King Lear **Once Again**

O golden-tongued Romance, with serene lute!
   Fair plumed syren, queen of far-away!
   Leave melodizing on this wintry day,
Shut up thine olden pages, and be mute.
Adieu! for, once again, the fierce dispute
   Betwixt damnation and impassion'd clay
   Must I burn through; once more humbly assay
The bitter-sweet of this Shaksperean fruit.
Chief Poet! and ye clouds of Albion,
   Begetters of our deep eternal theme!
When through the old oak forest I am gone,
   Let me not wander in a barren dream:
But, when I am consumed in the fire,
Give me new phoenix wings to fly at my desire.

Drama developed as an art form from several closely related human characteristics, most important of which perhaps are the urge to imitate and the love of make-believe. Such tendencies are often apparent in human activity—in the games children play and in the amusement and entertainment adults enjoy. To lose oneself for a while by assuming the identity of some imagined person seems to fulfill a human need. Both the urge to imitate and the love of make-believe culminate in drama—the impulse to make a story live through action, character, dialogue, and setting.

Whether the story of a play is based upon historical, scientific, or literary (imagined) truth, watching it come to life on a stage with actors is quite different from reading a poem, a novel or short story or, for that matter, the printed version of the play itself. However, plays may be read with great pleasure and emotional and intellectual satisfaction. In fact, if we are to know much about drama, we must read plays, for the opportunity to attend a live theatrical performance is, for most of us, limited. Moreover, quiet reading of a play can reveal much that the eye and ear failed to note during the performance.

History of Drama

The ancient Greeks met on semiannual feast days to honor the god Dionysus, ruler over vegetation and wine. At first, their worship of the wine god was expressed in choral songs and dances performed by elaborately trained and costumed choruses; but with time, more and more of the dramatic, the make-believe element, was added. During an intermission, perhaps, the leader of the chorus would tell of some exploit in the god's life; later on he came to represent Dionysus himself, and to tell his story in the first person. Finally, some minor member of the chorus answered the rhetorical utterances of Dionysus, and thus dramatic dialogue and impersonation came into being. To describe this activity, the word *drama*, derived from the Greek verb *dran*, "to act or do," was used. By its etymology, therefore, drama implies action, the essence of the traditional dramatic composition.

Greek comedy and tragedy both originated in seasonal festivals. From the broad jesting burlesque natural to a rustic carnival developed comedy. From the ritualized worship of Dionysus and Apollo developed tragedy, which reached its culmination in the three great Greek playwrights Aeschylus, Sophocles, and Euripides. The classical selection included here, Sophocles' *Antigonê*, represents one of the highest achievements in Greek tragedy. Only two authors of Greek comedy are known to us—Aristophanes, whose feminist play *Lysistrata* has great timeliness today, and Menander, of whose plays we possess only a few fragments.

Greek drama was lost during the political and social upheavals of the Middle Ages and another form of drama emerged in Europe—the morality plays of the Christian Church. Everywhere confronted by ignorance and lack of schooling, the priests found dramatic representations at Easter and Christmas the easiest and most successful way to tell biblical stories to their parishioners. What started as devices for religious instruction in the absence of printing, books, and mass education soon became so popular as entertainment that the cathedrals became too small for their presentation. When moved out of the cathedrals, these plays soon fell into secular hands; the trade guilds in certain cities produced an elaborate series of pageants telling the biblical story. Thus, drama has had two analogous beginnings in Europe—once in the pagan festivals of ancient Greece, and then a thousand years later, completely unaware of its earlier beginning, in the medieval Christian Church.

Out of these religious plays of the Middle Ages and out of the school and university revivals of the previously lost Greek and Roman dramas, rediscovered during the Renaissance, grew the new drama of Western Europe. While in the English tradition the dramas of William Shakespeare have gained general preeminence, many other playwrights, both in England and on the Continent, also contributed to the revitalized form. In France, Molière, who has been called France's Shakespeare, established the dramatic satire as an art form. Nevertheless, during the Renaissance, it was English drama that reached heights making it comparable with the drama of any period.

In 1642 the new Puritan government in England forced the closing of the theatres, indicting them on moral grounds, and performances of plays ceased there for the next eighteen years. The theatres opened again in 1660, presenting the polished plays of John Dryden and, toward the end of the century, those of William Congreve and others. After the plays of Oliver Goldsmith and Richard Brinsley Sheridan in the late eighteenth century, drama both in England and on the Continent entered a period of decline lasting until Henrik Ibsen, August Strindberg, and Anton Chekhov revolutionized the dramatic form in the last quarter of the nineteenth century. Profiting in part from these continental influences—from Ibsen especially—George Bernard Shaw reestablished English drama in the world's esteem, and so it has continued into our own day, aided notably by the works of John Galsworthy (who won the Nobel Prize for Literature in 1932 and through his play *Justice* helped reform the British penal system).

In the United States powerful and original drama did not completely emerge until after the First World War, when Eugene O'Neill, heavily influenced by Strindberg and Sigmund Freud, composed plays that were to win for him the Nobel Prize for Literature in 1936. By this time such writers as Maxwell Anderson, Lillian Hellman, Sidney Howard, Elmer Rice, Robert Sherwood, Thornton Wilder, and others clearly demonstrated that American writers could take their place among the best of the modern dramatists. Immediately after World War II, Arthur Miller, Tennessee Williams, Lorraine Hansberry, LeRoi Jones, Paddy Chayevsky, and others displayed the restored dynamic power of the American theatre.

Types of Drama

A traditional play is likely to be built about a central character involved in some conflict of will—the wills of two persons who oppose each other, or the will of one person who tries to win over unfavorable circumstances, or the internally conflicting will of one person torn between two irreconcilable forces. Of course a play seldom limits itself exclusively to only one of these conflicts. *Antigonê* and *King Lear* contain all three, and in most of the other plays included in this section, the reader can almost certainly find some evidence of each of these conflicts. An exception may be Strindberg's *The Stronger*, perhaps the first performable one-act play. This play illustrates the conflict of a character torn internally by irreconcilable forces and was Strindberg's experimental effort to reduce the structure of the play to a single internal conflict.

Conventionally, drama is broadly divided into two major types: *tragedy* and *comedy*. In general, if the central character loses in this conflict of wills discussed above, the play is labeled tragic; if the character triumphs, the play is called comic. Aristotle, the Greek philosopher, believed that tragedy must excite the emotions of pity and fear, followed by the purging of these emotions, which in turn enables the audience to experience "tragic pleasure." To accomplish this series of emotional reactions during the performance of the play, the play must present a single complete action; must show a reversal from happiness to misery through a surprising discovery; must involve persons of superior attainments and power; and, finally, must be written in poetic lines of the highest quality.

Later playwrights and critics have modified some of these classical requirements. Sophocles' *Antigonê*, Shakespeare's *King Lear*, and Miller's *The Crucible* represent three changing approaches to tragedy: that of the ancient Greeks, the Elizabethans, and the dramatists of the twentieth century. In *Antigonê*, Sophocles adheres closely to the Aristotelian requirements. In *King Lear*, Shakespeare relaxes Aristotle's rule for a single action, and interweaves several subplots throughout the play. And Arthur Miller, in his "Tragedy and the Common Man," takes violent issue with Aristotle's concept of tragedy. Miller, an admirer of Henrik Ibsen's plays, has continued Ibsen's use of common persons as tragic figures and of prose instead of poetry as the language of tragedy into the twentieth century. Miller's play *The Crucible* is a prose tragedy of the "common man." Although it is set in Salem, Massachusetts, during the witchcraft trials of the seventeenth century, it has a purposeful application to the social and psychological problems of today. In Miller's *Death of a Salesman* he further symbolizes his insistence that the protagonist can be of ordinary station in life by naming the central character Willie Loman (low man).

By conventional definition, comedy has the same serious conflict as tragedy, but the conflict is resolved happily for the main character. In plays where the dramatist is interested only in clever amusement rather than the serious entertainment of the audience—that is, when the ending is happy but the conflict is inconsequential and the characterization is exaggerated—the result is properly called *farce* (or *burlesque*) rather than comedy. When the possibility of a tragic ending is averted by some unusual twist of action so that the protagonist is saved from an unhappy fate, the proper term is *melodrama,* rather than either tragedy or comedy. Many plays, films, and television dramas fall into one of these categories. While both melodrama and farce have their places in the dramatic mode, they should not be mistaken for pure tragedy or comedy. Comedy at its best is scarcely less serious in creation or purpose than tragedy, and is equally exacting not only in ideas but in plot, dialogue, character, and setting.

The comic effect derives primarily from some kind of folly, thus exposing absurd, illogical, or pretentious speech, action, or character. The function, as George Meredith observed, is to evoke thoughtful laughter arising out of the realization of our human foibles and inconsistencies. Consequently, comedy lends itself well to satire and becomes a means whereby the dramatist chastises the audience (and society) for its vices, shortcomings, and hypocrisy. In seventeenth-century France, at the court of Louis XIV, Molière's *Tartuffe,* with its portrayal of the follies and idiosyncrasies of members of the court, began to pave the way for the critical, satirical comedy of George Bernard Shaw two centuries later. Both Molière and Shaw wanted to point out how irrational, hypocritical, and pretentious human beings seem. In *Arms and the Man* Shaw exemplified the satiric potential of comedy when he called for a realistic view of war, heroes, and love, and ridiculed the melodramatic mode that had been characteristic of the English theatre until the last quarter of the nineteenth century. Shaw's plays show the realistic treatment of the Norwegian dramatist Henrik Ibsen; but Shaw preferred the comic-satiric to the tragic, a significant break with the tradition of most European dramatists of his time.

Most contemporary dramatists have disavowed the traditional dichotomy between tragedy and comedy, insisting that a play may contain elements of both. This mixture is apparent in Thornton Wilder's *The Skin of Our Teeth,* which reflects the despair that rational scientific thought in the nineteenth century produced by the middle of the twentieth century. This play is often seen as the precursor of plays stimulated by the existentialist thinking of Sartre and Camus and, thus, the real beginning of what Martin Esslin, British critic, named "the theatre of the absurd." Wilder's attitude predates the post–World War II pessimism that energized the theatre and produced John Osborne's *Look Back in Anger* and the plays of Ionesco, Beckett, Genet, and Pinter and, in the United States, Kopit and Albee. Samuel Beckett's *Waiting for Godot* remains the primary example of the play of the absurd.

Harold Pinter is probably the chief dramatist now writing in English. *The Birthday Party* typifies his mixture of realism, naturalism, expressionism, and absurdism, but he disclaims all labels, saying, in effect, that he is simply writing plays which are suitable to the last decades of the twentieth century.

SOPHOCLES

Antigonê

Translation by Dudley Fitts and Robert Fitzgerald

Sophocles (c. 496–406 B.C.), born near Athens, Greece, to a family of wealth and position, was a contemporary of the two other great Greek writers of tragedy, Aeschylus and Euripides. Only seven of his 123 plays have come down to us in complete form. His first successful tragedy was *Ajax. Antigonê* followed, then *Oedipus Rex* and *Electra.* Among the Greek dramatists of his time Sophocles was known for his innovations: increasing the size of the chorus, adding more actors, and introducing painted scenery.

Antigonê is the third and last play in Sophocles' Oedipus cycle, which also includes *Oedipus Rex* and *Oedipus at Colonus.* According to Greek legend, King Laios of Thebes and his descendants have been doomed by the god Apollo. Oedipus, supposedly killed as a baby, has survived in exile. Not knowing that he is the son of Laios and Iocastê, he kills his father. Several years later he solves the riddle of the Sphinx for the Thebans and becomes their king, marrying his mother, the widow Iocastê. When the truth is revealed, Oedipus, in horror, blinds himself and proclaims his own exile. His two sons, Eteoclês and Polyneicês, quarrel over the succession; the Thebans favor Eteoclês, and Polyneicês is driven from the city. He returns with an army, but he and Eteoclês kill each other in battle, and Creon, brother of Iocastê, succeeds to the throne. Antigonê and Ismenê, daughters of Oedipus, are discussing Creon's first official decree as the play opens.

Antigonê contains some of Sophocles' finest characterizations. The characters are more human than those in his other plays; they are governed less by the gods than by their own wills. Antigonê does not seem an unwitting victim of the gods; her tragedy arises from actions based on her own deep beliefs and emotions.

PERSONS REPRESENTED

ANTIGONÊ
ISMENÊ
EURYDICÊ
CREON
HAIMON
TEIRESIAS

A SENTRY
A MESSENGER
A BOY
SERVANTS
GUARDS

    CHORUS (with a CHORAGOS, or Leader)

SCENE

Before the palace of CREON, King of Thebes. A central double door, and two lateral doors. A platform extends the length of the façade, and from this platform three steps lead down into the orchestra, or chorus-ground.

    TIME: Dawn of the day after the repulse of the Argive army from the assault on Thebes.

PROLOGUE

(ANTIGONÊ and ISMENÊ enter from the central door of the Palace.)

ANTIGONÊ:
Ismenê, dear sister,
You would think that we had already suffered enough
For the curse on Oedipus:
I cannot imagine any grief
That you and I have not gone through. And now—
Have they told you of the new decree of our King Creon?

ISMENÊ:
I have heard nothing: I know
That two sisters lost two brothers, a double death
In a single hour; and I know that the Argive army
Fled in the night; but beyond this, nothing.

ANTIGONÊ:
I thought so. And that is why I wanted you
To come out here with me. There is something we must do.

ISMENÊ:
Why do you speak so strangely?

ANTIGONÊ:
Listen, Ismenê:
Creon buried our brother Eteoclês
With military honors, gave him a soldier's funeral,
And it was right that he should; but Polyneicês,
Who fought as bravely and died as miserably,—
They say that Creon has sworn
No one shall bury him, no one mourn for him,
But his body must lie in the fields, a sweet treasure
For carrion birds to find as they search for food.
That is what they say, and our good Creon is coming here
To announce it publicly; and the penalty—
Stoning to death in the public square!
                    There it is,
And now you can prove what you are:
A true sister, or a traitor to your family.

ISMENÊ:
Antigonê, you are mad! What could I possibly do?

ANTIGONÊ:
You must decide whether you will help me or not.

ISMENÊ:
I do not understand you. Help you in what?

ANTIGONÊ:
Ismenê, I am going to bury him. Will you come?

ISMENÊ:
Bury him! You have just said the new law forbids it.

ANTIGONÊ:
He is my brother. And he is your brother, too.

ISMENÊ:
But think of the danger! Think what Creon will do!

ANTIGONÊ:
Creon is not strong enough to stand in my way.

ISMENÊ:
Ah sister!
Oedipus died, everyone hating him
For what his own search brought to light, his
    eyes
Ripped out by his own hand; and Iocastê died,
His mother and wife at once: she twisted the
    cords
That strangled her life; and our two brothers
    died,
Each killed by the other's sword. And we are left:
But oh, Antigonê,
Think how much more terrible than these
Our own death would be if we should go against
    Creon
And do what he has forbidden! We are only
    women,
We cannot fight with men, Antigonê!
The law is strong, we must give in to the law
In this thing, and in worse. I beg the Dead
To forgive me, but I am helpless: I must yield
To those in authority. And I think it is dangerous
    business
To be always meddling.

ANTIGONÊ:
                    If that is what you think,
I should not want you, even if you asked to come.
You have made your choice, you can be what
    you want to be.
But I will bury him; and if I must die,
I say that this crime is holy: I shall lie down
With him in death, and I shall be as dear
To him as he to me.
                    It is the dead,
Not the living, who make the longest demands:
We die for ever . . .
                    You may do as you like,
Since apparently the laws of the gods mean
    nothing to you.

ISMENÊ:
They mean a great deal to me; but I have no
    strength
To break laws that were made for the public
    good.

ANTIGONÊ:
That must be your excuse, I suppose. But as for
    me,
I will bury the brother I love.

ISMENÊ:
                    Antigonê,
I am so afraid for you!

ANTIGONÊ:
                    You need not be:
You have yourself to consider, after all.

ISMENÊ:
But no one must hear of this, you must tell no
    one!
I will keep it a secret, I promise!

ANTIGONÊ:
                    Oh tell it! Tell everyone!
Think how they'll hate you when it all comes
    out
If they learn that you knew about it all the time!

ISMENÊ:
So fiery! You should be cold with fear.

ANTIGONÊ:
Perhaps. But I am doing only what I must.

ISMENÊ:
But can you do it? I say that you cannot.

ANTIGONÊ:
Very well: when my strength gives out, I shall
    do no more.

ISMENÊ:
Impossible things should not be tried at all.

ANTIGONÊ:
Go away, Ismenê:
I shall be hating you soon, and the dead will too,
For your words are hateful. Leave me my foolish
    plan:
I am not afraid of the danger; if it means death,
It will not be the worst of deaths—death without
    honor.

ISMENÊ:
Go then, if you feel that you must.
You are unwise,
But a loyal friend indeed to those who love you.

(*Exit into the Palace.* ANTIGONÊ *goes off, L.
Enter the* CHORUS.)

PÁRODOS

STROPHE 1

CHORUS:
Now the long blade of the sun, lying
Level east to west, touches with glory
Thebes of the Seven Gates. Open, unlidded
Eye of golden day! O marching light
Across the eddy and rush of Dircê's stream,

Striking the white shields of the enemy
Thrown headlong backward from the blaze of
     morning!

CHORAGOS:
Polyneicês their commander
Roused them with windy phrases,
He the wild eagle screaming
Insults above our land,
His wings their shields of snow,
His crest their marshalled helms.

ANTISTROPHE 1

CHORUS:
Against our seven gates in a yawning ring
The famished spears came onward in the night;
But before his jaws were sated with our blood,
Or pinefire took the garland of our towers,
He was thrown back; and as he turned, great
     Thebes—
No tender victim for his noisy power—
Rose like a dragon behind him, shouting war.

CHORAGOS:
For God hates utterly
The bray of bragging tongues;
And when he beheld their smiling,
Their swagger of golden helms,
The frown of his thunder blasted
Their first man from our walls.

STROPHE 2

CHORUS:
We heard his shout of triumph high in the air
Turn to a scream; far out in a flaming arc
He fell with his windy torch, and the earth struck
     him.
And others storming in fury no less than his
Found shock of death in the dusty joy of battle.

CHORAGOS:
Seven captains at seven gates
Yielded their clanging arms to the god
That bends the battle-line and breaks it.
These two only, brothers in blood,
Face to face in matchless rage,
Mirroring each the other's death,
Clashed in long combat.

ANTISTROPHE 2

CHORUS:
But now in the beautiful morning of victory
Let Thebes of the many chariots sing for joy!

With hearts for dancing we'll take leave of war:
Our temples shall be sweet with hymns of praise,
And the long night shall echo with our chorus.

SCENE I

CHORAGOS:
But now at last our new King is coming:
Creon of Thebes, Menoikeus' son.
In this auspicious dawn of his reign
What are the new complexities
That shifting Fate has woven for him?
What is his counsel? Why has he summoned
The old men to hear him?

(*Enter* CREON *from the Palace, C. He addresses
the* CHORUS *from the top step.*)

CREON:
   Gentlemen: I have the honor to inform you
that our Ship of State, which recent storms have
threatened to destroy, has come safely to harbor
at last, guided by the merciful wisdom of
Heaven. I have summoned you here this morning
because I know that I can depend upon you: your
devotion to King Laios was absolute; you never
hesitated in your duty to our late ruler Oedipus;
and when Oedipus died, your loyalty was transferred to his children. Unfortunately, as you
know, his two sons, the princes Eteoclês and
Polyneicês, have killed each other in battle; and
I, as the next in blood, have succeeded to the
full power of the throne.
   I am aware, of course, that no Ruler can expect
complete loyalty from his subjects until he has
been tested in office. Nevertheless, I say to you
at the very outset that I have nothing but contempt for the kind of Governor who is afraid,
for whatever reason, to follow the course that
he knows is best for the State; and as for the man
who sets private friendship above the public
welfare,—I have no use for him, either. I call
God to witness that if I saw my country headed
for ruin, I should not be afraid to speak out
plainly; and I need hardly remind you that I
would never have any dealings with an enemy
of the people. No one values friendship more
highly than I; but we must remember that friends
made at the risk of wrecking our Ship are not
real friends at all.
   These are my principles, at any rate, and that
is why I have made the following decision concerning the sons of Oedipus: Eteoclês, who died

as a man should die, fighting for his country, is to be buried with full military honors, with all the ceremony that is usual when the greatest heroes die; but his brother Polyneicês, who broke his exile to come back with fire and sword against his native city and the shrines of his fathers' gods, whose one idea was to spill the blood of his blood and sell his own people into slavery—Polyneicês, I say, is to have no burial: no man is to touch him or say the least prayer for him; he shall lie on the plain, unburied; and the birds and the scavenging dogs can do with him whatever they like.

This is my command, and you can see the wisdom behind it. As long as I am King, no traitor is going to be honored with the loyal man. But whoever shows by word and deed that he is on the side of the State, he shall have my respect while he is living, and my reverence when he is dead.

CHORAGOS:
If that is your will, Creon son of Menoikeus,
You have the right to enforce it: we are yours.

CREON:
That is my will. Take care that you do your part.

CHORAGOS:
We are old men: let the younger ones carry it
    out.

CREON:
I do not mean that: the sentries have been ap-
    pointed.

CHORAGOS:
Then what is it that you would have us do? ·

CREON:
You will give no support to whoever breaks this
    law.

CHORAGOS:
Only a crazy man is in love with death!

CREON:
And death it is; yet money talks, and the wisest
Have sometimes been known to count a few
    coins too many.

(*Enter* SENTRY *from L.*)

SENTRY:
I'll not say that I'm out of breath from running,
King, because every time I stopped to think
about what I have to tell you, I felt like going

back. And all the time a voice kept saying, "You fool, don't you know you're walking straight into trouble?"; and then another voice: "Yes, but if you let somebody else get the news to Creon first, it will be even worse than that for you!" But good sense won out, at least I hope it was good sense, and here I am with a story that makes no sense at all; but I'll tell it anyhow, because, as they say, what's going to happen's going to hap-pen, and—

CREON:
Come to the point. What have you to say?

SENTRY:
I did not do it. I did not see who did it. You must not punish me for what someone else has done.

CREON:
A comprehensive defense! More effective, per-
    haps,
If I knew its purpose. Come: what is it?

SENTRY:
A dreadful thing . . . I don't know how to put
it—

CREON:
Out with it!

SENTRY:
                    Well, then;
The dead man—
                    Polyneicês—

(*Pause. The* SENTRY *is overcome, fumbles for words.* CREON *waits impassively.*)

                                    out there—
                                        someone,—
New dust on the slimy flesh!

(*Pause. No sign from* CREON.)

Someone has given it burial that way, and
Gone . . .

(*Long pause.* CREON *finally speaks with deadly control.*)

CREON:
And the man who dared do this?

SENTRY:
                                    I swear I
Do not know! You must believe me!
                                        Listen:
The ground was dry, not a sign of digging, no,

Not a wheeltrack in the dust, no trace of anyone.
It was when they relieved us this morning: and
    one of them,
The corporal, pointed to it.
                                        There it was,
The strangest—
                Look:
The body, just mounded over with light dust: you
    see?
Not buried really, but as if they'd covered it
Just enough for the ghost's peace. And no sign
Of dogs or any wild animal that had been there.

And then what a scene there was! Every man
    of us
Accusing the other: we all proved the other man
    did it,
We all had proof that we could not have done
    it.
We were ready to take hot iron in our hands,
Walk through fire, swear by all the gods,
It was not I!
I do not know who it was, but it was not I!

(CREON's *rage has been mounting steadily, but
the* SENTRY *is too intent upon his story to notice
it.*)

And then, when this came to nothing, someone
    said
A thing that silenced us and made us stare
Down at the ground: you had to be told the
    news,
And one of us had to do it! We threw the dice,
And the bad luck fell to me. So here I am,
No happier to be here than you are to have me:
Nobody likes the man who brings bad news.

CHORAGOS:
I have been wondering, King: can it be that the
    gods have done this?

CREON (*furiously*):
Stop!
Must you doddering wrecks
Go out of your heads entirely? "The gods!"
Intolerable!
The gods favor this corpse? Why? How had he
    served them?
Tried to loot their temples, burn their images,
Yes, and the whole State, and its laws with it!
Is it your senile opinion that the gods love to
    honor bad men?
A pious thought!—
                        No, from the very beginning

There have been those who have whispered to-
    gether,
Stiff-necked anarchists, putting their heads to-
    gether,
Scheming against me in alleys. These are the
    men,
And they have bribed my own guard to do this
    thing.

Money!
(*Sententiously*)
There's nothing in the world so demoralizing as
    money.
Down go your cities,
Homes gone, men gone, honest hearts corrupted,
Crookedness of all kinds, and all for money!
(*To* SENTRY)
                                        But you—!
I swear by God and by the throne of God,
The man who has done this thing shall pay for it!
Find that man, bring him here to me, or your
    death
Will be the least of your problems: I'll string you
    up
Alive, and there will be certain ways to make
    you
Discover your employer before you die;
And the process may teach you a lesson you seem
    to have missed:
The dearest profit is sometimes all too dear:
That depends on the source. Do you understand
    me?
A fortune won is often misfortune.

SENTRY:
King, may I speak?

CREON:
                        Your very voice distresses me.

SENTRY:
Are you sure that it is my voice, and not your
    conscience?

CREON:
By God, he wants to analyze me now!

SENTRY:
It is not what I say, but what has been done,
    that hurts you.

CREON:
You talk too much.

SENTRY:
                        Maybe; but I've done nothing.

CREON:
Sold your soul for some silver: that's all you've
    done.

SENTRY:
How dreadful it is when the right judge judges
    wrong!

CREON:
Your figures of speech
May entertain you now; but unless you bring me
    the man,
You will get little profit from them in the end.
    (*Exit* CREON *into the Palace.*)

SENTRY:
"Bring me the man"—!
I'd like nothing better than bringing him the
    man!
But bring him or not, you have seen the last of
    me here.
At any rate, I am safe!
    (*Exit* SENTRY.)

ODE I

STROPHE 1

CHORUS:
Numberless are the world's wonders, but none
More wonderful than man; the stormgray sea
Yields to his prows, the huge crests bear him
    high;
Earth, holy and inexhaustible, is graven
With shining furrows where his plows have gone
Year after year, the timeless labor of stallions.

ANTISTROPHE 1

The lightboned birds and beasts that cling to
    cover,
The lithe fish lighting their reaches of dim water,
All are taken, tamed in the net of his mind;
The lion on the hill, the wild horse windy-maned,
Resign to him; and his blunt yoke has broken
The sultry shoulders of the mountain bull.

STROPHE 2

Words also, and thought as rapid as air,
He fashions to his good use; statecraft is his,
And his the skill that deflects the arrows of snow,
The spears of winter rain: from every wind
He has made himself secure—from all but one:
In the late wind of death he cannot stand.

ANTISTROPHE 2

O clear intelligence, force beyond all measure!
O fate of man, working both good and evil!
When the laws are kept, how proudly his city
    stands!
When the laws are broken, what of his city then?
Never may the anarchic man find rest at my
    hearth,
Never be it said that my thoughts are his
    thoughts.

SCENE II

(*Re-enter* SENTRY *leading* ANTIGONÊ.)

CHORAGOS:
What does this mean? Surely this captive woman
Is the Princess Antigonê. Why should she be
    taken?

SENTRY:
Here is the one who did it! We caught her
In the very act of burying him.—Where is
    Creon?

CHORAGOS:
Just coming from the house.

    (*Enter* CREON, *C.*)

CREON:
                        What has happened?
Why have you come back so soon?

SENTRY (*expansively*):
                                    O King,
A man should never be too sure of anything:
I would have sworn
That you'd not see me here again: your anger
Frightened me so, and the things you threatened
    me with;
But how could I tell then
That I'd be able to solve the case so soon?

No dice-throwing this time: I was only too glad
    to come!

Here is this woman. She is the guilty one:
We found her trying to bury him.
Take her, then; question her; judge her as you
    will.
I am through with the whole thing now, and glad
    of it.

CREON:
But this is Antigonê! Why have you brought her
  here?

SENTRY:
She was burying him, I tell you!

CREON (*severely*):

Is this the truth?

SENTRY:
I saw her with my own eyes. Can I say more?

CREON:
The details: come, tell me quickly!

SENTRY:

It was like this:
After those terrible threats of yours, King,
We went back and brushed the dust away from
  the body.
The flesh was soft by now, and stinking,
So we sat on a hill to windward and kept guard.
No napping this time! We kept each other
  awake.
But nothing happened until the white round sun
Whirled in the center of the round sky over us:
Then, suddenly,
A storm of dust roared up from the earth, and
  the sky
Went out, the plain vanished with all its trees
In the stinging dark. We closed our eyes and
  endured it.
The whirlwind lasted a long time, but it passed;
And then we looked, and there was Antigonê!
I have seen
A mother bird come back to a stripped nest,
  heard
Her crying bitterly a broken note or two
For the young ones stolen. Just so, when this girl
Found the bare corpse, and all her love's work
  wasted,
She wept, and cried on heaven to damn the hands
That had done this thing.
                And then she brought more dust
And sprinkled wine three times for her brother's
  ghost.

We ran and took her at once. She was not afraid,
Not even when we charged her with what she
  had done.
She denied nothing.
                And this was a comfort to me,
And some uneasiness: for it is a good thing
To escape from death, but it is no great pleasure
To bring death to a friend.

Yet I always say
There is nothing so comfortable as your own safe
  skin!

CREON (*slowly, dangerously*):
And you, Antigonê,
You with your head hanging, do you confess this
  thing?

ANTIGONÊ:
I do. I deny nothing.

CREON (*to* SENTRY):

You may go.

(*Exit* SENTRY.)

(*To* ANTIGONÊ)
Tell me, tell me briefly:
Had you heard my proclamation touching this
  matter?

ANTIGONÊ:
It was public. Could I help hearing it?

CREON:
And yet you dared defy the law.

ANTIGONÊ:

I dared.
It was not God's proclamation. That final Justice
That rules the world below makes no such laws.

Your edict, King, was strong,
But all your strength is weakness itself against
The immortal unrecorded laws of God.
They are not merely now: they were, and shall
  be,
Operative for ever, beyond man utterly.

I knew I must die, even without your decree:
I am only mortal. And if I must die
Now, before it is my time to die,
Surely this is no hardship: can anyone
Living, as I live, with evil all about me,
Think Death less than a friend? This death of
  mine
Is of no importance; but if I had left my brother
Lying in death unburied, I should have suffered.
Now I do not.
                You smile at me. Ah Creon,
Think me a fool, if you like; but it may well be
That a fool convicts me of folly.

CHORAGOS:
Like father, like daughter: both headstrong, deaf
  to reason!
She has never learned to yield.

CREON:
                                        She has much to learn.
The inflexible heart breaks first, the toughest iron
Cracks first, and the wildest horses bend their
    necks
At the pull of the smallest curb.
                                        Pride? In a slave?
This girl is guilty of a double insolence,
Breaking the given laws and boasting of it.
Who is the man here,
She or I, if this crime goes unpunished?
Sister's child, or more than sister's child,
Or closer yet in blood—she and her sister
Win bitter death for this!
    (*To* SERVANTS)
                                        Go, some of you,
Arrest Ismenê. I accuse her equally.
Bring her: you will find her sniffling in the house
    there.

Her mind's a traitor: crimes kept in the dark
Cry for light, and the guardian brain shudders;
But how much worse than this
Is brazen boasting of barefaced anarchy!

ANTIGONÊ:
Creon, what more do you want than my death?

CREON:
                                        Nothing.
That gives me everything.

ANTIGONÊ:
                    Then I beg you: kill me.
This talking is a great weariness: your words
Are distasteful to me, and I am sure that mine
Seem so to you. And yet they should not seem
    so:
I should have praise and honor for what I have
    done.
All these men here would praise me
Were their lips not frozen shut with fear of
    you.
    (*Bitterly*)
Ah the good fortune of kings,
Licensed to say and do whatever they please!

CREON:
You are alone here in that opinion.

ANTIGONÊ:
No, they are with me. But they keep their tongues
    in leash.

CREON:
Maybe. But you are guilty, and they are not.

ANTIGONÊ:
There is no guilt in reverence for the dead.

CREON:
But Eteoclês—was he not your brother too?

ANTIGONÊ:
My brother too.

CREON:
                                And you insult his memory?

ANTIGONÊ (*softly*):
The dead man would not say that I insult it.

CREON:
He would: for you honor a traitor as much as
    him.

ANTIGONÊ:
His own brother, traitor or not, and equal in
    blood.

CREON:
He made war on his country. Eteoclês defended
    it.

ANTIGONÊ:
Nevertheless, there are honors due all the dead.

CREON:
But not the same for the wicked as for the just.

ANTIGONÊ:
Ah Creon, Creon,
Which of us can say what the gods hold wicked?

CREON:
An enemy is an enemy, even dead.

ANTIGONÊ:
It is my nature to join in love, not hate.

CREON (*finally losing patience*):
Go join them, then; if you must have your love,
Find it in hell!

CHORAGOS:
But see, Ismenê comes:

    (*Enter* ISMENÊ, *guarded.*)

Those tears are sisterly, the cloud
That shadows her eyes rains down gentle sorrow.

CREON:
You too, Ismenê,
Snake in my ordered house, sucking my blood
Stealthily—and all the time I never knew
That these two sisters were aiming at my throne!
                                        Ismenê,

Do you confess your share in this crime, or deny
  it?
Answer me.

ISMENÊ:
Yes, if she will let me say so. I am guilty.

ANTIGONÊ   (*coldly*):
No, Ismenê. You have no right to say so.
You would not help me, and I will not have you
  help me.

ISMENÊ:
But now I know what you meant; and I am here
To join you, to take my share of punishment.

ANTIGONÊ:
The dead man and the gods who rule the dead
Know whose act this was. Words are not friends.

ISMENÊ:
Do you refuse me, Antigonê? I want to die with
  you:
I too have a duty that I must discharge to the
  dead.

ANTIGONÊ:
You shall not lessen my death by sharing it.

ISMENÊ:
What do I care for life when you are dead?

ANTIGONÊ:
Ask Creon. You're always hanging on his opinions.

ISMENÊ:
You are laughing at me. Why, Antigonê?

ANTIGONÊ:
It's a joyless laughter, Ismenê.

ISMENÊ:
                    But can I do nothing?

ANTIGONÊ:
Yes. Save yourself. I shall not envy you.
There are those who will praise you; I shall have
  honor, too.

ISMENÊ:
But we are equally guilty!

ANTIGONÊ:
                    No more, Ismenê.
You are alive, but I belong to Death.

CREON (*to the* CHORUS):
Gentlemen, I beg you to observe these girls:
One has just now lost her mind; the other,
It seems, has never had a mind at all.

ISMENÊ:
Grief teaches the steadiest minds to waver, King.

CREON:
Yours certainly did, when you assumed guilt with
  the guilty!

ISMENÊ:
But how could I go on living without her?

CREON:
                                    You are.
She is already dead.

ISMENÊ:
                    But your own son's bride!

CREON:
There are places enough for him to push his
  plow.
I want no wicked women for my sons!

ISMENÊ:
O dearest Haimon, how your father wrongs you!

CREON:
I've had enough of your childish talk of marriage!

CHORAGOS:
Do you really intend to steal this girl from your
  son?

CREON:
No; Death will do that for me.

CHORAGOS:
                    Then she must die?

CREON (*ironically*):
You dazzle me.
            —But enough of this talk!
(*To* GUARDS)
You, there, take them away and guard them well:
For they are but women, and even brave men
  run
When they see Death coming.

(*Exeunt* ISMENÊ, ANTIGONÊ, *and* GUARDS.)

ODE II

STROPHE 1

CHORUS:
Fortunate is the man who has never tasted God's
  vengeance!
Where once the anger of heaven has struck, that
  house is shaken
For ever: damnation rises behind each child

Like a wave cresting out of the black northeast,
When the long darkness under sea roars up
And bursts drumming death upon the wind-
   whipped sand.

ANTISTROPHE 1

I have seen this gathering sorrow from time long
   past
Loom upon Oedipus' children: generation from
   generation
Takes the compulsive rage of the enemy god.
So lately this last flower of Oedipus' line
Drank the sunlight! but now a passionate word
And a handful of dust have closed up all its
   beauty.

STROPHE 2

What mortal arrogance
Transcends the wrath of Zeus?
Sleep cannot lull him, nor the effortless long
   months
Of the timeless gods: but he is young for ever,
And his house is the shining day of high Olympos.
   All that is and shall be,
   And all the past, is his.
No pride on earth is free of the curse of heaven.

ANTISTROPHE 2

The straying dreams of men
   May bring them ghosts of joy:
But as they drowse, the waking embers burn
   them;
Or they walk with fixed eyes, as blind men walk.
But the ancient wisdom speaks for our own time:
   Fate works most for woe
   With Folly's fairest show.
Man's little pleasure is the spring of sorrow.

SCENE III

CHORAGOS:
But here is Haimon, King, the last of all your
   sons.
Is it grief for Antigonê that brings him here,
And bitterness at being robbed of his bride?

(*Enter* HAIMON.)

CREON:
We shall soon see, and no need of diviners.

                                        —Son,

You have heard my final judgment on that girl:
Have you come here hating me, or have you
   come
With deference and with love, whatever I do?

HAIMON:
I am your son, father. You are my guide.
You make things clear for me, and I obey you.
No marriage means more to me than your con-
   tinuing wisdom.

CREON:
Good. That is the way to behave: subordinate
Everything else, my son, to your father's will.
This is what a man prays for, that he may get
Sons attentive and dutiful in his house,
Each one hating his father's enemies,
Honoring his father's friends. But if his sons
Fail him, if they turn out unprofitably,
What has he fathered but trouble for himself
And amusement for the malicious?
                              So you are right
Not to lose your head over this woman.
Your pleasure with her would soon grow cold,
   Haimon,
And then you'd have a hellcat in bed and else-
   where.
Let her find her husband in Hell!
Of all the people in this city, only she
Has had contempt for my law and broken it.

Do you want me to show myself weak before
   the people?
Or to break my sworn word? No, and I will not.
The woman dies.
I suppose she'll plead "family ties." Well, let her.
If I permit my own family to rebel,
How shall I earn the world's obedience?
Show me the man who keeps his house in hand,
He's fit for public authority.
                              I'll have no dealings
With law-breakers, critics of the government:
Whoever is chosen to govern should be obeyed—
Must be obeyed, in all things, great and small,
Just and unjust! O Haimon,
The man who knows how to obey, and that man
   only,
Knows how to give commands when the time
   comes.
You can depend on him, no matter how fast
The spears come: he's a good soldier, he'll stick
   it out.

Anarchy, anarchy! Show me a greater evil!

This is why cities tumble and the great houses
    rain down,
This is what scatters armies!
No, no: good lives are made so by discipline.
We keep the laws then, and the lawmakers,
And no woman shall seduce us. If we must lose,
Let's lose to a man, at least! Is a woman stronger
    than we?

CHORAGOS:
Unless time has rusted my wits,
What you say, King, is said with point and dig-
    nity.

HAIMON (*boyishly earnest*):
Father:
Reason is God's crowning gift to man, and you
    are right
To warn me against losing mine. I cannot say—
I hope that I shall never want to say!—that you
Have reasoned badly. Yet there are other men
Who can reason, too; and their opinions might
    be helpful.
You are not in a position to know everything
That people say or do, or what they feel:
Your temper terrifies them—everyone
Will tell you only what you like to hear.
But I, at any rate, can listen; and I have heard
    them
Muttering and whispering in the dark about this
    girl.
They say no woman has ever, so unreasonably,
Died so shameful a death for a generous act:
"She covered her brother's body. Is this inde-
    cent?
She kept him from dogs and vultures. Is this a
    crime?
Death?—She should have all the honor that we
    can give her!"

This is the way they talk out there in the city.

You must believe me:
Nothing is closer to me than your happiness.
What could be closer? Must not any son
Value his father's fortune as his father does his?
I beg you, do not be unchangeable:
Do not believe that you alone can be right.
The man who thinks that,
The man who maintains that only he has the
    power
To reason correctly, the gift to speak, the soul—
A man like that, when you know him, turns out
    empty.

It is not reason never to yield to reason!

In flood time you can see how some trees bend,
And because they bend, even their twigs are safe,
While stubborn trees are torn up, roots and all.
And the same thing happens in sailing:
Make your sheet fast, never slacken,—and over
    you go,
Head over heels and under: and there's your
    voyage.
Forget you are angry! Let yourself be moved!
I know I am young; but please let me say this:
The ideal condition
Would be, I admit, that men should be right by
    instinct;
But since we are all too likely to go astray,
The reasonable thing is to learn from those who
    can teach.

CHORAGOS:
You will do well to listen to him, King,
If what he says is sensible. And you, Haimon,
Must listen to your father.—Both speak well.

CREON:
You consider it right for a man of my years and
    experience
To go to school to a boy?

HAIMON:
                    It is not right
If I am wrong. But if I am young, and right,
What does my age matter?

CREON:
You think it right to stand up for an anarchist?

HAIMON:
Not at all. I pay no respect to criminals.

CREON:
Then she is not a criminal?

HAIMON:
The City would deny it, to a man.

CREON:
And the City proposes to teach me how to rule?

HAIMON:
Ah. Who is it that's talking like a boy now?

CREON:
My voice is the one voice giving orders in this
    City!

HAIMON:
It is no City if it takes orders from one voice.

CREON:
The State is the King!

HAIMON:

                              Yes, if the State is a desert.

(pause.)

CREON:
This boy, it seems, has sold out to a woman.

HAIMON:
If you are a woman: my concern is only for you.

CREON:
So? Your "concern"! In a public brawl with your
   father!

HAIMON:
How about you, in a public brawl with justice?

CREON:
With justice, when all that I do is within my
   rights?

HAIMON:
You have no right to trample on God's right.

CREON *(completely out of control)*:
Fool, adolescent fool! Taken in by a woman!

HAIMON:
You'll never see me taken in by anything vile.

CREON:
Every word you say is for her!

HAIMON *(quietly, darkly)*:

                              And for you.
And for me. And for the gods under the earth.

CREON:
You'll never marry her while she lives.

HAIMON:
Then she must die.—But her death will cause
   another.

CREON:
Another?
Have you lost your senses? Is this an open threat?

HAIMON:
There is no threat in speaking to emptiness.

CREON:
I swear you'll regret this superior tone of yours!
You are the empty one!

HAIMON:

                  If you were not my father,
I'd say you were perverse.

CREON:
You girlstruck fool, don't play at words with me!

HAIMON:
I am sorry. You prefer silence.

CREON.

                              Now, by God—!
I swear, by all the gods in heaven above us,
You'll watch it, I swear you shall!
   (To the SERVANTS)

                              Bring her out!
Bring the woman out! Let her die before his eyes!
Here, this instant, with her bridegroom beside
   her!

HAIMON:
Not here, no; she will not die here, King.
And you will never see my face again.
Go on raving as long as you've a friend to endure
   you.
   (Exit HAIMON.)

CHORAGOS:
Gone, gone.
Creon, a young man in a rage is dangerous!

CREON:
Let him do, or dream to do, more than a man
   can.
He shall not save these girls from death.

CHORAGOS:

                              These girls?
You have sentenced them both?

CREON:

                              No, you are right.
I will not kill the one whose hands are clean.

CHORAGOS:
But Antigonê?

CREON *(somberly)*:

                  I will carry her far away
Out there in the wilderness, and lock her
Living in a vault of stone. She shall have food,
As the custom is, to absolve the State of her
   death.
And there let her pray to the gods of hell:
They are her only gods:
Perhaps they will show her an escape from
   death,
Or she may learn,

                  though late,
That piety shown the dead is pity in vain.
   (Exit CREON.)

ODE III

STROPHE

CHORUS:
Love, unconquerable
Waster of rich men, keeper
Of warm lights and all-night vigil
In the soft face of a girl:
Sea-wanderer, forest-visitor!
Even the pure Immortals cannot escape you,
And mortal man, in his one day's dusk,
Trembles before your glory.

ANTISTROPHE

Surely you swerve upon ruin
The just man's consenting heart,
As here you have made bright anger
Strike between father and son—
And none has conquered but Love!
A girl's glance working the will of heaven:
Pleasure to her alone who mocks us,
Merciless Aphroditê.

SCENE IV

CHORAGOS (as ANTIGONÊ enters guarded):
But I can no longer stand in awe of this,
Nor, seeing what I see, keep back my tears.
Here is Antigonê, passing to that chamber
Where all find sleep at last.

STROPHE 1

ANTIGONÊ:
Look upon me, friends, and pity me
Turning back at the night's edge to say
Good-by to the sun that shines for me no longer;
Now sleepy Death
Summons me down to Acheron, that cold shore:
There is no bridesong there, nor any music.

CHORUS:
Yet not unpraised, not without a kind of honor,
You walk at last into the underworld;
Untouched by sickness, broken by no sword.
What woman has ever found your way to death?

ANTISTROPHE 1

ANTIGONÊ:
How often I have heard the story of Niobê,
Tantalos' wretched daughter, how the stone

Clung fast about her, ivy-close: and they say
The rain falls endlessly
And sifting soft snow; her tears are never done.
I feel the loneliness of her death in mine.

CHORUS:
But she was born of heaven, and you
Are woman, woman-born. If her death is yours,
A mortal woman's, is this not for you
Glory in our world and in the world beyond?

STROPHE 2

ANTIGONÊ:
You laugh at me. Ah, friends, friends,
Can you not wait until I am dead? O Thebes,
O men many-charioted, in love with Fortune,
Dear springs of Dircê, sacred Theban grove,
Be witnesses for me, denied all pity,
Unjustly judged! and think a word of love
For her whose path turns
Under dark earth, where there are no more tears.

CHORUS:
You have passed beyond human daring and come
   at last
Into a place of stone where Justice sits.
I cannot tell
What shape of your father's guilt appears in this.

ANTISTROPHE 2

ANTIGONÊ:
You have touched it at last: that bridal bed
Unspeakable, horror of son and mother mingling:
Their crime, infection of all our family!
O Oedipus, father and brother!
Your marriage strikes from the grave to murder
   mine.
I have been a stranger here in my own land:
All my life
The blasphemy of my birth has followed me.

CHORUS:
Reverence is a virtue, but strength
Lives in established law: that must prevail.
You have made your choice,
Your death is the doing of your conscious hand.

EPODE

ANTIGONÊ:
Then let me go, since all your words are bitter,
And the very light of the sun is cold to me.
Lead me to my vigil, where I must have

Neither love nor lamentation; no song, but
   silence.

(CREON *interrupts impatiently.*)

CREON:
If dirges and planned lamentations could put off
   death,
Men would be singing for ever.
   (*To the* SERVANTS)
                                    Take her, go!
You know your orders; take her to the vault
And leave her alone there. And if she lives or
   dies,
That's her affair, not ours: our hands are clean.

ANTIGONÊ:
O tomb, vaulted bride-bed in eternal rock,
Soon I shall be with my own again
Where Persephonê welcomes the thin ghosts
   underground:

And I shall see my father again, and you, mother,
And dearest Polyneicês—
                              dearest indeed
To me, since it was my hand
That washed him clean and poured the ritual
   wine:
And my reward is death before my time!

And yet, as men's hearts know, I have done no
   wrong,
I have not sinned before God. Or if I have,
I shall know the truth in death. But if the guilt
Lies upon Creon who judged me, then, I pray,
May his punishment equal my own.

CHORAGOS:
                              O passionate heart,
Unyielding, tormented still by the same winds!

CREON:
Her guards shall have good cause to regret their
   delaying.

ANTIGONÊ:
Ah! That voice is like the voice of death!

CREON:
I can give you no reason to think you are mistaken.

ANTIGONÊ:
Thebes, and you my father's gods,
And rulers of Thebes, you see me now, the last
Unhappy daughter of a line of kings,
Your kings, led away to death. You will remem-
   ber

What things I suffer, and at what men's hands,
Because I would not transgress the laws of
   heaven.
   (*To the* GUARDS, *simply*)
Come: let us wait no longer.

(*Exit* ANTIGONÊ, *L., guarded.*)

ODE IV

STROPHE 1

CHORUS:
All Danaê's beauty was locked away
In a brazen cell where the sunlight could not
   come:
A small room, still as any grave, enclosed her.
Yet she was a princess too,
And Zeus in a rain of gold poured love upon her.
O child, child,
No power in wealth or war
Or tough sea-blackened ships
Can prevail against untiring Destiny!

ANTISTROPHE 1

And Dryas' son also, that furious king,
Bore the god's prisoning anger for his pride:
Sealed up by Dionysos in deaf stone,
His madness died among echoes.
So at the last he learned what dreadful power
His tongue had mocked:
For he had profaned the revels,
And fired the wrath of the nine
Implacable Sisters that love the sound of the
   flute.

STROPHE 2

And old men tell a half-remembered tale
Of horror done where a dark ledge splits the sea
And a double surf beats on the gray shores:
How a king's new woman, sick
With hatred for the queen he had imprisoned,
Ripped out his two sons' eyes with her bloody
   hands
While grinning Arês watched the shuttle plunge
Four times: four blind wounds crying for re-
   venge,

ANTISTROPHE 2

Crying, tears and blood mingled.—Piteously
   born,

Those sons whose mother was of heavenly birth!
Her father was the god of the North Wind
And she was cradled by gales,
She raced with young colts on the glittering hills
And walked untrammeled in the open light:
But in her marriage deathless Fate found means
To build a tomb like yours for all her joy.

SCENE V

(*Enter blind* TEIRESIAS, *led by a* BOY. *The
opening speeches of* TEIRESIAS *should be in
singsong contrast to the realistic lines of*
CREON.)

TEIRESIAS:
This is the way the blind man comes, Princes,
  Princes,
Lock-step, two heads lit by the eyes of one.

CREON:
What new thing have you to tell us, old
  Teiresias?

TEIRESIAS:
I have much to tell you: listen to the prophet,
  Creon.

CREON:
I am not aware that I have ever failed to listen.

TEIRESIAS:
Then you have done wisely, King, and ruled well.

CREON:
I admit my debt to you. But what have you to
  say?

TEIRESIAS:
This, Creon: you stand once more on the edge
  of fate.

CREON:
What do you mean? Your words are a kind of
  dread.

TEIRESIAS:
Listen, Creon:
I was sitting in my chair of augury, at the place
Where the birds gather about me. They were all
  a-chatter,
As is their habit, when suddenly I heard
A strange note in their jangling, a scream, a
Whirring fury; I knew that they were fighting,
Tearing each other, dying
In a whirlwind of wings clashing. And I was
  afraid.

I began the rites of burnt-offering at the altar,
But Hephaistos failed me: instead of bright flame,
There was only the sputtering slime of the fat
  thigh-flesh
Melting: the entrails dissolved in gray smoke,
The bare bone burst from the welter. And no
  blaze!

This was a sign from heaven. My boy described
  it,
Seeing for me as I see for others.

I tell you, Creon, you yourself have brought
This new calamity upon us. Our hearths and
  altars
Are stained with the corruption of dogs and
  carrion birds
That glut themselves on the corpse of Oedipus'
  son.
The gods are deaf when we pray to them, their
  fire
Recoils from our offering, their birds of omen
Have no cry of comfort, for they are gorged
With the thick blood of the dead.
                                    O my son,
These are no trifles! Think: all men make mis-
  takes,
But a good man yields when he knows his course
  is wrong,
And repairs the evil. The only crime is pride.

Give in to the dead man, then: do not fight with
  a corpse—
What glory is it to kill a man who is dead?
Think, I beg you:
It is for your own good that I speak as I do.
You should be able to yield for your own good.

CREON:
It seems that prophets have made me their espe-
  cial province.
All my life long
I have been a kind of butt for the dull arrows
Of doddering fortune-tellers!
                              No, Teiresias:
If your birds—if the great eagles of God himself
Should carry him stinking bit by bit to heaven,
I would not yield. I am not afraid of pollution:
No man can defile the gods.
                            Do what you will,
Go into business, make money, speculate
In India gold or that synthetic gold from Sardis,
Get rich otherwise than by my consent to bury
  him.

Teiresias, it is a sorry thing when a wise man
Sells his wisdom, lets out his words for hire!

TEIRESIAS:
Ah Creon! Is there no man left in the world—

CREON:
To do what?—Come, let's have the aphorism!

TEIRESIAS:
No man who knows that wisdom outweighs any
    wealth?

CREON:
As surely as bribes are baser than any baseness.

TEIRESIAS:
You are sick, Creon! You are deathly sick!

CREON:
As you say: it is not my place to challenge a
    prophet.

TEIRESIAS:
Yet you have said my prophecy is for sale.

CREON:
The generation of prophets has always loved
    gold.

TEIRESIAS:
The generation of kings has always loved brass.

CREON:
You forget yourself! You are speaking to your
    King.

TEIRESIAS:
I know it. You are a king because of me.

CREON:
You have a certain skill; but you have sold out.

TEIRESIAS:
King, you will drive me to words that—

CREON:
                         Say them, say them!
Only remember: I will not pay you for them.

TEIRESIAS:
No, you will find them too costly.

CREON:
                         No doubt. Speak:
Whatever you say, you will not change my will.

TEIRESIAS:
Then take this, and take it to heart!
The time is not far off when you shall pay back
Corpse for corpse, flesh of your own flesh.

You have thrust the child of this world into living
    night,
You have kept from the gods below the child that
    is theirs:
The one in a grave before her death, the other,
Dead, denied the grave. This is your crime:
And the Furies and the dark gods of Hell
Are swift with terrible punishment for you.

Do you want to buy me now, Creon?

                                   Not many days,
And your house will be full of men and women
    weeping,
And curses will be hurled at you from far
Cities grieving for sons unburied, left to rot
Before the walls of Thebes.

These are my arrows, Creon: they are all for you.

    (*To* BOY)
But come, child: lead me home.
Let him waste his fine anger upon younger men.
Maybe he will learn at last
To control a wiser tongue in a better head.

    (*Exit* TEIRESIAS.)

CHORAGOS:
The old man has gone, King, but his words
Remain to plague us. I am old, too,
But I cannot remember that he was ever false.

CREON:
That is true. . . . It troubles me.
Oh it is hard to give in! but it is worse
To risk everything for stubborn pride.

CHORAGOS:
Creon: take my advice.

CREON:
                         What shall I do?

CHORAGOS:
Go quickly: free Antigonê from her vault
And build a tomb for the body of Polyneicês.

CREON:
You would have me do this?

CHORAGOS:
                         Creon, yes!
And it must be done at once: God moves
Swiftly to cancel the folly of stubborn men.

CREON:
It is hard to deny the heart! But I
Will do it: I will not fight with destiny.

CHORAGOS:
You must go yourself, you cannot leave it to others.

CREON:
I will go.
—Bring axes, servants.
Come with me to the tomb. I buried her, I
Will set her free.
Oh quickly!
My mind misgives—
The laws of the gods are mighty, and a man must serve them
To the last day of his life!
(*Exit* CREON.)

PAEAN

STROPHE 1

CHORAGOS:
God of many names

CHORUS:
O Iacchos
son
of Kadmeian Sémelê
O born of the Thunder!
Guardian of the West
Regent
of Eleusis' plain
O Prince of maenad Thebes
and the Dragon Field by rippling Ismenos:

ANTISTROPHE 1

CHORAGOS:
God of many names

CHORUS:
the flame of torches
flares on our hills
the nymphs of Iacchos
dance at the spring of Castalia:
from the vine-close mountain
come ah come in ivy:
Evohé evohé! sings through the streets of Thebes

STROPHE 2

CHORAGOS:
God of many names

CHORUS:
Iacchos of Thebes
heavenly Child
of Sémelê bride of the Thunderer!

The shadow of plague is upon us:
come
with clement feet
oh come from Parnasos
down the long slopes
across the lamenting water

ANTISTROPHE 2

CHORAGOS:
Iô Fire! Chorister of the throbbing stars!
O purest among the voices of the night!
Thou son of God, blaze for us!

CHORUS:
Come with choric rapture of circling Maenads
Who cry *Iô Iacche!*
God of many names!

ÉXODOS

(*Enter* MESSENGER, *L.*)

MESSENGER:
Men of the line of Kadmos, you who live
Near Amphion's citadel:
I cannot say
Of any condition of human life "This is fixed,
This is clearly good, or bad." Fate raises up,
And Fate casts down the happy and unhappy alike:
No man can foretell his Fate.
Take the case of Creon:
Creon was happy once, as I count happiness:
Victorious in battle, sole governor of the land,
Fortunate father of children nobly born.
And now it has all gone from him! Who can say
That a man is still alive when his life's joy fails?
He is a walking dead man. Grant him rich,
Let him live like a king in his great house:
If his pleasure is gone, I would not give
So much as the shadow of smoke for all he owns.

CHORAGOS:
Your words hint at sorrow: what is your news for us?

MESSENGER:
They are dead. The living are guilty of their death.

CHORAGOS:
Who is guilty? Who is dead? Speak!

MESSENGER:

Haimon.
Haimon is dead; and the hand that killed him
Is his own hand.

CHORAGOS:

His father's? or his own?

MESSENGER:
His own, driven mad by the murder his father
   had done.

CHORAGOS:
Teiresias, Teiresias, how clearly you saw it all!

MESSENGER:
This is my news: you must draw what conclusions
   you can from it.

CHORAGOS:
But look: Eurydicê, our Queen:
Has she overheard us?

(*Enter* EURYDICÊ *from the Palace, C.*)

EURYDICÊ:
I have heard something, friends:
As I was unlocking the gate of Pallas' shrine,
For I needed her help today, I heard a voice
Telling of some new sorrow. And I fainted
There at the temple with all my maidens about
   me.
But speak again: whatever it is, I can bear it:
Grief and I are no strangers.

MESSENGER:

Dearest Lady,
I will tell you plainly all that I have seen.
I shall not try to comfort you: what is the use,
Since comfort could lie only in what is not true?
The truth is always best.

I went with Creon
To the outer plain where Polyneicês was lying,
No friend to pity him, his body shredded by dogs.
We made our prayers in that place to Hecatê
And Pluto, that they would be merciful. And we
   bathed
The corpse with holy water, and we brought
Fresh-broken branches to burn what was left of
   it,
And upon the urn we heaped up a towering
   barrow
Of the earth of his own land.
When we were done, we ran
To the vault where Antigonê lay on her couch
   of stone.

One of the servants had gone ahead,
And while he was yet far off he heard a voice
Grieving within the chamber, and he came back
And told Creon. And as the King went closer,
The air was full of wailing, the words lost,
And he begged us to make all haste. "Am I a
   prophet?"
He said, weeping, "And must I walk this road,
The saddest of all that I have gone before?
My son's voice calls me on. Oh quickly, quickly!
Look through the crevice there, and tell me
If it is Haimon, or some deception of the gods!"

We obeyed; and in the cavern's farthest corner
We saw her lying:
She had made a noose of her fine linen veil
And hanged herself. Haimon lay beside her,
His arms about her waist, lamenting her,
His love lost under ground, crying out
That his father had stolen her away from him.

When Creon saw him the tears rushed to his eyes
And he called to him: "What have you done,
   child? Speak to me.
What are you thinking that makes your eyes so
   strange?
O my son, my son, I come to you on my knees!"
But Haimon spat in his face. He said not a word,
Staring—
And suddenly drew his sword
And lunged. Creon shrank back, the blade
   missed; and the boy,
Desperate against himself, drove it half its length
Into his own side, and fell. And as he died
He gathered Antigonê close in his arms again,
Choking, his blood bright red on her white
   cheek.
And now he lies dead with the dead, and she
   is his
At last, his bride in the houses of the dead.

(*Exit* EURYDICÊ *into the Palace.*)

CHORAGOS:
She has left us without a word. What can this
   mean?

MESSENGER:
It troubles me, too; yet she knows what is best,
Her grief is too great for public lamentation,
And doubtless she has gone to her chamber to
   weep
For her dead son, leading her maidens in his
   dirge.

CHORAGOS:
It may be so; but I fear this deep silence.

(*Pause.*)

MESSENGER:
I will see what she is doing. I will go in.
(*Exit* MESSENGER *into the Palace.*)

(*Enter* CREON *with* ATTENDANTS, *bearing* HAIMON's *body.*)

CHORAGOS:
But here is the King himself: oh look at him,
Bearing his own damnation in his arms.

CREON:
Nothing you say can touch me any more.
My own blind heart has brought me
From darkness to final darkness. Here you see
The father murdering, the murdered son—
And all my civic wisdom!

Haimon my son, so young, so young to die,
I was the fool, not you; and you died for me.

CHORAGOS:
That is the truth; but you were late in learning
it.

CREON:
This truth is hard to bear. Surely a god
Has crushed me beneath the hugest weight of
heaven,
And driven me headlong a barbaric way
To trample out the thing I held most dear.

The pains that men will take to come to pain!

(*Enter* MESSENGER *from the Palace.*)

MESSENGER:
The burden you carry in your hands is heavy,
But it is not all: you will find more in your house.

CREON:
What burden worse than this shall I find there?

MESSENGER:
The Queen is dead.

CREON:
O port of death, deaf world,
Is there no pity for me? And you, Angel of evil,
I was dead, and your words are death again.
Is it true, boy? Can it be true?
Is my wife dead? Has death bred death?

MESSENGER:
You can see for yourself.

(*The doors are opened, and the body of* EURYDICÊ *is disclosed within.*)

CREON:
Oh pity!
All true, all true, and more than I can bear!
O my wife, my son!

MESSENGER:
She stood before the altar, and her heart
Welcomed the knife her own hand guided,
And a great cry burst from her lips for Megareus
dead,
And for Haimon dead, her sons; and her last
breath
Was a curse for their father, the murderer of her
sons.
And she fell, and the dark flowed in through her
closing eyes.

CREON:
O God, I am sick with fear.
Are there no swords here? Has no one a blow
for me?

MESSENGER:
Her curse is upon you for the deaths of both.

CREON:
It is right that it should be. I alone am guilty.
I know it, and I say it. Lead me in,
Quickly, friends.
I have neither life nor substance. Lead me in.

CHORAGOS:
You are right, if there can be right in so much
wrong.
The briefest way is best in a world of sorrow.

CREON:
Let it come,
Let death come quickly, and be kind to me.
I would not ever see the sun again.

CHORAGOS:
All that will come when it will; but we, mean-
while,
Have much to do. Leave the future to itself.

CREON:
All my heart was in that prayer!

CHORAGOS:
Then do not pray any more: the sky is deaf.

CREON:
Lead me away. I have been rash and foolish.

I have killed my son and my wife.
I look for comfort; my comfort lies here dead.
Whatever my hands have touched has come to
nothing.
Fate has brought all my pride to a thought of
dust.

(As CREON *is being led into the house, the*
CHORAGOS *advances and speaks directly to the*
audience.)

CHORAGOS:
There is no happiness where there is no wisdom;
No wisdom but in submission to the gods.
Big words are always punished,
And proud men in old age learn to be wise.

TRANSLATORS' COMMENTARY

Et quod propriè dicitur in idiomate Picardorum
horrescit apud Burgundos, immò apud Gallicos
viciniores; quanto igitur magis accidet hoc
apud linguas diversas! Quapropter quod bene
factum est in unâ linguâ non est possibile ut
transferatur in aliam secundum ejus proprie-
tatem quam habuerit in priori.

—ROGER BACON

I

In the Commentary appended to our version of
Euripides' *Alcestis* we wrote:

Our object was to make the *Alcestis* clear and
credible in English. Since it is a poem, it had
to be made clear as a poem; and since it is
a play, it had to be made credible as a play.
We set for ourselves no fixed rules of translation
or of dramatic verse: often we found the best
English equivalent in a literalness which extended to the texture and rhythm of the Greek
phrasing; at other times we were forced to a
more or less free paraphrase in order to achieve
effects which the Greek conveyed in ways impossible to English. Consequently, this version
of the *Alcestis* is not a "translation" in the
classroom sense of the word. The careful
reader, comparing our text with the original,
will discover alterations, suppressions, expan-
sions—a word, perhaps, drawn out into a
phrase, or a phrase condensed to a word: a way
of saying things that is admittedly not Euripidean, if by Euripidean one means a translation *ad verbum expressa* of Euripides' poem.
In defense we can say only that our purpose
was to reach—and, if possible, to render precisely—the emotional and sensible meaning in
every speech in the play; we could not follow
the Greek word for word, where to do so would
have been weak and therefore false.

We have been guided by the same principles in
making this version of the *Antigonê*.

II

We have made cuts only when it seemed absolutely necessary. The most notable excision is
that of a passage of sixteen lines beginning with
904 (Antigonê's long speech near the end of
Scene IV), which has been bracketed as spurious,
either in whole or in part, by the best critics.
Aristotle quotes two verses from it, which proves,
as Professor Jebb points out, that if it is an interpolation it must have been made soon after
Sophocles' death, possibly by his son Iophon.
However that may be, it is dismal stuff. Antigonê
is made to interrupt her lamentation by a series
of limping verses whose sense is as discordant as
their sound. We quote the Oxford translation, the
style of which is for once wholly adequate to the
occasion:

And yet, in the opinion of those who have just
sentiments, I honoured you [Polyneicês] aright.
For neither, though I had been the mother of
children, nor though my husband dying, had
mouldered away, would I have undertaken this
toil against the will of the citizens. On account
of what law do I say this? There would have
been another husband for me if the first died,
and if I lost my child there would have been
another from another man! but my father and
my mother being laid in the grave, it is impossible a brother should ever be born to me. On
the principle of such a law, having preferred
you, my brother, to all other considerations, I
seemed to Creon to commit a sin, and to dare
what was dreadful. And now, seizing me by
force, he thus leads me away, having never
enjoyed the nuptial bed, nor heard the nuptial
lay, nor having gained the lot of marriage, nor

of rearing my children; but thus I, an unhappy
woman, deserted by my friends, go, while alive,
to the cavern of the dead.

There are other excisions of less importance.
Perhaps the discussion of one of them will serve
to explain them all. Near the end of the *Éxodos*,
Creon is told of his wife's suicide. The Messenger
has five very graphic lines describing Eurydicê's
suicide, to which Creon responds with an outburst of dread and grief; yet two lines later, as
if he had not heard the first time, he is asking
the Messenger how Eurydicê died. The Messenger replies that she stabbed herself to the heart.
There is no evidence that the question and reply
are interpolations: on the contrary, they serve
the definite purpose of filling out the iambic
interlude between two lyric strophes; but in a
modern version which does not attempt to reproduce the strophic structure of this *Kommos*
they merely clog the dialogue. Therefore we
have skipped them; and the occasional suppres-
sion of short passages throughout the play is
based upon similar considerations.

III

In a like manner, we have not hesitated to use
free paraphrase when a literal rendering of the
Greek would result in obscurity. Again, the discussion of a specific instance may illuminate the
whole question.

After Antigonê has been led away to death,
the Chorus, taking a hint from her having compared her own fate to that of Niobê, proceeds
to elaborate the stories of mythological persons
who have suffered similar punishment. The
Fourth Ode cites Danaê, Lycurgos, the son of
Dryas, and Cleopatra, the daughter of Boreas and
wife of the Thracian king Phineus. Only Danaê
is mentioned by name; the others are allusively
identified. The difficulty arises from the allusive
method. Sophocles' audience would be certain
to recognize the allusions, but that is not true
of ours. To what extent can we depend upon the
audience's recognition in a day when, to quote
Mr. I. A. Richards, "we can no longer refer with
any confidence to any episode in the Bible or
to any nursery tale or any piece of mythology"?
We can assume that the story of Danaê is still
current; but Lycurgos is forgotten now, and the
sordid Phineus-Cleopatra-Eidothea affair no

longer stirs so much as an echo. Nevertheless,
Sophocles devotes two of his four strophes to this
Cleopatra, and he does it in so oblique a manner
that "translation" is out of the question. We have
therefore rendered these strophes with such
slight additions to the Greek sense as might
convey an equivalent suggestion of fable to a
modern audience.

IV

The Chorus is composed, says the Scholiast, of
"certain old men of Thebes": leading citizens
("O men many-charioted, in love with Fortune")
to whom Creon addresses his fatal decree, and
from whom he later takes advice. Sophocles'
Chorus numbered fifteen, including the Choragos,
or Leader; its function was to chant the Odes
and, in the person of the Choragos, to participate in the action. In a version designed
for the modern stage certain changes are inevitable. It cannot be urged too strongly that the
words of the Odes must be intelligible to the
audience; and they are almost certain not to be
intelligible if they are chanted in unison by so
large a group, with or without musical accompaniment. It is suggested, then, that in producing
this play no attempt be made to follow the ancient choric method. There should be no dancing. The *Párodos*, for example, should be a solemn but almost unnoticeable evolution of
moving or still patterns accompanied by a
drum-beat whose rhythm may be derived from
the cadence of the Ode itself. The lines given
to the Chorus in the Odes should probably be
spoken by single voices. The only accompaniment should be percussion: we follow Allan Sly's
score of the *Alcestis* in suggesting a large side
drum, from which the snares have been removed,
to be struck with two felt-headed tympani sticks,
one hard, one soft.

V

A careful production might make successful use
of masks. They should be of the Benda type used
in the production of O'Neill's *The Great God
Brown*: lifelike, closely fitting the contours of the
face, and valuable only as they give the effect
of immobility to character. On no account should
there be any attempt to reproduce the Greek
mask, which was larger than life size and served
a function non-existent on the modern stage—the

amplification of voice and mood for projection to the distant seats of the outdoor theater.

If masks are used at all, they might well be allotted only to those characters who are somewhat depersonalized by official position or discipline: Creon, Teiresias, the Chorus and Choragos, possibly the Messenger. By this rule, Antigonê has no mask; neither has Ismenê, Haimon, nor Eurydicê. If Creon is masked, we see no objection, in art or feeling, to the symbolic removal of his mask before he returns with the dead body of his son.

INDEX OF NAMES IN *Antigonê*

The transliteration of Greek names is an uncertain and—ultimately, perhaps—subjective matter. Certain of the entries below have more than one form, the first being that used in this translation.

ACHERON: a river of Hades

AMPHION: a prince of Orchomenos who married NIOBÊ, *q.v.;* hence, an ancestor of Oedipus

ANTIGONÊ: a daughter of Oedipus; in *Antigonê* affianced to HAIMON, *q.v.*

APHRODITÊ: goddess of love

APOLLO: god of the sun

ARÊS: god of war

ARGIVE: Greek

ARGOS: capital of Argolis, in the Peloponnesos

ARTEMIS: goddess of the hunt, sister of Apollo

ATHENA, ATHENÊ: daughter of Zeus, tutelary goddess of Athens

CASTALIA: a spring sacred to the Muses, on Mount Parnassos

CREON, KREON: brother of IOCASTÊ, *q.v.;* father of HAIMON and MEGAREUS, *qq.v.;* King of Thebes after the death of Polyneicês and Eteoclês

DANAÊ: a princess of Argos, confined by her father in a brazen chamber underground (or, some say, in a brazen tower), where she was seduced by Zeus in the form of a golden rain and bore him Perseus

DELPHI, DELPHOI: a city of Phokis, seat of a celebrated Oracle of Apollo

DEMÉTER: a sister of Zeus, goddess of agriculture

DIONYSOS, DIONYSUS: son of Zeus and SÉMELÊ, *q.v.;* god of wine

DIRCÊ, DIRKÊ: a spring near Thebes

DRYAS: a king of Thrace; father of Lykûrgos, who was driven mad by Dionysos

ELEUSIS: a city in Attica, sacred to Deméter and Persephonê; hence the adjective ELEUSINIAN

ETEOCLÊS, ETEOKLÊS: a son of Oedipus and Iocastê; brother of POLYNEICÊS, *q.v.*

EURYDICÊ, EURYDIKÊ: wife of CREON, *q.v.*

FURIES: the infernal spirits of Divine Vengeance

HAIMON, HAEMON: a son of Creon; affianced to Antigonê

HECATÊ: a goddess of the Titan race; identified with various other deities, as Selenê in heaven, Artemis on earth, and Persephonê in Hades; generally, a goddess of sorcery and witchcraft

HEPHAISTOS, HEPHAESTUS: god of fire

IACCHOS: a name for DIONYSOS, *q.v.*

IOCASTÊ, JOCASTA: wife of LAÏOS, *q.v.;* after Laïos' death, wife of Oedipus, and, by him, mother of ANTIGONÊ, ISMENÊ, POLYNEICÊS and ETEOCLÊS, *qq.v.*

ISMENÊ: a daughter of Oedipus and Iocastê; sister of Antigonê

ISMENOS: a river of Thebes, sacred to Apollo

KADMOS, CADMUS: the legendary founder of Thebes; father of SÉMELÊ, *q.v.*

LAÏOS, LAIUS: a king of Thebes; father of Oedipus, killed by him in fulfillment of an oracle

MAENAD: a priestess of DIONYSOS, *q.v.*

MEGAREUS: a son of CREON, *q.v.;* died during the assault of the Seven against Thebes

MENOIKEUS: father of CREON and IOCASTÊ, *qq.v.*

MUSES: nine daughters of Zeus and the nymph Mnemosynê, goddesses presiding over the arts and sciences

NIOBÊ: wife of AMPHION, *q.v.;* mother of fourteen children killed, because of her pride, by Apollo and Artemis; transformed into a rock on Mt. Sipylos

OEDIPUS: son of LAÏOS and IOCASTÊ, *qq.v.*

OLYMPOS, OLYMPUS: a Thessalian mountain, the seat of the gods

PALLAS: an epithet of ATHENA, *q.v.*

PARNASSOS, PARNASOS, PARNASSUS: a mountain sacred to Apollo; at its foot are Delphi and the Castalian Spring

PELOPS: a son of Tantalos; father of Atreus

PERSEPHONÊ: daughter of DEMÉTER, *q.v.;* Queen of Hades

PHOKIS: a kingdom on the Gulf of Corinth

PLUTO: brother of Zeus and Poseidon; King of Hades

POLYNEICÊS, POLYNEIKÊS: a son of Oedipus and Iocastê; killed by his brother Eteoclês, whom he killed at the same time, during the assault upon Thebes

SARDIS: a city in Lydia

SÉMELÊ: a daughter of KADMOS, q.v.; mother, by Zeus, of the god Dionysos

SPHINX: a riddling she-monster who killed herself when Oedipus solved her riddle

TANTALOS, TANTALUS: a king of Phrygia, father of PELOPS and NIOBÊ, qq.v.

TEIRESIAS, TIRESIAS: a blind prophet of Thebes, counsellor of Oedipus and Creon

ZEUS: father of gods and men

D.F.
R.F.

WILLIAM SHAKESPEARE

King Lear

William Shakespeare (1564–1616) is England's greatest dramatist and, except for the ancient Greek writers of tragedy, he probably has no peer in world dramatic literature. Born at Stratford-on-Avon, he attended the grammar school there, married Anne Hathaway in 1582, and had three children. For a brief time he taught in Stratford before moving to London in 1586, where he became an actor at two theatres. Later he performed at the Curtain, the Globe, and Blackfriars Theatres, acting in Ben Jonson's *Every Man in His Humour*, 1598, and *Sejanus*, 1603. His own earliest play, probably written in 1591, was *Henry VI*, followed by *Richard III* and *The Comedy of Errors*, 1592–93. He then composed his greatest plays: *Hamlet*, 1602; *Othello*, 1604; *Macbeth*, 1606; *King Lear*, 1607. Shakespeare wrote 38 plays in all and a great deal of poetry, including a sequence of sonnets, which are the poems of his most often read today.

King Lear, often said to be Shakespeare's greatest play, is not necessarily his best known or most often read. Its grand scale and deep pessimism seem to be too forbidding for some readers and audiences, and its demands on actors for a great range of ability make it difficult to cast. Its story, which comes from an old fable often told in chronicles of early English history, contains parallel plots—the suffering of Lear and the destruction of Gloucester. One critic has said that it seemed as if Shakespeare wanted to show a world of men and women turned to beasts, with only a few redeemed from such a fate of nature.

DRAMATIS PERSONAE

LEAR, *King of Britain*
KING OF FRANCE
DUKE OF BURGUNDY
DUKE OF CORNWALL
DUKE OF ALBANY
EARL OF KENT
EARL OF GLOUCESTER
EDGAR, *son to Gloucester*
EDMUND, *bastard son to Gloucester*
CURAN, *a courtier*
OLD MAN, *tenant to Gloucester*
DOCTOR
FOOL

OSWALD, *steward to Goneril*
A CAPTAIN *employed by Edmund*
GENTLEMAN *attendant on Cordelia*
HERALD
SERVANTS *to Cornwall*

GONERIL
REGAN } *daughters to Lear*
CORDELIA

KNIGHTS *of Lear's train*, CAPTAINS, MESSENGERS, SOLDIERS, *and* ATTENDANTS

SCENE—*Britain.*

ACT I

SCENE I.° KING LEAR'S *palace.*

[*Enter* KENT, GLOUCESTER, *and* EDMUND.]

KENT: I thought the King had more affected°
the Duke of Albany than Cornwall.

GLO: It did always seem so to us. But now, in
the division of the kingdom, it appears not which
of the Dukes he values most, for equalities are so
weighed that curiosity in neither can make
choice of either's moiety.°   7

KENT: Is not this your son, my lord?

GLO: His breeding, sir, hath been at my
charge. I have so often blushed to acknowledge
him that now I am brazed° to it.   11

KENT: I cannot conceive° you.

GLO: Sir, this young fellow's mother could.
Whereupon she grew round-wombed, and had
indeed, sir, a son for her cradle ere she had a
husband for her bed. Do you smell a fault?   16

KENT: I cannot wish the fault undone, the
issue° of it being so proper.°

GLO: But I have, sir, a son by order of law,
some year elder than this, who yet is no dearer in
my account. Though this knave came something
saucily into the world before he was sent for, yet
was his mother fair, there was good sport at his
making, and the whoreson° must be acknowledged. Do you know this noble gentleman, Ed-
mund?   26

EDM: No, my lord.

GLO: My Lord of Kent. Remember him hereafter as my honorable friend.

EDM: My services to your lordship.   30

KENT: I must love you, and sue to know you
better.

EDM: Sir, I shall study deserving.°

GLO: He hath been out nine years, and away
he shall again. The King is coming.   35

[*Sennet.° Enter one bearing a coronet,°* KING
LEAR, CORNWALL, ALBANY, GONERIL, REGAN,
CORDELIA, *and* ATTENDANTS.]

LEAR: Attend° the lords of France and Burgundy, Gloucester.

GLO: I shall, my liege.

[*Exeunt* GLOUCESTER *and* EDMUND.]

LEAR: Meantime we shall express our darker
purpose.°   39
Give me the map there. Know that we have di-
vided
In three our kingdom. And 'tis our fast intent
To shake all cares and business from our age,
Conferring them on younger strengths while we
Unburdened crawl toward death. Our son° of
Cornwall,
And you, our no less loving son of Albany,   45
We have this hour a constant will° to publish
Our daughters' several° dowers, that future strife
May be prevented° now. The Princes, France
and Burgundy,
Great rivals in our youngest daughter's love,
Long in our Court have made their amorous so-
journ,   50
And here are to be answered. Tell me, my daugh-
ters,
Since now we will divest us both of rule,
Interest of territory, cares of state,
Which of you shall we say doth love us most?
That we our largest bounty may extend   55
Where nature doth with merit challenge.°
Goneril,
Our eldest-born, speak first.

GON: Sir, I love you more than words can
wield° the matter,
Dearer than eyesight, space, and liberty,
Beyond what can be valued, rich or rare,   60
No less than life, with grace, health, beauty,
honor,
As much as child e'er loved or father found—
A love that makes breath poor and speech un-
able—

Act I, Sc. i: As the opening words of this scene show, Lear
has already decided on the division of the kingdom. There
remains only the public and ceremonious announcement of
his abdication.   **1. more affected:** had more affection
for.   **5–7. equalities . . . moiety:** for their shares are so
equal that a close examination (*curiosity*) cannot decide
which share (*moiety*) is to be preferred.   **11. brazed:** become brazen; lit., brass-plated.   **12. conceive:** understand.   **18. issue:** result; i.e., child. **proper:** handsome.
24. whoreson: rogue; lit., son of a whore.   **33. I . . . deserving:** I shall do my best to deserve your favor.

---

35 s.d., Sennet: trumpet call used to announce the approach
of a procession. **coronet:** a small crown worn by those of lesser
rank than King.   **36. Attend:** wait on.   **39. we . . . purpose:** we will explain what we have hitherto kept dark. Lear,
speaking officially as King, uses the royal "we."   **44. son:**
son-in-law.   **46. constant will:** firm intention.   **47. several:** separate.   **48. prevented:** forestalled.   **56. Where
. . . challenge:** where natural affection and desert have an
equal claim on my bounty.   **58. wield:** declare.

Beyond all manner of so much° I love you.
  COR: [*Aside*] What shall Cordelia do? Love,
    and be silent.   65
  LEAR: Of all these bounds, even from this line
    to this,
With shadowy forests and with champaigns
    riched,°
With plenteous rivers and wide-skirted meads,°
We make thee lady. To thine and Albany's issue
Be this perpetual. What says our second daugh-
    ter,   70
Our dearest Regan, wife to Cornwall? Speak.
  REG: I am made of that self metal° as my sis-
    ter,
And prize me at her worth.° In my true heart
I find she names my very deed of love,
Only she comes too short. That I profess   75
Myself an enemy to all other joys
Which the most precious square of sense
    possesses,°
And find I am alone felicitate°
In your dear Highness' love.
  COR: [*Aside*] Then poor Cordelia!
And yet not so, since I am sure my love's   81
More ponderous than my tongue.°
  LEAR: To thee and thine hereditary ever
Remain this ample third of our fair kingdom,
No less in space, validity° and pleasure   85
Than that conferred on Goneril. Now, our joy,
Although the last, not least, to whose young love
The vines of France and milk of Burgundy
Strive to be interested,° what can you say to
    draw
A third more opulent than your sisters? Speak.
  COR: Nothing, my lord.   91
  LEAR: Nothing!
  COR: Nothing.
  LEAR: Nothing will come of nothing.° Speak
    again.
  COR: Unhappy that I am, I cannot heave   95
My heart into my mouth. I love your Majesty

According to my bond,° nor more nor less.
  LEAR: How, how, Cordelia! Mend your
    speech a little,
Lest it may mar your fortunes.
  COR: Good my lord,
You have begot me, bred me, loved me. I   101
Return those duties back as are right fit,
Obey you, love you, and most honor you.
Why have my sisters husbands if they say
They love you all? Haply,° when I shall wed,
That lord whose hand must take my plight° shall
    carry   106
Half my love with him, half my care and duty.
Sure, I shall never marry like my sisters,
To love my father all.
  LEAR: But goes thy heart with this?   110
  COR: Aye, good my lord.
  LEAR: So young, and so untender?
  COR: So young, my lord, and true.
  LEAR: Let it be so. Thy truth then be thy
    dower.
For, by the sacred radiance of the sun,   115
The mysteries of Hecate,° and the night,
By all the operation of the orbs°
From whom we do exist and cease to be,
Here I disclaim° all my paternal care,
Propinquity,° and property of blood,°   120
And as a stranger to my heart and me
Hold thee from this forever. The barbarous
    Scythian,°
Or he that makes his generation messes
To gorge his appetite° shall to my bosom
Be as well neighbored, pitied, and relieved° 125
As thou my sometime daughter.
  KENT: Good my liege—
  LEAR: Peace, Kent!
Come not between the dragon° and his wrath.
I loved her most, and thought to set my rest°

---

64. **Beyond . . . much:** i.e., beyond all these things.
67. **champaigns riched:** enriched with fertile fields.
68. **wide-skirted meads:** extensive pasture lands. 72. **self metal:** same material. 73. **prize . . . worth:** value me at the same price. 77. **most . . . possesses:** feeling in the highest degree possesses. **square:** the carpenter's rule; i.e., measurement. 78. **felicitate:** made happy. 81-82. **love's . . . tongue:** love is heavier than my words. 85. **validity:** value. 89. **interested:** have a share in. 94. **Nothing . . . nothing:** the old maxim *Ex nihilo nihil fit.*

97. **bond:** i.e., the tie of natural affection and duty which binds daughter to father. 105. **Haply:** it may happen. 106. **plight:** promise made at betrothal. 116. **Hecate:** goddess of witchcraft. 117. **orbs:** stars. 119. **disclaim:** renounce. 120. **Propinquity:** relationship. **property of blood:** claim which you have as being of my blood. 122. **Scythian:** inhabitant of South Russia, regarded as the worst kind of savage. 123-24. **Or . . . appetite:** or he that feeds gluttonously on his own children. 125. **relieved:** helped in distress. 129. **dragon:** the Dragon of Britain was Lear's heraldic device and also a symbol of his ferocity. 130. **set . . . my rest:** lit., to risk all—a term in the card game called primero. Lear uses it with the double meaning of "find rest."

On her kind nursery.° Hence, and avoid° my
    sight!   131
So be my grave my peace, as here I give
Her father's heart from her! Call France. Who
    stirs?
Call Burgundy. Cornwall and Albany,
With my two daughters' dowers digest° this
    third.   135
Let pride, which she calls plainness,° marry her.
I do invest you jointly with my power,
Pre-eminence,° and all the large effects
That troop with majesty.° Ourself, by monthly
    course,°
With reservation of a hundred knights   140
By you to be sustained, shall our abode
Make with you by due turns. Only we still retain
The name and all the additions° to a king.
The sway, revenue, execution of the rest,
Belovèd Sons, be yours, which to confirm, 145
This coronet° part betwixt you.
            KENT: Royal Lear,
Whom I have ever honored as my King,
Loved as my father, as my master followed,
As my great patron thought on in my prayers—
        LEAR: The bow is bent and drawn, make from
            the shaft.°   151
        KENT: Let it fall rather, though the fork° in-
            vade
The region of my heart. Be Kent unmannerly
When Lear is mad. What wouldst thou do, old
    man?°
Think'st thou that duty shall have dread to speak
When power to flattery bows? To plainness hon-
    or's bound   156
When majesty stoops to folly.° Reverse thy
    doom,°

And in thy best consideration check
This hideous rashness. Answer my life my judg-
    ment,
Thy youngest daughter does not love thee least,
Nor are those empty-hearted whose low sound
Reverbs° no hollowness.   162
        LEAR: Kent, on thy life, no
            more.
    KENT: My life I never held but as a pawn°
To wage against thy enemies, nor fear to lose it,
Thy safety being the motive.   166
        LEAR: Out of my sight!
    KENT: See better, Lear, and let me still remain
The true blank° of thine eye.
        LEAR: Now, by Apollo——   170
        KENT: Now, by Apollo, King,
Thou swear'st thy gods in vain.
        LEAR: O vassal!° Miscreant!°
            [Laying his hand on his sword.]
    ALB. & CORN: Dear sir, forbear.
    KENT: Do.   175
Kill thy physician, and the fee bestow
Upon the foul disease. Revoke thy doom,
Or whilst I can vent clamor° from my throat
I'll tell thee thou dost evil.   179
        LEAR: Hear me, recreant!°
On thy allegiance,° hear me!
Since thou hast sought to make us break our vow,
Which we durst never yet, and with strained°
    pride
To come between our sentence and our
    power°—   184
Which nor our nature nor our place can bear,
Our potency made good° —take thy reward.
Five days we do allot thee, for provision°
To shield thee from diseases of the world,
And on the sixth to turn thy hated back   189
Upon our kingdom. If on the tenth day following
Thy banished trunk° be found in our dominions,
The moment is thy death. Away! By Jupiter,

---

131. nursery: care. **avoid:** depart from. **135. digest:** absorb. **136. plainness:** honest plain speech. **138. Pre-eminence:** authority. **138–39. large . . . majesty:** the outward show of power that goes with rule. **139. course:** turn. **143. additions:** titles of honor. **146. coronet:** i.e., the coronet which was to have been the symbol of Cordelia's kingdom. **151. shaft:** arrow. **152. fork:** point of a forked arrow. **154. old man:** Kent, who is as quick-tempered as Lear, has lost control of his tongue. The phrase to a still ruling king is grossly insulting. **155–57. Think'st . . . folly:** This is one of many passages in *Lear* where the abstract is strikingly and effectively used for the person. It means: "Do you think that a man who keeps his sense of duty will be afraid to speak when he sees a king yielding to his flatterers? An honorable man is forced to speak plainly when a king becomes a fool." **157. doom:** sentence.

162. Reverbs: re-echoes. **164. pawn:** a pledge to be sacrificed. **169. blank:** aim; i.e., something which you look at. The blank is the center of the target. **173. vassal:** wretch. **Miscreant:** lit., misbeliever. **178. vent clamor:** utter a cry. **180. recreant:** traitor. **181. On . . . allegiance:** The most solemn form of command that can be laid upon a subject, for to disobey it is to commit high treason. **183. strained:** excessive. **184. To . . . power:** to interpose yourself between my decree and my royal will; i.e., to make me revoke an order. **186. Our . . . good:** my power being now asserted. **187. for provision:** for making your preparations. **191. trunk:** body.

This shall not be revoked.   193

KENT: Fare° thee well, King. Sith° thus thou
    wilt appear,

Freedom lives hence, and banishment is here.

[*To* CORDELIA] The gods to their dear shelter take
    thee, maid,

That justly think'st and hast most rightly said!

[*To* REGAN *and* GONERIL] And your large°
    speeches may your deeds approve,°

That good effects° may spring from words of
    love.

Thus Kent, O Princes, bids you all adieu.   200

He'll shape his old course in a country new.

                                              [*Exit.*]

[*Flourish.°   Re-enter* GLOUCESTER, *with*
    FRANCE, BURGUNDY, *and* ATTENDANTS.]

GLO: Here's France and Burgundy, my noble
    lord.

LEAR: My lord of Burgundy,   203

We first address toward you, who with this King
Hath rivaled for our daughter. What, in the least,
Will you require° in present° dower with her,
Or cease your quest of love?

BUR: Most royal Majesty,

I crave no more than what your Highness of-
    fered,

Nor will you tender° less.   210

LEAR: Right noble Burgundy,

When she was dear° to us, we did hold her
    so,

But now her price is fall'n. Sir, there she stands.
If aught within that little seeming substance,°
Or all of it, with our displeasure pieced°   215
And nothing more, may fitly like° your Grace,
She's there, and she is yours.

BUR: I know no answer.

LEAR: Will you, with those infirmities she
    owes,°

Unfriended, new-adopted to our hate,   220

Dowered with our curse and strangered with our
    oath,°

Take her, or leave her?

BUR: Pardon me, royal sir,

Election makes not up on such conditions.°

LEAR: Then leave her, sir. For, by the power
    that made me,   225

I tell you all her wealth. [*To* FRANCE] For you,
    great King,

I would not from your love make such a stray,°
To match you where I hate. Therefore beseech
    you

To avert your liking° a more worthier way
Than on a wretch whom Nature is ashamed
Almost to acknowledge hers.   231

FRANCE: This is most strange,

That she that even but now was your best object,
The argument° of your praise, balm of your age,
Most best, most dearest, should in this trice of
    time   235

Commit a thing so monstrous, to dismantle°
So many folds of favor. Sure, her offense
Must be of such unnatural degree
That monsters it,° or your forevouched° affec-
    tion

Fall'n into taint.° Which to believe of her   240
Must be a faith that reason without miracle
Could never plant in me.°

COR: I yet beseech your Majesty—

If for I want that glib and oily art,
To speak and purpose not,° since what I well
    intend   245

I'll do 't before I speak—that you make known
It is no vicious blot,° murder, or foulness,
No unchaste action or dishonored step,
That hath deprived me of your grace and favor,
But even for want of that for which I am richer,
A still-soliciting° eye, and such a tongue   251
As I am glad I have not, though not to have it

194-201. Fare . . . new: The rhyme in this passage and elsewhere in the play is used for the particular purpose of stiffening the speech and giving it a special prophetic or moral
significance; cf. III.vi.112-23.   **194. Sith:** since.
198. large: fine-sounding. **approve:** i.e., be shown in
deeds.   **199. effects:** results.   **201 s.d., Flourish:** trumpet
fanfare.   **206. require:** request. **present:** immediate.
210. tender: offer.   **212. dear:** in the double sense of "beloved" and "valuable."   **214. little . . . substance:** creature that seems so small. Part of Lear's anger with Cordelia is
that so small a body seems to hold so proud a heart.
215. pieced: added to it.   **216. fitly like:** suitably
please.   **219. owes:** possesses.

221. strangered . . . oath: made a stranger to me by my
oath.   **224. Election . . . conditions:** i.e., one does not
choose one's wife on such conditions.   **227. from . . . stray:**
remove myself so far from showing love to you.   **229. avert
. . . liking:** turn your affection.   **234. argument:** topic.
236. dismantle: lit., take off (as a cloak).   **239. monsters it:**
makes it a monster. **forevouched:** previously declared.
240. Fall'n . . . taint: become bad.   **240-42. Which . . .
me:** that is so contrary to reason that only a miracle could
make me believe it.   **245. and . . . not:** and not mean
it.   **247. vicious blot:** vicious act which blots my honor.
251. still-soliciting: always begging favors.

Hath lost me in° your liking.

LEAR: Better thou
Hadst not been born than not to have pleased me
better.   255

FRANCE: Is it but this? A tardiness in nature°
Which often leaves the history unspoke
That it intends to do? My Lord of Burgundy,
What say you to the lady? Love's not love
When it is mingled with regards that stand 260
Aloof from the entire point.° Will you have her?
She is herself a dowry.

BUR: Royal Lear,
Give but that portion which yourself proposed,
And here I take Cordelia by the hand,   265
Duchess of Burgundy.

LEAR: Nothing. I have sworn, I am firm.

BUR: I am sorry then you have so lost a father
That you must lose a husband.

COR: Peace be with Burgundy! 270
Since that respects of fortune° are his love,
I shall not be his wife.

FRANCE: Fairest Cordelia, that art most rich
being poor,
Most choice forsaken, and most loved despised,
Thee and thy virtues here I seize upon,   275
Be it lawful I take up what's cast away.
Gods, gods! 'Tis strange that from their cold'st
neglect
My love should kindle to inflamed respect.°
Thy dowerless daughter, King, thrown to my
chance,
Is Queen of us, of ours, and our fair France.
Not all the dukes of waterish° Burgundy   281
Can buy this unprized precious maid of me.
Bid them farewell, Cordelia, though unkind.
Thou losest here, a better where to find.

LEAR: Thou hast her, France. Let her be
thine, for we   285
Have no such daughter, nor shall ever see
That face of hers again. Therefore be gone
Without our grace, our love, our benison.°
Come, noble Burgundy. [Flourish. Exeunt all
but FRANCE, GONERIL, REGAN, and COR-
DELIA.]

FRANCE: Bid farewell to your sisters.   290

COR: The jewels of our father,° with washed°
eyes
Cordelia leaves you. I know you what you are,
And, like a sister, am most loath to call
Your faults as they are named. Use well our fa-
ther.
To your professèd° bosoms I commit him.   295
But yet, alas, stood I within his grace,°
I would prefer° him to a better place.
So farewell to you both.

REG: Prescribe not us our duties.   299

GON: Let your study
Be to content your lord, who hath received you
At   Fortune's   alms.°   You   have   obedience
scanted.°
And well are worth the want that you have
wanted.°

COR: Time shall unfold what plaited° cunning
hides.
Who cover faults, at last shame them derides.
Well may you prosper!   306

FRANCE: Come, my fair Cordelia.
[Exeunt FRANCE and CORDELIA.]

GON: Sister,° it is not a little I have to say of
what most nearly appertains to us both. I think
our father will hence tonight.   310

REG: That's most certain, and with you, next
month with us.

GON: You see how full of changes his age is,
the observation we have made of it hath not been
little. He always loved our sister most, and with
what poor judgment he hath now cast her off
appears too grossly.   317

REG: 'Tis the infirmity of his age. Yet he hath
ever but slenderly known himself.

GON: The best and soundest of his time hath
been but rash. Then must we look to receive
from his age not alone the imperfections of long-
ingrafted condition,° but therewithal the unruly

---

253. **lost me in:** deprived me of.   256. **tardiness in nature:**
natural slowness.   260–61. **When . . . point:** when it is
mixed with other motives (the amount of the dowry) which
have nothing to do with the thing itself (love).   271. **respects of fortune:** considerations of my dowry.   278. **inflamed respect:** warmer affection.   281. **waterish:** with the
double meaning of "with many rivers" and "feeble."
288. **benison:** blessing.

291. **The . . . father:** i.e., creatures whom my father values so
highly. **washed:** weeping, but also made clearsighted by
tears.   295. **professèd:** which profess such love.
296. **within . . . grace:** in his favor.   297. **prefer:** promote.   302. **At . . . alms:** as an act of charity from Fortune. **scanted:** neglected.   303. **And . . . wanted:** and well
deserve the same lack of love which you have shown.
304. **plaited:** pleated, enfolded. Cf. ll. 236–37.   308–34.
Sister . . . heat: The abrupt change from rhyme to prose
marks the change from the emotion of the previous episodes
to the cynical frankness of the two sisters.   322–23. **long-
ingrafted condition:** temper which has long been part of his
nature.

waywardness that infirm and choleric years
bring with them.   325

REG: Such unconstant starts° are we like to
have from him as this of Kent's banishment.

GON: There is further compliment° of leave-
taking between France and him. Pray you, let's
hit° together. If our father carry authority with
such dispositions° as he bears, this last surrender
of his will but offend us.   332

REG: We shall further think on 't.

GON: We must do something, and i' the heat.°
                                        [*Exeunt.*]

SCENE II. *The* EARL OF GLOUCESTER's *castle.*

[*Enter* EDMUND, *with a letter.*]

EDM: Thou, Nature,° art my goddess, to thy
    law
My services are bound. Wherefore should I
Stand in the plague of custom, and permit
The curiosity of nations to deprive me,
For that I am some twelve or fourteen
    moonshines   5
Lag of a brother?° Why bastard? Wherefore
    base?
When my dimensions are as well compact,°
My mind as generous° and my shape as true,
As honest madam's issue? Why brand they us
With base? With baseness? Bastardy? Base, base?
Who in the lusty stealth of nature take   11
More composition and fierce quality°
Than doth, within a dull, stale, tired bed,
Go to the creating a whole tribe of fops°
Got° 'tween asleep and wake? Well then,   15
Legitimate Edgar, I must have your land.
Our father's love is to the bastard Edmund
As to the legitimate—fine word, "legitimate"!
Well, my legitimate, if this letter speed°
And my invention° thrive, Edmund the base   20

Shall top the legitimate. I grow, I prosper.
Now, gods, stand up for bastards!
    [*Enter* GLOUCESTER.]
GLO: Kent banished thus! And France in
    choler parted!
And the King gone tonight! Subscribed° his
    power!
Confined to exhibition!° All this done   25
Upon the gad!° Edmund, how now! What news?

EDM: So please your lordship, none.
                            [*Putting up the letter.*]

GLO: Why so earnestly seek you to put up
    that letter?

EDM: I know no news, my lord.

GLO: What paper were you reading?   30

EDM: Nothing, my lord.°

GLO: No? What needed then that terrible
dispatch° of it into your pocket? The quality of
nothing hath not such need to hide itself. Let's
see. Come, if it be nothing, I shall not need spectacles.   36

EDM: I beseech you, sir, pardon me. It is
a letter from my brother that I have not all
o'erread, and for so much as I have perused, I find
it not fit for your o'erlooking.°   40

GLO: Give me the letter, sir.

EDM: I shall offend, either to detain or give it.
The contents, as in part I understand them, are to
blame.

GLO: Let's see, let's see.   45

EDM: I hope, for my brother's justification, he
wrote this but as an essay° or taste of my virtue.

GLO: [*Reads.*] "This policy and reverence of
age° makes the world bitter to the best of our
times,° keeps our fortunes from us till our oldness
cannot relish them. I begin to find an idle and
fond° bondage in the oppression of aged tyranny,
who sways not as it hath power, but as it is   53
suffered.° Come to me, that of this I may speak
more. If our father would sleep till I waked him,
you should enjoy half his revenue forever, and
live the beloved of your brother,   EDGAR."

---

326. **unconstant starts:** sudden outbursts.   **328. compli-**
ment: formality.   **330. hit:** agree.   **331. dispositions:**
frame of mind.   **334. i' the heat:** while the iron is hot.
  Sc. ii: 1. Thou, Nature: Edmund, the "natural" son of his
father, appeals to Nature, whose doctrine is every man ruthlessly for himself.   **2–6. Wherefore . . . brother:** Why
should I allow myself to be plagued by custom and nice distinctions (*curiosity*) which deprive me of my natural rights,
because I am a year younger (*lag:* lagging behind) than my
legitimate brother?   **7. compact:** put together, framed.
8. generous: noble.   **12. More . . . quality:** more fiber
and ferocity.   **14. fops:** fools.   **15. Got:** begotten.
19. speed: prosper.   **20. invention:** plan.

---

24. **Subscribed:** signed away.   **25. Confined to exhibition:**
reduced to a pension.   **26. gad:** prick of a goad; i.e., the
spur of the moment.   **31. Nothing, my lord:** Gloucester's
tragedy also begins with the word "nothing." See I.i.91.
32–33. terrible   dispatch: i.e.,   hasty   thrusting.
40. o'erlooking: reading.   **47. essay:** trial.   **48–9. policy**
. . . age: this custom of respecting old men.   **49–50. best**
. . . times: i.e., when we are still young.   **52. fond:** foolish.   **54. suffered:** allowed.

Hum! Conspiracy!—"Sleep till I waked him, you should enjoy half his revenue!"—My son Edgar! Had he a hand to write this? A heart and brain to breed it in? When came this to you? Who brought it? 62

EDM: It was not brought me, my lord, there's the cunning of it. I found it thrown in at the casement° of my closet.°

GLO: You know the character° to be your brother's?

EDM: If the matter were good, my lord, I durst swear it were his, but in respect of that, I would fain think it were not. 70

GLO: It is his.

EDM: It is his hand, my lord, but I hope his heart is not in the contents.

GLO: Hath he never heretofore sounded you in this business? 75

EDM: Never, my lord. But I have heard him oft maintain it to be fit that, sons at perfect age and fathers declining, the father should be as ward to the son, and the son manage his revenue.

GLO: Oh, villain, villain! His very opinion in the letter! Abhorred villain! Unnatural, detested, brutish villain! Worse than brutish! Go, sirrah, seek him—aye, apprehend him. Abominable villain! Where is he? 84

EDM: I do not well know, my lord. If it shall please you to suspend your indignation against my brother till you can derive from him better testimony of his intent, you should run a certain course.° Where, if you violently proceed against him, mistaking his purpose, it would make a great gap° in your own honor and shake in pieces the heart of his obedience.° I dare pawn down my life for him that he hath wrote this to feel° my affection to your honor and to no further pretense of danger. 95

GLO: Think you so?

EDM: If your honor judge it meet, I will place you where you shall hear us confer of this, and by an auricular assurance° have your satisfaction, and that without any further delay than this very evening. 101

GLO: He cannot be such a monster—

EDM: Nor is not, sure.

GLO: —to his father, that so tenderly and entirely loves him. Heaven and earth! Edmund, seek him out, wind me into him,° I pray you. Frame the business after your own wisdom. I would unstate myself, to be in a due resolution.°

EDM: I will seek him, sir, presently,° convey° the business as I shall find means, and acquaint you withal. 111

GLO: These late eclipses in the sun and moon portend no good to us. Though the wisdom of nature° can reason° it thus and thus, yet nature finds itself scourged by the sequent° effects. Love cools, friendship falls off, brothers divide. In cities, mutinies; in countries, discord; in palaces, treason; and the bond cracked 'twixt son and father. This villain of mine comes under the prediction, there's son against father. The King 120 falls from bias of nature,° there's father against child. We have seen the best of our time. Machinations, hollowness, treachery, and all ruinous disorders follow us disquietly to our graves. Find out this villain, Edmund, it shall lose thee nothing. Do it carefully. And the noble and truehearted Kent banished! His offense, honesty! 'Tis strange. 128

[Exit.]

EDM: This is the excellent foppery° of the world, that when we are sick in fortune—often the surfeit° of our own behavior—we make guilty of our disasters the sun, the moon, and the stars, as if we were villains by necessity, fools by heavenly compulsion; knaves, thieves, and 134 treachers by spherical predominance;° drunkards, liars, and adulterers by an enforced obedience of planetary influence;° and all that we are evil in, by a divine thrusting on—an admirable evasion of whoremaster° man, to lay his goatish disposition to the charge of a star!° My father

---

65. **casement:** window. 65. **closet:** room. 66. **character:** handwriting. 88–9. **certain course:** i.e., know where you are going. 91: **gap:** hole. 91–2. **shake . . . obedience:** cause him no longer to obey you loyally. 93. **feel:** test. 99. **auricular assurance:** proof heard with your own ears.

106. **wind . . . him:** worm your way into his confidence for me. 107–08. **I . . . resolution:** I would lose my earldom to learn the truth. This is one of many touches of bitter irony in this tragedy, for it is not until he has "unstated himself" that Gloucester does indeed learn the truth about his two sons. 109. **presently:** at once. **convey:** manage. 113–14. **wisdom of nature:** i.e., a rational explanation. 114. **reason:** explain. 115. **sequent:** subsequent. 121. **bias of nature:** natural inclination. 129. **foppery:** folly. 131. **surfeit:** lit., eating to excess and its results. 135. **treachers . . . predominance:** traitors because the stars so decreed when we were born. 136–37. **enforced . . . influence:** because we were forced to be so in obeying the influence of the stars. 139. **whoremaster:** lecherous. 140. **to . . . star:** to say that some star caused him to have the morals of a goat.

compounded with my mother under the dragon's tail, and my nativity° was under Ursa Major,° so that it follows I am rough and lecherous. Tut, I should have been that I am had the maidenliest star in the firmament twinkled on my bas- 145 tardizing. Edgar——[*Enter* EDGAR.] And pat he comes like the catastrophe° of the old comedy. My cue is villainous melancholy, with a sigh like Tom o' Bedlam.° Oh, these eclipses do portend these divisions! Fa, sol, la, mi.°   150

EDG: How now, Brother Edmund! What serious contemplation are you in?

EDM: I am thinking, Brother, of a prediction I read this other day, what should follow these eclipses.   155

EDG: Do you busy yourself about that?

EDM: I promise you the effects he writes of succeed° unhappily, as of unnaturalness between the child and the parent; death, dearth, dissolutions of ancient amities;° divisions in state, menaces and maledictions against King and nobles; needless diffidences,° banishment of friends, dissipation of cohorts,° nuptial breaches, and I know not what.   164

EDG: How long have you been a sectary astronomical?°°

EDM: Come, come, when saw you my father last?

EDG: Why, the night gone by.

EDM: Spake you with him?   170

EDG: Aye, two hours together.

EDM: Parted you in good terms? Found you no displeasure in him by word or countenance?

EDG: None at all.

EDM: Bethink yourself wherein you may have offended him. And at my entreaty forbear his presence till some little time hath qualified° the heat of his displeasure, which at this instant so rageth in him that with the mischief of your person it would scarcely allay.°   180

EDG: Some villain hath done me wrong.

EDM: That's my fear. I pray you have a continent forbearance° till the speed of his rage goes slower, and, as I say, retire with me to my lodging, from whence I will fitly bring you to hear my lord speak. Pray ye, go, there's my key. If you do stir abroad, go armed.   187

EDG: Armed, Brother!

EDM: Brother, I advise you to the best—go armed. I am no honest man if there be any good meaning toward you. I have told you what I have seen and heard, but faintly, nothing like the image and horror of it. Pray you, away.

EDG: Shall I hear from you anon?

EDM: I do serve you in this business.   195

[*Exit* EDGAR.]

A credulous father, and a brother noble,
Whose nature is so far from doing harms
That he suspects none, on whose foolish honesty
My practices° ride easy. I see the business.
Let me, if not by birth, have lands by wit. 200
All with me's meet° that I can fashion fit.°

[*Exit.*]

SCENE III. *The* DUKE OF ALBANY's *palace.*

[*Enter* GONERIL *and* OSWALD, *her steward.*]

GON: Did my father strike my gentleman for chiding of his fool?°

OSW: Yes, madam.

GON: By day and night he wrongs me. Every hour
He flashes into one gross crime or other
That sets us all at odds. I'll not endure it.   5
His knights grow riotous, and himself upbraids us
On every trifle. When he returns from hunting,
I will not speak with him. Say I am sick.
If you come slack of former services,°
You shall do well, the fault of it I'll answer. 10

OSW: He's coming, madam, I hear him.

[*Horns within.*]

GON: Put on what weary negligence you please,
You and your fellows, I'd have it come to question.°

---

142. **nativity:** moment of birth. 142. **Ursa Major:** the Great Bear.   147. **catastrophe:** the final episode. 148-49. **my . . . Bedlam:** I must now pretend to be a melancholic and sigh like a lunatic beggar. Tom o' Bedlam was a lunatic discharged from Bedlam (Bethlehem Hospital for lunatics). See II.iii.14.   150. **Fa . . . mi:** Edmund hums to himself.   158. **succeed:** follow.   160. **amities:** friendships.   162. **diffidences:** distrusts.   163. **dissipation of cohorts:** breaking-up of established friendships (lit., of troops of soldiers).   165-66. **sectary astronomical:** a follower of the sect of astrologers.   177. **qualified:** lessened.   179-80. **with . . . allay:** it would scarcely be lessened even if he did you some bodily injury.

182-83. **continent forbearance:** self-control which will keep you from any rash action.   199. **practices:** plots. 201. **meet:** suitable. **fashion fit:** make fit my purposes.
Sc. iii: 1. **fool:** professional jester.   9. **come . . . services:** do not wait on him as efficiently as you used to.   13. **to question:** or in modern slang, to a showdown.

If he distaste it, let him to our sister,
Whose mind and mine, I know, in that are one,
Not to be overruled. Idle old man,   16
That still would manage those authorities
That he hath given away! Now, by my life,
Old fools are babes again, and must be used
With checks as flatteries when they are seen
   abused.°   20
Remember what I tell you.
   OSW: Very well, madam.
   GON: And let his knights have colder looks
      among you.
What grows of it, no matter, advise your fellows so.
I would breed from hence occasions,° and I
   shall,
That I may speak. I'll write straight to my sister
To hold my very course. Prepare for dinner. 27
                                            [Exeunt.]

SCENE IV. A hall in the same.

   [Enter KENT, disguised.]
   KENT: If but as well I other accents borrow
That can my speech defuse,° my good intent
May carry through itself to that full issue
For which I razed° my likeness. Now, banished
   Kent,
If thou canst serve where thou dost stand con-
   demned,   5
So may it come, thy master whom thou lovest
Shall find thee full of labors.
   [Horns within.° Enter LEAR, KNIGHTS, and
      ATTENDANTS.]
   LEAR: Let me not stay a jot for dinner. Go get
it ready. [Exit an ATTENDANT.] How now! What
art thou?   10
   KENT: A man, sir.
   LEAR: What dost thou profess?° What
wouldst thou with us?
   KENT: I do profess to be no less than I seem—
to serve him truly that will put me in trust, to
love him that is honest, to converse with him that
is wise and says little, to fear judgment,° to fight

when I cannot choose, and to eat no fish.°   18
   LEAR: What art thou?
   KENT: A very honest-hearted fellow, and as
poor as the King.   21
   LEAR: If thou be as poor for a subject as he is
for a king, thou art poor enough. What wouldst
thou?
   KENT: Service.   25
   LEAR: Who wouldst thou serve?
   KENT: You.
   LEAR: Dost thou know me, fellow?
   KENT: No, sir, but you have that in your
countenance° which I would fain call master.
   LEAR: What's that?   31
   KENT: Authority.
   LEAR: What services canst thou do?
   KENT: I can keep honest counsel, ride, run,
mar a curious tale in telling it,° and deliver a
plain message bluntly. That which ordinary men
are fit for, I am qualified in, and the best of me is
diligence.   38
   LEAR: How old art thou?
   KENT: Not so young, sir, to love a woman for
singing, nor so old to dote on her for anything. I
have years on my back forty-eight.
   LEAR: Follow me, thou shalt serve me. If I
like thee no worse after dinner, I will not part
from thee yet. Dinner, ho, dinner! Where's my
knave? My fool? Go you, and call my fool hither.
[Exit an ATTENDANT. Enter OSWALD.] You, you,
sirrah, where's my daughter?   48
   OSW: So please you ——   [Exit.]
   LEAR: What says the fellow there? Call the
clotpoll° back. [Exit a KNIGHT.] Where's my fool,
ho? I think the world's asleep. [Re-enter KNIGHT.]
How now! Where's that mongrel?   53
   KNIGHT: He says, my lord, your daughter is
not well.
   LEAR: Why came not the slave back to me
when I called him?
   KNIGHT: Sir, he answered me, in the
roundest° manner, he would not.
   LEAR: He would not!   60

19–20. Old . . . abused: old men must be treated like babies, and scolded, not flattered, when they are naughty. 25. breed . . . occasions: find excuses for taking action. Sc. iv: 2. defuse: make indistinct, disguise. 4. razed: lit., shaved off, disguised. 7 s.d., within: off stage. 12. What . . . profess: what is your profession? 17. judgment: The Day of Judgment; i.e., I have a conscience.

18. eat no fish: I don't observe fast days, and am therefore no Catholic. 30. countenance: bearing. 35. mar . . . it: I'm not one to delight in overelaborate (curious) phrases when telling my tale; i.e., he will have none of the fantastic talk of the typical courtier—such as Shakespeare mocks in the character of Osric [in Hamlet]. Kent himself mimics this fashion later (II.ii.112–15). 51. clotpoll: clodpole, blockhead. 59. roundest: plainest.

KNIGHT: My lord, I know not what the matter is, but, to my judgment, your Highness is not entertained° with that ceremonious affection° as you were wont. There's a great abatement of kindness appears as well in the general dependents° as in the Duke himself also and your daughter.   67

LEAR: Ha! sayest thou so?

KNIGHT: I beseech you pardon me, my lord, if I be mistaken, for my duty cannot be silent when I think your Highness wronged.

LEAR: Thou but rememberest° me of mine own conception. I have perceived a most faint neglect° of late, which I have rather blamed as mine own jealous curiosity° than as a very pretense° and purpose of unkindness. I will look further into 't. But where's my fool? I have not seen him this two days.   78

KNIGHT: Since my young lady's going into France, sir, the fool hath much pined away.

LEAR: No more of that, I have noted it well. Go you, and tell my daughter I would speak with her. [Exit an ATTENDANT.] Go you, call hither my fool. [Exit an ATTENDANT. Re-enter OSWALD.] Oh, you sir, you, come you hither, sir. Who am I, sir?

OSW: My lady's father.   86

LEAR: My lady's father! My lord's knave. You whoreson dog! You slave! You cur!

OSW: I am none of these, my lord, I beseech your pardon.   90

LEAR: Do you bandy° looks with me, you rascal?   [Striking him.]

OSW: I'll not be struck, my lord.

KENT: Nor tripped neither, you base football player.   [Tripping up his heels.]

LEAR: I thank thee, fellow. Thou servest me, and I'll love thee.   97

KENT: Come, sir, arise, away! I'll teach you differences.° Away, away! If you will measure your lubber's length again, tarry. But away! Go to, have you wisdom? So. [Pushes OSWALD out.]

LEAR: Now, my friendly knave, I thank thee.

There's earnest° of thy service.   103
                        [Giving KENT money.]
[Enter FOOL.]

FOOL: Let me hire him too. Here's my coxcomb.°   [Offering KENT his cap.]

LEAR: How now, my pretty knave! How dost thou?

FOOL: Sirrah, you were best take my coxcomb.

KENT: Why, fool?   110

FOOL: Why, for taking one's part that's out of favor. Nay, an thou canst not smile as the wind sits,° thou'lt catch cold shortly. There, take my coxcomb. Why, this fellow hath banished two on 's daughters, and done the third a blessing against his will. If thou follow him, thou must needs wear my coxcomb. How now, Nuncle!° Would I had two coxcombs and two daughters!

LEAR: Why, my boy?   119

FOOL: If I gave them all my living, I'd keep my coxcombs myself. There's mine, beg another of thy daughters.

LEAR: Take heed, sirrah, the whip.°

FOOL: Truth's a dog must to kennel. He must be whipped out, when Lady the brach° may stand by the fire and stink.

LEAR: A pestilent gall to me!°

FOOL: Sirrah, I'll teach thee a speech.

LEAR: Do.

FOOL: Mark it, Nuncle: 130
    "Have more than thou showest,
     Speak less than thou knowest,
     Lend less than thou owest,°
     Ride more than thou goest,°
     Learn more than thou trowest,°   135
     Set less than thou throwest,°
     Leave thy drink and thy whore
     And keep in-a-door,

---

63. **entertained:** treated. **ceremonious affection:** affection which shows itself in ceremony. Manners even between children and parents were very formal. Neglect of courtesies to the ex-King shows deliberate disrespect.   66. **dependents:** servants of the house.   72. **rememberest:** remind. 73–4. **faint neglect:** i.e., the "weary negligence" commanded by Goneril (I.iii.12).   75. **jealous curiosity:** excessive suspicion.   76. **pretense:** deliberate intention.   91. **bandy:** lit., hit the ball to and fro as in tennis. 99. **differences:** of rank.

103. **earnest:** money given on account of services to be rendered. Lear thus formally engages Kent as his servant. 105. **coxcomb:** the cap shaped like a cock's comb (crest) worn by the professional fool.   112–13. **an . . . sits:** i.e., if you can't curry favor with those in power.   117. **Nuncle:** Uncle.   123. **the whip:** The fool's profession was precarious, and in real life too smart a joke brought its painful reward. In March 1605 Stone, a professional fool, was whipped for commenting on the diplomatic mission about to sail for Spain that "there went sixty fools into Spain, besides my Lord Admiral and his two sons."   125. **Lady . . . brach:** Lady the pet bitch.   127. **A . . . me:** this pestilent fool rubs me on a sore spot.   133. **owest:** possess.   134. **goest:** walk.   135. **trowest:** know.   136. **Set . . . throwest:** don't bet a larger stake than you can afford to lose.

And thou shalt have more
Than two tens to a score."° 140

KENT: This is nothing, fool.

FOOL: Then 'tis like the breath of an unfeed lawyer. You gave me nothing for 't. Can you make no use of nothing, Nuncle?

LEAR: Why, no, boy, nothing can be made out of nothing.° 146

FOOL: [To KENT] Prithee tell him so much the rent of his land comes to. He will not believe a fool.

LEAR: A bitter fool! 150

FOOL: Dost thou know the difference, my boy, between a bitter fool and a sweet fool?

LEAR: No, lad, teach me.

FOOL: "That lord that counseled thee
To give away thy land, 155
Come place him here by me,
Do thou for him stand.
The sweet and bitter fool
Will presently appear—
The one in motley° here, 160
The other found out there."

LEAR: Dost thou call me fool, boy?

FOOL: All thy other titles thou hast given away. That thou wast born with.

KENT: This is not altogether fool, my lord.

FOOL: No, faith, lords and great men will not let me.° If I had a monopoly° out, they would have part on 't. And ladies too, they will not let me have all the fool to myself, they'll be snatching. Give me an egg, Nuncle, and I'll give thee two crowns. 171

LEAR: What two crowns shall they be?

FOOL: Why, after I have cut the egg in the middle and eat up the meat, the two crowns of the egg. When thou clovest thy crown i' the middle and gavest away both parts, thou borest thine ass on thy back o'er the dirt.° Thou hadst little wit in thy bald crown when thou gavest thy golden one away. If I speak like myself° in this, let him be whipped that first finds it so. [Singing]

"Fools had ne'er less wit in a year, 181
For wise men are grown foppish,
And know not how their wits to wear,
Their manners are so apish."°

LEAR: When were you wont to be so full of songs, sirrah? 186

FOOL: I have used it, Nuncle, ever since thou madest thy daughters thy mother. For when thou gavest them the rod and puttest down thine own breeches, [Singing] 190

"Then they for sudden joy did weep,
And I for sorrow sung,
That such a king should play bopeep,
And go the fools among."

Prithee, Nuncle, keep a schoolmaster that can teach thy fool to lie. I would fain learn to lie.

LEAR: An° you lie, sirrah, we'll have you whipped. 198

FOOL: I marvel what kin thou and thy daughters are. They'll have me whipped for speaking true, thou'lt have me whipped for lying, and sometimes I am whipped for holding my peace. I had rather be any kind o' thing than a fool. And yet I would not be thee, Nuncle. Thou hast pared thy wit o' both sides and left nothing i' the middle. Here comes one o' the pairings. 206

[Enter GONERIL.]

LEAR: How now, Daughter! What makes that frontlet° on? Methinks you are too much of late i' the frown.

FOOL: Thou wast a pretty fellow when thou hadst no need to care for her frowning. Now thou art an O without a figure.° I am better than thou art now. I am a fool, thou art nothing. [To GONERIL] Yes, forsooth, I will hold my tongue, so your face bids me, though you say nothing. 215

"Mum, mum.
He that keeps nor crust nor crumb,°
Weary of all, shall want some."

[Pointing to LEAR] That's a shealed peascod.°

GON: Not only, sir, this your all-licensed° fool, But other of your insolent retinue 221
Do hourly carp° and quarrel, breaking forth In rank and not to be endurèd riots. Sir,

139–40. And . . . score: and then your money will increase. 145–46. nothing . . . nothing: Lear unconsciously repeats himself. See I.i.94. 160. motley: the particolored uniform worn by a fool. 166–67. will . . . me: i.e., keep all my folly to myself. 167. monopoly: a royal patent giving the holders the sole right to deal in some commodity. The granting of such monopolies to courtiers was one of the crying scandals of the time. 176–77. thine . . . dirt: an old tale of the typical simple-minded countryman. 179. like myself: i.e., like a fool.

181–84. Fools . . . apish: there's no job left for fools nowadays, because the wise men are so like them, apish: like apes, who always imitate. 197. An: if. 208. frontlet: frown; lit., a band worn on the forehead. 212. an . . . figure: a cipher. 217. crumb: inside of the loaf. 219. shealed peascod: a shelled peapod. 220. all-licensed: allowed to take all liberties. 222. carp: find fault.

I had thought, by making this well known unto
      you,
To have found a safe redress, but now grow fear-
      ful   225
By what yourself too late have spoke and done
That you protect this course and put it on°
By your allowance.° Which if you should, the
      fault
Would not 'scape censure, nor the redresses
      sleep,
Which, in the tender of a wholesome weal, 230
Might in their working do you that offense
Which else were shame, that then necessity
Will call discreet proceeding.°
    FOOL: For, you know, Nuncle,
      "The hedge sparrow fed the cuckoo so long
      That it had it head bit off by it young." 236
So out went the candle, and we were left
      darkling.°
    LEAR: Are you our daughter?
    GON: Come, sir,
I would you would make use of that good wis-
      dom   240
Whereof I know you are fraught,° and put away
These dispositions° that of late transform you
From what you rightly are.
    FOOL: May not an ass know when the cart
      draws the horse? Whoop, Jug! I love thee.°
    LEAR: Doth any here know me? This is not
      Lear.
Doth Lear walk thus? Speak thus? Where are
      his eyes?
Either his notion° weakens, his discernings 247
Are lethargied°——Ha! Waking? 'Tis not so.
Who is it that can tell me who I am?
    FOOL: Lear's shadow.
    LEAR: I would learn that, for, by the marks of
sovereignty,° knowledge, and reason, I should be
false persuaded I had daughters.
    FOOL: Which they will make an obedient fa-
      ther.   254

    LEAR: Your name, fair gentlewoman?   255
    GON: This admiration,° sir, is much o' the
      savor
Of° other your new pranks. I do beseech you
To understand my purposes aright.
As you are old and reverend, you should be wise.
Here do you keep a hundred knights and squires,
Men so disordered,° so deboshed° and bold,
That this our Court, infected with their manners,
Shows like a riotous inn. Epicurism° and lust
Make it more like a tavern or a brothel   264
Than a graced° palace. The shame itself doth
      speak
For instant remedy. Be then desired
By her that else will take the thing she begs
A little to disquantity your train,°
And the remainder that shall still depend,°
To be such men as may besort° your age,   270
Which know themselves and you.
    LEAR: Darkness and devils!
Saddle my horses, call my train together.
Degenerate bastard! I'll not trouble thee.
Yet have I left a daughter.   275
    GON: You strike my people, and your disor-
      dered rabble
Make servants of their betters.
    [*Enter* ALBANY.]
    LEAR: Woe, that too late repents.—[*To*
      ALBANY]
      Oh, sir, are you come?
Is it your will? Speak, sir. Prepare my horses.
Ingratitude, thou marble-hearted fiend,   281
More hideous when thou show'st thee in a child
Than the sea monster!
    ALB: Pray, sir, be patient.
    LEAR: [*To* GONERIL] Detested kite!° Thou
      liest.
My train are men of choice and rarest parts,°
That all particulars of duty know,   287
And in the most exact regard support
The worships of their name.° O most small fault,
How ugly didst thou in Cordelia show!

---

227. put it on: encourage it.   **228. allowance:** approval.   **230-33. Which . . . proceeding:** if you continue
to be a nuisance I shall be forced to keep my state peaceful by
taking measures which will annoy you and would at other
times be shameful toward a father, but would be justified
as mere discretion.   **237. darkling:** in the dark.   **241.
fraught:** stored, endowed.   **242. dispositions:** moods.
244. Whoop . . . thee: one of the meaningless cries made by
the fool to distract attention.   **247. notion:** understanding.   **248. lethargied:** paralyzed.   **251-52. marks of sovereignty:** the outward signs which show that I am King.

256. admiration: pretended   astonishment.   **256-
57. much . . . Of:** tastes much the same as.   **261. disordered:** disorderly. **deboshed:** debauched.   **263. Epicurism:**
self-indulgence, riotous living.   **265. graced:** gracious.
268. disquantity . . . train: diminish the number of your followers.   **269. depend:** be your dependents.   **270. be-
sort:** be suitable for.   **285. kite:** the lowest of the birds of
prey, an eater of offal.   **286. parts:** accomplishments.
288-89. in . . . name: and in every minute detail uphold
their honorable names.

That, like an engine, wrenched my frame of na-
  ture 291
From the fixed place,° drew from my heart all
  love
And added to the gall.° O Lear, Lear, Lear!
Beat at this gate, that let thy folly in
                  [*Striking his head*]
And thy dear judgment out!° Go, go, my people.
  ALB: My lord, I am guiltless, as I am ignorant
Of what hath moved you. 297
    LEAR: It may be so, my lord.
Hear, Nature, hear,° dear goddess, hear!
Suspend thy purpose if thou didst intend 300
To make this creature fruitful.
Into her womb convey sterility.
Dry up in her the organs of increase,°
And from her derogate° body never spring
A babe to honor her! If she must teem,° 305
Create her child of spleen,° that it may live
And be a thwart disnatured° torment to her.
Let it stamp wrinkles in her brow of youth,
With cadent° tears fret° channels in her cheeks,
Turn all her mother's pains and benefits 310
To laughter and contempt, that she may feel
How sharper than a serpent's tooth it is
To have a thankless child! Away, away! [*Exit.*]
  ALB: Now, gods that we adore, whereof
    comes this?
  GON: Never afflict yourself to know the cause,
But let his disposition have that scope 316
That dotage gives it.
    [*Re-enter* LEAR.]
  LEAR: What, fifty of my followers at a clap!°
Within a fortnight!°
    ALB: What's the matter, sir?
  LEAR: I'll tell thee. [*To* GONERIL] Life and
    death! I am ashamed 321
That thou hast power to shake my manhood°
    thus,

That these hot tears, which break from me per-
  force,
Should make thee worth them. Blasts and fogs
  upon thee!
The untented woundings° of a father's curse
Pierce every sense about thee! Old fond° eyes,
Beweep this cause again, I'll pluck ye out 327
And cast you with the waters that you lose
To temper° clay. Yea, is it come to this?
Let it be so. Yet have I left a daughter
Who I am sure is kind and comfortable.° 331
When she shall hear this of thee, with her nails
She'll flay thy wolvish visage. Thou shalt find
That I'll resume the shape which thou dost think
I have cast off forever. Thou shalt, I warrant
  thee. 335
  [*Exeunt* LEAR, KENT, *and* ATTENDANTS.]
  GON: Do you mark that, my lord?
  ALB: I° cannot be so partial, Goneril,
To the great love I bear you——
  GON: Pray you, content. What, Oswald, ho!
[*To the* FOOL] You, sir, more knave than fool, after
  your master. 340
  FOOL: Nuncle Lear, Nuncle Lear, tarry, take
the fool with thee.°
    "A fox, when one has caught her,
      And such a daughter,
      Should sure to the slaughter, 345
    If my cap would buy a halter.
    So the fool follows after." [*Exit.*]
  GON: This man hath had good counsel. A hun-
  dred knights!
'Tis politic° and safe to let him keep 349
At point° a hundred knights. Yes, that on every
  dream,
Each buzz,° each fancy, each complaint, dislike,
He may enguard his dotage with their powers
And hold our lives in mercy. Oswald, I say!
  ALB: Well, you may fear too far.
  GON: Safer than trust too far.
Let me still take away the harms I fear, 356
Not fear still to be taken.° I know his heart.
What he hath uttered I have writ my sister.

291-92. like . . . place: like a little instrument (e.g., a lever) dislodged my firm nature. **293. gall:** bitterness. **294-95. Beat . . . out:** the first signs of madness in Lear. **299. Hear . . . hear:** In making this terrible curse, Lear also calls on Nature, but as goddess of natural affection. Cf. I.ii.1–22. **303. increase:** childbearing. **304. derogate:** debased. **305. teem:** conceive. **306. spleen:** malice. **307. thwart disnatured:** perverse and unnatural. **309. cadent:** falling. **fret:** wear away. **318. at a clap:** at one blow. **318-19. What . . . fortnight:** as Lear goes out he learns that Goneril has herself already begun to take steps "a little to disquantity his train" by ordering that fifty of them shall depart within a fortnight. To a man who regards his own dignity so highly, this fresh blow is devastating. **322. shake my manhood:** i.e., with sobs.

325. untented woundings: raw wounds. A tent was a small roll of lint used to clean out a wound before it was bound up. **326. fond:** foolish. **329. temper:** mix. **331. comfortable:** full of comfort. **337-38. I . . . you:** i.e., although my love makes me partial to you, yet I must protest. **341-42. take . . . thee:** i.e., take your fool and your own folly. **349. politic:** good policy. **350. At point:** fully armed. **351. buzz:** rumor. **356-57. Let . . . taken:** let me always remove what I fear will harm me rather than live in perpetual fear.

If she sustain him and his hundred knights
When I have showed the unfitness——   360
  [*Re-enter* OSWALD.] How now, Oswald!
What, have you writ that letter to my sister?
  OSW: Yes, madam.
  GON: Take you some company, and away to
    horse.
Inform her full of my particular fear,   365
And thereto add such reasons of your own
As may compact it more.° Get you gone,
And hasten your return. [*Exit* OSWALD.] No, no,
  my lord,
This milky gentleness and course° of yours
Though I condemn not, yet, under pardon, 370
You are much more attasked° for want of wis-
  dom
Than praised for harmful mildness.°
  ALB: How far your eyes may pierce I cannot
    tell.
Striving to better, oft we mar what's well.
  GON: Nay, then——   375
  ALB: Well, well, the event.°   [*Exeunt.*]

SCENE V. *Court before the same.*

  [*Enter* LEAR, KENT, *and* FOOL.]
  LEAR: Go you before to Gloucester with these
letters. Acquaint my daughter no further with
anything you know than comes from her demand
out of the letter. If your diligence be not speedy,
I shall be there afore you.   5
  KENT: I will not sleep, my lord, till I have
delivered your letter.   [*Exit*]
  FOOL: If a man's brains were in 's heels, were
't not in danger of kibes?°
  LEAR: Aye, boy.   10
  FOOL: Then I prithee be merry. Thy wit shall
ne'er go slipshod.°
  LEAR: Ha, ha, ha!
  FOOL: Shalt see thy other daughter will use
thee kindly,° for though she's as like this as a
crab's° like an apple, yet I can tell what I can
tell.   17

  LEAR: Why, what canst thou tell, my boy?
  FOOL: She will taste as like this as a crab does
to a crab. Thou canst tell why one's nose stands i'
the middle on 's face?   21
  LEAR: No.
  FOOL: Why, to keep one's eyes of either side 's
nose, that what a man cannot smell out he may
spy into.   25
  LEAR: I did her wrong——
  FOOL: Canst tell how an oyster makes his
shell?
  LEAR: No.
  FOOL: Nor I neither, but I can tell why a snail
has a house.   31
  LEAR: Why?
  FOOL: Why, to put 's head in, not to give it
away to his daughters and leave his horns with-
out a case.   35
  LEAR: I will forget my nature.—So kind a fa-
ther!—Be my horses ready?
  FOOL: Thy asses are gone about 'em. The rea-
son why the seven stars are no more than seven is
a pretty reason.   40
  LEAR: Because they are not eight?
  FOOL: Yes, indeed. Thou wouldst make a good
fool.
  LEAR: To take 't again perforce!° Monster
ingratitude!   45
  FOOL: If thou wert my fool, Nuncle, I'd have
thee beaten for being old before thy time.
  LEAR: How's that?
  FOOL: Thou shouldst not have been old till
thou hadst been wise.   50
  LEAR: Oh, let me not be mad, not mad, sweet
    Heaven!
Keep me in temper.° I would not be mad!
[*Enter* GENTLEMAN.] How now! Are the horses
  ready?
  GENT: Ready, my lord.
  LEAR: Come, boy.   55
  FOOL: She that's a maid now and laughs at my
    departure
Shall not be a maid long, unless things be cut
    shorter.   [*Exeunt.*]

ACT II

SCENE I. *The* EARL OF GLOUCESTER's *castle.*

[*Enter* EDMUND *and* CURAN, *meeting.*]

---

367. **compact it more:** make my argument more convincing.   369. **milky . . . course:** this milksop behavior.
371. **attasked:** blamed.   372. **harmful mildness:** a mildness
which may prove harmful.   376. **the event:** i.e., we must
see what will happen.
  Sc. v: 9. **kibes:** chilblains.   11–12. **Thy . . . slipshod:**
i.e., you don't need slippers, for you have no brains to be
protected from chilblains.   15. **kindly:** after her kind; i.e.,
nature.   16. **crab:** crab apple.

44. **To . . . perforce:** I will take back my kingdom by
force.   52. **temper:** sanity.

EDM: Save thee,° Curan.

CUR: And you, sir. I have been with your father, and given him notice that the Duke of Cornwall and Regan his Duchess will be here with him this night.   5

EDM: How comes that?

CUR: Nay, I know not. You have heard of the news abroad—I mean the whispered ones, for they are yet but ear-kissing° arguments?

EDM: Not I. Pray you what are they?   10

CUR: Have you heard of no likely wars toward 'twixt the Dukes of Cornwall and Albany?

EDM: Not a word.

CUR: You may do, then, in time. Fare you well, sir.   [Exit.]

EDM: The Duke be here tonight? The better! Best!   16
This weaves itself perforce into my business.
My father hath set guard to take my brother,
And I have one thing, of a queasy question,°
Which I must act. Briefness and fortune, work!
Brother, a word, descend.° Brother, I say!
[Enter EDGAR.] My father watches. O sir, fly this place.   22
Intelligence° is given where you are hid.
You have now the good advantage of the night.
Have you not spoken 'gainst the Duke of Cornwall?
He's coming hither, now, i' the night, i' the haste,
And Regan with him. Have you nothing said
Upon his party 'gainst the Duke of Albany?
Advise yourself.   29

EDG: I am sure on 't, not a word.

EDM: I hear my father coming. Pardon me,
In cunning° I must draw my sword upon you.
Draw. Seem to defend yourself. Now quit you well.°
Yield. Come before my father. Light, ho, here!
Fly, Brother. Torches, torches! So farewell.
                                              [Exit EDGAR.]
Some blood drawn on me would beget opinion°
                                       [Wounds his arm.]
Of my more fierce endeavor. I have seen drunkards   37
Do more than this in sport. Father, Father!

Stop, stop! No help?
  [Enter GLOUCESTER and SERVANTS with torches.]

GLO: Now, Edmund, where's the villain?   40

EDM: Here stood he in the dark, his sharp sword out,
Mumbling° of wicked charms, conjuring the moon°
To stand 's auspicious° mistress.

GLO: But where is he?

EDM: Look, sir, I bleed.   45

GLO: Where is the villain, Edmund?

EDM: Fled this way, sir. When by no means he could——

GLO: Pursue him, ho!—Go after.
                            [Exeunt some SERVANTS.]
                            "By no means" what?

EDM: Persuade me to the murder of your lordship,   50
But that I told him the revenging gods
'Gainst parricides did all their thunders bend,
Spoke with how manifold and strong a bond
The child was bound to the father. Sir, in fine,°
Seeing how loathly opposite I stood°   55
To his unnatural purpose, in fell° motion
With his preparèd° sword he charges home
My unprovided° body, lanced mine arm.
But when he saw my best alarumed spirits°
Bold in the quarrel's right, roused to the encounter,   60
Or whether gasted° by the noise I made,
Full suddenly he fled.

GLO: Let him fly far.
Not in this land shall he remain uncaught,
And found—dispatch.° The noble Duke my master,   65
My worthy arch and patron,° comes tonight.
By his authority I will proclaim it,
That he which finds him shall deserve our thanks,
Bringing the murderous caitiff° to the stake.°

42-43. Mumbling . . . mistress: this is the kind of story which would especially appeal to Gloucester. Cf. I.ii.112.
42. conjuring . . . moon: calling on Hecate, goddess of witchcraft.   43. auspicious: favorable.   54. in fine: in short.   55. how . . . stood: with what loathing I opposed.   56. fell: fearful.   57. prepared: drawn.
58. unprovided: unguarded.   59. my . . . spirits: my stoutest spirits called out by the alarm.   61. gasted: terrified.   65. And . . . dispatch: and when he's found, kill him.   66. arch . . . patron: chief support and protector.   69. caitiff: wretch; lit., captive. to . . . stake: i.e., place of execution.

He that conceals him, death.   70
  EDM: When I dissuaded him from his intent
And found him pight° to do it, with curst°
  speech
I threatened to discover him. He replied,
"Thou unpossessing bastard! Does thou think,
If I would stand against thee, could the reposal
Of any trust, virtue, or worth in thee   76
Make thy words faithed?° No. What I should
  deny—
As this I would, aye, though thou didst produce
My very character°—I'd turn it all°
To thy suggestion,° plot, and damnèd practice.°
And thou must make° a dullard of the world
If they not thought the profits of my death
Were very pregnant and potential spurs°
To make thee seek it."
  GLO: Strong and fastened° vil-
  lain!   85
Would he deny his letter? I never got° him.
                    [*Tucket° within*]
Hark, the Duke's trumpets! I know not why he
  comes.
All ports I'll bar,° the villain shall not 'scape,
The Duke must grant me that. Besides, his pic-
  ture
I will send far and near, that all the kingdom
May have due note of him, and of my land,   91
Loyal and natural° boy, I'll work the means
To make thee capable.°
  [*Enter* CORNWALL, REGAN, *and* ATTENDANTS.]
  CORN: How now, my noble friend! Since I
  came hither,
Which I can call but now, I have heard strange
  news.   95
  REG: If it be true, all vengeance comes too
  short
Which can pursue the offender. How dost, my
  lord?

  GLO: Oh, madam, my old heart is cracked, is
  cracked!
  REG: What, did my father's godson seek your
  life? He whom my father named? Your
  Edgar?
  GLO: Oh, lady, lady, shame would have it hid!
  REG: Was he not companion with the riotous
  knights   101
That tend upon my father?
  GLO: I know not, madam. 'Tis too bad, too
  bad.
  EDM: Yes, madam, he was of that consort.°
  REG: No marvel then, though he were ill
  affected.°   105
'Tis they have put him on° the old man's death,
To have the waste and spoil of his revènues.
I have this present evening from my sister
Been well informed of them, and with such cau-
  tions
That if they come to sojourn at my house,   110
I'll not be there.
  CORN: Nor I, assure thee, Regan.
Edmund, I hear that you have shown your father
A childlike office.°
  EDM: 'Twas my duty, sir.   115
  GLO: He did bewray° his practice, and re-
  ceived
This hurt you see, striving to apprehend him.
  CORN: Is he pursued?
  GLO: Aye, my good lord.
  CORN: If he be taken, he shall never more
Be feared of doing° harm. Make your own pur-
  pose,   121
How in my strength you please.° For you, Ed-
  mund,
Whose virtue and obedience doth this instant
So much commend itself, you shall be ours.
Natures of such deep trust we shall much need.
You we first seize on.   126
  EDM: I shall serve you, sir,
Truly, however else.
  GLO: For him I thank your Grace.
  CORN: You know not why we came to visit
  you—   130
  REG: Thus out of season, threading dark-eyed
  night.°

---

72. pight: determined. **curst:** bitter.   **77. faithed:** believed.   **79. character:** handwriting. Cf. I.ii.66. **turn it all:**
make it appear to be.   **80. suggestion:** idea. **practice:**
plot.   **81–84. make . . . it:** you would have to make people
dull indeed before they would disbelieve that your chief motive was to benefit by my death.   **83. pregnant . . . spurs:**
obvious and powerful encouragements.   **85. fastened:** confirmed.   **86. got:** begot. **s.d., Tucket:** trumpet call.
88. ports . . . bar: I'll have the seaports watched to prevent
his escape.   **92. natural:** i.e., one who has the proper feelings of son to father. Gloucester does not as yet realize what
"nature" means to Edmund. See I.ii.1.   **93. capable:** i.e., legitimate; lit., capable of succeeding as my
heir.

104. consort: party.   **105. though . . . affected:** if he
had traitorous thoughts.   **106. put . . . on:** persuaded
him to cause.   **114. childlike office:** filial service.
116. bewray: reveal.   **121. of doing:** because he might
do.   **121–22. Make . . . please:** use my authority for any
action you care to take.   **131. threading . . . night:** making
our way through the darkness.

Occasions, noble Gloucester, of some poise,°
Wherein we must have use of your advice.
Our father he hath writ, so hath our sister,
Of differences, which I least thought it fit   135
To answer from° our home. The several messen-
    gers
From hence attend dispatch.° Our good old
    friend,
Lay comforts to your bosom, and bestow
Your needful counsel to our business,
Which craves the instant use.°   140
   GLO: I serve you, madam.
Your Graces are right welcome.

                            [Flourish. Exeunt.]

SCENE II. Before GLOUCESTER's *castle.*

[Enter KENT *and* OSWALD, *severally.°]*

   OSW: Good dawning to thee, friend. Art of
this house?
   KENT: Aye.
   OSW: Where may we set our horses?
   KENT: I' the mire.   5
   OSW: Prithee, if thou lovest me, tell me.
   KENT: I love thee not.
   OSW: Why, then I care not for thee.
   KENT: If I had thee in Lipsbury pinfold,° I
would make thee care for me.   10
   OSW: Why dost thou use me thus? I know
thee not.
   KENT: Fellow, I know thee.
   OSW: What dost thou know me for?   14
   KENT: A° knave, a rascal, an eater of broken
meats; a base, proud, shallow, beggarly, three-
suited, hundred-pound, filthy, worsted-stocking
knave; a lily-livered, action-taking knave; a

whoreson, glass-gazing, superserviceable, finical
rogue; one-trunk-inheriting slave; one that
wouldst be a bawd in way of good service, and
art nothing but the composition of a knave, beggar, coward, pander, and the son and heir of a
mongrel bitch—one whom I will beat into clam-
orous whining if thou deniest the least syllable of
thy addition.   26
   OSW: Why, what a monstrous fellow art thou,
thus to rail on one that is neither known of thee
nor knows thee!
   KENT: What a brazen-faced varlet art thou, to
deny thou knowest me! Is it two days ago since I
tripped up the heels and beat thee before the
King? Draw, you rogue. For though it be night,
yet the moon shines. I'll make a sop o' the moon-
shine of you.° Draw, you whoreson cullionly°
barber-monger,° draw. *[Drawing his sword.]*   36
   OSW: Away! I have nothing to do with thee.
   KENT: Draw, you rascal. You come with let-
ters against the King, and take vanity the pup-
pet's part° against the royalty of her father.
Draw, you rogue, or I'll so carbonado° your
shanks. Draw, you rascal, come your ways.
   OSW: Help, ho! Murder! Help!   43
   KENT: Strike, you slave. Stand, rogue, stand,
you neat slave, strike.   *[Beating him.]*
   OSW: Help, ho! Murder! Murder!
[Enter EDMUND, *with his rapier drawn,* CORN-
WALL, REGAN, GLOUCESTER, *and* SERVANTS.]
   EDM: How now! What's the matter?
                           [Parting them.]
   KENT: With you, goodman boy,° an you
please.   49

---

132. **poise:** weight.   136. **from:** away from.   137. **attend dispatch:** are waiting to be sent back.   140. **craves
. . . use:** requires immediate action.   **Sc. ii: s.d., severally:** by different entrances.
9. **Lipsbury pinfold:** This phrase has not been convincingly
explained. A pinfold is a village pound, a small enclosure in
which strayed beasts are kept until reclaimed by their owners; a pinfold was a good place for a fight whence neither side
could escape.   15–18. **A . . . addition:** Kent here sums up
the characteristics of the more unpleasant kind of gentleman
servingman of whom Oswald is a fair specimen. **broken
meats:** remains of food sent down from the high table. **three-
suited:** allowed three suits a year. **hundred-pound:** i.e., the
extent of his wealth. **worsted-stocking:** no gentleman, or he
would have worn silk. **lily-livered:** cowardly. **action-taking
knave:** one who goes to law instead of risking a fight.

19–26. **glass-gazing:** always looking at himself in a mirror.
superserviceable: too eager to do what his master wishes.
finical: finicky. **one-trunk-inheriting:** whose whole inheritance from his father will go into one trunk. **bawd . . . service:**
ready to serve his master's lusts if it will please him. **composition:** mixture. **pander:** pimp. **addition:** lit., title of honor
added to a man's name.   34–35. **sop . . . you:** Not satisfac-
torily explained, but obviously something unpleasant; probably Kent means no more than "I'll make a wet mess of
you."   35. **cullionly:** base.   36. **barber-monger:** a man
always in the barber's shop. Elizabethan gentlemen fre-
quented the beauty parlor as much as our modern ladies
do.   39–40. **vanity . . . part:** Vanity appeared as an evil
character in the old Morality plays of the early sixteenth
century, which still survived in a degenerate form in puppet
shows exhibited at fairs.   41. **carbonado:** lit., a steak
slashed for cooking, so "slice."   49. **goodman boy:** my
young man. Edmund is still a young man, but it was an insult
to call him boy.

Come, I'll flesh you,° come on, young master.

GLO: Weapons! Arms! What's the matter here?

CORN: Keep peace, upon your lives.
He dies that strikes again. What is the matter?

REG: The messengers from our sister and the King.   55

CORN: What is your difference?° Speak.

OSW: I am scarce in breath, my lord.

KENT: No marvel, you have so bestirred your valor. You cowardly rascal, Nature disclaims in thee. A tailor made thee.°   60

CORN: Thou art a strange fellow—a tailor make a man?

KENT: Aye, a tailor, sir. A stonecutter or a painter could not have made him so ill, though he had been but two hours at the trade.   65

CORN: Speak yet, how grew your quarrel?

OSW: This ancient ruffian, sir, whose life I have spared at suit of his gray beard——

KENT: Thou whoreson zed! Thou unnecessary letter!° My lord, if you will give me leave, I will tread this unbolted° villain into mortar, and daub the walls of a jakes° with him. Spare my gray beard, you wagtail?°   73

CORN: Peace, sirrah!
You beastly knave, know you no reverence?°

KENT: Yes, sir, but anger hath a privilege.°

CORN: Why art thou angry?

KENT: That such a slave as this should wear a sword,
Who wears no honesty. Such smiling rogues as these,
Like rats, oft bite the holy cords a-twain   80
Which are too intrinse to unloose;° smooth° every passion
That in the natures of their lords rebel;
Bring oil to fire, snow to their colder moods;

Renege, affirm,° and turn their halcyon° beaks
With every gale and vary of their masters,   85
Knowing naught, like dogs, but following.
A plague upon your epileptic visage!
Smile you my speeches, as I were a fool?
Goose,° if I had you upon Sarum° plain,
I'd drive ye cackling home to Camelot.°   90

CORN: What, art thou mad, old fellow?

GLO: How fell you out? Say that.

KENT: No contraries hold more antipathy
Than I and such a knave.

CORN: Why dost thou call him knave? What is his fault?   95

KENT: His countenance likes me not.°

CORN: No more perchance does mine, nor his, nor hers.

KENT: Sir, 'tis my occupation to be plain.
I have seen better faces in my time
Than stands on any shoulder that I see   100
Before me at this instant.

CORN: This is some fellow
Who, having been praised for bluntness, doth affect
A saucy roughness,° and constrains the garb
Quite from his nature.° He cannot flatter, he—
An honest mind and plain—he must speak truth!
An they will take it, so. If not, he's plain.   107
These kind of knaves I know, which in this plainness
Harbor more craft and more corrupter ends
Than twenty silly ducking observants   110
That stretch their duties nicely.°

KENT: Sir,° in good faith, in sincere verity,
Under the allowance of your great aspéct,
Whose influence, like the wreath of radiant fire
On flickering Phoebus'° front——   115

CORN: What mean'st by this?

KENT: To go out of my dialect, which you discommend so much. I know, sir, I am no

---

50. flesh you: give you your first fight.   **56. difference:** disagreement.   **59-60. Nature . . . thee:** Nature refuses to own you, you are nothing but clothes—from the English proverb "The tailor makes the man."   **69-70. zed . . . letter:** because z does not exist in Latin and is not necessary in the English alphabet, since s can usually take its place.
71. unbolted: unsifted, coarse.   **72. jakes:** privy.
73. wagtail: a small bird which wags its tail up and down as it struts.   **75. know . . . reverence:** i.e., do you have the impertinence to raise your voice in the presence of your betters?   **76. anger . . . privilege:** something must be allowed to a man who has lost temper.   **80-81. bite . . . unloose:** i.e., cause the bonds of holy matrimony to be broken by serving the lusts of their employers.   **81. smooth:** help to gratify.

84. Renege, affirm: deny or agree; i.e., a perfect "yes man."   **halcyon:** kingfisher. A kingfisher hung up by the neck was supposed to turn its bill into the prevailing wind.
89-90. Goose . . . Camelot: These lines cannot be explained.
Sarum: Salisbury Plain, in the south of England.
90. Camelot: the home of King Arthur and the knights of his Round Table.   **96. His . . . not:** I don't like his face.
104. saucy roughness: impudent rudeness.   **104-105. constrains . . . nature:** affects a manner which is quite unnatural.   **110-11. silly . . . nicely:** silly servants who are always bowing to their masters as they strain to carry out their orders.   **112-15. Sir . . . front:** Kent now changes his tone from the honest blunt man to the affected courtier. See I.iv. 34.   **115. Phoebus:** the sun god.

flatterer. He that beguiled you in a plain accent
was a plain knave, which, for my part, I will not
be, though I should win your displeasure to en-
treat me to 't.°   122
    CORN: What was the offense you gave him?
    OSW: I never gave him any.
It pleased the King his master very late
To strike at me, upon his misconstruction,°
When he, conjunct,° and flattering his displeas-
    ure,
Tripped me behind; being down, insulted, railed,
And put upon him such a deal of man
That worthied him,° got praises of the
    King   130
For him attempting° who was self-subdued,°
And in the fleshment° of this dread exploit
Drew on me here again.
    KENT: None of these rogues
    and cowards
But Ajax is their fool.°   135
    CORN: Fetch forth the stocks!
You stubborn° ancient knave, you reverend°
    braggart,
We'll teach you——
    KENT: Sir, I am too old to learn.
Call not your stocks for me. I serve the King,
On whose employment I was sent to you.   141
You shall do small respect, show too bold malice
Against the grace and person of my master,
Stocking his messenger.°
    CORN: Fetch forth the stocks! As I have life
    and honor,   145
There shall he sit till noon.

119-22. He . . . to 't: the man who posed as blunt and honest
and deceived you was simply a knave. I shall never be a
knave, ever if you ask me and are angry because I refuse.
126. upon . . . misconstruction: because he deliberately mis-
interpreted my words.   127. conjunct: i.e., joining with
the King.   130. worthied him: got him favor.   131. attempting: attacking. self-subdued: made no resistance.
132. fleshment: excitement.   134-35. None . . . fool: This
cryptic but devastating remark rouses Cornwall to fury, for
he realizes from Kent's insolent tone, manner, and gesture
that by "Ajax" he is himself intended. Ajax was the ridiculous
braggart of the Greek army whom Shakespeare had already
dramatized [in *Troilus and Cressida*]. The name Ajax had
further unsavory significances for the original audience, for
"Ajax" was a common synonym for a jakes—a very evil-
smelling place. Kent thus implies "All these knaves and cowards are fooling this stinking braggart."   137. stubborn:
rude. reverend: old.   142-44. You . . . messenger: As the
King's representative, Kent is entitled to respectful treatment; to put him in the stocks is to offer an intolerable insult
to the King. See ll. 153–63 below and II.iv.28–29.

    REG: Till noon! Till night, my lord, and all
    night too.
    KENT: Why, madam, if I were your father's
    dog,
You should not use me so.
    REG: Sir, being his knave, I
    will.   150
    CORN: This is a fellow of the selfsame color
Our sister speaks of. Come, bring away° the
    stocks!   [*Stocks brought out*]
    GLO: Let me beseech your Grace not to do so.
His fault is much, and the good King his master
Will check° him for 't. Your purposed low
    correction°   155
Is such as basest and contemned'st° wretches
For pilferings and most common trespasses
Are punished with. The King must take it ill
That he, so slightly valued in his messenger,
Should have him thus restrained.   160
    CORN: I'll answer that.
    REG: My sister may receive it much more
    worse
To have her gentleman abused, assaulted,
For following her affairs. Put in his legs.
              [KENT *is put in the stocks.*]
Come, my good lord, away.   165
    [*Exeunt all but* GLOUCESTER *and* KENT.]
    GLO: I am sorry for thee, friend. 'Tis the
    Duke's pleasure.
Whose disposition all the world well knows
Will not be rubbed° nor stopped. I'll entreat for
    thee.
    KENT: Pray do not, sir. I have watched and
    traveled hard,
Some time I shall sleep out, the rest I'll whistle.
A good man's fortune may grow out at heels.°
Give you good morrow!°   172
    GLO: The Duke's to blame in this, 'twill be
    ill-taken.   [*Exit.*]
    KENT: Good King, that must approve the
    common saw,°
Thou out of Heaven's benediction comest   175
To the warm sun!°

152. bring away: fetch out.   155. check: rebuke, punish.
purposed . . . correction: the degrading punishment which
you propose.   156. contemned'st: most despised.
168. rubbed: turned aside, a metaphor from the game of
bowls.   171. A . . . heels: even a good man may suffer a
shabby fate.   172. Give . . . morrow: a good morning to
you.   174. approve . . . saw: stress the truth of the common proverb.   175-76. Thou . . . sun: you are coming out
of the shade into the heat.

Approach, thou beacon to this underglobe,°
That by thy comfortable beams I may
Peruse this letter! Nothing almost sees miracles
But misery.° I know 'tis from Cordelia,   180
Who hath most fortunately been informed
Of my obscurèd course,° and shall find time
From this enormous state,° seeking to give
Losses their remedies. All weary and
 o'erwatched,
Take vantage, heavy eyes, not to behold   185
This shameful lodging.
Fortune, good night. Smile once more, turn thy
 wheel!   [*Sleeps.*]

SCENE III. A wood.

 [*Enter* EDGAR.]
 EDG: I heard myself proclaimed,°
And by the happy° hollow of a tree
Escaped the hunt. No port is free, no place,
That guard and most unusual vigilance
Does not attend my taking.° Whiles I may 'scape
I will preserve myself, and am bethought°   6
To take the basest and most poorest shape
That ever penury in contempt of man
Brought near to beast.° My face I'll grime with
 filth,
Blanket° my loins, elf° all my hair in knots, 10
And with presented nakedness° outface
The winds and persecutions of the sky.
The country gives me proof and precedent°
Of Bedlam beggars,° who with roaring voices
Strike in their numbed and mortified° bare arms
Pins, wooden pricks, nails, sprigs of rosemary,
And with this horrible object, from low° farms,
Poor pelting° villages, sheepcotes and mills, 18

Sometime with lunatic bans,° sometime with
 prayers,
Enforce their charity. Poor Turlygod! Poor
 Tom!°   20
That's something yet. Edgar I nothing am.°
         [*Exit.*]

SCENE IV. Before GLOUCESTER's *castle.* KENT *in
the stocks.*

 [*Enter* LEAR, FOOL, *and* GENTLEMAN.]
 LEAR: 'Tis strange that they should so depart
 from home
And not send back my messenger.
 GENT: As I learned,
The night before there was no purpose° in them
Of this remove.   5
 KENT: Hail to thee, noble master!
 LEAR: Ha!
Makest thou this shame thy pastime?°
 KENT: No, my lord.
 FOOL: Ha, ha! He wears cruel° garters.
Horses are tied by the heads, dogs and bears by
the neck, monkeys by the loins, and men by the
legs. When a man's overlusty at legs,° then he
wears wooden netherstocks.°   14
 LEAR: What's he that hath so much thy place
 mistook
To set thee here?
 KENT: It is both he and she,
Your son and daughter.
 LEAR: No.
 KENT: Yes.   20
 LEAR: No, I say.
 KENT: I say, yea.
 LEAR: No, no, they would not.
 KENT: Yes, they have.
 LEAR: By Jupiter, I swear no.   25
 KENT: By Juno, I swear aye.
 LEAR: They durst not
 do 't,
They could not, would not do 't. 'Tis worse than
 murder
To do upon respect° such violent outrage.

---

177. **beacon . . . underglobe:** the rising sun.   **179-
80. Nothing . . . misery:** only those who are wretched appreciate miracles.   **182. obscured course:** i.e., my actions in
disguise.   **183. this . . . state:** these wicked times.
 Sc. iii: 1. proclaimed: See II.i.88–91.   **2. happy:**
lucky.   **5. attend my taking:** watch to take me.   **6. am
bethought:** have decided.   **8-9. penury . . . beast:**
poverty, to show that man is a contemptible creature, reduced to the level of a beast.   **10. Blanket:** cover with only
a blanket. **elf:** mat. Matted hair was believed to be caused by
elves.   **11. with . . . nakedness:** bold in my nakedness.
13. proof . . . precedent: examples.   **14. Bedlam beggars:**
lunatics discharged from Bedlam (or Bethlehem) Hospital,
the London madhouse. These sturdy beggars were the terror
of the countryside. See I.ii.149.   **15. mortified:** numbed.
17. low: humble.   **18. pelting:** paltry.

19. **bans:** curses.   **20. Poor . . . Tom:** Edgar rehearses the
names which a bedlam calls himself.   **21. That's . . . am:**
there's still a chance for me; as Edgar I am a dead man.
 Sc. iv: 4. purpose: intention.   **8. Makest . . . pastime:**
are you sitting there for amusement?   **10. cruel:** with a
pun on "crewel"—worsted.   **13. overlusty at legs:** i.e., a
vagabond.   **14. netherstocks:** stockings.   **29. upon respect:** the respect due to me, their King and father.

Resolve° me with all modest haste which way
Thou mightest deserve, or they impose, this
   usage,   31
Coming from us.°
   KENT: My lord, when at their home
I did commend your Highness' letters to them,
Ere I was risen from the place that showed 35
My duty kneeling, came there a reeking post,°
Stewed in his haste, half-breathless, panting forth
From Goneril his mistress salutations,
Delivered letters, spite of intermission,°
Which presently° they read. On whose contents
They summoned up their meiny,° straight took
   horse,   41
Commanded me to follow and attend
The leisure of their answer, gave me cold looks.
And meeting here the other messenger,
Whose welcome, I perceived, had poisoned
   mine—   45
Being the very fellow that of late
Displayed so saucily° against your Highness—
Having more man than wit about me, drew.
He raised the house with loud and coward cries.
Your son and daughter found this trespass worth°
The shame which here it suffers.   51
   FOOL: Winter's not gone yet° if the wild
geese fly that way.
     "Fathers that wear rags
       Do make their children blind,   55
     But fathers that bear bags°
       Shall see their children kind.
     Fortune, that arrant whore,
       Ne'er turns the key° to the poor."
But for all this, thou shalt have as many dolors°
for thy daughters as thou canst tell° in a year.
   LEAR: Oh,° how this mother swells up toward
   my heart!   62
Hysterica passio, down, thou climbing sorrow,

Thy element's° below! Where is this daughter?
   KENT: With the Earl, sir, here within.
   LEAR: Follow me not, stay here.   [*Exit*]
   GENT: Made you no more offense but what
you speak of?   68
   KENT: None.
How chance the King comes with so small a
   train?
   FOOL: An thou hadst been set i' the stocks for
that question, thou hadst well deserved it.
   KENT: Why, fool?
   FOOL: We'll° set thee to school to an ant, to
teach thee there's no laboring i' the winter. All
that follow their noses° are led by their eyes but
blind men, and there's not a nose among twenty
but can smell him that's stinking. Let go thy hold
when a great wheels runs down a hill, lest it
break thy neck with following it, but the great
one that goes up the hill, let him draw thee after.
When a wise man gives thee better counsel, give
me mine again. I would have none but knaves
follow it, since a fool gives it.   84

  "That sir which serves and seeks for gain,
    And follows but for form,°
  Will pack° when it begins to rain,
    And leave thee in the storm.

  "But I will tarry, the fool will stay,
    And let the wise man fly.   90
  The knave turns fool that runs away,
    The fool no knave, perdy."°

   KENT: Where learned you this, fool?
   FOOL: Not i' the stocks, fool.
[*Re-enter* LEAR, *with* GLOUCESTER.]
   LEAR: Deny to speak with me? They are sick?
   They are weary?   95
They have traveled all the night? Mere fetches,°
The images° of revolt and flying off.
Fetch me a better answer.
   GLO: My dear lord,
You know the fiery quality° of the Duke, 100
How unremovable and fixed he is
In his own course.
   LEAR: Vengeance! Plague! Death! Confusion!

---

30. Resolve: inform.   **32. Coming . . . us:** Lear uses the
royal "we"—"from us, the King."   **36. reeking post:**
sweating messenger.   **39. spite of intermission:** in spite of
the delay in reading my letter (which should have come
first).   **40. presently:** immediately.   **41. meiny:** followers.   **47. Displayed so saucily:** behaved so insolently.
50. worth: deserving.   **52. Winter's . . . yet:** there's more
trouble to come.   **56. bear bags:** have money.
59. turns . . . key: opens the door.   **60. dolors:** with a pun
on "dollars."   **61. tell:** count.   **62–64. Oh . . . below:**
The *mother*, called also *hysterica passio*, was an overwhelming feeling of physical distress and suffocation. Lear's mental
suffering is now beginning to cause a physical breakdown.
This sensation, and the violent throbbing of his heart until
finally it ceases, can be traced in Lear's speeches. See ll. 129,
146, 219–20; III.iv.16.

64. element: natural place.   **74–84. We'll . . . it:** The fool
is so much amused at Kent's discomfiture that he strings off a
series of wise sayings to show his own clearer understanding
of Lear's state.   **76. follow . . . noses:** go straight
ahead.   **86. but . . . form:** merely for show.   **87. pack:**
clear out.   **92. perdy:** by God.   **96. fetches:** excuses.
97. images: exact likenesses.   **100. quality:** nature.

Fiery? What quality? Why, Gloucester, Glouces-
ter,
I'd speak with the Duke of Cornwall and his
   wife.   105
   GLO: Well, my good lord, I have informed
      them so.
   LEAR: Informed them! Dost thou understand
      me, man?
   GLO: Aye, my good lord.
   LEAR: The King would speak with Cornwall,
      the dear father
Would with his daughter speak, commands her
   service.   110
Are they informed of this? My breath and blood!
"Fiery"? "The fiery Duke"? Tell the hot Duke
   that——
No, but not yet. Maybe he is not well.
Infirmity doth still neglect all office
Whereto our health is bound.° We are not our-
   selves   115
When nature being oppressed commands the
   mind
To suffer with the body. I'll forbear,
And am fall'n out with my more headier will,°
To take the indisposed and sickly fit
For the sound man. [*Looking on* KENT] Death on
   my state! Wherefore   120
Should he sit here? This act persuades me
That this remotion° of the Duke and her
Is practice° only. Give me my servant forth.°
Go tell the Duke and 's wife I'd speak with them,
Now, presently. Bid them come forth and hear
   me,   125
Or at their chamber door I'll beat the drum
Till it cry sleep to death.°
   GLO: I would have all well betwixt you.
                                               [*Exit.*]
   LEAR: Oh, me, my heart, my rising heart! But
      down!°
   FOOL: Cry to it, Nuncle, as the cockney° did
to the eels when she put 'em i' the paste alive.
She knapped° 'em o' the coxcombs with a stick,
and cried "Down, wantons, down!" 'Twas her
brother that, in pure kindness to his horse, but-
tered his hay.   135

[*Re-enter* GLOUCESTER, *with* CORNWALL,
   REGAN, *and* SERVANTS.]
   LEAR: Good morrow to you both.
   CORN: Hail to your Grace!
                              [KENT *is set at liberty.*]
   REG: I am glad to see your Highness.
   LEAR: Regan, I think you are, I know what
      reason   139
I have to think so. If thou shouldst not be glad,
I would divorce me from thy mother's tomb,
Sepúlchring an adultress.° [*To* KENT] Oh, are you
   free?
Some other time for that. Belovèd Regan,
Thy sister's naught.° O Regan, she hath tied
Sharp-toothed unkindness, like a vulture, here.
                              [*Points to his heart.*]
I can scarce speak to thee, thou'lt not believe
With how depraved a quality——O Regan!
   REG: I pray you, sir, take patience. I have
      hope
You less know how to value her desert
Than she to scant her duty.   150
   LEAR: Say, how is that?
   REG: I cannot think my sister in the least
Would fail her obligation. If, sir, perchance
She have restrained the riots of your followers,
'Tis on such ground and to such wholesome end
As clears her from all blame.   156
   LEAR: My curses on her!
   REG: Oh, sir, you are old,
Nature in you stands on the very verge
Of her confine.° You should be ruled and led
By some discretion that discerns your state
Better than you yourself. Therefore I pray you
That to our sister you do make return.
Say you have wronged her, sir.   164
   LEAR: Ask her forgiveness?
Do you but mark how this becomes the
   house.°——   [*Kneeling*]
"Dear daughter, I confess that I am old,
Age is unnecessary. On my knees I beg
That you'll vouchsafe me raiment, bed, and
   food."
   REG: Good sir, no more, these are unsightly
      tricks.   170
Return you to my sister.
   LEAR: [*Rising*] Never, Regan.

114–15. **Infirmity . . . bound:** when a man is sick, he neglects
his proper duty.   **118. am . . . will:** regret my
hastiness.   **122. remotion:** removal.   **123. practice:** pretense. **Give . . . forth:** release my servant at once.
127. cry . . . death: kill sleep by its noise.   **129. Oh . . .
down:** See ll. 62–64.   **130. cockney:** Londoner.
132. knapped: cracked.

141–42. **divorce . . . adultress:** i.e., I would suspect that your
dead mother had been false to me.   **144. naught:**
wicked.   **160. confine:** boundary, edge.   **166. becomes
. . . house;** i.e., suits my dignity.

She hath abated me of half my train,
Looked black upon me, struck me with her
    tongue,
Most serpentlike, upon the very heart.   175
All the stored vengeances of Heaven fall
On her ingrateful top!° Strike her young bones,
You taking airs, with lameness.
    CORN: Fie, sir, fie!
    LEAR: You nimble lightnings, dart your blind-
    ing flames   180
Into her scornful eyes. Infect her beauty,
You fen-sucked fogs,° drawn by the powerful sun
To fall° and blast her pride.
    REG: Oh, the blest gods! So will you wish on
    me
When the rash mood is on.   185
    LEAR: No, Regan, thou shalt never have my
    curse.
Thy tender-hefted° nature shall not give
Thee o'er to harshness. Her eyes are fierce, but
    thine
Do comfort and not burn. 'Tis not in thee
To grudge my pleasures, to cut off my
    train,   190
To bandy hasty words, to scant my sizes,°
And in conclusion to oppose the bolt°
Against my coming in. Thou better know'st
The offices of nature, bond of childhood,
Effects of courtesy, dues of gratitude.   195
Thy half o' the kingdom hast thou not forgot,
Wherein I thee endowed.
    REG: Good sir, to the pur-
    pose.°
    LEAR: Who put my man i' the stocks?
                          [*Tucket within.*]
    CORN: What trumpet's that?   200
    REG: I know 't, my sister's. This approves° her
    letter,
That she would soon be here.
    [*Enter* OSWALD.]   Is your lady come?
    LEAR: This is a slave whose easy-borrowed
    pride
Dwells in the fickle grace of her he follows.°
Out, varlet,° from my sight!   205

    CORN: What means your Grace?
    LEAR: Who stocked my servant? Regan, I
    have good hope
Thou didst not know on 't. Who comes here?
[*Enter* GONERIL.]   O Heavens,
If you do love old men, if your sweet sway 211
Allow° obedience, if yourselves are old,
Make it your cause. Send down, and take my
    part!
[*To* GONERIL] Art not ashamed to look upon this
    beard?
O Regan, wilt thou take her by the hand?   215
    GON: Why not by the hand, sir? How have I
    offended?
All's not offense that indiscretion finds
And dotage terms so.°
    LEAR: O sides, you are too tough,
Will you yet hold?° How came my man i' the
    stocks?   220
    CORN: I set him there, sir. But his own dis-
    orders
Deserved much less advancement.°
    LEAR: You!   Did
    you?
    REG: I pray you, Father, being weak, seem
    so.°
If till the expiration of your month   225
You will return and sojourn with my sister,
Dismissing half your train, come then to me.
I am now from home and out of that provision
Which shall be needful for your entertainment.°
    LEAR: Return to her, and fifty men dismissed?
No, rather I abjure° all roofs, and choose   231
To wage against the enmity o' the air,
To be a comrade with the wolf and owl—
Necessity's sharp pinch! Return with her?
Why, the hot-blooded France, that dowerless
    took   235
Our youngest-born—I could as well be brought
To keep his throne and, squirelike,° pension beg
To keep base life afoot. Return with her?
Persuade me rather to be slave and sumpter°
To this detested groom.   [*Pointing at* OSWALD.]
    GON: At your choice, sir. 241

---

177. **top:** head.   182. **fen-sucked fogs:** Cf. I.iv. 324.
183. **fall:** fall upon.   187. **tender-hefted:** gently
framed.   191. **scant my sizes:** reduce my allowances.
192. **oppose . . . bolt:** bar the door.   198. **Good . . . purpose:** and in good time to; or, please talk sense.   201. **approves:** confirms.   204–05. **whose . . . follows:** who soon
puts on airs because his fickle mistress favors him.
206. **varlet:** knave.

212. **Allow:** approve of.   217–218. **that . . . so:** because a
silly old man says so. See I.i.155–57,n.   219–20. **O . . .
hold:** See II.iv. 62–64,n, above.   222. **advancement:** promotion.   224. **seem so:** i.e., behave suitably.   229. **entertainment:** maintenance.   231. **abjure:** refuse with an
oath.   237. **squirelike:** like a servant.   239. **sumpter:**
pack horse, beast of burden.

LEAR: I prithee, Daughter, do not make me
　　mad.
I will not trouble thee, my child. Farewell.
We'll no more meet, no more see one another.
But yet thou art my flesh, my blood, my daugh-
　　ter,　　　　　　　　　　　　　　　　　　　245
Or rather a disease that's in my flesh
Which I must needs call mine. Thou art a boil,
A plague sore, an embossed carbuncle,°
In my corrupted blood. But I'll not chide thee.
Let shame come when it will, I do not call it.
I do not bid the thunderbearer° shoot,　251
Nor tell tales of thee to high-judging Jove.
Mend when thou canst, be better at thy leisure.
I can be patient, I can stay with Regan,
I and my hundred knights.　　　　　　　255
　　REG:　　　　　　　Not altogether so.
I looked not for you yet, nor am provided
For your fit welcome. Give ear, sir, to my sister,
For those that mingle reason with your passion
Must be content to think you old,° and so——
But she knows what she does.　　　　　261
　　LEAR:　　　　　　　Is this well spo-
　　ken?
　　REG: I dare avouch° it, sir. What, fifty follow-
　　ers?
Is it not well? What should you need of more?
Yea, or so many, sith° that both charge and
　　danger°　　　　　　　　　　　　　　265
Speak 'gainst so great a number? How in one
　　house
Should many people under two commands
Hold amity? 'Tis hard, almost impossible.
　　GON: Why might not you, my lord, receive
　　attendance
From those that she calls servants or from mine?
　　REG: Why not, my lord? If then they chanced
　　to slack° you,　　　　　　　　　　　271
We could control them. If you will come to me,
For now I spy a danger, I entreat you
To bring but five and twenty. To no more
Will I give place or notice.　　　　　　275
　　LEAR: I gave you all——
　　REG:　　　　　And in good time you gave it.
　　LEAR: Made you my guardians, my
　　depositaries,°

But kept a reservation° to be followed　279
With such a number. What, must I come to you
With five and twenty, Regan? Said you so?
　　REG: And speak 't again, my lord, no more
　　with me.
　　LEAR: Those wicked creatures yet do look
　　well-favored,°
When others are more wicked. Not being the
　　worst
Stands in some rank of praise.° [To GONERIL] I'll
　　go with thee.　　　　　　　　　　285
Thy fifty yet doth double five and twenty,
And thou art twice her love.
　　GON:　　　　　　　Hear me, my lord.
What need you five and twenty, ten, or five,
To follow in a house where twice so many　290
Have a command to tend you?
　　REG:　　　　　　　What need one?
　　LEAR: Oh,° reason not the need. Our basest
　　beggars
Are in the poorest thing superfluous.°
Allow not nature more than nature needs,　295
Man's life's as cheap as beast's. Thou art a lady.
If only to go warm were gorgeous,
Why, nature needs not what thou gorgeous
　　wear'st,
Which scarcely keeps thee warm. But for true
　　need——
You Heavens, give me that patience, patience I
　　need!　　　　　　　　　　　　　　300
You see me here, you gods, a poor old man,
As full of grief as age, wretched in both.
If it be you that stirs these daughters' hearts
Against their father, fool me not so much
To bear it tamely.° Touch me with noble anger,
And let not women's weapons, water drops,
Stain my man's cheeks! No, you unnatural hags,
I will have such revenges on you both　308
That all the world shall——I will do such
　　things——
What they are, yet I know not, but they shall be
The terrors of the earth. You think I'll weep.
No, I'll not weep.°

---

248. **embossed carbuncle:** swollen boil.　251. **thunder-
bearer:** Jupiter.　259–60. **those . . . old:** those who consider your passion with reason realize that you are old—and
should be wise.　263. **avouch:** guarantee.　265. **sith:**
since. **charge . . . danger:** expense and risk of maintaining.　271. **slack:** neglect.　278. **depositaries:** trustees.

279. **reservation:** condition. See I.i.134–41.　283. **well-
favored:** handsome.　284–85. **Not . . . praise:** i.e., since
Goneril is not so bad as Regan, that is one thing in her
favor.　293–300. **Oh . . . need:** the needs of a beggar are
very different from the needs of a king—but above all Lear
needs not dignity but patience.　293–94. **Our . . . superfluous:** even the few possessions of a beggar are not absolutely
necessary.　304–05. **fool . . . tamely:** do not degrade me so
much that I just tamely endure it.

I have full cause of° weeping, but this heart
Shall break into a hundred thousand flaws°
Or ere I'll weep. O fool, I shall go mad!   315
    [*Exeunt* LEAR, GLOUCESTER, KENT, *and* FOOL.]
  CORN: Let us withdraw, 'twill be a storm.
                  [*Storm and tempest.*]
  REG: This house is little. The old man and his
    people
Cannot be well bestowed.
  GON: 'Tis his own blame. Hath put himself
    from rest,
And must needs taste his folly.   320
  REG: For his particular,° I'll receive him
    gladly,
But not one follower.
  GON: So am I purposed.
Where is my Lord of Gloucester?
  CORN: Followed the old man forth. He is re-
    turned.   325
    [*Re-enter* GLOUCESTER.]
  GLO: The King is in high rage.
  CORN: Whither is he going?
  GLO: He calls to horse, but will I know not
    whither.
  CORN: 'Tis best to give him way, he leads him-
    self.
  GON: My lord, entreat him by no means to
    stay.   330
  GLO: Alack, the night comes on, and the bleak
    winds
Do sorely ruffle. For many miles about
There's scarce a bush.
  REG: Oh, sir, to willful men
The injuries that they themselves procure   335
Must be their schoolmasters. Shut up your doors.
He is attended with a desperate train,
And what they may incense° him to, being apt°
To have his ear abused,° wisdom bids fear.
  CORN: Shut up your doors, my lord, 'tis a wild
    night.   340
My Regan counsels well. Come out o' the storm.
                    [*Exeunt.*]

ACT III

SCENE I. *A heath.*

  [*Storm still.° Enter* KENT *and a* GENTLEMAN,
    meeting.]

  KENT: Who's there, besides foul weather?
  GENT: One minded like the weather, most
    unquietly.
  KENT: I know you. Where's the King?
  GENT: Contending with the fretful elements.
Bids the wind blow the earth into the sea,   5
Or swell the curlèd waters 'bove the main,°
That things might change or cease; tears his
    white hair,
Which the impetuous blasts, with eyeless° rage,
Catch in their fury, and make nothing of;
Strives in his little world of man° to outscorn
The to-and-fro-conflicting wind and rain.   11
This night, wherein the cub-drawn bear° would
    couch,°
The lion and the belly-pinchèd° wolf
Keep their fur dry, unbonneted° he runs,
And bids what will take all.   15
  KENT: But who is with him?
  GENT: None but the fool, who labors to outjest
His heart-struck injuries.
  KENT: Sir, I do know you,
And dare, upon the warrant of my note,°   20
Commend a dear° thing to you. There is division,
Although as yet the face of it be covered
With mutual cunning, 'twixt Albany and Corn-
    wall,
Who have—as who have not that their great
    stars
Throned and set high?°—servants, who seem no
    less,   25
Which are to France the spies and speculations°
Intelligent of our state°—what hath been seen,
Either in snuffs and packings° of the Dukes,
Or the hard rein which both of them have borne
Against the old kind King, or something deeper,
Whereof perchance these are but furnish-
    ings°——   31
But true it is, from France there comes a power°

---

6. **main:** mainland.   8. **eyeless:** blind.   10. **little . . . man:** It was a common Elizabethan idea, sometimes elaborately worked out, that individual man was a little world (microcosm) and reproduced in himself the universe (macrocosm).   12. **cub-drawn bear:** she-bear sucked dry, and therefore hungry. **couch:** take shelter.   13. **belly-pinched:** ravenous.   14. **unbonneted:** without a hat.   20. **upon . . . note:** guaranteed by my observation of you.   21. **dear:** precious.   24–25. **that . . . high:** whom Fate has set in a great position.   26. **speculations:** informers.   27. **Intelligent . . . state:** report on the state of our affairs.   28. **snuffs . . . packings:** resentment and plotting against each other.   31. **furnishings:** excuses. The sentence is not finished.   32. **power:** army.

---

313. **of:** for.   314. **flaws:** broken pieces.   321. **his particular:** himself personally.   338. **incense:** incite. **apt:** ready.   339. **abused:** deceived.
    Act III, Sc. i: s.d., **still:** continuing.

Into this scattered kingdom, who already,
Wise in our negligence, have secret feet
In some of our best ports and are at point°   35
To show their open banner. Now to you.
If on my credit° you dare build so far
To make your speed to Dover, you shall find
Some that will thank you, making just report
Of how unnatural and bemadding sorrow   40
The King hath cause to plain.°
I am a gentleman of blood° and breeding,
And from some knowledge and assurance° offer
This office° to you.
    GENT: I will talk further with you.   45
    KENT: No, do not.
For confirmation that I am much more
Than my outwall,° open this purse and take
What it contains. If you shall see Cordelia—
As fear not but you shall—show her this ring,
And she will tell you who your fellow° is   51
That yet you do not know. Fie on this storm!
I will go seek the King.
    GENT: Give me your hand.
Have you no more to say?   55
    KENT: Few words, but, to effect, more than all
      yet—
That when we have found the King—in which
      your pain°
That way, I'll this—he that first lights on him
Holloa the other.   [*Exeunt severally.*]

SCENE II. *Another part of the heath. Storm still.*

[*Enter* LEAR *and* FOOL.]
    LEAR: Blow, winds, and crack your cheeks!
      Rage! Blow!
You cataracts and hurricanoes,° spout
Till you have drenched our steeples, drowned the
      cocks!°
You sulphurous and thought-executing° fires,
Vaunt-couriers° to oak-cleaving thunderbolts, 5
Singe my white head! And thou, all-shaking
      thunder,

Smite flat the thick rotundity o' the world!
Crack nature's molds,° all germens° spill at once
That make ingrateful man!   9
    FOOL: O Nuncle, Court holy water° in a dry
house is better than this rain water out o' door.
Good Nuncle, in, and ask thy daughters' blessing.
Here's a night pities neither wise man nor fool.
    LEAR: Rumble thy bellyful! Spit, fire! Spout,
      rain!   14
Nor rain, wind, thunder, fire, are my daughters.
I tax° not you, you elements, with unkindness.
I never gave you kingdom, called you children,
You owe me no subscription.° Then let fall
Your horrible pleasure. Here I stand, your slave,
A poor, infirm, weak, and despised old man.
But yet I call you servile ministers°   21
That have with two pernicious daughters joined
Your high-engendered battles° 'gainst a head
So old and white as this. Oh, oh! 'Tis foul!
    FOOL: He that has a house to put 's head in
      has a good headpiece.   25
      "The° codpiece° that will house
        Before the head has any,
      The head and he shall louse
        So beggars marry many.
      The man that makes his toe   30
        What he his heart should make
      Shall of a corn cry woe,
        And turn his sleep to wake."
For there was never yet fair woman but she made
mouths in a glass.°   35
    LEAR: No, I will be the pattern of all patience,
I will say nothing.
    [*Enter* KENT.]
    KENT: Who's there?
    FOOL: Marry,° here's grace and a codpiece—
      that's a wise man and a fool.
    KENT: Alas, sir, are you here? Things that love
      night   40

---

35. at point: on the point of, about to.   **37. credit:** trustworthiness.   **41. plain:** complain.   **42. blood:** noble family.   **43. knowledge . . . assurance:** sure knowledge.   **44. office:** undertaking.   **48. outwall:** outside.   **51. fellow:** companion.   **57. pain:** labor.
    Sc. ii: 2. hurricanoes: waterspouts.   **3. cocks:** weathercocks on top of the steeples.   **4. thought-executing:** killing as quick as thought.   **5. Vaunt-couriers:** forerunners.

8. nature's molds: the molds in which men are made. **germens:** seeds of life.   **10. Court . . . water:** flattery of great ones.   **16. tax:** accuse.   **18. subscription:** submission.   **21. servile ministers:** servants who slavishly obey your masters.   **23. high-engendered battles:** armies begotten on high.   **26–33. The . . . wake:** the man who goes wenching before he has a roof over his head will become a lousy beggar. The man who is kinder to his toe than to his heart will be kept awake by his corns—i.e., Lear has been kinder to his feet (his daughters) than to his heart (himself). The Fool's remarks, especially when cryptic and indecent, are not easy to paraphrase.   **26. codpiece:** lit., the opening in the hose.   **34–35. made . . . glass:** made faces in a mirror.   **39. Marry:** Mary, by the Virgin.

Love not such nights as these. The wrathful skies
Gallow° the very wanderers of the dark
And make them keep their caves. Since I was
    man,
Such sheets of fire, such bursts of horrid thunder,
Such groans of roaring wind and rain, I never
Remember to have heard. Man's nature cannot
    carry°   46
The affliction nor the fear.

LEAR: Let the great gods,
That keep this dreadful pother° o'er our heads,
Find out their enemies now. Tremble, thou
    wretch,   50
That hast within thee undivulgèd crimes
Unwhipped of justice. Hide thee, thou bloody
    hand,
Thou perjured, and thou simular man of virtue°
That art incestuous. Caitiff, to pieces shake,
That under covert and convenient seeming° 55
Hast practiced on man's life. Close pent-up
    guilts,
Rive your concealing continents° and cry
These dreadful summoners grace.° I am a man
More sinned against than sinning.

KENT: Alack, bare-
    headed!   60
Gracious my lord, hard by here is a hovel.
Some friendship will it lend you 'gainst the tem-
    pest.
Repose you there while I to this hard house—
More harder than the stones whereof 'tis raised,
Which even but now, demanding after you, 65
Denied me to come in—return, and force
Their scanted courtesy.

LEAR: My wits begin to turn.
Come on, my boy. How dost, my boy? Art cold?
I am cold myself. Where is this straw, my fellow?
The art of our necessities is strange,   71
That can make vile things precious.° Come, your
    hovel.
Poor fool and knave, I have one part in my heart
That's sorry yet for thee.

FOOL: [*Singing*]   75
  "He° that has and a little tiny wit—
    With hey, ho, the wind and the rain—
    Must make content with his fortunes fit,°
    For the rain it raineth every day."

LEAR: True, my good boy. Come, bring us to
  this hovel.   [*Exeunt* LEAR *and* KENT.]

FOOL: This is a brave night to cool a courte-
  san.   81
I'll speak a prophecy° ere I go:
"When priests are more in word than matter,
When brewers mar their malt with water,
When nobles are their tailors' tutors,°   85
No heretics burned, but wenches' suitors,
When every case in law is right,
No squire in debt, nor no poor knight,
When slanders do not live in tongues,
Nor cutpurses come not to throngs,   90
When usurers tell their gold i' the field,
And bawds and whores do churches build—
Then shall the realm of Albion°
Come to great confusion.
Then comes the time, who lives to see 't, 95
That going shall be used with feet."°
This prophecy Merlin shall make, for I live be-
  fore his time.°   [*Exit.*]

SCENE III. GLOUCESTER'S *castle.*

[*Enter* GLOUCESTER *and* EDMUND.]

GLO: Alack, alack, Edmund, I like not this
unnatural dealing. When I desired their leave
that I might pity him,° they took from me the
use of mine own house, charged me, on pain of
their perpetual displeasure, neither to speak of
him, entreat for him, nor any way sustain° him.

EDM: Most savage and unnatural!   7

GLO: Go to, say you nothing. There's a division betwixt the Dukes, and a worse matter than
that. I have received a letter this night, 'tis dan-

76–79. He . . . day: another stanza of the song which the
Fool in *Twelfth Night* sings at the end of the play.
78. Must . . . fit: i.e., must be content with a fortune as slim
as his wit.   **82–96. prophecy . . . feet:** The fool gives a list
of common events, pretending that they are never likely to
happen. The prophecy is a parody of riddling prophecies
popular at this time which were attributed to Merlin, the old
magician of King Arthur's Court.   **85. nobles . . . tutors:**
Young noblemen and gallants were very particular about the
fashion and cut of their clothes.   **93. Albion:** England.
96. going. . . feet: feet will be used for walking.   **97. This
. . . time:** A piece of mock pedantry, for—according to
Holinshed's *Chronicles*—King Lear died some generations
before King Arthur.
    Sc. iii: 3. him: Lear.   **6. sustain:** relieve.

---

42. Gallow: terrify.   **46. carry:** endure.   **49. pother:**
turmoil.   **53. simular . . . virtue:** a man who pretends to
be virtuous.   **55. under . . . seeming:** under a false appearance of propriety.   **57. Rive . . . continents:** split open
that which covers and conceals you.   **57–58. cry . . .
grace:** ask for mercy from these dreadful summoners. The
summoner was the officer of the ecclesiastical court who summoned a man to appear to answer a charge of immorality.
71–72. art . . . precious: our needs are like the art of the
alchemist (who was forever experimenting to try to trans-
mute base metal into gold).

gerous to be spoken.—I have locked the letter in my closet. These injuries the King now bears will be revenged home.° There is part of a power already footed.° We must incline to the King. I will seek him and privily° relieve him. Go 15 you, and maintain talk with the Duke, that my charity be not of him perceived. If he ask for me, I am ill and gone to bed. Though I die for it, as no less is threatened me, the King my old master must be relieved. There is some strange thing toward, Edmund. Pray you be careful.   [*Exit.*]

EDM: This courtesy, forbid thee,° shall the Duke
Instantly know, and of that letter too.
This seems a fair deserving,° and must draw me
That which my father loses, no less than all. 25
The younger rises when the old doth fall.

[*Exit.*]

SCENE IV. *The heath. Before a hovel.*

[*Enter* LEAR, KENT, *and* FOOL.]

KENT: Here is the place, my lord. Good my lord, enter.
The tyranny° of the open night's too rough
For nature to endure.   [*Storm still.*]

LEAR: Let me alone.

KENT: Good my lord, enter here.   5

LEAR: Wilt break my heart?

KENT: I had rather break mine own. Good my lord, enter.

LEAR: Thou think'st 'tis much that this contentious° storm
Invades us to the skin. So 'tis to thee,
But where the greater malady is fixed°   10
The lesser is scarce felt. Thou'dst shun a bear,
But if thy flight lay toward the raging sea
Thou'dst meet the bear i' the mouth. When the mind's free°
The body's delicate. The tempest in my mind
Doth from my senses take all feeling else   15
Save what beats there.° Filial ingratitude!
Is it not as this mouth should tear this hand
For lifting food to 't? But I will punish home.
No, I will weep no more. In such a night

To shut me out! Pour on, I will endure.   20
In such a night as this! O Regan, Goneril!
Your old kind father, whose frank heart gave all——
Oh, that way madness lies, let me shun that,
No more of that.

KENT: Good my lord, enter here.   25

LEAR: Prithee, go in thyself, seek thine own ease.
This tempest will not give me leave to ponder
On things would hurt me more. But I'll go in.
[*To the* FOOL] In, boy, go first. You houseless poverty°——
Nay, get thee in. I'll pray, and then I'll sleep.
[FOOL *goes in.*]
Poor naked wretches, wheresoe'er you are,
That bide° the pelting of this pitiless storm,
How shall your houseless heads and unfed sides,
Your looped and windowed° raggedness, defend you   34
From seasons such as these? Oh, I have ta'en
Too little care of this! Take physic, pomp.°
Expose thyself to feel what wretches feel,
That thou mayst shake the superflux° to them
And show the Heavens more just.

EDG: [*Within*] Fathom and half, fathom and half! Poor Tom!   41
[*The* FOOL *runs out from the hovel.*]

FOOL: Come not in here, Nuncle, here's a spirit. Help me, help me!

KENT: Give me thy hand. Who's there?

FOOL: A spirit, a spirit. He says his name's Poor Tom.   46

KENT: What art thou that dost grumble there i' the straw?
Come forth.

[*Enter* EDGAR *disguised as a madman.*]

EDG: Away! The foul fiend follows me!
"Through the sharp hawthorn blows the cold wind."   50
Hum! Go to thy cold bed and warm thee.

LEAR: Hast thou given all to thy two daughters?
And art thou come to this?°

EDG: Who gives anything to Poor Tom?

---

13. **home:** to the utmost.   14. **footed:** landed.
15. **privily:** secretly.   22. **forbid thee:** forbidden to thee.   24. **This . . . deserving:** i.e., by betraying my father, I shall deserve much of (be rewarded by) the Duke.
Sc. iv: 2. **tyranny:** cruelty.   8. **contentious:** striving against us.   10. **the . . . fixed:** i.e., in the mind.
13. **free:** i.e., from cares.   16. **what . . . there:** i.e., the mental anguish which is increased by the thumping of Lear's overtaxed heart.

29. **houseless poverty:** poor homeless people.   32. **bide:** endure.   34. **looped . . . windowed:** full of holes and gaps.   36. **Take . . . pomp:** i.e., cure yourselves, you great men.   38. **superflux:** superfluity, what you do not need.   52–53. **Hast . . . this:** At the sight of the supposed lunatic Lear goes quite mad. Such utter destitution, he says, can only have been caused by daughters as unkind as his own.

Whom the foul fiend hath led through fire and through flame, through ford and whirlpool, o'er bog and quagmire, that hath laid knives under his pillow and halters in his pew,° set ratsbane° by his porridge, made him proud of heart to ride on a bay trotting horse over four-inched° bridges, to course° his own shadow for a traitor. Bless thy five wits!° Tom's a-cold. Oh, do de, do de, do de. Bless thee from whirlwinds, star-blasting,° and taking!° Do Poor Tom some charity, whom the foul fiend vexes. There could I have him now, and there, and there again, and there.°   66
[*Storm still.*]

LEAR: What, have his daughters brought him to this pass?
Couldst thou save nothing? Didst thou give them all?

FOOL: Nay, he reserved a blanket,° else we had been all shamed.   70

LEAR: Now, all the plagues that in the pendulous° air
Hang fated o'er men's faults light on thy daughters!

KENT: He hath no daughters, sir.

LEAR: Death, traitor! Nothing could have subdued nature
To such a lowness but his unkind daughters. 75
Is it the fashion that discarded fathers
Should have thus little mercy on their flesh?
Judicious punishment! 'Twas this flesh begot
Those pelican° daughters.

EDG: "Pillicock sat on Pillicock Hill.   80
Halloo, halloo, loo, loo!"°

FOOL: This cold night will turn us all to fools and madmen.

EDG: Take heed o' the foul fiend. Obey thy parents, keep thy word justly, swear not, commit not with man's sworn spouse, set not thy sweet heart on proud array. Tom's a-cold.   87

LEAR: What hast thou been?

EDG: A servingman,° proud in heart and mind, that curled my hair, wore gloves in my cap, served the lust of my mistress's heart and did the act of darkness with her, swore as many oaths as I spake words and broke them in the sweet face of Heaven. One that slept in the contriving of lust and waked to do it. Wine loved I deeply, dice dearly, and in woman outparamoured° the Turk.° False of heart, light of ear, bloody of hand, hog in sloth, fox in stealth, wolf in greediness, dog in madness, lion in prey. Let not the creaking of shoes nor the rustling of silks betray thy poor heart to woman. Keep thy foot out of brothels, thy hand out of plackets,° thy pen from lenders' books,° and defy the foul fiend.   103
"Still through the hawthorn blows the cold wind.
Says suum, mun, ha, no, nonny.
Dolphin my boy, my boy, sessa! Let him trot by."   [*Storm still.*]

LEAR: Why, thou wert better in thy grave than to answer with thy uncovered body this extremity of the skies. Is man no more than this? Consider him well. Thou° owest the worm no silk, the beast no hide, the sheep no wool, the cat no perfume.° Ha! Here's three on 's are sophisticated. Thou art the thing itself. Unaccommodated man is no more but such a poor, bare, forked animal as thou art. Off, off, you lendings!° Come, unbutton here.   [*Tearing off his clothes.*]

FOOL: Prithee, Nuncle, be contented, 'tis a naughty night to swim in. Now a little fire in a wild field were like an old lecher's heart, a small spark, all the rest on 's body cold. Look, here comes a walking fire.   121

[*Enter GLOUCESTER, with a torch.*]

EDG: This is the foul fiend Flibbertigibbet. He begins at curfew° and walks till the first cock, he gives the web and the pin,° squints the eye and

58. **pew:** seat. **ratsbane:** rat poison.   60. **four-inched:** i.e., narrow.   61. **course:** hunt after.   62. **five wits:** i.e., common wit, imagination, fantasy, estimation, and memory.   63. **star-blasting:** evil caused by a planet.   64. **taking:** malignant influence of fairies.   65-66. **There . . . there:** Poor Tom is chasing his own vermin.   69. **blanket:** i.e., his only covering. See II.iii.10.   71. **pendulous:** overhanging.   79. **pelican:** The pelican was the pattern of devoted motherhood because it fed its young on its own blood; but when the young grew strong, they turned on their parents.   80-81. **Pillicock . . . loo:** an old rhyme.   89-99. **A servingman . . . prey:** This is another description of the gentleman servingman. See II.ii.15-26.

96. **outparamoured:** had more mistresses than.   96-97. **the Turk:** the Turkish Emperor.   102. **plackets:** openings in a petticoat.   102-103. **pen . . . books:** The debtor often acknowledged the debt by signing in the lender's account book.   110-116. **Thou . . . here:** There is usually an underlying sense in Lear's ravings. The bedlam, he says, has not borrowed silk from the silkworm, or furs from the beast, or wool from the sheep to cover himself. Kent, the fool, and he himself are therefore *sophisticated*—adulterated, wearing coverings not their own. Natural man, *unaccommodated* (i.e., not provided with such conveniences), is just a naked animal. Lear will therefore strip himself naked and cease to be artificial.   111-12. **cat . . . perfume:** a perfume taken from the civet cat, which has glands that function in the same manner as the skunk's.   115. **lendings:** things borrowed.   123. **curfew:** sounded at 9 P.M.   124. **web . . . pin:** eye diseases, cataract.

makes the harelip, mildews the white wheat and
hurts the poor creature of earth.   126
 "Saint° Withold footed thrice the 'old,°
  He met the nightmare° and her ninefold.°
   Bid her alight,
   And her troth plight,   130
  And aroint thee, witch, aroint° thee!"
KENT: How fares your Grace?
LEAR: What's he?
KENT: Who's there? What is 't you seek?
GLO: What are you there? Your names? 135
EDG: Poor Tom, that eats the swimming frog,
the toad, the tadpole, the wall newt, and the
water; that in the fury of his heart, when the foul
fiend rages, eats cow dung for sallets;° swallows
the old rat and the ditch dog;° drinks the green
mantle of the standing pool; who is whipped
from tithing to tithing,° and stock-punished, and
imprisoned; who hath had three suits° to his
back, six shirts to his body, horse to ride, and
weapon to wear.   145
 "But mice and rats and such small deer
 Have been Tom's food for seven long year."
Beware my follower. Peace, Smulkin,° peace,
 thou fiend!
GLO: What, hath your Grace no better com-
pany?
EDG: The Prince of Darkness is a gentleman.
Modo he's called, and Mahu.   151
GLO: Our flesh and blood is grown so vile, my
 lord,
That it doth hate what gets° it.
EDG: Poor Tom's a-cold.
GLO: Go in with me. My duty cannot suffer
To obey in all your daughters' hard commands.
Though their injunction be to bar my doors 157
And let this tyrannous night take hold upon you,
Yet have I ventured to come seek you out
And bring you where both fire and food is ready.
LEAR: First let me talk with this philosopher.
What is the cause of thunder?°   162
KENT: Good my lord, take his offer, go into
 the house.

LEAR: I'll talk a word with this same learnèd
 Theban.°
What is your study?°   165
EDG: How to prevent the fiend and to kill ver-
min.
LEAR: Let me ask you one word in private.
KENT: Impórtune him once more to go, my
 lord.
His wits begin to unsettle.
 GLO: Canst thou blame him? [Storm still.]
His daughters seek his death. Ah, that good Kent!
He said it would be thus, poor banished man!
Thou say'st the King grows mad. I'll tell thee,
 friend,   173
I am almost mad myself. I had a son,
Now outlawed from my blood. He sought my life
But lately, very late. I loved him, friend,
No father his son dearer. Truth to tell thee,
The grief hath crazed my wits. What a night's
 this!   178
I do beseech your Grace——
LEAR: Oh, cry you mercy, sir.
Noble philosopher, your company.
EDG: Tom's a-cold.
GLO: In, fellow, there, into the hovel. Keep
 thee warm.
LEAR: Come, let's in all.
KENT: This way, my lord.
LEAR: With him,
I will keep still with my philosopher.   187
KENT: Good my lord, soothe him, let him take
 the fellow.
GLO: Take him you on.
KENT: Sirrah, come on, go along with us.
LEAR: Come, good Athenian.°   191
GLO: No words, no words. Hush.
EDG: "Child° Rowland to the dark tower
 came.
  His word was still 'Fie, foh, and fum,
   I smell the blood of a British man.'" 195
          [Exeunt.]

SCENE V. GLOUCESTER's *castle*.

[*Enter* CORNWALL *and* EDMUND.]
CORN: I will have my revenge ere I depart his
house.

127–31. Saint . . . thee: a charm to keep horses from suffering from nightmare. **127. 'old:** wold, uncultivated
downland. **128. nightmare:** nightmare was believed to be
caused by a fiend. **ninefold:** nine young. **131. aroint:** be
gone. **139. sallets:** salads. **140. ditch dog:** dog
drowned in a ditch. **142. tithing:** district, parish.
143. three suits: See II.ii.16. **148–51. Smulkin . . . Mahu:**
familiar spirits. **153. gets:** begets. **162. cause of
thunder:** This was much disputed by philosophers of the
time.

164. Theban: i.e., Greek philosopher. **165. study:** particular interest, or in modern academic jargon, "special
field." **191. Athenian:** like "Theban," l. 164.
193–95. Child . . . man: jumbled snatches of old ballads.
Child in old ballads is used of young warriors who have not
yet been knighted.

EDM: How, my lord, I may be censured,° that nature° thus gives way to loyalty, something fears me to think of.   5

CORN: I now perceive it was not altogether your brother's evil disposition made him seek his death, but a provoking merit, set a-work by a reprovable badness in himself.°   9

EDM: How malicious is my fortune, that I must repent to be just!° This is the letter he spoke of, which approves° him an intelligent party° to the advantages of France. Oh heavens, that this treason were not, or not I the detector!

CORN: Go with me to the Duchess.   15

EDM: If the matter of this paper be certain, you have mighty business in hand.

CORN: True or false, it hath made thee Earl of Gloucester. Seek out where thy father is, that he may be ready for our apprehension.°   20

EDM: [Aside] If I find him comforting the King, it will stuff his suspicion more fully.—I will persever° in my course of loyalty, though the conflict be sore between that and my blood.

CORN: I will lay trust upon thee, and thou shalt find a dearer father in my love. [Exeunt.]

SCENE VI.° A chamber in a farmhouse adjoining the castle.

[Enter GLOUCESTER, LEAR, KENT, FOOL, and EDGAR.]

GLO: Here is better than the open air, take it thankfully. I will piece out the comfort with what addition I can. I will not be long from you.

KENT: All the power of his wits has given way to his impatience.° The gods reward your kindness!   [Exit GLOUCESTER.]

EDG: Frateretto° calls me, and tells me Nero° is an angler in the lake of darkness. Pray, innocent,° and beware the foul fiend.   9

FOOL: Prithee, Nuncle, tell me whether a madman be a gentleman or a yeoman.°

LEAR: A king, a king!

FOOL: No, he's a yeoman that has a gentleman to his son, for he's a mad yeoman that sees his son a gentleman before him.°   15

LEAR: To have a thousand with red burning spits°
Come hissing in upon 'em——

EDG: The foul fiend bites my back.

FOOL: He's mad that trusts in the tameness of a wolf, a horse's health, a boy's love, or a whore's oath.   21

LEAR: It shall be done, I will arraign them straight.°
[To EDGAR] Come, sit thou here, most learned justicer.°
[To the FOOL] Thou, sapient° sir, sit here. Now, you she-foxes!

EDG: Look where he stands and glares! Wantest thou eyes at trial,° madam?   26
   "Come o'er the bourn, Bessy, to me."

FOOL: "Her boat hath a leak,
         And she must not speak
         Why she dares not come over to
            thee."   31

EDG: The foul fiend haunts poor Tom in the voice of a nightingale. Hopdance cries in Tom's belly for two white herring. Croak not,° black angel, I have no food for thee.

KENT: How do you, sir? Stand you not so amazed.°   36
Will you lie down and rest upon the cushions?

LEAR: I'll see their trial first. Bring in the evidence.

Sc. v: 3. **censured:** judged.   4. **nature:** i.e., natural affection toward my father yielding to loyalty to my Duke. For Edmund's real sentiments on nature see I.ii.1–2.   8–9. **but . . . himself:** i.e., but a good quality in Edgar that provoked him to commit murder because of the reprehensible badness in Gloucester.   11. **repent . . . just:** be sorry because I have acted rightly (in betraying my father).   12. **approves:** proves.   12–13. **intelligent party:** spy, one with secret information.   20. **apprehension:** arrest.   23. **persever:** persevere.
   Sc. vi: In this scene Lear is completely mad, the Fool is half-witted, and Edgar is pretending to be a lunatic.   5. **impatience:** suffering.   7. **Frateretto:** . . . fiend's name. . . . **Nero:** the debauched Roman Emperor who fiddled while Rome burned.   9. **innocent:** fool.

10–11. **whether . . . yeoman:** The fool is much interested in the social status of a madman and proceeds to discuss the problem.   11. **yeoman:** farmer, a notoriously wealthy class at this time.   13–15. **No . . . him:** Many yeomen farmers who had become wealthy by profiteering from the wars and dearths sent their sons to London to learn to become gentlemen, as fifty years ago Chicago meat packers sent their sons to Harvard and their daughters to England, to be presented at Court. This social change was much commented on, and is illustrated in Jonson's comedy *Every Man out of His Humour.*   16. **spits:** thin iron rods thrust through meat on which the meat was turned before the fire in roasting; very useful weapons in emergency.   22. **straight:** straightway.   23. **justicer:** judge.   24. **sapient:** wise.   26. **Wantest . . . trial:** can you not see who is at your trial (i.e., this fiend)? But Edgar is deliberately talking madly.   34–35. **Croak not:** don't rumble in my empty belly. The correct Elizabethan word for this embarrassing manifestation is "wamble."   36. **amazed:** astonished—a strong word.

[*To* EDGAR] Thou robèd man of justice,° take thy
place.
[*To the* FOOL] And thou, his yokefellow of
equity,°   40
Bench° by his side. [*To* KENT] You are o' the
commission,°
Sit you too.
   EDG: Let us deal justly.
"Sleepest or wakest thou, jolly shepherd?
   Thy sheep be in the corn,   45
   And for one blast of thy minikin° mouth,
   Thy sheep shall take no harm."
Purr! The cat is gray.
   LEAR: Arraign her first. 'Tis Goneril. I here
take my oath before this honorable assembly, she
kicked the poor King her father.   51
   FOOL: Come hither, mistress. Is your name
Goneril?
   LEAR: She cannot deny it.
   FOOL: Cry you mercy,° I took you for a joint
stool.°   56
   LEAR: And here's another, whose warped°
   looks proclaim
What store° her heart is made on. Stop her there!
Arms, arms, sword, fire! Corruption° in the
   place!
False justicer, why hast thou let her 'scape?   60
   EDG: Bless thy five wits!
   KENT: Oh, pity! Sir, where is the patience
now,
That you so oft have boasted to retain?
   EDG: [*Aside*] My tears begin to take his part so
much
They'll mar my counterfeiting.°   65
   LEAR: The little dogs and all,
Tray, Blanch, and Sweetheart, see, they bark at
me.
   EDG: Tom will throw his head at them.
Avaunt, you curs!
   Be thy mouth or black or white,   70
   Tooth that poisons if it bite,
   Mastiff, greyhound, mongrel grim,

Hound or spaniel, brach° or lym,°
Or bobtail tike or trundletail,°
Tom will make them weep and wail.   75
For, with throwing thus my head,
Dogs leap the hatch, and all are fled.
Do de, de, de. Sessa! Come, march to wakes° and
fairs and market towns. Poor Tom, thy horn° is
dry.   80
   LEAR: Then let them anatomize° Regan, see
what breeds about her heart. Is there any cause
in nature that makes these hard hearts? [*To*
EDGAR] You, sir, I entertain° for one of my hundred, only I do not like the fashion of your garments. You will say they are Persian attire,° but
let them be changed.   87
   KENT: Now, good my lord, lie here and rest
awhile.
   LEAR: Make no noise, make no noise. Draw
the curtains. So, so, so.° We'll go to supper i' the
morning. So, so, so.   92
   FOOL: And I'll go to bed at noon.°
[*Re-enter* GLOUCESTER.]
   GLO: Come hither, friend. Where is the King
my master?
   KENT: Here, sir, but trouble him not. His wits
are gone.   95
   GLO: Good friend, I prithee take him in thy
arms.
I have o'erheard a plot of death upon him.
There is a litter° ready, lay him in 't,
And drive toward Dover, friend, where thou
shalt meet
Both welcome and protection. Take up thy mas-
ter.   100
If thou shouldst dally° half an hour, his life,
With thine and all that offer to defend him,
Stand in assurèd loss. Take up, take up,
And follow me, that will to some provision
Give thee quick conduct.   105

---

73. **brach:** bitch. **lym:** bloodhound.   74. **trundletail:**
curly tail.   78. **wakes:** merrymakings.   79. **horn:** a
horn bottle carried by beggars in which they stored the drink
given by the charitable.   81. **anatomize:** dissect.
84. **entertain:** engage.   86. **Persian attire:** i.e., of a magnificent and foreign fashion. There had been considerable interest in Persia for some years, especially after the return of
some of the followers of Sir Anthony Shirley from his famous
expedition.   91. **So . . . so:** In dialogue "so, so" usually
indicates action. Here Lear imagines the bed curtains are
being drawn.   93. **And . . . noon:** i.e., if it's suppertime in
the morning, it will be bedtime at noon. The fool disappears
after this scene.   98. **litter:** a form of bed or stretcher enclosed by curtains used for carrying the sick or the
wealthy.   101. **dally:** hesitate.

---

39. **robed . . . justice:** another glance at Edgar's blanket.   40. **yokefellow of equity:** partner, in the law.
41. **Bench:** sit on the judge's bench. **commission:** Persons
of high rank or those accused of extraordinary crimes were
not tried before the ordinary courts, but by a commission
specially appointed.   46. **minikin:** dainty.   55. **Cry
. . . mercy:** I beg your pardon.   55–56. **joint stool:**
wooden stool of joiner's work.   57. **warped:** malignant.
58. **store:** material.   59. **Corruption:** bribery.   64–65.
My . . . counterfeiting: i.e., I am so sorry for the King
that I can hardly keep up this pretense.

KENT: Oppressèd nature sleeps.
This rest might yet have balmed° thy broken sin-
    ews,
Which, if convenience will not allow,
Stand in hard cure.° [*To the* FOOL] Come, help to
    bear thy master.
Thou must not stay behind.   110
    GLO: Come, come, away.
                        [*Exeunt all but* EDGAR.]
    EDG: When we our betters see bearing our
        woes,
We scarcely think our miseries our foes.
Who alone suffers suffers most i' the mind,
Leaving free things and happy shows behind.
But then the mind much sufferance doth o'erskip
When grief hath mates, and bearing fellowship.°
How light and portable my pain seems now
When that which makes me bend makes the King
    bow,   119
He childed as I fathered! Tom, away!
Mark the high noises,° and thyself° bewray
When false opinion, whose wrong thought defiles
    thee,
In thy just proof repeals° and reconciles thee.
What will hap more tonight, safe 'scape the
    King!   124
Lurk,° lurk.   [*Exit.*]

SCENE VII. GLOUCESTER's *castle.*

[*Enter* CORNWALL, REGAN, GONERIL, EDMUND,
and SERVANTS.]
    CORN: Post speedily to my lord your hus-
band.° Show him this letter. The army of France
is landed. Seek out the traitor Gloucester.
                [*Exeunt some of the* SERVANTS.]
    REG: Hang him instantly.
    GON: Pluck out his eyes.   5

CORN: Leave him to my displeasure. Edmund,
keep you our sister company. The revenges we
are bound to take upon your traitorous father are
not fit for your beholding. Advise the Duke,
where you are going, to a most festinate° preparation. We are bound to the like. Our posts° shall
be swift and intelligent° betwixt us. Farewell,
dear Sister. Farewell, my Lord of Gloucester.°
[*Enter* OSWALD.] How now! Where's the King?
    OSW: My Lord of Gloucester° hath conveyed
        him hence.   15
Some five or six and thirty of his knights,
Hot questrists° after him, met him at gate,
Who, with some other of the lords dependents,°
Are gone with him toward Dover, where they
    boast
To have well-armèd friends.   20
    CORN: Get horses for your mistress.
    GON: Farewell, sweet lord, and Sister.
    CORN: Edmund, farewell.
[*Exeunt* GONERIL, EDMUND, *and* OSWALD.]
                        Go seek the traitor Gloucester.
Pinion him like a thief, bring him before us. 25
                        [*Exeunt other* SERVANTS.]
Though well we may not pass° upon his life
Without the form of justice, yet our power
Shall do a courtesy to our wrath,° which men
May blame but not control. Who's there? The
    traitor?
[*Enter* GLOUCESTER, *brought in by two or
    three.*]
    REG: Ungrateful fox! 'Tis he.   30
    CORN: Bind fast his corky° arms.
    GLO: What mean your Graces? Good my
    friends, consider
You are my guests. Do me no foul play, friends.
    CORN: Bind him, I say. [SERVANTS *bind him.*]
    REG: Hard, hard. O filthy traitor!
    GLO: Unmerciful lady as you are, I'm none.
    CORN: To this chair bind him. Villain, thou
        shalt find—— [REGAN *plucks his beard.*]
    GLO: By the kind gods, 'tis most ignobly done

---

107. **balmed:** soothed.   109. **Stand . . . cure:** will hardly
be cured.   112–17. **When . . . fellowship:** when we see
better men than ourselves suffering as we do, our sufferings
seem slight. The man who suffers endures most in his mind
because he contrasts his present misery with his happy past;
but when he has companions in misery (*bearing fellowship*),
his mind suffers less.   121. **high noises:** i.e., the "hue and
cry" of the pursuers.   121–23. **thyself . . . thee:** do not
reveal yourself until the belief in your guilt is proved wrong
and you are called back.   123. **repeals:** calls back from
banishment.   125. **Lurk:** lie hid.
    Sc. vii: 1–2. **Post . . . husband:** These words are addressed
to Goneril. **Post:** ride fast.

10. **festinate:** hasty.   11. **posts:** messengers.   12. **intelligent:** full of information.   13. **Lord of Gloucester:** i.e.,
Edmund, who has been promoted for his treachery.
15. **Lord of Gloucester:** i.e., the old Earl.   17. **questrists:**
seekers.   18. **lords dependents:** lords of his party.
26. **pass:** pass judgment on.   27–28. **yet . . . wrath:** yet
because we are all-powerful we will give way to our
wrath.   31. **corky:** dry and withered.

To pluck me by the beard.°

REG: So white, and such a traitor!   40

GLO: Naughty lady,
These hairs which thou dost ravish° from my
   chin
Will quicken° and accuse thee. I am your host.
With robbers' hands my hospitable favors°
You should not ruffle thus. What will you do?

CORN: Come, sir, what letters had you late
   from France?   46

REG: Be simple answerer, for we know the
   truth.

CORN: And what confederacy° have you with
   the traitors
Late footed in the kingdom?

REG: To whose hands have you sent the lunatic King?   50
Speak.

GLO: I have a letter guessingly set down,
Which came from one that's of a neutral heart,
And not from one opposed.

CORN: Cunning.   55

REG: And false

CORN: Where hast thou sent the King?

GLO: To Dover.

REG: Wherefore to Dover? Wast thou not
   charged at peril°——

CORN: Wherefore to Dover? Let him first answer that.   60

GLO: I am tied to the stake, and I must stand
   the course.°

REG: Wherefore to Dover, sir?

GLO: Because I would not see thy cruel nails
Pluck out his poor old eyes, nor thy fierce sister
In his anointed° flesh stick boarish fangs.   65
The sea, with such a storm as his bare head
In hell-black night endured, would have buoyed
   up,°
And quenched the stellèd fires.°
Yet, poor old heart, he holp° the heavens to rain.
If wolves had at thy gate howled that stern time,
Thou shouldst have said, "Good porter, turn the
   key,"°   71

All cruels else subscribed.° But I shall see
The wingèd vengeance overtake such children.

CORN: See 't shalt thou never. Fellows, hold
   the chair.
Upon these eyes of thine I'll set my foot.   75

GLO: He that will think to live till he be old,
Give me some help! Oh, cruel! Oh, you gods!

                 [GLOUCESTER's *eye is put out.*]

REG: One side will mock another, the other
   too.

CORN: If you see vengeance——

I. SERV: Hold your hand, my lord.
I have served you ever since I was a child,   81
But better service have I never done you
Than now to bid you hold.

REG: How now, you dog!

I. SERV: If you did wear a beard upon your
   chin,   85
I'd shake it on this quarrel. What do you mean?

CORN: My villain!

[*They draw and fight.* CORNWALL *is wounded.*]

I. SERV: Nay, then, come on, and take the
   chance of anger.

REG: Give me thy sword. A peasant stand up
   thus!

      [*Takes a sword and runs at him behind.*]

I. SERV: Oh, I am slain! My lord, you have
   one eye left   90
To see some mischief on him. Oh!   [*Dies.*]

CORN: Lest it see more, prevent it. Out, vile
   jelly!
Where is thy luster now?

          [*Puts out* GLOUCESTER's *other eye.*]

GLO: All dark and comfortless. Where's my
   son Edmund?
Edmund, enkindle all the sparks° of nature,   95
To quit° this horrid act.

REG: Out, treacherous villain!
Thou call'st on him that hates thee. It was he
That made the overture° of thy treasons to us,
Who is too good to pity thee.   100

GLO: Oh, my follies! Then Edgar was abused.
Kind gods, forgive me that, and prosper him!

REG: Go thrust him out at gates, and let him
   smell
His way to Dover. [*Exit one with* GLOUCESTER.]
        How is 't, my lord? How look you?

---

39. **pluck . . . beard:** the greatest indignity that could be offered.   **42. ravish:** seize.   **43. quicken:** come to life.   **44. hospitable favors:** the face of your host. **48. confederacy:** alliance, understanding.   **59. at peril:** under penalty.   **60. I . . . course:** like a bear in the bear pit I must endure the onslaught.   **65. anointed:** i.e., anointed as a king, and therefore holy.   **67. buoyed up:** swelled up.   **68. stelled fires:** the light of the stars.   **69. holp:** helped.   **71. turn . . . key:** open the gate.

72. **All . . . subscribed:** all other cruel things were on his side.   **95. enkindle . . . sparks:** i.e., blow into flame your natural love.   **96. quit:** requite.   **99. overture:** revelation.

CORN: I have received a hurt. Follow me,
lady.   106
Turn out that eyeless villain. Throw this slave
Upon the dunghill. Regan, I bleed apace.°
Untimely comes this hurt. Give me your arm.
                    [*Exit* CORNWALL, *led by* REGAN.]
    2. SERV: I'll never care what wickedness I do
If this man come to good.   111
    3. SERV: If she live long,
And in the end meet the old course of death,°
Women will all turn monsters.
    2. SERV: Let's follow the old Earl, and get the
    bedlam°   115
To lead him where he would. His roguish mad-
    ness
Allows itself to anything.
    3. SERV: Go thou. I'll fetch some flax and
    whites of eggs
To apply to his bleeding face. Now, Heaven help
    him!   [*Exeunt severally.*]

ACT IV

SCENE I. The heath.

[*Enter* EDGAR.]
    EDG: Yet better thus, and known to be
    contemned,°
Than still° contemned and flattered. To° be
    worst,
The lowest and most dejected thing of fortune,
Stands still in esperance, lives not in fear.
The lamentable change is from the best,   5
The worst returns to laughter. Welcome then,
Thou unsubstantial air that I embrace!
The wretch that thou hast blown unto the worst
Owes nothing to thy blasts.—But who comes
    here?
    [*Enter* GLOUCESTER, *led by an* OLD MAN.]

My father, poorly led?° World, world, O world!
But that thy strange mutations make us hate
    thee,   11
Life would not yield to age.
    OLD MAN: Oh, my good lord, I have been your
tenant, and your father's tenant, these fourscore
years.   15
    GLO: Away, get thee away. Good friend, be
gone.
Thy comforts can do me no good at all,
Thee they may hurt.
    OLD MAN: Alack, sir, you cannot see your
    way.
    GLO: I have no way and therefore want no
    eyes.   20
I stumbled when I saw. Full oft 'tis seen,
Our means secure us, and our mere defects
Prove our commodities.° Ah, dear Son Edgar,
The food° of thy abusèd father's wrath,
Might I but live to see thee in my touch,   25
I'd say I had eyes again!
    OLD MAN: How now! Who's there?
    EDG: [*Aside*] Oh gods! Who is 't can say "I am
    at the worst"?
I am worse than e'er I was.
    OLD MAN: 'Tis poor mad Tom.
    EDG: [*Aside*] And worse I may be yet. The
    worst is not   31
So long as we can say "This is the worst."°
    OLD MAN: Fellow, where goest?
    GLO: Is it a beg-
    garman?
    OLD MAN: Madman and beggar too.   35
    GLO: He has some reason, else he could not
    beg.
I' the last night's storm I such a fellow saw,
Which made me think a man a worm. My son
Came then into my mind, and yet my mind
Was then scarce friends with him. I have heard
    more since.   40
As flies to wanton boys are we to the gods,
They kill us for their sport.
    EDG: [*Aside*]   How should this be?

---

108. **apace:** quickly, profusely.   113. **old. . .death:** natural
death in old age.   115. **bedlam:** i.e., Poor Tom. See I.ii.149;
II.iii.14.
    Act IV, Sc. i: 1. contemned: despised; i.e., as a beggar.
2. still: always.   **2–12. To . . . age:** when a man has
reached the lowest state of misfortune, he has hope
(*esperance*) for the better, and no fear for the worse. The
change to be lamented is when the best things turn to bad;
the worst can only change to joy. After this poor consolation
that nothing worse can happen to him, Edgar sees his blinded
father and continues (l. 10): One would not trouble to live to
old age except to spite the world.

---

10. **poorly led:** led by one poor old man—and not accompanied by the usual party of servants.   **22–23. Our . . . commodities:** when we are well off we grow careless, and then
our misfortunes prove blessings.   **24. food:** object.   **31–
32. The . . . worst:** so long as a man is alive, he may yet reach
a lower depth of misery.

Bad is the trade that must play fool to sorrow,
Angering itself and others.° Bless thee, master!
   GLO: Is that the naked fellow?   46
   OLD MAN: Aye, my lord.
   GLO: Then, prithee get thee gone. If for my
     sake
Thou wilt o'ertake us hence a mile or twain
I' the way toward Dover, do it for ancient love,
And bring some covering for this naked soul,
Who I'll entreat to lead me.   52
   OLD MAN: Alack, sir, he is
     mad.
   GLO: 'Tis the times' plague° when madmen
     lead the blind.
Do as I bid thee, or rather do thy pleasure.
Above the rest, be gone.
   OLD MAN: I'll bring him the best 'parel° that I
     have,
Come on 't what will.   [*Exit.*]
   GLO: Sirrah, naked fellow——
   EDG: Poor Tom's a-cold. [*Aside*] I cannot
     daub° it further.   60
   GLO: Come hither, fellow.
   EDG: [*Aside*] And yet I must.—Bless thy sweet
     eyes, they bleed.
   GLO: Know'st thou the way to Dover?
   EDG: Both stile and gate, horseway and foot-
path. Poor Tom hath been scared out of his good
wits. Bless thee, good man's son, from the foul
fiend! Five fiends have been in Poor Tom at
once—of lust, as Obidicut; Hobbididence, prince
of dumbness; Mahu, of stealing; Modo, of mur-
der; Flibbertigibbet, of mopping and mowing,°
who since possesses chambermaids and waiting-
women. So, bless thee, master!   72
   GLO: Here, take this purse, thou whom the
     Heavens' plagues
Have humbled to all strokes.° That I am
     wretched
Makes thee the happier. Heavens, deal so still!
Let the superfluous and lust-dieted man,
That slaves your ordinance, that will not see 77
Because he doth not feel, feel your power

quickly.°
So distribution should undo excess°
And each man have enough. Dost thou know
     Dover?   80
   EDG: Aye, master.
   GLO: There is a cliff whose high and bending°
     head
Looks fearfully in the confinèd deep.
Bring me but to the very brim of it,
And I'll repair the misery thou dost bear 85
With something rich about me. From that place
I shall no leading need.
   EDG: Give me thy arm.
Poor Tom shall lead thee.   [*Exeunt.*]

SCENE II. *Before the* DUKE OF ALBANY'S *palace.*

   [*Enter* GONERIL *and* EDMUND.]
   GON: Welcome, my lord. I marvel our mild
     husband
Not met us on the way.
   [*Enter* OSWALD.] Now, where's your master?
   OSW: Madam, within, but never man so
     changed.
I told him of the army that was landed. 5
He smiled at it. I told him you were coming.
His answer was "The worse." Of Gloucester's
     treachery
And of the loyal service of his son
When I informed him, then he called me sot
And told me I had turned the wrong side out.
What most he should dislike seems pleasant to
     him,   11
What like, offensive.
   GON: [*To* EDMUND] Then shall you go no fur-
     ther.
It is the cowish° terror of his spirit,
That dares not undertake.° He'll not feel wrongs
Which tie° him to an answer. Our wishes on the
     way   16
May prove effects.° Back, Edmund, to my
     brother.

44–45. **Bad . . . others:** this business of pretending to be mad
and fooling a man in such distress as Gloucester is now hateful.   **54. times' plague:** a sign of these diseased times.
57. 'parel: apparel.   **60. daub:** plaster it over, pretend.
70. mopping . . . mowing: making faces and grimaces.
74. humbled . . . strokes: made so humble that you can endure anything.

75–78. **Heavens . . . quickly:** you gods, deal with others as
you have dealt with me; let the man who has too much and
pampers his own lusts, who regards your commands as contemptuously as he regards his slaves, that will not understand
until he is hurt, feel your power quickly. This passage echoes
Lear's words (III.iv. 36–39).   **79. So . . . excess:** then the
man with too much would distribute his excessive wealth.
82. bending: overhanging.
   Sc. ii: 14. cowish: cowardly.   **15. undertake:** show initiative, venture.   **16. tie:** force.   **16–17. Our . . . effects:**
our hopes (of love) as we rode together may be fulfilled.

Hasten his musters° and conduct his powers.°
I° must change arms at home and give the
distaff°
Into my husband's hands. This trusty servant 20
Shall pass between us. Ere long you are like to
hear,
If you dare venture in your own behalf,
A mistress's° command. Wear this. Spare speech.
[*Giving a favor.*]
Decline your head. This kiss, if it durst speak,
Would stretch thy spirits up into the air. 25
Conceive,° and fare thee well.
    EDM: Yours in the ranks of death.
    GON: My most dear Gloucester!
[*Exit* EDMUND.]
Oh, the difference of man and man!
To thee a woman's services are due, 30
My fool° usurps my body.
    OSW: Madam, here comes my lord. [*Exit.*]
[*Enter* ALBANY.]
    GON: I have been worth the whistle.°
    ALB: O Goneril!
You are not worth the dust which the rude wind
Blows in your face. I fear your disposition. 36
That° nature which contemns it origin
Cannot be bordered certain in itself.
She that herself will sliver° and disbranch
From her material sap,° perforce must wither
And come to deadly use. 41
    GON: No more, the text is foolish.°
    ALB: Wisdom and goodness to the vile seem
vile.
Filths savor but themselves.° What have you
done?

Tigers, not daughters, what have you performed?
A father, and a gracious agèd man 46
Whose reverence even the head-lugged bear°
would lick,
Most barbarous, most degenerate, have you
madded!
Could my good brother° suffer you to do it?
A man, a prince, by him so benefited! 50
If that the Heavens do not their visible spirits°
Send quickly down to tame these vile offenses,
It will come.
Humanity must perforce prey on itself,
Like monsters of the deep.° 55
    GON: Milk-livered° man!
That bear'st a cheek for blows, a head for
wrongs,
Who hast not in thy brows an eye discerning
Thine honor from thy suffering;° that not
know'st
Fools do those villains pity who are punished
Ere they have done their mischief.° Where's thy
drum? 61
France spreads his banners in our noiseless land,
With plumèd helm thy state begins to threat,
Whiles thou, a moral° fool, sit'st still and criest
"Alack, why does he so?" 65
    ALB: See thyself, devil!
Proper deformity° seems not in the fiend
So horrid as in woman.
    GON: O vain fool!
    ALB: Thou changèd and self-covered° thing,
for shame, 70
Bemonster not thy feature.° Were 't my fitness
To let these hands obey my blood,°
They are apt enough to dislocate and tear
Thy flesh and bones. Howe'er° thou art a fiend,
A woman's shape doth shield thee. 75

18. **musters:** troops which have been collected. **powers:** forces. **19-20. I . . . hands:** I must become the soldier and leave my husband to do the spinning. **19. distaff:** stick used in spinning, essentially the work of the housewife. **23. mistress's:** in the double sense of lady and lover. Edmund, having disposed of his brother and father, now looks higher; he will through Goneril become possessed of her half of the kingdom of Lear. **26. Conceive:** use your imagination. **31. My fool:** i.e., my husband is no more than a fool to me. **33. worth . . . whistle:** There is a proverb "'Tis a poor dog that is not worth the whistle." Goneril means: I was once worth being regarded as your dog. **37-41. That . . . use:** that creature which despises its father (*origin*) cannot be kept within bounds; she that cuts herself off from her family tree will perish and like a dead branch come to the burning. **39. sliver:** slice off. **40. material sap:** that sap which is part of herself. **42. text is foolish:** i.e., this is a silly sermon. **44. Filths . . . themselves:** the filthy like the taste only of filth.

47. **head-lugged bear:** a bear with its head torn by the hounds. **49. good brother:** Cornwall. **51. visible spirits:** avenging spirits in visible form. **54-55. Humanity . . . deep:** A thought more than once expressed by Shakespeare—that when natural law is broken, men will degenerate into beasts and prey on each other. **56. Milk-livered:** cowardly; the liver was regarded as the seat of courage. **58-59. Who . . . suffering:** who cannot see when the insults which you endure are dishonorable to you. **60-61. Fools . . . mischief:** only a fool pities a villain when he is punished to prevent his committing a crime. **64. moral:** moralizing. **67. Proper deformity:** deformity natural to a fiend. **70. self-covered:** hiding your true self (i.e., devil) under the guise of a woman. **71. Bemonster . . . feature:** do not change your shape into a fiend. **72. blood:** anger. **74. Howe'er:** although.

GON: Marry, your manhood!° Mew!°
[*Enter a* MESSENGER.]
ALB: What news?
MESS: O my good lord, the Duke of Cornwall's dead,
Slain by his servant, going to put out
The other eye of Gloucester.   80
ALB: Gloucester's eyes!
MESS: A servant that he bred, thrilled with remorse,°
Opposed against the act, bending his sword
To his great master, who thereat enraged
Flew on him and amongst them felled him dead,
But not without that harmful stroke which since
Hath plucked him after.   87
ALB: This shows you are above,
You justicers, that these our nether crimes°
So speedily can venge. But, oh, poor Gloucester!
Lost he his other eye?
MESS: Both, both, my lord.   92
This letter, madam, craves a speedy answer.
'Tis from your sister.
GON: [*Aside*]One way I like this well,
But being widow, and my Gloucester° with her,
May all the building in my fancy pluck°
Upon my hateful life. Another way,   98
The news is not so tart.—I'll read, and answer.
                                [*Exit.*]
ALB: Where was his son when they did take his eyes?
MESS: Come with my lady hither.
ALB: He is not here.
MESS: No, my good lord, I met him back again.°
ALB: Knows he the wickedness?
MESS: Aye, my good lord, 'twas he informed against him,   105
And quit the house on purpose, that their punishment
Might have the freer course.
ALB: Gloucester, I live
To thank thee for the love thou show'dst the King,   109

And to revenge thine eyes. Come hither, friend.
Tell me what more thou know'st.   [*Exeunt.*]

SCENE III. The French camp near Dover.

[*Enter* KENT *and a* GENTLEMAN.]
KENT: Why the King of France is so suddenly gone back know you the reason?
GENT: Something he left imperfect in the state which since his coming-forth is thought of, which imports to the kingdom so much fear and danger that his personal return was most required and necessary.   7
KENT: Who hath he left behind him general?
GENT: The Marshal of France, Monsieur La Far.
KENT: Did your letters pierce the Queen to any demonstration of grief?   11
GENT: Aye, sir. She took them, read them in my presence,
And now and then an ample tear trilled down
Her delicate cheek. It seemed she was a queen
Over her passion,° who most rebel-like
Sought to be king o'er her.   16
KENT: Oh, then it moved her.
GENT: Not to a rage. Patience and Sorrow strove
Who should express her goodliest.° You have seen
Sunshine and rain at once. Her smiles and tears
Were like a better way.° Those happy smilets°
That played on her ripe lip seemed not to know
What guests were in her eyes, which parted thence   23
As pearls from diamonds dropped. In brief,
Sorrow would be a rarity most beloved
If all could so become it.°
KENT: Made she no verbal question?
GENT: Faith, once or twice she heaved the name of "Father"   28
Pantingly forth, as if it pressed her heart,
Cried "Sisters! Sisters! Shame of ladies! Sisters!
Kent! Father! Sisters! What, i' the storm? i' the night?
Let pity not be believed!" There she shook
The holy water from her heavenly eyes,   33

---

76. Marry . . . manhood: you're a fine specimen of a man!
Mew: a catcall.   **82. thrilled . . . remorse:** trembling with
pity.   **89. nether crimes:** crimes committed on earth
below.   **96. my Gloucester:** i.e., Edmund.   **97. May
. . . pluck:** may pull down my castle in the air (i.e., her desire
to marry Edmund).   **103. met . . . again:** met him as he
was on his way back.

Sc. iii: 15. passion: emotion.   **19. express . . . goodliest:**
make her seem more beautiful.   **21. like . . . way:** even
more lovely. **smilets:** little smiles.   **25–26. Sorrow . . . it:** if
everyone looked so beautiful in sorrow, it would be a quality
much sought after.

And clamor-moistened.° Then away she started
To deal with grief alone.
  KENT: It is the stars,
The stars above us, govern our conditions,
Else one self° mate and mate could not beget
Such different issues.° You spoke not with her
  since?
  GENT: No.   40
  KENT: Was this before the King returned?
  GENT: No, since.
  KENT: Well, sir, the poor distressèd Lear's i'
  the town,
Who sometime in his better tune remembers
What we are come about, and by no means 45
Will yield to see his daughter.
  GENT: Why, good sir?
  KENT: A sovereign° shame so elbows° him.
  His own unkindness
That stripped her from his benediction, turned
  her
To foreign casualties,° gave her dear rights 50
To his doghearted daughters. These things sting
His mind so venomously that burning shame
Detains him from Cordelia.
  GENT: Alack, poor gentle-
  man!
  KENT: Of Albany's and Cornwall's powers you
  heard not?   55
  GENT: 'Tis so, they are afoot.
  KENT: Well, sir, I'll bring you to our master
  Lear,
And leave you to attend him. Some dear cause°
Will in concealment wrap me up awhile. 59
When I am known aright, you shall not grieve
Lending° me this acquaintance. I pray you, go
Along with me.   [Exeunt.]

SCENE IV. The same. A tent.

 [Enter, with drum and colors,° CORDELIA, DOC-
  TOR, and SOLDIERS.]
  COR: Alack, 'tis he. Why, he was met even
  now

As mad as the vexed sea, singing aloud,
Crowned with rank fumiter and furrow weeds,
With burdocks, hemlock, nettles, cuckoo flowers,
Darnel,° and all the idle weeds that grow 5
In our sustaining° corn. A century° send forth.
Search every acre in the high-grown° field,
And bring him to our eye. [Exit an OFFICER.]
  What can man's wisdom
In the restoring his bereavèd sense?
He that helps him take all my outward worth.°
  DOCT: There is means, madam. 11
Our foster nurse° of nature is repose,
The which he lacks. That to provoke in him
Are many simples operative,° whose power
Will close the eye of anguish.   15
  COR: All blest secrets,
All you unpublished virtues° of the earth,
Spring with my tears! Be aidant and remediate°
In the good man's distress! Seek, seek for him,
Lest his ungoverned rage dissolve the life 20
That wants the means to lead it.°
 [Enter a MESSENGER.]
  MESS: News, madam.
The British powers are marching hitherward.
  COR: 'Tis known before, our preparation stands
In expectation of them.° O dear Father, 25
It is thy business that I go about,
Therefore great France
My mourning and important° tears hath pitied.
No blown° ambition doth our arms incite, 29
But love, dear love, and our aged father's right.
Soon may I hear and see him! [Exeunt.]

SCENE V. GLOUCESTER's castle.

 [Enter REGAN and OSWALD.]
  REG: But are my brother's powers set forth?
  OSW: Aye, madam.
  REG: Himself in person there?
  OSW: Madam, with much ado.
Your sister is the better soldier.   5

---

34. clamor-moistened: wet her cries of grief with tears.
38. self: same. 39. issues: children. 48. sovereign:
overpowering. elbows: plucks him by the elbow, reminding
him of the past. 50. casualties: chances, accidents.
58. dear cause: important reason. 61. Lending: bestowing on.
 Sc. iv: s.d., drum . . . colors: a drummer and a soldier carrying a flag.

3–5. fumiter . . . Darnel: These are all English wild flowers
and weeds. 6. sustaining: which maintains life. century:
company of a hundred soldiers. 7. high-grown: The season is therefore late summer. 10. outward worth: visible
wealth. 12. foster nurse: the nurse who feeds.
14. simples operative: efficacious herbs. 17. unpublished
virtues: secret remedies. 18. aidant . . . remediate: helpful and remedial. 21. wants . . . it: that has no sense
to guide it. 24–25 our . . . them: our army is ready to
meet them. 28. important: importunate, pleading.
29. blown: puffed up.

REG: Lord Edmund spake not with your lord
     at home?

OSW: No, madam.

REG: What might import my sister's letter to
     him?

OSW: I know not, lady.

REG: Faith, he is posted° hence on serious
     matter.   10
It was great ignorance, Gloucester's eyes being
     out,
To let him live. Where he arrives he moves
All hearts against us. Edmund, I think, is gone,
In pity of his misery, to dispatch
His nighted° life, moreover to descry   15
The strength o' the enemy.

OSW: I must needs after him, madam, with my
     letter.

REG: Our troops set forth tomorrow. Stay
     with us,
The ways are dangerous.

OSW: I may not, madam.   20
My lady charged my duty° in this business.

REG: Why should she write to Edmund?
     Might not you
Transport her purposes by word? Belike,
Something—I know not what—I'll love thee
     much,
Let me unseal the letter.   25

OSW: Madam, I had rather——

REG: I know your lady does not love her hus-
     band,
I am sure of that. And at her late being here
She gave strange œillades° and most speaking
     looks
To noble Edmund. I know you are of her bosom.°

OSW: I, madam?   31

REG: I speak in understanding. You are, I
     know't.
Therefore I do advise you, take this note.°
My lord is dead, Edmund and I have talked,
And more convenient is he for my hand   35
Than for your lady's. You may gather more.
If you do find him, pray you give him this,
And when your mistress hears thus much from
     you,
I pray desire her call her wisdom to her.
So, fare you well.   40

If you do chance to hear of that blind traitor,
Preferment° falls on him that cuts him off.

OSW: Would I could meet him, madam! I
     should show
What party I do follow.   44

REG: Fare thee well.

                                        [*Exeunt.*]

SCENE VI. *Fields near Dover.*

[*Enter* GLOUCESTER, *and* EDGAR *dressed like a
     peasant.*]

GLO: When shall we come to the top of that
     same hill?

EDG: You do climb up it now. Look how we
     labor.

GLO: Methinks the ground is even.

EDG: Horrible
     steep.
Hark, do you hear the sea?   5

GLO: No, truly.

EDG: Why then your other senses grow im-
     perfect
By your eyes' anguish.

GLO: So may it be, indeed.
Methinks thy voice is altered, and thou speak'st
In better phrase and matter than thou didst. 11

EDG: You're much deceived. In nothing am I
     changed
But in my garments.

GLO: Methinks you're better-spoken.

EDG: Come on, sir, here's the place. Stand
     still. How° fearful   15
And dizzy 'tis to cast one's eyes so low!
The crows and choughs° that wing the midway
     air
Show scarce so gross as beetles. Halfway down
Hangs one that gathers samphire,° dreadful
     trade!
Methinks he seems no bigger than his head. 20
The fishermen that walk upon the beach
Appear like mice, and yond tall anchoring bark°
Diminished to her cock°—her cock, a buoy
Almost too small for sight. The murmuring surge

---

42. **Preferment:** promotion.
   Sc. vi: 15–28. How . . . headlong: This vivid description of
the cliffs at Dover seems to have been written from direct
observation. The King's Players visited Dover in September
1606.   17. **choughs:** jackdaws.   19. **samphire:** a strongly
perfumed plant which grows on the chalk cliffs of Dover.
22. **bark:** ship.   23. **cock:** cockboat, the small ship's boat,
usually towed behind.

Sc. v: 10. **is posted:** has ridden fast.   15. **nighted:**
blinded.   21. **charged my duty:** entrusted it to me as a
solemn duty.   29. **œillades:** loving looks.   30. **of . . .
bosom:** in her confidence.   33. **take . . . note:** observe this.

That on the unnumbered idle pebbles chafes 25
Cannot be heard so high. I'll look no more,
Lest my brain turn and the deficient sight
Topple down headlong.°
    GLO: Set me where you
    stand.
    EDG: Give me your hand. You are now within
    a foot   30
Of the extreme verge. For all beneath the moon
Would I not leap upright.
    GLO: Let go my hand.
Here, friend, 's another purse, in it a jewel
Well worth a poor man's taking. Fairies and
    gods°   35
Prosper it with thee! Go thou further off.
Bid me farewell, and let me hear thee going.
    EDG: Now fare you well, good sir.
    GLO: With all my heart.
    EDG: Why I do trifle thus with his despair
Is done to cure it.°   41
    GLO: [*Kneeling*] O you mighty gods!
This world I do renounce, and in your sights
Shake patiently my great affliction off.
If° I could bear it longer and not fall   45
To quarrel with your great opposeless wills,
My snuff° and loathèd part of nature should
Burn itself out. If Edgar live, oh, bless him!
Now, fellow, fare thee well. [*He falls forward.°*]
    EDG: Gone, sir. Fare-
    well.   50
And yet I know not how conceit° may rob
The treasury of life when life itself
Yields to the theft.° Had he been where he
    thought,
By this had thought been past. Alive or dead?
Ho, you sir! Friend! Hear you, sir! Speak!   55

27–28. **deficient . . . headlong:** my sight failing, cause me to topple headlong.   35. **Fairies . . . gods:** As this tale is pre-Christian, it is natural for the characters to call on the gods of the "elder world."   40–41. **Why . . . it:** Edgar's purpose is to persuade his blinded father to go on living by the thought that he has been miraculously preserved after falling from a great height. When Gloucester begins to recover from the shock, Edgar has dropped his pretense of being a bedlam and speaks in a natural (but still disguised) voice.   45–48. **If . . . out:** if I could endure my misery longer without quarreling with the wish of Heaven, I would wait for the rest of my hateful life to burn itself out.   47. **snuff:** lit., smoking end of a burnt out candle.   49 **s.d., falls forward.** To be effective this episode needs an actor who is not afraid of hurting himself, for unless Gloucester's fall is heavy it is quite unconvincing. After his fall, he lies stunned for a few moments.   51. **conceit:** imagination.   53. **Yields . . . theft:** i.e., is willing to die.

Thus might he pass° indeed. Yet he revives.
What are you, sir?
    GLO: Away, and let me die.
    EDG: Hadst thou been aught but gossamer,°
    feathers, air,
So many fathom down precipitating,   60
Thou'dst shivered like an egg. But thou dost
    breathe,
Hast heavy substance, bleed'st not, speak'st, art
    sound.
Ten masts at each° make not the altitude
Which thou hast perpendicularly fell.
Thy life's a miracle. Speak yet again.   65
    GLO: But have I fall'n, or no?
    EDG: From the dread summit of this chalky
    bourn.°
Look up a-height, the shrill-gorged°lark so far
Cannot be seen or heard. Do but look up.
    GLO: Alack, I have no eyes.   70
Is wretchedness deprived that benefit,
To end itself by death? 'Twas yet some comfort
When misery could beguile° the tyrant's rage
And frustrate his proud will.
    EDG: Give me your arm.
Up, so. How is 't? Feel you your legs? You stand.
    GLO: Too well, too well.   77
    EDG: This is above all strangeness.
Upon the crown o' the cliff, what thing was that
Which parted from you?
    GLO: A poor unfortunate beggar.
    EDG: As I stood here below, methought his
    eyes
Were two full moons, he had a thousand noses,
Horns whelked° and waved like the enridgèd°
    sea.   84
It was some fiend, therefore, thou happy father,
Think that the clearest° gods, who make them
    honors
Of men's impossibilities,° have preserved thee.
    GLO: I do remember now. Henceforth I'll
    bear
Affliction till it do cry out itself   89

56. **pass:** pass away, die.   59. **gossamer:** the parachute-like web made by a species of small spider by which it floats through the air.   63. **Ten . . . each:** ten masts, one on top of the other.   67. **bourn:** boundary.   68. **shrill-gorged:** shrill-throated. The lark is a small brown bird which flies to a great height and there remains fluttering and singing a shrill but beautiful song.   73. **beguile:** cheat (by death). 84. **whelked:** with spiral twists. **enridged:** wavy. 86. **clearest:** most glorious.   86–87. **who . . . impossibilities:** who cause themselves to be honored by performing miracles impossible to men.

"Enough, enough," and die. That thing you
    speak of,   90
I took it for a man. Often 'twould say
"The fiend, the fiend." He led me to that place.
    EDG: Bear free° and patient thoughts. But
    who comes here?
    [*Enter* LEAR, *fantastically dressed with wild
    flowers.*]
The safer sense will n'er accommodate
His master thus.°   95
    LEAR: No,° they cannot touch me for coining,
I am the King himself.
    EDG: O thou side-piercing sight!
    LEAR: Nature's above art in that respect.
There's your press money. That fellow handles
his bow like a crowkeeper,° draw me a clothier's
yard.° Look, look, a mouse! Peace, peace, this
piece of toasted cheese will do 't. There's my
gauntlet,° I'll prove it on a° giant. Bring up the
brown bills.° Oh, well-flown, bird! I' the clout,°
i' the clout. Hewgh!° Give the word.°   106
    EDG: Sweet marjoram.°
    LEAR: Pass.
    GLO: I know that voice.
    LEAR: Ha! Goneril, with a white beard! They
flattered me like a dog, and told me I had white
hairs in my beard ere the black ones were there.
To say "aye" and "no" to everything that I said!
"Aye" and "no" too was no good divinity.°
When the rain came to wet me once and the
wind to make me chatter, when the thunder

would not peace at my bidding, there I found
'em, there I smelt 'em out. Go to, they are not
men o' their words. They told me I was every-
thing. 'Tis a lie, I am not agueproof.   120
    GLO: The trick° of that voice I do well re-
member. Is 't not the King?
    LEAR: Aye, every inch a
    king.
When I do stare, see how the subject quakes.
I pardon that man's life. What was thy cause?
Adultery?   126
Thou shalt not die. Die for adultery! No.
The wren goes to 't, and the small gilded fly
Does lecher in my sight.
Let copulation thrive, for Gloucester's bastard
    son   130
Was kinder to his father than my daughters
Got 'tween the lawful sheets.
To 't, luxury,° pell-mell! For I lack soldiers.
Behold yond simpering dame,
Whose face between her forks° presages snow,
That minces virtue° and does shake the head
To hear of pleasure's name.   137
The fitchew,° nor the soilèd° horse, goes to 't
With a more riotous appetite.
Down from the waist they are Centaurs,°
Though women all above.
But to° the girdle do the gods inherit,
Beneath is all the fiends'.
There's Hell, there's darkness, there's the sul-
    phurous pit,
Burning, scalding, stench, consumption, fie, fie,
    fie!   145
Pah, pah! Give me an ounce of civet,° good
apothecary, to sweeten my imagination. There's
money for thee.
    GLO: Oh, let me kiss that hand!
    LEAR: Let me wipe it first, it smells of mor-
tality.   150
    GLO: O ruined piece of nature! This great
    world
Shall so wear out to naught.° Dost thou know
    me?
    LEAR: I remember thine eyes well enough.

---

93. free: innocent.   **94-95. The . . . thus:** a man in his
right senses would never adorn himself thus. Edgar with unconscious irony repeats Lear's "accommodated." See
III.iv.113.   **96-106. No . . . word:** Lear's madness has a
sort of logical coherence. He begins by saying that he cannot
be charged with coining, because it was his right as king to
issue the coin, a natural right. From coin his mind goes to the
use of coin as *press money* for soldiers (money given to a
conscripted recruit as token that he has been engaged),
thence to the recruits at archery practice. Then his mind is
distracted by a mouse, but comes back to his quarrel with his
sons-in-law. He will throw down his gauntlet as a challenge to
single combat against any odds. He comes back to the archery
range, and a good shot right in the bull's-eye.   **101. crowkeeper:** a man hired to scare away crows from the crop.
101-02. clothier's yard: The expert archer drew his arrow
back a full yard to the ear.   **104. gauntlet:** glove, token
of challenge.   **104. prove . . . a:** i.e., fight even a.
105. brown bills: i.e., the infantry. **brown:** varnished to keep
from rusting.   **105. clout:** the canvas target.
106. Hewgh: imitation of the whizz of the arrow.
106. word: password.   **107. marjoram:** a savory herb.
114. no . . . divinity: i.e., false doctrine.

121. trick: peculiar note.   **133. luxury:** lust.   **135.
forks:** legs.   **136. minces virtue:** walks with a great air of
virtue.   **138. fitchew:** polecat, a creature demonstratively
oversexed. **soiled:** fed on spring grass.   **140. Centaurs:**
creatures half man and half stallion.   **142. But to:** only
down to.   **146. civet:** perfume. See III.iv.111–12,n.
151–52. O . . . naught: O ruined masterpiece of nature, the
universe likewise will come to nothing.

Dost thou squiny° at me? No, do thy worst, blind
Cupid,° I'll not love. Read thou this challenge,
mark but the penning on 't.   156

GLO: Were all the letters suns, I could not see
one.

EDG: I would not take this from report. It is,
And my heart breaks at it.

LEAR: Read.   160

GLO: What, with the case of eyes?

LEAR: Oh ho, are you there with me?° No
eyes in your head, nor no money in your purse?
Your eyes are in a heavy case, your purse in a
light. Yet you see how this world goes.   165

GLO: I see it feelingly.

LEAR: What, art mad? A man may see how
this world goes with no eyes. Look with thine
ears. See how yond Justice rails upon yond simple thief. Hark, in thine ear. Change places and,
handy-dandy,° which is the Justice, which is the
thief? Thou hast seen a farmer's dog bark at a
beggar?   173

GLO: Aye, sir.

LEAR: And the creature run from the cur?
There thou mightst behold the great image of
authority.°
A dog's obeyed in office.
Thou rascal beadle,° hold thy bloody hand!
Why dost thou lash that whore? Strip thine own
back.   180
Thou hotly lust'st to use her in that kind°
For which thou whip'st her. The usurer hangs the
cozener.°
Through tattered clothes small vices do appear,
Robes and furred gowns hide all. Plate sin with
gold
And the strong lance of justice hurtless breaks.
Arm it in rags, a pigmy's straw does pierce it.
None does offend, none, I say, none, I'll able°
'em.   187
Take that of me, my friend, who have the power
To seal the accuser's lips. Get thee glass eyes°
And, like a scurvy° politician, seem
To see the things thou dost not.   191

Now, now, now, now. Pull off my boots. Harder,.
harder. So.

EDG: Oh, matter and impertinency° mixed!
Reason in madness!

LEAR: If thou wilt weep my fortunes, take my
eyes.   195
I know thee well enough. Thy name is Glouces-
ter.
Thou must be patient, we came crying hither.
Thou know'st the first time that we smell the air,
We wawl and cry. I will preach to thee. Mark.

GLO: Alack, alack the day!   200

LEAR: When we are born, we cry that we are
come
To this great stage of fools. This 's a good block.°
It were a delicate strategem to shoe
A troop of horse with felt. I'll put 't in proof,°
And when I have stol'n upon these sons-in-law,
Then, kill, kill, kill, kill, kill, kill!   206

[Enter a GENTLEMAN, with ATTENDANTS.]

GENT: Oh, here he is. Lay hand upon him. Sir,
Your most dear daughter——

LEAR: No rescue? What, a prisoner? I am
even
The natural fool of Fortune.° Use me well,   210
You shall have ransom.° Let me have a surgeon,
I am cut to the brains.

GENT: You shall have anything.

LEAR: No seconds?° All myself?
Why, this would make a man a man of salt,°
To use his eyes for garden waterpots,   216
Aye, and laying autumn's dust.

GENT: Good sir——

LEAR: I will die bravely, like a smug bride-
groom.° What!
I will be jovial. Come, come, I am a king,   220
My masters, know you that.

GENT: You are a royal one, and we obey you.

LEAR: Then there's life in 't. Nay, an you get
it, you shall get it by running. Sa, sa, sa, sa.°

[Exit running. ATTENDANTS follow.]

---

154. squiny: look sideways, like a prostitute.   **154-
55. blind Cupid:** the usual sign hung over a brothel.
162. are . . . me: do you agree with me?   **171. handy-
dandy:** the nursery game of "Handy-pandy, sugar candy,
which hand will you have?"   **176-77. image of authority:**
figure showing the true meaning of authority.   **179. beadle:** parish officer.   **181. kind:** manner.   **182. usurer
. . . cozener:** the swindler hangs the crook.   **187. able:**
give power to.   **189. glass eyes:** spectacles.
190. scurvy: lit., with skin disease, "lousy."

193. matter . . . impertinency: sense and nonsense.
202. block: hat; lit., the block on which a felt hat is molded.
From hat Lear's mind turns to *felt.*   **204. put . . . proof:**
try it out.   **210. natural . . . Fortune:** born to be fooled by
Fortune.   **211. ransom:** Prisoners of good family could buy
their freedom from their captors.   **214. No seconds:** no
one to help me.   **215. man of salt:** because tears are
salt.   **219. like . . . bridegroom:** It was said of Lord Grey of
Wilton, who was led out as if to be executed on December 9,
1603, that he "had such gaiety and cheer in his countenance
that he seemed a dapper young bridegroom."   **224. Sa . . .
sa:** a cry used sometimes in sudden action.

GENT: A sight most pitiful in the meanest
   wretch,   225
Past speaking of in a king! Thou hast one daugh-
   ter
Who redeems nature from the general curse
Which twain have brought her to.
   EDG: Hail, gentle sir.
   GENT: Sir, speed you. What's your will?
   EDG: Do you hear aught, sir, of a battle
   toward?°   231
   GENT: Most sure and vulgar.° Everyone hears
   that
Which can distinguish sound.
   EDG: But, by your favor,
How near's the other army?   235
   GENT: Near and on speedy foot, the main des-
   cry
Stands on the hourly thought.°
   EDG: I thank you, sir. That's all.
   GENT: Though that the Queen on special
   cause is here,
Her army is moved on.   240
   EDG: I thank you, sir. [*Exit* GENTLEMAN.]
   GLO: You ever-gentle gods, take my breath
   from me.
Let not my worser spirit tempt me again
To die before you please!
   EDG: Well pray you, Father.
   GLO: Now, good sir, what are you?   246
   EDG: A most poor man, made tame to for-
   tune's blows,
Who, by the art°of known and feeling sorrows,
Am pregnant to° good pity. Give me your hand.
I'll lead you to some biding.°   250
   GLO: Hearty thanks.
The bounty and the benison° of Heaven
To boot, and boot!°
   [*Enter* OSWALD.]
   OSW: A proclaimed° prize! Most happy!
That eyeless head of thine was first framed flesh
To raise my fortunes. Thou old unhappy traitor,
Briefly thyself remember.° The sword is out
That must destroy thee.   258
   GLO: Now let thy friendly
   hand

Put strength enough to 't.   [EDGAR *interposes.*]
   OSW: Wherefore, bold peasant,
Darest thou support a published° traitor? Hence,
Lest that the infection of his fortune take
Like hold on thee! Let go his arm.
   EDG: Chill° not let go, zir, without vurther
   'casion.°   265
   OSW: Let go, slave, or thou diest!
   EDG: Good gentleman, go your gait,° and let
poor volk pass. An chud° ha' been zwaggered out
of my life, 'twould not ha' been zo long as 'tis by
a vortnight. Nay, come not near th' old man,
keep out, che vor ye,° or I'se try whether your
costard° or my ballow° be the harder. Chill be
plain with you.
   OSW: Out, dunghill!   [*They fight.*]
   EDG: Chill pick your teeth, zir. Come, no
matter vor your foins.°   [OSWALD *falls.*]
   OSW: Slave, thou hast slain me. Villain, take
   my purse.   277
If ever thou wilt thrive, bury my body,
And give the letters which thou find'st about me
To Edmund Earl of Gloucester. Seek him out
Upon the British party. Oh, untimely death!
Death!   [*Dies.*]
   EDG: I know thee well—a serviceable° vil-
   lain,
As duteous to the vices of thy mistress
As badness would desire.   285
   GLO: What, is he dead?
   EDG: Sit you down, Father, rest you.
Let's see these pockets. The letters that he speaks
   of
May be my friends. He's dead. I am only sorry
He had no other deathsman. Let us see.   290
Leave, gentle wax,° and, manners, blame us not.
To know our enemies' minds, we'd rip their
   hearts,
Their papers is more lawful. [*Reads.*]
   "Let our reciprocal vows be remembered. You
have many opportunities to cut him off. If your
will want not,° time and place will be fruitfully
offered. There is nothing done if he return the
conqueror. Then am I the prisoner, and his bed

---

231. **toward:** at hand.   232. **vulgar:** common, in everyone's mouth.   236–37. **the . . . thought:** the main body is
expected to come into sight at any time now.   248. **art:**
long experience.   249. **pregnant to:** able to conceive.
250. **biding:** resting-place.   252. **benison:** blessing.
253. **To . . . boot:** in the highest degree.   254. **proclaimed:**
Cf. IV.v.41–2.   257. **thyself remember:** prepare for
death—by confessing your sins.

262. **published:** publicly proclaimed.   265–73. **Chill . . .
you:** Edgar speaks stage rustic dialect.   265. **Chill:** I'll.
vurther 'casion: further occasion, reason.   267. **go . . .
gait:** go your own way.   268. **chud:** should.   271. **che
. . . ye:** I warn ye.   272. **costard:** head; lit., apple. **ballow:**
cudgel.   276. **foins:** thrusts.   283. **serviceable:** diligent.   291. **Leave . . . wax:** Here he breaks the seal.
296. **will . . . not:** desire is not lacking. *Will* means both willingness and lust.

my jail, from the loathed warmth whereof de-
liver me, and supply the place for your labor.
    "Your—wife, so I would say—affectionate
servant,   GONERIL."
Oh, undistinguished space° of woman's will!
A plot upon her virtuous husband's life,   304
And the exchange my brother! Here, in the sands,
Thee I'll rake up,° the post unsanctified°
Of murderous lechers, and in the mature time
With this ungracious paper strike the sight
Of the death-practiced° Duke. For him 'tis well
That of thy death and business I can tell.   310
    GLO: The King is mad. How° stiff° is my vile
        sense,°
That I stand up, and have ingenious° feeling
Of my huge sorrows! Better I were distract.°
So should my thoughts be severed from my
        griefs,
And woes by wrong imaginations lose   315
The knowledge of themselves. [Drum afar off]
    EDG: Give me your
        hand.
Far off methinks I hear the beaten drum.
Come, Father, I'll bestow you with a friend.
                                   [Exeunt.]

SCENE VII. *A tent in the French camp.* LEAR *on
a bed asleep, soft music playing,* GENTLEMAN,
and others attending.

    [*Enter* CORDELIA, KENT, *and* DOCTOR.]
    COR: O thou good Kent, how shall I live and
        work,
To match thy goodness? My life will be too short,
And every measure fail me.
    KENT: To be acknowledged, madam, is o'er-
        paid.
All my reports go with the modest truth,   5
Nor more nor clipped, but so.°
    COR: Be better suited.°
These weeds° are memories of those worser
        hours.

---

303. **undistinguished space:** limitless, extending beyond the
range of sight.   306. **rake up:** hide in the dust. **post
unsanctified:** unholy messenger.   309. **death-practiced:**
whose death is plotted.   311–13. **How . . . sorrows:** i.e., if
only I could go mad and forget my sorrows.   311. **stiff:**
strong. **sense:** sanity, **ingenious:** sensitive. **distract:** mad.
Sc. vii: 6. **Nor . . . so:** neither exaggerated nor curtailed,
but exact.   7. **suited:** garbed.   8. **weeds:** garments; i.e.,
his livery as Lear's servant.

I prithee put them off.
    KENT: Pardon me, dear madam,
Yet to be known shortens my made intent.°   11
My boon° I make it that you know me not
Till time and I think meet.
    COR: Then be 't so, my good lord.
                            [*To the* DOCTOR]
    How does the King?
    DOCT: Madam, sleeps still.   15
    COR: O you kind gods,
Cure this great breach in his abusèd nature!
The untuned and jarring senses, oh, wind up°
Of this child-changèd° father!
    DOCT: So please your Majesty
That we may wake the King. He hath slept long.
    COR: Be governed by your knowledge, and
        proceed   22
I' the sway° of your own will. Is he arrayed?
    GENT: Aye, madam. In the heaviness of his
        sleep
We put fresh garments on him.
    DOCT: Be by, good madam, when we do
        awake him.
I doubt not of his temperance.°
    COR: Very well.
    DOCT: Please you, draw near. Louder the
        music there!
    COR: O my dear Father! Restoration hang 30
Thy medicine on my lips, and let this kiss
Repair those violent harms that my two sisters
Have in thy reverence made!
    KENT: Kind and dear Princess!
    COR: Had you not been their father, these
        white flakes   35
Had challenged pity of them. Was this a face
To be opposed against the warring winds?
To stand against the deep dread-bolted thunder?
In the most terrible and nimble stroke
Of quick, cross lightning?° To watch—poor
        perdu!°—   40
With this thin helm? Mine enemy's dog,
Though he had bit me, should have stood that
        night
Against my fire, and wast thou fain, poor Father,
To hovel thee with swine and rogues forlorn

---

11. **Yet . . . intent:** my plan will be frustrated if I am revealed
now.   12. **boon:** request for a favor.   18. **wind up:** i.e.,
as the loose string of a musical instrument is tightened.
19. **child-changed:** transformed by the treatment of his children.   23. **sway:** direction.   27. **temperance:** sanity.
40. **cross lightning:** forked lightning. **perdu:** sentry in an exposed position.

In short and musty straw? Alack, alack! 45
'Tis wonder that thy life and wits at once
Had not concluded all. He wakes. Speak to him.

DOCT: Madam, do you, 'tis fittest.

COR: How does my royal lord? How fares
your Majesty?

LEAR: You do me wrong to take me out o' the
grave. 50
Thou art a soul in bliss,° but I am bound
Upon a wheel of fire that mine own tears
Do scald like molten lead.

COR: Sir, do you know me?

LEAR: You are a spirit, I know. When did you
die? 55

COR: Still, still far wide!

DOCT: He's scarce awake. Let him alone
awhile.

LEAR: Where have I been? Where am I? Fair
daylight?
I am mightily abused. I should e'en die with pity
To see another thus. I know not what to
say. 60
I will not swear these are my hands. Let's see,
I feel this pin prick. Would I were assured
Of my condition!

COR: Oh, look upon me, sir,
And hold your hands in benediction o'er me. 65
No, sir, you must not kneel.

LEAR: Pray do not mock me.
I am a very foolish fond old man,
Fourscore and upward, not an hour more or less,
And, to deal plainly, 70
I fear I am not in my perfect mind.
Methinks I should know you and know this man,
Yet I am doubtful, for I am mainly ignorant
What place this is, and all the skill I have
Remembers not these garments, nor I know not
Where I did lodge last night. Do not laugh at me,
For, as I am a man, I think this lady 77
To be my child Cordelia.

COR: And so I am, I am.

LEAR: Be your tears wet? Yes, faith. I pray
weep not. 80
If you have poison for me, I will drink it.
I know you do not love me, for your sisters
Have, as I do remember, done me wrong.
You have some cause, they have not.

COR: No cause, no cause.

LEAR: Am I in France? 86

KENT: In your own kingdom, sir.

LEAR: Do not abuse me.

DOCT: Be comforted, good madam. The great
rage,
You see, is killed in him. And yet it is danger
To make him even o'er° the time he has lost.
Desire him to go in, trouble him no more 92
Till further settling.

COR: Will 't please your Highness walk?

LEAR: You must bear with me.
Pray you now, forget and forgive. I am old and
foolish.

[Exeunt all but KENT and GENTLEMAN.]

GENT: Holds it true, sir, that the Duke of
Cornwall was so slain?

KENT: Most certain, sir.

GENT: Who is conductor of his people? 100

KENT: As 'tis said, the bastard son of Gloucester.

GENT: They say Edgar, his banished son, is
with the Earl of Kent in Germany.

KENT: Report is changeable.° 'Tis time to
look about. The powers of the kingdom approach
apace. 106

GENT: The arbiterment° is like to be bloody.
Fare you well, sir.   [Exit.]

KENT: My point and period° will be
throughly° wrought,
Or well or ill, as this day's battle's fought.

[Exit.]

ACT V

SCENE I. The British camp near Dover.

[Enter, with drum and colors, EDMUND, REGAN,
GENTLEMEN, and SOLDIERS.]

EDM: Know° of the Duke if his last purpose
hold,
Or whether since he is advised by aught
To change the course. He's full of alteration
And self-reproving. Bring his constant° pleasure.
[To a GENTLEMAN, who goes out.]

REG: Our sister's man is certainly miscarried.

EDM: 'Tis to be doubted,° madam. 6

REG: Now, sweet lord,
You know the goodness I intend upon you.

---

51. bliss: Heaven.

91. even o'er: go over.   104. Report . . . changeable: rumors are not reliable.   107. arbiterment: decision.
109. point . . . period: lit., full stop; the end of my chapter.
throughly: thoroughly.
    Act V, Sc. i: 1. Know: learn.   4. constant: firm; i.e., final
decision.   6. doubted: feared.

Tell me, but truly, but then speak the truth,
Do you not love my sister?   10
   EDM: In honored love.
   REG: But have you never found my brother's
way
To the forfended° place?
   EDM: That thought abuses° you.
   REG: I am doubtful that you have been con-
junct   15
And bosomed with her, as far as we call hers.°
   EDM: No, by mine honor, madam.
   REG: I never shall endure her. Dear my lord,
Be not familiar with her.
   EDM: Fear me not.—   20
She and the Duke her husband!

[*Enter, with drum and colors,* ALBANY,
GONERIL, *and* SOLDIERS.]

   GON: [*Aside*] I had rather lose the battle than
that sister
Should loosen him and me.
   ALB: Our very loving sister, well bemet.
Sir, this I hear: The King is come to his daughter,
With others whom the rigor of our state°   26
Forced to cry out.° Where I could not be honest,
I never yet was valiant. For this business,
It toucheth us, as France invades our land,
Not bolds the King, with others, whom I fear
Most just and heavy causes make oppose.°
   EDM: Sir, you speak nobly.
   REG: Why is this rea-
soned?°
   GON: Combine together 'gainst the enemy,
For these domestic and particular broils   35
Are not the question here.
   ALB: Let's then determine
With the ancient of war° on our proceedings.
   EDM: I shall attend you presently at your tent.
   REG: Sister, you'll go with us?   40
   GON: No.
   REG: 'Tis most convenient. Pray you go with
us.
   GON: [*Aside*] Oh ho, I know the riddle.°—I
will go.

[*As they are going out, enter* EDGAR *disguised.*]
   EDG: If e'er your Grace had speech with man
so poor,
Hear me one word.   45
   ALB: I'll overtake you. Speak.
      [*Exeunt all but* ALBANY *and* EDGAR.]
   EDG: Before you fight the battle, ope this let-
ter.
If you have victory, let the trumpet sound
For him that brought it. Wretched though I
seem,
I can produce a champion that will prove   50
What is avouchèd° there. If you miscarry,
Your business of the world hath so an end,
And machination ceases. Fortune love you!
   ALB: Stay till I have read the letter.
   EDG: I was forbid it.
When time shall serve, let but the herald cry
And I'll appear again.   57
   ALB: Why, fare thee well. I will o'erlook° thy
paper.   [*Exit* EDGAR.]
   [*Re-enter* EDMUND.]
   EDM: The enemy's in view. Draw up your
powers.
Here is the guess° of their true strength and
forces   60
By diligent discovery, but your haste
Is now urged on you.
   ALB: We will greet the time.°   [*Exit.*]
   EDM: To° both these sisters have I sworn my
love,
Each jealous of the other, as the stung   65
Are of the adder. Which of them shall I take?
Both? One? Or neither? Neither can be enjoyed
If both remain alive. To take the widow
Exasperates, makes mad her sister Goneril,
And hardly shall I carry out my side,°   70
Her husband being alive. Now then we'll use
His countenance° for the battle, which being
done,
Let her who would be rid of him devise
His speedy taking-off. As for the mercy
Which he intends to Lear and to Cordelia,   75
The battle done, and they within our power,

---

13. **forfended:** forbidden.   14. **abuses:** wrongs; i.e., you
should not have such a thought.   15-16. **I . . . hers:** I am
afraid that you have been united in intimacy with her in
every way.   26. **rigor . . . state:** our harsh government.
27. **cry out:** protest   28-31. **For . . . oppose:** this business
concerns us particularly, not because France is encouraging
Lear and others who rightly oppose us, but because he is
invading our country.   33. **reasoned:** argued.   38. **ancient of war:** experienced commanders.   43. **Oh . . . riddle:** i.e., you are afraid to leave me alone with Edmund.

---

51. **avouched:** declared.   58. **o'erlook:** read.   60. **guess:**
estimate.   63. **greet . . . time:** i.e., go to meet our
enemy.   64-78. **To . . . debate:** Edmund has now reached
the crisis in his fortunes. Both sisters are in love with him, he
can have either. Or he can aim higher and, with Lear and
Cordelia out of the way, achieve the whole kingdom for himself.   70. **my side:** i.e., of the bargain.   72. **countenance:** authority.

Shall never see his pardon, for my state
Stands on me to defend, not to debate.° [*Exit.*]

SCENE II. A field between the two camps.

[*Alarum within. Enter, with drum and colors,*
LEAR, CORDELIA, *and* SOLDIERS, *over the
stage; and exeunt. Enter* EDGAR *and* GLOU-
CESTER.]
EDG: Here, Father, take the shadow of this
tree
For your good host. Pray that the right may
thrive.
If ever I return to you again,
I'll bring you comfort.
    GLO: Grace go with you, sir! [*Exit* EDGAR.]
[*Alarum and retreat within. Re-enter* EDGAR.]
EDG: Away, old man. Give me thy hand,
away!   6
King Lear hath lost, he and his daughter ta'en.°
Give me thy hand, come on.
    GLO: No farther, sir. A man may rot even
here.
EDG: What, in ill thoughts again? Men° must
endure   10
Their going hence, even as their coming hither.
Ripeness° is all. Come on.
    GLO: And that's true too. [*Exeunt.*]

SCENE III. The British camp near Dover.

[*Enter, in conquest, with drum and colors,* ED-
MUND, LEAR *and* CORDELIA, *as prisoners,*
CAPTAIN, SOLDIERS, *etc.*]
EDM: Some officers take them away. Good
guard,
Until their greater pleasures° first be known
That are to censure them.
    COR: We are not the first
Who with best meaning have incurred the worst.
For thee, oppressèd King, am I cast down.   6
Myself could else outfrown false fortune's
frown.°
Shall we not see these daughters and these sis-
ters?

LEAR: No, no, no, no! Come, let's away to
prison.
We two alone will sing like birds i' the
cage.   10
When thou dost ask me blessing, I'll kneel down
And ask of thee forgiveness. So we'll live,
And pray, and sing, and tell old tales, and laugh
At gilded butterflies,° and hear poor rogues
Talk of Court news. And we'll talk with them
too,   15
Who loses and who wins, who's in, who's out,
And take upon 's the mystery of things°
As if we were God's spies. And we'll wear out,
In a walled prison, packs and sects of great ones
That ebb and flow by the moon.°   20
    EDM: Take them away.
    LEAR: Upon such sacrifices, my Cordelia,
The gods themselves throw incense. Have I
caught thee?
He that parts us shall bring a brand° from
Heaven,
And fire us° hence like foxes. Wipe thine eyes.
The goodyears° shall devour them, flesh and
fell,°   26
Ere they shall make us weep. We'll see 'em starve
first.
Come. [*Exeunt* LEAR *and* CORDELIA, *guarded.*]
    EDM: Come hither, Captain, hark.
Take thou this note. Go follow them to prison.
One step I have advanced thee. If thou dost
As this instructs thee, thou dost make thy way
To noble fortunes. Know thou this, that men
Are as the time is.° To be tender-minded
Does not become a sword.° Thy great employ-
ment   35
Will not bear question.° Either say thou'lt do 't,
Or thrive by other means.
    CAPT: I'll do 't, my lord.
    EDM: About it, and write happy° when thou
hast done.
Mark, I say, instantly, and carry it so   40

77-78. **for . . . debate:** my fortune is now in such a state that
I must act, not argue.
  Sc. ii: 7. ta'en: taken.   **10-12. Men . . . all:** Shakespeare
had already expressed this stoical view of life [in *Hamlet*].
12. Ripeness: perfect readiness.
  Sc. iii: 2. their . . . pleasures: the will of my superiors.
4-7. We . . . frown: See I.i.194-201,n.

14. **gilded butterflies:** i.e., Court folk.   **17. take . . .
things:** pretend to understand deep secrets.   **19-20. packs
. . . moon:** parties at Court whose fortunes change
monthly.   **24. a brand:** fire.   **25. fire us:** drive us out by
fire.   **26. goodyears:** The phrase "what the goodyear"
meant "what the deuce"; hence "goodyear" means something vaguely evil. Lear is talking baby talk—"The bogey-
men shall have them." **fell:** skin.   **33-34. men . . . is:** i.e., in
brutal times men must be brutes.   **35. sword:** soldier.
35-36. Thy . . . question: the duty now laid on you is too
important and brutal to be argued about.
39. happy: fortunate.

As I have set it down.
    CAPT: I cannot draw a cart, nor eat dried oats.
If it be man's work, I'll do 't.   [*Exit.*]
    [*Flourish. Enter* ALBANY, GONERIL, REGAN, *another* CAPTAIN, *and* SOLDIERS.]
    ALB: Sir, you have shown today your valiant
       strain,°   44
And fortune led you well. You have the captives
That were the opposites° of this day's strife.
We do require them of you, so to use them
As we shall find their merits and our safety
May equally determine.
    EDM: Sir, I thought it fit   50
To send the old and miserable King
To some retention and appointed guard,°
Whose age has charms in it, whose title more,
To pluck the common bosom° on his side
And turn our impressed lances° in our eyes 55
Which do command them. With him I sent the
    Queen,
My reason all the same, and they are ready
Tomorrow or at further space to appear
Where you shall hold your session.° At this time
We sweat and bleed. The friend hath lost his
    friend,   60
And the best quarrels, in the heat, are cursed
By those that feel their sharpness.°
The question of Cordelia and her father
Requires a fitter place.
    ALB: Sir, by your patience, 65
I hold you but a subject° of this war,
Not as a brother.
    REG: That's as we list to grace him.
Methinks our pleasure might have been de-
    manded
Ere you had spoke so far. He led our powers,
Bore the commission of my place and person,°
The which immediacy may well stand up 72
And call itself your brother.°
    GON: Not so hot.
In his own grace he doth exalt himself

More than in your addition.°
    REG: In my rights,
By me invested, he compeers° the best.
    GON: That were the most, if he should hus-
    band you.
    REG: Jesters do oft prove prophets.   80
    GON: Holloa, holloa!
That eye that told you so looked but a-squint.
    REG: Lady, I am not well, else I should answer
From a full-flowing stomach.° General,
Take thou my soldiers, prisoners, patrimony, 85
Dispose of them, of me, the walls are thine.°
Witness the world that I create thee here
My lord and master.
    GON: Mean you to enjoy him?
    ALB: The let-alone° lies not in your goodwill.
    EDM: Nor in thine, lord.   91
    ALB: Half-blooded fellow, yes.
    REG: [*To* EDMUND] Let the drum strike, and
    prove my title thine.
    ALB: Stay yet, hear reason. Edmund, I arrest
    thee
On capital treason,° and in thine attaint° 95
This gilded serpent. [*Pointing to* GONERIL] For
    your claim, fair Sister,
I bar it in the interest of my wife.
'Tis she is subcontracted° to this lord,
And I, her husband, contradict your bans.°
If you will marry, make your loves to me. 100
My lady is bespoke.°
    GON: An interlude!°
    ALB: Thou art armed, Gloucester. Let the
    trumpet sound.
If none appear to prove upon thy person
Thy heinous,° manifest, and many treasons, 105
There is my pledge. [*Throwing down a glove*] I'll
    prove it on thy heart
Ere I taste bread, thou art in nothing less
Than I have here proclaimed thee.
    REG: Sick, oh, sick!

---

44. **strain:** blood, courage.   46. **opposites:** opponents.
52. **retention . . . guard:** where he can be kept and properly
guarded.   54. **common bosom:** the sympathies of our soldiers.   55. **impressed lances:** the soldiers we have conscripted.   59. **session:** trial.   61–62. **And . . . sharpness:**
i.e., with the battle hardly over we are in no condition to
judge this matter calmly.   66. **subject:** i.e., not one who
gives orders.   71. **commission . . . person:** commission
appointing him commander as my deputy.   72–73. **The
. . . brother:** since he is my general, he is fit to be considered
your equal.

76. **your addition:** the title which you have given him. See
I.i.143.   78. **compeers:** equals.   84. **full-flowing stomach:** in full wrath.   86. **walls . . . thine:** i.e., you have won
the outer defenses.   90. **let-alone:** power to prevent.
95. **capital treason:** treason deserving death. **and . . . attaint:**
and accused with you (*attaint:* impeachment).   98. **sub-
contracted:** already betrothed.   99. **bans:** notice of intention to marry, read out in church for three Sundays previous
to the marriage.   101. **bespoke:** already reserved.
102. **An interlude:** i.e., this is mere play-acting.   105. **heinous:** odious.

GON: [*Aside*] If not, I'll ne'er trust medicine.°

EDM: [*Throwing down a glove*] There's my exchange. What in the world he is   111
That names me traitor, villainlike he lies.°
Call by thy trumpet. He that dares approach,
On him, on you—who not?—I will maintain
My truth and honor firmly.   115

ALB: A herald, ho!

EDM: A herald, ho, a herald!

ALB: Trust to thy single° virtue, for thy soldiers,
All levied in my name, have in my name
Took their discharge.   120

REG: My sickness grows upon me.

ALB: She is not well. Convey her to my tent.

[*Exit* REGAN, *led.*]

[*Enter a* HERALD.] Come hither, herald.—Let the trumpet sound.—
And read out this.   124

CAPT: Sound, trumpet! [*A trumpet sounds.*]

HER: [*Reads.*] "If any man of quality or degree° within the lists° of the army will maintain upon Edmund, supposed Earl of Gloucester, that he is a manifold traitor, let him appear by the third sound of the trumpet. He is bold in his defense."   131

EDM: Sound!   [*First trumpet.*]

HER: Again!   [*Second trumpet.*]
Again!   [*Third trumpet.*]
[*Trumpet answers within.*]

[*Enter* EDGAR *at the third sound, armed, with a trumpet before him.*]

ALB: Ask him his purposes, why he appears
Upon this call o' the trumpet.°   136

HER: What are you?
Your name, your quality? And why you answer
This present summons?

EDG: Know my name is lost,
By treason's tooth bare-gnawn and canker-bit.°
Yet am I noble as the adversary   142
I come to cope.°

ALB: Which is that adversary?

EDG: What's he that speaks for Edmund, Earl of Gloucester?

EDM: Himself. What say'st thou to him?

EDG: Draw thy sword,
That if my speech offend a noble heart,
Thy arm may do thee justice. Here is mine.
Behold, it is the privilege of mine honors,   150
My oath, and my profession.° I protest,
Mauger° thy strength, youth, place, and eminence,
Despite thy victor sword and fire-new° fortune,
Thy valor and thy heart, thou art a traitor,
False to thy gods, thy brother, and thy father,
Conspirant° 'gainst this high illustrious Prince,
And from the extremest upward of thy head
To the descent and dust below thy foot   158
A most toad-spotted° traitor. Say thou "No,"
This sword, this arm, and my best spirits are bent
To prove upon thy heart, whereto I speak,
Thou liest.

EDM: In wisdom I should ask thy name,
But since thy outside looks so fair and warlike
And that thy tongue some say of breeding°
   breathes,   165
What safe and nicely° I might well delay
By rule of knighthood I disdain and spurn.
Back do I toss these treasons to thy head,
With the hell-hated lie o'erwhelm thy heart,
Which for they yet glance by and scarcely bruise,
This sword of mine shall give them instant way
Where they shall rest forever. Trumpets, speak!

[*Alarums. They fight.* EDMUND *falls.*]

ALB: Save him, save him!   173

GON: This is practice,° Gloucester.
By the law of arms thou wast not bound to answer
An unknown opposite. Thou art not vanquished,
But cozened° and beguiled.

ALB: Shut your mouth, dame,   178
Or with this paper° shall I stop it. Hold, sir,
Thou worse than any name, read thine own evil.
No tearing, lady. I perceive you know it.

GON: Say if I do, the laws are mine, not thine.
Who can arraign me for 't?   183

---

110. medicine: poison.   **112. villainlike . . . lies:** he lies like a villain. This is the lie direct, which was a direct challenge to mortal combat.   **118. single:** solitary, unaided. **126–127. quality or degree:** rank or high position. **127. lists:** roll call, roster.   **135–36. Ask . . . trumpet:** The combat follows the normal procedure of chivalry. Edgar is wearing full armor, his face concealed by his closed helmet.   **141. canker-bit:** corrupted by maggots.   **143. cope:** meet, encounter.

151. profession: i.e., as a knight.   **152. Mauger:** in spite of.   **153. fire-new:** brand-new—like a new coin. **156. Conspirant:** conspiring.   **159. toad-spotted:** i.e., venomous as a toad.   **165. say of breeding:** accent of a gentleman.   **166. nicely:** i.e., if I stood on niceties of procedure.   **174. practice:** treachery.   **177. cozened:** cheated.   **179. this paper:** her love letter to Edmund, which Edgar had taken from Oswald's corpse. See IV.vi.294–302.

ALB: Most monstrous!
Know'st thou this paper?   185
   GON: Ask me not what I know. [*Exit.*]
   ALB: Go after her. She's desperate, govern°
   her.
   EDM: What you have charged me with, that
   have I done,
And more, much more. The time will bring it
   out.
'Tis past, and so am I. But what art thou   190
That hast this fortune on me? If thou 'rt noble,
I do forgive thee.
   EDG: Let's exchange charity.
I am no less in blood than thou art, Edmund.
If more, the more thou hast wronged me.   195
My name is Edgar, and thy father's son.
The gods are just, and of our pleasant vices
Make instruments to plague us.°
The dark and vicious place where thee he got°
Cost him his eyes.   200
   EDM: Thou hast spoken right, 'tis
   true.
The wheel is come full circle,° I am here.
   ALB: Methought thy very gait did prophesy
A royal nobleness. I must embrace thee.
Let sorrow split my heart if ever I   205
Did hate thee or thy father!
   EDG: Worthy Prince, I know 't.
   ALB: Where have you hid yourself?
How have you known the miseries of your fa-
   ther?
   EDG: By nursing them, my lord. List a brief
   tale,   210
And when 'tis told, oh, that my heart would
   burst!
The bloody proclamation to escape°
That followed me so near—Oh, our lives' sweet-
   ness!
That we the pain of death would hourly
   die   214
Rather than die at once!°—taught me to shift
Into a madman's rags, to assume a semblance
That very dogs disdained. And in this habit
Met I my father with his bleeding rings,

Their precious stones new-lost, became his guide,
Led him, begged for him, saved him from de-
   spair,   220
Never—oh, fault!—revealed myself unto him
Until some half-hour past, when I was armed.
Not sure, though hoping, of this good success,
I asked his blessing, and from first to last
Told him my pilgrimage. But his flawed heart—
Alack, too weak the conflict to support!—   226
'Twixt two extremes of passion, joy and grief,
Burst smilingly.°
   EDM: This speech of yours hath moved me,
And shall perchance do good. But speak you on.
You look as you had something more to say.
   ALB: If there be more, more woeful, hold it in,
For I am almost ready to dissolve,
Hearing of this.   234
   EDG: This would have seemed a period°
To such as love not sorrow, but another,
To amplify too much, would make much more,
And top extremity.°
Whilst I was big in clamor,° came there in a man
Who, having seen me in my worst estate,   240
Shunned my abhorred society. But then, finding
Who 'twas that so endured, with his strong arms
He fastened on my neck, and bellowed out
As he'd burst heaven, threw him on my father,
Told the most piteous tale of Lear and him 245
That ever ear received. Which in recounting
His grief grew puissant,° and the strings of life°
Began to crack. Twice then the trumpets
   sounded,
And there I left him tranced.°   249
   ALB: But who was this?
   EDG: Kent, sir, the banished Kent, who in dis-
   guise
Followed his enemy King,° and did him service
Improper for a slave.
   [*Enter a* GENTLEMAN, *with a bloody knife.*]
   GENT: Help, help, oh, help!
   EDG: What kind of help?   255
   ALB: Speak, man.
   EDG: What means this bloody knife?

---

187. govern: control.   **197–98. of . . . us:** This is the answer to Gloucester's lighthearted words at the opening of the
play—"Do you smell a fault?" (I.i.16)   **199. got:** begot.
202. The . . . circle: i.e., I end as I began—an outcast of
fortune.   **212. The . . . escape:** in order to escape after the
proclamation for my arrest. See II.iii.1   **213–15. Oh . . .
once:** life is so sweet to us that we will endure the pains of
death hourly if only we can live.

225–28. But . . . smilingly: In the performance the significance of Edgar's speech can easily be missed. Gloucester has
died from excessive emotion (*passion*), and Kent is near his
end.   **235. period:** end.   **238. top extremity:** exceed
the extreme limit of what could be endured.   **239. clamor:** grief.   **247. puissant:** powerful, overwhelming.
strings of life: heartstrings.   **249. tranced:** in a faint.
252. enemy King: the King who had declared him an
enemy.

GENT: 'Tis hot, it smokes.
It came even from the heart of—oh, she's dead!
ALB: Who dead? Speak, man.   260
GENT: Your lady, sir, your lady. And her sister
By her is poisoned. She hath confessed it.
EDM: I was contracted° to them both. All
   three
Now marry in an instant.
EDG: Here comes Kent. 265
ALB: Produce the bodies, be they alive or
   dead.   [*Exit* GENTLEMAN.]
This judgment of the Heavens, that makes us
   tremble,
Touches us not with pity.
   [*Enter* KENT.] Oh, is this he?
The time will not allow the compliment   270
Which very manners urges.
KENT: I am come
To bid my King and master aye good night.
Is he not here?
ALB: Great thing of us forgot!   275
Speak, Edmund, where's the King? And where's
   Cordelia?
See's thou this object, Kent?
[*The bodies of* GONERIL *and* REGAN *are brought
   in.*]
KENT: Alack, why thus?
EDM: Yet Edmund was beloved.°
The one the other poisoned for my sake,   280
And after slew herself.
ALB: Even so. Cover their faces.
EDM: I pant for life. Some good I mean to do,
Despite of mine own nature. Quickly send—
Be brief in it—to the castle, for my writ   285
Is on the life of Lear and on Cordelia.
Nay, send in time.
ALB: Run, run, oh, run!
EDG: To who, my lord? Who hath the office?
   Send
Thy token of reprieve°   290
EDM: Well thought on. Take my sword.
Give it the Captain.
ALB: Haste thee, for thy life.   [*Exit* EDGAR.]
EDM: He hath commission from thy wife and
   me
To hang Cordelia in the prison and   295
To lay the blame upon her own despair,
That she fordid° herself.

ALB: The gods defend her! Bear him hence
   awhile.   [EDMUND *is borne off.*]
[*Re-enter* LEAR, *with* CORDELIA *dead in his
   arms,* EDGAR, CAPTAIN, *and others follow-
   ing.*]
LEAR: Howl, howl, howl, howl! Oh, you are
   men of stones.
Had I your tongues and eyes, I'd use them so
That heaven's vault should crack. She's gone for-
   ever!   301
I know when one is dead and when one lives.
She's dead as earth. Lend me a looking-glass.
If that her breath will mist or stain the stone,°
Why, then she lives.   305
KENT: Is this the promised end?°
EDG: Or image of that horror?
ALB: Fall and cease.°
LEAR: This feather stirs, she lives. If it be so,
It is a chance which does redeem all sorrows
That ever I have felt.   311
KENT: [*Kneeling*] Oh, my good master!
LEAR: Prithee, away.
EDG: 'Tis noble Kent, your
   friend.
LEAR: A plague upon you, murderers, traitors
   all!   315
I might have saved her. Now she's gone forever!
Cordelia, Cordelia! Stay a little. Ha!
What is 't thou say'st? Her voice was ever soft,
Gentle and low, an excellent thing in woman.
I killed the slave that was a-hanging thee.   320
CAPT: 'Tis true, my lords, he did.
LEAR: Did I not, fellow?
I have seen the day with my good biting fal-
   chion°
I would have made them skip. I am old now,
And these same crosses° spoil me. Who are you?
Mine eyes are not o' the best, I'll tell you straight.
KENT: If fortune brag of two she loved and
   hated,   327
One of them we behold.
LEAR: This is a dull sight. Are you not Kent?
KENT: The same,
Your servant Kent. Where is your servant Caius?
LEAR: He's a good fellow, I can tell you that.
He'll strike, and quickly too. He's dead and rot-
   ten.   333

---

263. contracted: betrothed.   **279. Yet . . . beloved:** The
bastard's last grim triumph—two women died for his
love.   **290. token of reprieve:** sign that they are
reprieved.   **297. fordid:** destroyed.

304. stone: glass.   **306. the . . . end:** i.e., Doomsday.
308. Fall . . . cease: i.e., let Doomsday come and the world
end.   **323. falchion:** curved sword.   **325. crosses:**
troubles.

KENT: No, my good lord, I am the very
man°——

LEAR: I'll see that straight.   335

KENT: That from your first of difference° and
decay

Have followed your sad steps.

LEAR: You are welcome hither.

KENT: Nor no man else. All's cheerless, dark,
and deadly.

Your eldest daughters have fordone themselves,
And desperately are dead.   341

LEAR: Aye, so I think.

ALB: He knows not what he says, and vain is it
That we present us to him.

EDG: Very bootless.°   345

[Enter a CAPTAIN.]

CAPT: Edmund is dead, my lord.

ALB: That's but a trifle here.

You lords and noble friends, know our intent.
What comfort to this great decay° may come
Shall be applied. For us, we will resign,   350
During the life of this old Majesty,
To him our absolute power.

[To EDGAR and KENT] You, to your rights,
With boot,° and such addition as your honors
Have more than merited. All friends shall taste
The wages of their virtue, and all foes   356
The cup of their deservings. Oh, see, see!°

LEAR: And my poor fool° is hanged! No, no,
no life!

Why should a dog, a horse, a rat, have life
And thou no breath at all? Thou'lt come no more,
Never, never, never, never, never!   361
Pray you, undo this button.° Thank you, sir.
Do you see this? Look on her, look, her lips,
Look there, look there!   [Dies.]

EDG: He faints. My lord, my lord!

KENT: Break, heart, I prithee break!   366

EDG: Look up, my lord.

KENT: Vex not his ghost. Oh, let him pass! He
hates him

That would upon the rack of this tough world
Stretch him out longer.   370

EDG: He is gone indeed.

KENT: The wonder is he hath endured so long.
He but usurped his life.

ALB: Bear them from hence. Our present business

Is general woe. [To KENT and EDGAR] Friends of
my soul, you twain   375
Rule in this realm and the gored state sustain.

KENT: I have a journey, sir, shortly to go.
My master calls me,° I must not say no.

ALB: The weight of this sad time we must
obey,

Speak what we feel, not what we ought to say.
The oldest hath borne most. We that are young
Shall never see so much, nor live so long.   382

[Exeunt, with a dead march.]

331–334. **Your . . . man:** This is the first and only mention of a Caius, which was apparently the name assumed by Kent in his disguise.   **336. difference:** changed state.   **345. bootless:** useless.   **349. decay:** i.e., Lear.   **354. boot:** advantage.   **357. Oh . . . see:** There is a sudden change in Lear.

358. **fool:** Cordelia; *fool* is often used as a term of affection.   **362. Pray . . . button:** For the last time Lear is oppressed by the violent beating of his heart before it is stilled forever.   **378. calls me:** i.e., to follow him into the darkness.

MOLIÈRE

Tartuffe

Molière is the pseudonym of Jean-Baptiste Poquelin (1622–1673), French dramatist to the court of Louis XIV. It was Molière's education in a Jesuit school, where he wrote and produced plays in Latin, that prompted his early love of the theatre. His family wanted him to be a lawyer, so he became a member of the Bar in 1641. In 1643 he joined a group of actors, however, but the organization soon failed and Molière was imprisoned for the debts. After his release, he again set out with a theatrical troupe to play the provincial towns, a tour that lasted twelve years. In 1658 his group performed one of Corneille's plays for King Louis XIV and his court and followed it with one of Molière's own plays, as a result of which he became an immediate success at court. From 1659 to 1673, he wrote many plays, ten of which are considered his masterpieces. Some of these are *The School for Wives*, 1662; *Tartuffe*, 1664; *The Misanthrope*, 1666, *The Miser*, 1668; and *The Imaginary Invalid*, 1673.

Tartuffe was not presented in a public performance until five years after it was written, and in 1667 a storm of protest so great that the audience rioted caused the King to forbid any more performances. Molière's critics accused the play for attacking religion, but he replied that instead it attacked hypocrisy—that the audience should have seen Tartuffe as a religious hypocrite, Molière's symbol of the irrational and unquestioning "true believer," who in fact is blind to the truth.

THE CHARACTERS

MADAME PERNELLE, *Orgon's mother*
ORGON, *Elmire's husband*
ELMIRE, *Orgon's wife*
DAMIS, *Orgon's son, Elmire's stepson*

MARIANE, *Orgon's daughter, Elmire's stepdaughter, in love with Valère*
VALERE, *in love with Mariane*
CLEANTE, *Orgon's brother-in-law*
TARTUFFE, *a hypocrite*
DORINE, *Mariane's lady's-maid*
M. LOYAL, *a bailiff*
A POLICE OFFICER
FLIPOTE, *Madame Pernelle's maid*

The scene throughout: Orgon's house in Paris.

TARTUFFE By Molière, translated and © 1961, 1962 by Richard Wilbur. Reprinted by permission of Harcourt Brace Jovanovich, Inc.

ACT I

SCENE I

(MADAME PERNELLE *and* FLIPOTE, *her maid,*
ELMIRE, MARIANE, DORINE, DAMIS, CLEANTE.)

MADAME PERNELLE:
Come, come, Flipote; it's time I left this place.
ELMIRE:
I can't keep up, you walk at such a pace.
MADAME PERNELLE:
Don't trouble, child; no need to show me out.
It's not your manners I'm concerned about.
ELMIRE:
We merely pay you the respect we owe.
But, Mother, why this hurry? Must you go?
MADAME PERNELLE:
I must. This house appalls me. No one in it
Will pay attention for a single minute.
Children, I take my leave much vexed in spirit.
I offer good advice, but you won't hear it.
You all break in and chatter on and on.
It's like a madhouse with the keeper gone.
DORINE:
If . . .
MADAME PERNELLE:
        Girl, you talk too much, and I'm afraid
You're far too saucy for a lady's-maid.
You push in everywhere and have your say.
DAMIS:
But . . .
MADAME PERNELLE:
        You, boy, grow more foolish every day.
To think my grandson should be such a dunce!
I've said a hundred times, if I've said it once,
That if you keep the course on which you've
        started,
You'll leave your worthy father broken-hearted.
MARIANE:
I think . . .
MADAME PERNELLE:
        And you, his sister, seem so pure,
So shy, so innocent, and so demure.
But you know what they say about still waters.
I pity parents with secretive daughters.
ELMIRE:
Now, Mother . . .
MADAME PERNELLE:
        And as for you, child, let me
    add
That your behavior is extremely bad,

And a poor example for these children, too.
Their dear, dead mother did far better than you.
You're much too free with money, and I'm dis-
    tressed
To see you so elaborately dressed.
When it's one's husband that one aims to please,
One has no need of costly fripperies.
CLEANTE:
Oh, Madam, really . . .
MADAME PERNELLE:
        You are her brother, Sir,
And I respect and love you; yet if I were
My son, this lady's good and pious spouse,
I wouldn't make you welcome in my house.
You're full of wordly counsels which, I fear,
Aren't suitable for decent folk to hear.
I've spoken bluntly, Sir; but it behooves us
Not to mince words when righteous fervor moves
    us.
DAMIS:
Your man Tartuffe is fully of holy speeches . . .
MADAME PERNELLE:
And practices precisely what he preaches.
He's a fine man, and should be listened to.
I will not hear him mocked by fools like you.
DAMIS:
Good God! Do you expect me to submit
To the tyranny of that carping hypocrite?
Must we forgo all joys and satisfactions
Because that bigot censures all our actions?
DORINE:
To hear him talk—and he talks all the time—
There's nothing one can do that's not a crime.
He rails at everything, your dear Tartuffe.
MADAME PERNELLE:
Whatever he reproves deserves reproof.
He's out to save your souls, and all of you
Must love him, as my son would have you do.
DAMIS:
Ah no, Grandmother, I could never take
To such a rascal, even for my father's sake.
That's how I feel, and I shall not dissemble.
His every action makes me seethe and tremble
With helpless anger, and I have no doubt
That he and I will shortly have it out.
DORINE:
Surely it is a shame and a disgrace
To see this man usurp the master's place—
To see this beggar who, when first he came,
Had not a shoe or shoestring to his name
So far forget himself that he behaves
As if the house were his, and we his slaves.

MADAME PERNELLE:
Well, mark my words, your souls would fare far
    better
If you obeyed his precept to the letter.

DORINE:
You see him as a saint. I'm far less awed;
In fact, I see right through him. He's a fraud.

MADAME PERNELLE:
Nonsense!

DORINE:
        His man Laurent's the same, or worse;
I'd not trust either with a penny purse.

MADAME PERNELLE:
I can't say what his servant's morals may be;
His own great goodness I can guarantee.
You all regard him with distaste and fear
Because he tells you what you're loath to hear,
Condemns your sins, points out your moral flaws,
And humbly strives to further Heaven's cause.

DORINE:
If sin is all that bothers him, why is it
He's so upset when folk drop in to visit?
Is Heaven so outraged by a social call
That he must prophesy against us all?
I'll tell you what I think: if you ask me,
He's jealous of my mistress' company.

MADAME PERNELLE:
Rubbish! (*To* ELMIRE.) He's not alone, child, in
    complaining
Of all of your promiscuous entertaining.
Why, the whole neighborhood's upset, I know,
By all these carriages that come and go,
With crowds of guests parading in and out
And noisy servants loitering about.
In all of this, I'm sure there's nothing vicious;
But why give people cause to be suspicious?

CLEANTE:
They need no cause; they'll talk in any case.
Madam, this world would be a joyless place
If, fearing what malicious tongues might say,
We locked our doors and turned our friends
    away.
And even if one did so dreary a thing,
D'you think those tongues would cease their
    chattering?
One can't fight slander; it's a losing battle;
Let us instead ignore their tittle-tattle.
Let's strive to live by conscience' clear decrees,
And let the gossips gossip as they please.

DORINE:
If there is talk against us, I know the source:
It's Daphne and her little husband, of course.

Those who have greatest cause for guilt and
    shame
Are quickest to besmirch a neighbor's name.
When there's a chance for libel, they never miss
    it;
When something can be made to seem illicit
They're off at once to spread the joyous news,
Adding to fact what fantasies they choose.
By talking up their neighbor's indiscretions
They seek to camouflage their own transgres-
    sions,
Hoping that others' innocent affairs
Will lend a hue of innocence to theirs,
Or that their own black guilt will come to seem
Part of a general shady color-scheme.

MADAME PERNELLE:
All that is quite irrelevant. I doubt
That anyone's more virtuous and devout
Than dear Orante; and I'm informed that she
Condemns your mode of life most vehemently.

DORINE:
Oh, yes, she's strict, devout, and has no taint
Of worldliness; in short, she seems a saint.
But it was time which taught her that disguise;
She's thus because she can't be otherwise.
So long as her attractions could enthrall,
She flounced and flirted and enjoyed it all,
But now that they're no longer what they were
She quits a world which fast is quitting her,
And wears a veil of virtue to conceal
Her bankrupt beauty and her lost appeal.
That's what becomes of old coquettes today:
Distressed when all their lovers fall away,
They see no recourse but to play the prude,
And so confer a style on solitude.
Thereafter, they're severe with everyone,
Condemning all our actions, pardoning none,
And claiming to be pure, austere, and zealous
When, if the truth were known, they're merely
    jealous,
And cannot bear to see another know
The pleasures time has forced them to forgo.

MADAME PERNELLE: (*Initially to* ELMIRE.)
That sort of talk is what you like to hear;
Therefore you'd have us all keep still, my dear,
While Madam rattles on the livelong day.
Nevertheless, I mean to have my say.
I tell you that you're blest to have Tartuffe
Dwelling, as my son's guest, beneath this roof;
That Heaven has sent him to forestall its wrath
By leading you, once more, to the true path;
That all he reprehends is reprehensible,

And that you'd better heed him, and be sensible.
These visits, balls, and parties in which you revel
Are nothing but inventions of the Devil.
One never hears a word that's edifying:
Nothing but chaff and foolishness and lying,
As well as vicious gossip in which one's neighbor
Is cut to bits with èpèe, foil, and saber.
People of sense are driven half-insane
At such affairs, where noise and folly reign
And reputations perish thick and fast.
As a wise preacher said on Sunday last,
Parties are Towers of Babylon, because
The guests all babble on with never a pause;
And then he told a story which, I think . . .

    (*To* CLEANTE.)

I heard that laugh, Sir, and I saw that wink!
Go find your silly friends and laugh some more!
Enough; I'm going; don't show me to the door.
I leave this household much dismayed and vexed;
I cannot say when I shall see you next.

    (*Slapping* FLIPOTE.)

Wake up, don't stand there gaping into space!
I'll slap some sense into that stupid face.
Move, move, you slut.

SCENE II

(CLEANTE, DORINE.)

CLEANTE:

            I think I'll stay behind;
I want no further pieces of her mind.
How that old lady . . .

DORINE:

            Oh, what wouldn't she
  say
If she could hear you speak of her that way!
She'd thank you for the *lady*, but I'm sure
She'd find the *old* a little premature.

CLEANTE:
My, what a scene she made, and what a din!
And how this man Tartuffe has taken her in!

DORINE:
Yes, but her son is even worse deceived;
His folly must be seen to be believed.
In the late troubles, he played an able part
And served his king with wise and loyal heart,
But he's quite lost his senses since he fell
Beneath Tartuffe's infatuating spell.
He calls him brother, and loves him as his life,
Preferring him to mother, child, or wife.
In him and him alone will he confide;
He's made him his confessor and his guide;

He pets and pampers him with love more tender
Than any pretty maiden could engender,
Gives him the place of honor when they dine,
Delights to see him gorging like a swine,
Stuffs him with dainties till his guts distend,
And when he belches, cries "God bless you,
    friend!"
In short, he's mad; he worships him; he dotes;
His deeds he marvels at, his words he quotes,
Thinking each act a miracle, each word
Oracular as those that Moses heard.
Tartuffe, much pleased to find so easy a victim,
Has in a hundred ways beguiled and tricked him,
Milked him of money, and with his permission
Established here a sort of Inquisition.
Even Laurent, his lackey, dares to give
Us arrogant advice on how to live;
He sermonizes us in thundering tones
And confiscates our ribbons and colognes.
Last week he tore a kerchief into pieces
Because he found it pressed in a *Life of Jesus:*
He said it was a sin to juxtapose
Unholy vanities and holy prose.

SCENE III

(ELMIRE, MARIANE, DAMIS, CLEANTE, DORINE.)

ELMIRE: (*To* CLEANTE.)
You did well not to follow; she stood in the door
And said *verbatim* all she's said before.
I saw my husband coming. I think I'd best
Go upstairs now, and take a little rest.

CLEANTE:
I'll wait and greet him here; then I must go.
I've really only time to say hello.

DAMIS:
Sound him about my sister's wedding, please.
I think Tartuffe's against it, and that he's
Been urging Father to withdraw his blessing.
As you well know, I'd find that most distressing.
Unless my sister and Valère can marry,
My hopes to wed *his* sister will miscarry,
And I'm determined . . .

DORINE:

            He's coming.

SCENE IV

(ORGON, CLEANTE, DORINE.)

ORGON:

            Ah, Brother, good-day.

CLEANTE:
Well, welcome back. I'm sorry I can't stay.
How was the country? Blooming, I trust, and
  green?
ORGON:
Excuse me, Brother; just one moment.
  (*To* DORINE.)

                              Dorine . . .
  (*To* CLEANTE.)
To put my mind at rest, I always learn
The household news the moment I return.
  (*To* DORINE.)
Has all been well, these two days I've been gone?
How are the family? What's been going on?
DORINE:
Your wife, two days ago, had a bad fever,
And a fierce headache which refused to leave
  her.
ORGON:
Ah. And Tartuffe?
DORINE:
                    Tartuffe? Why, he's round and
  red,
Bursting with health, and excellently fed.
ORGON:
Poor fellow!
DORINE:
              That night, the mistress was unable
To take a single bite at the dinner-table.
Her headache-pains, she said, were simply
  hellish.
ORGON:
Ah. And Tartuffe?
DORINE:
                    He ate his meal with relish,
And zealously devoured in her presence
A leg of mutton and a brace of pheasants.
ORGON:
Poor fellow!
DORINE:
              Well, the pains continued strong,
And so she tossed and tossed the whole night
  long,
Now icy-cold, now burning like a flame.
We sat beside her bed till morning came.
ORGON:
Ah. And Tartuffe?
DORINE:
                    Why, having eaten, he rose
And sought his room, already in a doze,
Got into his warm bed, and snored away
In perfect peace until the break of day.

ORGON:
Poor fellow!
DORINE:
              After much ado, we talked her
Into dispatching someone for the doctor.
He bled her, and the fever quickly fell.
ORGON:
Ah. And Tartuffe?
DORINE:
                    He bore it very well.
To keep his cheerfulness at any cost,
And make up for the blood *Madame* had lost,
He drank, at lunch, four beakers full of port.
ORGON:
Poor fellow!
DORINE:
              Both are doing well, in short.
I'll go and tell *Madame* that you've expressed
Keen sympathy and anxious interest.

SCENE V

(ORGON, CLEANTE.)

CLEANTE:
That girl was laughing in your face, and though
I've no wish to offend you, even so
I'm bound to say that she had some excuse.
How can you possibly be such a goose?
Are you so dazed by this man's hocus-pocus
That all the world, save him, is out of focus?
You've given him clothing, shelter, food, and
  care;
Why must you also . . .
ORGON:
                        Brother, stop right there.
You do not know the man of whom you speak.
CLEANTE:
I grant you that. But my judgment's not so weak
That I can't tell, by his effect on others . . .
ORGON:
Ah, when you meet him, you two will be like
  brothers!
There's been no loftier soul since time began.
He is a man who . . . a man who . . . an excellent
  man.
To keep his precepts is to be reborn,
And view this dunghill of a world with scorn.
Yes, thanks to him I'm a changed man indeed.
Under his tutelage my soul's been freed
From earthly loves, and every human tie:

My mother, children, brother, and wife could
    die,
And I'd not feel a single moment's pain.
CLEANTE:
That's a fine sentiment, Brother; most humane.
ORGON:
Oh, had you seen Tartuffe as I first knew him.
Your heart, like mine, would have surrendered to
    him.
He used to come into our church each day
And humbly kneel nearby, and start to pray.
He'd draw the eyes of everybody there
By the deep fervor of his heartfelt prayer;
He'd sigh and weep, and sometimes with a sound
Of rapture he would bend and kiss the ground;
And when I rose to go, he'd run before
To offer me holy-water at the door.
His serving-man, no less devout than he,
Informed me of his master's poverty;
I gave him gifts, but in his humbleness
He'd beg me every time to give him less.
"Oh, that's too much," he'd cry, "too much by
    twice!
I don't deserve it. The half, Sir, would suffice."
And when I wouldn't take it back, he'd share
Half of it with the poor, right then and there.
At length, Heaven prompted me to take him in
To dwell with us, and free our souls from sin.
He guides our lives, and to protect my honor
Stays by my wife, and keeps an eye upon her;
He tells me whom she sees, and all she does,
And seems more jealous than I ever was!
And how austere he is! Why, he can detect
A mortal sin where you would least suspect;
In smallest trifles, he's extremely strict.
Last week, his conscience was severely pricked
Because, while praying, he had caught a flea
And killed it, so he felt, too wrathfully.
CLEANTE:
Good God, man! Have you lost your common
    sense—
Or is this all some joke at my expense?
How can you stand there and in all sobriety . . .
ORGON:
Brother, your language savors of impiety.
Too much free-thinking's made your faith un-
    steady,
And as I've warned you many times already,
'Twill get you into trouble before you're through.
CLEANTE:
So I've been told before by dupes like you:
Being blind, you'd have all others blind as well;

The clear-eyed man you call an infidel,
And he who sees through humbug and pretense
Is charged, by you, with want of reverence.
Spare me your warnings, Brother; I have no fear
Of speaking out, for you and Heaven to hear,
Against affected zeal and pious knavery.
There's true and false in piety, as in bravery,
And just as those whose courage shines the most
In battle, are the least inclined to boast,
So those whose hearts are truly pure and lowly
Don't make a flashy show of being holy.
There's a vast difference, so it seems to me,
Between true piety and hypocrisy:
How do you fail to see it, may I ask?
Is not a face quite different from a mask?
Cannot sincerity and cunning art,
Reality and semblance, be told apart?
Are scarecrows just like men, and do you hold
That a false coin is just as good as gold?
Ah, Brother, man's a strangely fashioned creature
Who seldom is content to follow Nature,
But recklessly pursues his inclination
Beyond the narrow bounds of moderation,
And often, by transgressing Reason's laws,
Perverts a lofty aim or noble cause.
A passing observation, but it applies.
ORGON:
I see, dear Brother, that you're profoundly wise;
You harbor all the insight of the age.
You are our one clear mind, our only sage,
The era's oracle, its Cato too,
And all mankind are fools compared to you.
CLEANTE:
Brother, I don't pretend to be a sage.
Nor have I all the wisdom of the age.
There's just one insight I would dare to claim:
I know that true and false are not the same;
And just as there is nothing I more revere
Than a soul whose faith is steadfast and sincere,
Nothing that I more cherish and admire
Than honest zeal and true religious fire,
So there is nothing that I find more base
Than specious piety's dishonest face—
Than these bold mountebanks, these histrios
Whose impious mummeries and hollow shows
Exploit our love of Heaven, and make a jest
Of all that men think holiest and best;
These calculating souls who offer prayers
Not to their Maker, but as public wares,
And seek to buy respect and reputation
With lifted eyes and signs of exaltation;
These charlatans, I say, whose pilgrim souls

Proceed, by way of Heaven, toward earthly
    goals,
Who weep and pray and swindle and extort,
Who preach the monkish life, but haunt the
    court,
Who make their zeal the partner of their vice—
Such men are vengeful, sly, and cold as ice,
And when there is an enemy to defame
They cloak their spite in fair religion's name,
Their private spleen and malice being made
To seem a high and virtuous crusade,
Until, to mankind's reverent applause,
They crucify their foe in Heaven's cause.
Such knaves are all too common: yet, for the
    wise,
True piety isn't hard to recognize,
And, happily, these present times provide us
With bright examples to instruct and guide us.
Consider Ariston and Périandre;
Look at Oronte, Alcidamas, Clitandre;
Their virtue is acknowledged; who could doubt
    it?
But you won't hear them beat the drum about it.
They're never ostentatious, never vain,
And their religion's moderate and humane;
It's not their way to criticize and chide:
They think censoriousness a mark of pride,
And therefore, letting others preach and rave,
They show, by deeds, how Christians should be-
    have.
They think no evil of their fellow man,
But judge of him as kindly as they can.
They don't intrigue and wangle and conspire;
To lead a good life is their one desire;
The sinner wakes no rancorous hate in them;
It is the sin alone which they condemn;
Nor do they try to show a fiercer zeal
For Heaven's cause than Heaven itself could feel.
These men I honor, these men I advocate
As models for us all to emulate.
Your man is not their sort at all, I fear:
And, while your praise of him is quite sincere,
I think that you've been dreadfully deluded.

ORGON:
Now then, dear Brother, is your speech con-
    cluded?

CLEANTE:
Why, yes.

ORGON:
            Your servant, Sir. (*He turns to go.*)

CLEANTE:
                No, Brother; wait.

There's one more matter. You agreed of late
That young Valère might have your daughter's
    hand.

ORGON:
I did.

CLEANTE:
        And set the date, I understand.

ORGON:
Quite so.

CLEANTE:
            You've now postponed it; is that true?

ORGON:
No doubt.

CLEANTE:
            The match no longer pleases you?

ORGON:
Who knows?

CLEANTE:
                D'you mean to go back on your
    word?

ORGON:
I won't say that.

CLEANTE:
                Has anything occurred
Which might entitle you to break your pledge?

ORGON:
Perhaps.

CLEANTE:
            Why must you hem, and haw, and
    hedge?
The boy asked me to sound you in this affair . . .

ORGON:
It's been a pleasure.

CLEANTE:
                But what shall I tell Valère?

ORGON:
Whatever you like.

CLEANTE:
                But what have you decided?
What are your plans?

ORGON:
                I plan, Sir, to be guided
By Heaven's will.

CLEANTE:
                Come, Brother, don't talk rot.
You've given Valère your word; will you keep it,
    or not?

ORGON:
Good day.

CLEANTE:
            This looks like poor Valère's undoing;
I'll go and warn him that there's trouble brewing.

ACT II

SCENE I

(ORGON, MARIANE.)

ORGON:
Mariane.
MARIANE:
   Yes, Father?
ORGON:
     A word with you; come here.
MARIANE:
What are you looking for?
ORGON: (*Peering into a small closet.*)
      Eavesdroppers, dear.
I'm making sure we shan't be overheard.
Someone in there could catch our every word.
Ah, good, we're safe. Now, Mariane, my child,
You're a sweet girl who's tractable and mild,
Whom I hold dear, and think most highly of.
MARIANE:
I'm deeply grateful, Father, for your love.
ORGON:
That's well said, Daughter; and you can repay
 me
If, in all things, you'll cheerfully obey me.
MARIANE:
To please you, Sir, is what delights me best.
ORGON:
Good, good. Now, what d'you think of Tartuffe,
 our guest?
MARIANE:
I, Sir?
ORGON:
   Yes. Weigh your answer; think it through.
MARIANE:
Oh, dear. I'll say whatever you wish me to.
ORGON:
That's wisely said, my Daughter. Say of him,
 then,
That he's the very worthiest of men,
And that you're fond of him, and would rejoice
In being his wife, if that should be my choice.
Well?
MARIANE:
  What?
ORGON:
   What's that?
MARIANE:
     I . . .

ORGON:
       Well?
MARIANE:
       Forgive me,
 pray.
ORGON:
Did you not hear me?
MARIANE:
     Of *whom*, Sir, must I say
That I am fond of him, and would rejoice
In being his wife, if that should be your choice?
ORGON:
Why, of Tartuffe.
MARIANE:
    But, Father, that's false, you
 know.
Why would you have me say what isn't so?
ORGON:
Because I am resolved it shall be true.
That it's my wish should be enough for you.
MARIANE
You can't mean, Father . . .
ORGON:
     Yes, Tartuffe shall be
Allied by marriage to this family
And he's to be your husband, is that clear?
It's a father's privilege . . .

SCENE II

(DORINE, ORGON, MARIANE.)

ORGON: (*To* DORINE.)
      What are you doing
 in here?
Is curiosity so fierce a passion
With you, that you must eavesdrop in this fash-
 ion?
DORINE:
There's lately been a rumor going about—
Based on some hunch or chance remark, no
 doubt—
That you mean Mariane to wed Tartuffe.
I've laughed it off, of course, as just a spoof.
ORGON:
You find it so incredible?
DORINE:
     Yes, I do.
I won't accept that story, even from you.

ORGON:
Well, you'll believe it when the thing is done.
DORINE:
Yes, yes, of course. Go on and have your fun.
ORGON:
I've never been more serious in my life.
DORINE:
Ha!
ORGON:
    Daughter, I mean it; you're to be his wife.
DORINE:
No, don't believe your father; it's all a hoax.
ORGON:
See here, young woman . . .
DORINE:
                Come, Sir, no more
  jokes;
You can't fool us.
ORGON:
            How dare you talk that way?
DORINE:
All right, then: we believe you, sad to say.
But how a man like you, who looks so wise
And wears a moustache of such splendid size,
Can be so foolish as to . . .
ORGON:
              Silence, please!
My girl, you take too many liberties.
I'm master here, as you must not forget.
DORINE:
Do let's discuss this calmly; don't be upset.
You can't be serious, Sir, about this plan.
What should that bigot want with Mariane?
Praying and fasting ought to keep him busy.
And then, in terms of wealth and rank, what is
  he?
Why should a man of property like you
Pick out a beggar son-in-law?
ORGON:
            That will do.
Speak of his poverty with reverence.
His is a pure and saintly indigence
Which far transcends all wordly pride and pelf.
He lost his fortune, as he says himself,
Because he cared for Heaven alone, and so
Was careless of his interests here below.
I mean to get him out of his present straits
And help him to recover his estates—
Which, in his part of the world, have no small
  fame.
Poor though he is, he's a gentleman just the same.

DORINE:
Yes, so he tells us; and, Sir, it seems to me
Such pride goes very ill with piety.
A man whose spirit spurns this dungy earth
Ought not to brag of lands and noble birth;
Such worldly arrogance will hardly square
With meek devotion and the life of prayer.
. . . But this approach, I see, has drawn a blank;
Let's speak, then, of this person, not his rank.
Doesn't it seem to you a trifle grim
To give a girl like her to a man like him?
When two are so ill-suited, can't you see
What the sad consequence is bound to be?
A young girl's virtue is imperilled, Sir
When such a marriage is imposed on her;
For if one's bridegroom isn't to one's taste,
It's hardly an inducement to be chaste,
And many a man with horns upon his brow
Has made his wife the thing that she is now.
It's hard to be a faithful wife, in short,
To certain husbands of a certain sort,
And he who gives his daughter to a man she hates
Must answer for her sins at Heaven's gates.
Think, Sir, before you play so risky a role.
ORGON:
This servant-girl presumes to save my soul!
DORINE:
You would do well to ponder what I've said.
ORGON:
Daughter, we'll disregard this dunderhead.
Just trust your father's judgment. Oh, I'm aware
That I once promised you to young Valère;
But now I hear the gambles, which greatly
  shocks me;
What's more, I've doubts about his orthodoxy.
His visits to church, I note, are very few.
DORINE:
Would you have him go at the same hours as you,
And kneel nearby, to be sure of being seen?
ORGON:
I can dispense with such remarks, Dorine.
  (*To* MARIANE.)
Tartuffe, however, is sure of Heaven's blessing.
And that's the only treasure worth possessing.
This match will bring you joys beyond all meas-
  ure;
Your cup will overflow with every pleasure;
You two will interchange your faithful loves
Like two sweet cherubs, or two turtle-doves.
No harsh word shall be heard, no frown be seen,
And he shall make you happy as a queen.

DORINE:
And she'll make him a cuckold, just wait and see.

ORGON:
What language!

DORINE:
Oh, he's a man of destiny;
He's *made* for horns, and what the stars demand
Your daughter's virtue surely can't withstand.

ORGON:
Don't interrupt me further. Why can't you learn
That certain things are none of your concern?

DORINE:
It's for your own sake that I interfere.
(*She repeatedly interrupts* ORGON *just as he is turning to speak to his daughter.*)

ORGON:
Most kind of you. Now, hold your tongue, d'you hear?

DORINE:
If I didn't love you . . .

ORGON:
Spare me your affection.

DORINE:
I'll love you, Sir, in spite of your objection.

ORGON:
Blast!

DORINE:
I can't bear, Sir, for your honor's sake,
To let you make this ludicrous mistake.

ORGON:
You mean to go on talking?

DORINE:
If I didn't protest
This sinful marriage, my conscience couldn't rest.

ORGON:
If you don't hold your tongue, you little shrew . . .

DORINE:
What, lost your temper? A pious man like you?

ORGON:
Yes! Yes! You talk and talk. I'm maddened by it.
Once and for all, I tell you to be quiet.

DORINE:
Well, I'll be quiet. But I'll be thinking hard.

ORGON:
Think all you like, but you had better guard
That saucy tongue of yours, or I'll . . .
(*Turning back to* MARIANE.)
Now, child,
I've weighed this matter fully.

DORINE: (*Aside.*)
It drives me wild
That I can't speak.
(*Orgon turns his head, and she is silent.*)

ORGON:
Tartuffe is no young dandy,
But, still, his person . . .

DORINE: (*Aside.*)
Is as sweet as candy.

ORGON:
Is such that, even if you shouldn't care
For his other merits . . .
(*He turns and stands facing* DORINE, *arms crossed.*)

DORINE: (*Aside.*)
They'll make a lovely pair.
If I were she, no man would marry me
Against my inclination, and go scot-free.
He'd learn, before the wedding-day was over,
How readily a wife can find a lover.

ORGON: (*To* DORINE.)
It seems you treat my orders as a joke.

DORINE:
Why, what's the matter? 'Twas not to you I spoke.

ORGON:
What *were* you doing?

DORINE:
Talking to myself, that's all.

ORGON:
Ah! (*Aside.*) One more bit of impudence and gall,
And I shall give her a good slap in the face.
(*He puts himself in position to slap her;* DORINE, *whenever he glances at her, stands immobile and silent.*)
Daughter, you shall accept, and with good grace,
The husband I've selected . . . Your wedding-day . . .
(*To* DORINE.)
Why don't you talk to yourself?

DORINE:
I've nothing to say.

ORGON:
Come, just one word.

DORINE:
No thank you, Sir. I pass.

ORGON:
Come, speak; I'm waiting.

DORINE:

                                    I'd not be such an ass.

ORGON: (*Turning to* MARIANE.)

In short, dear Daughter, I mean to be obeyed,
And you must bow to the sound choice I've
      made.

DORINE: (*Moving away.*)

I'd not wed such a monster, even in jest.
   (ORGON *attempts to slap her, but misses.*)

ORGON:

Daughter, that maid of yours is a thorough pest;
She makes me sinfully annoyed and nettled.
I can't speak further; my nerves are too unset-
      tled.
She's so upset me by her insolent talk,
I'll calm myself by going for a walk.

SCENE III

(DORINE, MARIANE.)

DORINE: (*Returning.*)

Well, have you lost your tongue girl? Must I play
Your part, and say the lines you ought to say?
Faced with a fate so hideous and absurd,
Can you not utter one dissenting word?

MARIANE:

What good would it do? A father's power is
      great.

DORINE:

Resist him now, or it will be too late.

MARIANE:

But . . .

DORINE:

            Tell him one cannot love at a father's
      whim;
That you shall marry for yourself, not him;
That since it's you who are to be the bride,
It's you, not he, who must be satisfied;
And that if his Tartuffe is so sublime,
He's free to marry him at any time.

MARIANE:

I've bowed so long to Father's strict control,
I couldn't oppose him now, to save my soul.

DORINE:

Come, come, Mariane. Do listen to reason, won't
      you?
Valère has asked your hand. Do you love him, or
      don't you?

MARIANE:

Oh, how unjust of you! What can you mean
By asking such a question, dear Dorine?

You know the depth of my affection for him;
I've told you a hundred times how I adore him.

DORINE:

I don't believe in everything I hear;
Who knows if your professions were sincere?

MARIANE:

They were, Dorine, and you do me wrong to
      doubt it;
Heaven knows that I've been all too frank about
      it.

DORINE:

You love him, then?

MARIANE:

                  Oh, more than I can express.

DORINE:

And he, I take it, cares for you no less?

MARIANE:

I think so.

DORINE:

                  And you both, with equal fire,
Burn to be married?

MARIANE:

                        That is our one desire.

DORINE:

What of Tartuffe, then? What of your father's
      plan?

MARIANE:

I'll kill myself, if I'm forced to wed that man.

DORINE:

I hadn't thought of that recourse. How splendid!
Just die, and all your troubles will be ended!
A fine solution. Oh, it maddens me
To hear you talk in that self-pitying key.

MARIANE:

Dorine, how harsh you are! It's most unfair.
You have no sympathy for my despair.

DORINE:

I've none at all for people who talk drivel
And, faced with difficulties, whine and snivel.

MARIANE:

No doubt I'm timid, but it would be wrong . . .

DORINE:

True love requires a heart that's firm and strong.

MARIANE:

I'm strong in my affection for Valère,
But coping with my father is his affair.

DORINE:

But if your father's brain has grown so cracked
Over his dear Tartuffe that he can retract
His blessing, though your wedding-day was
      named,

It's surely not Valère who's to be blamed.
MARIANE:
If I defied my father, as you suggest,
Would it not seem unmaidenly, at best?
Shall I defend my love at the expense
Of brazenness and disobedience?
Shall I parade my heart's desires, and flaunt . . .
DORINE:
No, I ask nothing of you. Clearly you want
To be Madame Tartuffe, and I feel bound
Not to oppose a wish so very sound.
What right have I to criticize the match?
Indeed, my dear, the man's a brilliant catch.
Monsieur Tartuffe! Now, there's a man of
    weight!
Yes, yes, Monsieur Tartuffe, I'm bound to state,
Is quite a person; that's not to be denied;
'Twill be no little thing to be his bride.
The world already rings with his renown;
He's a great noble—in his native town;
His ears are red, he has a pink complexion,
And all in all, he'll suit you to perfection.
MARIANE:
Dear God!
DORINE:
                    Oh, how triumphant you will feel
At having caught a husband so ideal!
MARIANE:
Oh, do stop teasing, and use your cleverness
To get me out of this appalling mess.
Advise me, and I'll do whatever you say.
DORINE:
Ah, no, a dutiful daughter must obey
Her father, even if he weds her to an ape.
You've a bright future; why struggle to escape?
Tartuffe will take you back where his family
    lives,
To a small town aswarm with relatives—
Uncles and cousins whom you'll be charmed to
    meet.
You'll be received at once by the elite,
Calling upon the bailiff's wife, no less—
Even, perhaps, upon the mayoress,
Who'll sit you down in the *best* kitchen chair.
Then, once a year, you'll dance at the village fair
To the drone of bagpipes—two of them, in fact—
And see a puppet-show, or an animal act.
Your husband . . .
MARIANE:
                    Oh, you turn my blood to ice!
Stop torturing me, and give me your advice.
DORINE:(*Threatening to go.*)

Your servant, Madam.
MARIANE:
                    Dorine, I beg of you . . .
DORINE:
No, you deserve it, this marriage must go
    through.
MARIANE:
Dorine!
DORINE:
        No.
MARIANE:
            Not Tartuffe! You know I think him
    . . .
DORINE:
Tartuffe's your cup of tea, and you shall drink
    him.
MARIANE:
I've always told you everything, and relied . . .
DORINE:
No. You deserve to be tartuffified.
MARIANE:
Well, since you mock me and refuse to care,
I'll henceforth seek my solace in despair:
Despair shall be my counsellor and friend,
And help me bring my sorrows to an end.
    (*She starts to leave.*)
DORINE:
There now, come back; my anger has subsided.
You do deserve some pity, I've decided.
MARIANE:
Dorine, if Father makes me undergo
This dreadful martyrdom, I'll die, I know.
DORINE:
Don't fret; it won't be difficult to discover
Some plan of action . . . But here's Valère, your
    lover.

SCENE IV

(VALERE, MARIANE, DORINE.)

VALERE:
Madam, I've just received some wondrous news
Regarding which I'd like to hear your views,
MARIANE:
What news?
VALERE:
                    You're marrying Tartuffe.
MARIANE:
                                    I find
That father does have such a match in mind.
VALERE:
Your father, Madam . . .

MARIANE:

                 . . . has just this minute
said
That it's Tartuffe he wishes me to wed.

VALERE:
Can he be serious?

MARIANE:

               Oh, indeed he can;
He's clearly set his heart upon the plan.

VALERE:
And what position do you propose to take,
Madam?

MARIANE:

        Why—I don't know.

VALERE:

                  For heaven's
sake—
You don't know?

MARIANE:

           No.

VALERE:

            Well, well!

MARIANE:

                 Advise me, do.

VALERE:
Marry the man. That's my advice to you.

MARIANE:
That's your advice?

VALERE:

           Yes.

MARIANE:

        Truly?

VALERE:

                Oh, absolutely.
You couldn't choose more wisely, more astutely.

MARIANE:
Thanks for this counsel; I'll follow it, of course.

VALERE:
Do, do; I'm sure 'twill cost you no remorse.

MARIANE:
To give it didn't cause your heart to break.

VALERE:
I gave it, Madam, only for your sake.

MARIANE:
And it's for your sake that I take it, Sir.

DORINE: (*Withdrawing to the rear of the stage.*)
Let's see which fool will prove the stubborner.

VALERE:
So! I am nothing to you, and it was flat
Deception when you . . .

MARIANE:

               Please, enough of that.

You've told me plainly that I should agree
To wed the man my father's chosen for me,
And since you've designed to counsel me so
    wisely,
I promise, Sir, to do as you advise me.

VALERE:
Ah, no, 'twas not by me that you were swayed.
No, your decision was already made;
Though now, to save appearances, you protest
That you're betraying me at my behest.

MARIANE:
Just as you say.

VALERE:

             Quite so. And I now see
That you were never truly in love with me.

MARIANE:
Alas, you're free to think so if you choose.

VALERE:
I choose to think so, and here's a bit of news:
You've spurned my hand, but I know where to
    turn
For kinder treatment, as you shall quickly learn.

MARIANE:
I'm sure you do. Your noble qualities
Inspire affection . . .

VALERE:

             Forget my qualities, please.
They don't inspire you overmuch, I find.
But there's another lady I have in mind
Whose sweet and generous nature will not scorn
To compensate me for the loss I've borne.

MARIANE:
I'm no great loss, and I'm sure that you'll transfer
Your heart quite painlessly from me to her.

VALERIE:
I'll do my best to take it in my stride.
The pain I feel at being cast aside
Time and forgetfulness may put an end to.
Of if I can't forget, I shall pretend to.
No self-respecting person is expected
To go on loving once he's been rejected.

MARIANE:
Now, that's a fine, high-minded sentiment.

VALERIE:
One to which any sane man would assent.
Would you prefer it if I pined away
In hopeless passion till my dying day?
Am I to yield you to a rival's arms
And not console myself with other charms?

MARIANE:
Go then; console yourself; don't hesitate.
I wish you to; indeed, I cannot wait.

VALERE:
You wish me to?
MARIANE:
                    Yes.
VALERE:
                    That's the final straw.
Madam, farewell. Your wish shall be my law.
    (*He starts to leave, and then returns: this re-*
        peatedly.)
MARIANE:
Splendid.
VALERE: (*Coming back again.*)
          This breach, remember, is of your mak-
        ing;
It's you who've driven me to the step I'm taking.
MARIANE:
Of course.
VALERE: (*Coming back again.*)
          Remember, too, that I am merely
Following your example.
MARIANE:
                    I see that clearly.
VALERE:
Enough. I'll go and do your bidding, then.
MARIANE:
Good.
VALERE: (*Coming back again.*)
          You shall never see my face again.
MARIANE:
Excellent.
VALERE: (*Walking to the door, then turning
        about.*)
          Yes?
MARIANE:
              What?
VALERE:
              What's that? What did you say?
MARIANE:
Nothing. You're dreaming.
VALERE:
                    Ah, Well, I'm on my way.
Farewell, *Madame.*
    (*He moves slowly away.*)
MARIANE:
              Farewell.
DORINE: (*To* MARIANE.)
                    If you ask me,
Both of you are as mad as mad can be.
Do stop this nonsense, now. I've only let you
Squabble so long to see where it would get you.
Whoa there, Monsieur Valère!
    (*She goes and seizes* VALERE *by the arm; he
        makes a great show of resistance.*)

VALERE:
                              What's this, Dorine?
DORINE:
Come here.
VALERE:
              No, no, my heart's too full of spleen.
Don't hold me back; her wish must be obeyed.
DORINE:
Stop!
VALERE:
              It's too late now; my decision's made.
DORINE:
Oh, pooh!
MARIANE: (*Aside.*)
              He hates the sight of me, that's plain.
I'll go, and so deliver him from pain.
DORINE: (*Leaving* VALERE, *running after* MARIANE.)
And now *you* run away! Come back.
MARIANE:
                              No, no.
Nothing you say will keep me here. Let go!
VALERE: (*Aside.*)
She cannot bear my presence, I perceive.
To spare her further torment, I shall leave.
DORINE: (*Leaving* MARIANE, *running after* VALERE.)
Again! You'll not escape, Sir; don't you try it.
Come here, you two. Stop fussing, and be quiet.
    (*She takes* VALERE *by the hand, then* MARIANE,
        and draws them together.)
VALERE: (*To* DORINE.)
What do you want of me?
MARIANE: (*To* DORINE.)
                    What is the point of this?
DORINE:
We're going to have a little armistice.
    (*To* VALERE.)
Now, weren't you silly to get so overheated?
VALERE:
Didn't you see how badly I was treated?
DORINE: (*To* MARIANE.)
Aren't you a simpleton, to have lost your head?
MARIANE:
Didn't you hear the hateful things he said?
DORINE: (*To* VALERE.)
You're both great fools. Her sole desire, Valère,
Is to be yours in marriage. To that I'll swear.
    (*To* MARIANE.)
He loves you only, and he wants no wife
But you, Mariane. On that I'll stake my life.
MARIANE: (*To* VALERE.)
Then why you advised me so, I cannot see.
VALERE: (*To* MARIANE.)
On such a question, why ask advice of *me?*

DORINE:
Oh, you're impossible. Give me your hands, you
two.
    (*To* VALERE.)
Yours first.
VALERE: (*Giving* DORINE *his hand,*)
            But why?
DORINE: (*To* MARIANE.)
                And now a hand from you.
MARIANE: (*Also giving* DORINE *her hand.*)
What are you doing?
DORINE:
                    There: a perfect fit.
You suit each other better than you'll admit.
    (VALERE *and* MARIANE *hold hands for some
    time without looking at each other.*)
VALERE: (*Turning toward* MARIANE.)
Ah, come, don't be so haughty. Give a man
A look of kindness, won't you, Mariane?
    (MARIANE *turns toward* VALERE *and smiles.*)
DORINE:
I tell you, lovers are completely mad!
VALERE: (*To* MARIANE.)
Now come, confess that you were very bad
To hurt my feelings as you did just now.
I have a just complaint, you must allow.
MARIANE:
You must allow that you were most unpleasant
    . . .
DORINE:
Let's table that discussion for the present;
Your father has a plan which must be stopped.
MARIANE:
Advise us, then; what means must we adopt?
DORINE:
We'll use all manner of means, and all at once.
    (*To* MARIANE.)
Your father's addled; he's acting like a dunce.
Therefore you'd better humor the old fossil.
Pretend to yield to him, be sweet and docile.
And then postpone, as often as necessary,
The day on which you have agreed to marry.
You'll thus gain time, and time will turn the trick.
Sometimes, for instance, you'll be taken sick,
And that will seem good reason for delay;
Or some bad omen will make you change the
    day—
You'll dream of muddy water, or you'll pass
A dead man's hearse, or break a looking-glass.
If all else fails, no man can marry you
Unless you take his ring and say "I do."
But now, let's separate. If they should find
Us talking here, our plot might be divined.

    (*To* VALERE.)
Go to your friends, and tell them what's oc-
    curred,
And have them urge her father to keep his word.
Meanwhile, we'll stir her brother into action,
And get Elmire, as well, to join our faction.
Good-bye.
VALERE: (*To* MARIANE.)
            Though each of us will do his best,
It's your true heart on which my hopes shall rest.
MARIANE: (*To* VALERE.)
Regardless of what Father may decide,
None but Valère shall claim me as his bride.
VALERE:
Oh, how those words content me! Come what
will . . .
DORINE:
Oh, lovers, lovers! Their tongues are never still.
Be off, now.
VALERE: (*Turning to go, then turning back.*)
            One last word . . .
DORINE:
                    No time to chat:
You leave by this door; and *you* leave by that.
    (DORINE *pushes them, by the shoulders, toward
    opposing doors.*)

ACT III

SCENE I

(DAMIS, DORINE.)

DAMIS:
May lightning strike me even as I speak,
May all men call me cowardly and weak,
If any fear or scruple holds me back
From settling things, at once, with that great
    quack!
DORINE:
Now, don't give away to violent emotion.
Your father's merely talked about this notion,
And words and deeds are far from being one.
Much that is talked about is never done.
DAMIS:
No, I must stop that scoundrel's machinations;
I'll go and tell him off; I'm out of patience.
DORINE:
Do calm down and be practical. I had rather
My mistress dealt with him—and with your fa-
    ther.
She has some influence with Tartuffe, I've noted.
He hangs upon her words, seems most devoted,
And may, indeed, be smitten by her charm.

Pray Heaven it's true! 'Twould do our cause no
  harm.
She sent for him, just now, to sound him out
On this affair you're so incensed about;
She'll find out where he stands, and tell him, too,
What dreadful strife and trouble will ensue
If he lends countenance to your father's plan.
I couldn't get in to see him, but his man
Says that he's almost finished with his prayers.
Go, now. I'll catch him when he comes down-
  stairs.

DAMIS:
I want to hear this conference, and I will.

DORINE:
No, they must be alone.

DAMIS:
                              Oh, I'll keep still.

DORINE:
Not you. I know your temper. You'd start a
  brawl,
And shout and stamp your foot and spoil it all.
Go on.

DAMIS:
             I won't; I have a perfect right . . .

DORINE:
Lord, you're a nuisance! He's coming; get out of
  sight.
   (DAMIS *conceals himself in a closet at the rear
   of the stage.*)

SCENE II

(TARTUFFE, DORINE.)

TARTUFFE: (*Observing* DORINE, *and calling to his
  manservant offstage.*)
Hang up my hair-shirt, put my scourge in place,
And pray, Laurent, for Heaven's perpetual
  grace.
I'm going to the prison now, to share
My last few coins with the poor wretches there.

DORINE: (*Aside.*)
Dear God, what affectation! What a fake!

TARTUFFE:
You wished to see me?

DORINE:
                              Yes . . .

TARTUFFE: (*Taking a handkerchief from his
  pocket.*)
                              For mercy's sake,
Please, take this handkerchief, before you speak.

DORINE:
What?

TARTUFFE:
       Cover that bosom, girl. The flesh is weak,
And unclean thoughts are difficult to control.
Such sights as that can undermine the soul.

DORINE:
Your soul, it seems, has very poor defenses,
And flesh makes quite an impact on your senses.
It's strange that you're so easily excited;
My own desires are not so soon ignited,
And if I saw you naked as a beast,
Not all your hide would tempt me in the least.

TARTUFFE:
Girl, speak more modestly; unless you do,
I shall be forced to take my leave of you.

DORINE:
Oh, no, it's I who must be on my way;
I've just one little message to convey.
Madame is coming down, and begs you, Sir,
To wait and have a word or two with her.

TARTUFFE:
Gladly.

DORINE: (*Aside.*)
       That had a softening effect!
I think my guess about him was correct.

TARTUFFE:
Will she be long?

DORINE:
                              No: that's her step I hear.
Ah, here she is, and I shall disappear.

SCENE III

(ELMIRE, TARTUFFE.)

TARTUFFE:
May Heaven, whose infinite goodness we adore,
Preserve your body and soul forevermore,
And bless your days, and answer thus the plea
Of one who is its humblest votary.

ELMIRE:
I thank you for that pious wish. But please,
Do take a chair and let's be more at ease.
   (*They sit down.*)

TARTUFFE:
I trust that you are once more well and strong?

ELMIRE:
Oh, yes: the fever didn't last for long.

TARTUFFE:
My prayers are too unworthy, I am sure,
To have gained from Heaven this most gracious
  cure;

But lately, Madam, my every supplication
Has had for object your recuperation.

ELMIRE:
You shouldn't have troubled so. I don't deserve it.

TARTUFFE:
Your health is priceless, Madam, and to preserve
    it
I'd gladly give my own, in all sincerity.

ELMIRE:
Sir, you outdo us all in Christian charity.
You've been most kind. I count myself your
    debtor.

TARTUFFE:
'Twas nothing, Madam. I long to serve you bet-
    ter.

ELMIRE:
There's a private matter I'm anxious to discuss.
I'm glad there's no one here to hinder us.

TARTUFFE:
I too am glad; it floods my heart with bliss
To find myself alone with you like this.
For just this chance I've prayed with all my
    power—
But prayed in vain, until this happy hour.

ELMIRE:
This won't take long, Sir, and I hope you'll be
Entirely frank and unconstrained with me.

TARTUFFE:
Indeed, there's nothing I had rather do
Than bare my inmost heart and soul to you.
First, let me say that what remarks I've made
About the constant visits you are paid
Were prompted not by any mean emotion,
But rather by a pure and deep devotion,
A fervent zeal . . .

ELMIRE:
                    No need for explanation.
Your sole concern, I'm sure, was my salvation.

TARTUFFE: (*Taking* ELMIRE's *hand and pressing
    her fingertips.*)
Quite so; and such great fervor do I feel . . .

ELMIRE:
Ooh! Please! You're pinching!

TARTUFFE:
                            'Twas from excess
    of zeal.
I never meant to cause you pain, I swear.
I'd rather . . .
    (*He places his hand on* ELMIRE's *knee.*)

ELMIRE:
                What can your hand be doing
    there?

TARTUFFE:
Feeling your gown: what soft, fine-woven stuff!

ELMIRE:
Please, I'm extremely ticklish. That's enough.
    (*She draws her chair away;* TARTUFFE *pulls his
        after her.*)

TARTUFFE: (*Fondling the lace collar of her gown.*)
My, my, what lovely lacework on your dress!
The workmanship's miraculous, no less.
I've not seen anything to equal it.

ELMIRE:
Yes, quite. But let's talk business for a bit.
They say my husband means to break his word
And give his daughter to you, Sir. Had you
    heard?

TARTUFFE:
He did once mention it. But I confess
I dream of quite a different happiness.
It's elsewhere, Madam, that my eyes discern
The promise of that bliss for which I yearn.

ELMIRE:
I see: you care for nothing here below.

TARTUFFE:
Ah, well—my heart's not made of stone, you
    know.

ELMIRE:
All your desires mount heavenward, I'm sure.
In scorn of all that's earthly and impure.

TARTUFFE:
A love of heavenly beauty does not preclude
A proper love for earthly pulchritude;
Our senses are quite rightly captivated
By perfect works our Maker has created.
Some glory clings to all that Heaven has made;
In you, all Heaven's marvels are displayed.
On that fair face, such beauties have been lav-
    ished,
The eyes are dazzled and the heart is ravished;
How could I look on you, O flawless creature,
And not adore the Author of all Nature,
Feeling a love both passionate and pure
For you, his triumph of self-portraiture?
At first, I trembled lest that love should be
A subtle snare that Hell had laid for me;
I vowed to flee the sight of you, eschewing
A rapture that might prove my soul's undoing;
But soon, fair being, I became aware
That my deep passion could be made to square
With rectitude, and with my bounden duty.
I thereupon surrendered to your beauty.
It is, I know, presumptuous on my part
To bring you this poor offering of my heart,

And it is not my merit, Heaven knows,
But your compassion on which my hopes repose.
You are my peace, my solace, my salvation;
On you depends my bliss—or desolation;
I bide your judgment and, as you think best,
I shall be either miserable or blest.

ELMIRE:

Your declaration is most gallant, Sir,
But don't you think it's out of character?
You'd have done better to restrain your passion
And think before you spoke in such a fashion.
It ill becomes a pious man like you . . .

TARTUFFE:

I may be pious, but I'm human too:
With your celestial charms before his eyes,
A man has not the power to be wise.
I know such words sound strangely, coming from
     me,
But I'm no angel, nor was meant to be,
And if you blame my passion, you must needs
Reproach as well the charms on which it feeds.
Your loveliness I had no sooner seen
Than you became my soul's unrivalled queen;
Before your seraph glance, divinely sweet,
My heart's defenses crumbled in defeat,
And nothing fasting, prayer, or tears might do
Could stay my spirit from adoring you.
My eyes, my sighs have told you in the past
What now my lips make bold to say at last,
And if, in your great goodness, you will deign
To look upon your slave, and ease his pain,—
If, in compassion for my soul's distress,
You'll stoop to comfort my unworthiness,
I'll raise to you, in thanks for that sweet manna,
An endless hymn, an infinite hosanna.
With me, of course, there need be no anxiety,
No fear of scandal or of notoriety.
These young court gallants, whom all the ladies
     fancy,
Are vain in speech, in action rash and chancy;
When they succeed in love, the world soon
     knows it;
No favor's granted them but they disclose it
And by the looseness of their tongues profane
The very altar where their hearts have lain.
Men of my sort, however, love discreetly,
And one may trust our reticence completely.
My keen concern for my good name insures
The absolute security of yours;
In short, I offer you, my dear Elmire,
Love without scandal, pleasure without fear.

ELMIRE:

I've heard your well-turned speeches to the end,
And what you urge I clearly apprehend.
Aren't you afraid that I may take a notion
To tell my husband of your warm devotion,
And that, supposing he were duly told,
His feelings toward you might grow rather cold?

TARTUFFE:

I know, dear lady, that your exceeding charity
Will lead your heart to pardon my temerity;
That you'll excuse my violent affection
As human weakness, human imperfection;
And that—O fairest!—you will bear in mind
That I'm but flesh and blood, and am not blind.

ELMIRE:

Some women might do otherwise, perhaps,
But I shall be discreet about your lapse;
I'll tell my husband nothing of what's occurred
If, in return, you'll give your solemn word
To advocate as forcefully as you can
The marriage of Valère and Mariane,
Renouncing all desire to dispossess
Another of his rightful happiness,
And . . .

SCENE IV

(DAMIS, ELMIRE, TARTUFFE.)

DAMIS: (*Emerging from the closet where he has
     been hiding.*)
          No! We'll not hush up this vile affair;
I heard it all inside that closet there,
Where Heaven, in order to confound the pride
Of this great rascal, prompted me to hide.
Ah, now I have my long-awaited chance
To punish his deceit and arrogance,
And give my father clear and shocking proof
Of the black character of his dear Tartuffe.

ELMIRE:

Ah no, Damis; I'll be content if he
Will study to deserve my leniency.
I've promised silence—don't make me break my
     word;
To make a scandal would be too absurd.
Good wives laugh off such trifles, and forget
     them;
Why should they tell their husbands, and upset
     them?

DAMIS:

You have your reasons for taking such a course,
And I have reasons, too, of equal force.
To spare him now would be insanely wrong.
I've swallowed my just wrath for far too long.
And watched this insolent bigot bringing strife

And bitterness into our family life.
Too long he's meddled in my father's affairs,
Thwarting my marriage-hopes, and poor Valère's.
It's high time that my father was undeceived;
And now I've proof that can't be disbelieved—
Proof that was furnished me by Heaven above.
It's too good not to take advantage of.
This is my chance, and I deserve to lose it.
If, for one moment, I hesitate to use it.

ELMIRE:
Damis . . .

DAMIS:
        No, I must do what I think right.
Madam, my heart is bursting with delight,
And, say whatever you will, I'll not consent
To lose the sweet revenge on which I'm bent.
I'll settle matters without more ado;
And here, most opportunely, is my cue.

SCENE V

(ORGON, DAMIS, TARTUFFE, ELMIRE.)

DAMIS:
Father, I'm glad you've joined us. Let us advise
    you
Of some fresh news which doubtless will surprise
    you.
You've just now been repaid with interest
For all your loving-kindness to our guest.
He's proved his warm and grateful feelings to-
    ward you;
It's with a pair of horns he would reward you.
Yes, I surprised him with your wife, and heard
His whole adulterous offer, every word.
She, with her all too gentle disposition,
Would not have told you of his proposition;
But I shall not make terms with brazen lechery,
And feel that not to tell you would be treachery.

ELMIRE:
And I hold that one's husband's peace of mind
Should not be spoilt by tattle of this kind.
One's honor doesn't require it: to be proficient
In keeping men at bay is quite sufficient.
These are my sentiments, and I wish, Damis,
That you had heeded me and held your peace.

SCENE VI

(ORGON, DAMIS, TARTUFFE.)

ORGON:
Can it be true, this dreadful thing I hear?

TARTUFFE:
Yes, Brother, I'm a wicked man, I fear:
A wretched sinner, all depraved and twisted,
The greatest villain that has ever existed.
My life's one heap of crimes, which grows each
    minute;
There's naught but foulness and corruption in
    it;
And I perceive that heaven, outraged by me,
Has chosen this occasion to mortify me.
Charge me with any deed you wish to name;
I'll not defend myself, but take the blame.
Believe what you are told, and drive Tartuffe
Like some base criminal from beneath your roof;
Yes, drive me hence, and with a parting curse:
I shan't protest, for I deserve far worse.

ORGON: (To DAMIS.)
Ah, you deceitful boy, how dare you try
To stain his purity with so foul a lie?

DAMIS:
What! Are you taken in by such a bluff?
Did you not hear . . . ?

ORGON:
                Enough, you rogue,
    enough!

TARTUFFE:
Ah, Brother, let him speak: you're being unjust.
Believe his story; the boy deserves your trust.
Why, after all, should you have faith in me?
How can you know what I might do, or be?
Is it on my good actions that you base
Your favor? Do you trust my pious face?
Ah, no, don't be deceived by hollow shows;
I'm far, alas, from being what men suppose;
Though the world takes me for a man of worth,
I'm truly the most worthless man on earth.
    (To DAMIS.)
Yes, my dear son, speak out now: call me the
    chief
Of sinners, a wretch, a murderer, a thief;
Load me with all the names men most abhor;
I'll not complain; I've earned them all, and more;
I'll kneel here while you pour them on my head
As a just punishment for the life I've led.

ORGON: (To TARTUFFE.)
This is too much, dear Brother.
    (To DAMIS.)   Have you no
    heart?

DAMIS:
Are you so hoodwinked by this rascal's art . . . ?

ORGON:
Be still, you monster.
    (To TARTUFFE.)   Brother, I pray you, rise.

(*To* DAMIS.)
Villain!

DAMIS:
      But . . .

ORGON:
            Silence!

DAMIS:
                  Can't you realize . . . ?

ORGON:
Just one word more, and I'll tear you limb from
    limb.

TARTUFFE:
In God's name, Brother, don't be harsh with him.
I'd rather far be tortured at the stake
Than see him bear one scratch for my poor sake.

ORGON: (*To* DAMIS.)
Ingrate!

TARTUFFE:
      If I must beg you, on bended knee,
To pardon him . . .

ORGON: (*Falling to his knees, addressing* TARTUFFE.)
              Such goodness cannot be!

(*To* DAMIS.)
Now, *there's* true charity!

DAMIS:
                What, you . . . ?

ORGON:
                  Villain, be still!
I know your motives; I know you wish him ill:
Yes, all of you—wife, children, servants, all—
Conspire against him and desire his fall,
Employing every shameful trick you can
To alienate me from this saintly man.
Ah, but the more you seek to drive him away,
The more I'll do to keep him. Without delay,
I'll spite this household and confound its pride
By giving him my daughter as his bride.

DAMIS:
You're going to force her to accept his hand?

ORGON:
Yes, and this very night, d'you understand?
I shall defy you all, and make it clear
That I'm the one who gives the orders here.
Come, wretch, kneel down and clasp his blessed
    feet,
And ask his pardon for your black deceit.

DAMIS:
I ask that swindler's pardon? Why, I'd rather . . .

ORGON:
So! You insult him, and defy your father!
A stick! A stick! (*To* TARTUFFE.) No, no—release
    me, do.

(*To* DAMIS.)
Out of my house this minute! Be off with you,
And never dare set foot in it again.

DAMIS:
Well, I shall go, but . . .

ORGON:
                Well, go quickly, then.
I disinherit you; an empty purse
Is all you'll get from me—except my curse!

SCENE VII

(ORGON, TARTUFFE.)

ORGON:
How he blasphemed your goodness! What a son!

TARTUFFE:
Forgive him, Lord, as I've already done.
    (*To* ORGON.)
You can't know how it hurts when someone tries
To blacken me in my dear Brother's eyes.

ORGON:
Ahh!

TARTUFFE:
      The mere thought of such ingratitude
Plunges my soul into so dark a mood . . .
Such horrow grips my heart . . . I gasp for
    breath,
And cannot speak, and feel myself near death.

ORGON: (*He runs, in tears, to the door through
    which he has just driven his son.*)
You blackguard! Why did I spare you? Why did I
    not
Break you in little pieces on the spot?
Compose yourself, and don't be hurt, dear friend.

TARTUFFE:
These scenes, these dreadful quarrels, have got to
    end.
I've much upset your household, and I perceive
That the best thing will be for me to leave.

ORGON:
What are you saying!

TARTUFFE:
              They're all against me here;
They'd have you think me false and insincere.

ORGON:
Ah, what of that? Have I ceased believing in
    you?

TARTUFFE:
Their adverse talk will certainly continue,
And charges which you now repudiate

You may find credible at a later date.

ORGON:

No, Brother, never.

TARTUFFE:

           Brother, a wife can sway
Her husband's mind in many a subtle way.

ORGON:

No, no.

TARTUFFE:

      To leave at once is the solution;
Thus only can I end their persecution.

ORGON:

No, no, I'll not allow it; you shall remain.

TARTUFFE:

Ah, well; 'twill mean much martyrdom and pain,
But if you wish it . . .

ORGON:

          Ah!

TARTUFFE:

          Enough; so be it.
But one thing must be settled, as I see it.
For your dear honor, and for our friendship's
    sake,
There's one precaution I feel bound to take.
I shall avoid your wife, and keep away . . .

ORGON:

No, you shall not, whatever they may say.
It pleases me to vex them, and for spite
I'd have them see you with her day and night.
What's more, I'm going to drive them to despair
By making you my only son and heir;
This very day, I'll give to you alone
Clear deed and title to everything I own.
A dear, good friend and son-in-law-to-be
Is more than wife, or child, or kin to me.
Will you accept my offer, dearest son?

TARTUFFE:

In all things, let the will of Heaven be done.

ORGON:

Poor fellow! Come, we'll go draw up the deed.
Then let them burst with disappointed greed!

ACT IV

SCENE I

(CLEANTE, TARTUFFE.)

CLEANTE:

Yes, all the town's discussing it, and truly,
Their comments do not flatter you unduly.
I'm glad we've met, Sir, and I'll give my view
Of this sad matter in a word or two.
As for who's guilty, that I shan't discuss;
Let's say it was Damis who caused the fuss;
Assuming, then, that you have been ill-used
By young Damis, and groundlessly accused,
Ought not a Christian to forgive, and ought
He not to stifle every vengeful thought?
Should you stand by and watch a father make
His only son an exile for your sake?
Again I tell you frankly, be advised:
The whole town, high and low, is scandalized;
This quarrel must be mended, and my advice is
Not to push matters to a further crisis.
No, sacrifice your wrath to God above,
And help Damis regain his father's love.

TARTUFFE:

Alas, for my part I should take great joy
In doing so. I've nothing against the boy.
I pardon all, I harbor no resentment;
To serve him would afford me much content-
    ment.
But Heaven's interest will not have it so:
If he comes back, then I shall have to go.
After his conduct—so extreme, so vicious—
Our further intercourse would look suspicious.
God knows what people would think! Why,
    they'd describe
My goodness to him as a sort of bribe;
They'd say that out of guilt I made pretense
Of loving-kindness and benevolence—
That, fearing my accuser's tongue, I strove
To buy his silence with a show of love.

CLEANTE:

Your reasoning is badly warped and stretched,
And these excuses, Sir, are most far-fetched.
Why put yourself in charge of Heaven's cause?
Does Heaven need our help to enforce it's laws?
Leave vengeance to the Lord, Sir; while we live,
Our duty's not to punish, but forgive;
And what the Lord commands, we should obey
Without regard to what the world may say.
What! Shall the fear of being misunderstood
Prevent our doing what is right and good?
No, no: let's simply do what Heaven ordains,
And let no other thoughts perplex our brains.

TARTUFFE:

Again, Sir, let me say that I've forgiven
Damis, and thus obeyed the laws of Heaven;
But I am not commanded by the Bible
To live with one who smears my name with libel.

CLEANTE:
Were you commanded, Sir, to indulge the whim
Of poor Orgon, and to encourage him
In suddenly transferring to your name
A large estate to which you have no claim?

TARTUFFE:
'Twould never occur to those who know me best
To think I acted from self-interest.
The treasures of this world I quite despise;
Their specious glitter does not charm my eyes;
And if I have resigned myself to taking
The gift which my dear Brother insists on mak-
    ing,
I do so only, as he well understands,
Lest so much wealth fall into wicked hands,
Lest those to whom it might descend in time
Turn it to purposes of sin and crime,
And not, as I shall do, make use of it
For Heaven's glory and mankind's benefit.

CLEANTE:
Forget these trumped-up fears. Your argument
Is one the rightful heir might well resent;
It *is* a moral burden to inherit
Such wealth, but give Damis a chance to bear it.
And would it not be worse to be accused
Of swindling, than to see that wealth misused?
I'm shocked that you allowed Orgon to broach
This matter, and that you feel no self-reproach;
Does true religion teach that lawful heirs
May freely be deprived of what is theirs?
And if the Lord has told you in your heart
That you and young Damis must dwell apart,
Would it not be the decent thing to beat
A generous and honorable retreat,
Rather than let the son of the house be sent,
For your convenience, into banishment?
Sir, if you wish to prove the honesty
Of your intentions . . .

TARTUFFE:
                    Sir, it is half-past three.
I've certain pious duties to attend to,
And hope my prompt departure won't offend
    you.

CLEANTE: (*Alone.*)
Damn.

SCENE II

(ELMIRE, MARIANE, CLEANTE, DORINE.)

DORINE:
            Stay, Sir, and help Mariane, for Heaven's
sake!

She's suffering so, I fear her heart will break.
Her father's plan to marry her off tonight
Has put the poor child in a desperate plight.
I hear him coming. Let's stand together, now,
And see if we can't change his mind, somehow,
About this match we all deplore and fear.

SCENE III

(ORGON, ELMIRE, MARIANE, CLEANTE, DORINE.)

ORGON:
Hah! Glad to find you all assembled here.
    (*To* MARIANE.)
This contract, child, contains your happiness,
And what it says I think your heart can guess.

MARIANE: (*Falling to her knees.*)
Sir, by that Heaven which sees me here dis-
    tressed,
And by whatever else can move your breast,
Do not employ a father's power, I pray you,
To crush my heart and force it to obey you,
Nor by your harsh commands oppress me so
That I'll begrudge the duty which I owe—
And do not so embitter and enslave me
That I shall hate the very life you gave me.
If my sweet hopes must perish, if you refuse
To give me to the one I've dared to choose,
Spare me at least—I beg you, I implore—
The pain of wedding one whom I abhor;
And do not, by a heartless use of force,
Drive me to contemplate some desperate course.

ORGON: (*Feeling himself touched by her.*)
Be firm, my soul. No human weakness, now.

MARIANE:
I don't resent your love for him. Allow
Your heart free rein, Sir; give him your property,
And if that's not enough, take mine from me;
He's welcome to my money; take it, do,
But don't, I pray, include my person too.
Spare me, I beg you; and let me end the tale
Of my sad days behind a convent veil.

ORGON:
A convent! Hah! When crossed in their amours,
All lovesick girls have the same thought as yours.
Get up! The more you loathe the man, and dread
    him,
The more ennobling it will be to wed him.
Marry Tartuffe, and mortify your flesh!
Enough; don't start that whimpering afresh

DORINE:
But why . . . ?

ORGON:

            Be still, there. Speak when you're
    spoken to.
Not one more bit of impudence out of you.

CLEANTE:

If I may offer a word of counsel here . . .

ORGON:

Brother, in counselling you have no peer;
All your advice is forceful, sound, and clever;
I don't propose to follow it, however.

ELMIRE: (*To* ORGON.)

I am amazed, and don't know what to say;
Your blindness simply takes my breath away.
You are indeed bewitched, to take no warning
From our account of what occurred this morn-
    ing.

ORGON:

Madam, I know a few plain facts, and one
Is that you're partial to my rascal son;
Hence, when he sought to make Tartuffe the vic-
    tim
Of a base lie, you dared not contradict him.
Ah, but you underplayed your part, my pet;
You should have looked more angry, more upset.

ELMIRE:

When men make overtures, must we reply
With righteous anger and a battle-cry?
Must we turn back their amorous advances
With sharp reproaches and with fiery glances?
Myself, I find such offers merely amusing.
And make no scenes and fusses in refusing;
My taste is for good-natured rectitude,
And I dislike the savage sort of prude
Who guards her virtue with her teeth and
    claws,
And tears men's eyes out for the slightest cause:
The Lord preserve me from such honor as that,
Which bites and scratches like an alley-cat!
I've found that a polite and cool rebuff
Discourages a lover quite enough.

ORGON:

I know the facts, and I shall not be shaken.

ELMIRE:

I marvel at your power to be mistaken.
Would it, I wonder, carry weight with you
If I could *show* you that our tale was true?

ORGON:

Show me?

ELMIRE:

    Yes.

ORGON:

      Rot.

ELMIRE:

           Come, what if I found a way
To make you see the facts as plain as day?

ORGON:

Nonsense.

ELMIRE:

       Do answer me; don't be absurd.
I'm not now asking you to trust our word.
Suppose that from some hiding-place in here
You learned the whole sad truth by eye and ear—
What would you say of your good friend, after
    that?

ORGON:

Why, I'd say . . . nothing, by Jehoshaphat!
It can't be true.

ELMIRE:

         You've been too long deceived,
And I'm quite tired of being disbelieved.
Come now: let's put my statements to the test,
And you shall see the truth made manifest.

ORGON:

I'll take that challenge. Now do your uttermost.
We'll see how you make good your empty boast.

ELMIRE: (*To* DORINE.)

Send him to me.

DORINE:

         He's crafty; it may be hard
To catch the cunning scoundrel off his guard.

ELMIRE:

No, amorous men are gullible. Their conceit
So blinds them that they're never hard to cheat.
Have him come down. (*To* CLEANTE *and*
    MARIANE.) Please leave us, for a bit.

SCENE IV

(ELMIRE, ORGON.)

ELMIRE:

Pull up this table, and get under it.

ORGON:

What?

ELMIRE:

     It's essential that you be well-hidden.

ORGON:

Why there?

ELMIRE:

       Oh, Heavens! Just do as you are
    bidden.
I have my plans; we'll soon see how they fare.
Under the table, now; and once you're there,
Take care that you are neither seen nor heard.

ORGON:
Well, I'll indulge you, since I gave my word
To see you through this infantile charade.
ELMIRE:
Once it is over, you'll be glad we played.
      (*To her husband, who is now under the table.*)
I'm going to act quite strangely, now, and you
Must not be shocked at anything I do.
Whatever I may say, you must excuse
As part of that deceit I'm forced to use.
I shall employ sweet speeches in the task
Of making that impostor drop his mask;
I'll give encouragement to his bold desires,
And furnish fuel to his amorous fires.
Since it's for your sake, and for his destruction,
That I shall seem to yield to his seduction,
I'll gladly stop whenever you decide
That all your doubts are fully satisfied.
I'll count on you, as soon as you have seen
What sort of man he is, to intervene,
And not expose me to his odious lust
One moment longer than you feel you must.
Remember: you're to save me from my plight
Whenever . . . He's coming! Hush! Keep out of
      sight!

SCENE V

(TARTUFFE, ELMIRE, ORGON.)

TARTUFFE:
You wish to have a word with me, I'm told.
ELMIRE:
Yes. I've a little secret to unfold.
Before I speak, however, it would be wise
To close that door, and look about for spies.
      (TARTUFFE *goes to the door, closes it, and re-
      turns.*)
The very last thing that must happen now
Is a repetition of this morning's row.
I've never been so badly caught off guard.
Oh, how I feared for you! You saw how hard
I tried to make that troublesome Damis
Control his dreadful temper, and hold his peace.
In my confusion, I didn't have the sense
Simply to contradict his evidence;
But as it happened, that was for the best,
And all has worked out in our interest.
This storm has only bettered your position;
My husband doesn't have the least suspicion,
And now, in mockery of those who do,
He bids me be continually with you.

And that is why, quite fearless of reproof,
I now can be alone with my Tartuffe,
And why my heart—perhaps too quick to
      yield—
Feels free to let its passion be revealed.
TARTUFFE:
Madam, your words confuse me. Not long ago,
You spoke in quite a different style, you know.
ELMIRE:
Ah, Sir, if that refusal made you smart,
It's little that you know of woman's heart,
Or what that heart is trying to convey
When it resists in such a feeble way!
Always, at first, our modesty prevents
The frank avowal of tender sentiments;
However high the passion which inflames us,
Still, to confess its power somehow shames us.
Thus we reluct, at first, yet in a tone
Which tells you that our heart is overthrown,
That what our lips deny, our pulse confesses,
And that, in time, all noes will turn to yesses.
I fear my words are all too frank and free,
And a poor proof of woman's modesty;
But since I'm started, tell me, if you will—
Would I have tried to make Damis be still,
Would I have listened, calm and unoffended,
Until your lengthy offer of love was ended,
And been so very mild in my reaction,
Had your sweet words not given me satisfaction?
And when I tried to force you to undo
The marriage-plans my husband has in view,
What did my urgent pleading signify
If not that I admired you, and that I
Deplored the thought that someone else might
      own
Part of a heart I wished for mine alone?
TARTUFFE:
Madam, no happiness is so complete
As when, from lips we love, come words so
      sweet;
Their nectar floods my every sense, and drains
In honeyed rivulets through all my veins.
To please you is my joy, my only goal;
Your love is the restorer of my soul;
And yet I must beg leave, now, to confess
Some lingering doubts as to my happiness.
Might this not be a trick? Might not the catch
Be that you wish me to break off the match
With Mariane, and so have feigned to love me?
I shan't quite trust your fond opinion of me
Until the feelings you've expressed so sweetly
Are demonstrated somewhat more concretely,

And you have shown, by certain kind conces-
    sions,
That I may put my faith in your professions.
ELMIRE: (*She coughs, to warn her husband.*)
Why be in such a hurry? Must my heart
Exhaust its bounty at the very start?
To make that sweet admission cost me dear,
But you'll not be content, it would appear,
Unless my store of favors is disbursed
To the last farthing, and at the very first.
TARTUFFE:
The less we merit, the less we dare to hope,
And with our doubts, mere words can never
    cope.
We trust no promised bliss till we receive it;
Not till a joy is ours can we believe it.
I, who so little merit your esteem,
Can't credit this fulfillment of my dream,
And shan't believe it, Madam, until I savor
Some palpable assurance of your favor.
ELMIRE:
My, how tyrannical your love can be,
And how it flusters and perplexes me!
How furiously you take one's heart in hand,
And make your every wish a fierce command!
Come, must you hound and harry me to death?
Will you not give me time to catch my breath?
Can it be right to press me with such force,
Give me no quarter, show me no remorse,
And take advantage, by your stern insistence,
Of the fond feelings which weaken my resist-
    ance?
TARTUFFE:
Well, if you look with favor upon my love,
Why, then, begrudge me some clear proof
    thereof?
ELMIRE:
But how can I consent without offense
To Heaven, toward which you feel such rever-
    ence?
TARTUFFE:
If Heaven is all that holds you back, don't worry.
I can remove that hindrance in a hurry.
Nothing of that sort need obstruct our path.
ELMIRE:
Must one not be afraid of Heaven's wrath?
TARTUFFE:
Madam, forget such fears, and be my pupil,
And I shall teach you how to conquer scruple.
Some joys, it's true, are wrong in Heaven's eyes;
Yet Heaven is not averse to compromise;
There is a science, lately formulated,

Whereby one's conscience may be liberated,
And any wrongful act you care to mention
May be redeemed by purity of intention.
I'll teach you, Madam, the secrets of that science;
Meanwhile, just place on me your full reliance.
Assuage my keen desires, and feel no dread:
The sin, if any, shall be on my head.
    (ELMIRE *coughs, this time more loudly.*)
You've a bad cough.
ELMIRE:

              Yes, yes. It's bad indeed.
TARTUFFE: (*Producing a little paper bag.*)
A bit of licorice may be what you need.
ELMIRE:
No, I've a stubborn cold, it seems. I'm sure it
Will take much more than licorice to cure it.
TARTUFFE:
How aggravating.
ELMIRE:

           Oh, more than I can say.
TARTUFFE:
If you're still troubled, think of things this way:
No one shall know our joys, save us alone,
And there's no evil till the act is known;
It's scandal, Madam, which makes it an offense,
And it's no sin to sin in confidence.
ELMIRE: (*Having coughed once more.*)
Well, clearly I must do as you require,
And yield to your importunate desire.
It is apparent, now, that nothing less
Will satisfy you, and so I acquiesce.
To go so far is much against my will;
I'm vexed that it should come to this; but still,
Since you are so determined on it, since you
Will not allow mere language to convince you,
And since you ask for concrete evidence, I
See nothing for it, now, but to comply.
If this is sinful, if I'm wrong to do it,
So much the worse for him who drove me to
    it.
The fault can surely not be charged to me.
TARTUFFE:
Madam, the fault is mine, if fault there be,
And . . .
ELMIRE:

        Open the door a little, and peek out;
I wouldn't want my husband poking about.
TARTUFFE:
Why worry about the man? Each day he grows
More gullible; one can lead him by the nose.
To find us here would fill him with delight,
And if he saw the worst, he'd doubt his sight.

ELMIRE:
Nevertheless, do step out for a minute
Into the hall, and see that no one's in it.

SCENE VI

(ORGON, ELMIRE.)

ORGON: (*Coming out from under the table.*)
That man's a perfect monster, I must admit!
I'm simply stunned. I can't get over it.
ELMIRE:
What, coming out so soon? How premature?
Get back in hiding, and wait until you're sure.
Stay till the end, and be convinced completely;
We mustn't stop till things are proved con-
    cretely.
ORGON:
Hell never harbored anything so vicious!
ELMIRE:
Tut, don't be hasty. Try to be judicious.
Wait, and be certain that there's no mistake.
No jumping to conclusions, for Heaven's sake!
    (*She places* ORGON *behind her, as* TARTUFFE *re-
    enters.*)

SCENE VII

(TARTUFFE, ELMIRE, ORGON.)

TARTUFFE: (*Not seeing* ORGON.)
Madam, all things have worked out to perfec-
    tion;
I've given the neighboring rooms a full inspec-
    tion;
No one's about; and now I may at last . . .
ORGON: (*Intercepting him.*)
Hold on, my passionate fellow, not so fast!
I should advise a little more restraint.
Well, so you thought you'd fool me, my dear
    saint!
How soon you wearied of the saintly life—
Wedding my daughter, and coveting my wife!
I've long suspected you, and had a feeling
That soon I'd catch you at your double-dealing.
Just now, you've given me evidence galore;
It's quite enough; I have no wish for more.
ELMIRE: (*To* TARTUFFE.)
I'm sorry to have treated you so slyly,
But circumstances forced me to be wily.
TARTUFFE:
Brother, you can't think . . .

ORGON:
                                        No more talk from
    you;
Just leave this household, without more ado.
TARTUFFE:
What I intended . . .
ORGON:
                                That seems fairly clear.
Spare me your falsehoods and get out of here.
TARTUFFE:
No, I'm the master, and you're the one to go!
This house belongs to me, I'll have you know,
And I shall show you that you can't hurt *me*
By this contemptible conspiracy,
That those who cross me know not what they do,
And that I've means to expose and punish you,
Avenge offended Heaven, and make you grieve
That ever you dared order me to leave.

SCENE VIII

(ELMIRE, ORGON.)

ELMIRE:
What was the point of all that angry chatter?
ORGON:
Dear God, I'm worried. This is no laughing mat-
    ter.
ELMIRE:
How so?
ORGON:
            I fear I understood his drift.
I'm much distrubed about that deed of gift.
ELMIRE:
You gave him . . . ?
ORGON:
                    Yes, it's all been drawn and
    signed.
But one thing more is weighing on my mind.
ELMIRE:
What's that?
ORGON:
                        I'll tell you; but first let's see if
    there's
A certain strong-box in his room upstairs.

ACT V

SCENE I

(ORGON, CLEANTE.)

CLEANTE:
Where are you going so fast?

ORGON:

                        God knows!

CLEANTE:

                                Then
wait;
Let's have a conference, and deliberate
On how this situation's to be met.

ORGON:

That strong-box has me utterly upset;
This is the worst of many, many shocks.

CLEANTE:

Is there some fearful mystery in that box?

ORGON:

My poor friend Argas brought that box to me
With his own hands, in utmost secrecy;
'Twas on the very morning of his flight.
It's full of papers which, if they came to light,
Would ruin him—or such is my impression.

CLEANTE:

Then why did you let it out of your possession?

ORGON:

Those papers vexed my conscience, and it
    seemed best
To ask the counsel of my pious guest.
The cunning scoundrel got me to agree
To leave the strong-box in his custody
So that, in case of an investigation,
I could employ a slight equivocation
And swear I didn't have it, and thereby,
At no expense to conscience, tell a lie.

CLEANTE:

It looks to me as if you're out on a limb.
Trusting him with that box, and offering him
That deed of gift, were actions of a kind
Which scarcely indicate a prudent mind.
With two such weapons, he has the upper hand,
And since you're vulnerable, as matters stand,
You erred once more in bringing him to bay.
You should have acted in some subtler way.

ORGON:

Just think of it: behind that fervent face,
A heart so wicked, and a soul so base!
I took him in, a hungry beggar, and then . . .
Enough, by God! I'm through with pious men:
Henceforth I'll hate the whole false brotherhood,
And persecute them worse than Satan could.

CLEANTE:

Ah, there you go—extravagant as ever!
Why can you not be rational? You never
Manage to take the middle course, it seems,
But jump, instead, between absurd extremes.
You've recognized your recent grave mistake

In falling victim to a pious fake;
Now, to correct that error, must you embrace
An even greater error in its place,
And judge our worthy neighbors as a whole
By what you've learned of one corrupted soul?
Come, just because one rascal made you swallow
A show of zeal which turned out to be hollow,
Shall you conclude that all men are deceivers,
And that, today, there are no true believers?
Let atheists make that foolish inference;
Learn to distinguish virtue from pretense,
Be cautious in bestowing admiration,
And cultivate a sober moderation.
Don't humor fraud, but also don't asperse
True piety; the latter fault is worse,
And it is best to err, if err one must,
As you have done, upon the side of trust.

SCENE II

(DAMIS, ORGON, CLEANTE.)

DAMIS:

Father, I hear that scoundrel's uttered threats
Against you; that he pridefully forgets
How, in his need, he was befriended by you,
And means to use your gifts to crucify you.

ORGON:

It's true, my boy. I'm too distressed for tears.

DAMIS:

Leave it to me, Sir; let me trim his ears.
Faced with such insolence, we must not waver.
I shall rejoice in doing you the favor
Of cutting short his life, and your distress.

CLEANTE:

What a display of young hotheadedness!
Do learn to moderate your fits of rage.
In this just kingdom, this enlightened age,
One does not settle things by violence.

SCENE III

(MADAME PERNELLE, MARIANE, ELMIRE, DORINE,
    DAMIS, ORGON, CLEANTE.)

MADAME PERNELLE:

I hear strange tales of very strange events.

ORGON:

Yes, strange events which these two eyes beheld.
The man's ingratitude is unparalleled.
I save a wretched pauper from starvation,
House him, and treat him like a blood relation,

Shower him every day with my largesse,
Give him my daughter, and all that I possess;
And meanwhile the unconscionable knave
Tries to induce my wife to misbehave;
And not content with such extreme rascality,
Now threatens me with my own liberality,
And aims, by taking base advantage of
The gifts I gave him out of Christian love,
To drive me from my house, a ruined man,
And make me end a pauper, as he began.

DORINE:
Poor fellow!

MADAME PERNELLE:
           No, my son, I'll never bring
Myself to think him guilty of such a thing.

ORGON:
How's that?

MADAME PERNELLE:
           The righteous always were ma-
ligned.

ORGON:
Speak clearly, Mother. Say what's on your mind.

MADAME PERNELLE:
I mean that I can smell a rat, my dear.
You know how everybody hates him, here.

ORGON:
That has no bearing on the case at all.

MADAME PERNELLE:
I told you a hundred times, when you were small,
That virtue in this world is hated ever;
Malicious men may die, but malice never.

ORGON:
No doubt that's true, but how does it apply?

MADAME PERNELLE:
They've turned you against him by a clever lie.

ORGON:
I've told you, I was there and saw it done.

MADAME PERNELLE:
Ah, slanderers will stop at nothing, Son.

ORGON:
Mother, I'll lose my temper . . . For the last time,
I tell you I was witness to the crime.

MADAME PERNELLE:
The tongues of spite are busy night and noon,
And to their venom no man is immune.

ORGON:
You're talking nonsense. Can't you realize
I saw it; saw it; saw it with my eyes?
Saw, do you understand me? Must I shout it
Into your ears before you'll cease to doubt it?

MADAME PERNELLE:
Appearances can deceive, my son. Dear me,

We cannot always judge by what we see.

ORGON:
Drat! Drat!

MADAME PERNELLE:
           One often interprets things awry;
Good can seem evil to a suspicious eye.

ORGON:
Was I to see his pawing at Elmire
As an act of charity?

MADAME PERNELLE:
           Till his guilt is clear,
A man deserves the benefit of the doubt.
You should have waited, to see how things turned
    out.

ORGON:
Great God in Heaven, what more proof did I
    need?
Was I to sit there, watching, until he'd . . .
You drive me to the brink of impropriety.

MADAME PERNELLE:
No, no, a man of such surpassing piety
Could not do such a thing. You cannot shake me.
I don't believe it, and you shall not make me.

ORGON:
You vex me so that, if you weren't my mother,
I'd say to you . . . some dreadful thing or other.

DORINE:
It's your turn now, Sir, not to be listened to;
You'd not trust us, and now she won't trust you.

CLEANTE:
My friends, we're wasting time which should be
    spent
In facing up to our predicament.
I fear that scoundrel's threats weren't made in
    sport.

DAMIS:
Do you think he'd have the nerve to go to court?

ELMIRE:
I'm sure he won't: they'd find it all too crude
A case of swindling and ingratitude.

CLEANTE:
Don't be too sure. He won't be at a loss
To give his claims a high and righteous gloss;
And clever rogues with far less valid cause
Have trapped their victims in a web of laws.
I say again that to antagonize
A man so strongly armed was most unwise.

ORGON:
I know it; but the man's appalling cheek
Outraged me so, I couldn't control my pique.

CLEANTE:
I wish to Heaven that we could devise

Some truce between you, or some compromise.
ELMIRE:
If I had known what cards he held, I'd not
Have roused his anger by my little plot.
ORGON: (*To* DORINE, *as* M. LOYAL *enters.*)
What is that fellow looking for? Who is he?
Go talk to him—and tell him that I'm busy.

SCENE IV

(MONSIEUR LOYAL, MADAME PERNELLE, ORGON,
     DAMIS, MARIANE, DORINE, ELMIRE, CLEANTE.)

MONSIEUR LOYAL:
Good day, dear sister. Kindly let me see
Your master.
DORINE:
                He's involved with company,
And cannot be disturbed just now, I fear.
MONSIEUR LOYAL:
I hate to intrude; but what has brought me here
Will not disturb your master, in any event.
Indeed, my news will make him most content.
DORINE:
Your name?
MONSIEUR LOYAL:
          Just say that I bring greetings from
Monsieur Tartuffe, on whose behalf I've come.
DORINE: (*To* ORGON.)
Sir, he's a very gracious man, and bears
A message from Tartuffe, which, he declares,
Will make you most content.
CLEANTE:
                            Upon my word,
I think this man had best be seen, and heard.
ORGON:
Perhaps he has some settlement to suggest.
How shall I treat him? What manner would be
     best?
CLEANTE:
Control your anger, and if he should mention
Some fair adjustment, give him your full atten-
     tion.
MONSIEUR LOYAL:
Good health to you, good Sir. May heaven con-
     found
Your enemies, and may your joys abound.
ORGON: (*Aside, to* CLEANTE.)
A gentle salutation: It confirms
My guess that he is here to offer terms.
MONSIEUR LOYAL:
I've always held your family most dear;

I served your father, Sir, for many a year.
ORGON:
Sir, I must ask your pardon; to my shame,
I cannot now recall your face or name.
MONSIEUR LOYAL:
Loyal's my name; I come from Normandy,
And I'm a bailiff, in all modesty.
For forty years, praise God, it's been my boast
To serve with honor in that vital post,
And I am here, Sir, if you will permit
The liberty, to serve you with this writ . . .
ORGON:
To—*what?*
MONSIEUR LOYAL:
          Now, please, Sir, let us have no friction:
It's nothing but an order of eviction.
You are to move your goods and family out
And make way for new occupants, without
Deferment or delay, and give the keys . . .
ORGON:
I? Leave this house?
MONSIEUR LOYAL:
                    Why yes, Sir, if you please.
This house, Sir, from the cellar to the roof,
Belongs now to the good Monsieur Tartuffe,
And he is lord and master of your estate
By virtue of a deed of present date,
Drawn in due form, with clearest legal phras-
     ing . . .
DAMIS:
Your insolence is utterly amazing!
MONSIEUR LOYAL:
Young man, my business here is not with you,
But with your wise and temperate father, who,
Like every worthy citizen, stands in awe
Of justice, and would never obstruct the law.
ORGON:
But . . .
MONSIEUR LOYAL:
          Not for a million, Sir, would you rebel
Against authority; I know that well.
You'll not make trouble, Sir, or interfere
With the execution of my duties here.
DAMIS:
Someone may execute a smart tattoo
On that black jacket of yours, before you're
     through.
MONSIEUR LOYAL:
Sir, bid your son be silent. I'd much regret
Having to mention such a nasty threat
Of violence, in writing my report.
DORINE: (*Aside.*)

This man Loyal's a most disloyal sort!

MONSIEUR LOYAL:
I love all men of upright character,
And when I agreed to serve these papers, Sir,
It was your feelings that I had in mind.
I couldn't bear to see the case assigned
To someone else, who might esteem you less
And so subject you to unpleasantness.

ORGON:
What's more unpleasant than telling a man to
leave
His house and home?

MONSIEUR LOYAL:
                    You'd like a short reprieve?
If you desire it, Sir, I shall not press you,
But wait until tomorrow to dispossess you.
Splendid. I'll come and spend the night here,
then,
Most quietly, with half a score of men.
For form's sake, you might bring me, just before
You go to bed, the keys to the front door.
My men, I promise, will be on their best
Behavior, and will not disturb your rest.
But bright and early, Sir, you must be quick
And move out all your furniture, every stick:
The men I've chosen are both young and strong,
And with their help it shouldn't take you long.
In short, I'll make things pleasant and conven-
ient,
And since I'm being so extremely lenient,
Please show me, Sir, a like consideration,
And give me your entire cooperation.

ORGON: (Aside.)
I may be all but bankrupt, but I vow
I'd give a hundred louis, here and now,
Just for the pleasure of landing one good clout
Right on the end of that complacent snout.

CLEANTE:
Careful; don't make things worse.

DAMIS:
                              My bootsole
itches
To give that beggar a good kick in the breeches.

DORINE:
Monsieur Loyal, I'd love to hear the whack
Of a stout stick across your fine broad back.

MONSIEUR LOYAL:
Take care: a woman too may go to jail if
She uses threatening language to a bailiff.

CLEANTE:
Enough, enough, Sir. This must not go on.
Give me that paper, please, and then begone.

MONSIEUR LOYAL:
Well, *au revoir*. God give you all good cheer!

ORGON:
May God confound you, and him who sent you
here!

SCENE V

(ORGON, CLEANTE, MARIANE, ELMIRE, MADAME
PERNELLE, DORINE, DAMIS.)

ORGON:
Now, Mother, was I right or not? This writ
Should change your notion of Tartuffe a bit.
Do you perceive his villainy at last?

MADAME PERNELLE:
I'm thunderstruck. I'm utterly aghast.

DORINE:
Oh, come, be fair. You mustn't take offense
At this new proof of his benevolence.
He's acting out of selfless love, I know.
Material things enslave the soul, and so
He kindly has arranged your liberation
From all that might endanger your salvation.

ORGON:
Will you not ever hold your tongue, you dunce?

CLEANTE:
Come, you must take some action, and at once.

ELMIRE:
Go tell the world of the low trick he's tried.
The deed of gift is surely nullified
By such behavior, and public rage will not
Permit the wretch to carry out his plot.

SCENE VI

(VALERE, ORGON, CLEANTE, ELMIRE, MARIANE,
MADAME PERNELLE, DAMIS, DORINE.)

VALERE:
Sir, though I hate to bring you more bad news,
Such is the danger that I cannot choose.
A friend who is extremely close to me
And knows my interest in your family
Has, for my sake, presumed to violate
The secrecy that's due to things of state,
And sends me word that you are in a plight
From which your one salvation lies in flight.
That scoundrel who's imposed upon you so
Denounced you to the King an hour ago
And, as supporting evidence, displayed
The strong-box of a certain renegade
Whose secret papers, so he testified,

You had disloyally agreed to hide.
I don't know just what charges may be pressed,
But there's a warrant out for your arrest;
Tartuffe has been instructed, furthermore,
To guide the arresting officer to your door.

CLEANTE:
He's clearly done this to facilitate
His seizure of your house and your estate.

ORGON:
That man, I must say, is a vicious beast!

VALERE:
You can't afford to delay, Sir, in the least.
My carriage is outside, to take you hence;
This thousand louis should cover all expense.
Let's lose no time, or you shall be undone;
The sole defense, in this case, is to run.
I shall go with you all the way, and place you
In a safe refuge to which they'll never trace you.

ORGON:
Alas, dear boy, I wish that I could show you
My gratitude for everything I owe you.
But now is not the time; I pray the Lord
That I may live to give you your reward.
Farewell, my dears; be careful . . .

CLEANTE:
                              Brother, hurry.
We shall take care of things; you needn't worry.

SCENE VII

(THE OFFICER, TARTUFFE, VALERE, ORGON, ELMIRE,
    MARIANE, MADAME PERNELLE, DORINE,
    CLEANTE, DAMIS.)

TARTUFFE:
Gently, Sir, gently; stay right where you are.
No need for haste; your lodging isn't far.
You're off to prison, by order of the Prince.

ORGON:
This is the crowning blow, you wretch; and since
It means my total ruin and defeat,
Your villainy is now at last complete.

TARTUFFE:
You needn't try to provoke me; it's no use.
Those who serve Heaven must expect abuse.

CLEANTE:
You are indeed most patient, sweet, and blame-
    less.

DORINE:
How he exploits the name of Heaven! It's shame-
    less.

TARTUFFE:
Your taunts and mockeries are all for naught;
To do my duty is my only thought.

MARIANE:
Your love of duty is most meritorious,
And what you've done is little short of glorious.

TARTUFFE:
All deeds are glorious, Madam, which obey
The sovereign prince who sent me here today.

ORGON:
I rescued you when you were destitute;
Have you forgotten that, you thankless brute?

TARTUFFE:
No, no, I well remember everything;
But my first duty is to serve my King.
That obligation is so paramount
That other claims, beside it, do not count;
And for it I would sacrifice my wife,
My family, my friend, or my own life.

ELMIRE:
Hypocrite!

DORINE:
                  All that we most revere, he uses
To cloak his plots and camouflage his ruses.

CLEANTE:
If it is true that you are animated
By pure and loyal zeal, as you have stated,
Why was this zeal not roused until you'd sought
To make Orgon a cuckold, and been caught?
Why weren't you moved to give your evidence
Until your outraged host had driven you hence?
I shan't say that the gift of all his treasure
Ought to have damped your zeal in any measure;
But if he is a traitor, as you declare,
How could you condescend to be his heir?

TARTUFFE: (To the OFFICER.)
Sir, spare me all this clamor; it's growing shrill.
Please carry out your orders, if you will.

OFFICER:
Yes, I've delayed too long, Sir. Thank you kindly.
You're just the proper person to remind me.
Come, you are off to join the other boarders
In the King's prison, according to his orders.

TARTUFFE:
Who? I, Sir?

OFFICER:
                  Yes.

TARTUFFE:
                        To prison? This can't be true!

OFFICER:
I owe an explanation, but not to you.
    (To ORGON.)

Sir, all is well; rest easy, and be grateful.
We serve a Prince to whom all sham is hateful,
A Prince who sees into our inmost hearts,
And can't be fooled by any trickster's arts.
His royal soul, though generous and human,
Views all things with discernment and acumen;
His sovereign reason is not lightly swayed,
And all his judgments are discreetly weighed.
He honors righteous men of every kind,
And yet his zeal for virtue is not blind,
Nor does his love of piety numb his wits
And make him tolerant of hypocrites.
'Twas hardly likely that this man could cozen
A King who's foiled such liars by the dozen.
With one keen glance, the King perceived the
    whole
Perverseness and corruption of his soul,
And thus high Heaven's justice was displayed:
Betraying you, the rogue stood self-betrayed.
The King soon recognized Tartuffe as one
Notorious by another name, who'd done
So many vicious crimes that one could fill
Ten volumes with them, and be writing still.
But to be brief: our sovereign was appalled
By this man's treachery toward you, which he
    called
The last, worst villainy of a vile career,
And bade me follow the impostor here
To see how gross his impudence could be,
And force him to restore your property.
Your private papers, by the King's command,
I hereby seize and give into your hand.
The King, by royal order, invalidates
The deed which gave this rascal your estates,
And pardons, furthermore, your grave offense
In harboring an exile's documents.

By these decrees, our Prince rewards you for
Your loyal deeds in the late civil war,
And shows how heartfelt is his satisfaction
In recompensing any worthy action,
How much he prizes merit, and how he makes
More of men's virtues than of their mistakes.

DORINE:
Heaven be praised!

MADAME PERNELLE:
                    I breathe again, at last.

ELMIRE:
We're safe.

MARIANE:
                    I can't believe the danger's past.

ORGON: (*To* TARTUFFE.)
Well, traitor, now you see . . .

CLEANTE:
                    Ah, Brother, please.
Let's not descend to such indignities.
Leave the poor wretch to his unhappy fate,
And don't say anything to aggravate
His present woes; but rather hope that he
Will soon embrace an honest piety,
And mend his ways, and by a true repentance
Move our just King to moderate his sentence.
Meanwhile, go kneel before your sovereign's
    throne
And thank him for the mercies he has shown.

ORGON:
Well said: let's go at once and, gladly kneel-
    ing,
Express the gratitude which all are feeling.
Then, when that first great duty has been done,
We'll turn with pleasure to a second one,
And give Valère, whose love has proven so true,
The wedded happiness which is his due.

AUGUST STRINDBERG

The Stronger

TRANSLATION BY ANTS ORAS

August Strindberg (1849–1912) was one of the most influential dramatists of the late nineteenth century. Born in Stockholm, Sweden, he was the fourth in a family of eleven children, and his life, from the beginning, was filled with poverty, hardship, and fear. In 1867 he spent a term at the University of Upsala; then he briefly attended the University of Stockholm, left to try teaching and acting, but soon returned to study literature and science. Finally King Charles XV of Sweden gave him a financial reward for one of his plays, and he left the university for a writing career. Although his first full-length play, *Master Olof*, was rejected by publishers, he received for it an appointment to the Royal Library, where he read, studied Chinese, and wrote his first novel. Many short stories, novels, and plays followed. Among his most influential plays are *The Father*, 1887; *Miss Julie*, 1888; *There Are Crimes and Crimes*, 1898; and *A Dream Play*, 1902.

Although Strindberg began by writing realistic drama, he moved to the naturalistic and finally to the symbolistic. He became preoccupied with innovation in the structure of drama, reducing the amount of exposition included, relying more and more on dialogue to present the psychological conflict, and abolishing the division of the play into acts.

The Stronger, 1889, which represents a breaking away from the conventional dramatic form, displays Strindberg's concern with the presentation of psychological conflict through dialogue alone and with the reduction of a play's structure to its simplest form, the brief monologue.

PERSONS
MME. X, *actress, married*
MLLE. Y, *actress, single*
A WAITRESS

A corner in a ladies' café; two small iron tables, a red velvet sofa and some chairs. MME. X *enters in winter clothing, wearing a hat and a cloak and carrying a fine Japanese basket on her arm.* MLLE. Y *sits with a half-empty beer bottle in front of her, reading an illustrated paper, then changing it for another.*

MME. X: How are you, little Amelie?—You're sitting alone here on Christmas Eve like a disconsolate old bachelor.

(MLLE. Y *looks up from the paper, nods, goes on reading.*)

MME. X: You know, I am heartily sorry to see you like this, alone, all alone in a café on Christmas Eve. I feel quite as sorry as that evening in a Paris restaurant when I saw a bridal party, with the bride sitting and reading a comic paper and the groom playing billiards with the witnesses. Goodness, I thought, with such a beginning how is this to continue and to end!

He played billiards on his wedding evening!—Yes, and she read a comic paper! Well, but that is hardly the same situation as here.

(*The* WAITRESS *enters, places a cup of hot chocolate before* MME. X *and goes out.*)

MME. X: I tell you what, Amelie! Now I really believe you would have done better to have kept him. Remember, I was the first to urge you "Forgive him!" Don't you recall it?—You could have been married to him, with a home of your own. Don't you remember last Christmas, how happy you felt out in the country with your fiancé's parents; how you praised the happiness of a home and how you longed to get away from the theater?—Yes, darling Amelie, a home is the best of all things—next to the theater—a home and some brats too—but that you wouldn't understand.

(MLLE. Y *looks contemptuous.*)

MME. X (*drinks a few spoonfuls from her cup, opens her basket and shows her Christmas presents*): Now you'll see what I've bought for my piglets. (*Shows a doll*) Look at this. This is for Lisa. Look how it rolls its eyes and turns its neck. There! And here is Maja's pop gun. (*Loads it and shoots at* MLLE. Y.)

(MLLE. Y *makes a scared gesture.*)

MME. X: Did this startle you? Did you fear I'd shoot you? What?—Good heavens, I don't believe you could possibly have thought that. I'd be less surprised if you were shooting me, since I got in your way—I know you can't forget that—although I was completely innocent. You still believe I eased you out of the theater with my intrigues, but I didn't! I didn't, even though you think I did!—But what is the use of telling you, for you still believe I did it. (*Takes out a pair of embroidered slippers*) And these are for my old man. With tulips embroidered by myself—I abhor tulips, you understand, but he wants tulips on everything.

(MLLE. Y *looks up from her paper, ironically and with some curiosity.*)

MME. X (*puts a hand in each slipper*): Look how small Bob's feet are. Well? And you ought to see how daintily he walks. You've never seen him in his slippers.

(MLLE. Y *laughs aloud.*)

MME. X: Look, I'll show you. (*Makes the slippers walk along the table.*)

(MLLE. Y *laughs aloud.*)

MME. X: Now look, and when he is out of sorts he stamps with his foot like this. "What! Damn those servants, they'll never learn how to make coffee! Goodness! Now those morons haven't clipped the lamp wick properly." And then there's a draught from the floor and his feet freeze: "Blast it, how cold it is, and these unspeakable idiots can't keep the fire going." (*Rubs one slipper's sole against the other's upper.*)

(MLLE. Y *bursts out laughing.*)

MME. X: And then he comes home and has to search for his slippers, which Marie has put under the chiffonier . . . Oh, but it is sinful to sit thus and make a fool of one's old man. Whatever he is, he is nice, a decent little fellow—you ought to've had such a husband, Amelie.—Why are you laughing? Why? Why?—And look here, I know he is faithful to me; yes, I do know that, for he told me himself . . . What are you grinning at? . . . When I was on my Norway tour, that nasty Frédérique came and tried to seduce him—Could you imagine such an infamy? (*Pause.*) But I'd have scratched out her eyes if she'd come near me after my return! (*Pause.*) What a good thing Bob told me about it himself rather than let me hear it through gossip! (*Pause.*) But Frédérique was not the only one, believe me!

I don't know why, but the women are positively crazy about my husband—perhaps they think he has some say about theater engagements because he is in the government department!—Who knows but you yourself may have been chasing him!—I never trusted you more than just so much—but now I do know he doesn't care for you, and I always thought you were bearing him some grudge.

(*Pause. They view each other, both embarrassed.*)

MME. X: Come to see us in the evening, Amelie, and show you aren't cross with us, at least not with me! I don't know why, but it is so uncomfortable to be at loggerheads with you, of all people. Possibly because I got in your way that time—(*rallentando*) or—I just don't know why in particular!

(*Pause.* MLLE. Y *gazes curiously at* MME. X.)

MME. X (*pensively*): Our acquaintance was such an odd one—when I first saw you I was afraid of you, so afraid that I couldn't risk letting you out of my sight; whenever I came or went I was always near you—I couldn't afford to have you for an enemy, so I became your friend. But there was always something discordant in the air when you came to our home, for I saw my husband couldn't stand you—it all felt somehow awkward, like ill-fitting clothes—and I did what I could to make him take to you but to no purpose—until you got yourself engaged to be married! Then a violent friendship flared up so that for a moment it looked as though the two of you had only now ventured to show your real feelings because you were safe—and so what?—What happened?—I wasn't jealous—how queer!—And I recall the christening when you stood godmother to our baby—I made Bob kiss you—and he did, but you were so confused—that is to say, I didn't notice at the time—haven't thought about it since—not once until—this moment. (*Gets up furiously.*)

Why are you silent? You haven't said a word all this time, you've only let me sit and talk. You've been sitting and staring and making me unwind all these thoughts which lay like raw silk in their cocoon—thoughts—maybe suspicious ones—let me see.—Why did you break off your engagement? Why haven't you been to our house since that happened? Why aren't you coming to see us tonight?

(MLLE. Y *seems on the point of speaking.*)

MME. X: Be quiet! You needn't say a word, for now I grasp it all myself. It was because—because—because!—Yes indeed!—Every bit of it falls into its place! That's it!—Shame! Shame! I won't sit at the same table with you. (*Moves her things to the other table.*)

So that was why I had to embroider tulips on his slippers although I hate tulips—because you like them! That was why—(*throws the slippers on the floor*)—that was why we had to spend the summer on Lake Mälar—because you couldn't bear the sea at Saltsiö; that was why my son had to be christened Eskil—because such was the name of your father; that was why I had to wear your colors, read your authors, eat your favorite dishes, drink your drinks—your chocolate, for example; that was why—Oh, my God—this is frightful to think of, frightful!—Everything came from you to me, even your passions and addictions!—Your soul slithered into mine like a worm into an apple, eating and eating, digging and digging, until all that was left was a rind with some black, messy substance inside! I wanted to escape from you but couldn't; you lay like a snake bewitching me with your black eyes—I felt how my wings rose only to drag me down; I lay with tied feet in the water, and the harder my hands struck out, the more I worked myself down, down right to the bottom where you lay like an enormous crab in order to grip me with your claws—and this is where I now am.

Shame, shame! How I hate you, how I hate you, how I hate you! Yet you only sit, silent, calm, uncaring; not caring whether the moon is waxing or waning, whether it is Christmas or New Year's, whether people are happy or unhappy; incapable of love or hatred; rigid like a stork over a mousehole—unable to grab your quarry, unable to chase it, yet well able to wait until it comes into your clutches. Here you sit in your corner—do you know that it is because of you that it's called the Rat-trap?—Here you scan your paper to find out whether anybody has got into trouble or is wretched or must give up the theater; here you sit, watching out for victims, calculating your chances like a pilot planning a shipwreck, and collecting your tribute!

Poor Amelie, do you know that I pity you because you are unhappy, unhappy like a hurt beast and full of malice because you are hurt?—I can't feel angry with you although I would like to—you are the cornered one after all—well yes, that affair with Bob, why should I bother about it?—In what way does it harm me?—And whether it was you or somebody else who taught me to drink chocolate, what of it? (*Drinks a spoonful from her cup; knowingly*) After all, chocolate is good for one's health. And if I learned from you how to dress—*tant mieux*—that only strengthened my husband's affection for me—and so you lost what I won—Yes, there are indications that you really have lost him. Yet of course you intended me to fade out of the picture—as you have done, sitting here as you do and regretting what you did—but look here, I just won't do it!—We shan't be petty, don't you agree? And why should I take only what no one else wants!

Perhaps, all things considered, I may indeed be the stronger—for you never got anything out of me, you only gave—and now I am like that thief—as you woke up you found I had all the things you missed.

How else could it come about that everything turned worthless and barren in your hand? With all your tulips and fine affections you never managed to keep a man's love—as I have done; you never learned the art of living from your writers, as I did; nor did you ever get any little Eskil of your own, even though Eskil is the name of your father!

And why are you always silent, silent, silent? Yes, I mistook this for strength; but perhaps all it meant was that you hadn't anything to say— that you never were able to think a thought. (*Gets up and takes the slippers from the floor*) Now I'm going home—with the tulips—*your* tulips! You were unable to learn anything from people—unable to bend—and so you snapped like a dry stalk—but I won't snap.

Thanks ever so much, Amelie, for all your kind lessons; thanks for teaching my husband how to love! Now I'm going home to love him. (*Goes.*)

GEORGE BERNARD SHAW

Arms and the Man

George Bernard Shaw (1856–1950), one of the most provocative British playwrights, was born in Dublin, Ireland. Interested in music, politics, and drama, Shaw was influential in each of these areas. He inherited his love of music from his talented mother and, as a regular music critic first for the London *Star* and later for the *World*, Shaw championed the musical dramas of Richard Wagner. In 1898 he published *The Perfect Wagnerite,* a wry sociological interpretation of Wagner's epic *Ring* cycle. Shaw's interest in politics was no less profound. In 1884 he was one of the founders of the Fabian Society, a group that advocated a gradual change to socialism and that counted among its early members such notable figures as William Morris and H. G. Wells. Shaw also distinguished himself as a drama critic. In his drama reviews for the London *Saturday Review* and in the prefaces to his own plays, Shaw developed a lucid and sinuous prose. In 1891 he published *The Quintessence of Ibsenism,* a study of Henrik Ibsen, the Norwegian playwright who influenced Shaw's dramatic technique immensely. Five years of writing plays brought success with *Candida* in 1897. *Arms and the Man* was published in 1898 and many of his greatest works followed: *Caesar and Cleopatra,* 1901; *Man and Superman,* 1901; *Major Barbara,* 1907; *Pygmalion,* 1912; *Back to Methuselah,* 1921; and *Saint Joan,* 1924. In 1925 he received the Nobel Prize for Literature, and he continued to write until the day of his death at the age of ninety-four.

In *Arms and the Man* Shaw satirizes the excesses of romanticism and of the romantic melodrama that dominated the stage during the nineteenth century. The typical romantic situation, hero, and heroine, once established, are continually undercut by an intense irony, excessive clichés, and visual comedy. Shaw's title is derived from the first line of Virgil's *Aeneid,* the hero of which is a great warrior, lover, and the founder of Rome. The irony of Shaw's title reflects his satirical view of war and heroism present in this play.

CHARACTERS

MAJOR PETKOFF   NICOLA

CATHERINE PETKOFF   CAPTAIN BLUNTSCHLI

RAINA PETKOFF   MAJOR SERGIUS SARANOFF

LOUKA   RUSSIAN OFFICER

ACT I

Night. A lady's bedchamber in Bulgaria, in a small town near the Dragoman Pass, late in November in the year 1885. Through an open window with a little balcony, a peak of the Balkans, wonderfully white and beautiful in the starlit snow, seems quite close at hand, though it is really miles away. The interior of the room is not like anything to be seen in the east of Europe. It is half rich Bulgarian, half cheap Viennese. Above the head of the bed, which stands against a little wall cutting off the corner of the room diagonally, is a painted wooden shrine, blue and gold, with an ivory image of Christ, and a light hanging before it in a pierced metal ball suspended by three chains. The principal seat, placed towards the other side of the room and opposite the window, is a Turkish ottoman. The counterpane and hangings of the bed, the window curtains, the little carpet, and all the ornamental textile fabrics in the room are oriental and gorgeous: the paper on the walls is occidental and paltry. The washstand, against the wall on the side nearest the ottoman and window, consists of an enamelled iron basin with a pail beneath it in a painted metal frame, and a single towel on the rail at the side. A chair near it is of Austrian bent wood, with cane seat. The dressing table, between the bed and the window, is an ordinary pine table, covered with a cloth of many colors, with an expensive toilet mirror on it. The door is on the side nearest the bed; and there is a chest of drawers between. This chest of drawers is also covered by a variegated native cloth; and on it there is a pile of paper backed novels, a box of chocolate creams, and a miniature easel with a large photograph of an extremely handsome officer, whose lofty bearing and magnetic glance can be felt even from the portrait. The room is lighted by a candle on the chest of drawers, and another on the dressing table with a box of matches beside it.

The window is hinged doorwise and stands wide open. Outside, a pair of wooden shutters, opening outwards, also stand open. On the balcony a young lady, intensely conscious of the romantic beauty of the night, and of the fact that her own youth and beauty are part of it, is gazing at the snowy Balkans. She is covered by a long mantle of furs, worth, on a moderate estimate, about three times the furniture of her room.

Her reverie is interrupted by her mother, CATHERINE PETKOFF, a woman over forty, imperiously energetic, with magnificent black hair and eyes, who might be a very splendid specimen of the wife of a mountain farmer, but is determined to be a Viennese lady, and to that end wears a fashionable tea gown on all occasions.

CATHERINE (entering hastily, full of good news): Raina! (She pronounces it Rah-eena, with the stress on the ee.) Raina! (She goes to the bed, expecting to find RAINA there.) Why, where—? (RAINA looks into the room.) Heavens, child! are you out in the night air instead of in your bed? Youll catch your death. Louka told me you were asleep.

RAINA (coming in): I sent her away. I wanted to be alone. The stars are so beautiful! What is the matter?

CATHERINE: Such news! There has been a battle.

RAINA (her eyes dilating): Ah! (She throws the cloak on the ottoman and comes eagerly to CATHERINE in her nightgown, a pretty garment, but evidently the only one she has on.)

CATHERINE: A great battle at Slivnitza! A victory! And it was won by Sergius.

RAINA (with a cry of delight): Ah! (Rapturously) Oh, mother! (Then, with sudden anxiety) Is father safe?

CATHERINE: Of course: he sends me the news. Sergius is the hero of the hour, the idol of the regiment.

RAINA: Tell me, tell me. How was it? (Ecstatically) Oh, mother, mother, mother! (She pulls her mother down on the ottoman; and they kiss one another frantically.)

CATHERINE (with surging enthusiasm): You cant guess how splendid it is. A cavalry charge! think of that! He defied our Russian commanders—acted without orders—led a charge on his own responsibility—headed it himself—was the first man to sweep through their guns. Cant you see it, Raina: our gallant splendid Bulgarians with their swords and eyes flashing, thundering down like an avalanche and scattering the wretched Servians and their dandified Austrian officers like chaff. And you! you kept Sergius waiting a year before you would be betrothed to him. Oh, if you have a drop of Bulgarian blood in your veins, you will worship him when he comes back.

RAINA: What will he care for my poor little worship after the acclamations of a whole army of heroes? But no matter: I am so happy—so proud! (*She rises and walks about excitedly.*) It proves that all our ideas were real after all.

CATHERINE (*indignantly*): Our ideas real! What do you mean?

RAINA: Our ideas of what Sergius would do—our patriotism—our heroic ideals. I sometimes used to doubt whether they were anything but dreams. Oh, what faithless little creatures girls are! When I buckled on Sergius's sword he looked so noble: it was treason to think of disillusion or humiliation or failure. And yet—and yet—(*Quickly*) Promise me youll never tell him.

CATHERINE: Dont ask me for promises until I know what I'm promising.

RAINA: Well, it came into my head just as he was holding me in his arms and looking into my eyes, that perhaps we only had our heroic ideas because we are so fond of reading Byron and Pushkin, and because we were so delighted with the opera that season at Bucharest. Real life is so seldom like that!—indeed never, as far as I knew it then. (*Remorsefully*) Only think, mother, I doubted him: I wondered whether all his heroic qualities and his soldiership might not prove mere imagination when he went into a real battle. I had an uneasy fear that he might cut a poor figure there beside all those clever Russian officers.

CATHERINE: A poor figure! Shame on you! The Servians have Austrian officers who are just as clever as our Russians; but we have beaten them in every battle for all that.

RAINA (*laughing and sitting down again*): Yes: I was only a prosaic little coward. Oh, to think that it was all true—that Sergius is just as splendid and noble as he looks—that the world is really a glorious world for women who can see its glory and men who can act its romance! What happiness! what unspeakable fulfilment! Ah! (*She throws herself on her knees beside her mother and flings her arms passionately round her. They are interrupted by the entry of* LOUKA, *a handsome, proud girl in a pretty Bulgarian peasant's dress with double apron, so defiant that her servility to* RAINA *is almost insolent. She is afraid of* CATHERINE, *but even with her goes as far as she dares.*

She is just now excited like the others; but she has no sympathy with RAINA's *raptures, and looks contemptuously at the ecstasies of the two before she addresses them.*)

LOUKA: If you please, madam, all the windows are to be closed and the shutters made fast. They say there may be shooting in the streets. (RAINA *and* CATHERINE *rise together, alarmed.*) The Servians are being chased right back through the pass; and they say they may run into the town. Our calvary will be after them; and our people will be ready for them, you may be sure, now theyre running away. (*She goes out on the balcony, and pulls the outside shutters to; then steps back into the room.*)

RAINA: I wish our people were not so cruel. What glory is there in killing wretched fugitives?

CATHERINE (*businesslike, her housekeeping instincts aroused*): I must see that everything is made safe downstairs.

RAINA (*to* LOUKA): Leave the shutters so that I can just close them if I hear any noise.

CATHERINE (*authoritatively, turning on her way to the door*): Oh, no dear: you must keep them fastened. You would be sure to drop off to sleep and leave them open. Make them fast, Louka.

LOUKA: Yes, madam. (*She fastens them.*)

RAINA: Dont be anxious about me. The moment I hear a shot, I shall blow out the candles and roll myself up in bed with my ears well covered.

CATHERINE: Quite the wisest thing you can do, my love. Good-night.

RAINA: Good-night. (*They kiss one another; and* RAINA's *emotion comes back for a moment.*) Wish me joy of the happiest night of my life—if only there are no fugitives.

CATHERINE: Go to bed, dear; and dont think of them. (*She goes out.*)

LOUKA (*secretly, to* RAINA): If you would like the shutters open, just give them a push like this (*she pushes them: they open: she pulls them to again*). One of them ought to be bolted at the bottom; but the bolt's gone.

RAINA (*with dignity, reproving her*): Thanks, Louka; but we must do what we are told. (LOUKA *makes a grimace.*) Good-night.

LOUKA (*carelessly*): Good-night. (*She goes out, swaggering.*)

(RAINA, *left alone, goes to the chest of drawers, and adores the portrait there with feelings that are beyond all expresson. She does not kiss it or press it to her breast, or shew it any mark of bodily affection; but she takes it in her hands and elevates it, like a priestess.*)

RAINA (*looking up at the picture*): Oh, I shall never be unworthy of you any more, my soul's hero—never, never, never. (*She replaces it reverently. Then she selects a novel from the little pile of books. She turns over the leaves dreamily; finds her page; turns the book inside out at it; and, with a happy sigh, gets into bed and prepares to read herself to sleep. But before abandoning herself to fiction, she raises her eyes once more, thinking of the blessed reality, and murmurs*) My hero! my hero! (*A distant shot breaks the quiet of the night outside. She starts, listening; and two more shots, much nearer, follow, startling her so that she scrambles out of bed, and hastily blows out the candle on the chest of drawers. Then, putting her fingers in her ears, she runs to the dressing table, blows out the light there, and hurries back to bed in the dark, nothing being visible but the glimmer of the light in the pierced ball before the image, and the starlight seen through the slits at the top of the shutters. The firing breaks out again: there is a startling fusillade quite close at hand. Whilst it is still echoing, the shutters disappear, pulled open from without, and for an instant the rectangle of snowy starlight flashes out with the figure of a man silhouetted in black upon it. The shutters close immediately; and the room is dark again. But the silence is now broken by the sound of panting. Then there is a scratch; and the flame of a match is seen in the middle of the room.*)

RAINA (*crouching on the bed*): Who's there? (*The match is out instantly.*) Who's there? Who is that?

A MAN'S VOICE (*in the darkness, subduedly, but threateningly*): Sh—sh! Don't call out; or youll be shot. Be good; and no harm will happen to you. (*She is heard leaving her bed, and making for the door.*) Take care: it's no use trying to run away. Remember: if you raise your voice my revolver will go off. (*Commandingly*) Strike a light and let me see you. Do you hear. (*Another moment of silence and darkness as she retreats to the dressing-table. Then she lights a candle; and the mystery is at an end. He is a man of about 35, in a deplorable plight, bespattered with mud and blood and snow, his belt and the strap of his revolver case keeping together the torn ruins of the blue tunic of a Servian artillery officer. All that the candlelight and his unwashed, unkempt con-*

dition make it possible to discern is that he is of middling stature and undistinguished appearance, with strong neck and shoulders; a roundish, obstinate looking head covered with short, crisp bronze curls; clear quick blue eyes and good brows and mouth; a hopelessly prosaic nose like that of a strong minded baby; trim soldierlike carriage and energetic manner; and with all his wits about him in spite of his desperate predicament: even with a sense of the humor of it, without, however, the least intention of trifling with it or throwing away a chance. He reckons up what he can guess about RAINA—*her age, her social position, her character, the extent to which she is frightened—at a glance, and continues, more politely but still most determinedly.*) Excuse my disturbing you; but you recognise my uniform— Servian! If I'm caught I shall be killed. (*Menacingly*) Do you understand that?

RAINA: Yes.

MAN: Well, I dont intend to get killed if I can help it. (*Still more formidably*) Do you understand that? (*He locks the door with a snap.*)

RAINA (*disdainfully*): I suppose not. (*She draws herself up superbly, and looks him straight in the face, saying, with cutting emphasis*) Some soldiers, I know, are afraid of death.

MAN (*with grim goodhumor*): All of them, dear lady, all of them, believe me. It is our duty to live as long as we can. Now, if you raise an alarm—

RAINA (*cutting him short*): You will shoot me. How do you know that *I* am afraid to die?

MAN (*cunningly*): Ah; but suppose I dont shoot you, what will happen then? Why, a lot of your cavalry—the greatest blackguards in your army—will burst into this pretty room of yours and slaughter me here like a pig; for I'll fight like a demon: they shant get me into the street to amuse themselves with: I know what they are. Are you prepared to receive that sort of company in your present undress? (RAINA, *suddenly conscious of her nightgown, instinctively shrinks, and gathers it more closely about her. He watches her, and adds, pitilessly*) Hardly presentable, eh? (*She turns to the ottoman. He raises his pistol instantly, and cries*) Stop! (*She stops.*) Where are you going?

RAINA (*with dignified patience*): Only to get my cloak.

MAN (*crossing swiftly to the ottoman and snatching the cloak*): A good idea! No: I'll keep the cloak; and you will take care that nobody comes in and sees you without it. This is a better weapon than the revolver. (*He throws the pistol down on the ottoman.*)

RAINA (*revolted*): It is not the weapon of a gentleman!

MAN: It's good enough for a man with only you to stand between him and death. (*As they look at one another for a moment,* RAINA *hardly able to believe that even a Servian officer can be so cynically and selfishly unchivalrous, they are startled by a sharp fusillade in the street. The chill of imminent death hushes the man's voice as he adds*) Do you hear? If you are going to bring those scoundrels in on me you shall receive them as you are. (RAINA *meets his eye with unflinching scorn. Suddenly he starts, listening. There is a step outside. Someone tries the door, and then knocks hurriedly and urgently at it.* RAINA *looks at him, breathless. He throws up his head with the gesture of a man who sees that it is all over with him, and dropping the manner he has been assuming to intimidate her, flings the cloak to her, exclaiming, sincerely and kindly*) No use: I'm done for. Quick! wrap yourself up: theyre coming!

RAINA (*catching the cloak eagerly*): Oh, thank you. (*She wraps herself up with great relief. He draws his sabre and turns to the door, waiting.*)

LOUKA (*outside, knocking*): My lady, my lady! Get up, quick, and open the door.

RAINA (*anxiously*): What will you do?

MAN (*grimly*): Never mind. Keep out of the way. It will not last long.

RAINA (*impulsively*): I'll help you. Hide yourself, oh, hide yourself, quick, behind the curtain. (*She seizes him by a torn strip of his sleeve, and pulls him towards the window.*)

MAN (*yielding to her*): Theres just half a chance, if you keep your head. Remember: nine soldiers out of ten are born fools. (*He hides behind the curtain, looking out for a moment to say, finally*) If they find me, I promise you a fight—a devil of a fight! (*He disappears.* RAINA *takes off the cloak and throws it across the foot of the bed. Then, with a sleepy, disturbed air, she opens the door.* LOUKA *enters excitedly.*)

LOUKA: A man has been seen climbing up the waterpipe to your balcony—a Servian. The soldiers want to search for him; and they are so wild and drunk and furious. My lady says you are to dress at once.

RAINA (*as if annoyed at being disturbed*):

They shall not search here. Why have they been let in?

CATHERINE (*coming in hastily*): Raina, darling: are you safe? Have you seen anyone or heard anything?

RAINA: I heard the shooting. Surely the soldiers will not dare come in here?

CATHERINE: I have found a Russian officer, thank Heaven: he knows Sergius. (*Speaking through the door to someone outside*) Sir: will you come in now. My daughter will receive you.

A young Russian officer, in Bulgarian uniform, enters, sword in hand.

OFFICER (*with soft, feline politeness and stiff military carriage*): Good evening, gracious lady: I am sorry to intrude; but there is a fugitive hiding on the balcony. Will you and the gracious lady your mother please to withdraw whilst we search?

RAINA (*petulantly*): Nonsense, sir: you can see that there is no one on the balcony. (*She throws the shutters wide open and stands with her back to the curtain where the man is hidden, pointing to the moonlit balcony. A couple of shots are fired right under the window; and a bullet shatters the glass opposite* RAINA, *who winks and gasps, but stands her ground; whilst* CATHERINE *screams, and the* OFFICER, *with a cry of* Take care! *rushes to the balcony.*)

THE OFFICER (*on the balcony, shouting savagely down to the street*): Cease firing there, you fools: do you hear? Cease firing, damn you! (*He glares down for a moment; then turns to* RAINA, *trying to resume his polite manner.*) Could anyone have got in without your knowledge? Were you asleep?

RAINA: No: I have not been to bed.

THE OFFICER (*impatiently, coming back into the room*): Your neighbors have their heads so full of runaway Servians that they see them everywhere. (*Politely*) Gracious lady: a thousand pardons. Good-night. (*Military bow, which* RAINA *returns coldly. Another to* CATHERINE, *who follows him out.* RAINA *closes the shutters. She turns and sees* LOUKA, *who has been watching the scene curiously.*)

RAINA: Dont leave my mother, Louka, whilst the soldiers are here. (LOUKA *glances at* RAINA, *at the ottoman, at the curtain; then purses her lips secretively, laughs to herself, and goes out.* RAINA, *highly offended by this demonstration, follows her to the door, and shuts it behind her with a slam, locking it violently. The man immediately steps out from behind the curtain, sheathing his sabre, and dismissing the danger from his mind in a businesslike way.*)

MAN: A narrow shave; but a miss is as good as a mile. Dear young lady: your servant to the death. I wish for your sake I had joined the Bulgarian army instead of the Servian. I am not a native Servian.

RAINA (*haughtily*):   No: you are one of the Austrians who set the Servians on to rob us of our national liberty, and who officer their army for them. We hate them!

MAN: Austrian! not I. Dont hate me, dear young lady. I am a Swiss, fighting merely as a professional soldier. I joined Servia because it came first on the road from Switzerland. Be generous: youve beaten us hollow.

RAINA: Have I not been generous?

MAN: Noble!—heroic! But I'm not saved yet. This particular rush will soon pass through; but the pursuit will go on all night by fits and starts. I must take my chance to get off in a quiet interval. You dont mind my waiting just a minute or two, do you?

RAINA: Oh no: I am sorry you will have to go into danger again. (*Pointing to the ottoman*) Wont you sit—(*She breaks off with an irrepressible cry of alarm as she catches sight of the pistol. The man, all nerves, shies like a frightened horse.*)

MAN (*irritably*):   Dont frighten me like that. What is it?

RAINA: Your revolver! It was staring that officer in the face all the time. What an escape!

MAN (*vexed at being unnecessarily terrified*): Oh, is that all?

RAINA (*staring at him rather superciliously as she conceives a poorer and poorer opinion of him, and feels proportionately more and more at her ease*):   I am sorry I frightened you. (*She takes up the pistol and hands it to him.*) Pray take it to protect yourself against me.

MAN (*grinning wearily at the sarcasm as he takes the pistol*):   No use, dear young lady: theres nothing in it. It's not loaded. (*He makes a grimace at it, and drops it disparagingly into his revolver case.*)

RAINA: Load it by all means.

MAN: Ive no ammunition. What use are cartridges in battle? I always carry chocolate instead; and I finished the last cake of that hours ago.

RAINA (*outraged in her most cherished ideals of manhood*):   Chocolate! Do you stuff your pockets with sweets—like a schoolboy—even in the field?

MAN (*hungrily*):   I wish I had some now.

(RAINA *stares at him, unable to utter her feelings. Then she sails away scornfully to the chest of drawers, and returns with the box of confectionery in her hand.*)

RAINA: Allow me. I am sorry I have eaten them all except these. (*She offers him the box.*)

MAN (*ravenously*):   Youre an angel! (*He gobbles the comfits.*) Creams! Delicious! (*He looks anxiously to see whether there are any more. There are none. He accepts the inevitable with pathetic goodhumor, and says, with grateful emotion*) Bless you, dear lady! You can always tell an old soldier by the inside of his holsters and cartridge boxes. The young ones carry pistols and cartridges; the old ones, grub. Thank you. (*He hands back the box. She snatches it contemptuously from him and throws it away. He shies again, as if she had meant to strike him.*) Ugh! Dont do things so suddenly, gracious lady. It's mean to revenge yourself because I frightened you just now.

RAINA (*superbly*):   Frighten me! Do you know, sir, that though I am only a woman, I think I am at heart as brave as you.

MAN: I should think so. You havnt been under fire for three days as I have. I can stand two days without shewing it much; but no man can stand three days: I'm as nervous as a mouse. (*He sits down on the ottoman, and takes his head in his hands.*) Would you like to see me cry?

RAINA (*alarmed*):   No.

MAN: If you would, all you have to do is to scold me just as if I were a little boy and you my nurse. If I were in camp now, theyd play all sorts of tricks on me.

RAINA (*a little moved*):   I'm sorry. I wont scold you. (*Touched by the sympathy in her tone, he raises his head and looks gratefully at her: she immediately draws back and says stiffly*) You must excuse me: our soldiers are not like that. (*She moves away from the ottoman.*)

MAN: Oh yes they are. There are only two sorts of soldiers: old ones and young ones. Ive served fourteen years: half of your fellows never smelt powder before. Why, how is it that youve just beaten us? Sheer ignorance of the art of war, nothing else. (*Indignantly*) I never saw anything so unprofessional.

RAINA (*ironically*): Oh! was it unprofessional to beat you?

MAN: Well, come! is it professional to throw a regiment of cavalry on a battery of machine guns, with the dead certainty that if the guns go off not a horse or man will ever get within fifty yards of the fire? I couldnt believe my eyes when I saw it.

RAINA (*eagerly turning to him, as all her enthusiasm and her dreams of glory rush back on her*): Did you see the great cavalry charge? Oh, tell me about it. Describe it to me.

MAN: You never saw a cavalry charge, did you?

RAINA: How could I?

MAN: Ah, perhaps not—of course! Well, it's a funny sight. It's like slinging a handful of peas against a window pane: first one comes; then two or three close behind him; and then all the rest in a lump.

RAINA (*her eyes dilating as she raises her clasped hands ecstatically*): Yes, first One!—the bravest of the brave!

MAN (*prosaically*): Hm! you should see the poor devil pulling at his horse.

RAINA: Why should he pull at his horse?

MAN (*impatient of so stupid a question*): It's running away with him, of course: do you suppose the fellow wants to get there before the others and be killed? Then they all come. You can tell the young ones by their wildness and their slashing. The old ones come bunched up under the number one guard: they know that theyre mere projectiles, and that it's no use trying to fight. The wounds are mostly broken knees, from the horses cannoning together.

RAINA: Ugh! But I dont believe the first man is a coward. I believe he is a hero!

MAN (*goodhumoredly*): Thats what youd have said if youd seen the first man in the charge to-day.

RAINA (*breathless, forgiving him everything*): Ah, I knew it! Tell me—tell me about him.

MAN: He did it like an operatic tenor—a regular handsome fellow, with flashing eyes and lovely moustache, shouting his war-cry and charging like Don Quixote at the windmills. We nearly burst with laughter at him; but when the sergeant ran up as white as a sheet, and told us theyd sent us the wrong cartridges, and that we couldnt fire a shot for the next ten minutes, we laughed at the other side of our mouths. I never felt so sick in my life; though Ive been in one or two very tight places. And I hadnt even a revolver cartridge—nothing but chocolate. We'd no bayonets—nothing. Of course, they just cut us to bits. And there was Don Quixote flourishing like a drum major, thinking he'd done the cleverest thing ever known, whereas he ought to be courtmartialled for it. Of all the fools ever let loose on a field of battle, that man must be the very maddest. He and his regiment simply committed suicide—only the pistol missed fire: thats all.

RAINA (*deeply wounded, but steadfastly loyal to her ideals*): Indeed! Would you know him again if you saw him?

MAN: Shall I ever forget him! (*She again goes to the chest of drawers. He watches her with a vague hope that she may have something more for him to eat. She takes the portrait from its stand and brings it to him.*)

RAINA: That is a photograph of the gentleman—the patriot and hero—to whom I am betrothed.

MAN (*recognising it with a shock*): I'm really very sorry. (*Looking at her*) Was it fair to lead me on? (*He looks at the portrait again*) Yes: thats him: not a doubt of it. (*He stifles a laugh.*)

RAINA (*quickly*): Why do you laugh?

MAN (*shamefacedly, but still greatly tickled*): I didnt laugh, I assure you. At least I didnt mean to. But when I think of him charging the windmills and thinking he was doing the finest thing—(*He chokes with suppressed laughter.*)

RAINA (*sternly*): Give me back the portrait, sir.

MAN (*with sincere remorse*): Of course. Certainly. I'm really very sorry. (*She deliberately kisses it and looks him straight in the face before returning to the chest of drawers to replace it. He follows her, apologizing.*) Perhaps I'm quite wrong, you know: no doubt I am. Most likely he had got wind of the cartridge business somehow, and knew it was a safe job.

RAINA: That is to say, he was a pretender and a coward! You did not dare say that before.

MAN (*with a comic gesture of despair*): It's no use, dear lady: I cant make you see it from the professional point of view. (*As he turns away to get back to the ottoman, the firing begins again in the distance.*)

RAINA (*sternly, as she sees him listening to the shots*):   So much the better for you!

MAN (*turning*):   How?

RAINA: You are my enemy; and you are at my mercy. What would I do if I were a professional soldier?

MAN: Ah, true, dear young lady: youre always right. I know how good youve been to me: to my last hour I shall remember those three chocolate creams. It was unsoldierly; but it was angelic.

RAINA (*coldly*):   Thank you. And now I will do a soldierly thing. You cannot stay here after what you have just said about my future husband; but I will go out on the balcony and see whether it is safe for you to climb down into the street. (*She turns to the window.*)

MAN (*changing countenance*):   Down that waterpipe! Stop! Wait! I cant! I darent! The very thought of it makes me giddy. I came up it fast enough with death behind me. But to face it now in cold blood—! (*He sinks on the ottoman.*) It's no use: I give up: I'm beaten. Give the alarm. (*He drops his head on his hands in the deepest dejection.*)

RAINA (*disarmed by pity*):   Come: dont be disheartened. (*She stoops over him almost maternally: he shakes his head.*) Oh, you are a very poor soldier—a chocolate cream soldier! Come, cheer up: it takes less courage to climb down than to face capture: remember that.

MAN (*dreamily, lulled by her voice*):   No: capture only means death; and death is sleep—oh, sleep, sleep, sleep, undisturbed sleep! Climbing down the pipe means doing something—exerting myself—thinking! Death ten times over first.

RAINA (*softly and wonderingly, catching the rhythm of his weariness*):   Are you so sleepy as that?

MAN: Ive not had two hours undisturbed sleep since I joined. I'm on the staff: you dont know what that means. I havnt closed my eyes for forty-eight hours.

RAINA (*at her wit's end*):   But what am I to do with you?

MAN (*staggering up, roused by her desperation*):   Of course I must do something. (*He shakes himself; pulls himself together; and speaks with rallied vigor and courage.*) You see, sleep or no sleep, hunger or no hunger, tired or not tired, you can always do a thing when you know it must be done. Well, that pipe must be got down: (*he hits himself on the chest*) do you hear that, you chocolate cream soldier? (*He turns to the window.*)

RAINA (*anxiously*):   But if you fall?

MAN: I shall sleep as if the stones were a feather bed. Good-bye. (*He makes boldly for the window; and his hand is on the shutter when there is a terrible burst of firing in the street beneath.*)

RAINA (*rushing to him*):   Stop! (*She seizes him recklessly, and pulls him quite round.*) Theyll kill you.

MAN (*coolly, but attentively*):   Never mind: this sort of thing is all in my day's work. I'm bound to take my chance. (*Decisively*) Now do what I tell you. Put out the candles; so that they shant see the light when I open the shutters. And keep away from the window, whatever you do. If they see me, theyre sure to have a shot at me.

RAINA (*clinging to him*):   Theyre sure to see you: it's bright moonlight. I'll save you—oh, how can you be so indifferent! You want me to save you, dont you?

MAN: I really dont want to be troublesome. (*She shakes him in her impatience.*) I am not indifferent, dear young lady, I assure you. But how is it to be done?

RAINA: Come away from the window—please! (*She coaxes him back to the middle of the room. He submits humbly. She releases him, and addresses him patronizingly.*) Now listen. You must trust to our hospitality. You do not yet know in whose house you are. I am a Petkoff.

MAN: Whats that?

RAINA (*rather indignantly*):   I mean that I belong to the family of the Petkoffs, the richest and best known in our country.

MAN: Oh yes, of course. I beg your pardon. The Petkoffs, to be sure. How stupid of me!

RAINA: You know you never heard of them until this minute. How can you stoop to pretend!

MAN: Forgive me: I'm too tired to think; and the change of subject was too much for me. Dont scold me.

RAINA: I forgot. It might make you cry. (*He nods, quite seriously. She pouts and then resumes her patronizing tone.*) I must tell you that my father holds the highest command of any Bulgarian in our army. He is (*proudly*) a Major.

MAN (*pretending to be deeply impressed*):   A Major! Bless me! Think of that!

RAINA: You shewed great ignorance in thinking that it was necessary to climb up to the balcony because ours is the only private house that has two rows of windows. There is a flight of stairs inside to get up and down by.

MAN: Stairs! How grand! You live in great luxury indeed, dear young lady.

RAINA: Do you know what a library is?

MAN: A library? A roomful of books?

RAINA: Yes. We have one, the only one in Bulgaria.

MAN: Actually a real library! I should like to see that.

RAINA (affectedly): I tell you these things to shew you that you are not in the house of ignorant country folk who would kill you the moment they saw your Servian uniform, but among civilized people. We go to Bucharest every year for the opera season; and I have spent a whole month in Vienna.

MAN: I saw that, dear young lady. I saw at once that you knew the world.

RAINA: Have you ever seen the opera of Ernani?

MAN: Is that the one with the devil in it in red velvet, and a soldiers' chorus?

RAINA (contemptuously): No!

MAN (stifling a heavy sigh of weariness): Then I dont know it.

RAINA: I thought you might have remembered the great scene where Ernani, flying from his foes just as you are to-night, takes refuge in the castle of his bitterest enemy, an old Castilian noble. The noble refuses to give him up. His guest is sacred to him.

MAN (quickly, waking up a little): Have your people got that notion?

RAINA (with dignity): My mother and I can understand that notion, as you call it. And if instead of threatening me with your pistol as you did you had simply thrown yourself as a fugitive on our hospitality, you would have been as safe as in your father's house.

MAN: Quite sure?

RAINA (turning her back on him in disgust): Oh, it is useless to try to make you understand.

MAN: Dont be angry: you see how awkward it would be for me if there was any mistake. My father is a very hospitable man: he keeps six hotels; but I couldnt trust him as far as that. What about your father?

RAINA: He is away at Slivnitza fighting for his country. I answer for your safety. There is my hand in pledge of it. Will that reassure you? (She offers him her hand.)

MAN (looking dubiously at his own hand): Better not touch my hand, dear young lady. I must have a wash first.

RAINA (touched): That is very nice of you. I see that you are a gentleman.

MAN (puzzled): Eh?

RAINA: You must not think I am surprised. Bulgarians of really good standing—people in our position—wash their hands nearly every day. But I appreciate your delicacy. You may take my hand. (She offers it again.)

MAN (kissing it with his hands behind his back): Thanks, gracious young lady: I feel safe at last. And now would you mind breaking the news to your mother? I had better not stay here secretly longer than is necessary.

RAINA: If you will be so good as to keep perfectly still whilst I am away.

MAN: Certainly. (He sits down on the ottoman.)

(RAINA goes to the bed and wraps herself in the fur cloak. His eyes close. She goes to the door. Turning for a last look at him, she sees that he is dropping off to sleep.)

RAINA (at the door): You are not going asleep, are you? (He murmurs inarticulately: she runs to him and shakes him.) Do you hear? Wake up: you are falling asleep.

MAN: Eh? Falling aslee—? Oh no: not the least in the world: I was only thinking. It's all right: I'm wide awake.

RAINA (severely): Will you please stand up while I am away. (He rises reluctantly.) All the time, mind.

MAN (standing unsteadily): Certainly—certainly: you may depend on me.

(RAINA looks doubtfully at him. He smiles weakly. She goes reluctantly, turning again at the door, and almost catching him in the act of yawning. She goes out.)

MAN (drowsily): Sleep, sleep, sleep, sleep, slee—(The words trail off into a murmur. He wakes again with a shock on the point of falling.) Where am I? Thats what I want to know: where am I? Must keep awake. Nothing keeps me awake except danger—remember that—(intently) danger, danger, danger, dan—(trailing off again: another shock) Wheres danger? Mus' find it. (He starts off vaguely round the room in search of it.) What am I looking for? Sleep—danger—dont know. (He stumbles against the bed.) Ah yes: now I know. All right now. I'm to go to bed, but not to sleep—be sure not to sleep—because of danger. Not to lie down either, only sit down. (*He sits on the bed. A blissful expression comes into his face.*) Ah! (*With a happy sigh he sinks back at full length; lifts his boots into the bed with a final effort; and falls fast asleep instantly.*)

(CATHERINE *comes in, followed by* RAINA.)

RAINA (*looking at the ottoman*): He's gone! I left him here.

CATHERINE: Here! Then he must have climbed down from the—

RAINA (*seeing him*): Oh! (*She points.*)

CATHERINE (*scandalized*): Well! (*She strides to the bed,* RAINA *following and standing opposite her on the other side.*) He's fast asleep. The brute!

RAINA (*anxiously*): Sh!

CATHERINE (*shaking him*): Sir! (*Shaking him again, harder*) Sir!! (*Vehemently, shaking very hard*) Sir!!!

RAINA (*catching her arm*): Dont, mamma: the poor dear is worn out. Let him sleep.

CATHERINE (*letting him go, and turning amazed to* RAINA): The poor dear! Raina!!! (*She looks sternly at her daughter. The man sleeps profoundly.*)

ACT II

The sixth of March, 1886. In the garden of Major Petkoff's house. It is a fine spring morning; and the garden looks fresh and pretty. Beyond the paling the tops of a couple of minarets can be seen, shewing that there is a valley there, with the little town in it. A few miles further the Balkan mountains rise and shut in the landscape. Looking towards them from within the garden, the side of the house is seen on the left, with a garden door reached by a little flight of steps. On the right the stable yard, with its gateway, encroaches on the garden. There are fruit bushes along the paling and house, covered with washing spread out to dry. A path runs by the house, and rises by two steps at the corner, where it turns out of sight. In the middle, a small table, with two bent wood chairs at it, is laid for breakfast with Turkish coffee pot, cups, rolls, etc.; but the cups have been used and the bread broken. There is a wooden garden seat against the wall on the right.

LOUKA, *smoking a cigaret, is standing between the table and the house, turning her back with angry disdain on a manservant who is lecturing her. He is a middle-aged man of cool temperament and low but clear and keen intelligence, with the complacency of the servant who values himself on his rank in servitude, and the imperturbability of the accurate calculator who has no illusions. He wears a white Bulgarian costume: jacket with decorated border, sash, wide knickerbockers, and decorated gaiters. His head is shaved up to the crown, giving him a high Japanese forehead. His name is* NICOLA.

NICOLA: Be warned in time, Louka: mend your manners. I know the mistress. She is so grand that she never dreams that any servant could dare to be disrespectful to her; but if she once suspects that you are defying her, out you go.

LOUKA: I do defy her. I will defy her. What do I care for her?

NICOLA: If you quarrel with the family, I never can marry you. It's the same as if you quarrelled with me!

LOUKA: You take her part against me, do you?

NICOLA (*sedately*): I shall always be dependent on the good will of the family. When I leave their service and start a shop in Sofeea, their custom will be half my capital: their bad word would ruin me.

LOUKA: You have no spirit. I should like to see them dare say a word against me!

NICOLA (*pityingly*): I should have expected more sense from you, Louka. But youre young: youre young!

LOUKA: Yes; and you like me the better for it, dont you? But I know some family secrets they wouldnt care to have told, young as I am. Let them quarrel with me if they dare!

NICOLA (*with compassionate superiority*): Do you know what they would do if they heard you talk like that?

LOUKA: What could they do?

NICOLA: Discharge you for untruthfulness. Who would believe any stories you told after that? Who would give you another situation? Who in this house would dare be seen speaking to you ever again? How long would your father be left on his little farm? (*She impatiently throws away the end of her cigaret, and stamps on it.*) Child: you dont know the power such high people have over the like of you and me when we try to rise out of our poverty against them. (*He goes close to her and lowers his voice.*) Look at me, ten years in their service. Do you think I know no secrets? I know things about the mistress that she wouldnt have the master know for a thousand levas. I know things about him that she wouldnt let him hear the last of for six months if I blabbed them to her. I know things about Raina that would break off her match with Sergius if—

LOUKA (*turning on him quickly*): How do you know? I never told you!

NICOLA (*opening his eyes cunningly*): So thats your little secret, is it? I thought it might be something like that. Well, you take my advice and be respectful; and make the mistress feel that no matter what you know or dont know, she can depend on you to hold your tongue and serve the family faithfully. Thats what they like; and thats how youll make most out of them.

LOUKA (*with searching scorn*): You have the soul of a servant, Nicola.

NICOLA (*complacently*): Yes: thats the secret of success in service.

(*A loud knocking with a whip handle on a wooden door is heard from the stable yard.*)

MALE VOICE OUTSIDE: Hollo! Hollo there! Nicola!

LOUKA: Master! back from the war!

NICOLA (*quickly*): My word for it, Louka, the war's over. Off with you and get some fresh coffee. (*He runs out into the stable yard.*)

LOUKA (*as she collects the coffee pot and cups on the tray, and carries it into the house*): Youll never put the soul of a servant into me.

(MAJOR PETKOFF *comes from the stable yard, followed by* NICOLA. *He is a cheerful, excitable, insignificant, unpolished man of about 50, naturally unambitious except as to his income and his importance in local society, but just now greatly pleased with the military rank which the war has thrust on him as a man of consequence in his town. The fever of plucky patriotism which the Servian attack roused in all the Bulgarians has pulled him through the war; but he is obviously glad to be home again.*)

PETKOFF (*pointing to the table with his whip*): Breakfast out here, eh?

NICOLA: Yes, sir. The mistress and Miss Raina have just gone in.

PETKOFF (*sitting down and taking a roll*): Go in and say Ive come; and get me some fresh coffee.

NICOLA: It's coming, sir. (*He goes to the house door.* LOUKA, *with fresh coffee, a clean cup, and a brandy bottle on her tray, meets him.*) Have you told the mistress?

LOUKA: Yes, she's coming.

(NICOLA *goes into the house.* LOUKA *brings the coffee to the table.*)

PETKOFF: Well: the Servians havnt run away with you, have they?

LOUKA: No, sir.

PETKOFF: Thats right. Have you brought me some cognac?

LOUKA (*putting the bottle on the table*): Here, sir.

PETKOFF: Thats right. (*He pours some into his coffee.*)

(CATHERINE, *who, having at this early hour made only a very perfunctory toilet, wears a Bulgarian apron over a once brilliant but now half worn-out red dressing gown, and a colored handkerchief tied over her thick black hair, comes from the house with Turkish slippers on her bare feet, looking astonishingly handsome and stately under all the circumstances.* LOUKA *goes into the house.*)

CATHERINE: My dear Paul: what a surprise for us! (*She stoops over the back of his chair to kiss him.*) Have they brought you fresh coffee?

PETKOFF: Yes: Louka's been looking after me. The war's over. The treaty was signed three days ago at Bucharest; and the decree for our army to demobilize was issued yesterday.

CATHERINE (*springing erect, with flashing eyes*): The war over! Paul: have you let the Austrians force you to make peace?

PETKOFF (*submissively*): My dear: they didnt consult me. What could *I* do? (*She sits down and turns away from him.*) But of course we saw to it that the treaty was an honorable one. It declares peace—

CATHERINE (*outraged*): Peace!

PETKOFF (*appeasing her*): —but not friendly relations: remember that. They wanted to put that in; but I insisted on its being struck out. What more could I do?

CATHERINE: You could have annexed Servia and made Prince Alexander Emperor of the Balkans. Thats what I would have done.

PETKOFF: I dont doubt it in the least, my dear. But I should have had to subdue the whole Austrian Empire first; and that would have kept me too long away from you. I missed you greatly.

CATHERINE (*relenting*): Ah! (*She stretches her hand affectionately across the table to squeeze his.*)

PETKOFF: And how have you been, my dear?

CATHERINE: Oh, my usual sore throats: thats all.

PETKOFF (*with conviction*): That comes from washing your neck every day. I've often told you so.

CATHERINE: Nonsense, Paul!

PETKOFF (*over his coffee and cigaret*): I dont believe in going too far with these modern customs. All this washing cant be good for the health: it's not natural. There was an Englishman at Philippopolis who used to wet himself all over with cold water every morning when he got up. Disgusting! It all comes from the English: their climate makes them so dirty that they have to be perpetually washing themselves. Look at my father! he never had a bath in his life; and he lived to be ninety-eight, the healthiest man in Bulgaria. I dont mind a good wash once a week to keep up my position; but once a day is carrying the thing to a ridiculous extreme.

CATHERINE: You are a barbarian at heart still, Paul. I hope you behaved yourself before all those Russian officers.

PETKOFF: I did my best. I took care to let them know that we had a library.

CATHERINE: Ah; but you didnt tell them that we have an electric bell in it? I have had one put up.

PETKOFF: Whats an electric bell?

CATHERINE: You touch a button; something tinkles in the kitchen; and then Nicola comes up.

PETKOFF: Why not shout for him?

CATHERINE: Civilized people never shout for their servants. Ive learnt that while you were away.

PETKOFF: Well, I'll tell you something Ive learnt too. Civilized people dont hang out their washing to dry where visitors can see it; so youd better have all that (*indicating the clothes on the bushes*) put somewhere else.

CATHERINE: Oh, thats absurd, Paul: I dont believe really refined people notice such things.

(*Someone is heard knocking at the stable gates.*)

PETKOFF: Theres Sergius. (*Shouting*) Hollo, Nicola!

CATHERINE: Oh, dont shout, Paul: it really isnt nice.

PETKOFF: Bosh! (*He shouts louder than before*) Nicola!

NICOLA (*appearing at the house door*): Yes, sir.

PETKOFF: If that is Major Saranoff, bring him round this way. (*He pronounces the name with the stress on the second syllable—Sarahnoff.*)

NICOLA: Yes, sir. (*He goes into the stable yard.*)

PETKOFF: You must talk to him, my dear, until Raina takes him off our hands. He bores my life out about our not promoting him—over my head, if you please.

CATHERINE: He certainly ought to be promoted when he marries Raina. Besides, the country should insist on having at least one native general.

PETKOFF: Yes; so that he could throw away whole brigades instead of regiments. It's no use, my dear: he hasnt the slightest chance of promotion until we're quite sure that the peace will be a lasting one.

NICOLA (*at the gate, announcing*): Major Sergius Saranoff! (*He goes into the house and returns presently with a third chair, which he places at the table. He then withdraws.*)

(MAJOR SERGIUS SARANOFF, *the original of the portrait in Raina's room, is a tall, romantically handsome man, with the physical hardihood, the high spirit, and the susceptible imagination of an untamed mountaineer chieftain. But his remarkable personal distinction is of a characteristically civilized type. The ridges of his eyebrows, curving with a ram's-horn twist round the marked projections at the outer corners; his jealously observant eye; his nose, thin, keen, and apprehensive in spite of the pugnacious high bridge and large nostril; his assertive chin, would not be out of place in a Parisian salon, shewing that the clever, imaginative barbarian has an acute critical faculty which has been thrown into intense activity by the arrival of western civilization in the Balkans. The result is precisely what the advent of nineteenth century thought first produced in England: to wit, Byronism. By his brooding on the perpetual failure, not only of others, but of himself, to live up to his ideals; by his consequent cynical scorn for humanity; by his jejune credulity as to the absolute validity of his concepts and the unworthiness of the world in disregarding them; by his wincings and mockeries under the sting of the petty disillusions which every hour spent among men brings to his sensitive observa-*

tion, he has acquired the half tragic, half ironic air, the mysterious moodiness, the suggestion of a strange and terrible history that has left nothing but undying remorse, by which Childe Harold fascinated the grandmothers of his English contemporaries. It is clear that here or nowhere is Raina's ideal hero. CATHERINE *is hardly less enthusiastic about him than her daughter, and much less reserved in shewing her enthusiasm. As he enters from the stable gate, she rises effusively to greet him.* PETKOFF *is distinctly less disposed to make a fuss about him.*)

PETKOFF: Here already, Sergius! Glad to see you.

CATHERINE: My dear Sergius! (*She holds out both her hands.*)

SERGIUS (*kissing them with scrupulous gallantry*):   My dear mother, if I may call you so.

PETKOFF (*drily*):   Mother-in-law, Sergius: mother-in-law! Sit down; and have some coffee.

SERGIUS: Thank you, none for me. (*He gets away from the table with a certain distaste for Petkoff's enjoyment of it, and posts himself with conscious dignity against the rail of the steps leading to the house.*)

CATHERINE: You look superb—splendid. The campaign has improved you. Everybody here is mad about you. We were all wild with enthusiasm about that magnificent cavalry charge.

SERGIUS (*with grave irony*):   Madam: it was the cradle and the grave of my military reputation.

CATHERINE: How so?

SERGIUS: I won the battle the wrong way when our worthy Russian generals were losing it the right way. That upset their plans, and wounded their self-esteem. Two of their colonels got their regiments driven back on the correct principles of scientific warfare. Two major-generals got killed strictly according to military etiquette. Those two colonels are now major-generals; and I am still a simple major.

CATHERINE: You shall not remain so, Sergius. The women are on your side; and they will see that justice is done you.

SERGIUS: It is too late. I have only waited for the peace to send in my resignation.

PETKOFF (*dropping his cup in his amazement*):   Your resignation!

CATHERINE: Oh, you must withdraw it!

SERGIUS (*with resolute, measured emphasis, folding his arms*):   I never withdraw.

PETKOFF (*vexed*):   Now who could have supposed you were going to do such a thing?

SERGIUS (*with fire*):   Everyone that knew me. But enough of myself and my affairs. How is Raina; and where is Raina?

RAINA (*suddenly coming round the corner of the house and standing at the top of the steps in the path*):   Raina is here. (*She makes a charming picture as they all turn to look at her. She wears an underdress of pale green silk, draped with an overdress of thin ecru canvas embroidered with gold. On her head she wears a pretty Phrygian cap of gold tinsel.* SERGIUS, *with an exclamation of pleasure, goes impulsively to meet her. She stretches out her hand: he drops chivalrously on one knee and kisses it.*)

PETKOFF (*aside to Catherine, beaming with parental pride*):   Pretty, isn't it? She always appears at the right moment.

CATHERINE (*impatiently*):   Yes: she listens for it. It is an abominable habit.

(SERGIUS *leads* RAINA *forward with splendid gallantry, as if she were a queen. When they arrive at the table, she turns to him with a bend of the head: he bows; and thus they separate, he coming to his place, and she going behind her father's chair.*)

RAINA (*stooping and kissing her father*):   Dear father! Welcome home!

PETKOFF (*patting her cheek*):   My little pet girl. (*He kisses her. She goes to the chair left by* NICOLA *for* SERGIUS, *and sits down.*)

CATHERINE: And so youre no longer a soldier, Sergius.

SERGIUS: I am no longer a soldier. Soldiering, my dear madam, is the coward's art of attacking mercilessly when you are strong, and keeping out of harm's way when you are weak. That is the whole secret of successful fighting. Get your enemy at a disadvantage; and never, on any account, fight him on equal terms. Eh, Major!

PETKOFF: They wouldnt let us make a fair stand-up fight of it. However, I suppose soldiering has to be a trade like any other trade.

SERGIUS: Precisely. But I have no ambition to shine as a tradesman; so I have taken the advice of that bagman of a captain that settled the exchange of prisoners with us at Peerot, and given it up.

PETKOFF: What! that Swiss fellow? Sergius: Ive often thought of that exchange since. He over-reached us about those horses.

SERGIUS: Of course he over-reached us. His father was a hotel and livery stable keeper; and he owed his first step to his knowledge of horse-dealing. (*With mock enthusiasm*) Ah, he was a soldier—every inch a soldier! If only I had bought the horses for my regiment instead of foolishly leading it into danger, I should have been a field-marshal now!

CATHERINE: A Swiss? What was he doing in the Servian army?

PETKOFF: A volunteer, of course—keen on picking up his profession. (*Chuckling*) We shouldnt have been able to begin fighting if these foreigners hadnt shewn us how to do it: we knew nothing about it; and neither did the Servians. Egad, there'd have been no war without them!

RAINA: Are there many Swiss officers in the Servian Army?

PETKOFF: No—all Austrians, just as our officers were all Russians. This was the only Swiss I came across. I'll never trust a Swiss again. He cheated us—humbugged us into giving him fifty able-bodied men for two hundred confounded worn out chargers. They werent even eatable!

SERGIUS: We were two children in the hands of that consummate soldier, Major: simply two innocent little children.

RAINA: What was he like?

CATHERINE: Oh, Raina, what a silly question!

SERGIUS: He was like a commercial traveller in uniform. Bourgeois to his boots!

PETKOFF (*grinning*): Sergius: tell Catherine that queer story his friend told us about him—how he escaped after Slivnitza. You remember?—about his being hid by two women.

SERGIUS (*with bitter irony*): Oh yes: quite a romance! He was serving in the very battery I so unprofessionally charged. Being a thorough soldier, he ran away like the rest of them, with our cavalry at his heels. To escape their attentions, he had the good taste to take refuge in the chamber of some patriotic young Bulgarian lady. The young lady was enchanted by his persuasive commercial traveller's manners. She very modestly entertained him for an hour or so, and then called in her mother lest her conduct should appear unmaidenly. The old lady was equally fascinated; and the fugitive was sent on his way in the morning, disguised in an old coat belonging to the master of the house, who was away at the war.

RAINA (*rising with marked stateliness*): Your life in the camp has made you coarse, Sergius. I did not think you would have repeated such a story before me. (*She turns away coldly.*)

CATHERINE (*also rising*): She is right, Sergius. If such women exist, we should be spared the knowledge of them.

PETKOFF: Pooh! nonsense! what does it matter?

SERGIUS (*ashamed*): No, Petkoff: I was wrong. (*To* RAINA, *with earnest humility*) I beg your pardon. I have behaved abominably. Forgive me, Raina. (*She bows reservedly.*) And you too, madam. (CATHERINE *bows graciously and sits down. He proceeds solemnly, again addressing* RAINA.) The glimpses I have had of the seamy side of life during the last few months have made me cynical; but I should not have brought my cynicism here—least of all into your presence, Raina. I—(*Here, turning to the others, he is evidently going to begin a long speech when the* MAJOR *interrupts him.*)

PETKOFF: Stuff and nonsense, Sergius! Thats quite enough fuss about nothing: a soldier's daughter should be able to stand up without flinching to a little strong conversation. (*He rises.*) Come: it's time for us to get to business. We have to make up our minds how those three regiments are to get back to Philippopolis: theres no forage for them on the Sofeea route. (*He goes towards the house.*) Come along. (SERGIUS *is about to follow him when* CATHERINE *rises and intervenes.*)

CATHERINE: Oh, Paul, cant you spare Sergius for a few moments? Raina has hardly seen him yet. Perhaps I can help you to settle about the regiments.

SERGIUS (*protesting*): My dear madam, impossible: you—

CATHERINE (*stopping him playfully*): You stay here, my dear Sergius: theres no hurry. I have a word or two to say to Paul. (SERGIUS *instantly bows and steps back.*) Now, dear (*taking* PETKOFF's *arm*): come and see the electric bell.

PETKOFF: Oh, very well, very well. (*They go into the house together affectionately. Sergius, left alone with Raina, looks anxiously at her, fearing that she is still offended. She smiles, and stretches out her arms to him.*)

SERGIUS (*hastening to her*): Am I forgiven?

RAINA (*placing her hands on his shoulders as she looks up at him with admiration and worship*): My hero! My king!

SERGIUS: My queen! (*He kisses her on the forehead.*)

RAINA: How I have envied you, Sergius! You have been out in the world, on the field of battle, able to prove yourself there worthy of any woman in the world; whilst I have had to sit at home inactive—dreaming—useless—doing nothing that could give me the right to call myself worthy of any man.

SERGIUS: Dearest: all my deeds have been yours. You inspired me. I have gone through the war like a knight in a tournament with his lady looking down at him!

RAINA: And you have never been absent from my thoughts for a moment. (*Very solemnly*) Sergius: I think we two have found the higher love. When I think of you, I feel that I could never do a base deed, or think an ignoble thought.

SERGIUS: My lady, and my saint! (*He clasps her reverently.*)

RAINA (*returning his embrace*): My lord and my—

SERGIUS: Sh—sh! Let me be the worshipper, dear. You little know how unworthy even the best man is of a girl's pure passion!

RAINA: I trust you. I love you. You will never disappoint me, Sergius. (LOUKA *is heard singing within the house. They quickly release each other.*) I cant pretend to talk indifferently before her: my heart is too full. (LOUKA *comes from the house with her tray. She goes to the table, and begins to clear it, with her back turned to them.*) I will get my hat; and then we can go out until lunch time. Wouldnt you like that?

SERGIUS: Be quick. If you are away five minutes, it will seem five hours. (RAINA *runs to the top of the steps, and turns there to exchange looks with him and wave him a kiss with both hands. He looks after her with emotion for a moment; then turns slowly away, his face radiant with the loftiest exaltation. The movement shifts his field of vision, into the corner of which there now comes the tail of* LOUKA's *double apron. His attention is arrested at once. He takes a stealthy look at her, and begins to twirl his moustache mischievously, with his left hand akimbo on his hip. Finally, striking the ground with his heels in something of a cavalry swagger, he strolls over to the other side of the table, opposite her, and says*) Louka: do you know what the higher love is?

LOUKA (*astonished*): No, sir.

SERGIUS: Very fatiguing thing to keep up for any length of time, Louka. One feels the need of some relief after it.

LOUKA (*innocently*): Perhaps you would like some coffee, sir? (*She stretches her hand across the table for the coffee pot.*)

SERGIUS (*taking her hand*): Thank you, Louka.

LOUKA (*pretending to pull*): Oh, sir, you know I didnt mean that. I'm surprised at you!

SERGIUS (*coming clear of the table and drawing her with him*): I am surprised at myself, Louka. What would Sergius, the hero of Slivnitza, say if he saw me now? What would Sergius, the apostle of the higher love, say if he saw me now? What would the half dozen Sergiuses who keep popping in and out of this handsome figure of mine say if they caught us here? (*Letting go her hand and slipping his arm dexterously round her waist*) Do you consider my figure handsome, Louka?

LOUKA: Let me go, sir. I shall be disgraced. (*She struggles: he holds her inexorably.*) Oh, will you let go?

SERGIUS (*looking straight into her eyes*): No.

LOUKA: Then stand back where we cant be seen. Have you no common sense?

SERGIUS: Ah, thats reasonable. (*He takes her into the stableyard gateway, where they are hidden from the house.*)

LOUKA (*plaintively*): I may have been seen from the windows: Miss Raina is sure to be spying about after you.

SERGIUS (*stung—letting her go*): Take care, Louka. I may be worthless enough to betray the higher love; but do not you insult it.

LOUKA (*demurely*): Not for the world, sir, I'm sure. May I go on with my work, please, now?

SERGIUS (*again putting his arm round her*): You are a provoking little witch, Louka. If you were in love with me, would you spy out of windows on me?

LOUKA: Well, you see, sir, since you say you are half a dozen different gentlemen all at once, I should have a great deal to look after.

SERGIUS (*charmed*): Witty as well as pretty. (*He tries to kiss her.*)

LOUKA (*avoiding him*): No: I dont want your kisses. Gentlefolk are all alike: you making love to me behind Miss Raina's back; and she doing the same behind yours.

SERGIUS (*recoiling a step*): Louka!

LOUKA: It shews how little you really care.

SERGIUS (*dropping his familiarity, and speaking*

with freezing politeness):   If our conversation is to continue, Louka, you will please remember that a gentleman does not discuss the conduct of the lady he is engaged to with her maid.

LOUKA: It's so hard to know what a gentleman considers right. I thought from your trying to kiss me that you had given up being so particular.

SERGIUS (*turning from her and striking his forehead as he comes back into the garden from the gateway*):   Devil! devil!

LOUKA: Ha! ha! I expect one of the six of you is very like me, sir; though I am only Miss Raina's maid. (*She goes back to her work at the table, taking no further notice of him.*)

SERGIUS (*speaking to himself*):   Which of the six is the real man? thats the question that torments me. One of them is a hero, another a buffoon, another a humbug, another perhaps a bit of a blackguard. (*He pauses, and looks furtively at* LOUKA *as he adds, with deep bitterness*) And one, at least, is a coward—jealous, like all cowards. (*He goes to the table.*) Louka.

LOUKA: Yes?

SERGIUS: Who is my rival?

LOUKA: You shall never get that out of me, for love or money.

SERGIUS: Why?

LOUKA: Never mind why. Besides, you would tell that I told you; and I should lose my place.

SERGIUS (*holding out his right hand in affirmation*):   No; on the honor of a—(*He checks himself; and his hand drops, nerveless, as he concludes sardonically*)—of a man capable of behaving as I have been behaving for the last five minutes. Who is he?

LOUKA: I don't know. I never saw him. I only heard his voice through the door of her room.

SERGIUS: Damnation! How dare you?

LOUKA (*retreating*):   Oh, I mean no harm: youve no right to take up my words like that. The mistress knows all about it. And I tell you that if that gentleman ever comes here again, Miss Raina will marry him, whether he likes it or not. I know the difference between the sort of manner you and she put on before one another and the real manner. (SERGIUS *shivers as if she had stabbed him. Then, setting his face like iron, he strides grimly to her, and grips her above the elbows with both hands.*)

SERGIUS: Now listen you to me.

LOUKA (*wincing*):   Not so tight: youre hurting me.

SERGIUS: That doesnt matter. You have stained my honor by making me a party to your eavesdropping. And you have betrayed your mistress.

LOUKA (*writhing*):   Please—

SERGIUS: That shews that you are an abominable little clod of common clay, with the soul of a servant. (*He lets her go as if she were an unclean thing, and turns away, dusting his hands of her, to the bench by the wall, where he sits down with averted head, meditating gloomily.*)

LOUKA (*whimpering angrily with her hands up her sleeves, feeling her bruised arms*):   You know how to hurt with your tongue as well as with your hands. But I dont care, now Ive found out that whatever clay I'm made of, youre made of the same. As for her, she's a liar; and her fine airs are a cheat; and I'm worth six of her. (*She shakes the pain off hardily; tosses her head; and sets to work to put the things on the tray. He looks doubtfully at her once or twice. She finishes packing the tray, and laps the cloth over the edges, so as to carry all out together. As she stoops to lift it, he rises.*)

SERGIUS: Louka! (*She stops and looks defiantly at him.*) A gentleman has no right to hurt a woman under any circumstances. (*With profound humility, uncovering his head*) I beg your pardon.

LOUKA: That sort of apology may satisfy a lady. Of what use is it to a servant?

SERGIUS (*rudely crossed in his chivalry, throws it off with a bitter laugh, and says slightingly*):   Oh! you wish to be paid for the hurt? (*He puts on his shako, and takes some money from his pocket.*)

LOUKA (*her eyes filling with tears in spite of herself*):   No: I want my hurt made well.

SERGIUS (*sobered by her tone*):   How?

(*She rolls up her left sleeve; clasps her arm with the thumb and fingers of her right hand; and looks down at the bruise. Then she raises her head and looks straight at him. Finally, with a superb gesture, she presents her arm to be kissed. Amazed, he looks at her; at the arm; at her again; hesitates; and then, with shuddering intensity, exclaims* Never! *and gets away as far as possible from her.*

Her arm drops. Without a word, and with unaffected dignity, she takes her tray, and is approaching the house when RAINA *returns, wearing a hat and jacket in the height of the Vienna fashion of the previous year, 1885.* LOUKA *makes way proudly for her, and then goes into the house.)*

RAINA: I'm ready. Whats the matter? (*Gaily*) Have you been flirting with Louka?

SERGIUS (*hastily*):   No, no. How can you think such a thing?

RAINA (*ashamed of herself*):   Forgive me, dear: it was only a jest. I am so happy to-day.

(He goes quickly to her, and kisses her hand remorsefully. Catherine comes out and calls to them from the top of the steps.)

CATHERINE (*coming down to them*):   I am sorry to disturb you, children; but Paul is distracted over those three regiments. He doesnt know how to send them to Philippopolis; and he objects to every suggestion of mine. You must go and help him, Sergius. He is in the library.

RAINA (*disappointed*):   But we are just going out for a walk.

SERGIUS: I shall not be long. Wait for me just five minutes. (*He runs up the steps to the door.*)

RAINA (*following him to the foot of the steps and looking up at him with timid coquetry*):   I shall go round and wait in full view of the library windows. Be sure you draw father's attention to me. If you are a moment longer than five minutes, I shall go in and fetch you, regiments or no regiments.

SERGIUS (*laughing*):   Very well. (*He goes in. RAINA watches him until he is out of her sight. Then, with a perceptible relaxation of manner, she begins to pace up and down the garden in a brown study.*)

CATHERINE: Imagine their meeting that Swiss and hearing the whole story! The very first thing your father asked for was the old coat we sent him off in. A nice mess you have got us into!

RAINA (*gazing thoughtfully at the gravel as she walks*):   The little beast!

CATHERINE: Little beast! What little beast?

RAINA: To go and tell! Oh, if I had him here, I'd cram him with chocolate creams till he couldnt ever speak again!

CATHERINE: Dont talk such stuff. Tell me the truth, Raina. How long was he in your room before you came to me?

RAINA (*whisking round and recommencing her march in the opposite direction*):   Oh, I forget.

CATHERINE: You cannot forget! Did he really climb up after the soldiers were gone; or was he there when that officer searched the room?

RAINA: No. Yes: I think he must have been there then.

CATHERINE: You think! Oh, Raina, Raina! Will anything ever make you straightforward? If Sergius finds out, it is all over between you.

RAINA (*with cool impertinence*):   Oh, I know Sergius is your pet. I sometimes wish you could marry him instead of me. You would just suit him. You would pet him, and spoil him, and mother him to perfection.

CATHERINE (*opening her eyes very widely indeed*):   Well, upon my word!

RAINA (*capriciously—half to herself*):   I always feel a longing to do or say something dreadful to him—to shock his propriety—to scandalize the five senses out of him. (*To CATHERINE, perversely*) I dont care whether he finds out about the chocolate cream soldier or not. I half hope he may. (*She again turns and strolls flippantly away up the path to the corner of the house.*)

CATHERINE: And what should I be able to say to your father, pray?

RAINA (*over her shoulder, from the top of the two steps*):   Oh, poor father! As if he could help himself! (*She turns the corner and passes out of sight.*)

CATHERINE (*looking after her, her fingers itching*):   Oh, if you were only ten years younger! (*LOUKA comes from the house with a salver, which she carries hanging down by her side.*) Well?

LOUKA: Theres a gentleman just called, madam—a Servian officer—

CATHERINE (*flaming*):   A Servian! And how dare he—(*checking herself bitterly*) Oh, I forgot. We are at peace now. I suppose we shall have them calling every day to pay their compliments. Well: if he is an officer why dont you tell your master? He is in the library with Major Saranoff. Why do you come to me?

LOUKA: But he asks for you, madam. And I dont think he knows who you are: he said the lady of the house. He gave me this little ticket for you. (*She takes a card out of her bosom; puts it on the salver; and offers it to CATHERINE.*)

CATHERINE (*reading*):   "Captain Bluntschli"! Thats a German name.

LOUKA: Swiss, madam, I think.

CATHERINE (*with a bound that makes Louka jump back*):   Swiss! What is he like?

LOUKA (*timidly*):   He has a big carpet bag, madam.

CATHERINE: Oh Heavens: he's come to return the coat! Send him away—say we're not at home—ask him to leave his address and I'll write to him—Oh stop: that will never do. Wait! (*She throws herself into a chair to think it out.* LOUKA *waits.*) The master and Major Saranoff are busy in the library, arnt they?

LOUKA: Yes, madam.

CATHERINE (*decisively*): Bring the gentleman out here at once. (*Imperatively*) And be very polite to him. Dont delay. Here (*impatiently snatching the salver from her*): leave that here; and go straight back to him.

LOUKA: Yes, madam. (*Going.*)

CATHERINE: Louka!

LOUKA (*stopping*): Yes, madam.

CATHERINE: Is the library door shut?

LOUKA: I think so, madam.

CATHERINE: If not, shut it as you pass through.

LOUKA: Yes, madam. (*Going.*)

CATHERINE: Stop! (LOUKA *stops.*) He will have to go that way (*indicating the gate of the stable yard*). Tell Nicola to bring his bag here after him. Dont forget.

LOUKA (*surprised*): His bag?

CATHERINE: Yes: here, as soon as possible. (*Vehemently*) Be quick! (LOUKA *runs into the house.* CATHERINE *snatches her apron off and throws it behind a bush. She then takes up the salver and uses it as a mirror, with the result that the handkerchief tied round her head follows the apron. A touch to her hair and a shake to her dressing gown make her presentable.*) Oh, how—how—how can a man be such a fool! Such a moment to select! (LOUKA *appears at the door of the house, announcing* Captain Bluntschli. *She stands aside at the top of the steps to let him pass before she goes in again. He is the man of the midnight adventure in Raina's room, clean, well brushed, smartly uniformed, and out of trouble, but still unmistakably the same man. The moment* LOUKA's *back is turned,* CATHERINE *swoops on him with impetuous, urgent, coaxing appeal.*) Captain Bluntschli: I am very glad to see you; but you must leave this house at once. (*He raises his eyebrows.*) My husband has just returned, with my future son-in-law; and they know nothing. If they did, the consequences would be terrible. You are a foreigner: you do not feel our national animosities as we do. We still hate the Servians: the only effect of the peace on my husband is to make him feel like a lion baulked of his prey. If he discovered our secret, he would never forgive me; and my daughter's life would hardly be safe. Will you, like the chivalrous gentleman and soldier you are, leave at once before he finds you here?

BLUNTSCHLI (*disappointed, but philosophical*): At once, gracious lady. I only came to thank you and return the coat you lent me. If you will allow me to take it out of my bag and leave it with your servant as I pass out, I need detain you no further. (*He turns to go into the house.*)

CATHERINE (*catching him by the sleeve*): Oh, you must not think of going back that way. (*Coaxing him across to the stable gates*) This is the shortest way out. Many thanks. So glad to have been of service to you. Good-bye.

BLUNTSCHLI: But my bag?

CATHERINE: It shall be sent on. You will leave me your address.

BLUNTSCHLI: True. Allow me. (*He takes out his card-case, and stops to write his address, keeping* CATHERINE *in an agony of impatience. As he hands her the card,* PETKOFF, *hatless, rushes from the house in a fluster of hospitality, followed by* SERGIUS.)

PETKOFF (*as he hurries down the steps*): My dear Captain Bluntschli—

CATHERINE: Oh Heavens! (*She sinks on the seat against the wall.*)

PETKOFF (*too preoccupied to notice her as he shakes* BLUNTSCHLI's *hand heartily.*): Those stupid people of mine thought I was out here, instead of in the—haw!—library. (*He cannot mention the library without betraying how proud he is of it.*) I saw you through the window. I was wondering why you didnt come in. Saranoff is with me: you remember him, dont you?

SERGIUS (*saluting humorously, and then offering his hand with great charm of manner*): Welcome, our friend the enemy!

PETKOFF: No longer the enemy, happily. (*Rather anxiously*) I hope youve called as a friend, and not about horses or prisoners—eh?

CATHERINE: Oh, quite as a friend, Paul. I was just asking Captain Bluntschli to stay to lunch; but he declares he must go at once.

SERGIUS (*sardonically*): Impossible, Bluntschli. We want you here badly. We have to send on three cavalry regiments to Philippopolis; and we dont in the least know how to do it.

BLUNTSCHLI (*suddenly attentive and business-like*): Philippopolis? The forage is the trouble, I suppose.

PETKOFF (*eagerly*): Yes: thats it. (*To Sergius*) He sees the whole thing at once.

BLUNTSCHLI: I think I can shew you how to manage that.

SERGIUS: Invaluable man! Come along! (*Tow-*

ering over BLUNTSCHLI, *he puts his hand on his shoulder and takes him to the steps,* PETKOFF *following. As* BLUNTSCHLI *puts his foot on the first step,* RAINA *comes out of the house.*)

RAINA (*completely losing her presence of mind*): Oh! The chocolate cream soldier!

(BLUNTSCHLI *stands rigid.* SERGIUS, *amazed, looks at* RAINA, *then at* PETKOFF, *who looks back at him and then at his wife.*)

CATHERINE (*with commanding presence of mind*): My dear Raina, dont you see that we have a guest here?—Captain Bluntschli, one of our new Servian friends.

(RAINA *bows:* BLUNTSCHLI *bows.*)

RAINA: How silly of me! (*She comes down into the centre of the group, between* BLUNTSCHLI *and* PETKOFF.) I made a beautiful ornament this morning for the ice pudding; and that stupid Nicola has just put down a pile of plates on it and spoiled it. (*To* BLUNTSCHLI, *winningly*) I hope you didnt think that you were the chocolate cream soldier, Captain Bluntschli.

BLUNTSCHLI (*laughing*): I assure you I did. (*Stealing a whimsical glance at her*) Your explanation was a relief.

PETKOFF (*suspiciously, to* RAINA): And since when, pray, have you taken to cooking?

CATHERINE: Oh, whilst you were away. It is her latest fancy.

PETKOFF (*testily*): And has Nicola taken to drinking? He used to be careful enough. First he shews Captain Bluntschli out here when he knew quite well I was in the—hum!—library; and then he goes downstairs and breaks Raina's chocolate soldier. He must—(NICOLA *appears at the top of the steps with a carpet bag. He descends; places it respectfully before* BLUNTSCHLI; *and waits for further orders. General amazement.* NICOLA, *unconscious of the effect he is producing, looks perfectly satisfied with himself. When* PETKOFF *recovers his power of speech, he breaks out at him with*) Are you mad, Nicola?

NICOLA (*taken aback*): Sir?

PETKOFF: What have you brought that for?

NICOLA: My lady's orders, sir. Louka told me that—

CATHERINE (*interrupting him*): My orders! Why should I order you to bring Captain Bluntschli's luggage out here? What are you thinking of, Nicola?

NICOLA (*after a moment's bewilderment, picking up the bag as he addresses* BLUNTSCHLI *with the very perfection of servile discretion*): I beg your pardon, sir, I am sure. (*To* CATHERINE) My fault, madam: I hope youll overlook it. (*He bows, and is going to the steps with the bag, when* PETKOFF *addresses him angrily.*)

PETKOFF: Youd better go and slam that bag, too, down on Miss Raina's ice pudding! (*This is too much for* NICOLA. *The bag drops from his hand.*) Begone, you butterfingered donkey.

NICOLA (*snatching up the bag, and escaping into the house*): Yes, sir.

CATHERINE: Oh, never mind, Paul: dont be angry.

PETKOFF (*muttering*): Scoundrel! He's got out of hand while I was away. I'll teach him. (*Recollecting his guest*) Oh well, never mind. Come, Bluntschli: let's have no more nonsense about having to go away. You know very well youre not going back to Switzerland yet. Until you do go back youll stay with us.

RAINA: Oh, do, Captain Bluntschli.

PETKOFF (*to* CATHERINE): Now, Catherine: it's of you that he's afraid. Press him; and he'll stay.

CATHERINE: Of course I shall be only too delighted if (*appealingly*) Captain Bluntschli really wishes to stay. He knows my wishes.

BLUNTSCHLI (*in his driest military manner*): I am at madam's orders.

SERGIUS (*cordially*): That settles it!

PETKOFF (*heartily*): Of course!

RAINA: You see you must stay.

BLUNTSCHLI (*smiling*): Well, if I must, I must. (*Gesture of despair from* CATHERINE.)

ACT III

In the library after lunch. It is not much of a library. Its literary equipment consists of a single fixed shelf stocked with old paper covered novels, broken backed, coffee stained, torn and thumbed; and a couple of little hanging shelves with a few gift books on them: the rest of the wall space being occupied by trophies of war and the chase. But it is a most comfortable sitting room. A row of three large windows shews a mountain panorama, just now seen in one of its friendliest aspects in the mellowing afternoon light. In the corner next the right hand window a square earthenware stove, a perfect tower of colored pottery, rises nearly to the ceiling and guarantees plenty of warmth. The ottoman in the middle is a circular bank of decorated cushions; and the window seats are well upholstered divans. Little Turkish tables, one of them with an elaborate hookah on it, and a screen to match them, complete the handsome effect of the furnishing. There is one object, however, hopelessly out of keeping with its surroundings. This is a small kitchen table, much the worse for wear, fitted as a writing table with an old canister full of pens, an eggcup filled with ink, and a deplorable scrap of heavily used pink blotting paper.

At the side of this table, which stands opposite the left hand window, BLUNTSCHLI *is hard at work with a couple of maps before him, writing orders. At the head of it sits* SERGIUS, *who is also supposed to be at work, but who is actually gnawing the feather of a pen, and contemplating* BLUNTSCHLI'S *quick, sure, businesslike progress with a mixture of envious irritation at his own incapacity, and awestruck wonder at an ability which seems to him almost miraculous, though its prosaic character forbids him to esteem it. The* MAJOR *is comfortably established on the ottoman, with a newspaper in his hand and the tube of the hookah within his reach.* CATHERINE *sits at the stove, with her back to them, embroidering.* RAINA, *reclining on the divan under the right hand window, is gazing in a daydream out at the Balkan landscape, with a neglected novel in her lap.*

The door is on the same side as the stove, further from the window. The button of the electric bell is between the door and the stove.

PETKOFF (*looking up from his paper to watch how they are getting on at the table*): Are you sure I cant help you in any way, Bluntschli?

BLUNTSCHLI (*without interrupting his writing or looking up*): Quite sure, thank you. Saranoff and I will manage it.

SERGIUS (*grimly*): Yes: we'll manage it. He finds out what to do; draws up the orders; and I sign em. Division of labour, Major. (BLUNTSCHLI *passes him a paper.*) Another one? Thank you. (*He plants the paper squarely before him; sets his chair carefully parallel to it; and signs with the air of a man resolutely performing a difficult and dangerous feat.*) This hand is more accustomed to the sword than to the pen.

PETKOFF: It's very good of you, Bluntschli: it is indeed, to let yourself be put upon in this way. Now are you quite sure I can do nothing?

CATHERINE (*in a low warning tone*): You can stop interrupting, Paul.

PETKOFF (*starting and looking round at her*): Eh? Oh! Quite right, my love: quite right. (*He takes his newspaper up again, but presently lets it drop.*) Ah, you havnt been campaigning, Catherine: you dont know how pleasant it is for us to sit here, after a good lunch, with nothing to do but enjoy ourselves. Theres only one thing I want to make me thoroughly comfortable.

CATHERINE: What is that?

PETKOFF: My old coat. I'm not at home in this one: I feel as if I were on parade.

CATHERINE: My dear Paul, how absurd you are about that old coat! It must be hanging in the blue closet where you left it.

PETKOFF: My dear Catherine, I tell you Ive looked there. Am I to believe my own eyes or not? (CATHERINE *quietly rises and presses the button of the electric bell by the fireplace.*) What are you shewing off that bell for? (*She looks at him majestically, and silently resumes her chair and her needlework.*) My dear: if you think the obstinacy of your sex can make a coat out of two old dressing gowns of Raina's, your waterproof, and my mackintosh, youre mistaken. Thats exactly what the blue closet contains at present. (NICOLA *presents himself.*)

CATHERINE (*unmoved by Petkoff's sally*): Nicola: go to the blue closet and bring your master's old coat here—the braided one he usually wears in the house.

NICOLA: Yes, madame. (NICOLA *goes out.*)

PETKOFF: Catherine.

CATHERINE: Yes, Paul?

PETKOFF: I bet you any piece of jewellery you like to order from Sophia against a week's housekeeping money, that the coat isnt there.

CATHERINE: Done, Paul.

PETKOFF (*excited by the prospect of a gamble*): Come: here's an opportunity for some sport. Wholl bet on it? Bluntschli: I'll give you six to one.

BLUNTSCHLI (*imperturbably*): It would be robbing you, Major. Madame is sure to be right. (*Without looking up, he passes another batch of papers to* SERGIUS.)

SERGIUS (*also excited*): Bravo, Switzerland! Major: I bet my best charger against an Arab mare for Raina that Nicola finds the coat in the blue closet.

PETKOFF (*eagerly*): Your best char—

CATHERINE (*hastily interrupting him*): Dont be foolish, Paul. An Arabian mare will cost you 50,000 levas.

RAINA (*suddenly coming out of her picturesque revery*): Really, mother, if you are going to take the jewellery, I dont see why you should grudge me my Arab.

(NICOLA *comes back with the coat, and brings it to* PETKOFF, *who can hardly believe his eyes.*)

CATHERINE: Where was it, Nicola?

NICOLA: Hanging in the blue closet, madame.

PETKOFF: Well, I am d—

CATHERINE (*stopping him*): Paul!

PETKOFF: I could have sworn it wasnt there. Age is beginning to tell on me. I'm getting hallucinations. (*To* NICOLA) Here: help me to change. Excuse me, Bluntschli. (*He begins changing coats,* NICOLA *acting as valet.*) Remember: I didnt take that bet of yours, Sergius. Youd better give Raina that Arab steed yourself, since youve roused her expectations. Eh, Raina? (*He looks round at her; but she is again rapt in the landscape. With a little gush of parental affection and pride, he points her out to them, and says*) She's dreaming, as usual.

SERGIUS: Assuredly she shall not be the loser.

PETKOFF: So much the better for her. *I* shant come off so cheap, I expect. (*The change is now complete.* NICOLA *goes out with the discarded coat.*) Ah, now I feel at home at last. (*He sits down and takes his newspaper with a grunt of relief.*)

BLUNTSCHLI (*to* SERGIUS, *handing a paper*): Thats the last order.

PETKOFF (*jumping up*): What! finished?

BLUNTSCHLI: Finished. (PETKOFF *goes beside* SERGIUS; *looks curiously over his left shoulder as he signs; and says with childlike envy*) Havnt you anything for me to sign?

BLUNTSCHLI: Not necessary. His signature will do.

PETKOFF: Ah well, I think weve done a thundering good day's work. (*He goes away from the table.*) Can I do anything more?

BLUNTSCHLI: You had better both see the fellows that are to take these. (*To* SERGIUS) Pack them off at once; and shew them that Ive marked on the orders the time they should hand them in by. Tell them that if they stop to drink or tell stories—if theyre five minutes late, theyll have the skin taken off their backs.

SERGIUS (*rising indignantly*): I'll say so. And if

one of them is man enough to spit in my face for insulting him, I'll buy his discharge and give him a pension. (*He strides out, his humanity deeply outraged.*)

BLUNTSCHLI (*confidentially*): Just see that he talks to them properly, Major, will you?

PETKOFF (*officiously*): Quite right, Bluntschli, quite right. I'll see to it. (*He goes to the door importantly, but hesitates on the threshold.*) By the bye, Catherine, you may as well come too. Theyll be far more frightened of you than of me.

CATHERINE (*putting down her embroidery*): I daresay I had better. You will only splutter at them. (*She goes out,* PETKOFF *holding the door for her and following her.*)

BLUNTSCHLI: What a country! They make cannons out of cherry trees; and the officers send for their wives to keep discipline! (*He begins to fold and docket the papers.* RAINA, *who has risen from the divan, strolls down the room with her hands clasped behind her, and looks mischievously at him.*)

RAINA: You look ever so much nicer than when we last met. (*He looks up, surprised.*) What have you done to yourself?

BLUNTSCHLI: Washed; brushed; good night's sleep and breakfast. Thats all.

RAINA: Did you get back safely that morning?

BLUNTSCHLI: Quite, thanks.

RAINA: Were they angry with you for running away from Sergius's charge?

BLUNTSCHLI: No, they were glad; because theyd all just run away themselves.

RAINA (*going to the table, and leaning over it towards him*): It must have made a lovely story for them—all that about me and my room.

BLUNTSCHLI: Capital story. But I only told it to one of them—a particular friend.

RAINA: On whose discretion you could absolutely rely?

BLUNTSCHLI: Absolutely.

RAINA: Hm! He told it all to my father and Sergius the day you exchanged the prisoners. (*She turns away and strolls carelessly across to the other side of the room.*)

BLUNTSCHLI (*deeply concerned, and half incredulous*): No! you dont mean that, do you?

RAINA (*turning, with sudden earnestness*): I do indeed. But they dont know that it was in this house you took refuge. If Sergius knew, he would challenge you and kill you in a duel.

BLUNTSCHLI: Bless me! then dont tell him.

RAINA (*full of reproach for his levity*): Can you realize what it is to me to deceive him? I want to be quite perfect with Sergius—no meanness, no smallness, no deceit. My relation to him is the one really beautiful and noble part of my life. I hope you can understand that.

BLUNTSCHLI (*sceptically*): You mean that you wouldnt like him to find out that the story about the ice pudding was a — a — a — You know.

RAINA (*wincing*): Ah, dont talk of it in that flippant way. I lied: I know it. But I did it to save your life. He would have killed you. That was the second time I ever uttered a falsehood. (BLUNTSCHLI *rises quickly and looks doubtfully and somewhat severely at her.*) Do you remember the first time?

BLUNTSCHLI: I! No. Was I present?

RAINA: Yes; and I told the officer who was searching for you that you were not present.

BLUNTSCHLI: True. I should have remembered it.

RAINA (*greatly encouraged*): Ah, it is natural that you should forget it first. It cost you nothing: it cost me a lie!—a lie!! (*She sits down on the ottoman, looking straight before her with her hands clasped on her knee.* BLUNTSCHLI, *quite touched, goes to the ottoman with a particularly reassuring and considerate air, and sits down beside her.*)

BLUNTSCHLI: My dear young lady, dont let this worry you. Remember: I'm a soldier. Now what are the two things that happen to a soldier so often that he comes to think nothing of them? One is hearing people tell lies (RAINA *recoils*): the other is getting his life saved in all sorts of ways by all sorts of people.

RAINA (*rising in indignant protest*): And so he becomes a creature incapable of faith and of gratitude.

BLUNTSCHLI (*making a wry face*): Do you like gratitude? I dont. If pity is akin to love, gratitude is akin to the other thing.

RAINA: Gratitude! (*Turning on him*) If you are incapable of gratitude you are incapable of any noble sentiment. Even animals are grateful. Oh, I see now exactly what you think of me! You were not surprised to hear me lie. To you it was something I probably did every day—every hour. That is how men think of women. (*She walks up the room melodramatically.*)

BLUNTSCHLI (*dubiously*): Theres reason in everything. You said youd told only two lies in your whole life. Dear young lady: isnt that rather a short allowance? I'm quite a straightforward man myself; but it wouldnt last me a whole morning.

RAINA (*staring haughtily at him*): Do you know, sir, that you are insulting me?

BLUNTSCHLI: I cant help it. When you get into that noble attitude and speak in that thrilling voice, I admire you; but I find it impossible to believe a single word you say.

RAINA (*superbly*): Captain Bluntschli!

BLUNTSCHLI (*unmoved*): Yes?

RAINA (*coming a little towards him, as if she could not believe her senses*): Do you mean what you said just now? Do you know what you said just now?

BLUNTSCHLI: I do.

RAINA (*gasping*): I! I!!! (*She points to herself incredulously, meaning "I, Raina Petkoff, tell lies!" He meets her gaze unflinchingly. She suddenly sits down beside him, and adds, with a complete change of manner from the heroic to the familiar*) How did you find me out?

BLUNTSCHLI (*promptly*): Instinct, dear young lady. Instinct, and experience of the world.

RAINA (*wonderingly*): Do you know, you are the first man I ever met who did not take me seriously?

BLUNTSCHLI: You mean, dont you, that I am the first man that has ever taken you quite seriously?

RAINA: Yes, I suppose I do mean that. (*Cosily, quite at her ease with him*) How strange it is to be talked to in such a way! You know, Ive always gone on like that—I mean the noble attitude and the thrilling voice. I did it when I was a tiny child to my nurse. She believed in it. I do it before my parents. They believe in it. I do it before Sergius. He believes in it.

BLUNTSCHLI: Yes: he's a little in that line himself, isnt he?

RAINA (*startled*): Do you think so?

BLUNTSCHLI: You know him better than I do.

RAINA: I wonder—I wonder is he? If I thought that—! (*Discouraged*) Ah, well: what does it matter? I suppose, now youve found me out, you despise me.

BLUNTSCHLI (*warmly, rising*): No, my dear young lady, no, no, no a thousand times. It's part of your youth—part of your charm. I'm like all the rest of them—the nurse—your parents—Sergius: I'm your infatuated admirer.

RAINA (*pleased*): Really?

BLUNTSCHLI (*slapping his breast smartly with his hand, German fashion*): Hand aufs Herz! Really and truly.

RAINA (*very happy*): But what did you think of me for giving you my portrait?

BLUNTSCHLI (*astonished*): Your portrait! You never gave me your portrait.

RAINA (*quickly*): Do you mean to say you never got it?

BLUNTSCHLI: No. (*He sits down beside her, with renewed interest, and says, with some complacency*) When did you send it to me?

RAINA (*indignantly*): I did not send it to you. (*She turns her head away, and adds, reluctantly*) It was in the pocket of that coat.

BLUNTSCHLI (*pursing his lips and rounding his eyes*) Oh-o-oh! I never found it. It must be there still.

RAINA (*springing up*): There still!—for my father to find the first time he puts his hand in his pocket! Oh, how could you be so stupid?

BLUNTSCHLI (*rising also*): It doesn't matter: it's only a photograph: how can he tell who it was intended for? Tell him he put it there himself.

RAINA (*impatiently*): Yes: that is so clever—so clever! Oh, what shall I do!

BLUNTSCHLI: Ah, I see. You wrote something on it. That was rash.

RAINA (*annoyed almost to tears*): Oh, to have done such a thing for you, who care no more—except to laugh at me—oh! Are you sure nobod has touched it?

BLUNTSCHLI: Well, I cant be quite sure. You see, I couldnt carry it about with me all the time: one cant take much luggage on active service.

RAINA: What did you do with it?

BLUNTSCHLI: When I got through to Peerot I had to put it in safe keeping somehow. I thought of the railway cloak room; but thats the surest place to get looted in modern warfare. So I pawned it.

RAINA: Pawned it!!!

BLUNTSCHLI: I know it doesnt sound nice; but it was much the safest plan. I redeemed it the day before yesterday. Heaven only knows whether the pawnbroker cleared out the pockets or not.

RAINA (*furious—throwing the words right into his face*): You have a low, shopkeeping mind. You think of things that would never come into a gentleman's head.

BLUNTSCHLI (*phlegmatically*): Thats the Swiss national character, dear lady.

RAINA: Oh, I wish I had never met you. (*She flounces away, and sits at the window fuming.*)

(LOUKA *comes in with a heap of letters and telegrams on her salver, and crosses, with her bold, free gait, to the table. Her left sleeve is looped up to the shoulder with a brooch, shewing her naked arm, with a broad gilt bracelet covering the bruise.*)

LOUKA (*to* BLUNTSCHLI): For you. (*She empties the salver recklessly on to the table.*) The messenger is waiting. (*She is determined not to be civil to a Servian, even if she must bring him his letters.*)

BLUNTSCHLI (*to* RAINA): Will you excuse me: the last postal delivery that reached me was three weeks ago. These are the subsequent accumulations. Four telegrams—a week old. (*He opens one.*) Oho! Bad news!

RAINA (*rising and advancing a little remorsefully*): Bad news?

BLUNTSCHLI: My father's dead. (*He looks at the telegram with his lips pursed, musing on the unexpected change in his arrangements.*)

RAINA: Oh, how very sad!

BLUNTSCHLI: Yes: I shall have to start for home in an hour. He has left a lot of big hotels behind him to be looked after. (*He takes up a fat letter in a long blue envelope.*) Here's a whacking letter from the family solicitor. (*He pulls out the enclosures and glances over them.*) Great Heavens! Seventy! Two hundred! (*In a crescendo of dismay*) Four hundred! Four thousand!! Nine thousand six hundred!!! What on earth shall I do with them all!

RAINA (*timidly*): Nine thousand hotels?

BLUNTSCHLI: Hotels! nonsense. If you only knew!—oh, it's too ridiculous! Excuse me: I must give my fellow orders about starting. (*He leaves the room hastily, with the documents in his hand.*)

LOUKA (*tauntingly*): He has not much heart, that Swiss, though he is so fond of the Servians. He has not a word of grief for his poor father.

RAINA (*bitterly*): Grief!—a man who has been doing nothing but killing people for years! What does he care? what does any soldier care? (*She goes to the door, restraining her tears with difficulty.*)

LOUKA: Major Saranoff has been fighting too; and he has plenty of heart left. (RAINA, *at the door, looks haughtily at her and goes out.*) Aha! I thought you wouldnt get much feeling out of your soldier. (*She is following* RAINA *when* NICOLA *enters with an armful of logs for the fire.*)

NICOLA (*grinning amorously at her*): Ive been trying all the afternoon to get a minute alone with you, my girl. (*His countenance changes as he notices her arm.*) Why, what fashion is that of wearing your sleeve, child?

LOUKA (*proudly*): My own fashion.

NICOLA: Indeed! If the mistress catches you, she'll talk to you. (*He throws the logs down on the ottoman, and sits comfortably beside them.*)

LOUKA: Is that any reason why you should take it on yourself to talk to me?

NICOLA: Come: dont be so contrary with me. Ive some good news for you. (*He takes out some paper money.* LOUKA, *with an eager gleam in her eyes, comes close, to look at it.*) See! a twenty leva bill! Sergius gave me that, out of pure swagger. A fool and his money are soon parted. Theres ten levas more. The Swiss gave me that for backing up the mistress's and Raina's lies about him. He's no fool, he isnt. You should have heard old Catherine downstairs as polite as you please to me, telling me not to mind the Major being a little impatient; for they knew what a good servant I was—after making a fool and a liar of me before them all! The twenty will go to our savings; and you shall have the ten to spend if youll only talk to me so as to remind me I'm a human being. I get tired of being a servant occasionally.

LOUKA (*scornfully*): Yes: sell your manhood for 30 levas, and buy me for 10! Keep your money. You were born to be a servant. I was not. When you set up your shop you will only be everybody's servant instead of somebody's servant.

NICOLA (*picking up his logs, and going to the stove*): Ah, wait till you see. We shall have our evenings to ourselves; and I shall be master in my own house, I promise you. (*He throws the logs down and kneels at the stove.*)

LOUKA: You shall never be master in mine. (*She seats herself proudly on Sergius's chair.*)

NICOLA (*turning, still on his knees, and squatting down rather forlornly on his calves, daunted by her implacable disdain*): You have a great ambition in you, Louka. Remember: if any luck comes to you, it was I that made a woman of you.

LOUKA: You!

NICOLA (*with dogged self-assertion*): Yes, me. Who was it made you give up wearing a couple of pounds of false black hair on your head and reddening your lips and cheeks like any other Bulgarian girl? I did. Who taught you to trim your nails, and keep your hands clean, and be dainty about yourself, like a fine Russian lady? Me: do you hear that? me! (*She tosses her head defiantly; and he rises ill humoredly, adding, more coolly*) Ive often thought that if Raina were out of the way, and you just a little less of a fool and Sergius just a little more of one, you might come to be one of my grandest customers, instead of only being my wife and costing me money.

LOUKA: I believe you would rather be my servant than my husband. You would make more out of me. Oh, I know that soul of yours.

NICOLA (*going up close to her for greater emphasis*): Never you mind my soul; but just listen to my advice. If you want to be a lady, your present behaviour to me wont do at all, unless when we're alone. It's too sharp and impudent; and impudence is a sort of familiarity: it shews affection for me. And dont you try being high and mighty with me, either. Youre like all country girls: you think it's genteel to treat a servant the way I treat a stableboy. Thats only your ignorance; and dont you forget it. And dont be so ready to defy everybody. Act as if you expected to have your own way, not as if you expected to be ordered about. The way to get on as a lady is the same as the way to get on as a servant: youve got to know your place: thats the secret of it. And you may depend on me to know my place if you get promoted. Think over it, my girl. I'll stand by you: one servant should always stand by another.

LOUKA (*rising impatiently*): Oh, I must behave in my own way. You take all the courage out of me with your coldblooded wisdom. Go and put those logs on the fire: thats the sort of thing you understand. (*Before* NICOLA *can retort,* SERGIUS *comes in. He checks himself a moment on seeing* LOUKA; *then goes to the stove.*)

SERGIUS (*to Nicola*): I am not in the way of your work, I hope.

NICOLA (*in a smooth, elderly manner*): Oh no sir: thank you kindly. I was only speaking to this foolish girl about her habit of running up here to the library whenever she gets a chance, to look at the books. Thats the worst of her education, sir: it gives her habits above her station. (*To* LOUKA) Make that table tidy, Louka, for the Major. (*He goes out sedately.*)

(LOUKA, *without looking at* SERGIUS, *begins to*

arrange the papers on the table. He crosses slowly to her, and studies the arrangement of her sleeve reflectively.)

SERGIUS: Let me see: is there a mark there? (*He turns up the bracelet and sees the bruise made by his grasp. She stands motionless, not looking at him: fascinated, but on her guard.*) Ffff! Does it hurt?

LOUKA: Yes.

SERGIUS: Shall I cure it?

LOUKA (*instantly withdrawing herself proudly, but still not looking at him*): No. You cannot cure it now.

SERGIUS (*masterfully*): Quite sure? (*He makes a movement as if to take her in his arms.*)

LOUKA: Dont trifle with me, please. An officer should not trifle with a servant.

SERGIUS (*touching the arm with a merciless stroke of his forefinger*): That was no trifle, Louka.

LOUKA: No. (*Looking at him for the first time*) Are you sorry?

SERGIUS (*with measured emphasis, folding his arms*): I am never sorry.

LOUKA (*wistfully*): I wish I could believe a man could be so unlike a woman as that. I wonder are you really a brave man?

SERGIUS (*unaffectedly, relaxing his attitude*): Yes: I am a brave man. My heart jumped like a woman's at the first shot; but in the charge I found that I was brave. Yes: that at least is real about me.

LOUKA: Did you find in the charge that the men whose fathers are poor like mine were any less brave than the men who are rich like you.

SERGIUS (*with bitter levity*): Not a bit. They all slashed and cursed and yelled like heroes. Psha! the courage to rage and kill is cheap. I have an English bull terrier who has as much of that sort of courage as the whole Bulgarian nation, and the whole Russian nation at its back. But he lets my groom thrash him, all the same. Thats your soldier all over! No, Louka: your poor men can cut throats; but they are afraid of their officers; they put up with insults and blows; they stand by and see one another punished like children—aye, and help to do it when they are ordered. And the officers!—well (*with a short, bitter laugh*) I am an officer. Oh, (*fervently*) give me the man who will defy to the death any power on earth or in heaven that sets itself up against his own will and conscience: he alone is the brave man.

LOUKA: How easy it is to talk! Men never seem to me to grow up: they all have schoolboy's ideas. You dont know what true courage is.

SERGIUS (*ironically*): Indeed! I am willing to be instructed.

LOUKA: Look at me! how much am I allowed to have my own will? I have to get your room ready for you—to sweep and dust, to fetch and carry. How could that degrade me if it did not degrade you to have it done for you? But (*with subdued passion*) if I were Empress of Russia, above everyone in the world, then—ah then, though according to you I could shew no courge at all, you should see, you should see.

SERGIUS: What would you do, most noble Empress?

LOUKA: I would marry the man I loved, which no other queen in Europe has the courage to do. If I loved you, though you would be as far beneath me as I am beneath you, I would dare to be the equal of my inferior. Would you dare as much if you loved me? No: if you felt the beginnings of love for me you would not let it grow. You dare not: you would marry a rich man's daughter because you would be afraid of what other people would say of you.

SERGIUS (*carried away*): You lie: it is not so, by all the stars! If I loved you, and I were the Czar himself, I would set you on the throne by my side. You know that I love another woman, a woman as high above you as heaven is above earth. And you are jealous of her.

LOUKA: I have no reason to be. She will never marry you now. The man I told you of has come back. She will marry the Swiss.

SERGIUS (*recoiling*): The Swiss!

LOUKA: A man worth ten of you. Then you can come to me; and I will refuse you. You are not good enough for me. (*She turns to the door.*)

SERGIUS (*springing after her and catching her fiercely in his arms*): I will kill the Swiss; and afterwards I will do as I please with you.

LOUKA (*in his arms, passive and steadfast*): The Swiss will kill you, perhaps. He has beaten you in love. He may beat you in war.

SERGIUS (*tormentedly*): Do you think I believe that she—she! whose worst thoughts are higher than your best ones, is capable of trifling with another man behind my back?

LOUKA: Do you think she would believe the Swiss if he told her now that I am in your arms?

SERGIUS (*releasing her in despair*): Damnation! Oh, damnation! Mockery, mockery everywhere: everything I think is mocked by everything I do. (*He strikes himself frantically on the breast.*) Coward, liar, fool! Shall I kill myself like a man, or live and pretend to laugh at myself? (*She again turns to go.*) Louka! (*She stops near the door.*) Remember: you belong to me.

LOUKA (*quietly*):   What does that mean—an insult?

SERGIUS (*commandingly*):   It means that you love me, and that I have had you here in my arms, and will perhaps have you there again. Whether that is an insult I neither know or care: take it as you please. But (*vehemently*) I will not be a coward and a trifler. If I choose to love you, I dare marry you, in spite of all Bulgaria. If these hands ever touch you again, they shall touch my affianced bride.

LOUKA: We shall see whether you dare keep your word. But take care. I will not wait long.

SERGIUS (*again folding his arms and standing motionless in the middle of the room*):   Yes, we shall see. And you shall wait my pleasure.

(BLUNTSCHLI, *much preoccupied, with his papers still in his hand, enters, leaving the door open for* LOUKA *to go out. He goes across to the table, glancing at her as he passes.* SERGIUS, *without altering his resolute attitude, watches him steadily.* LOUKA *goes out, leaving the door open.*)

BLUNTSCHLI (*absently, sitting at the table as before, and putting down his papers*):   Thats a remarkable looking young woman.

SERGIUS (*gravely, without moving*):   Captain Bluntschli.

BLUNTSCHLI: Eh?

SERGIUS: You have deceived me. You are my rival. I brook no rivals. At six o'clock I shall be in the drilling-ground on the Klissoura road, alone, on horseback, with my sabre. Do you understand?

BLUNTSCHLI (*staring, but sitting quite at his ease*):   Oh, thank you: thats a cavalry man's proposal. I'm in the artillery; and I have the choice of weapons. If I go, I shall take a machine gun. And there shall be no mistake about the cartridges this time.

SERGIUS (*flushing, but with deadly coldness*):   Take care, sir. It is not our custom in Bulgaria to allow invitations of that kind to be trifled with.

BLUNTSCHLI (*warmly*):   Pooh! dont talk to me about Bulgaria. You dont know what fighting is. But have it your own way. Bring your sabre along. I'll meet you.

SERGIUS (*fiercely delighted to find his opponent a man of spirit*):   Well said, Switzer. Shall I lend you my best horse?

BLUNTSCHLI: No: damn your horse!—thank you all the same, my dear fellow. (RAINA *comes in, and hears the next sentence.*) I shall fight you on foot. Horseback's too dangerous: I dont want to kill you if I can help it.

RAINA (*hurrying forward anxiously*):   I have heard what Captain Bluntschli said, Sergius. You are going to fight. Why? (SERGIUS *turns away in silence, and goes to the stove, where he stands watching her as she continues, to* BLUNTSCHLI) What about?

BLUNTSCHLI: I dont know: he hasnt told me. Better not interfere, dear young lady. No harm will be done: Ive often acted as sword instructor. He wont be able to touch me; and I'll not hurt him. It will save explanations. In the morning I shall be off home; and youll never see me or hear of me again. You and he will then make it up and live happily ever after.

RAINA (*turning away deeply hurt, almost with a sob in her voice*):   I never said I wanted to see you again.

SERGIUS (*striding forward*):   Ha! That is a confession.

RAINA (*haughtily*):   What do you mean?

SERGIUS: You love that man!

RAINA (*scandalized*):   Sergius!

SERGIUS: You allow him to make love to you behind my back, just as you accept me as your affianced husband behind his. Bluntschli: you knew our relations; and you deceived me. It is for that that I call you to account, not for having received favors *I* never enjoyed.

BLUNTSCHLI (*jumping up indignantly*):   Stuff! Rubbish! I have received no favors. Why, the young lady doesnt even know whether I'm married or not.

RAINA (*forgetting herself*):   Oh! (*Collapsing on the ottoman*) Are you?

SERGIUS: You see the young lady's concern, Captain Bluntschli. Denial is useless. You have enjoyed the privilege of being received in her own room, late at night—

BLUNTSCHLI (*interrupting him pepperily*):   Yes, you blockhead! She received me with a pistol at her head. Your cavalry were at my heels. I'd have blown out her brains if she'd uttered a cry.

SERGIUS (*taken aback*):   Bluntschli! Raina: is this true?

RAINA (*rising in wrathful majesty*):   Oh, how dare you, how dare you?

BLUNTSCHLI: Apologize, man: apologize! (*He resumes his seat at the table.*)

SERGIUS (*with the old measured emphasis, folding his arms*): I never apologize!

RAINA (*passionately*): This is the doing of that friend of yours, Captain Bluntschli. It is he who is spreading this horrible story about me. (*She walks about excitedly.*)

BLUNTSCHLI: No: he's dead—burnt alive.

RAINA (*stopping, shocked*): Burnt alive!

BLUNTSHLI: Shot in the hip in a wood-yard. Couldnt drag himself out. Your fellows' shells set the timber on fire and burnt him, with half a dozen other poor devils in the same predicament.

RAINA: How horrible!

SERGIUS: And how ridiculous! Oh, war! war! the dream of patriots and heroes! A fraud, Bluntschli, a hollow sham, like love.

RAINA (*outraged*): Like love! You say that before me!

BLUNTSCHLI: Come, Saranoff: that matter is explained.

SERGIUS: A hollow sham, I say. Would you have come back here if nothing had passed between you except at the muzzle of your pistol? Raina is mistaken about our friend who was burnt. He was not my informant.

RAINA: Who, then? (*Suddenly guessing the truth*) Ah, Louka! my maid, my servant! You were with her this morning all that time after—after—Oh, what sort of god is this I have been worshipping! (*He meets her gaze with sardonic enjoyment of her disenchantment. Angered all the more, she goes closer to him, and says, in a lower, intenser tone*) Do you know that I looked out of the window as I went upstairs, to have another sight of my hero; and I saw something I did not understand then. I know now that you were making love to her.

SERGIUS (*with grim humor*): You saw that?

RAINA: Only too well. (*She turns away, and throws herself on the divan under the centre window, quite overcome.*)

SERGIUS (*cynically*): Raina: our romance is shattered. Life's a farce.

BLUNTSCHLI (*to* RAINA, *goodhumoredly*): You see: he's found himself out now.

SERGIUS: Bluntschli: I have allowed you to call me a blockhead. You may now call me a coward as well. I refuse to fight you. Do you know why?

BLUNTSCHLI: No; but it doesnt matter. I didnt ask the reason when you cried on; and I dont ask the reason now that you cry off. I'm a professional soldier: I fight when I have to, and am very glad to get out of it when I havnt to. Youre only an amateur: you think fighting's an amusement.

SERGIUS: You shall hear the reason all the same, my professional. The reason is that it takes two men—real men—men of heart, blood and honor—to make a genuine combat. I could no more fight with you than I could make love to an ugly woman. Youve no magnetism: youre not a man, youre a machine.

BLUNTSCHLI (*apologetically*): Quite true, quite true. I always was that sort of chap. I'm very sorry. But now that youve found that life isnt a farce, but something quite sensible and serious, what further obstacle is there to your happiness?

RAINA (*rising*): You are very solicitous about my happiness and his. Do you forget his new love—Louka? It is not you that he must fight now, but his rival, Nicola.

SERGIUS: Rival!! (*striking his forehead*).

RAINA: Dont you know that theyre engaged?

SERGIUS: Nicola! Are fresh abysses opening? Nicola!!

RAINA (*sarcastically*): A shocking sacrifice, isnt it? such beauty! such intellect! such modesty! wasted on a middle-aged servant man. Really, Sergius, you cannot stand by and allow such a thing. It would be unworthy of your chivalry.

SERGIUS (*losing all self-control*): Viper! Viper! (*He rushes to and fro, raging.*)

BLUNTSCHLI: Look here, Saranoff: youre getting the worst of this.

RAINA (*getting angrier*): Do you realize what he has done, Captain Bluntschli? He has set this girl as a spy on us; and her reward is that he makes love to her.

SERGIUS: False! Monstrous!

RAINA: Monstrous! (*Confronting him*) Do you deny that she told you about Captain Bluntschli being in my room?

SERGIUS: No; but—

RAINA (*interrupting*): Do you deny that you were making love to her when she told you?

SERGIUS: No; but I tell you—

RAINA (*cutting him short contemptuously*): It is unnecessary to tell us anything more. That is quite enough for us. (*She turns away from him and sweeps majestically back to the window.*)

BLUNTSCHLI (*quietly, as* SERGIUS, *in an agony of mortification, sinks on the ottoman, clutching his averted head between his fists*): I told you you were getting the worst of it, Saranoff.

SERGIUS: Tiger cat!

RAINA (*running excitedly to* BLUNTSCHLI): You hear this man calling me names, Captain Bluntschli?

BLUNTSCHLI: What else can he do, dear lady? He must defend himself somehow. Come (*very persuasively*): dont quarrel. What good does it do? (RAINA, *with a gasp, sits down on the ottoman, and after a vain effort to look vexedly at* BLUNTSCHLI, *falls a victim to her sense of humor, and can hardly help laughing.*)

SERGIUS: Engaged to Nicola! (*He rises.*) Ha! ha! (*Going to the stove and standing with his back to it*) Ah well, Bluntschli, you are right to take this huge imposture of a world coolly.

RAINA (*quaintly to* BLUNTSCHLI, *with an intuitive guess at his state of mind*): I daresay you think us a couple of grown-up babies, dont you?

SERGIUS (*grinning savagely*): He does, he does. Swiss civilization nursetending Bulgarian barbarism, eh?

BLUNTSCHLI (*blushing*): Not at all, I assure you. I'm only very glad to get you two quieted. There, there: let's be pleasant and talk it over in a friendly way. Where is this other young lady?

RAINA: Listening at the door, probably.

SERGIUS (*shivering as if a bullet had struck him, and speaking with quiet but deep indignation*): I will prove that that, at least, is a calumny. (*He goes with dignity to the door and opens it. A yell of fury bursts from him as he looks out. He darts into the passage, and returns dragging in* LOUKA, *whom he flings violently against the table, exclaiming*) Judge her, Bluntschli—you, the cool, impartial man: judge the eavesdropper.

(LOUKA *stands her ground, proud and silent.*)

BLUNTSCHLI (*shaking his head*): I musnt judge her. I once listened myself outside a tent when there was a mutiny brewing. It's all a question of the degree of provocation. My life was at stake.

LOUKA: My love was at stake. (SERGIUS *flinches, ashamed of her in spite of himself.*) I am not ashamed.

RAINA (*contemptuously*): Your love! Your curiosity, you mean.

LOUKA (*facing her and retorting her contempt with interest*): My love, stronger than anything you can feel, even for your chocolate cream soldier.

SERGIUS (*with quick suspicion, to* LOUKA): What does that mean?

LOUKA (*fiercely*): It means—

SERGIUS (*interrupting her slightingly*): Oh, I remember: the ice pudding. A paltry taunt, girl!

(MAJOR PETKOFF *enters, in his shirtsleeves.*)

PETKOFF: Excuse my shirtsleeves, gentlemen. Raina: somebody has been wearing that coat of mine: I'll swear it—somebody with bigger shoulders than mine. It's all burst open at the back. Your mother is mending it. I wish she'd make haste. I shall catch cold. (*He looks more attentively at them.*) Is anything the matter?

RAINA: No. (*She sits down at the stove, with a tranquil air.*)

SERGIUS: Oh, no. (*He sits down at the end of the table, as at first.*)

BLUNTSCHLI (*who is already seated*): Nothing, nothing.

PETKOFF (*sitting down on the ottoman in his old place*): Thats all right. (*He notices* LOUKA.) Anything the matter, Louka?

LOUKA: No, sir.

PETKOFF (*genially*): Thats all right. (*He sneezes.*) Go and ask your mistress for my coat, like a good girl, will you? (*She turns to obey; but* NICOLA *enters just then with the coat; and she makes a pretence of having business in the room by taking the little table with the hookah away to the wall near the windows.*)

RAINA (*rising quickly as she sees the coat on* NICOLA's *arm*): Here it is, papa. Give it to me, Nicola; and do you put some more wood on the fire. (*She takes the coat, and brings it to the* MAJOR, *who stands up to put it on.* NICOLA *attends to the fire.*)

PETKOFF (*to* RAINA, *teasing her affectionately*): Aha! Going to be very good to poor old papa just for one day after his return from the wars, eh?

RAINA (*with solemn reproach*): Ah, how can you say that to me, father?

PETKOFF: Well, well, only a joke, little one. Come: give me a kiss. (*She kisses him.*) Now give me the coat.

RAINA: No: I am going to put it on for you. Turn your back. (*He turns his back and feels behind him with his arms for the sleeves. She dexterously takes the photograph from the pocket and throws it on the table before* BLUNTSCHLI, *who covers it with a sheet of paper under the very nose of* SERGIUS, *who looks on amazed, with his suspicions roused in the highest degree. She then helps* PETKOFF *on with his coat.*) There, dear! Now you are comfortable?

PETKOFF: Quite, little love. Thanks. (*He sits down; and* RAINA *returns to her seat near the stove.*) Oh, by the bye, Ive found something funny. Whats the meaning of this? (*He puts his hand into the picked pocket.*) Eh? Hallo! (*He tries the other pocket.*) Well, I could have sworn—! (*Much puzzled, he tries the breast pocket.*) I wonder—(*trying the original pocket.*) Where can it—? (*A light flashes on him. He rises, exclaiming*) Your mother's taken it!

RAINA (*very red*): Taken what?

PETKOFF: Your photograph, with the inscription: "Raina, to her Chocolate Cream Soldier: a souvenir." Now you know theres something more in this than meets the eye; and I'm going to find it out. (*Shouting*) Nicola!

NICOLA (*dropping a log, and turning*): Sir!

PETKOFF: Did you spoil any pastry of Miss Raina's this morning?

NICOLA: You heard Miss Raina say that I did, sir.

PETKOFF: I know that, you idiot. Was it true?

NICOLA: I am sure Miss Raina is incapable of saying anything that is not true, sir.

PETKOFF: Are you? Then I'm not. (*Turning to the others*) Come: do you think I dont see it all? (*He goes to* SERGIUS, *and slaps him on the shoulder.*) Sergius: youre the chocolate cream soldier, arnt you?

SERGIUS (*starting up*): I! A chocolate cream soldier! Certainly not.

PETKOFF: Not! (*He looks at them. They are all very serious and very conscious.*) Do you mean to tell me that Raina sends photographic souvenirs to other men?

SERGIUS (*enigmatically*): The world is not such an innocent place as we used to think, Petkoff.

BLUNTSCHLI (*rising*): It's all right, Major. I'm the chocolate cream soldier. (PETKOFF *and* SERGIUS *are equally astonished.*) The gracious young lady saved my life by giving me chocolate creams when I was starving: shall I ever forget their flavour! My late friend Stolz told you the story at Peerot. I was the fugitive.

PETKOFF: You! (*He gasps.*) Sergius: do you remember how those two women went on this morning when we mentioned it? (SERGIUS *smiles cynically.* PETKOFF *confronts* RAINA *severely.*) Youre a nice young woman, arnt you?

RAINA (*bitterly*): Major Saranoff has changed his mind. And when I wrote that on the photograph, I did not know that Captain Bluntschli was married.

BLUNTSCHLI (*startled into vehement protest*): I'm not married.

RAINA (*with deep reproach*): You said you were.

BLUNTSCHLI: I did not. I positively did not. I never was married in my life.

PETKOFF (*exasperated*): Raina: will you kindly inform me, if I am not asking too much, which of these gentlemen you are engaged to?

RAINA: To neither of them. This young lady (*introducing* LOUKA, *who faces them all proudly*) is the object of Major Saranoff's affections at present.

PETKOFF: Louka! Are you mad, Sergius? Why, this girl's engaged to Nicola.

NICOLA (*coming forward*): I beg your pardon, sir. There is a mistake. Louka is not engaged to me.

PETKOFF: Not engaged to you, you scoundrel! Why, you had twenty-five levas from me on the day of your betrothal; and she had that gilt bracelet from Miss Raina.

NICOLA (*with cool unction*): We gave it out so, sir. But it was only to give Louka protection. She had a soul above her station; and I have been no more than her confidential servant. I intend, as you know, sir, to set up a shop later on in Sofeea; and I look forward to her custom and recommendation should she marry into the nobility. (*He goes out with impressive discretion, leaving them all staring after him.*)

PETKOFF (*breaking the silence*): Well, I am— hm!

SERGIUS: This is either the finest heroism or the most crawling baseness. Which is it, Bluntschli?

BLUNTSCHLI: Never mind whether it's heroism or baseness. Nicola's the ablest man Ive met in Bulgaria. I'll make him manager of a hotel if he can speak French and German.

LOUKA (*suddenly breaking out at* SERGIUS): I have been insulted by everyone here. You set them the example. You owe me an apology. (SERGIUS, *like a repeating clock of which the spring has been touched, immediately begins to fold his arms.*)

BLUNTSCHLI (*before he can speak*): It's no use. He never apologizes.

LOUKA: Not to you, his equal and his enemy. To me, his poor servant, he will not refuse to apologize.

SERGIUS (*approvingly*): You are right. (*He bends his knee in his grandest manner*) Forgive me.

LOUKA: I forgive you. (*She timidly gives him her hand, which he kisses.*) That touch makes me your affianced wife.

SERGIUS (*springing up*): Ah, I forgot that!

LOUKA (*coldly*): You can withdraw if you like.

SERGIUS: Withdraw! Never! You belong to me. (*He puts his arm about her.*)

(CATHERINE *comes in and finds* LOUKA *in* SERGIUS's *arms, with all the rest gazing at them in bewildered astonishment.*)

CATHERINE: What does this mean? (SERGIUS *releases* LOUKA.)

PETKOFF: Well, my dear, it appears that Sergius is going to marry Louka instead of Raina. (*She is about to break out indignantly at him: he stops her by exclaiming testily*) Dont blame me: Ive nothing to do with it. (*He retreats to the stove.*)

CATHERINE: Marry Louka! Sergius: you are bound by your word to us!

SERGIUS (*folding his arms*): Nothing binds me.

BLUNTSCHLI (*much pleased by this piece of common sense*): Saranoff: your hand. My congratulations. These heroics of yours have their practical side after all. (*To* LOUKA) Gracious young lady: the best wishes of a good Republican! (*He kisses her hand, to* RAINA's *great disgust.*)

CATHERINE (*threateningly*): Louka: you have been telling stories.

LOUKA: I have done Raina no harm.

CATHERINE (*haughtily*): Raina! (RAINA *is equally indignant at the liberty.*)

LOUKA: I have a right to call her Raina: she calls me Louka. I told Major Saranoff she would never marry him if the Swiss gentleman came back.

BLUNTSCHLI (*surprised*): Hallo!

LOUKA (*turning to* RAINA): I thought you were fonder of him than of Sergius. You know best whether I was right.

BLUNTSCHLI: What nonsense! I assure you, my dear Major, my dear Madame, the gracious young lady simply saved my life, nothing else. She never cared two straws for me. Why, bless my heart and soul, look at the young lady and look at me. She, rich, young, beautiful, with her imagination full of fairy princes and noble natures and cavalry charges and goodness knows what! And I, a commonplace Swiss soldier who hardly knows what a decent life is after fifteen years of barracks and battles: a vagabond, a man who has spoiled all his chances in life through an incurably romantic disposition, a man—

SERGIUS (*starting as if a needle had pricked him and interrupting* BLUNTSCHLI *in incredulous amazement*): Excuse me, Bluntschli: what did you say had spoiled your chances in life?

BLUNTSCHLI (*promptly*): An incurably romantic disposition. I ran away from home twice when I was a boy. I went into the army instead of into my father's business. I climbed the balcony of this house when a man of sense would have dived into the nearest cellar. I came sneaking back here to have another look at the young lady when any other man of my age would have sent the coat back—

PETKOFF: My coat!

BLUNTSCHLI: Yes: thats the coat I mean—would have sent it back and gone quietly home. Do you suppose I am the sort of fellow a young girl falls in love with? Why, look at our ages! I'm thirty-four; I dont suppose the young lady is much over seventeen. (*This estimate produces a marked sensation, all the rest turning and staring at one another. He proceeds innocently.*) All that adventure which was life or death to me, was only a schoolgirl's game to her—chocolate creams and hide and seek. Heres the proof! (*He takes the photograph from the table.*) Now, I ask you, would a woman who took the affair seriously have sent me this and written on it: "Raina, to her Chocolate Cream Soldier: a souvenir"? (*He exhibits the photograph triumphantly, as if it settled the matter beyond all possibility of refutation.*)

PETKOFF: Thats what I was looking for. How the deuce did it get there?

BLUNTSCHLI (*to* RAINA, *complacently*): I have put everything right, I hope, gracious young lady.

RAINA (*in uncontrollable vexation*): I quite agree with your account of yourself. You are a romantic idiot. (BLUNTSCHLI *is unspeakably taken aback.*) Next time, I hope you will know the difference between a schoolgirl of seventeen and a woman of twenty-three.

BLUNTSCHLI (*stupefied*): Twenty-three! (*She snaps the photograph contemptuously from his hand; tears it across; and throws the pieces at his feet.*)

SERGIUS (*with grim enjoyment of his rival's discomfiture*): Bluntschli: my one last belief is gone. Your sagacity is a fraud, like all the other things. You have less sense than even I have.

BLUNTSCHLI (*overwhelmed*): Twenty-three! Twenty-three!! (*He considers.*) Hm! (*Swiftly making up his mind*) In that case, Major Petkoff, I beg to propose formally to become a suitor for your daughter's hand, in place of Major Saranoff retired.

RAINA: You dare!

BLUNTSCHLI: If you were twenty-three when you said those things to me this afternoon, I shall take them seriously.

CATHERINE (*loftily polite*): I doubt, sir, whether you quite realize either my daughter's position or that of Major Sergius Saranoff, whose place you propose to take. The Petkoffs and the Saranoffs are known as the richest and most important families in the country. Our position is almost historical: we can go back for nearly twenty years.

PETKOFF: Oh, never mind that, Catherine. (*To* BLUNTSCHLI) We should be most happy, Bluntschli, if it were only a question of your position; but hang it, you know, Raina is accustomed to a very comfortable establishment. Sergius keeps twenty horses.

BLUNTSCHLI: But what on earth is the use of twenty horses? Why, it's a circus!

CATHERINE (*severely*): My daughter, sir, is accustomed to a first-rate stable.

RAINA: Hush, mother: youre making me ridiculous.

BLUNTSCHLI: Oh well, if it comes to a question of an establishment, here goes! (*He darts impetuously to the table and seizes the papers in the blue envelope.*) How many horses did you say?

SERGIUS: Twenty, noble Switzer.

BLUNTSCHLI: I have two hundred horses. (*They are amazed.*) How many carriages?

SERGIUS: Three.

BLUNTSCHLI: I have seventy. Twenty-four of them will hold twelve inside, besides two on the box, without counting the driver and conductor. How many tablecloths have you?

SERGIUS: How the deuce do I know?

BLUNTSCHLI: Have you four thousand?

SERGIUS: No.

BLUNTSCHLI: I have. I have nine thousand six hundred pairs of sheets and blankets, with two thousand four hundred eider-down quilts. I have ten thousand knives and forks, and the same quantity of dessert spoons. I have six hundred servants. I have six palatial establishments, besides two livery stables, a tea garden and a private house. I have four medals for distinguished services; I have the rank of an officer and the standing of a gentleman; and I have three native languages. Show me any man in Bulgaria that can offer as much!

PETKOFF (*with childish awe*): Are you Emperor of Switzerland?

BLUNTSCHLI: My rank is the highest known in Switzerland: I am a free citizen.

CATHERINE: Then, Captain Bluntschli, since you are my daughter's choice, I shall not stand in the way of her happiness. (PETKOFF *is about to speak.*) That is Major Petkoff's feeling also.

PETKOFF: Oh, I shall be only too glad. Two hundred horses! Whew!

SERGIUS: What says the lady?

RAINA (*pretending to sulk*): The lady says that he can keep his tablecloths and his omnibuses. I am not here to be sold to the highest bidder.

BLUNTSCHLI: I wont take that answer. I appealed to you as a fugitive, a beggar, and a starving man. You accepted me. You gave me your hand to kiss, your bed to sleep in, and your roof to shelter me—

RAINA (*interrupting him*): I did not give them to the Emperor of Switzerland.

BLUNTSCHLI: Thats just what I say. (*He catches her hand quickly and looks her straight in the face as he adds, with confident mastery*) Now tell us who you did give them to.

RAINA (*succumbing with a shy smile*): To my chocolate cream soldier.

BLUNTSCHLI (*with a boyish laugh of delight*): Thatll do. Thank you. (*He looks at his watch and suddenly becomes businesslike.*) Time's up, Major. Youve managed those regiments so well that youre sure to be asked to get rid of some of the Infantry of the Teemok division. Send them home by way of Lom Palanka. Saranoff: dont get married until I come back: I shall be here punctually at five in the evening on Tuesday fortnight. Gracious ladies—good evening. (*He makes them a military bow, and goes.*)

SERGIUS: What a man! What a man!

ARTHUR MILLER

The Crucible

Arthur Miller (1915–   ) was born to a middle-class Jewish family in the Harlem district of New York. While he was attending the University of Michigan, his talent for playwriting won him the Hopwood Prize for Drama in 1936. He won the Theatre Guild National Award in 1938, the year of his graduation.

In 1945 Miller wrote an ironic novel, *Focus,* about racial prejudice. His first successful play on Broadway was *All My Sons,* 1947, which deals with a father, who, during World War II, uses faulty parts in the airplane equipment that he supplies to the government. Like much of Miller's work, it is critical of a social evil—in this case, war profiteering. *Death of a Salesman,* 1949, has become one of the classics of the American theater. It has won five awards, including the New York Drama Critics' Circle Award and the Pulitzer Prize, and has been performed innumerable times by college drama departments and amateur little-theater groups. *Death of a Salesman* has grown in stature in the nearly two decades since its long Broadway run.

In 1950 Miller wrote an adaptation of Ibsen's *An Enemy of the People;* in 1953 he wrote *The Crucible.* In 1955 two one-act plays were produced under the title *A View from the Bridge,* which again won him the New York Drama Critics' Circle Award and the Pulitzer Prize. He then wrote and helped direct the successful movie *The Misfits,* 1961. Early in 1964 Miller's autobiographical drama *After the Fall* was the first play to be presented by the newly established Repertory Company of Lincoln Center in New York. In December 1964 Miller's play, *Incident at Vichy,* was produced in New York. His work *I Don't Need You Anymore,* 1967, is a collection of short stories that includes "The Misfits," from which the screen play of the movie was developed. Miller's most recent play, *The American Clock,* 1980, was not a success on Broadway.

A reader survey report in the London *Observer* in 1966 put *Death of a Salesman* and *The Crucible* on a list of twenty plays written since 1900 that show the main trends of the theater in this century.

The Crucible deals with that dark period of the Salem witch trials in seventeenth-century New England. Miller saw the so-called witch hunting of the post-World War II years, led by Senator Joseph McCarthy, as similar to the hysterical forces at work in Salem. The play is also a psychological and social dramatization of people destroyed by prejudice, guilt, and greed.

CAST OF CHARACTERS

REVEREND PARRIS   GILES COREY
BETTY PARRIS   REVEREND JOHN HALE
TITUBA   ELIZABETH PROCTOR
ABIGAIL WILLIAMS   FRANCIS NURSE
SUSANNA WALCOTT   EZEKIEL CHEEVER
MRS. ANN PUTNAM   MARSHAL HERRICK
THOMAS PUTNAM   JUDGE HATHORNE
MERCY LEWIS   DEPUTY GOVERNOR
MARY WARREN   DANFORTH
JOHN PROCTOR   SARAH GOOD
REBECCA NURSE   HOPKINS

A NOTE ON THE HISTORICAL ACCURACY OF THIS PLAY

This play is not history in the sense in which the word is used by the academic historian. Dramatic purposes have sometimes required many characters to be fused into one; the number of girls involved in the "crying-out" has been reduced; Abigail's age has been raised; while there were several judges of almost equal authority, I have symbolized them all in Hathorne and Danforth. However, I believe that the reader will discover here the essential nature of one of the strangest and most awful chapters in human history. The fate of each character is exactly that of his historical model, and there is no one in the drama who did not play a similar—and in some cases exactly the same—role in history.

As for the characters of the persons, little is known about most of them excepting what may be surmised from a few letters, the trial record, certain broadsides written at the time, and references to their conduct in sources of varying reliability. They may therefore be taken as crea-

tions of my own, drawn to the best of my ability in conformity with their known behavior, except as indicated in the commentary I have written for this text.

ACT ONE
(AN OVERTURE)

A small upper bedroom in the home of REVEREND SAMUEL PARRIS, *Salem, Massachusetts, in the spring of the year 1692.*

There is a narrow window at the left. Through its leaded panes the morning sunlight streams. A candle still burns near the bed, which is at the right. A chest, a chair, and a small table are the other furnishings. At the back a door opens on the landing of the stairway to the ground floor. The room gives off an air of clean spareness. The roof rafters are exposed, and the wood colors are raw and unmellowed.

As the curtain rises, REVEREND PARRIS *is discovered kneeling beside the bed, evidently in prayer. His daughter,* BETTY PARRIS, *aged ten, is lying on the bed, inert.*

At the time of these events Parris was in his middle forties. In history he cut a villainous path, and there is very little good to be said for him. He believed he was being persecuted wherever he went, despite his best efforts to win people and God to his side. In meeting, he felt insulted if someone rose to shut the door without first asking his permission. He was a widower with no interest in children, or talent with them. He regarded them as young adults, and until this strange crisis he, like the rest of Salem, never conceived that the children were anything but thankful for being permitted to walk straight, eyes slightly lowered, arms at the sides, and mouths shut until bidden to speak.

His house stood in the "town"—but we today would hardly call it a village. The meeting house was nearby, and from this point outward—toward the bay or inland—there were a few small-windowed, dark houses snuggling against the raw Massachusetts winter. Salem had been established hardly forty years before. To the European world the whole province was a barbaric frontier inhabited by a sect of fanatics who, nevertheless, were shipping out products of slowly increasing quantity and value.

No one can really know what their lives were like. They had no novelists—and would not have permitted anyone to read a novel if one were handy. Their creed forbade anything resembling a theater or "vain enjoyment." They did not celebrate Christmas, and a holiday from work meant only that they must concentrate even more upon prayer.

Which is not to say that nothing broke into this strict and somber way of life. When a new farmhouse was built, friends assembled to "raise the roof," and there would be special foods cooked and probably some potent cider passed around. There was a good supply of ne'er-do-wells in Salem, who dallied at the shovelboard in Bridget Bishop's tavern. Probably more than the creed, hard work kept the morals of the place from spoiling, for the people were forced to fight the land like heroes for every grain of corn, and no man had very much time for fooling around.

That there were some jokers, however, is indicated by the practice of appointing a two-man patrol whose duty was to "walk forth in the time of God's worship to take notice of such as either lye about the meeting house, without attending to the word and ordinances, or that lye at home or in the fields without giving good account thereof, and to take the names of such persons, and to present them to the magistrates, whereby they may be accordingly proceeded against." This predilection for minding other people's business was time-honored among the people of Salem, and it undoubtedly created many of the suspicions which were to feed the coming madness. It was also, in my opinion, one of the things that a John Proctor would rebel against, for the time of the armed camp had almost passed, and since the country was reasonably—although not

wholly—safe, the old disciplines were beginning to rankle. But, as in all such matters, the issue was not clearcut, for danger was still a possibility, and in unity still lay the best promise of safety.

The edge of the wilderness was close by. The American continent stretched endlessly west, and it was full of mystery for them. It stood, dark and threatening, over their shoulders night and day, for out of it Indian tribes marauded from time to time, and Reverend Parris had parishioners who had lost relatives to these heathen.

The parochial snobbery of these people was partly responsible for their failure to convert the Indians. Probably they also preferred to take land from heathens rather than from fellow Christians. At any rate, very few Indians were converted, and the Salem folk believed that the virgin forest was the Devil's last preserve, his home base and the citadel of his final stand. To the best of their knowledge the American forest was the last place on earth that was not paying homage to God.

For these reasons, among others, they carried about an air of innate resistance, even of persecution. Their fathers had, of course, been persecuted in England. So now they and their church found it necessary to deny any other sect its freedom, lest their New Jerusalem be defiled and corrupted by wrong ways and deceitful ideas.

They believed, in short, that they held in their steady hands the candle that would light the world. We have inherited this belief, and it has helped and hurt us. It helped them with the discipline it gave them. They were a dedicated folk, by and large, and they had to be to survive the life they had chosen or been born into in this country.

The proof of their belief's value to them may be taken from the opposite character of the first Jamestown settlement, farther south, in Virginia. The Englishmen who landed there were motivated mainly by a hunt for profit. They had thought to pick off the wealth of the new country and then return rich to England. They were a band of individualists, and a much more ingratiating group than the Massachusetts men. But Virginia destroyed them. Massachusetts tried to kill off the Puritans, but they combined; they set up a communal society which, in the beginning, was little more than an armed camp with an autocratic and very devoted leadership. It was, however, an autocracy by consent, for they were united from top to bottom by a commonly held ideology whose perpetuation was the reason and justification for all their sufferings. So their self-denial, their purposefulness, their suspicion of all vain pursuits, their hard-handed justice, were altogether perfect instruments for the conquest of this space so antagonistic to man.

But the people of Salem in 1692 were not quite the dedicated folk that arrived on the *Mayflower.* A vast differentiation had taken place, and in their own time a revolution had unseated the royal government and substituted a junta which was at this moment in power. The times, to their eyes, must have been out of joint, and to the common folk must have seemed as insoluble and complicated as do ours today. It is not hard to see how easily many could have been led to believe that the time of confusion had been brought upon them by deep and dark-ling forces. No hint of such speculation appears on the court record, but social disorder in any age breeds such mystical suspicions, and when, as in Salem, wonders are brought forth from below the social surface, it is too much to expect people to hold back very long from laying on the victims with all the force of their frustrations.

The Salem tragedy, which is about to begin in these pages, developed from a paradox. It is a paradox in whose grip we still live, and there is no prospect yet that we will discover its resolution. Simply, it was this: for good purposes, even high purposes, the people of Salem developed a theocracy, a combine of state and religious power whose function was to keep the community together, and to prevent any kind of disunity that might open it to destruction by material or ideological enemies. It was forged for a necessary purpose and accomplished that purpose. But all organization is and must be grounded on the idea of exclusion and prohibition, just as two objects cannot occupy the same space. Evidently the time came in New England when the repressions of order were heavier than seemed warranted by the dangers against which the order was organized. The witch-hunt was a perverse manifestation of the panic which set in among all classes when the balance began to turn toward greater individual freedom.

When one rises above the individual villainy displayed, one can only pity them all, just as we shall be pitied someday. It is still impossible for man to organize his social life without repres-sions, and the balance has yet to be struck between order and freedom.

The witch-hunt was not, however, a mere repression. It was also, and as importantly, a long overdue opportunity for everyone so inclined to express publicly his guilt and sins, under the cover of accusations against the victims. It suddenly became possible—and patriotic and holy—for a man to say that Martha Corey had come into his bedroom at night, and that, while his wife was sleeping at his side, Martha laid herself down on his chest and "nearly suffocated him." Of course it was her spirit only, but his satisfaction at confessing himself was no lighter than if it had been Martha herself. One could not ordinarily speak such things in public.

Long-held hatreds of neighbors could now be openly expressed, and vengeance taken, despite the Bible's charitable injunctions. Land-lust, which had been expressed before by constant bickering over boundaries and deeds, could now be elevated to the arena of morality; one could cry witch against one's neighbor and feel perfectly justified in the bargain. Old scores could be settled on a plane of heavenly combat between Lucifer and the Lord; suspicions and the envy of the miserable toward the happy could and did burst out in the general revenge.

REVEREND PARRIS *is praying now, and, though we cannot hear his words, a sense of his confusion hangs about him. He mumbles, then seems about to weep; then he weeps, then prays again; but his daughter does not stir on the bed.*

The door opens, and his Negro slave enters. TITUBA *is in her forties.* PARRIS *brought her with him from Barbados, where he spent some years as a merchant before entering the ministry. She enters as one does who can no longer bear to be barred from the sight of her beloved, but she is also very frightened because her slave sense has warned her that, as always, trouble in this house eventually lands on her back.*

TITUBA (*already taking a step backward*): My Betty be hearty soon?

PARRIS: Out of here!

TITUBA (*backing to the door*): My Betty not goin' die . . .

PARRIS (*scrambling to his feet in a fury*): Out of my sight! (*She is gone.*) Out of my—(*He is overcome with sobs. He clamps his teeth against*

*them and closes the door and leans against it,
exhausted.)* Oh, my God! God help me! (*Quaking
with fear, mumbling to himself through his sobs,
he goes to the bed and gently takes* BETTY's *hand.*)
Betty. Child. Dear child. Will you wake, will you
open up your eyes! Betty, little one . . .

(*He is bending to kneel again when his niece,*
ABIGAIL WILLIAMS, *seventeen, enters—a strikingly beautiful girl, an orphan, with an endless
capacity for dissembling. Now she is all worry
and apprehension and propriety.*)

ABIGAIL: Uncle? (*He looks to her.*) Susanna
Walcott's here from Doctor Griggs.

PARRIS: Oh? Let her come, let her come.

ABIGAIL (*leaning out the door to call to*
SUSANNA, *who is down the hall a few steps*):
Come in, Susanna.

(SUSANNA WALCOTT, *a little younger than*
ABIGAIL, *a nervous, hurried girl, enters.*)

PARRIS (*eagerly*):   What does the doctor say,
child?

SUSANNA (*craning around* PARRIS *to get a look
at* BETTY):   He bid me come and tell you,
reverend sir, that he cannot discover no medicine
for it in his books.

PARRIS: Then he must search on.

SUSANNA: Aye, sir, he have been searchin' his
books since he left you, sir. But he bid me tell
you, that you might look to unnatural things for
the cause of it.

PARRIS (*his eyes going wide*):   No—no. There
be no unnatural cause here. Tell him I have sent
for Reverend Hale of Beverly, and Mr. Hale will
surely confirm that. Let him look to medicine
and put out all thought of unnatural causes here.
There be none.

SUSANNA: Aye, sir. He bid me tell you. (*She
turns to go.*)

ABIGAIL: Speak nothin' of it in the village,
Susanna.

PARRIS: Go directly home and speak nothing
of unnatural causes.

SUSANNA: Aye, sir. I pray for her. (*She goes
out.*)

ABIGAIL: Uncle, the rumor of witchcraft is all
about; I think you'd best go down and deny it
yourself. The parlor's packed with people, sir.
I'll sit with her.

PARRIS (*pressed, turns on her*):   And what shall
I say to them? That my daughter and my
niece I discovered dancing like heathen in the
forest?

ABIGAIL: Uncle, we did dance; let you tell
them I confessed it—and I'll be whipped if I
must be. But they're speakin' of witchcraft.
Betty's not witched.

PARRIS: Abigail, I cannot go before the congregation when I know you have not opened
with me. What did you do with her in the
forest?

ABIGAIL: We did dance, uncle, and when you
leaped out of the bush so suddenly, Betty was
frightened and then she fainted. And there's the
whole of it.

PARRIS: Child. Sit you down.

ABIGAIL (*quavering, as she sits*):   I would
never hurt Betty. I love her dearly.

PARRIS: Now look you, child, your punishment will come in its time. But if you trafficked
with spirits in the forest I must know it now,
for surely my enemies will, and they will ruin
me with it.

ABIGAIL: But we never conjured spirits.

PARRIS: Then why can she not move herself
since midnight? This child is desperate! (ABIGAIL
lowers her eyes.) It must come out—my enemies
will bring it out. Let me know what you done
there. Abigail, do you understand that I have
many enemies?

ABIGAIL: I have heard of it, uncle.

PARRIS: There is a faction that is sworn to
drive me from my pulpit. Do you understand
that?

ABIGAIL: I think so, sir.

PARRIS: Now then, in the midst of such disruption, my own household is discovered to be
the very center of some obscene practice.
Abominations are done in the forest—

ABIGAIL: It were sport, uncle!

PARRIS (*pointing at* BETTY):   You call this
sport? (*She lowers her eyes. He pleads.*) Abigail,
if you know something that may help the doctor,
for God's sake tell it to me. (*She is silent.*) I saw
Tituba waving her arms over the fire when I
came on you. Why was she doing that? And I
heard a screeching and gibberish coming from
her mouth. She were swaying like a dumb beast
over that fire!

ABIGAIL: She always sings her Barbados songs,
and we dance.

PARRIS: I cannot blink what I saw, Abigail,
for my enemies will not blink it. I saw a dress
lying on the grass.

ABIGAIL (*innocently*):   A dress?

PARRIS (*It is very hard to say.*): Aye, a dress. And I thought I saw—someone naked running through the trees!

ABIGAIL (*in terror*): No one was naked! You mistake yourself, uncle!

PARRIS (*with anger*): I saw it! (*He moves from her. Then, resolved*) Now tell me true, Abigail. And I pray you feel the weight of truth upon you, for now my ministry's at stake, my ministry and perhaps your cousin's life. Whatever abomination you have done, give me all of it now, for I dare not be taken unaware when I go before them down there.

ABIGAIL: There is nothin' more. I swear it, uncle.

PARRIS (*studies her, then nods, half convinced*): Abigail, I have fought here three long years to bend these stiff-necked people to me, and now, just now when some good respect is rising for me in the parish, you compromise my very character. I have given you a home, child, I have put clothes upon your back—now give me upright answer. Your name in the town—it is entirely white, is it not?

ABIGAIL (*with an edge of resentment*): Why, I am sure it is, sir. There be no blush about my name.

PARRIS (*to the point*): Abigail, is there any other cause than you have told me, for your being discharged from Goody Proctor's service? I have heard it said, and I tell you as I heard it, that she comes so rarely to the church this year for she will not sit so close to something soiled. What signified that remark?

ABIGAIL: She hates me, uncle, she must, for I would not be her slave. It's a bitter woman, a lying, cold, sniveling woman, and I will not work for such a woman!

PARRIS: She may be. And yet it has troubled me that you are now seven month out of their house, and in all this time no other family has ever called for your service.

ABIGAIL: They want slaves, not such as I. Let them send to Barbados for that. I will not black my face for any of them! (*With ill-concealed resentment at him*) Do you begrudge my bed, uncle?

PARRIS: No—no.

ABIGAIL (*in a temper*): My name is good in the village! I will not have it said my name is soiled! Goody Proctor is a gossiping liar!

(*Enter* MRS. ANN PUTNAM. *She is a twisted soul of forty-five, a death-ridden woman, haunted by dreams.*)

PARRIS (*as soon as the door begins to open*): No—no, I cannot have anyone. (*He sees her, and a certain deference springs into him, although his worry remains.*) Why, Goody Putnam, come in.

MRS. PUTNAM (*full of breath, shiny-eyed*): It is a marvel. It is surely a stroke of hell upon you.

PARRIS: No, Goody Putnam, it is—

MRS. PUTNAM (*glancing at* BETTY): How high did she fly, how high?

PARRIS: No, no, she never flew—

MRS. PUTNAM (*very pleased with it*): Why, it's sure she did. Mr. Collins saw her goin' over Ingersoll's barn, and come down light as a bird, he says!

PARRIS: Now, look you, Goody Putnam, she never—(*Enter* THOMAS PUTNAM, *a well-to-do, hard-handed landowner, near fifty.*) Oh, good morning, Mr. Putnam.

PUTNAM: It is a providence the thing is out now! It is a providence. (*He goes directly to the bed.*)

PARRIS: What's out, sir, what's—?

(MRS. PUTNAM *goes to the bed.*)

PUTNAM (*looking down at Betty*): Why, *her* eyes is closed! Look you, Ann.

MRS. PUTNAM: Why, that's strange. (*To Parris*) Ours is open.

PARRIS (*shocked*): Your Ruth is sick?

MRS. PUTNAM (*with vicious certainty*): I'd not call it sick; the Devil's touch is heavier than sick. It's death, y'know, it's death drivin' into them, forked and hoofed.

PARRIS: Oh, pray not! Why, how does Ruth ail?

MRS. PUTNAM: She ails as she must—she never waked this morning, but her eyes open and she walks, and hears naught, sees naught, and cannot eat. Her soul is taken, surely.

(PARRIS *is struck.*)

PUTNAM (*as though for further details*): They say you've sent for Reverend Hale of Beverly?

PARRIS (*with dwindling conviction now*): A precaution only. He has much experience in all demonic arts, and I—

MRS. PUTNAM: He has indeed; and found a witch in Beverly last year, and let you remember that.

PARRIS: Now, Goody Ann, they only thought

that were a witch, and I am certain there be no element of witchcraft here.

PUTNAM: No witchcraft! Now look you, Mr. Parris—

PARRIS: Thomas, Thomas, I pray you, leap not to witchcraft. I know that you—you least of all, Thomas, would ever wish so disastrous a charge laid upon me. We cannot leap to witchcraft. They will howl me out of Salem for such corruption in my house.

A word about Thomas Putnam. He was a man with many grievances, at least one of which appears justified. Some time before, his wife's brother-in-law, James Bayley, had been turned down as minister at Salem. Bayley had all the qualifications, and a two-thirds vote into the bargain, but a faction stopped his acceptance, for reasons that are not clear.

Thomas Putnam was the eldest son of the richest man in the village. He had fought the Indians at Narragansett, and was deeply interested in parish affairs. He undoubtedly felt it poor payment that the village should so blatantly disregard his candidate for one of its more important offices, especially since he regarded himself as the intellectual superior of most of the people around him.

His vindictive nature was demonstrated long before the witchcraft began. Another former Salem minister, George Burroughs, had had to borrow money to pay for his wife's funeral, and, since the parish was remiss in his salary, he was soon bankrupt. Thomas and his brother John had Burroughs jailed for debts the man did not owe. The incident is important only in that Burroughs succeeded in becoming minister where Bayley, Thomas Putnam's brother-in-law, had been rejected; the motif of resentment is clear here. Thomas Putnam felt that his own name and the honor of his family had been smirched by the village, and he meant to right matters however he could.

Another reason to believe him a deeply embittered man was his attempt to break his father's will, which left a disproportionate amount to a stepbrother. As with every other public cause in which he tried to force his way, he failed in this.

So it is not surprising to find that so many accusations against people are in the handwriting of Thomas Putnam, or that his name is so often found as a witness corroborating the supernatural testimony, or that his daughter led the crying-out at the most opportune junctures of the trials, especially when—But we'll speak of that when we come to it.

PUTNAM (*At the moment he is intent upon getting* PARRIS, *for whom he has only contempt, to move toward the abyss.*): Mr. Parris, I have taken your part in all contention here, and I would continue; but I cannot if you hold back in this. There are hurtful, vengeful spirits layin' hands on these children.

PARRIS: But, Thomas, you cannot—

PUTNAM: Ann! Tell Mr. Parris what you have done.

MRS. PUTNAM: Reverend Parris, I have laid seven babies unbaptized in the earth. Believe me, sir, you never saw more hearty babies born. And yet, each would wither in my arms the very night of their birth. I have spoke nothin', but my heart has clamored intimations. And now, this year, my Ruth, my only—I see her turning strange. A secret child she has become this year, and shrivels like a sucking mouth were pullin' on her life too. And so I thought to send her to your Tituba—

PARRIS: To Tituba! What may Tituba—?

MRS. PUTNAM: Tituba knows how to speak to the dead, Mr. Parris.

PARRIS: Goody Ann, it is a formidable sin to conjure up the dead!

MRS. PUTNAM: I take it on my soul, but who else may surely tell us what person murdered my babies?

PARRIS (*horrified*): Woman!

MRS. PUTNAM: They were murdered, Mr. Parris! And mark this proof! Mark it! Last night my Ruth were ever so close to their little spirits; I know it, sir. For how else is she struck dumb now except some power of darkness would stop her mouth? It is a marvelous sign, Mr. Parris!

PUTNAM: Don't you understand it, sir? There is a murdering witch among us, bound to keep herself in the dark. (PARRIS *turns to* BETTY, *a frantic terror rising in him.*) Let your names make of it what they will, you cannot blink it more.

PARRIS (*to* ABIGAIL): Then you were conjuring spirits last night.

ABIGAIL (*whispering*): Not I, sir—Tituba and Ruth.

PARRIS (*turns now, with new fear, and goes to*

BETTY, *looks down at her, and then, gazing off*): Oh, Abigail, what proper payment for my charity! Now I am undone.

PUTNAM: You are not undone! Let you take hold here. Wait for no one to charge you—declare it yourself. You have discovered witchcraft—

PARRIS: In my house? In my house, Thomas? They will topple me with this! They will make of it a—

(*Enter* MERCY LEWIS, *the* PUTNAMS' *servant, a fat, sly, merciless girl of eighteen.*)

MERCY: Your pardons. I only thought to see how Betty is.

PUTNAM: Why aren't you home? Who's with Ruth?

MERCY: Her grandma come. She's improved a little, I think—she give a powerful sneeze before.

MRS. PUTNAM: Ah, there's a sign of life!

MERCY: I'd fear no more, Goody Putnam. It were a grand sneeze; another like it will shake her wits together, I'm sure. (*She goes to the bed to look.*)

PARRIS: Will you leave me now, Thomas? I would pray a while alone.

ABIGAIL: Uncle, you've prayed since midnight. Why do you not go down and—

PARRIS: No—no. (*To* PUTNAM) I have no answer for that crowd. I'll wait till Mr. Hale arrives. (*To get* MRS. PUTNAM *to leave*) If you will, Goody Ann . . .

PUTNAM: Now look you, sir. Let you strike out against the Devil, and the village will bless you for it! Come down, speak to them—pray with them. They're thirsting for your word, Mister! Surely you'll pray with them.

PARRIS (*swayed*): I'll lead them in a psalm, but let you say nothing of witchcraft yet. I will not discuss it. The cause is yet unknown. I have had enough contention since I came; I want no more.

MRS. PUTNAM: Mercy, you go home to Ruth, d'y'hear?

MERCY: Aye, mum.

(MRS. PUTNAM *goes out.*)

PARRIS (*to* ABIGAIL): If she starts for the window, cry for me at once.

ABIGAIL: I will, uncle.

PARRIS (*to* PUTNAM): There is a terrible power in her arms today. (*He goes out with* PUTNAM.)

ABIGAIL (*with hushed trepidation*): How is Ruth sick?

MERCY: It's weirdish, I know not—she seems to walk like a dead one since last night.

ABIGAIL (*turns at once and goes to* BETTY, *and now, with fear in her voice*): Betty? (BETTY *doesn't move. She shakes her.*) Now stop this! Betty! Sit up now!

(BETTY *doesn't stir.* MERCY *comes over.*)

MERCY: Have you tried beatin' her? I gave Ruth a good one and it waked her for a minute. Here, let me have her.

ABIGAIL (*holding* MERCY *back*): No, he'll be comin' up. Listen, now; if they be questioning us, tell them we danced—I told him as much already.

MERCY: Aye. And what more?

ABIGAIL: He knows Tituba conjured Ruth's sisters to come out of the grave.

MERCY: And what more?

ABIGAIL: He saw you naked.

MERCY (*clapping her hands together with a frightened laugh*): Oh, Jesus!

(*Enter* MARY WARREN, *breathless. She is seventeen, a subservient, naive, lonely girl.*)

MARY WARREN: What'll we do? The village is out! I just come from the farm; the whole country's talkin' witchcraft! They'll be callin' us witches, Abby!

MERCY (*pointing and looking at* MARY WARREN): She means to tell, I know it.

MARY WARREN: Abby, we've got to tell. Witchery's a hangin' error, a hangin' like they done in Boston two year ago! We must tell the truth, Abby! You'll only be whipped for dancin', and the other things!

ABIGAIL: Oh, *we'll* be whipped!

MARY WARREN: I never done none of it, Abby. I only looked!

MERCY (*moving menacingly toward* MARY): Oh, you're a great one for lookin', aren't you, Mary Warren? What a grand peeping courage you have!

(BETTY, *on the bed, whimpers.* ABIGAIL *turns to her at once.*)

ABIGAIL: Betty? (*She goes to* BETTY.) Now, Betty, dear, wake up now. It's Abigail. (*She sits* BETTY *up and furiously shakes her.*) I'll beat you, Betty! (BETTY *whimpers.*) My, you seem improving. I talked to your papa and I told him everything. So there's nothing to—

BETTY (*darts off the bed, frightened of* ABIGAIL,

and flattens herself against the wall): I want my mama!

ABIGAIL (*with alarm, as she cautiously approaches* BETTY): What ails you, Betty? Your mama's dead and buried.

BETTY: I'll fly to Mama. Let me fly! (*She raises her arms as though to fly, and streaks for the window, gets one leg out.*)

ABIGAIL (*pulling her away from the window*): I told him everything; he knows now, he knows everything we—

BETTY: You drank blood, Abby! You didn't tell him that!

ABIGAIL: Betty, you never say that again! You will never—

BETTY: You did, you did! You drank a charm to kill John Proctor's wife! You drank a charm to kill Goody Proctor!

ABIGAIL (*smashes her across the face*): Shut it! Now shut it!

BETTY (*collapsing on the bed*) Mama, Mama! (*She dissolves into sobs.*)

ABIGAIL: Now look you. All of you. We danced. And Tituba conjured Ruth Putnam's dead sisters. And that is all. And mark this. Let either of you breathe a word, or the edge of a word, about the other things, and I will come to you in the black of some terrible night and I will bring a pointy reckoning that will shudder you. And you know I can do it; I saw Indians smash my dear parents' heads on the pillow next to mine, and I have seen some reddish work done at night, and I can make you wish you had never seen the sun go down! (*She goes to* BETTY *and roughly sits her up.*) Now, you—sit up and stop this!

(*But* BETTY *collapses in her hands and lies inert on the bed.*)

MARY WARREN (*with hysterical fright*): What's got her? (ABIGAIL *stares in fright at* BETTY.) Abby, she's going to die! It's a sin to conjure, and we—

ABIGAIL (*starting for* MARY): I say shut it, Mary Warren!

(*Enter* JOHN PROCTOR. *On seeing him,* MARY WARREN *leaps in fright.*)

Proctor was a farmer in his middle thirties. He need not have been a partisan of any faction in the town, but there is evidence to suggest that he had a sharp and biting way with hypocrites. He was the kind of man—powerful of body, even-tempered, and not easily led—who cannot refuse support to partisans without drawing their deepest resentment. In Proctor's presence a fool felt his foolishness instantly—and a Proctor is always marked for calumny therefore.

But as we shall see, the steady manner he displays does not spring from an untroubled soul. He is a sinner, a sinner not only against the moral fashion of the time, but against his own vision of decent conduct. These people had no ritual for the washing away of sins. It is another trait we inherited from them, and it has helped to discipline us as well as to breed hypocrisy among us. Proctor, respected and even feared in Salem, has come to regard himself as a kind of fraud. But no hint of this has yet appeared on the surface, and as he enters from the crowded parlor below it is a man in his prime we see, with a quiet confidence and an unexpressed, hidden force. Mary Warren, his servant, can barely speak for embarrassment and fear.

MARY WARREN: Oh! I'm just going home, Mr. Proctor.

PROCTOR: Be you foolish, Mary Warren? Be you deaf? I forbid you leave the house, did I not? Why shall I pay you? I am looking for you more often than my cows!

MARY WARREN: I only come to see the great doings in the world.

PROCTOR: I'll show you a great doin' on your arse one of these days. Now get you home; my wife is waitin' with your work! (*Trying to retain a shred of dignity, she goes slowly out.*)

MERCY LEWIS (*both afraid of him and strangely titillated*): I'd best be off. I have my Ruth to watch. Good morning, Mr. Proctor.

(MERCY *sidles out. Since* PROCTOR'S *entrance,* ABIGAIL *has stood as though on tiptoe, absorbing his presence, wide-eyed. He glances at her then goes to* BETTY *on the bed.*)

ABIGAIL: Gad. I'd almost forgot how strong you are, John Proctor!

PROCTOR (*looking at* ABIGAIL *now, the faintest suggestion of a knowing smile on his face*): What's this mischief here?

ABIGAIL (*with a nervous laugh*): Oh, she's only gone silly somehow.

PROCTOR: The road past my house is a pilgrimage to Salem all morning. The town's mumbling witchcraft.

ABIGAIL: Oh, posh! (*Winningly she comes a little closer, with a confidential, wicked air.*) We were dancin' in the woods last night, and my uncle leaped in on us. She took fright, is all.

PROCTOR (*his smile widening*): Ah, you're wicked yet, aren't y'! (*A thrill of expectant laughter escapes her, and she dares come closer, feverishly looking into his eyes.*) You'll be clapped in the stocks before you're twenty.

(*He takes a step to go, and she springs into his path.*)

ABIGAIL: Give me a word, John. A soft word. (*Her concentrated desire destroys his smile.*)

PROCTOR: No, no, Abby. That's done with.

ABIGAIL (*tauntingly*): You come five mile to see a silly girl fly? I know you better.

PROCTOR (*setting her firmly out of his path*): I come to see what mischief your uncle's brewin' now. (*With final emphasis*) Put it out of mind, Abby.

ABIGAIL (*grasping his hand before he can release her*): John—I am waitin' for you every night.

PROCTOR: Abby, I never give you hope to wait for me.

ABIGAIL (*now beginning to anger—she can't believe it*): I have something better than hope, I think!

PROCTOR: Abby, you'll put it out of mind. I'll not be comin' for you more.

ABIGAIL: You're surely sportin' with me.

PROCTOR: You know me better.

ABIGAIL: I know how you clutched my back behind your house and sweated like a stallion whenever I come near! Or did I dream that? It's she put me out, you cannot pretend it were you. I saw your face when she put me out, and you loved me then and you do now!

PROCTOR: Abby, that's a wild thing to say—

ABIGAIL: A wild thing may say wild things. But not so wild, I think. I have seen you since she put me out; I have seen you nights.

PROCTOR: I have hardly stepped off my farm this seven-month.

ABIGAIL: I have a sense for heat, John, and yours has drawn me to my window, and I have seen you looking up, burning in your loneliness. Do you tell me you've never looked up at my window?

PROCTOR: I may have looked up.

ABIGAIL (*now softening*): And you must. You are no wintry man. I know you, John. I *know* you. (*She is weeping.*) I cannot sleep for dreamin'; I cannot dream but I wake and walk about the house as though I'd find you comin' through some door. (*She clutches him desperately.*)

PROCTOR (*gently pressing her from him, with great sympathy but firmly*): Child—

ABIGAIL (*with a flash of anger*): How do you call me child!

PROCTOR: Abby, I think of you softly from time to time. But I will cut off my hand before I'll ever reach for you again. Wipe it out of mind. We never touched, Abby.

ABIGAIL: Aye, but we did.

PROCTOR: Aye, but we did not.

ABIGAIL (*with a bitter anger*): Oh, I marvel how such a strong man may let such a sickly wife be—

PROCTOR (*angered—at himself as well*): You'll speak nothin' of Elizabeth!

ABIGAIL: She is blackening my name in the village! She is telling lies about me! She is a cold, sniveling woman, and you bend to her! Let her turn you like a—

PROCTOR (*shaking her*): Do you look for whippin'?

(*A psalm is heard being sung below.*)

ABIGAIL (*in tears*): I look for John Proctor that took me from my sleep and put knowledge in my heart! I never knew what pretense Salem was, I never knew the lying lessons I was taught by all these Christian women and their covenanted men! And now you bid me tear the light out of my eyes? I will not, I cannot! You loved me, John Proctor, and whatever sin it is, you love me yet! (*He turns abruptly to go out. She rushes to him.*) John, pity me, pity me!

(*The words "going up to Jesus" are heard in the psalm, and* BETTY *claps her ears suddenly and whines loudly.*)

ABIGAIL: Betty? (*She hurries to* BETTY, *who is now sitting up and screaming.* PROCTOR *goes to* BETTY *as* ABIGAIL *is trying to pull her hands down, calling "Betty!"*)

PROCTOR (*growing unnerved*): What's she doing? Girl, what ails you? Stop that wailing!

(*The singing has stopped in the midst of this, and now* PARRIS *rushes in.*)

PARRIS: What happened? What are you doing to her? Betty! (*He rushes to the bed, crying, "Betty, Betty!"* MRS. PUTNAM *enters, feverish with curiosity, and with her* THOMAS PUTNAM *and* MERCY LEWIS. PARRIS, *at the bed, keeps lightly slapping* BETTY's *face, while she moans and tries to get up.*)

ABIGAIL: She heard you singin' and suddenly she's up and screamin'.

MRS. PUTNAM: The psalm! The psalm! She cannot bear to hear the Lord's name!

PARRIS: No, God forbid. Mercy, run to the doctor! Tell him what's happened here! (MERCY LEWIS *rushes out.*)

MRS. PUTNAM: Mark it for a sign, mark it! (REBECCA NURSE, *seventy-two, enters. She is white-haired, leaning upon her walking-stick.*)

PUTNAM (*pointing at the whimpering* BETTY): That is a notorious sign of witchcraft afoot, Goody Nurse, a prodigious sign!

MRS. PUTNAM: My mother told me that! When they cannot bear to hear the name of—

PARRIS (*trembling*): Rebecca, Rebecca, go to her, we're lost. She suddenly cannot bear to hear the Lord's—

(GILES COREY, *eighty-three, enters. He is knotted with muscle, canny, inquisitive, and still powerful.*)

REBECCA: There is hard sickness here, Giles Cory, so please to keep the quiet.

GILES: I've not said a word. No one here can testify I've said a word. Is she going to fly again? I hear she flies.

PUTNAM: Man, be quiet now!

(*Everything is quiet.* REBECCA *walks across the room to the bed. Gentleness exudes from her.* BETTY *is quietly whimpering, eyes shut.* REBECCA *simply stands over the child, who gradually quiets.*)

And while they are so absorbed, we may put a word in for Rebecca. Rebecca was the wife of Francis Nurse, who, from all accounts, was one of those men for whom both sides of the argument had to have respect. He was called upon to arbitrate disputes as though he were an unofficial judge, and Rebecca also enjoyed the high opinion most people had for him. By the time of the delusion, they had three hundred acres, and their children were settled in separate homesteads within the same estate. However, Francis had originally rented the land, and one theory has it that, as he gradually paid for it and raised his social status, there were those who resented his rise.

Another suggestion to explain the systematic campaign against Rebecca, and inferentially against Francis, is the land war he fought with his neighbors, one of whom was a Putnam. This squabble grew to the proportions of a battle in the woods between partisans of both sides, and it is said to have lasted for two days. As for Rebecca herself, the general opinion of her character was so high that to explain how anyone dared cry her out for a witch—and more, how adults could bring themselves to lay hands on her—we must look to the fields and boundaries of that time.

As we have seen, Thomas Putnam's man for the Salem ministry was Bayley. The Nurse clan had been in the faction that prevented Bayley's taking office. In addition, certain families allied to the Nurses by blood or friendship, and whose farms were contiguous with the Nurse farm or close to it, combined to break away from the Salem town authority and set up Topsfield, a new and independent entity whose existence was resented by old Salemites.

That the guiding hand behind the outcry was Putnam's is indicated by the fact that, as soon as it began, this Topsfield-Nurse faction absented themselves from church in protest and disbelief. It was Edward and Jonathan Putnam who signed the first complaint against Rebecca; and Thomas Putnam's little daughter was the one who fell into a fit at the hearing and pointed to Rebecca as her attacker. To top it all, Mrs. Putnam—who is now staring at the bewitched child on the bed—soon accused Rebecca's spirit of "tempting her to iniquity," a charge that had more truth in it than Mrs. Putnam could know.

MRS. PUTNAM (*astonished*): What have you done?

(REBECCA, *in thought, now leaves the bedside and sits.*)

PARRIS (*wondrous and relieved*): What do you make of it, Rebecca?

PUTNAM (*eagerly*): Goody Nurse, will you go to my Ruth and see if you can wake her?

REBECCA (*sitting*): I think she'll wake in time. Pray calm yourselves. I have eleven children, and I am twenty-six times a grandma, and I have seen them all through their silly seasons, and when it comes on them they will run the Devil bow-legged keeping up with their mischief. I think she'll wake when she tires of it. A child's spirit is like a child, you can never catch it by running after it; you must stand still, and, for love, it will soon itself come back.

PROCTOR: Aye, that's the truth of it, Rebecca.

MRS. PUTNAM: This is no silly season, Rebecca. My Ruth is bewildered, Rebecca; she cannot eat.

REBECCA: Perhaps she is not hungered yet. (*To* PARRIS) I hope you are not decided to go in search of loose spirits, Mr. Parris. I've heard promise of that outside.

PARRIS: A wide opinion's running in the parish that the Devil may be among us, and I would satisfy them that they are wrong.

PROCTOR: Then let you come out and call them wrong. Did you consult the wardens before you called this minister to look for devils?

PARRIS: He is not coming to look for devils!

PROCTOR: Then what's he coming for?

PUTNAM: There be children dyin' in the village, Mister!

PROCTOR: I see none dyin'. This society will not be a bag to swing around your head, Mr. Putnam. (*To* PARRIS.) Did you call a meeting before you—?

PUTNAM: I am sick of meetings; cannot the man turn his head without he have a meeting?

PROCTOR: He may turn his head, but not to Hell!

REBECCA: Pray, John, be calm. (*Pause. He defers to her.*) Mr. Parris, I think you'd best send Reverend Hale back as soon as he come. This will set us all to arguin' again in the society, and we thought to have peace this year. I think we ought rely on the doctor now, and good prayer.

MRS. PUTNAM: Rebecca, the doctor's baffled!

REBECCA: If so he is, then let us go to God for the cause of it. There is prodigious danger in the seeking of loose spirits. I fear it, I fear it. Let us rather blame ourselves and—

PUTNAM: How may we blame ourselves? I am one of nine sons; the Putnam seed have peopled this province. And yet I have but one child left of eight—and now she shrivels!

REBECCA: I cannot fathom that.

MRS. PUTNAM (*with a growing edge of sarcasm*): But I must! You think it God's work you should never lose a child, nor grandchild either, and I bury all but one? There are wheels within wheels in this village, and fires within fires!

PUTNAM (*to* PARRIS): When Reverend Hale comes, you will proceed to look for signs of witchcraft here.

PROCTOR (*to* PUTNAM): You cannot command Mr. Parris. We vote by name in this society, not by acreage.

PUTNAM: I never heard you worried so on this society, Mr. Proctor. I do not think I saw you at Sabbath meeting since snow flew.

PROCTOR: I have trouble enough without I come five mile to hear him preach only hellfire and bloody damnation. Take it to heart, Mr. Parris. There are many others who stay away from church these days because you hardly ever mention God any more.

PARRIS (*now aroused*): Why, that's a drastic charge!

REBECCA: It's somewhat true; there are many that quail to bring their children—

PARRIS: I do not preach for children, Rebecca. It is not the children who are unmindful of their obligations toward this ministry.

REBECCA: Are there really those unmindful?

PARRIS: I should say the better half of Salem village—

PUTNAM: And more than that!

PARRIS: Where is my wood? My contract provides I be supplied with all my firewood. I am waiting since November for a stick, and even in November I had to show my frostbitten hands like some London beggar!

GILES: You are allowed six pound a year to buy your wood, Mr. Parris.

PARRIS: I regard that six pound as part of my salary. I am paid little enough without I spend six pound on firewood.

PROCTOR: Sixty, plus six for firewood—

PARRIS: The salary is sixty-six pound, Mr. Proctor! I am not some preaching farmer with a book under my arm; I am a graduate of Harvard College.

GILES: Aye, and well instructed in arithmetic!

PARRIS: Mr. Corey, you will look far for a man of my kind at sixty pound a year! I am not used to this poverty; I left a thrifty business in the Barbados to serve the Lord. I do not fathom it, why am I persecuted here? I cannot offer one proposition but there be a howling riot of argument. I have often wondered if the Devil be in it somewhere; I cannot understand you people otherwise.

PROCTOR: Mr. Parris, you are the first minister ever did demand the deed to this house—

PARRIS: Man! Don't a minister deserve a house to live in?

PROCTOR: To live in, yes. But to ask ownership is like you shall own the meeting house itself; the last meeting I were at you spoke so long on deeds and mortgages I thought it were an auction.

PARRIS: I want a mark of confidence, is all! I am your third preacher in seven years. I do not wish to be put out like the cat whenever some majority feels the whim. You people seem not to comprehend that a minister is the Lord's man in the parish; a minister is not to be so lightly crossed and contradicted—

PUTNAM: Aye!

PARRIS: There is either obedience or the church will burn like Hell is burning!

PROCTOR: Can you speak one minute without we land in Hell again? I am sick of Hell!

PARRIS: It is not for you to say what is good for you to hear!

PROCTOR: I may speak my heart, I think!

PARRIS (*in a fury*): What, are we Quakers? We are not Quakers here yet, Mr. Proctor. And you may tell that to your followers!

PROCTOR: My followers!

PARRIS (*Now he's out with it.*): There is a party in this church. I am not blind; there is a faction and a party.

PROCTOR: Against you?

PUTNAM: Against him and all authority!

PROCTOR: Why, then I must find it and join it.

(*There is shock among the others.*)

REBECCA: He does not mean that.

PUTNAM: He confessed it now!

PROCTOR: I mean it solemnly, Rebecca; I like not the smell of this "authority."

REBECCA: No, you cannot break charity with your minister. You are another kind, John. Clasp his hand, make your peace.

PROCTOR: I have a crop to sow and lumber to drag home. (*He goes angrily to the door and turns to* COREY *with a smile.*) What say you, Giles, let's find the party. He says there's a party.

GILES: I've changed my opinion of this man, John. Mr. Parris, I beg your pardon. I never thought you had so much iron in you.

PARRIS (*surprised*): Why, thank you, Giles!

GILES: It suggests to the mind what the trouble be among us all these years. (*To all*) Think on it. Wherefore is everybody suing everybody else? Think on it now, it's a deep thing, and dark as a pit. I have been six time in court this year—

PROCTOR (*familiarly, with warmth, although he knows he is approaching the edge of* GILES' *tolerance with this*): Is it the Devil's fault that a man cannot say you good morning without you clap him for defamation? You're old, Giles, and you're not hearin' so well as you did.

GILES (*He cannot be crossed.*): John Proctor, I have only last month collected four pound damages for you publicly sayin' I burned the roof off your house, and I—

PROCTOR (*laughing*): I never said no such thing, but I've paid you for it, so I hope I can call you deaf without charge. Now come along, Giles, and help me drag my lumber home.

PUTNAM: A moment, Mr. Proctor. What lumber is that you're draggin', if I may ask you?

PROCTOR: My lumber. From out my forest by the riverside.

PUTNAM: Why, we are surely gone wild this year. What anarchy is this? That tract is in my bounds, it's in my bounds, Mr. Proctor.

PROCTOR: In your bounds! (*Indicating* REBECCA) I bought that tract from Goody Nurse's husband five months ago.

PUTNAM: He had no right to sell it. It stands clear in my grandfather's will that all the land between the river and—

PROCTOR: Your grandfather had a habit of willing land that never belonged to him, if I may say it plain.

GILES: That's God's truth; he nearly willed away my north pasture but he knew I'd break his fingers before he'd set his name to it. Let's get your lumber home, John. I feel a sudden will to work coming on.

PUTNAM: You load one oak of mine and you'll fight to drag it home!

GILES: Aye, and we'll win too, Putnam—this fool and I. Come on! (*He turns to* PROCTOR *and starts out.*)

PUTNAM: I'll have my men on you, Corey! I'll clap a writ on you!

(*Enter* REVEREND JOHN HALE *of Beverly.*)

Mr. Hale is nearing forty, a tight-skinned, eager-eyed intellectual. This is a beloved errand for him; on being called here to ascertain witchcraft he felt the pride of the specialist whose unique knowledge has at last been publicly called for. Like almost all men of learning, he spent a good deal of his time pondering the invisible world, especially since he had himself encountered a witch in his parish not long before. That woman, however, turned into a mere pest under his searching scrutiny, and the child she had allegedly been afflicting recovered her normal behavior after Hale had given her his kindness and a few days of rest in his own house. However, that experience never raised a doubt in his mind as to the reality of the underworld or the existence of Lucifer's many-faced lieutenants. And his belief is not to his discredit. Better minds than Hale's were—and still are—convinced that there is a society of spirits beyond our ken. One cannot help noting that one of his lines has never yet raised a laugh in any audience that has seen this play; it is his assurance that "We cannot look to superstition in this. The Devil is precise." Evidently we are not quite certain even now whether diabolism is holy and not to be scoffed at. And it is no accident that we should be so bemused.

Like Reverend Hale and the others on this stage, we conceive the Devil as a necessary part of a respectable view of cosmology. Ours is a divided empire in which certain ideas and emotions and actions are of God, and their opposites are of Lucifer. It is as impossible for most men to conceive of a morality without sin as of an earth without "sky." Since 1692 a great but superficial change has wiped out God's beard and the Devil's horns, but the world is still gripped between two diametrically opposed absolutes. The concept of unity, in which positive and negative are attributes of the same force, in which good and evil are relative, ever-changing, and always joined to the same phenomenon—such a concept is still reserved to the physical sciences and to the few who have grasped the history of ideas. When it is recalled that until the Christian era the underworld was never regarded as a hostile area, that all gods were useful and essentially friendly to man despite occasional lapses; when we see the steady and methodical inculcation into humanity of the idea of man's worthlessness—until redeemed—the necessity of the Devil may become evident as a weapon, a weapon designed and used time and time again in every age to whip men into a surrender to a particular church or church-state.

Our difficulty in believing the—for want of a better word—political inspiration of the Devil is due in great part to the fact that he is called up and damned not only by our social antagonists but by our own side, whatever it may be. The Catholic Church, through its Inquisition, is famous for cultivating Lucifer as the arch-fiend, but the Church's enemies relied no less upon the Old Boy to keep the human mind enthralled. Luther was himself accused of alliance with Hell, and he in turn accused his enemies. To complicate matters further, he believed that he had had contact with the Devil and had argued theology with him. I am not surprised at this, for at my own university a professor of history—a Lutheran, by the way—used to assemble his graduate students, draw the shades, and commune in the classroom with Erasmus. He was never, to my knowledge, officially scoffed at for this, the reason being that the university officials, like most of us, are the children of a history which still sucks at the Devil's teats. At this writing, only England has held back before the temptations of contemporary diabolism. In the countries of the Communist ideology, all resistance of any import is linked to the totally malign capitalist succubi, and in America any man who is not reactionary in his views is open to the charge of alliance with the Red hell. Political opposition, thereby, is given an inhumane overlay which then justifies the abrogation of all normally applied customs of civilized intercourse. A political policy is equated with moral right, and opposition to it with diabolical malevolence. Once such an equation is effectively made, society becomes a congerie of plots and counterplots, and the main role of government changes from that of the arbiter to that of the scourge of God.

The results of this process are no different now from what they ever were, except sometimes in the degree of cruelty inflicted, and not always even in that department. Normally the actions and deeds of a man were all that society felt comfortable in judging. The secret intent of an action was left to the ministers, priests, and rabbis to deal with. When diabolism rises, however, actions are the least important manifests of the true nature of a man. The Devil, as Reverend Hale said, is a wily one, and until an hour before he fell, even God thought him beautiful in Heaven.

The analogy, however, seems to falter when one considers that, while there were no witches then, there are Communists and capitalists now, and in each camp there is certain proof that spies of each side are at work undermining the other. But this is a snobbish objection and not at all warranted by the facts. I have no doubt that people *were* communing with, and even worshiping, the Devil in Salem, and if the whole truth could be known in this case, as it is in others, we should discover a regular and conventionalized propitiation of the dark spirit. One certain evidence of this is the confession of Tituba, the slave of Reverend Parris, and another is the behavior of the children who were known to have indulged in sorceries with her.

There are accounts of similar *klatches* in Europe, where the daughters of the towns would assemble at night and, sometimes with fetishes, sometimes with a selected young man, give themselves to love, with some bastardly results. The Church, sharp-eyed as it must be when gods long dead are brought to life, condemned these orgies as witchcraft and interpreted them, rightly, as a resurgence of the Dionysiac forces it had crushed long before. Sex, sin, and the Devil were early linked, and so they continued to be in Salem, and are today. From all accounts there are no more puritanical mores in the world than those enforced by the Communists in Russia, where women's fashions, for instance, are as prudent and all-covering as any American Baptist would desire. The divorce laws lay a tremendous responsibility on the father for the care of his children. Even the laxity of divorce regulations in the early years of the revolution was undoubtedly a revulsion from the nineteenth-century Victorian immobility of marriage and the consequent hypocrisy that developed from it. If for no other reasons, a state so powerful, so jealous of the uniformity of its citizens, cannot long tolerate the atomization of the family. And yet, in American eyes at least, there remains the conviction that the Russian attitude toward women is lascivious. It is the Devil working again, just as he is working within the Slav who is shocked at the very idea of a woman's disrobing herself in a burlesque show. Our opposites are always robed in sexual sin, and it is from this unconscious conviction that demonology gains both its attractive sensuality and its capacity to infuriate and frighten.

Coming into Salem now, Reverend Hale conceives of himself much as a young doctor on his first call. His painfully acquired armory of symptoms, catchwords, and diagnostic procedures are now to be put to use at last. The road from Beverly is unusually busy this morning, and he has passed a hundred rumors that make him smile at the ignorance of the yeomanry in this most precise science. He feels himself allied with the best minds of Europe—kings, philosophers, scientists, and ecclesiasts of all churches. His goal is light, goodness and its preservation, and he knows the exaltation of the blessed whose intelligence, sharpened by minute examinations of enormous tracts, is finally called upon to face what may be a bloody fight with the Fiend himself.

(*He appears loaded down with half a dozen heavy books.*)

HALE: Pray you, someone take these!

PARRIS (*delighted*): Mr. Hale! Oh! it's good to see you again! (*Taking some books*) My, they're heavy!

HALE (*setting down his books*): They must be; they are weighted with authority.

PARRIS (*a little scared*): Well, you do come prepared!

HALE: We shall need hard study if it comes to tracking down the Old Boy. (*Noticing* REBECCA) You cannot be Rebecca Nurse?

REBECCA: I am, sir. Do you know me?

HALE: It's strange how I knew you, but I suppose you look as such a good soul should. We have all heard of your great charities in Beverly.

PARRIS: Do you know this gentleman? Mr. Thomas Putnam. And his good wife Ann.

HALE: Putnam! I had not expected such distinguished company, sir.

PUTNAM (*pleased*): It does not seem to help us today, Mr. Hale. We look to you to come to our house and save our child.

HALE: Your child ails too?

MRS. PUTNAM: Her soul, her soul seems flown away. She sleeps and yet she walks . . .

PUTNAM: She cannot eat.

HALE: Cannot eat! (*Thinks on it. Then, to* PROCTOR *and* GILES COREY) Do you men have afflicted children?

PARRIS: No, no, these are farmers John Proctor—

GILES COREY: He don't believe in witches.

PROCTOR (*to* HALE): I never spoke on witches one way or the other. Will you come, Giles?

GILES: No—no, John, I think not. I have some few queer questions of my own to ask this fellow.

PROCTOR: I've heard you to be a sensible man,

Mr. Hale. I hope you'll leave some of it in Salem.

(PROCTOR *goes.* HALE *stands embarrassed for an instant.*)

PARRIS (*quickly*):   Will you look at my daughter, sir? (*Leads* HALE *to the bed.*) She has tried to leap out the window; we discovered her this morning on the highroad, waving her arms as though she'd fly.

HALE (*narrowing his eyes*):   Tries to fly.

PUTNAM: She cannot bear to hear the Lord's name, Mr. Hale; that's a sure sign of witchcraft afloat.

HALE (*holding up his hands*):   No, no. Now let me instruct you. We cannot look to superstition in this. The Devil is precise; the marks of his presence are definite as stone, and I must tell you all that I shall not proceed unless you are prepared to believe me if I should find no bruise of hell upon her.

PARRIS: It is agreed, sir—it is agreed—we will abide by your judgment.

HALE: Good then. (*He goes to the bed, looks down at* BETTY. *To* PARRIS) Now, sir, what were your first warning of this strangeness?

PARRIS: Why, sir—I discovered her—(*indicating* ABIGAIL)—and my niece and ten or twelve of the other girls, dancing in the forest last night.

HALE (*surprised*):   You permit dancing?

PARRIS: No, no, it were secret—

MRS. PUTNAM (*unable to wait*):   Mr. Parris's slave has knowledge of conjurin', sir.

PARRIS (*to* MRS. PUTNAM):   We cannot be sure of that, Goody Ann—

MRS. PUTNAM (*frightened, very softly*):   I know it, sir. I sent my child—she should learn from Tituba who murdered her sisters.

REBECCA (*horrified*):   Goody Ann! You sent a child to conjure up the dead?

MRS. PUTNAM: Let God blame me, not you, not you, Rebecca! I'll not have you judging me any more! (*To* HALE) Is it a natural work to lose seven children before they live a day?

PARRIS: Ssh!

(REBECCA, *with great pain, turns her face away. There is a pause.*)

HALE: Seven dead in childbirth.

MRS. PUTNAM (*softly*):   Aye. (*Her voice breaks; she looks up at him. Silence.* HALE *is impressed.* PARRIS *looks to him. He goes to his books, opens one, turns pages, then reads. All wait, avidly.*)

PARRIS (*hushed*):   What book is that?

MRS. PUTNAM: What's there, sir?

HALE (*with a tasty love of intellectual pursuit*):   Here is all the invisible world, caught, defined, and calculated. In these books the Devil stands stripped of all his brute disguises. Here are all your familiar spirits—your incubi and succubi; your witches that go by land, by air, and by sea; your wizards of the night and of the day. Have no fear now—we shall find him out if he has come among us, and I mean to crush him utterly if he has shown his face! (*He starts for the bed.*)

REBECCA: Will it hurt the child, sir?

HALE: I cannot tell. If she is truly in the Devil's grip we may have to rip and tear to get her free.

REBECCA: I think I'll go, then. I am too old for this. (*She rises.*)

PARRIS (*striving for conviction*):   Why, Rebecca, we may open up the boil of all our troubles today!

REBECCA: Let us hope for that. I go to God for you, sir.

PARRIS (*with trepidation—and resentment*):   I hope you do not mean to go to Satan here! (*Slight pause.*)

REBECCA: I wish I knew. (*She goes out; they feel resentful of her note of moral superiority.*)

PUTNAM (*abruptly*):   Come, Mr. Hale, let's get on. Sit you here.

GILES: Mr. Hale, I have always wanted to ask a learned man—what signifies the readin' of strange books?

HALE: What books?

GILES: I cannot tell; she hides them.

HALE: Who does this?

GILES: Martha, my wife. I have waked at night many a time and found her in a corner, readin' of a book. Now what do you make of that?

HALE: Why, that's not necessarily—

GILES: It discomfits me! Last night—mark this—I tried and tried and could not say my prayers. And then she close her book and walks out of the house, and suddenly—mark this—I could pray again!

Old Giles must be spoken for, if only because his fate was to be so remarkable and so different from that of all the others. He was in his early eighties at this time, and was the most comical hero in the history. No man has ever been blamed for so much. If a cow was missed, the first thought was to look for her around Corey's house; a fire blazing up at night brought suspicion of arson to his door. He didn't give a hoot for public opinion, and only in his last years—after he had married Martha—did he bother much with the church. That she stopped his prayer is very probable, but he forgot to say that he'd only recently learned any prayers and it didn't take much to make him stumble over them. He was a crank and a nuisance, but withal a deeply innocent and brave man. In court, once, he was asked if it were true that he had been frightened by the strange behavior of a hog and had then said he knew it to be the Devil in an animal's shape. "What frighted you?" he was asked. He forgot everything but the word "frighted," and instantly replied, "I do not know that I ever spoke that word in my life."

HALE: Ah! The stoppage of prayer—that is strange. I'll speak further on that with you.

GILES: I'm not sayin' she's touched the Devil, now, but I'd admire to know what books she reads and why she hides them. She'll not answer me, y' see.

HALE: Aye, we'll discuss it. (*To all*) Now mark me, if the Devil is in her you will witness some frightful wonders in this room, so please to keep your wits about you. Mr. Putnam, stand close in case she flies. Now, Betty, dear, will you sit up? (PUTNAM *comes in closer, ready-handed.* HALE *sits* BETTY *up, but she hangs limp in his hands.*) Hmmm. (*He observes her carefully. The others watch breathlessly.*) Can you hear me? I am John Hale, minister of Beverly. I have come to help you, dear. Do you remember my two little girls in Beverly? (*She does not stir in his hands.*)

PARRIS (*in fright*):   How can it be the Devil? Why would he choose my house to strike? We have all manner of licentious people in the village!

HALE: What victory would the Devil have to win a soul already bad? It is the best the Devil wants, and who is better than the minister?

GILES: That's deep, Mr. Parris, deep, deep!

PARRIS (*with resolution now*):   Betty! Answer Mr. Hale! Betty!

HALE: Does someone afflict you, child? It need not be a woman, mind you, or a man. Perhaps some bird invisible to others comes to you—perhaps a pig, a mouse, or any beast at all. Is there some figure bids you fly? (*The child remains limp in his hands. In silence he lays her*

back on the pillow. Now, *holding out his hands toward her, he intones.*) In nomine Domini Sabaoth sui filiique ite ad infernos. (*She does not stir. He turns to* ABIGAIL, *his eyes narrowing.*) Abigail, what sort of dancing were you doing with her in the forest?

ABIGAIL: Why—common dancing is all.

PARRIS: I think I ought to say that I—I saw a kettle in the grass where they were dancing.

ABIGAIL: That were only soup.

HALE: What sort of soup were in this kettle, Abigail?

ABIGAIL: Why, it were beans—and lentils, I think, and—

HALE: Mr. Parris, you did not notice, did you, any living thing in the kettle? A mouse, perhaps, a spider, a frog—?

PARRIS (*fearfully*):   I—do believe there were some movement—in the soup.

ABIGAIL: That jumped in, we never put it in!

HALE (*quickly*):   What jumped in?

ABIGAIL: Why, a very little frog jumped—

PARRIS: A frog, Abby!

HALE (*grasping* ABIGAIL):   Abigail, it may be your cousin is dying. Did you call the Devil last night?

ABIGAIL: I never called him! Tituba, Tituba . . .

PARRIS (*blanched*):   She called the Devil?

HALE: I should like to speak with Tituba.

PARRIS: Goody Ann, will you bring her up? (MRS. PUTNAM *exits.*)

HALE: How did she call him?

ABIGAIL: I know not—she spoke Barbados.

HALE: Did you feel any strangeness when she called him? A sudden cold wind, perhaps? A trembling below the ground?

ABIGAIL: I didn't see no Devil! (*Shaking* BETTY) Betty, wake up. Betty! Betty!

HALE: You cannot evade me, Abigail. Did your cousin drink any of the brew in that kettle?

ABIGAIL: She never drank it!

HALE: Did you drink it?

ABIGAIL: No, sir!

HALE: Did Tituba ask you to drink it?

ABIGAIL: She tried, but I refused.

HALE: Why are you concealing? Have you sold yourself to Lucifer?

ABIGAIL: I never sold myself! I'm a good girl! I'm a proper girl!

(MRS. PUTNAM *enters with* TITUBA, *and instantly* ABIGAIL *points at* TITUBA.)

ABIGAIL: She made me do it! She made Betty do it!

TITUBA (*shocked and angry*):   Abby!

ABIGAIL: She makes me drink blood!

PARRIS   Blood!!

MRS. PUTNAM: My baby's blood?

TITUBA: No, no, chicken blood. I give she chicken blood!

HALE: Woman, have you enlisted these children for the Devil?

TITUBA: No, no, sir, I don't truck with no Devil!

HALE: Why can she not wake? Are you silencing this child?

TITUBA: I love me Betty!

HALE: You have sent your spirit out upon this child, have you not? Are you gathering souls for the Devil?

ABIGAIL: She sends her spirit on me in church; she makes me laugh at prayer!

PARRIS: She have often laughed at prayer!

ABIGAIL: She comes to me every night to go and drink blood!

TITUBA: You beg *me* to conjure! She beg *me* make charm—

ABIGAIL: Don't lie! (*To* HALE) She comes to me while I sleep; she's always making me dream corruptions!

TITUBA: Why you say that, Abby?

ABIGAIL: Sometimes I wake and find myself standing in the open doorway and not a stitch on my body! I always hear her laughing in my sleep. I hear her singing her Barbados songs and tempting me with—

TITUBA: Mister Reverend, I never—

HALE (*resolved now*):   Tituba, I want you to wake this child.

TITUBA: I have no power on this child, sir.

HALE: You most certainly do, and you will free her from it now! When did you compact with the Devil?

TITUBA: I don't compact with no Devil!

PARRIS: You will confess yourself or I will take you out and whip you to your death, Tituba!

PUTNAM: This woman must be hanged! She must be taken and hanged!

TITUBA (*terrified, falls to her knees*):   No, no, don't hang Tituba! I tell him I don't desire to work for him, sir.

PARRIS: The Devil?

HALE: Then you saw him! (*Tituba weeps.*) Now Tituba, I know that when we bind ourselves to Hell it is very hard to break with it. We are going to help you tear yourself free—

TITUBA (*frightened by the coming process*):   Mister Reverend, I do believe somebody else be witchin' these children.

HALE: Who?

TITUBA: I don't know, sir, but the Devil got him numerous witches.

HALE: Does he! (*It is a clue.*) Tituba, look into my eyes. Come, look into me. (*She raises her eyes to his fearfully.*) You would be a good Christian woman, would you not, Tituba?

TITUBA: Aye, sir, a good Christian woman.

HALE: And you love these little children?

TITUBA: Oh, yes, sir, I don't desire to hurt little children.

HALE: And you love God, Tituba?

TITUBA: I love God with all my bein'.

HALE: Now, in God's holy name—

TITUBA: Bless Him. Bless Him. (*She is rocking on her knees, sobbing in terror.*)

HALE: And to His glory—

TITUBA: Eternal glory. Bless Him—bless God . . .

HALE: Open yourself, Tituba—open yourself and let God's holy light shine on you.

TITUBA: Oh, bless the Lord.

HALE: When the Devil comes to you does he ever come—with another person? (*She stares up into his face.*) Perhaps another person in the village? Someone you know.

PARRIS: Who came with him?

PUTNAM: Sarah Good? Did you ever see Sarah Good with him? Or Osburn?

PARRIS: Was it man or woman came with him?

TITUBA: Man or woman. Was—was woman.

PARRIS: What woman? A woman, you said. What woman?

TITUBA: It was black dark, and I—

PARRIS: You could see him, why could you not see her?

TITUBA: Well, they was always talking; they was always runnin' round and carryin' on—

PARRIS: You mean out of Salem? Salem witches?

TITUBA: I believe so, yes, sir.

(*Now* HALE *takes her hand. She is surprised.*)

HALE: Tituba. You must have no fear to tell us who they are, do you understand? We will protect you. The Devil can never overcome a minister. You know that, do you not?

TITUBA (*kisses* HALE's *hand*):   Aye, sir, oh, I do.

HALE: You have confessed yourself to witchcraft, and that speaks a wish to come to Heaven's side. And we will bless you, Tituba.

TITUBA (*deeply relieved*):   Oh, God bless you, Mr. Hale!

HALE (*with rising exaltation*):   You are God's instrument put in our hands to discover the Devil's agent among us. You are selected, Tituba, you are chosen to help us cleanse our village. So speak utterly, Tituba, turn your back on him and face God—face God, Tituba, and God will protect you.

TITUBA (*joining with him*):   Oh, God, protect Tituba!

HALE (*kindly*):   Who came to you with the Devil? Two? Three? Four? How many?

(TITUBA *pants, and begins rocking back and forth again, staring ahead.*)

TITUBA: There was four. There was four.

PARRIS (*pressing in on her*):   Who? Who? Their names, their names!

TITUBA (*suddenly bursting out*):   Oh, how many times he bid me kill you, Mr. Parris!

PARRIS: Kill me!

TITUBA (*in a fury*):   He say Mr. Parris must be kill! Mr. Parris no goodly man, Mr. Parris mean man and no gentle man, and he bid me rise out of my bed and cut your throat! (*They gasp.*) But I tell him, "No! I don't hate that man. I don't want kill that man." But he say, "You work for me, Tituba, and I make you free! I give you pretty dress to wear, and put you way high up in the air, and you gone fly back to Barbados!" And I say, "You lie, Devil, you lie!" And then he come one stormy night to me, and he say, "Look! I have *white* people belong to me." And I look—and there was Goody Good.

PARRIS: Sarah Good!

TITUBA (*rocking and weeping*):   Aye, sir, and Goody Osburn.

MRS. PUTNAM: I knew it! Goody Osburn were midwife to me three times. I begged you, Thomas, did I not? I begged him not to call Osburn because I feared her. My babies always shriveled in her hands!

HALE: Take courage, you must give us all their names. How can you bear to see this child suffering? Look at her, Tituba. (*He is indicating* BETTY *on the bed.*) Look at her God-given innocence; her soul is so tender; we must protect her, Tituba; the Devil is out and preying on her like

a beast upon the flesh of the pure lamb. God will bless you for your help.

(ABIGAIL *rises, staring as though inspired, and cries out.*)

ABIGAIL: I want to open myself! (*They turn to her, startled. She is enraptured, as though in a pearly light.*) I want the light of God, I want the sweet love of Jesus! I danced for the Devil; I saw him; I wrote in this book; I go back to Jesus; I kiss His hand. I saw Sarah Good with the Devil! I saw Goody Osburn with the devil! I saw Bridget Bishop with the Devil!

(*As she is speaking,* BETTY *is rising from the bed, a fever in her eyes, and picks up the chant.*)

BETTY (*staring too*):   I saw George Jacobs with the Devil! I saw Goody Howe with the Devil!

PARRIS: She speaks! (*He rushes to embrace* BETTY.) She speaks!

HALE: Glory to God! It is broken, they are free!

BETTY (*calling out hysterically and with great relief*):   I saw Martha Bellows with the Devil!

ABIGAIL: I saw Goody Sibber with the Devil! (*It is rising to a great glee.*)

PUTNAM: The marshal, I'll call the marshal!

(PARRIS *is shouting a prayer of thanksgiving.*)

BETTY: I saw Alice Barrow with the Devil!

(*The curtain begins to fall.*)

HALE (*as* PUTNAM *goes out*):   Let the marshal bring irons!

ABIGAIL: I saw Goody Hawkins with the Devil!

BETTY: I saw Goody Bibber with the Devil!

ABIGAIL: I saw Goody Booth with the Devil!

(*On their ecstatic cries the curtain falls.*)

ACT TWO

The common room of PROCTOR's *house, eight days later.*

At the right is a door opening on the fields outside. A fireplace is at the left, and behind it a stairway leading upstairs. It is the low, dark, and rather long living room of the time. As the curtain rises, the room is empty. From above, ELIZABETH *is heard softly singing to the children. Presently the door opens and* JOHN PROCTOR *enters, carrying his gun. He glances about the room as he comes toward the fireplace, then halts for an instant as he hears her singing. He con-*

tinues on to the fireplace, leans the gun against the wall as he swings a pot out of the fire and smells it. Then he lifts out the ladle and tastes. He is not quite pleased. He reaches to a cupboard, takes a pinch of salt, and drops it into the pot. As he is tasting again, her footsteps are heard on the stair. He swings the pot into the fireplace and goes to a basin and washes his hands and face. ELIZABETH *enters.*

ELIZABETH: What keeps you so late? It's almost dark.

PROCTOR: I were planting far out to the forest edge.

ELIZABETH: Oh, you're done then.

PROCTOR: Aye, the farm is seeded. The boys asleep?

ELIZABETH: They will be soon. (*And she goes to the fireplace, proceeds to ladle up stew in a dish.*)

PROCTOR: Pray now for a fair summer.

ELIZABETH: Aye.

PROCTOR: Are you well today?

ELIZABETH: I am. (*She brings the plate to the table, and, indicating the food*) It is a rabbit.

PROCTOR: (*going to the table*):   Oh, is it! In Jonathan's trap?

ELIZABETH: No, she walked into the house this afternoon, I found her sittin' in the corner like she come to visit.

PROCTOR: Oh, that's a good sign walkin' in.

ELIZABETH: Pray God. It hurt my heart to strip her, poor rabbit. (*She sits and watches him taste it.*)

PROCTOR: It's well seasoned.

ELIZABETH (*blushing with pleasure*):   I took great care. She's tender?

PROCTOR: Aye. (*He eats. She watches him.*) I think we'll see green fields soon. It's warm as blood beneath the clods.

ELIZABETH: That's well.

(PROCTOR *eats, then looks up.*)

PROCTOR: If the crop is good I'll buy George Jacob's heifer. How would that please you?

ELIZABETH: Aye, it would.

PROCTOR (*with a grin*):   I mean to please you, Elizabeth.

ELIZABETH (*It is hard to say.*)   I know it, John.

(*He gets up, goes to her, kisses her. She receives it. With a certain disappointment, he returns to the table.*)

PROCTOR (*as gently as he can*):   Cider?

ELIZABETH (*with a sense of reprimanding her-self for having forgot*):   Aye! (*She gets up and goes and pours a glass for him. He now arches his back.*)

PROCTOR: This farm's a continent when you go foot by foot droppin' seeds in it.

ELIZABETH (*coming with the cider*):   It must be.

PROCTOR (*drinks a long draught, then, putting the glass down*):   You ought to bring some flowers in the house.

ELIZABETH: Oh! I forgot! I will tomorrow.

PROCTOR: It's winter in here yet. On Sunday let you come with me, and we'll walk the farm together; I never see such a load of flowers on the earth. (*With good feeling he goes and looks up at the sky through the open doorway.*) Lilacs have a purple smell. Lilac is the smell of night-fall, I think. Massachusetts is a beauty in the spring!

ELIZABETH: Aye, it is.

(*There is a pause. She is watching him from the table as he stands there absorbing the night. It is as though she would speak but cannot. Instead, now, she takes up his plate and glass and fork and goes with them to the basin. Her back is turned to him. He turns to her and watches her. A sense of their separation rises.*)

PROCTOR: I think you're sad again. Are you?

ELIZABETH (*She doesn't want friction, and yet she must.*):   You come so late I thought you'd gone to Salem this afternoon.

PROCTOR: Why? I have no business in Salem.

ELIZABETH: You did speak of going, earlier this week.

PROCTOR (*He knows what she means.*):   I thought better of it since.

ELIZABETH: Mary Warren's there today.

PROCTOR: Why'd you let her? You heard me forbid her go to Salem any more!

ELIZABETH: I couldn't stop her.

PROCTOR (*holding back a full condemnation of her*):   It is a fault, it is a fault, Elizabeth—you're the mistress here, not Mary Warren.

ELIZABETH: She frightened all my strength away.

PROCTOR: How may that mouse frighten you, Elizabeth? You—

ELIZABETH: It is a mouse no more. I forbid her go, and she raises up her chin like the daughter of a prince and says to me, "I must go to Salem, Goody Proctor; I am an official of the court!"

PROCTOR: Court! What court?

ELIZABETH: Aye, it is a proper court they have now. They've sent four judges out of Boston, she says, weighty magistrats of the General Court, and at the head sits the Deputy Governor of the Province.

PROCTOR (*astonished*): Why, she's mad.

ELIZABETH: I would to God she were. There be fourteen people in the jail now, she says. (PROCTOR *simply looks at her, unable to grasp it.*) And they'll be tried, and the court have power to hang them too, she says.

PROCTOR (*scoffing, but without conviction*): Ah, they'd never hang—

ELIZABETH: The Deputy Governor promise hangin' if they'll not confess, John. The town's gone wild, I think. She speak of Abigail, and I thought she were a saint, to hear her. Abigail brings the other girls into the court, and where she walks the crowd will part like the sea for Israel. And folks are brought before them, and if they scream and howl and fall to the floor—the person's clapped in the jail for bewitchin' them.

PROCTOR (*wide-eyed*): Oh, it is a black mischief.

ELIZABETH: I think you must go to Salem, John. (*He turns to her.*) I think so. You must tell them it is a fraud.

PROCTOR (*thinking beyond this*): Aye, it is, it is surely.

ELIZABETH: Let you go to Ezekiel Cheever—he knows you well. And tell him what she said to you last week in her uncle's house. She said it had naught to do with witchcraft, did she not?

PROCTOR (*in thought*): Aye, she did, she did. (*Now, a pause.*)

ELIZABETH (*quietly, fearing to anger him by prodding*): God forbid you keep that from the court, John. I think they must be told.

PROCTOR (*quietly, struggling with his thought*): Aye, they must, they must. It is a wonder they do believe her.

ELIZABETH: I would go to Salem now, John—let you go tonight.

PROCTOR: I'll think on it.

ELIZABETH (*with her courage now*): You cannot keep it, John.

PROCTOR (*angering*): I know I cannot keep it. I say I will think on it!

ELIZABETH (*hurt, and very coldly*): Good, then, let you think on it. (*She stands and starts to walk out of the room.*)

PROCTOR: I am only wondering how I may prove what she told me, Elizabeth. If the girl's a saint now, I think it is not easy to prove she's fraud, and the town gone so silly. She told it to me in a room alone—I have no proof for it.

ELIZABETH: You were alone with her?

PROCTOR (*stubbornly*): For a moment alone, aye.

ELIZABETH: Why, then, it is not as you told me.

PROCTOR (*his anger rising*): For a moment, I say. The others come in soon after.

ELIZABETH (*Quietly. She has suddenly lost all faith in him.*): Do as you wish, then. (*She starts to turn.*)

PROCTOR: Woman. (*She turns to him.*) I'll not have your suspicion any more.

ELIZABETH (*a little loftily*): I have no—

PROCTOR: I'll not have it!

ELIZABETH: Then let you not earn it.

PROCTOR (*with a violent undertone*): You doubt me yet?

ELIZABETH (*with a smile, to keep her dignity*): John, if it were not Abigail that you must go to hurt, would you falter now? I think not.

PROCTOR: Now look you—

ELIZABETH: I see what I see, John.

PROCTOR (*with solemn warning*): You will not judge me more, Elizabeth. I have good reason to think before I charge fraud on Abigail, and I will think on it. Let you look to your own improvement before you go to judge your husband any more. I have forgot Abigail, and—

ELIZABETH: And I.

PROCTOR: Spare me! You forget nothin' and forgive nothin'. Learn charity, woman. I have gone tiptoe in this house all seven month since she is gone. I have not moved from there to there without I think to please you, and still an everlasting funeral marches round your heart. I cannot speak but I am doubted, every moment judged for lies, as though I come into a court when I come into this house!

ELIZABETH: John, you are not open with me. You saw her with a crowd, you said. Now you—

PROCTOR: I'll plead my honesty no more, Elizabeth.

ELIZABETH (*Now she would justify herself.*): John, I am only—

PROCTOR: No more! I should have roared you down when first you told me your suspicion. But I wilted, and, like a Christian, I confessed. Confessed! Some dream I had must have mistaken you for God that day. But you're not, you're not, and let you remember it! Let you look sometimes for the goodness in me, and judge me not.

ELIZABETH: I do not judge you. The magistrate sits in your heart that judges you. I never thought you but a good man, John— (*with a smile*)—only somewhat bewildered.

PROCTOR (*laughing bitterly*): Oh, Elizabeth, your justice would freeze beer! (*He turns suddenly toward a sound outside. He starts for the door as* MARY WARREN *enters. As soon as he sees her, he goes directly to her and grabs her by the cloak, furious.*) How do you go to Salem when I forbid it? Do you mock me? (*Shaking her*) I'll whip you if you dare leave this house again!

(*Strangely, she doesn't resist him, but hangs limply by his grip.*)

MARY WARREN: I am sick, I am sick, Mr. Proctor. Pray, pray, hurt me not. (*Her strangeness throws him off, and her evident pallor and weakness. He frees her.*) My insides are all shuddery; I am in the proceedings all day, sir.

PROCTOR (*With draining anger—his curiosity is draining it.*): And what of these proceedings here? When will you proceed to keep this house, as you are paid nine pound a year to do—and my wife not wholly well?

(*As though to compensate,* MARY WARREN *goes to* ELIZABETH *with a small rag doll.*)

MARY WARREN: I made a gift for you today, Goody Proctor. I had to sit long hours in a chair, and passed the time with sewing.

ELIZABETH (*perplexed, looking at the doll*): Why, thank you, it's a fair poppet.

MARY WARREN (*with a trembling, decayed voice*): We must all love each other now, Goody Proctor.

ELIZABETH (*amazed at her strangeness*): Aye, indeed we must.

MARY WARREN (*glancing at the room*): I'll get up early in the morning and clean the house. I must sleep now. (*She turns and starts off.*)

PROCTOR: Mary. (*She halts.*) Is it true? There be fourteen women arrested?

MARY WARREN: No, sir. There be thirty-nine now—(*She suddenly breaks off and sobs and sits down, exhausted.*)

ELIZABETH: Why, she's weepin'! What ails you, child?

MARY WARREN: Goody Osburn—will hang! (*There is a shocked pause, while she sobs.*)

PROCTOR: Hang! (*He calls into her face.*) Hang, y'say?

MARY WARREN (*through her weeping*): Aye.

PROCTOR: The Deputy Governor will permit it?

MARY WARREN: He sentenced her. He must. (*To ameliorate it*) But not Sarah Good. For Sarah Good confessed, y'see.

PROCTOR: Confessed! To what?

MARY WARREN: That she—(*in horror at the memory*)—she sometimes made a compact with Lucifer, and wrote her name in his black book—with her blood—and bound herself to torment Christians till God's thrown down—and we all must worship Hell forevermore.

(*Pause.*)

PROCTOR: But—surely you know what a jabberer she is. Did you tell them that?

MARY WARREN: Mr. Proctor, in open court she near to choked us all to death.

PROCTOR: How, choked you?

MARY WARREN: She sent her spirit out.

ELIZABETH: Oh, Mary, Mary, surely you—

MARY WARREN (*with an indignant edge*): She tried to kill me many times, Goody Proctor!

ELIZABETH: Why, I never heard you mention that before.

MARY WARREN: I never knew it before. I never knew anything before. When she come into the court I say to myself, I must not accuse this woman, for she sleep in ditches, and so very old and poor. But then—then she sit there, denying and denying, and I feel a misty coldness climbin' up my back, and the skin on my skull begin to creep, and I feel a clamp around my neck and I cannot breathe air; and then—(*entranced*)—I hear a voice, a screamin' voice, and it were my voice—and all at once I remembered everything she done to me!

PROCTOR: Why? What did she do to you?

MARY WARREN (*like one awakened to a marvelous secret insight*): So many time, Mr. Proctor, she come to this very door, beggin' bread and a cup of cider—and mark this: whenever I turned her away empty, she *mumbled.*

ELIZABETH: Mumbled! She may mumble if she's hungry.

MARY WARREN: But *what* does she mumble? You must remember, Goody Proctor. Last month—a Monday, I think—she walked away, and I thought my guts would burst for two days after. Do you remember it?

ELIZABETH: Why—I do, I think, but—

MARY WARREN: And so I told that to Judge Hathorne, and he asks her so. "Goody Osburn," says he, "what curse do you mumble that this girl must fall sick after turning you away?" And then she replies—(*mimicking an old crone*)—"Why, your excellence, no curse at all. I only say my commandments; I hope I may say my commandments," says she!

ELIZABETH: And that's an upright answer.

MARY WARREN: Aye, but then Judge Hathorne say, "Recite for us your commandments!"—(*leaning avidly toward them*)—and of all the ten she could not say a single one. She never knew no commandments, and they had her in a flat lie!

PROCTOR: And so condemned her?

MARY WARREN (*now a little strained, seeing his stubborn doubt*):   Why, they must when she condemned herself.

PROCTOR: But the proof, the proof!

MARY WARREN (*with greater impatience with him*):   I told you the proof. It's hard proof, hard as rock, the judges said.

PROCTOR (*pauses an instant, then*):   You will not go to court again, Mary Warren.

MARY WARREN: I must tell you, sir, I will be gone every day now. I am amazed you do not see what weighty work we do.

PROCTOR: What work you do! It's strange work for a Christian girl to hang old women!

MARY WARREN: But, Mr. Proctor, they will not hang them if they confess. Sarah Good will only sit in jail some time—(*recalling*)—and here's a wonder for you; think on this. Goody Good is pregnant!

ELIZABETH: Pregnant! Are they mad? The woman's near to sixty!

MARY WARREN: They had Doctor Griggs examine her, and she's full to the brim. And smokin' a pipe all these years, and no husband either! But she's safe, thank God, for they'll not hurt the innocent child. But be that not a marvel? You must see it, sir, it's God's work we do. So I'll be gone every day for some time. I'm—I am an official of the court, they say, and I—(*She has been edging toward off-stage.*)

PROCTOR: I'll official you! (*He strides to the mantel, takes down the whip hanging there.*)

MARY WARREN (*terrified, but coming erect, striving for her authority*):   I'll not stand whipping any more!

ELIZABETH (*hurriedly, as* PROCTOR *approaches*): Mary, promise you'll stay at home—

MARY WARREN (*backing from him, but keeping her erect posture, striving, striving for her way*): The Devil's loose in Salem, Mr. Proctor; we must discover where he's hiding!

PROCTOR: I'll whip the Devil out of you! (*With whip raised he reaches out for her, and she streaks away and yells.*)

MARY WARREN (*pointing at* ELIZABETH):   I saved her life today!

(*Silence. His whip comes down.*)

ELIZABETH (*softly*):   I am accused?

MARY WARREN (*quaking*):   Somewhat mentioned. But I said I never see no sign you ever sent your spirit out to hurt no one, and seeing I do live so closely with you, they dismissed it.

ELIZABETH: Who accused me?

MARY WARREN: I am bound by law, I cannot tell it. (*To* PROCTOR) I only hope you'll not be so sarcastical no more. Four judges and the King's deputy sat to dinner with us but an hour ago. I—I would have you speak civilly to me, from this out.

PROCTOR (*in horror, muttering in disgust at her*):   Go to bed.

MARY WARREN (*with a stamp of her foot*):   I'll not be ordered to bed no more, Mr. Proctor! I am eighteen and a woman, however single!

PROCTOR: Do you wish to sit up? Then sit up.

MARY WARREN: I wish to go to bed!

PROCTOR (*in anger*):   Good night, then!

MARY WARREN: Good night. (*Dissatisfied, uncertain of herself, she goes out. Wide-eyed, both,* PROCTOR *and* ELIZABETH *stand staring.*)

ELIZABETH (*quietly*):   Oh, the noose, the noose is up!

PROCTOR: There'll be no noose.

ELIZABETH: She wants me dead. I knew all week it would come to this!

PROCTOR (*without conviction*):   They dismissed it. You heard her say—

ELIZABETH: And what of tomorrow? She will cry me out until they take me!

PROCTOR: Sit you down.

ELIZABETH: She wants me dead, John, you know it!

PROCTOR: I say sit down. (*She sits, trembling. He speaks quickly, trying to keep his wits.*) Now we must be wise, Elizabeth.

ELIZABETH (*with sarcasm, and a sense of being lost*):   Oh, indeed, indeed!

PROCTOR: Fear nothing. I'll find Ezekiel Cheever. I'll tell him she said it were all sport.

ELIZABETH: John, with so many in the jail, more than Cheever's help is needed now, I think. Would you favor me with this? Go to Abigail.

PROCTOR (*his soul hardening as he senses . . .*): What have I say to Abigail?

ELIZABETH (*delicately*): John—grant me this. You have a faulty understanding of young girls. There is a promise made in any bed—

PROCTOR (*striving against his anger*): What promise!

ELIZABETH: Spoke or silent, a promise is surely made. And she may dote on it now—I am sure she does—and thinks to kill me, then to take my place.

(PROCTOR*'s anger is rising; he cannot speak.*)

ELIZABETH: It is her dearest hope, John, I know it. There be a thousand names; why does she call mine? There be a certain danger in calling such a name—I am no Goody Good that sleeps in ditches, nor Osburn, drunk and half-witted. She'd dare not call out such a farmer's wife but there be monstrous profit in it. She thinks to take my place, John.

PROCTOR: She cannot think it! (*He knows it is true.*)

ELIZABETH ("*reasonably*"): John, have you ever shown her somewhat of contempt? She cannot pass you in the church but you will blush—

PROCTOR: I may blush for my sin.

ELIZABETH: I think she sees another meaning in that blush.

PROCTOR: And what see you? What see you, Elizabeth?

ELIZABETH ("*conceding*"): I think you be somewhat ashamed, for I am there, and she so close.

PROCTOR: When will you know me, woman? Were I stone I would have cracked for shame this seven month!

ELIZABETH: Then go and tell her she's a whore. Whatever promise she may sense—break it, John, break it.

PROCTOR (*between his teeth*): Good, then. I'll go. (*He starts for his rifle.*)

ELIZABETH (*trembling, fearfully*): Oh, how unwillingly!

PROCTOR (*turning on her, rifle in hand*): I will curse her hotter than the oldest cinder in hell. But pray, begrudge me not my anger!

ELIZABETH: Your anger! I only ask you—

PROCTOR: Woman, am I so base? Do you truly think me base?

ELIZABETH: I never called you base.

PROCTOR: Then how do you charge me with such a promise? The promise that a stallion gives a mare I gave that girl!

ELIZABETH: Then why do you anger with me when I bid you break it?

PROCTOR: Because it speaks deceit, and I am honest! But I'll plead no more! I see now your spirit twists around the single error of my life, and I will never tear it free!

ELIZABETH (*crying out*): You'll tear it free— when you come to know that I will be your only wife, or no wife at all! She has an arrow in you yet, John Proctor, and you know it well!

(*Quite suddenly, as though from the air, a figure appears in the doorway. They start slightly. It is* MR. HALE. *He is different now—drawn a little, and there is a quality of deference, even of guilt, about his manner now.*)

HALE: Good evening.

PROCTOR (*still in his shock*): Why, Mr. Hale! Good evening to you, sir. Come in, come in.

HALE (*to* ELIZABETH): I hope I do not startle you.

ELIZABETH: No, no, it's only that I heard no horse—

HALE: You are Goodwife Proctor.

PROCTOR: Aye; Elizabeth.

HALE (*nods, then*): I hope you're not off to bed yet.

PROCTOR (*setting down his gun*): No, no.

(HALE *comes further into the room. And* PROCTOR, *to explain his nervousness*) We are not used to visitors after dark, but you're welcome here. Will you sit you down, sir?

HALE: I will. (*He sits.*) Let you sit, Goodwife Proctor.

(*She does, never letting him out of her sight. There is a pause as* HALE *looks about the room.*)

PROCTOR (*to break the silence*): Will you drink cider, Mr. Hale?

HALE: No, it rebels my stomach; I have some further traveling yet tonight. Sit you down, sir. (PROCTOR *sits.*) I will not keep you long, but I have some business with you.

PROCTOR: Business of the court?

HALE: No—no, I come of my own, without the court's authority. Hear me. (*He wets his lips.*) I know not if you are aware, but your wife's name is—mentioned in the court.

PROCTOR: We know it, sir. Our Mary Warren told us. We are entirely amazed.

HALE: I am a stranger here, as you know. And in my ignorance I find it hard to draw a clear opinion of them that come accused before the court. And so this afternoon, and now tonight, I go from house to house—I come now from Rebecca Nurse's house and—

ELIZABETH (*shocked*): Rebecca's charged!

HALE: God forbid such a one be charged. She is, however—mentioned somewhat.

ELIZABETH (*with an attempt at a laugh*): You will never believe, I hope, that Rebecca trafficked with the Devil.

HALE: Woman, it is possible.

PROCTOR (*taken aback*): Surely you cannot think so.

HALE: This is a strange time, Mister. No man may longer doubt the powers of the dark are gathered in monstrous attack upon this village. There is too much evidence now to deny it. You will agree, sir?

PROCTOR (*evading*): I—have no knowledge in that line. But it's hard to think so pious a woman to be secretly a Devil's bitch after seventy year of such good prayer.

HALE: Aye. But the Devil is a wily one, you cannot deny it. However, she is far from accused, and I know she will not be. (*Pause.*) I thought, sir, to put some questions as to the Christian character of this house, if you'll permit me.

PROCTOR (*coldly, resentful*): Why, we—have no fear of questions, sir.

HALE: Good, then. (*He makes himself more comfortable.*) In the book of record that Mr. Parris keeps, I note that you are rarely in the church on Sabbath Day.

PROCTOR: No, sir, you are mistaken.

HALE: Twenty-six time in seventeen month, sir. I must call that rare. Will you tell me why you are so absent?

PROCTOR: Mr. Hale, I never knew I must account to that man for I come to church or stay at home. My wife were sick this winter.

HALE: So I am told. But you, Mister, why could you not come alone?

PROCTOR: I surely did come when I could, and when I could not I prayed in this house.

HALE: Mr. Proctor, your house is not a church; your theology must tell you that.

PROCTOR: It does, sir, it does; and it tells me that a minister may pray to God without he have golden candlesticks upon the altar.

HALE: What golden candlesticks?

PROCTOR: Since we built the church there were pewter candlesticks upon the altar; Francis Nurse made them, y'know, and a sweeter hand never touched the metal. But Parris came, and for twenty week he preach nothin' but golden candlesticks until he had them. I labor the earth from dawn of day to blink of night, and I tell you true, when I look to heaven and see my money glaring at his elbows—it hurt my prayer, sir, it hurt my prayer. I think, sometimes, the man dreams cathedrals, not clapboard meetin' houses.

HALE (*thinks, then*): And yet, Mister, a Christian on Sabbath Day must be in church. (*Pause.*) Tell me—you have three children?

PROCTOR: Aye, Boys.

HALE: How comes it that only two are baptized?

PROCTOR (*starts to speak, then stops, then, as though unable to restrain this*): I like it not that Mr. Parris should lay his hand upon my baby. I see no light of God in that man. I'll not conceal it.

HALE: I must say it, Mr. Proctor; that is not for you to decide. The man's ordained, therefore the light of God is in him.

PROCTOR (*flushed with resentment but trying to smile*): What's your suspicion, Mr. Hale?

HALE: No, no, I have no—

PROCTOR: I nailed the roof upon the church, I hung the door—

HALE: Oh, did you! That's a good sign, then.

PROCTOR: It may be I have been too quick to bring the man to book, but you cannot think we ever desired the destruction of religion. I think that's in your mind, is it not?

HALE (*not altogether giving way*): I—have—there is a softness in your record, sir, a softness.

ELIZABETH: I think, maybe, we have been too hard with Mr. Parris. I think so. But sure we never loved the Devil here.

HALE (*nods, deliberating this; then, with the voice of one administering a secret test*): Do you know your Commandments, Elizabeth?

ELIZABETH (*without hesitation, even eagerly*): I surely do. There be no mark of blame upon my life, Mr. Hale. I am a covenanted, Christian woman.

HALE: And you, Mister?

PROCTOR (*a trifle unsteadily*): I—am sure I do, sir.

HALE (*glances at her open face, then at* JOHN, *then*): Let you repeat them, if you will.

PROCTOR: The Commandments.

HALE: Aye.

PROCTOR (*looking off, beginning to sweat*): Thou shalt not kill.

HALE: Aye.

PROCTOR (*counting on his fingers*): Thou shalt not steal. Thou shalt not covet thy neighbor's goods, nor make unto thee any graven image. Thou shalt not take the name of the Lord in vain; thou shalt have no other gods before me. (*With some hesitation*) Thou shalt remember the Sabbath Day and keep it holy. (*Pause. Then*) Thou shalt honor thy father and mother. Thou shalt not bear false witness. (*He is stuck. He counts back on his fingers, knowing one is missing.*) Thou shalt not make unto thee any graven image.

HALE: You have said that twice, sir.

PROCTOR (*lost*): Aye. (*He is flailing for it.*)

ELIZABETH (*delicately*): Adultery, John.

PROCTOR (*as though a secret arrow had pained his heart*): Aye. (*Trying to grin it away—to* HALE) You see, sir, between the two of us we do know them all. (HALE *only looks at* PROCTOR, *deep in his attempt to define this man.* PROCTOR *grows more uneasy.*) I think it be a small fault.

HALE: Theology, sir, is a fortress; no crack in a fortress may be accounted small. (*He rises; he seems worried now. He paces a little, in deep thought.*)

PROCTOR: There be no love for Satan in this house, Mister.

HALE: I pray it, I pray it dearly. (*He looks to both of them, an attempt at a smile on his face, but his misgivings are clear.*) Well, then— I'll bid you good night.

ELIZABETH (*unable to restrain herself*): Mr. Hale. (*He turns.*) I do think you are suspecting me somewhat? Are you not?

HALE (*obviously disturbed—and evasive*): Goody Proctor, I do not judge you. My duty is to add what I may to the godly wisdom of the court. I pray you both good health and good fortune. (*To* JOHN) Good night, sir. (*He starts out.*)

ELIZABETH (*with a note of desperation*): I think you must tell him, John.

HALE: What's that?

ELIZABETH (*restraining a call*): Will you tell him?

(*Slight pause.* HALE *looks questioningly at* JOHN.)

PROCTOR (*with difficulty*): I—I have no witness and cannot prove it, except my word be taken. But I know the children's sickness had naught to do with witchcraft.

HALE (*stopped, struck*): Naught to do—?

PROCTOR: Mr. Parris discovered them sportin' in the woods. They were startled and took sick. (*Pause.*)

HALE: Who told you this?

PROCTOR (*hesitates, then*): Abigail Williams.

HALE: Abigail!

PROCTOR: Aye.

HALE (*his eyes wide*): Abigail Williams told you it had naught to do with witchcraft!

PROCTOR: She told me the day you came, sir.

HALE (*suspiciously*): Why—why did you keep this?

PROCTOR: I never knew until tonight that the world is gone daft with this nonsense.

HALE: Nonsense! Mister, I have myself examined Tituba, Sarah Good, and numerous others that have confessed to dealing with the Devil. They have *confessed* it.

PROCTOR: And why not, if they must hang for denyin' it? There are them that will swear to anything before they'll hang; have you never thought of that?

HALE: I have. I—I have indeed. (*It is his own suspicion, but he resists it. He glances at* ELIZABETH, *then at* JOHN.) And you—would you testify to this in court?

PROCTOR: I—had not reckoned with goin' into court. But if I must I will.

HALE: Do you falter here?

PROCTOR: I falter nothing, but I may wonder if my story will be credited in such a court. I do wonder on it, when such a steady-minded minister as you will suspicion such a woman that never lied, and cannot, and the world knows she cannot! I may falter somewhat, Mister; I am no fool.

HALE (*Quietly—it has impressed him.*): Proctor, let you open with me now, for I have a rumor that troubles me. It's said you hold no belief that there may even be witches in the world. Is that true, sir?

PROCTOR (*He knows this is critical, and is striving against his disgust with* HALE *and with himself for even answering.*): I know not what I have said, I may have said it. I have wondered if there be witches in the world—although I cannot believe they come among us now.

HALE: Then you do not believe—

PROCTOR: I have no knowledge of it; the Bible speaks of witches, and I will not deny them.

HALE: And you, woman?

ELIZABETH: I—I cannot believe it.

HALE (*shocked*): You cannot!

PROCTOR: Elizabeth, you bewilder him!

ELIZABETH (*to* HALE): I cannot think the Devil may own a woman's soul, Mr. Hale, when she keeps an upright way, as I have. I am a good woman, I know it; and if you believe I may do only good work in the world, and yet be secretly bound to Satan, then I must tell you, sir, I do not believe it.

HALE: But, woman, you do believe there are witches in—

ELIZABETH: If you think that I am one, then I say there are none.

HALE: You surely do not fly against the Gospel, the Gospel—

PROCTOR: She believe in the Gospel, every word!

ELIZABETH: Question Abigail Williams about the Gospel, not myself!

(HALE *stares at her.*)

PROCTOR: She do not mean to doubt the Gospel, sir, you cannot think it. This be a Christian house, sir, a Christian house.

HALE: God keep you both; let the third child be quickly baptized, and go you without fail each Sunday in to Sabbath prayer; and keep a solemn, quiet way among you. I think—

(GILES COREY *appears in doorway.*)

GILES: John!

PROCTOR: Giles! What's the matter?

GILES: They take my wife.

(FRANCIS NURSE *enters.*)

GILES: And his Rebecca!

PROCTOR (*to* FRANCIS): Rebecca's in the *jail!*

FRANCIS: Aye, Cheever come and take her in his wagon. We've only now come from the jail, and they'll not even let us in to see them.

ELIZABETH: They've surely gone wild now, Mr. Hale!

FRANCIS (*going to* HALE): Reverend Hale! Can you not speak to the Deputy Governor? I'm sure he mistakes these people—

HALE: Pray calm yourself, Mr. Nurse.

FRANCIS: My wife is the very brick and mortar of the church, Mr. Hale—(*indicating* Giles)—and Martha Corey, there cannot be a woman closer yet to God than Martha.

HALE: How is Rebecca charged, Mr. Nurse?

FRANCIS (*with a mocking, half-hearted laugh*): For murder, she's charged! (*Mockingly quoting the warrant*) "For the marvelous and supernatural murder of Goody Putnam's babies." What am I to do, Mr. Hale?

HALE (*turns from* FRANCIS, *deeply troubled, then*): Believe me, Mr. Nurse, if Rebecca Nurse be tainted, then nothing's left to stop the whole green world from burning. Let you rest upon the justice of the court; the court will send her home, I know it.

FRANCIS: You cannot mean she will be tried in court!

HALE (*pleading*): Nurse, though our hearts break, we cannot flinch; these are new times, sir. There is a misty plot afoot so subtle we should be criminal to cling to old respects and ancient friendships. I have seen too many frightful proofs in court—the Devil is alive in Salem, and we dare not quail to follow wherever the accusing finger points!

PROCTOR (*angered*): How may such a woman murder children?

HALE (*in great pain*): Man, remember, until an hour before the Devil fell, God thought him beautiful in Heaven.

GILES: I never said my wife were a witch, Mr. Hale; I only said she were reading books!

HALE: Mr. Corey, exactly what complaint were made on your wife?

GILES: That bloody mongrel Walcott charge her. Y'see, he buy a pig of my wife four or five year ago, and the pig died soon after. So he come dancin' in for his money back. So my Martha, she says to him, "Walcott, if you haven't the wit to feed a pig properly, you'll not live to own many," she says. Now he goes to court and claims that from that day to this he cannot keep a pig alive for more than four weeks because my Martha bewitch them with her books!

(*Enter* EZEKIEL CHEEVER. *A shocked silence.*)

CHEEVER: Good evening to you, Proctor.

PROCTOR: Why, Mr. Cheever. Good evening.

CHEEVER: Good evening, all. Good evening, Mr. Hale.

PROCTOR: I hope you come not on business of the court.

CHEEVER: I do, Proctor, aye, I am clerk of the court now, y'know.

(*Enter* MARSHAL HERRICK, *a man in his early*

thirties, who is somewhat shamefaced at the moment.)

GILES: It's a pity, Ezekiel, that an honest tailor might have gone to Heaven must burn in Hell. You'll burn for this, do you know it?

CHEEVER: You know yourself I must do as I'm told. You surely know that, Giles. And I'd as lief you'd not be sending me to Hell. I like not the sound of it, I tell you; I like not the sound of it. (*He fears* PROCTOR, *but starts to reach inside his coat.*) Now believe me, Proctor, how heavy be the law, all its tonnage I do carry on my back tonight. (*He takes out a warrant.*) I have a warrant for your wife.

PROCTOR (*to* HALE): You said she were not charged!

HALE: I know nothin' of it. (*To* CHEEVER) When were she charged?

CHEEVER: I am given sixteen warrant tonight, sir, and she is one.

PROCTOR: Who charged her?

CHEEVER: Why, Abigail Williams charge her.

PROCTOR: On what proof, what proof?

CHEEVER (*looking about the room*): Mr. Proctor, I have little time. The court bid me search your house, but I like not to search a house. So will you hand me any poppets that your wife may keep here?

PROCTOR: Poppets?

ELIZABETH: I never kept no poppets, not since I were a girl.

CHEEVER (*embarrassed, glancing toward the mantel where sits* MARY WARREN'*s poppet*): I spy a poppet, Goody Proctor.

ELIZABETH: Oh! (*Going for it*) Why, this is Mary's.

CHEEVER (*shyly*): Would you please to give it to me?

ELIZABETH (*handing it to him, asks* HALE): Has the court discovered a text in poppets now?

CHEEVER (*carefully holding the poppet*): Do you keep any others in this house?

PROCTOR: No, nor this one either till tonight. What signifies a poppet?

CHEEVER: Why, a poppet—(*he gingerly turns the poppet over*)—a poppet may signify—Now, woman, will you please to come with me?

PROCTOR: She will not! (*To* ELIZABETH) Fetch Mary here.

CHEEVER (*ineptly reaching toward* ELIZABETH): No, no, I am forbid to leave her from my sight.

PROCTOR (*pushing his arm away*): You'll leave her out of sight and out of mind, Mister. Fetch Mary, Elizabeth. (ELIZABETH *goes upstairs.*)

HALE: What signifies a poppet, Mr. Cheever?

CHEEVER (*turning the poppet over in his hands*): Why, they say it may signify that she—(*He has lifted the poppet's skirt, and his eyes widen in astonished fear.*) Why, this, this—

PROCTOR (*reaching for the poppet*): What's there?

CHEEVER: Why—(*he draws out a long needle from the poppet*)—it is a needle! Herrick, Herrick, it is a needle!

(HERRICK *comes toward him.*)

PROCTOR (*angrily, bewildered*): And what signifies a needle!

CHEEVER (*his hands shaking*): Why, this go hard with her, Proctor, this—I had my doubts, Proctor, I had my doubts, but here's calamity. (*To* HALE, *showing the needle*) You see it, sir, it is a needle!

HALE: Why? What meanin' has it?

CHEEVER (*wide-eyed, trembling*): The girl, the Williams girl, Abigail Williams, sir. She sat to dinner in Reverend Parris's house tonight, and without word nor warnin' she falls to the floor. Like a struck beast, he says, and screamed a scream that a bull would weep to hear. And he goes to save her, and, stuck two inches in the flesh of her belly, he draw a needle out. And demandin' of her how she come to be so stabbed, she—(*to* PROCTOR *now*)—testify it were your wife's familiar spirit pushed it in.

PROCTOR: Why, she done it herself! (*To* HALE): I hope you're not takin' this for proof, Mister!

CHEEVER: 'Tis hard proof! (*To* HALE) I find here a poppet Goody Proctor keeps. I have found it, sir. And in the belly of the poppet a needle's stuck. I tell you true, Proctor, I never warranted to see such proof of Hell, and I bid you obstruct me not, for I—

(*Enter* ELIZABETH *with* MARY WARREN. PROCTOR, *seeing* MARY WARREN, *draws her by the arm to* HALE.)

PROCTOR: Here now! Mary, how did this poppet come into my house?

MARY WARREN (*frightened for herself, her voice very small*): What poppet's that, sir?

PROCTOR (*impatiently, points at the doll in* CHEEVER'*s hand*): This poppet, this poppet.

MARY WARREN (*evasively, looking at it*): Why, I—I think it is mine.

PROCTOR: It is your poppet, is it not?

MARY WARREN (*not understanding the direction of this*): It—is, sir.

PROCTOR: And how did it come into this house?

MARY WARREN (*glancing about at the avid faces*): Why—I made it in the court, sir, and—give it to Goody Proctor tonight.

PROCTOR (*to* HALE): Now, sir—do you have it?

HALE: Mary Warren, a needle have been found inside this poppet.

MARY WARREN (*bewildered*): Why, I meant no harm by it, sir.

PROCTOR (*quickly*): You stuck that needle in yourself?

MARY WARREN: I—I believe I did, sir, I—

PROCTOR (*to* HALE): What say you now?

HALE (*watching* MARY WARREN *closely*): Child, you are certain this be your natural memory? May it be, perhaps, that someone conjures you even now to say this?

MARY WARREN: Conjures me? Why, no, sir, I am entirely myself, I think. Let you ask Susanna Walcott—she saw me sewin' it in court. (*Or better still*) Ask Abby, Abby sat beside me when I made it.

PROCTOR (*to* HALE, *of* CHEEVER): Bid him be-gone. Your mind is surely settled now. Bid him out, Mr. Hale.

ELIZABETH: What signifies a needle?

HALE: Mary—you charge a cold and cruel murder on Abigail.

MARY WARREN: Murder! I charge no—

HALE: Abigail were stabbed tonight; a needle were found stuck into her belly—

ELIZABETH: And she charges me?

HALE: Aye.

ELIZABETH (*her breath knocked out*): Why—! The girl is murder! She must be ripped out of the world!

CHEEVER (*pointing at* ELIZABETH): You've heard that, sir! Ripped out of the world! Herrick, you heard it!

PROCTOR (*suddenly snatching the warrant out of* CHEEVER'*s hands*): Out with you.

CHEEVER: Proctor, you dare not touch the warrant.

PROCTOR (*ripping the warrant*): Out with you!

CHEEVER: You've ripped the Deputy Governor's warrant, man!

PROCTOR: Damn the Deputy Governor! Out of my house!

HALE: Now, Proctor, Proctor!

PROCTOR: Get y'gone with them! You are a broken minister.

HALE: Proctor, if she is innocent, the court—

PROCTOR: If *she* is innocent! Why do you never wonder if Parris may be innocent, or Abigail? Is the accuser always holy now? Were they born this morning as clean as God's fingers? I'll tell you what's walking Salem—vengeance is walking Salem. We are what we always were in Salem, but now the little crazy children are jangling the keys of the kingdom, and common vengeance writes the law! This warrant's vengeance! I'll not give my wife to vengeance!

ELIZABETH: I'll go, John—

PROCTOR: You will not go!

HERRICK: I have nine men outside. You cannot keep her. The law binds me, John, I cannot budge.

PROCTOR (*to* HALE, *ready to break him*): Will you see her taken?

HALE: Proctor, the court is just—

PROCTOR: Pontius Pilate! God will not let you wash your hands of this!

ELIZABETH: John—I think I must go with them. (*He cannot bear to look at her.*) Mary, there is bread enough for the morning; you will bake, in the afternoon. Help Mr. Proctor as you were his daughter—you owe me that, and much more. (*She is fighting her weeping. To* PROCTOR) When the children wake, speak nothing of witchcraft—it will frighten them. (*She cannot go on.*)

PROCTOR: I will bring you home. I will bring you soon.

ELIZABETH: Oh, John, bring me soon!

PROCTOR: I will fall like an ocean on that court! Fear nothing, Elizabeth.

ELIZABETH (*with great fear*): I will fear nothing. (*She looks about the room, as though to fix it in her mind.*) Tell the children I have gone to visit someone sick.

(*She walks out the door,* HERRICK *and* CHEEVER *behind her. For a moment,* PROCTOR *watches from the doorway. The clank of chain is heard.*)

PROCTOR: Herrick! Herrick, don't chain her! (*He rushes out the door. From outside*) Damn you, man, you will not chain her! Off with them! I'll not have it! I will not have her chained!

(*There are other men's voices against his.* HALE, *in a fever of guilt and uncertainty, turns from the door to avoid the sight;* MARY WARREN *bursts into tears and sits weeping.* GILES COREY *calls to* HALE.)

GILES: And yet silent, minister? It is fraud, you know it is fraud! What keeps you, man?

(PROCTOR *is half braced, half pushed into the room by two deputies and* HERRICK.)

PROCTOR: I'll pay you, Herrick, I will surely pay you!

HERRICK (*panting*): In God's name, John, I cannot help myself. I must chain them all. Now let you keep inside this house till I am gone! (*He goes out with his deputies.*)

(PROCTOR *stands there, gulping air. Horses and a wagon creaking are heard.*)

HALE (*in great uncertainty*): Mr. Proctor—

PROCTOR: Out of my sight!

HALE: Charity, Proctor, charity. What I have heard in her favor, I will not fear to testify in court. God help me, I cannot judge her guilty or innocent—I know not. Only this consider: the world goes mad, and it profit nothing you should lay the cause to the vengeance of a little girl.

PROCTOR: You are a coward! Though you be ordained in God's own tears, you are a coward now!

HALE: Proctor, I cannot think God be provoked so grandly by such a petty cause. The jails are packed—our greatest judges sit in Salem now—and hangin's promised. Man, we must look to cause proportionate. Were there murder done, perhaps, and never brought to light? Abomination? Some secret blasphemy that stinks to Heaven? Think on cause, man, and let you help me to discover it. For there's your way, believe it, there is your only way, when such confusion strikes upon the world. (*He goes to* GILES *and* FRANCIS.) Let you counsel among yourselves; think on your village and what may have drawn from heaven such thundering wrath upon you all. I shall pray God open up our eyes.

(HALE *goes out.*)

FRANCIS (*struck by* HALE's *mood*): I never heard no murder done in Salem.

PROCTOR (*He has been reached by* HALE's *words.*): Leave me, Francis, leave me.

GILES (*shaken*): John—tell me, are we lost?

PROCTOR: Go home now, Giles. We'll speak on it tomorrow.

GILES: Let you think on it. We'll come early, eh?

PROCTOR: Aye. Go now, Giles.

GILES: Good night, then.

(GILES COREY *goes out. After a moment*)

MARY WARREN (*in a fearful squeak of a voice*): Mr. Proctor, very likely they'll let her come home once they're given proper evidence.

PROCTOR: You're coming to the court with me, Mary. You will tell it in the court.

MARY WARREN: I cannot charge murder on Abigail.

PROCTOR (*moving menacingly toward her*): You will tell the court how that poppet come here and who stuck the needle in.

MARY WARREN: She'll kill me for sayin' that! (PROCTOR *continues toward her.*) Abby'll charge lechery on you, Mr. Proctor!

PROCTOR (*halting*): She's told you!

MARY WARREN: I have known it, sir. She'll ruin you with it, I know she will.

PROCTOR (*hesitating, and with deep hatred of himself*): Good. Then her saintliness is done with. (MARY *backs from him.*) We will slide together into our pit; you will tell the court what you know.

MARY WARREN (*in terror*): I cannot, they'll turn on me—

(PROCTOR *strides and catches her, and she is repeating, "I cannot, I cannot!"*)

PROCTOR: My wife will never die for me! I will bring your guts into your mouth but that goodness will not die for me!

MARY WARREN (*struggling to escape him*): I cannot do it, I cannot!

PROCTOR (*grasping her by the throat as though he would strangle her*): Make your peace with it! Now Hell and Heaven grapple on our backs, and all our old pretense is ripped away—make your peace! (*He throws her to the floor, where she sobs, "I cannot, I cannot . . ." And now, half to himself, staring, and turning to the open door*) Peace. It is a providence, and no great change; we are only what we always were, but naked now. (*He walks as though toward a great horror, facing the open sky.*) Aye, naked! And the wind, God's icy wind, will blow!

(*And she is over and over again sobbing, "I cannot, I cannot, I cannot," as the curtain falls.*)

ACT THREE

The vestry room of the Salem meeting house, now serving as the anteroom of the General Court.

As the curtain rises, the room is empty, but for sunlight pouring through two high windows in the back wall. The room is solemn, even forbid-

ding. *Heavy beams jut out, boards of random widths make up the walls. At the right are two doors leading into the meeting house proper, where the court is being held. At the left another door leads outside.*

There is a plain bench at the left, and another at the right. In the center a rather long meeting table, with stools and a considerable armchair snugged up to it.

Through the partitioning wall at the right we hear a prosecutor's voice, JUDGE HATHORNE's, *asking a question; then a woman's voice,* MARTHA COREY's, *replying.*

HATHORNE'S VOICE: Now, Martha Corey, there is abundant evidence in our hands to show that you have given yourself to the reading of fortunes. Do you deny it?

MARTHA COREY'S VOICE: I am innocent to a witch. I know not what a witch is.

HATHORNE'S VOICE: How do you know, then, that you are not a witch?

MARTHA COREY'S VOICE: If I were, I would know it.

HATHORNE'S VOICE: Why do you hurt these children?

MARTHA COREY'S VOICE: I do not hurt them. I scorn it!

GILES' VOICE (*roaring*):   I have evidence for the court!

(*Voices of townspeople rise in excitement.*)

DANFORTH'S VOICE: You will keep your seat!

GILES' VOICE: Thomas Putnam is reaching out for land!

DANFORTH'S VOICE: Remove that man, Marshal!

GILES' VOICE: You're hearing lies, lies!

(*A roaring goes up from the people.*)

HATHORNE'S VOICE: Arrest him, excellency!

GILES' VOICE: I have evidence. Why will you not hear my evidence?

(*The door opens and* GILES *is half carried into the vestry room by* HERRICK.)

GILES: Hands off, damn you, let me go!

HERRICK: Giles, Giles!

GILES: Out of my way, Herrick! I bring evidence—

HERRICK: You cannot go in there, Giles! it's a court!

(*Enter* HALE *from the court.*)

HALE: Pray be calm a moment.

GILES: You, Mr. Hale, go in there and demand I speak.

HALE: A moment, sir, a moment.

GILES: They'll be hangin' my wife!

(JUDGE HATHORNE *enters. He is in his sixties, a bitter, remorseless Salem judge.*)

HATHORNE: How do you dare come roarin' into this court! Are you gone daft, Corey?

GILES: You're not a Boston judge, Hathorne. You'll not call me daft!

(*Enter* DEPUTY GOVERNOR DANFORTH *and, behind him,* EZEKIEL CHEEVER *and* PARRIS. *On his appearance, silence falls.* DANFORTH *is a grave man in his sixties, of some humor and sophistication that does not, however, interfere with an exact loyalty to his position and his cause. He comes down to* GILES, *who awaits his wrath.*)

DANFORTH (*looking directly at* GILES):   Who is this man?

PARRIS: Giles Corey, sir, and a more contentious—

GILES (*to* PARRIS):   I am asked the question, and I am old enough to answer it! (*To* DANFORTH, *who impresses him and to whom he smiles through his strain*) My name is Corey, sir, Giles Corey. I have six hundred acres, and timber in addition. It is my wife you be condemning now. (*He indicates the courtroom.*)

DANFORTH: And how do you imagine to help her cause with such contemptuous riot? Now be gone. Your old age alone keeps you out of jail for this.

GILES (*beginning to plead*):   They be tellin' lies about my wife, sir, I—

DANFORTH: Do you take it upon yourself to determine what this court shall believe and what it shall set aside?

GILES: Your Excellency, we mean no disrespect for—

DANFORTH: Disrespect indeed! It is disruption, Mister. This is the highest court of the supreme government of this province, do you know it?

GILES (*beginning to weep*):   Your Excellency, I only said she were readin' books, sir, and they come and take her out of my house for—

DANFORTH (*mystified*):   Books! What books?

GILES (*through helpless sobs*):   It is my third wife, sir; I never had no wife that be so taken with books, and I thought to find the cause of it, d'y'see, but it were no witch I blamed her for. (*He is openly weeping.*) I have broke charity with the woman, I have broke charity with her.

(*He covers his face, ashamed.* DANFORTH *is respectfully silent.*)

HALE: Excellency, he claims hard evidence for his wife's defense. I think that in all justice you must—

DANFORTH: Then let him submit his evidence in proper affidavit. You are certainly aware of our procedure here, Mr. Hale. (*To* HERRICK) Clear this room.

HERRICK: Come now, Giles. (*He gently pushes* COREY *out.*)

FRANCIS: We are desperate, sir; we come here three days now and cannot be heard.

DANFORTH: Who is this man?

FRANCIS: Francis Nurse, Your Excellency.

HALE: His wife's Rebecca that were condemned this morning.

DANFORTH: Indeed! I am amazed to find you in such uproar. I have only good report of your character, Mr. Nurse.

HATHORNE: I think they must both be arrested in contempt, sir.

DANFORTH (*to* FRANCIS): Let you write your plea, and in due time I will—

FRANCIS: Excellency, we have proof for your eyes; God forbid you shut them to it. The girls, sir, the girls are frauds.

DANFORTH: What's that?

FRANCIS: We have proof of it, sir. They are all deceiving you.

(DANFORTH *is shocked, but studying* FRANCIS.)

HATHORNE: This is contempt, sir, contempt!

DANFORTH: Peace, Judge Hathorne. Do you know who I am, Mr. Nurse?

FRANCIS: I surely do, sir, and I think you must be a wise judge to be what you are.

DANFORTH: And do you know that near to four hundred are in the jails from Marblehead to Lynn, and upon my signature?

FRANCIS: I—

DANFORTH: And seventy-two condemned to hang by that signature?

FRANCIS: Excellency, I never thought to say it to such a weighty judge, but you are deceived.

(*Enter* GILES COREY *from left. All turn to see as he beckons in* MARY WARREN *with* PROCTOR. MARY *is keeping her eyes to the ground;* PROCTOR *has her elbow as though she were near collapse.*)

PARRIS (*on seeing her, in shock*): Mary Warren! (*He goes directly to bend close to her face.*) What are you about here?

PROCTOR (*pressing* PARRIS *away from her with a gentle but firm motion of protectiveness*): She would speak with the Deputy Governor.

DANFORTH (*shocked by this, turns to* HERRICK): Did you not tell me Mary Warren were sick in bed?

HERRICK: She were, Your Honor. When I go to fetch her to the court last week, she said she were sick.

GILES: She has been strivin' with her soul all week, Your Honor; she comes now to tell the truth of this to you.

DANFORTH: Who is this?

PROCTOR: John Proctor, sir. Elizabeth Proctor is my wife.

PARRIS: Beware this man, Your Excellency, this man is mischief.

HALE (*excitedly*): I think you must hear the girl, sir, she—

DANFORTH (*who has become very interested in* MARY WARREN *and only raises a hand toward* HALE): Peace. What would you tell us, Mary Warren?

(PROCTOR *looks at her, but she cannot speak.*)

PROCTOR: She never saw no spirits, sir.

DANFORTH (*with great alarm and surprise, to* MARY): Never saw no spirits!

GILES (*eagerly*): Never.

PROCTOR (*reaching into his jacket*): She has signed a deposition, sir—

DANFORTH (*instantly*): No, no, I accept no depositions. (*He is rapidly calculating this; he turns from her to* PROCTOR.) Tell me, Mr. Proctor, have you given out this story in the village?

PROCTOR: We have not.

PARRIS: They've come to overthrow the court, sir! This man is—

DANFORTH: I pray you, Mr. Parris. Do you know, Mr. Proctor, that the entire contention of the state in these trials is that the voice of Heaven is speaking through the children?

PROCTOR: I know that, sir.

DANFORTH (*thinks, staring at* PROCTOR, *then turns to* MARY WARREN): And you, Mary Warren, how came you to cry out people for sending their spirits against you?

MARY WARREN: It were pretense, sir.

DANFORTH: I cannot hear you.

PROCTOR: It were pretense, she says.

DANFORTH: Ah? And the other girls? Susanna Walcott, and—the others? They are also pretending?

MARY WARREN: Aye, sir.

DANFORTH (*wide-eyed*): Indeed. (*Pause. He is baffled by this. He turns to study* PROCTOR's *face.*)

PARRIS (*in a sweat*): Excellency, you surely cannot think to let so vile a lie be spread in open court.

DANFORTH: Indeed not, but it strike hard upon me that she will dare come here with such a tale. Now, Mr. Proctor, before I decide whether I shall hear you or not, it is my duty to tell you this. We burn a hot fire here; it melts down all concealment.

PROCTOR: I know that, sir.

DANFORTH: Let me continue. I understand well, a husband's tenderness may drive him to extravagance in defense of a wife. Are you certain in your conscience, Mister, that your evidence is the truth?

PROCTOR: It is. And you will surely know it.

DANFORTH: And you thought to declare this revelation in the open court before the public?

PROCTOR: I thought I would, aye—with your permission.

DANFORTH (*his eyes narrowing*): Now, sir, what is your purpose in so doing?

PROCTOR: Why, I—I would free my wife, sir.

DANFORTH: There lurks nowhere in your heart, nor hidden in your spirit, any desire to undermine this court?

PROCTOR (*with the faintest faltering*): Why, no, sir.

CHEEVER (*clears his throat, awakening*): I—Your Excellency.

DANFORTH: Mr. Cheever.

CHEEVER: I think it be my duty, sir—(*Kindly, to* PROCTOR) You'll not deny it, John. (*To* DANFORTH) When we come to take his wife, he damned the court and ripped your warrant.

PARRIS: Now you have it!

DANFORTH: He did that, Mr. Hale?

HALE (*takes a breath*): Aye, he did.

PROCTOR: It were a temper, sir. I knew not what I did.

DANFORTH (*studying him*): Mr. Proctor.

PROCTOR: Aye, sir.

DANFORTH (*straight into his eyes*): Have you ever seen the Devil?

PROCTOR: No, sir.

DANFORTH: You are in all respects a Gospel Christian?

PROCTOR: I am, sir.

PARRIS: Such a Christian that will not come to church but once in a month!

DANFORTH (*Restrained—he is curious.*): Not come to church?

PROCTOR: I—I have no love for Mr. Parris. It is no secret. But God I surely love.

CHEEVER: He plow on Sunday, sir.

DANFORTH: Plow on Sunday!

CHEEVER (*apologetically*): I think it be evidence, John. I am an official of the court, I cannot keep it.

PROCTOR: I—I have once or twice plowed on Sunday. I have three children, sir, and until last year my land give little.

GILES: You'll find other Christians that do plow on Sunday if the truth be known.

HALE: Your Honor, I cannot think you may judge the man on such evidence.

DANFORTH: I judge nothing. (*Pause. He keeps watching* PROCTOR, *who tries to meet his gaze.*) I tell you straight, Mister—I have seen marvels in this court. I have seen people choked before my eyes by spirits; I have seen them stuck by pins and slashed by daggers. I have until this moment not the slightest reason to suspect that the children may be deceiving me. Do you understand my meaning?

PROCTOR: Excellency, does it not strike upon you that so many of these women have lived so long with such upright reputation, and—

PARRIS: Do you read the Gospel, Mr. Proctor?

PROCTOR: I read the Gospel.

PARRIS: I think not, or you should surely know that Cain were an upright man, and yet he did kill Abel.

PROCTOR: Aye, God tells us that. (*To* DANFORTH) But who tells us Rebecca Nurse murdered seven babies by sending out her spirit on them? It is the children only, and this one will swear she lied to you.

(DANFORTH *considers, then beckons* HATHORNE *to him.* HATHORNE *leans in, and he speaks in his ear.* HATHORNE *nods.*)

HATHORNE: Aye, she's the one.

DANFORTH: Mr. Proctor, this morning, your wife send me a claim in which she states that she is pregnant now.

PROCTOR: My wife pregnant!

DANFORTH: There be no sign of it—we have examined her body.

PROCTOR: But if she say she is pregnant, then she must be! That woman will never lie, Mr. Danforth.

DANFORTH: She will not?

PROCTOR: Never, sir, never.

DANFORTH: We have thought it too convenient to be credited. However, if I should tell you now that I will let her be kept another month; and if she begin to show her natural signs, you shall have her living yet another year until she is delivered—what say you to that? (JOHN PROCTOR *is struck silent.*) Come now. You say your only purpose is to save your wife. Good, then, she is saved at least this year, and a year is long. What say you, sir? It is done now. (*In conflict,* PROCTOR *glances at* FRANCIS *and* GILES.) Will you drop this charge?

PROCTOR: I—I think I cannot.

DANFORTH (*now an almost imperceptible hardness in his voice*): Then your purpose is somewhat larger.

PARRIS: He's come to overthrow this court, Your Honor!

PROCTOR: These are my friends. Their wives are also accused—

DANFORTH (*with a sudden briskness of manner*): I judge you not, sir. I am ready to hear your evidence.

PROCTOR: I come not to hurt the court; I only—

DANFORTH (*cutting him off*): Marshal, go into the court and bid Judge Stoughton and Judge Sewall declare recess for one hour. And let them go to the tavern, if they will. All witnesses and prisoners are to be kept in the building.

HERRICK: Aye, sir. (*Very deferentially*) If I may say it, sir, I know this man all my life. It is a good man, sir.

DANFORTH (*It is the reflection on himself he resents.*): I am sure of it, Marshal. (HERRICK *nods, then goes out.*) Now, what deposition do you have for us, Mr. Proctor? And I beg you be clear, open as the sky, and honest.

PROCTOR (*as he takes out several papers*): I am no lawyer, so I'll—

DANFORTH: The pure in heart need no lawyers. Proceed as you will.

PROCTOR (*handing* DANFORTH *a paper*): Will you read this first, sir? It's a sort of testament. The people signing it declare their good opinion of Rebecca, and my wife, and Martha Corey. (DANFORTH *looks down at the paper.*)

PARRIS (*to enlist* DANFORTH's *sarcasm*): Their good opinion! (*But* DANFORTH *goes on reading, and* PROCTOR *is heartened.*)

PROCTOR: These are all landholding farmers, members of the church. (*Delicately, trying to point out a paragraph*) If you'll notice, sir— they've known the women many years and never saw no sign they had dealings with the Devil.

(PARRIS *nervously moves over and reads over* DANFORTH's *shoulder.*)

DANFORTH (*glancing down a long list*): How many names are here?

FRANCIS: Ninety-one, Your Excellency.

PARRIS (*sweating*): These people should be summoned. (DANFORTH *looks up at him questioningly.*) For questioning.

FRANCIS (*trembling with anger*): Mr. Danforth, I gave them all my word no harm would come to them for signing this.

PARRIS: This is a clear attack upon the court!

HALE (*to* PARRIS, *trying to contain himself*): Is every defense an attack upon the court? Can no one—?

PARRIS: All innocent and Christian people are happy for the courts in Salem! These people are gloomy for it. (*To* DANFORTH *directly*) And I think you will want to know, from each and every one of them, what discontents them with you!

HATHORNE: I think they ought to be examined, sir.

DANFORTH: It is not necessarily an attack, I think. Yet—

FRANCIS: These are all covenanted Christians, sir.

DANFORTH: Then I am sure they may have nothing to fear. (*Hands* CHEEVER *the paper*) Mr. Cheever, have warrants drawn for all of these— arrest for examination. (*To* PROCTOR) Now, Mister, what other information do you have for us? (FRANCIS *is still standing, horrified.*) You may sit, Mr. Nurse.

FRANCIS: I have brought trouble on these people; I have—

DANFORTH: No, old man, you have not hurt these people if they are of good conscience. But you must understand, sir, that a person is either with this court or he must be counted against it, there be no road between. This is a sharp time, now, a precise time—we live no longer in the dusky afternoon when evil mixed itself with good and befuddled the world. Now, by God's grace, the shining sun is up, and them that fear not light will surely praise it. I hope you will be one of those. (MARY WARREN *suddenly sobs.*) She's not hearty, I see.

PROCTOR: No, she's not, sir. (*To* MARY, *bending*

to her, holding her hand, quietly) Now remember what the angel Raphael said to the boy Tobias. Remember it.

MARY WARREN (*hardly audible*): Aye.

PROCTOR: "Do that which is good, and no harm shall come to thee."

MARY WARREN: Aye.

DANFORTH: Come, man, we wait you.

(MARSHAL HERRICK *returns, and takes his post at the door.*)

GILES: John, my deposition, give him mine.

PROCTOR: Aye. (*He hands* DANFORTH *another paper.*) This is Mr. Corey's deposition.

DANFORTH: Oh? (*He looks down at it. Now* HATHORNE *comes behind him and reads with him.*)

HATHORNE (*suspiciously*): What lawyer drew this, Corey?

GILES: You know I never hired a lawyer in my life, Hathorne.

DANFORTH (*finishing the reading*): It is very well phrased. My compliments. Mr. Parris, if Mr. Putnam is in the court, will you bring him in? (HATHORNE *takes the deposition, and walks to the window with it.* PARRIS *goes into the court.*) You have no legal training, Mr. Corey?

GILES (*very pleased*): I have the best, sir—I am thirty-three time in court in my life. And always plaintiff, too.

DANFORTH: Oh, then you're much put-upon.

GILES: I am never put-upon; I know my rights, sir, and I will have them. You know, your father tried a case of mine—might be thirty-five year ago, I think.

DANFORTH: Indeed.

GILES: He never spoke to you of it?

DANFORTH: No, I cannot recall it.

GILES: That's strange, he give me nine pound damages. He were a fair judge, your father. Y'see, I had a white mare that time, and this fellow come to borrow the mare—(*Enter* PARRIS *with* THOMAS PUTNAM. *When he sees* PUTNAM, GILES' *ease goes; he is hard.*) Aye, there he is.

DANFORTH: Mr. Putnam, I have here an accusation by Mr. Corey against you. He states that you coldly prompted your daughter to cry witchery upon George Jacobs that is now in jail.

PUTNAM: It is a lie.

DANFORTH (*turning to* GILES): Mr. Putnam states your charge is a lie. What say you to that?

GILES (*furious, his fists clenched*): A fart on Thomas Putnam, that is what I say to that!

DANFORTH: What proof do you submit for your charge, sir?

GILES: My proof is there! (*Pointing to the paper*) If Jacobs hangs for a witch he forfeit up his property—that's law! And there is none but Putnam with the coin to buy so great a piece. This man is killing his neighbors for their land!

DANFORTH: But proof, sir, proof.

GILES (*pointing at his deposition*): The proof is there! I have it from an honest man who heard Putnam say it! The day his daughter cried out on Jacobs, he said she'd given him a fair gift of land.

HATHORNE: And the name of this man?

GILES (*taken aback*): What name?

HATHORNE: The man that give you this information.

GILES (*hesitates, then*): Why, I—I cannot give you his name.

HATHORNE: And why not?

GILES (*hesitates, then bursts out*): You know well why not! He'll lay in jail if I give his name!

HATHORNE: This is contempt of the court, Mr. Danforth!

DANFORTH (*to avoid that*): You will surely tell us the name.

GILES: I will not give you no name. I mentioned my wife's name once and I'll burn in hell long enough for that. I stand mute.

DANFORTH: In that case, I have no choice but to arrest you for contempt of this court, do you know that?

GILES: This is a hearing; you cannot clap me for contempt of a hearing.

DANFORTH: Oh, it is a proper lawyer! Do you wish me to declare the court in full session here? Or will you give me good reply?

GILES (*faltering*): I cannot give you no name, sir, I cannot.

DANFORTH: You are a foolish old man. Mr. Cheever, begin the record. The court is now in session. I ask you, Mr. Corey—

PROCTOR (*breaking in*): Your Honor—he has the story in confidence, sir, and he—

PARRIS: The Devil lives on such confidences! (*To* DANFORTH) Without confidences there could be no conspiracy, Your Honor!

HATHORNE: I think it must be broken, sir.

DANFORTH (*to* GILES): Old man, if your informant tells the truth let him come here openly like a decent man. But if he hide in anonymity I must know why. Now sir, the government and

central church demand of you the name of him
who reported Mr. Thomas Putnam a common
murderer.

HALE: Excellency—

DANFORTH: Mr. Hale.

HALE: We cannot blink it more. There is a
prodigious fear of this court in the country—

DANFORTH: Then there is a prodigious guilt
in the country. Are *you* afraid to be questioned
here?

HALE: I may only fear the Lord, sir, but there
is fear in the country nevertheless.

DANFORTH (*angered now*): Reproach me not
with the fear in the country; there is fear in the
country because there is a moving plot to topple
Christ in the country!

HALE: But it does not follow that everyone
accused is part of it.

DANFORTH: No uncorrupted man may fear
this court, Mr. Hale! None! (*To* GILES): You are
under arrest in contempt of this court. Now sit
you down and take counsel with yourself, or you
will be set in the jail until you decide to answer
all questions.

(GILES COREY *makes a rush for* PUTNAM.
PROCTOR *lunges and holds him.*)

PROCTOR: No, Giles!

GILES (*over* PROCTOR'S *shoulder at* PUTNAM): I'll
cut your throat, Putnam, I'll kill you yet!

PROCTOR (*forcing him into a chair*): Peace,
Giles, peace. (*Releasing him.*) We'll prove our-
selves. Now we will. (*He starts to turn to*
DANFORTH.)

GILES: Say nothin' more, John. (*Pointing at*
DANFORTH) He's only playin' you! He means to
hang us all!

(MARY WARREN *bursts into sobs.*)

DANFORTH: This is a court of law, Mister. I'll
have no effrontery here!

PROCTOR: Forgive him, sir, for his old age.
Peace, Giles, we'll prove it all now. (*He lifts up*
MARY'S *chin.*) You cannot weep, Mary. Remember the angel, what he say to the boy. Hold to
it, now; there is your rock. (MARY *quiets. He takes
out a paper, and turns to* DANFORTH.) This is
Mary Warren's deposition. I—I would ask you
remember, sir, while you read it, that until two
week ago she were no different than the other
children are today. (*He is speaking reasonably,
restraining all his fears, his anger, his anxiety.*)
You saw her scream, she howled, she swore familiar spirits choked her; she even testified that

Satan, in the form of women now in jail, tried
to win her soul away, and then when she refused—

DANFORTH: We know all this.

PROCTOR: Aye, sir. She swears now that she
never saw Satan; nor any spirit, vague or clear,
that Satan may have sent to hurt her. And she
declares her friends are lying now.

(PROCTOR *starts to hand* DANFORTH *the deposition, and* HALE *comes up to* DANFORTH *in a trembling state.*)

HALE: Excellency, a moment. I think this goes
to the heart of the matter.

DANFORTH (*with deep misgivings*): It surely
does.

HALE: I cannot say he is an honest man; I
know him little. But in all justice, sir, a claim
so weighty cannot be argued by a farmer. In
God's name, sir, stop here; send him home and
let him come again with a lawyer—

DANFORTH (*patiently*): Now look you, Mr.
Hale—

HALE: Excellency, I have signed seventy-two
death warrants; I am a minister of the Lord, and
I dare not take a life without there be a proof
so immaculate no slightest qualm of conscience
may doubt it.

DANFORTH: Mr. Hale, you surely do not doubt
my justice.

HALE: I have this morning signed away the
soul of Rebecca Nurse, Your Honor. I'll not conceal it, my hand shakes yet as with a wound! I
pray you, sir, *this* argument let lawyers present
to you.

DANFORTH: Mr. Hale, believe me; for a man
of such terrible learning you are most bewildered—I hope you will forgive me. I have been
thirty-two year at the bar, sir, and I should be
confounded were I called upon to defend these
people. Let you consider, now—(*To* PROCTOR
and the others) And I bid you all do likewise.
In an ordinary crime, how does one defend the
accused? One calls up witnesses to prove his
innocence. But witchcraft is *ipso facto*, on its face
and by its nature, an invisible crime, is it not?
Therefore, who may possibly be witness to it?
The witch and the victim. None other. Now we
cannot hope the witch will accuse herself;
granted? Therefore, we must rely upon her
victims--and they do testify, the children certainly do testify. As for the witches, none will
deny that we are most eager for all their confes-

sions. Therefore, what is left for a lawyer to bring out? I think I have made my point. Have I not?

HALE: But this child claims the girls are not truthful, and if they are not—

DANFORTH: That is precisely what I am about to consider, sir. What more may you ask of me? Unless you doubt my probity?

HALE (*defeated*):   I surely do not, sir. Let you consider it, then.

DANFORTH: And let you put your heart to rest. Her deposition, Mr. Proctor.

(PROCTOR *hands it to him.* HATHORNE *rises, goes beside* DANFORTH, *and starts reading.* PARRIS *comes to his other side.* DANFORTH *looks at* JOHN PROCTOR, *then proceeds to read.* HALE *gets up, finds position near the* JUDGE, *reads too.* PROCTOR *glances at* GILES. FRANCIS *prays silently, hands pressed together.* CHEEVER *waits placidly, the sublime official, dutiful.* MARY WARREN *sobs once.* JOHN PROCTOR *touches her head reassuringly. Presently* DANFORTH *lifts his eyes, stands up, takes out a kerchief and blows his nose. The others stand aside as he moves in thought toward the window.*)

PARRIS (*hardly able to contain his anger and fear*):   I should like to question—

DANFORTH (*his first real outburst, in which his contempt for* PARRIS *is clear*):   Mr. Parris, I bid you be silent! (*He stands in silence, looking out the window. Now, having established that he will set the gait*) Mr. Cheever, will you go into the court and bring the children here? (CHEEVER *gets up and goes out upstage.* DANFORTH *now turns to* MARY.) Mary Warren, how came you to this turnabout? Has Mr. Proctor threatened you for this deposition?

MARY WARREN: No, sir.

DANFORTH: Has he ever threatened you?

MARY WARREN (*weaker*):   No, sir.

DANFORTH (*sensing a weakening*):   Has he threatened you?

MARY WARREN: No, sir.

DANFORTH: Then you tell me that you sat in my court, callously lying, when you knew that people would hang by your evidence? (*She does not answer.*) Answer me!

MARY WARREN (*almost inaudibly*):   I did, sir.

DANFORTH: How were you instructed in your life? Do you not know that God damns all liars? (*She cannot speak.*) Or is it now that you lie?

MARY WARREN: No, sir—I am with God now.

DANFORTH: You are with God now.

MARY WARREN: Aye, sir.

DANFORTH (*containing himself*):   I will tell you this—you are either lying now, or you were lying in the court, and in either case you have committed perjury and you will go to jail for it. You cannot lightly say you lied, Mary. Do you know that?

MARY WARREN: I cannot lie no more. I am with God, I am with God.

(*But she breaks into sobs at the thought of it, and the right door opens, and enter* SUSANNA WALCOTT, MERCY LEWIS, BETTY PARRIS, *and finally* ABIGAIL. CHEEVER *comes to* DANFORTH.)

CHEEVER: Ruth Putnam's not in the court, sir, nor the other children.

DANFORTH: These will be sufficient. Sit you down, children. (*Silently they sit.*) Your friend, Mary Warren, has given us a deposition. In which she swears that she never saw familiar spirits, apparitions, nor any manifest of the Devil. She claims as well that none of you have seen these things either. (*Slight pause.*) Now, children, this is a court of law. The law, based upon the Bible, and the Bible, writ by Almighty God, forbid the practice of witchcraft, and describe death as the penalty thereof. But likewise, children, the law and Bible damn all bearers of false witness. (*Slight pause.*) Now then. It does not escape me that this deposition may be devised to blind us; it may well be that Mary Warren has been conquered by Satan, who sends her here to distract our sacred purpose. If so, her neck will break for it. But if she speak true, I bid you now drop your guile and confess your pretense, for a quick confession will go easier with you. (*Pause.*) Abigail Williams, rise. (*Abigail slowly rises.*) Is there any truth in this?

ABIGAIL: No, sir.

DANFORTH (*thinks, glances at* MARY, *then back to* ABIGAIL):   Children, a very augur bit will now be turned into your souls until your honesty is proved. Will either of you change your positions now, or do you force me to hard questioning?

ABIGAIL: I have naught to change, sir. She lies.

DANFORTH (*to* MARY):   You would still go on with this?

MARY WARREN (*faintly*):   Aye, sir.

DANFORTH (*turning to Abigail*):   A poppet were discovered in Mr. Proctor's house, stabbed by a needle. Mary Warren claims that you sat beside her in the court when she made it, and that you saw her make it and witnessed how she herself stuck the needle into it for safe-keeping. What say you to that?

ABIGAIL (*with a slight note of indignation*): It is a lie, sir.

DANFORTH (*after a slight pause*): While you worked for Mr. Proctor, did you see poppets in that house?

ABIGAIL: Goody Proctor always kept poppets.

PROCTOR: Your Honor, my wife never kept no poppets. Mary Warren confesses it was her poppet.

CHEEVER: Your Excellency.

DANFORTH: Mr. Cheever.

CHEEVER: When I spoke with Goody Proctor in that house, she said she never kept no poppets. But she said she did keep poppets when she were a girl.

PROCTOR: She has not been a girl these fifteen years, Your Honor.

HATHORNE: But a poppet will keep fifteen years, will it not?

PROCTOR: It will keep if it is kept, but Mary Warren swears she never saw no poppets in my house, nor anyone else.

PARRIS: Why could there not have been poppets hid where no one ever saw them?

PROCTOR (*furious*): There might also be a dragon with five legs in my house, but no one has ever seen it.

PARRIS: We are here, Your Honor, precisely to discover what no one has ever seen.

PROCTOR: Mr. Danforth, what profit this girl to turn herself about? What may Mary Warren gain but hard questioning and worse?

DANFORTH: You are charging Abigail Williams with a marvelous cool plot to murder, do you understand that?

PROCTOR: I do, sir. I believe she means to murder.

DANFORTH (*pointing at* ABIGAIL, *incredulously*): This child would murder your wife?

PROCTOR: It is not a child. Now hear me, sir. In the sight of the congregation she were twice this year put out of this meetin' house for laughter during prayer.

DANFORTH (*shocked, turning to* ABIGAIL): What's this? Laughter during—!

PARRIS: Excellency, she were under Tituba's power at that time, but she is solemn now.

GILES: Aye, now she is solemn and goes to hang people!

DANFORTH: Quiet, man.

HATHORNE: Surely it have no bearing on the question, sir. He charges contemplation of murder.

DANFORTH: Aye. (*He studies* ABIGAIL *for a moment. Then*) Continue, Mr. Proctor.

PROCTOR: Mary. Now tell the Governor how you danced in the woods.

PARRIS (*instantly*): Excellency, since I come to Salem this man is blackening my name. He—

DANFORTH: In a moment, sir. (*To* MARY WARREN, *sternly, and surprised*) What is this dancing?

MARY WARREN: I—(*She glances at* ABIGAIL, *who is staring down at her remorselessly. Then, appealing to* PROCTOR) Mr. Proctor—

PROCTOR (*taking it right up*): Abigail leads the girls to the woods, Your Honor, and they have danced there naked—

PARRIS: Your Honor, this—

PROCTOR (*at once*): Mr. Parris discovered them himself in the dead of night! There's the "child" she is!

DANFORTH (*It is growing into a nightmare, and he turns, astonished, to* PARRIS.): Mr. Parris—

PARRIS: I can only say, sir, that I never found any of them naked, and this man is—

DANFORTH: But you discovered them dancing in the woods? (*Eyes on Parris, he points at* ABIGAIL.) Abigail?

HALE: Excellency, when I first arrived from Beverly, Mr. Parris told me that.

DANFORTH: Do you deny it, Mr. Parris?

PARRIS: I do not, sir, but I never saw any of them naked.

DANFORTH: But she have *danced?*

PARRIS (*unwillingly*): Aye, sir.

(DANFORTH, *as though with new eyes, looks at* ABIGAIL.)

HATHORNE: Excellency, will you permit me? (*He points at* MARY WARREN.)

DANFORTH (*with great worry*): Pray, proceed.

HATHORNE: You say you never saw no spirits, Mary, were never threatened or afflicted by any manifest of the Devil or the Devil's agents.

MARY WARREN (*very faintly*): No, sir.

HATHORNE (*with a gleam of victory*): And yet, when people accused of witchery confronted you in court, you would faint, saying their spirits came out of their bodies and choked you—

MARY WARREN: That were pretense, sir.

DANFORTH: I cannot hear you.

MARY WARREN: Pretense, sir.

PARRIS: But you did turn cold, did you not? I myself picked you up many times, and your skin were icy. Mr. Danforth, you—

DANFORTH: I saw that many times.

PROCTOR: She only pretended to faint, Your Excellency. They're all marvelous pretenders.

HATHORNE: Then can she pretend to faint now?

PROCTOR: Now?

PARRIS: Why not? Now there are no spirits attacking her, for none in this room is accused of witchcraft. So let her turn herself cold now, let her pretend she is attacked now, let her faint. (*He turns to* MARY WARREN.) Faint!

MARY WARREN: Faint?

PARRIS: Aye, faint. Prove to us how you pretended in the court so many times.

MARY WARREN (*looking to* PROCTOR):   I—cannot faint now, sir.

PROCTOR (*alarmed, quietly*):   Can you not pretend it?

MARY WARREN: I—(*She looks about as though searching for the passion to faint.*) I—have no *sense* of it now, I—

DANFORTH: Why? What is lacking now?

MARY WARREN: I—cannot tell, sir, I—

DANFORTH: Might it be that here we have no afflicting spirit loose, but in the court there were some?

MARY WARREN: I never saw no spirits.

PARRIS: Then see no spirits now, and prove to us that you can faint by your own will, as you claim.

MARY WARREN (*stares, searching for the emotion of it, and then shakes her head*):   I—cannot do it.

PARRIS: Then you will confess, will you not? It were attacking spirits made you faint!

MARY WARREN: No, sir, I—

PARRIS: Your Excellency, this is a trick to blind the court!

MARY WARREN: It's not a trick! (*She stands.*) I—I used to faint because I—I thought I saw spirits.

DANFORTH: *Thought* you saw them!

MARY WARREN: But I did not, Your Honor.

HATHORNE: How could you think you saw them unless you saw them?

MARY WARREN: I—I cannot tell how, but I did. I—I heard the other girls screaming, and you, Your Honor, you seemed to believe them, and I—It were only sport in the beginning, sir, but then the whole world cried spirits, spirits, and I—I promise you, Mr. Danforth, I only thought I saw them but I did not.

(DANFORTH *peers at her.*)

PARRIS (*smiling, but nervous because* DANFORTH *seems to be struck by* MARY WARREN'*s story*):   Surely Your Excellency is not taken by this simple lie.

DANFORTH (*turning worriedly to* ABIGAIL):   Abigail. I bid you now search your heart and tell me this—and beware of it, child, to God every soul is precious and His vengeance is terrible on them that take life without cause. Is it possible, child, that the spirits you have seen are illusion only, some deception that may cross your mind when—

ABIGAIL: Why, this—this—is a base question, sir.

DANFORTH: Child, I would have you consider it—

ABIGAIL: I have been hurt, Mr. Danforth; I have seen my blood runnin' out! I have been near to murdered every day because I done my duty pointing out the Devil's people—and this is my reward? To be mistrusted, denied, questioned like a—

DANFORTH (*weakening*):   Child, I do not mistrust you—

ABIGAIL (*in an open threat*):   Let *you* beware, Mr. Danforth. Think you to be so mighty that the power of Hell may not turn *your* wits? Beware of it! There is—(*Suddenly, from an accusatory attitude, her face turns, looking into the air above—it is truly frightened.*)

DANFORTH (*apprehensively*):   What is it, child?

ABIGAIL (*looking about in the air, clasping her arms about her as though cold*):   I—I know not. A wind, a cold wind, has come. (*Her eyes fall on* MARY WARREN.)

MARY WARREN (*terrified, pleading*):   Abby!

MERCY LEWIS (*shivering*):   Your Honor, I freeze!

PROCTOR: They're pretending!

HATHORNE (*touching* ABIGAIL'*s hand*):   She is cold, Your Honor, touch her!

MERCY LEWIS (*through chattering teeth*):   Mary, do you send this shadow on me?

MARY WARREN: Lord, save me!

SUSANNA WALCOTT: I freeze, I freeze!

ABIGAIL (*shivering visibly*):   It is a wind, a wind!

MARY WARREN: Abby, don't do that!

DANFORTH (*himself engaged and entered by* ABIGAIL): Mary Warren, do you witch her? I say to you, do you send your spirit out?

(*With a hysterical cry* MARY WARREN *starts to run.* PROCTOR *catches her.*)

MARY WARREN (*almost collapsing*): Let me go, Mr. Proctor, I cannot, I cannot—

ABIGAIL (*crying to Heaven*): Oh, Heavenly Father, take away this shadow!

(*Without warning or hesitation,* PROCTOR *leaps at* ABIGAIL *and, grabbing her by the hair, pulls her to her feet. She screams in pain.* DANFORTH, *astonished, cries, "What are you about?" and* HATHORNE *and* PARRIS *call, "Take your hands off her!" and out of it all comes* PROCTOR'*s roaring voice.*)

PROCTOR: How do you call Heaven! Whore! Whore!

(HERRICK *breaks* PROCTOR *from her.*)

HERRICK: John!

DANFORTH: Man! Man, what do you—

PROCTOR (*breathless and in agony*): It is a whore!

DANFORTH (*dumfounded*): You charge—?

ABIGAIL: Mr. Danforth, he is lying!

PROCTOR: Mark her! Now she'll suck a scream to stab me with, but—

DANFORTH: You will prove this! This will not pass!

PROCTOR (*trembling, his life collapsing about him*): I have known her, sir. I have known her.

DANFORTH: You—you are a lecher?

FRANCIS (*horrified*): John, you cannot say such a—

PROCTOR: Oh, Francis, I wish you had some evil in you that you might know me! (*To* DANFORTH) A man will not cast away his good name. You surely know that.

DANFORTH (*dumfounded*): In—in what time? In what place?

PROCTOR (*his voice about to break, and his shame great*): In the proper place—where my beasts are bedded. On the last night of my joy, some eight months past. She used to serve me in my house, sir. (*He has to clamp his jaw to keep from weeping.*) A man may think God sleeps, but God sees everything. I know it now. I beg you, sir, I beg you—see her what she is. My wife, my dear good wife, took this girl soon after, sir, and put her out on the highroad. And being what she is, a lump of vanity, sir—(*He is being overcome.*)

Excellency, forgive me, forgive me. (*Angrily against himself, he turns away from the governor for a moment. Then, as though to cry out is his only means of speech left*) She thinks to dance with me on my wife's grave! And well she might, for I thought of her softly. God help me, I lusted, and there *is* a promise in such sweat. But it is a whore's vengeance, and you must see it; I set myself entirely in your hands. I know you must see it now.

DANFORTH (*blanched, in horror, turning to* ABIGAIL): You deny every scrap and tittle of this?

ABIGAIL: If I must answer that, I will leave and I will not come back again!

(DANFORTH *seems unsteady.*)

PROCTOR: I have a bell of my honor! I have rung the doom of my good name—you will believe me, Mr. Danforth! My wife is innocent, except she knew a whore when she saw one!

ABIGAIL (*stepping up to* DANFORTH): What look do you give me? (DANFORTH *cannot speak.*) I'll not have such looks! (*She turns and starts for the door.*)

DANFORTH: You will remain where you are! (HERRICK *steps into her path. She comes up short, fire in her eyes.*) Mr. Parris, go into the court and bring Goodwife Proctor out.

PARRIS (*objecting*): Your Honor, this is all a—

DANFORTH (*sharply to* PARRIS): Bring her out! And tell her not one word of what's been spoken here. And let you knock before you enter. (PARRIS *goes out.*) Now we shall touch the bottom of this swamp. (*To* PROCTOR) Your wife, you say, is an honest woman.

PROCTOR: In her life, sir, she have never lied. There are them that cannot sing, and them that cannot weep—my wife cannot lie. I have paid much to learn it, sir.

DANFORTH: And when she put this girl out of your house, she put her out for a harlot?

PROCTOR: Aye, sir.

DANFORTH: And knew her for a harlot?

PROCTOR: Aye, sir, she knew her for a harlot.

DANFORTH: Good then. (*To* ABIGAIL) And if she tell me, child, it were for harlotry, may God spread His mercy on you! (*There is a knock. He calls to the door.*) Hold! (*To* ABIGAIL) Turn your back. Turn your back. (*To* PROCTOR) Do likewise. (*Both turn their backs—*ABIGAIL *with indignant slowness.*) Now let neither of you turn to face Goody Proctor. No one in this room is to speak one word, or raise a gesture aye or nay. (*He turns toward the door, calls.*) Enter! (*The door opens.* ELIZABETH *enters with* PARRIS. PARRIS *leaves her. She stands alone, her eyes looking for* PROCTOR.) Mr. Cheever, report this testimony in all exactness. Are you ready?

CHEEVER: Ready, sir.

DANFORTH: Come here, woman. (ELIZABETH *comes to him, glancing at* PROCTOR's *back.*) Look at me only, not at your husband. In my eyes only.

ELIZABETH (*faintly*): Good, sir.

DANFORTH: We are given to understand that at one time you dismissed your servant, Abigail Williams.

ELIZABETH: That is true, sir.

DANFORTH: For what cause did you dismiss her? (*Slight pause. Then* ELIZABETH *tries to glance at* PROCTOR.) You will look in my eyes only and not at your husband. The answer is in your memory and you need no help to give it to me. Why did you dismiss Abigail Williams?

ELIZABETH (*not knowing what to say, sensing a situation, wetting her lips to stall for time*): She—dissatisfied me. (*Pause.*) And my husband.

DANFORTH: In what way dissatisfied you?

ELIZABETH: She were—(*She glances at* PROCTOR *for a cue.*)

DANFORTH: Woman, look at me! (ELIZABETH *does.*) Were she slovenly? Lazy? What disturbance did she cause?

ELIZABETH: Your Honor, I—in that time I were sick. And I—My husband is a good and righteous man. He is never drunk as some are, nor wastin' his time at the shovelboard, but always at his work. But in my sickness—you see, sir, I were a long time sick after my last baby, and I thought I saw my husband somewhat turning from me. And this girl—(*She turns to* ABIGAIL.)

DANFORTH: Look at me.

ELIZABETH: Aye, sir. Abigail Williams—(*She breaks off.*)

DANFORTH: What of Abigail Williams?

ELIZABETH: I came to think he fancied her. And so one night I lost my wits, I think, and put her out on the highroad.

DANFORTH: Your husband—did he indeed turn from you?

ELIZABETH (*in agony*): My husband—is a goodly man, sir.

DANFORTH: Then he did not turn from you.

ELIZABETH (*starting to glance at* Proctor): He—

DANFORTH (*reaches out and holds her face, then*): Look at me! To your own knowledge, has John Proctor ever committed the crime of lechery? (*In a crisis of indecision she cannot speak.*) Answer my question! Is your husband a lecher!

ELIZABETH (*faintly*): No, sir.

DANFORTH: Remove her, Marshal.

PROCTOR: Elizabeth, tell the truth!

DANFORTH: She has spoken. Remove her!

PROCTOR (*crying out*): Elizabeth, I have confessed it!

ELIZABETH: Oh, God! (*The door closes behind her.*)

PROCTOR: She only thought to save my name!

HALE: Excellency, it is a natural lie to tell; I beg you, stop now before another is condemned! I may shut my conscience to it no more—private vengeance is working through this testimony! From the beginning this man has struck me true. By my oath to Heaven, I believe him now, and I pray you call back his wife before we—

DANFORTH: She spoke nothing of lechery, and this man has lied!

HALE: I believe him! (*Pointing at* ABIGAIL) This girl has always struck me false! She has—

(ABIGAIL, *with a weird, wild, chilling cry, screams up to the ceiling.*)

ABIGAIL: You will not! Begone! Begone, I say!

DANFORTH: What is it, child? (*But* ABIGAIL, *pointing with fear, is now raising up her frightened eyes, her awed face, toward the ceiling—the girls are doing the same—and now* HATHORNE, HALE, PUTNAM, CHEEVER, HERRICK, *and* DANFORTH *do the same.*) What's there? (*He lowers his eyes from the ceiling, and now he is frightened; there is real tension in his voice.*) Child! (*She is transfixed—with all the girls, she is whimpering open-mouthed, agape at the ceiling.*) Girls! Why do you—?

MERCY LEWIS (*pointing*): It's on the beam! Behind the rafter!

DANFORTH (*looking up*): Where!

ABIGAIL: Why—? (*She gulps.*) Why do you come, yellow bird?

PROCTOR: Where's a bird? I see no bird!

ABIGAIL (*to the ceiling*): My face? My face?

PROCTOR: Mr. Hale—

DANFORTH: Be quiet!

PROCTOR (*to* HALE): Do you see a bird?

DANFORTH: Be quiet!!

ABIGAIL (*to the ceiling, in a genuine conversation with the "bird," as though trying to talk it out of attacking her*): But God made my face; you cannot want to tear my face. Envy is a deadly sin, Mary.

MARY WARREN (*on her feet with a spring, and horrified, pleading*): Abby!

ABIGAIL (*unperturbed, continuing to the "bird"*): Oh, Mary, this is a black art to change your shape. No, I cannot, I cannot stop my mouth; it's God's work I do.

MARY WARREN: Abby, I'm *here!*

PROCTOR (*frantically*): They're pretending, Mr. Danforth!

ABIGAIL (*Now she takes a backward step, as though in fear the bird will swoop down momentarily*): Oh, please, Mary! Don't come down.

SUSANNA WALCOTT: Her claws, she's stretching her claws!

PROCTOR: Lies, lies.

ABIGAIL (*backing further, eyes still fixed above*): Mary, please don't hurt me!

MARY WARREN (*to* DANFORTH): I'm not hurting her!

DANFORTH (*to* MARY WARREN): Why does she see this vision?

MARY WARREN: She sees nothin'!

ABIGAIL (*now staring full front as though hypnotized, and mimicking the exact tone of* MARY WARREN*'s cry*): She sees nothin'!

MARY WARREN (*pleading*): Abby, you mustn't!

ABIGAIL AND ALL THE GIRLS (*all transfixed*): Abby, you mustn't!

MARY WARREN (*to all the girls*): I'm here, I'm here!

GIRLS: I'm here, I'm here!

DANFORTH (*horrified*): Mary Warren! Draw back your spirit out of them!

MARY WARREN: Mr. Danforth!

GIRLS (*cutting her off*): Mr. Danforth!

DANFORTH: Have you compacted with the Devil? Have you?

MARY WARREN: Never, never!

GIRLS: Never, never!

DANFORTH (*growing hysterical*): Why can they only repeat you?

PROCTOR: Give me a whip—I'll stop it!

MARY WARREN: They're sporting. They—!

GIRLS: They're sporting!

MARY WARREN (*turning on them all hysterically and stamping her feet*): Abby, stop it!

GIRLS (*stamping their feet*): Abby, stop it!

MARY WARREN: Stop it!

GIRLS: Stop it!

MARY WARREN (*screaming it out at the top of her lungs, and raising her fists*): Stop it!!

GIRLS (*raising their fists*): Stop it!!

(MARY WARREN, *utterly confounded, and becoming overwhelmed by* ABIGAIL*'s—and the girls'—utter conviction, starts to whimper, hands half raised, powerless, and all the girls begin whimpering exactly as she does.*)

DANFORTH: A little while ago you were afflicted. Now it seems you afflict others; where did you find this power?

MARY WARREN (*staring at* ABIGAIL): I—have no power.

GIRLS: I have no power.

PROCTOR: They're gulling you, Mister!

DANFORTH: Why did you turn about this past two weeks? You have seen the Devil, have you not?

HALE (*indicating* ABIGAIL *and the girls*): You cannot believe them!

MARY WARREN: I—

PROCTOR (*sensing her weakening*): Mary, God damns all liars!

DANFORTH (*pounding it into her*): You have seen the Devil, you have made compact with Lucifer, have you not?

PROCTOR: God damns liars, Mary!

(MARY *utters something unintelligible, staring at* ABIGAIL, *who keeps watching the "bird" above.*)

DANFORTH: I cannot hear you. What do you say? (MARY *utters again unintelligibly.*) You will confess yourself or you will hang? (*He turns her roughly to face him.*) Do you know who I am? I say you will hang if you do not open with me!

PROCTOR: Mary, remember the angel Raphael—do that which is good and—

ABIGAIL (*pointing upward*): The wings! Her wings are spreading! Mary, please, don't, don't—!

HALE: I see nothing, Your Honor!

DANFORTH: Do you confess this power! (*He is an inch from her face.*) Speak!

ABIGAIL: She's going to come down! She's walking the beam!

DANFORTH: Will you speak!

MARY WARREN (*staring in horror*): I cannot!

GIRLS: I cannot!

PARRIS: Cast the Devil out! Look him in the face! Trample him! We'll save you, Mary, only stand fast against him and—

ABIGAIL (*looking up*): Look out! She's coming down!

(*She and all the girls run to one wall, shielding their eyes. And now, as though cornered, they let out a gigantic scream, and* MARY, *as though infected, opens her mouth and screams with them. Gradually* ABIGAIL *and the girls leave off, until only* MARY *is left there, staring up at the "bird," screaming madly. All watch her, horrified by this evident fit.* PROCTOR *strides to her.*)

PROCTOR: Mary, tell the Governor what they—(*He has hardly got a word out, when, seeing him coming for her, she rushes out of his reach, screaming in horror.*)

MARY WARREN: Don't touch me—don't touch me! (*At which the girls halt at the door.*)

PROCTOR (*astonished*): Mary!

MARY WARREN (*pointing at* PROCTOR): You're the Devil's man!

(*He is stopped in his tracks.*)

PARRIS: Praise God!

GIRLS: Praise God!

PROCTOR (*numbed*): Mary, how—?

MARY WARREN: I'll not hang with you! I love God, I love God.

DANFORTH (*to* MARY): He bid you do the Devil's work?

MARY WARREN (*hysterically, indicating* PROCTOR): He come at me by night and every day to sign, to sign, to—

DANFORTH: Sign what?

PARRIS: The Devil's book? He come with a book?

MARY WARREN (*hysterically, pointing at* PROCTOR, *fearful of him*): My name, he want my name. "I'll murder you," he says, "if my wife hangs! We must go and overthrow the court," he says!

(DANFORTH's *head jerks toward* PROCTOR, *shock and horror in his face.*)

PROCTOR (*turning, appealing to* HALE): Mr. Hale!

MARY WARREN (*her sobs beginning*): He wake me every night, his eyes were like coals and his fingers claw my neck, and I sign, I sign . . .

HALE: Excellency, this child's gone wild!

PROCTOR (*as* DANFORTH's *wide eyes pour on him*): Mary, Mary!

MARY WARREN (*screaming at him*): No, I love God; I go your way no more. I love God, I bless God. (*Sobbing, she rushes to* ABIGAIL.) Abby, Abby, I'll never hurt you more! (*They all watch, as* ABIGAIL, *out of her infinite charity, reaches out and draws the sobbing* MARY *to her, and then looks up to* DANFORTH.)

DANFORTH (*to* PROCTOR): What are you? (PROCTOR *is beyond speech in his anger.*) You are combined with anti-Christ, are you not? I have seen your power; you will not deny it! What say you, Mister?

HALE: Excellency—

DANFORTH: I will have nothing from you, Mr. Hale! (*To* PROCTOR) Will you confess yourself befouled with Hell, or do you keep that black allegiance yet? What say you?

PROCTOR (*his mind wild, breathless*): I say—I say—God is dead!

PARRIS: Hear it, hear it!

PROCTOR (*laughs insanely, then*): A fire, a fire is burning! I hear the boot of Lucifer, I see his filthy face! And it is my face, and yours, Danforth! For them that quail to bring men out of ignorance, as I have quailed, and as you quail now when you know in all your black hearts that this be fraud—God damns our kind especially, and we will burn, we will burn together.

DANFORTH: Marshal! Take him and Corey with him to the jail!

HALE (*starting across to the door*): I denounce these proceedings!

PROCTOR: You are pulling Heaven down and raising up a whore!

HALE: I denounce these proceedings, I quit this court! (*He slams the door to the outside behind him.*)

DANFORTH (*calling to him in a fury*): Mr. Hale! Mr. Hale!

(*The curtain falls.*)

ACT FOUR

A cell in Salem jail, that fall.

At the back is a high barred window; near it, a great, heavy door. Along the walls are two benches.

The place is in darkness but for the moonlight seeping through the bars. It appears empty. Pres-

ently footsteps are heard coming down a corridor beyond the wall, keys rattle, and the door swings open. MARSHAL HERRICK *enters with a lantern.*

He is nearly drunk, and heavy-footed. He goes to a bench and nudges a bundle of rags lying on it.

HERRICK: Sarah, wake up! Sarah Good! (*He then crosses to the other bench.*)

SARAH GOOD (*rising in her rags*): Oh, Majesty! Comin', comin'! Tituba, he's here, His Majesty's come!

HERRICK: Go to the north cell; this place is wanted now. (*He hangs his lantern on the wall.* TITUBA *sits up.*)

TITUBA: That don't look to me like His Majesty; look to me like the marshal.

HERRICK (*taking out a flask*): Get along with you now, clear this place. (*He drinks, and* SARAH GOOD *comes and peers up into his face.*)

SARAH GOOD: Oh, is it you, Marshal! I thought sure you be the devil comin' for us. Could I have a sip of cider for me goin'-away?

HERRICK (*handing her the flask*): And where are you off to, Sarah?

TITUBA (*as* SARAH *drinks*): We goin' to Barbados, soon the Devil gits here with the feathers and the wings.

HERRICK: Oh? A happy voyage to you.

SARAH GOOD: A pair of bluebirds wingin' southerly, the two of us! Oh, it be a grand transformation, Marshal! (*She raises the flask to drink again.*)

HERRICK (*taking the flask from her lips*): You'd best give me that or you'll never rise off the ground. Come along now.

TITUBA: I'll speak to him for you, if you desires to come along, Marshal.

HERRICK: I'd not refuse it, Tituba; it's the proper morning to fly into Hell.

TITUBA: Oh, it be no Hell in Barbados. Devil, him be pleasureman in Barbados, him be singin' and dancin' in Barbados. It's you folks—you riles him up 'round here; it be too cold 'round here for that Old Boy. He freeze his soul in Massachusetts, but in Barbados he just as sweet and—(*A bellowing cow is heard, and* TITUBA *leaps up and calls to the window.*) Aye, sir! That's him, Sarah!

SARAH GOOD: I'm here, Majesty! (*They hurriedly pick up their rags as* HOPKINS, *a guard, enters.*)

HOPKINS: The Deputy Governor's arrived.

HERRICK (*grabbing* TITUBA): Come along, come along.

TITUBA (*resisting him*): No, he comin' for me. I goin' home!

HERRICK (*pulling her to the door*): That's not Satan, just a poor old cow with a hatful of milk. Come along now, out with you!

TITUBA (*calling to the window*): Take me home, Devil! Take me home!

SARAH GOOD (*following the shouting* TITUBA *out*): Tell him I'm goin', Tituba! Now you tell him Sarah Good is goin' too!

(*In the corridor outside* TITUBA *calls on*—"Take me home, Devil; Devil take me home!" *and* HOPKINS' *voice orders her to move on.* HERRICK *returns and begins to push old rags and straw into a corner. Hearing footsteps, he turns, and enter* DANFORTH *and* JUDGE HATHORNE. *They are in greatcoats and wear hats against the bitter cold. They are followed in by* CHEEVER, *who carries a dispatch case and a flat wooden box containing his writing materials.*)

HERRICK: Good morning, Excellency.

DANFORTH: Where is Mr. Parris?

HERRICK: I'll fetch him. (*He starts for the door.*)

DANFORTH: Marshal. (HERRICK *stops.*) When did Reverend Hale arrive?

HERRICK: It were toward midnight, I think.

DANFORTH (*suspiciously*): What is he about here?

HERRICK: He goes among them that will hang, sir. And he prays with them. He sits with Goody Nurse now. And Mr. Parris with him.

DANFORTH: Indeed. That man have no authority to enter here, Marshal. Why have you let him in?

HERRICK: Why, Mr. Parris command me, sir. I cannot deny him.

DANFORTH: Are you drunk, Marshal?

HERRICK: No, sir; it is a bitter night, and I have no fire here.

DANFORTH (*containing his anger*): Fetch Mr. Parris.

HERRICK: Aye, sir.

DANFORTH: There is a prodigious stench in this place.

HERRICK: I have only now cleared the people out for you.

DANFORTH: Beware hard drink, Marshal.

HERRICK: Aye, sir. (*He waits an instant for further orders. But* DANFORTH, *in dissatisfaction, turns his back on him, and* HERRICK *goes out. There is a pause.* DANFORTH *stands in thought.*)

HATHORNE: Let you question Hale, Excellency; I should not be surprised he have been preaching in Andover lately.

DANFORTH: We'll come to that; speak nothing of Andover. Parris prays with him. That's strange. (*He blows on his hands, moves toward the window, and looks out.*)

HATHORNE: Excellency, I wonder if it be wise to let Mr. Parris so continuously with the prisoners. (DANFORTH *turns to him, interested.*) I think, sometimes, the man has a mad look these days.

DANFORTH: Mad?

HATHORNE: I met him yesterday coming out of his house, and I bid him good morning—and he wept and went his way. I think it is not well the village sees him so unsteady.

DANFORTH: Perhaps he have some sorrow.

CHEEVER (*stamping his feet against the cold*): I think it be the cows, sir.

DANFORTH: Cows?

CHEEVER: There be so many cows wanderin' the highroads, now their masters are in the jails, and much disagreement who they will belong to now. I know Mr. Parris be arguin' with farmers all yesterday—there is great contention, sir, about the cows. Contention make him weep, sir; it were always a man that weep for contention. (*He turns, as do* HATHORNE *and* DANFORTH, *hearing someone coming up the corridor.* DANFORTH *raises his head as* PARRIS *enters. He is gaunt, frightened, and sweating in his greatcoat.*)

PARRIS (*to* DANFORTH, *instantly*): Oh, good morning, sir, thank you for coming. I beg your pardon wakin' you so early. Good morning, Judge Hathorne.

DANFORTH: Reverend Hale have no right to enter this—

PARRIS: Excellency, a moment. (*He hurries back and shuts the door.*)

HATHORNE: Do you leave him alone with the prisoners?

DANFORTH: What's his business here?

PARRIS (*prayerfully holding up his hands*): Excellency, hear me. It is a providence. Reverend Hale has returned to bring Rebecca Nurse to God.

DANFORTH (*surprised*): He bids her confess?

PARRIS (*sitting*): Hear me. Rebecca have not given me a word this three month since she came. Now she sits with him, and her sister and Martha Corey and two or three others, and he pleads with them, confess their crimes and save their lives.

DANFORTH: Why—this is indeed a providence. And they soften, they soften?

PARRIS: Not yet, not yet. But I thought to summon you, sir, that we might think on whether it be not wise, to—(*He dares not say it.*) I had thought to put a question, sir, and I hope you will not—

DANFORTH: Mr. Parris, be plain, what troubles you?

PARRIS: There is news, sir, that the court—the court must reckon with. My niece, sir, my niece—I believe she has vanished.

DANFORTH: Vanished!

PARRIS: I had thought to advise you of it earlier in the week, but—

DANFORTH: Why? How long is she gone?

PARRIS: This be the third night. You see, sir, she told me she would stay a night with Mercy Lewis. And next day, when she does not return, I send to Mr. Lewis to inquire. Mercy told him she would sleep in *my* house for a night.

DANFORTH: They are both gone?!

PARRIS (*in fear of him*): They are, sir.

DANFORTH (*alarmed*): I will send a party for them. Where may they be?

PARRIS: Excellency, I think they be aboard a ship. (DANFORTH *stands agape.*) My daughter tells me how she heard them speaking of ships last week, and tonight I discover my—my strongbox is broke into. (*He presses his fingers against his eyes to keep back tears.*)

HATHORNE (*astonished*): She have robbed you?

PARRIS: Thirty-one pound is gone. I am penniless. (*He covers his face and sobs.*)

DANFORTH: Mr. Parris, you are a brainless man! (*He walks in thought, deeply worried.*)

PARRIS: Excellency, it profit nothing you should blame me. I cannot think they would run off except they fear to keep in Salem any more. (*He is pleading.*) Mark it, sir, Abigail had close knowledge of the town, and since the news of Andover has broken here—

DANFORTH: Andover is remedied. The court returns there on Friday, and will resume examinations.

PARRIS: I am sure of it, sir. But the rumor here speaks rebellion in Andover, and it—

DANFORTH: There is no rebellion in Andover!

PARRIS: I tell you what is said here, sir. Andover have thrown out the court, they say, and will have no part of witchcraft. There be a faction here, feeding on that news, and I tell you true, sir, I fear there will be riot here.

HATHORNE: Riot! Why at every execution I have seen naught but high satisfaction in the town.

PARRIS: Judge Hathorne—it were another sort that hanged till now. Rebecca Nurse is no Bridget that lived three year with Bishop before she married him. John Proctor is not Isaac Ward that drank his family to ruin. (*To* DANFORTH) I would to God it were not so, Excellency, but these people have great weight yet in the town. Let Rebecca stand upon the gibbet and send up some righteous prayer, and I fear she'll wake a vengeance on you.

HATHORNE: Excellency, she is condemned a witch. The court have—

DANFORTH (*in deep concern, raising a hand to* HATHORNE): Pray you. (*To* PARRIS) How do you propose, then?

PARRIS: Excellency, I would postpone these hangin's for a time.

DANFORTH: There will be no postponement.

PARRIS: Now Mr. Hale's returned, there is hope, I think—for if he bring even one of these to God, that confession surely damns the others in the public eye, and none may doubt more that they are all linked to Hell. This way, unconfessed and claiming innocence, doubts are multiplied, many honest people will weep for them, and our good purpose is lost in their tears.

DANFORTH (*after thinking a moment, then going to* CHEEVER): Give me the list.

(CHEEVER *opens the dispatch case, searches.*)

PARRIS: It cannot be forgot, sir, that when I summoned the congregation for John Proctor's excommunication there were hardly thirty people come to hear it. That speak a discontent, I think, and—

DANFORTH (*studying the list*): There will be no postponement.

PARRIS: Excellency—

DANFORTH: Now, sir—which of these in your opinion may be brought to God? I will myself strive with him till dawn. (*He hands the list to* PARRIS, *who merely glances at it.*)

PARRIS: There is not sufficient time till dawn.

DANFORTH: I shall do my utmost. Which of them do you have hope for?

PARRIS (*not even glancing at the list now, and in a quavering voice, quietly*): Excellency—a dagger—(*He chokes up.*)

DANFORTH: What do you say?

PARRIS: Tonight, when I open my door to leave my house—a dagger clattered to the ground. (*Silence.* DANFORTH *absorbs this. Now* PARRIS *cries out.*) You cannot hang this sort. There is danger for me. I dare not step outside at night!

(REVEREND HALE *enters. They look at him for an instant in silence. He is steeped in sorrow, exhausted, and more direct than he ever was.*)

DANFORTH: Accept my congratulations, Reverend Hale; we are gladdened to see you returned to your good work.

HALE (*coming to* DANFORTH *now*): You must pardon them. They will not budge.

(HERRICK *enters, waits.*)

DANFORTH (*conciliatory*): You misunderstand, sir; I cannot pardon these when twelve are already hanged for the same crime. It is not just.

PARRIS (*with failing heart*): Rebecca will not confess?

HALE: The sun will rise in a few minutes. Excellency, I must have more time.

DANFORTH: Now hear me, and beguile yourselves no more. I will not receive a single plea for pardon or postponement. Them that will not confess will hang. Twelve are already executed; the names of these seven are given out, and the village expects to see them die this morning. Postponement now speaks a floundering on my part; reprieve or pardon must cast doubt upon the guilt of them that died till now. While I speak God's law, I will not crack its voice with whimpering. If retaliation is your fear, know this—I should hang ten thousand that dared to rise against the law, and an ocean of salt tears could not melt the resolution of the statutes. Now draw yourselves up like men and help me, as you are bound by Heaven to do. Have you spoken with them all, Mr. Hale?

HALE: All but Proctor. He is in the dungeon.

DANFORTH (*to* HERRICK): What's Proctor's way now?

HERRICK: He sits like some great bird; you'd not know he lived except he will take food from time to time.

DANFORTH (*after thinking a moment*): His wife—his wife must be well on with child now.

HERRICK: She is, sir.

DANFORTH: What think you, Mr. Parris? You have closer knowledge of this man; might her presence soften him?

PARRIS: It is possible, sir. He have not laid eyes on her these three months. I should summon her.

DANFORTH (*to* HERRICK): Is he yet adamant? Has he struck at you again?

HERRICK: He cannot, sir, he is chained to the wall now.

DANFORTH (*after thinking on it*): Fetch Goody Proctor to me. Then let you bring him up.

HERRICK: Aye, sir. (HERRICK *goes. There is silence.*)

HALE: Excellency, if you postpone a week and publish to the town that you are striving for their confessions, that speak mercy on your part, not faltering.

DANFORTH: Mr. Hale, as God have not empowered me like Joshua to stop this sun from rising, so I cannot withhold from them the perfection of their punishment.

HALE (*harder now*): If you think God wills you to raise rebellion, Mr. Danforth, you are mistaken!

DANFORTH (*instantly*): You have heard rebellion spoken in the town?

HALE: Excellency, there are orphans wandering from house to house; abandoned cattle bellow on the highroads, the stink of rotting crops hangs everywhere, and no man knows when the harlots' cry will end his life—and you wonder yet if rebellion's spoke? Better you should marvel how they do not burn your province!

DANFORTH: Mr. Hale, have you preached in Andover this month?

HALE: Thank God they have no need of me in Andover.

DANFORTH: You baffle me, sir. Why have you returned here?

HALE: Why, it is all simple. I come to do the Devil's work. I come to counsel Christians they should belie themselves. (*His sarcasm collapses.*) There is blood on my head! Can you not see the blood on my head!

PARRIS: Hush! (*For he has heard footsteps. They all face the door.* HERRICK *enters with* ELIZABETH. *Her wrists are linked by heavy chain,* which HERRICK *now removes. Her clothes are dirty; her face is pale and gaunt.* HERRICK *goes out.*)

DANFORTH (*very politely*): Goody Proctor. (*She is silent.*) I hope you are hearty?

ELIZABETH (*as a warning reminder*): I am yet six months before my time.

DANFORTH: Pray be at your ease, we come not for your life. We—(*uncertain how to plead, for he is not accustomed to it*) Mr. Hale, will you speak with the woman?

HALE: Goody Proctor, your husband is marked to hang this morning.

(*Pause.*)

ELIZABETH (*quietly*): I have heard it.

HALE: You know, do you not, that I have no connection with the court? (*She seems to doubt it.*) I come of my own, Goody Proctor. I would save your husband's life, for if he is taken I count myself his murderer. Do you understand me?

ELIZABETH: What do you want of me?

HALE: Goody Proctor, I have gone this three month like our Lord into the wilderness. I have sought a Christian way, for damnation's doubled on a minister who counsels men to lie.

HATHORNE: It is no lie, you cannot speak of lies.

HALE: It is a lie! They are innocent!

DANFORTH: I'll hear no more of that!

HALE (*continuing to* ELIZABETH): Let you not mistake your duty as I mistook my own. I came into this village like a bridegroom to his beloved, bearing gifts of high religion; the very crowns of holy law I brought, and what I touched with my bright confidence, it died; and where I turned the eye of my great faith, blood flowed up. Beware, Goody Proctor—cleave to no faith when faith brings blood. It is mistaken law that leads you to sacrifice. Life, woman, life is God's most precious gift; no principle, however glorious, may justify the taking of it. I beg you, woman, prevail upon your husband to confess. Let him give his lie. Quail not before God's judgment in this, for it may well be God damns a liar less than he that throws his life away for pride. Will you plead with him? I cannot think he will listen to another.

ELIZABETH: (*quietly*): I think that be the Devil's argument.

HALE (*with a climactic desperation*): Woman, before the laws of God we are as swine! We cannot read His will!

ELIZABETH: I cannot dispute with you, sir; I lack learning for it.

DANFORTH (*going to her*): Goody Proctor, you are not summoned here for disputation. Be there no wifely tenderness within you? He will die with the sunrise. Your husband. Do you understand it? (*She only looks at him.*) What say you? Will you contend with him? (*She is silent.*) Are you stone? I tell you true, woman, had I no other proof of your unnatural life, your dry eyes now would be sufficient evidence that you delivered up your soul to Hell! A very ape would weep at such calamity! Have the devil dried up any tear of pity in you? (*She is silent.*) Take her out. It profit nothing she should speak to him!

ELIZABETH (*quietly*): Let me speak with him, Excellency.

PARRIS (*with hope*): You'll strive with him? (*She hesitates.*)

DANFORTH: Will you plead for his confession or will you not?

ELIZABETH: I promise nothing. Let me speak with him.

(*A sound—the sibilance of dragging feet on stone. They turn. A pause.* HERRICK *enters with* JOHN PROCTOR. *His wrists are chained. He is another man, bearded, filthy, his eyes misty as though webs had overgrown them. He halts inside the doorway, his eye caught by the sight of* ELIZABETH. *The emotion flowing between them prevents anyone from speaking for an instant. Now* HALE, *visibly affected, goes to* DANFORTH *and speaks quietly.*)

HALE: Pray, leave them, Excellency.

DANFORTH (*pressing* HALE *impatiently aside*): Mr. Proctor, you have been notified, have you not? (PROCTOR *is silent, staring at* ELIZABETH.) I see light in the sky, Mister; let you counsel with your wife, and may God help you turn your back on Hell. (PROCTOR *is silent, staring at* ELIZABETH.)

HALE (*quietly*): Excellency, let—

(DANFORTH *brushes past* HALE *and walks out.* HALE *follows.* CHEEVER *stands and follows,* HATHORNE *behind.* HERRICK *goes.* PARRIS, *from a safe distance, offers:*)

PARRIS: If you desire a cup of cider, Mr. Proctor, I am sure I—(PROCTOR *turns an icy stare at him, and he breaks off.* PARRIS *raises his palms toward* PROCTOR.) God lead you now. (PARRIS *goes out.*)

(*Alone.* PROCTOR *walks to her, halts. It is as though they stood in a spinning world. It is beyond sorrow, above it. He reaches out his hand as though toward an embodiment not quite real, and as he touches her, a strange soft sound, half laughter, half amazement, comes from his throat. He pats her hand. She covers his hand with hers. And then, weak, he sits. Then she sits, facing him.*)

PROCTOR: The child?

ELIZABETH: It grows.

PROCTOR: There is no word of the boys?

ELIZABETH: They're well. Rebecca's Samuel keeps them.

PROCTOR: You have not seen them?

ELIZABETH: I have not. (*She catches a weakening in herself and downs it.*)

PROCTOR: You are a—marvel, Elizabeth.

ELIZABETH: You—have been tortured?

PROCTOR: Aye. (*Pause. She will not let herself be drowned in the sea that threatens her.*) They come for my life now.

ELIZABETH: I know it.

(*Pause.*)

PROCTOR: None—have yet confessed?

ELIZABETH: There be many confessed.

PROCTOR: Who are they?

ELIZABETH: There be a hundred or more, they say. Goody Ballard is one; Isaiah Goodkind is one. There be many.

PROCTOR: Rebecca?

ELIZABETH: Not Rebecca. She is one foot in Heaven now; naught may hurt her more.

PROCTOR: And Giles?

ELIZABETH: You have not heard of it?

PROCTOR: I hear nothin', where I am kept.

ELIZABETH: Giles is dead.

(*He looks at her incredulously.*)

PROCTOR: When were he hanged?

ELIZABETH (*quietly, factually*): He were not hanged. He would not answer aye or nay to his indictment; for if he denied the charge they'd hang him surely, and auction out his property. So he stand mute, and died Christian under the law. And so his sons will have his farm. It is the law, for he could not be condemned a wizard without he answer the indictment, aye or nay.

PROCTOR: Then how does he die?

ELIZABETH (*gently*): They press him, John.

PROCTOR: Press?

ELIZABETH: Great stones they lay upon his chest until he plead aye or nay. (*With a tender smile for the old man*) They say he give them but two words. "More weight," he says. And died.

PROCTOR (*numbed—a thread to weave into his agony*): "More weight."

ELIZABETH: Aye. It were a fearsome man, Giles Corey.

(*Pause.*)

PROCTOR (*with great force of will, but not quite looking at her*):   I have been thinking I would confess to them, Elizabeth. (*She shows nothing.*) What say you? If I give them that?

ELIZABETH: I cannot judge you, John.

(*Pause.*)

PROCTOR (*simply—a pure question*):   What would you have me do?

ELIZABETH: As you will, I would have it. (*Slight pause*) I want you living, John. That's sure.

PROCTOR (*pauses, then with a flailing of hope*): Giles' wife? Have she confessed?

ELIZABETH: She will not.

(*Pause.*)

PROCTOR: It is a pretense, Elizabeth.

ELIZABETH: What is?

PROCTOR: I cannot mount the gibbet like a saint. It is a fraud. I am not that man. (*She is silent.*) My honesty is broke, Elizabeth; I am no good man. Nothing's spoiled by giving them this lie that were not rotten long before.

ELIZABETH: And yet you've not confessed till now. That speak goodness in you.

PROCTOR: Spite only keeps me silent. It is hard to give a lie to dogs. (*Pause. For the first time he turns directly to her.*) I would have your forgiveness, Elizabeth.

ELIZABETH: It is not for me to give, John, I am—

PROCTOR: I'd have you see some honesty in it. Let them that never lied die now to keep their souls. It is pretense for me, a vanity that will not blind God nor keep my children out of the wind. (*Pause.*) What say you?

ELIZABETH (*upon a heaving sob that always threatens*):   John, it come to naught that I should forgive you, if you'll not forgive yourself. (*Now he turns away a little, in great agony.*) It is not my soul, John, it is yours. (*He stands, as though in physical pain, slowly rising to his feet with a great immortal longing to find his answer. It is difficult to say, and she is on the verge of tears.*) Only be sure of this, for I know it now: Whatever

you will do, it is a good man does it. (*He turns his doubting, searching gaze upon her.*) I have read my heart this three month, John. (*Pause.*) I have sins of my own to count. It needs a cold wife to prompt lechery.

PROCTOR (*in great pain*):   Enough, enough—

ELIZABETH (*now pouring out her heart*): Better you should know me!

PROCTOR: I will not hear it! I know you!

ELIZABETH: You take my sins upon you, John—

PROCTOR (*in agony*):   No, I take my own, my own!

ELIZABETH: John, I counted myself so plain, so poorly made, no honest love could come to me! Suspicion kissed you when I did; I never knew how I should say my love. It were a cold house I kept! (*In fright, she swerves, as* HATHORNE *enters.*)

HATHORNE: What say you, Proctor? The sun is soon up.

(PROCTOR, *his chest heaving, stares, turns to* ELIZABETH. *She comes to him as though to plead, her voice quaking.*)

ELIZABETH: Do what you will. But let none be your judge. There be no higher judge under Heaven than Proctor is! Forgive me, forgive me, John—I never knew such goodness in the world! (*She covers her face, weeping.*)

(PROCTOR *turns from her to* HATHORNE; *he is off the earth, his voice hollow.*)

PROCTOR: I want my life.

HATHORNE (*electrified, surprised*):   You'll confess yourself?

PROCTOR: I will have my life.

HATHORNE (*with a mystical tone*):   God be praised! It is a providence! (*He rushes out the door, and his voice is heard calling down the corridor.*) He will confess! Proctor will confess!

PROCTOR (*with a cry, as he strides to the door*): Why do you cry it? (*In great pain he turns back to her.*) It is evil, is it not? It is evil.

ELIZABETH (*in terror, weeping*):   I cannot judge you, John, I cannot!

PROCTOR: Then who will judge me? (*Suddenly clasping his hands*) God in Heaven, what is John Proctor, what is John Proctor? (*He moves as an animal, and a fury is riding in him, a tantalized search.*) I think it is honest, I think so; I am no saint. (*As though she had denied this he calls angrily at her.*) Let Rebecca go like a saint; for me it is fraud!

(*Voices are heard in the hall, speaking together in suppressed excitement.*)

ELIZABETH: I am not your judge, I cannot be. (*As though giving him release*) Do as you will, do as you will!

PROCTOR: Would you give them such a lie? Say it. Would you ever give them this? (*She cannot answer.*) You would not; if tongs of fire were singeing you you would not! It is evil. Good, then—it is evil, and I do it!

(HATHORNE *enters with* DANFORTH, *and, with them,* CHEEVER, PARRIS, *and* HALE. *It is a businesslike, rapid entrance, as though the ice had been broken.*)

DANFORTH (*with great relief and gratitude*): Praise to God, man, praise to God; you shall be blessed in Heaven for this. (CHEEVER *has hurried to the bench with pen, ink, and paper.* PROCTOR *watches him.*) Now then, let us have it. Are you ready, Mr. Cheever?

PROCTOR (*with a cold, cold horror at their efficiency*): Why must it be written?

DANFORTH: Why, for the good instruction of the village, Mister; this we shall post upon the church door! (*To* PARRIS, *urgently*) Where is the marshal?

PARRIS (*runs to the door and calls down the corridor*): Marshal! Hurry!

DANFORTH: Now, then, Mister, will you speak slowly, and directly to the point, for Mr. Cheever's sake. (*He is on record now, and is really dictating to* CHEEVER, *who writes.*) Mr. Proctor, have you seen the Devil in your life? (PROCTOR's *jaws lock.*) Come, man, there is light in the sky; the town waits at the scaffold; I would give out this news. Did you see the Devil?

PROCTOR: I did.

PARRIS: Praise God!

DANFORTH: And when he come to you, what were his demand? (PROCTOR *is silent.* DANFORTH *helps.*) Did he bid you to do his work upon the earth?

PROCTOR: He did.

DANFORTH: And you bound yourself to his service? (DANFORTH *turns, as* REBECCA NURSE *enters, with* HERRICK *helping to support her. She is barely able to walk.*) Come in, come in, woman!

REBECCA (*brightening as she sees* PROCTOR): Ah, John! You are well, then, eh?

(PROCTOR *turns his face to the wall.*)

DANFORTH: Courage, man, courage—let her witness your good example that she may come to God herself. Now hear it, Goody Nurse! Say on, Mr. Proctor. Did you bind yourself to the Devil's service?

REBECCA (*astonished*): Why, John!

PROCTOR (*through his teeth, his face turned from* REBECCA): I did.

DANFORTH: Now, woman, you surely see it profit nothin' to keep this conspiracy any further. Will you confess yourself with him?

REBECCA: Oh, John—God send his mercy on you!

DANFORTH: I say, will you confess yourself, Goody Nurse?

REBECCA: Why, it is a lie, it is a lie; how may I damn myself? I cannot, I cannot.

DANFORTH: Mr. Proctor. When the Devil came to you did you see Rebecca Nurse in his company? (PROCTOR *is silent.*) Come, man, take courage—did you ever see her with the Devil?

PROCTOR (*almost inaudibly*): No.

(DANFORTH, *now sensing trouble, glances at* JOHN *and goes to the table, and picks up a sheet—the list of condemned.*)

DANFORTH: Did you ever see her sister, Mary Easty, with the Devil?

PROCTOR: No, I did not.

DANFORTH (*his eyes narrow on* PROCTOR): Did you ever see Martha Corey with the Devil?

PROCTOR: I did not.

DANFORTH (*realizing, slowly putting the sheet down*): Did you ever see anyone with the Devil?

PROCTOR: I did not.

DANFORTH: Proctor, you mistake me. I am not empowered to trade your life for a lie. You have most certainly seen some person with the Devil. (*Proctor is silent.*) Mr. Proctor, a score of people have already testified they saw this woman with the Devil.

PROCTOR: Then it is proved. Why must I say it?

DANFORTH: Why "must" you say it! Why, you should rejoice to say it if your soul is truly purged of any love for Hell!

PROCTOR: They think to go like saints. I like not to spoil their names.

DANFORTH (*inquiring, incredulous*): Mr. Proctor, do you think they go like saints?

PROCTOR (*evading*): This woman never thought she done the Devil's work.

DANFORTH: Look you, sir. I think you mistake your duty here. It matters nothing what she thought—she is convicted of the unnatural murder of children, and you for sending your spirit out upon Mary Warren. Your soul alone is the issue here, Mister, and you will prove its whiteness or you cannot live in a Christian country. Will you tell me now what persons conspired with you in the Devil's company? (PROCTOR *is silent.*) To your knowledge was Rebecca Nurse ever—

PROCTOR: I speak my own sins; I cannot judge another. (*Crying out, with hatred*) I have no tongue for it.

HALE (*quickly to* DANFORTH): Excellency, it is enough he confess himself. Let him sign it, let him sign it.

PARRIS (*feverishly*): It is a great service, sir. It is a weighty name; it will strike the village that Proctor confess. I beg you, let him sign it. The sun is up, Excellency!

DANFORTH (*considers; then with dissatisfaction*): Come, then, sign your testimony. (*To* CHEEVER) Give it to him. (CHEEVER *goes to* PROCTOR, *the confession and a pen in hand.* PROCTOR *does not look at it.*) Come, man, sign it.

PROCTOR (*after glancing at the confession*): You have all witnessed it—it is enough.

DANFORTH: You will not sign it?

PROCTOR: You have all witnessed it; what more is needed?

DANFORTH: Do you sport with me? You will sign your name or it is no confession, Mister! (*His breast heaving with agonized breathing,* PROCTOR *now lays the paper down and signs his name.*)

PARRIS: Praise be to the Lord!

(PROCTOR *has just finished signing when* DANFORTH *reaches for the paper. But* PROCTOR *snatches it up, and now a wild terror is rising in him, and a boundless anger.*)

DANFORTH (*perplexed, but politely extending his hand*): If you please, sir.

PROCTOR: No.

DANFORTH (*as though* PROCTOR *did not understand*): Mr. Proctor, I must have—

PROCTOR: No, no. I have signed it. You have seen me. It is done! You have no need for this.

PARRIS: Proctor, the village must have proof that—

PROCTOR: Damn the village! I confess to God, and God has seen my name on this! It is enough!

DANFORTH: No, sir, it is—

PROCTOR: You came to save my soul, did you

not? Here! I have confessed myself; it is enough!

DANFORTH: You have not con—

PROCTOR: I have confessed myself! Is there no good penitence but it be public? God does not need my name nailed upon the church! God sees my name; God knows how black my sins are! It is enough!

DANFORTH: Mr. Proctor—

PROCTOR: You will not use me! I am no Sarah Good or Tituba, I am John Proctor! You will not use me! It is no part of salvation that you should use me!

DANFORTH: I do not wish to—

PROCTOR: I have three children—how may I teach them to walk like men in the world, and I sold my friends?

DANFORTH: You have not sold your friends—

PROCTOR: Beguile me not! I blacken all of them when this is nailed to the church the very day they hang for silence!

DANFORTH: Mr. Proctor, I must have good and legal proof that you—

PROCTOR: You are the high court, your word is good enough! Tell them I confessed myself; say Proctor broke his knees and wept like a woman; say what you will, but my name cannot—

DANFORTH (*with suspicion*): It is the same, is it not? If I report it or you sign to it?

PROCTOR (*He knows it is insane.*): No, it is not the same! What others say and what I sign to is not the same!

DANFORTH: Why? Do you mean to deny this confession when you are free?

PROCTOR: I mean to deny nothing!

DANFORTH: Then explain to me, Mr. Proctor, why you will not let—

PROCTOR (*with a cry of his whole soul*): Because it is my name! Because I cannot have another in my life! Because I lie and sign myself to lies! Because I am not worth the dust on the feet of them that hang! How may I live without my name? I have given you my soul; leave me my name!

DANFORTH (*pointing at the confession in* PROCTOR's *hand*): Is that document a lie? If it is a lie I will not accept it! What say you? I will not deal in lies, Mister! (PROCTOR *is motionless.*) You will give me your honest confession in my hand, or I cannot keep you from the rope. (PROCTOR *does not reply.*) Which way do you go, Mister?

(*His breast heaving, his eyes staring,* PROCTOR *tears the paper and crumples it, and he is weeping in fury, but erect.*)

DANFORTH: Marshal!

PARRIS (*hysterically, as though the tearing paper were his life*): Proctor, Proctor!

HALE: Man, you will hang! You cannot!

PROCTOR (*his eyes full of tears*): I can. And there's your first marvel, that I can. You have made your magic now, for now I do think I see some shred of goodness in John Proctor. Not enough to weave a banner with, but white enough to keep it from such dogs. (ELIZABETH, *in a burst of terror, rushes to him and weeps against his hand.*) Give them no tear! Tears pleasure them! Show honor now, show a stony heart and sink them with it! (*He has lifted her, and kisses her now with great passion.*)

REBECCA: Let you fear nothing! Another judgment waits us all!

DANFORTH: Hang them high over the town! Who weeps for these, weeps for corruption! (*He sweeps out past them.* HERRICK *starts to lead* REBECCA, *who almost collapses, but* PROCTOR *catches her, and she glances up at him apologetically.*)

REBECCA: I've had no breakfast.

HERRICK: Come, man.

(HERRICK *escorts them out,* HATHORNE *and* CHEEVER *behind them.* ELIZABETH *stands staring at the empty doorway.*)

PARRIS (*in deadly fear, to* ELIZABETH): Go to him, Goody Proctor! There is yet time!

(*From outside a drumroll strikes the air.* PARRIS *is startled.* ELIZABETH *jerks about toward the window.*)

PARRIS: Go to him! (*He rushes out the door, as though to hold back his fate.*) Proctor! Proctor!

(*Again, a short burst of drums.*)

HALE: Woman, plead with him! (*He starts to rush out the door, and then goes back to her.*) Woman! It is pride, it is vanity. (*She avoids his eyes, and moves to the window. He drops to his knees.*) Be his helper!—What profit him to bleed? Shall the dust praise him? Shall the worms declare his truth? Go to him, take his shame away!

ELIZABETH (*supporting herself against collapse, grips the bars of the window, and with a cry*): He have his goodness now. God forbid I take it from him!

(*The final drumroll crashes, then heightens violently.* HALE *weeps in frantic prayer, and the new sun is pouring in upon her face, and the drums rattle like bones in the morning air. The curtain falls.*)

HAROLD PINTER

The Birthday Party

Harold Pinter (1930–   ), English actor, director, writer for film and television, poet, and eminent playwright, started his career in the theatre as an actor and then director. Since 1973 he has been the director of the National Theatre in London. The many honors given him include the Shakespeare Prize, 1970; the Austrian State Prize, 1973; the Pirandello Prize, 1980; and honorary degrees from Reading, 1970; Birmingham, 1971; and other universities.

Pinter's major plays are *The Dumb Waiter,* 1957; *The Hothouse,* 1958; *The Birthday Party,* 1958; *The Caretaker,* 1963; *The Homecoming,* 1964; and *Old Times,* 1971. And in 1981 he wrote the screen version of *The French Lieutenant's Woman,* which won him an Oscar. He has published two books outside the field of drama: *Poems and Prose, 1941–77,* 1978, and *Family Voices,* 1981.

Though Pinter would seem to belong to the group often referred to as "theatre of the absurd," he tends to disclaim being a part of any drama movement; he does say that Proust, Dostoevsky, Kafka, and Joyce have had an immense influence on him, and he is a great admirer of the plays of Robert Bolt, the best known of which is *A Man for All Seasons.* Originally, Pinter planned to be a poet, and obviously his plays are influenced by, in his words, the "non-rational strategies of poetry." Without doubt, he is one of the major dramatists of the post–World War II period.

Pinter has had the satisfaction of seeing *The Birthday Party* acclaimed at last, although it was considered unsuccessful in its first staging. One critic has said that in Pinter's plays everyone torments everyone else in some way but that the effect is mostly comic, because Pinter gets humor from a wide range of devices—from farce to clever linguistic tricks, often non sequiturs. All of these appear in "The Birthday Party," where realism is always clashing with the unreal and the sinister—a combination that makes contemporary drama at its best.

CAST OF CHARACTERS

PETEY, *a man in his sixties*

MEG, *a woman in her sixties*

STANLEY, *a man in his late thirties*

LULU, *a girl in her twenties*

GOLDBERG, *a man in his fifties*

MCCANN, *a man of thirty*

THE BIRTHDAY PARTY   Reprinted by permission of Grove Press, Inc. Copyright 1959 by Harold Pinter.

Act I   A morning in summer
Act II   Evening of the same day
Act III   The next morning

ACT ONE

The living-room of a house in a seaside town. A door leading to the hall down left. Back door and small window up left. Kitchen hatch, centre back. Kitchen door up right. Table and chairs, centre.

PETEY *enters from the door on the left with a paper and sits at the table. He begins to read.* MEG's *voice comes through the kitchen hatch.*

MEG: Is that you, Petey?
    Pause.
Petey, is that you?
    Pause.
Petey?
PETEY: What?
MEG: Is that you?
PETEY: Yes, it's me.
MEG: What? (*Her face appears at the hatch.*) Are you back?
PETEY: Yes.
MEG: I've got your cornflakes ready. (*She disappears and reappears.*) Here's your cornflakes.
    He rises and takes the plate from her, sits at the table, props up the paper and begins to eat. MEG *enters by the kitchen door.*
Are they nice?
PETEY: Very nice.
MEG: I thought they'd be nice. (*She sits at the table.*) You got your paper?
PETEY: Yes.
MEG: Is it good?
PETEY: Not bad.
MEG: What does it say?
PETEY: Nothing much.
MEG: You read me out some nice bits yesterday.
PETEY: Yes, well, I haven't finished this one yet.
MEG: Will you tell me when you come to something good?
PETEY: Yes.
    Pause.
MEG: Have you been working hard this morning?
PETEY: No. Just stacked a few of the old chairs. Cleaned up a bit.
MEG: Is it nice out?

PETEY: Very nice.
    Pause.
MEG: Is Stanley up yet?
PETEY: I don't know. Is he?
MEG: I don't know. I haven't seen him down yet.
PETEY: Well then, he can't be up.
MEG: Haven't you seen him down?
PETEY: I've only just come in.
MEG: He must be still asleep.
    She looks round the room, stands, goes to the sideboard and takes a pair of socks from a drawer, collects wool and a needle and goes back to the table.
What time did you go out this morning, Petey?
PETEY: Same time as usual.
MEG: Was it dark?
PETEY: No, it was light.
MEG (*beginning to darn*): But sometimes you go out in the morning and it's dark.
PETEY: That's in the winter.
MEG: Oh, in winter.
PETEY: Yes, it gets light later in winter.
MEG: Oh.
    Pause.
What are you reading?
PETEY: Someone's just had a baby.
MEG: Oh, they haven't! Who?
PETEY: Some girl.
MEG: Who, Petey, who?
PETEY: I don't think you'd know her.
MEG: What's her name?
PETEY: Lady Mary Splatt.
MEG: I don't know her.
PETEY: No.
MEG: What is it?
PETEY (*studying the paper*): Er—a girl.
MEG: Not a boy?
PETEY: No.
MEG: Oh, what a shame. I'd be sorry. I'd much rather have a little boy.
PETEY: A little girl's all right.
MEG: I'd much rather have a little boy.
    Pause . . . Vaguely.
PETEY: I've finished my cornflakes.
MEG: Were they nice?
PETEY: Very nice.
MEG: I've got something else for you.

PETEY: Good.

> *She rises, takes his plate and exits into the kitchen. She then appears at the hatch with two pieces of fried bread on a plate.*

MEG: Here you are, Petey.

> *He rises, collects the plate, looks at it, sits at the table.* MEG *re-enters.*

Is it nice?

PETEY: I haven't tasted it yet.

MEG: I bet you don't know what it is.

PETEY: Yes, I do.

MEG: What is it, then?

PETEY: Fried bread.

MEG: That's right.

> *He begins to eat.*
> *She watches him eat.*

PETEY: Very nice.

MEG: I knew it was.

PETEY (*turning to her*): Oh, Meg, two men came up to me on the beach last night.

MEG: Two men?

PETEY: Yes. They wanted to know if we could put them up for a couple of nights.

MEG: Put them up? Here?

PETEY: Yes.

MEG: How many men?

PETEY: Two.

MEG: What did you say?

PETEY: Well, I said I didn't know. So they said they'd come round to find out.

MEG: Are they coming?

PETEY: Well, they said they would.

MEG: Had they heard about us, Petey?

PETEY: They must have done.

MEG: Yes, they must have done. They must have heard this was a very good boarding house. It is. This house is on the list.

PETEY: It is.

MEG: I know it is.

PETEY: They might turn up today. Can you do it?

MEG: Oh, I've got that lovely room they can have.

PETEY: You've got a room ready?

MEG: I've got the room with the armchair all ready for visitors.

PETEY: You're sure?

MEG: Yes, that'll be all right then, if they come today.

PETEY: Good.

> *She takes the socks etc. back to the sideboard drawer.*

MEG: I'm going to wake that boy.

PETEY: There's a new show coming to the Palace.

MEG: On the pier?

PETEY: No. The Palace, in the town.

MEG: Stanley could have been in it, if it was on the pier.

PETEY: This is a straight show.

MEG: What do you mean?

PETEY: No dancing or singing.

MEG: What do they do then?

PETEY: They just talk.

> *Pause.*

MEG: Oh.

PETEY: You like a song, eh, Meg?

MEG: I like listening to the piano. I used to like watching Stanley play the piano. Of course, he didn't sing. (*Looking at the door.*) I'm going to call that boy.

PETEY: Didn't you take him up his cup of tea?

MEG: I always take him up his cup of tea. But that was a long time ago.

PETEY: Did he drink it?

MEG: I made him. I stood there till he did. I'm going to call him. (*She goes to the door.*) Stan! Stanny! (*She listens.*) Stan! I'm coming up to fetch you if you don't come down! I'm coming up! I'm going to count three! One! Two! Three! I'm coming to get you! (*She exits and goes upstairs. In a moment, shouts from* STANLEY, *wild laughter from* MEG. PETEY *takes his plate to the hatch. Shouts. Laughter.* PETEY *sits at the table. Silence. She returns.*) He's coming down. (*She is panting and arranges her hair.*) I told him if he didn't hurry up he'd get no breakfast.

PETEY: That did it, eh?

MEG: I'll get his cornflakes.

> MEG *exits to the kitchen.* PETEY *reads the paper.* STANLEY *enters. He is unshaven, in his pyjama jacket and wears glasses. He sits at the table.*

PETEY: Morning, Stanley.

STANLEY: Morning.

> *Silence.* MEG *enters with the bowl of cornflakes, which she sets on the table.*

MEG: So he's come down at last, has he? He's come down at last for his breakfast. But he doesn't deserve any, does he, Petey? (STANLEY *stares at the cornflakes.*) Did you sleep well?

STANLEY: I didn't sleep at all.

MEG: You didn't sleep at all? Did you hear that,

Petey? Too tired to eat your breakfast, I suppose? Now you eat up those cornflakes like a good boy. Go on.

He begins to eat.

STANLEY: What's it like out today?

PETEY: Very nice.

STANLEY: Warm?

PETEY: Well, there's a good breeze blowing.

STANLEY: Cold?

PETEY: No, no, I wouldn't say it was cold.

MEG: What are the cornflakes like, Stan?

STANLEY: Horrible.

MEG: Those flakes? Those lovely flakes? You're a liar, a little liar. They're refreshing. It says so. For people when they get up late.

STANLEY: The milk's off.

MEG: It's not. Petey ate his, didn't you, Petey?

PETEY: That's right.

MEG: There you are then.

STANLEY: All right, I'll go on to the second course.

MEG: He hasn't finished the first course and he wants to go on to the second course!

STANLEY: I feel like something cooked.

MEG: Well, I'm not going to give it to you.

PETEY: Give it to him.

MEG (*sitting at the table, right*): I'm not going to.
Pause.

STANLEY: No breakfast.
Pause.
All night long I've been dreaming about this breakfast.

MEG: I thought you said you didn't sleep.

STANLEY: Day-dreaming. All night long. And now she won't give me any. Not even a crust of bread on the table.
Pause.
Well, I can see I'll have to go down to one of those smart hotels on the front.

MEG (*rising quickly*): You won't get a better breakfast there than here.

She exits to the kitchen. STANLEY *yawns broadly.* MEG *appears at the hatch with a plate.*

Here you are. You'll like this.

PETEY *rises, collects the plate, brings it to the table, puts it in front of* STANLEY, *and sits.*

STANLEY: What's this?

PETEY: Fried bread.

MEG (*entering*): Well, I bet you don't know what it is.

STANLEY: Oh yes I do.

MEG: What?

STANLEY: Fried bread.

MEG: He knew.

STANLEY: What a wonderful surprise.

MEG: You didn't expect that, did you?

STANLEY: I bloody well didn't.

PETEY (*rising*): Well, I'm off.

MEG: You going back to work?

PETEY: Yes.

MEG: Your tea! You haven't had your tea!

PETEY: That's all right. No time now.

MEG: I've got it made inside.

PETEY: No, never mind. See you later. Ta-ta, Stan.

STANLEY: Ta-ta.

PETEY *exits, left.*

Tch, tch, tch, tch.

MEG (*defensively*): What do you mean?

STANLEY: You're a bad wife.

MEG: I'm not. Who said I am?

STANLEY: Not to make your husband a cup of tea. Terrible.

MEG: He knows I'm not a bad wife.

STANLEY: Giving him sour milk instead.

MEG: It wasn't sour.

STANLEY: Disgraceful.

MEG: You mind your own business, anyway. (STANLEY *eats.*) You won't find many better wives than me, I can tell you. I keep a very nice house and I keep it clean.

STANLEY: Whoo!

MEG: Yes! And this house is very well known, for a very good boarding house for visitors.

STANLEY: Visitors? Do you know how many visitors you've had since I've been here?

MEG: How many?

STANLEY: One.

MEG: Who?

STANLEY: Me! I'm your visitor.

MEG: You're a liar. This house is on the list.

STANLEY: I bet it is.

MEG: I know it is.

He pushes his plate away and picks up the paper.

Was it nice?

STANLEY: What?

MEG: The fried bread.

STANLEY: Succulent.

MEG: You shouldn't say that word.

STANLEY: What word?

MEG: That word you said.

STANLEY: What, succulent—?

MEG: Don't say it!

STANLEY: What's the matter with it?

MEG: You shouldn't say that word to a married woman.

STANLEY: Is that a fact?

MEG: Yes.

STANLEY: Well, I never knew that.

MEG: Well, it's true.

STANLEY: Who told you that?

MEG: Never you mind.

STANLEY: Well, if I can't say it to a married woman who can I say it to?

MEG: You're bad.

STANLEY: What about some tea?

MEG: Do you want some tea? (STANLEY *reads the paper.*) Say please.

STANLEY: Please.

MEG: Say sorry first.

STANLEY: Sorry first.

MEG: No. Just sorry.

STANLEY: Just sorry!

MEG: You deserve the strap.

STANLEY: Don't do that!

She takes his plate and ruffles his hair as she passes. STANLEY *exclaims and throws her arm away. She goes into the kitchen. He rubs his eyes under his glasses and picks up the paper. She enters.*

MEG: I brought the pot in.

STANLEY (*absently*):   I don't know what I'd do without you.

MEG: You don't deserve it though.

STANLEY: Why not?

MEG (*pouring the tea, coyly*):   Go on. Calling me that.

STANLEY: How long has that tea been in the pot?

MEG: It's good tea. Good strong tea.

STANLEY: This isn't tea. It's gravy!

MEG: It's not.

STANLEY: Get out of it. You succulent old washing bag.

MEG: I am not! And it isn't your place to tell me if I am!

STANLEY: And it isn't your place to come into a man's bedroom and—wake him up.

MEG: Stanny! Don't you like your cup of tea of a morning—the one I bring you?

STANLEY: I can't drink this muck. Didn't anyone ever tell you to warm the pot, at least?

MEG: That's good strong tea, that's all.

STANLEY (*putting his head in his hands*):   Oh God, I'm tired.

Silence. MEG *goes to the sideboard, collects a duster, and vaguely dusts the room, watching him. She comes to the table and dusts it.* Not the bloody table!

Pause.

MEG: Stan?

STANLEY: What?

MEG (*shyly*):   Am I really succulent?

STANLEY: Oh, you are. I'd rather have you than a cold in the nose any day.

MEG: You're just saying that.

STANLEY (*violently*):   Look, why don't you get this place cleared up! It's a pigsty. And another thing, what about my room? It needs sweeping. It needs papering. I need a new room!

MEG (*sensual, stroking his arm*):   Oh, Stan, that's a lovely room. I've had some lovely afternoons in that room.

He recoils from her hand in disgust, stands and exits quickly by the door on the left. She collects his cup and the teapot and takes them to the hatch shelf. The street door slams. STANLEY *returns.*

MEG: Is the sun shining? (*He crosses to the window, takes a cigarette and matches from his pyjama jacket, and lights his cigarette.*) What are you smoking?

STANLEY: A cigarette.

MEG: Are you going to give me one?

STANLEY: No.

MEG: I like cigarettes. (*He stands at the window, smoking. She crosses behind him and tickles the back of his neck.*) Tickle, tickle.

STANLEY (*pushing her*):   Get away from me.

MEG: Are you going out?

STANLEY: Not with you.

MEG: But I'm going shopping in a minute.

STANLEY: Go.

MEG: You'll be lonely, all by yourself.

STANLEY: Will I?

MEG: Without your old Meg. I've got to get things in for the two gentlemen.

A pause. STANLEY *slowly raises his head. He speaks without turning.*

STANLEY: What two gentlemen?

MEG: I'm expecting visitors.

He turns.

STANLEY: What?

MEG: You didn't know that, did you?

STANLEY: What are you talking about?

MEG: Two gentlemen asked Petey if they could

come and stay for a couple of nights. I'm expecting them. (*She picks up the duster and begins to wipe the cloth on the table.*)

STANLEY: I don't believe it.

MEG: It's true.

STANLEY (*moving to her*):   You're saying it on purpose.

MEG: Petey told me this morning.

STANLEY (*grinding his cigarette*):   When was this? When did he see them?

MEG: Last night.

STANLEY: Who are they?

MEG: I don't know.

STANLEY: Didn't he tell you their names?

MEG: No.

STANLEY (*pacing the room*):   Here? They wanted to come here?

MEG: Yes, they did. (*She takes the curlers out of her hair.*)

STANLEY: Why?

MEG: This house is on the list.

STANLEY: But who are they?

MEG: You'll see when they come.

STANLEY (*decisively*):   They won't come.

MEG: Why not?

STANLEY (*quickly*):   I tell you they won't come. Why didn't they come last night, if they were coming?

MEG: Perhaps they couldn't find the place in the dark. It's not easy to find in the dark.

STANLEY: They won't come. Someone's taking the Michael. Forget all about it. It's a false alarm. A false alarm. (*He sits at the table.*) Where's my tea?

MEG: I took it away. You didn't want it.

STANLEY: What do you mean, you took it away?

MEG: I took it away.

STANLEY: What did you take it away for?

MEG: You didn't want it!

STANLEY: Who said I didn't want it?

MEG: You did!

STANLEY: Who gave you the right to take away my tea?

MEG: You wouldn't drink it.

STANLEY *stares at her.*

STANLEY (*quietly*):   Who do you think you're talking to?

MEG (*uncertainly*):   What?

STANLEY: Come here.

MEG: What do you mean?

STANLEY: Come over here.

MEG: No.

STANLEY: I want to ask you something. (MEG *fidgets nervously. She does not go to him.*) Come on. (*Pause.*) All right. I can ask it from here just as well. (*Deliberately.*) Tell me, Mrs. Boles, when you address yourself to me, do you ever ask yourself who exactly you are talking to? Eh?

Silence. He groans, his trunk falls forward, his head falls into his hands.

MEG (*in a small voice*):   Didn't you enjoy your breakfast, Stan? (*She approaches the table.*) Stan? When are you going to play the piano again? (STANLEY *grunts.*) Like you used to? (STANLEY *grunts.*) I used to like watching you play the piano. When are you going to play it again?

STANLEY: I can't, can I?

MEG: Why not?

STANLEY: I haven't got a piano, have I?

MEG: No, I meant like when you were working. That piano.

STANLEY: Go and do your shopping.

MEG: But you wouldn't have to go away if you got a job, would you? You could play the piano on the pier.

He looks at her, then speaks airily.

STANLEY: I've . . . er . . . I've been offered a job, as a matter of fact.

MEG: What?

STANLEY: Yes. I'm considering a job at the moment.

MEG: You're not.

STANLEY: A good one, too. A night club. In Berlin.

MEG: Berlin?

STANLEY: Berlin. A night club. Playing the piano. A fabulous salary. And all found.

MEG: How long for?

STANLEY: We don't stay in Berlin. Then we go to Athens.

MEG: How long for?

STANLEY: Yes. Then we pay a flying visit to . . . er . . . whatsisname. . . .

MEG: Where?

STANLEY: Constantinople. Zagreb. Vladivostock. It's a round the world tour.

MEG (*sitting at the table*):   Have you played the piano in those places before?

STANLEY: Played the piano? I've played the piano all over the world. All over the country. (*Pause.*) I once gave a concert.

MEG: A concert?

STANLEY (*reflectively*): Yes. It was a good one, too. They were all there that night. Every single one of them. It was a great success. Yes. A concert. At Lower Edmonton.

MEG: What did you wear?

STANLEY (*to himself*): I had a unique touch. Absolutely unique. They came up to me. They came up to me and said they were grateful. Champagne we had that night, the lot. (*Pause.*) My father nearly came down to hear me. Well, I dropped him a card anyway. But I don't think he could make it. No, I—I lost the address, that was it. (*Pause.*) Yes. Lower Edmonton. Then after that, you know what they did? They carved me up. Carved me up. It was all arranged, it was all worked out. My next concert. Somewhere else it was. In winter. I went down there to play. Then, when I got there, the hall was closed, the place was shuttered up, not even a caretaker. They'd locked it up. (*Takes off his glasses and wipes them on his pyjama jacket.*) A fast one. They pulled a fast one. I'd like to know who was responsible for that. (*Bitterly.*) All right, Jack, I can take a tip. They want me to crawl down on my bended knees. Well I can take a tip . . . any day of the week. (*He replaces his glasses, then looks at* MEG.) Look at her. You're just an old piece of rock cake, aren't you? (*He rises and leans across the table to her.*) That's what you are, aren't you?

MEG: Don't you go away again, Stan. You stay here. You'll be better off. You stay with your old Meg. (*He groans and lies across the table.*) Aren't you feeling well this morning, Stan. Did you pay a visit this morning?

He stiffens, then lifts himself slowly, turns to face her and speaks lightly, casually.

STANLEY: Meg. Do you know what?

MEG: What?

STANLEY: Have you heard the latest?

MEG: No.

STANLEY: I'll bet you have.

MEG: I haven't.

STANLEY: Shall I tell you?

MEG: What latest?

STANLEY: You haven't heard it?

MEG: No.

STANLEY (*advancing*): They're coming today.

MEG: Who?

STANLEY: They're coming in a van.

MEG: Who?

STANLEY: And do you know what they've got in that van?

MEG: What?

STANLEY: They've got a wheelbarrow in that van.

MEG (*breathlessly*): They haven't.

STANLEY: Oh yes they have.

MEG: You're a liar.

STANLEY (*advancing upon her*): A big wheelbarrow. And when the van stops they wheel it out, and they wheel it up the garden path, and then they knock at the front door.

MEG: They don't.

STANLEY: They're looking for someone.

MEG: They're not.

STANLEY: They're looking for someone. A certain person.

MEG (*hoarsely*): No, they're not!

STANLEY: Shall I tell you who they're looking for?

MEG: No!

STANLEY: You don't want me to tell you?

MEG: You're a liar!

A sudden knock on the front door. LULU's *voice: Ooh-ooh!* MEG *edges past* STANLEY *and collects her shopping bag.* MEG *goes out.* STANLEY *sidles to the door and listens.*

VOICE (*through letter box*): Hullo, Mrs. Boles . . .

MEG: Oh, has it come?

VOICE: Yes, it's just come.

MEG: What, is that it?

VOICE: Yes. I thought I'd bring it round.

MEG: Is it nice?

VOICE: Very nice. What shall I do with it?

MEG: Well, I don't . . . (*Whispers.*)

VOICE: No, of course not . . . (*Whispers.*)

MEG: All right, but . . . (*Whispers.*)

VOICE: I won't . . . (*Whispers.*) Ta-ta, Mrs. Boles. STANLEY *quickly sits at the table. Enter* LULU.

LULU: Oh, hullo.

STANLEY: Ay-ay.

LULU: I just want to leave this in here.

STANLEY: Do. (LULU *crosses to the sideboard and puts a solid, round parcel upon it.*) That's a bulky object.

LULU: You're not to touch it.

STANLEY: Why would I want to touch it?

LULU: Well, you're not to, anyway.

LULU *walks upstage.*

LULU: Why don't you open the door? It's all stuffy in here.

She opens the back door.

STANLEY (*rising*): Stuffy? I disinfected the place this morning.

LULU (*at the door*): Oh, that's better.

STANLEY: I think it's going to rain to-day. What do you think?

LULU: I hope so. You could do with it.

STANLEY: Me! I was in the sea at half past six.

LULU: Were you?

STANLEY: I went right out to the headland and back before breakfast. Don't you believe me!

She sits, takes out a compact and powders her nose.

LULU (*offering him the compact*): Do you want to have a look at your face? (STANLEY *withdraws from the table.*) You could do with a shave, do you know that? (STANLEY *sits, right, at the table.*) Don't you ever go out? (*He does not answer.*) I mean, what do you do, just sit around the house like this all day long? (*Pause.*) Hasn't Mrs. Boles got enough to do without having you under her feet all day long?

STANLEY: I always stand on the table when she sweeps the floor.

LULU: Why don't you have a wash? You look terrible.

STANLEY: A wash wouldn't make any difference.

LULU (*rising*): Come out and get a bit of air. You depress me, looking like that.

STANLEY: Air? Oh, I don't know about that.

LULU: It's lovely out. And I've got a few sandwiches.

STANLEY: What sort of sandwiches?

LULU: Cheese.

STANLEY: I'm a big eater, you know.

LULU: That's all right. I'm not hungry.

STANLEY (*abruptly*): How would you like to go away with me?

LULU: Where?

STANLEY: Nowhere. Still, we could go.

LULU: But where could we go?

STANLEY: Nowhere. There's nowhere to go. So we could just go. It wouldn't matter.

LULU: We might as well stay here.

STANLEY: No. It's no good here.

LULU: Well, where else is there?

STANLEY: Nowhere.

LULU: Well, that's a charming proposal. (*He gets up.*) Do you have to wear those glasses?

STANLEY: Yes.

LULU: So you're not coming out for a walk?

STANLEY: I can't at the moment.

LULU: You're a bit of a washout, aren't you?

She exits, left. STANLEY *stands. He then goes to the mirror and looks in it. He goes into the kitchen, takes off his glasses and begins to wash his face. A pause. Enter, by the back door,* GOLDBERG *and* MCCANN. MCCANN *carries two suitcases,* GOLDBERG *a briefcase. They halt inside the door, then walk downstage.* STANLEY, *wiping his face, glimpses their backs through the hatch.* GOLDBERG *and* MCCANN *look round the room.* STANLEY *slips on his glasses, sidles through the kitchen door and out of the back door.*

MCCANN: Is this it?

GOLDBERG: This is it.

MCCANN: Are you sure?

GOLDBERG: Sure I'm sure.

Pause.

MCCANN: What now?

GOLDBERG: Don't worry yourself, McCann. Take a seat.

MCCANN: What about you?

GOLDBERG: What about me?

MCCANN: Are you going to take a seat?

GOLDBERG: We'll both take a seat. (MCCANN *puts down the suitcases and sits at the table, left.*) Sit back, McCann. Relax. What's the matter with you? I bring you down to the seaside. Take a holiday. Do yourself a favour. Learn to relax, McCann, or you'll never get anywhere.

MCCANN: Ah sure, I do try, Nat.

GOLDBERG (*sitting at the table, right*): The secret is breathing. Take my tip. It's a well-known fact. Breathe in, breathe out, take a chance, let yourself go, what can you lose? Look at me. When I was an apprentice yet, McCann, every second Friday of the month my Uncle Barney used to take me to the seaside, regular as clockwork. Brighton, Canvey Island, Rottingdean—Uncle Barney wasn't particular. After lunch on Shabbuss we'd go and sit in a couple of deck chairs—you know, the ones with canopies—we'd have a little paddle, we'd watch the tide coming in, going out, the sun coming down—golden days, believe me, McCann. (*Reminiscent.*) Uncle Barney. Of course, he was an impeccable dresser. One of the old school. He had a house just outside Basingstoke at the time. Respected by the whole community. Culture? Don't talk to me about culture. He was an all-round man, what do you mean? He was a cosmopolitan.

MCCANN: Hey, Nat. . . .

GOLDBERG (*reflectively*): Yes. One of the old school.

MCCANN: Nat. How do we know this is the right house?

GOLDBERG: What?

MCCANN: How do we know this is the right house?

GOLDBERG: What makes you think it's the wrong house?

MCCANN: I didn't see a number on the gate.

GOLDBERG: I wasn't looking for a number.

MCCANN: No?

GOLDBERG (*settling in the armchair*): You know one thing Uncle Barney taught me? Uncle Barney taught me that the word of a gentleman is enough. That's why, when I had to go away on business I never carried any money. One of my sons used to come with me. He used to carry a few coppers. For a paper, perhaps, to see how the M.C.C. was getting on overseas. Otherwise my name was good. Besides, I was a very busy man.

MCCANN: What about this, Nat? Isn't it about time someone came in?

GOLDBERG: McCann, what are you so nervous about? Pull yourself together. Everywhere you go these days it's like a funeral.

MCCANN: That's true.

GOLDBERG: True? Of course it's true. It's more than true. It's a fact.

MCCANN: You may be right.

GOLDBERG: What is it, McCann? You don't trust me like you did in the old days?

MCCANN: Sure I trust you, Nat.

GOLDBERG: But why is it that before you do a job you're all over the place, and when you're doing the job you're as cool as a whistle?

MCCANN: I don't know, Nat. I'm just all right once I know what I'm doing. When I know what I'm doing, I'm all right.

GOLDBERG: Well, you do it very well.

MCCANN: Thank you, Nat.

GOLDBERG: You know what I said when this job came up. I mean naturally they approached

me to take care of it. And you know who I asked for?

MCCANN: Who?

GOLDBERG: You.

MCCANN: That was very good of you, Nat.

GOLDBERG: No, it was nothing. You're a capable man, McCann.

MCCANN: That's a great compliment, Nat, coming from a man in your position.

GOLDBERG: Well, I've got a position, I won't deny it.

MCCANN: You certainly have.

GOLDBERG: I would never deny that I had a position.

MCCANN: And what a position!

GOLDBERG: It's not a thing I would deny.

MCCANN: Yes, it's true, you've done a lot for me. I appreciate it.

GOLDBERG: Say no more.

MCCANN: You've always been a true Christian.

GOLDBERG: In a way.

MCCANN: No, I just thought I'd tell you that I appreciate it.

GOLDBERG: It's unnecessary to recapitulate.

MCCANN: You're right there.

GOLDBERG: Quite unnecessary.

Pause. MCCANN *leans forward.*

MCCANN: Hey Nat, just one thing. . . .

GOLDBERG: What now?

MCCANN: This job—no, listen—this job, is it going to be like anything we've ever done before?

GOLDBERG: Tch, tch, tch.

MCCANN: No, just tell me that. Just that, and I won't ask any more.

GOLDBERG *sighs, stands, goes behind the table, ponders, looks at* MCCANN, *and then speaks in a quiet, fluent, official tone.*

GOLDBERG: The main issue is a singular issue and quite distinct from your previous work. Certain elements, however, might well approximate in points of procedure to some of your other activities. All is dependent on the attitude of our subject. At all events, McCann, I can assure you that the assignment will be carried out and the mission accomplished with no excessive aggravation to you or myself. Satisfied?

MCCANN: Sure. Thank you, Nat.

MEG *enters, left.*

GOLDBERG: Ah, Mrs. Boles?

MEG: Yes?

GOLDBERG: We spoke to your husband last night. Perhaps he mentioned us? We heard that you kindly let rooms for gentlemen. So I brought my friend along with me. We were after a nice place, you understand. So we came to you. I'm Mr. Goldberg and this is Mr. McCann.

MEG: Very pleased to meet you.

They shake hands.

GOLDBERG: We're pleased to meet you, too.

MEG: That's very nice.

GOLDBERG: You're right. How often do you meet someone it's a pleasure to meet?

MCCANN: Never.

GOLDBERG: But today it's different. How are you keeping, Mrs. Boles?

MEG: Oh, very well, thank you.

GOLDBERG: Yes? Really?

MEG: Oh yes, really.

GOLDBERG: I'm glad.

GOLDBERG *sits at the table, right.*

GOLDBERG: Well, so what do you say? You can manage to put us up, eh, Mrs. Boles?

MEG: Well, it would have been easier last week.

GOLDBERG: It would, eh?

MEG: Yes.

GOLDBERG: Why? How many have you got here at the moment?

MEG: Just one at the moment.

GOLDBERG: Just one?

MEG: Yes. Just one. Until you came.

GOLDBERG: And your husband, of course?

MEG: Yes, but he sleeps with me.

GOLDBERG: What does he do, your husband?

MEG: He's a deck-chair attendant.

GOLDBERG: Oh, very nice.

MEG: Yes, he's out in all weathers.

She begins to take her purchases from her bag.

GOLDBERG: Of course. And your guest? Is he a man?

MEG: A man?

GOLDBERG: Or a woman?

MEG: No. A man.

GOLDBERG: Been here long?

MEG: He's been here about a year now.

GOLDBERG: Oh yes. A resident. What's his name?

MEG: Stanley Webber.

GOLDBERG: Oh yes? Does he work here?

MEG: He used to work. He used to be a pianist. In a concert party on the pier.

GOLDBERG: Oh yes? On the pier, eh? Does he play a nice piano?

MEG: Oh, lovely. (*She sits at the table.*) He once gave a concert.

GOLDBERG: Oh? Where?

MEG (*falteringly*): In . . . a big hall. His father gave him champagne. But then they locked the place up and he couldn't get out. The caretaker had gone home. So he had to wait until the morning before he could get out. (*With confidence.*) They were very grateful. (*Pause.*) And then they all wanted to give him a tip. And so he took the tip. And then he got a fast train and he came down here.

GOLDBERG: Really?

MEG: Oh yes. Straight down.

Pause.

MEG: I wish he could have played tonight.

GOLDBERG: Why tonight?

MEG: It's his birthday today.

GOLDBERG: His birthday?

MEG: Yes. Today. But I'm not going to tell him until tonight.

GOLDBERG: Doesn't he know it's his birthday?

MEG: He hasn't mentioned it.

GOLDBERG (*thoughtfully*): Ah! Tell me. Are you going to have a party?

MEG: A party?

GOLDBERG: Weren't you going to have one?

MEG (*her eyes wide*): No.

GOLDBERG: Well, of course, you must have one. (*He stands.*) We'll have a party, eh? What do you say?

MEG: Oh yes!

GOLDBERG: Sure. We'll give him a party. Leave it to me.

MEG: Oh, that's wonderful, Mr. Gold—

GOLDBERG: Berg.

MEG: Berg.

GOLDBERG: You like the idea?

MEG: Oh, I'm so glad you came today.

GOLDBERG: If we hadn't come today we'd have come tomorrow. Still, I'm glad we came today. Just in time for his birthday.

MEG: I wanted to have a party. But you must have people for a party.

GOLDBERG: And now you've got McCann and me. McCann's the life and soul of any party.

MCCANN: What?

GOLDBERG: What do you think of that, Mc-Cann? There's a gentleman living here. He's got a birthday today, and he's forgotten all about it. So we're going to remind him. We're going to give him a party.

MCCANN: Oh, is that a fact?

MEG: Tonight.

GOLDBERG: Tonight.

MEG: I'll put on my party dress.

GOLDBERG: And I'll get some bottles.

MEG: And I'll invite Lulu this afternoon. Oh, this is going to cheer Stanley up. It will. He's been down in the dumps lately.

GOLDBERG: We'll bring him out of himself.

MEG: I hope I look nice in my dress.

GOLDBERG: Madam, you'll look like a tulip.

MEG: What colour?

GOLDBERG: Er—well, I'll have to see the dress first.

MCCANN: Could I go up to my room?

MEG: Oh, I've put you both together. Do you mind being both together?

GOLDBERG: I don't mind. Do you mind, Mc-Cann?

MCCANN: No.

MEG: What time shall we have the party?

GOLDBERG: Nine o'clock.

MCCANN (at the door):   Is this the way?

MEG (rising):   I'll show you. If you don't mind coming upstairs.

GOLDBERG: With a tulip? It's a pleasure.

MEG and GOLDBERG exit laughing, followed by MCCANN. STANLEY appears at the window. He enters by the back door. He goes to the door on the left, opens it and listens. Silence. He walks to the table. He stands. He sits, as MEG enters. She crosses and hangs her shopping bag on a hook. He lights a match and watches it burn.

STANLEY: Who is it?

MEG: The two gentlemen.

STANLEY: What two gentlemen?

MEG: The ones that were coming. I just took them to their room. They were thrilled with their room.

STANLEY: They've come?

MEG: They're very nice, Stan.

STANLEY: Why didn't they come last night?

MEG: They said the beds were wonderful.

STANLEY: Who are they?

MEG (sitting):   They're very nice, Stanley.

STANLEY: I said, who are they?

MEG: I've told you, the two gentlemen.

STANLEY: I didn't think they'd come.

He rises and walks to the window.

MEG: They have. They were here when I came in.

STANLEY: What do they want here?

MEG: They want to stay.

STANLEY: How long for?

MEG: They didn't say.

STANLEY (turning):   But why here? Why not somewhere else?

MEG: This house is on the list.

STANLEY (coming down):   What are they called? What are their names?

MEG: Oh, Stanley, I can't remember.

STANLEY: They told you, didn't they? Or didn't they tell you?

MEG: Yes, they. . . .

STANLEY: Then what are they? Come on. Try to remember.

MEG: Why, Stan? Do you know them?

STANLEY: How do I know if I know them until I know their names?

MEG: Well . . . he told me, I remember.

STANLEY: Well?

She thinks.

MEG: Gold—something.

STANLEY: Goldsomething?

MEG: Yes. Gold. . . .

STANLEY: Yes?

MEG: Goldberg.

STANLEY: Goldberg?

MEG: That's right. That was one of them.

STANLEY slowly sits at the table, left.

Do you know them?

STANLEY does not answer.

Stan, they won't wake you up, I promise. I'll tell them they must be quiet.

STANLEY sits still.

They won't be here long, Stan. I'll still bring you up your early morning tea.

STANLEY sits still.

You mustn't be sad today. It's your birthday.

A pause.

STANLEY (dumbly):   Uh?

MEG: It's your birthday, Stan. I was going to keep it a secret until tonight.

STANLEY: No.

MEG: It is. I've brought you a present. (*She goes

to the sideboard, picks up the parcel, and places it on the table in front of him.) Here. Go on. Open it.

STANLEY: What's this?

MEG: It's your present.

STANLEY: This isn't my birthday, Meg.

MEG: Of course it is. Open your present.

He stares at the parcel, slowly stands, and opens it. He takes out a boy's drum.

STANLEY (*flatly*): It's a drum. A boy's drum.

MEG (*tenderly*): It's because you haven't got a piano. (*He stares at her, then turns and walks towards the door, left.*) Aren't you going to give me a kiss? (*He turns sharply, and stops. He walks back towards her slowly. He stops at her chair, looking down upon her. Pause. His shoulders sag, he bends and kisses her on the cheek.*) There are some sticks in there. (STANLEY *looks into the parcel. He takes out two drumsticks. He taps them together. He looks at her.*)

STANLEY: Shall I put it round my neck?

She watches him, uncertainly. He hangs the drum around his neck, taps it gently with the sticks, then marches round the table, beating it regularly. MEG, *pleased, watches him. Still beating it regularly, he begins to go round the table a second time. Halfway round the beat becomes erratic, uncontrolled.* MEG *expresses dismay. He arrives at her chair, banging the drum, his face and the drumbeat now savage and possessed.*

Curtain

ACT TWO

MCCANN *is sitting at the table tearing a sheet of newspaper into five equal strips. It is evening. After a few moments* STANLEY *enters from the left. He stops upon seeing* MCCANN, *and watches him. He then walks towards the kitchen, stops, and speaks.*

STANLEY: Evening.

MCCANN: Evening.

Chuckles are heard from outside the back door, which is open.

STANLEY: Very warm tonight. (*He turns towards the back door, and back.*) Someone out there?

MCCANN *tears another length of paper.* STANLEY *goes into the kitchen and pours a glass of water. He drinks it looking through the hatch. He puts the glass down, comes out of the kitchen and walks quickly towards the door, left.* MCCANN *rises and intercepts him.*

MCCANN: I don't think we've met.

STANLEY: No, we haven't.

MCCANN: My name's McCann.

STANLEY: Staying here long?

MCCANN: Not long. What's your name?

STANLEY: Webber.

MCCANN: I'm glad to meet you, sir. (*He offers his hand.* STANLEY *takes it, and* MCCANN *holds the grip.*) Many happy returns of the day. (STANLEY *withdraws his hand. They face each other.*) Were you going out?

STANLEY: Yes.

MCCANN: On your birthday?

STANLEY: Yes. Why not?

MCCANN: But they're holding a party here for you tonight.

STANLEY: Oh really? That's unfortunate.

MCCANN: Ah no. It's very nice.

Voices from outside the back door.

STANLEY: I'm sorry. I'm not in the mood for a party tonight.

MCCANN: Oh, is that so? I'm sorry.

STANLEY: Yes, I'm going out to celebrate quietly, on my own.

MCCANN: That's a shame.

They stand.

STANLEY: Well, if you'd move out of my way—

MCCANN: But everything's laid on. The guests are expected.

STANLEY: Guests? What guests?

MCCANN: Myself for one. I had the honour of an invitation.

MCCANN *begins to whistle "The Mountains of Morne".*

STANLEY (*moving away*): I wouldn't call it an honour, would you? It'll just be another booze-up.

STANLEY *joins* MCCANN *in whistling "The Mountains of Morne." During the next five lines the whistling is continuous, one whistling while the other speaks, and both whistling together.*

MCCANN: But it is an honour.

STANLEY: I'd say you were exaggerating.

MCCANN: Oh no. I'd say it was an honour.

STANLEY: I'd say that was plain stupid.

MCCANN: Ah no.

They stare at each other.

STANLEY: Who are the other guests?

MCCANN: A young lady.

STANLEY: Oh yes? And. . . .?

MCCANN: My friend.

STANLEY: Your friend?

MCCANN: That's right. It's all laid on.

STANLEY *walks round the table towards the door.* MCCANN *meets him.*

STANLEY: Excuse me.

MCCANN: Where are you going?

STANLEY: I want to go out.

MCCANN: Why don't you stay here?

STANLEY *moves away, to the right of the table.*

STANLEY: So you're down here on holiday?

MCCANN: A short one. (STANLEY *picks up a strip of paper.* MCCANN *moves in.*) Mind that.

STANLEY: What is it?

MCCANN: Mind it. Leave it.

STANLEY: I've got a feeling we've met before.

MCCANN: No we haven't.

STANLEY: Ever been anywhere near Maidenhead?

MCCANN: No.

STANLEY: There's a Fuller's teashop. I used to have my tea there.

MCCANN: I don't know it.

STANLEY: And a Boots Library. I seem to connect you with the High Street.

MCCANN: Yes?

STANLEY: A charming town, don't you think?

MCCANN: I don't know it.

STANLEY: Oh no. A quiet, thriving community. I was born and brought up there. I lived well away from the main road.

MCCANN: Yes?

Pause.

STANLEY: You're here on a short stay?

MCCANN: That's right.

STANLEY: You'll find it very bracing.

MCCANN: Do you find it bracing?

STANLEY: Me? No. But you will. (*He sits at the table.*) I like it here, but I'll be moving soon. Back home. I'll stay there too, this time. No place like home. (*He laughs.*) I wouldn't have left, but business calls. Business called, and I had to leave for a bit. You know how it is.

MCCANN (*sitting at the table, left*):   You in business?

STANLEY: No. I think I'll give it up. I've got a small private income, you see. I think I'll give it up. Don't like being away from home. I used to live very quietly—played records, that's about all. Everything delivered to the door. Then I started a little private business, in a small way, and it compelled me to come down here—kept me longer than I expected. You never get used to living in someone else's house. Don't you agree? I lived so quietly. You can only appreciate what you've had when things change. That's what they say, isn't it? Cigarette?

MCCANN: I don't smoke.

STANLEY *lights a cigarette. Voices from the back.*

STANLEY: Who's out there?

MCCANN: My friend and the man of the house.

STANLEY: You know what? To look at me, I bet you wouldn't think I'd led such a quiet life. The lines on my face, eh? It's the drink. Been drinking a bit down here. But what I mean is . . . you know how it is . . . I'll be all right when I get back . . . but what I mean is, the way some people look at me you'd think I was a different person. I suppose I have changed, but I'm still the same man that I always was. I mean, you wouldn't think, to look at me, really . . . I mean, not really, that I was the sort of bloke to—to cause any trouble, would you? (MCCANN *looks at him.*) Do you know what I mean?

MCCANN: No. (*As* STANLEY *picks up a strip of paper.*) Mind that.

STANLEY (*quickly*):   Why are you down here?

MCCANN: A short holiday.

STANLEY: This is a ridiculous house to pick on. (*He rises.*)

MCCANN: Why?

STANLEY: Because it's not a boarding house. It never was.

MCCANN: Sure it is.

STANLEY: Why did you choose this house?

MCCANN: You know, sir, you're a bit depressed for a man on his birthday.

STANLEY (*sharply*):   Why do you call me sir?

MCCANN: You don't like it?

STANLEY (*to the table*):   Listen. Don't call me sir.

MCCANN: I won't, if you don't like it.

STANLEY (*moving away*): No. Anyway, this isn't my birthday.

MCCANN: No?

STANLEY: No. It's not till next month.

MCCANN: Not according to the lady.

STANLEY: Her? She's crazy. Round the bend.

MCCANN: That's a terrible thing to say.

STANLEY (*to the table*): Haven't you found that out yet? There's a lot you don't know. I think someone's leading you up the garden path.

MCCANN: Who would do that?

STANLEY (*leaning across the table*): That woman is mad!

MCCANN: That's slander.

STANLEY: And you don't know what you're doing.

MCCANN: Your cigarette is near that paper.
  Voices from the back.

STANLEY: Where the hell are they? (*Stubbing his cigarette.*) Why don't they come in? What are they doing out there?

MCCANN: You want to steady yourself.
  STANLEY *crosses to him and grips his arm.*

STANLEY (*urgently*): Look—

MCCANN: Don't touch me.

STANLEY: Look. Listen a minute.

MCCANN: Let go my arm.

STANLEY: Look. Sit down a minute.

MCCANN (*savagely, hitting his arm*): Don't do that!
  STANLEY *backs across the stage, holding his arm.*

STANLEY: Listen. You knew what I was talking about before, didn't you?

MCCANN: I don't know what you're at at all.

STANLEY: It's a mistake! Do you understand?

MCCANN: You're in a bad state, man.

STANLEY (*whispering, advancing*): Has he told you anything? Do you know what you're here for? Tell me. You needn't be frightened of me. Or hasn't he told you?

MCCANN: Told me what?

STANLEY (*hissing*): I've explained to you, damn you, that all those years I lived in Basingstoke I never stepped outside the door.

MCCANN: You know, I'm flabbergasted with you.

STANLEY (*reasonably*): Look. You look an honest man. You're being made a fool of, that's all. You understand? Where do you come from?

MCCANN: Where do you think?

STANLEY: I know Ireland very well. I've many friends there. I love that country and I admire and trust its people. I trust them. They respect the truth and they have a sense of humour. I think their policemen are wonderful. I've been there. I've never seen such sunsets. What about coming out to have a drink with me? There's a pub down the road serves draught Guinness. Very difficult to get in these parts— (*He breaks off. The voices draw nearer.* GOLDBERG *and* PETEY *enter from the back door.*)

GOLDBERG (*as he enters*): A mother in a million. (*He sees* STANLEY.) Ah.

PETEY: Oh hullo, Stan. You haven't met Stanley, have you, Mr. Goldberg?

GOLDBERG: I haven't had the pleasure.

PETEY: Oh well, this is Mr. Goldberg, this is Mr. Webber.

GOLDBERG: Pleased to meet you.

PETEY: We were just getting a bit of air in the garden.

GOLDBERG: I was telling Mr. Boles about my old mum. What days. (*He sits at the table, right.*) Yes. When I was a youngster, of a Friday, I used to go for a walk down the canal with a girl who lived down my road. A beautiful girl. What a voice that bird had! A nightingale, my word of honour. Good? Pure? She wasn't a Sunday school teacher for nothing. Anyway, I'd leave her with a little kiss on the cheek—I never took liberties—we weren't like the young men these days in those days. We knew the meaning of respect. So I'd give her a peck and I'd bowl back home. Humming away I'd be, past the children's playground. I'd tip my hat to the toddlers, I'd give a helping hand to a couple of stray dogs, everything came natural. I can see it like yesterday. The sun falling behind the dog stadium Ah! (*He leans back contentedly.*)

MCCANN: Like behind the town hall.

GOLDBERG: What town hall?

MCCANN: In Carrikmacross.

GOLDBERG: There's no comparison. Up the street, into my gate, inside the door, home. "Simey!" my old mum used to shout, "quick before it gets cold." And there on the table what would I see? The nicest piece of gefilte fish you could wish to find on a plate.

MCCANN: I thought your name was Nat.

GOLDBERG: She called me Simey.

PETEY: Yes, we all remember our childhood.

GOLDBERG: Too true. Eh, Mr. Weber, what do you say? Childhood. Hot water bottles. Hot milk. Pancakes. Soap suds. What a life.

Pause.

PETEY (*rising from the table*):   Well, I'll have to be off.

GOLDBERG: Off?

PETEY: It's my chess night.

GOLDBERG: You're not staying for the party?

PETEY: No, I'm sorry, Stan. I didn't know about it till just now. And we've got a game on. I'll try and get back early.

GOLDBERG: We'll save some drink for you, all right? Oh, that reminds me. You'd better go and collect the bottles.

MCCANN: Now?

GOLDBERG: Of course, now. Time's getting on. Round the corner, remember? Mention my name.

PETEY: I'm coming your way.

GOLDBERG: Beat him quick and come back, Mr. Boles.

PETEY: Do my best. See you later, Stan.

PETEY *and* MCCANN *go out, left.* STANLEY *moves to the centre.*

GOLDBERG: A warm night.

STANLEY (*turning*):   Don't mess me about!

GOLDBERG: I beg your pardon?

STANLEY (*moving downstage*):   I'm afraid there's been a mistake. We're booked out. Your room is taken. Mrs. Boles forgot to tell you. You'll have to find somewhere else.

GOLDBERG: Are you the manager here?

STANLEY: That's right.

GOLDBERG: Is it a good game?

STANLEY: I run the house. I'm afraid you and your friend will have to find other accommodation.

GOLDBERG (*rising*):   Oh, I forgot, I must congratulate you on your birthday. (*Offering his hand.*) Congratulations.

STANLEY (*ignoring hand*):   Perhaps you're deaf.

GOLDBERG: No, what makes you think that? As a matter of fact, every single one of my senses is at its peak. Not bad going, eh? For a man past fifty. But a birthday, I always feel, is a great occasion, taken too much for granted these days. What a thing to celebrate—birth! Like getting up in the morning. Marvellous! Some people don't like the idea of getting up in the morning. I've heard them. Getting up in the morning, they say, what is it? Your skin's crabby, you need a shave, your eyes are full of muck, your mouth is like a boghouse, the palms of your hands are full of sweat, your nose is clogged up, your feet stink, what are you but a corpse waiting to be washed? Whenever I hear that point of view I feel cheerful. Because I know what it is to wake up with the sun shining, to the sound of the lawnmower, all the little birds, the smell of the grass, church bells, tomato juice—

STANLEY: Get out.

Enter MCCANN, *with bottles.*

Get that drink out. These are unlicensed premises.

GOLDBERG: You're in a terrible humour today, Mr. Webber. And on your birthday too, with the good lady getting her strength up to give you a party.

MCCANN *puts the bottles on the sideboard.*

STANLEY: I told you to get those bottles out.

GOLDBERG: Mr. Webber, sit down a minute.

STANLEY: Let me—just make this clear. You don't bother me. To me, you're nothing but a dirty joke. But I have a responsibility towards the people in this house. They've been down here too long. They've lost their sense of smell. I haven't. And nobody's going to take advantage of them while I'm here. (*A little less forceful.*) Anyway, this house isn't your cup of tea. There's nothing here for you, from any angle, any angle. So why don't you just go, without any more fuss?

GOLDBERG: Mr. Webber, sit down.

STANLEY: It's no good starting any kind of trouble.

GOLDBERG: Sit down.

STANLEY: Why should I?

GOLDBERG: If you want to know the truth, Webber, you're beginning to get on my breasts.

STANLEY: Really? Well, that's—

GOLDBERG: Sit down.

STANLEY: No.

GOLDBERG *sighs, and sits at the table right.*

GOLDBERG: McCann.

MCCANN: Nat?

GOLDBRG: Ask him to sit down.

MCCANN: Yes, Nat. (MCCANN *moves to* STANLEY.) Do you mind sitting down?

STANLEY: Yes, I do mind.

MCCANN: Yes now, but—it'd be better if you did.

STANLEY: Why don't you sit down?

MCCANN: No, not me—you.

STANLEY: No thanks.

    Pause.

MCCANN: Nat.

GOLDBERG: What?

MCCANN: He won't sit down.

GOLDBERG: Well, ask him.

MCCANN: I've asked him.

GOLDBERG: Ask him again.

MCCANN (*to* STANLEY):   Sit down.

STANLEY: Why?

MCCANN: You'd be more comfortable.

STANLEY: So would you.

    Pause.

MCCANN: All right. If you will I will.

STANLEY: You first.

    MCCANN *slowly sits at the table, left.*

MCCANN: Well?

STANLEY: Right. Now you've both had a rest you can get out!

MCCANN (*rising*):   That's a dirty trick! I'll kick the shite out of him!

GOLDBERG (*rising*):   No! I have stood up.

MCCANN: Sit down again!

GOLDBERG: Once I'm up I'm up.

STANLEY: Same here.

MCCANN (*moving to* STANLEY):   You've made Mr. Goldberg stand up.

STANLEY (*his voice rising*):   It'll do him good!

MCCANN: Get in that seat.

GOLDBERG: McCann.

MCCANN: Get down in that seat!

GOLDBERG (*crossing to him*):   Webber. (*Quietly.*) SIT DOWN. (*Silence.* STANLEY *begins to whistle "The Mountains of Morne". He strolls casually to the chair at the table. They watch him. He stops whistling. Silence. He sits.*)

STANLEY: You'd better be careful.

GOLDBERG: Webber, what were you doing yesterday?

STANLEY: Yesterday?

GOLDBERG: And the day before. What did you do the day before that?

STANLEY: What do you mean?

GOLDBERG: Why are you wasting everybody's time, Webber? Why are you getting in everybody's way?

STANLEY: Me? What are you—

GOLDBERG: I'm telling you, Webber. You're a washout. Why are you getting on everybody's wick? Why are you driving that old lady off her conk?

MCCANN: He likes to do it!

GOLDBERG: Why do you behave so badly, Webber! Why do you force that old man out to play chess?

STANLEY: Me?

GOLDBERG: She's not the leper, Webber!

STANLEY: What the—

GOLDBERG: What did you wear last week, Webber? Where do you keep your suits?

MCCANN: Why did you leave the organization?

GOLDBERG: What would your old mum say, Webber?

MCCANN: Why did you betray us?

GOLDBERG: You hurt me, Webber. You're playing a dirty game.

MCCANN: That's a Black and Tan fact.

GOLDBERG: Who does he think he is?

MCCANN: Who do you think you are?

STANLEY: You're on the wrong horse.

GOLDBERG: When did you come to this place?

STANLEY: Last year.

GOLDBERG: Where did you come from?

STANLEY: Somewhere else.

GOLDBERG: Why did you come here?

STANLEY: My feet hurt!

GOLDBERG: Why did you stay?

STANLEY: I had a headache!

GOLDBERG: Did you take anything for it?

STANLEY: Yes.

GOLDBERG: What?

STANLEY: Fruit salts!

GOLDBERG: Enos or Andrews?

STANLEY: En— An—

GOLDBERG: Did you stir properly? Did they fizz?

STANLEY: Now, now, wait, you—

GOLDBERG: Did they fizz? Did they fizz or didn't they fizz?

MCCANN: He doesn't know!

GOLDBERG: You don't know. When did you last have a bath?

STANLEY: I have one every—

GOLDBERG: Don't lie.

MCCANN: You betrayed the organization. I know him!

STANLEY: You don't!

GOLDBERG: What can you see without your glasses?

STANLEY: Anything.

GOLDBERG: Take off his glasses.

    MCCANN *snatches his glasses and as* STANLEY *rises, reaching for them, takes his chair downstage centre, below the table,* STANLEY *stumbling as he follows.* STANLEY *clutches the chair and stays bent over it.*

Webber, you're a fake. (*They stand on each side of the chair.*)

When did you last wash up a cup?

STANLEY: The Christmas before last.

GOLDBERG: Where?

STANLEY: Lyons Corner House.

GOLDBERG: Which one?

STANLEY: Marble Arch.

GOLDBERG: Where was your wife?

STANLEY: In—

GOLDBERG: Answer.

STANLEY (*turning, crouched*): What wife?

GOLDBERG: What have you done with your wife?

MCCANN: He's killed his wife!

GOLDBERG: Why did you kill your wife?

STANLEY (*sitting, his back to the audience*): What wife?

MCCANN: How did he kill her?

GOLDBERG: How did you kill her?

MCCANN: You throttled her.

GOLDBERG: With arsenic.

MCCANN: There's your man!

GOLDBERG: Where's your old mum?

STANLEY: In the sanatorium.

MCCANN: Yes!

GOLDBERG: Why did you never get married?

MCCANN: She was waiting at the porch.

GOLDBERG: You skedaddled from the wedding.

MCCANN: He left her in the lurch.

GOLDBERG: You left her in the pudding club.

MCCANN: She was waiting at the church.

GOLDBERG: Webber! Why did you change your name?

STANLEY: I forgot the other one.

GOLDBERG: What's your name now?

STANLEY: Joe Soap.

GOLDBERG: You stink of sin.

MCCANN: I can smell it.

GOLDBERG: Do you recognise an external force?

STANLEY: What?

GOLDBERG: Do you recognise an external force?

MCCANN: That's the question!

GOLDBERG: Do you recognise an external force, responsible for you, suffering for you?

STANLEY: It's late.

GOLDBERG: Late! Late enough! When did you last pray?

MCCANN: He's sweating!

GOLDBERG: When did you last pray?

MCCANN: He's sweating!

GOLDBERG: Is the number 846 possible or necessary?

STANLEY: Neither.

GOLDBERG: Wrong! Is the number 846 possible or necessary?

STANLEY: Both.

GOLDBERG: Wrong! It's necessary but not possible.

STANLEY: Both.

GOLDBERG: Wrong! Why do you think the number 846 is necessarily possible?

STANLEY: Must be.

GOLDBERG: Wrong! It's only necessarily necessary! We admit possibility only after we grant necessity. It is possible because necessary but by no means necessary through possibility. The possibility can only be assumed after the proof of necessity.

MCCANN: Right!

GOLDBERG: Right? Of course right! We're right and you're wrong, Webber, all along the line.

MCCANN: All along the line!

GOLDBERG: Where is your lechery leading you?

MCCANN: You'll pay for this.

GOLDBERG: You stuff yourself with dry toast.

MCCANN: You contaminate womankind.

GOLDBERG: Why don't you pay the rent?

MCCANN: Mother defiler!

GOLDBERG: Why do you pick your nose?

MCCANN: I demand justice!

GOLDBERG: What's your trade?

MCCANN: What about Ireland?

GOLDBERG: What's your trade?

STANLEY: I play the piano.

GOLDBERG: How many fingers do you use?

STANLEY: No hands!

GOLDBERG: No society would touch you. Not even a building society.

MCCANN: You're a traitor to the cloth.

GOLDBERG: What do you use for pyjamas?

STANLEY: Nothing.

GOLDBERG: You verminate the sheet of your birth.

MCCANN: What about the Albigensenist heresy?

GOLDBERG: Who watered the wicket in Melbourne?

MCCANN: What about the blessed Oliver Plunkett?

GOLDBERG: Speak up Webber. Why did the chicken cross the road?

STANLEY: He wanted to—he wanted to—he wanted to. . . .

MCCANN: He doesn't know!

GOLDBERG: Why did the chicken cross the road?

STANLEY: He wanted to—he wanted to. . . .

GOLDBERG: Why did the chicken cross the road?

STANLEY: He wanted. . . .

MCCANN: He doesn't know. He doesn't know which came first!

GOLDBERG: Which came first?

MCCANN: Chicken? Egg? Which came first?

GOLDBERG and MCCANN: Which came first? Which came first? Which came first?

> STANLEY *screams.*

GOLDBERG: He doesn't know. Do you know your own face?

MCCANN: Wake him up. Stick a needle in his eye.

GOLDBERG: You're a plague, Webber. You're an overthrow.

MCCANN: You're what's left!

GOLDBERG: But we've got the answer to you. We can sterilise you.

MCCANN: What about Drogheda?

GOLDBERG: Your bite is dead. Only your pong is left.

MCCANN: You betrayed our land.

GOLDBERG: You betray our breed.

MCCANN: Who are you, Webber?

GOLDBERG: What makes you think you exist?

MCCANN: You're dead.

GOLDBERG: You're dead. You can't live, you can't think, you can't love. You're dead. You're a plague gone bad. There's no juice in you. You're nothing but an odour!

> *Silence. They stand over him. He is crouched in the chair. He looks up slowly and kicks* GOLDBERG *in the stomach.* GOLDBERG *falls.* STANLEY *stands.* MCCANN *seizes a chair and lifts it above his head.* STANLEY *seizes a chair and covers his head with it.* MCCANN *and* STANLEY *circle.*

GOLDBERG: Steady, McCann.

STANLEY (*circling*): Uuuuuhhhhh!

MCCANN: Right, Judas.

GOLDBERG: (*rising*): Steady, McCann.

MCCANN: Come on!

STANLEY: Uuuuuuuhhhhh!

MCCANN: He's sweating.

STANLEY: Uuuuuhhhhh!

GOLDBERG: Easy, McCann.

MCCANN: The bastard sweatpig is sweating.

> *A loud drumbeat off left, descending the stairs.* GOLDBERG *takes the chair from* STAN-LEY. *They put the chairs down. They stop still. Enter* MEG, *in evening dress, holding sticks and drum.*

MEG: I brought the drum down. I'm dressed for the party.

GOLDBERG: Wonderful.

MEG: You like my dress?

GOLDBERG: Wonderful. Out of this world.

MEG: I know. My father gave it to me. (*Placing drum on table.*) Doesn't it make a beautiful noise?

GOLDBERG: It's a fine piece of work. Maybe Stan'll play us a little tune afterwards.

MEG: Oh yes. Will you, Stan?

STANLEY: Could I have my glasses?

GOLDBERG: Ah yes. (*He holds his hand out to* MCCANN. MCCANN *passes him his glasses.*) Here they are. (*He holds them out for* STANLEY, *who reaches for them.*) Here they are. (STANLEY *takes them.*) Now. What have we got here? Enough to scuttle a liner. We've got four bottles of Scotch and one bottle of Irish.

MEG: Oh, Mr. Goldberg, what should I drink?

GOLDBERG: Glasses, glasses first. Open the Scotch, McCann.

MEG (*at the sideboard*): Here's my very best glasses in here.

MCCANN: I don't drink Scotch.

GOLDBERG: You've got the Irish.

MEG (*bringing the glasses*): Here they are.

GOLDBERG: Good. Mrs. Boles, I think Stanley should pour the toast, don't you?

MEG: Oh yes. Come on, Stanley. (STANLEY *walks slowly to the table.*) Do you like my dress, Mr. Goldberg?

GOLDBERG: It's out on its own. Turn yourself round a minute. I used to be in the business. Go on, walk up there.

MEG: Oh no.

GOLDBERG: Don't be shy. (*He slaps her bottom.*)

MEG: Ooooh!

GOLDBERG: Walk up the boulevard. Let's have a look at you. What a carriage. What's your opinion, McCann? Like a Countess, nothing less. Madam, now turn about and promanade to the kitchen. What a deportment!

MCCANN (*to* STANLEY): You can pour my Irish too.

GOLDBERG: You look like a Gladiola.

MEG: Stan, what about my dress?

GOLDBERG: One for the lady, one for the lady. Now madam—your glass.

MEG: Thank you.

GOLDBERG: Lift your glasses, ladies and gentlemen. We'll drink a toast.

MEG: Lulu isn't here.

GOLDBERG: It's past the hour. Now—who's going to propose the toast? Mrs. Boles, it can only be you.

MEG: Me?

GOLDBERG: Who else?

MEG: But what do I say?

GOLDBERG: Say what you feel. What you honestly feel. (MEG *looks uncertain.*) It's Stanley's birthday. Your Stanley. Look at him. Look at him and it'll come. Wait a minute, the light's too strong. Let's have proper lighting. McCann, have you got your torch?

MCCANN (*bringing a small torch from his pocket*): Here.

GOLDBERG: Switch out the light and put on your torch. (MCCANN *goes to the door, switches off the light, comes back, shines the torch on* MEG. *Outside the window there is still a faint light.*) Not on the lady, on the gentleman! You must shine it on the birthday boy. (MCCANN *shines the torch in* STANLEY's *face*) Now, Mrs. Boles, it's all yours.
Pause.

MEG: I don't know what to say.

GOLDBERG: Look at him. Just look at him.

MEG: Isn't the light in his eyes?

GOLDBERG: No, no. Go on.

MEG: Well—it's very, very nice to be here tonight, in my house, and I want to propose a toast to Stanley, because it's his birthday, and he's lived here for a long while now, and he's my Stanley now. And I think he's a good boy, although sometimes he's bad. (*An appreciative laugh from* GOLDBERG.) And he's the only Stanley I know, and I know him better than all the world, although he doesn't think so. ("*Hear— hear*" *from* GOLDBERG.) Well, I could cry because I'm so happy, having him here and not gone away, on his birthday, and there isn't anything I wouldn't do for him, and all you good people here tonight. . . . (*She sobs.*)

GOLDBERG: Beautiful! A beautiful speech. Put the light on, McCann. (MCCANN *goes to the door.* STANLEY *remains still.*) That was a lovely toast. (*The light goes on.* LULU *enters from the*

door, left. GOLDBERG comforts MEG.) Buck up now. Come on, smile at the birdy. That's better. Ah look who's here.

MEG: Lulu.

GOLDBERG: How do you do, Lulu? I'm Nat Goldberg.

LULU: Hallo.

GOLDBERG: Stanley, a drink for your guest. You just missed the toast, my dear, and what a toast.

LULU: Did I?

GOLDBERG: Stanley, a drink for your guest. Stanley. (STANLEY *hands a glass to* LULU.) Right. Now raise your glasses. Everyone standing up? No, not you, Stanley. You must sit down.

MCCANN: Yes, that's right. He must sit down.

GOLDBERG: You don't mind sitting down a minute? We're going to drink to you.

MEG: Come on!

LULU: Come on!
    STANLEY *sits in a chair at the table.*

GOLDBERG: Right. Now Stanley's sat down. (*Taking the stage.*) Well, I want to say first that I've never been so touched to the heart as by the toast we've just heard. How often, in this day and age, do you come across real, true warmth? Once in a lifetime. Until a few minutes ago, ladies and gentlemen, I, like all of you, was asking the same question. What's happened to the love, the bonhomie, the unashamed expression of affection of the day before yesterday, that our mums taught us in the nursery?

MCCANN: Gone with the wind.

GOLDBERG: That's what I thought, until today. I believe in a good laugh, a day's fishing, a bit of gardening. I was very proud of my old greenhouse, made out of my own spit and faith. That's the sort of man I am. Not size but quality. A little Austin, tea in Fullers, a library book from Boots, and I'm satisfied. But just now, I say just now, the lady of the house said her piece and I for one am knocked over by the sentiments she expressed. Lucky is the man who's at the receiving end, that's what I say. (*Pause.*) How can I put it to you? We all wander on our tod through this world. It's a lonely pillow to kip on. Right!

LULU (*admiringly*): Right!

GOLDBERG: Agreed. But tonight, Lulu, McCann, we've known a great fortune. We've heard a lady extend the sum total of her devotion, in all its pride, plume and peacock, to a member of her own living race. Stanley, my heartfelt congratulations. I wish you, on behalf of us all, a happy birthday. I'm sure you've never been a prouder man than you are today. Mazoltov! And may we only meet at Simchahs! (LULU *and* MEG *applaud.*) Turn out the light, McCann, while we drink the toast.

LULU: The was a wonderful speech.

> MCCANN *switches out the light, comes back, and shines the torch in* STANLEY's *face. The light outside the window is fainter.*

GOLDBERG: Lift your glasses. Stanley—happy birthday.

MCCANN: Happy birthday.

LULU: Happy birthday.

MEG: Many happy returns of the day, Stan.

GOLDBERG: And well over the fast.

> *They all drink.*

MEG (*kissing him*): Oh, Stanny. . . .

GOLDBERG: Lights!

MCCANN: Right! (*He switches on the lights.*)

MEG: Clink my glass, Stan.

LULU: Mr. Goldberg—

GOLDBERG: Call me Nat.

MEG (*to* MCCANN): You clink my glass.

LULU (*to* GOLDBERG): You're empty. Let me fill you up.

GOLDBERG: It's a pleasure.

LULU: You're a marvellous speaker, Nat, you know that? Where did you learn to speak like that?

GOLDBERG: You liked it, eh?

LULU: Oh yes!

GOLDBERG: Well, my first chance to stand up and give a lecture was at the Ethical Hall, Bayswater. A wonderful opportunity. I'll never forget it. They were all there that night. Charlotte Street was empty. Of course, that's a good while ago.

LULU: What did you speak about?

GOLDBERG: The Necessary and the Possible. It went like a bomb. Since then I always speak at weddings.

> STANLEY *is still.* GOLDBERG *sits left of the table.* MEG *joins* MCCANN *downstage, right,* LULU *is downstage, left.* MCCANN *pours more Irish from the bottle, which he carries, into his glass.*

MEG: Let's have some of yours.

MCCANN: In that?

MEG: Yes.

MCCANN: Are you used to mixing them?

MEG: No.

MCCANN: Give me your glass.

> MEG *sits on a shoe-box, downstage, right.* LULU, *at the table, pours more drink for* GOLDBERG *and herself, and gives* GOLDBERG *his glass.*

GOLDBERG: Thank you.

MEG (*to* MCCANN): Do you think I should?

GOLDBERG: Lulu, you're a big bouncy girl. Come and sit on my lap.

MCCANN: Why not?

LULU: Do you think I should?

GOLDBERG: Try it.

MEG (*sipping*): Very nice.

LULU: I'll bounce up to the ceiling.

MCCANN: I don't know how you can mix that stuff.

GOLDBERG: Take a chance.

MEG (*to* MCCANN): Sit down on this stool.

> LULU *sits on* GOLDBERG's *lap.*

MCCANN: This?

GOLDBERG: Comfortable?

LULU: Yes, thanks.

MCCANN (*sitting*): It's comfortable.

GOLDBERG: You know, there's a lot in your eyes.

LULU: And in yours, too.

GOLDBERG: Do you think so?

LULU (*giggling*): Go on!

MCCANN (*to* MEG): Where'd you get it?

MEG: My father gave it to me.

LULU: I didn't know I was going to meet you here tonight.

MCCANN (*to* MEG): Ever been to Carrikmacross?

MEG (*drinking*): I've been to King's Cross.

LULU: You came right out of the blue, you know that?

GOLDBERG (*as she moves*): Mind how you go. You're cracking a rib.

MEG (*standing*): I want to dance! (LULU *and* GOLDBERG *look into each other's eyes.* MCCANN *drinks.* MEG *crosses to* STANLEY.) Stanley. Dance. (STANLEY *sits still.* MEG *dances round the room alone, then comes back to* MCCANN, *who fills her glass. She sits.*)

LULU (*to* GOLDBERG): Shall I tell you something?

GOLDBERG: What?

LULU: I trust you.

GOLDBERG (*lifting his glass*): Gesundheit.

LULU: Have you got a wife?

GOLDBERG: I had a wife. What a wife. Listen to this. Friday, of an afternoon, I'd take myself for a little constitutional, down over the park. Eh, do me a favour, just sit on the table a minute, will you? (LULU *sits on the table. He stretches and continues*). A little constitutional. I'd say hullo to the little boys, the little girls—I never made distinctions—and then back I'd go, back to my bungalow with the flat roof. "Simey," my wife used to shout, "quick, before it gets cold!" And there on the table what would I see? The nicest piece of rollmop and pickled cucumber you could wish to find on a plate.

LULU: I thought your name was Nat.

GOLDBERG: She called me Simey.

LULU: I bet you were a good husband.

GOLDBERG: You should have seen her funeral.

LULU: Why?

GOLDBERG (*draws in his breath and wags head*): What a funeral.

MEG (*to* MCCANN):   My father was going to take me to Ireland once. But then he went away by himself.

LULU (*to* GOLDBERG):   Do you think you knew me when I was a little girl?

GOLDBERG: Were you a nice little girl?

LULU: I was.

MEG: I don't know if he went to Ireland.

GOLDBERG: Maybe I played piggy-back with you.

LULU: Maybe you did.

MEG: He didn't take me.

GOLDBERG: Or pop goes the weasel.

LULU: Is that a game?

GOLDBERG: Sure it's a game!

MCCANN: Why didn't he take you to Ireland?

LULU: You're tickling me!

GOLDBERG: You should worry.

LULU: I've always liked older men. They can soothe you.
        They embrace.

MCCANN: I know a place. Roscrea. Mother Nolan's.

MEG: There was a night-light in my room, when I was a little girl.

MCCANN: One time I stayed there all night with the boys. Singing and drinking all night.

MEG: And my Nanny used to sit up with me, and sing songs to me.

MCCANN: And a plate of fry in the morning. Now where am I?

MEG: My little room was pink. I had a pink car-

pet and pink curtains, and I had musical boxes all over the room. And they played me to sleep. And my father was a very big doctor. That's why I never had any complaints. I was cared for, and I had little sisters and brothers in other rooms, all different colours.

MCCANN: Tullamore, where are you?

MEG (*to* MCCANN):   Give us a drop more.

MCCANN (*filling her glass and singing*):   Glorio, Glorio, to the bold Fenian men!

MEG: Oh, what a lovely voice.

GOLDBERG: Give us a song, McCann.

LULU: A love song!

MCCANN (*reciting*):   The night that poor Paddy was stretched, the boys they all paid him a visit.

GOLDBERG: A love song!

MCCANN (*in a full voice, sings*):
    Oh, the Garden of Eden has vanished, they say,
    But I know the lie of it still.
    Just turn to the left at the foot of Ben Clay
    And stop when halfway to Coote Hill.
    It's there you will find it, I know sure enough,
    And it's whispering over to me:
    Come back, Paddy Reilly, to Bally-James-Duff,
    Come home, Paddy Reilly, to me!

LULU (*to* GOLDBERG):   You're the dead image of the first man I ever loved.

GOLDBERG: It goes without saying.

MEG (*rising*):   I want to play a game!

GOLDBERG: A game?

LULU: What game?

MEG: Any game.

LULU (*jumping up*):   Yes, let's play a game.

GOLDBERG: What game?

MCCANN: Hide and seek.

LULU: Blind man's buff.

MEG: Yes!

GOLDBERG: You want to play blind man's buff?

LULU and MEG: Yes!

GOLDBERG: All right. Blind man's buff. Come on! Everyone up! (*Rising.*) McCann. Stanley—Stanley!

MEG: Stanley. Up.

GOLDBERG: What's the matter with him?

MEG (*bending over him*):   Stanley, we're going to play a game. Oh, come on, don't be sulky, Stan.

LULU: Come on.
    STANLEY *rises*. MCCANN *rises*.

GOLDBERG: Right! Now—who's going to be blind first?

LULU: Mrs. Boles.

MEG: Not me.

GOLDBERG: Of course you.

MEG: Who, me?

LULU (*taking her scarf from her neck*): Here you are.

MCCANN: How do you play this game?

LULU (*tying her scarf round* MEG's *eyes*): Haven't you ever played blind man's buff? Keep still, Mrs. Boles. You mustn't be touched. But you can't move after she's blind. You must stay where you are after she's blind. And if she touches you then you become blind. Turn round. How many fingers am I holding up?

MEG: I can't see.

LULU: Right.

GOLDBERG: Right! Everyone move about. McCann. Stanley. Now stop. Now still. Off you go!

STANLEY *is downstage, right,* MEG *moves about the room.* GOLDBERG *fondles* LULU *at arm's length.* MEG *touches* MCCANN.

MEG: Caught you!

LULU: Take off your scarf.

MEG: What lovely hair!

LULU (*untying the scarf*): There.

MEG: It's you!

GOLDBERG: Put it on, McCann.

LULU (*tying it on* MCCANN). There. Turn round. How many fingers am I holding up?

MCCANN: I don't know.

GOLDBERG: Right! Everyone move about. Right. Stop! Still!

MCCANN *begins to move.*

MEG: Oh, this is lovely!

GOLDBERG: Quiet! Tch, tch, tch. Now—all move again. Stop! Still!

MCCANN *moves about.* GOLDBERG *fondles* LULU *at arm's length.* MCCANN *draws near* STANLEY. *He stretches his arm and touches* STANLEY's *glasses.*

MEG: It's Stanley!

GOLDBERG (*to* LULU). Enjoying the game?

MEG: It's your turn, Stan.

MCCANN *takes off the scarf.*

MCCANN (*to* STANLEY): I'll take your glasses.

MCCANN *takes* STANLEY's *glasses.*

MEG: Give me the scarf.

GOLDBERG (*holding* LULU): Tie his scarf, Mrs. Boles.

MEG: That's what I'm doing. (*To* STANLEY.) Can you see my nose?

GOLDBERG: He can't. Ready? Right! Everyone move. Stop! And still!

STANLEY *stands blindfold.* MCCANN *backs slowly across the stage to the left. He breaks* STANLEY's *glasses, snapping the frames.* MEG *is downstage, left,* LULU *and* GOLDBERG *upstage centre, close together.* STANLEY *begins to move, very slowly, across the stage to the left.* MCCANN *picks up the drum and places it sideways in* STANLEY's *path.* STANLEY *walks into the drum and falls over with his foot caught in it.*

MEG: Ooh!

GOLDBERG: Sssh!

STANLEY *rises. He begins to move towards* MEG, *dragging the drum on his foot. He reaches her and stops. His hands move towards her and they reach her throat. He begins to strangle her.* MCCANN *and* GOLDBERG *rush forward and throw him off.*

BLACKOUT

There is now no light at all through the window. The stage is in darkness.

LULU: The lights!

GOLDBERG: What's happened?

LULU: The lights!

MCCANN: Wait a minute.

GOLDBERG: Where is he?

MCCANN: Let go of me!

GOLDBERG: Who's this?

LULU: Someone's touching me!

MCCANN: Where is he?

MEG: Why has the light gone out?

GOLDBERG: Where's your torch? (MCCANN *shines the torch in* GOLDBERG's *face.*) Not on me! (MCCANN *shifts the torch. It is knocked from his hand and falls. It goes out.*)

MCCANN: My torch!

LULU: Oh God!

GOLDBERG: Where's your torch? Pick up your torch!

MCCANN: I can't find it.

LULU: Hold me. Hold me.

GOLDBERG: Get down on your knees. Help him find the torch.

LULU: I can't.

MCCANN: It's gone.

MEG: Why has the light gone out?

GOLDBERG: Everyone quiet! Help him find the torch.

> *Silence. Grunts from* MCCANN *and* GOLDBERG *on their knees. Suddenly there is a sharp, sustained rat-a-tat with a stick on the side of the drum from the back of the room. Silence. Whimpers from* LULU.

GOLDBERG: Over here. McCann!

MCCANN: Here.

GOLDBERG: Come to me, come to me. Easy. Over there.

> GOLDBERG *and* MCCANN *move up left of the table.* STANLEY *moves down right of the table.* LULU *suddenly perceives him moving towards her, screams and faints.* GOLDBERG *and* MCCANN *turn and stumble against each other.*

GOLDBERG: What is it?

MCCANN: Who's that?

GOLDBERG: What is it?

> *In the darkness* STANLEY *picks up* LULU *and places her on the table.*

MEG: It's Lulu!

> GOLDBERG *and* MCCANN *move downstage, right.*

GOLDBERG: Where is she?

MCCANN: She fell.

GOLDBERG: Where?

MCCANN: About here.

GOLDBERG: Help me pick her up.

MCCANN (*moving downstage, left*):   I can't find her.

GOLDBERG: She must be somewhere.

MCCANN: She's not here.

GOLDBERG (*moving downstage, left*):   She must be.

MCCANN: She's gone.

> MCCANN *finds the torch on the floor, shines it on the table and* STANLEY. LULU *is lying spread-eagled on the table,* STANLEY *bent over her.* STANLEY, *as soon as the torchlight hits him, begins to giggle.* GOLDBERG *and* MCCANN *move towards him. He backs, giggling, the torch on his face. They follow him upstage, left. He backs against the hatch, giggling. The torch draws closer. His giggle rises and grows as he flattens himself against the wall. Their figures converge upon him.*

> *Curtain*

ACT THREE

The next morning. PETEY *enters, left, with a newspaper and sits at the table. He begins to read.* MEG's *voice comes through the kitchen hatch.*

MEG: Is that you, Stan? (*Pause.*) Stanny?

PETEY: Yes?

MEG: Is that you?

PETEY: It's me.

MEG (*appearing at the hatch*):   Oh, it's you. I've run out of cornflakes.

PETEY: Well, what else have you got?

MEG: Nothing.

PETEY: Nothing?

MEG: Just a minute. (*She leaves the hatch and enters by the kitchen door.*) You got your paper?

PETEY: Yes.

MEG: Is it good?

PETEY: Not bad.

MEG: The two gentlemen had the last of the fry this morning.

PETEY: Oh, did they?

MEG: There's some tea in the pot though. (*She pours tea for him.*) I'm going out shopping in a minute. Get you something nice.

MEG: I've got a splitting headache.

PETEY (*reading*):   You slept like a log last night.

MEG: Did I?

PETEY: Dead out.

MEG: I must have been tired. (*She looks about the room and sees the broken drum in the fireplace.*) Oh, look. (*She rises and picks it up*). The drum's broken. (PETEY *looks up.*) Why is it broken?

PETEY: I don't know.

> *She hits it with her hand.*

MEG: It still makes a noise.

PETEY: You can always get another one.

MEG (*sadly*):   It was probably broken in the party. I don't remember it being broken though, in the party. (*She puts it down.*) What a shame.

PETEY: You can always get another one, Meg.

MEG: Well, at least he did have it on his birthday, didn't he? Like I wanted him to.

PETEY (*reading*):   Yes.

MEG: Have you seen him down yet? (PETEY *does not answer.*) Petey.

PETEY: What?

MEG: Have you seen him down?

PETEY: Who?

MEG: Stanley.

PETEY: No.

MEG: Nor have I. That boy should be up. He's late for his breakfast.

PETEY: There isn't any breakfast.

MEG: Yes, but he doesn't know that. I'm going to call him.

PETEY (*quickly*):   No, don't do that, Meg. Let him sleep.

MEG: But you say he stays in bed too much.

PETEY: Let him sleep . . . this morning. Leave him.

MEG: I've been up once, with his cup of tea. But Mr. McCann opened the door. He said they were talking. He said he'd made him one. He must have been up early. I don't know what they were talking about. I was surprised. Because Stanley's usually fast asleep when I wake him. But he wasn't this morning. I heard him talking. (*Pause.*) Do you think they know each other? I think they're old friends. Stanley had a lot of friends. I know he did. (*Pause.*) I didn't give him his tea. He'd already had one. I came down again and went on with my work. Then, after a bit, they came down to breakfast. Stanley must have gone to sleep again.

   Pause.

PETEY: When are you going to do your shopping, Meg?

MEG: Yes, I must. (*Collecting the bag.*) I've got a rotten headache. (*She goes to the back door, stops suddenly and turns.*) Did you see what's outside this morning?

PETEY: What?

MEG: That big car.

PETEY: Yes.

MEG: It wasn't there yesterday. Did you . . . did you have a look inside it?

PETEY: I had a peep.

MEG (*coming down tensely, and whispering*):   Is there anything in it?

PETEY: In it?

MEG: Yes.

PETEY: What do you mean, in it?

MEG: Inside it.

PETEY: What sort of thing?

MEG: Well . . . I mean . . . is there . . . is there a wheelbarrow in it?

PETEY: A wheelbarrow?

MEG: Yes.

PETEY: I didn't see one.

MEG: You didn't? Are you sure?

PETEY: What would Mr. Goldberg want with a wheelbarrow?

MEG: Mr. Goldberg?

PETEY: It's his car.

MEG (*relieved*):   His car? Oh, I didn't know it was his car.

PETEY: Of course it's his car.

MEG: Oh, I feel better.

PETEY: What are you on about?

MEG: Oh, I do feel better.

PETEY: You go and get a bit of air.

MEG: Yes, I will. I will. I'll go and get the shopping. (*She goes towards the back door. A door slams upstairs. She turns.*) It's Stanley! He's coming down—what am I going to do about his breakfast? (*She rushes into the kitchen.*) Petey, what shall I give him? (*She looks through the hatch.*) There's no cornflakes. (*They both gaze at the door. Enter* GOLDBERG. *He halts at the door, as he meets their gaze, then smiles.*)

GOLDBERG: A reception committee!

MEG: Oh, I thought it was Stanley.

GOLDBERG: You find a resemblance?

MEG: Oh no. You look quite different.

GOLDBERG (*coming into the room*):   Different build, of course.

MEG (*entering from the kitchen*):   I thought he was coming down for his breakfast. He hasn't had his breakfast yet.

GOLDBERG: Your wife makes a very nice cup of tea, Mr. Boles, you know that?

PETEY: Yes, she does sometimes. Sometimes she forgets.

MEG: Is he coming down?

GOLDBERG: Down? Of course he's coming down. On a lovely sunny day like this he shouldn't come down? He'll be up and about in next to no time. (*He sits at the table.*) And what a breakfast he's going to get.

MEG: Mr. Goldberg.

GOLDBERG: Yes?

MEG: I didn't know that was your car outside.

GOLDBERG: You like it?

MEG: Are you going to go for a ride?

GOLDBERG (*to* PETEY):   A smart car, eh?

PETEY: Nice shine on it all right.

GOLDBERG: What is old is good, take my tip. There's room there. Room in the front, and room in the back. (*He strokes the teapot.*) The pot's hot. More tea, Mr. Boles?

PETEY: No thanks.

GOLDBERG (*pouring tea*):   That car? That car's never let me down.

MEG: Are you going to go for a ride?

GOLDBERG (*ruminatively*):   And the boot. A beautiful boot. There's just room . . . for the right amount.

MEG: Well, I'd better be off now. (*She moves to the back door, and turns.*) Petey, when Stanley comes down. . . .

PETEY: Yes?

MEG: Tell him I won't be long.

PETEY: I'll tell him.

MEG (*vaguely*):   I won't be long. (*She exits.*)

GOLDBERG (*sipping his tea*):   A good woman. A charming woman. My mother was the same. My wife was identical.

PETEY: How is he this morning?

GOLDBERG: Who?

PETEY: Stanley. Is he any better?

GOLDBERG (*a little uncertainly*):   Oh . . . a little better, I think, a little better. Of course, I'm not really qualified to say, Mr. Boles. I mean, I haven't got the . . . the qualifications. The best thing would be if someone with the proper . . . mnn . . . qualifications . . . was to have a look at him. Someone with a few letters after his name. It makes all the difference.

PETEY: Yes.

GOLDBERG: Anyway, Dermot's with him at the moment. He's . . . keeping him company.

PETEY: Dermot?

GOLDBERG: Yes.

PETEY: It's a terrible thing.

GOLDBERG (*sighs*):   Yes. The birthday celebration was too much for him.

PETEY: What came over him?

GOLDBERG (*sharply*):   What came over him? Breakdown, Mr. Boles. Pure and simple. Nervous breakdown.

PETEY: But what brought it on so suddenly?

GOLDBERG (*rising, and moving upstage*):   Well, Mr. Boles, it can happen in all sorts of ways. A friend of mine was telling me about it only the other day. We'd both been concerned with another case—not entirely similar, of course, but . . . quite alike, quite alike. (*He pauses.*) Anyway, he was telling me, you see, this friend of mine, that sometimes it happens gradual—day by day it grows and grows and grows . . . day by day. And then other times it happens all at once. Poof! Like that! The nerves break. There's no guarantee how it's going to happen, but with certain people . . . it's a foregone conclusion.

PETEY: Really?

GOLDBERG: Yes. This friend of mine—he was telling me about it—only the other day. (*He stands uneasily for a moment, then brings out a cigarette case and takes a cigarette.*) Have an Abdullah.

PETEY: No, no, I don't take them.

GOLDBERG: Once in a while I treat myself to a cigarette. An Abdullah, perhaps, or a . . . (*He snaps his fingers.*)

PETEY: What a night. (GOLDBERG *lights his cigarette with a lighter.*) Came in the front door and all the lights were out. Put a shilling in the slot, came in here and the party was over.

GOLDBERG (*coming downstage*):   You put a shilling in the slot?

PETEY: Yes.

GOLDBERG: And the lights came on.

PETEY: Yes, then I came in here.

GOLDBERG (*with a short laugh*):   I could have sworn it was a fuse.

PETEY (*continuing*):   There was dead silence. Couldn't hear a thing. So I went upstairs and your friend—Dermot—met me on the landing. And he told me.

GOLDBERG (*sharply*):   Who?

PETEY: Your friend—Dermot.

GOLDBERG (*heavily*):   Dermot. Yes. (*He sits.*)

PETEY: They get over it sometimes though, don't they? I mean, they can recover from it, can't they?

GOLDBERG: Recover? Yes, sometimes they recover, in one way or another.

PETEY: I mean, he might have recovered by now, mightn't he?

GOLDBERG: It's conceivable. Conceivable.

PETEY *rises and picks up the teapot and cup.*

PETEY: Well, if he's no better by lunchtime I'll go and get hold of a doctor.

GOLDBERG (*briskly*):   It's all taken care of, Mr. Boles. Don't worry yourself.

PETEY (*dubiously*):   What do you mean? (*Enter* MCCANN *with two suitcases.*) All packed up?

PETEY *takes the teapot and cups into the*

kitchen. MCCANN *crosses left and puts down the suitcases. He goes up to the window and looks out.*

GOLDBERG: Well? (MCCANN *does not answer.*) McCann. I asked you well.

MCCANN (*without turning*): Well what?

GOLDBERG: What's what? (MCCANN *does not answer.*)

MCCANN (*turning to look at* GOLDBERG, *grimly*): I'm not going up there again.

GOLDBERG: Why not?

MCCANN: I'm not going up there again.

GOLDBERG: What's going on now?

MCCANN (*moving down*): He's quiet now. He stopped all that . . . talking a while ago.

PETEY *appears at the kitchen hatch, unnoticed.*

GOLDBERG: When will he be ready?

MCCANN (*sullenly*): You can go up yourself next time.

GOLDBERG: What's the matter with you?

MCCANN (*quietly*): I gave him. . . .

GOLDBERG: What?

MCCANN: I gave him his glasses.

GOLDBERG: Wasn't he glad to get them back?

MCCANN: The frames are bust.

GOLDBERG: How did that happen?

MCCANN: He tried to fit the eyeholes into his eyes. I left him doing it.

PETEY (*at the kitchen door*): There's some Sellotape somewhere. We can stick them together.

GOLDBERG *and* MCCANN *turn to see him. Pause.*

GOLDBERG: Sellotape? No, no, that's all right, Mr. Boles. It'll keep him quiet for the time being, keep his mind off other things.

PETEY (*moving downstage*): What about a doctor?

GOLDBERG: It's all taken care of.

MCCANN *moves over right to the shoe-box, and takes out a brush and brushes his shoes.*

PETEY (*moves to the table*): I think he needs one.

GOLDBERG: I agree with you. It's all taken care of. We'll give him a bit of time to settle down, and then I'll take him to Monty.

PETEY: You're going to take him to a doctor?

GOLDBERG (*staring at him*): Sure. Monty.

Pause. MCCANN *brushes his shoes.*

So Mrs. Boles has gone out to get us something nice for lunch?

PETEY: That's right.

GOLDBERG: Unfortunately we may be gone by then.

PETEY: Will you?

GOLDBERG: By then we may be gone.

Pause.

PETEY: Well, I think I'll see how my peas are getting on, in the meantime.

GOLDBERG: The meantime?

PETEY: While we're waiting.

GOLDBERG: Waiting for what? (PETEY *walks towards the back door.*) Aren't you going back to the beach?

PETEY: No, not yet. Give me a call when he comes down, will you, Mr. Goldberg?

GOLDBERG (*earnestly*): You'll have a crowded beach today . . . on a day like this. They'll be lying on their backs, swimming out to sea. My life. What about the deck-chairs? Are the deck-chairs ready?

PETEY: I put them all out this morning.

GOLDBERG: But what about the tickets? Who's going to take the tickets?

PETEY: That's all right. That'll be all right, Mr. Goldberg. Don't you worry about that. I'll be back.

He exits. GOLDBERG *rises, goes to the window and looks after him.* MCCANN *crosses to the table, left, sits, picks up the paper and begins to tear it into strips.*

GOLDBERG: Is everything ready?

MCCANN: Sure.

GOLDBERG *walks heavily, brooding, to the table. He sits right of it noticing what* MCCANN *is doing.*

GOLDBERG: Stop doing that!

MCCANN: What?

GOLDBERG: Why do you do that all the time? It's childish, it's pointless. It's without a solitary point.

MCCANN: What's the matter with you today?

GOLDBERG: Questions, questions. Stop asking me so many questions. What do you think I am?

MCCANN *studies him. He then folds the paper, leaving the strips inside.*

MCCANN: Well?

Pause. GOLDBERG *leans back in the chair, his eyes closed.*

MCCANN: Well?

GOLDBERG (*with fatigue*): Well what?

MCCANN: Do we wait or do we go and get him?

GOLDBERG (*slowly*): You want to go and get him?

MCCANN: I want to get it over.

GOLDBERG: That's understandable.

MCCANN: So do we wait or do we go and get him?

GOLDBERG (*interrupting*):   I don't know why, but I feel knocked out. I feel a bit . . . It's uncommon for me.

MCCANN: Is that so?

GOLDBERG: It's unusual.

MCCANN (*rising swiftly and going behind* GOLDBERG's *chair. Hissing*):   Let's finish and go. Let's get it over and go. Get the thing done. Let's finish the bloody thing. Let's get the thing done and go!

Pause.

Will I go up?

Pause.

Nat!

GOLDBERG *sits humped.* MCCANN *slips to his side.*

Simey!

GOLDBERG (*opening his eyes, regarding* MCCANN):   What—did—you—call—me?

MCCANN: Who?

GOLDBERG (*murderously*):   Don't call me that! (*He seizes* MCCANN *by the throat.*) NEVER CALL ME THAT!

MCCANN (*writhing*):   Nat, Nat, Nat, NAT! I called you Nat. I was asking you, Nat. Honest to God. Just a question, that's all, just a question, do you see, do you follow me?

GOLDBERG (*jerking him away*):   What question?

MCCANN: Will I go up?

GOLDBERG (*violently*):   Up? I thought you weren't going to go up there again?

MCCANN: What do you mean? Why not?

GOLDBERG: You said so!

MCCANN: I never said that!

GOLDBERG: No?

MCCANN (*from the floor, to the room at large*):   Who said that? I never said that! I'll go up now!

He jumps up and rushes to the door, left.

GOLDBERG: Wait!

He stretches his arms to the arms of the chair.

Come here.

MCCANN *approaches him very slowly.*

I want your opinion. Have a look in my mouth.

He opens his mouth wide.

Take a good look.

MCCANN *looks.*

You know what I mean?

MCCANN *peers.*

You know what? I've never lost a tooth. Not since the day I was born. Nothing's changed. (*He gets up.*) That's why I've reached my position, McCann. Because I've always been as fit as a fiddle. All my life I've said the same. Play up, play up, and play the game. Honour thy father and thy mother. All along the line. Follow the line, the line, McCann, and you can't go wrong. What do you think, I'm a self-made man? No! I sat where I was told to sit. I kept my eye on the ball. School? Don't talk to me about school. Top in all subjects. And for why? Because I'm telling you, I'm telling you, follow my line? Follow my mental? Learn by heart. Never write down a thing. And don't go too near the water. And you'll find—that what I say is true.

Because I believe that the world . . . (*Vacant.*). . . .

Because I believe that the world . . . (*Desperate.*). . . .

BECAUSE I BELIEVE THAT THE WORLD . . . (*Lost.*). . . .

He sits in chair.

Sit down, McCann, sit here where I can look at you.

MCCANN *kneels in front of the table.*

(*Intensely, with growing certainty.*) My father said to me, Benny, Benny, he said, come here. He was dying. I knelt down. By him day and night. Who else was there? Forgive, Benny, he said, and let live. Yes, Dad. Go home to your wife. I will, Dad. Keep an eye open for low-lives, for schnorrers and for layabouts. He didn't mention names. I lost my life in the service of others, he said, I'm not ashamed. Do your duty and keep your observations. Always bid good morning to the neighbours. Never, never forget your family, for they are the rock, the constitution and the core! If you're ever in any difficulties Uncle Barney will see you in the clear. I knelt down. (*He kneels, facing* MCCANN.) I swore on the good book. And I knew the word I had to remember—Respect! Because McCann— (*Gently.*) Seamus—who came before your father? His father. And who came before him? Before him? . . . (*Vacant— triumphant.*) Who came before your father's father but your father's father's mother! Your great-gran-granny.

Silence. He slowly rises.

And that's why I've reached my position, McCann. Because I've always been as fit as a fiddle. My motto. Work hard and play hard. Not a day's illness.

GOLDBERG *sits.*

GOLDBERG: All the same, give me a blow. (*Pause.*) Blow in my mouth.

MCCANN *stands, puts his hands on his knees, bends, and blows in* GOLDBERG'S *mouth.*

One for the road.

MCCANN *blows again in his mouth.* GOLDBERG *breathes deeply, smiles.*

GOLDBERG: Right!

Enter LULU. MCCANN *looks at them, and goes to the door.*

MCCANN (*at the door*):   I'll give you five minutes. (*He exits with the expander.*)

GOLDBERG: Come over here.

LULU: What's going to happen?

GOLDBERG: Come over here.

LULU: No, thank you.

GOLDBERG: What's the matter? You got the needle to Uncle Natey?

LULU: I'm going.

GOLDBERG: Have a game of pontoon first, for old time's sake.

LULU: I've had enough games.

GOLDBERG: A girl like you, at your age, at your time of health, and you don't take to games?

LULU: You're very smart.

GOLDBERG: Anyway, who says you don't take to them?

LULU: Do you think I'm like all the other girls?

GOLDBERG: Are all the other girls like that, too?

LULU: I don't know about any other girls.

GOLDBERG: Nor me. I've never touched another woman.

LULU (*distressed*):   What would my father say, if he knew? And what would Eddie say?

GOLDBERG: Eddie?

LULU: He was my first love, Eddie was. And whatever happened, it was pure. With him! He didn't come into my room at night with a briefcase!

GOLDBERG: Who opened the briefcase, me or you? Lulu, schmulu, let bygones be bygones, do me a turn. Kiss and make up.

LULU: I wouldn't touch you.

GOLDBERG: And today I'm leaving.

LULU: You're leaving?

GOLDBERG: Today.

LULU (*with growing anger*):   You used me for a night. A passing fancy.

GOLDBERG: Who used who?

LULU: You made use of me by cunning when my defences were down.

GOLDBERG: Who took them down?

LULU: That's what you did. You quenched your ugly thirst. You taught me things a girl shouldn't know before she's been married at least three times!

GOLDBERG: Now you're a jump ahead! What are you complaining about?

Enter MCCANN *quickly.*

LULU: You didn't appreciate me for myself. You took all those liberties only to satisfy your appetite. Oh Nat, why did you do it?

GOLDBERG: You wanted me to do it, Lulula, so I did it.

MCCANN: That's fair enough. (*Advancing.*) You had a long sleep, Miss.

LULU (*backing upstage left*):   Me?

MCCANN: Your sort, you spend too much time in bed.

LULU: What do you mean?

MCCANN: Have you got anything to confess?

LULU: What?

MCCANN (*savagely*):   Confess!

LULU: Confess what?

MCCANN: Down on your knees and confess!

LULU: What does he mean?

GOLDBERG: Confess. What can you lose?

LULU: What, to him?

GOLDBERG: He's only been unfrocked six months.

MCCANN: Kneel down, woman, and tell me the latest!

LULU (*retreating to the back door*):   I've seen everything that's happened. I know what's going on. I've got a pretty shrewd idea.

MCCANN (*advancing*):   I've seen you hanging about the Rock of Cashel, profaning the soil with your goings-on. Out of my sight!

LULU: I'm going.

She exits. MCCANN *goes to the door, left, and goes out. He ushers in* STANLEY, *who is dressed in a dark well cut suit and white collar. He holds his broken glasses in his hand. He is clean-shaven.* MCCANN *follows and closes the door.* GOLDBERG *meets* STANLEY, *seats him in a chair.*

GOLDBERG: How are you, Stan?

Pause.

Are you feeling any better?
> *Pause.*

What's the matter with your glasses?
> GOLDBERG *bends to look.*

They're broken. A pity.
> STANLEY *stares blankly at the floor.*

MCCANN (*at the table*): He looks better, doesn't he?

GOLDBERG: Much better.

MCCANN: A new man.

GOLDBERG: You know what we'll do?

MCCANN: What?

GOLDBERG: We'll buy him another pair.
> *They begin to woo him, gently and with rel-*
> *ish. During the following sequence* STANLEY
> *shows no reaction. He remains, with no*
> *movement, where he sits.*

MCCANN: Out of our own pockets.

GOLDBERG: It goes without saying. Between you and me, Stan, it's about time you had a new pair of glasses.

MCCANN: You can't see straight.

GOLDBERG: It's true. You've been cockeyed for years.

MCCANN: Now you're even more cockeyed.

GOLDBERG: He's right. You've gone from bad to worse.

MCCANN: Worse than worse.

GOLDBERG: You need a long convalescence.

MCCANN: A change of air.

GOLDBERG: Somewhere over the rainbow.

MCCANN: Where angels fear to tread.

GOLDBERG: Exactly.

MCCANN: You're in a rut.

GOLDBERG: You look anaemic.

MCCANN: Rheumatic.

GOLDBERG: Myopic.

MCCANN: Epileptic.

GOLDBERG: You're on the verge.

MCCANN: You're a dead duck.

GOLDBERG: But we can save you.

MCCANN: From a worse fate.

GOLDBERG: True.

MCCANN: Undeniable.

GOLDBERG: From now on, we'll be the hub of your wheel.

MCCANN: We'll renew your season ticket.

GOLDBERG: We'll take tuppence off your morning tea.

MCCANN: We'll give you a discount on all inflammable goods.

GOLDBERG: We'll watch over you.

MCCANN: Advise you.

GOLDBERG: Give you proper care and treatment.

MCCANN: Let you use the club bar.

GOLDBERG: Keep a table reserved.

MCCANN: Help you acknowledge the fast days.

GOLDBERG: Bake you cakes.

MCCANN: Help you kneel on kneeling days.

GOLDBERG: Give you a free pass.

MCCANN: Take you for constitutionals.

GOLDBERG: Give you hot tips.

MCCANN: We'll provide the skipping rope.

GOLDBERG: The vest and pants.

MCCANN: The ointment.

GOLDBERG: The hot poultice.

MCCANN: The fingerstall.

GOLDBERG: The abdomen belt.

MCCANN: The ear plugs.

GOLDBERG: The baby powder.

MCCANN: The back scratcher.

GOLDBERG: The spare tyre.

MCCANN: The stomach pump.

GOLDBERG: The oxygen tent.

MCCANN: The prayer wheel.

GOLDBERG: The plaster of Paris.

MCCANN: The crash helmet.

GOLDBERG: The crutches.

MCCANN: A day and night service.

GOLDBERG: All on the house.

MCCANN: That's it.

GOLDBERG: We'll make a man of you.

MCCANN: And a woman.

GOLDBERG: You'll be re-orientated.

MCCANN: You'll be rich.

GOLDBERG: You'll be adjusted.

MCCANN: You'll be our pride and joy.

GOLDBERG: You'll be a mensch.

MCCANN: You'll be a success.

GOLDBERG: You'll be integrated.

MCCANN: You'll give orders.

GOLDBERG: You'll make decisions.

MCCANN: You'll be a magnate.

GOLDBERG: A statesman.

MCCANN: You'll own yachts.

GOLDBERG: Animals.

MCCANN: Animals.
> GOLDBERG *looks at* MCCANN.

GOLDBERG: I said animals. (*He turns back to* STANLEY.) You'll be able to make or break, Stan. By my life. (*Silence.* STANLEY *is still.*) Well? What do you say?
> STANLEY's *head lifts very slowly and turns in* GOLDBERG's *direction.*

GOLDBERG: What do you think? Eh, boy?

STANLEY *begins to clench and unclench his eyes.*

MCCANN: What's your opinion, sir? Of this prospect, sir?

GOLDBERG: Prospect. Sure. Sure it's a prospect.

STANLEY'S *hands clutching his glasses begin to tremble.*

What's your opinion of such a prospect? Eh, Stanley?

STANLEY *concentrates, his mouth opens, he attempts to speak, fails and emits sounds from his throat.*

STANLEY: Uh-gug . . . uh-gug . . . eeehhh-gag . . . (*On the breath.*) Caahh . . . caahh. . . .

They watch him. He draws a long breath which shudders down his body. He concentrates.

GOLDBERG: Well, Stanny boy, what do you say, eh?

They watch. He concentrates. His head lowers, his chin draws into his chest, he crouches.

STANLEY: Uh-gughh . . . uh-gughh. . . .

MCCANN: What's your opinion, sir?

STANLEY: Caaahh . . . caaahhh. . . .

MCCANN: Mr. Webber! What's your opinion?

GOLDBERG: What do you say, Stan? What do you think of the prospect?

MCCANN: What's your opinion of the prospect?

STANLEY'S *body shudders, relaxes, his head drops, he becomes still again, stooped.* PETEY *enters from door, downstage, left.*

GOLDBERG: Still the same old Stan. Come with us. Come on, boy.

MCCANN: Come along with us.

PETEY: Where are you taking him?

They turn. Silence.

GOLDBERG: We're taking him to Monty.

PETEY: He can stay here.

GOLDBERG: Don't be silly.

PETEY: We can look after him here.

GOLDBERG: Why do you want to look after him?

PETEY: He's my guest.

GOLDBERG: He needs special treatment.

PETEY: We'll find someone.

GOLDBERG: No. Monty's the best there is. Bring him, McCann.

They help STANLEY *out of the chair.* GOLDBERG *puts the bowler hat on* STANLEY'S *head. They all three move towards the door, left.*

PETEY: Leave him alone!

They stop. GOLDBERG *studies him.*

GOLDBERG (*insidiously*): Why don't you come with us, Mr. Boles?

MCCANN: Yes, why don't you come with us?

GOLDBERG: Come with us to Monty. There's plenty of room in the car.

PETEY makes no move. They pass him and reach the door. MCCANN *opens the door and picks up the suitcases.*

PETEY (*broken*): Stan, don't let them tell you what to do!

They exit.

Silence. PETEY *stands. The front door slams. Sound of a car starting. Sound of a car going away. Silence.* PETEY *slowly goes to the table. He sits on a chair, left. He picks up the paper and opens it. The strips fall to the floor. He looks down at them.* MEG *comes past the window and enters by the back door.* PETEY *studies the front page of the paper.*

MEG (*coming downstage*): The car's gone.

PETEY: Yes.

MEG: Have they gone?

PETEY: Yes.

MEG: Won't they be in for lunch?

PETEY: No.

MEG: Oh, what a shame. (*She puts her bag on the table.*) It's hot out. (*She hangs her coat on a hook.*) What are you doing?

PETEY: Reading.

MEG: Is it good?

PETEY: All right.

She sits by the table.

MEG: Where's Stan?

Pause.

Is Stan down yet, Petey?

PETEY: No . . . he's. . . .

MEG: Is he still in bed?

PETEY: Yes, he's . . . still asleep.

MEG: Still? He'll be late for his breakfast.

PETEY: Let him . . . sleep.

Pause.

MEG: Wasn't it a lovely party last night?

PETEY: I wasn't there.

MEG: Weren't you?

PETEY: I came in afterwards.

MEG: Oh.

Pause.

It was a lovely party. I haven't laughed so much for years. We had dancing and singing.

And games. You should have been there.

PETEY: It was good, eh?

Pause.

MEG: I was the belle of the ball.

PETEY: Were you?

MEG: Oh yes. They all said I was.

PETEY: I bet you were, too.

MEG: Oh, it's true. I was.

Pause.

I know I was.

Curtain

PART 4
Poetry

ARCHIBALD MacLEISH

Ars Poetica

A poem should be palpable and mute
As a globed fruit,

Dumb
As old medallions to the thumb,

Silent as the sleeve-worn stone
Of casement ledges where the moss has grown—

A poem should be wordless
As the flight of birds.

        *   *   *

A poem should be motionless in time
As the moon climbs.   10

Leaving, as the moon releases
Twig by twig the night-entangled trees,

Leaving, as the moon behind the winter leaves,
Memory by memory the mind—

A poem should be motionless in time
As the moon climbs

        *   *   *

A poem should be equal to:
Not true

For all the history of grief
An empty doorway and a maple leaf   20

For love
The leaning grasses and the two lights above the
    sea—

A poem should not mean
But be

                                             1926

Poetry is a form of literature that many readers hold in a special kind of affectionate admiration. From the earliest times, probably even before the time of recorded language, poets have been the oracles and prophets of their peoples. Poets have always reflected the temper of the ages in which they live: Homer epitomizes a glorious epoch in Greek history, as Hardy epitomizes the perplexity and despair of late Victorian England.

THE NATURE OF POETRY

Poetry cannot be precisely defined, but some of its distinguishing characteristics can be described. Poetry deals in matters beyond direct statement—in meanings conditioned by emotional attitudes—and its intention is to evoke the full flavor and impact of experience. Poetry often achieves its effects by the selection of words that are suggestive not only of sensory experience but of emotional attitudes, by the use of figurative comparisons, and by rime and rhythm. Finally, the most distinctive feature of poetry is the organic quality achieved by the close organization of its component parts. The poet in a sense is a maker of experiences. (The Old English word for poet is *scop*, "the maker.") Life is so cluttered with detail that to most of us it often seems chaotic. Like other artists, the poet discards the confusing detail, selects and arranges the remainder to communicate his impression, and thereby creates a meaningful experience for his reader.

What one receives from a poem, then, is an experience. I. A. Richards, perhaps the most stimulating of the mid-century critics of poetry, has pointed out that a poem has a "Total Meaning" which is a blend of the poet's *sense* (what the poem is apparently about), his *feeling* (the poet's attitude toward his subject matter), his *tone* (attitude toward his reader), and his *intention* (aim, or effect). A poet is more or less aware of this fact and, as he writes, expresses all the meanings as fully as his ability and his medium will permit. The reader, in turn, will profit by considering all of them when trying to arrive at a full realization of a poem.

Consider, for example, the following occasional poem by Thomas Hardy, "On an Invitation to the United States." [1]

[1] Reprinted with permission of the publisher from *Collected Poems* by Thomas Hardy. Copyright 1925 by The Macmillan Company.

My ardours for emprize nigh lost
Since life has bared its bones to me,
I shrink to seek a modern coast
Whose riper times have yet to be;
For, wonning in these ancient lands,
Enchased and lettered as a tomb,
And scored with prints of perished
   hands,
And chronicled with dates of doom,

Where the new regions claim them
   free
From that long drip of human tears
Which peoples old in tragedy
Have left upon the centuried years.
Though my own Being bear no bloom
I trace the lives such scenes enshrine,
Give past exemplars present room,
And their experience count as mine.

Obviously, the poem is about Hardy's declining an invitation to visit the United States—his reaction to an invitation to come to a land with a more promising future but a less historic past. But statement of the *sense* of the poem is not the equivalent of the poem. In fact, even the following full paraphrase of the sense of the poem falls far short of the poem itself: "I have almost lost my taste for adventure since I discovered how grim life is; I hesitate to seek a new country that has not yet reached full fruition, and has not had a tragic-storied past. Living in this old land, which is much like a tombstone with its inscriptions, I—even though I do not prosper personally—study the lives of the great people of England's history and consider their experience as mine."

For full comprehension we need to absorb the poet's *feeling* about the material. Hardy presents that feeling by implying a contrast between the pasts of the United States and England and by suggesting a relationship between his own past and that of his country. He hints some mild doubt of the United States—a country raw and untried by a long history of adversities and tribulations, though perhaps with a promising future. Just as indirectly he communicates, without sentimentality, his love of England by imagery that pictures her long and tragic history, full of adversities, trials, and struggles; and he makes clear his desire to share what he feels is England's unhappy lot.

We need also to grasp his *tone*, or his attitude toward his reader. His tone, like his feeling, is complex, for, though he is addressing himself particularly to the people of the United States, the people who extended to him the invitation that occasioned the poem, in the background he includes among his audience English compatriots. With neither condescension to the inviters nor depreciation of the worth of their regard, he courteously declines. Though he reminds his background audience, the English, of their mournful history, and indirectly rededicates them as well as himself to his resolve to endure and to be proud of enduring, he steers as widely clear of national conceit and chauvinism as he does of a defensive attitude that would be uncomfortable to English and American alike.

Hardy's full poetic *intention* is to comment feelingly on the individual's relation to his country's history and on his goal in life. Furthermore, he intends to imply the judgment that to assume a share of the unhappy human lot may be a greater act than to achieve purely personal well-being, the attitude of a true pessimist.

The total meaning of "On an Invitation to the United States," therefore, depends on its *sense, feeling, tone,* and *intention.* Briefly, Hardy says that he cannot accept the invitation, acknowledges the favorable prospects of America and expresses his love of England, shows to those who invited him a courteous but not deferential appreciation, and takes the opportunity to comment on the value of tradition. In other words, the communication of this complex meaning provides an experience for the reader, an experience which *is* the poem.

THE METHOD OF POETRY

As "On an Invitation to the United States" reveals, there is more to a poem than the *sense* which can be translated into direct prose statement or paraphrase. Poets characteristically communicate by suggestion or implication; that is, they say more than their words and word combinations literally mean. Perhaps *indirection* is the best term to summarize the way by which poets say so much in so few words.

Diction   The words of poetry are for the most part the same words that people use to carry on the plain business of living. Individually those words stand for about the same things and have approximately the same sounds in poems as they have in everyday speech. But in poetry words are used more precisely and are ordered more carefully than in conversation. Moreover, a poem does not depend solely upon denotative meanings of words; what the words suggest—their connotative rather than their denotative values—may be even more important to its effect. Consider the implications of some of the words in "On an Invitation to the United States": *modern, riper, emprize, wonning*. In context *modern* has just a slightly unfavorable overtone; it suggests, though faintly, that Hardy had in mind an overmodernity, an excessive degree of modernity. Much the same is true of the word *riper* in its context here: Hardy seems to imply that the United States is presently lacking the maturity he cherishes in England. *Emprize* and *wonning* are also highly implicative words. Their effect here is to promote, by supplying atmosphere, Hardy's intention of getting the reader to understand and approve his cherishing of the past. Both are archaic—*emprize* having been supplanted by the modern form *enterprise* or *adventure;* and *wonning,* by *dwelling, residing, living.* By using these archaisms along with such other words as *old, centuried, ancient, chronicled, dates of doom,* Hardy reminds the reader of Norse and Norman invaders, the Anglo-Saxon Chronicle, Alfred and Harold, the Domesday Book, and Runnymede and Magna Charta.

Imagery   The selection of language in poetry is governed primarily by the poet's desire to give his reader sensory experience—as Coleridge says, "to instill that energy into the mind, which compels the imagination to produce the picture." By appealing to one or more of the physical senses, the poet arouses both the mind and the emotion of the reader so that he in a measure experiences physical sensation. These things imaginatively sensed are collectively known as *imagery*.

The Concrete Word   Doubtless the simplest device to evoke imagery is the single concrete word, a word such as *scored* or *chronicled* in Hardy's poem. Hardy might have written *marked* "with prints of perished hands" instead of "*scored* with prints of perished hands." But he chose *scored* because it supplies to the reader's imagination the image Hardy desired, that of signs much deeper and more permanent than mere surface "marks." So with *chronicled.* Hardy chose a word to suggest a whole complex of meaning, the Anglo-Saxon Chronicle and even England's whole history.

Figurative Language Another device poets use to create imagery is figurative language. Basically, most figures are comparisons, expressed or implied, of things not ordinarily thought of as being alike—comparisons that do not on the surface seem logical but that on closer inspection prove illuminating. For instance, Hardy says "life has bared its bones to me." He is using a *metaphor* here, an implied comparison that not only suggests his interpretation of the true character of life, but vividly reveals Hardy's state of mind. Again, Hardy, in a *simile,* directly compares England to a tomb—"ancient lands,/Enchased and lettered as a tomb." Thus he suggests to the reader the richness of England's past—the multitude of deeds and personages that make up England's history. As the inscriptions on tombs record the deeds and exploits (as well as the vital statistics) of the persons buried in the tombs, so England is filled with places, monuments, and shrines that recall the richness of her past.

Rhythm and Rime Another kind of indirection prominent in the method of poetry is the use of sound effects to intensify meaning. Along with the attempt to communicate his total meaning by choosing words and images which convey his sense, feeling, and tone, the poet attempts to organize his words into a pattern of sound that is a part of that total meaning. The sound of poetry, then, like the diction and the imagery, is to be considered only in relation to the total design of the poem.

Sound effects are the products of organized repetitions. *Rhythm* is the result of systematically *stressing* or *accenting* words and syllables, whereas *rime* repeats similar sounds in some apparent scheme. Both rhythm and rime arouse interest in the reader, for as soon as he grasps their pattern he unconsciously expects them to continue. Expecting their continuation, he is more attentive not only to the sound itself but to the sense, feeling, and tone of the poet.

Different rhythms tend to arouse different emotions.

> Scots, wha hae wi' Wallace bled,
> Scots, wham Bruce has aften led,
> Welcome to your gory bed,
>   Or to victory!
>
> Now's the day, and now's the hour:
> See the front o' battle lour;
> See approach proud Edward's power—
>   Chains and slavery![2]

The rhythmic beat here, along with the sense of the words, sounds a grim, determined battle cry and stirs the reader to a quicker beating of the blood.

[2]From "Scots, Wha Hae wi' Wallace Bled" by Robert Burns.

They sat them down upon the yellow sand,
Between the sun and moon upon the shore;
And sweet it was to dream of Fatherland,
Of child, and wife, and slave; but evermore
Most weary seemed the sea, weary the oar,
Weary the wandering fields of barren foam.
Then some one said, "We will return no more;"
And all at once they sang, "Our island home
Is far beyond the wave; we will no longer roam." [3]

Here the rhythm, aided by the heavy frequency of liquids and nasals, helps to induce in the reader a sense of the dreaminess and lack of ambition that, according to the myth, characterized all those who ate the lotus.

Rhythms exist for the full gamut of emotions, since the only limitation upon the variety of rhythms is that which word-meaning imposes. Thus rhythms can easily be found for those quieter emotions accompanying meditation and reflection:

"A cold coming we had of it,
Just the worst time of the year
For a journey, and such a long journey:
The ways deep and the weather sharp,
The very dead of winter."
And the camels galled, sore-footed, refractory,
Lying down in the melting snow. [4]

This rhythm is less patterned than the preceding two. The poet here has departed from a strict rhythmic movement much more frequently and prominently than has either of the two preceding poets. These departures, while preserving a reflective mood, make for informality and a conversational tone. Variation from a rigid metrical pattern is often found in poetry, especially in modern poetry.

Rime—a patterned recurrence of like or similar sounds—also functions indirectly to intensify meaning. It is a further impressing of design upon material in order to achieve an intention in sense, feeling, and tone. It serves as a binding and unifying element and lends continuity. It may also be used for emphasis, especially when, as often occurs, the rime word at the end of a line concludes a phrase or clause. And rime, like rhythm, affords pleasure at the fulfillment of a pattern the reader has unconsciously recognized. When Tennyson writes

They sat them down upon the yellow sand,

the reader recognizes the likelihood that Tennyson will somewhere, perhaps in the very next line, come back to a sound similar to the one on which he stopped the

[3] From "The Lotos-Eaters" by Alfred, Lord Tennyson. See page 566.
[4] From "Journey of the Magi" by T. S. Eliot. See pages 563–64 for the full text.

first, and is pleased when he finds that expectation fulfilled:

> They sat them down upon the yellow sand,
> Between the sun and moon upon the shore;
> And sweet it was to dream of Fatherland.

Closely allied to metrical and rime pattern are a number of textural devices—devices that are similar to rime in that they involve correspondence of sounds. These devices tend to occur within the line unit of poetry but affect the total sound pattern. *Alliteration, assonance, consonance* give ease and speed to pronunciation, stepping up melody and tempo. Such pleasantness of sound is called euphony. Not always, however, is euphony desirable. In fact, cacophony, its opposite, may better achieve the poet's intention. For instance, in Eliot's line

> And the camels galled, sore-footed, refractory

the last three words, *galled, sore-footed, refractory*, cause a sense of strain and slowing of tempo appropriate to the experience he is describing.

The nature of poetry and the method of poetry are so dependent upon each other that one cannot be conceived without the other. Their relationship is organic; it is not a mere mechanical association. In other words, the way of saying a thing is a large part of what is said. A poem does much more than say or state. It transmutes sense, feeling, tone, and intention into experience, into being itself.

ANONYMOUS
True Thomas

True Thomas lay on Huntlie bank;
   A ferlie[1] he spied wi' his e'e;
And there he saw a ladye bright
   Come riding down by the Eildon Tree.

Her skirt was of the grass-green silk,
   Her mantle of the velvet fine,
At ilka tett[2] of her horse's mane
   Hung fifty silver bells and nine.

True Thomas he took off his hat,
   And bowed him low down till his knee: 10
"Hail to thee, Mary, Queen of Heaven!
   For thy peer on earth I never did see."

"O no, O no, True Thomas," she says,
   "That name does not belong to me;
I am but the queen of fair Elfland,
   That am hither come to visit thee.

"Harp and carp,[3] Thomas," she said;
   "Harp and carp along wi' me;
And if ye dare to kiss my lips,
   Sure of your body I will be."   20

"Betide me weal, betide me woe,
   That doom shall never daunten me."
Syne he has kiss'd her rosy lips,
   All underneath the Eildon Tree.

"Now ye maun[4] go wi' me," she said,
   "True Thomas, ye maun go wi' me;
And ye maun serve me seven years,
   Thro' weal or woe as may chance to be."

She's mounted on her milk-white steed,
   She's ta'en True Thomas up behind;   30
And aye, whene'er her bridle rang,
   The steed gaed swifter than the wind.

[1]marvel.   [2]each lock.   [3]talk and play lightly.
[4]must.

O they rade on, and farther on,
   The steed gaed swifter than the wind;
Until they reach'd a desert wide,
   And living land was left behind.

"Light down, light down now, True Thomas,
   And lean your head upon my knee;
Abide ye there a little space,
   And I will show you ferlies three.   40

"O see ye not yon narrow road,
   So thick beset wi' thorns and briers?
That is the Path of Righteousness,
   Though after it but few inquires.

"And see ye not yon braid, braid road
   That lies across the lily leven?[5]
That is the Path of Wickedness,
   Though some call it the Road to Heaven.

"And see ye not yon bonny road
   That winds about the fernie brae?[6]   50
That is the Road to fair Elfland,
   Where thou and I this night maun gae.

"But, Thomas, ye sall haud your tongue,
   Whatever ye may hear or see;
For speak ye word in Elfin-land,
   Ye'll ne'er win back to your ain countrie."

O they rade on, and farther on,
   And they waded rivers abune the knee;
And they saw neither sun nor moon,
   But they heard the roaring of the sea.   60

It was mirk, mirk night, there was nae starlight,
   They waded thro' red blude to the knee;
For a' the blude that's shed on the earth
   Rins through the springs o' that countrie.

Syne they came to a garden green,
   And she pu'd an apple frae a tree:
"Take this for thy wages, True Thomas;
   It will give thee the tongue that can never lee."

[5]lovely meadow.   [6]fern-covered slope.

"My tongue is my ain," True Thomas he said;
  "A gudely gift ye wad gie to me!   70
I neither dought to buy or sell
  At fair or tryst where I might be.

"I dought neither speak to prince or peer,
  Nor ask of grace from fair ladye!"—
"Now haud thy peace, Thomas," she said,
  "For as I say, so must it be."

He has gotten a coat of the even cloth,
  And a pair o' shoon of the velvet green;
And till seven years were gane and past,
  True Thomas on earth was never seen.   80

ANONYMOUS

Bonny Barbara Allan

It was in and about the Martinmas time,
  When the green leaves were a falling,
That Sir John Graeme, in the West Country,
  Fell in love with Barbara Allan.

He sent his man down through the town,
  To the place where she was dwelling:
"O haste and come to my master dear,
  Gin[1] ye be Barbara Allan."

O hooly, hooly[2] rose she up,
  To the place where he was lying,   10
And when she drew the curtain by,
  "Young man, I think you're dying."

"O it's I'm sick, and very, very sick,
  And 'tis a' for Barbara Allan;"
"O the better for me ye's never be,
  Tho your heart's blood were a spilling.

"O dinna ye mind,[3] young man," said she,
  "When ye was in the tavern a drinking,
That ye made the healths gae round and round,
  And slighted Barbara Allan?"   20

He turned his face unto the wall,
  And death was with him dealing:
"Adieu, adieu, my dear friends all,
  And be kind to Barbara Allan."

[1]if.   [2]slowly and softly.   [3]remember.

And slowly, slowly raised she up,
  And slowly, slowly left him,
And sighing said, she could not stay,
  Since death of life had reft him.

She had not gane a mile but twa,
  When she heard the dead-bell ringing,   30
And every jow[4] that the dead-bell geid,[5]
  It cry'd "Woe to Barbara Allan!"

"O mother, mother, make my bed!
  O make it soft and narrow!
My love has died for me today,
  I'll die for him tomorrow."

WALTER DE LA MARE

The Listeners

'Is there anybody there?' said the Traveller,
  Knocking on the moonlit door;
And his horse in the silence champed the grasses
  Of the forest's ferny floor:
And a bird flew up out of the turret,
  Above the Traveller's head:
And he smote upon the door again a second time;
  'Is there anybody there?' he said.
But no one descended to the Traveller;
  No head from the leaf-fringed sill   10
Leaned over and looked into his grey eyes,
  Where he stood perplexed and still.
But only a host of phantom listeners
  That dwelt in the lone house then
Stood listening in the quiet of the moonlight
  To that voice from the world of men:
Stood thronging the faint moonbeams on the
    dark stair,
  That goes down to the empty hall,
Hearkening in an air stirred and shaken
  By the lonely Traveller's call.   20
And he felt in his heart their strangeness,
  Their stillness answering his cry,
While his horse moved, cropping the dark turf,
  'Neath the starred and leafy sky;
For he suddenly smote on the door, even
  Louder, and lifted his head:—
'Tell them I came, and no one answered,
  That I kept my word,' he said.

[4]stroke.   [5]gave.

THE LISTENERS Reprinted by permission of the Literary Trustees of Walter de la Mare and The Society of Authors as their representative.

Never the least stir made the listeners,
    Though every word he spake   30
Fell echoing through the shadowiness of the
    still house
From the one man left awake:
Ay, they heard his foot upon the stirrup,
    And the sound of iron on stone,
And how the silence surged softly backward,
    When the plunging hoofs were gone.

EZRA POUND

Ballad of the Goodly Fere[1]

*Simon Zelotes speaketh it somewhile after the
    Crucifixion.*

Ha' we lost the goodliest fere o' all
For the priests and the gallows tree?
Aye, lover he was of brawny men,
O' ships and the open sea.

When they came wi' a host to take Our Man
His smile was good to see;
"First let these go!" quo' our Goodly Fere,
"Or I'll see ye damned," says he.

Aye, he sent us out through the crossed high
    spears,
And the scorn of his laugh rang free;   10
"Why took ye not me when I walked about
Alone in the town?" says he.

Oh, we drunk his "Hale" in the good red wine
When we last made company;
No capon priest was the Goodly Fere
But a man o' men was he.

I ha' seen him drive a hundred men
Wi' a bundle o' cords swung free,
That they took the high and holy house
For their pawn and treasury.   20

They'll no' get him a' in a book I think,
Though they write it cunningly;

[1]friend, companion.

BALLAD OF THE GOODLY FERE From Ezra Pound, *Personae.*
Copyright 1926 by Ezra Pound. Reprinted by permission of
New Directions Publishing Corporation.

No mouse of the scrolls was the Goodly Fere
But aye loved the open sea.

If they think they ha' snared our Goodly Fere
They are fools to the last degree.
"I'll go to the feast," quo' our Goodly Fere,
"Though I go to the gallows tree."

"Ye ha' seen me heal the lame and blind,
And wake the dead," says he;   30
"Ye shall see one thing to master all:
'Tis how a brave man dies on the tree."

A son of God was the Goodly Fere
That bade us his brothers be.
I ha' seen him cow a thousand men.
I have seen him upon the tree.

He cried no cry when they drave the nails
And the blood gushed hot and free;
The hounds of the crimson sky gave tongue
But never a cry cried he.   40

I ha' seen him cow a thousand men
On the hills o' Galilee;
They whined as he walked out calm between,
Wi' his eyes like the grey o' the sea,

Like the sea that brooks no voyaging
With the winds unleashed and free,
Like the sea that he cowed at Genseret
Wi' twey words spoke' suddenly.

A master of men was the Goodly Fere,
A mate of the wind and sea;   50
If they think they ha' slain our Goodly Fere
They are fools eternally.

I ha' seen him eat o' the honey-comb
Sin' they nailed him to the tree.

DONALD FINKEL

Hunting Song

The fox came lolloping, lolloping,
Lolloping. His tongue hung out

HUNTING SONG From *The Clothing's New Emperor and
Other Poems* published by Charles Scribner's Sons; © 1955.
Reprinted by permission of the author.

And his ears were high.
He was like death at the end of a string
When he came to the hollow
Log. Ran in one side
And out of the other. O
He was sly.

The hounds came tumbling, tumbling,
Tumbling. Their heads were low   10
And their eyes were red.
The sound of their breath was louder than death
When they came to the hollow
Log. They held at one end
But a bitch found the scent. O
They were mad.

The hunter came galloping, galloping,
Galloping. All damp was his mare
From her hooves to her mane.
His coat and his mouth were redder than death   20
When he came to the hollow
Log. He took in the rein
And over he went. O
He was fine.

The log, he just lay there, alone in
The clearing. No fox nor hound
Nor mounted man
Saw his black round eyes in their perfect disguise
(As the ends of a hollow
Log). He watched death go through him,   30
Around him and over him. O
He was wise.

JOHN CROWE RANSOM

Captain Carpenter

Captain Carpenter rose up in his prime
Put on his pistols and went riding out
But had got wellnigh nowhere at that time
Till he fell in with ladies in a rout.

It was a pretty lady and all her train
That played with him so sweetly but before
An hour she'd taken a sword with all her main
And twined him of his nose for evermore.

Captain Carpenter mounted up one day
And rode straightway into a stranger rogue   10
That looked unchristian but be that as may
The Captain did not wait upon prologue.

But drew upon him out of his great heart
The other swung against him with a club
And cracked his two legs at the shinny part
And let him roll and stick like any tub.

Captain Carpenter rode many a time
From male and female took he sundry harms
He met the wife of Satan crying "I'm
The she-wolf bids you shall bear no more arms.   20

Their strokes and counters whistled in the wind
I wish he had delivered half his blows
But where she should have made off like a hind
The bitch bit off his arms at the elbows.

And Captain Carpenter parted with his ears
To a black devil that used him in this wise
O Jesus ere his threescore and ten years
Another had plucked out his sweet blue eyes.

Captain Carpenter got up on his roan
And sallied from the gate in hell's despite   30
I heard him asking in the grimmest tone
If any enemy yet there was to fight?

"To any adversary it is fame
If he risk to be wounded by my tongue
Or burnt in two beneath my red heart's flame
Such are the perils he is cast among.

"But if he can he has a pretty choice
From an anatomy with little to lose
Whether he cut my tongue and take my voice
Or whether it be my round red heart he
    choose."   40

It was the neatest knave that ever was seen
Stepping in perfume from his lady's bower
Who at this word put in his merry mien
And fell on Captain Carpenter like a tower.

I would not knock old fellows in the dust
But there lay Captain Carpenter on his back
His weapons were the old heart in his bust
And a blade shook between rotten teeth alack.

The rogue in scarlet and grey soon knew his
    mind
He wished to get his trophy and depart   50
With gentle apology and touch refined
He pierced him and produced the Captain's heart.

God's mercy rest on Captain Carpenter now
I thought him Sirs an honest gentleman
Citizen husband soldier and scholar enow
Let jangling kites eat of him if they can.

But God's deep curses follow after those
That shore him of his goodly nose and ears
His legs and strong arms at the two elbows
And eyes that had not watered seventy years.   60

The curse of hell upon the sleek upstart
That got the Captain finally on his back
And took the red red vitals of his heart
And made the kites to whet their beaks clack
    clack.

JOHN MANIFOLD

The Griesly[1] Wife

"Lie still, my newly married wife,
    Lie easy as you can.
You're young and ill accustomed yet
    To sleeping with a man."

The snow lay thick, the moon was full
    And shone across the floor.
The young wife went with never a word
    Barefooted to the door.

He up and followed sure and fast,
    The moon shone clear and white.   10
But before his coat was on his back
    His wife was out of sight.

He trod the trail wherever it turned
    By many a mound and scree,
And still the barefoot track led on,
    And an angry man was he.

He followed fast, he followed slow,
    And still he called her name,
But only the dingoes of the hills
    Yowled back at him again.   20

[1]ghastly, grisly, uncanny.

THE GRIESLY WIFE   Copyright © 1946 by The John Day
Company. Reprinted from *Selected Verse* by John Manifold
by permission of The John Day Company, Inc., publisher.

His hair stood up along his neck,
    His angry mood was gone,
For the track of the two bare feet gave out
    And a four-foot track went on.

Her nightgown lay upon the snow
    As it might upon the sheet,
But the track that led from where it lay
    Was never of human feet.

His heart turned over in his chest,
    He looked from side to side,   30
And he thought more of his gumwood fire
    Than he did of his griesly bride.

And first he started walking back
    And then began to run,
And his quarry wheeled at the end of her track
    And hunted him in turn.

Oh, long the fire may burn for him
    And open stand the door,
And long the bed may wait empty:
    He'll not be back any more.   40

T. S. ELIOT

Journey of the Magi

"A cold coming we had of it,
Just the worst time of the year
For a journey, and such a long journey:
The ways deep and the weather sharp,
The very dead of winter."
And the camels galled, sore-footed, refractory,
Lying down in the melting snow.
There were times we regretted
The summer palaces on slopes, the terraces,
And the silken girls bringing sherbet.   10
Then the camel men cursing and grumbling
And running away, and wanting their liquor
    and women,
And the night-fires going out, and the lack of
    shelters,
And the cities hostile and the towns unfriendly

JOURNEY OF THE MAGI   From *Collected Poems 1909–1962* by
T. S. Eliot, copyright, 1936, by Harcourt Brace Jovanovich,
Inc.; copyright, ©, 1963, 1964, by T. S. Eliot. Reprinted by
permission of the publisher.

And the villages dirty and charging high prices:
A hard time we had of it.
At the end we preferred to travel all night,
Sleeping in snatches,
With the voices singing in our ears, saying
That this was all folly.   20

Then at dawn we came down to a temperate
   valley,
Wet, below the snow line, smelling of
   vegetation;
With a running stream and a water-mill beating
   the darkness,
And three trees on the low sky,
And an old white horse galloped away in the
   meadow.
Then we came to a tavern with vine-leaves over
   the lintel,
Six hands at an open door dicing for pieces of
   silver,
And feet kicking the empty wine-skins.
But there was no information, and so we
   continued
And arrived at evening, not a moment too soon   30
Finding the place; it was (you may say)
   satisfactory.

All this was a long time ago, I remember,
And I would do it again, but set down
This set down
This: were we led all that way for
Birth or Death? There was a Birth, certainly,
We had evidence and no doubt. I had seen
   birth and death,
But had thought they were different; this Birth
   was
Hard and bitter agony for us, like Death, our
   death.
We returned to our places, these Kingdoms,   40
But no longer at ease here, in the old
   dispensation,
With an alien people clutching their gods.
I should be glad of another death.

W. H. AUDEN

O What Is That Sound?

O what is that sound which so thrills the ear
   Down in the valley drumming, drumming?

Only the scarlet soldiers, dear,
   The soldiers coming.

O what is that light I see flashing so clear
   Over the distance brightly, brightly?
Only the sun on their weapons, dear,
   As they step lightly.

O what are they doing with all that gear;
   What are they doing this morning, this
     morning?   10
Only the usual maneuvers, dear,
   Or perhaps a warning.

O why have they left the road down there;
   Why are they suddenly wheeling, wheeling?
Perhaps a change in the orders, dear;
   Why are you kneeling?

O haven't they stopped for the doctor's care;
   Haven't they reined their horses, their horses?
Why, they are none of them wounded, dear,
   None of these forces.   20

O is it the parson they want, with white hair;
   Is it the parson, is it, is it?
No, they are passing his gateway, dear,
   Without a visit.

O it must be the farmer who lives so near,
   It must be the farmer, so cunning, cunning;
They have passed the farm already, dear,
   And now they are running.

O where are you going? stay with me here.
   Were the vows you swore me deceiving,
     deceiving?   30
No, I promised to love you, my dear,
   But I must be leaving.

O it's broken the lock and splintered the door,
   O it's the gate where they're turning, turning;
Their feet are heavy on the floor
   And their eyes are burning.

JOHN KEATS

La Belle Dame sans Merci

O what can ail thee, knight-at-arms,
   Alone and palely loitering?
The sedge has wither'd from the lake,
   And no birds sing.

O what can ail thee, knight-at-arms!
  So haggard and so woe-begone?
The squirrel's granary is full,
  And the harvest's done.

I see a lilly on thy brow,
  With anguish moist and fever dew,   10
And on thy cheeks a fading rose
  Fast withereth too.

I met a lady in the meads,
  Full beautiful—a faery's child,
Her hair was long, her foot was light,
  And her eyes were wild.

I made a garland for her head,
  And bracelets too, and fragrant zone;
She look'd at me as she did love,
  And made sweet moan.   20

I set her on my pacing steed,
  And nothing else saw all day long,
For sidelong would she bend, and sing
  A faery's song.

She found me roots of relish sweet,
  And honey wild, and manna dew,
And sure in language strange she said—
  "I love thee true."

She took me to her elfin grot,
  And there she wept, and sigh'd full sore, 30
And there I shut her wild wild eyes
  With kisses four.

And there she lulled me asleep,
  And there I dream'd—Ah! woe betide!
The latest dream I ever dream'd
  On the cold hill's side.

I saw pale kings and princes too,
  Pale warriors, death-pale were they all;
They cried—"La Belle Dame sans Merci
  Hath thee in thrall!"   40

I saw their starved lips in the gloam,
  With horrid warning gaped wide,
And I awoke and found me here,
  On the cold hill's side.

And this is why I sojourn here,
  Alone and palely loitering,
Though the sedge is wither'd from the lake,
  And no birds sing.

JOHN FANDEL

The Bee

A zig-zag bee, *zzz* and *zzz*-ing, came
Out of the flowers in my room; his claim
For being there was he had been carried there
While he worked in a flower, unaware.

He swayed, buzzed toward a window where a screen
Stopped him, sieved the universe between
A green beyond and his desire for
A green beyond; he was neither/nor.

From flowers to screen, he hummed a sort of
    thunder—
Nothing, yet olympic to my wonder;   10
His song stopped when the network stopped the bee.
He inspected man's ingenuity.

The screen was there to keep him out, not in.
I wanted to let his ecstasy begin
Again—to let it continue as it was.
Let a bee have his summer: what he does

With his brief season is a song for hours;
Let a bee have his privilege of flowers,
I thought. Therefore, I took an envelope
(He did not know this was his one white hope)   20

And tried to maneuver him to crawl inside.
Something, maybe fear or maybe pride,
Prompted him to be difficult:
He had his bee-wise reason to consult

Whether this should be or should not be.
I learned some independence from the bee.
Yet, because I could not watch him strive
Futilely, and wanted him alive—

I could not let him die, with honeysuckle
Just in view—I nudged him with my knuckle,   30
Then carried him outside like a note for mailing.
I opened the envelope, and the bee went sailing

Into his freedom as his thunder began
Again. I felt aliveness as a man
Should. I felt the summer rise in me.
I saw a million flowers for the bee.

ALFRED, LORD TENNYSON

from The Lotos-Eaters

"Courage!" he said, and pointed toward the
  land,
"This mounting wave will roll us shoreward
  soon."
In the afternoon they came unto a land
In which it seemèd always afternoon.
All round the coast the languid air did swoon,
Breathing like one that hath a weary dream.
Full-faced above the valley stood the moon;
And, like a downward smoke, the slender
  stream
Along the cliff to fall and pause and fall did
  seem.

A land of streams! some, like a downward
  smoke,   10
Slow-drooping veils of thinnest lawn, did go;
And some through wavering lights and shadows
  broke,
Rolling a slumbrous sheet of foam below.
They saw the gleaming river seaward flow
From the inner land; far off, three
  mountain-tops,
Three silent pinnacles of aged snow,
Stood sunset-flushed; and, dewed with showery
  drops,
Up-clomb the shadowy pine above the woven
  copse.

The charmèd sunset lingered low adown
In the red West; through mountain clefts the
  dale   20
Was seen far inland, and the yellow down
Bordered with palm, and many a winding vale
And meadow, set with slender galingale;
A land where all things always seemed the
  same!
And round about the keel with faces pale,
Dark faces pale against that rosy flame,
The mild-eyed melancholy Lotos-eaters came.

Branches they bore of that enchanted stem,
Laden with flowers and fruit, whereof they gave
To each, but whoso did receive of them   30
And taste, to him the gushing of the wave
Far far away did seem to mourn and rave
On alien shores; and if his fellow spake,
His voice was thin, as voices from the grave;
And deep-asleep he seemed, yet all awake.
And music in his ears his beating heart did
  make.

They sat them down upon the yellow sand,
Between the sun and moon upon the shore;
And sweet it was to dream of Fatherland,
Of child, and wife, and slave; but evermore   40
Most weary seemed the sea, weary the oar,
Weary the wandering fields of barren foam.
Then some one said, "We will return no more";
And all at once they sang, "Our island home
Is far beyond the wave; we will no longer
  roam."

ROBERT FROST

The Aim Was Song

Before man came to blow it right
　The wind once blew itself untaught,
And did its loudest day and night
　In any rough place where it caught.

Man came to tell it what was wrong:
　It hadn't found the place to blow;
It blew too hard—the aim was song.
　And listen—how it ought to go!

He took a little in his mouth,
　And held it long enough for north　　　10
To be converted into south,
　And then by measure blew if forth.

By measure. It was word and note,
　The wind the wind had meant to be—
A little through the lips and throat.
　The aim was song—the wind could see.

THE AIM WAS SONG From *The Poetry of Robert Frost*, edited by Edward Connery Lathem. Copyright 1916, 1923, 1928, 1930, 1939, © 1969 by Holt, Rinehart and Winston. Copyright 1944, 1951, © 1956, 1958 by Robert Frost. Copyright © 1967 by Lesley Frost Ballantine. Reprinted by permission of Holt, Rinehart and Winston, Publishers.

LEONARD COHEN

Suzanne

Suzanne takes you down
to her place near the river,
you can hear the boats go by
you can stay the night beside her.
And you know that she's half crazy
but that's why you want to be there
and she feeds you tea and oranges
that come all the way from China.
Just when you mean to tell her
that you have no gifts to give her,　　　10
she gets you on her wave-length
and she lets the river answer
that you've always been her lover.
　　And you want to travel with her,
　　you want to travel blind
　　and you know that she can trust you
　　because you've touched her perfect body
　　with your mind.

Jesus was a sailor
when he walked upon the water　　　20
and he spent a long time watching
from a lonely wooden tower
and when he knew for certain
only drowning men could see him
he said All men will be sailors then
until the sea shall free them,
but he himself was broken
long before the sky would open,
forsaken, almost human,
he sank beneath your wisdom like a stone.　　　30
　　And you want to travel with him,
　　you want to travel blind
　　and you think maybe you'll trust him

SUZANNE Reprinted by permission of Project Seven Music Division, C.T.M.S. Inc., New York, N.Y., 1966.

because he touched your perfect body
with his mind.

Suzanne takes your hand
and she leads you to the river,
she is wearing rags and feathers
from Salvation Army counters.
The sun pours down like honey   40
on our lady of the harbour
as she shows you where to look
among the garbage and the flowers,
there are heroes in the seaweed
there are children in the morning,
they are leaning out for love
they will lean that way forever
while Suzanne she holds the mirror.
    And you want to travel with her
    and you want to travel blind   50
    and you're sure that she can find you
    because she's touched her perfect body
    with her mind.

WILLIAM BLAKE

Mad Song

The wild winds weep,
And the night is a-cold;
Come hither, Sleep,
And my griefs unfold:
But lo! the morning peeps
Over the eastern steeps,
And the rustling birds of dawn
The earth do scorn.

Lo! to the vault
Of paved heaven,   10
With sorrow fraught
My notes are driven:
They strike the ear of night,
Make weep the eyes of day;
They make mad the roaring winds,
And with tempests play.

Like a fiend in a cloud,
With howling woe
After night I do crowd,
And with night will go;   20
I turn my back to the east
From whence comforts have increased;
For light doth seize my brain
With frantic pain.

THOMAS HARDY

When I Set Out for Lyonnesse

When I set out for Lyonnesse,
  A hundred miles away,
   The rime was on the spray,
And starlight lit my lonesomeness
When I set out for Lyonnesse
  A hundred miles away.

What could bechance at Lyonnesse
  While I should sojourn there
   No prophet durst declare,
Nor did the wisest wizard guess   10
What would bechance at Lyonnesse
  While I should sojourn there.

When I came back from Lyonnesse
  With magic in my eyes,
   All marked with mute surmise
My radiance rare and fathomless,
When I came back from Lyonnesse
  With magic in my eyes.

GERARD MANLEY HOPKINS

Pied Beauty

test poem →

Glory be to God for dappled things—
  For skies of couple-color as a brindled cow;
   For rose-moles all in stipple upon trout
that swim;
Fresh-firecoal chestnut-falls; finches' wings;
  Landscape plotted and pieced—fold, fallow,
and plow;
   And áll trádes, their gear and tackle and
trim.

All things counter, original, spare, strange;
aliteration → Whatever is fickle, freckled (who knows how?)
   With swift, slow; sweet, sour; adazzle, dim;
He fathers-forth whose beauty is past change: 10
    Praise him.

WHEN I SET OUT FOR LYONNESSE   Reprinted with permission
of The Macmillan Company from _Collected Poems_ by
Thomas Hardy. Copyright 1925 by The Macmillan Company.
PIED BEAUTY   From _Poems of Gerard Manley Hopkins_, Third
Edition, edited by W. H. Gardner. Copyright 1948 by Oxford
University Press, Inc. Reprinted by permission.

WILLIAM BUTLER YEATS

Down by the Salley Gardens

Down by the salley gardens my love and I did
    meet;
She passed the salley gardens with little
    snow-white feet.
She bid me take love easy, as the leaves grow
    on the tree;
But I, being young and foolish, with her would
    not agree.

In a field by a river my love and I did stand,
And on my leaning shoulder she laid her
    snow-white hand.
She bid me take life easy, as the grass grows on
    the weirs
But I was young and foolish, and now am full of
    tears.

ROBERT HERRICK

Upon Julia's Clothes

Whenas in silks my Julia goes,
Then, then, methinks, how sweetly flows
The liquefaction of her clothes.

Next, when I cast mine eyes, and see
That brave vibration, each way free,
Oh, how that glittering taketh me!

JOHN SUCKLING

Song to a Lute

Hast thou seen the down i' th' air
    When wanton blasts have tossed it,
Or the ship upon the sea
    When ruder waves have crossed it?

DOWN BY THE SALLEY GARDENS Reprinted with permission
of The Macmillan Company from *Collected Poems* by
William Butler Yeats. Copyright 1906 by The Macmillan
Company, renewed 1934 by William Butler Yeats.

Hast thou marked the crocodile's weeping,
    Or the fox's sleeping?
Or hast viewed the peacock in his pride,
    Or the dove by his bride
When he courts for lechery?
O so fickle, O so vain, O so false, so false is she! 10

ANDREW MARVELL

To His Coy Mistress

Had we but world enough, and time,
This coyness, Lady, were no crime.
We would sit down and think which way
To walk and pass our long love's day.
Thou by the Indian Ganges' side
Shouldst rubies find; I by the tide
Of Humber would complain. I would
Love you ten years before the Flood,
And you should, if you please, refuse
Till the conversion of the Jews.   10
My vegetable love would grow
Vaster than empires, and more slow;
An hundred years would go to praise
Thine eyes and on thy forehead gaze;
Two hundred to adore each breast,
But thirty thousand to the rest;
An age at least to every part,
And the last age should show your heart.
For, Lady, you deserve this state,
Nor would I love at lower rate.   20

But at my back I always hear
Time's wingèd chariot hurrying near;
And yonder all before us lie
Deserts of vast eternity.
Thy beauty shall no more be found,
Nor, in thy marble vault, shall sound
My echoing song; then worms shall try
That long preserved virginity,
And your quaint honor turn to dust,
And into ashes all my lust: 30
The grave's a fine and private place,
But none, I think, do there embrace.
Now therefore, while the youthful hue
Sits on thy skin like morning dew,
And while thy willing soul transpires
At every pore with instant fires,
Now let us sport us while we may,
And now, like amorous birds of prey

Rather at once our time devour
Than languish in his slow-chapped power. 40
Let us roll all our strength and all
Our sweetness up into one ball,
And tear our pleasures with rough strife
Thorough the iron gates of life:
Thus, though we cannot make our sun
Stand still, yet we will make him run.

And Spain go under and the shore
Of Africa the gilded sand 30
And evening vanish and no more
The low pale light across that land

Nor now the long light on the sea—

And here face downward in the sun
To feel how swift how secretly
The shadow of the night comes on . . .

ARCHIBALD MacLEISH

You, Andrew Marvell

And here face down beneath the sun
And here upon earth's noonward height
To feel the always coming on
The always rising of the night

To feel creep up the curving east
The earthly chill of dusk and slow
Upon those under lands the vast
And ever-climbing shadow grow

And strange at Ecbatan the trees
Take leaf by leaf the evening strange 10
The flooding dark about their knees
The mountains over Persia change

And now at Kermanshah the gate
Dark empty and the withered grass
And through the twilight now the late
Few travelers in the westward pass

And Baghdad darken and the bridge
Across the silent river gone
And through Arabia the edge
Of evening widen and steal on 20

And deepen on Palmyra's street
The wheel rut in the ruined stone
And Lebanon fade out and Crete
High through the clouds and overblown

And over Sicily the air
Still flashing with the landward gulls
And loom and slowly disappear
The sails above the shadowy hulls

YOU, ANDREW MARVELL From *Collected Poems*, 1952, by
Archibald MacLeish. Reprinted by permission of Houghton
Mifflin Company.

ERNEST DOWSON

I Am Not What I Was under the Reign of the Lovely Cynara

Last night, ah, yesternight, betwixt her lips and
mine
There fell thy shadow, Cynara! thy breath was
shed
Upon my soul between the kisses and the wine;
And I was desolate and sick of an old passion,
Yea, I was desolate and bowed my head:
I have been faithful to thee, Cynara! in my
fashion.

All night upon mine heart I felt her warm heart
beat,
Night-long within mine arms in love and sleep
she lay;
Surely the kisses of her bought red mouth were
sweet;
But I was desolate and sick of an old passion, 10
When I awoke and found the dawn was gray:
I have been faithful to thee, Cynara! in my
fashion.

I have forgot much, Cynara! gone with the wind,
Flung roses, roses riotously with the throng,
Dancing, to put thy pale, lost lilies out of mind;
But I was desolate and sick of an old passion,
Yea, all the time, because the dance was long:
I have been faithful to thee, Cynara! in my
fashion.

I cried for madder music and for stronger wine,
But when the feast is finished and the lamps
expire, 20
Then falls thy shadow, Cynara! the night is thine;

And I am desolate and sick of an old passion,
Yea, hungry for the lips of my desire:
I have been faithful to thee, Cynara! in my
fashion.

WILLIAM SHAKESPEARE

Let Me Not to the Marriage of True Minds

Let me not to the marriage of true minds
Admit impediments. Love is not love
Which alters when it alteration finds,
Or bends with the remover to remove.
O, no! it is an ever-fixèd mark
That looks on tempests and is never shaken.
It is the star to every wand'ring bark,
Whose worth's unknown, although his height be
taken.
Love's not Time's fool, though rosy lips and
cheeks
Within his bending sickle's compass come.   10
Love alters not with his brief hours and weeks,
But bears it out even to the edge of doom.
    If this be error and upon me proved,
    I never writ, nor no man ever loved.

WILLIAM SHAKESPEARE

My Mistress' Eyes Are Nothing Like the Sun

My mistress' eyes are nothing like the sun;
Coral is far more red than her lips' red.
If snow be white, why then her breasts are dun;
If hairs be wires, black wires grow on her head.
I have seen roses damasked,[1] red and white,
But no such roses see I in her cheeks;
And in some perfumes is there more delight
Than in the breath that from my mistress reeks.
I love to hear her speak, yet well I know
That music hath a far more pleasing sound.   10
I grant I never saw a goddess go:
My mistress, when she walks, treads on the
ground.
    And yet, by heaven, I think my love as rare
    As any she[2] belied with false compare.

[1]mingled.   [2]any woman.

ELINOR WYLIE

I Hereby Swear that to Uphold Your House

I hereby swear that to uphold your house
I would lay my bones in quick destroying lime
Or turn my flesh to timber for all time;
Cut down my womanhood; lop off the boughs
Of that perpetual ecstasy that grows
From the heart's core; condemn it as a crime
If it be broader than a beam, or climb
Above the stature that your roof allows.
I am not the hearthstone nor the cornerstone
Within this noble fabric you have builded;   10
Not by my beauty was its cornice gilded;
Not on my courage were its arches thrown:
My lord, adjudge my strength, and set me
where
I bear a little more than I can bear.

THOM GUNN

On the Move

"Man, you gotta Go."

The blue jay scuffling in the bushes follows
Some hidden purpose, and the gust of birds
That spurts across the field, the wheeling
swallows,
Have nested in the trees and undergrowth.
Seeking their instinct, or their poise, or both,
One moves with an uncertain violence
Under the dust thrown by a baffled sense
Or the dull thunder of approximate words.

On motorcycles, up the road, they come:
Small, black, as flies hanging in heat, the Boys,   10
Until the distance throws them forth, their hum
Bulges to thunder held by calf and thigh.
In goggles, donned impersonality,
In gleaming jackets trophied with the dust,
They strap in doubt—by hiding it, robust—
And almost hear a meaning in their noise.

Exact conclusion of their hardiness
Has no shape yet, but from known whereabouts
They ride, direction where the tires press.
They scare a flight of birds across the field: 20
Much that is natural, to the will must yield.
Men manufacture both machine and soul,
And use what they imperfectly control
To dare a future from the taken routes.

It is a part solution, after all.
One is not necessarily discord
On earth; or damned because, half animal,
One lacks direct instinct, because one wakes
Afloat on movement that divides and breaks.
One joins the movement in a valueless world,   30
Choosing it, till, both hurler and the hurled,
One moves as well, always toward, toward.

A minute holds them, who have come to go:
The self-defined, astride the created will
They burst away; the towns they travel through
Are home for neither bird nor holiness,
For birds and saints complete their purposes.
At worst, one is in motion; and at best,
Reaching no absolute, in which to rest,
One is always nearer by not keeping still.   40

ROBERT FROST

A Leaf-Treader

I have been treading on leaves all day until I am
    autumn-tired.
God knows all the color and form of leaves I have
    trodden on and mired.
Perhaps I have put forth too much strength and
    been too fierce from fear.
I have safely trodden underfoot the leaves of an-
    other year.

All summer long they were overhead, more lifted
    up than I.
To come to their final place in earth they had to
    pass me by.
All summer long I thought I heard them threaten-
    ing under their breath.
And when they came it seemed with a will to
    carry me with them to death.

They spoke to the fugitive in my heart as if it
    were leaf to leaf.
They tapped at my eyelids and touched my lips
    with an invitation to grief.   10
But it was no reason I had to go because they had
    to go.
Now up, my knee, to keep on top of another year
    of snow.

WALLACE STEVENS

Domination of Black

At night, by the fire,
The colors of the bushes
And of the fallen leaves,
Repeating themselves,
Turned in the room,
Like the leaves themselves
Turning in the wind.
Yes: but the color of the heavy hemlocks
Came striding.
And I remembered the cry of the peacocks.   10
The colors of their tails
Were like the leaves themselves
Turning in the wind,
In the twilight wind.
They swept over the room,
Just as they flew from the boughs of the hemlocks
Down to the ground.
I heard them cry—the peacocks.
Was it a cry against the twilight
Or against the leaves themselves   20
Turning in the wind,
Turning as the flames
Turned in the fire,
Turning as the tails of the peacocks
Turned in the loud fire,
Loud as the hemlocks
Full of the cry of the peacocks?
Or was it a cry against the hemlocks?

Out of the window,
I saw how the planets gathered   30
Like the leaves themselves
Turning in the wind.
I saw how the night came,
Came striding like the color of the heavy hemlocks.
I felt afraid.
And I remembered the cry of the peacocks.

T. S. ELIOT

Usk

Do not suddenly break the branch, or
Hope to find
The white hart behind the white well.
Glance aside, not for lance, do not spell
Old enchantments. Let them sleep.
'Gently dip, but not too deep',
Lift your eyes
Where the roads dip and where the roads rise
Seek only there
Where the grey light meets the green air   10
The hermit's chapel, the pilgrim's prayer.

CONRAD AIKEN

Morning Song from Senlin

It is morning, Senlin says, and in the morning
When the light drips through the shutters like
   the dew,
I arise, I face the sunrise,
And do the things my fathers learned to do.
Stars in the purple dusk above the rooftops
Pale in a saffron mist and seem to die,
And I myself on a swiftly tilting planet
Stand before a glass and tie my tie.

Vine leaves tap my window,
Dew-drops sing to the garden stones,   10
The robin chirps in the chinaberry tree
Repeating three clear tones.

It is morning. I stand by the mirror
And tie my tie once more.
While waves far off in a pale rose twilight
Crash on a coral shore.
I stand by a mirror and comb my hair:
How small and white my face!—
The green earth tilts through a sphere of air
And bathes in a flame of space.   20

There are houses hanging above the stars
And stars hung under a sea.
And a sun far off in a shell of silence
Dapples my walls for me.

It is morning, Senlin says, and in the morning
Should I not pause in the light to remember
   god?
Upright and firm I stand on a star unstable,
He is immense and lonely as a cloud.
I will dedicate this moment before my mirror
To him alone, for him I will comb my hair.   30
Accept these humble offerings, cloud of silence!
I will think of you as I descend the stair.

Vine leaves tap my window,
The snail-track shines on the stones,
Dew-drops flash from the chinaberry tree
Repeating two clear tones.

It is morning, I awake from a bed of silence,
Shining I rise from the starless waters of sleep.
The walls are about me still as in the evening,
I am the same, and the same name still I keep.   40
The earth revolves with me, yet makes no
   motion,
The stars pale silently in a coral sky.
In a whistling void I stand before my mirror,
Unconcerned, and tie my tie.

There are horses neighing on far-off hills
Tossing their long white manes,
And mountains flash in the rose-white dusk,
Their shoulders black with rains.
It is morning. I stand by the mirror
And surprise my soul once more;   50
The blue air rushes above my ceiling,
There are suns beneath my floor.

. . . It is morning, Senlin says, I ascend from
   darkness
And depart on the winds of space for I know
   not where,
My watch is wound, a key is in my pocket,
And the sky is darkened as I descend the stair.
There are shadows across the windows, clouds
   in heaven,
And a god among the stars; and I will go
Thinking of him as I might think of daybreak
And humming a tune I know.   60

Vine leaves tap at the window,
Dew-drops sing to the garden stones,
The robin chirps in the chinaberry tree
Repeating three clear tones.

WALTER DE LA MARE

Silver

Slowly, silently, now the moon
Walks the night in her silver shoon;
This way, and that, she peers, and sees
Silver fruit upon silver trees;
One by one the casements catch
Her beams beneath the silvery thatch;
Couched in his kennel, like a log,
With paws of silver sleeps the dog;
From their shadowy cote the white breasts peep
Of doves in a silver-feathered sleep; 10
A harvest mouse goes scampering by,
With silver claws, and silver eye;
And moveless fish in the water gleam,
By silver reeds in a silver stream.

W. H. AUDEN

Look, Stranger,
on This Island Now

Look, stranger, on this island now
The leaping light for your delight discovers,
Stand stable here
And silent be,
That through the channels of the ear
May wander like a river
The swaying sound of the sea.

Here at the small field's ending pause
When the chalk wall falls to the foam and its
    tall ledges
Oppose the pluck 10
And knock of the tide,
And the shingle scrambles after the sucking
    surf,
And the gull lodges
A moment on its sheer side.

Far off like floating seeds the ships
Diverge on urgent voluntary errands,

And the full view
Indeed may enter
And move in memory as now these clouds do,
That pass the harbour mirror 20
And all the summer through the water saunter.

A. E. HOUSMAN

Loveliest of Trees

Loveliest of trees, the cherry now
Is hung with bloom along the bough,
And stands about the woodland ride
Wearing white for Eastertide.

Now, of my threescore years and ten,
Twenty will not come again,
And take from seventy springs a score,
It only leaves me fifty more.

And since to look at things in bloom
Fifty springs are little room, 10
About the woodlands I will go
To see the cherry hung with snow.

ELINOR WYLIE

August

Why should this Negro insolently stride
Down the red noonday on such noiseless feet?
Piled in his barrow, tawnier than wheat,
Lie heaps of smoldering daisies, somber-eyed,
Their copper petals shriveled up with pride,
Hot with a superfluity of heat,
Like a great brazier borne along the street
By captive leopards, black and burning pied.
Are there no water-lilies, smooth as cream,

SILVER From *Collected Poems*, 1920, by Walter de la Mare.
Reprinted by permission of The Literary Trustees of Walter
de la Mare and The Society of Authors as their representative.
LOOK, STRANGER, ON THIS ISLAND NOW Copyright 1937 and
renewed 1965 by W. H. Auden. Reprinted from *Collected
Shorter Poems 1927–1957*, by W. H. Auden, by permission
of Random House, Inc.

LOVELIEST OF TREES From *A Shropshire Lad*—Authorised
Edition—from *The Collected Poems of A. E. Housman.*
Copyright 1939, 1940, © 1959 by Holt, Rinehart and Wins-
ton, Inc. Copyright © 1967, 1968 by Robert E. Symons.
Reprinted by permission of Holt, Rinehart and Winston, Inc.
AUGUST Copyright 1921 by Alfred A. Knopf, Inc. Renewed
1949 by William Rose Benét. Reprinted from *Collected
Poems*, by Elinor Wylie, by permission of Alfred A. Knopf,
Inc.

With long stems dripping crystal? Are there
  none 10
Like those white lilies, luminous and cool,
Plucked from some hemlock-darkened northern
  stream
By fair-haired swimmers, diving where the sun
Scarce warms the surface of the deepest pool?

G. K. CHESTERTON

The Donkey

When fishes flew and forests walked
  And figs grew upon thorn,
Some moment when the moon was blood,
  Then surely I was born;

With monstrous head and sickening cry
  And ears like errant wings,
The devil's walking parody
  On all four-footed things.

The tattered outlaw of the earth,
  Of ancient crooked will;
Starve, scourge, deride me: I am dumb; 10
  I keep my secret still.

Fools! For I also had my hour;
  One far, fierce hour and sweet.
There was a shout about my ears,
  And palms before my feet.

EMILY DICKINSON

I Never Saw a Moor

I never saw a moor,
I never saw the sea;
Yet know I how the heather looks,
And what a wave must be.

I never spoke with God,
Nor visited in heaven;
Yet certain am I of the spot
As if the chart were given.

THE DONKEY From the book *The Wild Knight and Other Poems*, 1900, by G. K. Chesterton. Published by E. P. Dutton & Co., Inc., and reprinted with their permission.
I NEVER SAW A MOOR From *The Complete Poems of Emily Dickinson*, Little, Brown and Company, 1960.

JOHN DONNE

Death Be Not Proud

Death be not proud, though some have called
  thee
Mighty and dreadful, for, thou are not soe,
For, those, whom thou think'st, thou dost
  overthrow,
Die not, poore Death, nor yet canst thou kill
  mee;
From rest and sleepe, which but thy pictures
  bee,
Much pleasure, then from thee, much more
  must flow,
And soonest our best men with thee doe goe,
Rest of their bones, and soules deliverie.
Thou art slave to Fate, chance, kings, and
  desperate men,
And dost with poyson, warre, and sicknesse
  dwell, 10
And poppie, or charmes can make us sleepe as
  well,
And better than thy stroake; why swell'st thou
  then?
One short sleepe past, wee wake eternally,
And Death shall be no more, Death thou shalt
  die.

JOHN DONNE

The Triple Foole

   I am two fooles, I know,
For loving, and for saying so
   In whining Poetry;
But where's that wiseman, that would not be I,
   If she would not deny?
Then as th'earths inward narrow crooked lanes
Do purge sea waters fretfull salt away,
   I thought, if I could draw my paines,
Through Rimes vexation, I should them allay.
Griefe brought to numbers cannot be so fierce, 10
For, he tames it, that fetters it in verse.

   But when I have done so,
Some man, his art and voice to show,
   Doth Set and sing my paine,
And, by delighting many, frees againe
   Griefe, which verse did restraine.

To Love, and Griefe tribute of Verse belongs,
But not of such as pleases when 'tis read,
  Both are increased by such songs:
For both their triumphs so are published,   20
And I, which was two fooles, do so grow three;
Who are a little wise, the best fooles bee.

GEORGE GORDON, LORD BYRON
She Walks in Beauty

She walks in beauty, like the night
Of cloudless climes and starry skies,
And all that's best of dark and bright
Meet in her aspect and her eyes;
Thus mellowed to that tender light
Which heaven to gaudy day denies.

One shade the more, one ray the less,
Had half impaired the nameless grace
Which waves in every raven tress
Or softly lightens o'er her face,   10
Where thoughts serenely sweet express
How pure, how dear their dwelling-place.

And on that cheek and o'er that brow
So soft, so calm, yet eloquent,
The smiles that win, the tints that glow
But tell of days in goodness spent,
A mind at peace with all below,
A heart whose love is innocent.

EDGAR ALLAN POE
To Helen

Helen, thy beauty is to me
  Like those Nicéan barks of yore,
That gently, o'er a perfumed sea,
  The weary, way-worn wanderer bore
    To his own native shore.

On desperate seas long wont to roam,
  Thy hyacinth hair, thy classic face,
Thy Naiad airs have brought me home
  To the glory that was Greece,
    And the grandeur that was Rome.   10

Lo! in yon brilliant window-niche
  How statue-like I see thee stand,
The agate lamp within thy hand!
  Ah, Psyche, from the regions which
    Are Holy-Land!

WILLIAM WORDSWORTH
The Solitary Reaper

Behold her, single in the field,
Yon solitary highland lass!
Reaping and singing by herself;
Stop here, or gently pass!
Alone she cuts and binds the grain,
And sings a melancholy strain;
O listen! for the vale profound
Is overflowing with the sound.

No nightingale did ever chaunt
More welcome notes to weary bands   10
Of travelers in some shady haunt,
Among Arabian sands:
A voice so thrilling ne'er was heard
In spring-time from the cuckoo-bird,
Breaking the silence of the seas
Among the farthest Hebrides.

Will no one tell me what she sings?—
Perhaps the plaintive numbers flow
For old, unhappy, far-off things,
And battles long ago: 20
Or is it some more humble lay,
Familiar matter of today?
Some natural sorrow, loss, or pain,
That has been, and may be again?

Whate'er the theme, the maiden sang
As if her song could have no ending;
I saw her singing at her work,
And o'er the sickle bending;—
I listened, motionless and still;
And, as I mounted up the hill   30
The music in my heart I bore,
Long after it was heard no more.

JULIAN SYMONS

Pub

The glasses are raised, the voices drift into
    laughter,
The clock hands have stopped, the beer in the
    hands of the soldiers
Is blond, the faces are calm and the fingers can
    feel
The wet touch of glasses, the glasses print rings
    on the table,
The smoke rings curl and go up and dissolve
    near the ceiling,
        This moment exists and is real.

What is reality? Do not ask that. At this
    moment
Look at the butterfly eyes of the girls, watch
    the barmaid's
Precision in pouring a Scotch, and remember
    this day,
This day at this moment you were no longer an
    island,   10
People were friendly, the clock in the hands of
    the soldiers
        For this moment had nothing to say.

And nothing to say and the glasses are raised,
    we are happy
Drinking through time, and a world that is
    gentle and helpless
Survives in the pub and goes up in the smoke of
    our breath,
The regulars doze in the corner, the talkers are
    fluent;
Look now in the faces of those you love and
    remember
        That you are not thinking of death.

But thinking of death as the lights go out and
    the glasses
Are lowered, the people go out and the evening 20
Goes out, ah, goes out like a light and leaves
    you alone,
As the heart goes out, the door opens out into
    darkness,
The foot takes a step, and the moment, the
    moment of falling
        Is here, you go down like a stone,

Are you able to meet the disaster, able to meet
    the
Cold air of the street and the touch of
    corruption, the rotting
Fingers that murder your own in the grip of
    love?
Can you bear to find hateful the faces you once
    thought were lovely,
Can you bear to find comfort alone in the evil
    and stunted,
        Can you bear to abandon the dove?   30

The houses are shut and the people go home,
    we are left in
Our island of pain, the clocks start to move and
    the powerful
To act, there is nothing now, nothing at all
To be done: for the trouble is real: and the
    verdict is final
Against us. The clocks go round faster and
    faster. And fast as confetti
        The days are beginning to fall.

WILLIAM BUTLER YEATS

Sailing to Byzantium

1

That is no country for old men. The young
In one another's arms, birds in the trees,
—Those dying generations—at their song,
The salmon-falls, the mackerel-crowded seas,
Fish, flesh, or fowl, commend all summer long
Whatever is begotten, born, and dies.
Caught in that sensual music all neglect
Monuments of unaging intellect.

2

An aged man is but a paltry thing,
A tattered coat upon a stick, unless   10
Soul clap its hands and sing, and louder sing
For every tatter in its mortal dress,

PUB From *The Second Man* by Julian Symons, 1943. Reprinted by permission of Routledge & Kegan Paul Ltd.

SAILING TO BYZANTIUM Reprinted with permission of Mac-
millan Publishing Co., Inc. from *Collected Poems* by William
Butler Yeats. Copyright 1928 by Macmillan Publishing Co.,
Inc., renewed 1956 by Georgie Yeats.

Nor is there singing school but studying
Monuments of its own magnificence;
And therefore I have sailed the seas and come
To the holy city of Byzantium.

3

O sages standing in God's holy fire
As in the gold mosaic of a wall,
Come from the holy fire, perne in a gyre,
And be the singing-masters of my soul.   20
Consume my heart away; sick with desire
And fastened to a dying animal
It knows not what it is; and gather me
Into the artifice of eternity.

4

Once out of nature I shall never take
My bodily form from any natural thing,
But such a form as Grecian goldsmiths make
Of hammered gold and gold enameling
To keep a drowsy Emperor awake;
Or set upon a golden bough to sing   30
To lords and ladies of Byzantium
Of what is past, or passing, or to come.

JOHN MILTON

To the Nightingale

O Nightingale, that on yon bloomy spray
    Warblest at eve, when all the woods are still,
    Thou with fresh hope the lover's heart dost fill,
    While the jolly hours lead on propitious May,
Thy liquid notes that close the eye of day,
    First heard before the shallow cuckoo's bill,
    Portend success in love; O if Jove's will
    Have linked that amorous power to thy soft lay,
Now timely sing, ere the rude bird of hate
    Foretell my hopeless doom in some grove nigh   10
    As thou from year to year hast sung too late
For my relief, yet hadst no reason why:
    Whether the Muse, or Love call thee his mate,
    Both them I serve, and of their train am I.

SAMUEL TAYLOR COLERIDGE

Kubla Khan

In Xanadu did Kubla Khan
    A stately pleasure-dome decree:
Where Alph, the sacred river, ran
Through caverns measureless to man
    Down to a sunless sea.
So twice five miles of fertile ground
    With walls and towers were girdled round:
And there were gardens bright with sinuous rills
Where blossomed many an incense-bearing tree;
And here were forests ancient as the hills,   10
Enfolding sunny spots of greenery.
But O, that deep romantic chasm which slanted
Down the green hill athwart a cedarn cover!
A savage place! as holy and enchanted
As e'er beneath a waning moon was haunted
By woman wailing for her demon-lover!
And from this chasm, with ceaseless turmoil seething
As if this earth in fast thick pants were breathing,
A mighty fountain momently was forced;
Amid whose swift half-intermitted burst   20
Huge fragments vaulted like rebounding hail,
Or chaffy grain beneath the thresher's flail:
And 'mid these dancing rocks at once and ever
It flung up momently the sacred river.
Five miles meandering with a mazy motion
Through wood and dale the sacred river ran,
Then reached the caverns measureless to man,
And sank in tumult to a lifeless ocean:
And 'mid this tumult Kubla heard from far
Ancestral voices prophesying war!   30

    The shadow of the dome of pleasure
        Floated midway on the waves;
    Where was heard the mingled measure
        From the fountain and the caves.
It was a miracle of rare device,
A sunny pleasure-dome with caves of ice!

    A damsel with a dulcimer
        In a vision once I saw:
    It was an Abyssinian maid,
        And on her dulcimer she played,   40
    Singing of Mount Abora.
    Could I revive within me
        Her symphony and song,
To such a deep delight 'twould win me,
That with music loud and long,
I would build that dome in air,
That sunny dome! those caves of ice!
And all who heard should see them there,
And all should cry, Beware! Beware!
His flashing eyes, his floating hair!   50

Weave a circle round him thrice,
  And close your eyes with holy dread,
  For he on honey-dew hath fed,
And drunk the milk of Paradise.

T. S. ELIOT

The Love Song of J. Alfred Prufrock

Let us go then, you and I,
When the evening is spread out against the sky
Like a patient etherised upon a table;
Let us go, through certain half-deserted streets,
The muttering retreats
Of restless nights in one-night cheap hotels
And sawdust restaurants with oyster-shells:
Streets that follow like a tedious argument
Of insidious intent
To lead you to an overwhelming question . . .   10
Oh, do not ask, 'What is it?'
Let us go and make our visit.

In the room the women come and go
Talking of Michelangelo.

The yellow fog that rubs its back upon the window-
    panes,
The yellow smoke that rubs its muzzle on the
    window-panes
Licked its tongue into the corners of the evening,
Lingered upon the pools that stand in drains,
Let fall upon its back the soot that falls from
    chimneys,
Slipped by the terrace, made a sudden leap,   20
And seeing that it was a soft October night
Curled once about the house, and fell asleep.

And indeed there will be time
For the yellow smoke that slides along the street
Rubbing its back upon the window-panes;
There will be time, there will be time
To prepare a face to meet the faces that you meet;
There will be time to murder and create,
And time for all the works and days of hands

That lift and drop a question on your plate;   30
Time for you and time for me,
And time yet for a hundred indecisions,
And for a hundred visions and revisions,
Before the taking of a toast and tea.

In the room the women come and go
Talking of Michelangelo.

And indeed there will be time
To wonder, 'Do I dare.' and, 'Do I dare?'
Time to turn back and descend the stair,
With a bald spot in the middle of my hair—   40
(They will say: 'How his hair is growing thin!')
My morning coat, my collar mounting firmly to the
    chin,
My necktie rich and modest, but asserted by a simple
    pin—
('They will say: 'But how his arms and legs are thin!')
Do I dare
Disturb the universe?
In a minute there is time
For decisions and revisions which a minute will
    reverse.

For I have known them all already, known them all—
Have known the evenings, mornings, afternoons, 50
I have measured out my life with coffee spoons;
I know the voices dying with a dying fall
Beneath the music from a farther room.
  So how should I presume?

And I have known the eyes already, known them
    all—
The eyes that fix you in a formulated phrase,
And when I am formulated, sprawling on a pin,
When I am pinned and wriggling on the wall,
Then how should I begin
To spit out all the butt-ends of my days and
    ways?
                                                  60
  And how should I presume?

And I have known the arms already, known them
    all—
Arms that are braceleted and white and bare
(But in the lamplight, downed with light brown hair!)
Is it perfume from a dress
That makes me so digress?
Arms that lie along a table, or wrap about a shawl.
  And should I then presume?
  And how should I begin?

              .   .   .   .   .

Shall I say, I have gone at dusk through narrow
    streets
                                                  70
And watched the smoke that rises from the pipes

Of lonely men in shirt-sleeves, leaning out of
   windows? . . .

I should have been a pair of ragged claws
Scuttling across the floors of silent seas.

   .   .   .   .   .

And the afternoon, the evening, sleeps so peacefully!
Smoothed by long fingers,
Asleep . . . tired . . . or it malingers,
Stretched on the floor, here beside you and me.
Should I, after tea and cakes and ices,
Have the strength to force the moment to its
   crisis?   80
But though I have wept and fasted, wept and prayed,
Though I have seen my head (grown slightly bald)
   brought in upon a platter,
I am no prophet—and here's no great matter;
I have seen the moment of my greatness flicker,
And I have seen the eternal Footman hold my coat,
   and snicker,
And in short, I was afraid.

And would it have been worth it, after all,
After the cups, the marmalade, the tea,
Among the porcelain, among some talk of you and
   me,
Would it have been worth while,   90
To have bitten off the matter with a smile,
To have squeezed the universe into a ball
To roll it towards some overwhelming question,
To say: 'I am Lazarus, come from the dead,
Come back to tell you all, I shall tell you all'—
If one, settling a pillow by her head,
   Should say: 'That is not what I meant at all.
   That is not it, at all.'

And would it have been worth it, after all,   100
Would it have been worth while,
After the sunsets and the dooryards and the sprinkled
   streets,

After the novels, after the teacups, after the skirts
   that trail along the floor—
And this, and so much more?—
It is impossible to say just what I mean!
But as if a magic lantern threw the nerves in patterns
   on a screen:
Would it have been worth while
If one, settling a pillow or throwing off a shawl,
And turning toward the window, should say:
   'That is not it at all,
   That is not what I meant, at all.'   110

   .   .   .   .   .

No! I am not Prince Hamlet, nor was meant to be;
Am an attendant lord, one that will do
To swell a progress, start a scene or two,
Advise the prince; no doubt, an easy tool,
Deferential, glad to be of use,
Politic, cautious, and meticulous;
Full of high sentence, but a bit obtuse;
At times, indeed, almost ridiculous—
Almost, at times, the Fool.

I grow old . . . I grow old . . .   120
I shall wear the bottoms of my trousers rolled.

Shall I part my hair behind? Do I dare to eat a peach?
I shall wear white flannel trousers, and walk upon the
   beach.
I have heard the mermaids singing, each to each.

I do not think that they will sing to me.

I have seen them riding seaward on the waves
Combing the white hair of the waves blown back
When the wind blows the water white and black.

We have lingered in the chambers of the sea
By sea-girls wreathed with seaweed red and
   brown   130
Till human voices wake us, and we drown.

THE POET AS ELEGIST

HOWARD NEMEROV
During a Solar Eclipse

The darkening disc of the moon before the sun
All morning moves, turning our common day
A deep and iris blue, a daylight of dream
In which we stand bemused and looking on
Backward at shadow and reflected light,

While the two great wanderers among the worlds
Enter their transit with our third—a thing
So rare that in his time upon the earth
A man may see, as I have done, but four:
In childhood two, a third in youth, and this   10

In likelihood my last. We stand bemused
While grass and rock darken, and stillness grows,
Until the sun and moon slide out of phase
And light returns us to the common life
That is so long to do and so soon done.

ROBERT HERRICK
Upon a Child That Died

Here she lies, a pretty bud,
Lately made of flesh and blood,
Who as soon fell fast asleep
As her little eyes did peep.
Give her strewings, but not stir
The earth that lightly covers her.

X. J. KENNEDY
Little Elegy

For a child who skipped rope

Here lies resting, out of breath,
Out of turns, Elizabeth
Whose quicksilver toes not quite
Cleared the whirring edge of night.

Earth whose circles round us skim
Till they catch the lightest limb,
Shelter now Elizabeth
And for her sake trip up Death.

EMILY DICKINSON
Because I Could Not Stop for Death

Because I could not stop for Death,
He kindly stopped for me;
The carriage held but just ourselves
And Immortality.

We slowly drove; he knew no haste,
And I had put away
My labor and my leisure too,
For his civility.

We passed the school, where children strove,
At recess, in the ring,   10
We passed the fields of gazing grain,
We passed the setting sun.

LITTLE ELEGY   Copyright © by X. J. Kennedy; originally appeared in *The New Yorker*. From *Nude Descending a Staircase* by X. J. Kennedy. Reprinted by permission of Doubleday and Company.
BECAUSE I COULD NOT STOP FOR DEATH   From *The Complete Poems of Emily Dickinson*, Little, Brown and Company, 1960.

DURING A SOLAR ECLIPSE   From *Sentences*, University of Chicago Press, 1980. Reprinted by permission of the author.

Or rather, he passed us;
The dews drew quivering and chill;
For only gossamer, my gown;
My tippet, only tulle.

We paused before a house that seemed
A swelling of the ground;
The roof was scarcely visible,
The cornice, in the ground.   20

Since then, 'tis centuries, and yet
Feels shorter than the day
I first surmised the horses' heads
Were toward eternity.

DYLAN THOMAS

Do Not Go Gentle into That Good Night

Do not go gentle into that good night,
Old age should burn and rave at close of day;
Rage, rage against the dying of the light.

Though wise men at their end know dark is
    right,
Because their words had forked no lightning
    they
Do not go gentle into that good night.

Good men, the last wave by, crying how bright
Their frail deeds might have danced in a green
    bay,
Rage, rage against the dying of the light.

Wild men who caught and sang the sun in
    flight,   10
And learn, too late, they grieved it on its way,
Do not go gentle into that good night.

Grave men, near death, who see with blinding
    sight
Blind eyes could blaze like meteors and be gay,
Rage, rage against the dying of the light.

And you, my father, there on the sad height,
Curse, bless, me now with your fierce tears, I
    pray.
Do not go gentle into that good night.
Rage, rage against the dying of the light.

A. E. HOUSMAN

Epitaph on an Army of Mercenaries

These, in the day when heaven was falling,
    The hour when earth's foundations fled,
Followed their mercenary calling
    And took their wages and are dead.

Their shoulders held the sky suspended;
    They stood, and earth's foundations stay;
What God abandoned, these defended,
    And saved the sum of things for pay.

WILLIAM WORDSWORTH

A Slumber Did My Spirit Seal

A slumber did my spirit seal;
    I had no human fears:
She seemed a thing that could not feel
    The touch of earthly years.

No motion has she now, no force;
    She neither hears nor sees;
Rolled round in earth's diurnal course,
    With rocks, and stones, and trees.

JOHN CROWE RANSOM

Bells for John Whiteside's Daughter

There was such speed in her little body,
And such lightness in her footfall,
It is no wonder her brown study
Astonishes us all.

Her wars were bruited in our high window.
We looked among orchard trees and beyond,
Where she took arms against her shadow,
Or harried unto the pond

The lazy geese, like a snow cloud
Dripping their snow on the green grass,   10
Tricking and stopping, sleepy and proud,
Who cried in goose, Alas,

For the tireless heart within the little
Lady with rod that made them rise
From their noon apple-dreams and scuttle
Goose-fashion under the skies!

But now go the bells, and we are ready,
In one house we are sternly stopped
To say we are vexed at her brown study,
Lying so primly propped.   20

W. H. AUDEN

In Memory of W. B. Yeats

1

He disappeared in the dead of winter:
The brooks were frozen, the airports almost
   deserted,
The snow disfigured the public statues;
The mercury sank in the mouth of the dying
   day.
O all the instruments agree
The day of his death was a dark cold day.

Far from his illness
The wolves ran on through the evergreen
   forests,
The peasant river was untempted by the
   fashionable quays;
By mourning tongues   10
The death of the poet was kept from his poems.

But for him it was his last afternoon as himself,
An afternoon of nurses and rumors;
The provinces of his body revolted,
The squares of his mind were empty,
Silence invaded the suburbs,
The current of his feeling failed: he became his
   admirers.

Now he is scattered among a hundred cities
And wholly given over to unfamiliar affections;
To find his happiness in another kind of wood   20
And be punished under a foreign code of
   conscience.
The words of a dead man
Are modified in the guts of the living.
But in the importance and noise of tomorrow
When the brokers are roaring like beasts on the
   floor of the Bourse,
And the poor have the sufferings to which they
   are fairly accustomed,
And each in the cell of himself is almost
   convinced of his freedom;
A few thousand will think of this day
As one thinks of a day when one did something
   slightly unusual.

O all the instruments agree   30
The day of his death was a dark cold day.

2

You were silly like us: your gift survived it all;
The parish of rich women, physical decay,
Yourself; mad Ireland hurt you into poetry.
Now Ireland has her madness and her weather
   still,
For poetry makes nothing happen: it survives
In the valley of its saying where executives
Would never want to tamper; it flows south
From ranches of isolation and the busy griefs,
Raw towns that we believe and die in; it
   survives,   40
A way of happening, a mouth.

3

Earth, receive an honored guest;
William Yeats is laid to rest:
Let the Irish vessel lie
Emptied of its poetry.

Time that is intolerant
Of the brave and innocent,
And indifferent in a week
To a beautiful physique,

Worships language and forgives   50
Everyone by whom it lives;
Pardons cowardice, conceit,
Lays its honors at their feet.

Time that with this strange excuse
Pardoned Kipling and his views,
And will pardon Paul Claudel,
Pardons him for writing well.

In the nightmare of the dark
All the dogs of Europe bark,
And the living nations wait,   60
Each sequestered in its hate;

Intellectual disgrace
Stares from every human face,
And the seas of pity lie
Locked and frozen in each eye.

Follow, poet, follow right
To the bottom of the night,
With your unconstraining voice
Still persuade us to rejoice;

With the farming of a verse   70
Make a vineyard of the curse,
Sing of human unsuccess
In a rapture of distress;

In the deserts of the heart
Let the healing fountain start,
In the prison of his days
Teach the free man how to praise.

RICHARD EBERHART

The Groundhog

In June, amid the golden fields,
I saw a groundhog lying dead.
Dead lay he; my senses shook,
And mind outshot our naked frailty.
There lowly in the vigorous summer
His form began its senseless change,
And made my senses waver dim
Seeing nature ferocious in him.
Inspecting close his maggots' might
And seething cauldron of his being,   10
Half with loathing, half with a strange love,
I poked him with an angry stick.
The fever rose, became a flame
And Vigour circumscribed the skies,
Immense energy in the sun,
And through my frame a sunless trembling.
My stick had done nor good nor harm.
Then stood I silent in the day
Watching the object, as before;
And kept my reverence for knowledge   20
Trying for control, to be still,
To quell the passion of the blood;
Until I had bent down on my knees
Praying for joy in the sight of decay.
And so I left; and I returned
In Autumn strict of eye, to see
The sap gone out of the groundhog,
But the bony sodden hulk remained.
But the year had lost its meaning,
And in intellectual chains   30
I lost both love and loathing,
Mured up in the wall of wisdom.
Another summer took the fields again
Massive and burning, full of life,
But when I chanced upon the spot
There was only a little hair left,
And bones bleaching in the sunlight
Beautiful as architecture;
I watched them like a geometer,
And cut a walking stick from a birch.   40
It has been three years, now.
There is no sign of the groundhog.
I stood there in the whirling summer,
My hand capped a withered heart,
And thought of China and of Greece,
Of Alexander in his tent;
Of Montaigne in his tower,
Of Saint Theresa in her wild lament.

THE GROUNDHOG From *Collected Poems 1930–1960* by Richard Eberhart. © 1960 by Richard Eberhart. Reprinted by permission of Oxford University Press, Inc.

DYLAN THOMAS

Twenty-four Years

Twenty-four years remind the tears of my eyes.
(Bury the dead for fear that they walk to the grave
  in labour.)
In the groin of the natural doorway I crouched like
  a tailor
Sewing a shroud for a journey
By the light of the meat-eating sun.
Dressed to die, the sensual strut begun,
With my red veins full of money,
In the final direction of the elementary town
I advance for as long as forever is.

A. E. HOUSMAN

To an Athlete Dying Young

The time you won your town race
We chaired you through the market-place;
Man and boy stood cheering by,
And home we brought you shoulder-high.

Today, the road all runners come,
Shoulder-high we bring you home,
And set you at your threshold down,
Townsman of a stiller town.

Smart lad, to slip betimes away
From fields where glory does not stay,   10
And early though the laurel grows
It withers quicker than the rose.

Eyes the shady night has shut
Cannot see the record cut,
And silence sounds no worse than cheers
After earth has stopped the ears:

Now you will not swell the rout
Of lads that wore their honours out,
Runners whom renown outran
And the name died before the man.   20

So set, before its echoes fade,
The fleet foot on the sill of shade,
And hold to the low lintel up
The still-defended challenge-cup.

And round that early-laureled head
Will flock to gaze the strengthless dead,
And find unwithered on its curls
The garland briefer than a girl's.

THE POET AS WIT AND HUMORIST

RAYMOND GRIFFITH

Essay on Enjambment

Once clauses in poems weren't quartered and
   chopped;
At the ultimate pauses a reader's voice dropped,
Which was why such lines were called end-stopped.
But then assorted poets like Shakespeare started
To ignore line endings. Verbs and their objects parted
Company to face life divided and broken-hearted.
Now free versify-
ing is even deny-
ing the sacred unify-
ing bonds of words by pry-   10
ing them apart and si-
phoning end-stop off with endless hy-
phening. And going one b-
etter, poetic go-g-
etters are releasing l-
etters from traditional f-
etters. V-
Vhere, my friends, v-
vill this lust to lop
end? Stop!   20

L. L. MILLER

A Limerick

Ann bragged that her limericks were best—
A-a-b-b-a with a jest—
Whatever she'd hum
Would come out dĕe-dĕe-dúm,
And that, of course, made An(n)-a-pest!

ESSAY ON ENJAMBMENT From *College Composition and Communication*, February 1979. © 1979 by the National Council of Teachers of English. Reprinted by permission of the publisher and the author.
A LIMERICK. From *College Composition and Communication*, October 1979. © 1979 by the National Council of Teachers of English. Reprinted by permission of the publishers and the author.

RUPERT BROOKE

Heaven

Fish (fly-replete, in depth of June,
Dawdling away their wat'ry noon)
Ponder deep wisdom, dark or clear,
Each secret fishy hope or fear.
Fish say, they have their Stream and Pond;
But is there anything Beyond?
This life cannot be All, they swear,
For how unpleasant, if it were!
One may not doubt that, somehow, Good
Shall come of Water and of Mud;   10
And, sure, the reverent eye must see
A Purpose in Liquidity.
We darkly know, by Faith we cry,
The future is not Wholly Dry.
Mud unto mud!—Death eddies near—
Not here the appointed End, not here!
But somewhere, beyond Space and Time,
Is wetter water, slimier slime!
And there (they trust) there swimmeth One
Who swam ere rivers were begun,   20
Immense, of fishy form and mind,
Squamous, omnipotent, and kind;
And under that Almighty Fin,
The littlest fish may enter in.
Oh! never fly conceals a hook,
Fish say, in the Eternal Brook,
But more than mundane weeds are there,
And mud, celestially fair;
Fat caterpillars drift around,
And Paradisal grubs are found;   30
Unfading moths, immortal flies,
And the worm that never dies.
And in that Heaven of all their wish,
There shall be no more land, say fish.

HEAVEN Reprinted by permission of Dodd, Mead & Company, Inc. from *The Collected Poems of Rupert Brooke*. Copyright 1915 by Dodd, Mead & Company, Inc. Copyright renewed 1943 by Edward Marsh.

ROBERT FROST

Departmental

An ant on the tablecloth
Ran into a dormant moth
Of many times his size.
He showed not the least surprise.
His business wasn't with such.
He gave it scarcely a touch,
And was off on his duty run.
Yet if he encountered one
Of the hive's enquiry squad
Whose work is to find out God   10
And the nature of time and space,
He would put him onto the case.
Ants are a curious race;
One crossing with hurried tread
The body of one of their dead
Isn't given a moment's arrest—
Seems not even impressed.
But he no doubt reports to any
With whom he crosses antennae,
And they no doubt report   20
To the higher up at court.
Then word goes forth in Formic:
"Death's come to Jerry McCormic,
Our selfless forager Jerry.
Will the special Janizary
Whose office it is to bury
The dead of the commissary
Go bring him home to his people.
Lay him in state on a sepal.
Wrap him for shroud in a petal.   30
Embalm him with ichor of nettle.
This is the word of your Queen."
And presently on the scene
Appears a solemn mortician;
And taking formal position
With feelers calmly atwiddle,
Seizes the dead by the middle,
And heaving him high in air,
Carries him out of there.
No one stands round to stare.   40
It is nobody else's affair.

It couldn't be called ungentle.
But how thoroughly departmental.

DEPARTMENTAL From *The Poetry of Robert Frost*, edited by
Edward Connery Lathem. Copyright 1916, 1923, 1928, 1930,
1939, © 1969 by Holt, Rinehart and Winston. Copyright
1944, 1951, © 1956, 1958 by Robert Frost. Copyright © 1967
by Lesley Frost Ballantine. Reprinted by permission of Holt,
Rinehart and Winston, Publishers.

PHYLLIS McGINLEY

A Garland of Precepts

Though a seeker since my birth,
Here is all I've learned on earth,
This is the gist of what I know:
Give advice and buy a foe.
Random truths are all I find
Stuck like burs about my mind.
Salve a blister. Burn a letter.
Do not wash a cashmere sweater.
Tell a tale but seldom twice.
Give a stone before advice.   10

Pressed for rules and verities,
All I recollect are these:
Feed a cold to starve a fever.
Argue with no true believer.
Think-too-long is never-act.
Scratch a myth and find a fact.
Stitch in time saves twenty stitches.
Give the rich, to please them, riches.
Give to love your health and hall.
But do not give advice at all.   20

SIR PHILIP SIDNEY

O Grammar-Rules, O Now Your Virtues Show

O grammar-rules, O now your virtues show;
    So children still read you with awful eyes,
    As my young dove may, in your precepts
        wise,
    Her grant to me by her own virtue know;

A GARLAND OF PRECEPTS From *Times Three* by Phyllis
McGinley. Copyright 1952 by Phyllis McGinley. Copyright
renewed 1980 by Julie Elizabeth Hayden and Phyllis Hayden
Blake. Originally published in *The New Yorker*. Reprinted by
permission of Viking Penguin Inc.

For late, with heart most high, with eyes most
low,
  I craved the thing which ever she denies;
  She lightning Love displaying Venus' skies,
  Lest once should not be heard, twice said,
  No, No!
Sing then, my muse, now Io Pan sing;
  Heav'ns envy not at my high triumphing,   10
  But grammar's force with sweet success
  confirm;
For grammar says,—oh this, dear Stella,
  weigh,—
  For grammar says,—to grammar who says
  nay?—
  That in one speech two negatives affirm!

JOHN KEATS

On the Grasshopper and
the Cricket

The poetry of earth is never dead:
  When all the birds are faint with the hot
  sun,
  And hide in cooling trees, a voice will run
From hedge to hedge about the new-mown
  mead;
  That is the Grasshopper's—he takes the lead
  In summer luxury,—he has never done
  With his delights; for when tired out with
  fun
He rests at ease beneath some pleasant weed.
The poetry of earth is ceasing never:
  On a lone winter evening, when the frost   10
  Has wrought a silence, from the stove
  there shrills
The Cricket's song, in warmth increasing
  ever,
  And seems to one in drowsiness half lost,
  The Grasshopper's among some grassy
  hills.

DOROTHY PARKER

One Perfect Rose

A single flow'r he sent me, since we met.
  All tenderly his messenger he chose;
Deep-hearted, pure, with scented dew still
  wet—
  One perfect rose.

I knew the language of the floweret;
  "My fragile leaves," it said, "his heart
  enclose."
Love long has taken for his amulet
  One perfect rose.

Why is it no one ever sent me yet
  One perfect limousine, do you suppose?   10
Ah no, it's always just my luck to get
  One perfect rose.

E. B. WHITE

I Paint What I See

A Ballad of Artistic Integrity

"What do you paint, when you paint a wall?"
  Said John D.'s grandson Nelson.
"Do you paint just anything there at all?
"Will there be any doves, or a tree in fall?
"Or a hunting scene, like an English hall?"

  "I paint what I see," said Rivera.

"What are the colors you use when you paint?"
  Said John D.'s grandson Nelson.
"Do you use any red in the beard of a saint?
"If you do, is it terribly red, or faint?   10
"Do you use any blue? Is it Prussian?"

  "I paint what I paint," said Rivera.

"Whose is that head that I see on my wall?"
  Said John D.'s grandson Nelson.
"Is it anyone's head whom we know, at all?
"A Rensselaer, or a Saltonstall?
"Is it Franklin D.? Is it Mordaunt Hall?
"Or is it the head of a Russian?"

  "I paint what I paint," said Rivera.

"I paint what I paint, I paint what I see,   20
  "I paint what I think," said Rivera.
"And the thing that is dearest in life to me
"In a bourgeois hall is Integrity;
  "However . . .
"I'll take out a couple of people drinkin'
"And put in a picture of Abraham Lincoln,
"I could even give you McCormick's reaper
"And still not make my art much cheaper.
"But the head of Lenin has got to stay
"Or my friends will give me the bird today   30
  "The bird, the bird, forever."

"It's not good taste in a man like me,"
  Said John D.'s grandson Nelson,
"To question an artist's integrity
"Or mention a practical thing like a fee,
"But I know what I like to a large degree
  "Though art I hate to hamper;
"For twenty-one thousand conservative bucks
"You painted a radical. I say shucks,
  "I never could rent the offices—   40
  "The capitalistic offices.

"For this, as you know, is a public hall
"And people want doves, or a tree in fall,
"And though your art I dislike to hamper,
"I owe a *little* to God and Gramper,
  "And after all,
  "It's *my* wall . . ."

  "We'll see if it is," said Rivera.

JOHN BETJEMAN

In Westminster Abbey

Let me take this other glove off
  As the *vox humana* swells,
And the beauteous fields of Eden
  Bask beneath the Abbey bells.

Here, where England's statesmen lie,
Listen to a lady's cry.

Gracious Lord, oh bomb the Germans.
  Spare their women for Thy Sake,
And if that is not too easy
  We will pardon Thy Mistake.   10
But, gracious Lord, whate'er shall be,
Don't let anyone bomb me.

Keep our Empire undismembered
  Guide our Forces by Thy Hand,
Gallant blacks from far Jamaica,
  Honduras and Togoland;
Protect them Lord in all their fights,
And, even more, protect the whites.

Think of what our Nation stands for,
  Books from Boots' and country lanes,   20
Free speech, free passes, class distinction,
  Democracy and proper drains.
Lord, put beneath Thy special care
One-eighty-nine Cadogan Square.

Although dear Lord I am a sinner,
  I have done no major crime;
Now I'll come to Evening Service
  Whensoever I have the time.
So, Lord, reserve for me a crown,
And do not let my shares go down.   30

I will labour for Thy Kingdom,
  Help our lads to win the war,
Send white feathers to the cowards
  Join the Women's Army Corps,
Then wash the Steps around Thy Throne
In the Eternal Safety Zone.

Now I feel a little better,
  What a treat to hear Thy Word,
Where the bones of leading statesmen,
  Have so often been interr'd.   40
And now, dear Lord, I cannot wait
Because I have a luncheon date.

IN WESTMINSTER ABBEY From *Collected Poems* by John Betjeman. Reprinted by permission of the author and John Murray Publishers, Ltd.

LOUIS SIMPSON

The Custom of the World

O, we loved long and happily, God knows!
The ocean danced, the green leaves tossed, the
    air
Was filled with petals, and pale Venus rose
When we began to kiss. Kisses brought care,
And closeness caused the taking off of clothes,
O, we loved long and happily, God knows!

"The watchdogs are asleep, the doormen
    doze. . . ."
We huddled in the corners of the stair,
And then we climbed it. What had we to lose?
What would we gain? The best way to compare 10
And quickest, was by taking off our clothes.
O, we loved long and happily, God knows!

Between us two a silent treason grows,
Our pleasures have been changed into despair.
Wild is the wind, from a cold country blows,
In which these tender blossoms disappear.

And did this come of taking off our clothes?
O, we loved long and happily, God knows!

Mistress, my song is drawing to a close.
Put on your rumpled skirt and comb your hair,   20
And when we meet again let us suppose
We never loved or ever naked were.
For though this nakedness was good, God knows
The custom of the world is wearing clothes.

THE CUSTOM OF THE WORLD   Copyright © 1949 by Louis
Simpson. Reprinted from *A Dream of Governors*, by Louis
Simpson, by permission of Wesleyan University Press.

LUCIAN

On Magical Whiskers

TRANSLATED BY WILLIS BARNSTONE

If by growing a goatee you hope to come upon
    wisdom,
then, O wise friend, any smelly goat in
                    a handsome beard
is at once Plato.

ON MAGICAL WHISKERS   Reprinted by permission of Schocken
Books Inc. from *Greek Lyric Poetry*, translated by Willis
Barnstone. Copyright © 1962, 1967 by Willis Barnstone.

THE POET AS PORTRAYER OF CHARACTER

JOSEPH BRODSKY

Six Years Later

TRANSLATED FROM RUSSIAN BY RICHARD WILBUR

So long had life together been that now
The second of January fell again
On Tuesday, making her astonished brow
Lift like a windshield wiper in the rain,
   So that her misty sadness cleared, and
     showed
   A cloudless distance waiting up the road.

So long had life together been that once
The snow began to fall, it seemed unending;
That, lest the flakes should make her eyelids
   wince,
I'd shield them with my hand, and they, pre-
   tending   10
   Not to believe that cherishing of eyes,
   Would beat against my palm like butterflies.

So alien had all novelty become
That sleep's entanglements would put to
   shame
Whatever depths the analysts might plumb;
That when my lips blew out the candle flame,
   Her lips, fluttering from my shoulder, sought
   To join my own, without another thought.

So long had life together been that all
That tattered brood of papered roses went,   20
And a whole birch grove grew upon the wall,
And we had money, by some accident,
   And tonguelike on the sea, for thirty days,
   The sunset threatened Turkey with its blaze.

So long had life together been without
Books, chairs, utensils—only that ancient
   bed—
That the triangle, before it came about,
Had been a perpendicular, the head
   Of some acquaintance hovering above
   Two points which had been coalesced by
     love.   30

So long had life together been that she
And I, with our joint shadows, had composed
A double door, a door which, even if we
Were lost in work or sleep, was always closed:
   Somehow, it would appear, we drifted right
   On through it into the future, into the
     night.

ADRIENNE RICH

The Diamond Cutters

However legendary,
The stone is still a stone,
Though it had once resisted
The weight of Africa,
The hammer-blows of time
That wear to bits of rubble
The mountain and the pebble—
But not this coldest one.

Now, you intelligence
So late dredged up from dark　　　　　10
Upon whose smoky walls
Bison took fumbling form
Or flint was edged on flint—
Now, careful arriviste,
Delineate at will
Incisions in the ice.

Be serious, because
The stone may have contempt
For too-familiar hands,
And because all you do　　　　　20
Loses or gains by this:
Respect the adversary,
Meet it with tools refined,
And thereby set your price.

Be hard of heart, because
The stone must leave your hand.
Although you liberate
Pure and expensive fires
Fit to enamour Shebas,
Keep your desire apart.　　　　　30
Love only what you do,
And not what you have done.

Be proud, when you have set
The final spoke of flame
In that prismatic wheel,
And nothing's left this day
Except to see the sun
Shine on the false and the true,
And know that Africa
Will yield you more to do.　　　　　40

EDWIN ARLINGTON ROBINSON

Credo

I cannot find my way: there is no star
In all the shrouded heavens anywhere;
And there is not a whisper in the air
Of any living voice but one so far
That I can hear it only as a bar
Of lost, imperial music, played when fair
And angel fingers wove, and unaware,
Dead leaves to garlands where no roses are.

No, there is not a glimmer, nor a call,
For one that welcomes, welcomes when he
　　　fears,　　　　　10
The black and awful chaos of the night;
For through it all—above, beyond it all—
I know the far-sent message of the years,
I feel the coming glory of the Light.

EDWIN ARLINGTON ROBINSON

Mr. Flood's Party

Old Eben Flood, climbing alone one night
Over the hill between the town below
And the forsaken upland hermitage
That held as much as he should ever know
On earth again of home, paused warily.
The road was his with not a native near;
And Eben, having leisure, said aloud,
For no man else in Tilbury Town to hear:

"Well, Mr. Flood, we have the harvest moon
Again, and we may not have many more;　　　10
The bird is on the wing, the poet says,
And you and I have said it here before.
Drink to the bird." He raised up to the light
The jug that he had gone so far to fill,
And answered huskily: "Well, Mr. Flood,
Since you propose it, I believe I will."

Alone, as if enduring to the end
A valiant armor of scarred hopes outworn,
He stood there in the middle of the road
Like Roland's ghost winding a silent horn.　　20
Below him, in the town among the trees,
Where friends of other days had honored him,
A phantom salutation of the dead
Rang thinly till old Eben's eyes were dim.

Then, as a mother lays her sleeping child
Down tenderly, fearing it may awake,
He set the jug down slowly at his feet
With trembling care, knowing that most things
　　break;
And only when assured that on firm earth
It stood, as the uncertain lives of men　　　30
Assuredly did not, he paced away,
And with his hand extended paused again:

"Well, Mr. Flood, we have not met like this
In a long time; and many a change has come
To both of us, I fear, since last it was
We had a drop together. Welcome home!"
Convivially returning with himself,

Again he raised the jug up to the light;
And with an acquiescent quaver said:
"Well, Mr. Flood, if you insist, I might.   40

"Only a very little, Mr. Flood—
For auld lang syne. No more, sir; that will do."
So, for the time, apparently it did,
And Eben evidently thought so too;
For soon amid the silver loneliness
Of night he lifted up his voice and sang,
Secure, with only two moons listening,
Until the whole harmonious landscape rang—

"For auld lang syne." The weary throat gave
    out,
The last word wavered; and the song being
    done,   50
He raised again the jug regretfully
And shook his head, and was again alone.
There was not much that was ahead of him,
And there was nothing in the town below—
Where strangers would have shut the many
    doors
That many friends had opened long ago.

So on we worked, and waited for the light,
And went without the meat, and cursed the
    bread;
And Richard Cory, one calm summer night,
Went home and put a bullet through his head.

E. E. CUMMINGS

"next to of course god america i

"next to of course god america i
love you land of the pilgrims' and so forth oh
say can you see by the dawn's early my
country 'tis of centuries come and go
and are no more what of it we should worry
in every language even deafanddumb
thy sons acclaim your glorious name by gorry
by jingo by gee by gosh by gum
why talk of beauty what could be more beautiful than these heroic happy dead   10
who rushed like lions to the roaring slaughter
they did not stop to think they died instead
then shall the voice of liberty be mute?"

He spoke. And drank rapidly a glass of water

EDWIN ARLINGTON ROBINSON

Richard Cory

Whenever Richard Cory went down town,
We people on the pavement looked at him:
He was a gentleman from sole to crown,
Clean favored, and imperially slim.

And he was always quietly arrayed,
And he was always human when he talked;
But still he fluttered pulses when he said,
"Good-morning," and he glittered when he
    walked.

And he was rich—yes, richer than a king—
And admirably schooled in every grace: 10
In fine, we thought that he was everything
To make us wish that we were in his place.

EMILY DICKINSON

He Preached upon "Breadth"

He preached upon "breadth" til it argued him
    narrow,—
The broad are too broad to define;
And of "truth" until it proclaimed him a liar,—
The truth never flaunted a sign.

Simplicity fled from his counterfeit presence
As gold the pyrites would shun.
What confusion would cover the innocent Jesus
To meet so enabled a man!

MR. FLOOD'S PARTY   Reprinted with permission of The Macmillan Company from *Collected Poems* by Edward Arlington Robinson. Copyright 1921 by Edward Arlington Robinson, renewed 1949 by Ruth Nivison.

RICHARD CORY   From *The Children of the Night* by Edwin Arlington Robinson. (New York: Charles Scribner's Sons, 1897.) Reprinted courtesy Charles Scribner's Sons.
"NEXT TO OF COURSE GOD AMERICA I   Copyright, 1926, by Horace Liveright; renewed, 1954, by E. E. Cummings. Reprinted from *Poems 1923–1954*, by E. E. Cummings, by permission of Harcourt Brace Jovanovich, Inc.
HE PREACHED UPON "BREADTH"   From *The Complete Poems of Emily Dickinson*, Little, Brown and Company, 1960.

PHYLLIS McGINLEY

Simeon Stylites

On top of a pillar Simeon sat.
He wore no mantle,
He had no hat,
But bare as a bird
Sat night and day.
And hardly a word
Did Simeon say.

Under the sun of the desert sky.
He sat on a pillar
Nine feet high   10
When Fool and his brother
Came round to admire,
He raised it another
Nine feet high'r.

The seasons circled about his head.
He lived on water
And crusts of bread
(Or so one hears)
From pilgrims' store,
For thirty years   20
And a little more.

And why did Simeon sit like that,
Without a garment,
Without a hat,
In a holy rage
For the world to see?
It puzzles the age,
It puzzles me.
It puzzled many
A Desert Father.   30
And I think it puzzled the Good Lord, rather.

GWENDOLYN BROOKS

We Real Cool

The Pool Players.
Seven at the Golden Shovel.

We real cool. We
Left school. We

Lurk late. We
Strike straight. We

Sing sin. We
Thin gin. We

Jazz June. We
Die soon.

TED HUGHES

Hawk Roosting

I sit in the top of the wood, my eyes closed.
Inaction, no falsifying dream
Between my hooked head and hooked feet:
Or in sleep rehearse perfect kills and eat.

The convenience of the high trees!
The air's buoyancy and the sun's ray
Are of advantage to me;
And the earth's face upward for my inspection.

My feet are locked upon the rough bark.
It took the whole of Creation   10
To produce my foot, my each feather:
Now I hold Creation in my foot

Or fly up, and revolve it all slowly—
I kill where I please because it is all mine.
There is no sophistry in my body:
My manners are tearing off heads—

The allotment of death.
For the one path of my flight is direct
Through the bones of the living.
No arguments assert my right: 20

The sun is behind me.
Nothing has changed since I began.
My eye has permitted no change.
I am going to keep things like this.

LUCILLE CLIFTON

In the Inner City

in the inner city
or
like we call it
home
we think a lot about uptown
and the silent nights
and the houses straight as
dead men
and the pastel lights
and we hang on to our no place   10
happy to be alive
and in the inner city
or
like we call it
home

WILLIAM STAFFORD

So Long

At least at night, a streetlight
is better than a star.
And better good shoes on a
long walk than a good friend.

Often, in winter, with my old
cap, I slip away into the gloom
like a happy fish, at home
with all I touch, at the level of love.

No one can surface till far,
far on, and all that we'll have   10
to love may be what's near
in the cold, even then.

HAROLD WITT

Certainty

Certainty seems to be this person
at work on the roof,
who sped up the ladder as agilely urgent
as if in a circus,
and kneels there wearing a yellow helmet;
his pliers of purpose

flash as he grips them, and twists—just enough—
mysterious wires.
He's wristed with cleverness, belted with tools,
a lineman of light   10
who knows what he's doing (though we may be
    fools)
and does it right.

If only all darkness had such perfect workmen
risking the task—
to catch the tossed cable that can bring brightness
and nimbly attach
power where it's best to, then step down lithely,
without a scratch.

JOHN CIARDI

Suburban Homecoming

As far as most of what you call people, my
    darling, are
concerned, I don't care who or what gets into
    the phone. I
am not home and not expected and I even,
    considerably, doubt I live here.

I mean this town and its everlasting
    katzenjammer when-
ever whoever dials again, is going to hell, or to
    some other
perpetual buffet, in a wheelbarrowful of bad
    martinis: and you, my

legal sweet, forever in the act of putting your
    hat on
as I come in the door to be told I have exactly
    five—
or, on good days, ten—minutes to change in
    because here we go

again to some collection of never-quite-the-
    same-but-   10
always-no-different faces; you, my moth-brained
    flutter
from bright cup to cup, no matter what nothing
    is in them; you, my own

brand-named, laboratory-tested, fair-trade-
    priced, wedded
(as advertised in *Life*) feather-duster, may go
    jump into
twenty fathoms of Advice to the Lovelorn and
    pull it in after you—

but I have not arrived, am not in, the phone did
    not ring
and was not answered, we have not really, I
    believe, met, and
if we do and if I stay to be (I doubt it)
    introduced, I'm still not going.

EDWARD THOMAS

The Owl

Downhill I came, hungry, and yet not starved;
Cold, yet had heat within me that was proof
Against the North wind; tired, yet so that rest
Had seemed the sweetest thing under a roof.

Then at the inn I had food, fire, and rest,
Knowing how hungry, cold, and tired was I.
All of the night was quite barred out except
An owl's cry, a most melancholy cry

Shaken out long and clear upon the hill,
No merry note, nor cause of merriment,   10
But one telling me plain what I escaped
And others could not, that night, as in I went.

And salted was my food, and my repose,
Salted, and sobered, too, by the bird's voice
Speaking for all who lay under the stars,
Soldiers and poor, unable to rejoice.

ROBERT BROWNING

Soliloquy of the Spanish Cloister

Gr-r-r—there go, my heart's abhorrence!
    Water your damned flower-pots, do!
If hate killed men, Brother Lawrence,
    God's blood, would not mine kill you!
What? your myrtle-bush wants trimming?
    Oh, that rose has prior claims—
Needs its leaden vase filled brimming?
    Hell dry you up with its flames!

At the meal we sit together:
    Salve tibi! I must hear   10
Wise talk of the kind of weather,
    Sort of season, time of year:
Not a plenteous cork-crop: scarcely
    Dare we hope oak-galls, I doubt:
What's the Latin name for "parsley"?
    What's the Greek name for Swine's Snout?

Whew! We'll have our platter burnished,
    Laid with care on our own shelf!
With a fire-new spoon we're furnished,
    And a goblet for ourself,   20
Rinsed like something sacrificial
    Ere 'tis fit to touch our chaps—
Marked with L for our initial!
    (He-he! There his lily snaps!)

Saint, forsooth! While brown Dolores
    Squats outside the Convent bank
With Sanchicha, telling stories,
    Steeping tresses in the tank,
Blue-black, lustrous, thick like horse-hairs,
    —Can't I see his dead eye glow,   30
Bright as 'twere a Barbary corsair's?
    (That is, if he'd let it show!)

When he finishes refection,
    Knife and fork he never lays
Cross-wise, to my recollection,
    As do I, in Jesu's praise.
I the Trinity illustrate,
    Drinking watered orange-pulp—
In three sips the Arian frustrate;
    While he drains his at one gulp.   40

Oh, those melons! If he's able
    We're to have a feast! so nice!
One goes to the Abbot's table,
    All of us get each a slice.

How go on your flowers? None double?
  Not one fruit-sort can you spy?
Strange!—And I, too, at such trouble
  Keep them close-nipped on the sly!

There's a great text in Galatians,
  Once you trip on it, entails   50
Twenty-nine distinct damnations,
  One sure, if another fails:
If I trip him just a-dying,
  Sure of heaven as sure can be,
Spin him round and send him flying
  Off to hell, a Manichee!

Or, my scrofulous French novel
  On gray paper with blunt type!
Simply glance at it, you grovel
  Hand and foot in Belial's gripe: 60
If I double down its pages
  At the woeful sixteenth print,
When he gathers his greengages,
  Ope a sieve and slip it in't?

Or, there's Satan! one might venture
  Pledge one's soul to him, yet leave
Such a flaw in the indenture
  As he'd miss till, past retrieve,
Blasted lay that rose-acacia
  We're so proud of! Hy, Zy, Hine . . .   70
'St, there's Vespers! *Plena gratia,*
  Ave, Virgo! Gr-r-r—you swine!

CARL SANDBURG

Limited

I am riding on a limited express, one of the crack
  trains of the nation.
Hurtling across the prairie into blue haze and dark
  air go fifteen all-steel coaches holding a thousand
  people.
(All the coaches shall be scrap and rust and all the
  men and women laughing in the diners and
  sleepers shall pass to ashes.)
I ask a man in the smoker where he is going and
  he answers: "Omaha."

LIMITED From *Chicago Poems* by Carl Sandburg. Copyright 1916 by Holt, Rinehart and Winston, Inc. Copyright 1944 by Carl Sandburg. Reprinted by permission of Holt, Rinehart and Winston, Inc.

WILLIAM BUTLER YEATS

No Second Troy

Why should I blame her that she filled my days
With misery, or that she would of late
Have taught to ignorant men most violent ways,
Or hurled the little streets upon the great,
Had they but courage equal to desire?
What could have made her peaceful with a mind
That nobleness made simple as a fire,
With beauty like a tightened bow, a kind
That is not natural in an age like this,
Being high and solitary and most stern?   10
Why, what could she have done, being what
  she is?
Was there another Troy for her to burn?

WILLIAM BUTLER YEATS

That the Night Come

She lived in storm and strife,
Her soul had such desire
For what proud death may bring
That it could not endure
The common good of life,
But lived as 'twere a king
That packed his marriage day
With banneret and pennon,
Trumpet and kettle drum,
And the outrageous cannon   10
To bundle time away
That the night come.

NO SECOND TROY Reprinted with permission of The Macmillan Company from *Collected Poems* by William Butler Yeats. Copyright 1933 by The Macmillan Company, renewed 1961 by Bertha Georgie Yeats.
THAT THE NIGHT COME Reprinted with permission of The Macmillan Company from *Collected Poems* by William Butler Yeats. Copyright 1912 by The Macmillan Company, renewed 1940 by Bertha Georgie Yeats.

ROBERT FROST

The Silken Tent

She is as in a field a silken tent
At midday when a sunny summer breeze
Has dried the dew and all its ropes relent,
So that in guys it gently sways at ease,
And its supporting central cedar pole,
That is its pinnacle to heavenward
And signifies the sureness of the soul,
Seems to owe naught to any single cord,
But strictly held by none, is loosely bound
By countless silken ties of love and thought   10
To everything on earth the compass round,
And only by one's going slightly taut
In the capriciousness of summer air
Is of the slightest bondage made aware.

HENRY REED

Lessons of War:
Judging Distances

Not only how far away, but the way that you
    say it
Is very important. Perhaps you may never get
The knack of judging a distance, but at least
    you know
How to report on a landscape: the central
    sector,
The right of arc and that, which we had last
    Tuesday,
        And at least you know

That maps are of time, not place, so far as the
    army
Happens to be concerned—the reason being,
Is one which need not delay us. Again, you
    know

There are three kinds of tree, three only, the fir
    and the poplar,   10
And those which have bushy tops too; and
    lastly
        That things only seem to be things.

A barn is not called a barn, to put it more
    plainly,
Or a field in the distance, where sheep may be
    safely grazing.
You must never be over-sure. You must say,
    when reporting:
At five o'clock in the central sector is a dozen
Of what appear to be animals; whatever you do,
        Don't call the bleeders *sheep.*

I am sure that's quite clear; and suppose, for
    the sake of example,
The one at the end, asleep, endeavours to
    tell us   20
What he sees over there to the west, and how
    far away,
After first having come to attention. There to
    the west,
On the fields of summer the sun and the
    shadows bestow
        Vestments of purple and gold.

The still white dwellings are like a mirage in
    the heat,
And under the swaying elms a man and a
    woman
Lie gently together. Which is, perhaps, only to
    say
That there is a row of houses to the left of arc,
And that under some poplars a pair of what
    appears to be humans
        Appear to be loving.   30

Well that, for an answer, is what we might
    rightly call
Moderately satisfactory only, the reason being,
Is that two things have been omitted, and those
    are important.
The human beings, now: in what direction are
    they,
And how far away, would you say? And do not
    forget
        There may be dead ground in between.

There may be dead ground in between; and I
    may not have got
The knack of judging a distance; I will only
    venture

A guess that perhaps between me and the
    apparent lovers,
(Who, incidentally, appear by now to have
    finished,)
At seven o'clock from the houses, is roughly a   40
    distance
        Of about one year and a half.

WILLIAM WORDSWORTH

Personal Talk

I am not one who much or oft delight
    To season my fireside with personal talk,—
    Of friends, who live within an easy walk,
Or neighbours, daily, weekly, in my sight:
And, for my chance-acquaintance, ladies bright,
    Sons, mothers, maidens withering on the stalk,
    These all wear out of me, like forms, with
        chalk
Painted on rich men's floors, for one feast-night.
Better than such discourse doth silence long,
    Long, barren silence, square with my desire;   10
To sit without emotion, hope, or aim,
    In the loved presence of my cottage-fire,
And listen to the flapping of the flame,
Or kettle whispering its faint undersong.

JOHN FREDERICK NIMS

Love Poem

My clumsiest dear, whose hands shipwreck vases,
At whose quick touch all glasses chip and ring,
Whose palms are bulls in china, burs in linen,
And have no cunning with any soft thing

Except all ill-at-ease fidgeting people:
The refugee uncertain at the door
You make at home; deftly you steady
The drunk clambering on his undulant floor.

LOVE POEM From *The Iron Pastoral* by John Frederick Nims.
Reprinted by permission of William Sloane Associates.
Copyright © 1947 by John Frederick Nims.

Unpredictable dear, the taxi drivers' terror,
Shrinking from far headlights pale as a dime   10
Yet leaping before red apoplectic streetcars—
Misfit in any space. And never on time.

A wrench in clocks and the solar system. Only
With words and people and love you move at
    ease.
In traffic of wit expertly manoeuvre
And keep us, all devotion, at your knees.

Forgetting your coffee spreading on our flannel,
Your lipstick grinning on our coat,
So gayly in love's unbreakable heaven
Our souls on glory of spilt bourbon float.   20

Be with me, darling, early and late. Smash
    glasses—
I will study wry music for your sake.
For should your hands drop white and empty
All the toys of the world would break.

ELIZABETH BARRETT BROWNING

If Thou Must Love Me, Let It Be for Naught

If thou must love me, let it be for naught
    Except for love's sake only. Do not say,
    'I love her for her smile—her look—her way
Of speaking gently,—for a trick of thought
That falls in well with mine, and certes brought
    A sense of pleasant ease on such a day'—
    For these things in themselves, Beloved, may
Be changed, or change for thee—and love, so
    wrought,
May be unwrought so. Neither love me for
    Thine own dear pity's wiping my cheeks
    dry: 10
A creature might forget to weep, who bore
    Thy comfort long, and lose thy love thereby!
But love me for love's sake, that evermore
    Thou mayst love on, through love's eternity.

THEODORE ROETHKE

I Knew a Woman

I knew a woman, lovely in her bones,
When small birds sighed, she would sigh back
    at them;
Ah, when she moved, she moved more ways
    than one:
The shapes a bright container can contain!
Of her choice virtues only gods should speak,
Or English poets who grew up on Greek
(I'd have them sing in chorus, cheek to cheek).

How well her wishes went! She stroked my
    chin,
She taught me Turn, and Counter-turn, and
    Stand;
She taught me Touch, that undulant white skin; 10
I nibbled meekly from her proffered hand;
She was the sickle; I, poor I, the rake,
Coming behind her for her pretty sake
(But what prodigious mowing we did make).

Love likes a gander, and adores a goose:
Her full lips pursed, the errant note to seize;
She played it quick, she played it light and
    loose;
My eyes, they dazzled at her flowing knees;
Her several parts could keep a pure repose,
Or one hip quiver with a mobile nose   20
(She moved in circles, and those circles moved).

Let seed be grass, and grass turn into hay:
I'm martyr to a motion not my own;
What's freedom for? To know eternity.
I swear she cast a shadow white as stone.
But who would count eternity in days?
These old bones live to learn her wanton ways:
(I measure time by how a body sways).

EDNA ST. VINCENT MILLAY

Wild Swans

I looked in my heart while the wild swans went
    over.
And what did I see I had not seen before?

Only a question less or a question more;
Nothing to match the flight of wild birds flying.
Tiresome heart, forever living and dying,
House without air, I leave you and lock your door.
Wild swans, come over the town, come over
The town again, trailing your legs and crying!

ALEXANDER POPE

Ode on Solitude

Happy the man, whose wish and care
    A few paternal acres bound,
Content to breathe his native air,
                In his own ground.

Whose herds with milk, whose fields with bread,
    Whose flocks supply him with attire,
Whose trees in summer yield him shade,
                In winter fire.

Blest, who can unconcern'dly find
    Hours, days, and years slide soft away,   10
In health of body, peace of mind,
                Quiet by day;

Sound sleep by night; study and ease
    Together mixed; sweet recreation,
And innocence, which most does please,
                With meditation.

Thus let me live, unseen, unknown,
    Thus unlamented let me die,
Steal from the world, and not a stone
                Tell where I lie.   20

JOHN MILTON

On His Having Arrived at the Age of Twenty-three

How soon hath Time, the subtle thief of youth,
    Stol'n on his wing my three and twentieth
        year!
My hasting days fly on with full career,

But my late spring no bud or blossom shew'th.
Perhaps my semblance might deceive the truth,
  That I to manhood am arrived so near,
  And inward ripeness doth much less appear,
  That some more timely-happy spirits endu'th.
Yet be it less or more, or soon or slow,
  It shall be still in strictest measure even   10
  To that same lot, however mean or high,
Toward which Time leads me, and the will of
    Heaven;
  All is, if I have grace to use it so,
  As ever in my great task-Master's eye.

JOHN MILTON

On His Blindness

When I consider how my light is spent
  Ere half my days in this dark world and wide,
  And that one talent which is death to hide
  Lodged with me useless, though my soul
    more bent
To serve therewith my Maker, and present
  My true account, lest He returning chide,
  "Doth God exact day-labor, light denied?"
  I fondly ask. But Patience, to prevent
That murmur, soon replies, "God doth not need
  Either man's work or his own gifts. Who best 10
  Bear His mild yoke, they serve Him best. His
    state
Is kingly: thousands at His bidding speed
  And post o'er land and ocean without rest;
  They also serve who only stand and wait."

ROBERT FROST

The Road Not Taken

Two roads diverged in a yellow wood,
And sorry I could not travel both
And be one traveler, long I stood
And looked down one as far as I could
To where it bent in the undergrowth;

Then took the other, as just as fair,
And having perhaps the better claim,
Because it was grassy and wanted wear;
Though as for that the passing there
Had worn them really about the same,   10

And both that morning equally lay
In leaves no step had trodden black.
Oh, I kept the first for another day!
Yet knowing how way leads on to way,
I doubted if I should ever come back.

I shall be telling this with a sigh
Somewhere ages and ages hence:
Two roads diverged in a wood, and I—
I took the one less traveled by,
And that has made all the difference.   20

THE POET AS CRITIC AND PHILOSOPHER

ROBERT GRAVES

Warning to Children

Children, if you dare to think
Of the greatness, rareness, muchness,
Fewness of this precious only
Endless world in which you say
You live, you think of things like this:
Blocks of slate enclosing dappled
Red and green, enclosing tawny
Yellow nets, enclosing white
And black acres of dominoes,
Where a neat brown paper parcel
Tempts you to untie the string.
In the parcel a small island,
On the island a large tree,
On the tree a husky fruit.
Strip the husk and pare the rind off:
In the kernel you will see
Blocks of slate enclosed by dappled
Red and green, enclosed by tawny
Yellow nets, enclosed by white
And black acres of dominoes,
Where the same brown paper parcel—
Children, leave the string alone!
For who dares undo the parcel
Finds himself at once inside it,
On the island, in the fruit,
Blocks of slate about his head,
Finds himself enclosed by dappled
Green and red, enclosed by yellow
Tawny nets, enclosed by black
And white acres of dominoes,
With the same brown paper parcel
Still untied upon his knee.
And, if he then should dare to think
Of the fewness, muchness, rareness,
Greatness of this endless only
Precious world in which he says
He lives—he then unties the string.

JOHN UPDIKE

Energy: A Villanelle

The log gives back, in burning, solar fire
    green leaves imbibed and processed one by
        one;
nothing is lost but, still, the cost grows higher.

The ocean's tons of tide, to turn, require
    no more than time and moon; it's cosmic
        fun.
The log gives back, in burning, solar fire.

All microörganisms must expire
    and quite a few became petroleum;
nothing is lost but, still, the cost grows higher.

The oil rigs in Bahrain imply a buyer   10
    who counts no cost, when all is said and
        done.
The logs give back, in burning, solar fire

but Good Gulf gives it faster; every tire
    is by the fiery heavens lightly spun.
Nothing is lost but, still, the cost grows higher.

So guzzle gas, the leaden night draws nigher
    when cinders mark where stood the blazing
        sun.
The logs give back, in burning, solar fire;
nothing is lost but, still, the cost grows higher.

THOMAS HARDY

The Convergence of the Twain

(*Lines on the loss of the* Titanic)

In a solitude of the sea
Deep from human vanity,
And the Pride of Life that planned her, stilly
couches she.

Steel chambers, late the pyres
Of her salamandrine fires,
Cold currents thrid, and turn to rhythmic tidal
lyres.

Over the mirrors meant
To glass the opulent
The sea-worm crawls—grotesque, slimed, dumb,
indifferent.

Jewels in joy designed   10
To ravish the sensuous mind
Lie lightless, all their sparkles bleared and black
and blind.

Dim moon-eyed fishes near
Gaze at the gilded gear
And query: "What does this vaingloriousness
down here?" . . .

Well: while was fashioning
This creature of cleaving wing,
The Immanent Will that stirs and urges
everything

Prepared a sinister mate
For her—so gaily great—   20
A Shape of Ice, for the time far and dissociate.

And as the smart ship grew
In stature, grace, and hue,
In shadowy silent distance grew the Iceberg
too.

Alien they seemed to be:
No mortal eye could see
The intimate welding of their later history,

Or sign that they were bent
By paths coincident
On being anon twin halves of one august event,   30

Till the Spinner of the Years
Said "Now!" And each one hears,
And consummation comes, and jars two
hemispheres.

RICHARD SHELTON

Alone

what a word and I thought it would be
less disrespectful
old rotten tooth hanging on
there is no radius for this

so here I am
with the rusty motor of hope
sticking out of the sand like a dead arm
well it lasted
long enough it lasted until it was over

it ground the corn and did the dishes   10
and when it started to break down
where could I hide the pieces
with that repairman
looking at my uncouth hair
while I handed him tools always
the wrong one

now I can watch bushes
running their fingers over the legs
of strangers and say why not
let them have whatever   20
they get out of it

under the shadows are more
shadows and under those shadows
is nothing

I have my work to do
inventing new memories
and keeping verbs in the proper mood
somebody has to
and if I walk my defeated secrets
like a dog what's that to you   30
who left by way of the mirror
still believing that rain shows mercy

when how many times did I tell you
the fireflies are naked and cold
in the rags of their light

DONALD W. BAKER

Formal Application

"The poets apparently want to rejoin the human race."

I shall begin by learning to throw
the knife, first at trees, until it sticks
in the trunk and quivers every time,

next from a chair, using only wrist
and fingers, at a thing on the ground,
a fresh ant hill or a fallen leaf,

then at a moving object, perhaps
a pieplate swinging on twine, until
I pot it at least twice in three tries.

Meanwhile, I shall be teaching the birds   10
that the skinny fellow in sneakers
is a source of suet and bread crumbs,

first putting them on a shingle nailed
to a pine tree, next scattering them
on the needles, closer and closer

to my seat, until the proper bird,
a towhee, I think, in black and rust
and gray, takes tossed bread crumbs six feet away.

Finally, I shall coordinate
conditioned reflex and functional   20
form and qualify as Modern Man.

You see the splash of blood and feathers
and the blade pinning it to the tree?
It's called an "Audubon Crucifix."

The phrase has pleasing (even pious)
connotations, like *Arbeit Macht Frei*,
"Molotov Cocktail," and *Enola Gay*.

FORMAL APPLICATION From *Saturday Review* of May 11, 1963. Reprinted by permission of *Saturday Review*.
AT THE UN-NATIONAL MONUMENT ALONG THE CANADIAN BORDER Originally appeared in *Ladies Home Journal*, 1962. Reprinted by permission of the author.
TRIBUTE TO KAFKA FOR SOMEONE TAKEN From *Poems 1961* published by Yale University Press. Copyright 1961 by Alan Dugan. Reprinted by permission of the author.
MIRROR From *Crossing the Water* by Sylvia Plath, published by Faber and Faber and Harper & Row, 1971. The poem originally appeared in *The New Yorker*, August 3, 1963. Copyright © 1963 by Ted Hughes. Reprinted by permission of Harper & Row, Publishers, Inc.

WILLIAM STAFFORD

At the Un-National Monument along the Canadian Border

This is the field where the battle did not happen,
where the unknown soldier did not die.
This is the field where grass joined hands,
where no monument stands,
and the only heroic thing is the sky.

Birds fly here without any sound,
unfolding their wings across the open.
No people killed—or were killed—on this ground
hallowed by neglect and an air so tame
that people celebrate it by forgetting its name.   10

ALAN DUGAN

Tribute to Kafka for Someone Taken

The party is going strong.
The doorbell rings. It's
for someone named me.
I'm coming. I take
a last drink, a last
puff on a cigarette,
a last kiss at a girl,
and step into the hall,
                          bang,
shutting out the laughter. "Is   10
your name you?" "Yes."
"Well come along then."
"See here. See here. See here."

SYLVIA PLATH

Mirror

I am silver and exact. I have no preconceptions.
Whatever I see I swallow immediately
Just as it is, unmisted by love or dislike.
I am not cruel, only truthful—
The eye of a little god, four-cornered.
Most of the time I meditate on the opposite wall.

It is pink, with speckles. I have looked at it so long
I think it is a part of my heart. But it flickers.
Faces and darkness separate us over and over.

Now I am a lake. A woman bends over me,   10
Searching my reaches for what she really is.
Then she turns to those liars, the candles or the
  moon.
I see her back, and reflect it faithfully.
She rewards me with tears and an agitation of
  hands.
I am important to her. She comes and goes.
Each morning it is her face that replaces the dark-
  ness.
In me she has drowned a young girl, and in me an
  old woman
Rises toward her day after day, like a terrible fish.

PERCY BYSSHE SHELLEY

Ozymandias

I met a traveler from an antique land
Who said: Two vast and trunkless legs of stone
Stand in the desert. Near them, on the sand,
Half sunk, a shattered visage lies, whose frown,
And wrinkled lip, and sneer of cold command,
Tell that its sculptor well those passions read
Which yet survive, stamped on these lifeless
  things,
The hand that mocked them, and the heart that
  fed.
And on the pedestal these words appear:
"My name is Ozymandias, king of kings;   10
Look on my works, ye Mighty, and despair!"
Nothing beside remains. Round the decay
Of that colossal wreck, boundless and bare,
The lone and level sands stretch far away.

RANDALL JARRELL

The Death of the
Ball Turret Gunner

From my mother's sleep I fell into the State,
And I hunched in its belly till my wet fur froze.
Six miles from earth, loosed from its dream of life,
I woke to black flak and the nightmare fighters.
When I died they washed me out of the turret
  with a hose.

ROBINSON JEFFERS

Science

Man, introverted man, having crossed
In passage and but a little with the nature of
  things this latter century
Has begot giants; but being taken up
Like a maniac with self-love and inward
  conflicts cannot manage his hybrids.
Being used to deal with edgeless dreams,
Now he's bred knives on nature turns them also
  inward: they have thirsty points though.
His mind forebodes his own destruction;
Actaeon who saw the goddess naked among
  leaves and his hounds tore him.
A little knowledge, a pebble from the shingle,
A drop from the oceans: who would have
  dreamed this infinitely little too much?   10

MATTHEW ARNOLD

Dover Beach

The sea is calm tonight,
The tide is full, the moon lies fair
Upon the straits;—on the French coast the light
Gleams and is gone; the cliffs of England stand,
Glimmering and vast, out in the tranquil bay.
Come to the window, sweet is the night-air!
Only, from the long line of spray
Where the sea meets the moon-blanched land,
Listen! you hear the grating roar
Of pebbles which the waves draw back, and
  fling,   10
At their return, up the high strand,
Begin, and cease, and then again begin,
With tremulous cadence slow, and bring
The eternal note of sadness in.
Sophocles long ago
Heard it on the Aegean, and it brought
Into his mind the turbid ebb and flow
Of human misery; we
Find also in the sound a thought,
Hearing it by this distant northern sea.   20

The Sea of Faith
Was once, too, at the full, and round earth's
    shore
Lay like the folds of a bright girdle furled.
But now I only hear
Its melancholy, long, withdrawing roar,
Retreating, to the breath
Of the night-wind, down the vast edges drear
And naked shingles of the world.

Ah, love, let us be true
To one another! for the world, which seems   30
To lie before us like a land of dreams,
So various, so beautiful, so new,
Hath really neither joy, nor love, nor light,
Nor certitude, nor peace, nor help for pain;
And we are here as on a darkling plain
Swept with confused alarms of struggle and flight,
Where ignorant armies clash by night.

ANTHONY HECHT

The Dover Bitch

A Criticism of Life

So there stood Matthew Arnold and this girl
With the cliffs of England crumbling away
    behind them,
And he said to her, "Try to be true to me,
And I'll do the same for you, for things are
    bad
All over, etc., etc."
Well now, I knew this girl. It's true she had
    read
Sophocles in a fairly good translation
And caught that bitter allusion to the sea,
But all the time he was talking she had in
    mind
The notion of what his whiskers would feel
    like   10
On the back of her neck. She told me later on
That after a while she got to looking out
At the lights across the channel, and really felt
    sad,
Thinking of all the wine and enormous beds
And blandishments in French and the
    perfumes.

THE DOVER BITCH: A CRITICISM OF LIFE   From *The Hard Hours*
by Anthony Hecht. Copyright © 1967 by Anthony E. Hecht.
Reprinted with the permission of Atheneum Publishers.

And then she got really angry. To have been
    brought
All the way down from London, and then be
    addressed
As sort of a mournful cosmic last resort
Is really tough on a girl, and she was pretty.
Anyway, she watched him pace the room   20
And finger his watch-chain and seem to sweat
    a bit,
And then she said one or two unprintable
    things.
But you mustn't judge her by that. What I
    mean to say is,
She's really all right. I still see her once in a
    while
And she always treats me right. We have a
    drink
And I give her a good time, and perhaps it's a
    year
Before I see her again, but there she is,
Running to fat, but dependable as they come,
And sometimes I bring her a bottle of *Nuit
    d'Amour.*

THOMAS GRAY

Elegy

Written in a Country Churchyard

The curfew tolls the knell of parting day,
    The lowing herd wind slowly o'er the lea,
The plowman homeward plods his weary way,
    And leaves the world to darkness and to me.

Now fades the glimmering landscape on the
    sight,
    And all the air a solemn stillness holds,
Save where the beetle wheels his droning
    flight,
    And drowsy tinklings lull the distant folds;

Save that from yonder ivy-mantled tower
    The moping owl does to the moon complain   10
Of such, as wand'ring near her secret bower,
    Molest her ancient solitary reign.

Beneath those rugged elms, that yew-tree's
    shade,
    Where heaves the turf in many a mold'ring
    heap,
Each in his narrow cell forever laid,
    The rude forefathers of the hamlet sleep.

The breezy call of incense-breathing morn,
  The swallow twitt'ring from the straw-built
    shed,
The cock's shrill clarion, or the echoing horn,
  No more shall rouse them from their lowly
    bed.   20

For them no more the blazing hearth shall burn,
  Or busy housewife ply her evening care:
No children run to lisp their sire's return,
  Or climb his knees the envied kiss to share.

Oft did the harvest to their sickle yield;
  Their furrow oft the stubborn glebe has broke;
How jocund did they drive their team afield!
  How bowed the woods beneath their sturdy
    stroke!

Let not Ambition mock their useful toil,
  Their homely joys, and destiny obscure;   30
Nor Grandeur hear with a disdainful smile
  The short and simple annals of the poor.

The boast of heraldry, the pomp of power,
  And all that beauty, all that wealth e'er gave,
Awaits alike th' inevitable hour:
  The paths of glory lead but to the grave.

Nor you, ye proud, impute to these the fault,
  If Mem'ry o'er their tomb no trophies raise,
Where through the long-drawn aisle and fretted
    vault
  The pealing anthem swells the note of
    praise.   40

Can storied urn or animated bust
  Back to its mansion call the fleeting breath?
Can Honor's voice provoke the silent dust,
  Or Flatt'ry sooth the dull, cold ear of Death?

Perhaps in this neglected spot is laid
  Some heart once pregnant with celestial fire;
Hands that the rod of empire might have
    swayed,
  Or waked to ecstasy the living lyre.

But Knowledge to their eyes her ample page,
  Rich with the spoils of time, did ne'er
    unroll;
Chill Penury repressed their noble rage,   50
  And froze the genial current of the soul.

Full many a gem of purest ray serene,
  The dark unfathomed caves of ocean bear:
Full many a flower is born to blush unseen,
  And waste its sweetness on the desert air.

Some village Hampden, that with dauntless
    breast
  The little tyrant of his fields withstood;
Some mute, inglorious Milton here may rest,
  Some Cromwell, guiltless of his country's
    blood.   60

Th' applause of listening senates to command,
  The threats of pain and ruin to despise,
To scatter plenty o'er a smiling land,
  And read their history in a nation's eyes,

Their lot forbade: nor circumscribed alone
  Their growing virtues, but their crimes
    confined;
Forbade to wade through slaughter to a throne,
  And shut the gates of mercy on mankind;

The struggling pangs of conscious truth to
    hide,
  To quench the blushes of ingenuous shame, 70
Or heap the shrine of Luxury and Pride
  With incense kindled at the Muse's flame.

Far from the madding crowd's ignoble strife,
  Their sober wishes never learned to stray;
Along the cool, sequestered vale of life
  They kept the noiseless tenor of their way.

Yet e'en these bones from insult to protect,
  Some frail memorial still erected nigh,
With uncouth rhymes and shapeless sculpture
    decked,
  Implores the passing tribute of a sigh.   80

Their name, their years, spelt by th' unlettered
    Muse,
  The place of fame and elegy supply;
And many a holy text around she strews,
  That teach the rustic moralist to die.

For who, to dumb forgetfulness a prey,
  This pleasing anxious being e'er resigned,
Left the warm precincts of the cheerful day,
  Nor cast one longing lingering look behind?

On some fond breast the parting soul relies,
  Some pious drops the closing eye requires; 90
E'en from the tomb the voice of Nature cries,
  E'en in our ashes live their wonted fires.

For thee who, mindful of the unhonored dead
  Dost in these lines their artless tale relate;
If chance, by lonely contemplation led,
  Some kindred spirit shall inquire thy fate,

Haply some hoary-headed swain may say,
  "Oft have we seen him at the peep of dawn
Brushing with hasty steps the dews away,
  To meet the sun upon the upland lawn.   100

"There at the foot of yonder nodding beech
  That wreathes its old fantastic roots so high,
His listless length at noontide would he stretch,
  And pore upon the brook that babbles by.

"Hard by yon wood, now smiling as in scorn,
  Mutt'ring his wayward fancies he would
      rove;
Now drooping, woeful-wan, like one forlorn,
  Or crazed with care, or crossed in hopeless
      love.

"One morn I missed him on the customed hill,
  Along the heath, and near his fav'rite tree;   110
Another came; nor yet beside the rill,
  Nor up the lawn, nor at the wood was he;

"The next, with dirges due, in sad array,
  Slow through the church-way path we saw
      him borne.
Approach and read (for thou canst read) the
      lay,
  Graved on the stone beneath yon agèd
      thorn."

THE EPITAPH

Here rests his head upon the lap of earth
  A youth to Fortune and to Fame unknown;
Fair science frowned not on his humble birth,
  And Melancholy marked him for her own.   120

Large was his bounty, and his soul sincere;
  Heav'n did a recompense as largely send:
He gave to Mis'ry (all he had), a tear;
  He gained from Heav'n ('twas all he wished)
    a friend.

No farther seek his merits to disclose,
  Or draw his frailties from their dread abode
(There they alike in trembling hope repose),
  The bosom of his Father and his God.

DYLAN THOMAS

In My Craft or Sullen Art

In my craft or sullen art
Exercised in the still night
When only the moon rages

And the lovers lie abed
With all their griefs in their arms,
I labour by singing light
Not for ambition or bread
Or the strut and trade of charms
On the ivory stages
But for the common wages   10
Of their most secret heart.
Not for the proud man apart
From the raging moon I write
On these spindrift pages
Not for the towering dead
With their nightingales and psalms
But for the lovers, their arms
Round the griefs of the ages,
Who pay no praise or wages
Nor heed my craft or art.   20

STEPHEN SPENDER

I Think Continually of Those

I think continually of those who were truly
  great.
Who, from the womb, remembered the soul's
  history
Through corridors of light where the hours are
  suns
Endless and singing. Whose lovely ambition
Was that their lips, still touched with fire,
Should tell of the Spirit clothed from head to
  foot in song.
And who hoarded from the Spring branches
The desires falling across their bodies like blos-
  soms.

What is precious is never to forget
The essential delight of the blood drawn from
  ageless springs   10
Breaking through rocks in worlds before our
  earth.
Never to deny its pleasure in the morning
  simple light
Nor its grave evening demand for love.
Never to allow gradually the traffic to smother
With noise and fog the flowering of the spirit.

Near the snow, near the sun, in the highest
  fields
See how these names are fêted by the waving
  grass
And by the streamers of white cloud
And whispers of wind in the listening sky.
The names of those who in their lives fought
  for life   20
Who wore at their hearts the fire's centre.
Born of the sun they travelled a short while
  towards the sun,
And left the vivid air signed with their honor.

COUNTEE CULLEN

Ultimatum

I hold not with the fatalist creed
Of what must be must be;
There is enough to meet my need
In this most meagre me.

These two slim arms were made to rein
My steed, to ward and fend;
There is more gold in this small brain
Than I can ever spend.

The seed I plant is chosen well;
Ambushed by no sly sweven,   10
I plant it if it droops to hell,
Or if it blooms to heaven.

WILLIAM CARLOS WILLIAMS

Poem

As the cat
climbed over
the top of

ULTIMATUM From *On These I Stand* (1947) by Countee
Cullen. Copyright, 1927 by Harper & Row, Publishers, Inc.;
renewed 1955 by Ida M. Cullen. Reprinted by permission
of Harper & Row, Publishers.
POEM From William Carlos Williams, *Collected Earlier
Poems.* Copyright 1938 by William Carlos Williams. Reprinted by permission of New Directions Publishing Corporation.

the jamcloset
first the right
forefoot

carefully
then the hind
stepped down

into the pit of   10
the empty
flowerpot

WILLIAM CARLOS WILLIAMS

The Term

A rumpled sheet
of brown paper
about the length

and apparent bulk
of a man was
rolling with the

wind slowly over
and over in
the street as

a car drove down   10
upon it and
crushed it to

the ground. Unlike
a man it rose
again rolling

with the wind over
and over to be as
it was before.

HENRY WADSWORTH LONGFELLOW

Chaucer

An old man in a lodge within a park;
The chamber walls depicted all around

THE TERM From William Carlos Williams, *Collected Earlier
Poems.* Copyright 1938 by William Carlos Williams. Reprinted by permission of New Directions Publishing Corporation.

With portraitures of huntsman, hawk, and
   hound,
And the hurt deer. He listeneth to the lark,
Whose song comes with the sunshine through
   the dark   5
Of painted glass in leaden lattice bound;
He listeneth and he laugheth at the sound.
Then writeth in a book like any clerk.
He is the poet of the dawn, who wrote
The Canterbury Tales, and his old age   10
Made beautiful with song; and as I read
I hear the crowing cock, I hear the note
Of lark and linnet, and from every page
Rise odors of ploughed field or flowery mead.

JOHN MILTON

On Shakespeare

What needs my Shakespeare for his honored
   bones,
The labor of an age in piled stones,
Or that his hallowed reliques should be hid
Under a star-ypointing pyramid?
Dear son of memory, great heir of Fame,
What need'st thou such weak witness of thy
   name?
Thou in our wonder and astonishment
Hast built thyself a live-long monument.
For whilst to the shame of slow-endeavoring
   art,
Thy easy numbers flow, and that each heart   10
Hath from the leaves of thy unvalued book,
Those Delphic lines with deep impression
   took,
Then thou our fancy of itself bereaving,
Dost make us marble with too much conceiving;
And so sepulchered in such pomp dost lie,
That kings for such a tomb would wish to die.

RICHARD WILBUR

Year's End

Now winter downs the dying of the year,
And night is all a settlement of snow;
From the soft street the rooms of houses show
A gathered light, a shapen atmosphere,

Like frozen-over lakes whose ice is thin
And still allows some stirring down within.

I've known the wind by water banks to shake
The late leaves down, which frozen where they
   fell
And held in ice as dancers in a spell
Fluttered all winter long into a lake;   10
Graved on the dark in gestures of descent,
They seemed their own most perfect monument.

There was perfection in the death of ferns
Which laid their fragile cheeks against the
   stone
A million years. Great mammoths overthrown
Composedly have made their long sojourns,
Like palaces of patience, in the gray
And changeless lands of ice. And at Pompeii

The little dog lay curled and did not rise
But slept the deeper as the ashes rose   20
And found the people incomplete, and froze
The random hands, the loose unready eyes
Of men expecting yet another sun
To do the shapely thing they had not done.

These sudden ends of time must give us pause.
We fray into the future, rarely wrought
Save in the tapestries of afterthought.
More time, more time. Barrages of applause
Come muffled from a buried radio.
The New-year bells are wrangling with the
   snow.   30

ROBERT LOWELL

For Sale

Poor sheepish plaything,
organized with prodigal animosity,
lived in just a year—
my Father's cottage at Beverly Farms
was on the market the month he died.   5
Empty, open, intimate,
its town-house furniture

YEAR'S END From *Ceremony and Other Poems*, copyright, 1948, 1949, 1950, by Richard Wilbur. Reprinted by permission of Harcourt Brace Jovanovich, Inc.
FOR SALE From *Life Studies* by Robert Lowell. Reprinted by permission of Farrar, Straus & Giroux, Inc. Copyright © 1956, 1959 by Robert Lowell.

had an on tiptoe air
of waiting for the mover
on the heels of the undertaker.   10
Ready, afraid
of living alone till eighty,
Mother mooned in a window,
as if she had stayed on a train
one stop past her destination.   15

T. S. ELIOT

Animula

"Issues from the hand of God, the simple soul"
To a flat world of changing lights and noise,
To light, dark, dry or damp, chilly or warm;
Moving between the legs of tables and of
    chairs,
Rising or falling, grasping at kisses and toys,
Advancing boldly, sudden to take alarm,
Retreating to the corner of arm and knee,
Eager to be reassured, taking pleasure
In the fragrant brilliance of the Christmas tree,
Pleasure in the wind, the sunlight and the sea;   10
Studies the sunlit pattern on the floor
And running stags around a silver tray;
Confounds the actual and the fanciful,
Content with playing-cards and kings and
    queens,
What the fairies do and what the servants say.
The heavy burden of the growing soul
Perplexes and offends more, day by day;
Week by week, offends and perplexes more
With the imperatives of "is and seems"
And may and may not, desire and control.   20
The pain of living and the drug of dreams
Curl up the small soul in the window seat
Behind the *Encyclopaedia Britannica*.
Issues from the hand of time the simple soul
Irresolute and selfish, misshapen, lame,
Unable to fare forward or retreat,
Fearing the warm reality, the offered good,
Denying the importunity of the blood,
Shadow of its own shadows, spectre in its own
    gloom,
Leaving disordered papers in a dusty room;   30
Living first in the silence after the viaticum.

Pray for Guiterriez, avid of speed and power,
For Boudin, blown to pieces,
For this one who made a great fortune,
And that one who went his own way.
Pray for Floret, by the boarhound slain between
    the yew trees,
Pray for us now and at the hour of our birth.

RUDYARD KIPLING

The Way Through the Woods

They shut the road through the woods
Seventy years ago.
Weather and rain have undone it again,
And now you would never know
There was once a road through the woods
Before they planted the trees.
It is underneath the coppice and heath
And the thin anemones.
Only the keeper sees
That, where the ring-dove broods,   10
And the badgers roll at ease,
There was once a road through the woods.

Yet, if you enter the woods
Of a summer evening late,
When the night-air cools on the trout-ringed
    pools
Where the otter whistles his mate,
(They fear not men in the woods,
Because they see so few.)
You will hear the beat of a horse's feet,
And the swish of a skirt in the dew,   20
Steadily cantering through
The misty solitudes,
As though they perfectly knew
The old lost road through the woods. . . .
But there is no road through the woods.

THEODORE ROETHKE

The Waking

I wake to sleep, and take my waking slow.
I feel my fate in what I cannot fear.
I learn by going where I have to go.

We think by feeling. What is there to know?
I hear my being dance from ear to ear.
I wake to sleep, and take my waking slow.

Of those so close beside me, which are you?
God bless the ground! I shall walk softly there,
And learn by going where I have to go.

Light takes the tree; but who can tell us how?   10
The lowly worm climbs up a winding stair;
I wake to sleep, and take my waking slow.

Great Nature has another thing to do
To you and me; so take the lively air,
And, lovely, learn by going where to go.

This shaking keeps me steady. I should know.
What falls away is always. And is near.
I wake to sleep, and take my waking slow.
I learn by going where I have to go.

WALLACE STEVENS

Anecdote of the Jar

I placed a jar in Tennessee,
And round it was, upon a hill.
It made the slovenly wilderness
Surround that hill.

The wilderness rose up to it,
And sprawled around, no longer wild.
The jar was round upon the ground
And tall and of a port in air.

It took dominion everywhere.
The jar was gray and bare.   10
It did not give of bird or bush,
Like nothing else in Tennessee.

RICHARD EBERHART

Rumination

When I can hold a stone within my hand
And feel time make it sand and soil, and see
The roots of living things grow in this land,
Pushing between my fingers flower and tree,
Then I shall be as wise as death,
For death has done this and he will
Do this to me, and blow his breath
To fire my clay, when I am still.

ALFRED, LORD TENNYSON

Ulysses   1942

It little profits that an idle king,
By this still hearth, among these barren crags,
Match'd with an aged wife, I mete and dole
Unequal laws unto a savage race,
That hoard, and sleep, and feed, and know not
   me.
I cannot rest from travel: I will drink
Life to the lees: all times I have enjoy'd
Greatly, have suffer'd greatly, both with those
That loved me, and alone; on shore, and when
Through scudding drifts the rainy Hyades   10
Vext the dim sea: I am become a name;
For always roaming with a hungry heart
Much have I seen and known; cities of men
And manners, climates, councils, governments,
Myself not least, but honor'd of them all;
And drunk delight of battle with my peers,
Far on the ringing plains of windy Troy.
I am a part of all that I have met;
Yet all experience is an arch wherethrough
Gleams that untravel'd world, whose margin
   fades   20
For ever and for ever when I move.
How dull it is to pause, to make an end,
To rust unburnish'd, not to shine in use!
As though to breathe were life! Life piled on life
Were all too little, and of one to me
Little remains; but every hour is saved
From that eternal silence, something more,
A bringer of new things; and vile it were
For some three suns to store and hoard myself,
And this gray spirit yearning in desire   30
To follow knowledge, like a sinking star,
Beyond the utmost bound of human thought.

This is my son, mine own Telemachus,
To whom I leave the scepter and the isle—
Well-loved of me, discerning to fulfil
This labor, by slow prudence to make mild
A rugged people, and through soft degrees
Subdue them to the useful and the good.
Most blameless is he, centred in the sphere
Of common duties, decent not to fail
In offices of tenderness, and pay   40
Meet adoration to my household gods,
When I am gone. He works his work, I mine.
    There lies the port: the vessel puffs her sail:
There gloom the dark broad seas. My mariners,
Souls that have toil'd, and wrought, and thought
  with me—
That ever with a frolic welcome took
The thunder and the sunshine, and opposed
Free hearts, free foreheads—you and I are old;
Old age hath yet his honor and his toil.   50
Death closes all: but something ere the end,
Some work of noble note, may yet be done,
Not unbecoming men that strove with Gods.
The lights begin to twinkle from the rocks:
The long day wanes: the slow moon climbs:
  the deep
Moans round with many voices. Come, my
  friends,
'Tis not too late to seek a newer world.
Push off, and sitting well in order smite
The sounding furrows; for my purpose holds
To sail beyond the sunset, and the baths   60
Of all the western stars, until I die.
It may be that the gulfs will wash us down:
It may be we shall touch the Happy Isles,
And see the great Achilles, whom we knew.
Though much is taken, much abides; and though
We are not now that strength which in old days
Moved earth and heaven, that which we are, we
  are;—
One equal temper of heroic hearts,
Made weak by time and fate, but strong in will
To strive, to seek, to find, and not to yield.   70

WILLIAM BUTLER YEATS

The Second Coming

Turning and turning in the widening gyre
The falcon cannot hear the falconer;
Things fall apart; the centre cannot hold;
Mere anarchy is loosed upon the world,
The blood-dimmed tide is loosed, and
  everywhere

The ceremony of innocence is drowned;
The best lack all conviction, while the worst
Are full of passionate intensity.

Surely some revelation is at hand;
Surely the Second Coming is at hand.   10
The Second Coming! Hardly are those words
  out
When a vast image out of *Spiritus Mundi*
Troubles my sight: somewhere in sands of the
  desert
A shape with lion body and the head of a man,
A gaze blank and pitiless as the sun,
Is moving its slow thighs, while all about it
Reel shadows of the indignant desert birds.
The darkness drops again; but now I know
That twenty centuries of stony sleep
Were vexed to nightmare by a rocking cradle,   20
And what rough beast, its hour come round at
  last,
Slouches towards Bethlehem to be born?

E. E. CUMMINGS

pity this busy monster,manunkind

pity this busy monster,manunkind,

not. Progress is a comfortable disease:
your victim (death and life safely beyond)

plays with the bigness of his littleness
—electrons deify one razorblade
into a mountainrange;lenses extend

unwish through curving wherewhen till unwish
returns on its unself.
           A world of made
is not a world of born—pity poor flesh

and trees,poor stars and stones,but never this   10
fine specimen of hypermagical

ultraomnipotence. We doctors know

a hopeless case if—listen:there's a hell
of a good universe next door;let's go

THE SECOND COMING Reprinted with permission of The Macmillan Company from *Collected Poems* by William Butler Yeats. Copyright 1924 by The Macmillan Company, renewed 1952 by Bertha Georgie Yeats.
PITY THIS BUSY MONSTER,MANUNKIND Copyright 1944, by E. E. Cummings. Reprinted from his volume *Poems 1923—1954* by permission of Harcourt Brace Jovanovich, Inc.

GERARD MANLEY HOPKINS

Spring and Fall

To a Young Child

Márgarét, are you gríeving
Over Goldengrove unleaving?
Leáves, líke the things of man, you
With your fresh thoughts care for, can you?
Áh! ás the heart grows older
It will come to such sights colder
By and by, nor spare a sigh
Though worlds of wanwood leafmeal lie;
And yet you wíll weep and know why.
Now no matter, child, the name: 10
Sórrow's spríngs áre the same.
Nor mouth had, no nor mind, expressed
What heart heard of, ghost guessed:
It ís the blight man was born for,
It is Margaret you mourn for.

SAMUEL TAYLOR COLERIDGE

The Nightingale

No cloud, no relique of the sunken day
Distinguishes the West, no long thin slip
Of sullen light, no obscure trembling hues.
Come, we will rest on this old mossy bridge!
You see the glimmer of the stream beneath,
But hear no murmuring: it flows silently,
O'er its soft bed of verdure. All is still,
A balmy night! and though the stars be dim,
Yet let us think upon the vernal showers
That gladden the green earth, and we shall
    find   10
A pleasure in the dimness of the stars.
And hark! the Nightingale begins its song,
"Most musical, most melancholy" bird!
A melancholy bird? Oh! idle thought!
In Nature there is nothing melancholy.

GERARD MANLEY HOPKINS

As Kingfishers Catch Fire

As kingfishers catch fire, dragonflies dráw fláme;
As tumbled over rim in roundy wells
Stones ring; like each tucked string tells, each
    hung bell's
Bow swung finds tongue to fling out broad its
    name;
Each mortal thing does one thing and the same:
Deals out that being indoors each one dwells;
Selves—goes itself; *myself* it speaks and spells;
Crying *Whát I dó is me: for that I came.*

Í say móre: the just man justices;
Kéeps gráce: thát keeps all his goings graces;   10
Acts in God's eye what in God's eye he is—
Christ—for Christ plays in ten thousand places,
Lovely in limbs, and lovely in eyes not his
To the Father through the features of men's
    faces.

DELMORE SCHWARTZ

The Heavy Bear Who Goes with Me

"The withness of the body"—WHITEHEAD

The heavy bear who goes with me,
A manifold honey to smear his face,
Clumsy and lumbering here and there,
The central ton of every place,
The hungry beating brutish one
In love with candy, anger, and sleep,
Crazy factotum, dishevelling all,
Climbs the building, kicks the football,
Boxes his brother in the hate-ridden city.

Breathing at my side, that heavy animal,   10
That heavy bear who sleeps with me,
Howls in his sleep for a world of sugar,
A sweetness intimate as the water's clasp,
Howls in his sleep because the tight-rope
Trembles and shows the darkness beneath.

THE HEAVY BEAR WHO GOES WITH ME   From Delmore
Schwartz, *Selected Poems: Summer Knowledge.* Copyright
1938 by New Directions. Reprinted by permission of New
Directions Publishing Corporation.

—The strutting show-off is terrified,
Dressed in his dress-suit, bulging his pants,
Trembles to think that his quivering meat
Must finally wince to nothing at all.

That inescapable animal walks with me,   20
Has followed me since the black womb held,
Moves where I move, distorting my gesture,
A caricature, a swollen shadow,
A stupid clown of the spirit's motive,
Perplexes and affronts with his own darkness,
The secret life of belly and bone,
Opaque, too near, my private, yet unknown,
Stretches to embrace the very dear
With whom I would walk without him near,
Touches her grossly, although a word   30
Would bare my heart and make me clear,
Stumbles, flounders, and strives to be fed
Dragging me with him in his mouthing care,
Amid the hundred million of his kind,
The scrimmage of appetite everywhere.

WALT WHITMAN

When I Heard the Learn'd Astronomer

When I heard the learn'd astronomer,
When the proofs, the figures, were ranged in
    columns before me,
When I was shown the charts and diagrams, to
    add, divide, and measure them,
When I sitting heard the astronomer where he
    lectured with much applause in the lecture-
    room,
How soon unaccountable I became tired and
    sick,
Till rising and gliding out I wander'd off by   5
    myself,
In the mystical moist night air, and from time
    to time,
Look'd up in perfect silence at the stars.

ALEXANDER POPE

A Little Learning

A little learning is a dangerous thing;
Drink deep, or taste not the Pierian spring:

There shallow draughts intoxicate the brain,
And drinking largely sobers us again.
Fired at first sight with what the Muse imparts,
In fearless youth we tempt the heights of Arts;
While from the bounded level of our mind
Short views we take, nor see the lengths behind,
But, more advanced, behold with strange
    surprise
New distant scenes of endless science rise!   10
So pleased at first the towering Alps we try,
Mount o'er the vales, and seem to tread the sky;
The eternal snows appear already past,
And the first clouds and mountains seem the last:
But those attained, we tremble to survey
The growing labours of the lengthened way;
The increasing prospect tires our wandering eyes,
Hills peep o'er hills, and Alps on Alps arise!

ALEXANDER POPE

Know Thyself

Know then thyself, presume not God to scan;
The proper study of mankind is Man.
Placed on this isthmus of a middle state,
A being darkly wise and rudely great:
With too much knowledge for the Sceptic side,
With too much weakness for the Stoic's pride,
He hangs between; in doubt to act or rest,
In doubt to deem himself a God or Beast,
In doubt his mind or body to prefer;
Born but to die, and reasoning but to err;   10
Alike in ignorance, his reason such
Whether he thinks too little or too much:
Chaos of thought and passion, all confused;
Still by himself abused, or disabused;
Created half to rise and half to fall;
Great lord of all things, yet a prey to all;
Sole judge of truth, in endless error hurled:
The glory, jest, and riddle of the world!

ROBERT FROST

Sand Dunes

Sea waves are green and wet,
But up from where they die

SAND DUNES From *The Poetry of Robert Frost* edited by
Edward Connery Lathem. Copyright 1923, 1928, 1934, ©
1969 by Holt, Rinehart and Winston, Inc. Copyright 1936,
1942, 1951, © 1956, 1962 by Robert Frost. Copyright ©
1964, 1970 by Lesley Frost Ballantine. Reprinted by permission of Holt, Rinehart and Winston, Inc.

Rise others vaster yet,
And those are brown and dry.

They are the sea made land
To come at the fisher town
And bury in solid sand
The men she could not drown.

She may know cove and cape,
But she does not know mankind   10
If by any change of shape
She hopes to cut off mind.

Men left her a ship to sink:
They can leave her a hut as well;
And be but more free to think
For the one more cast-off shell.

WILFRED OWEN

Dulce et Decorum Est

Bent double, like old beggars under sacks,
Knock-kneed, coughing like hags, we cursed
    through sludge,
Till on the haunting flares we turned our backs,
And towards our distant rest began to trudge.
Men marched asleep. Many had lost their boots,
But limped on, blood-shod. All went lame, all
    blind;
Drunk with fatigue; deaf even to the hoots
Of gas-shells dropping softly behind.

Gas! Gas! Quick, boys!—An ecstasy of fumbling,   10
Fitting the clumsy helmets just in time,
But some one still was yelling out and stumbling
And flound'ring like a man in fire or lime.
Dim through the misty panes and thick green
    light,
As under a green sea, I saw him drowning.

In all my dreams before my helpless sight
He plunges at me, guttering, choking, drowning.

If in some smothering dreams, you too could pace
Behind the wagon that we flung him in,

And watch the white eyes wilting in his face,
His hanging face, like a devil's sick of sin,   20
If you could hear, at every jolt, the blood
Come gargling from the froth-corrupted lungs
Obscene as cancer, bitter as the cud
Of vile, incurable sores on innocent tongues,—
My friend, you would not tell with such high zest
To children ardent for some desperate glory,
The old lie: *Dulce et decorum est*
Pro patria mori.

ARTHUR HUGH CLOUGH

Say Not the Struggle Nought Availeth

Say not the struggle nought availeth,
    The labor and the wounds are vain,
The enemy faints not, nor faileth,
    And as things have been they remain.

If hopes were dupes, fears may be liars;
    It may be, in yon smoke concealed,
Your comrades chase e'en now the fliers,
    And, but for you, possess the field.

For while the tired waves, vainly breaking,
    Seem here no painful inch to gain,   10
Far back, through creeks and inlets making,
    Comes silent, flooding in, the main.

And not by eastern windows only,
    When daylight comes, comes in the light,
In front, the sun climbs slow, how slowly,
    But westward, look, the land is bright.

A. E. HOUSMAN

"Terence, This Is Stupid Stuff . . ."

"Terence, this is stupid stuff:
You eat your victuals fast enough;
There can't be much amiss, 'tis clear,

DULCE ET DECORUM EST From *The Collected Poems of Wilfred Owen*, by Wilfred Owen. Copyright © 1963 by Chatto and Windus Ltd. Reprinted by permission of New Directions.

To see the rate you drink your beer.
But oh, good Lord, the verse you make,
It gives a chap the belly-ache.
The cow, the old cow, she is dead;
It sleeps well, the horned head:
We poor lads, 'tis our turn now
To hear such tunes as killed the cow.   10
Pretty friendship 'tis to rhyme
Your friends to death before their time
Moping melancholy mad:
Come, pipe a tune to dance to, lad."

Why, if 'tis dancing you would be,
There's brisker pipes than poetry.
Say, for what were hop-yards meant,
Or why was Burton built on Trent?
Oh many a peer of England brews
Livelier liquor than the Muse,   20
And malt does more than Milton can
To justify God's ways to man.
Ale, man, ale's the stuff to drink
For fellows whom it hurts to think:
Look into the pewter pot
To see the world as the world's not.
And faith, 'tis pleasant till 'tis past:
The mischief is that 'twill not last.
Oh I have been to Ludlow fair
And left my necktie God knows where,   30
And carried half-way home, or near,
Pints and quarts of Ludlow beer:
Then the world seemed none so bad,
And I myself a sterling lad;
And down in lovely muck I've lain,
Happy till I woke again.
Then I saw the morning sky:
Heigho, the tale was all a lie;
The world, it was the old world yet,
I was I, my things were wet,   40
And nothing now remained to do
But begin the game anew.

Therefore, since the world has still
Much good, but much less good than ill,
And while the sun and moon endure
Luck's a chance, but trouble's sure,
I'd face it as a wise man would,
And train for ill and not for good.
'Tis true, the stuff I bring for sale
Is not so brisk a brew as ale: 50
Out of a stem that scored the hand

I wrung it in a weary land.
But take it: if the smack is sour,
The better for the embittered hour;
It should do good to heart and head
When your soul is in my soul's stead;
And I will friend you, if I may,
In the dark and cloudy day.

There was a king reigned in the East:
There, when kings will sit to feast,   60
They get their fill before they think
With poisoned meat and poisoned drink.
He gathered all that springs to birth
From the many-venomed earth;
First a little, thence to more,
He sampled all her killing store;
And easy, smiling, seasoned sound
Sate the king when healths went round.
They put arsenic in his meat
And stared aghast to watch him eat;   70
They poured strychnine in his cup
And shook to see him drink it up:
They shook, they stared as white's their shirt:
Them it was their poison hurt.
—I tell the tale that I heard told.
Mithridates, he died old.

ALFRED, LORD TENNYSON

The Eagle

He clasps the crag with crooked hands;
Close to the sun in lonely lands,
Ring'd with the azure world, he stands.

The wrinkled sea beneath him crawls;
He watches from his mountain walls,
And like a thunderbolt he falls.

WILLIAM WORDSWORTH

The World Is Too Much with Us

The world is too much with us; late and soon,
Getting and spending, we lay waste our powers:
Little we see in Nature that is ours;
We have given our hearts away, a sordid boon!
This Sea that bares her bosom to the moon;

The winds that will be howling at all hours,
And are up-gathered now like sleeping flowers;
For this, for everything, we are out of tune,
It moves us not.—Great God! I'd rather be
A Pagan suckled in a creed outworn;   10
So might I, standing on this pleasant lea,
Have glimpses that would make me less forlorn;
Have sight of Proteus rising from the sea;
Or hear old Triton blow his wreathed horn.

ROBERT FROST

Good-by and Keep Cold

This saying good-by on the edge of the dark
And cold to an orchard so young in the bark
Reminds me of all that can happen to harm
An orchard away at the end of the farm
All winter, cut off by a hill from the house.
I don't want it girdled by rabbit and mouse,
I don't want it dreamily nibbled for browse
By deer, and I don't want it budded by grouse.
(If certain it wouldn't be idle to call
I'd summon grouse, rabbit, and deer to the
    wall   10
And warn them away with a stick for a gun.)
I don't want it stirred by the heat of the sun.
(We made it secure against being, I hope,
By setting it out on a northerly slope.)
No orchard's the worse for the wintriest storm;
But one thing about it, it mustn't get warm.
"How often already you've had to be told,
Keep cold, young orchard. Good-by and keep
    cold.
Dread fifty above more than fifty below."
I have to be gone for a season or so.   20
My business awhile is with different trees,
Less carefully nourished, less fruitful than these,
And such as is done to their wood with an ax—
Maples and birches and tamaracks.
I wish I could promise to lie in the night
And think of an orchard's arboreal plight
When slowly (and nobody comes with a light)
Its heart sinks lower under the sod.
But something has to be left to God.

ROBERT FROST

Mending Wall

Something there is that doesn't love a wall,
That sends the frozen-ground-swell under it,
And spills the upper boulders in the sun;
And makes gaps even two can pass abreast.
The work of hunters is another thing:
I have come after them and made repair
Where they have left not one stone on a stone,
But they would have the rabbit out of hiding,
To please the yelping dogs. The gaps I mean,
No one has seen them made or heard them
    made,   10
But at spring mending-time we find them there.
I let my neighbor know beyond the hill;
And on a day we meet to walk the line
And set the wall between us once again.
We keep the wall between us as we go.
To each the boulders that have fallen to each.
And some are loaves and some so nearly balls
We have to use a spell to make them balance:
'Stay where you are until our backs are turned!'
We wear our fingers rough with handling
    them.   20
Oh, just another kind of outdoor game,
One on a side. It comes to little more:
There where it is we do not need the wall:
He is all pine and I am apple orchard.
My apple trees will never get across
And eat the cones under his pines, I tell him.
He only says, 'Good fences make good neighbors.'
Spring is the mischief in me, and I wonder
If I could put a notion in his head:
'*Why* do they make good neighbors? Isn't it   30
Where there are cows? But here there are no
    cows.
Before I built a wall I'd ask to know
What I was walling in or walling out,
And to whom I was like to give offense.
Something there is that doesn't love a wall,
That wants it down.' I could say 'Elves' to him,
But it's not elves exactly, and I'd rather
He said it for himself. I see him there
Bringing a stone grasped firmly by the top
In each hand, like an old-stone savage armed.   40

He moves in darkness as it seems to me,
Not of woods only and the shade of trees.
He will not go behind his father's saying,
And he likes having thought of it so well
He says again, 'Good fences make good neighbors.'

WILLIAM BLAKE

The Tyger

Tyger! Tyger! burning bright
In the forests of the night:
What immortal hand or eye,
Could frame thy fearful symmetry?

In what distant deeps or skies
Burnt the fire of thine eyes?

On what wings dare he aspire?
What the hand dare seize the fire?

And what shoulder, and what art,
Could twist the sinews of thy heart?   10
And when thy heart began to beat,
What dread hand? and what dread feet?

What the hammer? what the chain?
In what furnace was thy brain?
What the anvil? what dread grasp
Dare its deadly terrors clasp?

When the stars threw down their spears,
And water'd heaven with their tears,
Did he smile his work to see?
Did he who made the Lamb make thee?   20

Tyger! Tyger! burning bright
In the forests of the night:
What immortal hand or eye,
Dare frame thy fearful symmetry?

Notes on the Poets

Notes on the Poets

CONRAD AIKEN (1889–1973), born in Savannah, Georgia, was a poet, fiction writer and critic. A leader among American poets after World War I, he contributed to *The Dial*, the distinguished literary magazine that published works of young authors and supported new artistic movements. In 1930 he was awarded a Pulitzer Prize for his *Selected Poems*, and in 1950–51 he was consultant on poetry to the Library of Congress. His *Collected Poems* appeared in 1970 and his autobiographical work *Ushant* in 1971.

MATTHEW ARNOLD (1822–1888), an English poet and critic greatly interested in social and religious topics, was strongly affected by the science of his day. In both his poetry and his prose he revealed wide learning and a deep respect for culture, which he defined as "the best that has been thought and said in the world."

W. H. AUDEN (1907–1973), born in England and educated at Oxford University, was, in the 1930's, a leader of a group of young English poets writing about the political and social problems of the day. Auden, later a naturalized American citizen, subsequently turned to more religious and philosophical concerns in his poetry. Two of his later works are *About the Home*, 1965, and *Secondary Worlds*, 1968.

DONALD W. BAKER (1923–   ), an American poet and critic, has taught English at both Brown University and Wabash College. He has published critical reviews of various modern poets, including James Dickey.

JOHN BETJEMAN (1906–   ), English poet, attended Oxford University. Writing with the same polish and wit on architectural subjects as he does in his poetry, Betjeman has been a book critic for the *Daily Telegraph*, a weekly columnist for the *Spectator*, an essayist, and a radio and television performer. In 1972 he was appointed Poet Laureate of Great Britain.

Among his latest works are *Collected Poems*, 1971, and *A Pictorial History of English Architecture*, 1972.

WILLIAM BLAKE (1757–1827), the self-educated son of a London tradesman, was a rare combination of poet and painter. In his lyrics and in his highly original paintings, notably those for *The Book of Job*, he expressed a mystical awareness of the divine.

JOSEPH BRODSKY (1940–   ), one of the most promising Russian writers by the time he was 23, migrated to New York City, became an American citizen, and teaches poetry and writing courses at Columbia University and New York University. He once translated the poems of John Donne into Russian and taught himself Polish while he was imprisoned by the Soviets. He published *Selected Poems* in 1974 and *Modern Russian Poets on Poetry* in 1976. He appears regularly in the best periodicals and is now considered a major poet in both Western Europe and the United States.

RUPERT BROOKE (1887–1915), after a short but brilliant poetic career, enlisted in the British Army in World War I, and died of sunstroke. His best poems are probably his sonnets.

GWENDOLYN BROOKS (1917–   ), currently editor of *The Black Position*, won the Pulitzer Prize in 1949 for her second book of poems, *Annie Allen*. Since then she has published a novel, *Maud Martha*, 1953, an autobiography, *Report from Part One*, 1972, and further volumes of poetry. Her latest collections are *Family Pictures*, 1970, and *Aloneness*, 1971.

ELIZABETH BARRETT BROWNING (1806–1861), wife of the English poet Robert Browning and a major poet in her own right, wrote a classic volume of sonnets, *Sonnets from the Portuguese*, 1850. She and her husband lived for long periods in Florence, Italy, where she died.

ROBERT BROWNING (1812–1889), English poet of the Victorian period, wrote for many years without attracting public attention or critical approval, but he lived to become a hero in the literary world, with cults founded solely to study his works. He is especially known for his employment of the dramatic verse monologue to reveal character and personality.

GEORGE GORDON, LORD BYRON (1788–1824), poet, dramatist, critic, and soldier, was born in London and educated at Harrow and Trinity College, Cambridge University. A friend of Shelley's, he was a great force in the Romantic movement in poetry in the nineteenth century. He died of fever en route to join the Greeks in their fight for freedom in 1824.

G. K. CHESTERTON (1874–1936), often called the master of paradox, began his literary career as a critic of art books. A versatile writer, he published fiction (he is best remembered in this field as the creator of Father Brown, a whimsical priest-detective), biography, criticism, poetry, essays, and plays.

JOHN CIARDI (1916–   ), a major American poet and critic, won his first notable poetry prize while he was earning his M.A. at the University of Michigan. He has taught at several colleges in the United States and abroad. His translation of Dante's *Inferno* and *Purgatorio* won wide acclaim. At the *Saturday Review* he served for many years as poetry editor, and later as a columnist. He has published many volumes of poetry. *In Fact*, 1963, offers a good sampling of his verse.

LUCILLE CLIFTON (1936–   ) is currently artist-in-residence at Coppin State College, Baltimore, Maryland. Her first volume of poems, *Good Times*, appeared in 1969. More recently, she has written nonfiction as well as poetry. Her latest works include *An Ordinary Woman*, 1974, and *Generations*, 1976.

ARTHUR HUGH CLOUGH (1819–1861), poet and teacher, received his early education at Rugby, where he fell under the influence of Thomas Arnold, Rugby's great headmaster and Matthew Arnold's father. At Oxford he acquired religious doubts that influenced his later thinking and writing. Like Matthew Arnold, he was troubled by the effect of scientific discovery on traditional religious doctrines.

LEONARD COHEN (1934–   ), poet, novelist, musician, and songwriter, was born in Montreal, Quebec, and graduated from McGill University. *Let Us Compare Mythologies*, 1956, his first collection of poetry, was followed by five additional volumes. Then he published two novels, *The Favorite Game*, 1963, and *Beautiful Losers*, 1966.

SAMUEL TAYLOR COLERIDGE (1772–1834), was educated at Cambridge University. He became a major poet of the Romantic movement and was a friend of William Wordsworth's with whom he published *Lyrical Ballads*, 1798. His best-known poem is *"The Rime of the Ancient Mariner."*

COUNTEE CULLEN (1903–1946), a poet who was popular during the twenties and thirties, wrote seven volumes of verse (*Color*, 1925, was the first; *On These I Stand*, 1947, the last), largely about the feelings and aspirations of blacks.

E. E. CUMMINGS (1894–1962), was born in Cambridge, Massachusetts, and was educated at Harvard University. He published many volumes of verse and prose. The unconventional punctuation and form of his poetry are technical devices which indicate the way the poem should be read and which he felt gave purer and clearer expression of his thought. His *73 Poems* was published in 1963. A posthumous volume of his *Complete Poems* was issued in 1968.

WALTER DE LA MARE (1873–1956), English essayist, novelist, and poet, wrote for children and adults alike. Although his novel, *Memoirs of a Midget*, 1921, received the James Tait Black Award, de la Mare is remembered primarily for his mysterious and melodic poetry. His most famous collection of verse, *Come Hither*, appeared in 1923.

EMILY DICKINSON (1830–1886), now considered one of America's greatest poets, spent most of her life in self-imposed seclusion. She published only seven poems in her lifetime and did not win a wide audience until after her death. Though her poems are brief, they show close observation, intensity, and illuminating, often whimsical, metaphor.

JOHN DONNE (1572–1631), who, after an intense spiritual struggle, became the most famous Anglican preacher of his day, won his lasting reputation not so much for his *Sermons* as for two groups of poems, the love lyrics of his youth and the religious lyrics of his maturity.

ERNEST DOWSON (1867–1900), an English poet, whose single book of poems was published in 1896, is known for a poem entitled "Non Sum Qualis Eram Bonae Sub Regno Cynarae," or most often called "Cynara." Much of the fame of this poem rests on Margaret Mitchell's use of part of one of its lines as the title of her novel *Gone with the Wind*.

ALAN DUGAN (1923–   ), was born in Brooklyn, attended Olivet College and Mexico City College, and served in the U.S. Air Force in World War II. He received his first award for poetry in 1946. Since then he has received the National Book Award for Poetry in 1961, the Pulitzer Prize for Poetry in 1962, and a Guggenheim Fellowship in 1963–64. He has published *Poems*, 1961, and *Poems 2*, 1963. His *Collected Poems* appeared in 1969.

RICHARD EBERHART (1904–   ), is an American poet, playwright, and educator. In 1930 his *A Bravery of Earth* appeared. Since then he has published numerous volumes of poetry, including *Fields of Grace*, 1972, and *Poems to Poets*, 1975, and, in 1966, he was awarded the Pulitzer Prize. His *Collected Poems, 1930–1976* was published in 1976. He was named Poet Laureate of New Hampshire in 1979. *Of Poetry and Poets* and *Survivors* were published in 1979 and *Ways of Light* in 1980.

T. S. ELIOT (1888–1965), an American-born critic and poet who became a British citizen, influenced a whole generation of writers, particularly through his long poem *The Waste Land*. His major theme is the frustration and the consequent spiritual inadequacy of our times.

JOHN FANDEL (1925–   ), a professor of English at Manhattan College, is also poetry editor of *Commonweal*. His first collection of poems, *The Season's Difference*, was published while he was a college senior. In addition to privately issued works, he has published a further volume, *Testament*, 1959, and a sequel, *Body of Earth*, 1972.

DONALD FINKEL (1929–   ), currently poet-in-residence at Washington University in St. Louis, has published poetry in *The New Yorker*, *Atlantic Monthly*, and *Paris Review*, and in various anthologies. His published volumes of poetry include *The Clothing's New Emperor*, *A Joyful Noise*, and *Answer Back*.

ROBERT FROST (1874–1963), though born in San Francisco, was identified with the New England of his forebears. As a young man, he taught, farmed, and wrote poetry there—all with little initial success. Not until he went to England for the years 1912–15 did he come to

the attention of critics and public. After his return to New England, his reputation grew steadily. He won the Pulitzer Prize four times and is considered one of the greatest American poets.

ROBERT GRAVES (1895–   ), an English novelist, poet, and critic, was elected to the Chair of Poetry at Oxford University in 1961. Both as poet and as novelist, he displays a wide, thorough scholarship and an active imagination. His poetry often does not seem to be in either the American or British tradition. In 1961 his *Collected Poems* appeared. A later work is entitled *Poems 1968–1970*, 1971.

THOMAS GRAY (1716–1771) was born in London and educated at Eton and Cambridge University. He refused the poet laureateship in 1757 and became professor of history and modern languages at Cambridge. He wrote much poetry, the most often read of which is his "Elegy Written in a Country Churchyard," set in the churchyard at Stoke Poges, where he is buried.

RAYMOND GRIFFITH (1925–   ), professor of English at the University of Wisconsin at Whitewater, was educated at New York University and Loyola University in Chicago. He has taught at Punjab University in India, Kyung Hee University in Korea, and North Staffordshire Polytechnic University in England. His poems have been published in *Saturday Review*, *College Composition and Communication*, in journals in India, and in other anthologies.

THOM GUNN (1929–   ) is an English poet whose verse often deals with violence in the contemporary scene. He is a graduate of Cambridge University and has taught at the University of California at Berkeley. His fifth volume of poems, *Touch*, came out in 1968.

THOMAS HARDY (1840–1928), one of the two or three English writers who have produced both great poetry and great novels, was trained as an architect. His earliest writings were poems; about 1870 he turned to the novel and wrote all his novels in the succeeding twenty-six years. In 1896, discouraged by harsh criticism of *Jude the Obscure*, which he had written a year earlier, he returned to poetry. In this final period of his work he wrote *The Dynasts*, 1904–08, a great epic drama in verse and the most ambitious of his poems.

ANTHONY HECHT (1923–   ), a prolific poet and

translator, was educated at Bard College and Columbia University. He has translated the plays of Aeschylus, the essays of Voltaire, and poems of Joseph Brodsky. He has received many grants, fellowships, and honors, including a Pulitzer Prize and a fellowship in the American Academy of Poets. Many volumes of his poetry are in print, including *A Summoning of Stones*, 1954, and *Venetian Vespers*, 1979.

ROBERT HERRICK (1591–1674), the most popular of the Cavalier poets, was, like Donne, a churchman as well as a poet. Like Donne, too, he is best known for his love lyrics and religious lyrics. His graceful, light secular poems usually treat of the simple pleasures of life and of love.

GERARD MANLEY HOPKINS (1844–1889), a brilliant Oxford graduate, became converted to Roman Catholicism and entered the priesthood. His poetry, which was experimental in its imagery and rhythm, was not known until 1918, when Robert Bridges published a volume of his verse.

A. E. HOUSMAN (1859–1936), English scholar and poet, was not a prolific writer; he produced only three small volumes of lyrics. But the simplicity, irony, and flawlessness of these lyrics place him among the chief English poets.

TED HUGHES (1930–   ), born in Yorkshire, England, was married to the American poet Sylvia Plath. Since the appearance of his book of poems *Hawk in the Rain*, 1957, he has been considered by many as one of the foremost poetic talents of our day. *Wodwo*, 1967, is typical of his themes, attitudes, and arresting imagery. His books include *Crow*, 1971; *Under the North Star*, 1981; and *New Selected Poems*, 1982.

RANDALL JARRELL (1914–1965), American poet, taught at several universities; in 1956–58 he was poetry consultant to the Library of Congress. His poetry, greatly influenced by his experiences in World War II, shows his deep reaction to the tragedies of life and to the courage of many who face those tragedies. His *Complete Poems* was issued posthumously in 1968.

ROBINSON JEFFERS (1887–1962) has been called American poetry's apostle of negation. Jeffers' poetic line resembles Whitman's in length, vigor, and rhythm, but the philosophies of the two poets are at opposite poles. Jeffers' creed is the renunciation of humanity and the glorification of unspoiled nature.

JOHN KEATS (1795–1821) learned Latin, French, and history on his own and was apprenticed to an apothecary. Later he passed the examinations in surgery. But his love for literature caused him to turn to poetry, for which he is greatly known. His friend Shelley wrote the famous elegy "Adonais" upon Keats's untimely death.

X. J. KENNEDY (1929–   ), former editor of *Paris Review*, currently teaches at Tufts University. In 1961 his *Nude Descending a Staircase* won the Lamont Award for Poetry.

RUDYARD KIPLING (1865–1936), journalist, short-story writer, and poet, wrote largely of his stay in India, his love of the sea, the jungle, wild beasts, and his military experiences. His poetry has been variously judged, but during his time, at least, it was greatly liked.

HENRY WADSWORTH LONGFELLOW (1807–1882) was born in Maine and educated at Bowdoin College, where he was a classmate of Nathaniel Hawthorne. Later he was professor of modern languages at Bowdoin and Harvard University. He is best known for his long poems "Evangeline" and "Hiawatha" and for "Paul Revere's Ride."

ROBERT LOWELL (1917–1977), American poet, wrote much about New England, commemorating his ancestors who settled there and became influential in American life; he was a great-grandnephew of James Russell Lowell. In 1940 he converted to Catholicism, and many of his poems written since then reflect his religious thinking. He was awarded the Pulitzer Prize in 1947 for his volume of poetry *Lord Weary's Castle*. Lowell's recent work includes *The Old Glory* (three plays based on stories by Hawthorne and Melville), 1964; *Notebooks 1967–1968*, 1969; *History*, 1973; and *Day by Day*, 1977.

LUCIAN (c. 120–c. 200), Greek poet, satirist, and wit, came to literary notice after the Roman Empire had expanded to include Greece. He is considered the first classical writer to have composed satirical dialogue. His writing has been compared to that of Swift and Voltaire.

PHYLLIS MCGINLEY (1905–1978) was a writer of light verse. She published several volumes and contributed widely to national magazines.

In 1961 she won the Pulitzer Prize for Poetry. *Times Three*, one of her most popular volumes, first appeared in 1954; *A Wreath of Christmas Legends* appeared in 1967.

ARCHIBALD MACLEISH (1892–1982), an important public figure as well as a literary man, was Librarian of Congress and an undersecretary of state. In 1949, he was awarded the Boylston Professorship of Rhetoric and Oratory at Harvard University. He published many notable works in poetry and drama, including *The Great American Fourth of July Parade*, a verse play for radio, in 1975.

JOHN MANIFOLD (1915–   ), poet and musicologist, was born in Australia and educated at Cambridge University. Though he uses a variety of poetic forms, he shows a mature control of them; his poetry stresses action and lyricism. His volume, *Opus 8: Poems 1961–69*, appeared in 1971; his *Collected Verse* appeared in 1978.

ANDREW MARVELL (1621–1678) was educated at Cambridge University and became in 1657 assistant to John Milton, who was Latin secretary to the Council of State. His poetry at first was chiefly lyrical. Later he turned to political satire in verse.

EDNA ST. VINCENT MILLAY (1892–1950), Pulitzer Prize winner for poetry in 1923, was born in Rockland, Maine, attended school at Vassar College, and, after a varied career as journalist, actress, dramatist, and libretto writer, devoted the remainder of her life to writing poetry. Her verse is distinguished by its passionate zest for life, its revolt against Victorian prudery, and its intense emotions. *Renascence and Other Poems*, published in 1917, established her reputation among the brilliant poets of her generation.

L. L. MILLER (1923–   ), a native Kansan, is a professor of English at St. John's Lutheran College in Winfield, Kansas. His poems have been printed in several magazines, and he has been awarded prizes for his light verse. He is an officer of the Kansas Authors Club.

JOHN MILTON (1608–1674), one of the greatest poets of the late Renaissance, was educated at Christ's College, Cambridge. He served as Latin secretary to the Council of State under Oliver Cromwell, during which time he became blind. The Restoration of Charles II brought both political and financial reverses to Milton, who was an ardent Puritan and a champion of political freedom. Though he is best known as the author of the epic *Paradise Lost*, he was also an important sonnet writer.

HOWARD NEMEROV (1920–   ) is an American writer of poetry, short stories, and novels. He has published several volumes beginning in 1947 with a book of poems, *The Image and the Law*. His subsequent works include *The Blue Swallows*, 1967; *The Winter Lightning*, 1968; *Gnomes and Occasions*, 1973; and *The Western Approaches, Poems 1973–75*, 1975. *The Collected Poems of Howard Nemerov* appeared in 1977.

JOHN FREDERICK NIMS (1913–   ), is an American poet and teacher. He uses both traditional and modern verse forms and derives his symbols from the harshness and violence of the present-day world. *Of Flesh and Bone*, 1967, is a good representation of his work. His most recent volume, *Western Wind*, appeared in 1974.

WILFRED OWEN (1893–1918), British poet of World War I, returned to the Western Front after having been wounded and invalided home, was decorated for gallantry, and was killed in action one week before the Armistice.

DOROTHY PARKER (1893–1967), short-story writer, poet, and wit, is noted for her multi-faceted humor—ironic, sarcastic, tender, comic. She has been admired for the technical expertise of her verse as well as her candor and humor. Some critic once wrote that to read her poems is equivalent to seeing Dorothy Parker through the wrong end of a telescope. Two major works are *Not So Deep as a Well*, 1926, and *Here Lies*, 1930.

SYLVIA PLATH (1923–1963), a poet who was married to the British poet Ted Hughes, was a distinctive voice both in the intensely personal character of her poems and in her precise, vivid images. Her books of poems are *The Colossus*, 1962; *Uncollected Poems*, 1965; and *Ariel*, 1966, a posthumous volume. A novel, *The Bell Jar*, was published in 1962. She committed suicide in 1963.

EDGAR ALLAN POE (1809–1849) was born to actors, orphaned early, attended various schools here and in England, finally withdrawing from West Point to pursue a career in journalism. He is best known for his many short stories and for defining the form precisely. He also wrote some well-known poems, among them "The Raven," "Annabel Lee," and "Ulalume," and he is still much admired in France, where he was a strong influence on the imagist movement earlier in this century. See also the note preceding his story "The Tell-Tale Heart" in Part Two.

ALEXANDER POPE (1688–1744) was ill from the age of twelve and largely self-educated. He showed his poetic skill by the time he was sixteen and published his first poetry in 1709. He is famous for his verse essays "An Essay on Man" and "Essay on Criticism" and for his odes. He assisted many of the poets and dramatists of his day, so he was close to many of the other great writers of his time.

EZRA POUND (1885–1972), an expatriate American, published his first poetry in 1909. Though not widely popular, his work, especially the *Cantos*, has rivaled that of Eliot in its influence upon other poets. Moreover, Pound's suggestions and criticisms significantly affected Eliot's own masterwork, *The Wasteland*. Pound's *Selected Poems*, 1957, has perhaps the greatest interest for the general reader.

JOHN CROWE RANSOM (1888–1974), a native Tennessean, attended Vanderbilt and Oxford universities. Until his death he was Carnegie Professor of Poetry at Kenyon College. One of America's leading literary critics, Ransom founded and, until 1958, edited the *Kenyon Review*. Among his works are *Chills and Fever,* 1924; *Two Gentlemen in Bonds,* 1927; and *Collected Poems,* 1963.

HENRY REED (1914–   ) is an English poet, critic, and radio dramatist. In his first poems he satirized the bureaucracy during World War II and, in 1947, he adapted Melville's *Moby Dick* for radio.

ADRIENNE RICH (1929–   ) won the Yale Series of Younger Poets Prize in 1951 for her first collection of poems, A *Change of World*, published while she was still an undergraduate at Radcliffe. She has also received many awards for her other volumes of poetry, *The Diamond Cutters, Snapshots of a Daughter-in-Law,* and *Necessities of Life.* In 1976 she published *Of Woman Born*, a study of motherhood.

EDWIN ARLINGTON ROBINSON (1869–1935), three-time Pulitzer Prize winner, is in the first rank of American poets. He wrote character studies in verse, revealing the inner triumphs and outward failures of man.

THEODORE ROETHKE (1908–1963), born in Michi-

gan and educated at the University of Michigan and Harvard University, was a public relations counsel and a tennis coach, then a teacher of English at the University of Washington. His poetry was first published in 1930; later he held Guggenheim fellowships and received the Pulitzer Prize for Poetry in 1953.

CARL SANDBURG (1878–1967), poet, Lincoln biographer, and authority on American folk songs, worked as a barber, a dishwasher, and a harvest hand, among other jobs, before his thoughts turned to literature during his college days. This background equipped him well to write about the vitality and variety of American life. In 1940 Sandburg was awarded the Pulitzer Prize for History for *Abraham Lincoln: The War Years.* His volumes of poetry include *Smoke and Steel,* 1920; *Slabs of the Sunburnt West,* 1922; *The People, Yes,* 1936; *Honey and Salt,* 1963. In 1951 his *Complete Poems* won the Pulitzer Prize for Poetry. In line, language, and subject matter he extends the Whitman tradition.

DELMORE SCHWARTZ (1913–1966), born in Brooklyn and educated at the University of Wisconsin, New York University, and Harvard, was a poet, translator, critic, and fiction writer. He was editor of *Partisan Review* and poetry editor of the *New Republic.* Among his publications are a translation of Arthur Rimbaud's A *Season in Hell,* 1939; *The Imitation of Life and Other Problems of Literary Criticism,* 1941; *Summer Knowledge: New and Selected Poems 1938–58,* 1959; *Successful Love and Other Stories,* 1961.

WILLIAM SHAKESPEARE (1564–1616), England's, and perhaps the world's, greatest dramatic poet, produced some thirty plays, many of which contain memorable short songs. Apart from his plays, his chief work was a sonnet sequence.

PERCY BYSSHE SHELLEY (1792–1822), English Romantic poet, was an idealist who revolted against tyranny in all forms—political, social, and moral—and who led an unconventional life in accordance with his ideals. His major theme is the possibility of human perfection.

RICHARD SHELTON (1933–   ), currently a member of the English faculty at the University of Arizona, has contributed poems to numerous literary and popular periodicals, including *The New Yorker.* Among his published works are

Journal of Return, 1969; *Calendar,* 1972; *Of All the Dirty Words,* 1972; and *The Bus to Veracruz,* 1978.

SIR PHILIP SIDNEY (1554–1586) was educated at Oxford University and traveled on the Continent, meeting the painters Titian and Veronese in Venice. The author of a sonnet series, "Astrophel and Stella," he was interested in using classical meters from Greek and Latin poetry in English verse. Spenser dedicated "The Shepheardes Calendar" to Sidney and wrote an elegy to him upon his death.

LOUIS SIMPSON (1923–   ) is an American poet and novelist who migrated from the British West Indies to the United States in 1940. He is known for his editorial work on the two volumes of *New Poets of England and America,* 1957, and for several volumes of his own poetry, including *Selected Poems,* 1965. He has also written a novel and several critical works, the most recent of which, *Three on the Tower,* 1975, examines the lives and works of T. S. Eliot, Ezra Pound, and William Carlos Williams.

STEPHEN SPENDER (1907–   ), English poet, writer, and critic, was a fellow student of W. H. Auden at Oxford University and was much influenced by Auden in his political and social thought. He was also interested in painting and in printing, actually setting up a press and supporting himself by printing jobs. In 1933 his first noticed book of poetry, *Poems,* was published, followed by other volumes of poetry, drama, and criticism. Spender believes that literature should have a social purpose and deal with social values.

WILLIAM STAFFORD (1914–   ) is a college English professor. He has published much poetry. Among his later works are *Traveling Through the Dark,* 1962; *The Rescued Year,* 1966; and *Allegiances,* 1970.

WALLACE STEVENS (1879–1955) studied law at Harvard University and New York Law School and made his career in insurance, becoming vice president of the Hartford Accident and Indemnity Company. At the same time he was steadily publishing his poetry and gaining literary stature. He won a Pulitzer Prize in the last year of his life and is considered one of America's important poets.

SIR JOHN SUCKLING (1607–1642) was an English lyric poet, the inventor of cribbage, a politi-cal leader, and, above all, a bon vivant. He was a great wit and a highly gifted writer of lyric poetry.

JULIAN SYMONS (1912–   ) is an Englishman with an extremely versatile career as a writer. His thirty-some-odd books include poetry, criticism, biography, TV plays, and novels. His specialization is crime fiction and his most recent works include *The Plot Against Roger Rider,* 1973; *A Three Pipe Problem,* 1975; and *The Hungry Thirties,* 1976.

ALFRED, LORD TENNYSON (1809–1892) is in many ways the poet who best represents the spirit of Victoria's England. After an early period of neglect and adverse criticism, he won great public favor, which he held to his death. He became poet laureate in 1850.

DYLAN THOMAS (1914–1953), considered by many the greatest lyric poet of the younger generation of his time, was born in the Welsh seaport of Swansea. He was early steeped in Welsh lore and poetry and in the Bible, all of which left their mark on his rich, startling imagery and driving rhythm. He made his living by radio broadcasting, scenario writing, storytelling, and readings of his poetry. His first book, *Eighteen Poems,* was published when he was twenty. His *Collected Poems, 1934–1952* contains, in the poet's own words, "All, up to the present year, that I wish to preserve."

EDWARD THOMAS (1878–1907), English poet, whose work shows his special consciousness of language as the heart of his imagery, was a member of a group of English and American poets who adhered to the Romantic tradition of the nineteenth century, though the new spirit of the technological civilization was influencing many of their fellow poets.

JOHN UPDIKE (1932–   ), the well-known American author and poet, attended Harvard and Oxford universities. After a brief career as a reporter for *The New Yorker,* he became a free-lance writer in 1957. His second novel, *Rabbit, Run,* 1959, considered a major contemporary work, gained him wide recognition. In addition to contributing to many major national periodicals, Updike has recently published several works, including *Rabbit Redux,* 1971, *A Month of Sundays,* 1975, and *Rabbit Is Rich,* 1981.

E. B. WHITE (1899–   ) is an essayist, poet, short-story writer, and editor, widely known for his writing in *The New Yorker* and *Harper's*. Also, he has revised William Strunk's *Elements of Style,* a handbook White used as a student.

WALT WHITMAN (1819–1892) created the free verse form. His *Leaves of Grass,* published in 1855, was a revolutionary book. In it Whitman spoke as the prophet of democracy and a worshiper of the common man. His technique has influenced two generations of later poets, including Sandburg, MacLeish, and Jeffers.

RICHARD WILBUR (1921–   ) was born in New York City, grew up in New Jersey, attended Amherst College and Harvard University, and taught at Harvard. He has received a Guggenheim Fellowship, the Prix de Rome of the American Academy of Arts and Sciences, and, in 1957, a Pulitzer Prize. In addition to his own poetry, Wilbur has published translations of Molière's *The Misanthrope, Tartuffe,* and, most recently, *The School for Wives.*

WILLIAM CARLOS WILLIAMS (1883–1963), born in New Jersey and trained as a physician at the University of Pennsylvania and in Europe, combined the writing of poetry with the practice of medicine. His ability to find concrete images that convey his ideas and attitudes puts him in the first rank of American poets. His poetry achieves a clear artistic unity of idea and form.

HAROLD WITT (1923–   ) was born in California and studied at the University of California at Berkeley and the University of Michigan. He is a librarian and writer who has published several volumes of verse and contributed poems to *Saturday Review* and *The New Yorker.* His *Death of Venus,* 1958, won him the Hopwood Prize for Poetry and the Phelan Award for Narrative Poetry. Later, he wrote *Now, Swim,* 1974; and *Winesburg by the Sea: Poems,* 1979.

WILLIAM WORDSWORTH (1770–1850), English Romantic poet, found most of his subjects in nature and the life of simple people. He had the genius to see and record the beauty and wonder of the familiar.

ELINOR WYLIE (1885–1828), whose poems are always controlled, exact, and brilliant, was in her personal life a rebel against social convention. Her peak of popularity came in the early 1920's when, as the wife of William Rose Benét, she took an active part in the literary life of New York City.

WILLIAM BUTLER YEATS (1865–1939), foremost figure of the Irish literary renaissance and one of the great poets of our century, was also an editor, folklorist, and playwright and took an active interest in politics. His best poetry is sinewy, conversational, and musical.

Glossary

ABSURDISM: A post-World War II school of drama, based on existentialism, which rejects the realistic and naturalistic drama of the first half of the century in favor of an unstructured, non-rational, often actionless, highly verbal drama. The characters are portrayed as lost and lonely, feeling responsible only to and for themselves in a world that is "absurd." Samuel Beckett's *Waiting for Godot* is considered the finest example of absurdist theatre. Pinter's *The Birthday Party* is a more recent classic.

ACCENT: Stress or emphasis given to a poetic syllable or metrical foot. *See* Prosody.

ACT: A major devision in a play or opera, which is often further divided into scenes.

ACTION: The sequence of selected events or occurrences forming the narrative or plot of a short story, novel, play, or poem.

ALEXANDRINE: *See* Hexameter.

ALLEGORY: A narrative, often an elaborated metaphor, in which persons and objects stand for concepts beyond the narrative itself. *See* Figurative Language.

ALLITERATION: The repetition of initial consonant sounds or of accented consonant sounds. *See* Rime; Texture.

ALLUSION: An indirect reference to something beyond the denotation of the words spoken or written. Willie Morris in "The Awakening" alludes to "Ivy League colleges," by which he means a group of eight prestigious private Eastern colleges, which he contrasts to tax-supported state universities.

AMBIGUITY: A situation in which the words have more than one possible interpretation, with the intended meaning not indicated; ambiguity can also be used to create awareness of two or more meanings simultaneously.

ANALOGY: The pointing out of some areas of resemblance in two different things usually not thought of as being similar.

ANAPEST: A metrical foot consisting of two unstressed syllables followed by one stressed syllable.

ANTAGONIST: The opponent of the main character in a literary work.

ARGUMENTATION: One of the four types of discourse in rhetoric, argumentation is planned specifically to convince by giving reasons to prove that its thesis is valid. *See* Essay.

ARTICLE: A short piece of non-fiction that presents its views for a periodical. Often "article" is used as a synonym for "essay," but frequently it is also used to designate a piece of writing that does not have the quality of an essay. An article is often hastily written, intended to be timely rather than lasting; yet articles often achieve the status of literary essays.

ASIDE: A remark made by an actor on stage but directed to the audience and assumed not to be heard by anyone on stage. Its purpose is to provide information to the audience or to evoke some particular reaction from the audience to the action, characters, or setting.

ASSONANCE: Repetition of similar vowel sounds (such as *grave* and *gain*) which are not followed, as in rime, by similar consonants. *See* Texture.

BALLAD: In its original form a simple, highly concentrated narrative or story poem, often sung. The more polished "literary" ballad is a conscious artistic imitation by an identified writer. *See* Narrative Poetry.

BLANK VERSE: Unrimed iambic pentameter, as in Shakespeare's plays. *See* Prosody; Stanza.

BURLESQUE: The completely distorted treatment of a serious idea or conversely, the treatment of a trivial idea in a serious manner.

CACOPHONY: Harsh, unpleasant sound. *See* Euphony; Texture.

CADENCE: Rhythmic, though not regularly metrical, flow of language. Cadence is influenced by many of the factors that determine rhythm. *See* Rhythm.

CAESURA: A pause within a line of poetry. *See* Prosody.

CATASTROPHE: The last major scene following the climax of a tragic play, also called the *denouement*.

CATHARSIS: The positive emotional relief from the tension and anxiety of a tragic play when the final action makes the audience fully conscious of the protagonist's defeat and certain destruction. Essentially, it is that almost pleasurable feeling one has when a terrible event has occurred and is over. It is often referred to as "tragic catharsis."

CHARACTERIZATION: The shaping of characters by use of the dramatic devices: description, dialogue, circumstance, action, setting, and others. Along with plot and setting, it is the third of the basic components of drama.

CHORUS: In Greek drama a group led by the *choragos* in singing, dancing and declaiming to provide information and comment upon the theme, characters, and action of the play, as in Sophocles' *Antigonê* in Part Three.

CLIMAX: The point—a line, a sentence, a gesture, an action—in a piece of fiction, poetry, or drama when the greatest intensity is felt and the readers or viewers are most deeply moved because they now know how the work will end.

COMEDY: A drama that differs from tragedy primarily because the theme, problem, or conflict is resolved happily for the protagonist. Tragedy begins with the same kind of theme, problem, or conflict but ends in the destruction of the protagonist. Much of what is frequently labeled comedy in the mass media is technically farce or burlesque, and similarly, what is called comic is most often farcical. *See* Drama.

COMPLICATION: The increased complexity of plot, structure, or idea that thickens the plot and so involves the reader or viewer more and more.

CONCEIT: An impressive, unusual, or clever thought, perhaps in the form of an involved or distorted metaphor. The conceit is most often a device in Elizabethan poetry. In Part Four, Frost's "The Silken Tent" is a modern example of the use of a conceit.

CONFLICT: The struggle that a character has with another character, or with circumstance, fate, or self.

CONNOTATION: Those meanings developed by a word beyond its specific dictionary denotation. *Dogs* are "quadruped, carnivorous mammals," but dogs are sometimes "human feet," as in "my dogs are tired," or infantrymen ("dog-faces"), weapons ("dogs of war"), rascals or pranksters ("you dog!") or frankfurters ("hot dogs"). *See* Denotation.

CONSONANCE: Identity of consonants in non-riming words (such as *deer, door*); they are not rimes because the vowels differ. *See also* Texture.

COUPLET: The form of verse with two successive stanzas riming. *See* Stanza.

DACTYL: A metrical foot consisting of one stressed syllable followed by two unstressed syllables. *See* Meter; Prosody.

DENOTATION: A specific actual thing or idea as defined in a dictionary (such as *dog:* "a quadruped, carnivorous mammal") as opposed to connotation, the associative, emotive meanings implied by the context. Thus, one begins with a denotation and adds connotations as they evolve.

DENOUEMENT: That last point in a play when all the complications have been disentangled for a fortunate outcome (comedy), or when the audience realizes that no disentanglement is possible logically and an unfortunate outcome for the protagonist is a certainty (tragedy). *See* Comedy; Tragedy.

DESCRIPTION: One of the four types of discourse in rhetoric. Description is used generally to present character or setting. *See* Essay.

DEUS EX MACHINA (Latin for "the god from the machine"): In drama, the use of an unlikely or improbable literary, dramatic, or (in the case of the Greek drama) mechanical device to resolve an unfortunate situation in the plot of the play. In Greek drama it was an actual physical device by which a god could be lowered onto the stage to set things right for the protagonist by virtue of his divine authority. In melodrama the deus ex machina is essential to turn misfortune into a happy ending, even when the situation seems so desperate as to promise only a tragic ending. *See* Drama.

DIALOGUE: Conversation between two or more characters. The speech of a single character, as in Strindberg's *The Stronger* (Part Three) or

Browning's "Soliloquy of the Spanish Cloister" (Part Four), is called a *monologue*.

DIDACTIC: Instructive, often designed to provide a moral lesson.

DIMETER: A two-foot line of verse. *See* Meter; Prosody.

DRAMA: Generally, drama is divided into four main types: tragedy, comedy, melodrama, and farce. *Tragedy* is a serious, dignified play ending in catastrophe. It focuses on the struggle of a central protagonist moving toward an inevitable destiny. *Comedy*, also a serious form of drama, is written and performed to entertain by ending happily. It often deals with people in their "human" state, limited and made ridiculous by their faults and animal nature. *Melodrama* is serious drama with suggestion of the tragic turned comic by a trick: a *deus ex machina* or the interposition of a character or situation that makes the happy ending occur without acceptable motivation. *Farce* is drama concerned with amusement, so that any seeming seriousness disappears before the ending, and the outcome is not of any importance. In fact, farce results from the deliberate distortion of the tragic or comic to the point of being inconsequential to the audience, and the plot, characters, or setting are amusing because of their improbability. *See* Comedy; Tragedy.

DRAMATIC: Having the components or qualities associated with a play: plot, character, dialogue, scene, suspense, climax, etc. Fiction or poetry is classified as dramatic, or scenic, if it is primarily communicated through dialogue , as in Hemingway's "A Clean, Well-Lighted Place" in Part Two, or if it relies on suspense building to a climax. Some fine examples of dramatic poetry are Browning's monologues "My Last Duchess" and "Soliloquy of the Spanish Cloister" in Part Four.

DRAMATIS PERSONAE: Cast of characters in a play, usually provided in a list at the beginning of the text.

ELEGY: A subjective, meditative poem expressing emotions of grief, especially for the death of someone. The great elegies are songs of grief for the death of a close friend or great person: for example, Milton's "Lycidas," on the death of a classmate; and Auden's "In Memory of W. B. Yeats" (in Part Four), in honor of a great fellow-poet.

ELLIPSIS: The omission of a word or words that are grammatically necessary but not essential to meaning. In writing, three periods (. . .) signify an ellipsis.

EMPATHY: An audience's identifying with a dramatic situation on stage or in writing so completely that the emotion generated is mutually shared.

END-STOPPED LINE: A line whose metrical end coincides with the sentence structure and the meaning.

ENJAMBMENT: A term signifying the running on of the sense of a line into the next line, ignoring the metrical end of the line. See Raymond Griffith's poem "Essay on Enjambment" in Part Four.

ESSAY: A short non-fiction composition with a single thesis or topic. Essays are informal (familiar or personal) or formal, depending upon their topic, structure, diction, and tone. Having its origins in Greek rhetoric, generally the essay can be divided into four types: *Argumentation* is an attempt to prove the truth or falsity of some proposition; *description*, which is most often used in conjunction with another of the essay forms, provides a detailed description of a scene, setting, or situation; *exposition* explains the nature of an object, an idea, or a thesis; and *narration* relates the details of an event or the sequence of details in a series of events. *See* Argumentation; Description; Exposition; Narration; Rhetoric.

EUPHONY: Sound combinations that are pleasing to the ear, the opposite of cacophony. *See* Cacophony; Texture.

EXISTENTIALISM: A post-World War II philosophical movement which stresses that people are lonely but free, and are responsible for determining their own fate by the choices they make.

EXPOSITION: One of the four types of discourse in rhetoric, exposition is a kind of writing that "sets forth" or explains a thesis or topic. "To grow orchids successfully one needs to do the following four things" would be an example of a topic for an expository paper. Peter Woolfson in "Speech Is More than Language" (Part One) uses the expository mode. He does not argue; he simply presents the ideas that satisfy him that there is a difference between speech and language. *See* Essay.

EXPRESSIONISM: Any presentation that presents

life not realistically but by means of highly subjective symbols.

EYE-RIME: A terminal pairing of words or syllables that appear from the spelling to rime but in pronunciation do not, as *yea* and *tea.*

FABLE: A generally simple tale that points up some truth about human nature and sometimes makes a moral statement in its conclusion. Some of these are anonymous, handed down from one generation to the next, but some are conscious literary compositions.

FARCE: A play involving amusing, exaggerated situations and characters, where the outcome is unimportant and the actions and characterizations are of chief concern for their amusement value. *See* Comedy; Drama.

FICTION: A short story, novel, or play composed from the writer's stock of "literary" truth out of his imagination, but perhaps including historical and scientific truth also. *See* the Introduction to Part Two.

FIGURATIVE LANGUAGE: Words used out of their denotative sense and in their connotative senses to convey a special effect and meaning. Many figures of speech are based on comparison or intensification. The more common figures are simile and metaphor, which are based on comparison. Other figurative devices are symbol and allegory. Personification, hyperbole, synecdoche, understatement, and irony also provide figurative elements.

FLASHBACK: A passage that interrupts the forward time sequence of a short story, novel, or play to go back to a former time.

FOOT: A metrical unit composed of any of a variety of combinations of stressed and unstressed syllables, with the exception of the spondee, which has two stressed syllables.

FORESHADOWING: Giving the reader or viewer hints of action or outcome to follow.

FREE VERSE: Verse with irregularly patterned meter and length of line.

GENRE: A classification into which literary works are placed according to their form. For example, *short story, novel, poem,* and *play* are literary genres.

HEPTAMETER: A seven-foot line of verse. *See* Meter; Prosody.

HEXAMETER: A six-foot line of verse; also called *Alexandrine. See* Meter; Prosody.

HUBRIS: Excessive, uncontrollable pride and self-confidence in a protagonist, which enlarges the "tragic flaw" that ultimately destroys. King Creon in *Antigonê* and Lear in *King Lear* are examples of characters whose hubris causes their downfall.

HYPERBOLE: A figure of speech using intentional overstatement, not intended to be taken literally. *See* Understatement; Figurative Language.

IAMB: A metrical foot consisting of one unstressed syllable followed by one stressed syllable. *See* Meter; Prosody.

IMAGERY: The presentation of sensory experience in words, using allusions and figurative language. W. H. Auden's "Look, Stranger, on This Island Now" (Part Four) has some memorable imagery.

INTERNAL RIME: Rime occurring within a single line of poetry. *See* Rime.

IRONY: A broad term describing a contrast between what appears to be and reality. In *verbal irony,* a meaning opposite to the literal meaning of the words is intended; in *irony of situation,* a situation or effect opposite to the expected and normally appropriate one exists; and in *dramatic irony,* significant facts or events not known to the relevant characters on stage are given to the audience or reader.

ITALIAN SONNET: *See* Sonnet.

LIMERICK: Comic nonsense verse with five lines rimed *aabba,* usually with the *a* lines in anapestic trimeter and the *b* lines in anapestic dimeter.

LINE: A structural unit of verse. The poetic line is described by the predominant kind of metrical foot and the number of feet it contains. *See* Meter; Prosody.

LYRIC: A poem meant to be sung, or an especially musical or highly subjective poem; one of the three main types of poetry. *See* Poetry.

MASQUE: A staged entertainment of elaborate presentation but simple content. Ben Jonson produced masques for the court of Queen Elizabeth I.

MELODRAMA: *See* Drama.

METAPHOR: The figure of speech that compares or identifies an object in one class to an object in another class, without using *as* or *like.* Broadly, figurative language in general. *See* Simile.

METER: The relationship of stressed and unstressed syllables, designating both the kind of metrical foot and the number of feet in a line of verse. *See* Prosody; Rhythm.

METONYMY: A figurative device by which one thing is used to represent another because one is suggestive of the other, the two having a recognizable attribute in common. Byron in a poem refers to Belgium's "beauty" and "chivalry," suggesting Belgium's beautiful women and gallant men. Metonymy and synecdoche, which are closely related, are special kinds of metaphor. See Synecdoche; Metaphor.

MONOMETER: A one-foot line of verse. See Meter; Prosody.

MOOD: The overall atmosphere or emotional tone of a work. See Tone.

MOTIVATION: The inner causes or external situations that help shape character.

MYTH: Traditionally, an anonymous story of gods or superhuman characters that explains some phenomenon to primitive people. Common themes dealt with in myths are fertility and creation, temptation and fall, renewal and rebirth. Every culture has its own mythology, the best-known to English readers being the myths of the Greeks, Romans, and Norse.

NARRATION: One of the four types of discourse in rhetoric, narration relates an event or series of events. Though it may exist alone as a piece of writing, it is most often accompanied by description. See Essay; Rhetoric.

NARRATIVE: A true or fictional story that is *told*, not enacted; the term is also used to designate the *story poem*, one of the three main types of poetry.

NATURALISM: Chiefly, that type of fiction portraying man as a puppet of heredity and environment, as opposed to Realism or Expressionism.

NOVEL: Any extended work of prose fiction, usually dealing with well-established characters (either static or dynamic), situations, and settings. Henry Fielding's *Tom Jones* is an early example of the genre.

NOVELLA (NOUVELLE): A novelette or short novel, falling in length between a short story and a novel, and embodying many of the characteristics of both. See Novel; Short Story.

OCTAVE: An eight-line stanza; also, the first eight lines of a sonnet. See Sonnet.

ODE: Usually a long, formal lyric poem, complex in meter and form, commemorating a special occasion, object, or quality. The ode was originally a Greek form of dramatic poetry, choral in nature.

OMNISCIENCE: The point of view in which the author knows everything about every character's inner and outer being and circumstances.

ONOMATOPOEIA: Words formed in imitation of the natural sounds they name. See Texture.

PARABLE: A simple story with a rather obvious moral truth, usually conveyed by comparison with an actual situation. See Allegory.

PARADOX: A seemingly self-contradictory statement or circumstance.

PARODY: An imitation of the language, style, and ideas of another work for comic or critical effect.

PASTORAL: A type of classical poetry that deals with rural life; also, any favorable treatment of rural life. See Lyric; Poetry.

PATHOS: The quality that produces sympathy or pity; unlike tragedy, pathos is aroused by the unresisting and innocent, not by the active and struggling. *Bathos* is exaggerated pathos or a descent into the trivial and ridiculous.

PENTAMETER: A five-foot line of verse. See Meter; Prosody.

PERSONIFICATION: The figure of speech in which human qualities are given to nonhuman objects or abstractions. See Figurative Language.

PETRARCHAN SONNET: See Sonnet.

PLOT: In its simplest interpretation, plot is a series of sequential causally related episodes or actions used to achieve a desired effect or outcome. A plot's action usually centers on a conflict, which builds to a climax followed by a denouement or resolution. See Climax; Conflict; Crisis; Complication.

POETRY: Generally, poetry is divided into several main types: *narrative poetry* (story poems); *dramatic* poetry, which uses many of the methods of drama itself; and *lyric poetry*, which is highly musical, emotional, and subjective. Some types of dramatic poetry are the dramatic monologue and the verse-drama. Types of lyric poetry include the elegy, the hymn, the sonnet, and the ode. See Dramatic; Lyric; Narrative.

POINT OF VIEW: The "eye" through which the story is seen and the consciousness that reports and interprets the material. Briefly, there are two basic points of view, the *first-person* and the *omniscient*. In the former, a narrator, the "I" telling the story, can report only what the narrator knows of events and characters. The first-person narrator may be either a main character or a minor one; in either case, what can be reported is greatly limited. The second point of view, the omniscient, is a third-person point of view with three subdivisions, depending on how much omniscience is displayed and how much the narrator intrudes into the story. In the first subdivision, the *third-person* story, the author moves freely in and out of the minds of any and all characters. In the second, the *central intelligence* story, the author chooses to move in and out of the mind of only one character. And in the third, the *scenic* story, the author chooses to present the characters in their words and deeds without invading their consciousness at all. *See* the Introduction to Part Two.

PROSODY: In general, the art or study of metrical composition. A fuller discussion of prosody will be found at the end of this glossary, on pages 640–41.

PROTAGONIST: The main character in drama or fiction.

QUATRAIN: A four-line stanza with any of a number of end-rime schemes. *See* Prosody.

REALISM: A literary treatment meant to portray life as it is, generally by focusing on selected ordinary details and everyday human experience.

RHETORIC: The art of presenting facts and ideas in effectively organized and appealing language. Rhetoric may be classified into four forms of discourse: argumentation, description, exposition and narration. *See* Argumentation; Description; Exposition; Narration.

RHYTHM: Literally, measured movement. In language, rhythm results primarily from meter, the relationship of stressed and unstressed syllables or sounds, though pitch, tempo, syllabic length, and sentence structure are other influential factors. *See* Meter.

RIME: Usually refers to end rime, the similarity or correspondence of words or the terminal sounds of words at the end of a line of verse; but, in general, rime is any degree of correspondence of sound combinations in a line, whether terminal or internal. Slant or partial rime is an approximate correspondence of sounds. Textural effects—assonance, consonance, alliteration—are themselves forms of rime. *See* Prosody; Texture.

RIME SCHEME: The patterns of end rime in a stanza. *See* Prosody.

ROMANTICISM: Treatment in highly imaginative ways of varied, dynamic, even improbable materials. Often the term is used derogatorily to mean exaggerated, over-idealized material, especially as opposed to realism.

RUN-ON LINE: *See* Enjambment.

SATIRE: Material that focuses on human weaknesses and follies with humor and wit, sometimes lightly, sometimes bitterly.

SCANSION: *See* Prosody.

SCENE: A division of an act in a play; also, the setting or locale of an action.

SESTET: A six-line stanza; also, the last six lines of a sonnet. *See* Sonnet.

SETTING: The temporal and spatial background—especially the latter—in which the action of a story occurs.

SHAKESPEAREAN SONNET: *See* Sonnet.

SIMILE: The figure of speech that expresses with *as* or *like* a resemblance of an object of one class to an object of another class. *See* Figurative Language; Metaphor.

SLANT RIME: Loose or approximate rime (such as *run* and *tone*). *See* Rime.

SOLILOQUY: A dramatic monologue which is understood to be the speaker talking to himself or to the audience, but not to another character.

SONNET: A poem of fourteen lines in iambic pentameter. The Petrarchan or Italian sonnet commonly divides itself into an octave (eight lines) riming *abbaabba*, in which the theme is presented, and a sestet (six lines), usually riming *cdecde*, in which the conclusion to the theme is presented. The Shakespearean sonnet, riming *ababcdcdefefgg*, commonly develops the theme in three quatrains (four lines each) and concludes it in a couplet. *See* Prosody.

SPONDEE: A metrical foot consisting of two stressed syllables. *See* Meter; Prosody.

STANZA: A pattern of lines and rimes in verse. Stanzas are identified on the basis of the type of meter, number of metrical feet in each line, number of lines, and the pattern of rime when rime is employed. Many stanzaic patterns have been long established and have conventional names—for example, couplet, ballad quatrain, Spenserian. Blank verse (unrimed iambic pentameter) and other non-stanzaic verse forms (such as free verse) may be broken into verse paragraphs, which are determined more by content than by form. *See* Prosody.

STORY: Any account, either true or imaginary, of

actions or events. In fiction, a story is a collection of sequentially arranged events and as such is an essential ingredient of plot. In journalism, the term is used to designate a news account. "Story" is often erroneously used as a synonym for essay.

STREAM OF CONSCIOUSNESS: Flow of thought that is associational, elliptical, fragmented as it runs through a character's mind, not organized by exterior logic or thought.

STRESS: Emphasis given a syllable in poetry.

SUBPLOT: Minor series of events, which may reinforce or contrast with the events of the main plot.

SUPPORTING DATA: In an essay, the examples, evidence, explanation, comments, quotations, etc., that reinforce the main idea or thesis.

SYMBOL: In the broadest sense, something that suggests or stands for an idea, quality, or conception larger than itself (the lion as the symbol of courage, the flag as the symbol of a nation). In poetic usage, a symbol is a more central and pervasive comparison than either simile or metaphor, often providing the basic imagery of an entire poem. It represents a step beyond metaphor in that the first term of the comparison is not supplied. See Figurative Language.

SYMBOLISM: Any use of concrete story elements—things, situations, scenes, or characters—to signify something relatively abstract.

SYNECDOCHE: A figure of speech in which the part of a thing is made to represent the whole thing, or vice versa. In one poet's words "palm and pine" refer to the vast extent of the British Empire at its height (part for whole). In a headline like "America Beats Italy in Olympic Soccer," *America* and *Italy* mean the Olympic soccer teams from America and Italy (whole for part). Synecdoche is common in everyday speech and writing as well as in poetry. Synecdoche and metonymy are related as figures of association. See Metaphor; Metonymy.

TETRAMETER: A four-foot line of verse. See Meter; Prosody.

TEXTURE: As applied to poetry, texture is the general relationship of sounds, usually not including the more exact forms of rime. Important textural devices are cacophony, euphony, onomatopoeia, alliteration, assonance, and consonance. See Rime.

THEME: The central idea or underlying meaning of a literary work, which may be either implied or directly stated. See Thesis.

THESIS: The attitude or position toward an idea taken by a writer or speaker with the purpose of explaining, supporting, or proving it. In an essay, the thesis, or main idea, is often expressed explicitly in a thesis statement.

TONE: The attitude conveyed by the writer toward his or her subject.

TRAGEDY: In drama, a series of causally related events in the life of a protagonist which, treated in a dignified, serious manner, results in a catastrophe. Classical Greek tragedy emphasizes the noble protagonist's poor choice, dictated by a "tragic flaw," which results in downfall. Later tragedies departed in various ways from the classical definition of the form. See the Introduction to Part Three.

TRAGICOMEDY: A drama with all the characteristics of a tragedy, but which ends happily as in a comedy, after an "unexpected" intervention of a deus ex machina. See Drama.

TRAGIC FLAW: A weakness, though not necessarily a true moral defect, leading to an unfortunate choice, which results in the downfall of the hero.

TRIMETER: A three-foot line of verse. See Meter; Prosody.

TROCHEE: A metrical foot consisting of one stressed and one unstressed syllable. See Meter; Prosody.

UNDERSTATEMENT: The figure of speech also known as *litotes*, in which less is said than is meant and than might normally be expected. See Figurative Language; Irony.

UNITIES: The singleness of action, time, and place in a play. A play should have no secondary plot that is not directly relevant to the main action, should not cover a stretch of time greater than a day, and should be confined to a single setting.

VERSE: A single line of a poem; also, poetry in general as contrasted with prose. Sometimes the term is used disparagingly in reference to light poetry or to poetry of inferior quality.

VILLANELLE: A highly structured verse form with an intricate pattern of repeated lines, using only two rimes. Dylan Thomas's "Do Not Go Gentle into That Good Night" is a famous example. Another example is John Updike's "Energy: A Villanelle."

PROSODY

Prosody, generally defined as the "science of versification," rises above mere attention to the mechanical considerations of metrical structure to become an art of communication in which the sound furthers the sense and in which the sense intensifies the sound. Since English verse is primarily dependent upon emphasis given a syllable rather than on length of syllable), English prosody is much a matter of studying the occurrence of accents.

The prosodic structure of a stanza is analyzed by a process known as *scansion.* In scanning, one examines (1) the prevailing metrical foot; (2) the line length; (3) the placement of pauses; and (4) the number of lines and, if the verse is rimed, the pattern of end rime.

1. METRICAL FEET

Iamb: Unaccented syllable, accented syllable (a-gó).

Trochee: Accented syllable, unaccented syllable (dwél-ling).

Anapest: Two unaccented syllables, accented syllable (of the sún).

Dactyl: Accented syllable, two unaccented syllables (mér-ri-ly).

Spondee: A fifth kind of metrical foot, in which two consecutive accented syllables from different metrical feet occur or in which a primary and secondary accent occur consecutively (pláy-hóuse).

2. LINE

The line length in metrical feet is *monometer* if the line has one foot, *dimeter* if two feet, *trimeter* if three, *tetrameter* if four, *pentameter* if five, *hexameter* (*Alexandrine*) if six, *heptameter* if seven, *octameter* if eight. In theory there may be more than eight feet in a line, but in practice a line longer than heptameter tends to break up into two or more lines.

3. PAUSES

Also important, especially in blank verse, alliterative verse, and the heroic couplet, is the location of pauses ending sense units—phrases, clauses, sentences—within the line. A main pause, known as the *caesura,* and secondary pauses are common. (In scansion they are indicated by the symbols / / and / .) A line is termed *end-stopped* when it ends with a sense pause, *run-on* when the sense extends into the next line.

Little verse is metrically perfect, for metrical perfection does not permit the flexibility necessary to combine sense and sound most fittingly. Nearly all English verse is iambic, but substitution of another type of foot is common and substantial passages of trochee, dactyl, and anapest can be found.

4. PATTERN OF LINES AND RIMES

The number of lines and the rime pattern are described as *couplet* (*aa*); *tercet* or *triplet* (*terza rima, aba-bcb-cdc,* etc.); *quatrain* (*ballad, abcb; Rubáiyát, aaba; envelope quatrain, abba*); *octave;* and so forth.

Following are metrical descriptions of some common verse patterns.

Blank verse: Iambic pentameter unrimed.
The wórld|was áll|befóre|them, // whére|to chóose
Their pláce|of rést,| // and Próv|idénce|their guíde.
They,|hánd|in hánd,| // with wán|dering stéps|and slów,
Through É|den toók|their sol|itár|y wáy.

Heroic couplet: Iambic pentameter rimed (*aa*); first couplet below is run-on, second couplet end-stopped.
Of áll|the cáus|es whích|conspíre|to blínd
Man's ér|ring júdge|ment, ánd|misguíde|the mind,
Whát the|weák heád|with stróng|est bí|as rules,
Is Pride, // the nev́|er faíl|ing více|of foóls.

Ballad measure: Iambic, first and third lines tetrameter, second and fourth lines trimeter, and second and fourth lines riming (i.e., iambic, 4-3-4-3, *abcb*).
And soón|I heárd|a roár|ing wínd;
It díd|not cóme|anéar;
But wíth|its soúnd|it shoók|the saíls
That wére|so thín|and seár.

Rubáiyát quatrain: Iambic pentameter rimed *aaba.*

Come, fill | the cúp, | // and iń | the fiŕe | of Spŕing
Your Wiń | ter-gaŕ | ment of | Repén | tance flińg.
   The Biŕd | of Tiḿe | has buŕ | a liŕ | tle wáy
To flút | ter // —ańd | the Biŕd | is oń | the Wińg.

Spenserian stanza: Iambic pentameter rimed *ababbcbcc,* the last line being hexameter (Alexandrine).

And stíll | she slept | an aź | ure-líd | ded sleép,
In blán | chèd liń | en, / smóoth, | and láv | endeŕed,
While hé | from forŕh | the clós | et broúght | a heáp
Of cán | died ap | ple, quińce, | and plúm, | and
   goúrd;
With jél | lies soóth | er thán | the creám | y cuŕd,
And lú | cent sýr | ops, // tińct | with ciń | naḿon;
Mánna | and daŕes, | in aŕ | gosý | transferŕed
From Féz; | and spíc | èd dáin | ties, év | ery ońe,
From   sil | ken   Saḿ | arcańd | to   cé | dared
   Léb | anón.

Index of Authors and Titles

Index of Authors and Titles

John C. Hodges
late of the University of Tennessee

and

Mary E. Whitten
North Texas State University

HARBRACE COLLEGE HANDBOOK

Ninth Edition

Preface

The Ninth Edition of the *Harbrace College Handbook,* like its predecessors, is a reference guide for the individual writer and a textbook for use in class. A comprehensive yet concise summary of the principles of effective writing, the *Harbrace* provides an easily mastered system for the correction of student papers, and the directness and economy of its rules and examples make it a lasting resource for the writer.

A glance at the front endpapers shows that the organization of the Ninth Edition is very similar to that of the Eighth. Topics are treated in an orderly way, from the smallest elements to the largest. The book begins with a review of the essentials of grammar and ends with a glossary of grammatical terms. The former may be used as needed to introduce the other sections, and the latter may be used as a reference throughout the course. According to the requirements of a particular class, the book may be taught in any order. For example, some instructors may want to begin with Section **32, The Whole Composition,** others with Section **31, The Paragraph,** or with Sections **19–30,** which deal with diction and sentences. In every section, the large number and variety of exercises make it possible for instructors to select activities appropriate to the needs of their class.

The Revision / The Ninth Edition is the result of extensive revision—especially in the larger elements. In response to suggestions from many users and reviewers of the Eighth Edition, the following sections have been substantially revised and expanded: In Section **18,** the list of frequently misspelled words has almost tripled. Section **23 (Unity and Logical Thinking)** now includes discussions of formal and informal definition, deductive and inductive reasoning, and the most common fallacies. Section **31** includes expanded coverage of the topic sentence and methods of paragraph development, and Section **32** has been completely rewritten in terms of essay writing as a process—from choosing and limiting a topic, gathering ideas and formulating a thesis statement, to revising the second draft. Throughout the section, a single student essay is used to illustrate each step of the process. In Section **33,** the new research paper is accompanied by detailed annotations of both its structure and its documentation. All the documentation adheres to the style of the 1977 *MLA Handbook,* but other styles, such as those used in the social and physical sciences, are discussed and illustrated. Other additions to Section 33 include material on the computerization of library catalogs, a discussion of formal outlining, and an expanded discussion of plagiarism. Finally, Section **34** has been enlarged to include four sample business letters and two resumes.

Teaching Aids / For the first time, an *Instructor's Guide* (149 pages) is available to users of the *Harbrace College Handbook.* The Guide offers teaching strategies, classroom activities, and answers to exercises for each of the thirty-four sections; a set of criteria for grading papers; and an annotated bibliography of important titles in composition pedagogy and research. Other teaching aids include three forms of the *Harbrace College Workbook* by Sheila Y.

Graham: Form 9A, with sports used as the theme throughout; Form 9B (1983), an alternate version of 9A with a different theme; and Form 9C, with the theme of the world of work. A two-color *Instructor's Edition* is available for each workbook. Also available are a Correction Chart and a new Test Package with both diagnostic and achievement tests, scorable either manually or mechanically.

Acknowledgments / I did not work alone in the preparation of the Ninth Edition. Eileen B. Evans, Western Michigan University, wrote Section 32 and shared the writing of the *Instructor's Guide.* Peter T. Zoller, Wichita State University, revised most of Section 31 and all of Section 34. These contributors and I worked in close consultation with Natalie Bowen and Paul H. Nockleby, my editors at Harcourt Brace Jovanovich, who guided the scope and nature of change in this edition.

I am indebted to the following instructors and directors of freshman composition, who read all or part of various drafts of the manuscript and made valuable suggestions for its improvement: Percy Adams, University of Tennessee; Lois S. Anderson, Tennessee Technological University; Rance G. Baker, San Antonio College; Barbara J. Cicardo, University of Southwestern Louisiana; Bruce Chadwick, Long Island University; John J. Colaccio, Bergen Community College; William Connelly, Middle Tennessee State University; Richard J. Daigle, University of Bridgeport; Robert V. Dees, Orange Coast College; Kathleen E. Dubs, University of Oregon; Eileen B. Evans, Western Michigan University; Lynn Garrett, Louisiana State University; David Goslee, University of Tennessee; Sheila Y. Graham, University of Tennessee; Rosanna Grassi, Syracuse University; Stanley R. Hauer, University of Southern Mississippi; Dixie Elise Hickman, University of Southern Mississippi; Michael J. Hogan, University of New Mexico; Robert R. Hoyt, Hillsborough Community College; Marjorie Kirrie, Portland State University; G. Shelby Lee, Broward Community College; Gerald Levin, University of Akron; Donald V. Mehus, Fairleigh Dickinson University; Eleanor Drake Mitchell, Tennessee Technological University; James R. Moore, Mt. San Antonio College; James S. Mullican, Indiana State University; David Perlman; Barbara M. Roberts, James Madison University; Randal F. Robinson, Michigan State University; Martha A. Saunders, West Georgia College; Bain Tate Stewart, University of Tennessee, Knoxville; Ronald Strahl, Indiana University—Purdue University at Indianapolis; Margaret A. Strom, George Washington University; Virginia Thigpen, Volunteer State Community College; John W. Warren, Tennessee Technological University; Charles F. Whitaker, Eastern Kentucky University; David Yerkes, Columbia University; and Peter T. Zoller, Wichita State University.

In addition, I thank others who have contributed to the quality of the Ninth Edition, including Jean T. Davis, Marilyn Marcus, Gail O'Hare, and Elisa Turner, all of Harcourt Brace Jovanovich; Drake Bush; Sarah T. Hogan, North Texas State University; John J. Miniter, Texas Woman's University; and, especially, Audrey Ann Welch. And I continue to appreciate the work of those editors—particularly Karen H. Kirtley and the late William A. Pullin—who contributed to the success of the *Harbrace College Handbook* in its earlier editions.

Mary E. Whitten

To the Student

Numbers or Symbols / A number or a symbol written in the margin of your paper indicates a need for correction or improvement and calls for revision. If a number is used, turn directly to the corresponding number at the top of the page in the handbook. If a symbol is used, first consult the alphabetical list of symbols inside the back cover to find the number of the section to which you should turn. An appropriate letter after a number or symbol (such as **2c** or **frag/c**) will refer you to a specific part of a section.

References / Your instructor will ordinarily refer you to the number or symbol (**2** or **frag**, **9** or **cap**, **18** or **sp**, **28** or **ref**) appearing at the head of one of the thirty-four sections of the handbook. The rule given in color at the beginning of each section covers the whole section. One of the more specific rules given within the section will usually be needed to guide you in revision. Study the section to which you have been referred—the whole of the section if necessary—and master the specific part of the section that applies to your writing.

Correction and Revision / After you have studied the rules called to your attention, revise your paper carefully, as directed by your instructor. One method of revision is explained and illustrated in Section 8, page 694.

Contents

19 Good Usage and Glossary **723**

20 Exactness **734**

21 Wordiness **738**

22 Omission of Necessary Words **741**

EFFECTIVE SENTENCES

27 Shifts

28 Reference of Pronouns

29 Emphasis

30 Variety

LARGER ELEMENTS

31 The Paragraph

GRAMMAR

Sentence Sense

1

Master the essentials of the sentence as an aid to clear thinking and effective writing.

A key to good writing is to possess or develop sentence sense. Sentence sense is the awareness of what *makes* a sentence—the ability to recognize its grammatical essentials and to understand the relationships between its parts.

Observing the positions, forms, and meanings of words can help you to understand the relationship between parts of sentences. Notice below how meaning is expressed by the arrangement and the forms of words.

The hijacked plane has landed safely.

Note the importance of word order. Other arrangements of the same words are possible:

The hijacked plane has safely landed. [no appreciable difference in meaning]
Has the hijacked plane landed safely? [a change in meaning]

But not every arrangement of words is possible in an English sentence:

NONSENSICAL   Hijacked safely plane has landed the.

Note also that changing the forms of words affects sentence meaning:

The hijacked planes have landed safely. [a change in meaning]

Below are five simple sentences. In each, the vertical line separates the two basic grammatical parts of the sentence, the subject and the predicate. The first part functions as the complete subject (the subject and all words associated with it), and the second part functions as the complete predicate (the verb and all words associated with it). Most simple sentences follow this pattern:

```
Complete subject + complete predicate.
```

The hijacked **plane** | **has landed** safely.

Sandra | **gave** us three magnolia trees.

These **trees** | **should have been planted** in January.

The **tomato** | **is** a fruit.   **It** | **tastes** good in salads.

In each of these sentences, the subject (or simple subject) and the verb are in boldface. The subject is the part of a sentence about which something is asserted in the predicate. The predicate is the part that asserts something about the subject.

Expanding Sentences

Below are examples of ways that a simple sentence may be expanded.

SENTENCE   The plane has landed.   [subject + predicate]
EXPANSION

The hijacked plane | has landed safely.

The first hijacked plane to arrive at this airport | has landed safely in the south runway.

The first hijacked plane that we have ever seen at this airport | has landed safely in the south runway, which has been closed to traffic for a year.

The base of the expanded sentences may be isolated by striking out those words that have been added.

REDUCTION

The ~~first hijacked~~ plane ~~that we have ever seen at this airport~~ has landed ~~safely in the south runway, which has been closed to traffic for a year.~~

Combining Sentences

Speakers and writers combine sentences and in the process rearrange, add, delete, or substitute words:

The saying is old.   It has a new meaning.

VARIOUS COMBINATIONS

The saying is old, but it has a new meaning.
Although it has a new meaning, the saying is old.
The saying, which is old, has a new meaning.
The old saying has a new meaning.
It is an old saying with a new meaning.

A close study of this section can help you to develop or sharpen your sentence sense. Sentence sense is prerequisite to the intelligent use of this handbook—especially Sections **2** (Sentence Fragment), **3** (Comma Splice), **6** (Agreement), **12** (The Comma), **14** (The Semicolon), **23** (Unity), **24** (Subordination), **25** (Coherence), **26** (Parallelism), **29** (Emphasis), and **30** (Variety). For explanations of any unfamiliar grammatical terms, see the **Glossary of Grammatical Terms** beginning on page 815.

1a

Learn to recognize verbs and their subjects.

You can learn to recognize verbs and the subjects of verbs by observing their meaning, their form, and their position in sentences.

VERBS

Meaning   Verbs are words that express action, occurrence, or existence (a state of being).

Play ball!   The rain **stopped**.
They **exist**.   **Am** I right?

Function   A verb functions as the predicate of a sentence or as an essential part of the predicate.

Subject + PREDICATE.

William   **drives**.
William   usually **drives** his car to work.

Form   In the present tense, all verbs change form to indicate a singular subject in the third person (I *eat*—he *eats*). When converted from the present to the past tense, nearly all verbs change form (*eat*—*ate*).

PRESENT TENSE		PAST TENSE
I **ski**. Ray **skis**.		I **skied**.
You **win**. She **wins**.		You **won**.
We **quit**. He **quits**.	BUT	He **quit**.

In addition, certain suffixes, such as *-ize* and *-ify*, often indicate that a word is a verb (*legalize, classify*).

Verb phrases   A verb may consist of two or more words (*may see, should have been eaten, will be helping*), a unit called a *verb phrase*. When used with *have, has,* or *had,* most verbs end in *-d* or *-ed* (*have moved, had played*), but some have a special ending (*has been eaten*). Used with a form of *be*, all progressive verbs end in *-ing*, as in *was eating* (see page 687).

Tom **has moved**.   They **have taken** the tests.
He **is moving**.   We **had been taking** lessons.

Auxiliary verbs   A verb phrase like *has moved* or *was taking* follows this pattern: **auxiliary verb + main verb.** The following words are commonly used as auxiliaries: *have, has, had, am, is, are, was, were, be, been, do, does, did, will, shall, can, may, must, would, could, might.* Word groups like *am going to, is about to, ought to, used to, had better,* and *have to* may function as auxiliary verbs:

He **had gone** to London.
We **were enjoying** the game.   They **did** not **enjoy** it.
Ruth **is going to try**.   [Compare "Ruth *will try*."]

Other words may intervene between the auxiliary and the main verb:

Television **will** never completely **replace** the radio.   [The auxiliary *will* signals the approach of the verb *replace*.]

The contraction for *not* may be added to many auxiliaries: *haven't, doesn't, aren't, can't.*

Verbs with particles   Many verbs are used with particles like *away, across, in, off, on, down, for, out,* and *up with.* Notice how meaning can be changed by the addition of one of these uninflected words.

SINGLE-WORD VERBS	VERBS WITH PARTICLES
She **called** me.	She **called on** me.
I **put** his picture on my desk.	I **put up with** his picture on my desk.

Other words may intervene between the verb and the particle:

We **looked** José **up**.   Millie **handed** her report **in**.

SUBJECTS

Meaning   To identify a subject, find the verb; then use the verb in a question beginning with *who* or *what*, as shown in the following examples:

The dog in the cage ate.   The hut was built by Al.
Verb: **ate**   Verb: **was built**
WHO or WHAT ate? **The dog**   WHAT was built? **The hut**
   (not the cage) **ate**.   (not Al) **was built**.
Subject: **dog**   Subject: **hut**

Form   Although other words or word groups may function as subjects, nouns or pronouns are the most frequently used.

Many nouns (words used to name persons, places, things, ideas, animals, and so on) change their form to indicate number (*movement, movements; city, cities; woman, women*) and to indicate the possessive case (*John's* car, the *boys'* dogs, the *women's* vote). Such suffixes as *-ance, -ation, -ence, -ment, -ness,* and *-ship* frequently indicate that a word is a noun (*appearance, determination, reference, atonement, boldness, hardship*). The articles *a, an,* and *the* regularly signal that a noun is to follow (a *chair,* an *activity,* the last *race*).

Form makes it a simple matter to recognize some pronouns. Pronouns such as *I, we, she, he, they,* and *who* function as subjects; when used as objects, these words change to the forms *me, us, her, him, them,* and *whom.* Other pronouns—such as *you, it, mine, ours, yours, hers, his, theirs, that, which*—resemble nouns in that they function as either subjects or objects without a change in form.

Position   Subjects usually come before verbs in sentences.

SUBJECT—verb.
They disappeared.
The youngest **boy** did not smile very often.

Common exceptions to the *subject—verb* pattern occur when subjects are used in questions and after the expletive *there* (which is never the subject).

Was the **statement** true?   [verb—subject]
Did these **people survive**?   [auxiliary—subject—verb]
There **were** no **objections**.   [expletive—verb—subject]

Occasionally, verbs precede their subjects in sentences such as the following:

Over the door **were sprigs** of mistletoe.
Even more important **is** the **waste** of human resources.

Note: Subjects and verbs may be compound.

Cobras and **pythons** lay eggs.   [compound subject]
We **sat** by the pool and **waited**.   [compound verb]

■ **Exercise 1**   Underline the verbs (including any auxiliaries and particles) and their subjects in the following sentences (selected from *Reader's Digest*).

1. Lasting friendships develop.
2. Secrecy was another problem.
3. Rodgers constantly courts trouble with his boat-rocking comments.
4. The fire gobbled up some of the most expensive real estate on earth.
5. Answers to such questions may never be found.

6. Are vitamins important for sudden bursts of energy?
7. There are now about two million television sets in China.
8. John's simplicity gave his actions the force of parables.
9. Gnats and small flies invade the sheath and pollinate the blossoms.
10. He straightened his glasses, breathed a prayer of thanks, and swung his hoe at a nearby weed.

1b

Learn to recognize objects of verbs, as well as complements of subjects and objects.

You can learn to recognize objects of verbs, subject complements, and object complements by observing their meaning, their form, and their position in sentences.

DIRECT AND INDIRECT OBJECTS OF VERBS

Meaning   To identify a direct object, find the subject and the verb; then use them in a question ending with *whom* or *what* as shown in the following example:

Karen graciously invited the reporters to lunch.
Subject and verb: **Karen invited**
Karen invited WHOM or WHAT? **the reporters**
Direct object: **reporters**

A verb that has a direct object to complete its meaning is called a *transitive* verb. Notice that a direct object in a sentence like the following is directly affected by the action of the verb:

High winds leveled a *city* in West Texas. [The direct object is the receiver of the action.]

Some verbs (such as *give, offer, bring, take, lend, send, buy,* and *sell*) may have both a direct object and an indirect object. An indirect object states *to whom* or *for whom* (or *to what* or *for what*) something is done.

Richard sent Audrey an invitation.
Subject, verb, and direct object: **Richard sent invitation**
Richard sent an invitation TO WHOM? **Audrey**
Indirect object: **Audrey**

Form   Like the subjects of verbs, direct and indirect objects of verbs are generally nouns or pronouns: see **1a**, page 666. See also **1c**, pages 668–69.

Two women robbed the **taxi driver**. They robbed **him**.
Sam bought **Ann** a new **watch**. He bought **her that**.

Position   The following sentence patterns and examples show the usual word order of direct and indirect objects of verbs.

```
SUBJECT—VERB—OBJECT.
```

Mice frighten elephants.
Many **fans were hanging placards** in the stadium.

```
SUBJECT—VERB—INDIRECT OBJECT—DIRECT OBJECT.
```

Mary baked Timothy a cake.
The **company will** probably **send you** a small **refund.**

But in some sentences—especially questions—the direct object does not take the position indicated by the basic patterns.

What **placards did** the **fans hang** in the stadium?
[direct object—auxiliary—subject—verb]

A test for an object   Knowing how to change an active verb to the passive voice can also help you to identify an object, since the object of an active verb can usually be made the subject of a passive verb:

ACTIVE   The Eagles finally **defeated** the **Lions.**
[*Lions* is the direct object of *defeated.*]

PASSIVE   The **Lions were** finally **defeated** by the Eagles.
[*Lions* is the subject of *were defeated.*]

Notice above that a form of *be* is added when an active verb is changed to the passive.

SUBJECT AND OBJECT COMPLEMENTS

Meaning   A subject complement refers to, identifies, or qualifies the subject. Subject complements help to complete the meaning of intransitive linking verbs (*be, am, is, are, was, were, been, seem, become, feel, look, smell, sound, taste,* and so on). See also page 668.

Diane is my **cousin.**   [*cousin* identifies *Diane,* the subject.]
Several tourists became **homesick.**   [*Homesick* describes or qualifies *tourists,* the subject.]

In the sentences above, the relationship between the subject and its complement is so close that the words used as subject complements can be placed next to the subject. They can then, in different sentences, serve as an appositive (an added noun explaining or identifying another noun) or as a regular adjective (rather than a predicate adjective).

Diane, **my cousin,** dropped by.   [appositive]
Several **homesick** tourists did not enjoy the trip.   [adjective]

An object complement refers to, identifies, or qualifies the direct object. Object complements help to complete the meaning of such verbs as *make, name, elect, call, find, consider.*

We elected Phyllis **president.**
[Compare: Because of our votes, Phyllis became president.]

The dealer considered it **worthless.**
[Compare: According to the dealer, it was worthless.]

Form   Nouns, pronouns, and adjectives are used as subject and object complements. See **1a** for a discussion of the forms of nouns and pronouns. Adjectives (which modify or qualify a noun or pronoun) often change form to indicate comparison: *tall, taller, tallest.* In addition to *-er* and *-est,* such suffixes as *-al, -ful, -ish, -like, -ous,* and *-y* often indicate that a word is an adjective: *national, useful, greenish, childlike, famous, lumpy.*

Position   Although word order varies (especially in questions or exclamations), a study of the following basic patterns and examples will help you learn to recognize subject and object complements.

```
SUBJECT—LINKING VERB—SUBJECT COMPLEMENT.
```

His **nickname was Skippy.**
The **pie tasted** too **sweet** for me.

```
SUBJECT—VERB—DIRECT OBJECT—OBJECT COMPLEMENT.
```

We called him Skippy.
I found the **pie** too **sweet.**

The ability to recognize objects of verbs and complements of subjects will help you to understand differences in the use of transitive and intransitive verbs. A transitive verb takes an object, and it may be made passive. See also page 667.

> TRANSITIVE ACTIVE These statistics **deceive** many people. [The direct object is *people*.]
>
> TRANSITIVE PASSIVE Many people **are deceived** by these statistics. [*People* is now the subject of the passive verb *are deceived*.]

Some intransitive verbs take a subject complement; some are complete without a complement.

> INTRANSITIVE LINKING The data **seemed** reliable. [The subject complement is *reliable*.]
>
> INTRANSITIVE COMPLETE They **did** not **listen.** [No complement is necessary.]

Note: Direct and indirect objects of verbs, subject complements, and object complements may be compound.

> She likes **okra** and **spinach.** [compound direct object]
> They sent **Elyse** and **Mike** complimentary tickets. [compound indirect object]
> The cathedrals are **old** and **famous.** [compound subject complement]
> They will name the baby **Jude** or **Judith.** [compound object complement]

■ **Exercise 2** Underline all direct and indirect objects of verbs and the two subject complements in Exercise 1, page 666.

■ **Exercise 3** Label all subjects of verbs, subject complements, and object complements in the quotations below. Prepare for a class discussion of the basic sentence patterns (and any variations) and the types of verbs used.

1. The argument bruises old myths. —LANCE MORROW
2. Inventions are the hallmark of mankind. —JAKE PAGE
3. With their world a shambles, people fled. —RONALD SCHILLER
4. In the *Odyssey,* Homer gives us detailed information of wind and stars. —MAURICIO OBREGÓN
5. Sensible people find nothing useless. —LA FONTAINE
6. Neither intelligence nor integrity can be imposed by law. —CARL BECKER
7. America has not always been kind to its artists and scholars. —LYNDON B. JOHNSON
8. The multitude of books is making us ignorant. —VOLTAIRE
9. There is no little enemy. —BENJAMIN FRANKLIN
10. Only a moral idiot with a suicidal mania would press the button for a nuclear war. —WALTER LIPPMANN

1c
Learn to recognize all the parts of speech.

Two methods of classifying words in a sentence are shown below. The first method classifies words according to their function in a sentence; the second, according to their part of speech.

Waiters usually offer us free coffee at Joe's cafe.

	FUNCTION	PART OF SPEECH
Waiters	subject	noun
usually	modifier	adverb
offer	verb of predicate	verb
us	indirect object	pronoun
free	modifier	adjective
coffee	direct object	noun
at	preposition	preposition
Joe's	modifier	noun
cafe	object of preposition	noun

Notice here that one part of speech—the noun (a naming word with a typical form)—is used as a subject, a direct object, a modifier, and an object of a preposition.

Words are traditionally grouped into eight classes or parts of speech: *verbs, nouns, pronouns, adjectives, adverbs, prepositions, conjunctions,* and *interjections.* Verbs, nouns, adjectives, and adverbs (called vocabulary or content words) make up more than 99 percent of all words listed in the dictionary. But pronouns, prepositions, and conjunctions—although small in number—are important because they are used over and over in our speaking and writing. Prepositions and conjunctions (called function or structure words) connect and relate other parts of speech.

Of the eight word classes, only three—prepositions, conjunctions, and interjections—do not change their form. For a summary of the form changes of the other parts of speech, see **inflection**, page 819.

Carefully study the forms, meanings, and functions of each of the eight parts of speech listed on the following pages. For additional examples or more detailed information, see the corresponding entries in the **Glossary of Grammatical Terms** beginning on page 815.

VERBS   *notify, notifies, is notifying, notified*
    write, writes, is writing, wrote, has written

A verb functions as the predicate of a sentence or as an essential part of the predicate: see **1a**.

> Herman **writes.**
> He **has written** five poems.
> He **is** no longer **writing** those dull stories.

One frequently used verb-forming suffix is *-ize:*

> *terror, idols* (nouns)—*terrorize, idolize* (verbs)

Note: Verb forms classified as participles, gerunds, or infinitives (verbals) cannot function as the predicate of a sentence: see **1d.**

PARTICIPLES	The man **writing** the note is Bill. [modifier]
	She gave him **written** instructions. [modifier]
GERUND	His **writing** all night long disturbed his whole family. [subject]
INFINITIVES	Herman wants **to write**. [direct object]
	The urge **to write** left him. [modifier]

NOUNS

man, men; kindness, kindnesses
nation, nations; nation's, nations'
Carthage, United States, William, NASA
prudence, the *money,* an *understanding*

Nouns function as subjects, objects, complements, appositives, and modifiers, as well as in direct address and in absolute constructions. Nouns name persons, places, things, ideas, animals, and so on. See also **1a** and **1b** and page 820.

> **Marilyn** drives a **truck** for the **Salvation Army**.

Endings such as *-ation, -ism, -ity, -ment,* and *-ness* are called noun-forming suffixes:

> *relax, starve* (verbs)—*relaxation, starvation* (nouns)
> *kind, happy* (adjectives)—*kindness, happiness* (nouns)

Compound nouns   Words such as *father-in-law, Salvation Army, swimming pool, dropout,* and *breakthrough* are generally classified as compound nouns.

PRONOUNS

I, me, my, mine, myself; they, you, him, it
this, these; who, whose, whom; which, that
one, ones, one's; everybody, anyone

Pronouns serve the function of nouns in sentences:

> **They** bought **it** for **her**.   **Everyone** knows **this**.

ADJECTIVES

shy, sleepy, attractive, famous
three men, *this* class, *another* one
young, younger, youngest

The articles *a, an,* and *the* are variously classified as adjectives, determiners, or function words. Adjectives modify or qualify nouns and pronouns (and sometimes gerunds) and are generally placed near the words they modify:

> The **beautiful** and **famous** cathedrals no longer interest **homesick** tourists.
> **Thrifty** and **sensible**, he will be promoted soon.

Adjectives may function as complements of the subject or of the object: see **1b**.

> The Great Smoky Mountains are most **beautiful** in the fall.
> Her tennis serve made Joanne **famous**.

Suffixes such as *-al, -able, -ant, -ative, -ic, -ish, -less, -ous,* and *-y* may be added to certain verbs or nouns to form adjectives:

> *accept, repent* (verbs)—*acceptable, repentant* (adjectives)
> *angel, effort* (nouns)—*angelic, effortless* (adjectives)

ADVERBS

rarely saw, call *daily, soon* left, left *sooner*
very short, *too* angry, *never* shy, *not* fearful
practically never loses, *nearly always* cold

As the examples show, adverbs modify verbs, adjectives, and other adverbs. In addition, an adverb may modify a verbal, a phrase, a clause, or even the rest of the sentence in which it appears:

> I noticed a plane **slowly** circling overhead.
> **Honestly**, Ben did catch a big shark.

The *-ly* ending nearly always converts adjectives to adverbs:

> *rare, honest* (adjectives)—*rarely, honestly* (adverbs)

PREPOSITIONS

on a shelf, *between* us, *because of* rain
to the door, *by* them, *before* class

A preposition always has an object, which is usually a noun or a pronoun. The preposition links and relates its object to some other word in the sentence. The preposition with its object (and any modifiers) is called a *prepositional phrase:*

> Byron expressed **with great force** his love **of liberty**.

The preposition may follow rather than precede its object, and it may be placed at the end of the sentence:

> What are you selling it **for**?   Faith is what we live **by**.

Words commonly used as prepositions:

about	besides	inside	since
above	between	into	through
across	beyond	like	throughout
after	but	near	till
against	by	of	to
along	concerning	off	toward
among	despite	on	under
around	down	onto	underneath
at	during	out	until
before	except	outside	up
behind	excepting	over	upon
below	for	past	with
beneath	from	regarding	within
beside	in	round	without

Phrasal prepositions (two or more words):

according to	by way of	in spite of
along with	due to	instead of
apart from	except for	on account of
as for	in addition to	out of
as regards	in case of	up to
as to	in front of	with regard to
because of	in lieu of	with respect to
by means of	in place of	with reference to
by reason of	in regard to	with the exception of

CONJUNCTIONS

Amy *and* Bill, in *or* out
long *but* witty

> She acts **as if** she really cares.
> I worked, **for** my father needed money.

Conjunctions function as connectors of words, phrases, or clauses: see also **1d** and **1e**.

The coordinating conjunctions (*and, but, or, nor, for, so, yet*) and the correlatives (*both—and, either—or, neither—nor, not only—but also, whether—or*) connect sentence elements of equal grammatical rank.

The subordinating conjunctions (such as *after, as if, because, if, since, till, when, where, while*) connect subordinate clauses with main clauses: see **1d** and the list on page 672.

Conjunctive adverbs Words like *however, nevertheless, then,* and *therefore* (see the list on page 677) are used as conjunctive adverbs (or adverbial conjunctions):

> Don seemed bored in class; **however,** he did listen and learn.

INTERJECTIONS *Wow! Oh,* that's a surprise.

Interjections are exclamations, which may be followed by an exclamation point or by a comma: see **12b** and **17c**.

A dictionary labels words according to their part of speech. Some words have only one classification—for example, *notify* (verb), *sleepy* (adjective), *practically* (adverb). Other words have more than one label. The word *living,* for instance, is first treated as a form of the verb *live* and is then listed separately and defined as an adjective and as a noun. The actual classification depends on the use of the word in a given sentence:

> They were **living** wretchedly.   [verb]
> She is a **living** example of patience.   [adjective]
> He barely makes a **living**.   [noun]

Another example is the word *up:*

> Look **up**!   [adverb]
> They dragged the sled **up** the hill.   [preposition]
> The **up** escalator is jerking again.   [adjective]
> He follows the **ups** and downs of the market.   [noun]
> "They will **up** the rent again," he complained.   [verb]

■ **Exercise 4** Using your dictionary as an aid if you wish, classify each word in the following sentences according to its part of speech.

1. He struts with the gravity of a frozen penguin.   —TIME
2. Men are often taken, like rabbits, by the ears. And though the tongue has no bones, it can sometimes break millions of them.   —F. L. LUCAS
3. Awesome is the tyranny of the fixed idea.   —ERIC LARABEE
4. Of all persons, adolescents are the most intensely personal; their intensity is often uncomfortable to adults.
   —EDGAR Z. FRIEDENBERG
5. They pick a President and then for four years they pick on him.   —ADLAI STEVENSON

1d

Learn to recognize phrases and subordinate clauses.

The sentences below consist only of the basic grammatical parts along with the articles *the* and *a:* see the sentence patterns in **1a** and **1b**.

> We explored the beach. We used metal detectors.
> We found a doubloon. It was battered.

Most sentences, however, contain groups of words used as single parts of speech. Such word groups are either phrases or subordinate clauses.

SENTENCES COMBINED

Exploring the beach with metal detectors, we found **a battered doubloon.**   [phrases]

When we were exploring the beach with metal detectors, we found a battered doubloon.   [subordinate clause preceding a main clause—see **1e**]

PHRASES

A phrase is often defined as a group of related words without a subject and a predicate. Phrases are generally classified as follows:

VERB PHRASES   The rose **has wilted**.   **Did** you **see** it? Mr. Kelly **may run up** the bill.   The roof **used to leak**.

NOUN PHRASES   **The severe drought** struck **many Midwestern States**.   I introduced Greer, **a very interesting speaker**.

PREPOSITIONAL PHRASES   The oldest car **on campus** is mine. We were exploring the beach **with metal detectors**.

PARTICIPIAL PHRASES   **Exploring the beach**, we found many sand dollars.   The beach, **covered with seaweed**, looked uninviting.

GERUND PHRASES   **Exploring the beach** is fun.   They enjoyed **feeding the seagulls**.

INFINITIVE PHRASES   We wanted **to explore the beach**.   That is the problem **to be solved now**.   Vernon and I went to Boston **to visit relatives**.

ABSOLUTE PHRASES   **The van loaded**, we headed for the mountains.   The Nobel Prize winner left the room, **reporters clustering around him**.   [See also page 815].

Notice in the examples above that *exploring*—a verb form ending in *-ing*—is used as an adjective and also as a noun. The grammatical classification is not based on form but on use in the sentence: the participle functions as an adjective and the gerund functions as a noun.

Participles, gerunds, and infinitives are derived from verbs. (See also the note on pages 668–69 and **verbal** on page 823.) They are much like verbs in that they have different tenses, can take subjects and objects, and can be modified by adverbs. But they cannot serve as the only verb form in the predicate of a sentence. Participial, gerund, and infinitive phrases function as adjectives, nouns, or adverbs and are therefore only parts of sentences, as the following sentence combinations illustrate.

SENTENCES

Dr. Ford explained the process.   He drew simple illustrations.

PHRASES IN SENTENCES

Explaining the process, Dr. Ford drew simple illustrations.

OR

Simple illustrations **drawn by Dr. Ford** explained the process.   [participial phrases]

Dr. Ford explained the process by **drawing simple illustrations**.   [gerund phrase]

Dr. Ford drew simple illustrations **to explain the process**.   [infinitive phrase]

(1) Phrases used as nouns

Gerund phrases are always used as nouns. Infinitive phrases are often used as nouns (although they may also function as modifiers). Occasionally a prepositional phrase functions as a noun (as in "*After supper* is too late!").

NOUNS

The **decision** is important.

She likes the **job**.

His **action** prompted the **change**.

He uses my room for **storage**.

He wants two things: **money** and **power**.

PHRASES USED AS NOUNS

Choosing a major is important. [gerund phrase—subject]

She likes **to do the work**. [infinitive phrase—direct object]

His leaving the farm prompted **her to seek a job in town**. [gerund phrase—subject; infinitive phrase—direct object]

He uses my room for **storing all his auto parts**. [gerund phrase—object of a preposition]

He wants two things: **to make money** and **to gain power**. [infinitive phrases—a compound appositive]

■ **Exercise 5**   Underline the gerund phrases and the infinitive phrases used as nouns in the following sentences (selected from *Time*). Be sure to underline any prepositional phrases modifying words in the gerund or the infinitive phrases.

1. Successfully merchandising a product is creative.
2. Americans have always needed to know the point of it all.
3. They have also been getting tougher by enforcing strict new anti-litter laws.
4. Taking criticism from others is painful but useful.
5. Merely to argue for the preservation of park land is not enough.
6. Angry and proud, Claire resolved to fight back.
7. After giving birth, most women lapse into some sort of melancholy.
8. Workers managed to pipe the gas through a purifying plant and into a pipeline.
9. All human acts—even saving a stranger from drowning or donating a million dollars to the poor—may be ultimately selfish.
10. This method of growing plants without soil has long been known to scientists but has only recently begun to attract amateurs' attention.

(2) Phrases used as modifiers

Prepositional phrases nearly always function as adjectives or adverbs. Infinitive phrases are also used as adjectives or adverbs. Participial phrases are used as adjectives. Absolute phrases are used as adverbs.

ADJECTIVES

It is a **significant** idea.

Appropriate language is best.

Destructive storms lashed the Midwest.

The **icy** bridge was narrow.

PHRASES USED AS ADJECTIVES

It is an idea **of significance**. [prepositional phrase]

Language **to suit the occasion** is best. [infinitive phrase]

Destroying many crops of corn and oats, storms lashed the Midwest. [participial phrase containing a prepositional phrase]

The bridge **covered with ice** was narrow. [participial phrase containing a prepositional phrase]

ADVERBS

Drive **carefully**.

I nodded **respectfully**.

ADVERBS

Consequently, we could hardly see the road.

PHRASES USED AS ADVERBS

Drive **with care on wet streets**. [prepositional phrases]

I nodded **to show respect**. [infinitive phrase]

PHRASES USED AS ADVERBS

The rain coming down in torrents, we could hardly see the road. [absolute phrase—see page 815]

The preceding examples demonstrate how phrases function in the same way as single-word modifiers. Remember, however, that phrases are not merely substitutes for single words. Many times phrases express more than can be packed into a single word:

The gas gauge fluttered **from empty to full**.
He telephoned his wife **to tell her of his arrival**.
The firefighters **hosing down the adjacent buildings** had very little standing room.

■ **Exercise 6**   Underline each phrase used as a modifier in the following sentences. Then state whether the phrase functions as an adjective or as an adverb.

1. A moment like that one should last forever.
2. The fans blinded by the sun missed the best plays.
3. Crawling through the thicket, I suddenly remembered the box of shells left on top of the truck.
4. The people to watch closely are the ones ruling behind the political scene.
5. A motorcycle racing along the beach zoomed over our big sand castle.
6. The number on that ticket indicates a seat in the balcony.
7. I came to college to get a liberal education and to learn a trade.
8. They worked fast, one man sawing logs and the other loading the truck.
9. Not wanting to appear in court, Marilyn decided to pay the fine.
10. All told, fame is fickle.

SUBORDINATE CLAUSES

A clause is often defined as a group of related words that contains both a subject and a predicate. Like a phrase, a subordinate (or dependent) clause is not a sentence. The subordinate clause functions as a single part of speech—as a noun, an adjective, or an adverb. Notice the relationship of the sentences below to the clauses that follow.

SENTENCES   **That fact I must admit.**
Ralph was my first and only blind date.
I married him.

SUBORDINATE CLAUSES IN SENTENCES

I must admit **that Ralph was my first and only blind date**. [noun clause—direct object]

The first and only blind date **that I ever had** was Ralph. [adjective clause]

Ralph was my first and only blind date **because I married him**. [adverb clause]

In the examples above, *that* and *because* are used as *subordinators:* they subordinate the clauses they introduce, making these clauses dependent. The following words are commonly used to mark subordinate clauses.

RELATIVE PRONOUNS *that, what, which, who whoever, whom, whomever, whose*

SUBORDINATING CONJUNCTIONS *after, although, as, because, before, if, once, since, that, though, till, unless, until, when, whenever, where, wherever, while*

Subordinators may consist of more than one word:

as if, as soon as, as though, even though, in order that, in that, no matter how, so that

No matter how hard I try, I cannot float with my toes out of the water.
We bought three dozen doughnuts **so that everyone would be sure to have enough.**

(3) Subordinate clauses used as nouns

NOUNS	NOUN CLAUSES
The **news** may be false.	**What the newspapers say** may be false. [subject]
I do not know his **address.**	I do not know **where he lives.** [direct object]
Give the tools to **Rita.**	Give the tools to **whoever can use them best.** [object of a preposition]
That fact—Karen's **protest**—amazed me.	The fact **that Karen protested** amazed me. [appositive]

The conjunction *that* before a noun clause may be omitted in some sentences:

I know **she is right.** [Compare "I know *that she is right.*"]

(4) Subordinate clauses used as modifiers

Two types of subordinate clauses, the adjective clause and the adverb clause, are used as modifiers.

Adjective clauses   Any clause that modifies a noun or a pronoun is an adjective clause. Adjective clauses, which nearly always follow the words modified, are most frequently introduced by a relative pronoun but may begin with such words as *when, where,* or *why.*

ADJECTIVES	ADJECTIVE CLAUSES
Everyone needs **loyal** friends.	Everyone needs friends **who are loyal.**
The **golden** window reflects the sun.	The window, **which shines like gold,** reflects the sun.
Peaceful countrysides no longer exist.	Countrysides **where one can find peace of mind** no longer exist.

If it is not used as a subject, the relative pronoun in an adjective clause may sometimes be omitted:

He is a man **I admire.**
[Compare "He is a man *whom I admire.*"]

Adverb clauses   An adverb clause usually modifies a verb but may modify an adjective, an adverb, or even the rest of the sentence in which it appears. Many adverb clauses can take various positions in a sentence: see **12b** and **12d.** Adverb clauses are ordinarily introduced by subordinating conjunctions.

ADVERBS	ADVERB CLAUSES
Soon the lights went out.	**When the windstorm hit,** the lights went out.
No alcoholic beverages are sold **locally.**	No alcoholic beverages are sold **where I live.**
The price is **too** high for me.	The price is higher **than I can afford.**
Speak **very** distinctly.	Speak as distinctly **as you can.**

Some adverb clauses may be elliptical. See also **25b.**

If I can save enough money, I'll go to Alaska next summer. **If not,** I'll take a trip to St. Louis. [Omitted words are clearly implied.]

■ **Exercise 7**   Find each subordinate clause in the following sentences (selected from the *New York Times Magazine*) and label it as a noun clause, an adjective clause, or an adverb clause.

1. Food manufacturers contend that modern processing often robs food of its natural color.
2. What my son wants to wear or be or try to be is now almost entirely his business.
3. Grocers today must deal with shoppers whose basic attitudes are drastically changed.
4. As I talked to my neighbors, I found that all of them did depend on a world that stretched far beyond their property lines.
5. As it declines in value, money becomes more of an obsession.
6. If a pitcher who throws only a fastball and a curveball is in a tight situation, the batter can reasonably expect the fastball.
7. Bloodhounds do not follow tracks as people often believe. . . . Because a trail so often hangs several inches or sometimes feet above the ground, hounds can follow a person even if he wades through water.
8. At present, computers are rapidly moving into offices around the world to take over secretarial chores that involve processing words.
9. We are a plugged-in society—plugged in to the tube, which all but assumes the role of parent, or teacher, or lover.
10. The language is what it is, and not what you want it to be.

1e

Learn to recognize main clauses and the various types of sentences.

A main clause can stand alone as a sentence, a grammatically independent unit of expression, although it may require other sentences to complete its meaning. Coordinating conjunctions (*and, but, or, nor, for, so, yet*) often connect and relate main clauses.

MAIN CLAUSES IN SENTENCES

I had lost my passport, but I did not worry about it.
[A coordinating conjunction links the two main clauses.]

Although I had lost my passport, **I did not worry about it.**
[A subordinate clause precedes the main clause.]

MAIN CLAUSES CONVERTED TO SENTENCES

I had lost my passport.
I did not worry about it. OR **But I did not worry about it.**

Unlike main clauses, subordinate clauses become fragments if isolated and written as sentences: see **2b**.

Sentences may be classified according to their structure as *simple, compound, complex,* or *compound-complex.*

1. A simple sentence has only one subject and one predicate (either or both of which may be compound):

Dick started a coin collection. [SUBJECT—VERB—OBJECT. See also the various patterns of the simple sentence in **1a** and **1b**.]

2. A compound sentence consists of at least two main clauses:

Dick started a coin collection, and his wife bought an album of rare stamps. [MAIN CLAUSE, and MAIN CLAUSE. See **12a**.]

3. A complex sentence has one main clause and at least one subordinate clause:

As soon as Dick started a coin collection, his wife bought an album of rare stamps. [ADVERB CLAUSE, MAIN CLAUSE. See **12b**.]

4. A compound-complex sentence consists of at least two main clauses and at least one subordinate clause:

As soon as Dick started a coin collection, his wife bought an album of rare stamps; on Christmas morning they exchanged coins and stamps. [ADVERB CLAUSE, MAIN CLAUSE; MAIN CLAUSE. See **14a**.]

Sentences may also be classified according to their purpose as *statements, commands* or *requests, questions,* or *exclamations* and are punctuated accordingly:

STATEMENT   He refused the offer.

COMMAND OR REQUEST   Refuse the offer.

QUESTIONS   Did he refuse the offer? He refused, didn't he? He refused it?

EXCLAMATIONS   What an offer! He refused it! Refuse it!

■ **Exercise 8**   Underline the main clauses in the following sentences (selected from *Natural History*). Put subordinate clauses in brackets: see **1d**. (Noun clauses may be an integral part of the basic pattern of a main clause, as in the second sentence.)

1. Practice never really makes perfect, and a great deal of frustration invariably accompanies juggling.
2. Nature is his passion in life, and colleagues say he is a skilled naturalist and outdoorsman.
3. The two clouds have a common envelope of atomic hydrogen gas, which ties them firmly together.
4. Transportation comes to a halt as the steadily falling snow, accumulating faster than snowplows can clear it away, is blown into deep drifts along the highways.
5. Agriculture is the world's most basic industry; its success depends in large part on an adequate supply of water.
6. Probably because their whirling sails were new and strange to Cervantes, windmills outraged the gallant Don Quixote.
7. There have been several attempts to explain this rhythm, but when each hypothesis was experimentally explored, it had to be discarded.
8. Allegiance to a group may be confirmed or denied by the use or disuse of a particular handshake, as Carl's experience indicates.

9. Some black stem rust of wheat has been controlled by elimination of barberry, a plant that harbored the rust.
10. We know that innocent victims have been executed; fortunately, others condemned to death have been found innocent prior to execution.

■ **Exercise 9**   Classify the sentences in Exercise 8 as *compound* (there are two), *complex* (five), or *compound-complex* (three).

■ **Exercise 10**   First identify the main and subordinate clauses in the sentences in the following paragraph; then classify each sentence according to structure.

[1] Jim angrily called himself a fool, as he had been doing all the way to the swamp. [2] Why had he listened to Fred's mad idea? [3] What did ghosts and family legends mean to him, in this age of computers and solar-energy converters? [4] He had enough mysteries of his own, of a highly complex sort, which involved an intricate search for values. [5] But now he was chasing down ghosts, and this chase in the middle of the night was absurd. [6] It was lunacy! [7] The legends that surrounded the ghosts had horrified him as a child, and they were a horror still. [8] As he approached the dark trail that would lead him to the old mansion, he felt almost sick. [9] The safe, sure things of every day had become distant fantasies. [10] Only this grotesque night—and whatever ghosts might be lurking in the shadows—seemed hideously real.

■ **Exercise 11**   Observing differences in emphasis, convert each pair of sentences below to (a) a simple sentence, (b) a compound sentence consisting of two main clauses, and (c) a complex sentence with one main clause and one subordinate clause.

EXAMPLE

Male sperm whales occasionally attack ships. These whales jealously guard their territory.

a. *Jealously guarding their territory, male sperm whales occasionally attack ships.*
b. *Male sperm whales occasionally attack ships; these whales jealously guard their territory.*
c. *Since male sperm whales jealously guard their territory, they occasionally attack ships.*

1. The men smuggled marijuana into Spain. They were sentenced to six years in prison.
2. The council first condemned the property. Then it ordered the owner's eviction.
3. Uncle Oliver applied for a patent on his invention. He learned of three hundred such devices already on the market.
4. The border guards delayed every tourist. They carefully examined passports and luggage.

Sentence Fragments

2

As a rule, do not write sentence fragments.

A fragment is a nonsentence. It is a part of a sentence—such as a phrase or subordinate clause—written as if it were a sentence.

FRAGMENTS	SENTENCES
My father always planting a spring garden.	My father always plants a spring garden.
Because he likes to eat vegetables.	He likes to eat vegetables.
That help the body to combat infection.	He eats foods that help the body to combat infection—
For example, yellow and green vegetables.	for example, yellow and green vegetables.

Recognizing intonation patterns may help you avoid some types of fragments in your writing. Read the following sentences aloud, and note how your voice indicates the end of each complete statement.

> We saw that.   We saw that movie.
> We saw that movie on TV last summer.

The best way to avoid fragments, however, is to recognize the structural differences between sentences and non-sentences. Remember that a complete statement is an independent unit containing at least one subject and predicate. Study Section **1**, especially **1d** and **1e**.

Not all fragments are to be avoided. Some types of fragments are standard. Exclamations, as well as questions and their answers, are often single words, phrases, or subordinate clauses written as sentences:

> Why? **Because governments cannot establish heaven on earth.**
> Where does Peg begin a mystery story? **On the last page. Always!**

Written dialogue that mirrors speech habits often contains grammatically incomplete sentences or elliptical expressions within the quotation marks: see **9e**. Occasionally, professional writers deliberately use fragments for rhetorical effect:

> The American grain calls for plain talk, for the unvarnished truth. **Better to err a little in the cause of bluntness than soften the mind with congenial drivel. Better a challenging half-truth than a discredited cliché.** —WRIGHT MORRIS [The reader can readily supply omitted words in the two bold-faced fragments. Note the effective repetition and the parallel structure.]

Despite their suitability for some purposes, sentence fragments are comparatively rare in formal expository writing. In formal papers, sentence fragments are to be used—if at all—sparingly and with care. College students are often advised to learn the fundamentals of English composition before permitting themselves to take liberties with the accepted patterns of the complete sentence.

Test for Sentence Completeness

Before handing in a composition, proofread each word group written as a sentence. Test each one for completeness. First, be sure that it has at least one subject and one predicate.

FRAGMENTS MISSING EITHER A SUBJECT OR A PREDICATE

> And for days tried to change my mind. [no subject]
> Water sparkling in the moonlight. [no predicate]

Next, be sure that the word group is not a dependent clause beginning with a subordinating conjunction or a relative pronoun (see page 672).

FRAGMENTS WITH SUBJECT AND PREDICATE

> When he tried for days to change my mind. [subject and verb: *he tried;* subordinating conjunction: *When*]
> Which sparkles in the moonlight. [subject and verb: *Which sparkles;* relative pronoun: *Which*]

Revision of a Sentence Fragment

Since a fragment is often an isolated, mispunctuated part of an adjacent sentence, one way to revise a fragment is to make it a part of the complete sentence. Another way to revise a fragment is to make it into a sentence. Revisions need not alter the meaning.

FRAGMENT	Henry smiled self-consciously. **Like a politician before a camera.** [an isolated phrase]
REVISED	Henry smiled self-consciously, like a politician before a camera. [phrase included in sentence]
	OR
	Henry smiled self-consciously—like a politician before a camera. [The use of the dash instead of the comma tends to emphasize the material that follows.]
	OR
	Henry smiled self-consciously. He looked like a politician before a camera. [fragment made into a sentence]

Caution: When revising fragments, do not misuse the semicolon between parts of unequal grammatical rank: see **14c.**

2a

Do not carelessly capitalize and punctuate a phrase as you would a sentence.

FRAGMENT	Soon I began to work for the company. **First in the rock pit and later on the highway.** [prepositional phrases]
REVISED	Soon I began to work for the company, first in the rock pit and later on the highway. [fragment included in the preceding sentence]
FRAGMENT	He will have a chance to go home next weekend. **And to meet his new stepfather.** [infinitive phrase]
REVISED	He will have a chance to go home next weekend and to meet his new stepfather. [fragment included in the preceding sentence]
FRAGMENT	Astronauts venturing deep into space may not come back to earth for fifty years. **Returning only to discover an uninhabitable planet.** [participial phrase]
REVISED	Astronauts venturing deep into space may not come back to earth for fifty years. They may return only to discover an uninhabitable planet. [fragment made into a sentence]
FRAGMENT	The children finally arrived at camp. **Many dancing for joy, and some crying for their parents.** [absolute phrases]
REVISED	The children finally arrived at camp. Many were dancing for joy, and some were crying for their parents. [fragment made into a sentence]

■ **Exercise 1** Eliminate each fragment below by including it in the adjacent sentence or by making it into a sentence.

1. They enjoy reading a few types of novels. Such as science fiction.
2. The pampered Dennis finally left home. Earnestly seeking to become an individual in his own right.
3. It is wise to ignore her sarcasm. Or to make a quick exit.
4. She did not recognize Gary. His beard gone and hair cut.
5. Louise likes to pretend that she is very old. And to speak of the "days of her youth."
6. They will visit our campus soon. Maybe next month.
7. These commercials have a hypnotic effect. Not only on children but on adults too.
8. A few minutes later. A news bulletin interrupted the show.
9. Eric just stood there speechless. His face turning redder by the minute.
10. He killed six flies with one swat. Against the law of averages but possible.

2b

Do not carelessly capitalize and punctuate a subordinate clause as you would a sentence.

FRAGMENT   Thousands of young people became active workers in the community. **After this social gospel had changed their apathy to concern.** [subordinate clause]

REVISED   Thousands of young people became active workers in the community after this social gospel had changed their apathy to concern. [fragment included in the preceding sentence]

FRAGMENT   I didn't know where he came from. **Or who he was.** [subordinate clause]

REVISED   I didn't know where he came from or who he was. [fragment included in the preceding sentence]

FRAGMENT   I was trying to read the directions. **Which were confusing and absurd.** [subordinate clause]

REVISED   I was trying to read the directions, which were confusing and absurd. [fragment included in the preceding sentence]

OR

I was trying to read the directions. They were confusing and absurd. [fragment made into a sentence]

OR

I was trying to read the confusing, absurd directions. [fragment reduced to adjectivals that are included in the preceding sentence]

■ **Exercise 2** Eliminate each fragment below by including it in the preceding sentence or by making it into a sentence.

1. I decided to give skiing a try. After I had grown tired of watching other people fall.
2. Pat believes that everyone should go to college. And that all tests for admission should be abolished.
3. Many students were obviously victims of spring fever. Which affected class attendance.
4. Paul faints whenever he sees blood. And whenever he climbs into a dentist's chair.
5. I am making a study of cigarette advertisements. That use such slogans as "less tar, more taste" and "the lowest in tar and nicotine."

2c

Do not carelessly capitalize and punctuate any other fragment (such as an appositive or a part of a compound predicate) as you would a sentence.

FRAGMENT   The new lawyer needed a secretary. **A secretary with intelligence and experience.**

REVISED   The new lawyer needed a secretary—a secretary with intelligence and experience.

OR

The new lawyer needed a secretary with intelligence and experience.

FRAGMENT   He lost the gold watch. **The one which had belonged to his grandfather.**

REVISED   He lost the gold watch, the one which had belonged to his grandfather. [fragment included in the preceding sentence]

OR

He lost the gold watch which had belonged to his grandfather.

FRAGMENT   Sarah was elected president of her class. **And was made a member of the National Honor Society.** [detached part of a compound predicate]

REVISED   Sarah was elected president of her class and was made a member of the National Honor Society.

■ **Exercise 3** Eliminate each fragment below by including it in the preceding sentence or by making it into a sentence.

1. My roommate keeps all her shoes, scuba gear, books, and clothes in one closet. The worst disaster area on campus.
2. According to Macaulay, half-knowledge is bad. Even worse than ignorance.
3. The group met during the summer and made plans. And decided on the dates for action in the fall.
4. The hydraulic lift raises the plows out of the ground. And lowers them again.
5. I had a feeling that some sinister spirit brooded over the place. A feeling that I could not analyze.

■ **Exercise 4** Find the nine fragments in the following paragraph. Revise each fragment by attaching it logically to an adjacent sentence or by rewriting the fragment so that it stands by itself as a sentence.

[1] The little paperback almanac I found at the newsstand has given me some fascinating information. [2] Not just about the weather and changes in the moon. [3] There are also intriguing statistics. [4] A tub bath, for example, requires more water than a shower. [5] In all probability, ten or twelve gallons more, depending on how dirty the bather is. [6] And one of the Montezumas downed fifty jars of cocoa every day. [7] Which seems a bit exaggerated to me. [8] To say the least. [9] I also learned that an average beard has thirteen thousand whiskers. [10] That, in the course of a lifetime, a man could shave off more than nine yards of whiskers, over twenty-seven feet. [11] If my math is correct. [12] Some other interesting facts in the almanac. [13] Suppose a person was born on Sunday, February 29, 1976. [14] Another birthday not celebrated on Sunday until the year 2004. [15] Because February 29 falls on weekdays till then—twenty-eight birthdays later. [16] As I laid the almanac aside, I remembered that line in *Slaughterhouse-Five:* "And so it goes."

Comma Splice and Fused Sentence

3

Do not carelessly link two sentences with only a comma (comma splice) or run two sentences together without any punctuation (fused sentence).

Carefully observe how three sentences have been linked to make the one long sentence below.

> SENTENCES SEPARATED These are mysteries performed in broad daylight before our very eyes. We can see every detail. And yet they are still mysteries.

> SENTENCES LINKED These are mysteries performed in broad daylight before our very eyes; we can see every detail, and yet they are still mysteries. —ANNIE DILLARD

> [MAIN CLAUSE; MAIN CLAUSE, *and* MAIN CLAUSE.]

When you connect the end of one sentence to the beginning of another, be especially careful about punctuation.

> NOT The current was swift, he could not swim to shore. [comma splice—sentences are linked with only a comma]

> NOT The current was swift he could not swim to shore. [fused sentence—sentences are run together with no punctuation]

> VARIOUS METHODS OF REVISION

Because the current was swift, he could not swim to shore. [first main clause subordinated: see **12b**]

The current was so swift that he could not swim to shore. [second main clause subordinated]

Because of the swift current he could not swim to shore. [first clause reduced to an introductory phrase]

The current was swift. He could not swim to shore. [each main clause converted to a sentence]

The current was swift; he could not swim to shore. [main clauses separated by a semicolon: see **14a**]

The current was swift, so he could not swim to shore. [comma preceding the connective *so:* see **12a**]

He could not swim to shore, for the current was swift. [comma preceding the coordinating conjunction *for*]

When you revise carelessly connected sentences, choose a method that achieves the emphasis you want.

If you cannot always recognize a main clause and distinguish it from a phrase or from a subordinate clause, study **1d** and **1e**.

3a

Use a comma between main clauses *only* when they are linked by the coordinating conjunctions *and, but, or, for, nor, so,* or *yet*. See also **12a**.

> COMMA SPLICE Our country observed its Bicentennial in 1976, my hometown celebrated its fiftieth anniversary the same year.

> REVISED Our country observed its Bicentennial in 1976, **and** my hometown celebrated its fiftieth anniversary the same year. [the coordinating conjunction *and* added after the comma]
> OR
> Our country observed its Bicentennial in 1976; my hometown celebrated its fiftieth anniversary the same year. [A semicolon separates the main clauses. See **14a**.]

> COMMA SPLICE Her first novel was not a best seller, it was not a complete failure either.

> REVISED Her first novel was not a best seller, **nor** was it a complete failure. [Note the shift in the word order of subject and verb after the coordinating conjunction *nor.*]
> OR
> Her first novel was **neither** a best seller **nor** a complete failure. [a simple sentence with a compound complement]

> COMMA SPLICE The old tree stumps grated against the bottom of our boat, they did not damage the propeller.

> REVISED The old tree stumps grated against the bottom of our boat, **but** they did not damage the propeller. [the coordinating conjunction *but* added after the comma]
> OR
> **Although** the old tree stumps grated against the bottom of our boat, they did not damage the propeller. [Addition of *although* makes the first clause subordinate: see **12b**.]

Caution: Do not omit punctuation between main clauses not linked by *and, but, or, for, nor, so,* and *yet*.

> FUSED SENTENCE She wrote him a love letter he answered it in person.

> REVISED She wrote him a love letter. He answered it in person. [each main clause written as a sentence]
> OR
> She wrote him a love letter; he answered it in person. [main clauses separated by a semicolon: see **14a**]

Note 1: Either a comma or a semicolon may be used between short main clauses not linked by *and, but, or, for, nor, so,* or *yet* when the clauses are parallel in form and unified in thought:

> School bores them, preaching bores them, even television bores them. —ARTHUR MILLER
> One is the reality; the other is the symbol. —NANCY HALE

Note 2: The comma is used to separate a statement from a tag question:

He votes, doesn't he? [affirmative statement, negative question]

You can't change it, can you? [negative statement, affirmative question]

■ **Exercise 1** Connect each pair of sentences below in two ways, first with a semicolon and then with one of these coordinating conjunctions: *and, but, for, or, nor, so, or yet.*

EXAMPLE

I could have walked up the steep trail. I preferred to rent a horse.

a. *I could have walked up the steep trail; I preferred to rent a horse.*

b. *I could have walked up the steep trail, **but** I preferred to rent a horse.*

1. Dexter goes hunting. He carries his Leica instead of his Winchester.
2. The stakes were high in the political game. She played to win.
3. The belt was too small for him. She had to exchange it.
4. At the drive-in, they watched the musical comedy on one screen. We enjoyed the horror movie on the other.

■ **Exercise 2** Use a subordinating conjunction (see the list on page 672) to combine each of the four pairs of sentences in Exercise 1. For the use of the comma, refer to **12b**.

EXAMPLE

Although *I could have walked up the steep trail, I preferred to rent a horse.*

■ **Exercise 3** Proofread the following sentences (selected and adapted from *National Geographic*). Place a checkmark after a sentence with a comma splice and an X after a fused sentence. Do not mark correctly punctuated sentences.

1. The second-home craze has hit hard, everyone wants a piece of the wilderness.
2. The orchid needs particular soil microbes those microbes vanished when the virgin prairie was plowed.
3. Ty fought back the urge to push hard on the accelerator, which might have wrecked or disabled the van on the rough road.
4. Attempts to extinguish such fires have often failed some have been burning for decades.
5. Some of them had never seen an automobile, the war had bred familiarity with aircraft.
6. When the mining machines rumbled away, the ruined mountain was left barren and ugly.
7. The winds lashed our tents all night, by morning we had to dig ourselves out from under a snowdrift.
8. South Pass country is still short on roads and people, and so I was delighted to discover an experienced guide in Charley Wilson, son of Pony Express rider Nick Wilson.
9. The song that awakened me carried an incredible sense of mournfulness, it seemed to be the prolonged cry of a lone animal calling in the night.
10. I had thought that the illegal aliens headed mostly to farms, a sub-rosa international work force consigned to the meanest stoop labor, some do, but many bring blue-collar skills to the cities.

■ **Exercise 4** Use various methods of revision (see page 676) as you correct the comma splices or fused sentences in Exercise 3.

3b

Be sure to use a semicolon before a conjunctive adverb or transitional phrase placed between main clauses. See also 14a.

COMMA SPLICE   TV weather maps have various symbols, for example, a big apostrophe means drizzle.

REVISED   TV weather maps have various symbols; for example, a big apostrophe means drizzle. [MAIN CLAUSE; *transitional expression,* MAIN CLAUSE.]

FUSED SENTENCE   The tiny storms cannot be identified as hurricanes therefore they are called neutercanes.

REVISED   The tiny storms cannot be identified as hurricanes; therefore they are called neutercanes.
[MAIN CLAUSE; *conjunctive adverb* MAIN CLAUSE.]

Below is a list of frequently used conjunctive adverbs and transitional phrases; they function as both an adverb and a conjunctive:

CONJUNCTIVE ADVERBS

also	incidentally	nonetheless
anyway	indeed	otherwise
besides	instead	still
consequently	likewise	then
finally	meanwhile	therefore
furthermore	moreover	thus
hence	nevertheless	
however	next	

TRANSITIONAL PHRASES

after all	even so	in the second place
as a result	for example	on the contrary
at any rate	in addition	on the other hand
at the same time	in fact	
by the way	in other words	

Expressions such as *that is* and *what is more* also function as adverbials connecting main clauses:

The new members have paid their dues; **what is more,** they are all eager to work hard for our organization.

Conjunctive adverbs and transitional phrases are not grammatically equivalent to coordinating conjunctions. A coordinating conjunction has a fixed position between the main clauses it links, but many conjunctive adverbs and transitional phrases may either begin the second main clause or take another position in it:

She doubted the value of daily meditation, **but** she decided to try it.   [The coordinating conjunction has a fixed position.]

She doubted the value of daily meditation; **however,** she decided to try it.   [The conjunctive adverb begins the second main clause.]

She doubted the value of daily meditation; she decided, **however,** to try it.   [The conjunctive adverb appears later in the clause.]

Caution: Do not let a divided quotation trick you into making a comma splice.

COMMA SPLICE	"Marry her," Martin said, "after all, she's very rich."
REVISED	"Marry her," Martin said. "After all, she's very rich."
COMMA SPLICE	"Who won?" Elizabeth asked, "what was the score?"
REVISED	"Who won?" Elizabeth asked. "What was the score?"

Compare:

CORRECT	"The Rams led at the half," she said, "by twenty-one points." [See **12d(3)**.]
CORRECT	"The Rams led at the half," she said. "By twenty-one points." [See **9e**.]

■ **Exercise 5** Connect each pair of sentences below, following the pattern of the example.

> EXAMPLE
> At first the slogan shocked. After a year or two, however, it became a platitude.
> *At first the slogan shocked; however, after a year or two it became a platitude.*

1. The art company sent a sample collection of famous American paintings. The work of Norman Rockwell, however, was carelessly omitted.
2. The loud arguments sounded convincing. The majority, therefore, voted for the motion.
3. I don't mind lending him money. He is, after all, my favorite cousin.
4. India is not poor. It has, as a matter of fact, a huge amount of coal and iron reserves.

■ **Exercise 6** Divide the following quotations without creating a comma splice, as shown in the example below.

> EXAMPLE
> Eric Sevareid has said, "Let those who wish compare America with Rome. Rome lasted a thousand years."
> *"Let those who wish compare America with Rome," Eric Sevareid has said. "Rome lasted a thousand years."*

1. "I never saw her again. In fact, no one ever saw her again," wrote Kenneth Bernard.
2. W. C. Fields once said, "I am free of all prejudice. I hate everyone equally."
3. "I am saddest when I sing. So are those who hear me," Artemus Ward commented.
4. Gene Marine asked ironically, "What good is a salt marsh? Who needs a swamp?"
5. Pablo Picasso stated, "There is no abstract art. You must always start with something. Afterward you can remove all traces of reality."

■ **Exercise 7** Correct the comma splices and fused sentences in the following paragraph. Do not revise a correctly punctuated sentence.

¹ "Age is just a frame of mind," Nellie often says, "you're as old or as young as you think you are." ² Does she really believe this, or is she just making conversation? ³Well, when she was sixteen, her father said, "Baby Nell, you're not old enough to marry Johnny, besides he's a Democrat." ⁴ So Nellie ran away from her Missouri home in Oklahoma she found another Democrat, Frank, and married him. ⁵ When Nellie was thirty-nine, Frank died. ⁶ A year later she shocked everyone by marrying a Texan named William, he was a seventy-year-old veteran of the Spanish-American War. ⁷ "Billy thinks young," Nellie explained, "and he's just as young as he thinks he is." ⁸ Maybe she was right that happy marriage lasted eighteen years. ⁹ Nellie celebrated her seventieth birthday by going to Illinois, there she married Tom, who in her opinion was a youngster in his late sixties. ¹⁰ But her third marriage didn't last long, because Tom soon got hardening of the arteries and died of a heart attack, however, Nellie's arteries were fine. ¹¹ In 1975, when Nellie was eighty-three, she found and finally married her old Missouri sweetheart, then eighty-seven-year-old Johnny whisked her away to his soybean farm in Arkansas. ¹² Nellie's fourth wedding made front-page news, and then the whole town echoed Nellie's words: "Life doesn't begin at sixteen or at forty. It begins when you want it to, age is just a frame of mind."

■ **Exercise 8** First review Section **2** and study Section **3**. Then proofread the following for sentence fragments, comma splices, and fused sentences. Make appropriate revisions. Put a checkmark after each sentence that needs no revision.

1. Juan first enrolled for morning classes only, then he went job-hunting.
2. The cabin was originally built to house four people a family of ten lives in it now. Not to mention all the dogs and cats.
3. Becky signed up for the swimming relay, however, she is not really interested in competitive sports.
4. The Optimists Club sponsors a flea market every year, it is not, however, an easy way to make money.
5. Edgar Allan Poe attended West Point, where he was not a success.
6. Mr. Jordan requires us clerks to be on time for work. The reason being that bargain hunters start shopping early, almost before the doors open.
7. Our choir will go to Holland in May, when the tulip gardens are especially beautiful.
8. A long article in the magazine describes botulism, this is just another name for food poisoning.
9. That is absurd. It's nonsense. An argument that is riddled with stupid assumptions.
10. After class, I often drop by the college bookstore. Usually buying best-selling paperbacks, then never getting around to reading any of them.

Adjectives and Adverbs

4

Distinguish between adjectives and adverbs and use the appropriate forms.

Adjectives and adverbs function as modifiers; that is, they qualify or restrict the meaning of other words. Adjectives modify nouns and pronouns. Adverbs modify verbs (or verbals), adjectives, and other adverbs.

ADJECTIVES	ADVERBS
the **sudden** change	changed **suddenly**

a **probable** cause
an **unusual, large** one

probably caused
an **unusually** large one

The *-ly* ending can be an adjective-forming suffix as well as an adverb-forming one.

NOUNS TO ADJECTIVES   earth—earthly, ghost—ghostly
ADJECTIVES TO ADVERBS   rapid—rapidly, lucky—luckily

A number of words ending in *-ly* (such as *deadly, cowardly*), as well as many not ending in *-ly* (such as *far, fast, little, well*), may function either as adjectives or as adverbs. Some adverbs have two forms (such as *loud, loudly; quick, quickly; slow, slowly*).

When in doubt about the correct form of a given modifier—such as *slow* or *slowly*—consult your dictionary. Look for the labels *adj.* and *adv.* and for examples of usage. Read any usage notes.

I drove through the water **slowly.** Fry it **slowly.**
Drive **slow.** Fry it **slow.**   [limited usage]

Also consult your dictionary when in doubt about the forms of comparison and their spellings.

Present and past participles function as adjectives: "a *startling* comment," "the *startled* coach." Do not carelessly omit the *-d* or *-ed* of a past participle: "injured players," "a prejudiced person," "the experienced driver."

Caution: Do not use the double negative: see also page 819.

NONSTANDARD   They don't have no home.
STANDARD   They don't have any home.
OR   They have no home.

4a

Use adverbs to modify verbs, adjectives, and other adverbs.

His clothes fit him **perfectly.**   [The adverb modifies the verb *fit*.]
We have a **reasonably** secure future.   [The adverb modifies the adjective *secure*.]
Jean eats **exceptionally** fast.   [The adverb *exceptionally* modifies the adverb *fast*.]

Most dictionaries still label the following as informal usage: *sure* for *surely, real* for *really,* and *good* for the adverb *well.*

INFORMAL   I played **good.**
GENERAL   I played **well.**   [appropriate in both formal and informal usage]

■ **Exercise 1**   In the phrases below, convert adjectives into adverbs, following the pattern of the examples.

EXAMPLE
abrupt reply   *replied abruptly*   [OR   *abruptly replied*]

1. vague answer
2. safe travel
3. fierce fight
4. quick refusal
5. hearty welcome
6. blind conformity

EXAMPLE
complete happiness   *completely happy*

7. clear possibility
8. unusual anger
9. sudden popularity
10. strange sadness

■ **Exercise 2**   In the following sentences, convert any non-standard or informal modifier into an adverb form. Put a checkmark after each sentence that needs no revision.

1. A pocket calculator sure does help.
2. He took the joke serious.
3. Our team played well but did not win.
4. He was lucky to escape as easy as he did.
5. I do not practice as regular as I should.
6. It all happened very sudden.
7. The price will probable come down eventually.
8. Last night Venus seemed exceptional bright.
9. He talks very loudly when he is not sure of himself.
10. My notes are hard to read when I have to write that rapid.

4b

Use adjectives (not adverbs) for complements modifying the subject or the object. See 1b.

As subject complements (predicate adjectives), adjectives always modify the subject. Subject complements are used with such verbs as *feel, look, smell, sound,* and *taste,* which are called *linking verbs* when they connect a subject with its predicate adjective.

The soup tastes **different** with these herbs in it.
The speech sounded **bold.**

As object complements, adjectives always modify the object.

These herbs make the soup **different.**
He considered the speech **bold.**

Note: Both *bad* and *badly* are now standard when used with *feel* as a subject complement, but writers generally prefer *bad: They felt bad.*

Compare the meaning of the adjectives and adverbs below.

Jo looked **angry** to me.   [adjective—subject complement]
Jo looked **angrily** at me.   [adverb modifying *looked*]
He considered Jane **happy.**   [adjective—object complement]
He considered Jane **happily.**   [adverb modifying *considered*]

■ **Exercise 3**   Using adjectives as complements, write two sentences that illustrate each of the following patterns.

Subject—linking verb—subject complement.

Subject—verb—direct object—object complement.

4c

Use the appropriate forms for the comparative and the superlative.

In general, the shorter adjectives (and a few adverbs) form the comparative degree by adding *-er* and the superlative by adding *-est.* The longer adjectives and most adverbs form the comparative by the use of *more* (*less*) and the superlative by the use of *most* (*least*). A few modifiers have irregular comparatives and superlatives.

POSITIVE	COMPARATIVE	SUPERLATIVE
warm	warmer	warmest
warmly	more warmly	most warmly
helpful	less helpful	least helpful
good, well	better	best
bad, badly	worse	worst

Many writers prefer to use the comparative degree for two persons or things and the superlative for three or more:

COMPARATIVE	Was Monday or Tuesday **warmer**?	
	James was the **taller** of the two.	
SUPERLATIVE	Today is the **warmest** day of the year.	
	William was the **tallest** of the three.	

Caution: Do not use a double comparative or superlative: NOT more busier BUT busier; NOT least busiest BUT least busy.

Note: Current usage, however illogical it may seem, accepts comparisons of many adjectives or adverbs with absolute meanings, such as "a *more perfect* society," "the *deadest* campus," and "*less completely* exhausted." But many writers make an exception of *unique*—using "*more nearly* unique" rather than "more unique." They consider *unique* an absolute adjective—one without degrees of comparison.

Be sure to make your comparisons complete: see **22c**.

4d

Avoid awkward or ambiguous use of a noun form as an adjective.

Many noun forms are used effectively to modify other nouns (as in *boat* race, *show* business, *college* student and so on), especially when appropriate adjectives are not available. But such forms should be avoided when they are either awkward or confusing.

AWKWARD	Many candidates entered the president race.
BETTER	Many candidates entered the presidential race.
CONFUSING	The Representative Landor recess maneuvers led to victory.
BETTER	Representative Landor's maneuvers during the recess led to victory.

■ **Exercise 4** Correct all errors in the use of adjectives or adverbs. Also eliminate any awkward use of nouns as adjectives. Put a checkmark after any sentence that needs no revision.

1. The repair estimates mechanic was out to lunch.
2. She was even more livelier than her daughter.
3. The class enjoyed writing autobiography compositions.
4. The magazine has been published continuous since 1951, but it does not sell good now.
5. Baseball is more easy followed than football.
6. The older of the two is doing well in school.
7. Maribeth lives in a reasonable exclusive Kansas City resident area.
8. That food, I thought, can't taste as bad as it looks.
9. That is the worse grade I have ever received.
10. The recession and inflation kept getting worser.

Case

5

Choose the case form that shows the function of pronouns or nouns in sentences.

Case refers to the form of a word that indicates its use in a sentence as the subject of a verb, the object of a preposition, and so on. The English language has three cases: subjective, possessive, objective. Most nouns, many indefinite pronouns, and the personal pronouns *it* and *you* have a distinctive case form only for the possessive: *Rebecca's* coat, *someone's* dog, *its* color, *your* hands: see **15a**. But six common pronouns—*I, we, he, she, they, who*—have distinctive forms in all three cases:

Case forms

SUBJECTIVE	I	we	he, she	they	who
POSSESSIVE	my	our	his, her	their	whose
	(mine)	(ours)	(hers)	(theirs)	
OBJECTIVE	me	us	him, her	them	whom

SUBJECTIVE CASE *I, we, he, she, they, who*

Frank and **I** met in Paris. [subject of verb]
The only ones on stage were Lola and **she**. [subject complement]
Morris met the man **who** invented it. [subject in clause—see **5b**]
These people—**he** and **they**—remained silent. [appositives identifying the subject—see **5a**]

Subjects of verbs (but not of infinitives) are put in the subjective case.

POSSESSIVE CASE *my, our, his, her, their, whose, its, your, mine, ours, hers, theirs, yours*

Their dog finally learned to obey **its** master. [before a noun]
Theirs is better than **ours** is. [in the noun position]
Whose car did Terry drive? [before a noun]
His telling the story was a good idea. [before a gerund—see **5d**]

Note: The possessive forms *his* and *their* are nonstandard when made a part of a *-self* pronoun. Use *himself, themselves*. (See also *myself*: **19i**, page 731.)

OBJECTIVE CASE *me, us, him, her, them, whom*

Fran likes Glenda and **me**. [direct object]
Weston sends **them** a package now and then. [indirect object]
The man did check the tires for **us**. [object of preposition]
Potter, for **whom** the party was given, did not want to make a speech. [object of preposition in clause—see **5c**]
The officer ticketed us both, Rita and **me**. [appositive identifying the object of the verb, the pronoun *us*—see **5a**]
Our guests expected **us** to entertain **them**. [subject and object of the verbal *to entertain*, an infinitive—see **5e**]

Ignoring Hank and **me**, the twins talked about old times.
[object of the verbal *ignoring*, a participle]

Note: Use *who, whose,* or *whom* [NOT *which*] to refer to people: see page 733.

CASE IN COMBINED SENTENCES

Observe that the case (subjective or objective) of the italicized pronouns does not change when the following pairs of sentences are combined.

We need this.   **We** are students.
We students need this.

Don told **us** that.
Don told **us** students that.

[The insertion of a plural noun after the boldface pronoun does not affect the form of the pronoun.]

My wife saw it.   **I** saw it.
My wife and **I** saw it.

He wrote to Al.   He wrote to **me**.
He wrote to Al and **me**.

[See also **5a**. Formal English does not accept *myself* as a substitute for *me* or *I*: see **19i**, page 731.]

I eat fast.   She eats faster.
She eats faster than **I**.

I met Ed.   I think **he** is shy.
I met Ed, **who** I think is shy.

[See also **5b**.]

Then I called on Warren.   I can always depend on **him**.
Then I called on Warren, **whom** I can always depend on. [OR on **whom** I can always depend]

[See also **5c**.]

Observe the change in the case of the boldface pronouns in these sentences:

I grew up fast.   New responsibilities caused this.
New responsibilities caused **me** to grow up fast.
[*I* is subject of *grew up* (verb with particle); *me* is subject of *to grow up* (an infinitive). See **5e**.]
He smokes a smelly pipe.   She complains about it.
She complains about **his** smoking a smelly pipe.
[*He* is subject of *smokes* (a verb). *His* (the possessive case) is used before *smoking* (a gerund). See **5d** and page 819.]

In sentences such as the following, subjects and subject complements are interchangeable.

You and I are the losers.   The losers are **you and I**.
[See also **5f**.]

5a

Take special care with pronouns in compound constructions (including compound appositives).

She and her brother played golf. [subject]
Clara may ask **you or me** about it. [object of verb]
They sat in front of **her and me**. [object of preposition]
My best friends are **Bob and he**. [subject complement—see **5f**]

Notice below that the form of the pronoun used as an appositive depends on the function of the noun that the appositive explains or identifies.

Two members of the cast, **he and I**, assist the director.
[Compare "*He and I,* members of the cast, assist the director."]

The director often calls on her assistants: **him and me**.
[Compare "The director often calls on *him and me,* her assistants."]

In general usage, *me* is the appropriate form in the expression *Let's you and me* (although *Let's you and I* is used informally). Compare "Let *us*—just you and *me*." Be sure to use objective pronouns as objects of prepositions:

between you and **me**   like you and **me**
for you and **her**   to her brother and **her**
except Elmer and **him**   with Carla and **him**

■ **Exercise 1**   Choose the correct pronoun within the parentheses in each sentence below.

1. (He, Him) and (I, me) wrote and directed three one-act plays.
2. Joe and (I, me, myself) arrived an hour early.
3. It was Oliver and (they, them) who volunteered to address the envelopes.
4. (He, Him) and his brother are looking for part-time jobs.
5. Between Charlotte and (she, her) there is a friendly rivalry.
6. Mr. Rodriguez will hire a new engineer, either Williams or (he, him).
7. Leaving James and (he, him) at home, they went to the airport to meet the actor and (she, her).
8. My family and (I, me, myself) expected Frank and (she, her) to support (theirselves, themselves).
9. Two players on our team, Tom and (he, him), talked with the coach after the game.
10. After the game the coach talked with two players on our team, Tom and (he, him).

5b

Determine the case of each pronoun by its use in its own clause.

(1) *Who* or *whoever* as the subject of a clause

The subject of a verb in a subordinate clause takes the subjective case, even when the whole clause is used as an object:

I forgot **who** won the Superbowl in 1980. [In its own clause, *who* is the subject of the verb *won*. The complete clause *who won the Superbowl in 1980* is the object of the verb *forgot*.]

He has respect for **whoever** is in power. [*Whoever* is the subject of *is*. The complete clause *whoever is in power* is the object of the preposition *for*.]

(2) *Who* or *whom* before *I think, he says,* and so on

Such expressions as *I think, he says, she believes,* and *we know* may follow either *who* or *whom*. The choice depends on the use of *who* or *whom* in its own clause:

Gene is a man **whom** we know well. [*Whom* is the direct object of *know*. Compare "We know him well."]

Gene is a man **who** we know is honest. [*Who* is the subject of the second *is*. Compare "We know that Gene is a man *who* is honest."]

(3) Pronoun after *than* or *as*

In sentences such as the following, which have implied (rather than stated) elements, the choice of the pronoun form is important to meaning:

> She admires Kurt more than **I**. [meaning "more than I do"]
> She admires Kurt more than **me**. [meaning "more than she admires me"]
>
> He talks about food as much as **she**. [meaning "as much as she does"]
> He talks about food as much as **her**. [meaning "as much as he talks about her"]

Formal usage still requires the use of the subjective case of pronouns in sentences such as the following:

> Mr. Ames is older than **I**. [Compare "older than I am."]
> Aristotle is not so often quoted as **they**. [Compare "as they are."]

■ **Exercise 2** In sentences 1, 2, and 3 below, insert *I think* after each *who;* then read each sentence aloud. Notice that *who,* not *whom,* is still the correct case form. In sentences 4 and 5, complete each comparison by using first *they* and then *them.* Prepare to explain the differences in meaning.

1. George Eliot, who was a woman, wrote *Adam Bede.*
2. It was Elizabeth Holland who served as the eighth president of the university.
3. Maugham, who was an Englishman, died in 1965.
4. My roommate likes you as much as _____.
5. The director praised her more than _____.

5c

In formal writing use *whom* for all objects. See also **5b**.

In sentences:

> **Whom** do they recommend? [object of the verb *do recommend*]
> For **whom** did the board of directors vote? [object of the preposition *for*]
> Danny told Chet **whom** to call. Danny told Chet to call **whom**? [object of the infinitive *to call*—see also **5e**]

In subordinate clauses:

> The artist **whom** she loved has gone away. [object of the verb *loved* in the adjective clause]
> This is a friend **whom** I write to once a year. [object of the preposition *to* in the adjective clause]

Formal and informal English accept the omission of *whom* in sentences such as the following:

> The artist she loved has gone away.
> This is a friend I write to once a year.

Note: Informal English accepts *who* rather than *whom,* except after a preposition:

> Who do they recommend?   She told me who to call.

■ **Exercise 3** Using the case form in parentheses, convert each pair of sentences below into a single sentence.

EXAMPLES
I understand the daredevil. He motorcycled across the Grand Canyon. (*who*)
I understand the daredevil who motorcycled across the Grand Canyon.

Evelyn consulted an astrologer. She had met him in San Francisco. (*whom*)
Evelyn consulted an astrologer whom she had met in San Francisco.

1. Hercule Poirot is a famous detective. Agatha Christie finally kills him off in *Curtain*. (*whom*)
2. Some parents make an introvert out of an only child. They think they are protecting their offspring. (*who*)
3. Does anyone remember the name of the Frenchman? He built a helicopter in 1784. (*who*)
4. One of the officials called for a severe penalty. The players had quarreled with the officials earlier. (*whom*)

■ **Exercise 4** Formalize usage by changing *who* to *whom* when the pronoun functions as an object. Put a checkmark after sentences containing *who* correctly used as the subject of a verb or as a subject complement.

1. Who do they suspect?
2. Who could doubt that?
3. He knows who they will promote.
4. He knows who will be promoted.
5. The witness who the lawyer questioned next could remember nothing.
6. Guess who I ran into at the airport.
7. No one cares who they are or what they stand for.
8. In a crowded emergency room she knows exactly who to help first.
9. To find out who deceived who, be sure to tune in for the next episode.
10. During registration whoever I asked for directions gave me a map of the campus.

5d

As a rule, use the possessive case immediately before a gerund.

> I resented **his** criticizing our every move. [Compare "I resented his criticism, not him."]
> **Harry's** refusing the offer was a surprise. [Compare "Harry's refusal was a surprise."]

The *-ing* form of a verb can be used as a noun (gerund) or as an adjective (participle). The possessive case is not used before participles:

> **Caroline's** radioing the Coast Guard solved our problem. [*Radioing* is a gerund. Compare "*Her action* solved our problem."]
> The **man** sitting at the desk solved our problem. [*Sitting* is a participle. Compare "*He* solved our problem."]

Note: Do not use an awkward possessive before a gerund.

AWKWARD   The board approved of something's being sent to the poor overseas.
BETTER   The board approved of sending something to the poor overseas.

5e

Use the objective case for the subject or the object of an infinitive.

> They expected Nancy and **me** to do the scriptwriting. [subject of the infinitive *to do*]
>
> I did not want to challenge Victor or **him**. [object of the infinitive *to challenge*]

5f

Use the subjective case for the complement of the verb *be*.

> It was **she** who called. [Compare "She was the one who called."]
>
> The man who will get all the credit is no doubt Blevins or **he**. [Compare "Blevins or he is no doubt the man who will get all the credit."]

It's me (*him, her, us*, and *them*) is standard in informal speech or writing:

> If there had to be just one saved, I'm glad it was him.
> —JAMES HERRIOT

But many writers avoid this structure.

■ **Exercise 5** Find and revise in the sentences below all case forms that would be inappropriate in formal writing. Put a check-mark after each sentence that needs no revision.

1. I soon became acquainted with Ruth and her, whom I thought were agitators.
2. It was Doris and she who I blamed for me not making that sale.
3. Jack's racing the motor did not hurry Tom or me.
4. Between you and I, I prefer woodblock prints.
5. Who do you suppose will ever change Earth to Eden?
6. Since Joan eats less than I, I weigh more than she.
7. Let's you and I plan the curriculum of an ideal university.
8. The attorney who I interviewed yesterday is going to make public the records of three men who she believes are guilty of tax evasion.
9. We players always cooperate with our assistant coach, who we respect and who respects us.
10. The librarian wanted us—Kurt Jacobs and I—to choose Schlesinger's *The Bitter Heritage*.

Agreement

6

Make a verb agree in number with its subject; make a pronoun agree in number with its antecedent.

Verb and subject

In sentences such as those below, the forms of the verb and the subject (a noun or a noun substitute) agree grammatically:

SINGULAR	The **list** of items **was** long.
PLURAL	The **lists** of items **were** long.

Singular subjects take singular verbs (*list was*), and plural subjects take plural verbs (*lists were*).

The *-s* (or *-es*) suffix

Remember that *-s* (or *-es*) is (1) a plural-forming suffix for most nouns and (2) a singular-forming suffix for verbs—those present-tense verbs taking third-person singular subjects.

THIRD-PERSON SUBJECTS WITH PRESENT-TENSE VERBS

SINGULAR	PLURAL
The bell rings.	The bells ring.
The rope stretches.	The ropes stretch.

SINGULAR	PLURAL
The church remains.	The churches remain.
A hero doesn't.	Heroes don't.

All present-tense verbs change form to agree with third-person singular subjects: *I remain, he remains; I do, it does; I have, she has*. (See also **person**, page 821.) The verb *be* is the most irregular verb in the language: *I am, you are, she is* (present); *I was, you were, he was* (past). (See also **conjugation**, page 817.)

Probably the best way for you to eliminate errors in subject-verb agreement in your writing is to proofread carefully. But if you find it difficult to distinguish verbs and relate them to their subjects, review **1a**.

Pronoun and antecedent

As a rule, a pronoun and its antecedent (the word the pronoun refers to) also agree in number:

SINGULAR	Even an **animal** has **its** own territory.
PLURAL	Even **animals** have **their** own territory.

Singular antecedents are referred to by singular pronouns (*animal ← its*); plural antecedents, by plural pronouns (*animals ← their*). See also Section **28**.

Note: A pronoun also agrees with its antecedent in person and in gender. Lack of agreement in person causes a shift in point of view: see **27b**.

NOT	**One** reads for pleasure during **our** spare time. [shift from third person to first person]
BUT	**We** read for pleasure during **our** spare time. [first person]
OR	**You** read for pleasure during **your** spare time. [second person]
OR	**People** read for pleasure during **their** spare time. [third person]

Agreement in gender is usually easy and natural: "the *boy* and *his* dog," "the *girl* and *her* dog." The masculine pronoun may be used to refer to common gender:

> **One** reads for pleasure if **he** has the time.

Two pronouns may refer to paired antecedents of different genders: "Every father and mother makes *his* or *her* mistakes." See also page 685.

6a

Make a verb agree in number with its subject.

(1) Do not be misled by nouns or pronouns intervening between the subject and the verb or by subjects and verbs with endings difficult to pronounce.

The **repetition** of the drumbeats **helps** to stir emotions.
Every **one** of you **is invited** to the panel discussion.
Scientists sift the facts.
The **scientist asks** several pertinent questions.

As a rule, the grammatical number of the subject is not changed by the addition of expressions beginning with such words as *accompanied by, along with, as well as, in addition to, including, no less than, not to mention, together with.*

Unemployment as well as taxes **influences** votes.
Taxes, not to mention unemployment, **influence** votes.

(2) Subjects joined by *and* are usually plural.

My **parents** and my **uncle do** not **understand** this.
The **band** and the **team were leading** the parade.
Building a good marriage and **building** a good log **fire** are similar in many ways. —JOSEPHINE LOWMAN [gerund phrases—Compare ''Two actions are similar.'']

Exceptions: Occasionally, such a compound subject takes a singular verb because the subject denotes one person or a single unit.

Its **inventor** and chief **practitioner is** a native son of Boston, Robert Coles. —MARTHA BAYLES
Pushing and **shoving** in public places **is** characteristic of Middle Eastern culture. —EDWARD T. HALL

Every or *each* preceding singular subjects joined by *and* calls for a singular verb:

Every silver knife, fork, and spoon **has** to be counted.
Each cat and each dog **has** its own toy.

Placed after a plural subject, *each* does not affect the verb form. Some writers use a singular verb when *each* follows a compound subject:

The cat and the dog each **have** their own toys.
[Or, sometimes, ''The cat and the dog each *has* its own toy.'']

(3) Singular subjects joined by *or, either . . . or,* or *neither . . . nor* usually take a singular verb.

Paula or her secretary **answers** the phone on Saturday.
Either the mayor or the governor **is** the keynote speaker.
Neither criticism nor praise **affects** them. [Informal ''Neither criticism nor praise affect them.'']

If one subject is singular and one is plural, the verb usually agrees with the nearer subject:

Neither the quality nor the prices **have** changed.
Neither the prices nor the quality **has** changed.
[Compare ''The prices *and* the quality *have not* changed.'']

The verb also agrees with the nearer subject in person in sentences like those below. (See also pages 683 and 821.)

Doesn't **he** or I deserve it?
Don't **I** or he deserve it?

Pat or **you were** supposed to call.
You or **Pat was** supposed to call.

(4) Do not let inverted word order (VERB + SUBJECT) or the structure *there* + VERB + SUBJECT cause you to make a mistake in agreement.

VERB + SUBJECT

Hardest hit by the high temperatures and the drought **were** American **farmers.** —TIME
Among our grandest and longest-lived illusions **is** the **notion** of the noble savage. —JOHN PFEIFFER
Neither **do vegetarians** eat only vegetables. —CONSUMER REPORTS
[Here *neither* is a conjunction meaning *nor yet*. See 6a(6).]

There + VERB + SUBJECT

There **were** Vietnam War **protests**, draft-card **burnings**, and civil rights **marches.** —LOUISE LEVATHES
There **were anger** and **hatred** in that voice. —JOHN CIARDI
[Compare ''Why *are* there fewer *quasars* now than there *were* in the past?'' —ADRIAN WEBSTER (verb + *there* + subject . . . *there* + verb)]

(5) A relative pronoun (*who, which, that*) used as subject has the same number as its antecedent.

It is the **pharmacist who** often **suggests** a new brand.
Tonsillitis is among those **diseases that are** curable.
This is the **one** of the local papers **that prints** a daily horoscope. [*That* refers to *one* because only one paper prints a daily horoscope; the other papers do not.]
It is not better things but better **people that make** better living. —CARLL TUCKER [Compare ''Better people (not better things) make better living.'']

(6) When used as subjects, such words as *each, either, neither, one, everybody,* and *anyone* regularly take singular verbs.

Neither likes the friends of the other.
Each of them **does have** political ambitions.
Everybody in the office **has** tickets.

Subjects such as *all, any, half, most, none,* and *some* may take a singular or a plural verb; the context generally determines the choice of the verb form.

Evelyn collects stamps; **some are** worth a lot. [Compare ''Some of them are worth a lot.'']
The honey was marked down because **some was** sugary. [Compare ''Some of it was sugary.'']

(7) Collective nouns (and phrases denoting a fixed quantity) take a singular verb when they refer to the group as a unit and take a plural verb when they refer to individuals or parts of the group.

Singular (regarded as a unit)

My **family has** its traditions.

The **number is** very small.
A **billion dollars is** a lot of money.
The **majority** of it **was** wasted.
Two-thirds of this **has** been finished.

Plural (regarded as individuals or parts)

A **number were** absent.
The **majority** of us **are** for it.
Two-thirds of these **have** been finished.

OPTIONS

Ten gallons of gas is/are expensive.
A thousand bushels of grain was/were crated.
The data is/are being studied.

(8) A linking verb agrees with its subject, not with its complement (predicate noun).

His **problem is** frequent headaches.
Frequent **headaches are** his problem.

Note: Because the number of the pronoun *what* depends on the number of the word (or word group) referred to, the verb does agree with its complement in sentences like these:

Of course, what you see in the final commercial **are** pretty pictures—the bear in a canoe, the bear in a Jeep, the bear padding behind the man.   —JONATHAN PRICE
[Compare "Pretty pictures are what you see."]

What I do, at these times, **is** to change the way the system works.   —LEWIS THOMAS
[Compare "That is what I do."]

(9) Nouns plural in form but singular in meaning usually take singular verbs. In all doubtful cases, consult a good dictionary.

Nouns that are regularly treated as singular include *economics, electronics, measles, mumps, news, physics,* and *tactics.*

News **is traveling** faster than ever before.
Physics **has fascinated** my roommate for months.

Some nouns ending in *-ics* (such as *athletics, politics,* and *statistics*) are considered singular when referring to an organized body of knowledge and plural when referring to activities, qualities, or individual facts:

Athletics **is required** of every student. [Compare "Participation in games *is required* of every student."]
Athletics **provide** good recreation. [Compare "Various games *provide* good recreation."]

(10) The title of a single work or a word spoken of as a word, even when plural in form, takes a singular verb.

Romeo and Juliet never **grows** old. [The play, not the characters, never grows old.]
"Autumn Leaves" **is** a beautiful song.
Children certainly **does** have an interesting history.

■ **Exercise 1** The following sentences are all correct. Read them aloud, stressing the italicized words. If any sentence sounds wrong to you, read it aloud two or three more times so that you will gain practice in saying and hearing the correct forms.

1. The *timing* of these strikes *was* poorly planned.
2. There *are* a few *cookies* and *pickles* left.
3. A *wrench* and a *hubcap were* missing.
4. *Every one* of my cousins, including Larry, *has* brown eyes.
5. Sandy was the *only one* of the singers *who was* off-key.
6. *Doesn't it* make sense?
7. *Each* of the episodes *is* exciting.
8. Every *one* of you *is* invited.
9. *A number* in this group *are* affected.
10. There *were* several *reasons* for this.

■ **Exercise 2** Choose the correct form of the verb within parentheses in each sentence below. Make sure that the verb agrees with its subject according to the rules of formal English.

1. Neither Anita nor Leon (feels, feel) that the evidence is circumstantial.
2. Tastes in reading, of course, (differs, differ).
3. Every one of the figures (was, were) checked at least twice.
4. A fountain and a hanging basket (adorns, adorn) the entrance.
5. Neither of them ever (asks, ask) for a second helping.
6. There (comes, come) to my mind now the names of the two or three people who were most influential in my life.
7. The booby prize (was, were) green apples.
8. A rustic lodge, as well as a game refuge and fishing waters, (is, are) close by.
9. Hidden cameras, which (invades, invade) the privacy of the unwary few, (provides, provide) entertainment for thousands.
10. The study of words (is, are) facilitated by breaking them down into prefixes, suffixes, and roots.

6b

Make a pronoun agree in number with its antecedent.

A singular antecedent (one that would take a singular verb) is referred to by a singular pronoun; a plural antecedent (one that would take a plural verb) is referred to by a plural pronoun:

SINGULAR   An **actor** during early rehearsals often **forgets his** lines.
PLURAL   **Actors** during early rehearsals often **forget their** lines.

(1) As a rule, use a singular pronoun to refer to such antecedents as *each, either, neither, one, anyone, everybody, a person.*

Each of these companies had **its** books audited. [NOT *their*]
One has to live with **oneself.** [NOT *themselves*]

Usage varies regarding the choice of pronoun referring to such antecedents as *everyone* or *a person* when the meaning includes both sexes or either sex (common gender):

A **person** needs to see **his** dentist twice a year. [OR *his or her*]

Every man and woman shows his/her essence by reaction to the soil.   —ROBERT S. De ROPP

So everybody gets married—unmarried—and married, but they're all married to somebody most of the time.
—MARGARET MEAD

In fact, the fear of growing old is so great that every aged person is an insult and a threat to the society. They remind us of our own death. . . .   —SHARON CURTIN

(2) Two or more antecedents joined by *and* are referred to by a plural pronoun; two or more singular antecedents joined by *or* or *nor* are referred to by a singular pronoun.

> **Andrew and Roger** lost **their** self-confidence.
> Did **Andrew or Roger** lose **his** self-confidence?

If one of two antecedents joined by *or* or *nor* is singular and one is plural, the pronoun usually agrees with the nearer antecedent:

> Neither the **package** nor the **letters** had reached **their** destination. [*Their* is closer to the plural antecedent *letters*.]
> Stray **kittens** or even an abandoned grown **cat** has **its** problems finding enough food to survive long. [*Its* is closer to the singular antecedent *cat*.]

(3) Collective nouns are referred to by singular or plural pronouns, depending on whether the collective noun is used in a singular or plural sense. See also 6a(7).

Special care should be taken to avoid treating a collective noun as both singular and plural within the same sentence.

INCONSISTENT	The choir **is** writing **their** own music. [singular verb, plural pronoun]
CONSISTENT	The choir **is** writing **its** own music. [both singular]
CONSISTENT	The group of students **do** not agree on methods, but **they** unite on basic aims. [both plural]

■ **Exercise 3**   Choose the correct pronoun or verb form within parentheses in each sentence below; follow the rules of formal English usage.

1. A number of people, such as Kate Swift and Warren Farrell, (has, have) offered (his, her and his, their) suggestions for a "human" singular pronoun, like *te* for *he or she* to refer to the antecedent *a person*.
2. If any one of the sisters (needs, need) a ride to church, (she, they) can call Trudy.
3. Neither the pilot nor the flight attendants mentioned the incident when (he, they) talked to reporters.
4. The Washington team (was, were) opportunistic; (it, they) took advantage of every break.
5. If the board of directors (controls, control) the company, (it, they) may vote (itself, themselves) bonuses.

■ **Exercise 4**   All the following sentences are correct. Change them as directed in parentheses, revising other parts of the sentence to secure agreement of subject and verb, pronoun and antecedent.

1. Everyone in our Latin class thoroughly enjoys the full hour. (Change *Everyone* to *The students*.)
2. Every activity in that class seems not only instructive but amusing. (Change *Every activity* to *The activities*.)
3. Since the students eat their lunch just before the class, the Latin professor keeps coffee on hand to revive any sluggish thinkers. (Change *the students* to *nearly every student*.)
4. Yesterday one of the students was called on to translate some Latin sentences. (Change *one* to *two*.)

5. We were busily following the oral translation in our textbooks. (Change *We* to *Everyone else*.)
6. One or perhaps two in the class were not paying attention when the student, Jim Melton, said, "Who do you see?" (Use *Two or perhaps only one* instead of *One or perhaps two*.)
7. The Latin professor ordered, "Look at those inflections that indicate case! *Whom! Whom* do you see! Not *who!*" (Change *those inflections* to *the inflection*.)
8. Nobody in the room was inattentive as Jim translated the sentence again: "*Whom* do *youm* see?" (Change *Nobody* to *Few*.)
9. The students, who understood Jim's problem with inflections, were smiling as the professor exclaimed, "*Youm!* Whoever heard of *youm!*" (Change *The students* to *Everyone*.)
10. A student who sometimes poses questions that provoke thought about the nature of language, Jim politely replied, "But, sir, whoever heard of *whom?*" (Change *questions* to *a question*.)

Verb Forms

7

Use the appropriate form of the verb. (See also 6a.)

Verb forms indicate tense, number and person, voice, and mood.

Tense

Tense refers to the form of the verb that indicates time:

> We often **ask** questions. [present tense]
> After the lecture we **asked** questions. [past tense]
>
> I **see** the point now. [present tense]
> I finally **saw** the point. [past tense]

The suffix *-ed* or *-d* marks the past tense of regular verbs: *asked, hoped*. Irregular verbs do not form their past tense by the addition of *-ed* or *-d*: *saw, went, gave, flew*.

Various auxiliary verbs indicate time in verb phrases:

will see	**had** asked	**do** hope	**were** going
can see	**have** asked	**did** hope	**has been** going

There are six tenses. Single-word verbs are used for two of these (the simple present and the simple past), and auxiliary verbs are used for the other four:

SIMPLE TENSES

present:	ask (asks)	see (sees)
past:	asked	saw
future:	will (shall) ask	will (shall) see

PERFECT TENSES

present:	have (has) asked	have (has) seen
past:	had asked	had seen
future:	will (shall) have asked	will (shall) have seen

The six tenses are based on primary forms called principal parts (*see, saw, seen*). See **7a**.

Number and Person

Verb forms also indicate the number of their subjects:

SINGULAR   Only one question **was** asked.
PLURAL   Many questions **were** asked.

In the present tense, all verbs change form to agree grammatically with third-person singular subjects: *I see, he sees.* See Section **6**, page 683.

Voice

Voice is the form of a transitive verb that indicates whether or not the subject named performs the action denoted by the verb. There are two voices, active and passive. Only transitive verbs have voice. Transitive active verbs take direct objects (see **1b**).

ACTIVE   Burglars often **steal** jewelry.   [The subject acts. The object is *jewelry.*]

The object of a transitive active verb can usually be converted into the subject of a transitive passive verb. When an active verb is made passive, a form of *be* is used.

PASSIVE   Jewelry **is** often **stolen** by burglars.   [The prepositional phrase *by burglars* could be omitted.]

Compare the active and the passive forms of the verb *see* in the conjugation on page 817. See also **29d**.

Note: Intransitive verbs do not take objects: see page 667.

The rookies **did** not **go.**
Carol **became** an engineer.   [a linking verb with subject complement]

Mood

Verbs change form to indicate mood, or the way an assertion is conceived. There are three moods: indicative, imperative, and subjunctive.

INDICATIVE   She usually **rents** a car.   [a factual statement]
              Does she usually **rent** a car?   [a question]

IMPERATIVE   **Rent** a car.   [a command or request]

SUBJUNCTIVE   If **I were** she, **I would rent** a car.   [a condition contrary to fact]
              I suggested that she **rent** a car.   [a recommendation]

See **7c** and **7d**.

Progressive Forms

The English language also has progressive verb forms, which are verb phrases consisting of a form of *be* plus an *-ing* verb (the present participle). These phrases denote an action in progress.

PRESENT   am (is, are) seeing
PAST   was (were) seeing
FUTURE   will be seeing
PRESENT PERFECT have (has) been seeing
PAST PERFECT   had been seeing
FUTURE PERFECT   will have been seeing

Passive progressive forms include *am (is, are) being seen, was (were) being seen,* and so on.

Note: Infinitives, participles, and gerunds (verbals) also have progressive forms, as well as tense—but not all six tenses.

	Infinitives
PRESENT	to see, to be seen, to be seeing
PRESENT PERFECT	to have seen, to have been seen, to have been seeing

	Participles
PRESENT	seeing, being seen
PAST	seen
PRESENT PERFECT	having seen, having been seen

	Gerunds
PRESENT	seeing, being seen
PRESENT PERFECT	having seen, having been seen

Forms of *be*

Be is the most irregular verb in the English language. This verb has eight forms: *am, are, is, was, were, be, been, being.*

They **are** happy.   That **may be** true.
We **will be** leaving soon.   He **was being** difficult.
His shoulder **had been** injured before.

Below is a list of forms of *be* used with various subjects in the simple tenses.

PRESENT	I am	you are	he/she/it is	[singular]
	we are	you are	they are	[plural]
PAST	I was	you were	he/she/it was	[singular]
	we were	you were	they were	[plural]
FUTURE	will be OR shall be	[all subjects, singular or plural]		

The perfect-tense forms are *have (has) been, had been,* and *will (shall) have been.*

7a

Avoid misusing the principal parts of verbs and confusing similar verbs.

(1) Avoid misusing the principal parts of verbs.

The principal parts of a verb include the *present* form (which is also the stem of the infinitive), the *past* form, and the *past participle.*

PRESENT STEM (INFINITIVE)	PAST TENSE	PAST PARTICIPLE
ask	asked	asked
begin	began	begun

Note: The *present participle* (the present form plus *-ing: asking, beginning*) is sometimes considered as a fourth principal part.

The *present* form may function as a single-word verb or may be preceded by words such as *will, do, may, could, have to, ought to,* or *used to.*

I **ask,** he **does ask,** we **begin,** it **used to begin**

The *past* form functions as a single-word verb.

He **asked** questions.
The show **began** at eight.

The *past participle*, when used as a part of a verb phrase, always has at least one auxiliary.

they **have asked**, she **was asked**, he **has been asked**
it **has begun**, the work **will be begun**, we **have begun**

Caution: Do not omit a needed *-d* or *-ed* because of the pronunciation. For example, although it is easy to remember a clearly pronounced *-d* or *-ed* (*faded, repeated*), it is sometimes difficult to add a needed *-d* or *-ed* in such expressions as *hoped to* or *opened the*. Observe the use of the *-ed* or *-d* ending in these sentences:

Yesterday I ask**ed** David.   Then I talk**ed** to her.
Perhaps we had pric**ed** our vegetables too high.
It had happen**ed** before.   She was not experienc**ed**.
He us**ed** to smoke.   I am not suppos**ed** to do it.
A judge may be prejudic**ed**.   [Compare ''a prejudic**ed** judge.'']

When in doubt about the forms of a verb, consult a good dictionary. (If forms are not listed after an entry, the verb is generally a regular one, taking the *-d* or *-ed* ending.)

The following list gives the principal parts of a number of verbs that are sometimes misused. Give special attention to any forms unfamiliar to you.

Principal Parts of Verbs

PRESENT STEM (INFINITIVE)	PAST TENSE	PAST PARTICIPLE
become	became	become
begin	began	begun
blow	blew	blown
break	broke	broken
bring	brought	brought
burst	burst	burst
catch	caught	caught
choose	chose	chosen
cling	clung	clung
come	came	come
dive	dived OR dove	dived
do	did	done
draw	drew	drawn
drink	drank	drunk
drive	drove	driven
eat	ate	eaten
fall	fell	fallen
fly	flew	flown
forgive	forgave	forgiven
freeze	froze	frozen
give	gave	given
go	went	gone
grow	grew	grown
know	knew	known
ride	rode	ridden
ring	rang	rung
rise	rose	risen
run	ran	run
see	saw	seen
shake	shook	shaken
sing	sang OR sung	sung
sink	sank OR sunk	sunk
speak	spoke	spoken

PRESENT STEM (INFINITIVE)	PAST TENSE	PAST PARTICIPLE
spin	spun	spun
steal	stole	stolen
swear	swore	sworn
swim	swam	swum
swing	swung	swung
take	took	taken
tear	tore	torn
throw	threw	thrown
wear	wore	worn
write	wrote	written

Note: Mistakes with verbs sometimes involve spelling errors. Use care when you write troublesome verb forms such as the following:

PRESENT STEM (INFINITIVE)	PAST TENSE	PAST PARTICIPLE	PRESENT PARTICIPLE
lead	led	led	leading
loosen	loosened	loosened	loosening
lose	lost	lost	losing
pay	paid	paid	paying
study	studied	studied	studying

■ **Exercise 1**   Respond to the questions in the past tense with a past tense verb; respond to the questions in the future tense with a present perfect verb (*have* or *has* + a past participle). Follow the pattern of the examples.

EXAMPLES   Did she criticize Don?   *Yes, she criticized Don.*
Will they take it?   *They have already taken it.*

1. Did he give it away?
2. Will you run a mile?
3. Did the man drown?
4. Will they begin that?
5. Did the wind blow?
6. Will she choose it?
7. Did it really happen?
8. Will the river rise?
9. Did you do that?
10. Will they steal it?
11. Did you spin your wheels?
12. Will they freeze it?
13. Did he cling to that belief?
14. Will they go to the police?
15. Did she know them?
16. Will the fire alarm ring?
17. Did the sack burst?
18. Will he eat it?
19. Did you grow these?
20. Will Bert speak out?

(2) Do not confuse *set* with *sit* or *lay* with *lie*.

Sit means "be seated," and *lie down* means "rest in or get into a horizontal position." To *set* or *lay* something down is to place it or put it somewhere.

Learn the distinctions between the forms of *sit* and *set* and those of *lie* and *lay*.

PRESENT STEM (INFINITIVE)	PAST TENSE	PAST PARTICIPLE	PRESENT PARTICIPLE
(to) sit	sat	sat	sitting
(to) set	set	set	setting
(to) lie	lay	lain	lying
(to) lay	laid	laid	laying

As a rule, the verbs (or verbals) *set* and *lay* take objects; *sit* and *lie* do not.

She had **laid** the book aside.   [*Book* is the object.]
I wanted to **lie** in the sun.   [*To lie* has no object.]
After asking me to **sit** down, she seemed to forget I was there.   [*To sit* has no object.]

Study the examples below, noting the absence of objects.

I did not sit down.   You should lie down.

Al sat up straight.   He lay down awhile.
She had sat too long.   It has lain here a week.
It was sitting here.   The coat was lying there.

Note: Because they take objects, the verbs *set* and *lay* may be passive as well as active.

Somebody **had set** the pup in the cart. [active]
The pup **had been set** in the cart. [passive]

We **ought to lay** our prejudices aside. [active]
Our prejudices **ought to be laid** aside. [passive]

■ **Exercise 2** Substitute the correct forms of *sit* and *lie* for the italicized word in each sentence. Follow the pattern of the example. Do not change the tense of the verb.

EXAMPLE   I *remained* in that position for twenty minutes.

*I **sat** in that position for twenty minutes.*
*I **lay** in that position for twenty minutes.*

1. Jack doesn't ever want to *get* down.
2. The dog *stayed* near the luggage.
3. The toy soldier has been *rusting* in the yard.
4. He often *sleeps* on a park bench.
5. Has it *been* there all along?

■ **Exercise 3** Choose the correct verb form within the parentheses.

1. After lunch I wanted to (lie, lay) down for a few minutes.
2. Yesterday we (lay, laid) the rest of the tiles ourselves.
3. The garden hose has (lain, laid) there for weeks.
4. The money for the tickets was still (lying, laying) on my desk.
5. He had just (lain, laid) the child down.
6. Alice and Dawn were (sitting, setting) up watching a late movie.
7. Alice and Dawn were (sitting, setting) up chairs for the concert.
8. They came in and (sat, set) down for a chat.
9. How long had the visitors (sat, set) there?
10. Sometimes I just (sit, set) there and watch the tide come in.

7b

Learn the meaning of tense forms. Use logical tense forms in sequence.

The six tenses are based on the three principal parts of verbs: the *present* (stem of the infinitive—to *see*, to *use*); the *past* (*saw*, *used*); and the *past participle* (*seen*, *used*). See **7a**.

(1) Learn the meaning of the six tense forms.

Although tense indicates time (see pages 686–87), the tense forms of verbs do not always agree with divisions of actual time. The present tense, for example, is by no means limited to the present time. .

PRESENT TENSE

I **see** what you meant by that remark. [now, present time]
He **uses** common sense. [habitual action]
Human beings **make** mistakes. [a timeless truth]
In the fall of 1939 Hitler **attacks** Poland. [historical present]
Officially winter **begins** next week. [present form (used with the adverbial *next week*) indicating future time]

Note: Auxiliaries indicate present tense in the following verb phrases.

He **does** use common sense. [emphatic present]
I **am** learning from my mistakes. [a progressive form indicating past, present, and (probably) future time]
Mistakes **are** often made. [passive form, habitual action]

PAST TENSE—past time, not extending to the present
I **saw** the accident. [at a definite time before now]
We **used** makeshift tools. [action completed in the past]

Note: Auxiliaries also indicate past tense:

I **did** see the accident. [emphatic]
We **were** using makeshift tools. [progressive]
The accident **was** seen by three people. [passive]
Talk shows **used to** be worse than they are now. [Compare ''*were* worse then.'']

FUTURE TENSE—at a future time, sometime after now
He **will** see his lawyer.
We **will** use a different strategy.

The auxiliary *will* also indicates future time in progressive and passive forms of the verb:

He **will be seeing** his lawyer. [progressive]
A different strategy **will be used**. [passive]

PRESENT PERFECT TENSE—sometime before now, up to now
I **have seen** the movie. [sometime before now]
He **has used** his savings wisely. [up to now]

PAST PERFECT TENSE—before an indicated time in the past
She **had seen** me before the game started.
When he **had used** his savings, he applied for a loan.

Note: Sometimes the simple past is used for the past perfect: "She *saw* me before the game started."

FUTURE PERFECT TENSE—after now and before an indicated time in the future
They **will have seen** the report by next week.

Speakers and writers often substitute the simple future for the future perfect:

They **will see** the report by next week.

Examples of progressive and passive forms in the present perfect tense follow.

Kevin **has been using** the money wisely.
The Crawfords **have been seeing** deer in the woods.
The money **has been used** wisely.
Deer **have been seen** in the woods.

Again, the simple future usually replaces the future perfect:

By 1990 they **will have been seeing** their dreams in action. [USUAL: ''they *will be seeing*'']
By 1990 their dreams **will have been seen** in action. [USUAL: ''their dreams *will be seen* in action'']

■ **Exercise 4** Be prepared to explain the differences in the meaning of tense forms separated by slashes in the following sentences.

1. It *has rained* / *had rained* for days.
2. Mary *waxed* / *did wax* / *was waxing* the car.
3. Walter *teaches* / *is teaching* Spanish.
4. I *spoke* / *have spoken* to him about this.
5. The Bowens *had sold* / *will have sold* their house by then.

6. Time *passes / does pass / has passed / had been passing* rapidly.
7. In 1840 Thomas Carlyle *calls / called* time a great mystery, a miracle.

(2) Use logical tense forms in sequence.

Verbs

Notice in the examples below the relationship of each verb form to actual time:

When the speaker **entered**, the audience **rose**. [Both actions took place at the same definite time in the past.]

I **have ceased** worrying because I **have heard** no more rumors. [Both verb forms indicate action at some time before now.]

When I **had been** at camp four weeks, I **received** word that my application **had been accepted**. [The *had* before *been* indicates a time prior to that of *received*.]

Infinitives

Use the present infinitive to express action occurring at the same time as, or later than, that of the main verb; use the present perfect infinitive for action prior to that of the main verb:

I would have liked **to live** (NOT *to have lived*) in Shakespeare's time. [present infinitive—for the same time as that of the main verb]

She wanted **to win**. She wants **to win**. [present infinitives—for time later than *wanted* or *wants*]

I would like **to have won** that prize. [present perfect infinitive—for time prior to that of the main verb. Compare "I wish I *had won*."]

Participles

Use the present form of participles to express action occurring at the same time as that of the main verb; use the present perfect form for action prior to that of the main verb:

Walking along the streets, he met many old friends. [The walking and the meeting were simultaneous.]

Having climbed that mountain they felt a real sense of achievement. [The climbing took place first; then came their sense of achievement.]

■ **Exercise 5** Choose the verb form inside parentheses that is the logical tense form in sequence.

1. When the fire sale (ended, had ended), the store closed.
2. Fans cheered as the goal (had been made, was made).
3. The team plans (to celebrate, to have celebrated) tomorrow.
4. We should have planned (to have gone, to go) by bus.
5. (Having finished, Finishing) the test, Leslie left the room.
6. (Having bought, Buying) the tickets, Mr. Selby took the children to the circus.
7. The president had left the meeting before it (had adjourned, adjourned).
8. It is customary for ranchers (to brand, to have branded) their cattle.
9. Marilyn had not expected (to see, to have seen) her cousin at the rally.
10. The pond has begun freezing because the temperature (dropped, has dropped).

7c

Use the subjunctive mood in the few types of expressions in which it is still appropriate.

Distinctive forms for the subjunctive occur only in the present and past tenses of *be* and in the present tense of other verbs used with third-person singular subjects.

INDICATIVE	I **am**, you **are**, he **is**, others **are** [present]
SUBJUNCTIVE	I **was**, you **were**, he **was**, others **were** [past]
	(with all subjects) **be** [present], **were** [past]
INDICATIVE	he **sees**, others **see** [present]
SUBJUNCTIVE	(that) he **see**, (that) others **see** [present]

The subjunctive has been largely displaced by the indicative. Compare the following optional usages:

Suppose he **were** to die.	Suppose he dies.
I will ask that he **do** this.	I will ask him to do this.
It is necessary that she **be** there on time.	She must be there on time.

Especially in formal English, however, the subjunctive is still used to express a contrary-to-fact condition.

Drive as if every other car on the road **were** out to kill you.
—ESQUIRE

The subjunctive is required (1) in *that* clauses of motion, resolution, recommendation, command, or demand and (2) in a few idiomatic expressions.

I move that the report **be** approved.
Resolved, that dues for the coming year **be** doubled.
I recommend (order, demand) that the prisoner **see** his lawyer.
I demand (request, insist) that the messenger **go** alone.
If need **be** . . . **Suffice** it to say . . . **Come** what may . . . [fixed subjunctive in idiomatic expressions]

■ **Exercise 6** Prepare for a class discussion of the use of the subjunctive and of the indicative used informally in the following sentences.

1. If Linda was here, she would explain everything.
2. We insist that he be punished.
3. I wish that peace were possible.
4. Americans now speak of Spain as though it were just across the river.
5. Present-day problems demand that we be ready for any emergency.
6. If there was time, I could finish my report.
7. Come what may, we will never choose anarchy.
8. I demand that he make amends.
9. If I were you, I would apply tomorrow.
10. The man acts as though he were the owner.

■ **Exercise 7** Compose five sentences in which the subjunctive is required.

7d

Avoid needless shifts in tense or mood. See also 27a.

INCONSISTENT He **walked** up to me in the cafeteria and **tries** to start a fight. [Tense shifts from past to present.]

BETTER He **walked** up to me in the cafeteria and **tried** to start a fight.

INCONSISTENT It is necessary to restrain an occasional fool-hardy park visitor. If a female bear **were** to mistake his friendly intentions and **supposes** him a menace to her cubs, he would be in trouble. [Mood shifts from subjunctive to indicative.] But females with cubs **were** only one of the dangers. [a correct sentence if standing alone, but here inconsistent with present tense of preceding sentence and therefore misleading] One **has** to remember that all bears **were** wild animals and not domesticated pets. [Tense shifts from present to past.] Though a bear **may seem** altogether peaceable and harmless, he **might** not **remain** peaceable, and he is never harmless. [Tense shifts from present to past.] It **is** therefore an important part of the park ranger's duty to **watch** the tourists and above all **don't** let anyone try to feed the bears. [Mood shifts from indicative to imperative.]

BETTER It is necessary to restrain an occasional foolhardy park visitor. If a female bear **were** to mistake his friendly intentions and **suppose** him a menace to her cubs, he would be in trouble. But females with cubs **are** only one of the dangers. One **has** to remember that all bears **are** wild animals and not domesticated pets. Though a bear **may seem** altogether peaceable and harmless, he **may** not **remain** peaceable, and he is never harmless. It **is** therefore an important part of the park ranger's duty to **watch** the tourists and above all not to **let** anyone try to feed the bears.

■ **Exercise 8** In the following passage correct all errors and inconsistencies in tense and mood as well as any other errors in verb usage. Put a checkmark after any sentence that is satisfactory as it stands.

[1] Charles Dickens creates many memorable characters in *David Copperfield.* [2] He give many of his characters names that suggest their personalities. [3] Mr. Murdstone is unfeeling, Little Emily is shy, and Dr. Strong is virtuous. [4] Dickens also tags his characters with recurring peculiarities of speech; these may even be call their trademarks. [5] For example, Barkis continues to have proposed marriage with these words: ''Barkis is willin'.'' [6] The proud Uriah Heep, a hypocrite, keeps calling himself a humble man. [7] Over and over Mr. Micawber rambled on and then concludes, ''In short—'' [8] When he owed debts, this character shrugs off what he terms his ''pecuniary difficulties.'' [9] With cheerful certainty, he repeats his favorite prophecy: ''Something is bound to turn up.'' [10] Set down and read *David Copperfield* through to become acquainted with these interesting people.

7e

Observe such distinctions as exist between *should* **and** *would.*

(1) Use *should* **to express a mild obligation or a condition.**

I (You, He, We, They) **should** help the needy.
If I (you, he, we, they) **should** resign, the program would not be continued.

(2) Use *would* **to express a customary action.**

I (You, He, We, They) **would** spend hours lying on the beach every summer.

Caution: Do not use *would have* as a substitute for *had.*

If you **had** (NOT *would have*) arrived earlier, you would have seen the president.

■ **Exercise 9** Revise any incorrect verb forms in the sentences below. Put a checkmark after any sentence that needs no revision. Prepare to explain the reason for each change you make.

1. If he would have registered later, he would have had night classes.
2. If Leslie enrolled in the class at the beginning, she could have made good grades.
3. A stone lying in one position for a long time may gather moss.
4. The members recommended that all delinquents be fined.
5. It was reported that there use to be very few delinquents.
6. After Douglas entered the room, he sat down at the desk and begins to write rapidly.
7. Until I received that letter, I was hoping to have had a visit from Marty.
8. Follow the main road for a mile; then you need to take the next road on the left.
9. The two suspects could not deny that they had stole the tapes.
10. I would have liked to have been with the team on the trip to New Orleans.

MECHANICS

Manuscript Form

8

Put your manuscript in acceptable form. Divide words at the ends of lines according to standard practices. Revise and proofread with care.

8a

Use the proper materials.

Unless you are given other instructions, follow these general practices.

(1) Handwritten papers Use regular notebook paper, size $8\frac{1}{2} \times 11$ inches, with widely spaced lines. (Narrow spaces between lines do not allow sufficient room for corrections.) Use black or blue ink. Write on only one side of the paper.

(2) **Typewritten papers**   Use regular white typing paper (not sheets torn from a spiral notebook), size $8\frac{1}{2} \times 11$ inches. Or use a good grade of bond paper (not onion-skin). Use a black ribbon. Double-space between lines. Type on only one side of the paper.

8b

Arrange your writing in clear and orderly fashion on the page.

(1) **Margins**   Leave sufficient margins—about an inch and a half at the left and top, an inch at the right and at the bottom—to prevent a crowded appearance. The ruled vertical line on notebook paper marks the left margin.

(2) **Indention**   Indent the first lines of paragraphs uniformly, about an inch in handwritten copy and five spaces in typewritten copy.

(3) **Paging**   Use Arabic numerals—without parentheses or periods—in the upper right-hand corner to mark all pages after the first.

(4) **Title**   *Do not put quotation marks around the title or underline it* (unless it is a quotation or the title of a book), and use no period after the title. Capitalize the first and last words of the title and all other words except articles, short conjunctions, and short prepositions. See also **9c**.

When you do not use a title page, center the title on the page about an inch and a half from the top or on the first ruled line. Leave the next line blank and begin the first paragraph on the third line. In this way the title will stand off from the text. When you do use a title page, attractively space the following information on the separate sheet of paper: the title of your paper, your name, the course title and number, the instructor's name, and the date. See the example on page 799.

(5) **Quoted lines**   When you quote over four lines of another's writing to explain or support your ideas, set the quotation off by indention and single-spacing: see **16a(1)** and **(2)**. Acknowledge the source of quotations: see Section **33**, pages 795–97.

(6) **Punctuation**   Never begin a line with a comma, a colon, a semicolon, or a terminal mark of punctuation; never end a line with the first of a set of brackets, parentheses, or quotation marks.

(7) **Identification**   Usually papers carry the name of the student, the course title and number, the instructor's name, and the date. Often the number of the assignment is given.

8c

Write or type your manuscript so that it can be read easily and accurately.

(1) **Legible handwriting**   Form each letter clearly; distinguish between each *o* and *a*, *i* and *e*, *t* and *l*, *b* and *f*. Be sure that capital letters differ from lower-case letters.

Use firm dots, not circles, for periods. Make each word a distinct unit. Avoid flourishes.

(2) **Legible typing**   Before typing your final draft, check the quality of the ribbon and the cleanness of the type. Do not forget to double-space between lines. Do not strike over an incorrect letter; make neat corrections. Leave one space after a comma or a semicolon, one or two after a colon, two after a period, a question mark, or an exclamation point. To indicate a dash, use two hyphens without spacing before, between, or after. Use a pen to insert marks that are not on your typewriter, such as accent marks, mathematical symbols, or brackets.

8d

Whenever possible avoid the division of a word at the end of a line. When a division is necessary, make the break only between syllables and according to standard practices.

You will seldom need to divide words if you leave a reasonably wide right margin. Remember that the reader expects a somewhat uneven right margin but may be distracted or slowed down by a series of word divisions at the ends of consecutive lines.

When you do need to divide a word at the end of a line, use a hyphen to mark the separation of syllables. In college dictionaries, dots usually divide the syllables of words:

re · al · ly   pre · fer   pref · er · ence

sell · ing   set · ting

But not every division between syllables is an appropriate place for dividing a word at the end of a line. The following principles are useful guidelines:

(1) **One-letter syllables**   Do not put the first or last letter of a word at the end or beginning of a line. Do not divide:

o · mit   a · ble   spunk · y   bo · a

(2) **Two-letter endings**   Do not put the last two letters of a word at the beginning of a line. Do not divide:

dat · ed   does · n't   safe · ly   grav · el   tax · is

(3) **Misleading divisions**   Do not make divisions that may cause a misreading. Do not divide:

sour · ces   on · ions   an · gel   colo · nel

The red vertical line in the examples of the next three guidelines marks an appropriate end-of-the-line division.

(4) **Hyphenated words**   Divide hyphenated words only at the hyphen.

mass-| produced
father-| in-law   OR   father-in-| law

(5) -ing words   Divide words ending in -ing between those consonants that you double when adding -ing.

set-| ting   jam-| ming   plan-| ning
[Compare sell-| ing]

(6) Consonants between vowels   Divide words between two consonants that come between vowels—except when the division does not reflect pronunciation.

pic-| nic   dis-| cuss   thun-| der

(7) Abbreviations and acronyms   Do not divide abbreviations, initials, or capitalized acronyms like

B. A. [degree],   U.S.A.F.,   CBS,   UCLA,   UNESCO.

(8) Caution: Do not divide one-syllable words, such as *twelfth, through,* or *grabbed.*

■ **Exercise 1**   First put a checkmark after the words below that should not be divided at the end of a line; then, with the aid of your dictionary, write out the other words by syllables and insert hyphens followed by a vertical line to indicate appropriate end-of-the-line divisions.

1. cross-reference	11. seacoast
2. economic	12. eventual
3. fifteenth	13. recline
4. NATO	14. C.P.A.
5. gripped	15. magical
6. gripping	16. WFAA-FM
7. guessing	17. matches
8. against	18. dissolve
9. present (gift)	19. cobwebs
10. present (give)	20. cobras

8e

Revise and proofread your manuscript with care.

(1) Revise and proofread your paper before submitting it to the instructor.

When doing in-class papers, use the last few minutes for proofreading and making corrections. When doing out-of-class papers, write a first draft, put the paper aside for a few hours or a day, and then revise it. You will be able to see more objectively what parts need to be expanded or changed.

As you revise, focus your attention on content and style. Use the Reviser's Checklist in Section **32**, page **782**. As you proofread, focus your attention on manuscript form—on mechanics, punctuation, spelling. Use the Proofreader's Checklist on the next page.

If only a few changes are needed, the paper may be handed in—after clear, legible corrections have been made—without rewriting. Changes may be made as follows:

(a) Deletion of words

*Billboards ~~along the highway~~
can save travelers time.*

(b) Addition of words

*These samples ^often^ last for weeks.
They save ^the consumer^ money.*

(c) Correction of misspellings, substitution of words

*~~Those~~ Those who ~~damn~~ damn advertising ~~talk~~ stress
~~about~~ its disadvantages.*

(d) Changes in capitalization and in punctuation

*^C^consumers should appreciate
advertising, ^n^not condemn it.*

Proofreader's Checklist

1. **Title**   Is there any unnecessary punctuation in the title? Is it centered on the line? Are key words capitalized? See **8b(4)**.

2. **Indention**   Is the first line of each paragraph indented? Is any lengthy quoted passage set off from the text? See **8b(2)** and **16a(1)–(2)**.

3. **Sentences**   Does each sentence begin with a capital and end with the appropriate end mark? Are there any fragments, comma splices, or fused sentences? See **9e**, **17a–c**, and Sections **2–3**.

4. **Spelling, mechanics**   Are there any misspellings or mistakes in typing or handwriting? Are capitals and underlining (italics) used correctly? Should any abbreviations or numbers be spelled out? See **8c** and Sections **9–11** and **18**.

5. **Punctuation**   Have any end marks been omitted? Are apostrophes correctly placed? Are there any superfluous commas? See Sections **12–17**.

Caution: Do not put words to be deleted in parentheses or make unsightly erasures. Do not forget to use a caret (∧) at the point in the line where an addition is made:

and ^a^ present for Ma͞rtha.

If extensive changes are necessary, make a full, clean copy to submit to the instructor.

(2) Revise your paper after the instructor has marked it.

One of the best ways to learn how to write is to revise returned papers carefully. Give special attention to any comment on content or style, and become familiar with the numbers or abbreviations used by your instructor to indicate specific errors or suggested changes.

Unless directed otherwise, follow this procedure as you revise a marked paper:

(a) Find in this handbook the exact principle that deals with each error or recommended change.

(b) After the instructor's mark in the margin, write the letter designating the appropriate principle, such as **a** or **c**.

(c) Rather than rewrite the composition, make the corrections on the marked paper. To make the corrections stand out distinctly from the original, use ink of a different color or a no. 2 pencil.

The purpose of this method of revision is to help you not only to understand why a change is desirable but to avoid repetition of the same mistakes.

On the following page are examples of a paragraph marked by an instructor and the same paragraph corrected by a student.

A Paragraph Marked by an Instructor

Those who damn advertising stress its

3   disadvantages, however, it saves consumers time,

labor, and money. Billboards can save travelers

12   time for many billboards tell where to find a meal

18   or a bed. TV commercials announce new labor-saveing

2   products. Such as a spray or a cleaner. In

addition, some advertisers give away free samples

19   of shampoo, toothpaste, soap flakes, and etc.

24   These samples often last for weeks. They save the

consumer money. Consumers should appreciate

advertising, not condemn it.

The Same Paragraph Corrected by a Student

Those who damn advertising stress its

3 *b*   disadvantages ; however, it saves consumers time,

labor, and money. Billboards can save travelers

12 *a*   time for many billboards tell where to find a meal

18 *c*   or a bed. TV commercials announce new labor-~~saveing~~ *saving*

2 *c*   products , ~~Such~~ *such* as a spray or a cleaner. In

addition, some advertisers give away free samples

19 *i*   of shampoo, toothpaste, soap flakes, ~~and~~ etc.

24 *a*   These samples *which* often last for weeks , ~~They~~ save the

consumer money. Consumers should appreciate

advertising, not condemn it.

The method of revision shown opposite works equally well if your instructor uses abbreviations or other symbols instead of numbers. In that case, instead of putting **c** after **18**, for example, you would put **c** or **18c** after **sp**.

Individual Record of Errors

You may find that keeping a record of your errors will help you to check the improvement in your writing. A clear record of the symbols on your revised papers will show your progress at a glance. As you write each paper, keep your record in mind; avoid mistakes that have already been pointed out and corrected.

One way to record your errors is to write them down as they occur in each paper, grouping them in columns according to the seven major divisions of the handbook, as illustrated below. In the spaces for paper no. 1 are the numbers and letters from the margin of the revised paragraph on the opposite page. In the spelling column is the correctly spelled word rather than **18c**. You may wish to add on your record sheet other columns for date, grade, and instructor's comments.

RECORD OF ERRORS

Paper No.	Grammar 1-7	Mechanics 8-11	Punctuation 12-17	Words Misspelled 18	Diction 19-22	Effective- ness 23-30	Larger Elements 31-34
1	3b 2c		12a	*saving*	19i	24a	

■ **Exercise 2** Proofread the following composition; circle mistakes. Prepare to discuss in class the changes that you would make.

Programmed People.

A lot of people in the workaday world is a machine—an insensitive, unhearing, unseeing, unthinking, unfeeling mechanism. They act like they are programmed, all their movements or responses triggered by clocks. Take, for example my brother. At 7:30 A.M. he automatically shuts off the alarm, then for the next hour he grumbles and sputter around like the cold, sluggish motor that he is.

On the way to work he did not see the glorious sky or notice ambulance at his neighbor's house. At 8:20 he unlocks his store and starts selling auto parts; however, all mourning long he never once really sees a customers' face. While eating lunch at Joe's cafe, the same music he spent a half dollar for yesterday is playing again. he does not hear it. At one o'clock my brother is back working with invoices and punching at a calculator; The clock and him ticks on and on.

When the hour hand hits five, it pushes the "move" button of my brother: lock store, take bus, pet dog at front door, kiss wife and baby, eat supper, read paper, watch TV, and during the 10-o'clock news he starts his nodding. His wife interrupts his light snoring to say that thier neighbor had a mild heart attach while mowing the lawn. My brother jerks and snorts. Then he mumbles, "Tell me tomorrow. I'm to tired now."

Capitals

9

Capitalize words according to standard conventions. Avoid unnecessary capitals.

A study of the principles in this section should help you use capitals correctly. When special problems arise with individual words or phrases, consult a good recent college dictionary. Dictionary entries of words that are regularly capitalized begin with capitals:

Satanism	Milky Way	Statue of Liberty
Halloween	Library of Congress	Buckeye State

Dictionaries also list capitalized abbreviations, along with options if usage is divided:

Dr., Mrs.	Ph.D.	A.M., a.m., AM
AMA, A.M.A.	M.A.	uhf, UHF

A recent dictionary is an especially useful guide when a trademark (such as *Band-Aid*, *Frisbee*, or *Kleenex*) begins to function as a common noun (*bandaid*, *frisbee*, *kleenex*), and when a generally uncapitalized word is capitalized because of a specific meaning in a given sentence:

These are **mosaic** pictures. [having a certain design]
These are **Mosaic** laws. [of or pertaining to Moses]

Most capitalized words fall into three main categories: proper names, key words in titles, and the first words of sentences.

9a

Capitalize proper names, words used as an essential part of proper names, and, usually, derivatives and abbreviations of proper names.

Proper names begin with capitals, but names of classes of persons, places, or things do not:

T. H. Brady, Jr.	on Main Street	the Constitution
a sophomore	a main street	any constitution

(1) Proper names

Capitalize the names of specific persons, places, and things; peoples and their languages; religions and their adherents; members of national, political, racial, social, civic, and athletic groups; geographical names and regions; organizations and institutions; historical documents, periods, and events; calendar designations; trademarks; holy books and words denoting the Supreme Being.

Tom Evans, Europe, the Olympics, Jews, English
Christianity, a Christian, Americans, Southern Democrat
a Methodist, the Jaycees, Detroit Lions, Los Angeles
Arctic Ocean, the Midwest, the Red Cross, Newman Club
the U.S. Senate, Indiana University, the Fifth Amendment
the Middle Ages, the Haymarket Riot, Monday, September
Labor Day, Masonite, the Bible, Koran, God, Allah, Yahweh

Note 1: Some writers still capitalize pronouns (except *who*, *whom*, *whose*) referring to the Deity. Many writers capitalize such pronouns only when the capital is needed to prevent ambiguity, as in the following sentence:

The Lord commanded the prophet to warn **His** people.

Note 2: Capitalize names of objects, animals, or ideas when they are personified. See also **20a(4)**.

I could feel **Old Man Time** breathing down the back of my neck.
—PATRICK McMANUS

(2) Words used as an essential part of proper names

Words like *college, river, park, memorial, street,* and *company* are capitalized only when they are part of proper names:

Yale University	Cape Cod Bay	Grand Canyon
Long Island City	Madison Avenue	A&M Feed Store

[Compare Norwegian elkhounds, a Honda hatchback, Parkinson's disease, Quaker guns.]

Note: In instances such as the following, capitalization depends on word placement:

on the Erie and Huron lakes   on Lakes Erie and Huron

(3) Derivatives

Words derived from proper names are usually capitalized:

Americanize   Israelite   Stalinism   Arabic   Orwellian

(4) Abbreviations

As a rule, capitalize abbreviations of (or acronyms formed from) capitalized words. See also **17a(2)**.

D.C.   G. B. Shaw   NBC   USMC   NATO   MIRV

Note 1: Both *no.* and *No.* are correct abbreviations for *number*, as in *No. 444* or *no. 444*.

Note 2: When proper names and their derivatives become names of a general class, they are no longer capitalized.

malapropism [derived from *Mrs. Malaprop*]
chauvinistic [derived from *Nicholas Chauvin*]

9b

In ordinary writing, capitalize titles that precede a proper name, but not those that follow it.

> Governor Paul Smith, Captain Palmer, Aunt Edith
> Paul Smith, our governor; Palmer, the captain; Edith, my aunt

Note: Usage is divided regarding the capitalization of titles indicating high rank or distinction when not followed by a proper name, or of words denoting family relationship when used as substitutes for proper names.

> Who was the President (OR president) of the United States?
> "Oh, Dad (OR dad)!" I said. "Tell Mother (OR mother)."

9c

In titles of books, plays, student papers, and so on, capitalize the first and last words and all other words except articles (*a, an, the*), short conjunctions, and short prepositions.

> *Crime and Punishment, Midnight on the Desert*
> "A Code to Live By," "Journalists Who Influence Elections"

Note 1: In titles a conjunction or a preposition of five or more letters is usually capitalized.

> *The Man Without a Country, Coming Through the Rye*

Note 2: In a title capitalize the first word of a hyphenated compound. As a rule, capitalize the word following the hyphen if it is a noun or a proper adjective or if it is equal in importance to the first word.

> *A Substitute for the H-Bomb* [noun]
> *The Arab-Israeli Dilemma* [proper adjective]
> "Hit-and-Run Accidents" [parallel words]

Usage varies with respect to the capitalization of words following such prefixes as *anti-, ex-, re-,* and *self-*:

> *The Anti-Poverty Program*, "Re-covering Old Sofas"

9d

Capitalize the pronoun *I* and the interjection *O* (but not *oh,* except when it begins a sentence).

> David sings, "Out of the depths I cry to thee, O Lord."

9e

Capitalize the first word of every sentence and the first word of directly quoted speech.

> She asked me what time it was.
> The reply is always "Not today."
> "Wow, college is great," I said. "Especially on weekends." [The first word of a fragment in dialogue is capitalized.]
> COMPARE "Wow, college is great," I said, "especially on weekends." [See also **12d(3)**.]

In the lobby we had a chance to get reacquainted. (It was a fifteen-minute intermission.) We talked about how much fun we had in high school. [a parenthetical sentence between sentences]

COMPARE In the lobby we had a chance to get reacquainted (it was a fifteen-minute intermission), and we talked about how much fun we had in high school. [a parenthetical main clause within a sentence]

Option:

> One thing is certain: we are still a free people. [regular usage]
> One thing is certain: We are still a free people. [used for emphasis] [See also **17d**.]

Note: For the treatment of directly quoted written material, see Section **33**, page 793.

9f

Avoid unnecessary capitals.

If you have a tendency to overuse capitals, review **9a** through **9e**. Also keep in mind this rule: common nouns may be preceded by the indefinite articles (*a, an*) and by such limiting modifiers as *every* or *several*.

> a speech course in radio and television writing
> COMPARE Speech 245: Radio and Television Writing
> every university, several schools of medicine
> COMPARE the University of Colorado School of Medicine

When preceded by *a, an,* or modifiers like *every* or *several,* capitalized nouns name one or many of the members of a class: *a St. Bernard, an Iowan, several Catholics.*
Study the following style sheet:

Style Sheet for Capitalization

CAPITALS	NO CAPITALS
Dr. Freda E. Watts	every doctor, my doctor
the War of 1812	a space war in 1999
English, Spanish, French	the language requirement
Harvard University	a university like Harvard
the U.S. Navy	a strong navy
December, Christmas	winter, holiday
the West, Westerners	to fly west, western regions
the Student Association	an association for students
Parkinson's disease	flu, asthma, leukemia
a Chihuahua, Ford trucks	a beagle, pickup trucks
two Democratic candidates	democratic procedures
our Bill of Rights	a kind of bill of rights

■ **Exercise 1** Write brief sentences correctly using each of the following words.

(1) professor (2) Professor (3) college (4) College (5) south (6) South (7) avenue (8) Avenue (9) theater (10) Theater

■ **Exercise 2** Supply capitals wherever needed below.

1. Trying to raise my grade average in both english and history, i spent my thanksgiving holidays reading articles on recently proposed amendments to the u.s. constitution.
2. The west offers grand sights for tourists: the carlsbad caverns, yellowstone national park, the painted desert, the rockies, the pacific ocean.

3. At the end of his sermon on god's social justice as set forth in the bible, he said, "we democrats really ought to reelect senator attebury."
4. The full title of robert sherrill's book is *the saturday night special and other guns with which americans won the west, protected bootleg franchises, slew wildlife, robbed countless banks, shot husbands purposely and by mistake, and killed presidents—together with the debate over continuing same.*

Italics

10

To indicate italics, underline words and phrases (along with the punctuation) in accordance with customary practices. Use italics sparingly for emphasis.

In handwritten or typewritten papers, italics are indicated by underlining. Printers set underlined words in italic type.

TYPEWRITTEN	PRINTED
It was on <u>60 Minutes</u>.	It was on *60 Minutes*.

10a

Titles of separate publications (books, magazines, newspapers, pamphlets, long musical works) and titles of plays, films, radio and television programs, and long poems are underlined (italicized).

Kaplan's *O My America!* is a funny novel.   [The italicized punctuation is a part of the title.]

Tickets to *The Homecoming* were easy to find.   [An initial *a, an,* or *the* is italicized and capitalized in a title.]

I had never before heard Beethoven's *Moonlight Sonata.* [Note that the composer's name is not italicized.]

He pored over *Time,* the *Atlantic Monthly,* and the *New York Times* (OR the New York *Times*).   [An initial *the* in titles of periodicals is usually not italicized; the name of the city in titles of newspapers is sometimes not italicized.]

Occasionally quotation marks are used for titles of separate publications and of radio and television programs. The usual practice, however, is to reserve quotation marks for titles of the individual parts of longer works (such as short stories, essays, songs, short poems) and for titles of episodes of a radio or television series. See **16b**.

"Human Character as a Vital Lie" is one of the best chapters in *The Denial of Death.*

I switched the channel to *M*A*S*H* and watched a rerun of an episode called "Dreams."

Exceptions

Neither italics nor quotation marks are used in references to the Bible and its parts or to legal documents.

The Bible begins with the Book of Genesis.

How many Americans have actually read the Bill of Rights?

10b

Foreign words and phrases are usually underlined (italicized) in the context of an English sentence.

It is an open-and-shut case of *caveat emptor,* and the FTC ought to stay out of it.   —BARRY FARRELL

The rice water weevil (*Lissorhoptrus oryzophilus*) is a potential threat to the California rice crop.   —SCIENTIFIC AMERICAN

Countless words borrowed from other languages are a part of the English vocabulary and are therefore not italicized:

amigo (Spanish)   dilemma (Greek)   karate (Japanese)
alumni (Latin)   disco (French)   pizza (Italian)

Dictionaries that label certain words and phrases as foreign are fairly dependable guides to the writer in doubt about the use of italics. The labels, however, are not always up-to-date, and writers must depend on their own judgment after considering current practices.

10c

Names of ships, airplanes, and trains and titles of works of art are underlined (italicized).

The U.S.S. *Enterprise* was the first aircraft carrier of its kind. The artist named the portrait *Innocence.*

Note: Names of spacecraft like the *Eagle* or *Columbia* are generally italicized. Practice varies, however, with names like Apollo 14 and Skylab 3.

Skylab's fall during the week of the Voyager 3 flyby was a serious event.   —SMITHSONIAN

Voyagers 1 and *2* carried antennae more than four times the diameter of *Mariner 4*'s.   —SCIENCE 80

10d

Words, letters, or figures spoken of as such or used as illustrations are usually underlined (italicized).

In no other language could a foreigner be tricked into pronouncing *manslaughter* as *man's laughter.*   —MARIO PEI

The letters *qu* replaced *cw* in such words as *queen, quoth,* and *quick.*   —CHARLES C. FRIES

The first *3* and the final *0* of the serial number are barely legible.

10e

Use underlining (italics) sparingly for emphasis. Do not underline the title of your own paper.

Writers occasionally use italics to show stress, especially in dialogue:

Out comes the jeer-gun again: "Whose side are *you* on?"
—GEORGE P. ELLIOTT

Sometimes italics are used to emphasize the meaning of a word, especially when the exact meaning might be missed without the italics.

To *do* justice means to treat all men with respect and human dignity—Negroes, whites, cops, and all of creation.
—DICK GREGORY

But overuse of italics for emphasis (like overuse of the exclamation point) defeats its own purpose. If you overuse italics to stress ideas, study Section **29**. Also try substituting more specific or more forceful words for those you are tempted to underline.

A title is not italicized when it stands at the head of a book or article. Accordingly, the title at the head of your paper (unless the title happens to be also that of a book) should not be underlined. See also **8b(4)**.

■ **Exercise**   Underline all words in the following sentences that should be italicized.

1. While waiting for the dentist, I thumbed through an old issue of U.S. News & World Report and scanned an article on ''Changes in Grading Policies.''
2. On the Queen Mary from New York to London, Eleanor said she was so bored that she read all three books of Dante's The Divine Comedy!
3. Spelling errors involving the substitution of d for t in such words as partner and pretty reflect a tendency in pronunciation.
4. In Paris my young cousin attended a performance of Mozart's opera The Magic Flute, which she characterized in her letter as très magnifique.
5. Michelangelo's Battle of the Centaurs and his Madonna of the Steps are among the world's finest sculptures.

Abbreviations and Numbers

11

In ordinary writing use abbreviations only when appropriate, and spell out numbers that can be expressed simply.

Abbreviations and figures are desirable in tables, footnotes, and bibliographies (see the list on page 795) and in some kinds of special or technical writing. In ordinary writing, however, only certain abbreviations are appropriate, and numbers that can be expressed in one word or two (like *forty-two* or *five hundred*) are usually spelled out.

All the principles in this section apply to ordinary writing, which of course includes the kind of writing often required in college.

Abbreviations

11a

In ordinary writing use the abbreviations *Mr., Mrs., Ms., Dr.,* and *St.* (for *Saint*). Spell out *doctor* and *saint* when not followed by proper names.

Mr. W. W. Kirtley, Mrs. Kay Gibbs, Dr. Bell, St. Francis
the young doctor, the early life of the saint

Note 1: The period is sometimes omitted after *Ms* (a shortened, combined form of *Miss* and *Mrs.*).

Caution: Do not use redundant titles: NOT Dr. E. T. Fulton, M.D. BUT Dr. E. T. Fulton OR E. T. Fulton, M.D. See also page 699.

Note 2: Such abbreviations as *Prof., Sen., Rep., Gen.,* and *Capt.* may be used before full names or before initials and last names, but not before last names alone.

Sen. John Sherman Cooper   Senator Cooper
Capt. P. T. Gaines   Captain Gaines

11b

In ordinary writing spell out names of states, countries, continents, months, days of the week, and units of measurement.

On Sunday, October 10, we spent the night in Tulsa, Oklahoma; the next day we flew to South America.
Only four feet tall, Susan weighs ninety-one pounds.
An acre is 4,047 square meters.

11c

In ordinary writing spell out *Street, Avenue, Road, Park, Mount, River, Company,* and similar words used as an essential part of proper names.

Fifth Avenue is east of Central Park.
The Ford Motor Company does not expect a strike soon.

Note: Avoid the use of & (for *and*) and such abbreviations as *Bros.* or *Inc.*, except in copying official titles.

AT&T   Gold Bros.   Lord & Taylor   G. Bell & Sons, Ltd.

11d

In ordinary writing spell out the words *volume, chapter,* and *page* and the names of courses of study.

The chart is on page 46 of chapter 9.
I registered for physical education and for child psychology.

Permissible Abbreviations

In addition to the abbreviations listed in **11a**, the following abbreviations and symbols are permissible and usually desirable.

1. *Titles and degrees after proper names:*

   E. R. Ames, Sr.   Alice Johnson, D.V.M.   Sam Jones, C.P.A.

2. *Certain words used with dates or figures:*

   in 586 B.C., in A.D. 70 $14.25, £349   25.5 mpg
   at 8:00 A.M. [OR a.m.]   No. 13 [OR no. 13]
   8:30 EST [OR E.S.T. OR e.s.t.]

3. *The District of Columbia and the United States used adjectivally:*

   Washington, D.C.   the U.S. Navy   U.S.-French relations

4. *The names of organizations, agencies, countries, persons, or things usually referred to by their capitalized initials:*

NAACP   NBC   IBM   OAS   IRS   USMC   CIA
FDA   JFK   U.S.S.R.   TV   CB   DNA   GNP

5. *Certain common Latin expressions* (although the English term is usually spelled out in formal writing, as indicated in brackets below):

cf.   [compare]
e.g.   [for example]
et al.   [and others]
etc.   [and so forth]
i.e.   [that is]
vs. OR v.   [versus]

For a list of abbreviations used in bibliographies, see page 795.

Note: Periods are not used with clipped forms (such as *math* or *prep school*) or acronyms (such as CORE or UNICEF). Before using an acronym, writers often spell out the phrase the acronym stands for to make the meaning of the acronym clear.

> Then there is the anti-satellite intercepter (ASAT). Consider ASAT's cost and value.

■ **Exercise 1**   Strike out any form below that is not appropriate in formal writing. (In a few items two forms are appropriate.)

1. Ms. Janet Hogan; a dr. but not a saint
2. in the U.S. Senate; in the United States; in the U.S.
3. 21 mpg; on TV; in Calif. and Ill.
4. on Magnolia St.; on Magnolia Street
5. Washington, D.C.; Charleston, S.C.
6. FBI; Federal Bureau of Investigation
7. on Aug. 15; on August 15
8. for Jr.; for John Evans, Jr.
9. e.g.; for example
10. before 6 A.M.; before six in the A.M.

Numbers

11e

Although usage varies, writers tend to spell out numbers that can be expressed in one word or two; they regularly use figures for other numbers.

after twenty-two years	after 124 years
only thirty dollars	only $29.99
five thousand voters	5,261 voters
ten million bushels	10,402,317 bushels
over three liters	3.785 liters

Special Usage Regarding Numbers

1. *Specific time of day*

   2 A.M.   OR   2:00 A.M.   OR   two o'clock in the morning
   4:30 P.M.   OR   half-past four in the afternoon

2. *Dates*

   May 7, 1977   OR   7 May 1977   [NOT May 7th, 1977]

May sixth   OR   the sixth of May   OR   May 6 OR   May 6th
the eighties   OR   the 1980's   OR   the 1980s
the twentieth century
in 1900   in 1981–1982   OR   in 1981–82
from 1980 to 1985   OR   1980–1985   OR   1980–85
   [NOT from 1980–1985, from 1980–85]

3. *Addresses*

   Apartment 3C, 8 Redwood Drive, Prescott, Arizona 86301
      [OR   Apt. 3c, 8 Redwood Dr., Prescott, AZ 86301]
   16 Tenth Street
   350 West 114 Street   OR   350 West 114th Street

4. *Identification numbers*

   Channel 13   Interstate 35   Henry VIII   Room 10

5. *Pages and divisions of books and plays*

   page 30   chapter 6   part 4
   in act 3, scene 2   OR   in Act III, Scene ii

6. *Decimals and percentages*

   a 2.5 average   12½ percent   0.907 metric ton

7. *Numbers in series and statistics*

   two cows, five pigs, and forty-two chickens
   125 feet long, 50 feet wide, and 12 feet deep
   scores of 17 to 13 and 42 to 3   OR   scores of 17–13 and 42–3
   The members voted 99 to 23 against it.

8. *Large round numbers*

   four billion dollars   OR $4 billion   OR $4,000,000,000
      [Figures are used for emphasis only.]
   12,500,000   OR   12.5 million

9. *Numbers beginning sentences*

   Six percent of the students voted.   [NOT 6 percent of the students voted.]

10. *Repeated numbers (in legal or commercial writing)*

   The agent's fee will not exceed one hundred (100) dollars.
   OR
   The agent's fee will not exceed one hundred dollars ($100).

■ **Exercise 2**   All items below are appropriate in formal writing. Using desirable abbreviations and figures, change each item to an acceptable shortened form.

EXAMPLES
Jude, the saint   *St. Jude*
at two o'clock that afternoon   *at 2 P.M.*

1. on the fifteenth of June
2. Ernest Threadgill, a doctor
3. thirty million dollars
4. Janine Keith, a certified public accountant
5. the United Nations
6. one o'clock in the afternoon
7. by the first of December, 1985
8. at the bottom of the fifteenth page
9. the Navy of the United States
10. four hundred years before Christ
11. in the second scene of the first act
12. a five-year plan (from 1985 to 1990)

PUNCTUATION

Read Exercise The Comma

12

Use the comma (which ordinarily indicates a pause and a variation in voice pitch) where it is required by the structure of the sentence.

Just as pauses and variations in voice pitch help to convey the meaning of spoken sentences, commas help to clarify the meaning of written sentences.

> When the lightning struck, James Harvey fainted.
> When the lightning struck James, Harvey fainted.

The sound of a sentence can serve as a guide in using commas.

But many times sound is not a dependable guide. The use of the comma is primarily determined by the structure of the sentence. If you understand this structure (see Section **1**), you can learn to apply the basic principles governing comma usage. The following rules cover the usual practices of the best modern writers:

Commas—

a precede the coordinating conjunctions *and, but, or, nor, for* and the connectives *so* and *yet* between main clauses;
b follow certain introductory elements;
c separate items in a series (including coordinate adjectives);
d set off nonrestrictive, parenthetical, and miscellaneous elements.

Between Main Clauses

12a

Use a comma before *and, but, or, nor, for, so,* and *yet* when they link main clauses. See also **1e**.

Study the sentence structure of the examples that follow the pattern below.

```
                    ⎧ and ⎫
                    ⎪ but ⎪
                    ⎪ or  ⎪
MAIN CLAUSE, ⎨ nor ⎬ MAIN CLAUSE.
                    ⎪ for ⎪
                    ⎪ so  ⎪
                    ⎩ yet ⎭
```

We are here on the planet only once, and we might as well get a feel for the place.   —ANNIE DILLARD

Serious automation remains largely a myth here, but in Japan it is quickly becoming reality.   —JOHN HILTON

Justice stands upon Power, or there is no justice.
—WILLIAM S. WHITE

The peoples of the Sahara have never been united, nor have they even considered uniting in any common cause.
—JAMES R. NEWMAN
[Note the word order: *nor + auxiliary + subject.*]

No one watches the performance, for everybody is taking part.   —JAN KOTT

They are hopeless and humble, so he loves them.
—E. M. FORSTER

Here is a great mass of people, yet it takes an effort of intellect and will even to see them.   —MICHAEL HARRINGTON

The pattern and examples illustrate the punctuation of a compound sentence. The rule also applies to coordinating conjunctions that link the main clauses of a compound-complex sentence (that is, a sentence with at least two main clauses and one subordinate clause):

> Men who are engaged in a daily struggle for survival do not think of old age, for they do not expect to see it.
> —JOHN KENNETH GALBRAITH

Exceptions to 12a

1. *Omission of the comma*

   The comma may be omitted when there is no possibility of confusing the reader or when the comma is not needed to make reading easier.

   > The next night the wind shifted and the thaw began.
   > —RACHEL CARSON

   Either the answer was true or it was false.

2. *Substitution of the semicolon*

   Occasionally, especially when the main clauses are long or when the second main clause reveals a striking contrast, a semicolon is used instead of the usual comma.

   > Unfortunately, society says that winning is everything ; but I would be foolish to believe that.   —WILLIAM FULLER RUSSELL

   A semicolon is often preferred when one of the main clauses contains commas. Sharply dividing the main clauses contributes to readability. See also **14a**.

   > Everyone there made allowances, of course; but being young is no excuse.
   > Readings must be taken while the strip is in place; so, if you're taking your own temperature, you'll have to use a mirror.   —CONSUMER REPORTS

Note: When linking main clauses with coordinating conjunctions, be aware of the various meanings of these connectives as you relate the clauses:

> **and**—in addition, also, moreover, besides
> **but** OR **yet**—nevertheless, however, still
> **for**—because, seeing that, since
> **or**—as an alternative, otherwise
> **nor**—and not, or not, not either   [used after a negative]
> **so**—therefore, as a result

When in doubt about the meaning of any connective, consult the dictionary. See also **3b** and **31c(4)**.

■ **Exercise 1** Following the punctuation pattern of **12a**, link the sentences in the items below with an appropriate *and, but, or, nor, for, so,* or *yet.*

EXAMPLE

We cannot win the battle. We cannot afford to lose it.
We cannot win the battle, nor can we afford to lose it.

1. A crisis strikes. Another presidential fact-finding committee is born.
2. The new leash law did not put all dogs behind bars. It did not make the streets safe for cats.
3. Motorists may admit their guilt and pay a fine immediately. They may choose to appear in court within thirty days and plead not guilty.
4. They decided not to take a vacation. They needed the money to remodel their kitchen.
5. The band leader can sing and dance and whistle. She cannot play the trombone.

■ **Exercise 2** Follow rule **12a** as you insert commas before connectives linking main clauses in the sentences below. (Remember that not all coordinating conjunctions link main clauses and that *but, for, so,* and *yet* do not always function as coordinating conjunctions.)

1. The students had finished taking the various tests and answering the long questionnaires and they had gone to lunch.
2. There are now special shoes for someone to fill for Bob has resigned and is going to business school.
3. I decided to withdraw from that eight-o'clock class so that I could sleep later but I plan to enroll again for the same class in January.
4. We had seen the stage play and the movie and the College Players' performance was the best of all.
5. Everyone in our group was invited to the party but Gary and Irene decided to go to the hockey game.

After Introductory Elements

12b

Use a comma after introductory elements such as adverb clauses, long phrases, transitional expressions, interjections, and an introductory *yes* or *no.*

(1) Introductory adverb clauses

Introductory adverb clauses begin with such subordinators as *after, although, as, as far as, as long as, as soon as, because, before, if, inasmuch as, insofar as, lest, no matter how, now that, once, provided, since, supposing, though, unless, until, when, whenever, where, wherever, whether or not, while.*

> ADVERB CLAUSE, MAIN CLAUSE.

When Americans are not happy, they feel guilty.
—JOHN LEONARD
Once these sea floors are thrust up by the natural forces that create mountains, the sculpting process begins.
—ROY A. GALLANT

Note 1: Rule **12b** also applies to elliptical adverb clauses and to introductory adverbial phrases that are parenthetical. See also **12d(3)**.

While writing his last novel, James recognized and faced his solitude. —LEON EDEL [Compare "While he was writing. . . ." See also **25b(3)**.]
These differences aside, the resemblance between 1972 and 1980 is very striking. —NORMAN PODHORETZ [Compare "Even when these differences are put aside. . . ." See also page 815.]

A writer may omit the comma after an introductory adverb clause, especially when the clause is short, if the omission does not make for difficult reading.

When we talk to people we always mean something quite different from what we say. —ANTHONY BURGESS

Note 2: When the adverb clause *follows* the main clause, there is usually no pause and no need for a comma.

She moved as if she owned the earth and conferred grace upon it. —JAMES A. MICHENER

Adverb clauses in this position, however, may be preceded by a comma if they are loosely connected with the rest of the sentence, especially if the subordinating conjunction seems equivalent to a coordinating conjunction.

Marine life is concentrated in about 4 percent of the ocean's total body of water, whereas roughly 96 percent is just about as poor in life as is a desert ashore. —THOR HEYERDAHL

(2) Long introductory phrases

Within this iron regime of dollars and ratings, a few ghettos of do-goodism exist. —DOUGLASS CATER
In a country with a frontier tradition and a deep-rooted enthusiasm for hunting and target shooting, firearms have long been part of the national scene. —TREVOR ARMBRISTER

Sometimes commas are omitted after long introductory phrases when no misreading would result:

After months of listening for some meager clue he suddenly began to talk in torrents. —ARTHUR L. KOPIT

Introductory phrases containing a gerund, a participle, or an infinitive, even though short, must often be followed by a comma to prevent misreading.

Before leaving, the soldiers demolished the fort.
Because of his effort to escape, his punishment was increased.

Short introductory prepositional phrases, except when they are distinctly parenthetical expressions (such as *in fact* or *for example*), are usually not followed by a comma.

Through the Middle Ages the Church was not an agent of oppression. —RICHARD N. GOODWIN

(3) Introductory transitional expressions, interjections, and an introductory *yes* or *no.*

Interjections, transitional expressions (such as *for example, in fact, on the other hand, in the second place*), and an introductory *yes* or *no* are generally considered parenthetical: see **12d(3)**. When used as introductory elements, they are ordinarily followed by commas:

Intelligent she was not. In fact, she veered in the opposite direction. —MAX SHULMAN
"Well, move the ball or move the body." —ALLEN JACKSON
Yes, every vote counts. No, it is not illegal.

■ **Exercise 3** In sentences 1–4 and 7–8 below, find the main clause and identify the preceding element as an adverb clause or as a phrase. Then determine whether or not to use a comma after the introductory element.

¹ If you walk into any bookstore these days you will notice a relatively new category of books prominently displayed. ² For example you will see titles like *Looking Out for Number One, How to Increase Your Personal Effectiveness, How to Deal with Almost Anything.* ³ In my opinion their message is the same: "Read me, enjoy me, and improve yourself." ⁴ With about as much subtlety as a sledgehammer these titles imply that there are short cuts to nearly anything your heart desires. ⁵ Do you lack confidence? ⁶ Do you crave success, riches, recognition? ⁷ If you do buy this book—or that book—and read it. ⁸ In a matter of hours you will be on your way. ⁹ The life you change will be your own.

Between Items in a Series

12c

Use commas to separate items in a series (including coordinate adjectives).

The punctuation of a series depends on its form:

The air was *raw, dank, gray.* [*a, b, c*]
The air was *raw, dank,* and *gray.* [*a, b,* and *c*]
The air was *raw* and *dank* and *gray.* [*a* and *b* and *c*]

(1) Words, phrases, and clauses in a series

A miner's life is a long series of wanderings, searchings, booms, and blow-outs. —DAVID JOHN THOMAS

He's as steady as a weather vane—liberal today, conservative tomorrow, reactionary next week. —WALTER F. MURPHY
[Note the parallel structure of the phrases: see also **26a(1)**.]

Go to your favorite drugstore tomorrow, buy yourself a bottle of the American Dream in the new economy size, shake well before using, and live luxuriously ever afterward.
—DAVID L. COHN

The comma before the conjunction may be omitted in the series *a, b,* and *c* if there is no danger of misreading:

Women still account for a very small percentage of the nation's lawyers, physicians and clergy.
—U.S. NEWS & WORLD REPORT

(2) Coordinate adjectives

Adjectives are coordinate when they modify the same word or word group. Use a comma between coordinate adjectives not linked by a coordinating conjunction:

It is a waiting, silent, limp room. —EUDORA WELTY
[*Waiting, silent,* and *limp* all modify *room.* Compare "It is a silent, limp waiting room."]

They are young, alert social workers.
[*Young* and *alert* modify the word group *social workers.* Compare "They are young, social, alert workers."]

She was a frowsy, middle-aged woman with wispy, drab-brown hair. She sat behind a long wooden table on a high platform overlooking her disciples with her narrow, piercing eyes. —EVELYN KOSSOFF

Exception to 12c

If the items in a series contain internal punctuation, semicolons are used instead of commas for clarity: see **14b**.

■ **Exercise 4** Using commas as needed, supply coordinate adjectives to modify any six of the following twelve word groups.

EXAMPLE
metric system   *the familiar, sensible metric system*

1. apple pie
2. social climbers
3. electronic music
4. pop art
5. minimum wage
6. traveler's checks
7. Baltimore oriole
8. rhetorical question
9. apartment buildings
10. major oil companies
11. blue cheese
12. secondary school

With Parenthetical and Miscellaneous Elements

12d

Use commas to set off nonrestrictive clauses and phrases and other parenthetical and miscellaneous elements, such as transitional expressions, items in dates, words used in direct address, and so on. Restrictive clauses and phrases are not set off by commas.

To set off a word or a word group with commas, use two commas unless the element is placed at the beginning of the sentence or at the end:

Darwin's *Origin of Species,* as Robert Ardrey points out, explains everything except the origin of species.
—F. W. HOLIDAY

Socially, death is as taboo as Victorian sex.
—OSBORN SEGERBERGER, JR.

Just take a look around El Barrio, the section where so many Puerto Ricans live. —OSCAR LEWIS

Caution: When two commas are needed to set off an element, do not forget one of the commas.

CONFUSING   An experienced driver generally speaking, does not fear the open road.
CLEAR   An experienced driver, generally speaking, does not fear the open road.

(1) Nonrestrictive clauses and phrases are set off by commas. Restrictive clauses and phrases are not set off.

Adjective clauses and phrases are classified as nonrestrictive (parenthetical) or restrictive (not parenthetical).

NONRESTRICTIVE CLAUSES AND PHRASES

Nonrestrictive clauses and phrases are not essential to the meaning of the main clause and may be omitted. Such modifiers are parenthetical and are set off by commas.

There are many Pygmalion-style directors, **who like to discover new people (even amateurs) and mold them into actors.** —ABE BURROWS
[The *who-* clause does not restrict or limit the meaning of directors (already identified) but does provide a parenthetical explanation of what is meant by *Pygmalion-style.*]

Solar energy, **which is safe, renewable, environmentally benign,** has serious disadvantages, too. —STEPHEN CHAPMAN [The *which*-clause is informative but nonessential.]

Huge cranes, **delicate as a dinosaur's head,** moved over the street. —BELVA PLAIN [Compare "Huge cranes, *which looked as* delicate as a dinosaur's head, moved over the street."]

He tossed the letter aside and pulled his apple pie, **topped with a melting scoop of vanilla ice cream,** toward him. —TRUMAN CAPOTE [The parenthetical phrase describes but does not identify the pie.]

Claud got up, **groaning and growling,** and limped off. —FLANNERY·O'CONNOR [Compare "Claud got up (*he was* groaning and growling) and limped off."]

RESTRICTIVE CLAUSES AND PHRASES

Restrictive clauses and phrases follow and limit the words they modify. They are essential to the meaning of the main clause and are not set off by commas.

We punish those **who hurt us** by making them feel guilty. —WILLARD GAYLIN [The adjective clause identifies the kind of people we punish. Contrast "He punishes his only daughter, who hurts him, by making her feel guilty."]

Couponing is merely the latest way **Americans have found to beat the system.** —WILL STANTON [This is a contact clause (with the connective *that* or *which* omitted—see page 817). Contact clauses used as adjectives are restrictive.]

The poor live on a diet **heavy in bread.** —NOEL GRAVE [The phrase identifies the kind of diet.]

The two things **most universally desired** are power and admiration. —BERTRAND RUSSELL [The essential phrase can be expanded to a restrictive clause: "*that* (OR *which*) are most universally desired."]

Note: Although some writers prefer to use the connective *that* at the beginning of restrictive clauses, *which* is also acceptable.

Sometimes a clause or phrase may be either nonrestrictive or restrictive. The writer signifies the meaning by using or by omitting commas.

NONRESTRICTIVE He spent hours nursing the Indian guides, **who were sick with malaria.** [He cared for all the Indian guides. They were all sick with malaria.]

RESTRICTIVE He spent hours nursing the Indian guides **who were sick with malaria.** [Some of the Indian guides were sick with malaria. He cared only for the sick ones.]

■ **Exercise 5** Use commas to set off nonrestrictive clauses and phrases in the following sentences. Put a checkmark after any sentence that needs no further punctuation.

1. Red snapper fried in butter is better than baked red snapper.
2. The smoke that filled the room is now gone.
3. My hometown which no one around here has ever heard of is a little place called Crossroads.
4. All players who broke the rules will sit on the bench next Saturday.
5. Martha Thompson sitting near the window smiled knowingly.
6. The coach chewing gum and clapping his hands is Teddy.
7. Venice which he visited next was torn by rival factions.
8. Venice is a city he likes to visit.
9. I will interview Mary Smith who manages the bank.
10. I will interview the Mary Smith who manages the bank.

(2) Use commas to set off nonrestrictive appositives, contrasted elements, geographical names, and most items in dates and addresses.

NONRESTRICTIVE APPOSITIVES

Fun, **a rare jewel,** is hard to find. —SUZANNE BRITT JORDAN

The most visible victims of pollution, fish are only a link in a chain from microscopic life to man. —GEORGE GOODMAN [The appositive precedes rather than follows *fish.*]

The peaks float in the sky, **fantastic pyramids of flame.** —ARTHUR C. CLARKE [Notice that the appositive could be shifted to the beginning of the sentence.]

Was the letter from Frances Evans, **Ph.D.,** or from F. H. Evans, **M.D.?** [Abbreviations after names are treated like nonrestrictive appositives.]

Note: Commas do not set off restrictive appositives.

His son *James* is sick. [*James,* not his son William] The word *malapropism* is derived from Sheridan's *The Rivals.* Do you refer to Samuel Butler *the poet* or to Samuel Butler *the novelist?*

CONTRASTED ELEMENTS

Racing is supposed to be a test of skill, **not a dice game with death.** —SONNY KLEINFIELD

His phrases dribbled off, **but not his memories.** —JAMES A. MICHENER

The goal was achievement, **not adjustment;** the young were taught to work, **not to socialize.** —ALLEN WHEELIS [Only one comma sets off an element before a semicolon.]

Note: Usage is divided regarding the placement of a comma before *but* in such structures as the following:

Other citizens who disagree with me base their disagreement, not on facts different from the ones I know, but on a different set of values. —RENÉ DUBOS

Today the Black Hills are being invaded again, not for gold but for uranium. —PETER MATTHIESSEN

GEOGRAPHICAL NAMES, ITEMS IN DATES AND ADDRESSES

Pasadena, California, is the site of the Rose Bowl.

The letter was addressed to Mr. J. L. Karnes, Clayton, Delaware 19938. [The zip code is not separated by a comma from the name of the state.]

Leslie applied for the job in October, 1981, and accepted it on Friday, March 5, 1982. OR

Leslie applied for the job in October 1981 and accepted it on Friday, 5 March 1982. [Note that commas may be omitted when the day of the month is not given or when the day of the month precedes rather than follows the month.]

■ **Exercise 6** Combine each pair of sentences by reducing the second sentence to an appositive or to a contrasted element set off by commas. Insert commas where needed to set off items in dates or addresses.

EXAMPLES
Michael Roger was born on January 7 1982 in Alabama. He is my only son.
Michael Roger, my only son, was born on January 7, 1982, in Alabama.
Carla's social security number is 452-25-7648. It is not 152-25-7648.
Carla's social security number is 452-25-7648, not 152-25-7648.

1. The General Sherman Tree is about 270 feet tall. It is a giant sequoia in California.
2. Those are pill bugs. They are not insects.
3. On April 1 1980 his divorced wife married his lawyer. His lawyer was Bill Wynne.
4. The publisher's address is 757 Third Avenue New York New York 10017. It is not 757 Madison Avenue.
5. We moved to Taos New Mexico on 30 September 1978. New Mexico is one of the popular sun states.

(3) Use commas to set off parenthetical elements.

The term *parenthetical* is correctly applied to all nonrestrictive elements discussed under **12d**. But it may also be applied to such transitional expressions as *however, first of all, in fact, to summarize,* or *that is* and to such expressions as *I believe* or *experts argue* (often called interrupters). Expressions that come at the beginning of a sentence are treated by both **12b** and **12d**.

PARENTHETICAL ELEMENTS

Finally, banks devise means of protecting the money.
——MALCOLM BRADBURY

Language, **then,** sets the tone of our society.
——EDWIN NEWMAN

Many farmers, **for example,** would like direct access to the detailed forecast maps.   ——SCIENCE 80

Well, global peace may be a dream.   [mild interjection]
Animal lovers, write letters of protest.   [direct address]
Science, **at its best,** is unifying.   ——STEPHEN JAY GOULD [parenthetical phrase]
No, the "characters" are vanishing in Velva, **just as they are vanishing in our cities.**   ——ERIC SEVAREID [introductory *no* and a parenthetical clause]
The Age of Television has dawned in China, **a generation later than in the West.**   ——LINDA MATHEWS [appended element]
He was thumping at a book, **his voice growing louder and louder.**   ——JOYCE CAROL OATES [absolute phrase]

Note 1: Expressions such as *also, too, of course, perhaps, at least, therefore,* and *likewise,* when they cause little or no pause in reading, are frequently not set off by commas.

The times **also** have changed in ways that soften the rhetoric.
——HENRY FAIRLIE

Study circles are **therefore** the most pervasive method of bringing education to Swedes of all ages and walks of life.   ——WILLIAM L. ABBOTT

Note 2: With direct quotations, such expressions as *he said, she asked, I replied,* and *we shouted* are set off by commas. See also **16a(4)**.

He said, "My opinion is really different."
"My opinion," he said, "is really different."
"My opinion is really different," he said.

12e

Occasionally a comma, although not called for by any of the major principles already discussed, may be needed to prevent misreading.

Use **12e** sparingly to justify your commas. In a general sense, nearly all commas are used to prevent misreading or to make reading easier. Your mastery of the comma will come through application of the more specific major principles (**a, b, c, d**) to the structure of your sentences.

CONFUSING	A few weeks before I had seen him in an off-Broadway play.
BETTER	A few weeks before, I had seen him in an off-Broadway play. [The comma clearly indicates intonation.]
CONFUSING	Those who can pay and forego consumption of other essential goods.
BETTER	Those who can, pay and forego consumption of other essential goods. ——ERIK P. ECKHOLM

■ **Exercise 7** All commas in the following paragraphs are correctly used. Explain the reason for each comma by referring to one of the principles discussed in this section (**12a, 12b, 12c,** or **12d**).

[1] Conflicts would not be restricted to conventional warfare. [2] True, we do have a treaty forbidding the use of "weapons of mass destruction" in outer space.   [3] However, the treaty does not define "weapons of mass destruction," and although it does require inspection of all installations on celestial bodies, it says nothing about stations or space colonies in orbit.   [4] In any case, the moral force of this treaty, all by itself, is hardly likely to deter the greedy ones, the bullies, the maniacs, the suicidal types, or the various champions of human "progress," "liberation," or "rejuvenation."
[5] Every colony, as well as the Earth itself, would be in danger from outer space at all times.   [6] No matter how many problems we may have today, we can still look at the stars with fair assurance that they constitute no immediate threat to us.   [7] But with millions of space colonies roaming the solar system, life could degenerate into a series of preparations for and recoveries from attacks—an updated version of the life-style of centuries past when raids of the Normans, Berbers and other seafaring people depopulated Europe's coastline—except that this time the weaponry would be a great deal more destructive.
——PAUL L. CSONKA, *"Space Colonization: An Invitation to Disaster?"*

■ **Exercise 8** Insert commas where needed in the following sentences (selected and adapted from the works of modern writers). Be prepared to explain the reason for each comma used. Also be prepared to point out where optional commas might be placed as a matter of stylistic preference.

1. Police action in arresting drunks will never prevent drunkenness nor can it cure an alcoholic. —RAMSEY CLARK
2. Fifty years ago *Hazel Beverly Marian Frances* and *Shirley* were all perfectly acceptable boys' names.
   —ALLEEN PACE NILSEN
3. Thus the ocean floors far from being the oldest features on earth were relatively young. —ALLISON R. PALMER
4. When language does change the alteration first occurs in the spoken not the written form. —ROBERT BURCHFIELD
5. Hooper said "Look Chief you can't go off half-cocked looking for vengeance against a fish. That shark isn't evil."
   —PETER BENCHLEY
6. Incidentally supporting the tobacco habit is very expensive some adults having been known to sacrifice much-needed family grocery money for a carton of cigarettes.
   —DAVID TATELMAN
7. The crowd's answer was polite almost dainty applause the kind that has a lot of coughing at the end instead of a release of spirit. —ANTHONY TUTTLE
8. Hard as it is for many of us to believe women are not really superior to men in intelligence or humanity—they are only equal. —ANNE ROIPHE
9. The earth breathes in a certain sense. —LEWIS THOMAS
10. December is the most violent month the time of murder robbery assault suicide and Christmas. —EARL SHORRIS
11. They can stand just so much eh Doctor? —E. B. WHITE
12. As if to celebrate the arrival of the Antarctic spring a brilliant flash of light illuminated the date of September 22 1979 in the southern hemisphere. —S. T. COHEN
13. In Detroit weather weighs heavily upon everyone.
    —JOYCE CAROL OATES
14. The temptation in describing a film like this one is to string together several adjectives—witless ugly brutal insensate stupid. —TIME
15. As almost everyone outside Texas understands Alaska is a very big place. —JOHN G. MITCHELL
16. I stand in the moonlight the hot desert at my back.
    —MARK KRAMER
17. He disliked being categorized no matter what the category. —IRWIN SHAW
18. "I had to see where J.R. lived" said Mick Pattemore his accent revealing not Sweetwater Texas but Somerset England. —JANE HALL
19. If there was ever an American boy who was saved by sports it was I. —JAMES A. MICHENER
20. Theirs has been described as a love/hate relationship smooth and pliable when they are of a mind and roof-shaking when they are not. —JOY G. SPIEGEL

■ **Exercise 9** For humorous effect, the writer of the following paragraph deliberately omits commas that can be justified by rules **12a**, **b**, or **d**. Be prepared for a discussion of the paragraph. Where could commas be inserted to contribute to ease in reading?

The commas are the most useful and usable of all the stops. It is highly important to put them in place as you go along. If you try to come back after doing a paragraph and stick them in the various spots that tempt you you will discover that they tend to swarm like minnows into all sorts of crevices whose existence you hadn't realized and before you know it the whole long sentence becomes immobilized and lashed up squirming in commas. Better to use them sparingly, and with affection, precisely when the need for each one arises, nicely, by itself. —LEWIS THOMAS, *The Medusa and the Snail*

Superfluous Commas

13

Do not use superfluous commas.

Unnecessary or misplaced commas are false or awkward signals that may confuse the reader. If you tend to use too many commas, remember that although the comma ordinarily signals a pause, not every pause calls for a comma. As you read each sentence in the following paragraph aloud, you may pause naturally at places other than those marked by a period, but no commas are necessary.

> Springboard divers routinely execute maneuvers in which their body rotates in space. The basic maneuvers are the somersault and the twist. In the somersault the body rotates head over heels as if the athlete were rotating about an axis extending from his left side to his right side through his waist. In the twist the body spins or pirouettes in midair as if the athlete were rotating about an axis extending from his head to his toes.
> —CLIFF FROHLICH, *"The Physics of Somersaulting and Twisting"*

To avoid using unnecessary commas, first review Section **12** and then study and observe the following rules.

13a

Do not use a comma to separate the subject from its verb or the verb from its object.

The commas circled below should be omitted.

> Even people with unlisted telephone numbers⊙ receive crank calls.
> [needless separation of subject and verb]

> The man said⊙ that the old tires were guaranteed.
> [needless separation of verb and object (a noun clause)]

13b

Do not misuse a comma before or after a coordinating conjunction. See 12a.

The commas circled below should be omitted.

> The facts were selected⊙ and organized with care.
> The USAF debunked UFO sightings, but⊙ millions of Americans didn't listen.

13c

Do not use commas to set off words and short phrases (especially introductory ones) that are not parenthetical or that are very slightly so.

The commas circled below should be omitted.

> Art Tatum was born⊙ in Toledo⊙ in 1910
> Maybe⊙ the battery cables needed cleaning.

13d

Do not use commas to set off restrictive (necessary) clauses, restrictive phrases, and restrictive appositives.

The commas circled below should be omitted.

> Everyone⊙ who smokes cigarettes⊙ risks losing about ten years of life.   [restrictive clause: see **12d(1)**]
>
> For years she has not eaten anything⊙ seasoned with onions or garlic.   [restrictive phrase: see **12d(1)**]
>
> The word⊙ *nope*⊙ is an interesting substitute for *no.* [restrictive appositive: see **12d(2)**]

13e

Do not use a comma before the first item or after the last item of a series (including a series of coordinate adjectives).

The commas circled below should be omitted.

> Field trips were required in a few courses, such as , botany, geology, and sociology.
>
> The company hires talented, smart, ambitious , women.

■ **Exercise 1**   Study the structure of the sentence below; then answer the question that follows by giving a specific rule number (such as **13a**, **13d**) for each item. Be prepared to explain your answers in class.

> Now when you say "newly rich" you picture a middle-aged and corpulent man who has a tendency to remove his collar at formal dinners and is in perpetual hot water with his ambitious wife and her titled friends.   —F. SCOTT FITZGERALD

Why is there no comma after (1) *Now,* (2) *say,* (3) *middle-aged,* (4) *man,* (5) *collar,* (6) *dinners,* or (7) *wife?*

■ **Exercise 2**   Change the structure and the punctuation of the following sentences according to the pattern of the examples.

> EXAMPLE
> A motorcyclist saw our flashing lights**,** and he stopped to offer aid.   [an appropriate comma: see **12a**]
> *A motorcyclist saw our flashing lights and stopped to offer aid.* [second main clause reduced to a part of compound predicate—comma no longer needed]

1. The hail stripped leaves from trees, and it pounded early gardens.
2. Some science fiction presents newly discovered facts, and it predicts the future accurately.
3. Rob likes the work, and he may make a career of it.

> EXAMPLE
> If any students destroyed public property**,** they were expelled.   [an appropriate comma: see **12b**]
> *Any students who destroyed public property were expelled.* [introductory adverb clause converted to restrictive clause—comma no longer needed]

4. When people lead rather than demand, they often get good results.
5. If a boy is willing to work, he can get a job here.

■ **Exercise 3**   In the following paragraph some of the commas are needed and some are superfluous. Circle all unnecessary commas. Be prepared to explain (see Section **12**) each comma that you allow to stand.

[1] There are, at least, three kinds of fishermen. [2] First, is the boat owner. [3] He usually gets up at 4 a.m., grabs a thermos of coffee, picks up his favorite, fishing buddy, and goes to the exact spot, where the trout or bass are striking. [4] Fishing for a certain kind of fish, is his specialty, and he, generally, gets exactly the kind he goes after. [5] Next is the person, who fishes with friends on a crowded pier, jetty, or barge. [6] He expects the fish to come to him, and is happy to catch anything, fit to eat, such as, perch or carp. [7] The third type is the loner, the one who fishes in some out-of-the-way place on the bank, by himself. [8] After he anchors one, great big, wad of bait on his hook, he throws his line out, and props up his pole, so that he doesn't have to hold it. [9] Then, he leans back, watches the cloud formations, or lazily examines a leaf or flower. [10] He, sometimes, dozes. [11] Also, he daydreams. [12] Lounging there with a kind of half smile on his face, he enjoys his solitude. [13] His fishing pole is merely an excuse for being there. [14] He forgets to watch his line, and, to rebait his hook.

The Semicolon

14

Use the semicolon (a) between main clauses not linked by *and, but, or, nor, for, so,* or *yet* and (b) between coordinate elements containing commas. Do not use the semicolon between parts of unequal grammatical rank.

Read aloud the following sentences; notice the way your voice reflects the differences in punctuation.

> The letters did not arrive until Thursday, although I had mailed them early Monday morning.
> The letters did not arrive until Thursday; however, I had mailed them early Monday morning.

A stronger mark of punctuation than the comma, the semicolon is sometimes called a weak period.

If you can distinguish between main and subordinate clauses and between phrases and clauses (see **1d** and **1e**), you should have little trouble using the semicolon. As you study the rules in this section, notice that the semicolon is used *only* between closely related coordinate elements.

14a

Use the semicolon between two main clauses not linked by *and, but, or, nor, for, so, yet.* See also **12a**.

MAIN CLAUSES LINKED WITHOUT A CONNECTIVE

> MAIN CLAUSE**;** MAIN CLAUSE.

The dark is not mysterious**;** it is merely dark.
—ARCHIBALD MacLEISH

No person is born arrogant; arrogance must be taught.
—CLARA M. DOBAY

She will say something; he will disagree; she will nod and let him have the last word.   —ROBERT COLES

Observe that each main clause above could be written as a separate sentence: see also **1e**, pages 672–73.

Rule **14a** also applies in compound-complex sentences:

A close friend of mine lived on a farm; I assumed he would always be there.   —WILLIAM MUELLER   [two main clauses and one subordinate clause]

Curing is a process in which harvested tobacco is slowly dried; it removes excess starch and permits other chemical reactions, which lead to a milder smoke.   —WILLIAM BENNETT   [two main clauses and two subordinate clauses]

MAIN CLAUSES LINKED BY ADVERBIALS   See also 3b.

Be sure to use a semicolon before conjunctive adverbs (*however, therefore, then,* and so on) and transitional phrases (*for example, on the contrary,* and so on) when these adverbial connectives are placed between main clauses. See the lists on page 677.

MAIN CLAUSE; {conjunctive adverb *or* transitional phrase} (,) MAIN CLAUSE.

In the pattern the comma (in parentheses) is generally omitted after an adverbial connective when the connective is not considered parenthetical or when the comma is not needed to prevent misreading or to mark intonation. See also **12d(3)**.

New Orleans is unique among American cities; indeed in many ways it is scarcely American.   —PHELPS GAY

Many farms do not require a labor input every day; hence commuting could be lessened.   —MARION CLAWSON

We no longer confide in each other; in fact, there are many things I could not mention to her.   —SAUL BELLOW

They have not yet been molded by experience; therefore, the immediate moment makes a great impression on them because that is all they know.   —WILLIAM J. HARRIS

Caution: Do not overwork the semicolon. Often it is better to revise compound sentences according to the principles of subordination: see Section **24** and also **14c**.

Exceptions to 14a:

1. A semicolon (instead of the usual comma) may precede *and, but, or, nor, for, so,* and *yet* when a main clause has internal commas or when the writer wishes to make a sharp division of the two main clauses. See also **12a**, page 700.

I was, if anything, disintegrated; and I was puzzled.
—WILLIAM GOLDING

Food is obviously necessary for survival; so you might pay more for it than you would for almost anything else.
—HARRY BROWNE

2. Sometimes a comma (instead of the usual semicolon) separates short main clauses like those below: see also **3a**, pages 676–77.

He isn't funny, he isn't romantic, he is neither urbane nor fancy free.   —PHILIP TERIGAN

3. A colon (instead of the usual semicolon) appears between main clauses when the second main clause explains or amplifies the first. See also **17d**, page 714.

This type of construction is like building a house of cards or of children's blocks: slabs of stone are set upright (orthostats) and other slabs are laid across the uprights as capstones.
—GLYN DANIEL

■ **Exercise 1**   Change each of the following items to conform to pattern **14a**, as shown in the examples below.

EXAMPLES
An engagement is not a marriage. Nor is a family quarrel a broken home.
An engagement is not a marriage; a family quarrel is not a broken home.
All members of my family save things they will never use. My sister, for example, saves old calendars and bent or rusty nails.
All members of my family save things they will never use; for example, my sister saves old calendars and bent or rusty nails.

1. The scientists did not accept this theory. Nor did they ridicule it.
2. Popular TV comedy series occasionally have spinoffs. From *The Mary Tyler Moore Show,* for instance, there came *Rhoda, Lou Grant,* and *Too Close for Comfort.*
3. He took a course in the art of self-defense. But later, during a class demonstration, he broke his wrist.
4. Tony himself cut and polished the turquoise. And it is a beauty.
5. The team kept on losing. And, as a result, the morale of the whole school was low.

14b

Use the semicolon to separate a series of items which themselves contain commas.

This use of the semicolon instead of the comma in a series is for clarity. The semicolon sharply separates the items so that the reader can distinguish the main divisions of the series at a glance.

A board is elected or appointed from each of three general categories of citizens: for example, a judge or lawyer of good repute; a professor of art, literature, or one of the humanities; and a social worker, psychologist, or clergyman.
—GEORGE P. ELLIOTT

Note: Occasionally, for emphasis, semicolons may divide a series of items that do not contain internal punctuation—especially a series of main clauses.

Among scholars there are discoverers; there are critics; and there are teachers.   —GILBERT HIGHET

■ **Exercise 2**   Combine the following sentences by deleting words and using a series of items separated by semicolons. Use the colon to introduce each series, as in the example.

EXAMPLE
On stage all set to fight were three debaters. One was Eric

Dunn, a zero-population-growth advocate. Another was Susan Miles, a theologian. And the third was K. C. Osborn, president of the freshman class.

On stage all set to fight were three debaters: Eric Dunn, a zero-population-growth advocate; Susan Miles, a theologian; and K. C. Osborn, president of the freshman class.

1. On the talk show were three guests. One was T. J. Ott, a psychic. Another was Charles Shelton, a local ufologist. And the third was Abbish Ludah, a guru.
2. We sold everything at our benefit flea market. We sold many dishes and vases, old and cracked. We also sold fishing gear, garden tools, and half-used tubes of lipstick.

14c

Do not use a semicolon between parts of unequal grammatical rank, such as a clause and a phrase or a main clause and a subordinate clause.

NOT   Along came Harvey; the dormitory clown.
BUT   Along came Harvey, the dormitory clown.   [a parenthetical appositive phrase—see **12d(2)**]

NOT   We took a detour; the reason being that the bridge was under construction.
BUT   We took a detour, the reason being that the bridge was under construction.   [a parenthetical phrase, an absolute—see **12d(3)**]

NOT   Lucy has three topics of conversation; her courses, her career, and her travels.
BUT   Lucy has three topics of conversation: her courses, her career, and her travels.   [series—see **17d(1)**]

NOT   If this report is true; then we should act now.
BUT   If this report is true, then we should act now. [introductory adverb clause—see **12b**]

NOT   We heard about the final decision; which really surprised us.
BUT   We heard about the final decision, which really surprised us.   [nonrestrictive clause—see **12d(1)**]

NOT   The truck needed a valve job; although it would still run.
BUT   The truck needed a valve job, although it would still run. [parenthetical clause—see note 2 on page 701 and **12d(3)**]

■ **Exercise 3**   Find the semicolons used between parts of unequal rank and substitute a correct mark of punctuation. Do not change properly placed semicolons.

1. Don went jogging one afternoon; never returning; then he was numbered among the tens of thousands who disappear every year.
2. Although the educational TV channel is sometimes a bore; at least tedious ads do not interrupt the programs.
3. I have two main pet peeves; jokes that are pointless and animals that get on furniture.
4. Before the derby she will take the motor apart and overhaul it; her supervisor will be an ace mechanic; her sister Alicia.
5. The tormented bull lowered his head in readiness for another charge; the one-sided contest not being over yet.

■ **Exercise 4**   Compose four sentences to illustrate various uses of the semicolon.

General Exercise on the Comma
and the Semicolon

■ **Exercise 5**   First, review Sections **12** and **14**. Then, using the following examples as guides, punctuate sentences 1–10 appropriately.

12a   Pat poured gasoline into the hot tank, for he had not read the warning in his tractor manual.
12b   Since Pat had not read the warning in his tractor manual, he poured gasoline into the hot tank.
In very large print in the tractor manual, the warning is conspicuous.
12c   Pat did not read the tractor manual, observe the warning, or wait for the tank to cool.
Pat was a rash, impatient young mechanic.
12d   Pat did not read his tractor manual, which warned against pouring gasoline into a hot tank.
Pat, a careless young man, poured gasoline into the hot tank of his tractor.
First, warnings should be read.
12e   A week before, he had glanced at the manual.
14a   Pat ignored the warning in the tractor manual; he poured gasoline into the hot tank.
Pat poured gasoline into the hot tank; thus he caused the explosion.
14b   At the hospital Pat said that he had not read the warning; that he had, of course, been careless; and that he would never again, under any circumstances, pour gasoline into a hot tank.

1. Many students were unhappy in the early 1980s for draft registration threatened their future plans.
2. Dr. Felipe a visiting professor from Kenya says that often it is not fun to learn but that it is always fun to know.
3. The stalls of the open market along the wharf were filled with tray after tray of glassy-eyed fish slender stalks of pink rhubarb mounds of home-grown tomatoes and jars of bronze honey.
4. Two or three scrawny mangy-looking hounds lay sprawled in the shade of the cabin.
5. While Diana was unpacking the cooking gear and Grace was chopping firewood I began to put up our shelter.
6. Slamming the door of his four-wheel drive to cut short the argument with his wife Jerry grabbed the grocery list from her and stalked into the supermarket.
7. Still in high school we had to memorize dates and facts such as 1066 the Battle of Hastings 1914–1918 World War I 1939–1945 World War II and 1969 the first moon landing.
8. The dream home that they often talk about is a retreat in the Rockies to tell the truth however they seem perfectly happy in their mobile home on the outskirts of Kansas City.
9. The criminal was asking for mercy his victim was pleading for justice.
10. Chris and I felt that our blustery argument would never end however my weather-watching roommate reminded us that thunderstorms are usually of short duration.

The Apostrophe

15

Use the apostrophe to indicate the possessive case (except for personal pronouns), to mark omissions in contracted words or numerals, and to form certain plurals.

15a

Use the apostrophe to indicate the possessive case of nouns and indefinite pronouns.

The possessive (or genitive) case shows ownership or a comparable relationship: *Donald's* car, two *weeks'* pay. The possessive case of nouns and of indefinite pronouns may be indicated by the use of *'s* (or by the apostrophe alone) or by an *of*-phrase.

    everybody's friend   OR   the friend of everybody
    the students' laughter   OR   the laughter of students

Occasionally, the possessive is indicated by the use of both an *of*-phrase and *'s:*

    that pie **of Al's** [a double possessive]
    COMPARE   this description of Al [Al is described.]
                this description of Al's [Al did the describing.]

A possessive noun or pronoun may be related to a word (or word group) that precedes it or that is clearly implied.

    Is that old broken-down dune buggy **Frank's** or **Jane's?**

(1) For singular nouns and indefinite pronouns, add the apostrophe and *s*.

    Laura's idea   a week's work   a dime's worth
    anyone's guess   somebody's coat   one's choices

Option: If a singular noun ends in *s*, add the apostrophe and *s* or only the apostrophe.

    Keats's poetry   OR   Keats' poetry
    a waitress's tips   OR   a waitress' tips

When a singular word ends in *s*, many writers use the apostrophe and *s* to reflect pronunciation, but they prefer to use only the apostrophe when the word following begins with an *s* or a *z* sound.

    Chris's enthusiasm   BUT   Chris' zeal
    the hostess's idea   BUT   for the hostess' sake

(2) For plural nouns ending in *s,* add only the apostrophe. For plurals not ending in *s,* add the apostrophe and *s.*

    boys' shoes (shoes for *boys*)   two dollars' worth
    babies' toes (toes of *babies*)   the Joneses' reunion
    BUT   men's clothing   women's job   children's rights

(3) For compounds or word groups, add the apostrophe and *s* only to the last word.

    my sister-in-law's shop   someone else's turn
    the Secretary of Labor's idea   George Heming, Jr.'s reply

(4) To indicate individual ownership, add the apostrophe and *s* to each name.

    Al's and Sue's cars [Note that *cars* is plural.]
    the doctor's and the dentist's offices

Note: To indicate joint ownership, add the apostrophe and *s* only to the last name or to each name.

    Al and Sue's car   OR   Al's and Sue's car

Variation to 15a

The use of the apostrophe or the possessive form varies with proper names (organizations, geographical designations, and so on).

    Devil's Island   Devils Tower   Devil Mountain

■ **Exercise 1** Change the modifier after the noun to a possessive form before the noun, following the pattern of the examples.

    EXAMPLES

    the laughter of the crowd   *the crowd's laughter*
    suggestions made by James   *James's suggestions*
                             OR *James' suggestions*

1. the tape decks belonging to Johnny
2. the boat bought by the Weinsteins
3. the voices of Bess and Mary
4. the efforts of the editor-in-chief
5. the strategy that Doris uses
6. worth a quarter
7. ideas of somebody else
8. stories by Dickens
9. shoes for women
10. a song written by Henry and Ross

15b

Use an apostrophe to mark omissions in contracted words or numerals.

    didn't   he'll   they're   there's   class of '85
    o'clock [reduction of "of the clock"]

Note: Contractions in writing mirror speech. As a rule, they are avoided in formal writing: see **19d.** But they are common (and often preferable) both in informal writing and in dialogue.

    INFORMAL

With all the books he reads, how come the guy is so illiterate? And why do people just naturally assume that you'll know what they're talking about? No, I don't know, and nobody knows. The planets don't, the stars don't, infinite space doesn't. —SAUL BELLOW

    DIALOGUE

"Well, Curley's pretty handy," the swamper said skeptically. "Never did seem right to me. S'pose Curley jumps a big guy an' licks him. Ever'body says what a game guy Curley is." —JOHN STEINBECK

15c

Use the apostrophe and *s* to form the plural of lower-case letters and of abbreviations followed by periods. When needed to prevent confusion, use the apostrophe and *s* to form the plural of capital letters, of symbols, of abbreviations not followed by periods, and of words referred to as words.

His *a*'s look like *o*'s. [The *'s* is not italicized (underlined). See also **10d.**]
Over half of the Ph.D.'s were still looking for jobs.
Her *I*'s are illegible, and her *miss*'s appear to be *mess*'s.

Either *'s* or *s* may be used to form such plurals as the following:

the 1900's OR the 1900s	his 7's OR his 7s
two *B*'s OR two *B*s	the *&*'s OR the *&*s
her *and*'s OR her *and*s	the VFW's OR the VFWs

15d

Do not use the apostrophe with the pronouns *his, hers, its, ours, yours, theirs,* or *whose* or with plural nouns not in the possessive case.

His parents sent money; **ours** sent food.
A friend of **theirs** knows a cousin of **yours**.
The **sisters** design **clothes** for **babies**.

Caution: Do not confuse *its* with *it's* or *whose* with *who's*:

Its motor is small.   [the motor *of it*]
It's a small motor.   [*It is* a small motor.]
Whose is that?   [*Who owns* that?]
Who's that?   [*Who is* that?]

■ **Exercise 2**   Insert apostrophes where needed in the following sentences. Put a checkmark after any sentence that needs no change in punctuation.

1. Many students attitudes changed completely in the mid-1970s.
2. Some students dropped these courses because of the stiff requirements.
3. Those newsstands sell Marian Rosss homemade candy.
4. Theyre not interested in hockey; its roughness repels them.
5. Snapshots of everyone in the class of 84 cover Jerrys bulletin board.
6. "Its just one C.P.A.s opinion, isnt it?" Otis commented.
7. Is that dog yours or theirs?
8. There are two *e*s and two *d*s in Hildegardes name, but not any *u*s.
9. The computer confused my account with somebody elses.
10. Marnie often quotes her Granddads favorite expression: "Everybodys useful, but nobodys indispensable!"
11. Its an expensive book, but its cover came unglued.
12. Theres nothing wrong with her attitude or idea, but theirs is not like hers.

Quotation Marks

16

Use quotation marks to set off all direct quotations, some titles, and words used in a special sense. Place other marks of punctuation in proper relation to quotation marks.

Quotations usually consist of passages borrowed from the written work of others or the direct speech of individuals, especially dialogue (conversation).

QUOTED WRITING   Thomas Griffith has written: "We have become a no-fault society, and it is adolescent to look for

villains."   [The words and punctuation within quotation marks are exactly as they appear in "Party of One: Bigger than Politics," *The Atlantic* (Jan. 1980), p. 22.]

QUOTED SPEECH   "Sure enough, I'd like to own a slave," Donna explained. "A compact, push-button robot!" [Within quotation marks are the exactly recorded words of the speaker; the punctuation is supplied by the writer.]

Notice that quotation marks are used in pairs: the first one marks the beginning of the quotation, and the second marks the end. Be careful not to omit or misplace the second one. Remember that the speaker and the verb of saying (such as *Donna explained*) should be outside the quotation marks.

16a

Use double quotation marks to enclose direct (but not indirect) quotations; use single marks to enclose a quotation within a quotation.

Double quotation marks:

Making fun of Cooper, Mark Twain said, "He saw nearly all things as through a glass eye, darkly."   [a directly quoted sentence]
According to Mark Twain, Cooper "saw nearly all things as through a glass eye, darkly."   [part of a sentence quoted directly]
Mark Twain said that Cooper saw nearly everything darkly, as if he were looking through a glass eye.   [indirect quotation—no quotation marks]

Single quotation marks within double:

She said, "Earl keeps calling my idea 'an impossible dream.'"   [a quotation within a quotation]

Note: The double quotation marks enclosing a minor title (see **16b**) are reduced to single marks when the title appears within a direct quotation:

"Edgar Allan Poe's 'A Predicament' is one of the funniest short stories I've ever read!" Chet exclaimed.   [a title within a quotation]

(1) Long prose quotations (not dialogue)   In printed matter, quoted material of ten or more lines is usually set off from the rest of the text by the use of smaller type, indention, or both. Quotation marks are used only if they appear in the original. In typewritten papers, lengthy quoted passages (more than four lines) are single-spaced and indented from the left margin (sometimes from both margins) five spaces. The first line is indented an additional five spaces when it marks the beginning of a paragraph.

```
Most people say that spring or summer is their

favorite season.  As an art major, I like all the

seasons because as Emerson (in his essay

"Nature") observed,

     To the attentive eye, each moment of the year
     has its own beauty, and in the same field, it
     beholds, every hour, a picture which was
```

never seen before, and which shall never be
seen again. The heavens change every moment,
and reflect their glory or gloom on the
plains beneath.

I read and marked these lines last summer, when I
had time to read a book given to me months before.

For the proper documentation of sources in a research paper, see Section **33**.

(2) Poetry   In both printed matter and typewritten papers, except for very special emphasis, a single line of poetry or less is handled like other short quotations—run in with the text and enclosed in quotation marks. A two-line quotation may be run in with the text, with a slash marking the end of the first line. Or it may be set off from the text like longer quotations and quoted line by line exactly as it appears in the original:

The poet asks, "If there were dreams to
sell, / What would you buy?"

OR

The poet asks,

    If there were dreams to sell,
    What would you buy?

In printed matter, longer passages (sometimes italicized) are usually set off by smaller type. In typewritten papers, they are single-spaced and indented from the left five spaces. (The numbers in parentheses indicate the line numbers of the poem.)

    Persons who angered the czar were
sent to Siberia. James Mangan describes
in "Siberia" the land and its effect on
the exiled:

        In Siberia's wastes
          Are sands and rocks.
        Nothing blooms of green or soft,
        But the snowpeaks rise aloft
          And the gaunt ice-blocks.

        And the exile there
          Is one with those;
        They are part, and he is part,
        For the sands are in his heart,
          And the killing snows. (21-30)

(3) Dialogue (conversation)   Written dialogue represents the directly quoted speech of two or more persons talking together. Standard practice is to write each person's speech, no matter how short, as a separate paragraph. Verbs of saying, as well as closely related bits of narrative, are included in the paragraph along with the speech:

Through an interpreter, I spoke with a Bedouin man tending nearby olive trees.

"Do you own this land? " I asked him.
He shook his head. "The land belongs to Allah, " he said.
"What about the trees? " I asked. He had just harvested a basket of green olives, and I assumed that at least the trees were his.
"The trees, too, are Allah's, " he replied.
I marveled at this man who seemed unencumbered by material considerations . . . or so I was thinking when, as if in afterthought, he said, "Of course, I own the *olives!* "
—HARVEY ARDEN, "In Search of Moses"

(4) Punctuation of dialogue   Commas are used to set off expressions such as *he said* and *she asked* in quoted dialogue: see **12d(3)**.

He said, "Pro football is like nuclear warfare."
"Pro football," he said, "is like nuclear warfare."
"Pro football is like nuclear warfare," he said.

When the quoted speech is a question or an exclamation, the question mark or exclamation point replaces the usual comma.

"Pro football?" she asked. "Like nuclear warfare!" she added.

When an expression such as *he said* introduces a quotation of two or more sentences, it is often followed by a colon: see **17d(1)**.

It is as Frank Gifford said: "Pro football is like nuclear warfare. There are no winners, only survivors."

■ **Exercise 1**   In the following sentences, change each indirect quotation to a direct quotation and each direct quotation to an indirect one.

1. Doris said that she had a theory about me.
2. Allen announced that he had read "The Sunless Sea."
3. A Weight Watcher, Eileen explained that she could eat as much as she wanted—of vegetables like spinach, eggplant, and zucchini.
4. Clyde asked, "Will you go to the opera with me?"
5. Last night Pruett said that he thought that Amanda's favorite quotation was "Tomorrow belongs to me."

16b

Use quotation marks for minor titles (short stories, essays, short poems, songs, episodes of a radio or television series, articles in periodicals) and subdivisions of books.

"She Loves Me" was part of the BBC *Great Performances* series.

Gregg Easterbrook's "The Spruce Goose of Outer Space," in the April 1980 issue of *The Washington Monthly*, is about an expensive but grounded flying machine.

Max Shulman's *Guided Tour of Campus Humor* contains numerous poems and short stories, including "Tears from One Who Didn't Realize How Good He Had It" and "Love Is a Fallacy."

Note: Quotation marks are sometimes used to enclose titles of books, periodicals, and newspapers, but italics are generally preferred: see **10a**.

16c

Words used in a special sense are sometimes enclosed in quotation marks.

> Such "prophecy" is intelligent guessing.
> His "castle" was in reality a cozy little rattrap.

Note: Either quotation marks or italics may be used in definitions such as the following. See also **10d**.

> "Puritanical" means "marked by stern morality."
> *Puritanical* means "marked by stern morality."
> *Puritanical* means *marked by stern morality.*

16d

Do not overuse quotation marks.

Do not use quotation marks to enclose the title of your composition: see **8b(4)**. In general, do not enclose in quotation marks common nicknames, bits of humor, technical terms, or trite or well-known expressions. Instead of using slang and colloquialisms within quotation marks, use more formal English. Do not use quotation marks for emphasis.

> NEEDLESS PUNCTUATION   "Kitty" will not "cop out."
> BETTER   Kitty will not quit.

■ **Exercise 2**   Add correctly placed quotation marks below.

1. In a poem entitled 2001, scientists turn one Einstein into three Einsteins.
2. Here, stoked means fantastically happy on a surfboard.
3. David enjoyed reading the short story A Circle in the Fire.
4. *Learning to Live Without Cigarettes* opens with a chapter entitled Sighting the Target.
5. Bernice replied, Thomas Jefferson once said, Never spend your money before you have it.

16e

When using various marks of punctuation with quoted words, phrases, or sentences, follow the conventions of American printers.

(1) Place the period and the comma within the quotation marks.

> "Jenny," he said, "let's have lunch."
> She replied, "OK, but first I want to finish 'The Machine Stops.'"

Exception:

> The author states: "Time alone reveals the just" (p. 471).
> [The period follows the reference to the source of the direct quotation.]

(2) Place the colon and the semicolon outside the quotation marks.

> She spoke of "the protagonists"; yet I remembered only one in "The Tell-Tale Heart": the mad murderer.

(3) Place the dash, the question mark, and the exclamation point within the quotation marks when they apply only to the quoted matter; place them outside when they apply to the whole sentence.

> Pilate asked, "What is truth?" [The question mark applies only to the quoted matter.]
> What is the meaning of the term "half truth"? [The question mark applies to the whole sentence.]
> Why did he ask, "What is truth?" [Both the quoted matter and the sentence as a whole are questions, but a second question mark does not follow the quotation marks.]
> Gordon answered, "No way!" [The exclamation point applies only to the quoted matter.]
> Stop whistling "All I Do Is Dream of You"! [The whole sentence, not the song title, is an exclamation.]

■ **Exercise 3**   Insert quotation marks where they are needed in the following sentences.

1. At the beginning of *All in the Family*, Archie and Edith always sang Those Were the Days.
2. Get aholt, instead of get ahold, is still heard occasionally in that region.
3. No, Peg said, I didn't agree to do that for her. I may be a softie, but I haven't gone bananas yet!
4. It was then that I discovered Housman's poem Loveliest of Trees.
5. Why cry over spilled milk? my grandmother used to ask. Be glad that you had the milk to spill.
6. As for me, Socrates said, all I know is that I know nothing.
7. Wasn't it on the *Phil Donahue in Denver* show that Shirley MacLaine asked Isn't travel the best form of self-search?
8. The Old Folks is one of the funniest of Carol Burnett's regular skits.
9. Who wrote The Star-Spangled Banner?
10. Catherine said, Do the townspeople ever say to me You're a born leader? Yes, lots of times, and when they do, I just tell them my motto is Lead, follow, or get the heck out of the way!

The Period and Other Marks

17

Use the period, the question mark, the exclamation point, the colon, the dash, parentheses, brackets, the slash, and the ellipsis mark according to standard practices. (For the use of the hyphen, see **18f**.)

Read the following sentences aloud. Observe how the punctuation in color signals intonation (pitch, stress, stops) and helps to reveal sentence meaning:

> "Why are you so depressed?" they want to know. "The universe is expanding!" he explains.   —ALBERT ROSENFELD
> In *Lady Windermere's Fan* (1892) is this famous line: "I [Lord Darlington] can resist everything except temptation."

No day / night cycle exists there. The inhabitants have no way of measuring time—even years—by our standards.
—JOHN A. KEEL

The pilot had "abnormally low blood sugar. The effects . . . include subtle mental confusion . . . and decrease of psycho-motor ability." —SATURDAY REVIEW

This section covers the main principles of usage of these punctuation marks in ordinary (rather than technical or special) writing.

The Period

17a

Use the period after declarative and mildly imperative sentences, after indirect questions, and after most abbreviations.

(1) Use the period to mark the end of a declarative sentence, a mildly imperative sentence, and an indirect question.

Everyone should drive defensively. [declarative]

Learn how to drive defensively. [mild imperative]

She asks how drivers can cross the city without driving offensively. [indirect question]

"What is that?" she asked. [declarative containing a direct question]

"Get with it!" he hollered. [declarative containing an exclamation]

(2) Use periods after most abbreviations.

Mrs.   an M.D.   R.S.V.P.   No. 444   etc.
1:10 p.m.

In current usage the period is frequently omitted after many abbreviations: see also Section **11**, page 698.

IRS   RR   USAF   APO   ASCAP   mpg   mph

Do not use periods after shortened or clipped forms:

2nd   10th   math   premed   gym   lab   psych

When in doubt about the punctuation of an abbreviation, consult a good college dictionary. Dictionaries often list a range of choices (for example, *A.W.O.L.*, *a.w.o.l.*, *AWOL*, *awol*).

Caution: When an abbreviation ending in a period appears last in the sentence, do not add a second period:

Someday I hope to be an R.N.

The Question Mark

17b

Use the question mark after direct (but not indirect) questions.

Who started the rumor?

Did he ask **who started the rumor?** [The sentence as a whole is a direct question despite the indirect question at the end.]

Did you hear her ask, "Are you accusing me of starting the rumor?" [double direct question followed by a single question mark]

Declarative sentences may contain direct questions:

"Who started the rumor?" he asked.   [No comma follows the question mark.]

He asked, "Who started the rumor?"   [No period follows the question mark.]

She told me—did I hear her correctly?—who started the rumor.   [interpolated question]

A declarative or an imperative sentence may be converted into a question:

He drove to Boston?

Drive to Boston?

Question marks may be used between the parts of a series:

Did he rent the house? buy the house? buy the adjoining land? [Question marks cause full stops and emphasize each part. Compare "Did he rent the house, buy the house, and buy the adjoining land?"]

Note: A question mark within parentheses is used to express the writer's uncertainty as to the correctness of the preceding word, figure, or date:

Chaucer was born in 1340 (?) and died in 1400.

Caution: Do not use a comma or a period after a question mark.

"Are *gobbledygook* and *Jabberwocky* synonyms?" he asked.

He asked, "Are *gobbledygook* and *Jabberwocky* synonyms?"

The Exclamation Point

17c

Use the exclamation point after an emphatic interjection and after a phrase, clause, or sentence to express a high degree of surprise, incredulity, or other strong emotion.

Wow! What a desperation pass!

"Man! We've been conned!" he said.

Act now! Get involved!

Caution 1: Avoid overuse of the exclamation point. Use a comma after mild interjections, and end mildly exclamatory sentences and mild imperatives with a period. See also **17a(1)**.

Oh, don't get involved.

How quiet the lake was.

Caution 2: Do not use a comma or a period after an exclamation point.

"Get off the road!" he yelled.

He yelled, "Get off the road!"

■ **Exercise 1**   Illustrate the chief uses of the period, the question mark, and the exclamation point by composing and correctly punctuating brief sentences of the types specified.

EXAMPLE

a declarative sentence containing a quoted direct question

"*What does fennel taste like?*" she asked.

1. a direct question
2. a mild imperative
3. a declarative sentence containing a quoted exclamation
4. a declarative sentence containing an indirect question
5. a declarative sentence containing an interpolated question

The Colon

17d

Use the colon as a formal introducer to call attention to what follows and as a mark of separation in scriptural and time references and in certain titles.

(1) The colon may direct attention to an explanation or summary, an appositive, a series, or a quotation.

One thing only was equivalent in value to a man: another man.   —HERBERT GOLD

Three times he drags me over to the bulletin board to show me his team's enviable record: five straight league titles.   —HAROLD BRODKEY

Theories which try to explain the secret of fire walking fall into three categories: physical, psychological, and religious.   —LEONARD FEINBERG

The sense of unity with nature is vividly shown in Zen Buddhist paintings and poetry: "An old pine tree preaches wisdom. And a wild bird is crying out truth."   —ANNE MORROW LINDBERGH

The colon may separate two main clauses or sentences when the second explains or amplifies the first:

The sorrow was laced with violence: In the first week of demolition, vandals struck every night.   —SMITHSONIAN

The American conceives of fishing as more than a sport: it is his personal contest against nature.   —JOHN STEINBECK

Note: After the colon, quoted sentences regularly begin with a capital, but other sentences (as the preceding examples show) may begin with either a capital letter or a lower-case letter, although the latter is generally preferred.

(2) Use the colon between figures in scriptural and time references and between titles and subtitles.

The text of the sermon was Matthew 6:10.
At 2:15 A.M. the phone rang.
I had just read *On Being Funny: Woody Allen and Comedy* by Eric Lax.

Note: The colon is also used after the salutation of a business letter and in bibliographical data: see **33b(4)** and **34a(3)**.

(3) Do not use superfluous colons.

As a rule, superfluous or unnecessary colons interrupt the sentence base. Sometimes they follow *such as.*

SUPERFLUOUS   These handicapped people can repair almost anything, such as: old lawnmowers, broken clocks, frayed wires, cracked vases.

REVISED   These handicapped people can repair almost anything, such as old lawnmowers, broken clocks, frayed wires, cracked vases. [colon omitted]

OR   These handicapped people can repair almost anything: old lawnmowers, broken clocks, frayed wires, cracked vases. [*such as* omitted]

SUPERFLUOUS   The six survivors were: one man, two women, and three children.

REVISED   The six survivors were one man, two women, and three children.

OR   There were six survivors: one man, two women, and three children.

OR   The six survivors were as follows: one man, two women, and three children. [Although *survivors* is plural, *as follows* (not *as follow*) is standard usage.]

■ **Exercise 2** Punctuate the following sentences by adding colons. Put a checkmark after any sentence that needs no change.

1. At 1230 A.M. he was still repeating his favorite quotation "TV is the opiate of the people."
2. The downtown streets are narrow, rough, and junky.
3. Even people in rural areas were not safe many criminals had left the cities and the suburbs.
4. During our tour of the library, our guide recommended that we find one of the following periodicals *Intellect, Smithsonian, Commentary,* or *The Chronicle of Higher Education.*
5. All their thoughts were centered on equal pay for equal work.

■ **Exercise 3** Decide whether to use a colon or a semicolon between the main clauses of the following sentences. See also **14a**.

1. These laws all have the same purpose they protect us from ourselves.
2. Some of these laws have an obvious purpose others seem senseless.
3. Few things in life are certain perhaps we could name them all on one hand.
4. One thing is certain the future looks bright.

The Dash

17e

Use the dash to mark a sudden break in thought; to set off (for emphasis or clarity) an added explanation, or illustration, or parenthetical element; and to mark the end of an introductory series.

On the typewriter, the dash is indicated by two hyphens without spacing before, between, or after. In handwriting, the dash is an unbroken line about the length of two or three hyphens.

(1) Use the dash to mark a sudden break in thought, an abrupt change in tone, or faltering speech.

A hypocrite is a person who—but who isn't?
   —DON MARQUIS

When I was six I made my mother a little hat—out of her new blouse.   —LILLY DACHÉ

In most food products—not many, *most*—two to four corporations already have seized control of the market.
   —DANIEL ZWERDLING

Quickly regaining speech, but still in a state of disbelief, I stammered: "No. Uh, yes. Uh—it's all right."
—DOROTHY K. DUFFEY

(2) Use the dash to set off (for emphasis or clarity) an added explanation or illustration.

Lightning is an electrical discharge—an enormous spark.
—RICHARD E. ORVILLE

Some do not succeed in shedding their old problems—such as an ailing marriage, for instance—when they get to Columbia. —VANCE PACKARD

The other course—to give trust, in the hope of being trusted—carries the promise of mutual benefit and survival. —SIDNEY LENS

She did not have a particularly light touch with flavors and textures—her roasts were dredged with flour, her seasonings heavily dependent on cayenne, parsley, and tomato.
—LAURA SHAPIRO

[A colon, which might be used here instead of the dash, would be more formal.]

(3) Use the dash to set off a parenthetical element for emphasis or (if it contains commas) for clarity.

Maybe a third of the thefts from libraries are—and always have been—inside jobs. —DAVID LAMPE

All change—I hesitate to call it progress—is bought at a price. —PAUL A. SAMUELSON

A true book is a report upon the mystery of existence; it tells what has been seen in a man's life in the world—touched there, thought of, tasted. —ARCHIBALD MacLEISH

Sentiments that human shyness will not always allow one to convey in conversation—sentiments of gratitude, of apology, of love—can often be more easily conveyed in a letter.
—ARISTIDES

(4) Use the dash between an introductory series and the main part of the sentence that explains or amplifies the series.

Items in an introductory series are often referents of *all, everything, none, such,* or *these* in the main part of the sentence.

Patience, diligence, painstaking attention to detail—these are the requirements. —MARK TWAIN

Keen, calculating, perspicacious, acute and astute—I was all of these. —MAX SHULMAN

Marble-topped tables, two Singer sewing machines, a big vase of pampas grass—everything was rich and grand.
—CARSON McCULLERS

Caution: Use the dash carefully in formal writing. Do not use dashes as awkward substitutes for commas, semicolons, or end marks.

Parentheses

17f

Use parentheses to set off parenthetical, supplementary, or illustrative matter and to enclose figures or letters when used for enumeration within a sentence.

I can still tell a ripsaw from a crosscut saw by what was taught me (by a lady carpentry teacher, Miss Sprague) in the fourth grade. —THEODORE H. WHITE

Some states (New York, for instance) outlaw the use of *any* electronic eavesdropping device by private individuals.
—MYRON BRENTON

When confronted with ambiguities, we are not certain as to how we should interpret (1) single words or phrases, (2) the sense of a sentence, (3) the emphases or accents desired by the writer or speaker, or (4) the significance of a statement.
—LIONEL RUBY

Each entry will be judged on the basis of (*a*) its artistic value, (*b*) its technical competence, and (*c*) its originality.

Note: In sentences such as the following, the commas and periods are placed after the closing parenthesis, not before the opening parenthesis.

Cuban schools, especially on the Isle of Youth (formerly the Isle of Pines), bear names of prominent African figures (Agostinho Neto, Eduardo Mondlane). —MARY LOU SUHOR

If a whole sentence beginning with a capital is in parentheses, the period or other end mark is placed just before the closing parenthesis. See also **9e.**

Whatever else may be happening, Madame Colette is never *really* unaware, never *really* confused, never *really* afraid. (She can get mighty irritated sometimes.) —STEPHEN KOCH

Punctuation of Parenthetical Matter

Dashes, parentheses, commas—all are used to set off parenthetical matter. Dashes set off parenthetical elements sharply and usually emphasize them:

Man's mind is indeed—as Luther said—a factory busy with making idols. —HARVEY COX [See **17e(3)**.]

Parentheses generally minimize the importance of the elements they enclose:

Man's mind is indeed (as Luther said) a factory busy with making idols. [See **17f**.]

Commas are the most commonly used separators:

Man's mind is indeed, as Luther said, a factory busy with making idols. [See **12d**.]

Brackets

17g

Use brackets to set off interpolations in quoted matter and to replace parentheses within parentheses.

The *Home Herald* printed the beginning of the mayor's speech: "My dear fiends [sic] and fellow citizens." [A bracketed *sic*—meaning "thus"—tells the reader that the error appears in the original.]

There is a pair of sentences that anyone over thirty heard with guaranteed regularity during his childhood. With only slight variations the pattern was: "Why aren't you eating your spinach? Think of the poor starving children of Armenia [China, Turkey, India]!" —RUTH GAY

She recommended several source books (for example, Jules H. Guilder's *Computer Programs in Science and Engineering* [Rochelle Park, N.J.: Hayden, 1980]).

The Slash

17h

Use the slash between terms to indicate that either term is applicable and to mark the end of a line of quoted poetry. See also 16a(2).

Note that the slash is used unspaced between terms, but with a space before and after it between lines of poetry.

> Today visions of the checkless / cashless society are not quite as popular as they used to be. —KATHRYN H. HUMES
>
> Equally rare is a first-rate adventure story designed for those who enjoy a smartly told tale that isn't steeped in blood and / or sex. —JUDITH CRIST
>
> When in "Mr. Flood's Party" the hero sets down his jug at his feet, "as a mother lays her sleeping child / Down tenderly, fearing it may awake," one feels Robinson's heart to be quite simply on his sleeve. —WILLIAM H. PITCHARD

■ **Exercise 4** Correctly punctuate each of the following sentences by supplying commas, dashes, parentheses, brackets, or the slash. Be prepared to explain the reason for all marks you add, especially those you choose for setting off parenthetical matter.

1. Gordon Gibbs or is it his twin brother? plays the drums.
2. Joseph who is Gordon's brother is a lifeguard at the Beachfront Hotel.
3. "I admit that I" he began, but his voice broke; he could say no more.
4. This organization needs more of everything more money, brains, initiative.
5. Some of my courses for example, French and biology demand a great deal of work outside the classroom.
6. In the TV version of *The Lone Ranger,* Jay Silverheels 1918–1980 played the role of Tonto.
7. This ridiculous sentence appeared in the school paper: "Because of a personal fool sic the Cougars failed to cross the goal line during the last seconds of the game."
8. The word *zipper* once a trademark like Polaroid is now a common noun.
9. Gently rolling hills, rich valleys, beautiful lakes these things impress the tourist in Connecticut.
10. Some innovations for example the pass fail system did not contribute to grade inflation.

The Ellipsis Mark

17i

Use three spaced periods (the ellipsis mark) to indicate an omission within a quoted passage and to mark a reflective pause or hesitation.

It is generally considered unnecessary to use the ellipsis mark at the beginning or the end of a quoted passage.

OMISSION WITHIN A QUOTED PASSAGE

> Clinton Rossiter writes: "My own answer to the question 'What is liberty?' is essentially this: Liberty . . . cannot be defined but can be understood." [Note the use of single quotation marks: see **16a**.]

Compare the quoted passage above with the original:

> My own answer to the question "What is liberty?" is essentially this: Liberty, like truth and justice and all the other great abstractions, cannot be defined but can be understood, and the first step toward understanding is to identify the most important uses of the word. —CLINTON ROSSITER

If a complete sentence in the quotation precedes the omission, use a period before the ellipsis mark:

> "Nevertheless, inflation really is a horror," Martin Mayer contends, "because it demeans work. In a developed economy, people necessarily work for money. If the money they receive in return for their labors is continually diminishing in value, they feel an insult to themselves and to their function in society, even if as installment debtors they benefit by it." [Note that no space precedes the period before the ellipsis mark.]

Compare the quotation with the original:

> Nevertheless, inflation really is a horror, because it demeans work. In a developed economy, people necessarily work for money. Obviously, they want money to buy something, but at the time of work, and of thinking about work, they do not normally have in their heads the idea of what they are going to buy with the proceeds. If the money they receive in return for their labors is continually diminishing in value, they feel an insult to themselves and to their function in society, even if as installment debtors they benefit by it. —MARTIN MAYER

The ellipsis mark indicates that a part of a sentence, one or more sentences, or (sometimes) a full paragraph or more has been left out. Spaced periods covering a whole line mark the omission of at least one paragraph in prose or a full line in poetry.

> All I can say is—I saw it!
> ● ● ● ● ● ● ● ●
> Impossible! Only—I saw it! —ROBERT BROWNING

A REFLECTIVE PAUSE OR HESITATION

The ellipsis mark is also used to indicate a pensive or thought-filled pause, deliberate hesitation, or an intentionally unfinished statement (not an interruption).

> Love, like other emotions, has causes . . . and consequences. —LAWRENCE CASLER
>
> It's a bird . . . it's a plane . . . well, it's the Gossamer Penguin, a 68-pound flying machine fueled only by the sun. —CATHLEEN McGUIGAN
>
> "It's well for you . . ." began Lucille. She bit the remark off. —ELIZABETH BOWEN
> [a deliberately unfinished statement]

The ellipsis mark may come after a period marking the end of a sentence:

> All channels are open. The meditation is about to begin. . . . —TOM ROBBINS

■ **Exercise 5** Beginning with *According to John Donne,* or with *As John Donne has written,* quote the following passage, omitting the words placed in brackets. Use three or four periods as needed to indicate omissions.

No man is an island [entire of itself;] every man is a piece of the continent, a part of the main. [If a clod be washed away by the sea, Europe is the less, as well as if a promontory were, as well as if a manor of thy friend's or of thine own were]. Any man's death diminishes me because I am involved in mankind [and therefore never send to know for whom the bell tolls; it tolls for thee].   —JOHN DONNE

■ **Exercise 6**   First, observing differences in meaning and emphasis, use an ellipsis mark in place of the dash, commas, and the italicized words below. Then write two sentences of your own to illustrate the use of the ellipsis mark to indicate a pause or hesitation.

1. My father was dying—*and, I wondered,* what would happen to us?
2. Our lives would have been different if *he had lived.*

■ **Exercise 7**   Punctuate the following sentences (selected and adapted from *The Atlantic*) by supplying appropriate end marks, commas, colons, dashes, and parentheses. Do not use unnecessary punctuation. Be prepared to explain the reason for each

mark you add, especially when you have a choice of correct marks (for example, commas, dashes, or parentheses).

1. Freeways in America are all the same aluminum guardrails green signs white lettering
2. "Is it is it the green light then" was all I managed to say
3. I tell you again What is alive and young and throbbing with historic current in America is musical theater
4. Things aren't helped by the following typo "The second study involved 177,106 of the approximately 130,000 refugees"
5. "Judy" she exploded "Judy that's an awful thing to say" She raised an arm to slap her daughter but it wouldn't reach
6. Emily formerly Mrs. Goyette caught McAndless' sleeve where no one could see and tugged it briefly but urgently
7. At last she had become what she had always wished to be a professional dancer
8. My own guess is that sociobiology will offer no comfort to thinkers conservatives or liberals who favor tidy ideas about what it means to be human
9. As one man put it "Rose Bowl Sugar Bowl and Orange Bowl all are gravy bowls"
10. "Good and" can mean "very" "I am good and mad" and "a hot cup of coffee" means that the coffee not the cup is hot

SPELLING AND DICTION

Spelling and Hyphenation

18

Spell every word according to established usage as shown by your dictionary. Hyphenate words in accordance with current usage.

Spelling

Spelling is a highly individual problem. You can improve your spelling by following these six suggestions:

1. Proofread to detect misspellings. Many misspellings are a result of mistakes in typing or in handwriting. Below are samples of a proofreader's corrections of typical misspellings:

a lot   doesn't   during   therefore

whatever   worldly

2. Make good use of your dictionary. When you consult the dictionary for a correct spelling, give attention to syllabication, pronunciation, and (when helpful) etymology.

Check meaning to be sure that you have found the exact word you have in mind.

Look for any labels that may restrict the use of a given spelling—like *British* or *chiefly British.*

BRITISH	AMERICAN
connexion	connection
humour	humor
jeweller	jeweler
offence	offense
realise	realize

Check for labels like *obsolete* or *archaic* (*compleat* for *complete*), *regional* or *dialectal* (*heighth* for *height*), or *slang* (*weirdy, weirdo*).

If your dictionary lists unlabeled optional spellings—such as *likable/likeable, theater/theatre,* or *tornados/tornadoes*—either form is correct.

3. Study in context pairs of spellings (like *device, devise*) that you confuse. Visualize the words as you pronounce them. Practice writing them in phrases that bring out their denotations.

4. Spell by rule. Take time to analyze the structure of a word. Learn regular patterns of spellings (as well as exceptions) to avoid repetition of similar errors.

5. Study word lists. The lists in this section consist of hundreds of frequently misspelled words. Single out for special study those words that you find troublesome.

6. Keep an individual spelling list. List for study those words that you have misspelled or tend to misspell. Be sure that each word on your list is correctly written.

18a

Do not allow pronunciation (whether incorrect or correct) to cause you to misspell words by omitting, adding, or transposing letters.

Mispronunciation often leads to the misspelling of such words as those listed below. To avoid difficulties resulting from mispronunciation, pronounce problem words aloud several times, clearly and distinctly, in accordance with the pronunciation shown by a dictionary. Be careful not to omit, add, or transpose any letter or syllable.

athlete	drowned	modern	quantity
barbarous	escape	pertain	recognize
candidate	everything	prescribe	represent
disastrous	gratitude	probable	umbrella

A word that is difficult to spell may have two correct pronunciations. Of these, one may be a better guide to spelling. For example, the person who correctly leaves out the first /n/ when saying *government* or the first /r/ when saying *surprise* may be more likely to omit the *n* or *r* when writing these words than one who, again correctly, pronounces these sounds.

Each word in the following list has more than one correct pronunciation. If you tend to misspell any of these words because of the way you say them, then depend on your vision and memory to learn their correct spellings.

arctic	hundred	sophomore
boundary	interest	temperature
February	literature	veteran
generally	perhaps	where

As you check pronunciations in the dictionary, give special attention to /ə/, the symbol for a neutral vowel sound in unaccented syllables, usually an indistinct *uh* sound (as in *confidence*). Be especially careful not to omit letters representing /ə/. (The term *schwa* is used to refer to the vowel sound or to its phonetic symbol.)

Caution: Do not misspell words like *and, have,* or *than* because they are not stressed in context.

> We had ham and [NOT *an*] eggs.
> I should have [NOT *of*] won.
> The movie is even more exciting than [NOT *then*] the book.

18b

Distinguish between words of similar sound and spelling; use the spelling required by the meaning.

Words such as *forth* and *fourth* or *sole* and *soul* sound alike but have vastly different meanings. Always be sure to choose the right word for your context.

A number of frequently confused spellings may be studied in groups:

Contractions and possessive pronouns:

It's best to wait.	The team did **its** best.
You're required to attend.	**Your** attendance is required.
There's a change in plans.	**Theirs** have changed.

Single words and two-word phrases:

It's an **everyday** event.	It happens nearly **every day.**
Maybe that is true.	That **may be** true.
I ran **into** trouble.	I ran **in to** get it.
Nobody cared.	The ghost had **no body.**

Singular nouns ending in **nce** *and plural nouns ending in* **nts:**

not much **assistance**	too many **assistants**
for **instance**	just **instants** ago
even less **patience** with	several **patients**

As you study the list of words below, use your dictionary to check the meaning of words not thoroughly familiar to you. You may find it helpful to devise examples of usage such as these:

breath—a deep breath	**breathe**—to breathe deeply
passed—had passed	**past**—in the past

Words Frequently Confused

accept, except		envelop, envelope
access, excess		fair, fare
advice, advise		formerly, formally
affect, effect	40	forth, fourth
aisle, isle		gorilla, guerrilla
alley, ally		hear, here
allude, elude		heard, herd
already, all ready		hole, whole
altar, alter		holy, wholly
altogether, all together	10	human, humane
always, all ways		its, it's
angel, angle		later, latter
ascent, assent		lead, led
assistance, assistants	50	lesson, lessen
bare, bear		lightning, lightening
birth, berth		lose, loose
board, bored		maybe, may be
born, borne		minor, miner
breath, breathe		moral, morale
canvas, canvass	20	of, off
Calvary, cavalry		passed, past
capital, capitol		patience, patients
censor, censure		peace, piece
choose, chose	60	personal, personnel
cite, sight, site		plain, plane
clothes, cloths		precede, proceed
coarse, course		presence, presents
complement, compliment		principle, principal
conscience, conscious		prophecy, prophesy
council, counsel	30	purpose, propose
descent, dissent		quiet, quite, quit
dam, damn		respectfully, respectively
desert, dessert		reverend, reverent
device, devise	70	right, rite, -wright, write
dominant, dominate		sense, since
dyeing, dying		stationary, stationery

statue, stature, statute
straight, strait
taut, taunt
than, then
their, there, they're
through, thorough

80

to, too, two
tract, track
weather, whether
were, where
who's, whose
your, you're

EXAMPLES

-ing: rise, lose, guide *rising, losing, guiding*
-ly, -er, -ness: late *lately, later, lateness*

1. -ly: like, safe, sure
2. -able, -ing, -ment: excite
3. -ful: care, hope, use
4. -ing, -ment, -able: argue
5. -ing: come, notice, hope

6. -ing, -less: use
7. -ous: continue, courage
8. -ly, -ing: complete
9. -able: desire, notice
10. -ing, -ment: manage

18c

Apply the rules for spelling when adding prefixes and suffixes to the root.

The root is the base to which the prefix or the suffix is added.

PREFIXES

(1) Add the prefix to the root without doubling or dropping letters.

Do not double the last letter of the prefix when it is different from the first letter of the root (as in *disappear*). Do not drop the last letter of the prefix when the root begins with the same letter (as in *immortal*).

dis + agree = disagree
un + usual = unusual
mis + used = misused
re + do = redo

dis + satisfied = dissatisfied
un + noted = unnoted
mis + spent = misspent
re + elect = reelect [OR re-elect]

SUFFIXES

(2) Drop an unpronounced final *e* before a suffix beginning with a vowel but not before a suffix beginning with a consonant.

like → liking BUT likely, likeness, likelihood
use → usage, using BUT useful, useless

Dropped -e before vowel:
age aging
combine combination
desire desirable
fame famous
scarce scarcity

Retained -e before consonant:
care careful
entire entirely
manage management
rude rudeness
safe safety

Caution: To keep the sound /s/ of *-ce* or /j/ of *-ge*, do not drop the final *e* before *-able* or *-ous*:

noticing BUT noticeable
changing BUT changeable
raging BUT outrageous
engaging BUT courageous

Similarly, keep the *e* before *-ance*, as in *vengeance*.

Other exceptions:

acreage hoeing lineage mileage [-e kept before vowel]
argument ninth truly wholly [-e dropped before consonant]

■ **Exercise 1** Practice adding suffixes to words ending in an unpronounced *e*.

(3) Double a final single consonant before a suffix beginning with a vowel (*a*) if the consonant ends a stressed syllable or a word of one syllable and (*b*) if the consonant is preceded by a single vowel. Otherwise, do not double the consonant.

One-syllable words:
drag dragged
hid hidden
shop shoppers
stun stunning
wet wettest

Words stressed on last syllable:
abhor abhorrent
begin beginning
occur occurrence
regret regrettable
unwrap unwrapped

Compare: benefited, reference [stressed on first syllable]

■ **Exercise 2** Write the present participle (*-ing* form) and the past tense of each verb: *rob*—robbing, robbed.

admit conceal hope plan stop
brag grip jog rebel audit

(4) As a rule, change final *y* to *i* before adding a suffix, but keep the *y* before *-ing*.

apply → applies, applied, appliance BUT applying
study → studies, studied BUT studying
happy → happily, happiness, happier, happiest

Exceptions: Verbs ending in *y* preceded by a vowel do not change the *y* before *-s* or *-ed: stay, stays, stayed.* Following the same pattern of spelling, nouns like *joys* or *days* have *y* before *s*. The following irregularities in spelling are especially troublesome:

lays, laid pays, paid [*Compare:* says, said.]

(5) Do not drop a final *l* when you add *-ly*.

formal formally usual usually
real really wool woolly

■ **Exercise 3** Add the designated suffixes to the following words.

1. -able: vary, ply
2. -er: funny, carry
3. -ous: vary, luxury
4. -ly: easy, final
5. -ed: supply, stay

6. -ing: study, worry
7. -d: pay, lay
8. -hood: lively, likely
9. -ness: friendly, lonely
10. -ly: usual, cool

18d

Apply the rules for spelling to avoid confusion of *ei* and *ie*.

When the sound is /ē/ (*ee*), write *ie* (except after *c*, in which case write *ei*).

				(after *c*)	
chief	grief	pierce	wield	ceiling	deceive
field	niece	relief	yield	conceit	perceive

When the sound is other than /ē/ (*ee*), usually write *ei*.

counterfeit	foreign	heifer	heir	sleigh	vein
forfeit	freight	height	neighbor	stein	weigh

Exceptions: friend, mischief, seize, sheik

■ **Exercise 4** Fill in the blanks with the appropriate letters: *ei* or *ie*.

1. p____ce
2. ach____ve
3. rec____ve
4. n____gh
5. fr____ght
6. ap____ce
7. bel____f
8. conc____ve
9. th____r
10. dec____t
11. n____ce
12. sh____ld
13. w____rd
14. shr____k
15. pr____st

18e

As a rule, form the plural of nouns by adding *s* or *es* to the singular.

(1) Form the plural of most nouns by adding *s* to the singular:

two boys	many nations	a few scientists
several safes	three cupfuls	all the radios

both sisters-in-law [chief word pluralized]
the Dudleys and the Berrys [proper names]

Note: To form the plural of some nouns ending in *f* or *fe*, change the ending to *ve* before adding the *s*: *a thief, two thieves; one life, our lives.*

(2) Add *es* to singular nouns ending in *s, ch, sh,* or *x.*

many losses	these mailboxes	the Rogerses
two approaches	a lot of ashes	two Dorises

[Note that each plural above makes an extra syllable.]

(3) Add *es* to singular nouns ending in *y* preceded by a consonant, after changing the *y* to *i*.

eighty—eighties
strawberry—strawberries
company—companies
industry—industries

Note: Although *es* is often added to a singular noun ending in *o* preceded by a consonant, usage varies:

echoes	heroes	potatoes	vetoes	[-*es* only]
autos	memos	pimentos	pros	[-*s* only]
nos/noes	mottos/mottoes	zeros/zeroes		[-*s* or -*es*]

Exceptions: Irregular plurals (including retained foreign spellings) are not formed by adding *s* or *es*.

SINGULAR	woman	goose	analysis	alga	species
PLURAL	women	geese	analyses	algae	species

■ **Exercise 5** Supply plural forms (including any optional spelling) for the following words, applying rule **18e**. (If a word is not covered by the rule, use your dictionary.)

1.	belief	6.	bath	11.	radius	16.	phenomenon
2.	theory	7.	hero	12.	scarf	17.	halo
3.	church	8.	story	13.	wife	18.	child
4.	genius	9.	wish	14.	speech	19.	handful
5.	Kelly	10.	forty	15.	tomato	20.	rodeo

A List of Words Frequently Misspelled

Like the words discussed in Section **18b**, the following list may be studied in groups of ten or twenty at a time. Blank spaces are provided at the end of the list for the addition of other words which you may wish to master (possibly those from your special field of interest) or which your instructor may recommend.

	absence		apparent		carrying
	acceptable		appearance		category
	accessible		appoint		cemetery
	accidentally		appreciate		census
	accommodate		appropriate		certain
	accompanied		approximately		challenge
	accomplish		arguing		changeable
	accordion		argument		changing
	accuracy		arrest		channel
10	accustomed	50	article	90	characteristic
	achievement		aspirin		chief
	acquainted		assassination		children
	acquire		associate		chocolate
	acreage		atheist		chosen
	across		athletics		Christianity
	actually		attached		coarsely
	address		attacked		commercial
	admission		attendance		commitment
	adolescent		authentic		committee
20	advice	60	average	100	competent
	advised		barbarous		competition
	affected		bargain		completely
	affectionately		basically		conceited
	aggravate		beautiful		conceive
	aggression		beginning		concentrate
	aisles		belief		condemn
	alcohol		believed		confident
	all right		beneficial		conscience
	a lot of		benefited		conscientious
30	always	70	biggest	110	consensus
	amateur		birthday		consistent
	among		boundary		continuous
	analysis		breath		contradict
	ancestry		breathe		controlled
	angel		bulletin		controversial
	annihilate		bureaucracy		convenient
	announcement		business		coolly
	anywhere		cafeteria		courses
	apiece		calculator		courteous
40	apology	80	calendar	120	criticism

criticize	everything	humane	likelihood	occurrence	prejudice
crowd	evidently	humorous	listening	occurring	prepare
cruelty	exaggerate	hundred	liveliest	off	preparation
curiosity	excellent	hungry	lose	official	pretty
curious	except	hurriedly	luxury	omission	prevail
dealt	exercise	hypocrisy	lying	omit	prevalent
deceive	exhaust	hypocrite	magazine	omitted	principle
decision	existence	ideally	magnificent	omitting	prisoner
decorate	expense	idiosyncrasy	maintenance	opponent	privilege
130 definitely	180 experience	230 ignorant	280 manageable	330 opportunity	380 probably

delicate	experiment	illogical	management	opposite	procedure
descend	explanation	imaginary	maneuver	oppression	proceed
description	extremely	imagine	manual	optimism	processes
desirable	familiar	imitate	marriage	ordinarily	professor
despair	family	immediately	material	originally	prominent
desperate	fascinate	immensely	mathematics	paid	pronunciation
despicable	favorite	incalculable	meanness	pamphlet	propaganda
destroy	February	incidentally	meant	parallel	prophecy
develop	finally	incredible	medicine	paralleled	prophesy
140 different	190 financially	240 independent	290 mere	340 parole	390 psychology

disagree	fluorine	indispensable	miniature	particle	publicly
disappear	foreign	individually	minor	particularly	pumpkin
disappoint	foresee	influential	minutes	past	purpose
disapprove	foretell	initiative	mirror	pastime	pursue
disastrous	forty	innocuous	mischievous	peaceable	pursuing
discipline	forward	instead	missile	peculiar	pursuit
discussion	friend	insurance	morale	penetrate	quandary
disease	fulfill	intelligent	morals	perceive	quantity
dispel	gauge	interest	mortgage	performance	questionnaire
150 distinct	200 generally	250 interference	300 morning	350 perhaps	400 quiet

disturb	government	integrate	muscle	permanent	quite
divide	governor	interrupt	mysterious	permissible	quizzes
divine	grammar	introduce	narrative	persuade	rarity
doctor	group	involve	naturally	pertain	reality
dormitory	gruesome	irrelevant	necessary	phase	realize
easily	guaranteed	irresistible	nevertheless	physical	really
ecstasy	guard	irritated	nickel	pigeon	rebel
effect	guerrilla	jealousy	niece	pitiful	receipt
efficient	guidance	jewelry	nineteen	planned	receive
160 eighth	210 happened	260 knowledge	310 ninety	360 pleasant	410 recession

elaborately	happily	laboratory	ninth	poison	recipe
embarrass	harass	laid	noticeable	politician	recognize
empty	heard	led	noticing	pollute	recommend
enemy	height	leisure	nowadays	possession	referring
entirely	here	length	nuclear	possibly	regular
environment	heroes	lenient	nuisance	practical	regulate
equipment	hindrance	liable	numerous	practically	rehearsal
equipped	holiday	library	occasion	precede	relief
escape	hoping	license	occasionally	predominant	relieve
170 especially	220 human	270 lightning	320 occurred	370 preferred	420 religious

	remember	stayed	transferred	
	remembrance	stepped	tremendous	
	reminisce	stopped	trouble	
	repetition	straight	truly	
	representative	strategy	twelfth	
	reproduce	strength	typical	
	resemblance	strenuous	tyranny	
	resistance	stretch	unanimous	
	resources	strict	unconscious	
430	restaurant	480 stubbornness	530 undoubtedly	

	review	studies	until	
	rhythm	studying	usage	
	ridiculous	suburban	using	
	roommate	succeed	usually	
	sacrifice	succession	vacuum	
	safety	sufficient	valuable	
	sandwich	suicide	various	
	satellite	summary	vegetable	
	Saturday	superintendent	vengeance	
440	saxophone	490 supersede	540 vice	

	scarcity	suppose	view	
	scenery	suppress	villain	
	schedule	surely	violence	
	secede	surprise	visible	
	secretary	surround	vitamins	
	seize	suspicious	warrant	
	senseless	susceptible	warring	
	sentence	swimming	weather	
	separate	symbol	Wednesday	
450	sergeant	500 technical	550 weird	

	several	technique	where	
	sheriff	temperature	wherever	
	shining	temporary	whether	
	shoulder	tendency	whichever	
	shrubbery	than	wholly	
	significant	their	whose	
	similar	theirs	without	
	simply	themselves	woman	
	since	then	women	
460	sincerely	510 therefore	560 writing	

	ski	thorough	written	
	skiing	though	yield	
	sophomore	thought	_____	
	source	through	_____	
	souvenir	till	_____	
	speak	tobacco	_____	
	speeches	together	_____	
	specimen	tomorrow	_____	
	sponsor	too	_____	
470	statistics	520 tragedy	_____	

Hyphenation

18f

Hyphenate words chiefly to express the idea of a unit and to avoid ambiguity. For the division of words at the end of a line, see **8d.**

Words forming a compound may be written separately, written as one word, or connected by hyphens. For example, three modern dictionaries all have the same listings of these compounds:

> hair stylist   hairsplitter   hair-raiser

Another modern dictionary, however, lists *hairstylist*, not *hair stylist*. Compounding is in such a state of flux that authorities do not always agree.

(1) Use the hyphen to join two or more words serving as a single adjective before a noun.

> the bluish-green sea   chocolate-covered peanuts
> peace-loving natives   his know-it-all glance
> the twenty-two-year-old laboratory technician
> [Note the singular form of the noun *year* after the numeral in the hyphenated modifier.]

Notice that in the examples below the modifiers after the noun are not hyphenated:

> The sea was bluish green.
> The peanuts, which were chocolate covered, tasted stale.
> The laboratory technician was twenty-two years old.
> [Numbers like *twenty-two* are hyphenated wherever they appear in a sentence.]

More than one hyphenated adjectival, of course, may precede the noun modified:

> "I reject get-it-done, make-it-happen thinking," he says.
> —THE ATLANTIC

"Suspension" hyphens are used in such series as the following:

> two-, three-, and four-hour classes

Note: The hyphen is generally omitted after an adverb ending in *-ly* in such phrases as the following:

> a hopelessly lost cause   a frequently used example

■ **Exercise 6**   Convert the following word groups according to the pattern of the examples.

> EXAMPLES
> an initiation lasting two months   *a two-month initiation*
> ideas that shake the world   *world-shaking ideas*

1. an apartment with six rooms
2. examinations that exhaust the mind
3. fingers stained with ink
4. a voter who is eighteen years old
5. shoppers who are budget minded
6. tents costing a hundred dollars
7. peace talks that last all night
8. a program that trains teachers
9. a hitchhiker who was waving a flag
10. ponds covered with lilies

(2) Use the hyphen with compound numbers from twenty-one to ninety-nine (or twenty-first to ninety-ninth).

forty=six, fifty=eighth   BUT   three hundred twenty

Note: Usage varies regarding the hyphenation of fractions. The hyphen is required, however, only when the fraction functions as a compound modifier. See also **18f(1)**.

almost one=half full   BUT   eating only one half of it
a two=thirds vote   BUT   two thirds of the voters

(3) Use the hyphen to avoid ambiguity or an awkward combination of letters or syllables between prefix and root or suffix and root.

a dirty movie=theater   [Compare ''a dirty=movie theater.'']
to re=sign a petition   [Compare ''to resign a position.'']
semi=independent, shell=like   BUT   semifluid, childlike

(4) Use the hyphen with the prefixes *ex-* (''former''), *self-, all-;* with the suffix *-elect;* and between a prefix and a capitalized word.

ex=wife   self=help   all=inclusive   mayor=elect
mid=September   non=Biblical   anti=American

Note: The hyphen is also used with figures or letters such as *mid=1980s* or *T=shirt.*

■ **Exercise 7**   Refer to **18f** and to your dictionary as you convert each phrase (or words within each phrase) to a compound or to a word with a prefix. Use hyphens when needed.

EXAMPLES

glasses used for water   *water glasses*   OR   *waterglasses*
not Communistic   *non-Communistic*
a man who makes   *a $75,000-a-year man*
  $75,000 a year

1. respect for oneself
2. persons keeping the score
3. bacon cured with sugar
4. a plan for sharing the profit
5. a latch used at night
6. four and twenty
7. a cleaner for all purposes
8. a woman who is ninety-two years old
9. in the shape of a V
10. fences that are covered with snow
11. the flight from Montreal to Portland
12. a sale lasting two or three days

Good Usage and Glossary

19

Use a good dictionary to help you select the words that express your ideas exactly.

You can find valuable information about words by referring to a good college dictionary, such as one of the following:

Funk & Wagnalls Standard College Dictionary
The American Heritage Dictionary
The Random House Dictionary
Webster's New Collegiate Dictionary
Webster's New World Dictionary

Occasionally you may need to refer to an unabridged dictionary or to a special dictionary: see the two lists on page 786.

19a

Use a good dictionary intelligently.

Intelligent use of a dictionary requires some understanding of its plan and of the special abbreviations given in the introductory matter. Knowing how the dictionary arranges and presents material will enable you to interpret much of the information provided in its entries.

Below is a sample dictionary entry. First, note the various definitions of *empty* as an adjective, as a transitive verb, as an intransitive verb, as a noun, and as part of an idiomatic phrase (with *of*). Next, observe the examples of usage. Finally, note the various other kinds of information (labeled in color) that the dictionary provides.

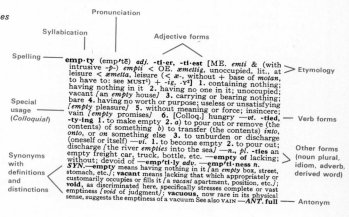

(1) Spelling, syllabication, and pronunciation   As a writer, use your dictionary not only to check spelling but also to find where words may be divided at the end of a line: see **8d**. As a speaker, check the pronunciation of unfamiliar words in your dictionary. Keys to the sound symbols are at the bottom of each two-page spread as well as in the introductory matter at the front of the dictionary. A primary stress mark (′) normally follows the syllable that is most heavily accented. Secondary stress marks follow lightly accented syllables.

■ **Exercise 1** With the aid of your dictionary, write out the following words using sound symbols and stress marks to indicate the correct pronunciation (or a correct one if options are given).

1. harass	6. interest
2. incongruous	7. egalitarian
3. performance	8. advertisement
4. Mozart	9. pogonip
5. pica	10. oceanography

(2) Parts of speech and inflected forms Your dictionary provides labels indicating the possible uses of words in sentences—for instance, *adj.* (adjective), *adv.* (adverb), *v.t.* (verb, transitive). It also lists ways that nouns, verbs, and modifiers change form to indicate number, tense, or comparison or to serve as another part of speech (for example, under *repress, v.t.,* may appear *repressible, adj.*).

■ **Exercise 2** With the aid of your dictionary, classify each of the following words as a verb (transitive or intransitive), a noun, an adjective, an adverb, a preposition, or a conjunction. Give the principal parts of each verb, the plural (or plurals) of each noun, and the comparative and superlative of each adjective and adverb. (Note that some words are used as two or more parts of speech.)

1. permit	3. sweet-talk	5. subtle	7. late	9. crisis
2. lonely	4. tattoo	6. for	8. bring	10. fine

(3) Definitions and examples of usage Observe how your dictionary arranges the definitions of a word: whether the most common meaning is given first or whether the definitions are listed in historical order. Notice also that an illustration of the usage of a word often clarifies a definition.

■ **Exercise 3** Study the definitions of any five of the following pairs of words, paying special attention to any examples of usage in your dictionary; then write sentences to illustrate the shades of difference in meaning.

1. rot—putrefy	6. charisma—charm
2. sensual—sensuous	7. burgoo—gumbo
3. viable—practicable	8. free—liberate
4. yukking—guffawing	9. jaded—a jade
5. mercy—clemency	10. draw—draft

(4) Synonyms and antonyms Lists and discussions of synonyms in dictionaries often help to clarify the meaning of closely related words. By studying the denotations and connotations of words with similar meanings, you will find that you are able to choose your words more exactly and to convey more subtle shades of meaning. Lists of antonyms can help you to find a word that is the direct opposite of another in meaning.

Note: For more complete lists of synonyms, antonyms, related and contrasted words, refer to a special dictionary or thesaurus. Below is a sample thesaurus entry.

empty *adj* **1** lacking contents that could or should be present <an *empty* apartment> <the whole book is *empty* of meaning>

Synonyms ———— **syn** bare, clear, stark, vacant, vacuous, void

Related words —— **rel** barren, blank; abandoned, deserted, emptied, forsaken, godforsaken, unfilled, unfurnished uninhabited, untenanted, vacated; destitute, devoid; depleted, drained, exhausted

Contrasted words — **con** complete, replete; filled, occupied, packed, teeming

Antonym —— **ant** full

2 syn VAIN 1, hollow, idle, nugatory, otiose
rel paltry, petty, trifling, trivial; banal, flat, inane, ineffectual, insipid, jejune, vapid; dumb, fatuous, foolish, ignorant, silly, simple
con meaningful, pregnant, significant; authentic, bona fide, genuine, veritable
3 syn EXPRESSIONLESS, blank, deadpan, inexpressive, unexpressive, vacant
4 syn DEVOID, innocent, void

Before choosing a synonym or closely related word from such a list, look it up in the dictionary to make sure that it expresses your meaning exactly. Although *stark, idle,* and *inexpressive* are all listed above as synonyms of *empty,* they have vastly different connotations.

■ **Exercise 4** With the aid of your dictionary or thesaurus, list two synonyms and one antonym for each of the following words. (1) hatred (2) pleasure (3) false (4) oppose (5) stingy

(5) Origin: development of the language In college dictionaries the origin of the word—also called its *derivation* or *etymology*—is shown in square brackets. For example, after *expel* might be this information: "[< L *expellere* < *ex-* out + *pellere* to drive, thrust]." This means that *expel* is derived from (<) the Latin (L) word *expellere,* which is made up of *ex-,* meaning "out," and *pellere,* meaning "to drive or thrust." Breaking up a word, when possible, into *prefix—root—suffix* will often help to get at the basic meaning of a word.

	prefix		root		suffix
dependent	de- down	+	pend to hang	+	-ent one who
interruption	inter- between	+	rupt to break	+	-ion act of
preference	pre- before	+	fer to carry	+	-ence state of

The bracketed information given by a good dictionary is especially rich in meaning when considered in relation to the historical development of our language. English is one of the Indo-European (IE) languages, a group of languages apparently derived from a common source.* Within this group of languages, many of the more familiar words are remarkably alike. Our word *mother,* for example, is *mater* in Latin (L), *meter* in Greek (Gk.), and *matar* in ancient Persian and in the Sanskrit (Skt.) of India. Words in different languages that apparently descend from a common parent language are called *cognates.* The large number of cognates and the many correspondences in sound and structure in most of the languages of Europe and some languages of Asia indicate that they are derived from the common language that linguists call Indo-European, which it is believed was spoken in parts of Europe about six thousand years ago. By the opening of the Christian era the speakers of this language had spread over most of Europe and as far east as India, and the original Indo-European had developed into eight or nine language families. Of these, the chief ones that influenced English were the Hellenic (Greek) group on the eastern Mediterra-

---

*The parenthetical abbreviations for languages here and on the next few pages are those commonly used in bracketed derivations in dictionaries.

nean, the Italic (Latin) on the central and western Mediterranean, and the Germanic in northwestern Europe. English is descended from the Germanic.

Two thousand years ago the Hellenic, the Italic, and the Germanic branches of Indo-European each comprised a more or less unified language group. After the fall of the Roman Empire in the fifth century, the several Latin-speaking divisions developed independently into the modern Romance languages, chief of which are Italian, French, and Spanish. Long before the fall of Rome the Germanic group was breaking up into three families: (1) East Germanic, represented by the Goths, who were to play a large part in the history of the last century of the Roman Empire before losing themselves in its ruins; (2) North Germanic, or Old Norse (ON), from which modern Danish (Dan.), Swedish (Sw.), Norwegian (Norw.), and Icelandic (Icel.) derive; and (3) West Germanic, the direct ancestor of English, Dutch (Du.), and German (Ger.).

The English language may be said to have begun about the middle of the fifth century, when the West Germanic Angles, Saxons, and Jutes began the conquest of what is now England and either absorbed or drove out the Celtic-speaking inhabitants. (Celtic—from which Scots Gaelic, Irish Gaelic, Welsh, and other languages later developed—is another member of the Indo-European family.) The next six or seven hundred years are known as the Old English (OE) or Anglo-Saxon (AS) period of the English language. The fifty or sixty thousand words then in the language were chiefly Anglo-Saxon, with a small mixture of Old Norse words as a result of the Danish (Viking) conquests of England beginning in the eighth century. But the Old Norse words were so much like the Anglo-Saxon that they cannot always be distinguished.

The transitional period from Old English to Modern English—about 1100 to 1500—is known as Middle English (ME). The Norman Conquest began in 1066. The Normans, or "Northmen," had settled in northern France during the Viking invasions and had adopted Old French (OF) in place of their native Old Norse. Then, crossing over to England by the thousands, they made French the language of the king's court in London and of the ruling classes—both French and English—throughout the land, while the masses continued to speak English. Only toward the end of the fifteenth century did English become once more the common language of all classes. But the language that emerged at that time had lost most of its Anglo-Saxon inflections and had taken on thousands of French words (derived originally from Latin). Nonetheless, it was still basically English, not French, in its structure.

The marked and steady development of the English language (until it was partly stabilized by printing, introduced in London in 1476) is suggested by the following passages, two from Old English and two from Middle English.

Hē ǣrest scēop	eorðan bearnum
He first created	*for earth's children*
heofon tō hrōfe,	hālig Scyppend.
heaven as a roof,	*holy creator.*

From the "Hymn of Cædmon"
(middle of the Old English period)

Ēalā, hū lēas and hū unwrest is þysses middan-eardes wēla!
Alas! how false and how unstable is this midworld's weal!

Sē þe wæs ǣrur rīce cyng and maniges landes hlāford,
He that was before powerful king and of many lands lord,

hē næfde þā ealles landes būton seofon fōt mæl.
he had not then of all land but seven foot space.

From the *Anglo-Saxon Chronicle*, A.D 1087
(end of the Old English period)

A knight ther was, and that a worthy man,
That fro the tyme that he first bigan
To ryden out, he loved chivalrye,
Trouthe and honour, fredom and curteisye.

From Chaucer's Prologue to the
Canterbury Tales, about 1385

Thenne within two yeres king Uther felle seke of a grete maladye. And in the meane whyle hys enemyes usurpped upon hym, and dyd a grete bataylle upon his men, and slewe many of his peple.

From Sir Thomas Malory's *Morte d'Arthur*,
printed 1485

A striking feature of Modern English (that is, English since 1500) is its immense vocabulary. As already noted, Old English used some fifty or sixty thousand words, very largely native Anglo-Saxon; Middle English used perhaps a hundred thousand words, many taken through the French from Latin and others taken directly from Latin; and unabridged dictionaries today list over four times as many. To make up this tremendous word hoard, we have borrowed most heavily from Latin, but we have drawn some words from almost every known language. English writers of the sixteenth century were especially eager to interlace their works with words from Latin authors. And, as the English pushed out to colonize and to trade in many parts of the globe, they brought home new words as well as goods. Modern science and technology have drawn heavily from the Greek. As a result of all this borrowing, English has become one of the richest and most cosmopolitan of languages.

In the process of enlarging our vocabulary we have lost most of our original Anglo-Saxon words. But those that are left make up the most familiar, most useful part of our vocabulary. Practically all our simple verbs, our articles, conjunctions, prepositions, and pronouns are native Anglo-Saxon; and so are many of our familiar nouns, adjectives, and adverbs. Every speaker and writer uses these native words over and over, much more frequently than the borrowed words. Indeed, if every word is counted every time it is used, the percentage of native words runs very high—usually between 70 and 90 percent. Milton's percentage was 81, Tennyson's 88, Shakespeare's about 90, and that of the King James Bible about 94. English has been enriched by its extensive borrowings without losing its individuality; it is still fundamentally the *English* language.

■ **Exercise 5** With the aid of your dictionary, give the etymology of each of the following words:

1. aspirin	6. helicopter
2. ecology	7. laser
3. gardenia	8. OK
4. geriatrics	9. polyester
5. guerrilla	10. Teflon

(6) Special usage labels Dictionaries ordinarily carry no usage labels for the bulk of English words. Unlabeled, or general, words range from the learned words appropriate in the most formal situations to the words used every day in both formal and informal situations.

Most dictionaries, however, provide a variety of special usage labels for words or for particular definitions of words. These labels indicate varieties of usage that differ from the general. Here is a sampling of labeled definitions, each of them found in two or more college dictionaries:

unalienable	*Archaic, Obsolete*	inalienable
lift	*Informal, Colloquial*	plagiarize
nowheres	*Nonstandard, Dialect, Colloquial*	not anywhere, nowhere
stink	*Slang*	to be of low quality

As the examples above indicate, the classification of words is often difficult and controversial because our language is constantly changing. Good writers try to choose the words, whatever their labels, that exactly fit the audience and the occasion, informal or formal.

■ **Exercise 6** Classify the following words and phrases according to the usage labels in your dictionary. If a word has no special usage label, classify it as *General*. If a given definition of a word has a usage label, give the meaning after the label.

EXAMPLES
tote bag—general
aholt—dialectal
nutty—informal for *silly,* slang for *insane*

1. doll
2. dude
3. funky
4. holler
5. irregardless
6. junk
7. macho
8. rube
9. snigger
10. unto

19b

Avoid informal words in formal writing.

Words or expressions labeled *Informal* or *Colloquial* in college dictionaries are standard English and are used by speakers and writers every day. These words are thus appropriate in informal writing, especially in dialogue. But informal words or expressions are usually inappropriate in formal expository compositions. In formal writing, use instead the general English vocabulary, the unlabeled words in your dictionary.

INFORMAL In class the teacher gave a definition of *polyunsaturated,* but I didn't **get it.**

FORMAL In class the teacher gave a definition of *polyunsaturated,* but I did not **understand it.**

Contractions are common in informal English, especially in dialogue: see the examples on page 709. But contracted forms (like *won't* or *there's*) are usually written out (*will not, there is*) in a formal composition—which is not as casual or spontaneous as conversational English is.

■ **Exercise 7** Make a list of ten words that you would consider informal in your writing. Then check your dictionary to see how (or if) each definition you have in mind is labeled.

19c

Use slang and jargon only when appropriate to the audience.

Slang words, including certain coinages and figures of speech, are variously considered as breezy, racy, extremely informal, nonstandard, facetious, taboo, offbeat, or vigorous. On occasion, slang can be used effectively, even in formal writing. Below is an example of the effective use of the word *spiel,* still labeled by dictionaries as *Slang:*

Here comes election year. Here come the hopefuls, the conventions, the candidates, the spiels, the postures, the press releases, and the TV performances. Here comes the year of the hoopla. —JOHN CIARDI

A few years ago the word *hoopla* was also generally considered as slang, but now dictionaries disagree: one classifies this word *Standard* (unlabeled); another, *Colloquial (Informal)*; still another, *Slang.* Like *hoopla,* words such as *spiel, uptight, paddy wagon, raunchy, schlep,* and *party pooper* have a particularly vivid quality; they soon may join former slang words such as *sham* and *mob* as part of the general English vocabulary.

But much slang is trite, tasteless, and inexact. For instance, when used to describe almost anything disapproved of, *gross* becomes inexact, flat.

Caution: As you avoid the use of ineffective slang in your writing, remember that many of the most vivid short words in our language are general, standard words. Certain long words can be as inexact and as drab as trite slang. For examples of the ineffective use of big words, see Exercise 9, page 727.

■ **Exercise 8** Replace the italicized words in the following sentences with more exact words or specific phrases.

1. After dress rehearsal the whole cast *goofed off.*
2. Lately the weather has been *lousy* on weekends.
3. Jean's new haircut is *dynamite.*
4. That *wisecrack ticked* him *off.*

19d

Use regional words only when appropriate to the audience.

Regional, or *dialectal,* words (also called *localisms* or *provincialisms*) should normally be avoided in speaking and writing outside the region where they are current. Speakers and writers may, however, safely use regional words known to the audience they are addressing.

REGIONAL Monty was **fixing to** feed his steak to the **critter.**
GENERAL Monty was **about to** feed his steak to the **dog.**
[OR *animal* OR *creature*]

19e

Avoid nonstandard words and usages.

Words and expressions labeled by dictionaries as *Nonstandard* or *Illiterate* should be avoided in most writing and speaking. Many common illiteracies are not listed in college dictionaries.

NONSTANDARD	**They's** no use asking them.
STANDARD	**There's** no use asking them.

19f

Avoid archaic and obsolete words.

All dictionaries list words (and meanings for words) that have long since passed out of general use. Such words as *ort* (fragment of food) and *yestreen* (last evening) are still found in dictionaries because these words, once the standard vocabulary of great authors, occur in our older literature and must be defined for the modern reader.

A number of obsolete or archaic words—such as *worser* (for *worse*) or *holp* (for *helped*)—are still in use but are now nonstandard.

19g

Use technical words only when appropriate to the audience.

When you are writing for the general reader, avoid all unnecessary technical language. Since the ideal of good writing is to make one's thought clear to as many people as possible, the careful writer will not describe an apple tree as a *Malus pumila* or a high fever as *hyperpyrexia*. (Of course, technical language, with its greater precision, is highly desirable when one is addressing an audience that can understand it, as when a physician addresses a group of physicians.)

19h

Avoid overwriting, an ornate or flowery style. Do not needlessly combine distracting sounds.

Overwriting, as well as the combination of distracting sounds, calls attention to words rather than to ideas. Such writing is generally fuzzy and repetitious, or carelessly indifferent to the importance of sound and its relationship to meaning.

ORNATE	Since the halcyon days of my early youth I have always anticipated with eagerness and pleasure the exciting vistas of distant climes and mysterious horizons.
BETTER	Since childhood I have looked forward to seeing the world.
DISTRACTING	The use of catalytic converters is just one contribution to the solution of the problem of air pollution.
BETTER	The use of catalytic converters is just one way to help solve the problem of air pollution.

Equally unpleasing to the average reader is the overuse of alliteration (repetition of the same consonant sound), as in "Some people *sh*un the *sea*shore."

■ **Exercise 9** Using simple, formal, straightforward English, rewrite the following sentences (from Stuart Chase's *Power of Words*).

1. It is obvious from the difference in elevation with relation to the short depth of the property that the contour is such as to preclude any reasonable developmental potential for active recreation.

2. Verbal contact with Mr. Blank regarding the attached notification of promotion has elicited the attached representation intimating that he prefers to decline the assignment.

3. Voucherable expenditures necessary to provide adequate dental treatment required as adjunct to medical treatment being rendered a pay patient in in-patient status may be incurred as required at the expense of the Public Health Service.

4. I hereby give and convey to you, all and singular, my estate and interests, right, title, claim and advantages of and in said orange, together with all rind, juice, pulp and pits, and all rights and advantages therein.

5. I prefer an abbreviated phraseology, distinguished for its lucidity.

6. Realization has grown that the curriculum or the experiences of learners change and improve only as those who are most directly involved examine their goals, improve their understandings and increase their skill in performing the tasks necessary to reach newly defined goals.

Glossary of Usage

19i

Consult the following glossary to determine the standing of a word or phrase and its appropriateness to your purpose.

The entries in the following glossary are authoritative only to the extent that they describe current usage. The usage labels included do not duplicate the descriptions in any one dictionary, but justification for each can usually be found in at least two of the leading dictionaries.

For a discussion of the special usage labels used in dictionaries, see **19a(6)**. The following labels appear most frequently in this glossary:

General Words in the standard English vocabulary, listed in dictionaries without special usage labels and appropriate in both formal and informal writing and speaking.

Informal Words or expressions labeled *Informal* or *Colloquial* in dictionaries—words widely used by educated as well as uneducated writers and speakers but not appropriate in a formal context. See also **19b**.

Standard All general and informal words or expressions.

Nonstandard Words or expressions labeled in dictionaries as *Archaic, Illiterate, Nonstandard, Obsolete, Slang,* or *Substandard*—words not considered a part of the standard English vocabulary. See also **19c, e,** and **f**.

Of course, the following glossary can include only a few of the words likely to cause difficulty. If the word you are looking for is not included, or if you need more information about any word in the list, consult a good college dictionary.

a, an Use *a* before a consonant sound, *an* before a vowel sound.

a history	a union	a one-dollar bill	a new dress	a C
an hour	an uncle	an only child	an NBA game	an F

accept See **except, accept**.

accidentally, incidentally When using these adverbs, remember that *-ly* is added to the adjective forms *accidental* and *incidental*, not to the noun forms *accident* and *incident*.

NONSTANDARD   Mr. Kent **accidently** overheard the report.
STANDARD   Mr. Kent **accidentally** overheard the report.

adapt, adopt   Do not confuse. To *adapt* is to adjust or make suitable. To *adopt* is to select as one's own or to choose to use or follow.

> We **adapted** the guidelines to our needs.   [made them fit]
> The company **adopted** new guidelines.   [chose to use]

advice, advise   Pronounced and spelled differently, *advice* is a noun, *advise* a verb.

> Patients should follow their doctors' **advice**.
> Patients should do what their doctors **advise**.

affect, effect   Do not confuse the verb *affect* with the noun *effect*. To *affect* is to rouse the emotions or to influence, change. An *effect* is a result, an outcome. (When used as a verb, *effect* means "bring about" or "accomplish": "The medicine *effected* a complete cure.")

> His tears **affected** her deeply.   The **effect** surprised me.
> The drug **affects** one's appetite.   The drug has side **effects**.

aggravate   Informally *aggravate* means "to annoy or to irritate." In general usage it means "to make worse" or "to intensify."

INFORMAL   Undisciplined children **aggravate** baby sitters.
GENERAL   Lack of water **aggravated** the suffering.

a half a   Informal for *half a* or *a half*.

ain't   A nonstandard contraction generally avoided in writing, unless used in dialogue or for humorous effect.

all the farther, all the faster   Regional, or dialectal, for *as far as, as fast as*.

NONSTANDARD   A mile is all the farther Mae can jog.
STANDARD   A mile is **as far as** Mae can jog.

allude, elude   See **elude, allude**.

allusion, illusion   Do not confuse. An *allusion* is a casual or indirect reference. An *illusion* is a false idea or an unreal image.

> The author's **allusion** to a heaven on earth amused me.
> The author's concept of a heaven on earth is an **illusion**.

almost, most   See **most**.

a lot   Sometimes misspelled as *alot*.

already, all ready   *Already* means "before or by the time specified." *All ready* means "completely prepared."

> The theater was **already** full by seven o'clock.
> The cast was **all ready** for the curtain call.

alright   Not yet a generally accepted spelling of *all right*.

altogether, all together   *Altogether* means "wholly, thoroughly." *All together* means "in a group."

> That law is **altogether** unnecessary.
> They were **all together** in the lobby.

A.M., P.M. (OR **a.m., p.m.**)   Use only with figures.

NOT   The wedding begins at ten thirty in the **a.m.**
BUT   The wedding begins at 10:30 A.M. [OR at ten thirty in the morning]

among, between   Prepositions with plural objects (including collective nouns). As a rule, use *among* with objects denoting three or more (a group), and use *between* with those denoting only two (or twos).

> walked **among** the crowd, quarreling **among** themselves
> a choice **between** war and peace, reading **between** the lines

amount of, number of   *Amount of* is followed by singular nouns; *number of*, by plural nouns.

> an **amount of** money, light, work, or postage   [singular]
> a **number of** coins, lights, jobs, or stamps   [plural]

See also **a number, the number**.

an   See **a, an**.

and etc.   Omit the redundant *and*. *Etc.* is an abbreviation of *et* ("and") *cetera* ("other things"). See also **etc.**

ante-, anti-   Do not confuse these prefixes. *Ante-* means "before, in front of." The more frequently used *anti-* means "against, opposite to" or "hostile to."

> antedate, anteroom, antenatal, antebellum, antecedent
> antiwar, anticlimax, antichrist, anti-Semitic, antidote, antibiotic

a number, the number   As subjects, *a number* is generally plural and *the number* is singular. Make sure that the verb agrees with the subject.

> **A number** of options **are** available.
> **The number** of options **is** limited.

anyone, any one   *Anyone* means "any person at all." *Any one* refers to a specific person or thing in a group. Similar forms are *everyone, every one; someone, some one*.

> **Anyone** can wax a floor.
> **Any one** of those men can wax a floor.

anyways, anywheres   Dialectal or colloquial for *anyway, anywhere*.

as   (1) Do not use *as* in place of the preposition *like* in making a comparison.

NOT   Natalie, as her mother, stands tall.
BUT   Natalie, **like** her mother, stands tall.

See also **like**.

(2) In your formal writing, do not use *as* in place of *whether, if,* or *that* after such verbs as *feel, know, say,* or *see*.

INFORMAL   I do not know as the President's adviser is right.
GENERAL   I do not know **whether** the President's adviser is right.

(3) If there is even a slight chance of ambiguity, many writers prefer not to use *as* for *because, since,* or *while*.

GENERAL   As it was raining, we watched TV.   [probably clear in context but possibly not]
PREFERRED   **While** it was raining, we watched TV.
OR   **Because** it was raining, we watched TV.

at   Redundant after *where*. See **where at, where to**.

awful   An overworked word for *ugly, shocking, very bad*. Informal as a substitute for *very*, as in "awful pretty" or "awful important."

awhile, a while   Distinguish between the adverb *awhile* and the article and noun *a while* (ordinarily used as an object of a preposition).

> After our long swim, we rested **awhile**.
> After our long swim, we rested for **a while**.

bad, badly   The adverb *badly* is preferred after most verbs. But either *bad* or *badly* is now standard in the sense of "ill" or "sorry," and writers now usually prefer *bad* after such verbs as *feel* or *look*.

> The organist plays **badly**.
> Charles feels **bad**.

be sure and   Write *be sure to* in such sentences as "*Be sure to* consult a lawyer."

because   See **reason . . . because.**

being as, being that   Nonstandard for *since, because.*

beside, besides   Always a preposition, *beside* usually means "next to," sometimes "apart from." As a preposition meaning "in addition to" or "other than," *besides* is now more common in writing than *beside.* When used adverbially, *besides* means "also" or "moreover."

> Marvin was sitting **beside** Bunny.
> **Besides** countless toys, these children have their own TV set.
> The burglars stole our silver—and my stereo **besides.**

better, had better   In the sense of an emphatic "ought to," *better* is an informal shortening of *had better.*

> INFORMAL   He better watch out!
> GENERAL   He **had** better watch out!   [OR He**'d** better watch out!]

between   See **among, between.**

boys   See **girls, boys.**

broke   Archaic for *broken.*

> STANDARD   Only my little finger was **broken**   [NOT broke].

bug   Slang if used as a verb. As a noun, *bug* is slang in the sense of "fan, enthusiast."

> SLANG   Loud noises bug her.   I am a tennis bug.
> STANDARD   Loud noises bother her.   I love tennis.

bunch   Informal if used to refer to people.

bust, busted, bursted   The principal parts of *burst* are *burst, burst, burst. Bursted* is archaic. *Bust* and *busted* are still considered slang. When *burst* does not fit the context, use a different verb, such as a form of *break* (NOT "busted the record" BUT "broke the record").

but what   Informal after *no* or *not* following such expressions as "no doubt" or "did not know."

> INFORMAL   There was no doubt but what they would win.
> GENERAL   There was no doubt **that** they would win.

can, may   Formal English still distinguishes between *can* referring to ability and *may* referring to permission.

> **Can** student nurses give injections?   [Are they able to?]
> **May** student nurses give injections?   [Are they permitted to?]

can't hardly, can't scarcely   Double negatives in implication. Use *can hardly, can scarcely.* See also **hardly, scarcely.**

case, line   Often used in wordy expressions.

> WORDY   In the case of Jones there were good intentions.
> CONCISE   Jones had good intentions.
> WORDY   Buy something in the line of fruit.
> CONCISE   Buy some fruit.

cause of . . . on account of, due to   Redundant. Omit the *on account of* or *due to;* or recast to avoid wordiness.

> WORDY   One cause of misunderstandings is on account of lack of communication.
> BETTER   One cause of misunderstandings is lack of communication.
> CONCISE   Lack of communication causes misunderstandings.

compare to, compare with   Formal English prefers *compare to* for the meaning "regard as similar" and *compare with* for the meaning "examine to discover similarities or differences."

> The speaker **compared** the earth **to** a lopsided baseball.
> Putting one under the other, the expert **compared** the forged signature **with** the authentic one.

complementary, complimentary   Do not confuse. *Complementary* means "completing" or "supplying needs." *Complimentary* means "expressing praise" or "given free."

> His talents and hers are **complementary.**
> Admiring the performance, he made several **complimentary** remarks.

conscious, conscience   Do not confuse. An adjective, *conscious* means "aware, able to feel and think." A noun, *conscience* means "the sense of right and wrong."

> After the accident, when I became **conscious** of my guilt, my **conscience** started bothering me.

could of   Nonstandard for *could have.* See **of.**

couple, couple of   Informal for *two* or for *several* in such phrases as "a couple aspirin," "a couple more gallons of paint," or "in just a couple of seconds."

data, criteria, phenomena   The plurals of *datum* (rarely used), *criterion*, and *phenomenon. Criterion* and *phenomenon* have alternate plurals: *criterions, phenomenons.* The plural *data* is often construed as a collective noun: "This *data has* been verified."

different from   In the United States the preferred preposition after *different* is *from.* But the less formal *different than* is accepted by many writers if the expression is followed by a clause.

> The Stoic philosophy is **different from** the Epicurean.
> The outcome was **different from** what I expected   OR   The outcome was **different than** I had expected.

differ from, differ with   *Differ from* means "to stand apart because of unlikeness." *Differ with* means "to disagree."

disinterested, uninterested   Often used interchangeably. Some authorities, however, do not accept *disinterested* ("impartial") as a substitute for *uninterested* ("indifferent").

done   Standard as an adjective and as the past participle of the verb *do.* Nonstandard as an adverb and as a substitute for *did.*

> NONSTANDARD   The bread is done sold.
> STANDARD   The bread is **already** sold. The bread is **done.**
> NONSTANDARD   Do the police know who done it?
> STANDARD   Do they know who **did** it? Who **has done** it?

don't   A contraction of *do not* rather than of *does not.*

> NONSTANDARD   He don't smoke. (He do not smoke.)
> STANDARD   He **doesn't** smoke. (He *does not* smoke.)
> STANDARD   They **don't** smoke. (They *do not* smoke.)

each and every   Redundant.

effect   See **affect, effect.**

elicit, illicit   A verb, *elicit* means "bring out or evoke," as in "to *elicit* information." An adjective, *illicit* means "illegal or improper," as in "an *illicit* sale."

elude, allude   To *elude* is to escape the notice of. To *allude* is to refer to casually or indirectly. The corresponding adjectives are *elusive* and *allusive.*

> Exact dates often **elude** me.
> Carol likes to **allude** to the ghost of Hamlet's father.

See also **allusion, illusion.**

emigrate from, immigrate to   The prefix *e-* (a variant of *ex-*) means "out of"; *im-* (a variant of *in-*) means "into." To *emigrate* is to go out of one's own country to settle in another. To *immigrate* is to come into a different country to settle there. The corresponding adjective or noun forms are *emigrant* and *immigrant*. (Compare: *export, import*.)

> Many workers **emigrated from** Mexico. The number of **emigrants** increased during the 1970s.
> Many Mexicans **immigrated to** the United States. These **immigrant** workers contributed to the growth of our economy.

eminent, imminent   *Eminent* means "distinguished." *Imminent* means "about to happen, threatening."

> Charlotte is an **eminent** scientist.
> Bankruptcy seemed **imminent.**

enthuse, enthused   *Enthuse* is informal as a verb meaning "to show enthusiasm." *Enthused* is informal as a synonym for *enthusiastic*.

> INFORMAL   We were all **enthused** about the new club.
> GENERAL   We were all **enthusiastic** about the new club.

etc.   Appropriate informally but used sparingly in formal writing. Many writers prefer to substitute *and so on* or *and so forth*. (Since *etc.* means "and other things," *and etc.* is redundant.)

> NEEDLESS   Ordinary games like Monopoly, backgammon, etc., did not interest these electronics hobbyists.
> REVISED   Ordinary games like Monopoly and backgammon did not interest these electronics hobbyists.

ever so often, every so often   Do not confuse. *Ever so often* means "very often, frequently." *Every so often* means "every now and then, occasionally."

everyone, every one   See **anyone, any one.**

except, accept   Do not confuse. To *except* is to exclude or make an exception of. To *accept* is to approve of or receive.

> These laws **except**   Present company
> juveniles.   **excepted!**
> These schools **accept**   I **accepted** their
> juveniles.   apologies.

explicit, implicit   *Explicit* means "expressed directly or precisely." *Implicit* means "implied or expressed indirectly."

> The advertisement was **explicit**: "All sales final."
> Reading between the lines, I understood the **implicit** message.

farther, further   Used interchangeably. Some writers, however, prefer *farther* in references to geographic distance (as in "six miles *farther*"). *Further* is used as a synonym for *additional* in more abstract references (such as "without *further* delay," "*further* proof").

fewer, less   Informally used interchangeably in the sense of "not many." Formally, *fewer* refers to numbers (how many), and *less* refers to amount, extent, or collective quantity (how much).

> fewer seeds   fewer hours   fewer than twenty students
> less seed   less time   less than $7,500 a year

fine   Informal for *very well*, as in "did fine on that test." Use sparingly as a vague word of approval.

fixing to   Regional or dialectal for "about to" or "getting ready to."

> REGIONAL   Congress is fixing to adjourn.
> GENERAL   Congress is about to adjourn.

folks   Informal for *parents, relatives*.

former   Refers to the first named of two. If three or more items are named, use *first* and *last* instead of *former* or *latter*.

> The Folger and the Huntington are two famous libraries; the

former is in Washington, D.C., and the latter is in San Marino, California.

fun   Informal if used adjectivally, as in "a fun person," "a fun car."

further   See **farther, further.**

get   Useful in numerous idioms but not appropriate formally in such expressions as "get with the times," "always gets in with his instructors," and "a stubborn attitude that gets me."

girls, boys   Informal if used to refer to grown people of any age.

good   Informal if used adverbially.

> INFORMAL   Watson plays good under pressure.
> GENERAL   Watson plays **well** under pressure.

great   Overworked informally for *skillful, good, clever, enthusiastic*, or *very well*, as in "really great at guessing the answers" or "with everything going great for us."

guy(s)   Informal for *any person(s)*.

had of, had have   Nonstandard for *had*.

> NONSTANDARD   I wish I had of [OR had have] said that.
> STANDARD   I wish I **had** said that.

had ought, hadn't ought   Nonstandard for *ought, ought not* or *oughtn't*.

hang   Useful in numerous idioms but slang in such expressions as "his hang-up about marriage" and "to hang out in discos."

hanged, hung   Informally interchangeable in the sense of "put to death by hanging." Formally, it is *hanged* (often used figuratively nowadays) that refers to such an act.

> Whenever my parents supplied enough rope, I usually **hanged** myself—but not always.

hardly, scarcely   Words with negative force, usually considered nonstandard if used with an unnecessary negative like *not, nothing*, or *without*.

> NOT   I couldn't hardly quit then.
> BUT   I **could hardly** quit then.
> NOT   Hardly nothing was in order.
> BUT   **Hardly anything** was in order.
> NOT   The motion passed without scarcely a protest.
> BUT   The motion passed **with scarcely** a protest.

hisself   Nonstandard for *himself*.

hooked on   Slang for *addicted to* or *obsessed with*.

hopefully   Still questionable for *it is hoped*.

how come   Informally used as a substitute for *why*.

> INFORMAL   I do not know how come they did that.
> GENERAL   I do not know **why** they did that.

illusion   See **allusion, illusion.**

immigrate   See **emigrate from, immigrate to.**

imply, infer   Used interchangeably as synonyms for *hint at, intimate, suggest*. Most writers, however, carefully distinguish between *infer* (meaning "draw a conclusion based on evidence") and *imply* ("suggest without actually stating").

> His attitude **implies** that money is no problem.
> I **infer** from his attitude that money is no problem.

incredible, incredulous   *Incredible* means "unbelievable, improbable." *Incredulous* means "skeptical, doubting."

> The witness's story was **incredible**.
> The judge gave the witness an **incredulous** look.

inferior than   Use *inferior to* or *worse than.*

ingenious, ingenuous   *Ingenious* means "clever, resourceful"; *ingenuous* means "open, frank," "artless."

This electric can opener is an **ingenious** device.
Don's **ingenuous** smile disarms the critics.

in regards to   Nonstandard for *in regard to* or *as regards.*

irregardless   Nonstandard for *regardless.*

is when, is where   Do not use *when* or *where* after *is* in giving definitions.

NOT	Begging the question is when [OR is where] a person argues by taking the conclusion for granted.
BUT	Begging the question is taking the conclusion for granted in an argument.
OR	A person begs the question by taking the conclusion for granted in an argument.

its, it's   *Its* is a possessive pronoun ("for *its* beauty"). *It's* is a contraction of *it is* (*It's* beautiful!") or of *it has* ("*It's* been a beautiful day!").

kick   Slang or very informal in such expressions as "to kick in my share," "on another kick," "just for kicks," "always kicking about grades," "gets kicked out of class," "just kicking around town."

kind, sort   Singular forms, which may be modified by *this* or *that.* The use of *these* or *those* is increasingly common but is still questionable.

QUESTIONABLE	These kind of arguments are deceptive.
PREFERRED	**These kinds** of arguments are deceptive.
OR	**This kind** of argument is deceptive.

kind of, sort of   Informal when used adverbially in the sense of "to a degree, somewhat, a bit" or "in a way" (as in "kind of silly," "sort of hesitated," or "kind of enjoying it").

kind of a, sort of a   Omit the *a* in your formal writing: NOT "this kind of a tour"   BUT   "this *kind of* tour."

later, latter   Comparative forms of *late* often confused in writing. In modern English, *later* (like *sooner*) refers to time; *latter* (like *former*) refers to one of two—to the second one (but not to the last of several).

We set a **later** date.   They arrived **later** than usual.
She wrote a song and a play. The **latter** won a prize.

See also **former.**

lay (laying, laid)   Nonstandard for *lie* (*lying, lay, lain*) meaning "to rest or recline." See also **7a(2).**

NONSTANDARD	I did lay down awhile. Had he laid down? The truck was laying on its side.
STANDARD	I did **lie** down awhile. Had he **lain** down? The truck was **lying** on its side.
NONSTANDARD	After lunch, I laid down awhile.
STANDARD	After lunch, I **lay** down awhile. [past of *lie*]

learn   Nonstandard for *teach, instruct, inform.*

NOT	That'll learn him!
BUT	That'll **teach** him!

leave   Nonstandard for *let* except when followed by an object and *alone,* as in "*Leave* [OR Let] them alone."

NONSTANDARD	He won't leave me go now.
STANDARD	He won't **let** me go now. [OR let me leave]
NONSTANDARD	Leave us not protest too much.
STANDARD	**Let** us not protest too much.

less   See **fewer, less.**

let's us   Redundant. Use *let's* or *let us.*

liable to   Informally used in place of *likely to* in reference to mere probability. Formally, *liable to* not only denotes likelihood or possibility but also suggests the idea of harm or danger.

INFORMAL	It's liable to be cooler soon. [mere likelihood]
GENERAL	The roof is **liable** to collapse. [likelihood + danger]

lie (lying, lay, lain)   Nonstandard for *lay* (*laying, laid*) in the sense of "put, place." See also **7a(2).**

NONSTANDARD	Onion slices are then lain on the fillets.
STANDARD	Onion slices are then **laid** on the fillets.
NONSTANDARD	Last night I lay my homework aside.
STANDARD	Last night I **laid** my homework aside.

like   Widely used as a conjunction (in place of *as, as if,* or *as though*) in conversation and in public speaking. Formal English, however, still rejects the use of *like* as a conjunction.

FORMAL	He drives **as** [NOT like] I did before my accident. OR He drives **the way** I did before my accident.
FORMAL	They acted **as though** [NOT like] they owned the town.

line   See **case, line.**

lose, loose   Do not confuse. *Lose* is a verb: *to lose, did lose, will lose. Loose* is chiefly an adjective: "a *loose* sentence," "to become *loose*," "at *loose* ends."

lousy   Slang, overworked informally, for *mean, bad, painful, inferior, nasty, messy.*

may be, maybe   Do not confuse the verb phrase *may be,* with the adverb *maybe.*

The story **may be** [OR might be] true.
Maybe [OR Perhaps] the story is true.

me and   Nonstandard as part of a compound subject. See also **5a.**

NONSTANDARD	Me and Drake took an early flight.
STANDARD	Drake and I took an early flight.

mighty   Informal for *very* or *extremely* (as in "mighty fine" or "mighty big").

morale, moral   Do not confuse. *Morale* (a noun) refers to mood or spirit. *Moral* (chiefly an adjective) refers to right conduct or ethical character.

the **morale** of our team, affecting **morale**, low **morale**
a **moral** person, **moral** judgments, an im**moral** act

most   Informal if used in place of *almost.*

INFORMAL	Most everyone needs to take a daily walk.
GENERAL	**Almost** everyone needs to take a daily walk.

myself   Standard as an intensive or a reflexive pronoun: "I *myself* saw a UFO" (intensive). "Momentarily I hated *myself*" (reflexive). Not acceptable formally and still questionable informally as a replacement for the subjective form *I* or the objective *me.*

My sister and **I** [NOT myself] prefer soccer.
He confided in Hayden as well as **me** [NOT myself].

neither   Nonstandard for *either* in double negatives such as "I don't like spinach neither." See **not . . . no/none/nothing.**

no-account, no-count, no-good   Informal for *worthless, good-for-nothing.*

nohow   Nonstandard for *not at all, in no way, anyway.*

no such a   Omit the *a:*   NOT "no such a place"   BUT "no such place."

not . . . no/none/nothing   A nonstandard construction when the two negatives have a negative meaning.

NONSTANDARD	He did not keep no records. [double negative]
STANDARD	He did not keep any records. [one negative: *not*]
	OR He kept no records. [one negative: *no*]
NONSTANDARD	We needed gas but couldn't buy none.
STANDARD	We needed gas but couldn't buy any.
	OR We needed gas but could buy none.
NONSTANDARD	I cannot do nothing about it.
STANDARD	I cannot do anything about it.
	OR I can do nothing about it.

nowheres   Nonstandard or regional for *nowhere*.

number   See **amount of, number of; a number, the number.**

of   Do not write *of* for an unstressed *have*.

COMPARE	I could have it done. [stressed]
	I could have done it. [unstressed]
NONSTANDARD	I might of [may of, could of, would of, must of, should of, ought to of] said that.
STANDARD	I might **have** [may *have*, could *have*, would *have*, must *have*, should *have*, ought to *have*] said that.

See also **had of.**

off of   In formal writing, omit the *of* after *off* in such phrases as "fell off of the ladder."

OK, O.K., okay   All three are accepted as standard forms expressing general approval. However, a more specific word usually replaces *OK* in a formal context.

per   Used especially in commercial writing. Many authors prefer to use *per* only in Latinisms ("per capita," "per se," or "per cent/ percent").

COMMERCIAL	over $1.50 per gallon	as per regulations
PREFERRED	over $1.50 **a** gallon	**according to** regulations

phenomena   See **data.**

plenty   Informal when used adverbially to mean *quite* or *sufficiently* (as in "plenty good enough") or adjectivally for *plenty of* ("in plenty time").

plus   Informal if used as a substitute for *and* between main clauses or if used as a conjunctive adverb (for *moreover, besides, in addition*) between main clauses or sentences. See also **12a** and **14a.**

INFORMAL	Barbara is taking five courses, plus she has to work three hours a day.
GENERAL	Barbara is taking five courses, **and** she has to work three hours a day.
INFORMAL	Barbara is taking five courses; plus, she has to work three hours a day. [OR . . . courses. Plus, she has to work. . . .]
GENERAL	Barbara is taking five courses; **moreover**, she has to work three hours a day. [OR . . . courses. *Moreover*, she has to work. . . .]

P.M., A.M.   See **A.M., P.M.**

practical, practicable   *Practical* means "useful, sensible" or "not theoretical." *Practicable* means "feasible, capable of being put into practice."

The sponsors are **practical** people. These plans are **practicable.**

principal, principle   Distinguish between *principal*, an adjective or noun meaning "chief" or "chief official," and the noun *principle*, meaning "fundamental truth."

A **principal** factor in his decision was his belief in the **principle** that men are born equal.

quote   Still considered chiefly informal for *quotation* (as in "a quote from Chaucer").

raise, rise   Do not confuse. *Raise (raised, raising)* means "to lift or cause to move upward, to bring up or increase." *Rise (rose, risen, rising)* means "to get up, to move or extend upward, ascend." *Raise* (a transitive verb) takes an object; *rise* (an intransitive verb) does not.

Retailers **raised** prices.   Retail prices **rose** sharply.

rap   Informal for *chat, discuss*, or *talk*. Slang in such expressions as "to beat a murder rap" or "took the rap for cheating."

rarely ever   In formal writing, either omit the *ever*, or use *hardly* instead of *rarely*.

NOT	He rarely ever mentioned money.
BUT	He **rarely** mentioned money.
	OR He **hardly ever** mentioned money.

real   Informal when used as an adverb meaning "very, extremely."

INFORMAL	The victorious team was **real** tired.
GENERAL	The victorious team was **extremely** tired.

reason . . . because   Informal redundancy. Use *that* instead of *because* or recast the sentence.

INFORMAL	The reason why he missed his class was because he overslept.
GENERAL	The **reason** why he missed his class was **that** he overslept.
	OR He missed his class **because** he overslept.

reckon   Informal for *guess, think*.

respectively, respectfully   Do not confuse. *Respectively* means "in the order given." *Respectfully* means "in a courteous manner."

I considered becoming a farmer, a landscape artist, and a florist, **respectively.**
I considered the rabbi's suggestion **respectfully.**

right   Archaic or dialectal for *very* (as in "a right nice apartment").

rise   See **raise, rise.**

said   Except in legal writing, questionable as an adjectival meaning "already specified or mentioned before." Substitute a demonstrative like *this* or *these* for *the said*.

LEGAL	The said machines were defective.
GENERAL	**These** machines were defective.

same   Used as a pronoun without *the* chiefly in commercial or legal writing. General usage prefers *it, this*, or *that*.

COMMERCIAL	I had a service policy but did not renew same.
GENERAL	I had a service policy but did not renew **it.**

says   Avoid the use of *says* for *said* after a past-tense verb: NOT "stood up and says" BUT "stood up and *said*." See also **27a.**

scarcely   See **hardly, scarcely.**

seldom ever   Omit the *ever* in your formal writing.

set, setting   Nonstandard for *sit* or *sat, sitting*. It is the verb *sit* (NOT *set*) that means "be seated or be situated." See also **7a(2).**

NONSTANDARD	I didn't even set down. He yawned and set up.

Some cabins were setting in two feet of water.

STANDARD   I didn't even **sit** down. He yawned and **sat** up. Some cabins were **sitting** in two feet of water.

show up   Informal for *arrive* or *come* and for *outdo* (as in "might show up at the party" and "trying to show me up").

sit   Occasionally misused for *set* (*put, place*): NOT "to sit something" BUT "to *set* something." See also **7a(2)**.

so   Often overworked as an intensive (as in "so very pleased") and as a connective between main clauses (see **24b**).

some   Informal for *remarkable, extraordinary* and for *somewhat, a little* (as in "was some dog," "is some better," and "was talking some").

someone, some one   See **anyone, any one**.

somewheres   Nonstandard for *somewhere*.

sort   See **kind, sort**.

sort of a   Omit the *a* in your formal writing.

stationary, stationery   *Stationary* means "in a fixed position"; *stationery* means "writing paper and envelopes."

superior than   Nonstandard. Use *superior to* or *better than*.

suppose to   Be sure to add the -*d*.

Who is **supposed to** be in charge?
You were **supposed to** read this chapter.

sure   Informal for *surely* or *certainly*.

INFORMAL   The sunrise **sure** was beautiful.
GENERAL   The sunrise **certainly** was beautiful.

sure and   See **be sure and**.

their, there, they're   Do not confuse. *Their* is the possessive form of *they*; *there* is ordinarily an adverb or an expletive; *they're* is a contraction of *they are*.

There is no explanation for **their** refusal.
They're installing a traffic light **there**.

theirself, theirselves   Nonstandard for *themselves*.

them   Nonstandard when used adjectivally: NOT them apples BUT *those* [OR *these*] apples.

then   Sometimes incorrectly used for *than*. See also pages 192–93. Unlike *then, than* does not relate to time.

Last summer, we paid more **than** that.   [Compare "We paid more *then.*"]
Other **than** a social-security check, they had no income.

these kind, these sort, those kind, those sort   See **kind, sort**.

thing   Often used in wordy constructions.

WORDY   One thing that we need is a map.
CONCISE   We need a map.

this here, that there, these here, them there   Nonstandard expressions. Use *this, that, these, those*.

thusly   Grammatically redundant. Write *thus* (already an adverb without the -*ly*).

to, too, two   Distinguish the preposition *to* from the adverb *too* and the numeral *two*.

If it isn't **too** cold, I will take my **two** poodles **to** the park.

try and   Informal for *try to*.

type   Informal for *type of* (as in "that type program").

use to, used to   Be sure to add the -*d* to *use* unless the auxiliary is accompanied by *did* in questions or in negative constructions.

NOT   Our coins use to contain silver.
BUT   Our coins **used to** contain silver.
NOT   Did he used to smoke?   He didn't used to smoke.
BUT   Did he **use to** smoke?   He didn't **use to** smoke.

used to could   Nonstandard for *used to be able*.

very   Omit when superfluous (as in "very unique" or "very terrified"). If you tend to overuse *very* as an intensifier, try using more exact words; in place of "very strange," for example, try *outlandish, grotesque*, or *bizarre*.

wait on   Informal for *wait for*.

INFORMAL   The taxi was waiting on him.
GENERAL   The taxi was **waiting for** him.

want for   Omit the nonstandard *for* in such sentences as "I want for you to quit."

want in, out, down, up, off, through   Informal or regional for *want to get in, out, down, up, off, through*.

want that   Nonstandard when a *that* clause is the object of *want*.

NONSTANDARD   I want that he should have a chance.
STANDARD   I **want** him to have a chance.

ways   Informal for *way* when referring to distance.

INFORMAL   It's a long ways to Chicago.
GENERAL   It's a long **way** to Chicago.

what   Nonstandard for *who* or *that*.

NOT   The man what did it got away.
BUT   The man **who** did it got away.

where   Informal for *that*.

INFORMAL   I saw in the newspaper where the strike had been settled.
GENERAL   I saw in the newspaper **that** the strike had been settled.

where . . . at, where . . . to   Omit the superfluous *at, to*.

NOT   Where is she at?   Where is she going to?
BUT   Where is she?   Where is she going?

which, who   Use *who* or *that* instead of *which* to refer to persons.

while   Do not overuse as a substitute for *and* or *but*. The conjunction *while* usually refers to time.

would of   Nonstandard for *would have*. See **of**.

Xmas   Standard for *Christmas* but used chiefly in commercial or informal writing.

you was   Nonstandard for *you were*.

your, you're   Do not confuse. *You're* is a contraction: "You're [*You are*] always right!" *Your* is the possessive form of *you*: "Your idea is a good one."

Exactness

20

Select words that are exact, idiomatic, and fresh.

Note: Sections **20** and **21** of this handbook deal with diction, the term used to refer to a writer's or speaker's choice of words.

Especially when writing, you should strive to choose words which express your ideas and feelings exactly. The choice of a right word will depend on your purpose, your point of view, and your reader.

If you can make effective use of the words you already know, you need not have a huge vocabulary. In fact, as shown by the following example, good writing often consists of short, familiar words.

> The ball was loose, rolling free near the line of scrimmage. I raced for the fumble, bent over, scooped up the ball on the dead run, and turned downfield. With a sudden burst of speed, I bolted past the line and past the linebackers. Only two defensive backs stood between me and the goal line. One came up fast, and I gave him a hip feint, stuck out my left arm in a classic straight-arm, caught him on the helmet, and shoved him to the ground. The final defender moved toward me, and I cut to the sidelines, swung sharply back to the middle for three steps, braked again, and reversed my direction once more. The defender tripped over his own feet in confusion. I trotted into the end zone, having covered seventy-eight yards on my touchdown run, happily flipped the football into the stands, turned and loped casually toward the sidelines. Then I woke up.
>
> —JERRY KRAMER, *Farewell to Football*

Of course, as you gain experience in writing, you will become increasingly aware of the need to add to your vocabulary. When you discover a valuable new word, make it your own by mastering its spelling, meaning, and exact use.

20a

Select the exact word needed to express your idea.

(1) Select the word that precisely denotes what you have in mind.

WRONG	A loud radio does not detract me when I am reading a good novel. [*Detract* means "to subtract a part of" or "to remove something desirable."]
RIGHT	A loud radio does not **distract** me when I am reading a good novel. [*Distract* means "to draw the attention away."]
INEXACT	Arnold was willing to pay the bill, and his billfold was empty. [*And* adds or continues.]
EXACT	Arnold was willing to pay the bill, **but** his billfold was empty. [*But* contrasts.]
WRONG	What they did was unjustful.
RIGHT	What they did was **unjust**.
WRONG	He never reverts to himself as an expert.
RIGHT	He never **refers** to himself as an expert.
OR	He never **reminds** anyone that he is an expert.

■ **Exercise 1** The italicized words in the following sentences are wrong or inexact. Correct the errors in diction and replace inexact words with exact ones.

1. Every gardener should have a *compote* bin.
2. Bo was interested in photography, *and* I bought her a new camera.
3. They did not do anything about this *disjustice*.
4. The lyrics are perfectly *adopted* to the music.
5. Strangers on campus are *awfully nice*.
6. Perhaps she just missed getting that job by some *misfortunate* chance.
7. I frequently consult the classified ads, *and* I can seldom find what I want.
8. She didn't say it but she *intimidated* it.
9. Hurricanes are *seasonable*.
10. Liquor *effects* the brain and nervous system.

■ **Exercise 2** With the aid of your dictionary, give the exact meaning of each italicized word in the quotations below. (Italics have been added.)

1. Ignorance of *history* is dangerous. —JEFFREY RECORD

   Those who cannot remember *the past* are condemned to repeat it. —GEORGE SANTAYANA

2. The capacity for rage, spite and aggression is part of our endowment as *human beings*. —KENNETH KENISTON

   Man, all down his history, has defended his uniqueness like a point of honor. —RUTH BENEDICT

3. Travel is no cure for melancholia; space-ships and time machines are no *escape* from the human condition.
   —ARTHUR KOESTLER

   Well, Columbus was probably regarded as an *escapist* when he set forth for the New World. —ARTHUR C. CLARKE

4. Once, a full high school education was the best achievement of a minority; today, it is the *barest minimum* for decent employment or self-respect. —ERIC SEVAREID

   Study and planning are an *absolute prerequisite* for any kind of intelligent action. —EDWARD BROOKE

5. We had a *permissive* father. He *permitted* us to work.
   —SAM LEVENSON

■ **Exercise 3** Prepare for a class discussion of diction. After the first quotation below are several series of words that the author might have used but did not select. Note the differences in meaning when an italicized word is substituted for the related word at the head of each series. Be prepared to supply your own alternatives for each of the words that follow the other four quotations.

1. Creeping gloom hits us all. The symptoms are usually the same: not wanting to get out of bed to start the day, failing to smile at ironies, failing to laugh at oneself.
   —CHRISTOPHER BUCKLEY
   a. gloom: *sadness, depression, dismals* (hit), *melancholy*
   b. hits: *strikes, assaults, infects, zaps*
   c. usually: *often, frequently, consistently, as a rule*
   d. failing: *too blue, unable, neglecting, too far gone*

2. Our plane rocked in a rain squall, bobbed about, then slipped into a patch of sun. —THEODORE H. WHITE
   a. rocked   b. bobbed   c. slipped   d. patch

3. A raw fall wind swirled leaves and dust in small tornadoes and sent pedestrians scurrying for indoor warmth.
   —ARTHUR HAILEY
   a. raw   b. swirled   c. small   d. scurrying

4. The most wonderful thing about the Moon is that it is there. —ISAAC ASIMOV
    a. wonderful   b. there

5. No emotion is so corrosive of the system and the soul as acute envy. —HARRY STEIN
    a. corrosive   b. system   c. soul   d. acute   e. envy

(2) Select the word with the connotation, as well as the denotation, appropriate to the idea you wish to express.

The denotation of a word is what the word actually signifies. According to the dictionary, the word *hair* denotes "one of the fine, threadlike structures that grow from the skin of most mammals." The connotation of a word is what the word suggests or implies. *Hair*, for instance, may connote beauty, fertility, nudity, strength, uncleanliness, temptation, rebellion, or primitivism.

The connotation of a word includes the emotions or associations that surround it. For instance, *taxi, tin lizzie, limousine, dune buggy, station wagon, dump truck, hot rod*—all denote much the same thing. But to various readers, and in various contexts, each word may have a special connotation. *Taxi* may suggest a city rush hour; *tin lizzie*, a historical museum; *limousine*, an airport; *dune buggy*, a seaside vacation; *station wagon*, children and dogs; *dump truck*, highway construction; *hot rod*, noise and racing. Similarly, *hatchback, bus, clunker, bookmobile, moving van, ambulance, squad car*—all denote a means of transportation, but each word carries a variety of connotations.

A word may be right in one situation, wrong in another. *Female parent*, for instance, is a proper expression in a biology laboratory, but it would be very inappropriate to say "John wept because of the death of his female human parent." *Female human parent* used in this sense is literally correct, but the connotation is wrong. The more appropriate word, *mother*, conveys not only the meaning denoted by *female human parent* but also the reason why John wept. The first expression simply implies a biological relationship; the second includes emotional suggestions.

■ **Exercise 4** Give one denotation and one connotation for each of the following words.

1. blue
2. mountain
3. astrology
4. Miami
5. conservative
6. law
7. dog
8. tennis shoes
9. technology
10. Saudi Arabia

(3) Select the specific and concrete word rather than the general and abstract.

A *general* word is all-inclusive, indefinite, sweeping in scope. A *specific* word is precise, definite, limited in scope.

GENERAL	SPECIFIC	MORE SPECIFIC / CONCRETE
food	dessert	apple pie
prose	fiction	short stories
people	Americans	the Smiths

An *abstract* word deals with concepts, with ideas, with what cannot be touched, heard, or seen. A *concrete* word has to do with particular objects, with the practical, with what can be touched, heard, or seen.

| ABSTRACT WORDS | democracy, loyal, evil, hate, charity |
| CONCRETE WORDS | mosquito, spotted, crunch, wedding |

All writers must sometimes use abstract words and must occasionally resort to generalizations, as in the following sentence:

I still believe that a liberal education, even if it will not solve the problems of individuals or the world, will help us to understand those problems. —CONRAD A. BALLIET

In a case like this, abstractions and generalizations are vital to the communication of ideas and theories. To be effective, however, the use of these words must be based upon clearly understood and well-thought-out ideas.

Experienced writers may have little difficulty handling general and abstract words. Many inexperienced writers, however, tend to use too many such words, leaving their writing drab and lifeless due to the lack of specific, concrete words. As you select words to fit your context, be as specific as you can. For example, instead of the word *bad*, consider using a more precise adjective (or adjectival) in phrases such as the following:

bad planks: rotten, warped, scorched, knotty, termite-eaten
bad children: rowdy, rude, ungrateful, selfish, perverse
bad meat: tough, tainted, overcooked, contaminated

To test whether or not a word is specific, ask one or more of these questions about what you want to say: Exactly who? Exactly what? Exactly when? Exactly where? Exactly how? As you study the examples below, notice what a difference specific, concrete words can make in the expression of an idea. Notice, too, how specific details can be used to expand or develop ideas.

VAGUE	I always think of a good museum as one that is very big.
SPECIFIC	I always think of a good museum as one I get lost in. —EDWARD PARKS
VAGUE	After a tolerably long practice as a mechanic, I firmly believe that a lot of auto parts that are sold are not needed.
SPECIFIC	After a tolerably long practice as a mechanic, I firmly believe that at least two-thirds of the batteries, starters, alternators, ignition coils, carburetors, and water pumps that are sold are not needed. —DON SHARP
VAGUE	I remember my pleasure at discovering new things about language.
SPECIFIC	I remember my real joy at discovering for the first time how language worked, at discovering, for example, that the central line of Joseph Conrad's *Heart of Darkness* was in parentheses. —JOAN DIDION

Notice in the second sentence below how specific details can be used to develop an idea.

Much of a Cuban's day is spent waiting. People wait for taxis, for buses, for newspapers, for ice cream, for cakes, for restaurants, for movies, for picture postcards. —STANLEY MEISLER

■ **Exercise 5** Replace the general words and phrases in italics with specific ones.

1. I always think of a pawn shop as *very small*.
2. *A lot of people* are threatened by *pollution*.
3. The *movie* was *great*.

4. Every Monday he has *the same thing* in his lunch box.
5. Our history professor suggested that we subscribe to *some magazines.*
6. Backpacking has *numerous advantages.*
7. The *dog walked* over to his *food.*
8. My father looked at my grade in science and said *what I least expected to hear.*
9. *Various aspects of the television show* were criticized *in the newspaper.*
10. *Cities* have their *problems.*

(4) Use appropriate figurative language to create an imaginative or emotional impression.

A figure of speech is a word or words used in an imaginative rather than in a literal sense. The two chief figures of speech are the *simile* and the *metaphor.* A *simile* is an explicit comparison between two things of a different kind or quality, usually introduced by *like* or *as.* A *metaphor* is an implied comparison of dissimilar things. In a metaphor, words of comparison, such as *like* or *as,* are not used.

SIMILES

The first thing people remember about failing at math is that it felt like sudden death.   —SHEILA TOBIAS

She shot me a glance that would have made a laser beam seem like a birthday candle.   —LARRY SERVAIS

The bowie knife is as American as a half-ton pickup truck.   —GEOFFREY NORMAN

The two men passed through the crowd as easily as the Israelites through the Red Sea.   —WILLIAM X. KIENZLE

You should learn to scan a menu (especially the big ostentatious ones) the way you examine a medical insurance policy.   —JAMES VILLAS   [*The way* is used in place of *as* or *like* (informal): see **19i**, page 731.]

METAPHORS

Dress is language.   —LANCE MORROW

Sucessful living is a journey toward simplicity and a triumph over confusion.   —MARTIN E. MARTY

Wolf pups make a frothy ribbon of sound like fat bubbling.   —EDWARD HOAGLAND   [a metaphor and a simile]

Single words are often used metaphorically:

These roses must be **planted** in good soil. [literal]

A man's feet must be **planted** in his country, but his eyes should survey the world.   —GEORGE SANTAYANA   [metaphorical]

Similes and metaphors are especially valuable when they are concrete and tend to point up essential relationships that cannot otherwise be communicated. (For faulty metaphors, see **23c**.) Sometimes writers extend a metaphor beyond a sentence:

Some women have managed to shape up and ship out into the mainstream of life, handling the currents and the rapids and the quiet pools with a gracious, confident ease. Others are trapped in one eddy after another, going nowhere at all, hung up in swirling pockets of confusion. Everyone gets sidetracked once in a while, and requires a rescue operation. That's the way life is. But some have been caught in an eddy or a piece of dead wood for so long that they have forgotten that life was meant to be lived in the mainstream.
   —GLADYS HUNT, *Ms. Means Myself*

Two other frequently used figures of speech are *hyperbole* and *personification. Hyperbole* is deliberate overstatement or fanciful exaggeration. *Personification* is the attribution to the nonhuman (objects, animals, ideas) of characteristics possessed only by the human.

HYPERBOLE

I, for one, don't expect till I die to be so good a man as I am at this minute, for just now I'm fifty thousand feet high—a tower with all the trumpets shouting.   —G. K. CHESTERTON

PERSONIFICATION

Time talks. It speaks more plainly than words. . . . It can shout the truth where words lie.   —EDWARD T. HALL

Due 5

■ **Exercise 6**   Complete each of the following sentences by using a simile, a metaphor, hyperbole, or personification. Use vivid and effective figures of speech.

EXAMPLES

The grass rolls out to the bleachers like *a freshly brushed billiard table*.   —JAY WRIGHT

As dam builders, Americans are a nation of *beavers*.
   —THOMAS Y. CANBY

1. Sightseers flocked around the TV crew like _____.
2. Viewed from outer space, the earth is _____.
3. The mosquitoes in those weeds _____.
4. The third hurricane of the season slashed through Louisiana swamps _____.
5. Death in a hovel or in a penthouse is _____.
6. Like _____, the class sat speechless.
7. The lecture was as _____.
8. Her eyes looked like _____.
9. Surging forward, the crowd _____.
10. Constant bickering is as _____.
11. She was as self-confident as _____.
12. The alarm sounded like _____.

20b

Select words that are idiomatic.

An idiomatic expression—such as *many a man, Sunday week,* or *hang fire*—means something beyond the simple combination of the definitions of its individual words. An idiom may be metaphorical: *He gets under my skin.* Such expressions cannot be meaningfully translated word for word into another language. Used every day, they are at the very heart of the English language.

Be careful to use idiomatic English, not unidiomatic approximations. *Many a man* is idiomatic; *many the man* is not. Ordinarily, native speakers use idiomatic English naturally and effectively, but once in a while they may have difficulty choosing idiomatic prepositions. When you are in doubt about what preposition to use after a given word, look up that word in the dictionary. For instance, *agree* may be followed by *about, on, to,* or *with.* The choice depends on the context. Below is a list of troublesome idioms for study.

FAULTY	IDIOMATIC
according with	according to
accuse with	accuse of
adverse against	adverse to
comply to	comply with

FAULTY	IDIOMATIC
conform in	conform to/with
desirous to	desirous of
die with	die of
in accordance to	in accordance with
independent from	independent of
inferior than	inferior to
jealous for	jealous of
prior than	prior to
superior than	superior to

■ **Exercise 7** Using your dictionary, classify the following expressions as idiomatic or unidiomatic. Revise any expressions that are unidiomatic. Classify idiomatic expressions according to the usage labels in your dictionary, using *General* as the classification for unlabeled expressions.

EXAMPLES
similar with *Unidiomatic—similar to*
to let on *Idiomatic, Informal*

1. oblivious about
2. to go at
3. to dress down
4. capable to
5. in search for
6. to compare against
7. to break with
8. prior than
9. to drop in
10. plan on going

20c

Select fresh expressions instead of trite, worn-out ones.

Such trite expressions as *to the bitter end, get it all together,* and *clean as a hound's tooth* were once striking and effective. Excessive use, however, has drained them of their original force and made them clichés. Some euphemisms (pleasant-sounding substitutions for more explicit but possibly offensive words) are not only trite but wordy—for example, *laid to rest* for *buried* or *sanitary engineer* for *janitor.* Many political slogans and the catchy phraseology of advertisements soon become hackneyed. Faddish or trendy words—like *impacted on, viable, upbeat,* or *be into* (as in "I am into dieting")—are so overused (or misused) that they quickly become trite and lose their force.

Nearly every writer uses clichés from time to time because they are so much a part of the language, especially of spoken English, and do contribute to the clear expression of ideas in written English.

We feel free when we escape—even if it be but **from the frying pan into the fire.** —ERIC HOFFER

It is not unusual for a professional writer to give a new twist to an old saying or a well-known literary passage.

If a thing is worth doing, it is worth doing badly.
—G. K. CHESTERTON

Into each life a little sun must fall. —L. E. SISSMAN

Washington is Thunder City—full of the sound and fury signifying power. —TOM BETHELL [Compare Shakespeare's "full of sound and fury,/Signifying nothing." —*Macbeth*]

Many writers use familiar lines from literature or the Bible and quote proverbs.

Our lives are empty of belief. They are **lives of quiet desperation.** —ARTHUR M. SCHLESINGER, JR. [Compare Thoreau's *Walden:* "The mass of men lead lives of quiet desperation."]

Slowly but steadily, in the following years, a new vision began gradually to replace the dream of political power—a powerful movement, the rise of another ideal to guide the unguided, another **pillar of fire by night** after a clouded day. —W. E. B. DU BOIS [Compare Exodus 13:21: "And the Lord went before them . . . by night in a pillar of fire, to give them light."]

Good writers, however, do not rely heavily on the phraseology of others; they choose their own words to communicate their own ideas.

■ **Exercise 8** Below is a list of trite expressions—only a sampling of the many in current use. Select ten that you often use or hear, and rewrite them in carefully chosen words.

EXAMPLES
a bolt from the blue   *a shock*
beyond the shadow of a doubt   *undoubtedly*

1. a brilliant performance
2. a chip off the old block
3. a crying shame
4. a good Samaritan
5. abreast of the times
6. after all is said and done
7. as cold as ice
8. as happy as a lark
9. at a complete loss for words
10. at the crack of dawn
11. at one fell swoop
12. beating around/about the bush
13. bite the bullet
14. bored to tears/death
15. few and far between
16. follow in the footsteps of
17. hightailed/hotfooted it out of there
18. hoping against hope
19. in the last analysis
20. in this day and age
21. it goes without saying
22. like a bull in a china shop/hog on ice
23. like water off a duck's back
24. little bundle of joy
25. makes my blood boil
26. nipped in the bud
27. no thinking man
28. over and done with
29. selling like hot cakes
30. slept like a top/log
31. stick to your guns
32. straight from the shoulder/hip
33. the depths of despair
34. the powers that be
35. the spitting image of
36. the very picture of health
37. water under the bridge/over the dam
38. went in one ear and out the other
39. working like a Trojan
40. wouldn't touch it with a ten-foot pole

■ **Exercise 9** Choose five of the ten items below as the basis for five original sentences. Use language that is exact, idiomatic, and fresh.

EXAMPLES
the appearance of her hair
Her hair poked through a broken net like stunted antlers.
—J. F. POWERS
OR
Her dark hair was gathered up in a coil like a crown on her head. —D. H. LAWRENCE

1. the look on his face
2. her response to fear
3. the way she walks
4. the condition of the streets
5. spring in the air
6. the noises of the city
7. the appearance of the room
8. the scene of the accident
9. the final minutes of play
10. the approaching storm

■ **Exercise 10**   Read the three paragraphs below in preparation for a class discussion of the authors' choice of words—their use of exact, specific language to communicate their ideas.

¹ I'd expected Oregon to be filled with trees, bearded loggers with friendly smiles, joggers, and hip college types.   ² We found, instead, hundreds of miles of desolate ranchland, will-cracking blizzards, hundred-mile spaces between towns of a thousand people, and frozen slush spraying us from passing logging trucks.   —PETER JENKINS, *"A Walk Across America"*

¹ Eating artichokes is a somewhat slow and serious business. ² You must concentrate, focusing on each leaf as you break it off at its fleshy base, dip it in its sauce and draw it carefully to your mouth (being careful not to drip).   ³ Between your front teeth it goes, and you scrape off the deliciously blanketed flesh. ⁴ Languorously you work this combination of flavors and sensations to the back of your mouth, where all the subtleties of the artichoke unfold and mingle with the sharp, rich sauce; and now your taste buds get the full, exciting impact.   ⁵ Down it goes, and you pluck another leaf, sometimes methodically, working around the base of this thistle bud, sometimes with abandon. ⁶ Yet you can never really "bolt" an artichoke; there is always a measure of pause with each leaf, as it is torn, dipped and tasted.
—MARTHA ROSE SHULMAN, *"An Artichoke Memoir"*

¹ The biblical story does not present the departure from Egypt as an everyday occurrence, but rather as an event accompanied by violent upheavals of nature.   ² Grave and ominous signs preceded the Exodus: clouds of dust and smoke darkened the sky and colored the water they fell upon with a bloody hue.   ³ The dust tore wounds in the skin of man and beast; in the torrid glow vermin and reptiles bred and filled air and earth; wild beasts, plagued by sand and ashes, came from the ravines of the wasteland to the abodes of men.   ⁴ A terrible torrent of hailstones fell, and a wild fire ran upon the ground; a gust of wind brought swarms of locusts, which obscured the light; blasts of cinders blew in wave after wave, day and night, night and day, and the gloom grew to a prolonged night, and blackness extinguished every ray of light.   ⁵ Then came the tenth and most mysterious plague: the Angel of the Lord "passed over the houses of the children of Israel . . . when he smote the Egyptians, and delivered our houses" (Exodus 12:27).   ⁶ The slaves, spared by the angel of destruction, were implored amid groaning and weeping to leave the land the same night.   ⁷ In the ash-gray dawn the multitude moved, leaving behind scorched fields and ruins where a few hours before had been urban and rural habitations.
—IMMANUEL VELIKOVSKY, *Ages in Chaos*

Wordiness

21

To avoid wordiness, use direct, economical diction. Repeat a word or phrase only when it is needed for emphasis or clarity.

The use of more words than necessary to express meaning is an offense against exact diction: see Section **20**. As you proofread and revise your compositions, delete unneeded words but keep or add exact ones. In this way, you can say more in fewer words.

WORDY FIRST DRAFT
In the early part of the month of August there was a really mean hurricane with very high winds that was moving threateningly toward Port Arthur.

FIRST REVISION
In ~~the~~ early ~~part of the month of~~ August ~~there was~~ a really mean hurricane with very high winds ~~that~~ was moving threateningly toward Port Arthur.

SECOND REVISION

In early August a ~~really mean~~ *vicious* hurricane with *93-mile-an-hour* ~~very high~~ winds was ~~moving threateningly~~ *threatening* ~~toward~~ Port Arthur.

FINISHED COPY

In early August a vicious hurricane with 93-mile-an-hour winds was threatening Port Arthur.

21a

Make every word count; omit words or phrases that add nothing to the meaning.

(1) **Avoid tautology (the use of different words to say the same thing).**

WORDY   Commuters going back and forth to work or school formed carpools.
CONCISE   Commuters formed carpools.
WORDY   Each writer has a distinctive style, and he or she uses this in his or her own works.
CONCISE   Each writer has a distinctive style.

Notice below that the useless words in brackets serve only to echo meaning. Avoid such wordiness in your own writing.

yellow [in color]   circular [in shape]
at 9:45 P.M. [that night]   return [back]
[basic] essentials   rich [and wealthy] nations
bitter [-tasting] salad   small [-size] potatoes
but [though]   to apply [or utilize] rules
connect [up together]   [true] facts

Caution: Be sure to avoid double comparisons, the double subject (subject + nominative pronoun referring to the subject), and the double negative.

[more] easier than, the [most] farthest
my sister [she] is, the victims [they] are
could[n't] hardly, did[n't do] nothing [See also *not . . . no*, **19i**.]

(2) **Do not use many words when a few will express the idea well. Omit unnecessary words.**

WORDY   **In the event that** the grading system is changed, expect complaints **on the part of** the students.

CONCISE   **If** the grading system is changed, expect complaints **from** the students. [Two words take the place of eight.]

WORDY   **As far as sexism is concerned, it seems to me that** a woman can be as guilty of sexism as a man.

CONCISE   A woman can be as guilty of sexism as a man. [Unnecessary words are deleted.]

WORDY   **The reason why** we honor Lincoln **in these various ways** is because he saved the Union.

CONCISE   We honor Lincoln because he saved the Union.

One or two words can replace such expressions as these:

at this point in time	**now**
bring all this to a conclusion	**conclude**
during the same time that	**while**
has a tendency to break	**breaks easily**
has the ability to sing	**can sing**
in a great many instances	**often**
made contact by personal visits	**visited**
on account of the fact that	**because**
situated in the vicinity of	**near**
was of the opinion that	**believed**

Note: One exact word can say as much as many. (See also 20a.)

spoke in such a low and hard-to-hear voice	**mumbled**
persons who really know their particular field	**experts**

Notice below that the words in brackets are not necessary.

because [of the fact that]	was [more or less] hinting
[really and truly] fearless	by [virtue of] his authority
fans [who were] watching TV	the oil [that exists] in shale

■ **Exercise 1**   Revise the following sentences to elimate wordiness.

1. As a usual rule, government officials express concern about public interest, but though it takes a crisis to get them to act.
2. Good health is essential. This is one of the most important things.
3. During the last two innings, many senseless mistakes occurred without any apparent reason for them.
4. When combined together, these ingredients they make a nutritious one-dish meal.
5. The exact date has not been determined and is not known to us.
6. Long lines of starving refugees in need of food were helped by Red Cross volunteer people.
7. Judy delights in giving parties; she really likes to be a hostess.
8. Perhaps maybe the chief cause of or reason for obesity in people who are overweight is lack of exercise.
9. Only beginners, those who are inexperienced, can enter that contest.
10. The tall skyscraper buildings form a dark silhouette against the evening sky.

■ **Exercise 2**   Substitute one or two words for each item below.

1. prior to the time that
2. in this day and age
3. did put in an appearance
4. has the capability of working
5. passed away OR met his maker
6. in the not too distant future
7. similar in character to
8. involving a great deal of expense
9. in a more or less serious manner
10. somewhere in the neighborhood of $2500

■ **Exercise 3**   Strike out unnecessary words in the following sentences.

1. It seems to me to be obvious.
2. The reason why I stayed behind was because I had no money.
3. Last weekend, on Saturday afternoon to be exact, I bought a sailboat, which to all intents and purposes is a nice yellow-colored toy that is really a whole lot of fun to play with.
4. Other things being equal, it is my opinion that all of these oil slicks, whether they are massive or not so big, do damage to the environment to a greater or lesser degree.
5. As for the nature of biased newscasts, I can only say that I realize that reporters have to do some editing, though they may not use the finest type of judgment when they are underscoring, as it were, some of the stories and downplaying others.

21b

Eliminate needless words by combining sentences or by simplifying phrases and clauses.

Note differences in emphasis as you study the following examples.

WORDY   He has a special way of telling a story. He makes a big to-do over little details. They sound like they are very important.

CONCISE   When telling a story, he makes little details sound important.

WORDY   A few of the listeners who had become angry called in so that they would have the opportunity of refuting the arguments set forth by Ian.

CONCISE   A few angry listeners called in to refute Ian's arguments.

WORDY   It is within the realm of possibility that what is earned by individual persons, the part that is surplus, will be subject to special taxation as a windfall.

CONCISE   Perhaps an individual's surplus earnings will be subject to a windfall-profits tax.

■ **Exercise 4**   Following the pattern of the examples, condense the sentences below.

EXAMPLE
These were theories which were, in essence, concerned with politics.
These were political theories.

1. These are pitfalls that do, of course, pose a real danger.
2. This is an act which, in truth, partakes of the nature of aggression.

EXAMPLE
It was a house built with cheap materials.
It was a cheaply built house.

3. It was a garden planned with a great deal of care.
4. It was a speech delivered with a lot of passion.

EXAMPLE
The stories written by Carson McCullers are different from those composed by Flannery O'Connor.
Carson McCullers' stories are different from Flannery O'Connor's.

5. The dishes prepared by her husband are not as good as those fixed by her father.
6. The ideas shared by the students were different from those promoted by the advertiser.

   EXAMPLE
   It is unfortunate. A few come to college so that they can avoid work.
   Unfortunately, a few come to college to avoid work.

7. It is inevitable. Corporations produce goods so that they can make a profit.
8. It is predictable. Before an election legislators reduce taxation so that they can win the approval of voters.

   EXAMPLE
   The forces that were against gun control ran an advertisement that covered two pages.
   The anti-gun control forces ran a two-page advertisement.

9. A group that is in favor of labor wants vacations that last two months.
10. One editorial against "nukes" stressed the need for plants that are state controlled.

■ **Exercise 5** Restructure or combine sentences to reduce the number of words.

1. These hazards are not visible, and they cause accidents, many of which are fatal ones.
2. The United States was being invaded. What I mean by that is a takeover of land. Foreign investors were buying up farms.
3. In spite of the fact that my parents did not approve of it, I was married to Evelyn last June.
4. The fire chief made the recommendation saying that wooden shingles should not be used on homes now being built or in the future.
5. The lawyer that was defending Smith was considered incompetent by many of those who were serving on the jury.

21c

Avoid careless or needless repetition of a word or phrase.

Sometimes a repeated word or phrase, by calling attention to itself rather than to its meaning, can be distracting.

> FAULTY   This interesting instructor knows how to make an uninteresting subject interesting.

Such repetition is not always easy to avoid or eliminate. But as a rule, you can quickly revise awkward repetition of words by making judicious substitutions or omissions.

> REVISED   This instructor knows how to make a dull subject interesting.

At times, however, synonyms can be clumsy, needlessly repeating an idea. It may be necessary to rewrite sentences to avoid repetition that weakens your writing.

Note: For the effective use of repetition in parallel structures, for emphasis, and as a transitional device, see **26b, 29e,** and **31c(3).**

Avoid careless or needless repetition of a word.

> CARELESS   We had problems solving those problems.
> REVISED   We had a hard time solving those problems.
> NEEDLESS   I think that he knows that that girl is not the one for him to marry.

> REVISED   I think he knows he should not marry that girl.
> NEEDLESS   His uncle is not like her uncle. Her uncle takes more chances than his uncle does.
> REVISED   Their uncles are different. Hers takes more chances than his.

Avoid carelessly repeating a root or a word base.

> CARELESS   I got the impression that his expression of sympathy was insincere.
> REVISED   I felt that his expression of sympathy was insincere.

Do not unintentionally use the same word or root in different senses.

> CARELESS   Even at the graveside services, the brothers kept quarreling. It was a grave situation.
> BETTER   . . . It was a **serious** situation.

Eliminate careless jingles (like "compared the fares there") and other distracting repetition of sounds: see **19h.**

Use a pronoun instead of needlessly repeating a noun or substituting a clumsy synonym. As long as the reference is clear, several pronouns in succession may refer to the same noun antecedent.

> NEEDLESS   The hall outside these offices was empty. The hall had dirty floors, and the walls of this corridor were full of gaudy portraits.
> REVISED   The hall outside these offices was empty. It had dirty floors, and its walls were full of gaudy portraits.

Judiciously use elliptical constructions to avoid needless repetition of words. The writers of the sentences below omitted the words in brackets, choosing not to repeat clearly understood phrases.

> Prosperity is the goal for some people, fame [is the goal] for others, and complete independence [is the goal] for still others. . . .   —RENÉ DUBOS

> Photography was developed as a means of recording appearances; cinema [was developed] as a vehicle for public entertainment.   —EDWARD T. CONE

Sometimes, as an aid to clarity, commas are used to mark omissions that avoid repetition.

> Family life in my parents' home was based upon a cosmic order: Papa was the sun; Mamma, the moon; and we kids, minor satellites.   —SAM LEVENSON

■ **Exercise 6** Revise or rewrite the following sentences to eliminate careless or needless repetition and any clumsy synonyms.

1. The President's recommendation to Congress sounded like an outlandish recommendation.
2. The condition of the floors after I had painted the ceiling floored my wife.
3. Abrupt interruptions like that disrupt my thoughts.
4. A comedy of intrigue (or a comedy of situation) is a comedy that relies on action instead of characterization for its comedy.
5. We had to wait late at Gate 13.
6. *Brunch* is a blend of the words *breakfast* and *lunch; fantabulous* is a blend of *fantastic* and *fabulous.*
7. A new addition was added at the side of the house. This addition was used for storage.

8. When debating, a debater should make the best use of time.
9. Leslie likes to go to the mountains to ski, Marcia enjoys going there to fish, and Joseph likes to go to the same type of high country to meditate.
10. Numerous products can be made from tobacco. The nicotine from this plant is used in pesticides. A sugar extracted from tobacco helps control blood pressure.

■ **Exercise 7**   Revise the following sentences to eliminate wordiness and careless or needless repetition.

1. The manager returned the application back because of illegible handwriting that could not be read.
2. In this day and time, it is difficult today to find in the field of science a chemist who shows as much promise for the future as Joseph Blake shows.
3. From time to time during one's life, one needs to remember that one who is learning to walk has to put one foot before the other one.
4. A distant hurricane or a seaquake can cause a tidal wave. This wave can form when either occurs.
5. The National Gallery of Art, which is in Washington, D.C., and which houses the Mellon, Kress, and Widener collections, is one of the largest marble structures in the entire world.
6. In my family, schoolwork came first, chores came second, fun and games came next, and discussions came last.
7. The auto industry, not to mention the steel industry, did not relish the thought of Americans importing tens of thousands of foreign cars.
8. The backlash that followed as a result of the Supreme Court ruling was stronger, or more pronounced, than I myself had expected that it would be.
9. When the fans in the stadium shout and yell, the shouting and yelling is deafening, and so the total effect of all this is that it is a contributing factor in decisions to stay home and watch the games on TV.
10. I am of the opinion that one reason why these two newspapers have such power is because so many people are happy to let the reporters and editors tell them what to think and let them form their opinions for them.

Omission of Necessary Words

22

Do not omit a word or phrase necessary to the meaning of the sentence.

In many instances a word or a phrase is optional; a writer may use it or omit it without changing the meaning of the sentence. In the following example, optional words are in brackets:

It seems [that] the security force on [the] campus overreacted.

In other instances a word like *that* or *the* is necessary or desirable for clarity:

I know **that** the security force on **the** other campus overreacted.

If you omit necessary words in your compositions, your mind may be racing ahead of your pen, or your writing may reflect omissions in your spoken English.

The analyst talked about the tax dollar goes.   [The writer thought "talked about where" but did not write *where*.]
You better be there on time!   [When speaking, the writer omits *had* before *better*.]

To avoid omitting necessary words, proofread your compositions carefully and study **22a–c**.

22a

Do not omit a necessary article, pronoun, conjunction, or preposition. See also **26b**.

(1) Omitted article or pronoun

INCOMPLETE	Feelings of inferiority are at bottom of person's jealousy.
COMPLETE	Feelings of inferiority are at **the** bottom of **a** person's jealousy.
INCOMPLETE	Beth knows a woman had a lawyer like that.
COMPLETE	Beth knows a woman **who** had a lawyer like that.

To avoid ambiguity, it is often necessary to repeat a pronoun or an article before the second part of a compound.

AMBIGUOUS	A friend and helper stood nearby. [One person or two?]
CLEAR	A friend and **a** helper stood nearby. [two persons clearly indicated by repetition of *a*]
ALSO CLEAR	My mother and father were there. [clearly two persons—repetition of *my* before *father* not necessary]

(2) Omitted conjunction or preposition

CONFUSING	Fran noticed the passenger who was sleeping soundly had dropped his wallet in the aisle. [The reader may be momentarily confused by "noticed the passenger."]
BETTER	Fran noticed **that** the passenger who was sleeping soundly had dropped his wallet in the aisle.
INFORMAL	I had never seen that type movie before.
GENERAL	I had never seen that type **of** movie before.
INCOMPLETE	Such comments neither contribute nor detract from his reputation.
COMPLETE	Such comments neither contribute **to** nor detract from his reputation. [When two verbs requiring different prepositions are used together, do not omit the first preposition. See also **20b**.]

In sentences such as the following, if you omit the conjunction, use a comma in its place.

The English used the paints chiefly on churches at first , then later on public buildings and the homes of the wealthy. —E. M. FISHER   [Compare "on churches at first *and* then later on public buildings."]

The fact is , very few people in this society make a habit of thinking in ethical terms.   —HARRY STEIN   [Compare "The fact is *that* very few people. . . ."]

■ **Exercise 1**   Insert needed words below.

1. A revolution was brewing the Panama Canal Zone.
2. Gary reminded Sheila Richard might not approve.
3. What kind course to take is the big question.
4. Winter and spring breaks the campus is dead.
5. The trouble was my good pair shoes got stolen.
6. Boynton will not ask nor listen to any advice.
7. Fires had burned for weeks were still not out.
8. She lent me a dollar then decided to take it back.

9. The book which the professor referred was not in our library.
10. The recipe calls for a variety spices.
11. She saw the boy finally obeyed her.
12. It is always the exception proves the rule.

■ **Exercise 2** Fill in the blanks below with appropriate articles, pronouns, conjunctions, or prepositions.

1. _____ good are not always rewarded; _____ evil often prosper. Life is not _____ morality play. —MICHAEL NOVAK
2. The battle left him untouched: it was the peace _____ undid him. —VIRGINIA WOOLF
3. Quarrelling means trying to show _____ the other man is in the wrong. —C. S. LEWIS
4. To me, there are two kinds of liberals: the type _____ fellow _____ would take off his coat in a snowstorm and put it around my shoulders, and the type _____ fellow _____ would caution me to wear a coat against the snow. —JAMES ALAN McPHERSON

22b

Avoid awkward omission of verbs and auxiliaries.

AWKWARD	Preston has never and cannot be wholly honest with himself.
BETTER	Preston has never **been** and cannot be wholly honest with himself.
INCOMPLETE	Since I been in college, some of my values have changed.
COMPLETE	Since I **have** been in college, some of my values have changed.

Usage is divided regarding the inclusion or the omission of verbs in such sentences as the following:

The Lions are overwhelming; the event is unavoidable. —E. B. WHITE [Plural *are* is used with *Lions,* and singular *is* with *event.*]

The sounds were angry, the manner violent. —A. E. VAN VOGT [Plural *were* is used with *sounds,* but singular *was* after *manner* is omitted.]

22c

Do not omit words needed to complete comparisons.

INCOMPLETE	Broken bottles around a swimming area are more dangerous than picnic tables.
COMPLETE	Broken bottles around a swimming area are more dangerous than **around** picnic tables.
INCOMPLETE	Snow here is as scarce as Miami.
COMPLETE	Snow here is as scarce as **it is in** Miami.
INCOMPLETE	The equipment of a soldier is heavier than a sailor.
COMPLETE	The equipment of a soldier is heavier than **that of** a sailor.
	OR A **soldier's** equipment is heavier than a **sailor's.**
CONFUSING	Sometimes a counselor helps an alcoholic less than the rest of the family.
CLEAR	Sometimes a counselor helps an alcoholic less than he or she **does** the rest of the family.
	OR Sometimes a counselor helps an alcoholic less than the rest of the family **does.**
INCOMPLETE	The amateur's performance was as good, possibly even better than, the professional's.
COMPLETE	The amateur's performance was as good **as,** possibly even better than, the professional's.

In a comparison such as the following, the word *other* may indicate a difference in meaning:

O'Brien runs faster than any player on the team. [O'Brien is apparently not on the team. In context, however, this may be an informal sentence meaning that O'Brien is the fastest of the players on the team.]

O'Brien runs faster than any **other** player on the team. [*Other* clearly indicates that O'Brien is on the team.]

■ **Exercise 3** Supply needed words in verb phrases and in comparisons.

1. They been trying to make small cars safe.
2. The consumers better listen to these warnings.
3. Ed's income is less than his wife.
4. Bruce admires Cathy more than Aline.
5. Fiberglass roofs are better.
6. The scenery here is as beautiful as any place.
7. I always have and always will like to read the comics.
8. One argument was as bad, maybe even worse than, the other.
9. The ordinance never has and never will be enforced.
10. The crusty old man irritates his roommate more than the cranky young nurse.

22d

When used as intensifiers in formal writing, *so, such,* **and** *too* **are generally (but not always) followed by a completing phrase or clause.**

The grand hotels were **so** grand **that they were known as palaces.** —HORACE SUTTON

Elizabeth has **such** beautiful hands **that nearly everyone she meets comments on them.**

Many a man is praised for his reserve and so-called shyness when he is simply **too** proud **to risk making a fool of himself.** —J. B. PRIESTLEY

■ **Exercise 4** Supply needed words in the following sentences.

1. I had my senior year a strange type virus.
2. As far as Boston, I could see the people were proud of their history.
3. The group is opposed and angered by these attempts to amend the Constitution.
4. I wish I been able to play football at university.
5. It's good to talk with a person has a similar problem.
6. His assistant and close friend considered only themselves.
7. The trouble is a good water-purifier costs so much.
8. He entered American Institute for Foreign Trade 1949.
9. Mr. Carter paid me more than Jim.
10. Nick announced the winner of the debate had not yet been voted on.
11. In our state the winter is as mild as Louisiana.
12. The mystery of the stolen jewels reminds me of mysteries like Sherlock Holmes.
13. Here is the hole which the rabbit escaped.
14. If Jack goes into a profession which he is not trained, he will fail.
15. The lawyer had to prove whatever the witness said was false.
16. I been concerned because the tuition is too high.
17. These trainees know they better study.
18. The large stadium was already filled with people and still coming.
19. Nobody interested their problems.
20. Elizabeth saw Nell was not in room.

EFFECTIVE SENTENCES

Unity
and
Logical Thinking

Unity, coherence, emphasis, variety—these are fundamental qualities of effective writing. Unity and coherence in sentences help to make ideas clear. Emphasis makes them forceful. Variety lends interest. But the final test of effective writing is the soundness of its reasoning.

23

Write unified sentences. Base your writing on sound logic.

A study of this section should help you write sentences that are neither cluttered with unrelated ideas or excessive detail, nor marred by mixed or awkward constructions. It should also help you avoid faulty definitions and illogical arguments, two very common mistakes in reasoning.

Unity

A sentence is unified when all its parts contribute to making one clear idea or impression. The parts of an ideal sentence form a perfect whole, so that a clause, a phrase, or even a word cannot be changed without disturbing the clarity of the thought or the focus of the impression.

23a

Bring into a sentence only related thoughts; use two or more sentences for thoughts not closely related.

Unrelated ideas should be developed in separate sentences. If the ideas in a sentence are related, they should be expressed in such a way that the relationship is immediately clear to the reader.

> UNRELATED   Yesterday Ted sprained his ankle, and he could not find his chemistry notes anywhere.
> RELATED   Accident-prone all day yesterday, Ted not only sprained his ankle but also lost his chemistry notes. [The relationship of the two ideas is made clear by the addition of the opening phrase.]

■ **Exercise 1**   All the sentences below contain ideas that are apparently unrelated. Adding words when necessary, rewrite each of the sentences to indicate clearly a relationship between ideas. If you cannot establish a close relationship, put the ideas in separate sentences.

1. Although the visiting professor has different and refreshing views, I played badminton on September 20.
2. I hate strong windstorms, and pecans pelted my bedroom roof all night.
3. The fence and barn need repairs, and why are property taxes so high?
4. There are many types of bores at social gatherings, but personally I prefer a quiet evening at home.
5. A telephone lineman who works during heavy storms can prove a hero, and cowards can be found in any walk of life.
6. Jones was advised to hire a tutor in French immediately, but the long hours of work at a service station kept his grades low.
7. Macbeth was not the only man to succumb to ambition, and Professor Stetson, for example, likes to draw parallels between modern men and literary characters.
8. Brad sent his sister a dozen red roses, and she sang on a fifteen-minute program over KTUV.
9. The food in the cafeteria has been the subject of many jokes, and most of the students do not look underfed.
10. Birds migrate to the warmer countries in the fall and in summer get food by eating worms and insects that are pests to the farmer.

23b

Do not allow excessive detail to obscure the central thought of the sentence.

If the detail of an overloaded sentence is important, it should be developed in separate sentences; otherwise it should be omitted.

> EXCESSIVE DETAIL   In 1788, when Andrew Jackson, then a young man of twenty-one years who had been living in the Carolinas, still a virgin country, came into Tennessee, a turbulent place of unknown opportunities, to enforce the law as the new prosecuting attorney, he had the qualifications that would make him equal to the task.
> ADEQUATE DETAIL   In 1788, when Andrew Jackson came into Tennessee as the new prosecuting attorney, he had the necessary qualifications for the task.

As you strive to eliminate excessive detail, remember that length alone does not make a sentence ineffective. Good writers can compose very long sentences, sometimes of paragraph length, without loss of unity. Parallel structure, balance, rhythm, effectively repeated connectives, and careful punctuation can bind a sentence into an emphatic unit, as in the following example:

> The rediscovery of fresh air, of home-grown food, of the delights of the apple orchard under a summer sun, of the swimming pool made by damming the creek that flows through the meadow, of fishing for sun perch or catfish from an ancient rowboat, or of an early morning walk down a country lane when the air is cool—all of these things can stir memories of a simpler time and a less troubled world.
> —CASKIE STINNETT, "The Wary Traveler"

Exercise 2 Recast the following sentences to eliminate excessive detail.

1. During the first period last Monday in room 206 of the English building, we freshmen enjoyed discussing the implications of language in various advertisements.
2. The fan that Joan bought for her brother, who frets about any temperature that exceeds seventy and insists that he can't stand the heat, arrived today.
3. When I was only four, living in a house built during the colonial period, little of which remains today, I often walked alone the two miles between my house and the lake.
4. Four cars of various designs and makes piled up on the freeway, which cost the state over $2 million.
5. In a firm voice and in a straight chair, the senator advocated drastic reforms, occasionally taking time out for a sip of water.
6. The dilapidated boat, seaworthy ten years ago but badly in need of repairs now, moved out into the bay.
7. Flames from the gas heater that was given to us three years ago by friends who were moving to Canada licked at the chintz curtains.
8. After finishing breakfast, which consisted of oatmeal, toast, and coffee, Sigrid called the tree surgeon, a cheerful man approximately fifty years old.
9. At last I returned the book that I had used for the report which I made Tuesday to the library.
10. A course in business methods helps undergraduates to get jobs and in addition helps them to find out whether they are fitted for business and thus to avoid postponing the crucial test, as so many do, until it is too late.

23c

Avoid mixed or awkward constructions.

(1) Do not mix metaphors by changing rapidly from one to another. See also 20a(4).

MIXED   Playing with fire can get a person into deep water.
BETTER   Playing with fire can result in burned fingers.
MIXED   Her plans to paint the town red were nipped in the bud.
BETTER   Her plans to paint the town red were thwarted. OR Her plans for a gala evening were nipped in the bud.

(2) Do not mix constructions. See also Section 1.

MIXED   When Howard plays the hypochondriac taxes his wife's patience. [adverb clause + predicate]
CLEAR   When Howard plays the hypochondriac, **he** taxes his wife's patience. [adverb clause, main clause]
CLEAR   Howard's playing the hypochondriac taxes his wife's patience. [subject + predicate]

(3) Avoid awkward or obscure sentences. Complete every construction clearly and sensibly.

OBSCURE   An example of discrimination is a cafe owner, especially after he has refused to serve foreigners. [It is the refusal, not the cafe owner, that is an example of discrimination.]
CLEAR   An example of discrimination is a cafe owner's refusal to serve foreigners.

In defining words, careful writers tell *what* a thing is, not when it is or where it is. See also **23d**.

AWKWARD   A sonnet is when a poem has fourteen lines.
BETTER   A sonnet is a poem of fourteen lines.

AWKWARD   Banishing a man is where he is driven out of his country.
BETTER   Banishing a man is driving him out of his country.

Often a sentence is flawed by a confusion of singular and plural words.

AWKWARD   Hundreds who attended the convention drove their own car.
BETTER   Hundreds who attended the convention drove their own cars.

Exercise 3 Revise the following sentences to eliminate mixed or awkward constructions.

1. For Don, money does grow on trees, and it also goes down the drain quickly.
2. Because his feet are not the same size explains the difficulty he has finding shoes that fit.
3. Friction is when one surface rubs against another.
4. Several of the applicants brought their resumé with them.
5. One example of a ripoff would be a butcher, because he could weigh his heavy thumb with the steak.
6. Like a bat guided by radar, Mark never skated on thin ice.
7. To be discreet is where a person carefully avoids saying or doing something tactless.
8. Does anyone here know why George resigned or where did he find a better job?
9. Tourists are not permitted to bring their camera indoors.
10. When children need glasses causes them to make mistakes in reading and writing.

Logical Thinking

Be sure that your sentences are well thought out and contain no slips or weaknesses of logic. The following principles of sound thinking may help you avoid the most common errors.

23d

Formulate definitions with care. See also 31b(6).

Errors and misunderstanding result when meanings of words and concepts are not clear. The two main types of definition are *formal* and *informal*. Either type can extend to the length of a paragraph, an essay, or even a book.

Formal definition. In formal writing you may sometimes need to use a technical or unfamiliar term to express your thought precisely. If the exact meaning of such a term is essential to your reader's understanding or interpretation, it may be necessary for you to define it formally. In a formal definition the essential nature of the term to be defined is expressed first by saying what the term *is* and then, implicitly or explicitly, what it is *not*. That is, first the class or category to which the word belongs is identified. Then the term being defined is distinguished from other members of that class or category. The first process is called *classification*, and the second is called *differentiation*.

TERM   An *invertebrate* is

CLASSIFICATION   an animal

DIFFERENTIATION   with no spinal column, ranging in size from minute protozoans to giant squids, and accounting for more than 90 percent of all living animal species.

TERM	A *sonnet* is
CLASSIFICATION	a lyric poem
DIFFERENTIATION	written in a single stanza, consisting of fourteen iambic pentameter lines linked by an intricate rhyme scheme.

As a rule, you can strengthen a definition by sharply restricting the classification. For example, "A sonnet is a lyric poem" is better than "A sonnet is a poem."

Informal definition. The demands of clarity and precision in writing are frequently satisfied by informal definition, in which synonyms or examples are commonly used.

SYNONYMS

Magendo, or black-market corruption, is flourishing.

—KEN ADELMAN [a lexical definition of a foreign term]

The bicycle, formerly a Christmas-tree item or a Sunday diversion, has become a serious vehicle of transportation in some American cities. —LANCE MORROW [a distinction between former connotative meanings and present denotation]

If you press your forefinger gently against your closed eyelid for a minute or less, you will probably start to see phosphenes: shapes and colors that march and swirl across your darkened field of view. —JEARL WALKER [word substitutions with restrictive details]

EXAMPLES

Many homophones (*be* and *bee, in* and *inn, see* and *sea*) are not common problems for spellers.

For the most part, the "external" arts, such as judo and karate, emphasize the acquisition of physical skills—speed, balance, accuracy, coordination, power. —DON ETHAN MILLER

Read

23e

Base your arguments on sound reasoning.

In compositions an argument is a group of statements that present evidence in support of a thesis. Each argument thus consists of a set of propositions, or premises, offered as justification for the thesis, or conclusion. A valid argument has two characteristics that must always be present: (a) all premises must be true; and (b) the form (or pattern) of the argument must itself be valid. If the premises are true and the form of the argument is valid, the conclusion must be true. Conclusions derived in this way are based on *deductive logic.*

IF	all dogs have four legs, and	[premise]
IF	Bruno is a dog	[premise]
THEN	Bruno must have four legs.	[conclusion]

If a premise is false or only partially true, the conclusion does not necessarily follow. If the form is invalid, then the argument is also faulty.

FALSE PREMISE	All dogs have four ears, and Bruno is a dog; therefore, Bruno has four ears.
INVALID FORM	All cats have four legs, and Bruno has four legs; therefore, Bruno is a cat.

Note: *Inductive logic* goes from specific observations or particular instances to a general conclusion that is probably—but not necessarily—valid. You should carefully state such

generalizations (avoiding qualifiers like *all, never, always*) and should support them with sufficient and relevant evidence. See Falacies of Induction, below.

in class

■ **Exercise 4** *Read* Be prepared for a class discussion of the premises and the conclusions in the following items.

1. First, many situations in real life have unhappy endings; therefore, if fiction is to illuminate life, it must present defeat as well as triumph. —LAURENCE PERRINE

2. Creationists say that evolutionary theory, because it seeks not to predict but only to explain what happened already, is not proper science but merely a belief system, which is to say, a religion. And the First Amendment says that no religion shall be fostered over another by the Federal Government; therefore, evolution should only be taught in schools with the caveat that it is theory. —JAKE PAGE

3. Standardized test scores are down, reading test scores are down, and students don't write as well as they used to. So, obviously, we have to go back to the basics.
   This may sound like compelling logic, but in a society that stands on the brink of a communications revolution, I would suggest that equating "the basics" with "the three R's" is a grievous and short-sighted error. —PETER H. WAGSCHAL

23f   *Read*

Avoid common fallacies or mistakes in reasoning.

FALLACIES OF DEDUCTION (OR INFERENCE)
See also 23e.

(1) **Non sequitur** ("It does not follow"): an argument in which the conclusion is not a necessary consequence of the premises.

FAULTY	Billy Joe is honest; therefore, he will get a good job.
BETTER	Billy Joe is honest; this characteristic should help him get a good job.

(2) **Self-contradiction:** an argument that contains mutually exclusive premises.

FAULTY	The government should control this unmanageable situation.
BETTER	We cannot expect government to control the uncontrollable, but it should try to do something about this situation.

(3) **Circular Reasoning, or Begging the Question:** a deductive argument in which the conclusion is contained in one of the premises.

FAULTY	I believe that this is an evil because society has always condemned it; society has always condemned it because it is evil.
BETTER	Society has always condemned this as an evil, and I believe society's judgment is correct.

FALLACIES OF INDUCTION

The following fallacies contain patterns of reasoning that misuse evidence or fail to support the general conclusion. See also the note opposite.

Read prepare by 4ts to do in class [handwritten]

(4) Confusion of Fact and Value Judgment. What can be observed, measured, and tested is a fact. Whether we like the fact or not, whether we believe it should be changed or not, these are value judgments—opinions or personal preferences. Both value judgments and facts are important, but they should not be confused.

FACT AND VALUE CONFUSED Your hair is too long. ["Too" indicates a personal preference, not a fact.]
FACT Your hair is long.
VALUE I don't like your hair long.

(5) Hasty Generalization: a generalization offered on the basis of too little evidence or evidence that is exceptional or biased in some way. *Enough* evidence must be gathered to warrant generalizing, and the evidence must not be exceptional or unusual.

INSUFFICIENT EVIDENCE None of the children in my family drink coffee; therefore, children don't like coffee. [More evidence is needed before this generalization is warranted.]
EXCEPTIONAL OR UNUSUAL EVIDENCE The increasing number of subway riders in Boston, New York, and Washington shows that urban dwellers in this country prefer mass transit to the automobile. [These three cities are unique in that their geographic area favors mass transit. Cities like Los Angeles or Oklahoma City whose geographic area is very large and whose population density is sparse might not favor mass transit.]

(6) Post hoc, ergo propter hoc ("After this, therefore because of this"): the mistake of assuming that because one event followed another, the first must be the cause of the second.

FAULTY Liz got wet and cold in the rain, so now she has a cold. [Many people become cold and wet in the rain and do not catch a cold.]
BETTER Liz came in contact with and was susceptible to cold germs, so now she has a cold.

(7) False Analogy: a weak, far-fetched comparison.

FAULTY The new mayor is not even the head of his own household, so I do not expect him to be a good civic leader or to have much influence on the city council.
BETTER Because he was indecisive during his campaign, I do not expect the new mayor to be a good civic leader or to have much influence on the city council.

FALLACIES OF IRRELEVANCE

(8) Ignoring the Question, or Rambling: presenting details or facts that are off the point and do not support the thesis.

FAULTY We should do more to help the poor help themselves. Of course, the Bible says we'll always have the poor with us, even though it does not say we should give them everything we have. [The writer loses sight of the main point: "We should help the poor help themselves.]

(9) Ad hominem ("To the person"): an attempt to disprove an argument by attacking the person who presents it. Do not evade the facts by attacking your opponent's economic, social, philosophical, or ethnic background.

FAULTY That merchant is allegedly a thief and a liar; his arguments against a sales tax are worthless. [The merchant might steal and lie and yet have excellent views on economic matters such as a sales tax. The evidence is not relevant to the assertion.]

(10) Ad populum ("To the people"): an appeal to popular emotions, prejudices, or beliefs.

FAULTY The majority of Americans today are a generous, compassionate, and freedom-loving people; to reflect the will of the people, immigration laws should not be changed but abolished.

(11) Bandwagon, or Join the Crowd: an argument saying, in effect, "Everyone's doing or saying or thinking this, so you should too."

FAULTY This novel has been No. 1 on the best-seller list for weeks. You must read it!

(12) Appeal to Authority, or Appeal to Prestige: an argument relying not on facts but on opinions, beliefs, or theories of experts or on testimonials of famous people.

FAULTY Both the *Washington Post* and the *New York Times* have predicted his reelection, so he will represent us again. [Predictions, even by experts, may or may not be accurate.]
FAULTY One of the greatest athletes eats this cereal, so it is probably more nutritious than the others.
BETTER A comparison of nutrition information printed on the boxes indicates that this cereal is probably more nutritious than the others.

FALLACIES OF IMPRECISION

(13) Ambiguity: a statement or argument in which the meaning is unclear; two or more different interpretations are therefore possible.

AMBIGUOUS "John is a poor mechanic." [This statement could be interpreted as "John is not a competent mechanic" or as "John's financial resources are limited."]

(14) Equivocation: a statement or argument in which an expression or word is used in two different senses.

FAULTY We Americans have the right to pursue happiness, and we should want to do what is right. So let's make happiness our goal in life. [The word *right* is used in two different senses.]

FALLACIES OF MISREPRESENTATION

(15) Oversimplification: a statement or argument that leaves out relevant considerations about an issue.

FAULTY People who pass tests are usually lucky.
BETTER People who pass tests are usually lucky, although they are prepared to answer most questions well.
FAULTY World War I was caused by the assassination of Archduke Francis Ferdinand in June, 1914.

BETTER   World War I had many causes, but the immediate precipitating event was the assassination of Archduke Francis Ferdinand in June, 1914.

(16) **False Division, or Either-Or:** any attempt to eliminate the middle ground by drawing a sharp distinction between parts of a complex whole when the facts show a gradation between the parts.

FAULTY   All living things are either plants or animals.
FAULTY   A nation is either at war or at peace.

■ **Exercise 5** Prepare for a class discussion of the faulty logic in the sentences below.

1. Everyone goes to Florida in the winter.
2. Breaking a mirror brings seven years of bad luck.
3. Do not elect my opponent to the Senate; his parents were not born in America.
4. Young people today do not obey their parents.
5. Jacqueline will be a good class president because all her classmates like her.
6. The other car was at fault, for the driver was a teenager.
7. All Germans like opera; I have never met a German who did not.
8. Gertrude has a migraine headache because she ate popcorn last night and got that phone call.
9. These razor blades give the smoothest shave; all the baseball players use them.
10. After that oil spill, the fish I caught tasted greasy. The report from the marine lab is wrong. Those fish are contaminated!
11. It is a fact that traveling by air is not safe. Within forty-eight hours eleven persons have been killed in air crashes.
12. If you do not lock your car, someone may steal it. Since someone stole your car, it must not have been locked up.
13. When an automobile accident occurs in the city, the police are never on hand.
14. It is a fact that our nation has become, or is becoming, a police state.
15. Either the train is late or my watch is wrong. Since the train is on time, my watch must be accurate.
16. Poor people cannot afford to go to the doctor, so we can say that poverty causes ill health. But sick people cannot work, so we can also say that ill health causes poverty. Since both ill health and poverty cause each other, if we wipe out one we'll wipe out the other.
17. That night we had our traditional bonfire to hex them, and so they lost the game the next day.
18. Susan is not qualified to talk about honesty in government because only last year she was accused of bribery and extortion.
19. A successful politician must be either a lion or a fox.
20. Frank was not advised of his rights prior to his arrest on charges of drunken driving. It is therefore not right to prosecute him.

Subordination

24

Use subordination to relate ideas concisely and effectively; use coordination only to give ideas equal emphasis.

One of the marks of a mature writing style is the ability to connect and relate ideas effectively, either by coordination or by subordination. *Coordination* means "being of equal structural rank." Coordination gives equal grammatical emphasis to two or more ideas. See also Section **26**.

COORDINATE ELEMENTS
tactless, **abrasive** language   [coordinate adjectives]
not only **sings** but also **dances**   [verbs]
chicken livers **slowly fried in butter** and **heavily seasoned with garlic**   [participial phrases]
a person **whose last name I do not know** and **whom I have never met.**   [coordinate adjective clauses]
If they do get to the Super Bowl, **they will lose the game**, or **they will win it because of lucky breaks.**   [main clauses]
These kindnesses did not go unnoticed. Nor were they unappreciated.   [simple sentences]

Notice in these examples that coordinating conjunctions and correlatives link words, phrases, clauses, and sentences of equal grammatical rank.

Subordination means "being of lower structural rank." It is the use of dependent elements—such as modifiers—that are of less importance grammatically than independent elements. Clauses functioning as nouns, adjectives, or adverbs are called subordinate because they are grammatically secondary to main clauses. Subordinate elements are parts of sentences, not sentences.

SUBORDINATE ELEMENTS
It was **tactless, abrasive** language.   [The modifiers are of less importance grammatically than the sentence base: *It was language.*]
Chicken livers **slowly fried in butter and heavily seasoned with garlic** are good with rice.   [The compound phrase functions as modifier.]
Gail is a person **whose last name I do not know and whom I have never met.**   [The adjective clauses (linked by the coordinating conjunction *and*) are secondary to the main clause: *Gail is a person.*]

In the following sentence, the main clause (*subject + compound predicate*) is in boldface. All other elements in the sentence are grammatically subordinate to the main clause.

Since I was sixteen years old at the time and had been graduated from high school, **I knew a great deal and had opinions** on a variety of subjects that I thought anyone else in the office would consider it a privilege to hear.   —EDWIN NEWMAN

As this example shows, grammatically subordinate structures may contain very important ideas.

Inexperienced writers tend to use too much coordination—too many short simple sentences or stringy compound ones. To express relationships between ideas, do not overwork coordinating connectives like *so* or *and* or conjunctive adverbs like *then* or *however*. Use relative pronouns (*who, which, that*) appropriately as subordinators. Also use subordinating conjunctions to indicate such relationships as cause (*because, since*), concession (*although, though*), time (*after, as, before, since, when, whenever, while, until*), place (*where, wherever*), condition (*if, unless*), and comparison (*as if*). Notice the differences in emphasis in the following sentences:

Clem had finished the pre-employment course, *and* he was ready for an on-the-job experience.
Clem, *who* had finished the pre-employment course, was ready for an on-the-job experience.

Because Clem had finished the pre-employment course, **he was ready for an on-the-job experience**.

If you cannot distinguish between phrases and clauses and between subordinate and main clauses, study **1d** and **1e**.

24a

Use subordination to combine a related series of short sentences into longer, more effective units.

When combining a series of related sentences, first choose one complete idea for your sentence base; then use subordinate structures (such as modifiers, parenthetical elements, and appositives) to relate the ideas in the other simple sentences to the base.

As you study the following examples of combined sentences, notice that the use of subordinate elements contributes to the concise expression of ideas. See also Section **21**.

CHOPPY   Douglas wrote a quick note. It was to Nora. She is his former employer.

BETTER   Douglas wrote a quick note to Nora, his former employer.

CHOPPY   Two days passed. Then helicopters headed for the mountaintop. The blizzard had stranded several climbers.

BETTER   After two days, helicopters headed for the mountaintop because the blizzard had stranded several climbers.

CHOPPY   The limbs were covered with ice. They sparkled in the sunlight. They were beautiful.

BETTER   Sparkling in the sunlight, the ice-covered limbs were beautiful.

Exercise 1   Combine the following short sentences into longer sentences by using effective subordination as well as coordination. (If you wish, keep one short sentence for emphasis: see **29h**.)

[1] I have just read "The Idea of a University" by John Henry Newman.   [2] I am especially interested in his views regarding knowledge.   [3] He says that knowledge is its own reward.   [4] It is not just a means to an end.   [5] Newman says knowledge is a treasure in itself.   [6] I had looked upon knowledge only in terms of practical results.   [7] One result would be financial security.   [8] But that was before I read this essay.   [9] Now I accept Newman's definition of knowledge.   [10] Such knowledge is worth pursuing for its own sake.

24b

Do not string main clauses together with *and, so,* or *but* when ideas should be subordinated. Use coordination only to give ideas equal emphasis. See also **30c**.

AWKWARD   I wanted to go to college, so I mowed and trimmed lawns all summer, and that way I could earn enough money to pay my tuition.

BETTER   Because I wanted to go to college, I mowed and trimmed lawns all summer to earn enough money for my tuition.

AWKWARD   Burns won, and it was a landslide vote, but he had rigged the election.

BETTER   Burns, who had rigged the election, won by a landslide vote.
OR
Having rigged the election, Burns won by a landslide vote.

COORDINATION   The offer was tempting, but I did not accept it. [equal grammatical stress on the offer and the refusal]

SUBORDINATION   Although the offer was tempting, I did not accept it. [stress on the refusal]
OR
Although I did not accept it, the offer was tempting. [stress on the offer]

Exercise 2   To improve sentence unity, revise the following sentences by using effective subordination and, when needed, coordination.

1. First she selected a lancet and sterilized it, and then she gave the patient a local anesthetic and lanced the infected flesh.
2. Yesterday I was taking a shower, so I did not hear the telephone ring, but I got the message in time to go to the party.
3. Two ambulances tore by, and an oncoming bus crowded a truckload of laborers off the road, but nobody got hurt.
4. Jean Henri Dunant was a citizen of Switzerland, and he felt sorry for Austrian soldiers wounded in the Napoleonic Wars; therefore, he started an organization, and it was later named the Red Cross.
5. The administrators stressed career education, and not only did they require back-to-basics courses, but they also kept students informed about job opportunities.

24c

Avoid excessive or overlapping subordination.

AWKWARD   I have never before known a man like Ernie, my friend who is always ready to help anybody who is in trouble that involves finances.

BETTER   I have never before known a man like my friend Ernie, who is always ready to help anybody in financial trouble.

AWKWARD   These were the voters who were concerned about unemployment that kept rising, who were worried about the dollar, which was diminishing in value.

BETTER   These were the voters concerned about rising unemployment and the diminishing value of the dollar.

Exercise 3   Prepare to contribute to a class discussion of the subordination and the coordination of ideas in the following paragraph.

[1] Going by canoe is often the best—and sometimes the only—way to go.   [2] Some difficult country can't be reached any other way, and once you arrive, the aches of paddling and sitting unsupported on a canoe seat seem a small price to pay for being there.   [3] One such place is the Boundary Waters area along the border of northeastern Minnesota and Ontario.   [4] The terrain is rolling and pocked by thousands of glacier lakes.   [5] Some are no more than bowls of rock that hold the accumulated clear green water; others are spring-fed and dark.   [6] The maze of lakes, islands, and portage trails is inhabited by all sorts of wildlife: beaver, otter, loons, and bear.   [7] It is a landscape suited to the

canoe and has in fact been canoe country since the time of the fur-trading voyageurs—hard Frenchmen whose freighters were up to twenty-five feet long and required eight paddlers.

—GEOFFREY NORMAN, "Rapid Transit"

■ **Exercise 4**   Combine choppy sentences and tighten loose ones. Use exact conjunctions (see pages 747–48) as you make a main clause subordinate or convert a sentence into a main clause.

1. I was walking across the campus. I found a twenty-dollar bill.
2. I was musing on the pleasures of loafing, and the idea struck me: complete idleness is hard work.
3. Growth stops. Insects eat the plant off. They do their eating just below the soil.
4. The little boy slept through it all, and so he was unconscious of our worries and fears.
5. I felt bad. I didn't tell anybody. I didn't want to go to the hospital again.
6. The yearbook had predicted it. Within a year the twins were married. They married twins.
7. The price of peace may be high. The price of war is higher.
8. An intention is not the deed. A blueprint is not a home.
9. The battle is worth fighting, and success is inevitable, or so the optimist believes.
10. Oliver is a bantam boxer, and he likes to throw his weight around, and so he keeps on picking fights.

■ **Exercise 5**   Relating your ideas precisely, use each connective below in a sentence. When necessary, consult the dictionary for exact meanings.

as	once	whether
besides	since	where
except for	so	whereas
like	thus	till/until

Coherence: Misplaced Parts, Dangling Modifiers

25

Avoid needless separation of related parts of the sentence. Avoid dangling modifiers.

Since the meaning of most English sentences depends largely on word order, the position of the parts of a sentence is especially important to clear communication.

MISPLACED   The doctor said that there was nothing seriously wrong **with a smile**.
BETTER   **With a smile** the doctor said that there was nothing seriously wrong.
            OR
            The doctor said **with a smile** that there was nothing seriously wrong.

DANGLING   **When discussing creativity**, a person's ability to finish a pun is stressed by John E. Gibson.

BETTER   **When discussing creativity, John E. Gibson** stresses a person's ability to finish a pun.

The parts of a sentence should be placed to convey the precise emphasis or meaning desired. Note how the meaning of the following sentences changes according to the position of the modifiers:

Rex **just** died with his boots on.
Rex died with **just** his boots on.
Just Rex died with his boots on.

The man **who drowned** had tried to help the child.
The man had tried to help the child **who drowned**.

Normally the modifier should be placed as near the word modified as idiomatic English will permit.

Misplaced Parts

25a

Avoid needless separation of related parts of the sentence.

(1) In standard written English, modifiers such as *almost, only, just, even, hardly, nearly,* and *merely* are regularly placed immediately before the words they modify.

In speech such modifiers are often put before the verb.

SPOKEN   The hut only costs $450.   [OR   costs *only* $450]
WRITTEN   The hut costs **only** $450.

SPOKEN   Stacey will not even write us a postcard.
          [OR   write us *even* a postcard]
WRITTEN   Stacey will not write us **even** a postcard.

■ **Exercise 1**   Revise the following sentences, placing the modifiers in correct relation to the words they modify.

1. The bomb of the terrorists only killed one student.
2. Bruce polished his silver dollars almost until they looked like new.
3. The transistor nearly cost fifty dollars.
4. He even works during his vacation.
5. Some contemporary poets hardly show any interest in making their poems intelligible.
6. On Thanksgiving Day the guests almost ate all the turkey.
7. I barely had enough to pay my tuition.

(2) The position of a modifying prepositional phrase should clearly indicate what the phrase modifies.

A prepositional phrase used as an adjective nearly always comes immediately after the word modified. (When used as an adjective before the noun modified, a prepositional phrase is hyphenated: "on-the-job training." See **18f**.)

MISPLACED   A garish poster attracts the visitor's eye **on the east wall**.
BETTER   A garish poster **on the east wall** attracts the visitor's eye.

Adverb phrases may be placed near the word modified or at

the beginning or end of a sentence. Sometimes, however, the usual placement can be awkward or unclear.

MISPLACED	One student said that such singing was not music but a throat ailment **in class**.
BETTER	**In class** one student **said** that such singing was not music but a throat ailment. OR One student **said in class** that such singing was not music but a throat ailment.

■ **Exercise 2**   Revise the following sentences to correct undesirable separation of related parts.

1. Newspapers carried the story of the quarterback's fumbling in every part of the country.
2. Lucille bakes date muffins just for her friends with pecans in them.
3. At the picnic Gertrude served sundaes to hungry guests in paper cups.
4. The professor made it clear why plagiarism is wrong on Monday.

(3) Adjective clauses should be placed near the words they modify.

MISPLACED	We bought gasoline in Arkansas at a small country store **which cost $10.25**.
BETTER	At a small country store in Arkansas, we bought gasoline **which cost $10.25**.

(4) Avoid "squinting" constructions—modifiers that may refer to either a preceding or a following word.

SQUINTING	Jogging **often** relaxes her.
BETTER	**Often**, jogging relaxes her.
	OR
	It relaxes her **to jog often**.

(5) Avoid the awkward separation of the sentence base and the awkward splitting of an infinitive.

AWKWARD	I **had** in spite of my not living in a neighborhood as fine as Jane's **pride**. [awkward separation of a verb from its object]
BETTER	In spite of my not living in a neighborhood as fine as Jane's, I **had pride**.
AWKWARD	Hawkins is the man **to**, whether you are a liberal, conservative, or moderate, **vote for**. [awkward splitting of an infinitive]
BETTER	Whether you are a liberal, conservative, or moderate, Hawkins is the man **to vote for**.

Note: Many times, though, splitting an infinitive is not only natural but also desirable.

> For her to **never** complain seems unreal.
> I wished to **properly** understand meditating.

■ **Exercise 3**   Revise the following sentences to eliminate squinting modifiers or needless separation of related sentence parts.

1. An official warned the hunter not to carry a rifle in a car that was loaded.
2. Selby said in the evening he would go.
3. Marvin wanted to, even during the 6:15 P.M. sports news, finish our game of checkers.

4. Harriet promised when she was on her way home to stop at the library.
5. The car was advertised in last night's paper which is only two years old and is in excellent condition.

Dangling Modifiers

25b
Avoid dangling modifiers.

Although any misplaced word, phrase, or clause can be said to dangle, the term *dangling* is applied primarily to verbal phrases that do not refer clearly and logically to another word or phrase in the sentence.

To correct a dangling modifier, rearrange the words in the sentence to make the modifier clearly refer to the right word, or add words to make the meaning clear and logical.

(1) Avoid dangling participial phrases.

DANGLING	**Discouraged by low grades**, dropping out made sense.
REVISED	**Because I was discouraged by low grades**, dropping out made sense. OR
	Discouraged by low grades, I thought dropping out made sense.

The second revision above follows this pattern:

> PARTICIPIAL PHRASE, SUBJECT—PREDICATE.

In the following sentence, the participial phrase is placed after the sentence base.

DANGLING	The evening passed very pleasantly, **playing backgammon and swapping jokes**.
REVISED	**They** passed the evening very pleasantly, **playing backgammon and swapping jokes**.

In the revision above, the participial phrase refers to the subject, as the following pattern illustrates:

> SUBJECT—PREDICATE, PARTICIPIAL PHRASE.

(2) Avoid dangling phrases containing gerunds or infinitives.

DANGLING	**Instead of watching** *The Late Show*, a novel was read.
REVISED	**Instead of watching** *The Late Show*, **Nancy** read a novel.
DANGLING	**Not able to swim that far**, a lifeguard came to my rescue.
REVISED	**I was not able to swim that far**, so a lifeguard came to my rescue.
	OR **Because I was not able to swim that far**, a lifeguard came to my rescue.

(3) Avoid dangling elliptical adverb clauses.

Elliptical clauses have words that are implied rather than stated.

DANGLING	**When confronted with these facts**, not one word was said.
REVISED	**When confronted with these facts**, **nobody** said a word.
	OR **When they were confronted with these facts**, not one word was said.
DANGLING	**Although only a small boy**, my father expected me to do a man's work.
REVISED	**Although I was only a small boy**, my father expected me to do a man's work.

Note: Verbal phrases such as the following (often called *sentence modifiers* because they qualify a whole clause or the rest of the sentence) are not classified as dangling modifiers but are considered standard usage.

> **To judge from reports**, all must be going well.
> His health is fairly good, **considering his age**.

■ **Exercise 4** Revise the following sentences to eliminate dangling modifiers. Put a checkmark after any sentence that needs no revision.

1. While wondering about this phenomenon, the sun sank from view.
2. By standing and repeating the pledge, the meeting came to an end.
3. Once made, you must execute the decision promptly.
4. Prepare to make an incision in the abdomen as soon as completely anesthetized.
5. After sitting there awhile, it began to snow, and we went indoors.
6. Darkness having come, we stopped for the night.
7. Having taken his seat, we began to question the witness.
8. Ready to pitch camp, the windstorm hit.
9. The convicts did not yield, thinking they could attract the support of the press.
10. Burned to the ground, the Welches had to build a new house.

■ **Exercise 5** Combine the two sentences in each item below into a single sentence. Use an appropriately placed verbal phrase or elliptical clause as an introductory parenthetical element.

EXAMPLES
We were in a hurry to leave Yellowstone. The dented fender was not noticed.
Being in a hurry to leave Yellowstone, we did not notice the dented fender.
A person may sometimes be confused. At such times he ought to ask questions.
When confused, a person ought to ask questions.

1. The statue has a broken arm and nose. I think it is an interesting antique.
2. James sometimes worried about the world situation. At such times joining the Peace Corps seemed to him a good idea.
3. I read the first three questions on the test. The test covered materials that I had not studied.
4. Larry was only twelve years old. His teachers noticed his inventive abilities.
5. I turned on the flashers and lifted the hood. A passing motorist, I thought, might see my predicament, slow down, and offer me a ride.

Parallelism

26

Use parallel structure as an aid to coherence.

Parallel (grammatically equal) sentence elements regularly appear in lists, series, and compound structures. Connectives like *and, or, but, yet* link and relate balanced sentence elements. (See also Section **24**.) Faulty parallelism disrupts the balance.

AWKWARD	What do the super-rich know about disease, those who are hungry, and poverty?
PARALLEL	What do the super-rich know about **disease, hunger,** and **poverty**? [nouns in series]
PARALLEL	What do the super-rich know about those who are **sick, hungry, and poor**? [adjectives in series]

If you cannot readily distinguish between parts of speech and between types of phrases and clauses, study Section **1**.

26a

For parallel structure, balance nouns with nouns, prepositional phrases with prepositional phrases, main clauses with main clauses, and so on.

As you study the parallel words, phrases, clauses, and sentences that follow, notice that repetition can be used to emphasize the balanced structure.

(1) Parallel words and phrases

People begin to feel ‖ **faceless**
and ‖ **insignificant**. ——S. L. HALLECK

The two most powerful words in the world today are
not ‖ **guns and money,**
but ‖ **wheat and oil**. ——FREDERIC BIRMINGHAM

She had ‖ **no time to be human,**
‖ **no time to be happy**. ——SEAN O'FAOLAIN

(2) Parallel clauses

‖ **What we say**
and ‖ **what we do**
somehow seem out of joint. ——NORMAN COUSINS

‖ **Top soil, once blown away, can never be returned;**
‖ **virgin prairie, once plowed, can never be reclaimed.**
——MARILYN COFFEY

(3) Parallel sentences

‖ **When I breathed in, I squeaked.**
‖ **When I breathed out, I rattled.** ——JOHN CARENEN

‖ **The danger of the past was that men became slaves.**
‖ **The danger of the future is that men may become robots.**
——ERICH FROMM

■ **Exercise 1** Underline the parallel structures. Then write sentences containing parallel (1) words, (2) phrases, (3) clauses, and (4) sentences.

1. In English, there are countless situations, moods, and relationships for which there is no single word.
   —THOMAS H. MIDDLETON
2. Imagine America without baseball, Europe without soccer, England without cricket, the Italians without bocci, China without Ping-Pong, and tennis for no one.
   —BARBARA W. TUCHMAN
3. To say that some truths are simple is not to say they are unimportant. —WILLIAM J. BENNETT
4. Reading through *The Origin* is like eating Cracker Jacks and finding an I O U note at the bottom of the box.
   —JOHN FLUDAS
5. The earth's nearest neighbor has mountains taller than Everest, valleys deeper than the Dead Sea rift, and highlands bigger than Australia. —NEWSWEEK
6. She completed her page, ornamented the foot of it with a rattling row of fancy lines and dots, threw over the release, spun the roller, twitching the foolscap sheets from under it in vicious haste, flung the carbons into the basket, shuffled the copies into order, slapped them vigorously on all four edges to bring them into symmetry, and bounced with them into the inner office. —DOROTHY SAYERS
7. There might be some people in the world who do not need flowers, who cannot be surprised by joy, but I haven't met them. —GLORIA EMERSON
8. Broadly speaking, human beings may be divided into three classes: those who are toiled to death, those who are worried to death, and those who are bored to death.
   —WINSTON CHURCHILL
9. Booms typically attract an oversupply of trained specialists; busts generate an undersupply. —CHRIS WELLES
10. Not for thirty years has political tension reached so dangerous a point as it has attained today. Not in all this time has there been so high a degree of misunderstanding, of suspicion, of bewilderment, and of sheer military fear.
    —GEORGE F. KENNAN

26b

To make the parallel clear, repeat a preposition, an article, the *to* of the infinitive, or the introductory word of a phrase or clause.

The reward rests not ‖ **in the task**
　　　　　　　but ‖ **in the pay.**　—JOHN K. GALBRAITH

Life is ‖ **a mystery**
　and ‖ **an adventure**
which he shares with all living things.
　　　　　　　—JOSEPH WOOD KRUTCH

It is easier ‖ **to love humanity as a whole**
　　than ‖ **to love one's neighbor.**　—ERIC HOFFER

It is the things we think we know—
　　　　‖ **because** they are so elementary
or ‖ **because** they surround us—
that often present the greatest difficulties when we are actually challenged to explain them. —STEPHEN JAY GOULD

■ **Exercise 2**　Insert words needed to bring out the parallel structure in the following sentences.

1. They would lie on the battlefield without medical attention for an hour or day.
2. Two things I intend to do: to try and succeed.

3. I told him politely that I could not go and I had reasons.
4. I finally realized that one can learn much more by studying than worrying.
5. On the safari Eva took photographs of a tiger and elephant.

26c

Correlatives (*both . . . and; either . . . or; neither . . . nor; not only . . . but also; whether . . . or*) usually connect parallel structures.

AWKWARD	We judge our friends both by what they say and actions.
PARALLEL	We judge our friends both ‖ **by their words** and ‖ **by their actions.**
PARALLEL	We judge our friends both ‖ **by what they say** and ‖ **by how they act.**
AWKWARD	Not only practicing at 6 a.m. during the week, but the team also scrimmages on Sunday afternoons.
PARALLEL	The team not only ‖ **practices at 6 a.m. during the week** but also ‖ **scrimmages on Sunday afternoons.**
OR	Not only does the team practice at 6 a.m. during the week, but it also scrimmages on Sunday afternoons. [The *also* may be omitted.]
AWKWARD	Either they obey the manager or get fired.
PARALLEL	Either ‖ **they obey the manager** or ‖ **they get fired.**
PARALLEL	They either ‖ **obey the manager** or ‖ **get fired.**
AWKWARD	Whether drunk or when he was sober, he liked to pick a fight.
PARALLEL	Whether ‖ **drunk** or ‖ **sober,** he liked to pick a fight.

26d

Be sure that a *who, whom,* or *which* clause precedes *and who, and whom,* or *and which.*

AWKWARD	Inez Santos is a woman with an open mind and who is seeking office. [A *who* clause does not precede the *and who*.]
PARALLEL	Inez Santos is a woman ‖ **who has an open mind** and ‖ **who is seeking office.**

■ **Exercise 3**　Revise the following sentences by using parallel structure to express parallel ideas. Put a checkmark after any sentence that needs no revision.

1. It is a rare disease and which is hard to diagnose.
2. Shirley likes to play tennis and watching basketball.
3. Our personalities are shaped by both heredity and what type of environment we have.
4. Someone has said that Americans cannot enjoy life without a TV set, an automobile, and a summer cottage.

5. My friend told me that the trip would be delayed but to be ready to start on Friday.
6. William is a man with the best intentions and who has the highest principles.
7. A seal watches carefully the way his fellows act and how they obey their trainer.
8. He was quiet and in a serious mood after the talk.
9. The secretary must attend all meetings, call the roll, and keep the minutes.
10. People fall naturally into two classes: the workers and those who like to depend on others.

■ **Exercise 4** First study the parallelism in the sentences below. Then use one of the sentences as a structural model for a sentence of your own.

1. All peoples, past and present, civilized and barbarian, share at least one thing in common: when the need arises, or the humor is upon them, they swear. —EDWARD C. ECHOLS

2. In the ghetto everybody gets a piece of the action: those who are Jews and those who are Christians; those who are white and those who are black; those who run the numbers and those who operate the churches; those—black and white—who own tenements and those—black and white—who own businesses.
   —BAYARD RUSTIN
   [Note that semicolons sharply divide the long, compound items in the series and contribute to clarity.]

3. If American English is to be saved, it will, in my view, have to be saved by individuals, or by small guerrilla groups that refuse to accept nonsense, send back unclear and pompous letters with a request for translation, and insist that organizations they are a part of speak plainly. —EDWIN NEWMAN

Shifts

27

Avoid needless shifts in grammatical structures, in tone or style, and in viewpoint.

Abrupt, unnecessary shifts—for example, from past to present, from singular to plural, from formal diction to slang, from one perspective to another—tend to obscure a writer's meaning and thus to cause needless difficulty in reading.

27a

Avoid needless shifts in tense, mood, and voice. See also Section 7.

SHIFT   During their talk Harvey **complained** about the idiocy of overkill while his father **discusses** the dangers of overlive. [shift from past to present tense]

BETTER   During their talk Harvey **complained** about the idiocy of overkill while his father **discussed** the dangers of overlive. [both verbs in the past tense]

SHIFT   If I **were** rich and if my father **was** still alive, my life would be different. [shift from subjunctive to indicative mood]

BETTER   If I **were** rich and if my father **were** still alive, my life would be different. [verbs in the subjunctive mood]

SHIFT   The old man finally **had to enter** a nursing home, but it **was** not **liked** by him. [The voice shifts from active to passive.]

BETTER   The old man finally **had to enter** a nursing home, but he **did** not **like** it. [Both verbs are active.]

When the literary present is used, as in summarizing plots of novels and plays, care should be taken to avoid slipping from the present tense into the past tense.

Romeo and Juliet fall in love at first sight, marry secretly, and die (NOT *died*) together in the tomb within the same hour.

27b

Avoid needless shifts in person and in number. See also **6b**.

SHIFT   A man has to expect criticism when you succeed. [shift in person]

BETTER   A **man** has to expect criticism when **he** succeeds.
         OR
         You have to expect criticism when **you** succeed.
         OR
         One has to expect criticism when **one** [OR he OR he or she] succeeds.
         OR
         Successful people have to expect criticism.

SHIFT   Every **student** in favor of the legalization of marijuana **was** asked to sign **their names** on a master ditto sheet. [shift in number]

BETTER   All **students** in favor of the legalization of marijuana **were** asked to sign **their names** on a master ditto sheet.

■ **Exercise 1** Correct all needless shifts in tense, mood, voice, person, and number in the following sentences.

1. After his easy victory, Kurt strutted over to me and asks a smart-aleck question.
2. Martínez recommended that property taxes be raised and spend wisely for the poor.
3. Marvin added meat to the frozen pizza, and then it was baked fifteen minutes by him.
4. Every bystander was suspect, so they were taken away for questioning.
5. I was told that billions of germs live on one's skin and that you should bathe often.

27c

Avoid needless shifts from indirect to direct discourse. See also **26a**.

SHIFT   The Gordons wonder **how the thief got the car keys** and **why didn't he or she steal the tapes**? [shift from indirect to direct discourse—a mixture of indirect and direct questions]

BETTER   The Gordons wonder **how the thief got the car keys** and **why he or she didn't steal the tapes**. [two indirect questions]
         OR
         The Gordons asked, "**How did the thief get the car

keys? Why didn't they steal the tapes?" [The shift in number from *thief* to *they* is typical of conversational English.]

SHIFT   The secretary said **that he was sick** and **would I please read the minutes.** [shift from indirect to direct discourse]

BETTER   The secretary said **that he was sick** and **asked me to read the minutes.** [indirect discourse]

27d

Avoid needless shifts in tone or style throughout the sentence (as well as throughout the larger elements of the composition).

INAPPROPRIATE   Journalists who contend that the inefficiency of our courts will lead to the total elimination of the jury system are **nuts.** [a shift from formal to colloquial diction; replace *nuts* with a word like *wrong, uninformed,* or *alarmists.*]

INAPPROPRIATE   After distributing the grass seed evenly over the lawn, rake the ground at least twice and then **gently bedew it with fine spray.** [The boldfaced expression is too "poetic" in a sentence with a prosaic purpose. Substitute something like *water it lightly.*]

27e

Avoid needless shifts in perspective or viewpoint throughout the sentence (as well as throughout the larger elements of the composition).

FAULTY PERSPECTIVE   The underwater scene was dark and mysterious; the willows lining the shore dipped gracefully into the water. [The perspective abruptly shifts from beneath the surface of the water to above it.]

BETTER   The underwater scene was dark and mysterious; **above,** the willows lining the shore dipped gracefully into the water.

■ **Exercise 2**   Correct all needless shifts in the following sentences. Put a checkmark after any sentence that needs no revision.

1. A woman stepped forward, grabs the mugger's belt, snatches the purses, and got lost in the crowd.
2. A vacation is enjoyed by all because it refreshes the mind and the body.
3. Aunt Leila spent her summers in Wisconsin but flew to Arizona for the winters.
4. Jim wondered whether Jack had left and did he say when he would return?
5. Every cook has their own recipes for making chili.
6. He told his aunt that there is someone in the room.
7. If she really likes someone, she would make any sacrifice for them.
8. Take your raincoat. They will be needed.
9. The outside of the building looks like a fortress; the comfortable furnishings seem out of place.
10. The darkness of the auditorium, the monotony of the ballet, and the strains of music drifting sleepily from the orchestra aroused in me a great desire to sack out.

■ **Exercise 3**   Revise the following paragraph to eliminate all needless shifts.

[1] He was a shrewd businessman, or so it had always seemed to me. [2] He has innocent-looking eyes, which are in a baby face, and swaggered when he walks. [3] When questioned about his recent windfall, he up and says, "I'm lucky enough to have the right contacts." [4] Not one name was mentioned by him; moreover, his reluctance to discuss his business transactions was evident. [5] Take these comments for what they are worth; they may help one in your dealings with this big shot.

Reference of Pronouns

28

Make a pronoun refer unmistakably to its antecedent. See also **6b.**

Each boldfaced pronoun below clearly refers to its italicized antecedent, a single word or a word group:

Languages are not invented; **they** grow with our need for expression.   —SUSANNE K. LANGER

There is no *country* in the world **whose** population is stationary.   —KENNETH BOULDING

Thus, *being busy* is more than merely a national passion; **it** is a national excuse.   —NORMAN COUSINS

A pronoun may clearly refer to a whole clause:

Some people think that *the fall of man had something to do with sex,* but **that**'s a mistake.   —C. S. LEWIS [Compare "*To think this* is a mistake."]

As you proofread your compositions, check to see that the meaning of each pronoun is immediately obvious. If there is any chance of confusion, repeat the antecedent, use a synonym for it, or recast your sentence.

Note: For the sake of clarity, you may find it necessary to establish a point of reference for acronyms and abbreviations (although they are not pronouns).

UNCLEAR   Some types of MIRVs face special restrictions. [What, a reader may ask, are MIRVs?]

CLEAR   These mainly are the multiwarheads known as **MIRVs,** the acronym for **multiple independently targetable re-entry vehicles.** . . . Some types of **MIRVs** face special restrictions.   —TIME

UNCLEAR   The second promising program is the E.G.S. of the state of Maharashtra. . . . The E.G.S. approach should be extended to all parts of the country. [What is the E.G.S.?]

CLEAR   The second promising program is the **Employment Guarantee Scheme** (**E.G.S.**) of the state of Maharashtra.

. . . The **E.G.S.** approach should be extended to all parts of the country.   —SCIENTIFIC AMERICAN

28a

Avoid an ambiguous reference.

A pronoun, of course, may clearly refer to two or more antecedents: *"Jack* and *Jill* met *their* Waterloo." Ambiguous reference, however, causes the reader to be unsure of the meaning of a pronoun because it could refer to one antecedent or to another.

AMBIGUOUS	Lisa wrote to Jennifer every day when she was in the hospital.
CLEAR	When Lisa was in the hospital, she wrote to Jennifer every day. OR
	When Jennifer was in the hospital, Lisa wrote to her every day.
AMBIGUOUS	After listening to Ray's proposal and to Sam's objections, I liked his ideas better.
CLEAR	I agreed with Sam after listening to his objections to Ray's proposal.

28b

Avoid a remote or an obscure reference.

Do not run the risk of your reader's momentarily losing track of the antecedent of a pronoun because you have placed the pronoun too far from its antecedent. Also avoid an obscure reference to an antecedent in the possessive case.

REMOTE	A freshman found herself the unanimously elected president of a group of enthusiastic reformers, mostly townspeople, **who** was not a joiner of organizations. [*Who* is too far removed from the antecedent *freshman*. See also **25a(3)**.]
BETTER	A **freshman who** was not a joiner of organizations found herself the unanimously elected president of a group of enthusiastic reformers, mostly townspeople.
OBSCURE	When Johnson's club was organized, **he** asked Goldsmith to become a member. [reference to antecedent in the possessive case]
BETTER	When **Johnson** organized his club, **he** asked Goldsmith to become a member.

Note: As a rule, writers avoid using a pronoun like *it, this,* or *he* to refer to the title of a composition or to a word in the title.

Title: Death with Dignity

AWKWARD FIRST SENTENCE	How can this ever be?
BETTER	How can death ever be dignified?

■ **Exercise 1**   Revise each sentence below to eliminate ambiguous, remote, or obscure pronoun reference.

1. The misunderstanding between the Kemps and the Dixons did not end until they invited them over for a swim in their new pool.
2. On the dashboard the various buttons and knobs seldom cause confusion on the part of the driver that are clearly labeled.
3. After Martin's advertising campaign was launched, he had more business than he could handle.
4. The lake covers many acres. Near the shore, water lilies grow in profusion, spreading out their green leaves and sending up white blossoms on slender stems. It is well stocked with fish.
5. Elaine waved to Mrs. Edwards as she was coming down the ramp.

28c

Use broad reference only with discretion.

Pronouns such as *it, this, that, which,* and *such* may refer to a specific word or phrase or to the general idea of a whole clause, sentence, or paragraph:

SPECIFIC REFERENCE   His nose was absolutely covered with warts of different sizes; it looked like a sponge, or some other kind of marine growth.   —DAN JACOBSON [*It* refers to *nose.*]

BROAD REFERENCE   This was One World now—and he owned a Volkswagen and a Japanese camera to prove it. —ARNOLD M. AUERBACH [*It* refers to *This was One World now.*]

When used carelessly, however, broad reference can interfere with clear communication. To ensure clarity, inexperienced writers may be advised to make each of their pronouns refer to a specific word.

(1) Avoid reference to the general idea of a preceding clause or sentence unless the meaning is clear.

VAGUE	Although the story referred to James, Henry misapplied it to himself, which is true in real life.
CLEAR	Although the story referred to James, Henry misapplied it to himself. Such mistakes occur in real life.

(2) As a rule, do not refer to a word or an idea not expressed but merely implied.

VAGUE	Eileen said that she would stay in Miami for at least a month. This explains her happiness. [*This* does not refer to a single stated word or idea in the preceding sentence.]
CLEAR	Eileen said that she would stay in Miami for at least a month. This remark suggests that she is happy there.
VAGUE	He wanted his teachers to think he was above average, as he could have been if he had used it to advantage. [*It* has no expressed antecedent.]
CLEAR	He wanted his teachers to think he was above average, as he could have been if he had used his ability to advantage.

(3) Avoid awkward use of the indefinite *you* or *it.*

AWKWARD	When one cannot swim, you fear deep, stormy waters. [See also **27b**.]
BETTER	The person who cannot swim fears deep, stormy waters.
AWKWARD	In the book **it** says that many mushrooms are edible.
BETTER	The book says that many mushrooms are edible.

Note: In some contexts, the use of the impersonal, or indefinite, *you* is both natural and acceptable. Notice in the example below that *you* is equivalent in meaning to "people in general" or "the reader."

The study of dreams has become a significant and respectable scientific exploration, one that can directly benefit **you.**
—PATRICIA GARFIELD

Some writers, however, prefer not to use *you* in a formal context.

28d

Avoid the awkward placement of *it* near another *it* with a different meaning.

AWKWARD	Although it was very hot on the beach, it was a beautiful place. [The first *it* is the indefinite or unspecified *it*. The second *it* refers to beach.]
BETTER	Although it was very hot on the beach, the place was beautiful.
AWKWARD	It would be unwise to buy the new model now, but it is a beautiful machine. [The first *it* is an expletive. The second *it* refers to *model.*]
BETTER	Buying the new model now would be unwise, but it is a beautiful machine.

■ **Exercise 2** Revise the following sentences as necessary to correct faults in reference. Put a checkmark after any sentence that needs no revision.

1. At the Chinese restaurant, the Meltons had a hard time eating with chopsticks, but that is their favorite food.
2. Apparently the dishwasher was out of order; it leaked all over the kitchen floor.
3. Copiers and other fine modern office machines enable business executives to accomplish more work because their assistants can manage them easily and quickly.
4. In the book it states that Mrs. Garrett can see through her fingertips.
5. Our language is rich in connectives that express fine distinctions of meaning.
6. I did not even buy a season ticket, which was very disloyal to my school.
7. Mary told Ann that she had to read *Shogun.*
8. When building roads the Romans tried to detour around valleys as much as possible for fear that flood waters might cover them and make them useless.
9. The extra fees surprised many freshmen that seemed unreasonably high.
10. In Frank's suitcase he packs only wash-and-wear clothes.

Emphasis

29

Select words and arrange the parts of the sentence to give emphasis to important ideas.

Since ideas vary in importance, expression of them should vary in emphasis. You may emphasize ideas through the use of exact diction (see Section **20**), through economy of language (see Section **21**), and through effective subordination and coordination (see Section **24**). You may also gain emphasis—

a by placing important words at the beginning or at the end of the sentence;

b by changing loose sentences into periodic sentences;

c by arranging ideas in the order of climax;

d by using the active voice instead of the passive voice;

e by repeating important words;

f by putting a word or phrase out of its usual order;

g by using balanced sentence construction;

h by abruptly changing sentence length.

29a

Gain emphasis by placing important words at the beginning or end of the sentence—especially at the end.

UNEMPHATIC	Total deafness is worse than total blindness, however, in many ways. [Parenthetical elements in an important position weaken the sentence.]
EMPHATIC	Total deafness, however, is in many ways worse than total blindness.
UNEMPHATIC	There was an underground blast that rocked the whole area. [Unemphatic words begin the sentence.]
EMPHATIC	An underground blast rocked the whole area.

The colon and the dash often precede an emphatic ending.

We have developed something new in politics: the professional amateur.   ——MEG GREENFIELD

Most commercial television stations talk about helping their communities, but it is in the main just that—talk.

——JEFF GREENFIELD

Since the semicolon, sometimes called a weak period, is a strong punctuation mark when used between main clauses, words placed before and after a semicolon have an important position. See also **14a.**

A penny saved used to be a penny earned; now, after five years, it is only half a penny.   ——ROBERT FRIEDMAN

Note: Introductory transitional expressions do not ordinarily weaken a sentence beginning.

Above all, the spirit of science is the spirit of progress.
——HERMANN J. MULLER

■ **Exercise 1** Revise the following sentences to make them more emphatic. Change the word order when desirable, and delete unnecessary words and phrases.

1. Music has the power to hypnotize, so they say.
2. In fact, only one person could have written all these articles because of their same political slant, I am convinced.
3. There is one stunt woman who earns five thousand dollars for two hours of work.
4. Lewisville finally decided to enforce the old ordinance; there were nearby towns that revived similar laws and began clean-up campaigns, also.
5. It had never before entered her mind to resent her husband's complacent ignorance or to ignore his unreasonable demands, however.

29b

Gain emphasis by changing loose sentences into periodic sentences.

In a *loose* sentence, the main idea (grammatically a main clause or sentence base) comes first; less important ideas or details (a subordinate clause, parenthetical phrase, an appended element) follow. In a *periodic* sentence, however, the main idea comes last, just before the period.

LOOSE | Hair has always been a statement for men, variously representing strength (Samson), fashionable virtue (King Charles I of England, whose wigs were long-locked and elaborate), bravado (General Custer), and genius (Einstein). —OWEN EDWARDS [The main idea comes first.]

PERIODIC | When you die, when you get a divorce, when you buy a house, when you have an auto accident, not to mention the hundreds of times during your lifetime when you are fleeced in your role as a consumer, a lawyer either must or should be involved. —DAVID HAPGOOD [The main idea comes last.]

Both types of sentences can be effective. The loose sentence is, and should be, the more commonly used. Although the periodic sentence is often the more emphatic, you should take care in your writing not to overuse it to the point of making your style unnatural. Variety is desirable: see Section **30**.

LOOSE | Such sticky labels do not accurately describe any generation—for example, labels like *lost, beat, now, silent, unlucky,* or *found.*

PERIODIC | Such sticky labels as *lost, beat, now, silent, unlucky,* or *found* do not accurately describe any generation.

LOOSE | In 1980 Alaska received more federal aid than any other state, if the report indicating the per capita distribution is correct.

PERIODIC | If the report indicating the per capita distribution is correct, in 1980 Alaska received more federal aid than any other state.

■ **Exercise 2** Convert the loose sentences to periodic sentences, and the periodic to loose. Notice how your revisions make for varying emphasis.

1. Italy remains cheerful, despite everything.
   —AUBERON WAUGH
2. Even where people want better relations, old habits and reflexes persist. —HEDRICK SMITH
3. The Milky Way Galaxy is entirely unremarkable, one of billions of other galaxies strewn through the vastness of space. —CARL SAGAN
4. And then she was sweet and apologetic, as always, as she had been all her life, nervously backing away from the arguments she should have had with my father, turning aside from the talks she should have had with me.
   —JOYCE CAROL OATES
5. As Mays told me, almost with pride, "If I don't know anything about something, or if I don't understand it, I just oppose it." —BERKELEY RICE

29c

Gain emphasis by arranging ideas in the order of climax.

Notice in the following examples that the ideas are arranged in the order of importance, with the strongest idea last:

Urban life is unhealthy, morally corrupt, and fundamentally inhuman. —RENÉ DUBOS [adjectives in the series arranged in climactic order]

They could hear the roar of artillery, the crash of falling timbers, the shrieks of the wounded. [sentence climax reached with *shrieks of the wounded*]

In the language of screen comedians four of the main grades of laugh are the titter, the yowl, the belly laugh and the boffo. The titter is just a titter. The yowl is a runaway titter. Anyone who has ever had the pleasure knows all about a belly laugh. The boffo is the laugh that kills. —JAMES AGEE [First, words are placed in climactic order, then sentences.]

In a sentence like the following, the order of climax depends on the writer's judgment:

Summing up for the defense of the small diesel, one can say that it offers excellent fuel consumption, it is long-lasting, it has no ignition system to cause trouble, and its level of pollution is low. —TONY HOGG

Note: Anticlimax—an unexpected shift from the dignified to the trivial or from the serious to the comic—is sometimes used for special effect.

But I still fear it will all end badly, this Protective Syndrome. I see a future in which the government has stripped us of all worldly goods worth having: clothes hangers, toothpaste, Alka-Seltzer, toasters, pencil sharpeners, and maybe even thumb tacks. —S. L. VARNADO

■ **Exercise 3** Arrange the ideas in the sentences below in what you consider to be the order of climax.

1. Franklin used the ant as a symbol of industry, wisdom, and efficiency.
2. Among the images in the poem are sun-drenched orchards, diamond-eyed children, and golden-flecked birds.
3. He left the city because his health was failing, his taxes were going up, and his pet dog was tired of the leash.
4. Something must be done at once. Unless we act now, the city will be bankrupt in five years. The commission is faced with a deficit.
5. The would-be governor attended a community festival, autographed books for teenagers, promised prosperity to all, and wrote letters to senior citizens.

29d

Gain emphasis by using the active voice instead of the passive voice.

UNEMPHATIC | Little attention is being paid to cheap, nutritious foods by the average shopper.

EMPHATIC | The average shopper is paying little attention to cheap, nutritious foods.

Exception: If the receiver of the action is more important than the doer, the passive voice is more effective.

There in the tin factory, in the first moment of the atomic age, a human being was crushed by books. —JOHN HERSEY

Freedom can be squashed by the tyrant or suffocated by the bureaucrat. —WILLIAM F. RICKENBACKER

■ **Exercise 4**   Make each sentence below more emphatic by substituting the active for the passive voice.

1. Pennies are often thrown into the fountain by tourists.
2. Every Saturday morning, television is being watched by easily influenced children.
3. The wastebasket was being filled with illegible photocopies by a student about to run out of coins.
4. When the play was brought to an end, the actors were greeted with a loud burst of applause by the audience.
5. It is greatly feared by the citizens that adequate punishment will not be meted out by the judge.

29e

Gain emphasis by repeating important words.

> It is impossible to be simultaneously blasted by a revolution in energy, a revolution in technology, a revolution in family life, a revolution in sexual roles, and a worldwide revolution in communications without also facing—sooner or later—a potentially explosive political revolution.   —ALVIN TOFFLER
>
> COMPARE
> It is impossible to be simultaneously blasted by a revolution in energy, in technology, in family life, in sexual roles, and in world communications without also facing—sooner or later—a potentially explosive political insurrection.

■ **Exercise 5**   First make each sentence below more emphatic by substituting repetition for the use of synonyms; then write two sentences of your own using repetition for emphasis.

1. Sometimes we lie to avoid hurting someone's feelings; occasionally we prevaricate to make another person like us.
2. He gripes all the time: he complains about the weather, fusses in heavy traffic, grumbles about high prices, and is critical of his meals.

29f

Gain emphasis by occasionally inverting the word order of a sentence. See also 30b.

> Only recently has this human deficiency been turned into law.   —GERALD GRAFF   [Compare "This human deficiency has only recently been turned into law."]
>
> Basic to all the Greek achievement was freedom.
> —EDITH HAMILTON   [Compare "Freedom was basic to all the Greek achievement."]

Caution: This method of gaining emphasis, if overused, will make the style distinctly artificial. And of course the order of the parts of the sentence should never be such as to cause ambiguity: see **25a**.

29g

Gain emphasis by using balanced sentence construction.

A sentence is balanced when grammatically equal structures—usually main clauses with parallel elements—are used to express contrasted (or similar) ideas: see Section **26**.

A balanced sentence emphasizes the contrast (or similarity) between parts of equal length and movement.

> To be French is to be like no one else; to be American is to be like everyone else.   —PETER USTINOV
>
> Love is positive; tolerance negative. Love involves passion; tolerance is humdrum and dull.   —E. M. FORSTER

■ **Exercise 6**   Write emphatic sentences using balanced construction to show the contrast between the following:

1. summer and winter
2. youth and age
3. town and city
4. hypocrisy and candor

29h

Gain emphasis by abruptly changing sentence length.

> In the last two decades there has occurred a series of changes in American life, the extent, durability, and significance of which no one has yet measured. No one can.   —IRVING HOWE   [The short sentence, which abruptly follows a much longer one, is emphatic.]

■ **Exercise 7**   Write a short, emphatic sentence to follow each long sentence below. Then write another pair of sentences—one long and one short—of your own.

1. According to some minor prophets of doom, the next century will be a push-button era, a computer-controlled and robot-dominated one with life dependent on the movement of a forefinger.
2. In sequined costumes the skaters glide into the huge arena, smile at the applauding spectators, strike a brief pose, and then race into a series of intricate leaps and spins, their feet perfectly balanced on thin wedges of shining steel.

■ **Exercise 8**   Prepare for a class discussion of emphasis in the following passages.

1. Opportunity for purposeful activity, opportunity for self-realization, opportunity for work and rest and love and play—this is what men think of as liberty today.
   —CLINTON ROSSITER
2. No one reads anymore—blame television. Families are breaking up—blame television. High culture is being despoiled—blame television. . . . What a splendid all-purpose explanation television has become.   —ARISTIDES
3. With the exception of the Civil War period, never before had the sense of hopefulness traditionally associated with the American experience been so damaged.   —JOHN LYTELL

■ **Exercise 9**   Revise the following sentences for greater emphasis.

1. I think that experimenting on fetuses should stop, whether they are dead or alive.
2. These retirees fear death, illness, poverty.
3. Fields of wild flowers were all around us.
4. Fools talk about each other; ideas fill the conversations of the wise.
5. At any rate, the gun fired when the fleeing youth tripped over the patrolman's foot.
6. The storm broke in all its fury at the close of a hot day.
7. A fast pass was caught by Milburn, and a thirty-yard gain was made by him before the whistle was blown by the referee.

8. I asked her to marry me, two years ago, in a shop on Tremont Street, late in the fall.
9. The art of the people was crude, but a great deal of originality was shown by some of them.
10. I can identify the guilty person in every Agatha Christie novel by the simple device of choosing the least likely suspect whose alibi is airtight.

Variety

30

Vary the structure and the length of your sentences to make your whole composition pleasing and effective.

Compare the two paragraphs below. Both use good sentences; both use virtually the same diction. It is varied structure and sentence length that make the difference.

NOT VARIED
> Yellowstone National Park is traffic congestion to millions of people. It is also crowds and a few hours or days in July. A different kind of Yellowstone, however, begins to appear later. This happens by early September. The nights are growing colder then, and workmen are boarding up lodges and curio shops. [five sentences, four simple and one compound—each beginning with the subject and followed by the verb]

VARIED
> To millions of people Yellowstone National Park is traffic congestion, crowds, a few hours or days in July. But by early September, when the nights are growing colder and workmen are boarding up lodges and curio shops, a different kind of Yellowstone begins to appear. —R. STEVEN FULLER [two sentences, one simple and one complex—neither beginning with the subject]

Inexperienced writers tend to rely too heavily—regardless of content or purpose—on a few comfortable, familiar structures. For that reason, Section **30** recommends sentence variety and cautions against monotonous repetition of any one type of sentence.

Note: If you have difficulty distinguishing various types of structures, review the fundamentals of the sentence treated in Section **1**, especially **1d**.

30a

As a rule, avoid a series of short simple sentences. Vary the length. See also **29h**.

Rather than present your ideas in a series of choppy, ineffective sentences, learn how to relate your ideas precisely in a longer sentence. See Section **24**.

CHOPPY An urban songwriter celebrates the simple values. These are to be found only in small towns. This songwriter probably wouldn't live in one.

EFFECTIVE The urban songwriter who celebrates the simple values to be found only in small towns probably wouldn't live in one. —THOMAS GRIFFITH

CHOPPY Wyoming is a state I cherish. It is one of the truly distinctive areas of the United States. Its university has a proud history.

EFFECTIVE Wyoming is a state I cherish, one of the truly distinctive areas of the United States, and its university has a proud history. —JAMES A. MICHENER

CHOPPY Maybe the video revolution is not materially affecting the mass. It is at least presenting more options. The options are for those on the fringes.

EFFECTIVE If the video revolution is not materially affecting the mass, it is at least presenting more options for those on the fringes. —CHRIS WELLES

CHOPPY Some people simply put coffee in an enamel saucepan. Next, they pour very hot water over it. Then they wait until flavor develops. Finally, they add eggshell or a small amount of cold water. The idea is to get the floating grounds to settle to the bottom.

EFFECTIVE Some people simply put coffee in an enamel saucepan, pour very hot water over it, wait until flavor develops, and get the floating grounds to settle to the bottom by adding eggshell or a small amount of cold water.

Note: Occasionally, as the example below illustrates, a series of brief, subject-first sentences may be used for special effect:

> He stumbled, recovered, picked up his pace. Now he was running. He broke out of the ring. People were throwing things at him. An egg hurtled past his head. A tomato hit someone nearby and splattered onto his suit. —GERRY NADEL [The short sentences suggest staccato action.]

■ **Exercise 1**   Study the structure of the sentences below, giving special attention to the variety of sentence lengths.

> As she picked her way toward the garden chairs beside the front porch, she poured out a customary torrent of complaint. Her eyesight was failing. She found herself swatting raisins on the kitchen table, thinking they were flies, and bringing her stick down on spiders that turned out to be scurrying tufts of lint. Her hearing was going, and she suffered from head noises. She imagined she heard drums beating.
> —PETER DE VRIES

■ **Exercise 2**   Convert each of the following series of short simple sentences to one long sentence in which ideas are carefully related.

1. There were thirty seconds of play left. Harrison intercepted the pass and raced downfield. He dropped the ball at the five-yard line.
2. Her speech had an interesting thesis. Salespersons should solve the existing problems of their customers. They should also point out new problems in order to solve them.
3. Bennett's Comet appeared in 1969. It disappeared again in 1970. It will not be visible again for thousands of years.
4. Ellen Dolan did not buy a second car. She bought a Piper. It is a cub plane. It flies at almost a hundred miles an hour.
5. J. Allen Boone is the author of *Kinship with All Life*. In his book Boone describes his ability to communicate with animals. He converses mentally with a dog. He orders ants to leave his home. They obey his orders. He even tames an ordinary housefly.

30b

Avoid a long series of sentences beginning with the subject. Vary the beginning.

Most writers begin about half their sentences with the subject—far more than the number of sentences begun in any other one way. But overuse of the subject-first beginning results in monotonous writing.

(1) Begin with an adverb or an adverb clause.

Suddenly a hissing and clattering came from the heights around us. —DOUGLAS LEE [adverb]

Even though baseball is essentially the same, the strategy of play then and now is different. —JAMES T. FARRELL [adverb clause]

(2) Begin with a prepositional phrase or a participial phrase.

For chain stores, price information can be stored in a central computer serving an entire city. —IRENE MALBIN [prepositional phrase]

Disturbed by the discord of American life in recent decades, Manchester took flight for the Pacific Islands. —JAMES SLOAN ALLEN [participial phrase]

(3) Begin with a sentence connective—a coordinating conjunction, a conjunctive adverb, or a transitional expression.

Notice below how each sentence connective relates the ideas in each set of sentences. See also **31c(4).**

It's slow. **But** it's democracy, and it works. —DAVID S. BOYER [The coordinating conjunction *but* makes a contrast. Compare "slow but efficient."]

We cut him off. We denounce. **And,** whenever possible, we diagnose. —WALTER REICH [Compare the less emphatic "We cut him off, denounce, and diagnose."]

Engine speed also affected the heater's output. **Nonetheless,** the system did manage to keep us warm enough throughout a New England winter. —CONSUMER REPORTS [conjunctive adverb]

The nuclei of atoms become radioactive when they absorb neutrons. **That is,** they decay by giving off some kind of radiation. —ROBERT HOFSTADTER [transitional expression]

(4) Begin with an appositive or with an absolute.

A city of ancient origins, Varna lies on the Black Sea coast. —COLIN RENFREW [appositive referring to the subject]

True, we have occasional debates, but they do not tell us much. —TERRY SANFORD [single-word absolute]

His eyebrows raised high in resignation, he began to examine his hand. —LIONEL TRILLING [absolute phrase]

Note: An occasional declarative sentence with inverted word order can contribute to sentence variety. See also **29f.**

At the feet of the tallest and plushiest offices lie the crummiest slums. —E. B. WHITE [Compare "The crummiest slums lie at the feet of the tallest and plushiest offices."]

■ **Exercise 3**   Prepare for a class discussion of the types of sentence beginnings in the following paragraph.

[1] No longer do we Americans want to destroy wantonly, but our new-found sources of power—to take the burden of work from our shoulders, to warm us, and cool us, and give us light, to transport us quickly, and to make the things we use and wear and eat—these power sources spew pollution in our country, so that the rivers and streams are becoming poisonous and lifeless. [2] The birds die for lack of food; a noxious cloud hangs over our cities that burns our lungs and reddens our eyes. [3] Our ability to conserve has not grown with our power to create, but this slow and sullen poisoning is no longer ignored or justified. [4] Almost daily, the pressure of outrage among Americans grows. [5] We are no longer content to destroy our beloved country. [6] We are slow to learn; but we learn. [7] When a superhighway was proposed in California which would trample the redwood trees in its path, an outcry arose all over the land, so strident and fierce that the plan was put aside. [8] And we no longer believe that a man, by owning a piece of America, is free to outrage it.

—JOHN STEINBECK, *America and Americans*

■ **Exercise 4**   Each of the sentences below begins with the subject. Recast each sentence twice to vary the beginning.

EXAMPLE
Two businessmen dropped by the dean's office and requested reasons for the inefficiency of the school's graduates.
a. *Dropping by the dean's office, two businessmen requested reasons for the inefficiency of the school's graduates.*
b. *In the dean's office, two businessmen requested reasons for the inefficiency of the school's graduates.*

1. We still need a better understanding between the members of our sororities and fraternities.
2. Reporters interviewed the newly appointed ambassador and asked him some tricky questions about world affairs.
3. Hundreds of students will line up in order to register in a floating university, the *Queen Victoria*.
4. Jesse enjoyed the course in science-fiction literature most of all.
5. The green fireballs traveled at great speed and fascinated sky watchers throughout the Southwest.

30c

Avoid loose, stringy compound sentences. See also **24b.**

To revise an ineffective compound sentence, try one of the following methods.

(1) Convert a compound sentence into a complex sentence.

COMPOUND   The Mississippi River is one of the longest rivers in the world, and in the springtime it often overflows its banks, and the lives of many people are endangered.

COMPLEX   The Mississippi River, which is one of the long-est rivers in the world, often overflows its banks in the springtime, endangering the lives of many people.

(2) Use a compound predicate in a simple sentence.

COMPOUND   He put on his coat, and next he picked up his hat and umbrella, and then he hurried from the house.

SIMPLE   He put on his coat, picked up his hat and umbrella, and hurried from the house.

(3) Use a modifier or an appositive in a simple sentence.

COMPOUND   The town was north of the Red River, and a tornado struck it, and it was practically demolished.

SIMPLE   The town, located north of the Red River, was struck by a tornado and practically demolished.

COMPOUND   She was the mayor of the town, and she was an amiable person, and she invited the four students into her office.

SIMPLE   The mayor of the town, an amiable person, invited the four students into her office.

(4) Use phrases in a simple sentence.

COMPOUND   The streets were icy, and we could not drive the car.

SIMPLE   Because of the icy streets, we could not drive the car.

COMPOUND   He arrived in Fresno at 1:30 A.M., and then he made the toll-free call.

SIMPLE   After arriving in Fresno at 1:30 A.M., he made the toll-free call.

■ **Exercise 5** Using the methods illustrated in **30c**, revise the loose, stringy compound sentences below.

1. The small car hugs the road, and it is easy to drive in traffic, but it is not comfortable.
2. The Johnsons grew tired of city smog and noise pollution, so they moved to the country, but there they had no fire department or police protection.
3. Americans at first traded their products, and then they began to use money and bank checks, and now they use the all-inclusive plastic credit card.
4. Harvey kept criticizing middle-class values, and he mentioned such things as marriage and two-car garages, but he did not define upper-class or lower-class values.

30d

Vary the conventional subject–verb sequence by occasionally separating subject and verb with words or phrases.

SUBJECT–VERB   **The auditorium is** across from the park, and **it is** a gift of the alumni. [compound sentence]

VARIED   **The auditorium,** across from the park, **is** a gift of the alumni. [simple sentence]

SUBJECT–VERB   **The crowd sympathized** with the visitors and **applauded** every good play.

VARIED   **The crowd,** sympathizing with the visitors, **applauded** every good play.

SUBJECT–VERB   **Her ability to listen is** an acquired skill that attracts many friends.

VARIED   **Her ability to listen,** an acquired skill, **attracts** many friends.

■ **Exercise 6** Using the methods illustrated in **30d**, vary the conventional subject-verb sequence.

1. Roger is like his mother, and he is an excellent conversationalist.
2. Rhode Island is east of Connecticut, and it has a forty-mile coastline.
3. My grandparents valued strong family ties and encouraged us young ones "to always keep in touch."
4. Margaret was racing back to the dormitory to avoid getting wet, and she fell broadside into a big puddle of water.
5. Wizzard Wells was a popular resort once, but it is a ghost town now.

30e

Occasionally, instead of the usual declarative sentence, use a question, an exclamation, or a command.

How can anybody assert that "growth" is a good thing? If my children grow, it is a very good thing; if I should suddenly start growing, it would be a disaster. —E. F. SCHUMACHER [Here a rhetorical question is followed by the usual declarative statement.]

Their eyes appear covered. One shudders for them. At the same time, what courage! —ALEXANDER ELIOT [The exclamation concludes a discussion of a Japanese print, Hakuin Ekaku's *Two Blind Men Crossing a Log Bridge*.]

All sentences in the following paragraph are declarative except for the third one, an imperative.

For our hypothetical family, the estimated annual saving with solar would be roughly $69 at today's prices. That's not a very dramatic yield. Note, however, that our calculations do not take into account any increases in the cost of conventional energy. Obviously, a change in the price of conventional energy would make a substantial difference in the saving. —CONSUMER REPORTS

■ **Exercise 7** Prepare for a class discussion of sentence variety in the following paragraph.

[1] Some people collect stamps or coins or antique cars. [2] I collect practically useless scraps of information without really wanting to. [3] Things that most people don't bother to remember accumulate in my mind like unused wire hangers in a coat closet. [4] For instance, hardly anybody except me remembers the names of the four models of the Edsel (Pacer, Ranger, Corsair and Citation), or the name of the only New York newspaper that supported Harry Truman in 1948 (the now-defunct New York *Star*). [5] Do you know there's enough concrete in Boulder Dam to build a six-lane highway from Seattle to Miami? [6] I do. [7] I also know the origin of the word *hitchhike* (two people traveling with one horse), and that the Japanese word for first lieutenant (*chūi*) is the same as the Swahili word for leopard. [8] Just don't ask me why. —WILLIAM ATTWOOD, "The Birth of the Bikini"

LARGER ELEMENTS

The Paragraph

31

Write paragraphs that are coherent, adequately developed, and unified.

The paragraph is the essential unit of thought in writing. Although it may consist of a single sentence, it is usually a group of sentences that develop one main point or controlling idea. The form of a paragraph is distinctive: the first line is indented, about one inch in handwriting and five spaces in typewritten copy.

Certain conventions or rules govern the construction of a paragraph. The reader expects a paragraph to be *coherent* (with its organization following a definite plan), *developed* (with its sentences adequately explaining or qualifying the main point), and *unified* (with all its sentences relevant to the main point). In general, most paragraphs are between 100 and 250 words long and usually consist of five to ten sentences.

Paragraph 1 observes the three conventions of coherence, development, and unity. Each of its sentences supports the controlling idea of the paragraph (called the *topic sentence*)—the fact that people have certain "curious experiences" when they fall asleep.

1   A number of curious experiences occur at the onset of sleep. A person just about to go to sleep may experience an electric shock, a flash of light, or a crash of thunder—but the most common sensation is that of floating or falling, which is why "falling alseep" is a scientifically valid description. A nearly universal occurrence at the beginning of sleep (although not everyone recalls it) is a sudden, uncoordinated jerk of the head, the limbs, or even the entire body. Most people tend to think of going to sleep as a slow slippage into oblivion, but the onset of sleep is not gradual at all. It happens in an instant. One moment the individual is awake, the next moment not.   —PETER FARB, *Humankind*

31a

Construct coherent paragraphs.

To construct a coherent paragraph you must have a controlling idea, usually expressed in the form of a question or statement, and a plan or pattern for organizing the supporting material.

(1) Construct a clear topic sentence and restrict it carefully.

The paragraph consists of a topic sentence (the controlling idea) and sentences that elaborate or qualify the topic sentence, much as modifiers do in a sentence. The first step in constructing a coherent paragraph is to formulate a clear, restricted topic sentence that tells the reader what the paragraph will be about.

One method of constructing a topic sentence is to put the controlling idea into the form of a question. If you wanted to write about draft registration, for example, you might ask a question like the following, which could be the topic sentence of your paragraph: Should draft registration be universal?

A second method of constructing a topic sentence is to think of your controlling idea as if it were a problem and to state the problem as clearly as possible. For example, if you wanted to write about the physics of light, you might state the idea in a topic sentence like the following:

> A problem in discussing the physics of light is that two different theories account for certain aspects of light but neither theory accounts for all the aspects of light.

A third method of constructing a topic sentence is to start with a general statement and then to restate it in a more particular way in a second sentence. These two sentences may then be combined into an introductory clause (general) and a main clause (more particular). If you wanted to write about communication, for example, you might arrive at a topic sentence as follows:

1. Many members of the animal kingdom communicate. [general statement]
   But humans communicate in the most sophisticated way. [particular statement]
2. While many members of the animal kingdom communicate, humans communicate in the most sophisticated way. [topic sentence]

This method of presenting a topic sentence has the advantage of orienting the reader in a general way and then directing the reader to the particular aspect of the general statement the writer intends to discuss.

Because paragraphs are short, the more precise or restricted the topic sentence, the better. The more general the topic sentence, the more difficulty you will have in constructing a coherent paragraph. Thus the question "What is love?" is not as good a topic sentence as "What is love among teenagers?" Although almost any statement or question can be made into a topic sentence, to be an effective topic sentence it must be precise enough to control every sentence in the paragraph.

In paragraph 2 the topic sentence begins with reasons why the author would like to know more about the yeti (the Abominable Snowman), but it concludes with the statement that the author would be saddened if the yeti were to be discovered. This topic sentence, in turn, controls all the remaining sentences. They explain why the author would be sad.

2   Even though I am intrigued with the yeti, both for its scientific importance and for what it says about our own interests and biases, I would be deeply saddened to have it discovered. If it were to be found and captured, studied and confined, we might well slay our nightmares. But the mystery and imagination it evokes would also be slain. If the yeti is an old form that we have driven into the mountains, now we would be driving it into the zoos. We would gain another possession, another ragged exhibit in the concrete world or the zoological park, another Latin name to enter on our scientific ledgers. But what about the wild creature that now roams free of man in the forests of the Himalayas? Every time man asserts his mastery over nature, he gains something in knowledge, but loses something in spirit.

—EDWARD W. CRONIN, "The Yeti"

■ **Exercise 1** Construct carefully restricted topic sentences from the following list of ideas. The more specific your topic sentences, the better.

1. Campus parking
2. Censoring television programs
3. The price of college textbooks
4. Competition for graduate school admissions
5. Reduced federal spending for student aid
6. Technical education

(2) Place the topic sentence where the reader can find it.

The topic sentence is usually the first or second sentence in the paragraph. Stated immediately, it thus provides the reader with the key idea that shapes the paragraph. At times, when the controlling idea is stated early in the paragraph, it may also be restated at the end, to point up its importance. In paragraph 3 compare "the intolerable has become normal" with the final "Ugliness is accepted, no longer even noticed."

3   In the towns and cities of Ulster, the intolerable has become normal. The civic environment is scarred. In Belfast and Derry, it is hard to find a shop with windows; shopkeepers have had so many broken that they are content to leave the boards up. Burned-out houses and shops are left as abandoned hulks. The army has run out its barbed wire, concrete and corrugated iron in dozens of checkpoints, barricades and gun emplacements. Ugliness is accepted, no longer even noticed.

—PAUL HARRISON, "The Dark Age of Ulster"

Occasionally, as in paragraph 4, the topic sentence is the last sentence, especially when the writer progresses from particulars or from a specific example to a generalization.

4   Imagine waking up and glancing at your clock, which reads 8:55 a.m. This information means nothing, until you apply your perception to it. If it's a weekday, you're due at work at 9 a.m., and being punctual is important, 8:55 becomes a negative stressor. If it's Saturday, your perception of 8:55 may result in a feeling of luxurious anticipation of a lazy day. The information in both cases was the same. Your perception of it determined your response.

—JENNIFER BOLCH, "How to Manage Stress"

Note: In many paragraphs the controlling idea is not expressly stated in a topic sentence, but in a unified paragraph it is implied distinctly. The implied idea of paragraph 5 ("These are steps in the embalming process") can be clearly understood in the context of Jessica Mitford's description. (The quotations are from an embalming textbook.)

5   About three to six gallons of a dyed and perfumed solution of formaldehyde, glycerin, borax, phenol, alcohol and water is soon circulating through Mr. Jones, whose mouth has been sewn together with a "needle directed upward between the upper lip and gum and brought out through the left nostril," with the corners raised slightly "for a more pleasant expression." If he should be bucktoothed, his teeth are cleaned with Bon Ami and coated with colorless nail polish. His eyes, meanwhile, are closed with flesh-tinted eye caps and eye cement.

—JESSICA MITFORD, The American Way of Death

■ **Exercise 2** Identify the topic sentences in paragraphs 6–8. If the topic sentence is implied, construct one.

6   Certainly the [U.S.] political problems, difficult and delicate though they may be, are not insoluble. Some, like the control or the liquidation of monopolies which stand in the way of individual initiative, have a long history in this country. Others, like the struggle to liberate individuals from the degrading fear of unemployment or old age or sickness, are less familiar—at least in the United States. Still others, like the overriding question of the relation between individual freedom and the intervention of the state, have a meaning for our generation which they did not have for generations before. But only a man who did not wish to find an answer to questions such as these would argue that no answer can be found.

—ARCHIBALD MacLEISH, "The Conquest of America"

7   When we watch a person walk away from us, his image shrinks in size. But since we know for a fact that he is not shrinking, we make an unconscious correcting and "see" him as retaining his full stature. Past experience tells us what his true stature is with respect to our own. Any sane and dependable expectation of the future requires that he have the same true stature when we next encounter him. Our perception is thus a prediction; it embraces the past and the future as well as the present.

—WARREN J. WITTREICH, "Visual Perception & Personality"

8   A TV set stood close to a wall in the small living room crowded with an assortment of chairs and tables. An aquarium crowded the mantelpiece of a fake fireplace. A lighted bulb inside the tank showed many colored fish swimming about in a haze of fish food. Some of it lay scattered on the edge of the shelf. The carpet underneath was sodden black. Old magazines and tabloids lay just about everywhere.

—BIENVENIDO SANTOS, "Immigration Blues"

(3) Organize paragraphs according to a definite pattern.

Most paragraphs are organized according to one of these three patterns: question-answer; problem-solution; topic-restriction-illustration.

a. **Question-answer pattern**

In this pattern the topic sentence asks a question and the supporting sentences answer it, as in paragraph 9.

9   Why did the Civil Rights movement arise? There are several possible reasons. Although the Supreme Court had

ruled in 1954 that segregated schools were inherently un-equal, the United States made little progress toward inte-gration in the next few years. Therefore, American blacks began to believe that their equality could come only through their own actions. Another reason may be that the late 1950's and 1960's provided the right climate for direct social action. Finally, it is possible that the social and eco-nomic condition of the blacks had become sufficiently good by the late fifties to enable them to act on their own.

—STUDENT

b. Problem-solution pattern

In this pattern the topic sentence states a problem, and the supporting sentences offer a solution, as in paragraph 10.

10   The trouble with the clans and tribes many of us were born into is not that they consist of meddlesome ogres but that they are too far away. [*problem*] In emergencies we rush across continents and if need be oceans to their sides, as they do to ours. Maybe we even make a habit of seeing them, once or twice a year, for the sheer pleasure of it. But blood ties seldom dictate our addresses. Our blood kin are often too remote to ease us from our Tuesdays to our Wed-nesdays. [*restatement of the problem*] For this we must rely on our families of friends. If our relatives are not, do not wish to be, or for whatever reasons cannot be our friends, then by some complex alchemy we must try to transform our friends into our relatives. If blood and roots don't do the job, then we must look to water and branches, and sort ourselves into new constellations, new families.

—JANE HOWARD, "All Happy Clans Are Alike"

c. Topic-restriction-illustration pattern

In this pattern, the writer announces the topic, then restricts or qualifies it in the same sentence or in the next sentence. Then the writer illustrates the restriction in the remaining sentences of the paragraph. In paragraph 11 the general topic "the fascination of lost worlds" begins the paragraph. The next sentence restates the general topic. The third sen-tence restricts the topic to "the scholar," and two illustrations are given, Jefferson and the unnamed South American trav-eler.

11   The fascination of lost worlds has long preoccupied humanity. It is inevitable that transitory man, student of the galaxies and computer of light-years, should entertain nos-talgic yearnings for some island outside of time, some Ava-lon untouched by human loss. Even the scholar has not been averse to searching for the living past on islands or preci-pice-guarded plateaus. Jefferson repeated the story of a trapper who had heard of the mammoth roaring in the Vir-ginia woods; in 1823 a South American traveler imagina-tively viewed through his spyglass mastodons grazing in remote Andean valleys.

—LOREN EISELEY, *The Immense Journey*

These patterns can be varied to suit your intention. The question-answer pattern, for example, can be rearranged as answer-question. Topic-restriction-illustration can be varied in a number of ways. The topic may be such that restriction is unnecessary and can be omitted. Or illustration can be first in the paragraph with the topic saved for last.

■ **Exercise 3**   In paragraphs 12–15, identify the pattern of each paragraph as question-answer, problem-solution, or topic-restriction-illustration. Remember that the patterns can be re-arranged.

12   What's wrong with the student-union bookshop? Everything. It's interested in selling sweatshirts and college mugs rather than good books. Its staff often is incompetent and uncivil. The manager may not be intelligent enough even to order a sufficient number of copies of required text-books for the beginning of a term. As for more lively books—why, there are masses of paperbacks, perhaps, that could be procured at any drugstore; there are a few shelves or racks of volumes labeled "Gift Books," usually lavishly illustrated and inordinately costly, intended as presents to fond parents; but there are virtually no *book* books, of the sort that students might like to buy.

—RUSSELL KIRK, "From the Academy: Campus Bookshops"

13   What a day that 11th of November [1918] was! It was not quite three o'clock in the morning when the State De-partment gave out to the dozing newspaper men the news that the Armistice had really been signed. Four days before, a false report of the end of hostilities had thrown the whole United States into a delirium of joy. People had poured out of offices and shops and paraded the streets singing and shouting, ringing bells, blowing tin horns, smashing one another's hats, cheering soldiers in uniform, draping them-selves in American flags, gathering in closely packed crowds before the newspaper bulletin boards, making a wild and hilarious holiday; in New York, Fifth Avenue had been closed to traffic and packed solid with surging men and women, while down from the windows of the city fluttered 155 tons of ticker tape and torn paper. It did not seem possible that such an outburst could be repeated. But it was.

—FREDERICK LEWIS ALLEN, *Only Yesterday*

14   I started this diary as a personal document after com-ing into teaching from a Wall Street brokerage firm. I felt that I wanted to become a part of a larger human experi-ence and in some small way to make a contribution to that experience. I was soon to discover that under the then pres-ent and still going strong bureaucracy, doing that was al-most impossible unless one was willing to become a part of that bureaucracy. I chose not to and in short order found myself, along with a few other young teachers, alienated, our hands tied, unable to offer suggestions or bring about change. After grappling with the decision to remain or get out I decided to record this diary, hoping it would help calm my frustrations.

—JIM HASKINS, *Diary of a Harlem Schoolteacher*

15   Our most important environmental problem, certainly the most urgent, is the burning of fossil fuels, which has significantly increased the carbon dioxide in the atmos-phere. It is important to get rid of it because as the CO_2 concentration goes up, it acts as a sort of greenhouse. If we increase the CO_2 in the atmosphere at the rate it's been going, atmospheric warming has been predicted to be as much as a degree and a half or so over the next ten to fifteen years. This will have major consequences for the climate, and could start to melt the icecaps.

—DEREK SPENCER, "Is the World Getting Warmer?"

31b

Construct well-developed paragraphs.

Once you have decided on a pattern for your paragraph (question-answer, problem-solution, topic-restriction-illustration), you must then consider how to develop the answer, the solution, or the illustrations. The method of paragraph development that you choose depends upon your purpose. Do you want to tell a story? Use a chronological order. Do you want to say how something is done? Explain a step-by-step process.

(1) Narration

Narrative paragraphs present a series of events that begin at a particular time and are organized chronologically. Narrative writing longer than a paragraph often uses a flashback (a jump back in time), but in a paragraph the reader expects that the material will be arranged in time order.

In paragraph 16, Charles Schulz's narrative begins with second grade and proceeds chronologically through high school. Often the topic sentence in a narrative paragraph is a kind of frame that pulls the various series of incidents of the paragraph together. Schulz begins his paragraph with a topic sentence that serves as such a frame. The paragraph follows the pattern of topic-restriction-illustration.

16   My scholastic career got off to a good start when I was very young. I received a special diploma in the second grade for being the outstanding boy student, and in the third and fifth grades I was moved ahead so suddenly that I was the smallest kid in the class. Somehow, I survived the early years of grade school, but when I entered junior high school, I failed everything in sight. High school proved not much better. There was no doubt that I was absolutely the worst physics student in the history of St. Paul Central High School. It was not until I became a senior that I earned any respectable grades at all. I have often felt that some semblance of maturity began to arrive at last. I saved that final report card because it was the only one that seemed to justify those long years of agony.
                                    —CHARLES M. SCHULZ, *Peanuts Jubilee*

(2) Process

Process paragraphs explain how something is done or made. For this reason, they often have a temporal element that makes a step-by-step chronological arrangement both possible and natural, as in paragraph 17.

17   The best of all scientific tricks with an egg is the well-known one in which air pressure forces a peeled hard-boiled egg into a glass milk bottle and then forces it out again undamaged. The mouth of the bottle must be only slightly smaller than the egg, and so you must be careful not to use too large an egg or too small a bottle. It is impossible to push the egg into the bottle. To get the egg through the mouth you must heat the air in the bottle. That is best done by standing the bottle in boiling water for a few minutes. Put the egg upright on the mouth and take the bottle off the stove. As the air in the bottle cools it contracts, creating a partial vacuum that draws the peeled egg inside. To get the egg out again invert the bottle so that the egg falls into the neck. Place the opening of the bottle against your mouth and blow vigorously. This will compress the air in the bot-

tle. When you stop blowing, the air expands, pushing the egg through the neck of the bottle and into your waiting hands.
                                    —MARTIN GARDNER, "Mathematical Games"

(3) Description

Description requires a sequential arrangement of details that move in a consistent way: from near to far, from general to particular, from right to left, from top to bottom, and so forth. As the description moves in one of these ways, it provides a framework for individual details. Thus, the reader has an orderly scheme to use as he or she visualizes what you are describing.

In paragraph 18, using a near-to-far movement, Thomas Merton describes the monastery that was to become his home.

18   I looked at the rolling country, and at the pale ribbon of road in front of us, stretching out as grey as lead in the light of the moon. Then suddenly I saw a steeple that shone like silver in the moonlight, growing into sight from behind a rounded knoll. The tires sang on the empty road, and, breathless, I looked at the monastery that was revealed before me as we came over the rise. At the end of an avenue of trees was a big rectangular block of buildings, all dark, with a church crowned by a tower and a steeple and a cross: and the steeple was as bright as platinum and the whole place was as quiet as midnight and lost in the all-absorbing silence and solitude of the fields. Behind the monastery was a dark curtain of woods, and over to the west was a wooded valley, and beyond that a rampart of wooded hills, a barrier and a defense against the world.
                                    —THOMAS MERTON, *The Seven Storey Mountain*

(4) Classification

Classification paragraphs divide a group or class of things into parts that will explain the group or class for the reader. In paragraph 19, the class is "book owners." Adler divides book owners into three types, not according to how many books they own, but according to how thoroughly they read their books.

19   There are three kinds of book owners. The first has all the standard sets and best-sellers—unread, untouched. (This deluded individual owns woodpulp and ink, not books.) The second has a great many books—a few of them read through, most of them dipped into, but all of them as clean and shiny as the day they were bought. (This person would probably like to make books his own, but is restrained by a false respect for their physical appearance.) The third has a few books or many—every one of them dog-eared and dilapidated, shaken and loosened by continual use, marked and scribbled in from front to back. (This man owns books.)
                                    —MORTIMER J. ADLER, "How To Mark A Book"

Once you have decided on the parts of the class you are dividing, you must decide what order you want to describe them in and maintain that order throughout. Depending on the purpose of the classification, the system of ordering might be from first to last, from largest to smallest, or from least important to most important.

(5) Analysis

Analysis is similar to classification in that the subject of the analysis is divided into parts. However, the purpose of the analysis is to suggest that the parts are related as causes or effects of the thing analyzed. In paragraph 20 the authors analyze the causes of a volcanic eruption.

20 Volcanic eruptions are the final stage of a process that begins with the melting of rock in a planet's interior, the "source region." The most usual source of the heat that leads to melting is energy released by the decay of radioactive elements. The material in the source region is generally only partially molten, being made up of magma, or liquid rock, and unmelted crystals. The lighter liquid gradually rises above the denser crystals through the action of gravity and collects in magma chambers. The segregation process that drives the liquid upward can take anywhere from hundreds of years to hundreds of millions, depending primarily on the force of gravity, which varies with depth and the planet's size, on the nature of the crystals in the source region, on the amount of liquid produced by the heat available and on the viscosity of the liquid.

—HARRY Y. McSWEEN, JR., and EDWARD M. STOLPER, "Basaltic Meteorites"

(6) Definition   See also **23d.**

Paragraphs of definition attempt to explain who a person is or what a place or thing is. Definitions can be formal or informal depending on your purpose. A *formal* definition is used in academic writing to explain as precisely as possible what a thing is by putting it in its class (in biology, its *genus*) and then by distinguishing it from other members of that genus. Paragraph 21 illustrates formal definition.

21 The purple martin (*Progne subis*) is locally common where proper multicelled nesting boxes or gourds are provided. No other North American swallow is dark all over. Females, young, and first-year males are light-bellied and could be confused with smaller swallows. Watch for purple iridescence on head and top of wings. Note the broad wings, and more soaring flight of martins. In late summer flocks of thousands roost together in shade trees of some cities. Song and calls are a distinctive, low-pitched, liquid, rolling twitter.   —*A Guide to Field Identification: Birds of North America*

Paragraph 22 illustrates an *informal* definition, which is designed to explain a term or idea for the general reader, often by providing examples or synonyms.

22 Biofeedback, Dr. Green said, means getting immediate, ongoing information about one's own biological processes or conditions—such as heart behavior, temperature, brain-wave activity, blood pressure or muscle tension—and using the information to change and control voluntarily the specific process or response being monitored.

—THOMAS W. PEW JR., "Biofeedback seeks new medical uses for concept of yoga"

A less common type of definition, but one that you may need to use from time to time, is a form of *historical* definition. In this type of definition you explain the meaning of a thing at a particular time in history. Paragraph 23 defines *English* in a historical setting.

23 English, in its original form, is Anglo-Saxon, a Low German dialect of the western sub-branch of the Germanic branch of Indo-European. Perhaps 25 per cent of our words (at least 50 per cent, however, of our words of most frequent

occurrence) go back to Anglo-Saxon or to Middle English (when the dictionary describes a word as being of Middle English origin, it means that it cannot be traced all the way back to Anglo-Saxon, but also that there is no evidence that it was borrowed from any other source; this means that it is more likely to be of native, or Anglo-Saxon, origin than of any other).   —MARIO PEI, *The Families of Words*

(7) Comparison/Contrast

A comparison points out the similarities of two things; a contrast points out the differences. The important thing to remember is to compare or contrast the thing with something else the reader knows better. For example, to tell the reader how large England is, you might say that it is about the size of Virginia. You can then contrast the two in terms of climate, population density, and so forth. Paragraph 24 is an example of contrast—the differences between two kinds of terror.

24 Most of us enjoy the gooseflesh and the tingle along the spine produced by the successful ghost story. There is something agreeable in letting our blood be chilled by bats in the moonlight, guttering candles, creaking doors, eerie shadows, piercing screams, inexplicable bloodstains, and weird noises. But the terror aroused by tricks and external "machinery" is a far cry from the terror evoked by some terrifying treatment of the human situation. The horror we experience in watching the Werewolf or Dracula or Frankenstein is far less significant than that we get from watching the bloody ambition of Macbeth or the jealousy of Othello. In the first, terror is the end-product; in the second, it is the natural accompaniment of a powerful revelation of life. In the first, we are always aware of a basic unreality; in the second, reality is terrifying.   —LAURENCE PERRINE, *Literature: Structure, Sound, and Sense,* 3rd edition

The comparison in paragraph 25 is between language and games.

25 The language game shares certain characteristics with all other true games. First of all, it has a minimum of two players (the private, incomprehensible speech of a schizophrenic is no more a true game than is solitaire). Second, a person within speaking distance of any stranger can be forced by social pressure to commit himself to play, in the same way that a bystander in the vicinity of any other kind of game may be asked to play or to look on. Third, something must be at stake and both players must strive to win it—whether the reward be a tangible gain like convincing an employer of the need for a raise or an intangible one like the satisfaction of besting someone in an argument. Fourth, a player of any game has a particular style that distinguishes him as well as the ability to shift styles depending upon where the game is played and who the other players are. In the case of the language game, the style might be a preference for certain expressions or a folksy way of speaking, and the style shift might be the bringing into play of different verbal strategies when speaking in the home, at the office, on the street, or in a place of worship.

—PETER FARB, *Word Play*

(8) Example

A paragraph developed by example is very common. In this type of paragraph you make a statement and then supply one or more examples to illustrate it. Paragraph 26 illustrates this technique.

26 In the past decade, however, "facts" have blossomed into a fad. The sales of *Guinness Book of World Records* rival those of the Bible. The popularity of *The People's Almanac, Fascinating Facts, Isaac Asimov's Book of Facts, Easy Answers to Hard Questions, Dictionary of Misinformation, Encyclopedia of Ignorance,* as well as of television shows such as *Real People,* testifies to the public's growing appetite for mental snacks. —CARLL TUCKER, "In the Matter of Facts"

■ **Exercise 4** Identify the pattern and the method of development in paragraphs 27–29.

27 Without doubt the most famous of all megalithic monuments is Stonehenge, on the Wiltshire plain of southern Britain. Visited by thousands yearly, it is second only to the Tower of London as a tourist attraction. It has a larger literature than any other archaeological site in the world, including the pyramids of Egypt and the great statues of Easter Island, as well as mythical sites such as Atlantis. The number of books on Stonehenge and on other megalithic monuments that have poured from the presses in the past decade or so is a measure of the continued interest in these antiquities. —GLYN DANIEL, "Megalithic Monuments"

28 Watching a millipede crawl slowly, softly over decaying humus is like watching a symphony in movement. Children marvel that this thousand-legged worm can coordinate so many legs without getting them all tangled up. Of course, millipedes do not have a thousand legs, nor are they worms. Careful observation reveals that each body block, or segment, has two pairs of legs, in contrast with the one pair per body block in centipedes. Though they have more legs than centipedes, they move much more slowly, feeding mainly on decaying plant tissues. —CECIL E. JOHNSON, "The Wild World of Compost"

29 The electronic revolution in data processing, which dominated the '70s, is anything but over. A decade ago, for instance, sixteen "bits," or pieces of information, could be packed on one chip of silicon inside a computer. Within five years, the capacity of a single chip will be 256,000 bits and rising, with no increase in price. This means that ever-smaller computers can deal with ever-larger amounts of data. Portable minicomputers may well become almost as commonplace in ten years as handheld calculators are now. —NEWSWEEK

31c

Construct unified paragraphs.

(1) Make each sentence contribute to the main idea.

A paragraph has unity when every sentence is relevant to the main or controlling idea. Any sentence that violates this unity should be deleted. Paragraph 30 is unified because every sentence contributes to the main idea—the high profits of the popular-music industry.

30 Popular music in America now outgrosses the combined revenue of movies, theater, opera, ballet, and sport. The recording industry produces 1,000 new songs each week, the sole purpose being for a few to become hits and make money. It is a staggeringly competitive business, for the profits are staggeringly high: in 1979, sales of LP and single records totaled $2.5 billion. With sales of taped cartridges of record albums added to this figure, total revenues approach $3.25 billion. —ROBERT RICHMAN, "Trash Theory"

To check the unity of your paragraph, you may find it helpful to write down its plan, so that any irrelevant sentences will be apparent. The preceding paragraph reveals this plan:

Topic:
  Popular music outgrosses other entertainments.

Illustration:
  number of songs produced, size of record sales

Caution: Do not make rambling statements that are only vaguely related to your topic. As you write a paragraph, hold to the main idea. For example, if the controlling idea of your paragraph is "My roommate Bill Jones cannot keep a secret," irrelevant sentences about Bill's sense of humor or about secrecy in general will disrupt the unity. Every sentence should pertain to Bill's inability to keep a secret.

■ **Exercise 5** Revise the following student paragraph to improve unity. Be prepared to give reasons for your revisions.

31 The expression "environmental problems" encompasses a wide range. Since the beginning of time, human beings have struggled against elements in their environment. They have always attempted to protect themselves against such natural disasters as fire and flood. As time went on, and the human population grew, abuse of land, overcrowding of cities, famine, and the extinction of various animal species became environmental problems. Human beings progressed, gaining more control over their environment and creating more problems in it. They were less dependent on environmental conditions for their lives: if it was dark, they could snap on a light, and if it was cold, they could turn up the furnace. People became very mobile, able to hop into a car and drive practically anywhere. Life was made easier by new products. But all of this "progress" had negative effects on the environment. It became increasingly more difficult to find efficient methods of disposing of waste, and air and water pollution resulted. Land, energy, and food became more scarce. Progress began as we defended ourselves against what often seemed a hostile environment, but somewhere along the way we not only gained control over—but also began to destroy—our environment.

TRANSITIONS BETWEEN SENTENCES

Sentences linked by transitional devices such as pronouns, repeated key words, transitional expressions, or parallel structure help create a unified paragraph.

(2) Link sentences by your use of pronouns.

In paragraph 32 Carin Rubenstein links her sentences by using the pronouns *their* and *they.* Although these same two pronouns are used repeatedly, their referent, "easy victims," is always clear.

32   Several movements characterized easy victims: their strides were either very long or very short; they moved awkwardly, raising their left legs with their left arms (instead of alternating them); on each step, they tended to lift their whole foot up and then place it down (less muggable sorts took steps in which their feet rocked from heel to toe). Overall, the people rated most muggable walked as if they were in conflict with themselves; they seemed to make each move in the most difficult way possible.

    —CARIN RUBENSTEIN,
"Body Language That Speaks to Muggers"

(3) Link sentences by repeating key words or ideas.

In paragraph 33, the repetition of the key word "no" links the sentences. (The repetition also serves to provide emphasis: see **29e**.)

33   If you ask the American people what they detest most, it will probably be the word *"no."* We have been brainwashed into thinking that if we wrap our lips around that nasty little word, we will immediately turn into kill-joys, grouches, nags, villains, tightwads, ogres, prudes or fanatics. I would like to say yes to *no* once again. *No* is a good word, especially if you can be brave and swashbuckling and reasonably sane about using it. I know people who say *no* just because. I want my kids and their kids to have something left to say *no* about. *No* is, after all, a part of life.

    —SUZANNE JORDAN, "The Joy of Abstinence"
(italics added)

Notice in paragraph 34 how repetition of key words binds together the sentences.

34
    Social change takes many forms in modern society, and people are affected by it in several different ways. For example, in the past, a man's prestige as well as much of his life satisfaction lay in his occupation and in his work. However, signs indicate that the traditional basis for satisfaction is changing. Now, the source often lies outside of "work." The satisfaction formerly obtained in an occupation is being pursued in clubs, sports, and many kinds of projects. This change in attitude toward work stems not only from the character of job duties, but also from shorter work hours and higher incomes.

(margin labels: change; satisfaction; occupation, work, job)

    —THERON ALEXANDER, "The Individual and Social Change"

(4) Link sentences by using transitional expressions.

Below is a list of various transitional expressions:

1. *Addition:* moreover, further, furthermore, besides, and, and then, likewise, also, nor, too, again, in addition, equally important, next, first, second, third, in the first place, in the second place, finally, last.
2. *Comparison:* similarly, likewise, in like manner.
3. *Contrast:* but, yet, and yet, however, still, nevertheless, on the other hand, on the contrary, even so, notwithstanding, for all that, in contrast to this, at the same time, although this may be true, otherwise, nonetheless. (Note: Addition, comparison, and contrast are used for items of equal importance.)
4. *Place:* here, beyond, nearby, opposite to, adjacent to, on the opposite side.
5. *Purpose:* to this end, for this purpose, with this object.
6. *Result:* hence, therefore, accordingly, consequently, thus, thereupon, as a result, then.
7. *Summary, repetition, exemplification, intensification:* to sum up, in brief, on the whole, in sum, in short, as I have said, in other words, that is, to be sure, as has been noted, for example, for instance, in fact, indeed, to tell the truth, in any event.
8. *Time:* meanwhile, at length, soon, after a few days, in the meantime, afterward, later, now, in the past.

Notice the various ways that transitional expressions connect and relate ideas in the sentences of paragraphs 9 and 25.

(5) Link sentences by means of parallel structure.

Parallelism is the repetition of the sentence pattern or of other grammatical structures. See also Section **26**.

    In paragraph 35 notice the parallelism in the second and third sentences, which develop the topic stated in the first sentence. The repeated pattern is *adverb clause, main clause.* This parallelism serves as a unifying force. See also **26a(3)**.

35   You must give up believing that all the riches of life will come from reaching the goals of your idealized self. If your ideal self is evidently not going to be attainable and you refuse to adjust down, you will go the route of chronic depression. On the other hand, if you recognize that you will never be president of the big-city bank, you can get on with becoming branch manager in your favorite community and maybe find your greatest pleasure in becoming a Little League coach or starting a choir.   —GAIL SHEEHY, *Passages*

In the series of paragraphs below, paragraph 36 states and explains the controlling idea, and 37–39 repeat parallel structures in the question-answer pattern that serves as a unifying force. For effective variety, the final emphatic one-sentence paragraph breaks the parallel pattern.

36   Somehow this nation has become caught in what I call the mire of "technofix": the belief, reinforced in us by the highest corporate and political forces, that all our current crises can be solved, or at least significantly eased, by the application of modern high technology. In the words of former Atomic Energy Commission chairman Glenn Seaborg: "We must pursue the idea that it is more science, better science, more wisely applied that is going to free us from [our] predicaments."

37   Energy crisis? Try synfuels. Never mind that they will require billions—eventually trillions—of dollars transferred out of the public coffers into the energy companies' pockets, or that nobody has yet fully explored, much less solved, the problems of environmental damage, pollution, hazardous-waste disposal and occupational dangers their production will create. Never mind—it's technofix.

38   Food for the hungry world? Try the "Green Revolution." Never mind that such farming is far more energy- and chemical-intensive than any other method known, and therefore generally too expensive for the poor countries that are supposed to benefit from it, or that its principle of monoculture over crop diversity places whole regions, even whole countries, at the risk of a single breed of disease or pest. Never mind—it's scientific.

39   Diseases? Try wonder drugs. Never mind that few of the thousands of drugs introduced every year have ever been fully tested for long-range effects, or that they are vastly overprescribed and overused, or that nearly half of them prove to be totally ineffective in treating the ailments they are administered for and half of the rest produce unintended side effects. Never mind—it's progress.

40   And progress, God help us all, may be our most important product. —KIRKPATRICK SALE, "The 'Miracle' of Technofix"

■ **Exercise 6**   Prepare for a class discussion of the specific linking devices (pronouns, transitional words, repetition, parallelism) used in paragraph 41.

41   Electronic music is a new departure from orthodox, or generally accepted, music in that it is electrically originated or modified sound. This sound is the output of electric pianos, organs, synthesizers, saxophones, guitars, flutes, violins, trumpets, and many other instruments. It is the product of composers who use tape recorders and tape manipulation to distort, for better or worse, conventional sounds. Also, it is the sounds we hear in concerts and on records that use amplification to boost or alter the volume of instruments. —MERRILL C. LEHRER, "The Electronic Music Revolution"

■ **Exercise 7**   Revise the sentences in paragraph 42, the work of a student, so that the thought flows smoothly from one sentence to the next.

42   When we hear the word "environment," one of the first words that comes to mind is the weather. We cannot control our climate; however we have created an artificial environment which can be either hot or cool to suit our needs. But no one can make a substitute for the sun. We depend on the sun for both heat and ultraviolet radiation, which forms the Vitamin D in man's body. The sun is the catalyst which continues our never-ending food chain, and now we have changed the sun's light to a form of heating called solar energy. Without the sun, we could not survive.

31d

Provide clear transitions between paragraphs.

Transitions from one paragraph to the next are just as necessary as those between sentences within the paragraph because the reader needs to be reminded of the direction of the writer's thought.

For example, read paragraph 43, which sets forth a claim made by those who promote transcendental meditation(TM).

Then observe the two types of transitional devices used in the first sentences of subsequent paragraphs that refute this claim.

43   As the saying goes, "You can prove anything with statistics." TM promoters claim that the higher the meditation rate, the lower the crime rate, and specifically that in cities where one percent of the population practice TM, the crime rate is lower than in other cities.

transitional expressions —First, a correlation does not necessarily indicate a cause and effect relationship. . . .

—Second, in large samples it is easy to get correlations. . . .

—Third, the one percent may not represent a cross section of each city's populace. . . . *repetition of words/ideas*

—RANDAL MONTGOMERY, "TM and Science: Friends or Foes?"

The closely related words in each group below are often placed at or near the beginnings of sentences to link ideas in separate paragraphs (as illustrated in paragraph 43) or within a paragraph (as in paragraph 25).

1. First. . . . Second. . . . Third. . . .
2. First. . . . Then. . . . Next. . . . Finally. . . .
3. Then. . . . Now. . . . Soon. . . . Later. . . .
4. One. . . . Another. . . . Still another. . . .
5. Some. . . . Others. . . . Still others. . . .
6. A few. . . . Many. . . . More. . . . Most. . . .
7. Just as significant. . . . more important. . . . most important of all. . . .

Sometimes a transitional paragraph (usually short, often consisting of only one sentence) serves as a bridge between two paragraphs. Notice below that the first noun phrase in the transitional paragraph 45 echoes the preceding key idea and that the second noun phrase points to a fact to be explained next.

44   Indeed, instead of seeing evolution as a smooth process, many of today's life scientists and archaeologists are studying the "theory of catastrophes" to explain "gaps" and "jumps" in the multiple branches of the evolutionary record. Others are studying small changes that may have been amplified through feedback into sudden structural transformations. Heated controversies divide the scientific community over every one of these issues.

45   But all such controversies are dwarfed by a single history-changing fact.

46   One day in 1953 at Cambridge in England a young biologist, James Watson, was sitting in the Eagle pub when his colleague, Francis Crick, ran excitedly in and announced to "everyone within hearing distance that we had found the secret of life." They had. Watson and Crick had unraveled the structure of DNA.

—ALVIN TOFFLER, *The Third Wave*

31e

Construct effective opening, concluding, and transitional paragraphs.

(1) Opening paragraphs

An opening paragraph, the one that begins an essay, functions as the writer's game plan. It must guide both writer and reader through the rest of the essay. The topic sentence of the opening paragraph is usually the thesis statement that will control all the remaining paragraphs of the essay. (See Section **32**.) The other sentences in the opening paragraph, the ones that support the topic sentence, are often used later in the essay, usually reworded, as the topic sentences of separate paragraphs.

The second function of the opening paragraph is to interest the reader. Often a writer will begin with a specific example or illustration, a quotation, an interesting statistic—whatever the writer believes will encourage the reader to read further. In magazines and newspapers, the first paragraph is often called "the hooker" because it acts like a baited hook. In academic writing, the first paragraph can be less enticing, but the writer still needs to attract the reader's attention and to focus the problem under discussion.

Paragraph 47, from a student essay, is an example of a beginning paragraph that attracts the reader's attention.

47   The faded yellow 5 × 8-inch card, taped at the head of the plain pine coffin, read: "Ronnie A. Ward, 51960573, died from wounds received during an armed conflict with the enemy, September 14, 1967, Republic of Viet Nam." Ronnie had now given all of himself.

(2) Concluding paragraphs

A concluding paragraph, the one that ends an essay, is the writer's final opportunity to restate the main idea of the essay. Often the concluding paragraph repeats in other words what was stated in the opening paragraph. In a short essay, the concluding paragraph may be no more than a sentence, but the longer the essay or the more complex its ideas, the more developed the concluding paragraph will need to be. The topic sentence of a concluding paragraph is usually a restatement of the main idea of the essay, and its supporting sentences are often reworded versions of the topic sentences of earlier paragraphs.

Checklist for Paragraph Revision

Coherence

1. Is the topic sentence effectively placed?
2. Is the topic sentence carefully restricted?
3. Is the paragraph pattern appropriate?

Development

4. Is the method of development appropriate?
5. Is the paragraph adequately developed?

Unity

6. Does each sentence support the main idea in the topic sentence?
7. Are the sentences smoothly linked?

Special types of paragraphs

8. If an opening paragraph, does it indicate the subject of the essay? Is it designed to interest the reader?
9. If a concluding paragraph, does it sum up the major ideas of the essay? Does it provide a convincing ending?
10. If a transitional paragraph, does it link what has gone before with what is to come?

---

(3) Transitional paragraphs

Paragraphs sometimes serve as transitions from one idea to another. As you saw in paragraph 45, transitional paragraphs may be as short as one sentence that sums up what went before (usually in a subordinate clause) and shows where the thought will now lead (usually in the main clause). Such a paragraph is usually short because the writer intends it to be merely a signpost.

■ **Exercise 8**   Revise the following student paragraph.

48   My friend Michelle often lends her textbooks, her class notes, and even her clothes. Borrowers seldom return them. Of course, some people are luckier than Michelle. The other day, when two "hungry" boys asked my roommate for spare dimes, he quickly reached for his billfold, but they beat him to it and ran off. Again, a motorist ran out of gasoline: and when my sister Alicia stopped to help him, she parked too near the mainstream of traffic. Her brand new Honda got sideswiped.

■ **Exercise 9**   The following student essay appears without paragraphs. Indicate where the essay might be divided into paragraphs.

Ronnie A. Ward

The faded yellow 5 × 8-inch card, taped at the head of the plain pine coffin, read: "Ronnie A. Ward, 51960573, died from wounds received during an armed conflict with the enemy, September 14, 1967, Republic of Viet Nam." Ronnie had now given all of himself. Ronnie A. Ward, born July 10, 1949, Wichita, Kansas, was the first of four children. Most people considered Ronnie as being short for a boy. At eighteen he was only 5'5" tall and weighed 110 pounds, but what he lacked in height, Ronnie made up for with his warm smile, soft voice, and patience and understanding. He had brown eyes and short brown hair that complemented his fair skin. The first time I met Ronnie was in 1957, in grade school. Even then Ronnie was different from most kids his age. Ronnie would be playing with the kids in the neighborhood, and his mother would call him home to help with the house work or to watch his sisters and brothers. Ronnie never complained about having to help at home. He was twelve when his father died of Hodgkin's disease. Without being told or asked, Ronnie assumed the task of "man of the house." He helped by taking care of the house and by watching the younger kids in the evening, while his mother worked. When Ronnie was sixteen, he quit school and took on a full-time job because his mother's health was poor, and she could no longer work. Ronnie enjoyed school and was active in sports and dramatics, but gave these up knowing the family needed his help. He thought first about the family's needs before his own. On payday, Ronnie always managed to bring home some small gift for his sister and brothers to make their life a little more enjoyable. When

Ronnie turned eighteen, he decided to enlist in the Army, hoping to make more money in the service to send home for the family. I saw Ronnie two days before I left home myself to join the Army. The next time I saw Ronnie was August 1967, Quang Tri, South Viet Nam. Ronnie had been attached to the unit I was in. It was good to have a long-time friend in the same outfit. We talked often of the good times we had together during our early years in Wichita. Ronnie hadn't changed, still quiet-spoken, friendly, and considerate to all. With a smile on his face he was usually doing something for someone else, without asking or wanting anything in return. That was Ronnie's way for as long as I had known him. September 14, 1967, started out like any other day. Our unit had been on many ''sweep and destroy'' missions in the past. When word was given that today's mission was to advance on a village in Quang Tri Province, suspected of being a Viet Cong stronghold, everything seemed superficially routine. On the outskirts of the village our unit stopped its advance to wait for nightfall. As Ronnie and I lay in the hot and humid stench of rot and decay in the woven wall-like underbrush of the jungle, we talked of home. Ronnie said he was going to send his mother some extra money this month, because his sister needed braces. He was worried that his sister's good looks would be spoiled if she did not get braces. At dusk our unit entered the village and started a hut-to-hut search for the Viet Cong. Ronnie entered one hut in which we heard a baby crying. He saw the half-naked baby lying in a homemade cradle, picked it up, and headed for the door, unaware that the cradle was a booby trap. I saw Ronnie standing in the doorway of the hut holding the baby in his arms when the booby trap exploded. Ronnie was blown out of the hut with the baby still in his arms and held tight to his chest. His left arm was blown off at the shoulder from the explosion. Blood was pouring across his face as I ran to him. He looked up at me with a half-frightened and sad look on his face. He didn't ask ''Am I going to die?'' Ronnie didn't complain about the pain either; instead he asked in a shallow soft voice, ''Is the baby all right? Is the baby alive?'' I picked up the still crying baby and held it out for Ronnie to see. Ronnie didn't say anything. He just smiled, reached for the baby, then died. All his life, Ronnie gave what he could of himself to others; and, in the end, he gave more than most. Ronnie gave his life.
—NICHOLAS J. WEBER

■ **Exercise 10**   Prepare for a class discussion of the strengths and weaknesses of the following professional and student paragraphs.

49   Can hailstorms be suppressed? Attempts to modify them have been made throughout history. The Romans shot arrows toward the storm. In medieval Europe, church bells were rung—a practice that tended to increase the casualty rate because lightning often struck the unprotected belfry, electrocuting the bell ringer. With advancing technology, the hail cannon, a device that fired a ring of smoke and gas instead of a solid missile, became popular. The sound of the discharge was supposed to break up the hailstones. It at least provided some psychological comfort. Cannons were later replaced by rockets, which exploded aloft with a resounding bang. None of these remedies had any obvious success.
—JOHN HALLETT, ''When Hail Breaks Loose''

50   Among the things I find hardest to do is to let a ringing telephone go unanswered. Suppose, for example, I have a good reason for not answering it. The first two rings I can easily endure, and then I start counting the rings. After I hit six, I wonder why it keeps ringing. Could it be that Dad has had another heart attack? When I finally do lift the receiver, no one is there. For the rest of the day or until it rings again and I answer it on the first ring, I have no peace of mind.
—STUDENT

51   Whatever their calling, most people spend most of their time doing chores. A chore may be defined as a somewhat disagreeable or boring task that must be done in order to accomplish one's real objective. The detective has his legwork and endless checking of details. The athlete and the musician practice what they already know. The politician makes his appearances; the lawyer prepares his briefs. Most human achievements conceal a vast, hidden background of chores, a world of routine humdrum that no one really likes but that everyone recognizes as necessary.   —STUDENT

52   A soap opera deals with the plights and problems brought about in the lives of its permanent principal characters by the advent and interference of one group of individuals after another. Thus, a soap opera is an endless sequence of narratives whose only cohesive element is the eternal presence of its bedeviled and beleaguered principal characters. A narrative, or story sequence, may run from eight weeks to several months. The ending of one plot is always hooked up with the beginning of the next, but the connection is unimportant and soon forgotten. Almost all the villains in the small-town daytime serials are émigrés from the cities—gangsters, white-collar criminals, designing women, unnatural mothers, cold wives, and selfish, ruthless, and just plain cussed rich men. They always come up against a shrewdness that outwits them or destroys them, or a kindness that wins them over to the good way of life.
—E. B. WHITE, ''Soapland''

The Whole Composition

32

Arrange and express your ideas effectively.

An essay (also called a theme or paper) is a short nonfiction composition, the content and organization of which are guided by a single controlling idea, the *thesis*. Just as a topic sentence directs the development of a paragraph, the thesis, or controlling statement, limits and sums up the point of the essay. And just as a paragraph is a series of sentences developing one topic, an essay is a series of paragraphs arranged to elaborate and support the thesis. Both an essay and a paragraph contain similar parts: a controlling sentence, supporting explanation and details, logical transitions, and a conclusion. Both consist of a beginning, a middle, and an end; both are unified and coherent.

An essay has a *purpose*. Depending on what that purpose is, the writer will choose one of the four basic kinds of writing:

Narration. The purpose of a narrative essay is to tell a story—to relate a sequence of events in chronological order. Usually the writer's further purpose is to make a stated or implied point about the significance of the events.

Description. In a descriptive essay, the purpose is to evoke a mood or create a dominant impression about a person, place, or object. Using concrete, vivid images that appeal to the reader's senses, the writer tries to make the reader see, hear, or feel what the writer saw, heard, or felt.

Exposition. Here the purpose is to inform, clarify, define, explain, or analyze. Most college writing—themes, research papers, essay examinations, lab reports—is expository, that is, students are asked to explain or clarify their ideas. Essays that explain the causes of stress, that classify types of students, that contrast solar heating and wood-burning stoves, that define the word *romantic,* or that analyze the effects of television on family meals—all are examples of exposition.

Argumentation. An argumentative essay attempts to convince, bring about an event, or move the reader to action. In an orderly way the writer analyzes a problem, offers a solution, acknowledges opposing solutions, and restates the one given in the essay. The appeal to the reader may be strictly logical or it may involve the reader's emotions.

Essays have many purposes, such as to entertain, inspire, or persuade, so the writer usually combines several kinds of writing, with one of them predominant. For example, an essay persuading legislators to require helmets for all motorcycle riders might include a description of a car-motorcycle collision, the story of how the accident happened, and an explanation of how helmets are designed to absorb the shock of impact.

An essay is designed for a particular *audience.* Both its content and its diction must be appropriate to the background, needs, and interests of that audience. If the topic is the pros and cons of buying a condominium in California, the audience does not want to read about the difficulties of moving from Omaha to Los Angeles, either along with or in place of the topic. If the writer is a specialist, and the audience shares the writer's expertise, the essay can have a more sophisticated thesis and use more specialized language than an essay on the same subject written for a general audience that knows little or nothing about the subject.

Writing an essay is a *process*—a series of steps in which writers expand and organize their ideas according to their central purpose and their audience. First, they choose and limit their subject **(32a).** Then, after they have collected ideas about their subject **(32b),** they arrange the main ideas into a pattern **(32c).** Their next step is to shape the sentence that controls the entire essay—the thesis statement **(32d)**—a step in which choosing and evaluating their audience **(32e)** is a crucial factor. Finally, they prepare a rough or working outline **(32f)** as an aid in writing the various drafts of the essay **(32 g–i).** As writers move through each of these steps, they may need to repeat one or more of them. For example, they may need to collect more ideas. Or they may write their essay only to discover that it does not develop the ideas announced in the thesis. They may thus have to revise their thesis, their paragraphs, or both; they may even have to choose another thesis.

No matter how much repetition of the steps is necessary, the goal is a clear statement of the thesis, developed with coherent and unified supporting information. Beginning writers sometimes think that experienced writers produce a single draft of flawless prose—that they start with the title

and proceed from the introduction through the conclusion without ever stopping to rearrange the order of ideas, to eliminate wordiness, or to revise diction. The fact is that experienced writers follow the same steps described above—selecting, writing, and revising again and again—until the essay is a unified, coherent, and well-developed statement of ideas.

■ **Exercise 1**   Prepare for a discussion of the following essay by deciding which of the four kinds of writing predominates and which kinds, if any, are secondary.

Some Preservation Definitions

1   Preserved. This is the word a lot of people use to describe what they have done to a building or area of a certain age. They "preserved" the colonial village, although only half of it was around before the Revolution (and the second half not until yesterday). They "preserved" the home of the town founder, even though they first had to go out and buy the bricks and the mortar and the framing and the windows and the roof. They "preserved" the old factory by gutting the interior and making three floors where only one had existed, the better to put in more boutiques. They "preserved" the bank by sandblasting its façade. They "preserved" the old house, after moving it, by stripping the Victorian additions and ordering out for colonial-style replacements. And they "preserved" the neighborhood by demanding that the new building down the street be Federal-style and not that avant-garde thing, even if it would have been the right size and its materials would have fit right in with all the others on the block.

2   Demolition is not just a wrecking ball swinging against brick and mortar. Any building or structure or site that is not being cared for properly is being demolished. Demolition can be inaction; in fact, it often is, destroying buildings and their environments by neglect. Demolition can also take place when people think they are preserving. Out of slavish devotion to what they believe or have been told the past is, they strip real structures and put on deceptive masks, or tear down the really old and construct new "old" buildings, actions that stem from misconceptions of what preservation is and can be.

3   At one time, everyone who thought about it had a fairly sure idea of what constituted historic preservation: it was an effort to save buildings that were considered important for one reason or another in the development of the country. But because preservation now covers a broad spectrum of activities, what "preserving" means is not as simple any more. In its dictionary sense, preservation means saving something pretty much the way it is. This often takes much work to accomplish. On the most basic level, it means keeping things in good condition by maintaining them. According to general priorities supported by the National Trust for Historic Preservation and other preservationists: "It is better to preserve than repair, better to repair than restore, better to restore than reconstruct." In other words, the less done to good structures the better, and if it is done in time, more extensive work will not be necessary.

4   By the time most preservationists enter the picture, a structure has usually passed the point of needing only the status quo—preservation in its literal meaning. Because the world is not static, buildings too must adapt to change, especially if they are to continue their prime function of use. Thus, preservation means not stasis but an effort to ward off detrimental changes—to maintain the qualities and contributions that made a structure or area a candidate for protection in the first place.

5   Maintenance of existing buildings is a vital means of preservation. Old farms can be maintained by being farmed, old business structures by being rented, and old houses by being lived in. Preservation by maintenance is taking place in areas like East Baltimore, where householders scrub the marble steps of their row houses, proud of a trademark that is both useful and beautiful and that gives residents a sense of identity. Preservation is taking place in towns where county courthouses and city halls are maintained in use either as courthouses or for other services because they are recognized as unique symbols of civic success and continuity. Some department store and business owners are proud of their landmarks and take steps to assure their preservation because the condition they are in serves as a visible statement of the continuing success of the owners' enterprises. Preservation is also happening where civic organizations keep the park bandstand painted and in use or where they persuade their government to exercise control over the kinds of commercial signs used in a downtown area.

6   Although some may not even know the term, all of the people involved in these activities may properly be called preservationists. They value their property, the structures and sites they have collectively inherited, and appreciate them as factors that create the quality of life in their environment. The stabilization and the maintenance of older buildings without undue change is a holding action against the tooth of time. —TONY P. WRENN and ELIZABETH D. MULLOY

32a

Choose a subject that interests you and limit it properly.

(1) Choosing a subject.

Whether you have been assigned a subject for an essay or must choose one, you should ask yourself what you know about it, for writers write best about what they know best. While every writer brings a unique set of experiences to the writing task, not all of those experiences will generate a good essay. Although writers often discover what they know as they write, they are also able to gauge the extent of their knowledge as they list possible subjects.

These following questions will suggest some areas to explore as you discover what subjects you are interested in and know most about:

1. If you weren't writing an essay, what would you rather be doing? Why?
2. What things are you good at?
3. What subjects are you least interested in writing about?
4. If you could solve any one problem, what would it be? Why? How would you solve it?
5. Which of the following areas do you enjoy talking or reading about?

sports	ecology	famous people
hobbies	space exploration	marriage
politics	money	drama
religion	parenting	psychology
television	careers	philosophy
advertising	movies	energy
food	music	travel

The answers to some of these questions may suggest subjects. One student, Shawn Redfield, answered as follows:

I'd rather be—sleeping, stripping that old rocking chair, drawing political cartoons, washing and waxing the car
I'm good at—finding bargains, listening to other people's problems, coaching soccer, cutting firewood

I like talking about—my favorite country-western bands, my job in the antique shop, my plans to run for Congress

Ideas that occur in more than one answer are usually a logical starting point. In addition to Shawn's obvious interest in politics, the answers above suggest an essay on antiques (stripping a rocking chair, finding bargains, working in an antique shop). But what about antiques? One subject can produce many possible topics. *Antiques* names a general category, and to write one essay that treats every aspect of it is impossible—not even a whole book is sufficient for a thorough discussion.

(2) Limiting the subject.

How can an essay subject—in this case, antiques—be limited or narrowed? One way is to reduce the general category (subject) to increasingly restricted ones (topics). The more restricted the category, the more specific the idea. Shawn Redfield came up with three possible topics by limiting the general category of antiques in three different ways:

1. *Antiques*

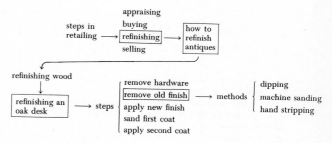

Limited topic: the factors that determine whether a refinisher uses dipping, sanding, or hand stripping to remove the finish from an old desk.

2. *Antiques*

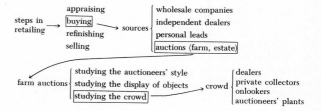

Limited topic: the motivation of bidders at farm auctions—why are they bidding? Who is most likely to drive the bidding beyond the appraised price? Why?

3. *Antiques* (Note how the two false starts below lead Shawn to his third topic.)

(a) American vs. European $\begin{cases} \text{expense} \\ \text{availability} \\ \text{condition} \end{cases}$

all American and European antiques? (no—too many to cover, and I don't know anything about European antiques)

(b) American antiques

		business	
	home		
17th century	furniture	professional	trades
18th century	decorations	surveyors' instruments	firemen's badges
19th century	utensils	pharmacists' mortars	carpenters' planes
		and pestles	blacksmiths' bellows
		dentists' cabinets	

all types for all three centuries?
(no—too many categories)

(c) American 19th-century antiques

manufactured			handmade (primitives)		
china			butter molds		wooden rakes
glassware	kitchen	bowls	farm	plows
	utensils	spatulas	tools	wagon seats
		measuring cups		horseshoes

Limited topic: the reasons for collecting American primitives

Another way to narrow the subject is to consider the four kinds of writing. Narration, description, exposition, argumentation—each of these is more appropriate to certain subjects than to others, and each suggests limits for an essay. When these four kinds are applied to the subject of antiques, the following topics might result:

1. *Narration:* a story relating how cleaning out an attic created an instant collection; a story about an elderly woman's preference for the objects of her youth rather than for modern things
2. *Description:* a description of an antique shop crammed with hundreds of items; a description of the apparent restraint of bidders at a formal auction
3. *Exposition:* an explanation of how to distinguish fakes and reproductions from genuine antique furniture; an explanation of the training programs for people who want to become auctioneers
4. *Argumentation:* an argument against buying antiques as a means of financial investment; an argument for developing a bidding strategy to use at auctions

■ **Exercise 2**   Draw up a list of six subjects that interest you and about which you know something. Ask questions to produce two properly limited topics for one of the subjects. Apply the four kinds of writing to produce two limited topics for another subject.

32b

Collect ideas about your topic.

From his three possible topics about antiques, Shawn Redfield has decided to explore the reasons people collect primitives—antique handmade objects. To generate ideas for the explanations and supporting details he needs, he may use one or all of the following methods.

(1) List-making.

Like grocery lists and lists of things to do, lists of ideas to include in an essay help you accomplish a task. Just as you jot down grocery items as they occur to you—not according to the order of the aisles at the store—you list ideas without regard to their order in the essay. And just as you delete some foods and add others during the walk through the store, you will delete some ideas and add others as you work out a plan of organization. The important thing, however, is to have ideas to organize. Write down every idea that occurs to you; save their organization for later.

Here is Shawn Redfield's list for his primitives topic:

antiques that are handmade or handcrafted = primitives
sometimes made at home, sometimes not
not very smoothly finished
practical furniture—beds, dressers, dry sinks, pie safes, rocking chairs, chests, cupboards
household things—butter molds, bowls
functional
also handcrafted metal things (usually not homemade)
blacksmiths—candlesticks, flatirons, pots, skillets, tools, horseshoes, nails, axles
tinsmiths—pie-safe panels, candlesticks—?
pewtersmiths—such a word?—candlesticks, spoons, picture frames, mugs, plates, pitchers, ladles, teaspoons, porridge bowls
brasssmiths(?)—pots, kettles, keys, teakettles, ladles, candlesticks, bells
copper—teakettles, pitchers, wash boilers
craftsmanship of unique pieces not all that polished
antique—defined how?
primitive—defined how?
estate or farm auctions—a good place to look
prices cheaper than really fine furniture, but prices on both keep going up
they remind me of stories Grandpa told me about using them
what did they use to mow grass—were there lawns?
go with furniture today; can still be used today
some are used for decoration, others are put to work—old dough bowl now a centerpiece, flatirons = bookends, etc.
inexpensive—lots of them around
they're popular
they'll increase in value

(2) Asking who, what, why, where, when, and how.

To be sure they have covered all aspects of a story, reporters ask the six questions above. The same questions can help you explore your topic. Here are some of the ideas Shawn came up with, asking himself the journalist's questions:

Who?	Who collects handcrafted antiques? Who appraises primitives?
What?	What items appeal most to me? What's the difference between a primitive and a collectible?
Why?	Why is collecting primitives popular? Why are there more pieces of primitive furniture than fine furniture around?
Where?	Where can the novice collector find out about the different kinds of primitives? Where in the United States are primitives most likely to be found?
When?	When is the best time, if there is one, to buy primitives? When did the interest in primitives start?
How?	How is *primitive* defined? How can a collection of farm implements be displayed? How does a person begin collecting? How do I re-cane a chair or clean up a pair of candlesticks?

(3) Asking questions based on paragraph-developing methods (see Section 31).

The same strategies that are used to expand a paragraph may suggest some ways to approach a topic. For example:

Narration—How do I respond to something I've just added to my collection? What do I remember about starting my collection?

Process—How was a rocking chair made? How were fields plowed? How is market value determined?

Description—How can the antique shop I work in be described? What is the chief impression conveyed by a kitchen decorated with primitives?

Classification—What types of people attend auctions? What types of primitives can I use in my home?

Analysis—What are the parts of the collecting process? What was the function of some of the farm tools?

Definition—What does *primitive* mean? What does *antique* mean?

Comparison and contrast—What's the difference between a cupboard and a hutch? How do Shaker furniture and Pennsylvania Dutch furniture differ in style?

Example—What objects represent the typical farmhouse of the mid-1800's? What objects were made at home? What objects were made by craftsmen?

Cause and effect—What causes people to collect primitives? What effect has the popularity of primitives had on buying them? How can the popularity of collecting primitives be interpreted? What effects did daily use have on primitives?

■ **Exercise 3**   From the narrowed topics you produced in Exercise 2, select the two you know most about. Use list-making, the journalist's questions, and methods of development to collect ideas for both.

32c

Arrange your ideas into a general pattern.

To make sense out of all the information you gather, you will need to identify your main ideas. Once those are clear, you can match details, facts, examples, definitions, and explanations with the corresponding main points. Set aside anything unrelated, no matter how proud or fond of it you may be. The object is to sift through the abundance of ideas you have collected, distinguishing the main ones first, and then the supporting ones.

Shawn Redfield has decided that he will try to explain why collecting primitives appeals as a hobby. On his list of ideas are these eight reasons:

1. craftsmanship of unique pieces not all that polished
2. prices cheaper than fine furniture
3. reminders of Grandpa's things and stories
4. go with furniture today
5. some are used decoratively, others put to work
6. inexpensive—lots of them around
7. they're popular
8. they'll increase in value

Essentially these boil down to three main reasons:

1. moderate expense (reasons 2, 6, 8)

2. the contrast of tradition and novelty (reasons 1, 3)
3. scope for individual taste—lots to choose from (reasons 4, 5, 6)

Notice that reason 7 is redundant and has been omitted, and that reason 8 is only indirectly related to expense. Working through the list and adding details suggested by the key words, Shawn now begins to supply information for each reason.

1. inexpensive
   prices of primitives vs. prices of antiques
   produced in quantity, common in every household
   mahogany desk ($5,000) vs. teakettle ($50), butter bowl ($30), tin candlestick ($15)
2. craftsmanship of pieces offers contrast of tradition and novelty
   homemade, not smoothly finished vs. polished, skilled finish of modern things
   durable
   reminders of Grandpa's stories
3. suit individual tastes
   lots to choose from, relatively little duplication—candlesticks of pewter, brass, iron, tin
   appropriate for either decorative or functional use
   decorative—butter mold, spoon set
   functional then, functional now
   functional—flatirons as bookends, chests as coffee tables, quilts as tablecloths

Shawn will continue to add supporting ideas as he writes, but only if they develop the points he is making. Whether an idea was in his original list or suggested by the process of writing, he will have to discard it if it does not belong with the three main ideas.

■ **Exercise 4**   For each of the following topics, identify the unrelated material.

1. arranging for house care during a two-week vacation—stopping the mail; vacuuming and dusting; locking the doors; mowing the lawn.
2. definition of *friend*—distinction between a friend and a neighbor; anecdote of someone who smuggled bacon and doughnuts through your bedroom window so you could feed unexpected visitors; titles of three essays on friendship.
3. story showing the value of budgeting money—definition of *money*; having to pass up a stereo system at 40 percent off; peace of mind from knowing the rent is paid.

■ **Exercise 5**   For one of the topics for which you have collected information, arrange your ideas into a general pattern.

32d

Shape a thesis statement.

The thesis statement is a single declarative sentence that announces the writer's attitude toward the subject and suggests the essay's overall pattern of organization. It is the single most important sentence in the entire essay. If it is lucid and precise, the essay usually is too. Although a thesis statement may be implied or delayed until the closing paragraph, as a rule it is stated as the final sentence of the introduction. If the introduction is a single paragraph, then the thesis concludes it; if the introduction is two or more paragraphs long, the thesis ends the final introductory paragraph. Placing a sentence after the thesis may weaken its emphasis, and open-

through the center of topic [handwritten annotation]

ing the essay with the thesis seldom prepares the reader for either the topic or the writer's approach.

Like a road map showing a driver's route on interstate highways, a thesis statement directs the movement of ideas through an essay. An effective thesis statement is incisive, offering specific guidelines to the essay's content and organization. It limits the scope of the topic so that the thesis is appropriate for the length of the paper. An effective thesis statement does not state the obvious. Nor does it use vague, abstract terms (such as *really, things, great, nice, very*), weak verbs (*to be, to have, to seem*), or the passive voice (as in "Primitives have been called the poor person's antiques"), which weaken the force of the thesis.

Compare the following thesis statements:

1. It's really interesting to collect things.
2. There are three reasons to collect primitives.
3. Weekends are spent bidding against other collectors when you collect primitives.
4. Bidding successfully for a sugar scoop indicates that the collector of primitives knows both the value of the prize and the limits of the competition.
5. Stripping a painted table by using ammonia and steel wool is easy, but it exposes the wood to a harsh chemical; using a power sander saves time, but it requires an even, light touch to avoid gouging the wood.

The first thesis statement gives no indication of either the topic or the approach; it is an all-purpose, say-nothing sentence that could lead to any number of different essays—which is exactly why it is useless. A thesis should suit only the essay it governs. Thesis statement 2 is weak for the same reason. It could fit several different essays with entirely different sets of reasons. Including the three reasons in the thesis would provide a more definite focus.

Thesis statement 3 provides only a general subject and no idea of the essay's organization. The reader might well ask: Who is meant by *you*? Are the other collectors also collectors of primitives? Under what conditions are they bidding against each other? Why is the competition limited to weekends?

Just as a general subject is narrowed, a general thesis statement can also be revised to make it more specific. Thesis statement 4 is appropriate for an essay on human behavior, while thesis statement 5 is appropriate for an essay on the advantages and disadvantages of two methods of stripping furniture.

Shawn Redfield produced the following thesis statements for his essay, and rightly decided that the fifth was the best of them all:

1. Primitives are inexpensive and adaptable. [weak verb, inexact topic, imprecise adjectives]
2. Inexpensive primitives are a combination of the traditional and the personal. [unclear whether all primitives are inexpensive or only inexpensive ones combine the two features]
3. Collecting primitives offers an inexpensive way to express individuality. [unclear what a "way to express individuality" means]
4. There are three reasons for the popularity of collecting primitives. [reasons not specified]
5. Collecting primitives will grow in popularity because primitives are relatively inexpensive, blend well with current trends in home decorating, and adapt to individual tastes. [contains an assertion and offers supporting reasons; clearest of the five]

Once you have created a clear and precise thesis statement, you have done the most difficult part of the job, for the thesis now determines what you will discuss when, and you have simply to fulfill your announced commitment to ideas and structure.

■ **Exercise 6** Improve each of the following thesis statements.

1. Baseball and softball are different but fun.
2. My summer job taught me I could do anything as well as a man could.
3. Photography is an interesting hobby for anyone who doesn't know anything about it.
4. Many factors must be considered when deciding to become a pharmacist.
5. It's the car to buy for high gas mileage and low maintenance costs.
6. For a fun vacation that tests your ingenuity, try wilderness camping.

■ **Exercise 7** Create a thesis statement for your topic.

32e

Choose and evaluate your audience.

Your audience deserves your respect. Whether generalists or specialists on the topic, your readers are entitled to a clear thesis statement, coherent explanations, logical transitions, and exact diction. The more precisely you define your audience, the more you can show your respect for their intelligence and curiosity. Writers who know their audience can develop examples or draw comparisons from their shared experiences. And such writers also know which terms, if any, must be defined and how fully. Further, if they know their audience is indifferent or hostile toward the subject, they will consider that too.

In short, establishing the audience for your essay helps to determine your tone and attitude. Only after you have evaluated your audience should you decide to be witty or ironic, reverent or impudent, for an inappropriate tone will offend your readers and reduce their willingness to consider your ideas.

Use the following guidelines for evaluating your audience:

1. What does the audience already know about the topic?
2. What is the attitude of the audience toward the topic?
3. Is the audience interested in the topic? Why? Why not?
4. For what purpose is the audience likely to read about the topic?
5. What kind of information will the audience accept as convincing support?

You can assume that most of the writing you do in college is for a *general* audience—educated and intellectually curious adults with a variety of political, ethnic, religious, and social backgrounds. Such an audience is potentially interested in any subject, so it does not need to have its interest aroused. It does expect, however, that the writer will present the subject in nontechnical language and will define or illustrate any specialized terms. For example, a general audience interested in the subatomic particles known as quarks wants a thorough but nontechnical explanation of how they function, but it does *not* want to read an academic research report to find out. (On the other hand, a group of physicists debating the evidence for quarks would expect a thorough and highly technical argument from a colleague writing an essay for a professional journal.)

Any topic can be shaped for any audience—general or specialized—depending on the knowledge of the writer and the background of the audience. But it is not possible to write for both kinds of audience at once, since their needs and expectations are entirely different. Here, for example, are two thesis statements on the topic of opening moves in chess:

GENERAL

Having mastered the moves of the pieces, the novice chess player needs to learn several standard openings, such as Ruy Lopez, Sicilian Defense, and Queen's Gambit. [appropriate for a chess beginner, who needs to have each of these strategies described]

SPECIALIZED

Although some modern chess theorists argue that if White opens P-K4, White's game is lost, this opening provides more flexibility than P-Q3. [appropriate for a reader who knows chess notation, who understands what the two moves involve, and who is interested in a controversial defense of P-K4]

■ **Exercise 8** Prepare to discuss how to shape each of the following topics for the audiences specified.

1. rock music: college students, country-western fans, composers
2. your school: state taxpayers, high school seniors, alumni
3. off-campus housing: city commissioners, school administrators, students, property owners
4. potatoes: home gardeners, commercial growers, nutritionists
5. changing attitudes toward marriage and the family: general audience, religious groups, sociologists

■ **Exercise 9** Read Wilfrid Sheed's essay "A Thought a Day Isn't Enough." Be prepared to discuss his attitude toward his subject and his audience (college seniors).

A Thought a Day Isn't Enough

1   When I was, say, twenty I thought I was a pretty bright and interesting fellow, although I was much too polite to show it. And I wondered why people of, say, forty were not twice as bright and interesting and so on up the line. A few, very few, of them were. Most of them seemed to get a little bit duller every year. They had fewer and fewer things to talk about—who are you going to vote for; how about those Yankees, etc. Their minds actually seemed to have shrunk and they preferred the company of people in the same boat, fellow dentists or morticians, who would never bring up anything new. This meant that there was either some dreadful biological law at work whereby old age sets in on the very day you leave campus or else there was a massive national act of laziness, of just giving up, performed every year at this time. Only later when I tried it myself did I come to realize how difficult it is to remain alive when nobody's watching and making you. Because we have this quaint custom of getting all our education over with early in life, we find ourselves fussed over excessively for sixteen years and then just like that abandoned and left for dead. This process is known as graduation, and welcome to it.

2   Of course, only in extreme cases do graduates become dull immediately. I've seen some of them do it on the way out of the final examinations but usually the first little gray hairs of the mind don't begin to show for ten years or so. At first, new jobs, marriages, relocations, etc., are stimulating enough. You don't need books or new ideas for a while. So you learn to live without them and you learn all too well. The world of work actually encourages this narrowness if you let it. Outside interests only slow you down in the rat race anyway. So the professional world becomes a kind of Franz Kafka mansion where the rooms get spiritually smaller and grayer the further up the stairs you go, and this is known as promotion.

3   You start out in a large bright space with lots of friends and lots of windows to look out of, but the windows are removed one by one so you can concentrate better on your work until you reach top management where you live, to judge from the conversation, in almost total darkness. Since this is the exact opposite of the way it looks, because the offices actually seem to get bigger, many people sometimes go right to the top without knowing what's happening to them. I have met some quite prominent businessmen who had less to say for themselves than New York taxi drivers. Perhaps that's too high a standard but these people hadn't read anything or heard of anybody outside their own tiny world in years and years. Even their politics were simple-minded. They would be ashamed to know so little about football. I don't read novels they say—clank, there's a window gone. I never get to the movies, theater, opera.

4   As my father used to say about people who don't read poetry—neither does a cow. I should add that I'm not just talking about business businessmen but about doctors, lawyers, the works. In every case, they claim that the pressure of work is walling them in. Yet in every field you're likely to find that the very best people do miraculously make time for books and the arts and it's the second-raters who don't. So time isn't the real problem. The problem is character. Character, once upon a time, referred exclusively to work. It can also be applied to play. It requires will power to stay playful, to keep your mind open. It takes character to stay alive. And it is not only between nine and five that people age. There are plenty of unemployed bores who work at it around the clock. Whenever you find yourself repeating the same thoughts in exactly the same words, you're jogging along with Father Time and gaining. Listen in on any barroom or even executive lunch and you will find people eagerly looking for ways to say the things they said a million times before. If you pull something new on them, they will look stunned and then drag it back somehow to their old turf. "As I always say" is their motto, and did you ever find yourself using this phrase yourself? You are in the club. And the next generation will be thinking, how did he get to be so dull?

5   The fact is that staying intellectually alive is very hard work. They made you do it in school, so you did it. But now that nobody's making you do it, you'll probably stop. Nobody marches you into the bookstore anymore, so you stop attending as with church. After all, what do books know anyway? You'll learn from life itself. But your particular life would fill no more than one slim volume in a library, and all around it there would be oceans of life in the other books. A book is just a stranger talking brilliantly; he's probably better company than you'll meet in a saloon. After all, he's usually sober and giving you the best hours of his day and he's forcing you to look at things in a new way and face new experience. It's no use saying, "As I was saying," to a book; incidentally, the fact that I happen to be in the book business myself has nothing to do with all this, nor the fact that I'm counting on this generation to keep me in cigars and caviar. You can read other people's books if you insist. I'm sure equally impassioned cases can be made for music and painting, and there's no need to quarrel.

6   An educated European assumes, often to my own embarrassment, that a college man will at least know the names of the world's leading composers, painters, architects and what they've been up to lately. So, since a patriotic note is also appropriate to these occasions, I call on you simply as Americans to stop being the Mortimer Snerds of the Western world, the Fred Flintstones, and to pick up your hem of the Western tradition. It is not too late to recover from your rotten educations, not the one you got here in this excellent place, but from the tube and lesser schools. Simply read a book. If not today, well at least by the end of next year. And if you repeat the dose often enough, you will have done more to stay young than all the jogging and rolling put together. And not just stay young. You will have pulled that one-in-a-million trick—growing up. And you will be twice as good twenty years from now as you think you are today.

—WILFRID SHEED

32f

Develop a working plan or rough outline.

You will find it easier to shape an essay from all the elements discussed thus far—subject, narrowed topic, thesis, audience, tone, attitude—by preparing a rough outline that shows the pattern in which you will develop your ideas as well as the sequence in which you will arrange them. (To develop a topic or sentence outline see **33d**.)

(1) Choosing a sequence for your ideas.

One of the patterns in **31a(3)**—question-answer, problem-solution, or topic-restriction-illustration—will give you a structure for your ideas. But you must also consider the sequence of ideas and paragraphs in the essay. If you choose the problem-solution pattern, for example, you must also consider in what order to present the elements of the problem and then the steps in the solution.

Your choice of sequence depends on the subject and purpose of your essay. In a description, for example, *spatial* order is useful to create an exact and orderly picture that enables the audience to recreate the scene: details move from left to right, from foreground to background, from top to bottom, and from inside to outside.

Exposition often uses *chronological* order, which presents events or details in a time sequence—from first to last, from past to present, and so forth. A chronological sequence would be appropriate in explaining how to make sourdough bread or in recounting the events that caused the Civil Rights movement.

The sequence of *climax* or *emphasis* moves from least important to most important. Just as the most emphatic point in a sentence occurs before the period, so the most emphatic point in an essay occurs before the conclusion. Thus, for example, a writer may choose to list the effects of a sunburn from the least dangerous to the most dangerous. Sometimes, however, when one item is of such immediate importance that it cannot be delayed, the order must be revised.

Finally, a writer may order ideas from general to specific or specific to general. An essay on the effects of the Mount St. Helens eruptions might proceed from specific, immediately recognized effects, such as volcanic ash in the streets, to general ones, such as long-term changes in weather patterns. Or an essay comparing two methods of decision-making might move from a discussion of general aims and appropriate situations for their use to the specific steps in each method.

(2) Preparing the rough outline.

In addition to listing the sequence of ideas, a rough outline should show the thesis, the audience, the purpose, and the general pattern.

Read "Do Animals Really Play?" by Eugene J. Walter, Jr., and then compare it with the rough outline that follows the essay.

Do Animals Really Play?

1   Do animals really "play"? Yes, and sometimes it's nothing more than fun and games, as when a monkey swings from a vine and tosses a stick, or when polar bears amuse themselves with stones, which they sometimes balance on their heads. Often, though, the seemingly frivolous antics we interpret as "play" are serious.

2   Play can be viewed as a pleasurable way of developing survival skills. The next time you're at a zoo, watch how the lion cubs frolic. One will crouch low against the ground, stalk slowly toward its littermate and then pounce on the surprised "victim." That usually touches off a knockabout wrestling match, with the cubs cuffing each other harmlessly. Such roughhouse sessions occur frequently among most carnivores such as wolves, tigers, cheetahs, raccoons, and coyotes. As they play, these young develop the abilities they need to become efficient predators.

3   Among monkeys and apes, playing helps lay the foundation for social order—a requirement for the survival of primate communities. Through play-fighting, a young monkey learns—in a harmless way—where it stands among its peers. The individuals that are most often victorious in the "matches" of infancy are most likely to assume a dominant role when they mature. Others that are lower on the social ladder learn their places early in life. This reduces more violent clashes among the monkeys as adults.

4   Many hoofed mammals engage in play, too. In herds of Mongolian wild horses, the breeding stallion will play-fight with his offspring, thereby helping the youngsters develop the agility they will need when confronted by predators or other stallions.

5   It appears that even whales play. A calf will perform all sorts of acrobatic gyrations on and around its mother, sliding over her tail, standing on its head or slapping its tail or flipper against the water's surface. It's possible that such play helps cement the bond between mother and offspring.

6   And what of birds—do they play? Some ornithologists are convinced that a few of the brainier ones do. The subject needs further inquiry. At this point, it's the mammals who appear to dominate the animal playground.

—EUGENE J. WALTER, JR.

Rough outline for "Do Animals Really Play?"

Thesis: The seemingly frivolous antics of animals' "play" prepare the young for adult life.

Audience: general (no specialized knowledge of animal behavior required)

Purpose: to explain why animals play by classifying types of play

Pattern: question-answer

1. Play develops survival skills.
    carnivores (lion cubs, wolves, tigers, cheetahs, raccoons, coyotes)
2. Play lays the foundation for social order.
    primates (monkeys)
3. Play develops agility.
    hoofed mammals (Mongolian wild horses)
4. Play develops mother-offspring bond
    marine mammals (whales)

5. Basis for choosing examples—mammals

Before Walters could write his essay, he took the following steps: he chose a subject (animal behavior), narrowed it (animal "play"), collected ideas (types of play and animals that engage in each type), chose a pattern (question-answer), and chose a sequence of ideas (general to specific—from a species-wide focus on survival skills to a narrow focus on the mother-offspring bond). Finally, he decided to shape his thesis for a general audience. Notice too that point 5 of the outline calls attention to the principle for choosing examples, which becomes an idea for the conclusion.

Here is Shawn Redfield's rough outline for his essay:

Rough outline for primitives essay

Thesis: Collecting primitives will grow in popularity because they are relatively inexpensive, they blend well with current home-decorating trends, and they adapt to individual tastes.

Audience: young couples beginning to decorate a home

Purpose: to explain the appeal of primitives to young homemakers

Pattern: question-answer—What explains the growing popularity of primitives?

1. primitives = common antiques of rural homes; hand-crafted if not homemade
   furniture—chairs, tables, cupboards, dressers, chests
   kitchen tools—spatulas, butter paddles, spoons, dough bowls, measuring cups, candlesticks, etc.
   farm tools—rakes, plows, scythes, axes
2. comparison of readily available primitives vs. hard-to-find antiques
   any of the above vs. paintings
   teakettles vs. secretary desks
3. home decoration trends today
   chrome and glass—contrasts in texture, style
   eclectic—primitives go with most things
   oak and calico—the appeal of tradition
4. primitives as collected by one person
   a unique collection possible because so many items available
   kinds of candlesticks
   original use or invented use
   quilt, flatiron, crock

■ **Exercise 10** Write a rough outline for your essay. (You may find that typing it rather than handwriting it helps you to see the essay's emerging structure.)

32g

Write and revise the first draft.

In this first draft Shawn Redfield concentrates on explaining each of the three parts of his thesis statement. He has kept his main ideas in mind by including the thesis and by underlining his topic sentences, and he has adhered to his outline. However, he has made no attempt to write an introduction or a conclusion nor has he supplied transitions from paragraph to paragraph. Read through the first draft and then look at Shawn's comments to himself.

FIRST DRAFT

Thesis statement: (Collecting primitives) will *awk* grow in popularity because (they) are relatively inexpensive, they blend well with current home-decorating trends, and they adapt to individual tastes.

1 intro needed

weak verb

Primitives (are) relatively inexpensive. Compared to collecting art or fine furniture, collecting primitives is very inexpensive. The current *clarify* economic crunch makes this feature more important now than ever. Primitives are the common handcrafted or homemade utensils of the rural home. *They* they were high priced when they *can I prove?* were new and are not expensive now. These *Does it belong?* objects were produced in quantity, which makes collecting them a hobby suitable to a large number of participants. Candlesticks, a skillet, a butter paddle, or a chest—compared *check sp.* to a silver tea service or a mahogony buffet these things are *show #* inexpensive but satisfying to collect.

2

Primitives (blend) well with current home- *right word?* decorating trends. Whether decorators choose sleek chrome and glass contemporary or cozy oak-and-calico decors, primitives add the contrast of tradition and the novelty of another lifestyle. The growing nostalgia *right word?* (infatuation) is well served by primitives. A 1929 Sears and Roebuck catalog among magazines of the day provides a nostalgic link with days *Why?* gone by. There is a certain air of security which surrounds the tools of people's ancestors. There is security in a child's toy made of cast iron, a barrel with walls of three-inch oak, or hatracks made of brass, security which is missing in today's disposable, plastic world. Besides security, primitives provide an interesting contrast in decor. The contrast between an iron dutch oven that came to this country in a wagon and a microwave oven flown in from Japan can add character to a kitchen. A coal scuttle as a magazine holder can supply the same character of contrast to an electrically heated living room. Home-decorating trends reflect people's needs. Tradition and novelty

3   **It's**
~~Its~~ a hobby that allows for "mass individuality"; Because of the way these objects were
produced, today *a lot* a lot of people could collect
the same thing, say candlesticks, yet no two
collections would be the same. *One person* ~~You~~ might
collect only brass candlesticks while *a second* ~~somebody~~
~~else~~ collected only pewter, and *a third* ~~somebody else~~
collected candlesticks of any metal. How do
primitives adapt to ~~your~~ individual tastes?
They serve a function in today's home, often a
function quite different from the original one.
An old crock may become a planter or a magazine
holder; it may even serve its original purpose.
A patchwork quilt may become a cushion, a chair
cover, a wall hanging, or a tablecloth. A flat-
iron may become a door stop, a bookend, or a
paperweight.   *Summary needed*

Primitives adapt to individual tastes.

The first draft of Shawn Redfield's essay is a preliminary
sketch of the essay under construction. Each paragraph has a
topic sentence and the order of the paragraphs follows that
announced in the thesis statement, but the answers to the
questions implied by the topic sentences are general and the
supporting examples few.

In revising this draft, Shawn needs to analyze every
word—beginning with the thesis—for clarity, coherence,
and adequate support. Shawn's notes to himself and your
own analysis might suggest the following revisions:

OVERALL
1. creating an introduction and a conclusion
2. rewording the thesis to avoid the awkwardness of *collecting primitives—they*
3. revising topic sentences so that they are not mechanical restatements of sections of the thesis

PARAGRAPH 1
4. choosing a strong verb for the topic sentence
5. defining *primitives* before beginning a discussion of their appeal
6. replacing general categories that illustrate the definition with specific examples
7. providing market values to prove the relative expenses
8. omitting *satisfying* if the idea isn't proven in the paragraph

PARAGRAPH 2
9. clarifying the topic sentence by deciding whether objects blend with trends or with other objects
10. considering whether the discussions of tradition and novelty are ordered in the paragraph according to emphasis

PARAGRAPH 3
11. deciding whether primitives adapt to one's tastes or reflect them and then, if necessary, revising the topic sentence
12. clarifying the relationship between the making of objects and their availability
13. adding a summary sentence

■ **Exercise 11** Reread the first draft of Shawn Redfield's
essay, marking everything that is unclear to you or that you think
needs revision. Compare your questions and comments with
those of your classmates.

■ **Exercise 12** Write the first draft of your essay.

32h
Write and revise the second draft.

Shawn Redfield's notes for changes to be made in the first
draft create guidelines for the writing of the second draft.
Using the rough outline (but not being rigidly committed to
it), the first draft, his comments on that draft, and new ideas
that occur as he writes, he creates a second version, which
begins to look like a conventional essay.

SECOND DRAFT   *add title*

1   *weak*
(There) exists an ever-growing concern about
people's leisure time. Since Clarence Darrow
opened the way for labor unions, the work week
has declined steadily. What will people do with
all this extra time? Photography, gardening,
and collecting are past(t)imes that have recently
grown in interest. Collecting what? Anything
and everything, from the expensive to the
inexpensive, from the useful to the useless--
rare coins, Edsels, duck decoys, mechanical
banks, and Beatles albums. Yet the would-be
collector with little money to spend need not
feel left out, for collecting primitives is an
inexpensive way to decorate an apartment or
house. Primitives are the common handcrafted or
homemade antique utensils of the rural home;
but they
they were high priced when they were new ~~and~~ are
not very expensive now. Because primitives are
relatively inexpensive, adapt to individual
tastes, and blend with current decorating
schemes, collecting primitives will continue to
(increase in popularity.) *Do I prove this? No,
I'm explaining the advantages of collecting.*

2   *Compared to collecting art or fine*
still weak
furniture, collecting primitives (is) very
inexpensive. Because (they) were produced in
quantity, they are now more common--and less
expensive--than one-of-a-kind items or objects
of limited use. A fifteen dollar vase or a *effec.*
potato digger does not require floating a loan, *examples?*
but (it) can make a unique addition to a
collector's home. ~~Cleaning~~ up an old horse
collar is not a major project, but (it) may result

*Cut—
takes
too
long
to get
to
thesis*

*prepare
reader
for this*

*in terms
of both
time and
money
awk.*

*awk. use
of it*

in a handsome frame for a mirror. Refinishing
an oak keg won't necessitate canceling the
bowling league membership, but it can provide a
one-of-a-kind end table. Collecting primitives
is not a hobby of kings, but it can be one for
anyone with an <u>average income.</u> *What's average?* 5

3 *individual taste shown by:*
1. selection
2. distinctive use

Collecting primitives not only suits modest
budgets but also individual tastes. In fact, it
allows for "mass individuality." While today
twenty international corporations may
manufacture the same item, in 1890 perhaps as
many as one hundred small but independent
companies made the same object, each company
crafting a distinctive design. Thus, today
hundreds of people may collect teakettles, for
example, yet a high degree of duplication would
be unlikely. ¶ While collectors are gathering
objects which say something about their likes
and dislikes and their knowledge of antiques and
history, they are also choosing objects which
may serve a function in today's home, though
often not the original function. An old crock
may become a planter or a magazine holder; a
patchwork quilt, a chair cover, a wall hanging
or a tablecloth; a flatiron, a door stop or a
bookend. <u>A collection of primitives is in some
ways a definition of the person who has
assembled them; they are chosen and used
according to the tastes of their owner.</u>

4   <u>Whether the collector prefers a sleek
chrome-and-glass or a cozy oak-and-calico decor,
primitives add the contrast of tradition and the
novelty of another lifestyle.</u> The cover of a
1929 Sears and Roebuck catalog among magazines
of <u>the day</u>, for instance, provides a nostalgic
link with days gone by. The <u>contrast</u> between an
iron dutch oven that ~~came to this country~~ *crossed the plains* in a
wagon and a microwave oven flown in from Japan
adds character to a kitchen. A coal scuttle
used as a magazine holder supplies the same
character of <u>contrast</u> to an electrically heated
living room. The preservation of these articles
from the past continues to fill the need for
<u>contrast</u> as it also reassures the need for
tradition. There is security in a child's toy
of cast iron, a barrel with walls of three-inch

unclear

overuse of contrast

oak, or a hat rack made of brass--security which
is missing in today's disposable, plastic world.
At once <u>removed from the present and a part of
it</u>, primitives satisfy decorating needs and, in
a large sense, family needs. → *clarify*

good idea

To sum up, collecting primitives is a
thriving, inexpensive pastime which allows
collectors to be at once individuals with unique
tastes and a part of the cultural tradition from
which their objects come. Whether the objects
are from the best of times or worst, collectors
delight in (their) history. Even as they dust and
arrange, sort and catalog, they are making room
for more.

not proven

fix ambiguous reference

After setting this second draft aside for a day or two,
Shawn Redfield once again analyzes his work, checking matters of content, organization, sentence structure, paragraph
unity, and diction. At this point, he is still more interested in
revising (that is, rethinking the scope and shape of his ideas
and how they relate to the thesis) than in proofreading (that
is, looking for errors in spelling, grammar, punctuation, and
mechanics).

New ¶?

When you revise your own work, use the checklist on
page 782, which will help you to evaluate all of the ideas in
your essay.

■ **Exercise 13**   Compare the first and second drafts of Shawn
Redfield's essay to see whether the revisions have answered your
questions. Are there any points that the writer made a note to
revise but did not? Which questions on the checklist still need
Shawn's attention?

■ **Exercise 14**   Write the second draft of your essay and then
answer all the questions on the revision checklist.

After using the revision checklist, Shawn makes three
major decisions:

1. to begin the introduction with collecting instead of with
   increased leisure time
2. to revise the thesis so that it clearly defines the three
   points covered in the essay
3. to divide the paragraph on individual tastes and to reserve
   the topic sentence until the second part

He will also select a title and correct errors in spelling, punctuation, grammar, and mechanics. The result is the final draft
on pages 782-83.

Overall considerations

1. Is every idea in the thesis stated clearly and given appropriate emphasis?
2. Does the thesis statement indicate the structure of the essay?
3. Does the sequence of paragraphs follow the order established in the thesis?
4. Do any terms require definition? If so, where should the definition(s) be introduced?
5. Do the body paragraphs prove the assertion of the thesis?
6. Are the ideas in the introduction logically related to the thesis?
7. Does the introduction attract the audience and prepare for the thesis?
8. Is there sufficient information to develop specific ideas?
9. Do the details, examples, and illustrations adequately support the ideas?
10. Is the conclusion complete without being abrupt?
11. Are all statements logically sound?
12. Is the tone consistent and appropriate for the audience?
13. Is the diction appropriate for both the content and the thesis?

Paragraphs

14. Is every paragraph controlled by a topic sentence, either stated or implied?
15. Does each paragraph explain and support its main idea? Are transitions within the paragraph clear and smooth?
16. Does each paragraph have a beginning, a middle, and an end?
17. Are the transitions between paragraphs adequate?

Sentences

18. Are the sentences varied in length? type? means of emphasis?
19. Are any words overused?
20. Are ideas within sentences given proper emphasis?
21. Are sentences grammatically correct?

Punctuation, Spelling, Mechanics

22. Are capitalization and abbreviations used correctly?
23. Have words at the ends of lines been divided correctly?
24. Are all words spelled correctly?
25. Are marks of punctuation used correctly and effectively?

32i

Prepare the final draft.

Now that Shawn Redfield has revised and proofread the second draft of his essay, he is ready to prepare a final copy. He is careful to extend the same conscientious effort that went into the writing process to the neatness and accuracy of his manuscript, for he thinks his ideas are significant, and he wants to convey that view by the appearance of his essay.

FINAL DRAFT

Primitives for the Present

1   What are at least one third of Americans doing with part of their leisure time? They are collecting anything and everything, from the expensive to the inexpensive, from the useful to the useless—— typewriters, jukeboxes, fishing tackle, fruit-crate labels, Edsels. Collecting some things, like jukeboxes or Edsels, is both expensive and time-consuming. Yet the would-be collector with limited money or time need not feel left out, for collecting primitives is an inexpensive and practical way to decorate a home. Primitives are the common antique utensils associated with nineteenth-century rural life; handcrafted or homemade rather than manufactured, primitives may be wooden, pottery, or leather. But kitchen tools and farm implements——butter bowls, skillets, candlesticks, wooden rakes, and scythes——most often come to mind. While they are relatively inexpensive, primitives reflect the tastes of the collector and complement modern lifestyles.

2   Compared to collecting fine furniture, collecting primitives costs little in either money or time. Like pieces of furniture, primitives were common to every household; yet they are still common——and thus less expensive than pieces of elaborate furniture. For example, a mahogany desk with inlaid panel doors may cost as much as five thousand dollars; while an iron teakettle with a porcelain finish may cost fifty. An afternoon spent cleaning great-grandmother's spoon set does not necessitate rescheduling the family vacation, but it does produce a grouping for the kitchen wall. Cleaning up an old horse collar is not a major project, but the result is a handsome mirror frame. Refinishing an oak keg won't mean cancelling the bowling league membership, but it does produce a rugged end table. Thus, collecting primitives is an economical pastime for anyone with limited money and time.

3   Collecting primitives suits not only modest budgets but also individual tastes. In fact, it allows for mass individuality. Unlike international corporations today, the small, independent companies of yesterday relied on the skills of their craftsmen. Because many companies made the same utensil, each company using a distinctive design (not to mention the work of self-employed craftsmen), today duplication among collections is relatively rare. Collections of candlesticks, for example, may contain only a few of the same most common ones. One person might collect only brass candlesticks while another collects only pewter and a third collects candlesticks of all kinds.

4   At the same time that collectors are gathering pieces which suit their taste, they are also choosing items they can use in a distinctive way, though the use is sometimes not the original one. For instance, an old crock becomes a planter or a magazine holder (it may even be used to make pickles or sauerkraut); a patchwork quilt may become a chair cover or a wall hanging; a flat-iron, a door stop or a bookend. Thus, a collection of primitives defines the person who has assembled them; they are chosen and used according to the tastes of their owner.

5   Whether collectors prefer the sleekness of chrome and glass or the coziness of oak and calico, primitives add the novelty of another lifestyle. An iron dutch oven that was brought to the .frontier in a wagon contrasts with a microwave flown in from Japan. A coal scuttle used as a magazine holder emphasizes the same contrast in an electrically heated living room. As preserving these articles from past life fills a need for variety, it also fills a need for continuity and tradition. There is security in a child's toy of cast iron, a barrel with walls of three-inch oak, or hat-racks made of brass--security which is missing in today's disposable, plastic world. At once removed from the present but a part of it, primitives satisfy decorating and personnel needs.

6   To sum up, collecting primitives allows collectors to be at once individuals with unique tastes and a part of the cultural tradition from which their objects came. Whether the primitives come from the best of times or the worst, collectors delight in the history of these objects and in the contrast they provide with the modern world. Even as collectors dust and arrange, sort and catalog, they are making room for more.

■ **Exercise 15**   Revise the final draft of Shawn Redfield's essay for emphasis and sentence variety. Notice, for example, that every sentence except the first is declarative, and that all but a few are either simple or complex. Try also to vary sentence lengths. What other changes would you suggest? Finally, proofread for any errors in spelling, punctuation, grammar, and mechanics.

■ **Exercise 16**   Prepare the final draft of your essay.

The Research Paper

33

Learn how to prepare a research paper.

A research paper (also called a library paper or term paper) is like a short expository composition (see Section **32**) in that it is an organized series of paragraphs developing a controlling idea or thesis. A research paper differs from a short composition in that it involves the use of library sources from which facts, quotations, and the opinions of others are drawn to explain, support, or authenticate ideas in the paper. These sources are identified by numbered notes, placed at the end of the text or at the bottom of the page. A research paper concludes with a bibliography, an alphabetical list of all sources cited.

The rules in this section describe the usual steps in the preparation of a research paper:

1. Selecting and limiting the subject
2. Preparing the bibliography
3. Developing the outline
4. Taking notes
5. Writing and documenting the paper

Each of these steps is illustrated in the preparation of a sample research paper, which is then given in full at the end of the section.

33a

Choose a subject that is suitable for a research paper and then limit it appropriately. See also 32a.

Not all subjects are suitable for a paper that relies on source materials found in the library. For example, you would probably find it difficult to document adequately a paper on your favorite childhood fantasies or on your opinions of an event so recent that little or nothing has yet been written on it.

Select a subject that you want to learn more about through reading. You might begin by selecting a general topic like literature, music, organic farming, cults, the media, or electronics.

Then start reading about your subject and decide what facets of it you could develop in a research paper. How much you limit your subject depends on the assigned length of the paper and on the availability and the adequacy of relevant books, newspapers, magazines, and so on. Below are examples of possible ways a general subject may be limited:

GENERAL   literature → fiction → futuristic novels

LIMITED   three futuristic novels: Orwell's *1984*, Huxley's *Brave New World*, Wells' *War of the Worlds*

MORE LIMITED   Big Brother (in *1984*) and Mustapha Mond (in *Brave New World*) as world controllers

EVEN MORE LIMITED   Big Brother's propaganda in the totalitarian world of *1984*

Note: You should be aware of the differences between a city or public library and a university or college library. A public library, which is designed for general use, contains mostly popular books and magazines. A university library is designed for research. It contains specialized journals, indexes, and critical works not found in a public library. For research papers, a university or college library is an indispensable tool.

■ **Exercise 1**   Select a subject that would be suitable for a library paper. Then check the availability of materials. (If you cannot find enough books, periodicals, and so on, try another subject.) As you skim through the information, perhaps beginning with an encyclopedia, single out facets of the subject that you would like to investigate further. Finally, limit the subject so that you can develop it in a paper of the assigned length.

33b

Making good use of the materials in the library, prepare a preliminary bibliography. Learn an acceptable form for bibliographical entries.

A preliminary bibliography contains information (titles, authors, dates, and so on) about the materials (books, magazines, newspapers, videotapes, audiodiscs, and so on) that you are likely to use as sources. Use the main catalog, indexes to periodicals, and reference books (as explained on the following pages) to make a preliminary bibliography by writing down the most promising titles you can find. Copy each title on a separate card (generally 3 × 5 inches) in an acceptable form: see page 789. You should keep these cards in alphabetical order until you complete your paper, adding useful titles as you find them and discarding those that prove useless. The final bibliography, to be typed at the end of your paper, will most often include only the works that help in the actual writing—usually only those cited in the endnotes (or footnotes).

A computer-aided search generally saves time in preparing a preliminary bibliography. Check to see whether your library has a terminal, or "on-line" system, connected with data bases.

(1) Learn to use library catalogs.

When first established, libraries in America used a book catalog as the main index to library holdings, updating it with supplements. As the number of holdings grew larger, librarians began using a file of 3 × 5-inch cards for catalog purposes. In 1902, the Library of Congress started selling printed cards to libraries, and in time the card catalog replaced the book catalog.

SAMPLE CATALOG CARDS

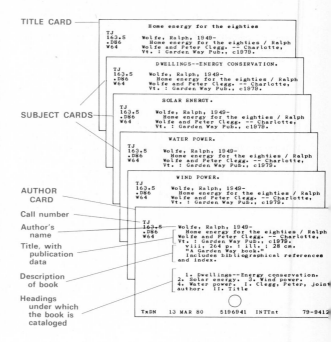

The card catalog

Still an active file in many libraries, the card catalog is the index to the whole library. It lists all books and all bound magazines, whether they are housed in the stacks, on the open shelves of the reference room, or in any other part of the building. In many libraries one general card catalog lists all books owned by the college or university and shows whether the book is in the general library or in a special collection in another building.

Usually the card catalog consists of cards arranged alphabetically in drawers. These may be "author" cards, "title" cards, or "subject" cards, for in most libraries each book is listed alphabetically in at least three places, once according to its author, again according to its title, and again according to its subject or subjects. These cards are identical except that the title card and the subject card have extra headings. As book collections in libraries mushroomed, the card catalog became costly and cumbersome. Since 1960, many libraries have turned to the microfilm or microfiche catalog, which photographically reproduces basically the same information found on the familiar cards.

The microfilm or microfiche catalog

When using a microfilm catalog housed in cartridges or cassettes, you need a microfilm viewer to read the record of library holdings. Since formats vary, you also need to find out if one alphabet covers all entries or if there are separate sections for author, title, and subject. Basically the microfiche catalog is the microfilm entry or record arranged in rows on small (usually 4 × 6 inches) sheets. As a rule, the microfiche catalog indexes authors, titles, and subjects separately.

A newer development in micrographics is the COM or Computer Output Microfilm catalog. Microimages on film are exact records of output from a computer. Formatted in different ways, the COM catalog is flexible and easy to use, although the user does need a microfilm or microfiche reader.

The computer catalog

Today, more and more college and university libraries are computerizing their library catalogs. To query the computer, students use typewriter-like terminals (located in the library and usually elsewhere on campus). By pressing a few lettered keys, users have instant access to information about an author, a title, a subject, an editor, and so on. The computer also indicates whether the library owns a particular work. Printouts provide copies of the information given on the video screen.

SAMPLE PRINTOUT

```
INT - FOR OTHER HOLDINGS, ENTER dh DEPRESS DISPLAY RECD SEND
OCLC: 5196941      Rec stat: c Entrd: 790703      Used: 800523
Type: a Bib lvl: m Govt pub:   Lang: eng Source:   Illus: a
Repr:   Enc lvl:   Conf pub: 0 Ctry: vtu Dat tp: s M/F/B: 10
Index: 1 Mod rec:   Festschr: 0 Cont: b
Desc: i Int lvl:   Dates: 1979,
 1 010    79-9412
 2 040    DLC c DLC d OCL
 3 020    0882661582 : c $10.95
 4 050 0  TJ163.5.D86 b W64
 5 082    696
 6 049    INTT
 7 100 10 Wolfe, Ralph, d 1949-
 8 245 10 Home energy for the eighties / c Ralph Wolfe
          and Peter Clegg.
 9 260 0  Charlotte, Vt. : b Garden Way Pub., c c1979.
10 300    viii, 264 p. : b ill. ; c 28 cm.
11 500    "A Garden Way book."
12 504    Includes bibliographical references and index.
13 650 0  Dwellings x Energy conservation.
14 650 0  Solar energy.
15 650 0  Wind power.
16 650 0  Water-power.
```

Note: After using the main catalog, you may wish to refer to the *Cumulative Book Index, Books in Print,* and *Paperbound Books in Print* to find titles that are closely related to your subject. Or you may wish to read what others have written about a book, perhaps one your library does not have, in the *Book Review Digest* or in a periodical referred to by a book such as *Book Review Index.*

(2) Use indexes to periodicals.

When preparing your bibliography, remember that the periodical indexes do for articles what the main catalog does for books in the library. You will probably find the *Readers' Guide to Periodical Literature* (an index to over one hundred periodicals) the most useful of these indexes. The front matter of each issue of the *Readers' Guide* provides an explanation of a sample entry as well as a key to abbreviations.

SUBJECT HEADING
(May 10, 1980 issue)

NINETEEN hundred and eighty-four
  Fighting 1984. M. Maddocks. Current 221:14-18
    Mr/Ap '80
  Was Orwell right? D. Ingram. il World Press **R**
    27:37-8 Mr '80

This issue contains an entry for George Orwell's *1984:* an illustrated article entitled "Was Orwell Right?" by D. Ingram—published in Vol. 27 of the *World Press Review* on pages 37–38 of the March 1980 issue.

AUTHOR HEADING
(March 1979–February 1980)

ORWELL, George, pseud
  Countdown to 1984: Big Brother may be right
    on schedule. D. Goodman; discussion. Futurist
    13:110-17 Ap; 291-3+ Ag '79 •
  1984: how close to reality? G. E. Jones. U.S.
    News 86:49-50 F 5 '79 •

This issue contains two entries for Orwell: a two-part discussion to be found in the April and August 1979 issues of *The Futurist* magazine, and an article in the February 5, 1979 issue of *U.S. News & World Report.*

Indexes to Periodicals

General

Poole's Index. 1802–1907. (subject index only)
Nineteenth Century Readers' Guide. 1890–99. (author, subject)
Readers' Guide. 1900–. (author, title, subject)
New York Times Index. 1913–. (a useful guide for finding the dates of important events, which can then be looked up in the *Times,* often available on microfilm, or in other newspapers)

Special

Applied Science and Technology Index. 1958–. Formerly *Industrial Arts Index.* 1913–57.
Art Index. 1929–.
Biography Index. 1946–.
Biological and Agricultural Index. 1964–. Formerly *Agricultural Index.* 1916–64.
Business Periodicals Index. 1958–.
Current Index to Journals in Education. 1969–.
Education Index. 1929–.
Engineering Index. 1884–.
Humanities Index. 1974–. Formerly *Social Sciences and Humanities Index.* 1965–73. *International Index.* 1907–65.
Index to Legal Periodicals. 1908–.
Music Index. 1949–.
Public Affairs Information Service (Bulletin). 1915–.
Social Sciences Index. 1974–. Formerly *Social Sciences and Humanities Index.* 1965–73. *International Index.* 1907–65.
United States Government Publications (Monthly Catalogue). 1895–.
See also the various abstracts, such as *Chemical Abstracts,* 1907–; *Abstracts of English Studies,* 1958–; *Abstracts of Popular Culture,* 1976–.

(3) Use reference books.

Learn the general location of the chief classes of reference books in order that you may turn to them without loss of time. For a detailed list of such books, with a short description of each, consult *Guide to Reference Books* by Eugene P. Sheehy (formerly by Constance M. Winchell) and *American Reference Books Annual (ARBA)*, edited by Janet H. Littlefield. Since many reference books, especially some of the encyclopedias, are kept up to date by frequent revisions, you should remember to cite the latest copyright date of the edition you are using. A few of the more important reference books are listed on the following pages (with abbreviated bibliographical information).

Reference Books

General dictionaries (unabridged)

A Dictionary of American English on Historical Principles. 4 vols. 1938–44.
Century Dictionary and Cyclopedia. 12 vols. 1911. 3 vols. 1927–33.
New Standard Dictionary of the English Language. 1947, 1952, 1966.
The Oxford English Dictionary. 13 vols. 1933. Originally issued as *A New English Dictionary on Historical Principles.* 10 vols. and Supplement. 1888–1933. (Supplements)
The Random House Dictionary of the English Language. 1967.
Webster's Third New International Dictionary. 1961. (Supplement, 6000 words, 1976)

Special dictionaries

Cowie, A. P., and R. Mackin. *Oxford Dictionary of Current Idiomatic English.* Vol. I–. 1975–.
Fowler, H. W. *Dictionary of Modern English Usage.* 2nd ed. Rev. Sir Ernest Gowers. 1965.
Hayakawa, S. I., and the Funk & Wagnalls dictionary staff. *Modern Guide to Synonyms and Related Words.* 1968.
Mawson, C. O. S. *Dictionary of Foreign Terms.* 2nd ed. Rev. Charles Berlitz. 1975.
Morris, William, and Mary Morris. *Harper Dictionary of Contemporary Usage.* 1975.
Onions, C. T. *Oxford Dictionary of English Etymology.* 1967.
Partridge, Eric. *Dictionary of Catch Phrases.* 1979.
————. *Dictionary of Slang and Unconventional English.* 7th ed. 1970.
Roget's International Thesaurus. 4th ed. 1977.
Webster's Collegiate Thesaurus. 1976.
Wentworth, Harold, and Stuart B. Flexner. *Dictionary of American Slang.* 2nd ed. 1975.

General encyclopedias

Academic American Encyclopedia. 21 vols.
Chambers's Encyclopaedia. 15 vols.
Collier's Encyclopedia. 24 vols.
Encyclopedia Americana. 30 vols.
Encyclopaedia Britannica. 30 vols.

Special encyclopedias

Adams, James T. *Dictionary of American History.* Rev. ed. 8 vols. 1976.
Cambridge Encyclopaedia of Astronomy. Ed. Simon Mitton. 1977.
Dictionary of the History of Ideas. Ed. Philip P. Wiener et al. 5 vols. 1973.

Encyclopedia of American Foreign Policy. Ed. Alexander DeConde. 3 vols. 1978.
Encyclopedia of Computers and Data Processing. Vol. I–. 1978–.
Encyclopedia of Philosophy. Ed. Paul Edwards et al. 4 vols. 1973.
Encyclopedia of Psychology. 2nd ed. Ed. Hans Jurgen Eysenck et al. 1979.
Encyclopedia of World Art. 15 vols. 1959–68.
Focal Encyclopedia of Photography. Rev. ed. 1969.
Grzimek's Animal Life Encyclopedia. 13 vols. 1972–75.
International Encyclopedia of Higher Education. Ed. Asa K. Knowles. 10 vols. 1977.
International Encyclopedia of the Social Sciences. Ed. D. E. Sills. 17 vols. 1968. Supplements.
Klein, Barry, and D. Icolari. *Reference Encyclopedia of the American Indian.* 3rd ed. 1978.
Kurian, George Thomas. *Encyclopedia of the Third World.* 2 vols. 1978.
Langer, William L. *An Encyclopedia of World History.* 5th ed. 1972.
McGraw-Hill Encyclopedia of Science & Technology. 15 vols. 4th ed. 1977. Yearbooks.
Munn, Glenn G. *Encyclopedia of Banking and Finance.* 7th rev. ed. Ed. Ferdinand L. Garcia. 1973.
The New Grove Dictionary of Music and Musicians. Ed. Stanley Sadie. 20 vols. 1980.
Stierlin, Henri. *Encyclopedia of World Architecture.* 2 vols. 2nd ed. 1979.
Thompson, Oscar. *International Cyclopedia of Music and Musicians.* 10th ed. Rev. ed. [Ed. Bruce Bohle]. 1975.

Atlases

Commercial Atlas and Marketing Guide (Rand McNally). 1981.
Cosmopolitan World Atlas (Rand McNally). Rev. ed. 1978.
Hammond Medallion World Atlas. 1977.
National Geographic Atlas of the World. 4th ed. 1975.
Oxford Economic Atlas of the World. 4th ed. 1972.
The Times (London) Atlas of the World: Comprehensive Edition. 5th ed. 1975.
U.S. Department of the Interior Geological Survey. *The National Atlas of the United States of America.* 1970.

Yearbooks—current events

Americana Annual. 1923–.
Annual Register. 1758–.
Britannica Book of the Year. 1938–.
Facts on File. 1940–.
Information Please Almanac. 1947–.
Reader's Digest Almanac and Yearbook. 1966–.
Statesman's Year-Book. 1864–.
Statistical Abstract of the United States. 1878–.
World Almanac and Book of Facts. 1868–.

Biography

Contemporary Authors. 1962–.
Current Biography. 1940–.
Dictionary of American Biography. 16 vols. and index. 1927–80. Supplements.
Dictionary of National Biography (British). 22 vols. 1882–1953. Supplements.
Dictionary of Scientific Biography. 16 vols. 1970–80.
International Who's Who (London). 1935–.
McGraw-Hill Encyclopedia of World Biography. 12 vols. 1973.
Webster's Biographical Dictionary. 1976.
Who's Who in America. 1899–. [See also *Marquis Who's Who Publications: Index to All Books* (revised annually).]

Literature

Bartlett's Familiar Quotations. 15th ed. 1980.
Benét, William Rose. The Reader's Encyclopedia. 2nd ed. 1965.
Cambridge History of American Literature. 3 vols. in 1. 1943.
Cambridge History of English Literature. 15 vols. 1907–33.
Essay and General Literature Index. 1900–.
Evans, Bergen. Dictionary of Quotations. 1968.
Fiction Catalog. 9th ed. 1976. Supplements.
Fleischman, W. B. Encyclopedia of World Literature in the 20th Century. 4 vols. 1967–75.
Granger's Index to Poetry. 6th ed. 1973.
Hart, James D. Oxford Companion to American Literature. 4th ed. 1965.
Harvey, Sir Paul. Oxford Companion to Classical Literature. 2nd ed. 1937.
————. Oxford Companion to English Literature. 4th ed. 1967.
Holman, C. Hugh. Handbook to Literature. 4th ed. 1980.
New Cambridge Bibliography of English Literature. 4 vols. 1973. Index, 1977.
Oxford Dictionary of Quotations. 3rd ed. 1979.
Play Index (Wilson). 1949–.
Seymour-Smith, Martin. Funk and Wagnalls Guide to Modern World Literature. 1975.
Short Story Index (Wilson). 1953. Supplements.
Smith, Horatio. Columbia Dictionary of Modern European Literature. 1947.
Spiller, Robert E., et al. Literary History of the United States. 4th ed. 2 vols. 1974.

(4) Use a standard bibliographical form.

Put each item of your bibliography on a separate card (preferably 3 × 5 inches) so that you can readily drop or add a card and can arrange the list alphabetically without recopying it. Follow exactly and consistently the bibliographical form you are instructed to use. The form illustrated by the samples below (and by the note forms on pages 795–97) closely follows the *MLA Handbook* (New York: Modern Language Association, 1977).

Bibliographical entries often consist of only three units, which are separated by periods:

Toffler, Alvin. <u>The</u> <u>Third</u> <u>Wave</u>. New York: Morrow, 1980.

1. *Name of the author.* Give the last name first to make alphabetization easy.

2. *Title of the book.* Underline (italicize) the title, and capitalize it in accordance with **9c**. Always include the book's subtitle.

3. *Publication data.* Include the place of publication, the publisher, and the latest copyright date as shown on the copyright page. You may give a shortened form of the publisher's name as long as it is clear.

Some entries, however, require more than three units. These must be given special treatment. As you study the following model bibliographical entries, which cover most of the special problems you are likely to encounter, observe both the punctuation and the arrangement of information. See also page 795 for a list of abbreviations that are permissible in bibliographies, notes, and tables.°

Sample Bibliographical Entries

Books

One author

Bird, Caroline. <u>The</u> <u>Two-Paycheck</u> <u>Marriage</u>: <u>How</u> <u>Women</u> <u>at</u> <u>Work</u> <u>Are</u> <u>Changing</u> <u>Life</u> <u>in</u> <u>America</u>. New York: Rawson, Wade, 1979.

Notice that the subtitle is always included in bibliographical entries.

Michener, James A. <u>Sports</u> <u>in</u> <u>America</u>. New York: Random House, 1976.

Two authors

Cutlip, Scott M., and Allen H. Center. <u>Effective</u> <u>Public</u> <u>Relations</u>. 5th ed. Englewood Cliffs, N.J.: Prentice-Hall, 1978.

Three authors

Aiken, Michael, Lewis A. Ferman, and Harold L. Sheppard. <u>Economic</u> <u>Failure</u>, <u>Alienation</u>, <u>and</u> <u>Extremism</u>. Ann Arbor: Univ. of Michigan Press, 1968.

More than three authors

Bailyn, Bernard, et al. <u>The</u> <u>Great</u> <u>Republic</u>: <u>A</u> <u>History</u> <u>of</u> <u>the</u> <u>American</u> <u>People</u>. Lexington, Mass.: Heath, 1977.

Notice that the state in which the book was published is given along with the city to avoid confusion with other cities named Lexington.

Corporate author

American Red Cross. <u>Standard</u> <u>First</u> <u>Aid</u> <u>&</u> <u>Personal</u> <u>Safety</u>. 2nd ed. Garden City, N.Y.: Doubleday, 1979.

Edition after the first

Grout, Donald Jay. <u>A</u> <u>History</u> <u>of</u> <u>Western</u> <u>Music</u>. 3rd ed. New York: Norton, 1980.

See also sample bibliographical entries directly above and below.

Editors

Barnet, Sylvan, Morton Berman, and William Burto, eds. <u>An</u> <u>Introduction</u> <u>to</u> <u>Literature</u>. 7th ed. Boston: Little, Brown, 1981.

Story or article from an anthology

Bond, Nelson. "The Voice from the Curious Cube." In <u>100</u> <u>Great</u> <u>Science</u> <u>Fiction</u> <u>Short</u> <u>Stories</u>. Ed. Isaac Asimov, Martin Harry Greenberg, and Joseph D. Olander. New York: Doubleday, 1978.

Translation

Laborit, Henri. <u>Decoding</u> <u>the</u> <u>Human</u> <u>Message</u>. Trans. Stephen Bodington and Alison Wilson. New York: St. Martin's Press, 1977.

° To save space, the sample bibliographical entries and note forms in this section are shown single-spaced. You should double-space both, however, as shown in the sample research paper, pages 807–10.

Reprint

Sheehy, Gail. <u>Passages</u>: <u>Predictable</u> <u>Crises</u> <u>of</u> <u>Adult</u>
    <u>Life</u>. 1976; rpt. New York: Bantam Books, 1977.

The original hard-cover edition was published a year earlier
than this paperback version.

Zimmern, Alfred. <u>America</u> <u>and</u> <u>Europe</u> <u>and</u> <u>Other</u>
    <u>Essays</u>. 1920; rpt. Freeport, N.Y.: Books for
    Libraries Press, 1969.

A work in more than one volume

Odell, George C. D. <u>Annals</u> <u>of</u> <u>the</u> <u>New</u> <u>York</u> <u>Stage</u>.
    15 vols. New York: Columbia Univ. Press, 1927–49.

The multivolume work was published over a period of years.

Sandburg, Carl. <u>Abraham</u> <u>Lincoln</u>: <u>The</u> <u>War</u> <u>Years</u>.
    4 vols. New York: Harcourt, 1939.

The work consists of four volumes published in the same
year.

A work in a series

Bebout, John E., and Ronald J. Grele. <u>Where</u> <u>Cities</u>
    <u>Meet</u>: <u>The</u> <u>Urbanization</u> <u>of</u> <u>New</u> <u>Jersey</u>. New
    Jersey Historical Series, Vol. 22. Princeton:
    Van Nostrand, 1964.

The volume number of a book in a series is given in Arabic
rather than Roman numerals.

Gillin, John Lewis, et al. <u>Social</u> <u>Problems</u>. 3rd ed.
    Century Social Science Series. New York:
    Appleton, 1943.

Green, Otis Howard. <u>The</u> <u>Literary</u> <u>Mind</u> <u>of</u> <u>Medieval</u>
    <u>and</u> <u>Renaissance</u> <u>Spain</u>. Studies in Romance
    Languages, No. 1. Introd. John E. Keller.
    Lexington: Univ. Press of Kentucky, 1970.

Notice that a separate author wrote the introduction.

Magazines and newspapers

Unsigned article

"Fertilizing Trees and Shrubs." <u>Southern</u> <u>Living</u>,
    Feb. 1980, pp. 170–71.

The names of months consisting of over five letters are usually abbreviated.

Daily newspaper

"Study Labels Alcohol Fuel as Threat to Food Supply."
    <u>Dallas</u> <u>Times</u> <u>Herald</u>, 16 March 1980, Sec. A,
    p. 14, cols. 1–2.

When not part of the newspaper's name, the city's name
may be given in brackets after the title.

Weekly magazine or newspaper

Clark, Matt, Sharon Begley, and Mary Hager. "The
    Miracles of Spliced Genes." <u>Newsweek</u>, 17 March
    1980, pp. 62–71.

Munro, Julie W. "A New Elitism in China?" <u>Chronicle</u>
    <u>of</u> <u>Higher</u> <u>Education</u>, 28 Nov. 1977, pp. 3–4.

Notice that no period is used with the question mark (or with
an exclamation point) after a title.

Monthly magazine

Frohlich, Cliff. "The Physics of Somersaulting and
    Twisting." <u>Scientific</u> <u>American</u>, March 1980, pp.
    154–64.

Journal—continuous pagination

Wurmser, Leon. "Drug Abuse: Nemesis of Psychiatry."
    <u>American</u> <u>Scholar</u>, 41 (1972), 393–407.

The pages of the journal issues are numbered continuously
throughout each year. Notice that both *Vol.* and *pp.* are
omitted when both the volume and the page numbers are
given.

Journal—separate pagination

Graham, Loren R. "Concerns about Science and
    Attempts to Regulate Inquiry." <u>Daedalus</u>, 107
    (Spring 1978), 1–21.

The pages of each issue of the journal are numbered separately. If the name of the season or month is not given by the
journal, put the issue number after the volume number: *NEA
Journal*, 55, No. 3 (1966), 35.

Editorial

"Elections in Rhodesia." Editorial. <u>San</u> <u>Francisco</u>
    <u>Chronicle</u>, 5 March 1980, p. 64, col. 1.

Book review

Wolfe, Alan. "Turning Economics to Dust." Rev. of
    <u>Free</u> <u>to</u> <u>Choose</u>: <u>A</u> <u>Personal</u> <u>Statement</u>, by Milton
    and Rose Friedman. <u>Saturday</u> <u>Review</u>, 2 Feb.
    1980, pp. 35–36.

Note: Sometimes a magazine article is printed on pages that
are separated by other articles; for example, the first part
appears on pages 137–39, the last on pages 188–203. As a
rule, list all the page numbers in a bibliography entry, using
a comma to indicate the interruption: pp. 137–39, 188–203.
But if there are more than two such sets of numbers, give
only the number of the first page: p. 137.

Encyclopedias and almanacs

Signed with name or initials

Allen, Frederick G. "Leyden Jar." <u>Encyclopedia</u>
    <u>Americana</u>. 1977 ed.

Full publication information is not required for a familiar
reference work.

R[asmussen], J[ohn] O., [Jr.] "Radioactivity."
    <u>Encyclopaedia</u> <u>Britannica</u>: <u>Macropaedia</u>. 1974 ed.

Brackets enclose the added parts of the name. A list of contributors is ordinarily supplied in the index volume or in the
front matter of an encyclopedia.

Unsigned

"New Words." In "Language." <u>Reader's</u> <u>Digest</u> <u>Almanac</u>
    <u>and</u> <u>Yearbook</u>. 1980 ed.

In this almanac main sections (like "Language") are arranged alphabetically in the text.

"Portsmouth, Treaty of." <u>Columbia</u> <u>Encyclopedia</u>.
    1975 ed.

The title indicates that the article is listed under *P.*

"Pulitzer Prizes in Journalism, Letters, and Music."
    <u>World</u> <u>Almanac</u> <u>and</u> <u>Book</u> <u>of</u> <u>Facts</u>. 1979 ed., pp.
    409–14.

Notice that page numbers are supplied for ease of reference,
though the front matter of this almanac does list topics alphabetically.

Pamphlets and bulletins

<u>Safety</u> <u>Data</u> <u>Sheet</u>—<u>Kitchen</u> <u>Machines</u>. Pamphlet 690.
    Chicago: National Restaurant Association, 1970.

Titles of pamphlets are italicized (underlined).

U.S. Bureau of Labor Statistics. <u>Tomorrow's</u> <u>Manpower</u>
    <u>Needs</u>. Washington, D.C.: GPO, 1973.

The publisher is the Government Printing Office.

Unpublished dissertation

Woodall, Guy Ramon. "Robert Walsh, Jr., as an Editor
    and Literary Critic: 1797–1836." Diss. Univ. of
    Tennessee 1966.

Micropublications

Document a book or periodical photographically reproduced in miniature form as though the work were in its original form. Rarely is it necessary to refer to a microform as
such in a bibliography entry.

Nonprint sources

Motion picture

<u>The</u> <u>Empire</u> <u>Strikes</u> <u>Back</u>. Twentieth-Century Fox,
    1980.

Television or radio program

"Paul's Case." <u>The</u> <u>American</u> <u>Short</u> <u>Story</u>. PBS, 11
    Feb. 1980.

White, Jim. <u>At</u> <u>Your</u> <u>Service</u>. KMOX, St. Louis, 13
    March 1981.

Stage play

<u>Morning's</u> <u>at</u> <u>Seven</u>. Lyceum Theatre, New York. 16
    April 1980.

Recording

Newhart, Bob. "Merchandising the Wright Brothers."
    <u>The</u> <u>Button-Down</u> <u>Mind</u> <u>of</u> <u>Bob</u> <u>Newhart</u>. Warner
    Bros., WS 1379, 1960.

Lecture

Dumas, Annette. "Shirley Jackson's 'The Lottery.'"
    Fine Arts Lecture Series, Mount St. Clare
    College, 15 Feb. 1981.

Interview

Young, Mary W. Personal interview. 22 Oct. 1981.

For samples of citations of other nonprint sources—such as
games, globes, filmstrips, microscope slides, and transparen-
cies—consult Eugene B. Fleischer's *A Style Manual for Citing Microform and Nonprint Media* (Chicago: American Library Association, 1978).

NOTES ON THE FINAL BIBLIOGRAPHY

Note 1: If you use two or more works by the same author in
your paper, list each work separately in your final bibliography, but do not repeat the author's name. To indicate the
omission of the name, use ten hyphens (or a straight line)
followed by a period. Notice that entries of this type are
alphabetized by title.

Thomas, Lewis. <u>The</u> <u>Lives</u> <u>of</u> <u>a</u> <u>Cell</u>: <u>Notes</u> <u>of</u> <u>a</u>
    <u>Biology</u> <u>Watcher</u>. 1974; rpt. New York: Bantam
    Books, 1975.

——————. <u>The</u> <u>Medusa</u> <u>and</u> <u>the</u> <u>Snail</u>: <u>More</u> <u>Notes</u> <u>of</u>
    <u>a</u> <u>Biology</u> <u>Watcher</u>. New York: Viking, 1979.

Note 2: Although the final form may not be required for
preliminary-bibliography cards, it is a helpful practice to use
from the beginning a complete form that is appropriate for
the final bibliography. (You may wish to add a call number to
help you relocate a book in the library.)

BIBLIOGRAPHY CARDS

Kanfer, Stefan. "Orwell 25 Years Later:
Future Imperfect." *Time*, 24 March
1975, pp. 77–78.

Meyers, Jeffrey. *A Reader's Guide to
George Orwell.* Totowa, N.J.:
Littlefield, Adams, 1977.

■ **Exercise 2** Select a subject (the one you chose for Exercise 1 on page 784 or a different one) and prepare a preliminary
bibliography. (Often you will find helpful bibliographies in the
books that you consult, especially in encyclopedias and other
reference works.)

Varying Styles of Documentation

Each department of a college or university ordinarily suggests a particular style for bibliographies and notes. As previ-

ously stated, the style of the *MLA Handbook* is used for the bibliographical and note models on pages 787–89 and 795–97 and in the sample research paper (pages 807–10), and you may use that style unless your instructor specifies a different one. Instructors in the sciences, business, economics, and so forth, may recommend a documentation form in one of the style books listed below, which are available in most university and public libraries. If you are asked to use one of these manuals, study it carefully, and make sure your bibliography and notes correspond exactly to the examples it provides. Following the list are some examples of documentation in the style of the American Psychological Association (APA), a style commonly used in the social and behavioral sciences.

Style books and manuals

American Institute of Physics. *Style Manual for Guidance in the Preparation of Papers.* 3rd ed. New York: American Institute of Physics, 1978.

American Chemical Society. *Handbook for Authors.* Washington, D.C.: American Chemical Society Publications, 1978.

American Mathematical Society. "Manual for Authors of Mathematical Papers." Reprinted from *Bulletin of the American Mathematical Society,* 68, No. 5, 1962.

Associated Press. *The Associated Press Stylebook.* Dayton, Ohio: Lorenz Press, 1980.

American Psychological Association. *Publication Manual.* 2nd ed. Washington, D.C.: American Psychological Association, 1974.

Conference of Biological Editors. *Style Manual for Biological Journals.* 2nd ed. Washington, D.C.: American Institute of Biological Sciences, 1964.

Turabian, Kate L. *A Manual for Writers of Term Papers, Theses, and Dissertations.* 4th ed. Chicago: University of Chicago Press, 1973.

Harvard Law Review. *A Uniform System of Citation.* 12th ed. Cambridge, Mass.: Harvard Law Review Association, 1976.

United States Government Printing Office. *Style Manual.* Rev. ed. Washington, D.C.: Government Printing Office, 1967.

Citations in APA style

In APA style, footnotes or endnotes are replaced by parenthetical author-date citations within the text, or date alone if the author's name is mentioned in the text. In the three examples below, note the details of punctuation and the treatment of the page number.

Short quotation

    One writer has stated, "Prisons can be divided
    into specific social groups organized by type of
    crime" (Liptz, 1979, p. 235), an observation with
    which many criminologists agree.

Long quotation (*four lines or more*)

    Liptz (1979) has stated the following:

        Prisons can be divided into specific social
        groups organized by types of crime. Social
        structures reflecting theft, arson, white-
        collar crime, and so on, were discovered
        within the prison walls. (p. 235)

Paraphrase

    Liptz (1979) discovered that the social groups
    established by prisoners within a prison are
    organized according to the type of crime. For
    example, thieves tend to congregate and so do
    arsonists. (p. 235)

Notice that, unlike a footnote or endnote, a citation in APA style does not include the title. The reader can easily find the title, however, by checking the reference list (see below) to find the entry with the same author and date.

Reference lists in APA style

In APA style, the alphabetical list of sources cited in the text is called a reference list, with the term *bibliography* used for lists of background materials and works for further reading. In the sample reference list entries below, note carefully all details of indention, spacing, punctuation, and mechanics.

Book—one author

    Liptz, A. Prisons as social structures. Los
        Angeles: Scholarly Press, 1979.

Book—two authors

    Klein, D. F., & Wender, P. H. Mind, mood, and
        medicine: A guide to the new biological
        psychiatry. New York: Farrar, Straus & Giroux,
        1981.

Journal—one author

    Pinker, S. Mental imagery and the third dimension.
        Journal of Experimental Psychology: General,
        1980, 109, 354–371.

Journal—multiple authors

    Johnson, M. K., Raye, C. L., Hasher, L., & Chromiak,
        W. Are there developmental differences in
        reality monitoring? Journal of Experimental
        Child Psychology, 1979, 27, 120, 128.

33c

Make a preliminary outline and develop it as you take notes on readings and as you write your research paper. See also 32f.

After completing a preliminary bibliography and a minimum of general reading on your subject (an encyclopedia article and parts of one or two other works may suffice), make a preliminary outline that will give direction to your investigation. The outline will enable you to discard irrelevant material from your bibliography and to begin spotting valuable passages on which you will want to take notes. If you attempt to take notes without first knowing what you are looking for, your efforts will lead only to frustration.

Be careful, however, not to adhere too rigidly to your preliminary outline. For although the outline will direct your reading, your reading will almost certainly suggest ways in which the outline may be improved. No outline should be regarded as complete until the research paper has been finished. As you take notes, you will probably revise your original outline frequently, adding subheadings to it, changing subheadings to major headings, perhaps dropping some headings entirely.

You may wish to compare the form and the content of the following preliminary outline with that of the final outline on page 800.

Preliminary Outline

Big Brother and His Propaganda Machine

Thesis: Used just for the sake of power, BB's propaganda is a particularly dangerous type.

George Orwell as propagandist and 1984 as propaganda

1. BB's totalitarian government related to propaganda:

    Its impact on Oceanians

    Their Leader—propagandist myth

    Pyramidal power structure

    Political machinery—the ministries

2. BB's use of propaganda to get uniformity

    Totally controls media

    History falsified

3. Newspeak—related to propaganda

    Why

    How

4. Main teachings of BB's propaganda:

    Love BB and hate his enemies.

    All else falls into place—no need to fear!

33d

Learn how to prepare a final outline.

Once you have developed and revised your preliminary outline as part of the process of organizing information, you are ready to select one of the conventional outline forms with standard notation so that your final outline shows the relationship of your main ideas and supporting information to the thesis.

First decide whether to use a topic outline, a sentence outline, or a paragraph outline. A topic outline presents information in parallel phrases or single words (see page 800). A sentence outline presents the same ideas in complete grammatically parallel declarative statements (see pages 797–98). And a paragraph outline presents ideas in paragraph form, as in the example below for Tracy Monahan's paper:

PARAGRAPH OUTLINE

Big Brother's Propaganda

Thesis: Big Brother disseminates the most dangerous kind of propaganda.

Introduction: In Nineteen Eighty-Four, Orwell (a propagandist) satirizes totalitarian propaganda as he presents his vision of life—in reverse.

I. The Oceanians are propaganda targets. They act like a stupid herd, and they revere a mythical leader. They even accept the hierarchy in a "classless" society.

II. Big Brother's bureaucracy serves as a propaganda machine. Its housing is a symbol, and its parts are interrelated.

III. Big Brother has complete control of the media. He supplies all materials, and he propagates the Party's ideal.

IV. The State falsifies history to control the past and make it fit the present. Winston's use of the memory hole and the clerks' rectifying old propaganda are evidence of this efficient, systematic, frightening attack on the past.

V. Totalitarian propaganda manipulates thought and emotion. Just as the State uses Newspeak to prevent thought, it also controls love and hate by teaching love for Big Brother and hate for his enemies.

Conclusion: Much of Big Brother's propaganda is outdated, but Nineteen Eighty-Four is still widely read as a warning.

Formal outlines use a system of notation that divides ideas and ranks them according to their level of importance. In the humanities, this system consists of Roman numerals, capital letters, Arabic numerals, and lower-case letters. Thus, for instance, ideas numbered with Roman numerals are of equal rank; they are also more important than ideas lettered A and B. The equality and relative importance of ideas are also shown by indention. Major ideas are flush with the left margin with each succeeding level indented as shown below:

Thesis:
I. Major idea
   A. Supporting idea
      1. Example or illustration for supporting idea
      2. Example or illustration for supporting idea
         a. Detail for example or illustration
         b. Detail for example or illustration
   B. Supporting idea
II. Major idea

Notice that:

1. The thesis statement is not marked with a Roman numeral because it is the single most important idea in the essay; it therefore has no equal.

2. The closer to the left margin an idea is, the more important it is.

3. At least two parts are required for the division of ideas at every level used.

4. Ideas at each level are cast in grammatically parallel structures, but it is not necessary to have parallel structure between levels. (See Section 26.)

As you can see, the form of an outline—the system of notation, the pattern of indention, and the parallel structure within ranks—emphasizes the order of and relationships among ideas.

As mentioned earlier, the system of numbers and letters discussed above is used for papers in the humanities. In the social and behavioral sciences, physical sciences, business, and engineering, a system of Arabic numerals alone is preferred:

1. Major idea
   1.1 Supporting idea
   1.2 Supporting idea
      1.2.1 Example or illustration for supporting idea
      1.2.2 Example or illustration for supporting idea
         1.2.2.1 Detail for example or illustration
         1.2.2.2 Detail for example or illustration

As you can see, both systems of notation emphasize the order of ideas and the relationships among them. Both are designed to provide a blueprint for the paper, and both serve as a table of contents for the reader.

33e

Take notes on readings (after evaluating the sources).

As you take notes on your readings, learn how to find and evaluate useful passages with a minimum of time and effort. Seldom will a whole book, or even a whole article, be of use as subject matter for any given research paper. To get what is needed for your paper, you will find that you must turn to many books and articles, rejecting most of them altogether and using from others only a section here and there. You cannot take the time to read each book completely. Use the table of contents and the index of a book, and learn to skim the pages rapidly until you find the passages you need.

One important consideration always is the reliability of the source. Do others speak of the writer as an authority? As you read, do you find evidence that the author is competent, well-informed, not prejudiced in any way? Is the work recent enough to provide up-to-date information? Is the edition the latest one available? Use your best judgment to determine the most dependable sources for your paper. You may find in the *Book Review Digest* convenient summaries of critical opinion on a book in your bibliography.

One of the best ways to take notes is on cards of uniform size, preferably 4 × 6 inches. (A smaller card may be used for the bibliography.) Each card must show the source of the note, including the exact page from which it is drawn. (When information is taken from more than one page, be sure to indicate in your notes exactly where one page ends and another begins.) It is a good idea to put a single note on one card (or ideas from a single source on a set of cards) with a heading keyed to a word or phrase in the outline. You can then easily arrange your note cards as you make changes in organization.

BIBLIOGRAPHY CARD WITH SOURCE

> Voorhees, Richard J. *The Paradox of
> George Orwell*. Humanities Series.
> Lafayette, Ind.: Purdue Univ.
> Studies, 1961.

SOURCE (from page 87)

From the middle thirties until his death Orwell was a propagandist harping on the significance of totalitarianism because he knew that thousands upon thousands of people in democratic countries were only remotely aware of it, and still more thousands thought that there was a lot to be said for it in one form or another. *Nineteen Eighty-Four* is his fiercest piece of propaganda.

NOTE CARD

> Orwell as propagandist (introduction)
> Voorhees, p. 87
>
> Orwell a propagandist from mid 1930s on—
> kept "harping on" totalitarianism.
>
> Why? He knew many people didn't know about its evils.
>
> "*Nineteen Eighty-Four* is his fiercest piece of propaganda."

For other examples of note cards, see pages 802, 803, 806.

Another way to take notes is to use regular notebook paper, perhaps adding photocopies of short excerpts from materials you think you may quote directly. On a photocopy you may mark quotable material and jot down your own ideas as you study the source.

PHOTOCOPIED SOURCE WITH NOTES

from Vol. IV – Orwell's <u>Essays</u>

Politics and the English Language   (137) ✓

covering up all the details. The great enemy of clear language is
insincerity. When there is a gap between one's real and one's declared   *NEWSPEAK*
aims, one turns as it were instinctively to long words and exhausted
idioms, like a cuttlefish squirting out ink. <u>In our age there is no such
thing as "keeping out of politics". All issues are political issues, and
politics itself is a mass of lies, evasions, folly, hatred and schizo-</u> ← *1984*
phrenia. When the general atmosphere is bad, language must suffer. ✓
I should expect to find—this is a guess which I have not sufficient
knowledge to verify—that the German, Russian and Italian languages
have all deteriorated in the last ten or fifteen years, as a result of
dictatorship. → *like Big Brother's*

[But] if thought corrupts language, language can also corrupt ⎫ *debatable*
thought. A bad usage can spread by tradition and imitation, even ⎬ *BUT*
among people who should and do know better. The debased lan- ⎭ *quotable*
guage that I have been discussing is in some ways very convenient.

Direct quotations

Any quotations that you use in your paper should be convincing and important ones. They should be made an integral part of your text. (For examples of ways this can be
done, see pages 801, 803.) When you discover a quotable
passage in your reading, you should take it down verbatim—that is, copy every word, every capital letter, and
every mark of punctuation exactly as in the original. Be sure
to enclose the quoted passage in quotation marks. When you
are quoting, quote accurately. When you are not quoting,
use your own sentence structure and phraseology, not a
slightly altered version of your source. Any conscious quotation (except well-known or proverbial passages) of the words
of another should be placed inside quotation marks (or indented if over four lines in length), and exact sources should
be cited.

In Nineteen Eighty-Four, Orwell defines doublethink

as "the power of holding two contradictory beliefs in

one's mind simultaneously, and accepting both of

them" (p. 215).

[Quotation marks enclose copied words, and internal documentation indicates the source.]

For other examples of the use and the documentation of
direct quotations, see the sample research paper on pages
801–07 (for instance, the long single-spaced direct quotation
on page 807 and its documentation on page 809 and the
shorter direct quotation on page 803 and note 9 on page 808).

As you write your research paper, keep a few guidelines in
mind when you are quoting the exact words of another. Pay
close attention to form, punctuation, and spacing: see **16a**.
Use periods appropriately to indicate ellipsis: see **17i**. But do
not use ellipsis periods before quotations that are only parts
of sentences. To avoid these periods at the beginning of a
quotation (especially one that begins a paragraph), use a
word like *that* or an introductory word group before the
quotation. You may use a period to end a quotation that is a
grammatically complete sentence, even though the source
may have a semicolon or another mark of punctuation.

Paraphrase

A paraphrase is a restatement of the source in about the
same number of words. As you compare the source with the
paraphrase below, notice differences in sentence structure
and word choice.

SOURCE

The aim of modern propaganda is no longer to modify ideas,
but to provoke action. It is no longer to change adherence to
a doctrine, but to make the individual cling irrationally to a
process of action. —JACQUES ELLUL

PARAPHRASE

Jacques Ellul (Propaganda, trans. Konrad Kellen and

Jean Lerner [New York: Knopf, 1965], p. 25) states

that modern propaganda does not try any longer to

change a person's ideas or loyalties to certain

principles; instead, it seeks to make individuals

irrationally follow a given procedure.

[Notice that the necessary documentation appears in parentheses in the text itself rather than in notes. This type of internal
documentation is generally used in papers with comparatively
few citations of sources.]

For examples of the use and documentation of paraphrases
in a research paper, see page 806.

Précis

A précis is a concise summary (shorter than the source).
When you make a paraphrase or write a précis, avoid copying not only the actual words but also the writer's style or
sentence structure. If you cannot do this, much of the material may be worth quoting directly.

SOURCE

From *Nineteen Eighty-Four* (N.Y.: Harcourt, 1949) by George
Orwell

. . . the subtlest practitioners of *doublethink* are those who
invented *doublethink* and know that it is a vast system of
mental cheating. In our society, those who have the best
knowledge of what is happening are also those who are fur-
thest from seeing the world as it is. In general, the greater the
understanding, the greater the delusion: the more intelligent,
the less sane (p. 216).

PRÉCIS

As Orwell observed, it is the inventors of

doublethink who are best at using their brand of

"mental cheating." In modern times, he contends,

even the best-informed do not see realities;

generally speaking, "the greater the understanding,

the greater the delusion: the more intelligent, the

less sane" (p. 216).

■ **Exercise 3** Carefully read paragraphs 1 (page 762) and 20 (page 766) in Section 31. First write a paraphrase of one of these paragraphs. Then write a précis of the same paragraph. Unless you are quoting directly, avoid using the sentence patterns of the source. To convey the ideas in the source exactly, choose your words carefully.

PLAGIARISM

You must acknowledge all material quoted, paraphrased, or summarized from any work. If you fail to cite a source, whether deliberately or accidentally, you are guilty of plagiarism—of presenting as your own work the words or ideas of another. As the *MLA Handbook* (New York: Modern Language Association, 1977) states:

> Plagiarism may take the form of repeating another's sentences as your own, adopting a particularly apt phrase as your own, paraphrasing someone else's argument as your own, or even presenting someone else's line of thinking in the development of a thesis as though it were your own. (p. 4)

After you have done a good deal of reading about a given subject, you will be able to distinguish between common knowledge in that field—facts, dates, and figures—and the distinctive ideas or interpretations of specific writers. When you use the ideas or information that these writers provide, be sure to cite the exact source of the material used.

NOT   In *Nineteen Eighty-Four*, doublethink is defined as the power of holding two contradictory beliefs in one's mind simultaneously, and accepting both of them. [undocumented copying]

BUT   In *Nineteen Eighty-Four*, Orwell defines doublethink as "the power of holding two contradictory beliefs in one's mind simultaneously, and accepting both of them" (p. 215). [Quotation marks enclose copied words, and the page number in parentheses cites the source.]

NOT   In fact, *Nineteen Eighty-Four* is Orwell's most ferocious propaganda. [an undocumented idea from the work of another writer]

BUT   In fact, *Nineteen Eighty-Four* has been called Orwell's most ferocious propaganda.[1]
OR
In fact, Richard J. Voorhees states: "*Nineteen Eighty-Four* is his [Orwell's] fiercest piece of propaganda."[1] [Note 1 cites the exact source of the idea or of the direct quotation: see page 792.]

If you are in doubt about whether you need to cite a source, ask your instructor before you hand in your paper.

33f

Using the outline, the bibliography, and the notes, write a properly documented research paper.

After you have made your outline as complete as possible and have taken notes on major headings and subheadings of the outline, you are ready to begin writing. Arrange your notes in the order of the outline, and then use them as the basis of your paper. Naturally you will need to expand some parts and to cut others, and you will need to provide transitional sentences—sometimes even transitional paragraphs. Write the material in the best way you can—in your own style, in your own words.

(1) Endnotes (or footnotes)

Since the material in your research paper comes largely from the work of others, you will need to give proper credit by citing your sources in notes numbered consecutively throughout the paper. These notes are called *endnotes* when they are placed in one list at the end of the text (see pages 807–09), or *footnotes* when they are placed at the bottom of the appropriate pages (see page 810). In this discussion, they will be called simply notes. Note numerals in the text should come immediately after the part of the sentence to which the note refers and should come *after* all punctuation except the dash.

Another purpose of notes is to present information that is related to the central idea of the paper but that does not directly support it, as in note 9 on page 808.

The following sample forms show how the first reference to a source differs from the bibliography entry for that source. Observe differences in indention and punctuation. Notice also that the author's name is inverted in the bibliography entry but not in the note reference. The subtitle of a book is always included in bibliography entries but may be omitted in the notes.

A book

Daiches, David. <u>Moses</u>: <u>The Man and His Vision</u>. New York: Praeger, 1975.

[1] David Daiches, <u>Moses</u> (New York: Praeger, 1975), pp. 60–61.

A newspaper

"Satellite-to-Homes TV Transmissions Seen Growing Fast." <u>Wall Street Journal</u>, Southwest Ed., 2 April 1980, p. 29, cols. 3–4.

[1] "Satellite-to-Homes TV Transmissions Seen Growing Fast," <u>Wall Street Journal</u>, Southwest Ed., 2 April 1980, p. 29, col. 3.

A magazine

Ellenton, Gloria. "Snow Belt of the Great Lakes." <u>Natural History</u>, Nov. 1979, pp. 108–15.

[1] Gloria Ellenton, "Snow Belt of the Great Lakes," <u>Natural History</u>, Nov. 1979, p. 113.

Points to Remember About First References

1. Notes are typed double-spaced.
2. The note numerals are typed slightly above the line, followed by a space.
3. The first line is indented five spaces. (Normal paragraph indention is used instead of the hanging indention used to make each entry stand out in a bibliography.)
4. The names of authors and editors are given in the normal order, first names first. (Since the notes are never alphabetized, there is no need to give the last name first.)

5. Commas are used between the main items (but not before parentheses).

6. In references to books, parentheses enclose the publication data. In references to journals, parentheses enclose the year of publication (preceded by the month or season if each issue is paginated separately) except when the day of the month is given.

7. Each note ends with a period.

8. Such abbreviations as the following may be used. (These abbreviations are also appropriate in bibliographies and in tables, but they are inappropriate in the text of a research paper.)

Assn.	Association
bk., bks.	book, books
c.	*circa,* "about" (for example, "c. 1966")
cf.	compare
ch., chs.	chapter, chapters
col., cols.	column, columns
dept.	department
diss.	dissertation
ed., eds.	edition(s) OR editor(s)
et al.	*et alii,* "and others"
f., ff.	and the following page, pages (Inclusive page numbers are preferred: "pp. 5–13" instead of "pp. 5 ff.")
ibid.	in the same place; in the source cited in the immediately preceding note
introd.	[author of] introduction, introduced by
l., ll.	line, lines
ms., mss.	manuscript, manuscripts
n.d.	no date [of publication]
n., nn.	note, notes (for example, "p. 6, n. 2")
no., nos.	number [of issue], numbers
n.p.	no place [of publication]; no publisher
p., pp.	page, pages
pt., pts.	part, parts
rev.	revision, revised, revised by OR review, reviewed by
rpt.	reprinted, reprint
sec., secs.	section, sections
trans.	translated by, translator, translation
Univ.	University
vol., vols.	volume, volumes

Standard abbreviations for months of publication and for names of states and countries (sometimes given to prevent confusion of cities such as Cambridge, Mass., and Cambridge, Eng.)

Compare the following note forms with the corresponding sample bibliographical entries on pages 787–89 to see exactly how the treatment differs.

Sample First References

Books

One author

[1] Caroline Bird, *The Two-Paycheck Marriage* (New York: Rawson, Wade, 1979), pp. 48–49.

Notice that the subtitle, *How Women at Work Are Changing Life in America,* is omitted.

[2] *Sports in America* (New York: Random House, 1976), p. 355.

The author's name may be omitted if it appears in full in the text of the paper.

Two authors

[3] Scott M. Cutlip and Allen H. Center, *Effective Public Relations,* 5th ed. (Englewood Cliffs, N.J.: Prentice-Hall, 1978), p. 73.

Three authors

[4] Michael Aiken, Lewis A. Ferman, and Harold L. Sheppard, *Economic Failure, Alienation, and Extremism* (Ann Arbor: Univ. of Michigan Press, 1968), pp. 184–86.

More than three authors

[5] Bernard Bailyn et al., *The Great Republic* (Lexington, Mass.: Heath, 1977), p. 45.

Corporate author

[6] American Red Cross, *Standard First Aid & Personal Safety,* 2nd ed. (Garden City, N.Y.: Doubleday, 1979), p. 127.

Edition after the first

[7] Donald Jay Grout, *A History of Western Music,* 3rd ed. (New York: Norton, 1980), p. 669.

Editors

[8] Sylvan Barnet, Morton Berman, and William Burto, eds., *An Introduction to Literature,* 7th ed. (Boston: Little, Brown, 1981), p. 4.

Story or article from an anthology

[9] Nelson Bond, "The Voice from the Curious Cube," in *100 Great Science Fiction Stories,* ed. Isaac Asimov, Martin Harry Greenberg, and Joseph D. Olander (New York: Doubleday, 1978), pp. 172–73.

Translation

[10] Henri Laborit, *Decoding the Human Message,* trans. Stephen Bodington and Alison Wilson (New York: St. Martin's Press, 1977), p. 57.

Reprint

[11] Gail Sheehy, *Passages* (1976; rpt. New York: Bantam Books, 1977), pp. 49–50.

[12] Alfred Zimmern, *America and Europe and Other Essays* (1920; rpt. Freeport, N.Y.: Books for Libraries Press, 1969), p. 23.

A work in more than one volume

[13] George C. D. Odell, *Annals of the New York Stage,* IX (New York: Columbia Univ. Press, 1937), 347–48.

The volume number (a Roman numeral) precedes the publishing information when the various volumes of the work have been published in different years. Notice that both *Vol.* and *pp.* are omitted when both the volume and the page numbers are given.

14 Carl Sandburg, Abraham Lincoln (New York: Harcourt, 1939), IV, 103.

Notice that the volume number follows the publishing information when the various volumes of a multivolume work were published in the same year.

A work in a series

15 John E. Bebout and Ronald J. Grele, Where Cities Meet, New Jersey Historical Series, Vol. 22 (Princeton: Van Nostrand, 1964), pp. 61–62.

Notice that the volume number of a book in a series is given in Arabic rather than Roman numerals.

16 John Lewis Gillin et al., Social Problems, 3rd ed., Century Social Science Series (New York: Appleton, 1943), pp. 320–21.

17 Otis Howard Green, The Literary Mind of Medieval and Renaissance Spain, Studies in Romance Languages, No. 1, introd. John E. Keller (Lexington: Univ. Press of Kentucky, 1970), p. 231.

Magazines and newspapers

Unsigned article

18 "Fertilizing Trees and Shrubs," Southern Living, Feb. 1980, p. 171.

Newspaper or weekly magazine

19 Matt Clark, Sharon Begley, and Mary Hager, "The Miracles of Spliced Genes," Newsweek, 17 March 1980, p. 69.

20 Julie W. Munro, "A New Elitism in China?" Chronicle of Higher Education, 28 Nov. 1977, p. 3.

Notice that no comma is used with the question mark.

Monthly magazine

21 Cliff Frohlich, "The Physics of Somersaulting and Twisting," Scientific American, March 1980, p. 157.

Daily newspaper

22 "Study Labels Alcohol Fuel as Threat to Food Supply," Dallas Times Herald, 16 March 1980, Sec. A, p. 14, col. 2.

Journal—continuous pagination

23 Leon Wurmser, "Drug Abuse: Nemesis of Psychiatry," American Scholar, 41 (1972), 397.

The pages of the journal issues are numbered continuously throughout each year.

Journal—separate pagination

24 Loren R. Graham, "Concerns about Science and Attempts to Regulate Inquiry," Daedalus, 107 (Spring 1978), 7.

The pages of each issue of the journal are numbered separately.

Editorial

25 "Elections in Rhodesia," Editorial, San Francisco Chronicle, 5 March 1980, p. 64, col. 1.

Book review

26 Alan Wolfe, "Turning Economics to Dust," rev. of Free to Choose: A Personal Statement, by Milton and Rose Friedman, Saturday Review, 2 Feb. 1980, p. 35.

Encyclopedias and almanacs

Signed with name or initials

27 Frederick G. Allen, "Leyden Jar," Encyclopedia Americana, 1977 ed.

Volume and page numbers are omitted in references to short articles (one page or less) alphabetically arranged.

28 J[ohn] O. R[asmussen], [Jr.], "Radioactivity," Encyclopaedia Britannica: Macropaedia, 1974 ed., XV, 441.

Notice that the volume and page numbers are given for the specific reference to one page of a multi-page article.

Unsigned

29 "New Words," in "Language," Reader's Digest Almanac and Yearbook, 1980 ed., p. 430.

The page number is required in the reference to one page of a multi-page article.

30 "Portsmouth, Treaty of," Columbia Encyclopedia, 1975 ed.

31 "Pulitzer Prizes in Journalism, Letters, and Music," World Almanac and Book of Facts, 1979 ed., p. 411.

Pamphlets and bulletins

32 Safety Data Sheet, Pamphlet 690 (Chicago: National Restaurant Association, 1970), p. 2.

33 U.S. Bureau of Labor Statistics, Tomorrow's Manpower Needs (Washington, D.C.: GPO, 1973), pp. 45–46.

Unpublished dissertation

34 Guy Ramon Woodall, "Robert Walsh, Jr., as an Editor and Literary Critic: 1797–1836," Diss. Univ. of Tennessee 1966, p. 186.

Nonprint sources

Motion picture

35 The Empire Strikes Back, Twentieth-Century Fox, 1980.

Television or radio program

36 "Paul's Case," The American Short Story, PBS, 11 Feb. 1980.

[37] Jim White, At Your Service, KMOX, St. Louis, 13 March 1981.

Stage play

[38] Morning's at Seven, Lyceum Theatre, New York, 16 April 1980.

Recording

[39] Bob Newhart, "Merchandising the Wright Brothers," The Button-Down Mind of Bob Newhart, Warner Bros., WS 1379, 1960.

Interview

[40] Personal interview with Mary W. Young, 22 Dec. 1981.

Lecture

[41] Annette Dumas, "Shirley Jackson's 'The Lottery,'" Fine Arts Lecture Series, Mount St. Clare College, 15 Feb. 1981.

The notes below show second (or later) references in an appropriately abbreviated form. Compare them with the first references to see exactly how they have been shortened.

Sample Second References

Books

[42] Bird, p. 48.

[43] Cutlip and Center, pp. 50–51.

[44] Bailyn et al., pp. 20–21.

[45] First Aid, p. 35.

[46] First Aid, p. 41.

[47] Odell, IX, 350.

Magazines and newspapers

[48] Clark, Begley, and Hager, p. 71.

[49] "A New Elitism in China?" p. 3.

Encyclopedias and almanacs

[50] Allen, "Leyden Jar."

[51] R[asmussen], XV, 442.

[52] "Pulitzer Prizes," p. 410.

Pamphlets and bulletins

[53] Safety Data, p. 1.

[54] U.S. Bureau, p. 45.

Dissertation

[55] Woodall, pp. 12–13.

Nonprint sources

[56] "Paul's Case."

[57] Interview with Young.

[58] Dumas, "Jackson's 'Lottery.'"

If you refer in your paper to two or more works by the same author, include titles (in shortened form if the title is long) in your second references.

[59] Lewis, Lives, p. 50.

[60] Lewis, Medusa, pp. 89–90.

If you refer to works by two authors with the same last name, repeat the full name of the author in second references.

[61] Caroline Bird, p. 79.

[62] George Lloyd Bird, pp. 13–14.

If you use articles with the same title from two or more encyclopedias, include the name of the encyclopedia in your note.

[63] "Portsmouth, Treaty of," Columbia Encyclopedia, 1975 ed.

[64] "Portsmouth, Treaty of," Encyclopedia Americana, 1977 ed.

(2) Final outline

The content of your outline should have been developing steadily throughout your note-taking and writing of the paper, and you should now be ready to prepare a final copy. Before you do, however, correlate the ideas in your outline with those in your text, and make any needed revisions. Also check the form of your outline: see **33d**, page 792. As you study the sample research paper on pages 801–07, notice that the arrangement of paragraphs accords with that of the divisions of the sentence outline below.

OUTLINE

Title: Big Brother's Propaganda

¶1   Introduction: In Nineteen Eighty-Four, Orwell (a propagandist) satirizes totalitarian propaganda as he presents his vision of life—in reverse.

2   Thesis: Big Brother disseminates the most dangerous kind of propaganda.

    I. The Oceanians are propaganda targets.

3   A. They act like a stupid herd.

4   B. They revere a mythical leader.

5   C. They accept the hierarchy in a "classless" society.

    II. Big Brother's bureaucracy serves as a propaganda machine.

6   A. Its very housing is a symbol.

7   B. Its parts are interrelated.

    III. Big Brother has complete control of the media.

8   A. He supplies all materials.

9   B. He propagates the Party's ideal.

    IV. The State falsifies history.

10–11   A. The purpose is to control the past and make it fit the present.

        B. The method is efficient.

12   1. Winston uses the memory hole.

13   2. Clerks "rectify" old propaganda.

14   C. The systematic attack on the past is frightening.

    V. Totalitarian propaganda manipulates thought and emotion.

15   A. The state uses Newspeak to prevent thought.

16   B. Love and hate are state-controlled.

17   1. One must love Big Brother.

18   2. One must hate his enemies.

19–20   Conclusion: Much of Big Brother's propaganda is outdated, but Nineteen Eighty-Four is still widely read as a warning.

The outline serves primarily as a guide to writing an organized and carefully developed composition; but it can also serve, when submitted in its final state along with the finished paper, as a kind of table of contents.

(3) Final revision and proofreading

After writing and carefully documenting the first draft of your paper, make needed revisions. To make your writing as clear and effective as possible, you will probably need to rewrite some sentences, and strike out or add others. Use the Reviser's Checklist on page 782. (You may wish to review pages 779–82 of Section **32**.) Refer to **8b** as you put your paper in final form. Even when writing final copy, you will probably continue to make changes in phraseology and to correct occasional errors in spelling, mechanics, or grammar. Type or write legibly. Proofread your final revision before handing it in, using the Proofreader's Checklist on page 693.

(4) Final bibliography

You should have assembled a preliminary bibliography early in your research. As you pursued your investigation, you probably eliminated some items and added others. Not until you have completed your paper can you know which items should make up your final bibliography. Once your paper is complete, look through your notes. Every book, article, or nonprint work quoted or cited as a source in a note (even if it appears only once) belongs in the bibliography. Once you have determined which items should be included, you can easily arrange the bibliography cards in alphabetical order and copy them, either in one alphabetical list or in a list classified according to your instructor's directions.

    Students are often asked to submit, along with the completed paper, both the final and the preliminary outlines; the notes, on cards; and the rough draft of the documented paper.

Sample Research Paper

On the following pages is a completed sample research paper. For purposes of comparison, the pages facing those of the paper contain not only selected passages from the sources but also note cards used in preparing the paper. Comments on content and form are also provided. Notice, as you read the paper, how Tracy Monahan credits other authors.

■ **Exercise 4** Prepare for a class discussion of the strengths and the weaknesses of the following research paper. Give special attention to content and form, organization, and documentation.

COMMENTS

This research paper consists of five parts:

1. *Title page.* The title page usually gives the title of the paper, the author, the name of the course and its section number, the instructor's name, and the date. (See also **8b**.)

2. *Final outline.* The final outline serves as a table of contents. Since the outline occupies only one page, it is not numbered. (In outlines occupying more than one page, all pages after the first are numbered with small Roman numerals in the upper right-hand corner of the page.) Notice that a topic outline is used here. If your instructor specifies a sentence outline, see the sample one on pages 797–98.

3. *Text of the paper.* The title is repeated on the first page of the text, which is not numbered. All pages after the first are numbered with Arabic numerals in the upper right-hand corner of the page. Notice that no period follows the page numbers.

4. *Notes.* The notes begin on a new page, following the text and preceding the bibliography; they are numbered consecutively with the text. (For example of notes placed at the bottom of the page, see page 810.)

5. *Bibliography.* The bibliography begins on a new page following the notes, and is numbered consecutively with the text and notes.

BIG BROTHER'S PROPAGANDA

by

Tracy Monahan

English 131, Section 3

Mr. Richards

March 12, 1982

OUTLINE

<u>Thesis</u>: Big Brother disseminates the most dangerous
         kind of propaganda.

<u>Introduction</u>: In <u>Nineteen Eighty-Four</u>, Orwell (a
      propagandist) satirizes totalitarian propaganda
      as he presents his vision of life--in reverse.

  I. The propagandized Oceanians

      A. Their loss of individuality
      B. Their reverence for Big Brother
      C. Their use of doublethink

 II. The bureaucratic propaganda machine

      A. Its housing--symbolic
      B. Its parts--interrelated

III. The media in a totalitarian world

      A. All materials supplied
      B. The Party's ideal propagated

 IV. The falsification of history

      A. Purpose of changes
      B. Methods of "rectification"

          1. Use of memory hole
          2. Use of clerical teams

      C. Effect on Winston

  V. The manipulation of thought and emotion

      A. Preventing thought--Newspeak
      B. Rousing the emotions

          1. Love for Big Brother
          2. Hatred of his enemies

<u>Conclusion</u>: Much of Big Brother's propaganda is
      outdated, but <u>Nineteen Eighty-Four</u> is still
      widely read as a warning.

COMMENTS

1. Paragraph 1 is the introduction.

2. Notes 1 and 3 credit the sources of ideas; note 2, of the quoted passage. See the endnotes on page 807.

3. Observe the way direct quotations are made an integral part of the text. The first one is introduced by *that*, the second by an introductory clause followed by a comma.

4. On the title page of the hard-cover edition of Orwell's novel is *Nineteen Eighty-Four*. On the title page of the Signet paperback edition is *1984*, the form used by Ralph Ranald and copied exactly by Tracy Monahan.

SOURCE

For note 2:

ORWELL: "I have always maïntained that every artist is a propagandist. I don't mean a political propagandist. If he has any honesty or talent at all he cannot be that. Most political propaganda is a matter of telling lies, not only about the facts but about your own feelings. But every artist is a propagandist in the sense that he is trying, directly or indirectly, to impose a vision of life that seems to him desirable. I think that we are broadly agreed about the vision of life that proletarian literature is trying to impose."

COMMENTS

1. Paragraph 2 states the thesis, or central idea. Paragraph 3 begins the discussion of point I of the outline: The propagandized Oceanians.

2. In the single-spaced quotation (over four lines in length), the interpolation in brackets supplies a subject and verb to complete the shortened sentence. See also **17g.**

3. Notice that the punctuation before the first ellipsis mark is retained to insure clarity. See also **17i.**

SOURCE

For note 4:

Orwell's *1984* is about religion reversed, law and government reversed, and above all, language reversed: not simply corrupted, but reversed. In the mad world of *1984*, the mad world which Orwell sought by his writing to lead men to *avoid*—for he was a political activist not interested in simple prediction—in this world, which I call Orwell's "antiuniverse," because of his conversion of all the positives of Western civilization into their negatives, all the channels of communication are systematically being closed down, restricted to just the minimums necessary for the technical functioning of society.

—RALPH A. RANALD

BIG BROTHER'S PROPAGANDA

1   Nineteen Eighty-Four has been called George Orwell's most ferocious propaganda.[1] Orwell was quick to admit that he was a propagandist. In fact, in 1940, during a BBC radio discussion, he said that "every artist is a propagandist in the sense that he is trying, directly or indirectly, to impose a vision of life that seems to him desirable."[2] But Orwell hated political propaganda which deliberately falsifies reality, especially the hypocritical kind used solely for the purpose of keeping totalitarian regimes in power. During the 1930s and 1940s he was repelled by the propaganda machines of dictators like Hitler and Stalin.[3] It is this variety of propaganda that Orwell satirizes in Nineteen Eighty-Four, a novel that presents his vision of life—in reverse. As Ralph A. Ranald has observed,

> Orwell's 1984 is about religion reversed, law and government reversed, and above all, language reversed: not simply corrupted, but reversed. In the world of 1984, the mad world which Orwell sought by his writing to lead men to avoid—for he was a political activist not interested in simple prediction—in this world, which I call Orwell's "antiuniverse," . . . [Orwell converts] all the positives of Western civilization into their negatives.[4]

And in Orwell's crazy world, it is Big Brother's political propaganda that helps to sustain and perpetuate this reversal of values.

2   To control society, to sustain the awesome power of the State, Big Brother uses what Oliver Thompson calls the most dangerous kind of propaganda: a "steady drip, drip" of toxic, power-oriented ideas not recognized as propaganda. These ideas pollute the environment and saturate all art forms. Such propaganda deadens the awareness of its targets.[5]

3   Big Brother is always watching, and his hypnotic eyes have cast a spell over the inhabitants of Oceánia. Thoroughly propagandized, they act like a stupid herd. They mechanically respond to every command, no matter how illogical it is. If any person dares to act or even think

COMMENTS

1. Paragraphs 4 and 5 continue point I of the outline.
2. Read note 6 (page 808) and observe the use of the page reference after the direct quotation ending the first sentence of paragraph 5.
3. As you read the source for note 6, observe how Tracy Monahan has combined paraphrase and direct quotation.

SOURCE

For note 6: *Nineteen Eighty-Four* (p. 209).

> Given this background, one could infer, if one did not know it already, the general structure of Oceanic society. At the apex of the pyramid comes Big Brother. Big Brother is infallible and all-powerful. Every success, every achievement, every victory, every scientific discovery, all knowledge, all wisdom, all happiness, all virtue, are held to issue directly from his leadership and inspiration. Nobody has ever seen Big Brother. He is a face on the hoardings, a voice on the telescreen. We may be reasonably sure that he will never die, and there is already considerable uncertainty as to when he was born. Big Brother is the guise in which the Party chooses to exhibit itself to the world. His function is to act as a focusing point for love, fear, and reverence, emotions which are more easily felt toward an individual than toward an organization.

COMMENT

Paragraph 6 begins point II of the outline: The bureaucratic propaganda machine.

BIBLIOGRAPHY CARD USED FOR NOTES 5 and 7

> Thomson, Oliver. *Mass Persuasion* in *History*. New York: Crane, Russak, 1977.

NOTE CARD USED FOR PARAGRAPH 6

> Big Brother's pyramidal power structure
> Thomson, p. 41
>
> T. thinks architecture is an important propagandist medium that people don't pay much attention to.
> A building can be "graphic communication."
> Can inspire awe and power—with long-term impact.
>
> "... the pyramids projected the massive dominance of the Pharaohs."

like an independent human being, Big Brother resorts to liquidation or re-education. Such an individual either becomes an "unperson," one who has never existed, or a reprogramed android, one who again loves and serves the State.

4   Ironically enough, the Oceanians have never seen Big Brother—just big pictures of him. In fact, Big Brother does not exist. He is the mythical Leader so often created by propagandists. His image is projected by the Inner Party to maintain its ruling powers. Propaganda depicts Big Brother as a deity. He is omnipresent, omniscient, omnipotent: "Every success, every achievement, every victory, every scientific discovery, all knowledge, all wisdom, all happiness, all virtue, are held to issue directly from his leadership and inspiration."[6]

5   Oceanians are programed in the art of doublethink, which Orwell defines as "the power of holding two contradictory beliefs in one's mind simultaneously, and accepting both of them" (p. 215). The Oceanians, not aware of their loss of human rights, firmly believe that everybody is equal in their society, but they serve their king and accept the State's rigid hierarchy. The pyramidal power structure is the natural order of things in their classless society. Naturally, Big Brother sits on top of the pyramid; he represents the Inner Party, less than two percent of society. Just below him or them is the Outer Party, the bureaucratic toadies, about thirteen percent. At the base of the pyramid are the proles—"the dumb masses" (p. 209)—about eighty-five percent.

6   Big Brother's bureaucracy consists of four ministries. These ministries are housed in huge white buildings, enormous pyramidal structures dominating London, the capital of Airstrip One, a province of Oceania. These towers contrast sharply with the run-down stores and shabby houses of the rest of the city. The very architecture of Big Brother's government buildings is an important propagandistic symbol because it is a "graphic communication" of awesomeness. Like the great

COMMENTS

1. The discussion of point II continues. Paragraph 8 turns to point III: The media in a totalitarian world.

2. Note 9: No ellipsis mark precedes the quoted *part* of the sentence.

3. In paragraph 8, the use of such phrases as "According to Richard S. Lambert," "knows *this*," and "Jacques Ellul writes" helps make direct quotations fit smoothly into the text.

NOTE CARD

Notice below that Tracy Monahan's own ideas are placed in brackets.

Propaganda machine

Thomson, *7 TYPES OF PROPAGANDA* listed. [Five seem closely related to Big Brother's machine.]

p. 11 political — rhetoric, subtle images
    economic — promotes confidence in economy

p. 12 war/military — concerned with morale. Uses war films, military music, etc.
    ideological — "spread of complete idea systems"

pp. 12-13 escapist — media entertainment distracts, gets "social acquiescence"

[Relate this to the proles?]

COMMENTS

As a rule, a comma or a colon precedes an introduced quotation. Examples from the paper:

¶1   As Ralph A. Ranald has observed,

¶4   He is . . . omnipotent:

In paragraph 8, however, are two illustrations of a different way to make a quotation an integral part of the text. Notice that the first indented quotation provides an object for the preposition *with;* the second, an object for the verb *supplies.*

Read the source, and notice the way Tracy Monahan combines paraphrase with quotation.

Egyptian pyramids, they project a political image of massive, lasting power.[7]

7   All four ministries are active, interrelated parts of Big Brother's massive propaganda machine. For example, they work together when grinding out materials for Hate Week. Each cog, however, has its particular job to do. The Ministry of Plenty (Miniplenty), specializes in economic propaganda; the Ministry of Peace (Minipax) in the military type. The Ministry of Love (Miniluv) reinforces or intensifies ideological propaganda.[8] Perhaps the biggest, most responsible cog in the machine, however, is the Ministry of Truth (Minitrue). Minitrue—with its slogans WAR IS PEACE, FREEDOM IS SLAVERY, IGNORANCE IS STRENGTH—not only produces political images and rhetoric in accordance with Big Brother's input but also coordinates and edits the propagandistic output of Miniplenty and Minipax. The huge machine never stops its propagandizing, and its perpetual, continuous noise has a mesmerizing effect on the whole society.

8   According to Richard S. Lambert, the internal propaganda of a totalitarian government "seeks to impose complete uniformity of thought, as well as of action, upon its citizens."[9] All-wise Big Brother knows this. "Where film production, the press, and radio transmission are not centrally controlled," Jacques Ellul writes, "no propaganda is possible."[10] Big Brother knows this too. In fact, he harnesses every channel of communication, holding tight reins on the Party specialists who run the Ministry of Truth. Minitrue provides Oceanic society with all its

> newspapers, films, textbooks, telescreen
> programs, plays, novels—with every
> conceivable kind of information, instruction,
> or entertainment, from a statue to a slogan,
> from a lyric poem to a biological treatise,
> and from a child's spelling book to a Newspeak
> dictionary. (pp. 43–44)

Those outside the Party—the proles—have such limited intelligence that Big Brother has to adapt his communication to their level. For their benefit, Minitrue supplies

    rubbishy newspapers containing almost nothing

except sport, crime, and astrology,
sensational five-cent novelettes, films oozing
with sex, and sentimental songs which were
composed entirely by mechanical means on a
special kind of kaleidoscope known as a
versificator. (p. 44)

This kind of escapist material, along with the
state lottery and numerous pubs, not only
contributes to the contentment of the proles but
also keeps their minds busy with things other than
the impact of power politics on their lives.

9   Big Brother uses the media for mass hypnosis.
He disseminates misinformation (largely lies but a
number of selected, twisted truths) that goes un-
recognized as propaganda. His propaganda preaches
only one gospel: the Party's ideal.

> The ideal set up by the Party was something
> huge, terrible, and glittering—a world of
> steel and concrete, of monstrous machines and
> terrifying weapons—a nation of warriors and
> fanatics, marching forward in perfect unity,
> all thinking the same thoughts and shouting
> the same slogans, perpetually working, fight-
> ing, triumphing, persecuting—three hundred
> million people all with the same face. (p. 74)

With the exception of a few characters like the
lovers Winston and Julia, the doublethinkers of
Oceania parrot the media's message; and, putting no
gods before Big Brother, they—as one body—live
their religion.

10   Orwell considered "the disappearance of objective history and the willingness of individuals to
work toward its elimination" as the "most frightening propagandistic achievement of the twentieth
century."[11] In Nineteen Eighty-Four, the work of
the Records Department in Minitrue is the control
of history. A Party slogan declares: "Who controls
the past controls the future: who controls the
present controls the past" (p. 35). Always tamper-
ing with records, Big Brother distorts, re-creates,
or destroys the past. As one critic has noted:

> No matter how intolerable the present is, the
> sense of alternative possibilities that objec-
> tive history inevitably presents can still
> liberate the imagination and perhaps lead to
> significant change. But once the past is per-
> petually "rectified" to conform to the pres-
> ent, this escape is no longer possible.[12]

11   Thousands working in the Records Department
look upon such "rectification" as daily routine.

SOURCE

Nineteen Eighty-Four (pp. 43–44)

> And the Records Department, after all, was itself only a
> single branch of the Ministry of Truth, whose primary job was
> not to reconstruct the past but to supply the citizens of
> Oceania with newspapers, films, textbooks, telescreen pro-
> grams, plays, novels—with every conceivable kind of infor-
> mation, instruction, or entertainment, from a statue to a slo-
> gan, from a lyric poem to a biological treatise and from a
> child's spelling book to a Newspeak dictionary. And the Min-
> istry had not only to supply the multifarious needs of the
> Party, but also to repeat the whole operation at a lower level
> for the benefit of the proletariat. There was a whole chain of
> separate departments dealing with proletarian literature,
> music, drama, and entertainment generally. Here were pro-
> duced rubbishy newspapers containing almost nothing except
> sport, crime, and astrology, sensational five-cent novelettes,
> films oozing with sex, and sentimental songs which were com-
> posed entirely by mechanical means on a special kind of ka-
> leidoscope known as a versificator.

COMMENTS

1. Observe Tracy Monahan's use of repetition as a transitional device in paragraph 9. The introduction to the long
quotation ends with "the Party's ideal," and the quotation
begins with "The ideal set up by the Party."

2. Paragraph 9 discusses point III(B) of the outline: Big
Brother's use of the media to propagate the Party's ideal.

COMMENTS

1. Paragraphs 10–14 develop point IV of the outline: The falsification of history. Observe the unified flow of Tracy Monahan's ideas as you read these paragraphs, paying special attention to the selection and arrangement of the three quotations, the first and third from Orwell, the second from Zwerdling.

2. Reread paragraphs 10–14 and carefully observe interrelations, a few of which are connected by arrows on page 805.

IV. The falsification of history

¶10   a reference to propagandistic achievement

Orwell: Two things are frightening:

    (1) the disappearance of history
    (2) the willingness of people
         to eliminate history

Zwerdling: A "rectified" past makes escape from present impossible.

11   a transitional paragraph echoing Zwerdling and referring to "rectification" as routine in the Records Department

12   One example of "rectification":

    Winston makes history disappear—a routine part of his job.

13   Another example:

    Many individuals work to eliminate history—a constant chore.

14   a reference to totalitarian propaganda

Winston thinks that wiping out the past is "more terrifying than torture and death."

Even Winston's thought may remind the reader of what Zwerdling said. Why this analogy? Does Winston sense, like Zwerdling, that no escape is possible except torture and death?

COMMENT

"As might be expected" provides the transition from point IV to point V. Paragraph 15 covers point V(A): Newspeak as a thought preventive.

This department falsifies the past to make it fit changes in present government policies.

12   False promises must be changed to suit present conditions. A clerk at the Speakwrite machine, Winston Smith "rectifies" materials sent to him through a pneumatic tube. Proficient in Newspeak (the official language), he reads a message: "times 14. 2. 84 miniplenty malquoted chocolate rectify" (p. 39). Winston dials on the telescreen for the copy of the *Times* (February 14, 1984) that carries Miniplenty's promise not to reduce the chocolate ration in 1984. He changes the optimistic promise to a pessimistic prediction: rationing may be necessary in April. He returns the altered version for filing and destroys the original by putting it into the memory hole, a kind of incinerator for irrelevant history, outdated information about vaporized persons, and other trash.

13   It is the state's policy to be in a constant state of war either with Eurasia or with Eastasia. Yet the Party insists that the present enemy has always been the enemy. When roles are reversed, the former enemy has never been an enemy but always an ally. Record clerks work frantically to make expedient changes in mountains of references to Eurasia and Eastasia. Minipax's military propaganda must constantly be "rectified" to protect the vital interest of the State: maintenance of power.

14   Eventually, Winston's experiences teach him to recognize totalitarian propaganda for what it is. Very disturbed by the systematic attack on the past, he thinks: "If the Party could thrust its hand into the past and say of this or that event, it never happened—that, surely, was more terrifying than torture and death" (p. 35).

15   As might be expected, Big Brother manipulates language to suit his purpose. His aim is to destroy words—the material for expressing ideas—and to eventually wipe out completely the necessity for thought. The words in Newspeak are formed in various ways: for example, by compounding (thoughtcrime, duckspeak, prolefeed, Minipax) and by adding prefixes or suffixes (ungood, thinkful).

Doubleplusgood gets rid of superlatives like <u>best</u> or <u>finest</u> and synonyms like <u>superb</u> or <u>excellent</u>. According to William Steinhoff, Newspeak is "the principal intellectual means by which doublethink is transformed into a conditioned reflex."[13] Doublethink is Big Brother's "reality control" (indeed "the occupational disease of propagandists").[14] Working in the Research Department as a compiler of the Newspeak dictionary, a clerk remarks that, unlike Oldspeak, the new language has a vocabulary that grows smaller, not larger. He says, "We're destroying words—scores of them, hundreds of them every day. . . . It's a beautiful thing, the destruction of words" (pp. 51–52).

COMMENTS

1. Four paragraphs (15–18) develop point V of the outline: The manipulation of thought and emotion.

2. Of these, three (16–18) develop parts of the second subheading: Rousing the emotions.

3. Notes 15 and 16 acknowledge the sources of ideas that are expressed in paraphrases (rather than in the exact words of the authors).

SOURCES

For note 15:

Oceania seeks to blot out spontaneous affection because it assumes, for good reason, that whatever is uncalculated is subversive. —IRVING HOWE

For note 16:

For the faithful [in Oceania], sexual energy is transformed into political hysteria. —IRVING HOWE

NOTE CARDS

Newspeak   ②

Steinhoff, p. 166: "Newspeak is the principal intellectual means by which doublethink is transformed into a conditioned reflex."

Newspeak—doublethink   ③

Zwerdling, p. 54: from a discussion of schizophrenic thinking in 1984: "an occupational disease of propagandists that is called 'reality control' or 'doublethink.'"

Newspeak   ①

In 1984 — p. 51 AND the appendix — aim, nature, etc.

Newspeak words—compounding, adding prefixes and suffixes

   bellyfeel, prolefeed, Minitrue, Pornosec, facecrime, sexcrime, crimestop, thought-crime — ungood, doubleplusgood, goodwise, gooder — duckspeaking

a duckspeaker, a fast talker in love with own voice, keeps quacking on and on.

16   Big Brother's propaganda not only straight-jackets thought but also manipulates emotions. Doublethinking Oceanians know that unqualified hatred of the State's enemies is a social necessity in their kingdom of love—love for Big Brother. Though living in a police state and (except for proles) under constant surveillance by Thought Police and Junior Spies, <u>loyal</u> citizens have nothing to fear, for they love their Leader and hate his enemies.

17   Those who love their leader, however, must have no room in their hearts for anyone else. When affection for others rises spontaneously, that love is considered subversive, something to be eliminated.[15] Though necessary for child-bearing, the sex act must be state-controlled. Winston's affair with Julia is a capital offense; the State must purify his heart in Miniluv's torture chambers.

18   Big Brother wisely turns the sex drive into political hysteria.[16] The fanatical Oceanians stand ready to strike terror into the hearts of any enemies. To stimulate hatred, Big Brother not only sets up a mythical Adversary but also uses such propaganda techniques as exciting rituals, stirring military music, barbaric rhythms, noisy rallies, slogan-chanting mobs, rabble-rousing war films, staged hangings. The Two Minute Hate and Hate Week intensify the mood. Like many another propagandist, Big Brother knows the unifying value of hate.

19   In <u>Nineteen Eighty-Four</u>, Orwell uses artistic exaggeration to help make his warning clear.[17] The reader can easily recognize Big Brother's propaganda for what it is——an obvious mixture of absurd lies and gross distortions of truth. Today's propaganda, however, is not always so easily recognized, for it tells the truth——convincing parts of it. By cleverly manipulating carefully selected facts, propagandists today either ignore or downplay any evidence that might effectively refute their one-sided arguments——the old card-stacking trick.[18] Modern propaganda has various names, such as government "publicity," political "advertising," or even official "communication packages." Such propaganda, like Big Brother's, often eulogizes the Leaders, hiding their mistakes and magnifying their successes.[19]

20   It has been said that Orwell's <u>Animal Farm</u> and <u>Nineteen Eighty-Four</u> "are probably the most widely read literary/political polemics ever written in English."[20] Of the two novels, perhaps <u>Nineteen Eighty-Four</u> is more likely to be remembered. It is a kind of nightmare that haunts the memory because its world looks much like our own. Readers of this novel ask questions like these: Was 1984 in 1948? Is 1984 almost here? Will it come soon? Maybe in 1994? Fortunately, the nightmare has not yet become reality.

> For it can be said that, so long as we can talk about <u>1984</u> and discuss whether it has come or not, then certainly it has not come: the one thing certain is that when 1984 is actually here and we are living in the kind of world that Orwell described as a warning, we shall be unconscious of it, and the very title of his book, which has become a monitory symbol for us, will have ceased to have any of its present meaning.[21]

COMMENTS

1. The main discussion ends with paragraph 18. The conclusion begins with paragraph 19.

2. Reread the first paragraph of the paper. Notice there the words and ideas that are repeated in paragraph 19. References to the title of Orwell's novel and to the nature of totalitarian propaganda are two examples of repetition. Linking the ideas in the introduction and those in the conclusion contributes to the unity of the paper.

SOURCE

For note 20:

> Orwell was never very clear about what sort of political system might work, nor was he particularly sophisticated about the peculiarities of *any* political organization. But he knew what he didn't like, and he knew why; the two short novels that emerged from this metamorphosis—*Animal Farm* and *1984*—are probably the most widely read literary/political polemics ever written in English. —ATLANTIC MONTHLY

COMMENTS

Note 1   Documentation of an unnumbered series. Not finding the place of publication on the title page of this book, Tracy Monahan asked a librarian about it and was referred to the *Cumulative Book Index*, which provides publication information.

Note 2   Reference to one volume of a four-volume work. The separate title appears before the main title. Compare the bibliography entry of Orwell's multivolume work.

NOTES

[1] Richard J. Voorhees, <u>The Paradox of George Orwell</u>, Humanities Series (Lafayette, Ind.: Purdue Univ. Studies, 1961), p. 87.

[2] Printed in <u>My Country Right or Left</u>, Vol. II of <u>The Collected Essays, Journalism and Letters of</u>

COMMENTS

Note 3   Tracy Monahan copies the title exactly as it is given on the title page of Colmer's book. For the usual treatment of titles within underlined titles, see notes 13 and 15.

Note 4   Reference to a continuously paginated issue of a journal. Omissions: the name of the season (Autumn) and the initial *The* in the title of the journal. (See also **10a** and page 796.) Notice also that the abbreviation for *pages* is omitted because of the presence of a volume number.

Note 6   A note providing more information than a simple citation of a source.

Note 7   A second reference. For clarity, a shortened title is supplied because Thomson's name does not appear in note 5.

Note 9   If the words *external* and *internal* had not been italicized in Lambert's original text, Tracy Monahan would have noted the change in emphasis as follows:

with their <u>internal</u> organization" (p. 138) (emphasis added).

Note 10   Here *trans.* means "translated by," not "translator." (In note 2, *ed.* means "edited by.")

Note 13   Observe that the title of Orwell's novel (underlined in the text) is not underlined because it appears within an italicized title.

George <u>Orwell</u>, ed. Sonia Orwell and Ian Angus (New York: Harcourt, 1968), 41.

3 John Colmer, <u>Coleridge to Catch–22</u> (New York: St. Martin's Press, 1978), p. 183.

4 "George Orwell and the Mad World: The Anti-Universe of <u>1984</u>," <u>South Atlantic Quarterly</u>, 66 (1967), 544–45.

5 <u>Mass Persuasion in History</u> (New York: Crane, Russak, 1977), p. 132.

6 George Orwell, <u>Nineteen Eighty–Four</u> (New York: Harcourt, 1949), p. 209. Subsequent references to pages of this edition are in the text. Other editions are as follows: Irving Howe, <u>Orwell's Nineteen Eighty–Four: Text, Sources, Criticism</u>, 2nd ed. (New York: Harcourt, 1982); <u>1984, A Novel by George Orwell</u> (1949; rpt. New York: New American Library, Signet Classic, 1971).

7 Thomson, <u>Mass Persuasion</u>, p. 41.

8 For a description of seven types of propaganda, see Thomson, pp. 11–13.

9 <u>Propaganda</u>, Discussion Books, No. 13 (London: Thomas Nelson, 1938), p. 138. Lambert also points out that the totalitarian state is more concerned with internal propaganda than with external: "But great as have been the <u>external</u> propagandist efforts of the dictator–ruled countries, they are half–hearted and indirect as compared with their <u>internal</u> organization" (p. 138).

10 <u>Propaganda</u>, trans. Konrad Kellen and Jean Lerner (New York: Knopf, 1965), p. 102.

11 Alex Zwerdling, <u>Orwell and the Left</u> (New Haven: Yale Univ. Press, 1974), p. 52.

12 Zwerdling, p. 53.

13 William Steinhoff, <u>George Orwell and the Origins of</u> 1984 (Ann Arbor: Univ. of Michigan Press, 1975), p. 166.

14 Zwerdling, p. 54.

15 Irving Howe, "1984: History as Nightmare," in <u>Twentieth Century Interpretations of</u> 1984, ed. Samuel Hynes (Englewood Cliffs, N.J.: Prentice-Hall, 1971), p. 48.

16 Howe, p. 49.

COMMENTS

Note 18 Reference to one page of a multi-page article in an encyclopedia.

Note 19 Observe the retention of the ampersand in the title of the magazine.

Note 20 Documentation of an unsigned, untitled review.

[17] Orwell also warns us about "veiled censorship" in a free press. See "The Freedom of the Press," New York Times Magazine, 8 Oct. 1972, p. 12.

[18] Hadley Cantril and Clyde W. Hart, "Propaganda," World Book Encyclopedia, 1975 ed., XV, 727.

[19] John S. Lang, "The Great American Bureaucratic Propaganda Machine," U.S. News & World Report, 27 Aug. 1979, p. 43.

[20] Rev. of The Transformation, by Peter Stansky and William Abrahams, Atlantic Monthly, April 1980, pp. 126–27.

[21] Christopher Small, The Road to Miniluv (Pittsburgh: Univ. of Pittsburgh Press, 1975), p. 21.

COMMENTS

1. All works cited as sources should be included in the bibliography.

2. A commonly used heading, BIBLIOGRAPHY generally refers to printed material only. Other possible headings are:

   WORKS CITED   A listing of all works (including nonprint materials such as audiodiscs) cited in the paper.

   WORKS CONSULTED   A listing not only of works cited but those consulted but not cited.

3. If the specimen research paper had included works consulted but not cited, entries such as the following would have been added.

   Myers, Jeffrey and Valerie. *George Orwell: An Annotated Bibliography of Criticism.* Garland Reference Library of the Humanities, 54. New York: Garland Publishing, 1977.

   Pohl, Fredrik, et al. "George Orwell's Vision of the Future: Pro and Con." *The Futurist,* April 1979, pp. 100–17.

Note: The Myers entry above lists a book by two authors with the same last name—stated as printed on the title page. Compare:

Gibson, Walter B., and Litzka R. Gibson. *The Psychic Sciences.* New York: Doubleday, 1966. [The last name appears twice on the title page.]

BIBLIOGRAPHY

Cantril, Hadley, and Clyde W. Hart. "Propaganda." World Book Encyclopedia. 1975 ed.

Colmer, John. Coleridge to Catch–22: Images of Society. New York: St. Martin's Press, 1978.

Ellul, Jacques. Propaganda: The Formation of Men's Attitudes. Trans. Konrad Kellen and Jean Lerner. New York: Knopf, 1965.

Howe, Irving. "1984: History as Nightmare." In Twentieth Century Interpretations of 1984: A Collection of Critical Essays. Ed. Samuel Hynes. Englewood Cliffs, N.J.: Prentice–Hall, 1971.

Lambert, Richard S. Propaganda. Discussion Books, No. 13. London: Thomas Nelson, 1938.

Lang, John S. "The Great American Bureaucratic Propaganda Machine." U.S. News & World Report, 27 Aug. 1979, pp. 43–47.

Orwell, George. The Collected Essays, Journalism and Letters of George Orwell. Ed. Sonia Orwell and Ian Angus. 4 vols. New York: Harcourt, 1968.

——————. "The Freedom of the Press." New York Times Magazine, 8 Oct. 1972, p. 12.

——————. Nineteen Eighty–Four. New York: Harcourt, 1949.

Ranald, Ralph A. "George Orwell and the Mad World: The Anti–Universe of 1984." South Atlantic

COMMENTS

1. Alphabetization: Initial articles (*A*, *An*, *The*) are ignored in alphabetizing. For example, Orwell's *The Collected Essays* precedes *Nineteen Eighty-Four* (*C* before *N*).

2. Punctuation: Observe the use and placement of periods and commas, especially in relation to parentheses and quotation marks. A colon separates titles from subtitles.

3. Annotation: If you are asked to submit an annotated bibliography, supply a brief description of each entry, as in this example:

Spoehr, Luther. Rev. of <u>A People's History of the United States</u>, by Howard Zinn. <u>Saturday Review</u>, 2 Feb. 1980, p. 37.

Considered a radical historian, Zinn describes a kind of pyramidal power structure (the powerful elite, their servile "guards," and the oppressed underclass) and advocates "decentralized socialism that will run society 'from the bottom up.'"

<u>Quarterly</u>, 66 (1967), 544–53.

Rev. of <u>The Transformation</u>, by Peter Stansky and William Abrahams. <u>Atlantic Monthly</u>, April 1980, pp. 126–27.

Small, Christopher. <u>The Road to Miniluv: George Orwell, the State, and God</u>. Pittsburgh: Univ. of Pittsburgh Press, 1975.

Steinhoff, William. <u>George Orwell and the Origins of 1984</u>. Ann Arbor: Univ. of Michigan Press, 1975.

Thomson, Oliver. <u>Mass Persuasion in History: An Historical Analysis of the Development of Propaganda Techniques</u>. New York: Crane, Russak, 1977.

Voorhees, Richard J. <u>The Paradox of George Orwell</u>. Humanities Series. Lafayette, Ind.: Purdue Univ. Studies, 1961.

Zwerdling, Alex. <u>Orwell and the Left</u>. New Haven: Yale Univ. Press, 1974.

Note: Some instructors prefer to receive handwritten rather than typewritten papers. Below is a sample page from a handwritten research paper in which footnotes were used instead of endnotes.

"Where film production, the press, and radio transmission are not centrally controlled," writes Jacques Ellul, "no propaganda is possible."[10] Knowing this, Big Brother holds tight reins on the Party specialists who run the Ministry of Truth. Minitrue provides Oceania with all its

newspapers, films, textbooks, telescreen programs, plays, novels — with every conceivable kind of information, instruction, or entertainment, from a statue to a slogan, from a lyric poem to a biological treatise, and from a child's spelling book to a Newspeak dictionary. (pp. 43-44)

Those outside the Party have such limited intelligence that Big Brother has to adapt his communication to their level. For their benefit,

[10] *Propaganda*, trans. Konrad Kellen and Jean Lerner (New York: Knopf, 1965), p. 102.

Business Writing

34

Write effective business letters and resumés.

Business letters are usually typed on only one side of white, unlined, $8\frac{1}{2} \times 11$ inch paper. Standard business envelopes measure about $3\frac{1}{2} \times 6\frac{1}{2}$ inches or 4×10 inches. (Letterhead stationery and envelopes vary in both size and color.)

34a

Business Letters

A business letter has six parts: (1) the heading, (2) the inside address, (3) the salutation, (4) the body of the letter, (5) the closing, which consists of the complimentary close and the signature (handwritten and then typed), and (6) any added notations.

BUSINESS LETTER FORMATS

If you work for a company, you should check to see if it has a policy about the format for business letters. Many do. Most companies use one of three styles: full block, modified block, or indented. In full block, the most formal style, all parts of the letter, including the first lines of paragraphs, are flush with the left margin. The model letter on page 812 is in full-block style. In modified-block style, shown in the letter on pages 812–13, the heading and the complimentary close are moved to the right. The indented format (pages 813 and 814) also moves the heading and the closing to the right and uses paragraph indention. This format is the least formal, the most like a personal letter. By and large, businesses or officials use the modified block, whereas individuals use the indented format.

(1) The heading of the letter gives the full address of the writer and the date of the letter.

If letterhead stationery is used, the date is typed beneath it in the center of the page. If plain stationery is used, the address of the writer followed by the date is put at the top of the page, flush with the right-hand margin, as in the letters on page 813. Notice that the heading is blocked and has no end punctuation.

(2) The inside address gives the name and full address of the addressee.

Four to six lines usually separate the heading from the inside address, depending on how much space is needed to center the body of the letter on the page.

(3) The salutation greets the addressee appropriately.

The salutation is written flush with the left margin, two

spaces below the inside address, and is followed by a colon. The salutation should be consistent with the tone of the letter, the first line of the inside address, and the complimentary close.

When the surname of the addressee is known, it is used in the salutation of a business letter, as in the following examples.

Dear Dr. Davis:	Dear Mayor Rodriguez:
Dear Mrs. Greissman:	Dear Ms. Joseph:

Note: Use *Miss* or *Mrs.* if the woman you are addressing has indicated a preference. Otherwise, use *Ms.*, which is always appropriate and which is preferred by many businesswomen, whatever their marital status.

In letters to organizations, or to persons whose name and sex are unknown, such salutations as the following are customary:

Dear Sir or Madam:	Dear L. L. Bean:
Dear Subscription Manager:	Dear Registrar:

If you do not know the name of the addressee, but you do know the sex, use either *Dear Sir* or *Dear Madam*.

For the appropriate forms of salutations and addresses in letters to government officials, military personnel, and so on, check an etiquette book or the front or back of your college dictionary.

(4) The body of the letter should follow the principles of good writing.

Typewritten letters are usually single-spaced, with double spacing between paragraphs. All paragraphs should begin flush with the left margin (in full block or modified block) or should be indented five to ten spaces (in indented format). The subject matter should be organized so that the reader can grasp immediately what is wanted, and the style should be clear and direct. Do not use stilted or abbreviated phrasing:

NOT	"The aforementioned letter"	BUT	"Your letter"
NOT	"Please send me it ASAP"	BUT	"Please send it to me as soon as possible."

(5) The closing ends the letter.

In full-block style, the closing is typed flush with the left-hand margin. In modified block and indented style, it is typed to the right of the letter, in alignment with the heading. The parts of the closing are as follows:

The complimentary close: This conventional ending is typed three lines below the last paragraph of the body of the letter. Among the endings commonly used in business letters are the following:

FORMAL	LESS FORMAL
Very truly yours,	Sincerely,
Sincerely yours,	Cordially,

The typed name: The name (as it will be written) is typed four lines below the closing.

Title of sender: This line, following the typed name, indicates the sender's position, if he or she is acting in an official capacity.

> Manager, Employee Relations
> Chairperson, Search Committee

Signature: The letter is signed between the complimentary close and the typed name.

(6) Notations supply additional information.

Notations are typed below the closing, flush with the left margin. They indicate, among other things, whether anything is enclosed with or attached to the letter (*enc., att.*); to whom copies of the letter have been sent (*cc: AAW, PTN*); and the initials of the sender and the typist (*DM/cll*).

MODEL BUSINESS LETTER

MIRACLE MILE COMMUNITY LEAGUE

1992 South Cochran Avenue   Los Angeles, CA 90036

February 1, 1982

```
Dr. Nathan T. Swift       ⎫
Community Health Center   ⎬ INSIDE ADDRESS
1101 Figueroa Street      ⎪
Los Angeles, CA  90027    ⎭
```

Dear Dr. Swift: **SALUTATION**

BODY
```
We have completed our evaluation of the nutrition
education program being conducted by your organi-
zation.  While the results are encouraging,
some aspects of the program might be modified.
Awareness training for the staff, a few schedule
changes, and greater involvement of the parents
could significantly improve the results of the
program.

We have prepared a study outlining the problems as
we see them and our recommendations for improving
the program. Angel Chavez, our Vice President for
Management Development, has agreed to work with you,
if you would like his assistance.

We look forward to hearing from you soon.
```

```
Sincerely,          Complimentary close  ⎫
                                         ⎪
  [signature:       Signature            ⎬ CLOSING
  Dorothy Muir]                          ⎪
Dorothy Muir        Typed name           ⎪
Chairman, Advisory Committee   Title     ⎭
```

DM/ewl   **NOTATION**

TYPES OF BUSINESS LETTERS

(1) Thank-you letter

Thank-you letters are written often in private life, but they are also used in business. If a representative of a company has been helpful or done more than you expected, a thank-

you letter or note is an appropriate way of showing appreciation. A gift, recommendation, award, or prize should also be acknowledged with a letter of thanks.

Usually, thank-you letters are in the informal indented style. It is not necessary to include an inside address, and a comma replaces the colon after the salutation. There are some who think thank-you letters should be handwritten, but typewritten ones are equally correct.

THANK-YOU LETTER

```
                           107 Kentin Drive
                           Mobile, AL  21304
                           December 12, 1981

Dear Dean Rutledge,

    Thank you very much for recommending me for The
Honor Society of Phi Kappa Phi.  I was chosen as one of
the members and attended the installation ceremony last
Tuesday evening.  I told my parents about your
recommendation, and they are as pleased as I am.

                           Sincerely,

                           [signature: John Trevant]

                           John Trevant
```

(2) Claim and adjustment letter

One of the most common business letters is the letter of claim and adjustment, which should include the following information.

Your claim: Describe exactly what is wrong. The more specific your description, the easier and quicker it will be to correct the situation. If an airline has lost your suitcase, for example, describe it fully and also include the flight number, date, and your destination. If an appliance is faulty, include the model and serial numbers in addition to the brand name and style.

Your request: Often a company will do exactly what you suggest, as long as it is possible. Again, the more specific your request—and the more reasonable and courteous your tone—the better your chance of getting what you want.

CLAIM AND
ADJUSTMENT LETTER
```
                           742 Rock Street
                           Chicago, IL  60646
                           February 11, 1982

Mr. Norman Huckley
Huckley Electronics, Inc.
235 Central Avenue
Chicago, IL  60637

Dear Mr. Huckley:

A week ago today I bought a 19" Supersonic color
television set from you, model number 0300-B, serial
number 0137-8112-77.  All week the set has worked
perfectly, but when I turned it on today, nothing
happened.  The trouble is not with the electrical
outlet, which I checked by plugging in another
appliance.
```

I would like you to examine the set here in my apartment, and either repair it free of charge or replace it with another 19" Supersonic. My telephone number is 689-4140, and you can call me any day from noon to 5:00 p.m.

Sincerely,

Thomas McNally

Thomas McNally

(3) Order letter

In an order letter, supply the following information as exactly as possible:

Description: Indicate the name of the product, the model or stock number if you know it, the page of the catalog from which you are ordering, the quantity of each item, and the price.

Destination: State whether you want the order shipped to the inside address at the top of your letter or to another address.

Any special circumstances: State such things as whether you need the order by a particular date, whether you want it sent a particular way (air freight, for example), or whether you will not pay more than a certain price.

Payment information: Include payment or indicate how you plan to pay for the merchandise.

ORDER LETTER

736 Minette Avenue
Cary, NC 27511
February 5, 1982

Trailblazers, Inc.
4200 West Washington Boulevard
Tacoma, WA 90876

Dear Trailblazers:

I wish to order the following merchandise from your Fall 1981 catalog:

1 Western camp shirt, #007, p. 5, size 10, blue, $18.95
2 Ragg sweaters, #095, p. 7, size 36, tan and navy, $19.95 each
1 Greenleaf sleeping bag, #432, p. 34, $43.00
1 Trailblazers dome tent, #212, p. 46, $112.00

Please ship this merchandise by surface carrier to my address as shown at the top of this letter.

I have enclosed a check for $230.00, which includes the $16.15 parcel post and handling charges specified in your ordering instructions.

Sincerely,

Susan Walters

Susan Walters

enc.

(4) Application letter

The purpose of an application letter is to convince the reader that he or she should examine your resumé. In it you should indicate the job you want and, briefly, your qualifications. In the last paragraph you should indicate when you are available for an interview. A letter of application is usually accompanied by a resumé (page 815), which gives more information about you than your letter can. Neither your letter nor your resumé should be longer than one typed page.

BUSINESS ENVELOPES

The address that appears on the envelope is identical to the inside address. The return address regularly gives the full name and address of the writer. With the zip code, special postal abbreviations not followed by periods may be used for names of states.

MODEL ADDRESSED ENVELOPE

Diane Bellows
1830 Lexington Avenue
Louisville, KY 40227

Mr. Aaron Navik
Personnel Manager
Echo Electronics
627 East 3rd Street
Louisville, KY 40223

APPLICATION LETTER

1830 Lexington Avenue
Louisville, KY 40227
June 8, 1981

Mr. Aaron Navik
Personnel Manager
Echo Electronics
627 East 3rd Street
Louisville, KY 40223

Dear Mr. Navik:

Please consider me for the position of Assistant Director of Employee Benefits in the Personnel Division of Echo Electronics. I was an administrative intern with Echo last summer and, now that I have graduated from the University of Louisville, I would like to join your company.

As you can see from the attached resumé, my major was Business Administration with special emphasis in personnel management. Whenever possible, I have looked for jobs and campus activities that would give me experience in dealing with people. As an assistant in the Admissions Office, I dealt with students, parents, alumni, and faculty. The position required both a knowledge of university regulations and sympathy for other people.

As an intern with Echo, I learned about the management of a company at first hand and gained a firmer grasp of the contribution personnel management makes to the overall objectives of the company. Participants in the intern program were required to write a paper analyzing the company where we were placed. If you are interested, I will be happy to send you a copy of my paper.

I would very much like to put my interests and my training to work for Echo Electronics, and I am available for an interview at your convenience.

                    Sincerely,

                    Diane Bellows

                    Diane Bellows

enc.

34b

The Resumé

A resumé is a list of a person's qualifications for a job and is enclosed with a letter of application. It is made up of four categories of information:

(1) Personal data: name, mailing address, telephone number
(2) Educational background
(3) Work experience
(4) Location of credentials file, which includes letters of recommendation

Like the letter of application, the resumé is a form of persuasion designed to emphasize your qualifications for a job and to get you an interview. Since there is usually more than one applicant for every job, your resumé should make the most of your qualifications. After reading all the letters and resumés received, a potential employer usually decides to interview only the three or four strongest candidates.

Writing a resumé requires the same planning and attention to detail that writing a paper does. First, make a list of the jobs you have had, the activities and clubs you have been part of, and the offices you have held. Amplify these items by adding dates, job titles and responsibilities, and a brief statement about what you learned from each of them. Arrange these items with the most recent first: March 1981–present, September 1979–February 1981. Remember that activities that do not appear to be relevant to the job you want may be explained to show that you learned important things from them. The resumés on pages 814–15 illustrate the points in the list at the top of the page.

You may find it helpful to consult one of the following books for further information on application letters, resumés, and interviews:

Juvenal L. Angel. *The Complete Resume Book and Job-Getter's Guide.* New York: Pocket Books, 1980.
Richard N. Bolles. *What Color Is Your Parachute? A Practical Manual for Job-Hunters and Career Changers.* 5th edition. Berkeley: Ten Speed Press, 1979.
John J. Komar. *The Interview Game: Winning Strategies for the Job Seeker.* New York: Follett, 1979.
Michael H. Smith. *The Resumé Writer's Handbook.* 2nd edition. New York: Barnes and Noble, 1980.

RESUMÉ DO'S AND DON'TS

DON'T	DO
1. Don't include personal material—age, marital status, photograph, etc.—that is not relevant to the job.	1. Do include your address and telephone number.
2. Don't mention specific courses unless they are directly relevant to the job.	2. Do mention your degree and the *areas* in which you received special training.
3. Don't include career goals. You may wish to change them or raise them.	3. Do *think* about your career goals so that you can discuss them during the interview.
4. Don't include salary unless you will not accept less.	4. Do *think* about the salary you will accept so that you can discuss it during the interview.
5. Don't mention jobs and activities unless you can make them relevant to the job.	5. Do explain briefly how each job and activity included pertains to the job you want.
6. Don't use a cluttered, sprawling format. It looks inefficient and unprofessional.	6. Do use a clear, crisp format. It shows the reader you are efficient and professional.

RESUMÉ 1 — DON'T

Diane Bellows   Marital status: Single
1830 Lexington Avenue   Health: Excellent
Louisville, KY 40227   Date of birth: 3/29/57

Education:

        University of Louisville, B.A., 1981
            Major: Business Administration--Personnel
            Management.
                Courses: Labor Relations, Personnel
                Management, etc.
            Minor: Economics.
                Courses: Money and Banking, Production
                Analysis, etc.

Career goal: To be personnel manager for a large company.

Salary desired: $1500/mo.

Experience:

        Volunteer worker for Arthur Schneider's School
        Board campaign, Summer, 1979.

        Academic Committee for Alpha Phi Sorority, 1979–81.

        Advertising Manager for University Yearbook, 1980.

        Student Worker in Admissions Office, 1979–81.

        Intern, Echo Electronics, Louisville, KY, 1980.

Activities:

        Active in Alpha Phi Sorority, 1979–81.

        Member of Heights Christian Church.

Coach, Girls' Softball League.

Cheerleader, Southeast High School.

| PHOTOGRAPH |

References: Placement Office
            University of Louisville
            Louisville, KY 40222

RESUMÉ 2 — DO

                              Diane Bellows
                              1830 Lexington Avenue
                              Louisville, KY 40227
                              (502) 689-3137

EDUCATION   University of Louisville, B.A., 1981

               Major: Business Administration with
                      emphasis in personnel management
               Minor: Economics with emphasis in
                      corporate finance

EXPERIENCE

  College   Orientation Leader, University Admissions
               Office, 1979–81. Met with prospective
               students and their parents; conducted tours
               of campus; answered questions; wrote reports
               for each orientation meeting.

               Academic Committee, Alpha Phi Sorority,
               1979–81. Organized study halls and tutoring
               services for disadvantaged students.

               Advertising Manager, University Yearbook,
               1980. Responsible for securing advertising
               that made the Yearbook self-supporting;
               wrote monthly progress report.

  Summers   Intern, Echo Electronics, June, 1980.
               Spent two weeks learning about pension plans,
               health care benefits, employee associations,
               and work regulations as they affect employee
               relations and personnel management.

               Volunteer Worker, Arthur Schneider's
               School Board reelection campaign, 1979.
               Wrote press releases, campaign brochures,
               direct mailers; researched information on
               teacher competence.

REFERENCES   Placement Office
               University of Louisville
               Louisville, KY 40222
               (502) 744-3219

■ **Exercise**

1. Prepare a resumé and then write a letter of application for a position you are competent to fill.
2. Write to the principal of the high school you graduated from, thanking her for recommending you for a summer job.
3. Call the attention of your representative in city government to repairs that are needed in your neighborhood playground.
4. Write to a national record company complaining about the technical quality of the record you ordered from them.
5. Order a particular ten-speed bicycle part from a bicycle warehouse.

Glossary of Grammatical Terms

This glossary presents brief explanations of frequently used grammatical terms. Consult the index for references to further discussion of most of the terms and for a number of terms not listed.

absolute   A parenthetical word or phrase that qualifies the rest of the sentence and is not related to it by a connective. An absolute does not modify a specific word or phrase in the sentence.

> **True**, Rome was not built in a day.
> **Considering the risks**, giving up cigarettes is sensible.

The term *absolute phrase* is often used for the type of absolute illustrated below.

> **The hostages free at last**, Americans rejoiced.
> COMPARE   The hostages *were* free at last. Americans rejoiced.
> **The expressway jammed with rush-hour traffic**, we were delayed two hours.
> COMPARE   The expressway **was** jammed with rush-hour traffic, **so** we were delayed two hours.
> I do not get much studying done in my dormitory room— **students running up and down the hall and yelling at one another and TV sets and stereos outblaring my FM music.**
> COMPARE   I do not get much studying done in my dormitory room **because** students **run** up and down the hall and **yell** at one another and TV sets and stereos **outblare** my FM music.

See **2a**. See also **parenthetical element**, **phrase**, and **participle**.

abstract noun   See **noun**.

acronym   A word made up of the first letter or two of a series of words.

> scuba   [self-contained underwater breathing apparatus]
> radar   [radio detecting and ranging]
> NASA   [National Aeronautics Space Administration]

active voice   See **voice**.

adjectival   Any word or word group functioning as an adjective: "*happy* people," "those *living on a fixed income*." The term is especially useful when it refers to a modifier without degrees of comparison.

> **this** one, **subscription** TV, **its** value, **an OPEC** decision
> people **on the street**, Nancy's **end-of-term** jitters
> one **who has a good sense of humor**, films **I like best**

See also **comparison**.

adjective   A part of speech regularly used to modify (describe or limit) a noun or a pronoun. Descriptive adjectives, unlike limiting adjectives, can usually be compared. See **comparison** and **adjectival**.

> **blue** sky, **newer** car, **best** joke, **beautiful** art [descriptive]
> **a** boy, **that** one, **its** nest, **both** men—**Whose** idea? [limiting]

Proper adjectives are capitalized. See **9a(3)**.

> **Christlike** figure   **Irish** humor   **Victorian** styles

Predicate adjectives function as complements of linking verbs (such as *feel, look, smell, sound, taste,* and forms of *be*). See **linking verb**.

> The milk tasted **sour**. They may be **lucky**. How **tall** is he?

See Section **4**.

adjective clause An adjectival containing a subject and verb. See also **adjectival** and **clause**.

> We usually like the people **who like us**.

adverb A part of speech regularly used to modify (describe or limit) a verb, an adjective, or another adverb.

> **slowly** ate, **too** tall, entered **very quietly** [*Slowly* modifies the verb *ate; too* the adjective *tall; very* the adverb *quietly; quietly* the verb *entered.*]

An adverb may also modify a verbal, or a whole phrase, clause, or sentence.

> **Naturally,** the villain succeeds at first by **completely** outwitting the hero. [*Naturally* modifies the rest of the sentence, and *completely* modifies the gerund *outwitting.*]

See Section **4**. See also **intensifier**.

adverb clause An adverbial containing a subject and a verb. See also **adverbial** and **clause**.

> **Although George Mason is not famous,** his ideas were used in our Bill of Rights.
> Cartoonists make at least eighteen drawings **so that Woody Woodpecker can laugh victoriously.**

adverbial A word (an adverb, but especially a noun, a conjunction, or an interjection), phrase, or clause functioning as an adverb.

> **Wow,** I forgot to ask; **however,** I'll see him **Friday**.
> **When the hail started,** we ran **into the library**.

adverbial conjunction See **conjunctive adverb**.

agreement The correspondence in form of one word with another to indicate number, person, or gender.

> NUMBER   the boy asks, boys ask   this type, these types
> PERSON   I am, you are, he is   I was, you were, he was
> GENDER   the man himself, the woman herself, the book itself

See Section **6**.

antecedent A word or word group that a pronoun refers to.

> Before **Ron** left, **he** paid the **man** and **woman who** delivered the firewood. [*Ron* is the antecedent of the personal pronoun *he; man* and *woman* are the antecedents of the relative pronoun *who.*]

See **6b** and Section **28**.

appositive A noun or noun substitute set beside another noun or noun substitute and identifying or explaining it.

> Davis, our **guide**, did not see the grizzly. [Compare "Davis was our guide." See also page 667.]
> A tasty **preservative**, salt is nutritious. [*Preservative* is in apposition with *salt.*]

See also **12d(2)**.

article *The, a,* or *an,* used adjectivally before nouns (**the** cups, **a** cup, **an** apple). *The* is a definite article. *A* and *an* are indefinite articles: see **19i** and **indefinite**.

attributive A noun used as an adjective (**examination** *questions*) or an adjective placed beside the word it modifies (**difficult** *questions* OR *questions,* **difficult** *but* **clear**). See **adjectival**; contrast **predicate adjective**.

auxiliary verb A verb (like *be, have, do*) used with a main verb in a verb phrase. An auxiliary regularly indicates tense but may also indicate voice, mood, person, number.

> **are** eating   **will be** eating   **was** eaten
> **has** eaten   **Do** eat with us.   **have been** eaten

Modal auxiliaries (such as *will, would, shall, should, may, might, must, can, could*) do not take such inflectional endings as *-s, -ing,* or *-en.*
See also **1a** and Section **7**.

case The form or position of a word that shows its use or relationship to other words in a sentence. The three cases in English are the *subjective* (or nominative), the *possessive* (or genitive), and the *objective.* Pronouns and nouns have case: see Section **5** and **15a**.

clause A group of related words that contains both a subject and a predicate and that functions as a part of a sentence. A clause is either *main* (independent) or *subordinate* (dependent).

> SENTENCES
> Only a few stars came out.   The moon was bright.
> I know Herb.   He will run for office.

> MAIN CLAUSES
> **Only a few stars came out,** for **the moon was bright.**
> **I know Herb;** he will run for office.
> [sentences connected by using the coordinating conjunction *for* and by using a semicolon and lower case for *he*]

> SUBORDINATE CLAUSES
> Only a few stars came out **because the moon was bright.** [adverb clause]
> I know Herb, **who will run for office.** [adjective clause]
> I know **that Herb will run for office.** [noun clause—direct object]
> [sentences converted to subordinate clauses by using the subordinating conjunctions *because* and *that* and the relative pronoun *who,* a subordinator]

Elliptical clauses have omitted elements that are clearly understood: see **elliptical construction**.

clipped form A shortened word like [tele]*phone, ad*[vertisement], or [in]*flu*[enza]. Dictionaries include no usage labels for many clipped forms; they label many others *informal* or *slang*.

collective noun See **noun**.

comma splice Misuse of a comma between main clauses not connected by a coordinating conjunction. See Section **3**.

common noun See **noun**.

comparative See **comparison**.

comparison The inflection or modification of an adjective or adverb to indicate degrees in quality, quantity, or manner. There are three degrees: positive, comparative, and superlative.

> POSITIVE   COMPARATIVE   SUPERLATIVE
> good, well   better   best

POSITIVE	COMPARATIVE	SUPERLATIVE
high	higher	highest
quickly	more quickly	most quickly
active	less active	least active

See **4c**.

complement   A word or words used to complete the sense of a verb. Although the term may refer to a direct or an indirect object, it usually refers to a subject complement, an object complement, or the complement of a verbal like *to be*.

> The lasagna tasted **delicious**. [subject complement]
> We made the ferret our **mascot**. [object complement]
> To be a good **leader**, one must learn how to follow. [complement of the infinitive *to be*]

complete predicate   See **predicate**.

complete subject   See **subject**.

complex sentence   See **sentence**.

compound   A word or word group with two or more parts that function as a unit.

> COMPOUND NOUNS   dropout, hunger strike, sister-in-law
> COMPOUND SUBJECT **Republicans**, **Democrats**, and **Independents** are working together.
> COMPOUND PREDICATE   Kate **has tried** but **has** not **succeeded**.

See also **sentence**.

compound-complex sentence   See **sentence**.

compound predicate   See **compound**.

compound sentence   See **sentence**.

compound subject   See **compound**.

concrete noun   See **noun**.

A set or table of the inflected forms of a verb that indicate tense, person, number, voice, and mood.

PRINCIPAL PARTS

see   saw   seen

Active voice   *Passive voice*

INDICATIVE MOOD

PRESENT TENSE

I / you / we / they *see*   I *am seen*
he / she / it *sees*   he / she / it *is seen*
                                   you / we / they *are seen*

PAST TENSE

I / he / you / we / they *saw*   I / he *was seen*
                                   you / we / they *were seen*

FUTURE TENSE

I / he / you / we / they *will*   I / he / you / we / they *will*
(OR *shall*) *see*   (OR *shall*) *be seen*

PRESENT PERFECT TENSE

I / you / we / they *have seen*   I / you / we / they *have been*
he *has seen*   *seen*
                                   he *has been seen*

PAST PERFECT TENSE

I / he / you / we / they *had*   I / he / you / we / they *had*
seen   *been seen*

FUTURE PERFECT TENSE

I / he / you / we / they *will*   I / he / you / we / they *will*
(OR *shall*) *have seen*   (OR *shall*) *have been seen*

Active voice   *Passive voice*

SUBJUNCTIVE MOOD

PRESENT TENSE

that he / I / you / we / they   that he / I / you / we / they
see   *be seen*

PAST TENSE

that he / I / you / we / they   that he / I / you / we / they
saw   *were seen*

PRESENT PERFECT TENSE

that he / I / you / we / they   that he / I / you / we / they
have seen   *have been seen*

PAST PERFECT TENSE

(same as the indicative)

IMPERATIVE MOOD

PRESENT TENSE

see   be seen

See page 687 for a synopsis of the progressive forms.

conjunction   A part of speech used to connect and relate words, phrases, clauses, or sentences. There are two kinds of conjunctions: coordinating and subordinating.

Coordinating conjunctions connect words and word groups of equal grammatical rank: *and, but, or, nor, for, so,* and *yet*.

> Dick **and** Mario will go into politics **or** social work.
> Not only did the temperature fall below zero, **but** the wind was blowing.

See also Section **26** and **correlatives**.

Subordinating conjunctions mark a dependent clause and connect it with a main clause: *after, although, as, as if, because, before, if, since, unless, until, when, while,* and so forth.

> **When** Frank does not wish to hear, he acts **as if** he were deaf.

conjunctive adverb   An adverbial connective, such as *consequently, then, nonetheless.* See the list on page 677.

> Inflation and recession affect the purchasing power of the dollar; **moreover**, they have an impact on the consumer's buying habits.

connective   A word or phrase that links and relates words, phrases, clauses, or sentences, such as *and, although, otherwise, finally, on the contrary, which, not only . . . but also.* Conjunctions, conjunctive adverbs, transitional expressions, relative pronouns, and correlatives function as connectives. See also **31c(4)**.

construction   A grammatical unit (such as a sentence, clause, or phrase) or the arrangement of related words in a grammatical unit.

contact clause   One clause, usually subordinate, attached to another clause without the use of a connective. A contact clause that functions as an adjective is restrictive.

> Luke did not have a friend **he could fully trust**.   [*whom* or *that* omitted after *friend*]
> The trivia **I am interested in** can be found in newspaper fillers.   [*which* or *that* omitted after *trivia*]

See also **restrictive**.

coordinating conjunction   See **conjunction**.

correlatives   Connectives used in pairs: *both . . . and; either . . . or; neither . . . nor; not only . . . but also; whether . . . or*. See also **26c** and **coordinating conjunctions**.

count noun   See **noun**.

dangling modifier   A word or word group that does not modify (or modify clearly) another word or word group in the sentence. An absolute expression is not a dangling modifier.

> DANGLING   **Racing to class**, that open manhole went unnoticed.   [*Racing* modifies nothing in the sentence. The reader expects *racing* to modify the subject—which is *manhole*.]
> REVISED   **Racing** to class, **I** did not notice that open manhole.   [*Racing* clearly modifies the subject *I*.]

See also **25b**.

declension   A set or table of inflected forms of nouns or pronouns. As the following table shows, nouns are inflected only in the possessive case. The personal pronouns and the relative/interrogative pronoun *who* are inflected in all three cases.

NOUN

	Subjective	*Possessive*	*Objective*
SINGULAR	day	day's	day
PLURAL	days	days'	days

PRONOUNS

	Subjective	*Possessive*	*Objective*
		Singular	
FIRST PERSON	I	my, mine	me
SECOND PERSON	you	your, yours	you
THIRD PERSON	he, she, it	his, her, hers, its	him, her, it
		Plural	
FIRST PERSON	we	our, ours	us
SECOND PERSON	you	your, yours	you
THIRD PERSON	they	their, theirs	them
	Subjective	*Possessive*	*Objective*
		Singular and Plural	
	who	whose	whom

demonstrative pronoun   One of the four pronouns that point out: *this, that, these, those*. These words often function in sentences as adjectives.

> **This** brand is as good as **that**.

dependent clause   A subordinate clause: see **clause**.

descriptive adjective   See **adjective**.

determiner   A word (such as *a, an, the, my, their,* or *our*) which signals the approach of a noun.

diagraming   A graphic means of showing relationships within the sentence. Various forms are used; any form is serviceable if it helps to show how the sentence works. Illustrations of three kinds of diagrams follow:

The dark clouds on the horizon had appeared suddenly.

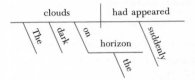

The key to the diagram:

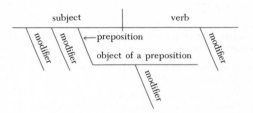

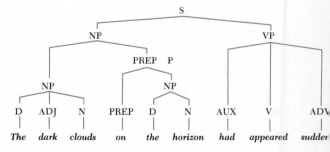

The key to the abbreviations:

ADJ	Adjective	PREP	Preposition
ADV	Adverb	PREP P	Prepositional Phrase
AUX	Auxiliary	S	Sentence
D	Determiner	V	Verb
N	Noun	VP	Verb Phrase
NP	Noun Phrase		

A key to the diagram below (which shows the layers of structure) is not provided. Terminology is left to the analyst's choice. (For example, one analyst might write *complete subject* on the line connecting *on the horizon* with *The dark clouds*, but another might prefer *noun phrase*.)

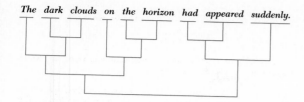

The dark clouds on the horizon had appeared suddenly.

direct address   A parenthetical word or phrase naming or denoting the person(s) spoken to.

> Falstaff enters and exclaims, "Well said, **Hal!**"
> Don't forget, **backseat passengers**, to use those seatbelts.

direct object   See **object.**

direct quotation   The exact spoken or written words of others.

> DIRECT QUOTATION   John asked, "Why haven't you joined the group, Martha?"
> INDIRECT QUOTATION   John asked Martha why she had not joined the group.

See also **16a.**

double negative   A nonstandard construction containing two negatives and having a negative meaning, such as *I didn't have no change with me.* See **not . . . no**, page 732.

elliptical construction   A construction in which words are omitted but clearly understood.

> The curtains are newer than the carpet [is].
> Whenever [it is] possible, get a full night's sleep.
> His hair is black; his face [is] deeply tanned.

expletive   The word *there* or *it* used as a structural filler and not adding to the meaning of the sentence.

> **There** were only a few ballet tickets left.   [Compare "Only a few ballet tickets were left."]
> **It** is obvious that they do not like us.   [Compare "That they do not like us is obvious."]

finite verb   The principal verb of a sentence or a clause. A finite verb can serve as the only verb of a sentence. Verb forms classified as gerunds, infinitives, and participles (verbals) are nonfinite verbs.

> One prisoner **escaped.**   Clyde **will read** the book.

See also **nonfinite verb.**

form change   See **inflection.**

fragment   See **sentence fragment.**

function words   Words (such as prepositions, conjunctions, auxiliaries, and articles) that indicate the functions of other words (*vocabulary words*) in a sentence and the grammatical relationships between them. See also **vocabulary words.**

fused sentence   Two sentences run together without any punctuation or a coordinating conjunction. See Section **3.**

gerund   A verbal (nonfinite verb) that ends in *-ing* and functions as a noun. Gerunds may take objects, complements, or modifiers.

> He escaped by *swimming* **rapidly.**   [The gerund *swimming* is the object of the preposition *by* and is modified by the adverb *rapidly.*]

Borrowing **money** is a mistake.   [The gerund phrase—the gerund *borrowing* and its object, *money*—serves as the subject of the sentence.]

A possessive noun or pronoun before a gerund may be classified either as an adjectival (modifying the noun element of the verbal) or as the subject of the gerund.

> **His borrowing** money is a mistake.   [Compare "*his* action" and "*He borrowed* the money."]

See also **nonfinite verb.**

idiom   An expression in good use that is characteristic of or peculiar to a language. Perfectly acceptable idioms may seem illogical if taken literally or may violate established rules of grammar.

> He **gave himself away** by smiling.
> I have known him for **many a year.**

imperative   See **mood.**

indefinite   An article (*a, an*), a pronoun (*anybody, everyone,* and so on) or an adjective (*any* book, *a few* friends, *several* replies, and so on) that does not specify distinct limits.

independent clause   A main clause: see **clause.**

indicative   See **mood.**

indirect object   See **object.**

indirect quotation   See **direct quotation.**

infinitive   A verbal (nonfinite verb) used chiefly as a noun, less frequently as an adjective or an adverb. The infinitive is usually made up of the word *to* plus the present form of a verb (called the *stem* of the infinitive), but the *to* may be omitted after such verbs as *let, make,* and *dare.* Infinitives may have subjects, objects, complements, or modifiers.

> Hal wanted **to open** the present.   [*Present* is the object of the infinitive *to open;* the whole infinitive phrase is the object of the verb *wanted.*]
> The work **to be done** overwhelms me.   [The infinitive is used adjectivally to modify the noun *work.*]
> **To tell** the truth, our team almost lost.   [The infinitive phrase is used adverbially to modify the rest of the sentence.]

See also **nonfinite verb.**

inflection   A change in the form of a word to show a specific meaning or grammatical relationship to some other word or group of words.

> VERBS   drink, drinks, drank, drunk; grasp, grasps, grasped
> PRONOUNS   **I**, **my** life, a gift for **me**
> NOUNS   dog, dogs; dog's, dogs'
> ADJECTIVES   a **good** one, a **better** one, the **best** one
> ADVERBS   carefully, **more** carefully, **most** carefully

See also **conjugation, declension,** and **comparison.**

intensifier (intensive)   A modifier used for emphasis. Such adverbs as "*very* boring," "*certainly* did," and "*so* pleased" are intensifiers. See also **qualifier.**

intensive pronoun   A *-self* pronoun used to emphasize another word in the sentence.

> The president **himself** answered my letter.   [The pronoun *himself* refers to and emphasizes *president.*]

interjection A part of speech used for simple exclamations: *Oh! Ouch! Whew!* When used in sentences, mild interjections are set off by commas.

intransitive See **verb**.

interrogative pronoun A pronoun (*which, what, who, whom, whose*) used to ask a question. An interrogative pronoun may function as a noun or as an adjective.

> **What** happened? **Which** did he choose? **Whose** car is it?

inversion A change in the usual word order of a sentence.

> Up go the referee's hands.
> In the middle of the lake is a small island.

irregular verb A verb that does not form its past tense and past participle in the standard way—that is, by the addition of *-d* or *-ed* to the stem of the infinitive (as with the regular verbs *hope, hoped; look, looked*). The principal parts of five common types of irregular verbs are given below.

> swim, swam, swum [vowels changed]
> beat, beat, beaten [*-en* added]
> feel, felt, felt [vowel shortened, *ee* changed to *e*]
> send, sent, sent [*-d* changed to *-t*]
> set, set, set [no change]

lexical words See **vocabulary words**.

linking verb A verb which relates the subject to the subject complement. Words commonly used as linking verbs are *become, seem, appear, feel, look, taste, smell, sound,* and the forms of the verb *be*.

> She **is** a pharmacist. The panels **feel** rough.

main clause An independent clause: see **clause**.

mass noun See **noun**.

misplaced modifier An adjectival or adverbial in an awkward position—usually, far away from what it modifies. Sometimes a misplaced modifier confuses the reader because it could qualify either of two words.

> MISPLACED I heard how to make catsup flow out of the bottle **on the radio**.
> REVISED I heard **on the radio** how to make catsup flow out of the bottle.
>
> MISPLACED To do one's best **sometimes** is not enough.
> REVISED To do one's best is **sometimes** not enough.
> OR It is not enough to do one's best **sometimes**.

See also **25a**.

modal auxiliary See **auxiliary verb**.

modifier An adjective or adverb (adjectival or adverbial), which describes, limits, or qualifies another word or word group: see Section **4**.

mood (mode) The way a speaker or writer regards an assertion—that is, as a declarative statement or a question (*indicative* mood), as a command or request (*imperative*), or as a supposition, hypothesis, recommendation, or condition contrary to fact (*subjunctive*). Verb forms indicate mood.

> INDICATIVE Joe **was** a winner. **Does** he drop by?
> IMPERATIVE **Be** a winner. **Do** drop by!
> SUBJUNCTIVE Joe talked as though he **were** a loser.
> I recommend that he **do** this soon.

See Section **7**.

nominal A word (such as a pronoun or gerund), phrase, or clause used as a noun.

> **Repairing that machine** was not easy.
> He contends **that selfless love is power**.

nominative See **case**.

nonfinite verb A verbal functioning as a noun, an adjective, or an adverb. A nonfinite verb cannot stand as the only verb in a sentence.

> NONFINITE VERBS IN PHRASES
> **to take** a vacation together
> shoppers **milling** around
> by just **remaining** silent
>
> NONFINITE VERBS IN SENTENCES
> My family wanted **to take** a vacation together.
> Shoppers **milling** around did not buy much.
> Some people win arguments by just **remaining** silent.

See also **verbal** and **finite verb**.

nonrestrictive Nonessential to the meaning of a sentence. A phrase or clause is nonrestrictive (parenthetical) when it is not necessary to the meaning of the main clause and may be omitted: see **12d**.

> The old horse, **slow but confident**, plodded on. [phrase]
> The airplane, **now being manufactured in large numbers**, is of immense commercial value. [phrase]
> The airplane, **which is now being manufactured in large numbers**, is of immense commercial value. [clause]

See also **restrictive**.

noun A part of speech that names a person, place, thing, idea, animal, quality, or action: *Mary, America, apples, justice, goose, strength, departure*. A noun usually changes form to indicate the plural and the possessive case, as in *man, men; man's, men's*.

> Types of nouns
>
> COMMON a **man**, the **cities**, some **trout** [general classes]
> PROPER **Mr. Ford**, in **Boston**, the **Forum** [capitalized, specific names]
> COLLECTIVE a **flock**, the **jury**, my **family** [groups]
> CONCRETE an **egg**, the **bus**, his **ear**, two **trees** [tangibles]
> ABSTRACT **honor**, **jealousy**, **pity**, **hatred** [ideas, qualities]
> COUNT one **dime**, ten **dollars**, a **job**, many **times** [singular or plural—often preceded by adjectivals telling how many]
> MASS much **money**, more **work**, less **time** [singular in meaning—often preceded by adjectivals telling how much]
>
> Functions of nouns
>
> SUBJECT OF FINITE VERB **Dogs** barked.
> OBJECT OF FINITE VERB OR OF PREPOSITION He gave **Jane** the **key** to the **house**.
> SUBJECT COMPLEMENT (PREDICATE NOUN) She is a **nurse**.
> OBJECT COMPLEMENT They named him **Jonathan**.
> SUBJECT OF NONFINITE VERB I want **Ed** to be here.
> OBJECT OF NONFINITE VERB I prefer to drive a **truck**.
> APPOSITIVE Moses, a **prophet**, saw the promised land.
> ADVERBIAL **Yesterday** they went **home**.
> ADJECTIVAL The **mountain** laurel is the **state** flower of Connecticut and Pennsylvania.

DIRECT ADDRESS   What do you think, **Angela**?

KEY WORD OF ABSOLUTE PHRASE   The **food** being cold, no one really enjoyed the meal.

noun clause   A subordinate clause used as a noun.

> **Whoever comes** will be welcome.   [subject]
> I hope **that he will recover.**   [direct object]
> I will give **whoever comes first** the best seat.   [indirect object]
> Spend it for **whatever seems best.**   [object of a preposition]
> This is **what you need.**   [subject complement]
> I loved it, **whatever it was.**   [appositive]
> **Whoever you are**, show yourself!   [direct address]

See also **nominal** and **clause**.

noun phrase   See **phrase**.

number   The inflectional form of a noun, a pronoun, a demonstrative adjective, or a verb that indicates number, either singular (one) or plural (more than one). See Section **6** and **18e**.

object   A noun or noun substitute governed by a transitive active verb, by a nonfinite verb, or by a preposition.

A *direct object*, or the *object of a finite verb*, is any noun or noun substitute that answers the question *What?* or *Whom?* after a transitive active verb. A direct object frequently receives, or is in some way affected by, the action of the verb.

> William raked **leaves.**   **What** did he say?
> The Andersons do not know **where we live.**

As a rule, a direct object may be converted into a subject with a passive verb: see **voice**.

An *object of a nonfinite verb* is any noun or its equivalent that follows and completes the meaning of a participle, a gerund, or an infinitive.

> Washing a **car** takes time.   He likes to wear a **tie.**
> Following the **truck**, a bus rounded the bend.

An *indirect object* is any noun or noun substitute that states *to whom* or *for whom* (or *to what* or *for what*) something is done. An indirect object ordinarily precedes a direct object.

> He bought **her** a watch.
> I gave the **floor** a second coat of varnish.

It is usually possible to substitute a prepositional phrase beginning with *to* or *for* for the indirect object.

> He bought a watch for her.

An *object of a preposition* is any noun or noun substitute which a preposition relates to another word or word group.

> Cedars grow tall in these **hills.**   [*Hills* is the object of *in.*]
> **What** am I responsible for?   [*What* is the object of *for.*]

object complement   See **complement**.

objective   See **case**.

parenthetical element   Nonessential matter (such as an aside or interpolation) that is set off by commas, dashes, or parentheses to mark pauses and intonation. A word, phrase, clause, or sentence may be parenthetical.

> **Granted**, over eighty million people, **according to that estimate**, did watch one episode.
> **In fact**, the parachute ride—**believe it or not**—is as safe as the ferris wheel.

See also **12d**, **17e**, and **17f**.

participle   A verb form that may function as part of a verb phrase (was *laughing*, had *finished*), as an adjective (the *laughing* children, the *finished* product), or as a nonfinite verb (The children, *laughing* loudly, left).

The present participle ends in *-ing* (the form also used for verbal nouns: see **gerund**. The past participle of regular verbs ends in *-d* or *-ed;* for a list of past participles of irregular verbs, see page 688.

Functioning as nonfinite verbs in *participial phrases*, participles may take objects, complements, modifiers:

> The prisoner **carrying the heaviest load** toppled forward. [The participle *carrying* takes the object *load;* the whole participial phrase modifies *prisoner.*]
> The telephone operator, **very confused by my request**, suggested that I place the call later. [The participle *confused* is modified by the adverb *very* and by the prepositional phrase *by my request;* the participial phrase modifies *telephone operator.*]

See also **nonfinite verb**.

particle with verb   A phrasal unit consisting of a verb plus one or two uninflected words like *after, in, up, off,* or *out* and having the force of a single-word verb.

> We **ran out on** them.   [Compare "We deserted them."]
> He **cut** me **off** without a cent.   [Compare "He disinherited me."]

parts of speech   The eight classes into which most grammarians group words according to their form changes and their position, meaning, and use in the sentence: *verbs, nouns, pronouns, adjectives, adverbs, prepositions, conjunctions,* and *interjections.* Each of these is discussed separately in this glossary. See also **1c**.

passive voice   See **voice**.

person   Changes in the form of pronouns and verbs denoting or indicating whether one is speaking (*I am*—first person), spoken to (*you are*—second person), or spoken about (*it is*—third person). In the present tense, a verb changes its form to agree grammatically with a third-person singular subject (*a bird eats, everybody does*). See **6a** and **27b**.

personal pronoun   Any one of a group of pronouns—*I, you, he, she, it* and their inflected forms—referring to the one (or ones) speaking, spoken to, or spoken about. See **declension**.

phrase   A group of related words without both a subject and a (finite) verb.

> NOUN PHRASE   A **young stranger** stepped forward.
> VERB PHRASE   All day long they **had been worrying.**
> PREPOSITIONAL PHRASES   **By seven o'clock**, the lines stretched **from the box office to the corner.**
> GERUND PHRASE   **Building a sun deck** can be fun.
> INFINITIVE PHRASE   Do you want **to use your time that way**?
> PARTICIPIAL PHRASE   My friends **traveling in Italy** felt the earthquake.
> APPOSITIVE PHRASE   I introduced her to Bob, **my roommate.**
> ABSOLUTE PHRASE   **The game over**, we shook hands.

positive   See **comparison**.

possessive   See **case**.

predicate   A basic grammatical division of a sentence. A predicate is the part of the sentence comprising what is said about the subject. The *complete predicate* consists of the main verb along with its auxiliaries (the *simple predicate*) and any complements and modifiers.

We *used* a patriotic theme for our homecoming **parade that year**. [*Used* is the simple predicate. *Used* and all the words that follow it make up the complete predicate.]
Had the team **already** *been preparing* themselves **psychologically**? [The simple predicate is the verb phrase *had been preparing*.]

predicate adjective An adjective functioning as a subject complement: see **complement** and **linking verb**.

predicate noun A noun functioning as a subject complement: see **complement** and **linking verb**.

prefix An added syllable or group of syllables attached to the beginning of a base or root (or another prefix). A prefix changes the meaning or creates a new word: *meditated, premeditated, unpremeditated*. See **18c**. See also **suffix**.

preposition A part of speech (a function word) that links and relates a vocabulary word to some other word in the sentence. See page 669 for a list of words commonly used as prepositions.

These paintings hung **in** the hall. [The preposition *in* connects and relates *hall* (the object of the preposition *in*) to the verb *hung*.]

prepositional phrase See **phrase**.

principal parts The forms of any verb from which the various tenses are derived: the present infinitive (*take, laugh*), the past (*took, laughed*), and the past participle (*taken, laughed*).

See also Section **7**.

progressive verb A verb phrase consisting of a present participle (ending in *-ing*) used with a form of *be* and denoting continuous action.

I **have been playing** tennis all afternoon.

See also page 687.

pronoun One of the eight parts of speech. Pronouns take the position of nouns and function as nouns do.

NOUNS	The old **house** was sold to Fred's aunt.
PRONOUNS	**It** was sold to **his** aunt.
	OR
	That was sold to **her**.

Types of pronouns

PERSONAL	**She** and **I** will see **him** in St. Paul.
INTERROGATIVE	**Who** are they? **What** is right?
	Which car is better?
RELATIVE	Leslie is the one **who** likes to bowl.
	A dog **that** barks may bite.
DEMONSTRATIVE	**This** is better than **that**.
INDEFINITE	**Each** of you should help **someone**.
RECIPROCAL	Help **each other**. They like **one another**.
REFLEXIVE	Carl blames **himself**.
	Did you injure **yourself**?
INTENSIVE	We need a vacation **ourselves**.
	I **myself** saw the crash.

See Sections **5**, **6**, and **28**.

See also the separate entry for each type of pronoun: **personal pronoun, interrogative pronoun**, and so on.

proper adjective A capitalized adjective (*a **Scottish** tune*) derived from a proper noun (*Scotland*).

See also **adjective**.

proper noun See **noun**.

qualifier Any modifier, descriptive or limiting. Frequently, however, the term refers only to those modifiers that restrict or intensify the meaning of other words.

Many thieves lie. **Almost all** of them do. [Compare "Thieves lie."]
Sometimes children are **too** selfish to share.

See also **intensifier**.

quotation See **direct quotation**.

reciprocal pronoun A compound pronoun expressing an interchangeable or mutual action or relationship: *each other* or *one another*.

They compete with **each other**.
We respect **one another**.

reflexive pronoun A *-self* pronoun used as an object or a complement and referring to the individual or individuals named by the subject.

They denied **themselves** nothing.   I am not **myself** today.

regular verb A verb that forms its past tense and past participle by adding *-d* or *-ed* to the stem of the infinitive: *love, loved; laugh, laughed*.

relative pronoun One of a small group of noun substitutes (*who, whom, whose, that, which, what, whoever, whomever, whichever, whatever*) used to introduce subordinate clauses.

He has a son *who* **is a genius**. [adjective clause introduced by the relative pronoun *who*]
Whoever **wins the prize** must have talent. [noun clause introduced by the relative pronoun *whoever*]

restrictive Essential to sentence meaning. A phrase or clause is restrictive when it is necessary to the meaning of the main clause and cannot be omitted: see **12d**.

Every drug **condemned by doctors** should be taken off the market. [restrictive phrase]
Every drug **that doctors condemn** should be taken off the market. [restrictive clause]

See also **nonrestrictive**.

sentence An independent unit of expression. A simple sentence follows the pattern **SUBJECT—PREDICATE**. Sentences are often classified according to structure as *simple, compound, complex*, or *compound-complex*.

SIMPLE   We won. [subject—predicate]
COMPOUND   They outplayed us, but we won. [two main clauses]
COMPLEX   Although we did win, they outplayed us. [subordinate clause, main clause]
COMPOUND-COMPLEX   I know that they outplayed us, but we did win. [two main clauses—the first of which contains a subordinate clause]

Sentences are also classified according to their purpose.

DECLARATIVE	We will fly to Portland.	[statement]
IMPERATIVE	Fly to Portland.	[command]
INTERROGATIVE	Shall we fly to Portland?	[question]
EXCLAMATORY	Would we like to fly to Portland!	[exclamation]

See Section **1**.

sentence fragment A nonsentence written as though it were a sentence. The term generally refers to a grammatically incomplete declarative sentence. See Section **2**.

sentence modifier A word or word group that modifies the rest of the sentence.

Yes, the bus arrived late.
Fortunately, no one was hurt.
The best professional teams win important games, **as a rule**.

subject A basic grammatical division of a sentence. The subject is a noun or noun substitute about which something is asserted or asked in the predicate. It usually precedes the predicate. (Imperative sentences have subjects that are not stated but are implied.) The *complete subject* consists of the *simple subject* and the words associated with it.

The dog locked in the hot car needed air. [*Dog* is the simple subject. *The dog locked in the hot car* is the complete subject.]

See also **1a**.

subject complement See **complement**.

subjective See **case**.

subjunctive See **mood**.

subordinating conjunction See **conjunction**.

subordinate clause A dependent clause: see **clause**.

subordinator A word that marks a dependent, or subordinate, clause: see pages 671–72.

suffix An added sound, syllable, or group of syllables attached to the end of a base or root (or another suffix). Suffixes change meanings, create new words, and indicate grammatical functions.

the play**s**	play**er**	play**er's**	play**ing**
play**ed**	play**ful**	play**fully**	play**fulness**

See also **inflection** and **18c**.

superlative See **comparison**.

syntax Sentence structure. The grammatical arrangement of words, phrases, and clauses.

tense The form of the verb which indicates its relation to time. Inflection (*eat, eats, eating, ate, eaten*) and the use of auxiliaries (*will* eat, *have* eaten, *had* eaten, *will have* eaten, and so on) show the tense of a verb. See **conjugation** and Section **7**.

transitive See **verb**.

verb A part of speech denoting action, occurrence, or existence (state of being). Inflections indicate tense (and sometimes person and number) and mood of a verb: see **inflection**, **mood**, **voice**, and Section **7**.
A *transitive verb* is a verb that requires an object to complete its

meaning. Transitive verbs can usually be changed from the active to the passive voice: see **object** and **voice**.

Sid **hung** a wreath on his door. [direct object: *wreath*]

An *intransitive verb* is a verb (such as *go* or *sit*) that does not have an object to complete its meaning. Linking verbs, which take subject complements, are intransitive.

She **has been waiting** patiently for hours.
I **was** sick last Christmas.

The same verb may be transitive in one sentence and intransitive in another.

TRANSITIVE   Dee **reads** novels. [direct object: *novels*]
INTRANSITIVE Dee **reads** well.

verb phrase See **phrase**.

verbal A nonfinite verb used as a noun, an adjective, or an adverb. Infinitives, participles, and gerunds are verbals. Verbals (like finite verbs) may take objects, complements, modifiers, and sometimes subjects.

Mr. Nelson went *to see* his daughter. [*To see*, an infinitive, functions as an adverb modifying the verb *went*. The object of the infinitive is *daughter*.]
Cars *parked* in the loading zone will be towed away. [*Parked*, a participle, modifies cars.]
Studying dialects in our area was fun. [*Studying*, a gerund, heads the phrase that is the subject of the verb *was*.]

See also **nonfinite verb** and **gerund**, **infinitive**, **participle**.

vocabulary (lexical) words Nouns, verbs, and most modifiers—those words found in vocabulary-building lists. See also **function words**.

voice The form of a transitive verb that indicates whether or not the subject performs the action denoted by the verb. A verb with a direct object is in the *active voice*. When the direct object is converted into a subject, the verb is in the *passive voice*. A passive verb is always a verb phrase consisting of a form of the verb *be* (or sometimes *get*) followed by a past participle.

ACTIVE   Priscilla **chose** John. [The subject (*Priscilla*) acts.]
PASSIVE John **was chosen** by Priscilla. [The subject (John) does not act.]

Speakers and writers often omit the *by*-phrase after a passive verb, especially when the performer of the action is not known or is not the focus of attention.

Those flowers **were picked** yesterday.
The guilty ones **should be punished** severely.
We just heard that a new secretary **was hired**.

See also **29d**.

word order The arrangement of words in sentences. Because of lost inflections, modern English depends heavily on word order to convey meaning.

Nancy gave Henry $14,000.
Henry gave Nancy $14,000.

Tony had built a barbecue pit.
Tony had a barbecue pit built.

Index

Numbers in **boldface** refer to rules; other numbers refer to pages. A colon is used after each boldface number to indicate that the following pages refer to the rule or the part of the rule concerned. The **boldface** rule is given in detail—**9a(4)** or **20a(3),** for example—in order to pinpoint a needed correction, but a less detailed reference (**9** or **9a**) will usually be sufficient for the student.

meaning, of words
connotative, **20a(2):** 735
denotative, **20a(1):** 734–35
metaphorical, 736
meanwhile, as conjunctive adverb,
3b: 677
merely, position of, **25a(1):** 749
metaphors
effective use of, **20a(4):** 736
mixed, **23c(1):** 744
microfilm or microfiche catalog in
library, 785
micropublications, citation of, 789
Middle English, 725
mighty, **19i:** 731
misplaced modifier, defined, 820
misplaced parts, **25a:** 749–50
clauses, **25a(3):** 750
phrases, **25a(2):** 749–50
single-word modifiers, **25a(1):** 749
split infinitives, **25a(5):** 750
squinting modifiers, **25a(4):** 750
misrepresentation, fallacies of, **23f:**
746–47
misspelling, **18:** 717–23
See also *spelling.*
mixed constructions, **23c(2):** 744
mixed metaphors, **23c(1):** 744
MLA style
in bibliography, 787–89
in notes, 795–97
modal auxiliaries, 816
mode, defined, 820
See also *mood.*
modifiers
adjectives and adverbs, **4:** 678–80
after *feel, look,* etc., **4b:** 679
coordinate, **12c(2):** 702
dangling, **25b:** 750–51
defined, 678, 820
hyphenated, **18f(1):** 722
misplaced, **25a:** 749–50, 820
nonrestrictive, **12d(1):** 702–3
position of, 749
restrictive, **12d(1):** 702–3
squinting, **25a(4):** 750
mood
defined, 687, 820
imperative, **7:** 687, 820
indicated by verb form, **7:** 687
indicative, **7:** 687, 820
shift in, **7d:** 691; **27a:** 753
subjunctive, **7:** 687; **7c:** 690
moral, morale, **19i:** 731
moreover, as conjunctive adverb, **3b:**
677
most
agreement of verb with, **6a:** 684
for *almost,* **19i:** 731
motion pictures
form for bibliography, 789
form for notes, 796
italics for titles of, **10a:** 697

Mr., Dr., etc., **11a:** 698
Mrs., Miss, Ms, use of in business
letters, 811
myself, for *I* or *me,* **19i:** 731

N
narration
in essay, 771, 774, 775
in paragraph development, 765
nce, nts, in spelling, **18b:** 718
nearly, position of, **25a(1):** 749
negative. See *double negative.*
neither
in double negative, **19i:** 731
pronoun with, **6b(1):** 685–86
verb with, **6a(6):** 684
neither . . . nor
linking antecedents, **6b(2):** 686
linking subjects, **6a(3):** 684
parallel structure with, **26c:** 752
nevertheless, as conjunctive adverb,
3b: 677
newspapers
form for bibliography, 788
forms for notes, 796, 797
italics for titles of, **10a:** 697
nicknames, avoiding quotation marks
with, **16d:** 712
no
in double negative, **19i:** 732
introductory, comma after, **12b(3):**
701
no such a, **19i:** 731
no-account, no-count, no-good, **19i:**
731
nobody, no body, **18b:** 718
nohow, **19i:** 731
nominal, defined, 820
nominative case, 816
See also *subjective case.*
none
agreement of verb with, **6a:** 684–
85
in double negative, **19i:** 732
nonetheless, as conjunctive adverb,
3b: 677
nonfinite verb, defined, 820
nonprint sources
forms for bibliography, 789
forms for notes, 796–97, 797
nonrestrictive elements
appositives, **12d(2):** 703
defined, 820
modifiers, **12d(1):** 702–3
non sequitur, **23f(1):** 745
nonstandard English, **19e:** 726
nor
antecedents joined by, **6b(2):** 686
as coordinating conjunction, 669
main clauses linked by, **12a:** 700,
700–1
subjects joined by, **6a(3):** 684

not . . . no/none/nothing, **19i:** 732
not only . . . but also, parallel structure with, **26c:** 752
notation
in business letters, 812
in outlines, 792
notes (endnotes/footnotes)
abbreviations in, 795
as first reference, 795–97
as second reference, 797
distinguished from bibliography
entries, 794
placement of, in manuscript, 794
purpose of, 794
note-taking
evaluation of sources for, 792
keyed to outline, 792
on cards, 792
on photocopies, 793
paraphrasing in, 793
précis in, 793
quoting directly in, 793
selection of material for, 792,
793
noun clause
defined, 671–72, 816
recognition of, 671–72
noun phrase
defined, 669, 821
denoting quantity, agreement of
verb with **6a(7):** 684–85
recognition of, 670–71
nouns
among parts of speech, 669
attributive, 816
case of, 680, **15a:** 709
collective, number of, **6a(7):** 684–
85
compound, 669
declension of, 818
defined and classified, 820
functions of, 669, 820–21
plural forms of, **18e:** 719–20
proper, capitalized, **9a:** 695
nowheres, **19i:** 732
nts, nce, in spelling, **18b:** 718
number
agreement in, **6:** 683
defined, 821
shifts in, **27b:** 753
number
abbreviation of, 695
distinguished from *amount,* **19i:**
728
preceded by *a* or *the,* verb agreement with, **19i:** 728
numbers
as figures or words, **11e:** 699
compound, hyphenated, **18f(2):**
723
plural form of, **15c:** 709–10
special usage of, **11e:** 699
when to use italics for, **10d:** 697

CONTENTS

Introduction

ONE WITH THE ELEMENTS

As far as automobiles go, "ragtops" are the ultimate in romance. Convertibles are the closest real life gets to a magic carpet ride. For many drivers during the second half of the twentieth century, the thrill of driving wasn't complete without the sun on their necks and the wind in their hair.

As an outgrowth of the post–World War II West-Coast chic, the convertible—which had been around as long as there had been cars—became the ultimate symbol of the laid-back, California "beautiful person" lifestyle. Many American men and women found that their favorite fantasy involved a tall blonde, a straight stretch of open road, and a hot car with the top down.

Since 1945, Detroit's car manufacturers, as well as car companies all around the world, have been keeping those fantasies alive by producing cars that are so sleek, so sexy, that they belong in a world of make-believe. Hollywood has certainly done its fair share to further glamorize the open-top automobile in countless movies and television programs.

On a more practical note, convertibles were never produced in great numbers, making them valuable commodities to car collectors! This book focuses on these fantasy automobiles, magic carpets reserved exclusively for life's best moments.

The Rolls Royce
Phantom I
was a formal
town car built
between 1925
and 1929. It
had a 6-cylinder,
7,695-cubic-
centimeter
engine and
rode on a 144-
inch wheelbase.

The 1932 Imperial Sedan was among the first Chryslers to have fully flexible rubber engine mountings (called "floating power"), an automatic clutch, and free wheels.

One of Chrysler's best, the 1931 Imperial Roadster had a chassis frame made of 8-inch-deep pressed steel, further strengthened by six cross members. Engine vibration was almost completely eliminated by a nine-bearing crankshaft, counterweighted at eight points.

Fred and August Duesenberg had built four Indianapolis 500 winners before engineering the 1933 Duesenberg SJ Roadster for road use by the general public. As you can see, it's a lot more than a Sunday-goin'-to-church car.

FOLLOWING PAGE:
The 1931 Duesenberg J Boattail Speedster lived up to its nickname when supercharged up to 320 horsepower. The car's actual name—the one given to it by its builder, Walter Murphy of Pasadena, California—was the Disappearing Top Torpedo Convertible Coupe.

*A synchromesh gearbox
and vacuum-servo brakes
were featured on this
1933 Packard V-12 Coupe.*

Chapter One

THE GOLDEN AGE OF RAGTOPS: 1928–1949

The term "convertible," meaning a car that could convert itself from enclosed to open-topped, was not standardized in the auto industry until 1928. Before that, cars with removable tops were known as roadsters, runabouts, or touring cars. The term was formally adopted in 1928, however, by the Society of Automotive Engineers.

1929, the year following this earth-shaking event, brought to the United States the stock-market crash and the Great Depression. Ironically, since the only folks who could afford a car were the untouchably rich, these harsh economic times gave birth to the era of the ultra-luxurious touring car.

Packard Twelve

Such a touring car was the Packard Twelve convertible of 1933, which had a massive 7,300-cubic-centimeter, 12-cylinder, centrifugal-pump, water-cooled engine. It had syncromesh gears, semi-elliptic leaf-spring suspension on rigid axles, mechanical drum brakes on all wheels, and a maximum speed of 100 miles per hour. So it had muscle, alright—long before anyone ever thought to call it that—but the thing that made it art was its convertible roof, designed by Count Alexis de Akro Sakroffsky. That roof transformed the vehicle, with its donning, into a limousine.

All of Packard's cars during this time were marvelous. The 1934 Packard convertible was designated a "classic" by the Classic Car Club of America (CCCA). Mint-condition convertibles manufactured by Packard in 1934 have sold for as much as $120,000 in today's collectors' market. But Packard merged with Studebaker in 1954, and the name was last used on a car four years later.

Other cars of the 1930s that typified the gorgeous convertibles of the era were the rag-top editions of the 1934 Pontiac Series 603 Cabriolet, the 1937 Ford DeLuxe Convertible Sedan, the 1937 Packard Super 8 Convertible Coupe, the 1940 Buick Roadmaster Convertible Sedan, and the 1940 Ford Deluxe Convertible Coupe.

The War

For the most part, the manufacturing of civilian production automobiles came to a halt during World War II, as the world's car factories were almost all being used for the war effort. Some "1942" convertibles were built in the United States during the weeks before

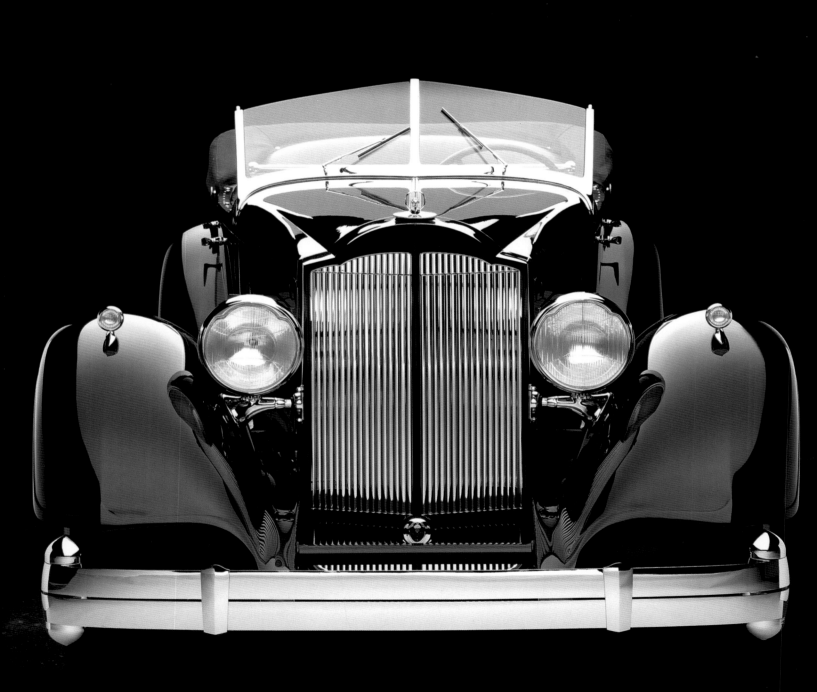

The 1939 Ford Deluxe Convertible had a V-8 engine and was one of the first Fords to have hydraulic brakes.

The 1940 Ford Convertible came with a new and improved steering column.

The 1937 Packard 8 Convertible had an 8-cylinder engine, as its name would imply, and was among the first Packards to have hydraulic brakes and independent front suspension.

The 1934 Custom Packard had the trademark V-shaped radiator and a 12-cylinder engine that displaced seven liters.

and after the Japanese bombed Pearl Harbor on December 7, 1941, bringing the United States into the war.

The 1942 Cadillac Dual Cowl Phaeton was one of the most unusual cars ever built. The dual cowls of its name referred to windshields. The back seat had its own windshield, mounted behind the front seat. The car had many features which were not, as of yet, available to the public, including automatic transmission and power windows.

Another 1942 model was the DeSoto Convertible, made by the Chrysler Corporation. It could be had with an optional four-speed semi-automatic transmission.

The 1940 Packard Darrin Victoria was designed by H "Dutch" Darrin, a Parisian car-builder who frequently did side jobs for car companies in Detroit. This old-money car used the standard Packard grille, bumpers, and lights, with an elongated and lowered hood. It had a 127-inch wheelbase and used engines ranging in size from 282 to 356 cubic inches of displacement. Prices ranged from $3,819 to $4,593.

The 1936 Cord 810 Convertible Phaeton—produced at Auburn's second factory in Connersville, Indiana—made quite a splash at its debut at the National Automobile Show at the Grand Central Palace in New York City in November of 1935. Some still call it the greatest car ever made.

Ah, classic architecture! The 1937 BMW Cabriolet was made by the Bayerische-Motoren-Werke of Munich, Germany, and helped lay the foundation for the famous BMW sports cars to come.

During the Second World War, body dies of Packard cars, like this 1941 Coupe 160 Deluxe Convertible, were sold to the Soviet government.

The Cadillac convertible of 1941— the first Caddy to have automatic transmission.

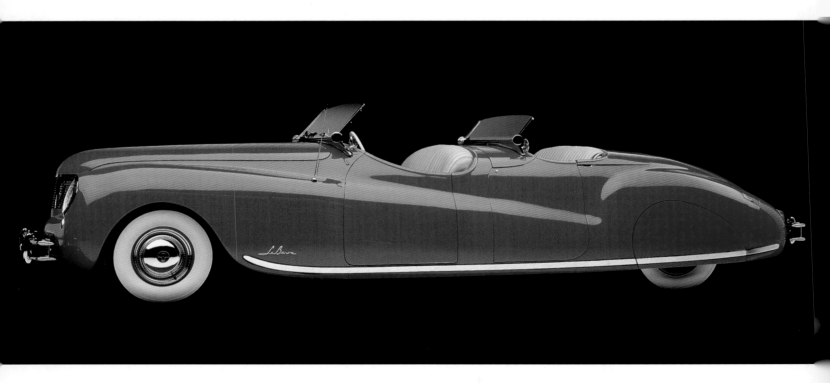

*Among the movie stars
who drove the 1940
Lincoln Continental
MK1 were Jackie Cooper
and Mickey Rooney.*

*Dan Topping, one-time
owner of the New York
Yankees, bought a 1941
Chrysler Newport new,
had his name cast upon the
heads, hubcaps, and grille,
and then gave the car to
movie star Lana Turner.*

The Post-War Era: A Slow Comeback

When the Axis powers surrendered in 1945, bringing the Second World War to an end, the world did not immediately bounce back to normal. During the first few years of the post-war era, new convertibles were nowhere to be seen. Car manufactures were too busy making cars that ran and successfully got their owners to their destinations to worry about a luxury item like roof convertibility.

In 1946, Packard once again began to produce its two lines of convertibles, each of which was almost exactly like the 1942 model, the last to be offered before the war halted production.

Oldsmobile offered a convertible in 1946, with styling practically identical to the cars that Olds had been making before the war. The first really new convertible of the post-war era was the 1947 Cadillac Series 62 Convertible Coupe. It had a 346-cubic-inch flathead V-8 engine which developed 150 horsepower at 3,400 revolutions per minute.

Over in the other General Motors division, the 1947 Buick Super Convertible Coupe, Model 56-C, had a base price of $2,333 and weighed 4,050 pounds. It sold 25,796 units in the United States, and 501 units abroad.

Cars of 1948–49

By 1948, things were back in gear. Business was good everywhere. World War II, with all of its horror, had fixed the United States' depressed economy. Accordingly, the convertible was back.

Options on the 1948 Chevrolet Fleetmaster Cabriolet, Model 2134, included bumper tip wing guards, rear fender stainless gravel deflectors, radio, side mirror, and wide whitewall tires. The base cost for the Fleetmaster was $1,750. But only slowly would Detroit relearn how to build and market a car for Middle America. Some lessons were learned the hard way.

The 1948 Lincoln Continental Convertible Cabriolet—along with having a name that is both redundant and makes your mouth hurt—was the most expensive Lincoln that year at $4,746. It weighed 4,135 pounds; only 738 were

Perfect for roadblocks, the 1948 Lincoln Continental Convertible Cabriolet was identical to the 1947 version. It weighed 4,135 pounds and cost $4,746.

On the 1949 Buick Roadmaster Convertible Coupe, the hydraulic top, windows, and seat were standard equipment. It weighed 4,370 pounds and cost $3,150.

The 1946 Hudson Super Six Convertible weighed 3,195 pounds and sold for $1,879. The car had a 121-inch wheelbase and was 207⅜ inches long overall. The 6-cylinder engine displaced 212 cubic inches and produced 102 horsepower.

made. High production costs for Ford meant low profits, and 1948 would be the last year that the Lincoln Continental was sold. Again, the seeming contradiction: Now that people had money again, they didn't want something quite that rich.

The Chrysler Town-Country Convertible was built from 1946 to 1949; during that time, 936 were manufactured. The price of the car rose rapidly over that stretch: $2,743 in 1946, $2,998 in 1947, $3,420 in 1948, and $3,995 in 1949. The wheelbase was 127.5 inches long. The engine was an 8-cylinder worth 135 horsepower.

The Packard Custom Eight Victoria Convertible of 1948–49 was that company's first post-war ragtop. Its 356-cubic-inch powerplant produced 160 horsepower at 3,600 revolutions per minute. The wheelbase was 127 inches long. It weighed 4,380 pounds, and sold for $4,295.

The 1949 Chrysler Town & Country Convertible had a kind of a big-city feel. Maybe that's because it was built atop the Chrysler New Yorker's chassis. The weight of the car that year was 4,630 pounds.

The 1947 Ford Sportsman convertible had wooden side body panels. That year, no Ford was more expensive ($2,285) and none sold worse.

*The Chrysler Town &
Country Convertible
(shown top & bottom) rode
on a 127½-inch wheelbase
and had an 8-cylinder
engine producing 135
horsepower. This 1948
edition weighed 4,332
pounds and cost $3,420.*

In the 1940s, our cars reflected our roads. The United States was known for its straight-aways—therefore Detroit cars tended toward the powerful. England was known for her curves, thus the 1946 MG TC. Top speed was only 73 miles per hour, but oooh, that handling! It was unbeatable on its winding home turf.

In Europe . . .

The MG TC was one of the first cars to come out of England after World War II. In fact, the first models came rolling off the assembly line in September of 1945, only a month after the Japanese surrendered and brought hostilities to an end.

The sports car was a fantastic combination of the classical and the progressive—cutting edge, yet almost nostalgic. The best of all jalopies, it was a driver's car, meant to be zoomed along winding country roads—with the top down.

Between 1947 and 1949, ten thousand MG TCs were built, all of them two-door, two-seater sports cars. The MG TC had a channel-section ladder-type chassis and an ash-framed steel body. It ran off a 4-cylinder, overhead-valve 1,250-cubic-centimeter powerplant with twin carburetors, all worth 54 horsepower at 5,200 revolutions per minute.

The four-speed gearbox had syncromesh on the top three gears. The suspension consisted of rigid axles on semi-elliptic springs with lever-type shocks. The hydraulic-drum brakes were made by Lockheed. Never really meant for the straightaways, it had a maximum speed of 73 miles per hour. It could go from 0 to 60 in a little over 22 seconds, and it got 28 miles per gallon.

Perhaps the most remarkable thing about the MG TC was its success as an export, selling two units in other countries for every one sold at home.

Out of Great Britain, designed by Alec Issigonia, came the 1948 Morris Minor Tourer. Manufactured by Morris Motors Ltd. of Oxford, England, it was the first car to have a unit chassis/body construction. It could be purchased as a two- or four-door sedan, a wagon called the Traveler, a van, or a pickup.

Including all of the versions, the Morris Minor was the first British car to ever sell a million units. The engine was a straight 4-cylinder and the transmission was a four-speed manual. The suspension in front was torsion-bar independent, and live-axle leaf-spring in the rear; all four wheels had drum brakes. It had a maximum speed of 75 miles per hour.

The Morris Minor was known for its great handling. The company was named after William Morris, a mechanic and used-car salesman from Longwall, Oxford, who designed his own car, the Morris Oxford, in 1912.

Olds 88

The 1950 Olds 88—from Oldsmobile, of course—was the first factory-made, high-performance car of the post-war era. Founder and master car-builder Ransom E. Olds accomplished this by taking the largest engine from his Olds 98 model (then the top of the line) and putting it under the hood of the smaller Olds 88.

The first stock-car races, including those run right on the sand at Daytona Beach—long before the smoothly paved tri-oval superspeedway was built there—were dominated by the Olds 88.

This car was also influential stylistically, with a lower hood line and fenders that were more smoothly blended with the body. When new, the Olds 88 convertible of 1950 went for $2,160.

Five years later, the 88 started a style trend by coming with an optional "Tu-tone" paint job.

The concept started a fad until, by 1958, cars that were painted more than one color, and sometimes as many as four, were all over the place.

Back at the Brickyard . . .

The 1951 Indianapolis 500 pace car was the Chrysler New Yorker, which came with the company's brand-new "Firepower V-8" engine. The motor displaced 331 cubic inches and produced 180 horsepower at 4,000 revolutions per minute. So that everyone would know what kind of engine the New Yorker had in it, a big chrome "V" was placed on the front. It weighed 4,460 pounds. Base cost was $3,941.

The 1952 Indy 500 pace car was the Studebaker Commander. Three thousand and eleven of them were made, each with a V-8 engine, weighing 3,230 pounds, and costing, without frills—$2,548.

The 1948 Jaguar had a drophead engine displacing 3,500 cubic centimeters. This was the last Jaguar to be built before the introduction of the XK120—which changed everything.

Chapter Two

A GRAND MOMENT IN HISTORY: CONVERTIBLES OF THE '50s AND '60s

In 1950, Packard, for the first time, offered convertibles in two models: the Super Eight and the Custom Eight, the latter being 7 inches longer in the wheelbase, 127 to 120 inches.

The Super Eight cost $3,250 in 1950, while the Custom Eight went for $4,295. Collectors should keep in mind that only 614 Super Eight convertibles were built, while a downright rare eighty-five of the Custom Eight convertibles were manufactured.

1951: The Year of the Power Option

Power options started out as an attempt to woo the ever-increasing number of female drivers, but the powers-that-be soon found out that everyone liked the pampered and futuristic feel of power-operated everything.

The 1951 Cadillac convertible became the first ragtop to come with power-operated seats, windows, trunk lid, and antenna.

On the other hand, Chrysler changed the way driving feels forever with the first power-steering option. That wasn't Chrysler's only change of the year, as they also debuted their new 180-horsepower hemihead V-8 engine, which out-muscled the Cadillac by 20 horsepower.

Also new as an option in the Cadillac was the automatic transmission. The early automatic was less than perfect. It shifted with a clunk, broke down frequently, and mystified mechanics when it did.

At this time, Ford lagged behind the other companies. Their convertibles still held powerplants that rated under 100 horsepower. Worse yet, Ford was still using the same bodies on its cars that had been designed in 1949. The

The 1952 MG TD was a direct descendant of the MG TC,
but sold three times as many units as its predecessor.

The 1950 Studebaker Convertible might have been funny looking, but it was the first to come with an automatic-transmission option. Studebaker sold 11,627 convertibles that year.

These days, folks in warm-weather areas are chopping down shock absorbers left and right to create "totally slammed" low-riders. In 1953, the Plymouth Belmont had that slammed look right off the factory line.

company was, for the time being, seemingly uninterested in getting with the post-war era's fashions and improvements.

In 1951, 140,000 convertibles were built by the United States automobile industry, representing three percent of all of the American motor vehicles built that year.

1951 Porsche 356

In Italy, the 1952 Bugatti Type 101 was named after its founding genius, Ettore "The Patron" Bugatti, who built racing and road cars during the 1920s. During that decade, Bugatti-built cars won close to two thousand races. Despite the great cars turned out by Bugatti, he was never financially successful. He took all profits and immediately re-invested them into whatever cutting-edge technology he was refining at the time.

In 1951, the Molsheim Works brought back the Bugatti name, with the Type 101 and 102 models. The 101 was the ragtop.

The Jaguar XK 120 of 1950. The "120" stood for maximum miles per hour. The model started out in 1948 as an attention-getter at the Earl's Court Motor Show in London. It caused such a stir that Jaguar went on to make twelve thousand of them.

The 1953 Packard Caribbean has been called Packard's answer to the Cadillac Eldorado. Under the hood was a 327-cubic-inch engine worth 212 horsepower. This was Packard's heaviest and most expensive car of the year. It weighed 4,265 pounds and cost $5,210. Wire wheels were standard. Seven hundred and fifty were built.

Siata was a small Italian car manufacturer in business from 1949 until 1970. Like a ray of sunshine, this Siata Spyder 208-S hit the roads in 1952.

The 1954 Sunbeam Talbot Alpine MK3—which had a 4-cylinder, 2.3-liter engine—was the first car to bear the Sunbeam name since 1939.

The Great American Sports Car

In 1953, Chevrolet introduced the car that was to become the great American sports car—the Corvette. The Corvette was immediately stunning to behold, of course, but it didn't start out with a heck of a lot punch under the hood. The 6-cylinder engine displaced 235.5 cubic inches and mustered only 150 horsepower.

The 1953 Chevrolet Corvette, a Harley Earl concept implemented by Chevrolet chief engineer Ed Cole, entered the market in mid-season and was available in only one color: Polo White. The design featured dual exhausts and taillights integrated into the fenders. The body was made of Fiberglas, primarily to keep costs down. It was the first time ever that that material was used in a production car.

Other classic design touches included a removable side-screen instead of the normal wind-up windows, and wire-mesh stone guards built in to protect the recessed headlights.

Only 315 Corvettes were built in 1953, and they sold for $3,513 apiece. The car was considered experimental—and its primary duty was to draw crowds to the General Motors traveling auto show known as the G.M. Motorama. Dual exhausts were mounted through the fiberglass body panels, which looked great when the car was brand new, but caused body discoloration quickly enough unless the owner tenaciously cleaned that area.

The 1956 Corvette SR-2 convertible had a V-8 engine capable of 265 horsepower. It had a wheelbase of 102 inches, an overall length of 168 inches, and it weighed 2,750 pounds. Its top speed was 120 miles per hour and it could go from zero-to-sixty in 7.5 seconds.

The 1961 Corvette, painted for stealth cruising. By that year, the number of naysayers was dwindling. The last of them would be silenced two years later by the introduction of the Sting Ray.

The car had other problems that needed to be ironed out. Since Chevrolet claimed that they couldn't come up with a manual transmission that could handle the wild Corvette, the car was equipped with a wimpy two-speed Powerglide automatic. The 1953 model also had the ancient recirculating ball steering rather than the preferred rack-and-pinion steering. The initial Corvette sold for $3,513, about the same price as the Jaguar XK120.

It wouldn't be until the 1955 Corvette that the engine, steering system, and transmission were as hot as the styling. By that time, the Corvette was well on its way to becoming an icon of the American road. And the model's power continued to grow.

The 1959 Corvette had a camshaft designed by ex-race driver Zora Arkus Duntov, a Belgian-born Russian who thought the Corvette's power should be just as important as its styling. The standard 283-cubic-inch V-8 engine rated 230 horsepower, while optional boosts in power went as high as 290 horsepower.

That year's Corvette Roadster set a record for the most chrome on a Corvette's snout. Interlocking tubes of chrome formed the grille, license-plate frame, and fenders.

The 1961 Roadster was the first Corvette to have a speedometer that went as high as 160 miles per hour. The standard V-8 engine rated 275 horsepower. The interior was molded so that the two bucket seats appeared to have been scooped out of the body. In that body, a crease ran backward from the top of the rear wheel arch. This was the flattest and most squared-off of all the Corvettes.

The 1962 Roadster had a standard 327-cubic-inch engine worth 300 horsepower. Optional engines were rated as high as 360 horsepower.

The 1967 Corvette Sting Ray Convertible not only had the big 427-cubic-inch, 425-horsepower engine, but also a solid chrome ball at the end of the four-on-the-floor stick shift to boot!

Pandering to the Customer's Tush

Since people who drive or ride in convertibles are, with the obvious exceptions, usually sitting, it is not unusual that car manufacturers have frequently pandered to the customer's tush.

The 1953 Cadillac Eldorado not only had both a power top and an automatic all-steel tonneau cover, but its most interesting option was a bun-warming heated front seat.

When the car first hit the streets it was known for its "fins." Today, they are hardly noticeable. Those fins were dwarfed by the massive wings to come out of Detroit over the next five years.

Surfing the Dial

The Buick Skylark convertible of 1953 had the new General Motors V-8 engine (rated at 188 horsepower), and every power option imaginable. The most eccentric luxury item was a foot control for the radio.

The interior of the Skylark was done up in two-tone leather, with the owner's initials—along with the Buick emblem—encased in the steering-wheel hub and protected in plastic.

Indy Honors: 1953–54

The 1953 Indianapolis 500 pace car, the Ford Crestline Sunliner Convertible, sold for $2,230 and weighed 3,334 pounds. There were 40,861 of them produced. Contemporary ad copy for the car read: "Terrific is the word . . . A glance will tell you it's your dream car—come true. For this new Ford with its longer, lower, wider look is undoubtedly the style-setter of the '53 season. Here's beauty that's terrific . . ."

Honors for the 1954 Indy 500 pace car went to the 3,575-pound Dodge Royal Lancer, of which only 701 were produced—perhaps one per dealer, so everyone got a show model. The standard engine was the 241-cubic-inch, 150-horsepower V-8. Standard were the wire wheels and the "Continental" tire kit—that is, a spare tire could be mounted on the back. The base price for the Royal Lancer was $2,632.

1955: A Sloppy Year

More than seven million motor vehicles were produced in Detroit in 1955. Of those, 212,000 were convertibles. Because of the demand for new cars, Detroit was churning out cars a little bit too fast. Construction became sloppy, with production managers telling their workers, in essence, "We don't want it good, we want it Tuesday."

Fords produced in 1955 are notorious rusters. Chevys from that year have front-end trouble. The 1955 Buicks leaked. The law of supply and demand took care of the quality-control problem. Sales dropped, and more care went into both the research and development of, and the construction of, American automobiles.

The 1954 Studebaker Commander had stainless side molding rub rails as standard equipment. Optional were large wheel discs and whitewall tires. It weighed 3,120 pounds and cost $2,287.

Ford or Fantasy?

The all-time American fantasy car? Look no further. Ford took Chevrolet's little sports-car experiment, the Corvette, and blew it right off the road in 1955 with the introduction of the Thunderbird—offering power, wealth, and youth all wrapped up in one package. There had never been an American car anything like it. It was named for a figure from Native American mythology, symbolizing power, speed, and wealth.

In its first year, the Thunderbird sold twenty-four units for every one Corvette. This was a hot-looking car, and it had get-up-and-go—a claim the Chevy counterpart couldn't make . . . yet—and it was almost $500 cheaper. The cost of the Thunderbird with no frills was $3,151.

All 31,786 of the first production run (1955–56) were two-seaters. Optional was a detachable hard top. In 1956, the hard top came with porthole windows. A windshield washer and power windows were among the "convenience" options.

The sports car had a steel-ladder chassis construction, and a (standard) V-8, 292-cubic-inch engine mustered 200 horsepower at 4,400 revolutions per minute. For an extra $123, you could get the "Special V-8," which displaced 321 cubic inches and produced 215 horsepower. The transmission was a three-speed manual. Overdrive and an automatic were optional. The Thunderbird had coil-spring suspension in the front and leaf springs in the rear. Drum brakes were featured in both front and rear.

Its maximum speed was 114 miles per hour. It could go from 0 to 60 miles per hour in 9.5 seconds and from 0 to 100 miles per hour in 21 seconds. The first T-Bird got 18 miles to the gallon. An interesting style element consisted of the twin jet exhausts present on all 1955 and some 1956 models. Exhaust was routed through the bumper overriders.

The 1955, 1956, and 1957 Ford Thunderbirds. Frank Hershey, the Ford designer responsible for the first Thunderbird (1955), said, "Our philosophy was to make a car that, while it was a sports car, a banker for instance, could drive it up to his bank in the morning with a certain amount of dignity."

The 1955 Ford Thunderbird, with its combination of sportiness and luxury, has been called the greatest convertible of all time. In the mood to get your kicks on Route 66? Here's your wheels.

The 1956 Ford Fairlane Sunliner Convertible sold for $2,460. It weighed 3,312 pounds. A healthy 58,147 were sold.

The 1956 Thunderbird came with an optional detachable hard top. Trouble was, if you wanted to take it off, you had better be home at the time, since the car offered no place to store it while on the road. The 1957 T-Bird had some design changes in the rear: There were now angled fins, and the twin exhausts were built into the bumper.

In 1958, Ford debuted the four-seater Thunderbird. Styling elements included uniquely molded doors. Ads for the new model read: "You've driven this [car] many times—in your dreams." The four-seater used Ford's brand-new "big block" engines. The standard was the V-8 332-cubic-incher, with an optional 352-cubic-incher available. The optional muscle manifested 375 horsepower.

The car was much bigger and bulkier than its two-seater predecessor. Known as "Big Bird"—in days long before *Sesame Street*—the four-seater Thunderbird had a wheelbase that was 11 inches longer than the two-seater's. The new model was 20 inches longer overall and 815 pounds heavier than the sports car. The spare wheel was mounted—Lincoln-Continental style—externally in the rear, adding 10 inches to the length. The reasoning was that the externally mounted spare left more room in the trunk for cargo.

The interior was not as lavish as the exterior. The dashboard was simple. The console was covered with vinyl and for the first time in a Thunderbird, there were bucket seats in the front. As was the case with the sports car, the standard transmission was a three-speed manual, but an automatic was optional.

The 1959 Thunderbird, also a four-seater, had several cosmetic changes over the 1958 version. The honeycomb front grille had been replaced with a horizontal-bar grille. The four stripes on the door—which some thought gave the car a heavy look—were replaced with a sharp chrome arrow, incorporated into the design molded into the door.

The Thunderbird grew larger every year after that, and, as its sales figures prove, it grew in popularity over the same time span. The 1958 model, the first four-seater, sold 37,892 cars. The 1959 Thunderbird had 67,446 customers, and 92,798 were sold of the 1960 T-Bird.

The 1956 Bentley S1 Continental Convertible had a standard automatic transmission, a 4.9-liter engine, and an impressive top speed of 120 miles per hour.

The 1956 Buick Special was powered by a 322-cubic-inch engine with a 2-barrel carburetor. The motor produced 255 horsepower and could go from 0 to 60 miles per hour in 11.7 seconds. With a wheelbase of 122 inches, it had a top speed of 110 miles per hour.

The fuel-injected V-8 that roared under the hood of this 1957 Chevrolet Bel Air was designed by engineers Ed Cole and Harry Barr.

The First Hot Chevy

The 1956 Chevrolet Bel Air became one of General Motors' all-time most popular cars, and it's no wonder. This was the Chevy that introduced the new Chevrolet V-8 engine. Here was a Chevrolet convertible that could sound and look most impressive as it peeled out of the drive-in.

This was a first for Chevy, which had long been considered a car that was perfect for Grandma to go to church in on Sunday.

Even with the new V-8 engine, Chevrolet's top standard engine was still less powerful than those of Ford and Plymouth: The Plymouth V-8 got 197 horsepower, the Ford V-8 was rated at 190 horsepower, while Chevy's new-and-improved V-8 measured at only 162 horsepower.

Cars of 1957

In 1957, 266,000 American convertibles were made. That was four percent of all the cars made that year in the U.S. The most awesome combination of really big fins and really big muscles had to be the 1957 Chrysler 300-C. The standard 392-cubic-inch engine produced 375 horsepower at 5,200 revolutions per minute. Options could boost that serious get-up-and-go all the way to 390 horsepower at 5,400 revolutions per minute. It was—and the point was proven repeatedly on the straightaways of the American highway system, trust us— the most powerful car of the year. And, oh yeah, the roof came off.

The 300-C weighed 4,340 pounds, and cost a then-hefty $5,359. There were 484 300-Cs manufactured, and all but five of them were sold domestically. Of course, the exporting of American cars at this point was minimal across the board. Detroit's big boats didn't even fit down some European streets.

That year's DeSoto Fireflite Convertible had a 341-cubic-inch engine, capable of cranking out 295 horsepower. Automatic transmission was standard, with three speeds and reverse, chosen by the driver with push buttons at the far left-hand side of the instrument panel.

The Pontiac Star Chief of 1957 changed Pontiac's image but good. Thought of as a car manufacturer for older folks who wanted comfort but not necessarily performance, Pontiac added *varoom* to its repertoire with the Star Chief. The car was designed by Simon "Bunkie" Knudson, and was a real dazzler. One reporter wrote: "My God, it's three-toned: red and white and chrome." The Star Chief—souped up to NASCAR rather than road limits, of course—won both of the big races at Daytona Beach that year. In the Daytona convertible race, the winning Star Chief was driven by the colorfully named Banjo Mathews.

LEFT AND FOLLOWING PAGE: Two views of the 1955 Pontiac Star Chief. This car had a 4-barrel carburetor worth 227 horsepower. Style touches included a Continental-style spare tire, wire wheel covers, and a special grille guard.

For Plymouth, the 1960 Fury represented a royal break- away from their usual stolid family automobiles.

The 1958 Chevro- let Impala was Chevy's attempt to catch Ford and Plymouth, who had restyled their cars the year be- fore. It worked. Including hard- tops, 181,500 Im- palas were sold in the first year of production.

This was the year that Ford debuted a convertible that was not a ragtop. The Skyliner was a steel-top. Lowering the hard top involved a mechanism that included ten solenoids, nine circuit breakers, five electric motors, thirteen switches, and 610 feet of wire. Because of this extra machinery, the car was heavy—both in mass and price tag. The trouble with the setup was that, once the steel top telescoped down into the trunk to let the sun shine in, there was no room left in the trunk for anything else. The same car with a normal soft top was available and called the Sunliner. Both cars had the standard Ford V-8 engine that produced 190 horsepower.

As an experiment, Pontiac introduced the 1957 Bonneville when that year's selling season was already half through. Only 630 were made and no more than one car was sent to any dealer. Obviously, the experiment was a successful one, as the longevity of the Bonneville line proves. The car debuted in 1957, but it was the 1958 version of the Bonneville—a Tri-Power Bonneville, to be exact—that had the honor of being the pace car at the 1958 Indianapolis 500. The pace car for the 1957 running of the "Greatest Spectacle in Racing" was the Mercury Turnpike Cruiser convertible.

There were 266,000 convertibles built in the United States in 1957, representing four percent of the total number of motor vehicles manufactured. The accepted front-runner was the Chrysler 300. This was the car that every company (or division of General Motors) wanted to imitate with their convertible. By this time, a pattern had been set that would remain in place for the next ten years: Each auto manufacturer chose to offer as a convertible their top model, and upon their convertibles they heaped their most exotic options. When Americans were ready to splurge to buy their fantasy car, they bought a ragtop.

Though it was the year of rocket-ship styling, in convertibles as well as hardtops, sales of American cars plummeted in 1958, a symptom of an economic recession then in progress. Less than four million cars were sold that year, down from more than seven million only a few years before.

Of the twenty-two models offered by Ford in 1959, the Galaxie Skyliner Retractable Hardtop was the most expensive, costing $3,350 per unit. It's easy to see why. The car needed two motors, one to move the wheels and the other to reconfigure itself.

There were 11,130 Cadillac Convertibles built in 1959. All were two-door, six-seaters. The car had an X-frame chassis and a steel body. The transmission was a General Motors Hydra-Matic three-speed automatic. It had coil-spring suspension on all four wheels. Freon-12 gas suspension was offered as an option. There were four-wheel, hydraulic, power-assisted drum brakes. And, oh yeah, they came in pink.

All-Time Biggest Fins

The largest fins in the history of production cars? That's an easy one. They would be the 42-inchers that grace the rear quarters of the 1959 Cadillac. And, yeah, the car came in pink!

The '59 Caddy weighed exactly two tons and its massive 390-cubic-inch V-8 engine got a whopping 8 miles per gallon. That engine also got 345 horsepower at 4,800 revolutions per minute. The car was 20 feet long and 6 feet wide. Obviously, because of its length and width, the 1959 Caddy was not known for its handling.

Wanna make a U-turn? Forget about it! This Caddy had a 24-foot turning radius. The wings, which were made to look even larger by the low profile of the front half of the car, had (simulated in chrome) "jet engines" mounted on them, with the bullet-shaped taillights becoming the "flame" from those

protruding "engines." The curved windshield could have been taken from something supersonic.

One of the unusual items temporarily available as an option was the "Autronic Eye," which cost an extra $55 and, mounted on the hood, sensed oncoming headlights and automatically dimmed its own. As it turned out, no one wanted it, so the option was quickly discontinued.

The maximum speed was 112 miles per hour. It took this monster 10.3 seconds to get from 0 to 60 miles per hour and 23.1 seconds to get from 0 to 100 miles per hour.

The interior, which was big enough to throw a party in, had automatic everything: seats, windows, locks, and internal control of the side mirrors. Everything was shiny, detailed in chrome. The trunk was large enough to hold five spare tires.

The Series 62 Cadillac— this one was manufactured in 1962—was the last Caddy to be designed by the legendary Harley Earl.

The 1962 MGA 1600 Mark 2 was the last of the long-running British series, which was about to evolve into the MGB.

The 1960 Austin-Healy 3000 had a 6-cylinder engine displacing just shy of 3 liters. The 3000 was the first Austin-Healy to have disc brakes.

The 1964 Aston Martin DB5 Convertible had a 4-liter engine, an alternator ignition, diaphragm clutch, and a transmission option with five forward speeds. Contrary to popular belief, an ejector seat was not an option.

The 1964 Chevelle Malibu convertible was part of Chevrolet's response to the muscle-car phenomenon started by John DeLorean's Pontiac GTO.

The 1962 Chevrolet Impala SS (Super Sports) had a big enough engine to get the job done, but lacked strong engineering development.

"Built To Go Places . . . Fast!"

That was the 1959 Daimler SP250 Dart's great sales pitch. The Dart was an attempt by Daimler to sell a car that would be popular in America. Indeed, among the 2,644 that were built between 1959 and 1964, 1,415 of them had the steering wheel on the left. All of those made, however, were two-door, two-seater sports convertibles.

The body was fiberglass and sat on a steel-girder chassis. The engine was an iron-block 2,548-cubic-centimeter V-8, rated at 140 horsepower at 5,800 revolutions per minute.

The transmission was either a four-speed manual or a three-speed Borg-Warner Model 8. The independent front suspension was done with wishbones and coil springs. The rear suspension consisted of a live axle with leaf springs. Girling discs on all four wheels provided the brakes.

The Dart had a maximum speed of 125 miles per hour. It could go from 0 to 60 miles per hour in 8.5 seconds and from 0 to 100 miles per hour in 19.1 seconds. It got 25 miles per gallon.

Giantism: Prelude to Extinction

The year 1959 signaled the peak of the style eccentricities of the decade, the year when all of the elements that distinguished the cars of the 1950s reached their most extreme: Fins were biggest, the most chrome was used—and mileage was at an all-time low.

More than 5.5 million Americans bought new cars in 1959, a comeback year for Detroit, and, of those, five percent bought convertibles. But the Detroit brain trust seemed to realize that giantism was the prelude to extinction, and the following year American cars did something they hadn't done in a long time—they got smaller.

Thunderbirds of the '60s

The 1960s saw the Thunderbird continue its transition from a sports car into a luxury car—all the way into a car that was no longer appropriate for a convertible option.

In 1960, 11,860 Thunderbird convertibles were sold at a $4,222 base cost each. Vinyl convertible tops came in black, white, and blue. Two engines were available: a 352-cubic-inch, 300-horsepower V-8, or a 430-cubic-inch, 350-horsepower V-8. New design elements included three groups of triple hash marks which decorated the rear fenders.

Sigmund Freud said that sometimes a cigar is a cigar. Well, we suspect that was not the case when the designers penciled in the shape of the 1961 Thunderbird, the pace car for that year's Indy 500. Freud also said something about a man's *accouterment* being designed to extend his anatomy, and here we suspect he may have had a point. When a man "wore" the 1961 T-Bird, he was huge. And, of course—though claiming that it didn't make any difference—women liked the car, too.

The 1961 Thunderbird was the largest, lowest, widest, and heaviest in the history of the line. The car was 205 inches long, had a wheelbase 113 inches long, weighed 4,222 pounds, was 75.9 inches wide, and had a top speed of 130 miles per hour. The standard engine was a 390-cubic-inch V-8, rated at 300 horsepower at 4,600 revolutions per minute. It was capable of going from 0 to 60 miles per hour in 8.5 seconds.

In 1962, the base cost of the T-Bird ragtop was $4,788. A new option on the ragtop was the Sports Roadster, which came with a removable fiberglass tonneau that transformed the car from a four-seater into a two-seater. The tonneau was easy to put on and take off, but a pain in the neck to store.

The 1963 Thunderbird convertible cost $4,912 without frills, and 5,913 were sold. Another 455 Sports Roadsters were sold at $5,563. Convertible Thunderbird sales rose to 9,198 in 1964, a year in which the base cost went down to $4,853. The Sports Roadster model was discontinued.

In 1965, sequential taillights were added. Only 6,846 convertibles were sold at a list price of $4,851 apiece—the second year in a row that the cost went down. The price dropped again in 1966 to $4,845, but so did the total number of Thunderbird ragtops sold, down to 5,049. Without fanfare, the convertible was discontinued after the 1966 selling season.

Mustangs of 1970–71

Although it is universally agreed that a Ford Motor Company committee was responsible, Lido Anthony "Lee" Iacocca is the individual most often credited with the spark of an idea that flamed into the Mustang.

It was Iacocca who pushed hardest, beginning in 1961, for Ford to build a sporty little car to fill the void formed when the Thunderbird evolved from a two-seater into a four-seater. (When the first Mustang was still on the drawing board, it was known as the T-5 project, which explains why the car was later known as the T-5 in Germany, where the name "Mustang" had already been trademarked.)

The first Mustang production model came in 1964. Both the convertible and the hardtop had 108-inch wheelbases and were 181.6 inches long overall. The convertible outweighed the hardtop, 2,615 to 2,449 pounds. Base cost for the ragtop was $2,614.

The standard engine for the inaugural Mustang was the mega-wimpy, 170-cubic-inch putt-putt worth 101 horsepower. Ford was smart though. They offered a tempting optional engine at not that much more money, and thus assured themselves that customers would take the frill every time. For only a few extra bucks, the debut Mustang could be had with none-too-shabby 225-cubic-inch, slant 6-cylinder capable of producing 145 horsepower. The top engine offered, for more than a couple extra bucks, was the 289-cubic-inch, 210-horsepower V-8 powerplant.

The first thirty-seven Mustangs off the assembly line were identical to the one that had paced the parade laps at the Indianapolis 500 in 1964, only minutes before a fiery crash killed two drivers and hospitalized several others right in front of a horrified and fire-threatened grandstand. Because of the accident, that pace car didn't get the same positive publicity from the race as the pace cars that came before and after. The first thirty-seven Mustangs off the assembly line, like the pace car, had the 289-cubic-inch engine, necessitated by the original's duties.

The first Mustang won the 1964 Tiffany Award, presented by Tiffany & Company for excellence in American design. The car sold 263,434 units in its first year. More than half of those customers were under the age of thirty-five.

The 1965 Mustang had several new options: a "GT" package, luxury interiors, and front disc brakes. The GT package included a 225-horsepower V-8 engine, a three-speed fully synchronized stick shift, and dual exhaust.

Resting on a wheelbase 121 inches long, the 1964 Polara 500 was one of the bigger Dodges. The biggest engine offered displaced 7,200 cubic centimeters.

A sort of super GT package was also available, and it included a high-performance V-8 worth 271 horsepower. The GT package cost $165 extra, while the super-GT package boosted the base price by $276. That car won the Industrial Institute's Bronze Medal Award.

The 1966 Mustang convertible was practically identical to the previous year's version, with the exception of the front grille on the GT, which now included "fog lamps," an inner second set of headlights inside the grille. Ford would experiment with different versions of this "four-eyes" look for the Mustang over the next few years.

The top engine option for the new, re-styled Mustang in 1967 was a 390-cubic-inch, 320-horsepower V-8. That option added $264 to the base price. GT-option cars with automatic transmissions were known as "GTAs." New options included a tilt-away steering wheel and a stereo tape system. The no-frills price tag read $2,698. It weighed 2,738 pounds. Ford sold 44,808 Mustang ragtops in 1967, a little less than ten percent of all of the Mustangs sold that year.

The largest big-block engine option got even bigger in 1968, with the top-of-the-line Mustang powerplant being pumped up to a 428-cubic-inch Cobra-Jet V-8 rated at 335 horsepower.

The Mustang was once again re-styled for 1969, with a new, sharply raked windshield and quad headlights—again one set was outside the grille and the other set inside. The outboard lamps were sunk into the fender openings while the inboard lights were embedded in the grille ends. Another new style element on that year's convertible was the rear-facing, simulated air vent in front of the rear wheel opening. The 428-cubic-inch engine remained the top option. Ford built 14,746 convertibles in 1969.

The 1964½ Mustang was a unanimous choice for rookie of the year. By the time the pony car celebrated its first birthday, it had sold 418,000 units—a record for a new model.

For those who think ragtops and luxury cars are mutually exclusive groups, note the 1961 Lincoln Continental convertible. The Lincoln convertible was produced, with the same body shell, until 1967.

Porsche 356B

Ferry Porsche—son of the legendary car designer Ferdinand Porsche—in conjunction with Karl Rube, designed the Porsche 356B convertible. The car looked and ran like an elongated and finely tuned Volkswagen Beetle.

First produced in 1959, the rear-engine 356B had unit-steel body construction with an integral pressed-steel platform chassis. The engine was a 1,582-cubic-centimeter, air-cooled, horizontally opposed flat 4-cylinder, capable of 90 horsepower at 5,500 revolutions per minute. Because of that rating, the engine was known as the "Super 90."

The car had a four-speed manual, all syncromesh, rear-wheel-drive transmission. The independent suspension in the front consisted of trailing arms with transverse torsion bars and an anti-roll bar. The rear suspension, also independent, consisted of swing half axles, radius arms, and transverse torsion bars. The shocks were telescopic. There were hydraulic drum brakes on all four wheels. When the 356B was replaced by the 356C in 1963, front and rear brakes were changed to discs.

The 356B's maximum speed was 90 miles per hour. It could go from 0 to 60 miles per hour in 10 seconds. For the time, the car ran with extraordinary economy, getting between 30 and 35 miles per gallon.

The rear-view mirror was attached to a slender chrome bar, giving the windshield a "split screen" look from the front. In the cockpit, there was a padded dash, with green-on-black instruments. The steering wheel, larger and closer to the vertical than most, was noted for its light feel in the hands. There were twin exhausts and a convenient access cover allowed oh-so-blue roadside mechanics easy retrieval of the torsion bars.

Rear Window

A problem from day one of convertibles was the poor quality of rear vision for the driver when the top was up. Because glass could not fold up with the rest of the ragtop when the weather was nice, rear windows on convertibles were made of plastic, which inevitably became cracked, scratched, and discolored.

One attempt to solve this problem came with the 1960 Lincoln Continental Mark V. On the Mark V, the rear window was glass, part of the car's body structure, not part of the roof. The rear window remained in place even when the roof was off, and could be raised and lowered just like the side windows.

The 1960 Lincoln Continental Mark V was one of the first American cars to have a list price in five figures.

Citroën DS 21 Decapotable

The Citroën DS 21 Decapotable, nicknamed "The Shark" because of the shape of its proboscis, was manufactured from 1960 to 1971. During that time, 1,365 of them were built. All of them sat five—two in the front and three in the back—and had an all-steel body with innovative detachable panels. The steel-platform chassis had welded box section side members. The sharky, streamlined body pierced the air with great aerodynamic efficiency. The detachable body panels came in very handy when the car needed maintenance or repair work. The rear fenders were also removable, making it much easier to change the rear tires.

The Paris car-builder Henri Chapron designed the DS 21's body, basing it on a chassis previously used in the Citroën Safari Estate model. One of the car's most noteworthy features was the hydraulic fluid suspension—independent all around with hydropneumatic struts—that could be raised or lowered depending on conditions. The bumpier the road, the higher the suspension would be raised. Because of the sophisticated suspension, this car was considered to offer the world's smoothest ride.

The transmission was a four-speed clutchless semi-automatic. Gear changes were accomplished by hydraulic servo motors when the driver moved the gear lever. The interior was completely padded with foam rubber, even the floor. The dashboard gave the interior a futuristic look and this car, like other Citroën models, had a one-spoke steering wheel.

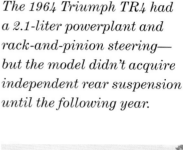

The 1964 Triumph TR4 had a 2.1-liter powerplant and rack-and-pinion steering— but the model didn't acquire independent rear suspension until the following year.

This 1966 Citroën DS21 Cabroilet Convertible could go from 0 to 60 miles per hour in (ho-hum) 11.2 seconds and from 0 to 100 miles per hour in a don't-hold-your-breath 40.4 seconds. The car did, however, get an impressive (for that era) 24 miles per gallon.

The engine on the 1962 Jaguar E Roadster was kept cool through the combined effort of a radiator header tank and twin electric fans. It had a four-speed, all synchromesh transmission, a four-wheel independent suspension with coil springs, and four-wheel disc brakes. The polished windshield frame was handmade. The bumpers were tiny and for show only. Real bumpers, the designer felt, would have been prohibitively heavy.

The engine, though not horrible, was still probably the weakest link on this classic. While the rest of the car appeared to have been sent back from the future, the engine was pretty obviously linked to the past—a descendent of the powerplant that had been used before World War II in the Citroën Traction Avant. The 4-cylinder engine displaced 2,175 cubic centimeters and generated 109 horsepower at 5,550 revolutions per minute. With disc brakes in the front and drum brakes in the rear, the DS 21 Decapotable could go as fast as 116 miles per hour—adequate in most circles.

Jaguar E

When you talk about the greatest performance convertibles ever, you have to talk about the Jaguar E-Type Roadster, made in Great Britain from 1959 until 1974; during that time 72,520 were constructed. It had a steel monocoque body, and purchasers had a choice of three engines: a 3,781-cubic-centimeter straight 6-cylinder, a 4,235-cubic-centimeter straight 6-cylinder, and a

5,343-cubic-centimeter V-12. Power output ranged between awesome and mega-awesome—from 265 to 272 horsepower. The transmission was a four-speed manual, although, after 1966, an automatic transmission was optional. It had disc brakes all around, and independent front suspension, with wishbones and torsion bar. The rear suspension was also independent, of the coil-and-radius-arm variety.

The maximum speed was (and, yes, this was the number for the production model) 150 miles per hour. These Jags could go from 0 to 60 miles per hour in 7 seconds, and from 0 to 100 miles per hour in only 16.2 seconds. Considering the kind of acceleration and potential velocity, this Jag's mileage was not bad: 16 to 20 miles per gallon.

1963—A Peak Year

There were 7.6 million American cars sold in 1963. Of these, seven percent—the greatest percentage of all years—were convertibles. After that, there was a steady decline until 1976, when American car-makers decided to stop manufacturing convertibles entirely.

Though there has not been any research done on the subject, the decline's commencement coincided with the November 22, 1963, assassination of the President of the United States, John F. Kennedy, who, after all, was murdered in a convertible. "Should have had the top up," some said. Bullets had turned the American Dream into *A Nightmare on Elm Street*.

The decline of the convertible was sped up in the 1970s by the increasing cost of gasoline. The new economy of transportation greatly diminished the amount of "driving for fun" that was going on.

Also assisting in the downfall of the ragtop was the fact that the world was becoming an increasingly safety-conscious place. Those faceless crash-test dummies never fared well in crashes involving convertibles—especially when the car rolled over.

Attention: Rude Playboys

A collaboration between AC Cars of Great Britain and Texas race-car builder Carroll Shelby brought forth the AC Cobra 427 (1965–68). A massive Ford engine—meant for a Mustang—was stuffed into a tiny British sports car, thus creating the perfect automobile for a somewhat rude playboy. The car was designed to win the 24 Hours of LeMans endurance race, a feat it never accomplished.

During the AC Cobra 427's production run, 316 of these beauties were created. All of them were two-door two-seaters with a light aluminum body, separate tubular-steel chassis with aluminum panels, and a 6,989-cubic-centimeter V-8 engine developing 425 horsepower at 6,000 revolutions per minute. Yowsah! That's like putting Arnold Schwarzenegger's arms on Twiggy's body and asking her to climb a rope. The top speed of the AC Cobra 427: 165 miles per hour.

The RG/SS Camero 396 was available as a convertible only between 1967 and 1969. This is a '68. They went exclusively hardtop in 1970 because of fears that legislation was about to be passed in the United States banning ragtops from the roads.

Go Go GTO!

The original American GTO, the Pontiac Tempest GTO, was, like, definitely a child of '60s sunshine. Introduced in 1964, during the most feverish pitch of Beatlemania, it came with a 389-cubic-inch engine with special HO heads, a high-lift cam, and high-performance valve springs. It is considered today to be the first full-sized muscle car. It was in this car that the Hurst shifter debuted, as an option. In contrast to the designs of the previous decade, the GTO was born chrome-free. It had two huge scoops on the hood that have been likened to nostrils.

Here's to You, Mrs. Robinson

1968 was the year of Robert Kennedy's and Martin Luther King's assassinations, political-convention riots, and hippies. The first edition of the Alfa Romeo 1300 Junior Spider was made famous that year, along with Dustin Hoffman, as one of the stars of the movie *The Graduate*. Though some of us can't imagine owning a sports car with "Junior" in its name, the car remained in production until 1978, and during that time 7,237 units were produced. It had all-steel monocoque body construction and a twin-cam, all-aluminum 1,290-cubic-centimeter engine.

That powerplant produced 89 horsepower at 6,000 revolutions per minute. The Spider had a five-speed transmission. There was independent suspension in the front. The suspension in the rear consisted of a live axle with coil springs. There were disc brakes on all four wheels.

The Spider's maximum speed was 106 miles per hour. It could go from 0 to 60 miles per hour in 11.2 seconds, and from 0 to 100 miles per hour in 21.3 seconds. That's not that much oomph—but quite enough for the sheltered Benjamin in the movie. The Spider got 29 miles to the gallon.

The 1968 Pontiac GTO was the winner of Motor Trend *magazine's "Car of the Year" award—and for good reason. The body was all new from the '67 version, sleeker with horizontal headlights, an Enduro bumper, and functional hood scoops. The optional 400-cubic-inch "Ram Air" engine was rated at 360 horses. It was updated midseason and renamed "Ram Air II."*

*The 1976 Cadillac Eldorado Bicentennial
was the last mass-produced, American-made
convertible of the decade. By 1978, these cars were
selling at auctions for twice their original price.*

Chapter Three

DEATH—AND REBIRTH

While the Mustang thrived into the '70s, the convertible struggled. Rock and roll was suitable in public but sex and drugs sometimes required privacy. In many ways, the van was becoming the fantasy car of the era, with its capacity to function as a motel room—whether on the road or near home.

After a few years of quad headlights, Mustang returned to two headlights in 1970. Both lamps were now located inside an enlarged grille. The engine options remained the same as they had been in 1969, except the 390-cubic-inch V-8 option was discontinued. Only 7,673 convertibles were sold, one-sixth of the number sold only four years before.

Every Mustang until 1971 had had a wheelbase exactly 108 inches long. That measurement increased by an inch for the 1971 model. The overall length of that car was 190 inches, almost 8 inches longer than the original Mustang in 1964. The 1971 ragtop—which went on sale on September 18, 1970—had increased back-seat room—a move designed exclusively for passenger comfort. There was still nowhere near enough room for romance back there. Again, trust us.

The End: 1976

With the exception of two-seater sports cars, there were no American-built convertibles between 1976, when Cadillac stopped manufacturing the Eldorado convertible, until the 1982 car season when Dodge, Buick, and Chrysler debuted the first American ragtops of the 1980s.

Not all of the new American ragtops were successful, however—and, in some cases, sales were horrendous. By 1987, Buick was once again making nothing but hardtops. Dodge scrapped their convertible program the following year.

With high compression despite governmental restrictions, the 1991 Corvette ZR1 has duel overhead cams, with four valves per cylinder. The engine's electronic control module directs the three-stage throttle control.

Optional engines for the 1970 Dodge RT Challenger ranged from the 340-cubic-inch 275-horsepower standard all the way up to a 425-horsepower Hemi.

The 1970 Oldsmobile Cutlass came with the famous "W-31" engine. Only 350-cubic-inches in displacement, but with power like a rocket, the W-31 made the Cutlass a potential winner on any strip. In 1970, the Cutlass, for the first time, could be driven with the massive 455-cubic-inch, "Rochester" 4-barrel carburetor engine capable of 365 horsepower.

By 1972, the Oldsmobile H/O Cutlass was already diminished, in terms of power, from previous years—but it now had front disc brakes.

In 1971, Ferrari race cars won five Grand Prix events. On the roads, Ferrari was winning less formal competitions with this 365/GTS Daytona.

*The 1970 Fiat (*Fabbrica
Italiana Automobili Torino*) Dino
had a 2.4-liter engine and strut-
type rear suspension.*

T-Tops Whistle

From 1977 to 1982, just about the only open-topped cars made in the United States were T-tops. These cars had removable panels in their hard roofs, which allowed the sun to shine in while a T-shaped frame remained above. That T-frame also functioned as a roll cage in case of an accident in which the car flipped over. T-top models included the Oldsmobile, Corvette, Pontiac Trans Am Turbo, Mustang (where it was called the "T-Roof"), Buick Regal, and Camaro Z-28.

Although Detroit's marketing departments tried to emphasize the convertible-like qualities of the T-tops, these cars were never considered true convertibles. One of the drawbacks of the T-top was that the wind would get under the skeletal roof and cause an annoying whistle.

Honey, I Shrunk the Ragtop

Chevrolet and Pontiac re-entered the ragtop market in 1983. The first pop-top Cadillac of the decade came the following year. AMC introduced the Alliance in 1985, a tiny car modeled after France's Renault sedan. Oldsmobile almost skipped the decade—they didn't make a ragtop until 1989.

The difference between the convertibles of the 1980s and the classics from previous decades was obvious: size. Cars were smaller in general, as Detroit reacted to a world of expensive gasoline, and—in almost every case—car

Try as it might, the Camaro never became the sporting icon that its stable-mate, the Corvette, did. The 1981 T-top model is a Z-28.

The 1987 Mazda RX7 Elford got more respect than the average Japanese convertible because of its high-performance, rotary-type Wankel engine.

The 1980 Pontiac Trans Am had a curb weight of 3,540 pounds. It sat on a 108.2-inch wheelbase. The standard engine was a 301-cubic-incher capable of 170 horsepower at 4,400 revolutions per minute.

manufacturers chose their smallest or next-to-smallest model to offer as a convertible. Oddly enough, *images* of large convertibles became extremely fashionable at this time as a nostalgic icon of "simpler times."

Mustangs of the 1980s

The ragtop also returned to the Mustang line midway through the 1983 selling season, when the 1983 Mustang GLX was introduced. It had an electric top and a real glass rear window. Ads claimed that there was room for four, but this assumed that the two who rode in the back were willing to grow well acquainted with their knees. The base cost was $12,467. The GT option, with a 5-liter V-8 engine, cost $13,560. Twenty-thousand Mustang convertibles were sold that year. Sales of the Mustang—with engine options ranging from the 2.3-liter, 4-cylinder to the 5-liter V-8—remained steady until 1988, when the number of Mustangs sold ballooned up to 33,344.

In 1993, the best-selling German make in the United States was the BMW, and it wasn't just because—and this is true—the cars were manufactured to be eighty percent recyclable when scrapped. Here's part of the reason why: the BMW Nazca CZ Spider.

On May 28, 1978, this 'Vette paced the thirty-three starting race cars around the warm-up laps before the sixty-second annual Indianapolis 500.

The Mercedes 300 SL (Sports Light) has been around since 1952— when the premiere version won the Swiss Grand Prix at Bern. This red beauty was built in 1981.

Fifty-six years after Alfieri Maserati founded the company with speed in mind, Maserati was still making lightning-quick cars, like the 1988 BI Turbo.

What kind of car would you buy if you had a zillion dollars? The legacy of Ferdinand Porche lives on in this 1987 model from the 900 series.

1990 Corvette

It was often said in 1990 that American ragtops "ain't what they used to be." But this was not quite a universal truth. The 1990 Corvette convertible was everything it once was—and more.

It had a new, flexible backlight made out of a revolutionary material that the scientists at GM decided to call "ultrashield." The product was a joint-development effort between the Corvette group, ASC, Inc., and O'Sullivan Manufacturers. The laminated electro-sealable material not only delivered good heat stability but also had nearly double the ultraviolet resistance of the existing material. Tests showed no apparent loss of light transmission and a minimal increase in haze.

1990 Mustang

Safety received more emphasis than ever as the new decade dawned. A driver-side air bag and rear shoulder belts became standard in all Mustang convertibles in 1990. Prices now ranged from the basic $9,456 to the top-of-the-line $15,141. Standard equipment on all Mustangs now included a teeny 2.3-liter 4-cylinder engine with electronic fuel injection, power front disc brakes, five-speed manual-overdrive transmission, block sidewall tires, sport bucket seats, and a tachometer on the instrument panel. The wheelbase was now 100.5 inches long and the ragtop was 179.6 inches in length overall. The car stood 52.1 inches high and was 68.3 inches wide. It had unitized body construction and modified McPherson strut suspension in the front.

Return to the Open Road

There is a healthy market of hot convertibles out there today, but most of them are beyond the means of the average driver. Ragtops now come almost exclusively on high-performance sports cars. The days of the roadhog boat-like gas-guzzling ragtop—or the topless Beetle, for that matter—are over. Also, a greater proportion of the convertibles made today are non-American.

Let's start with BMW, where the 1997 Z3 has a two-tone leather interior and a 2.8-liter engine. That powerplant conjures up 189 horsepower when working at 5,300 revolutions per minute.

Corvette-lovers tend to be music lovers as well, so it only stands to reason that there has always been an effort to provide the car's internal environment with fantastic sound. In this 1990 Calloway Corvette, that sound came in the form of an optional and newly improved Delco/Bose "Gold" sound system. Available in either cassette, digital disc, or tape configurations, the system —with a power output of 200 watts— was twice as powerful as the 1989 version.

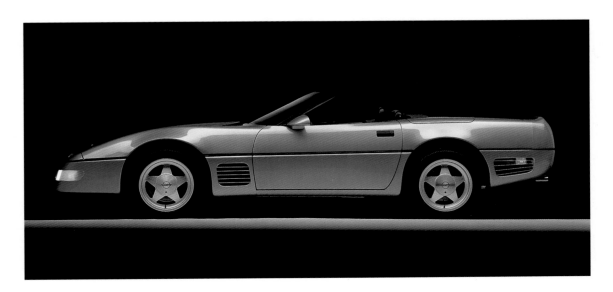

The 1996 BMW Z3 went from 0 to 60 in 6.3 seconds thanks to its 2.8-liter duel over-head-cam, 6-cylinder engine.

Excaliber—never a mass-market manufacturer to begin with—was one of the few companies to continue to produce convertibles throughout the 1970s. Their designs were always elegant yet nostalgic. Retro, some would say. This 1981 Excaliber Roadster was built five years before the company filed for bankruptcy.

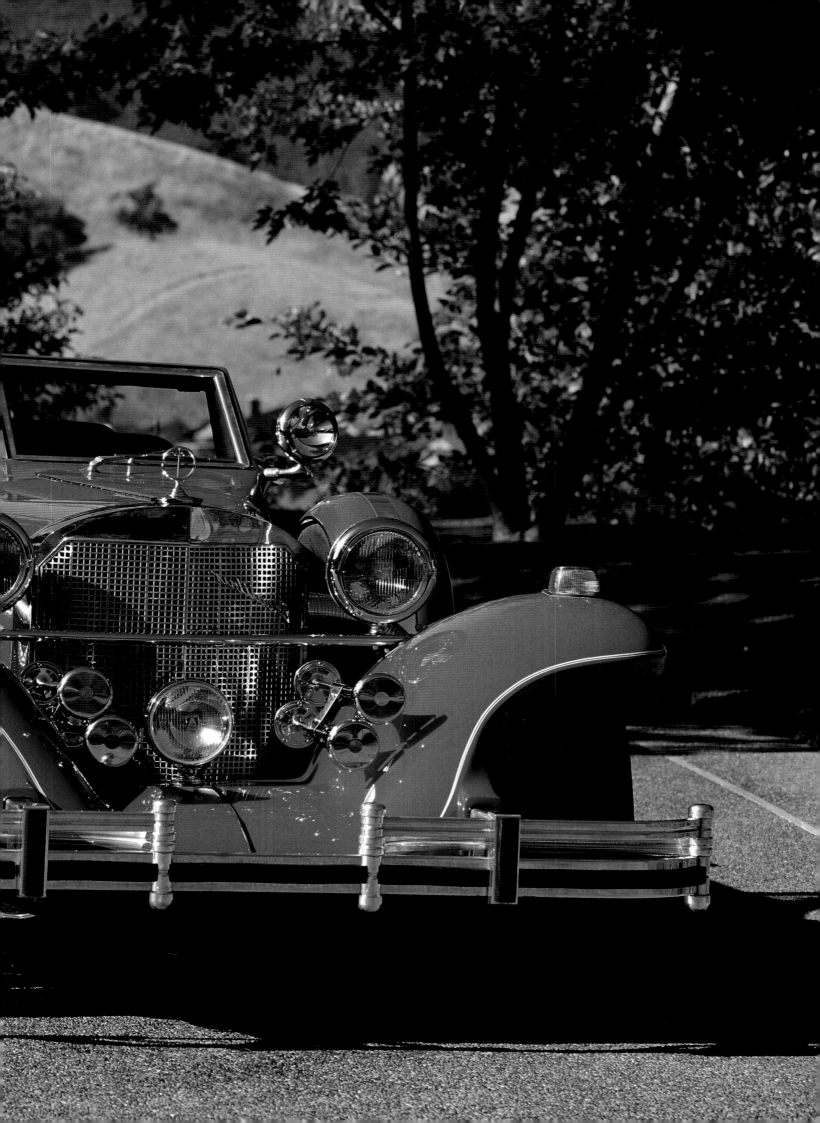

Unlike several Porsche models that preceded it, the 1992 Porsche 968 has a front-mounted engine.

This Jaguar XJS Sport was built in 1990, but the model had been around since 1975. Top speed was 150 miles per hour, and it went from 0 to 60 in 6.7 seconds.

The debut of the Fifth Generation of Corvettes came in 1997—stronger than ever, with its 5.7-liter V-8 engine producing 345 horsepower.

The 2,870-pounder is 158.5 inches long, 68.5 inches wide and just shy of 60 inches tall. The body sits on a 96.3-inch wheelbase. It gets from 0 to 60 miles per hour in 6.5 seconds, and the standard package has a list price of $35,900.

Mercedes-Benz SLK230 Kompressor

In a world where rack-and-pinion steering is practically universal among high-performance automobiles, Mercedes Benz still uses the recirculating ball—and the steering mechanism in the 1998 SLK230 Kompressor is no exception.

This hot little number has a supercharged 4-cylinder engine that displaces 2,295 cubic centimeters. The powerplant is rated at 185 horsepower when turning 5,300 revolutions per minute.

The two-seater has a five-speed automatic transmission and can go from 0 to 60 miles per hour in 6.6 seconds. Because of its size—3,025 pounds—the Kompressor gets only 19.6 miles per gallon. Economy's got nothin' to do with it.

The base price for the Kompressor is $39,700. The car measures 157.3 inches long, 67.5 inches wide, and 50.8 inches high. It sits atop a 95.5 inch wheelbase.

In the Clearing Stands the Boxster

Here it comes, there it goes! What was that blur? Must have been the 1997 Porsche Boxster, which has a top speed of 149 miles per hour, thanks to its 6-cylinder, 2,480-cubic-centimeter engine, capable of 201 horsepower at 6,000 revolutions per minute.

The two-seater weighs only 2,755 pounds. It is 169.9 inches long, 70 inches wide, and just shy of 51 inches high. The wheelbase measures 95.1 inches. The Boxster goes from a standstill to 60 miles per hour in a super-quick 6.1 seconds. It gets 22 miles per gallon, on the average, and has a no-frills list price of $39,900.

A Thoroughly Modern Mustang

Today's Mustang convertible, the 1997 model, has a base 3.8-liter engine (150 horsepower), and a top option 4.6-liter engine (producing a "pump-you-up" 305 horsepower). The wheelbase measures 101.3 inches. The two-door is 71.8 inches wide and 53.2 inches tall. It weighs between 3,084 and 3,264 pounds, depending on options. It gets 20 miles per gallon in the city and 30 miles per gallon on the highway. The base cost (no muscle) is $15,000. Bulk up under the hood and your price tag reads in the $31,000 neighborhood.

Latest 'Vette: 172 Miles Per Hour!

The 1997 Corvette comes with a removable hard top. It has standard dual air bags and optional dual-zone climate control (for when the top is on), foglamps, a compact disc player that can handle twelve discs at a time, and a power passenger seat.

The newest Corvette has a wheelbase 104.5 inches long. It is 179.7 inches long overall, 73.6 inches wide, and 47.7 inches high. The engine is a liquid-cooled V-8 with cast-aluminum block and heads. That powerplant displaces 347 cubic inches and delivers 345 horsepower at 5,600 revolutions per minute.

There is a six-speed manual transaxle transmission and rack-and-pinion steering. The car has speed-sensitive, magnetic variable-effort, power-assisted steering, and vented disc brakes on all four wheels.

The 1997 Corvette can get from 0 to 60 miles per hour in a blistering 4.7 seconds—and from 0 to 100 miles per hour in 11.6 seconds! With a top speed of, get this, 172 miles per hour, today's Corvette gets 18 miles per gallon in the city and a fairly amazing 28 miles per gallon on the highway. The base cost is $38,550, now a typical convertible price.

Painted to match the finest burgundy wine, this 1995 Camero Convertible had a wheelbase of 101.1 inches and weighed 3,251 pounds.

Elsewhere in Chevy-Land

The 1997 Chevrolet Camaro convertible now comes with three engine options. The standard powerplant is the modest 3.8-liter 6-cylinder worth, 200 horsepower at 5,200 revolutions per minute. The big engine is the 5.7-liter 8-cylinder rated at, depending on accouterments, 285 horsepower at 5,200 revolutions per minute, or the top-of-the-line 310 horsepower at 5,200 revolutions per minute.

The two-door convertible has a 101.1-inch wheelbase. The car is 193.2 inches long, 74.1 inches wide, and just under 52 inches high. The Camaro currently gets 19 miles per gallon in the city and 30 miles per gallon along the straightaways outside town. The price range is a real reasonable $18,000 to $31,000—that's about as cheap as a rag-top comes in this day and age.

British Intelligence has Already Ordered a Thousand

The 1997 Aston Martin DB7, the great-great-granddaughter of the original James Bond car, has a super-charged 6-cylinder engine that produces 335 horsepower at 5,750 revolutions per minute.

A five-speed manual transmission is standard, but there is an option for a four-speed automatic. The DB7, which seats four as long as two are midgets, has a wheelbase of 102 inches and weighs 3,804 pounds. Overall, the car is 182.9 inches long. The DB7 accelerates from motionless to 60 miles per hour in 5.7 seconds. Base cost is, no kidding, $125,000—but that price goes up if you want frills.

Little Cat Feet

If you don't want to spend that much money on your next car, then may we suggest the 1997 Jaguar XK8 convertible, which can be had for a base cost of $70,000. For that mere pittance, you get a 244-cubic-inch 8-cylinder engine, and a powerplant that brings forth 290 horsepower at 6,100 revolutions per minute.

A five-speed automatic transmission is standard. The wheelbase measures 102 inches long and this car weighs a demure 3,862 pounds. The latest Jag goes from 0 to 60 miles per hour in 6.7 seconds. It gets 16 miles to the gallon in stop-and-go driving and 24 miles per gallon on the open road.

The Camden Yards of Cars

For readers who don't know baseball, Oriole Park at Camden Yards is a brand-new baseball facility in Baltimore, Maryland, that was built to resemble the more quaint and fan-friendly ballparks of the past. In this modern-convenience-with-nostalgic-styling vein comes the 1997 Plymouth Prowler, purposely built to resemble "hotrods" of the past.

Chrysler's old-fashioned two-seater looks like it should have had a Beach Boys' song written about it, something about prowling past the hamburger stand. The wedge-shaped two-seater can be had for $35,000. There are no options. That's the price.

The engine is a 2,165-cubic-inch 6-cylinder with a cast-iron block and aluminum heads. The Prowler powerplant produces 214 horsepower at 5,850 revolutions per minute. There's a four-speed transaxle transmission with a stick shift. The suspension has unequal-length control arms, pushrod-operated coil springs, and an anti-roll bar on both ends.

The Prowler accelerates from 0 to 60 miles per hour in 7.1 seconds and from 0 to 100 miles per hour in 23.6 seconds. It gets 20 miles to the gallon in the city and 28 miles per gallon along the open blacktop.

Audi Cabriolet

The 1997 Audi Cabriolet can be had for $34,500. This five-passenger, two-door convertible has a 2.8-liter 6-cylinder engine that is rated at 172 horsepower.

The wheelbase for this German ragtop is 100.6 inches long. The Cabriolet is 176 inches long overall. It weighs 3,364 pounds. It gets 18 miles per gallon in the city and 20 miles per gallon on Interstate 80.

In 1991, Alfa Romeo became an operative division of Fiat. Three years later, this Spider came off the production line.

Bentley Brooklands

The Bentley Brooklands costs only $329,000. Of course, they'll divvy that up for you into several easy-to-make payments. Besides, that's the price only if you want all of the extras. A base model of the 1997 Brooklands would run you mere dog-track change—$150,000. But for the wealthy driver who wants some unbelievable muscle, this car is worth it!

The Brooklands gets an estimated 300 horsepower from its standard, turbo-charged overhead-valve, 6.8-liter, 8-cylinder powerplant. That's standard. The top option engine is the Turbo R, which delivers 385 horsepower.

The Brooklands has a 116.5-inch wheelbase and weighs between 5,180 and 5,750 pounds, depending on options. This Bentley gets muscle-car mileage, too: 11 miles per gallon in the city and 18 miles per gallon on the major thoroughfare.

Ferrari F355

From England to Italy we go for the 1997 Ferrari F355, which—for $127,000—could be parked in your driveway. This 2,980-pound, two-passenger sports car has its 3.5-liter V-8 engine—rated at 375 horsepower at 8,250 revolutions per minute—mounted in the rear.

There's a six-speed manual transmission. The wheelbase is only 96.5 inches long, and the car is 167.2 inches long overall. Don't get too far away from the nearest gas station, however. The F355 gets 15 miles per gallon on the open road and only 10 miles per gallon heading cross-town.

Ragtop of the Future: Sssssssssss

What's on Detroit's drawing board for the American convertible future? Well, one clue comes from Chrysler, where a pop-top prototype called the Dodge Copperhead made its public debut at the 1997 Detroit Auto Show—where it took the breath away with its sexy body, reminiscent, to some, of the Austin-Healey 3000. That body was designed by Metalcrafters of Southern California.

The engine is a 2.7-liter aluminum 6-cylinder rated at 220 horsepower. It comes with a five-speed manual gearbox and independent suspension at both ends. The Copperhead does give the impression that it is slithering along the ground, like the snake for which it's named. It's 72 inches wide, 167 inches long, and has a 110-inch wheelbase.

If the Copperhead ever goes into production—and, as this is written, no money has been allocated for that purpose—it will list in the $40,000 to $50,000 range. Considering that it's apt to be a 2000 model, that's a pretty reasonable price. Reader, drive on.

The 1994 Nissan 300ZX had a 3-liter, 6-cylinder engine—but is best known for its excellent handling.